CASES AND MATERIALS

ON

COMMERCIAL LAW

By

E. ALLAN FARNSWORTH
Alfred McCormack Professor of Law
Columbia University School of Law

JOHN O. HONNOLD
William A. Schnader Professor of Commercial Law Emeritus
University of Pennsylvania Law School

STEVEN L. HARRIS
Professor of Law
University of Illinois College of Law

CHARLES W. MOONEY, JR.
Professor of Law
University of Pennsylvania Law School

CURTIS R. REITZ
Algernon Sydney Biddle Professor of Law
University of Pennsylvania Law School

FIFTH EDITION

Westbury, New York
THE FOUNDATION PRESS, INC.
1993

Reprinted in part from Honnold, Harris, Mooney and Reitz's The Law of Sales and Secured Financing, Sixth Edition © 1993 By The Foundation Press, Inc.

COPYRIGHT © 1965, 1968, 1976, 1985 THE FOUNDATION PRESS, INC.
COPYRIGHT © 1993 By THE FOUNDATION PRESS, INC.
615 Merrick Ave.
Westbury, N.Y. 11590–6607
(516) 832–6950

Library of Congress Cataloging-in-Publication Data

Cases and materials on commercial law / by E. Allan Farnsworth ... [et al.]. — 5th ed.
    p.   cm. — (University casebook series)
  Rev. ed. of: Cases and materials on commercial law / by E. Allan Farnsworth and John Honnold. 4th ed. 1985.
  Includes index.
  ISBN 1–56662–069–4
  1. Commercial law—United States—Cases. I. Farnsworth, E. Allan (Edward Allan), 1928–   . II. Farnsworth, E. Allan (Edward Allan), 1928–   Cases and materials on commercial law. III. Series.
KF888.F3 1993
346.73'07—dc20
[347.3067]
                                        93–23774

Farnsworth, et al. Comm.Law 5th Ed. UCS
2nd Reprint—1998

*To the students
who for four decades
have shared the exploration
that led to this book*

*

PREFACE

This book, like its predecessors, is intended for use in an integrated course in commercial law. It deals with sales, leases, negotiable instruments, bank deposits and collections, electronic funds transfers, letters of credit, bulk sales, documents of title and secured transactions—in short, all of the subjects covered by the Uniform Commercial Code except investment securities.

The book's general structure is similar to that of the last edition. The book is divided into four Parts: I. Good Faith Purchase; II. Payment of the Price: The Check; III. Responsibility for and Power over Goods; IV. Financing the Sale.

We grant that there is no unique solution to the problem of how to organize the subject matter for classroom presentation, but experience has caused us to adhere to our decision to put much of the material on negotiable instruments at the outset. One reason for this, elaborated in the General Introduction, is that the student has already some acquaintance with sales problems from a first-year course in contracts; material on negotiable instruments is needed early to fill the largest gap in the student's understanding of basic principles involved in commercial transactions. What is learned about checks in Part II is soon put to use in the consideration of the draft in the documentary sale of goods in Part III. Furthermore, typical problems involving negotiable instruments fall into patterns standardized by banking practice, so that the statutory provisions governing them tend to be particularly precise and definite. On the other hand, problems involving goods vary more widely reflecting the wide variety of commodities and of buyers and sellers, so that the statutory provision governing them tend to be more flexible and "open-ended." Since one of the principal skills involved in the course is in the use of statutory language, there is merit in beginning to develop this skill in an atmosphere of precision and definiteness before moving on to flexibility and "open-endedness."

Much of the material in this edition is new, with many cases selected from the substantial body of recent litigation under the Code. Special attention is given to new Articles 2A and 4A, to revised Articles 3 and 4, and to possible future amendments to Article 9. Except for a few landmark decisions, historical background is provided by explanatory text. The ever-increasing flow of cases has included numerous decisions that have sharpened issues that had only been subjects of academic speculation or of inconclusive judicial work. Recent years have also seen the establishment of significant protection for consumers and efforts to adapt the law to new payment systems. The Bankruptcy Code recasts the language that controls the effectiveness of security interests and makes basic changes of unsettled portent that call for close attention. This edition includes materials designed to introduce students to these new developments.

The use of problems also calls for a few words of explanation. Problems are often employed at the outset of a topic to help students get off on the right foot and quickly come to grips with basic issues. These analytical, introductory problems are followed by cases that show judicial response to situations where the text of the Code does not provide a compelling answer, and sometimes by problems of the more conventional sort that add refinements to the basic presentation. Instructors who do not wish to use the problems can focus their attention of the cases without seriously impairing the continuity of the materials. Prototype transactions and forms illustrate the mechanics of check collections, documentary sales, and letters of credit. When practicable, problems have been framed in terms of the prototypes in order to examine legal problems in a realistic commercial context.

Our thanks go to the colleagues, business people, law librarians, research assistants, secretaries and students who have contributed to this edition, including Professor Cynthia Starnes of the Detroit College of Law for most of the material on Regulation CC, to Ms. Michelle Brownlee, Mr. Michael R. Conway, Jr., Ms. Meryl S. Icove, Mr. William E. Markstein, Mr. Andrew Pribe, and Ms. Adina Weiss for help in research and editing, and to Ms. Brenda Fox and Mrs. Margaret Ulrich for secretarial assistance.

E. ALLAN FARNSWORTH
JOHN O. HONNOLD
STEVEN L. HARRIS
CHARLES W. MOONEY, JR.
CURTIS R. REITZ

June, 1993

NOTE ON SOURCES

We appreciate the kindness of the authors and publishers who have permitted us to reproduce portions of the following copyrighted works.

- Baird & Jackson, Possession and Ownership: An Examination of the Scope of Article 9, 35 Stanford Law Review 175 (1983).

- Boss, The History of Article 2A: A Lesson for Practitioner and Scholar Alike, 39 Alabama Law Review 575 (1988).

- Brandel & Oliff, The Electronic Fund Transfer Act: A Primer, 40 Ohio St.L.J. 531 (1979).

- Chafee, Acceleration Provisions in Time Paper, 32 Harv.L.Rev. 747 (1919).

- Cohen, Suretyship Principles in the New Article 3: Clarifications and Substantive Changes, 42 Ala.L.Rev. 595 (1991).

- Cohen & Gerber, The After-Acquired Property Clause, 87 University of Pennsylvania Law Review 635 (1939).

- Cooter & Rubin, A Theory of Loss Allocation for Consumer Payments, 66 Tex.L.Rev. 63 (1987).

- Farnsworth, Insurance Against Check Forgery, 60 Colum.L.Rev. 284 (1960).

- Farnsworth, Documentary Drafts Under the Uniform Commercial Code, 22 Bus.Law. 479 (1967).

- Gilmore, The Commercial Doctrine of Good Faith Purchase, 63 Yale Law Journal 1057 (1954).

- Gilmore, Security Interests in Personal Property (1965).

- Herbert, The Uncommon Law (1936). Reprinted with the permission of the Estate of Sir Alan Herbert.

- Hillman, McDonnell & Nickles, Common Law and Equity Under the Uniform Commercial Code (1985). Reprinted with the permission of Warren Gorham Lamont, a division of Research Institute of America, 210 South Street, Boston, MA 02111. All rights reserved.

- Jackson & Kronman, A Plea for the Financing Buyer, 85 Yale Law Journal 1 (1975).

- Jordan & Warren, Introduction to Symposium: Revised Articles 3 & 4 and New Article 4A, 42 Ala.L.Rev. 373 (1991).

- Keeton & Widiss, Insurance Law (1988).

- Kripke, A Draftsman's Wishes That He Could Do Things Over Again—U.C.C. Article 9, 26 San Diego Law Review 1 (1989).

- Kripke, Should Section 9–307(1) of the Uniform Commercial Code Apply Against a Secured Party in Possession?, 35 The Business Lawyer 153 (1977).

- Kupfer, Accounts Receivable Financing: A Legal and Practical Look-See, The Practicing Lawyer, November 1956.

- Mooney, Beyond Negotiability: A New Model for Transfer and Pledge of Interests in Securities Controlled by Intermediaries, 12 Cardozo Law Review 305 (1990).

- Penney, New York Revisits the Code: Some Variations in the New York Enactment of the Uniform Commercial Code, 62 Colum.L.Rev. 992 (1962).

- Peters, Suretyship Under Article 3 of the Uniform Commercial Code, 77 Yale L.J. 833 (1968).

- The Philadelphia Inquirer, "They're the Night Stalkers" (November 20, 1988).

- Report of the American Bar Association Stock Certificate Committee (1975).

- Rudow, Determining the Commercial Reasonableness of the Sale of Repossessed Collateral, 19 Uniform Commercial Code Law Journal 139 (1986).

- Schwartz, Structured Finance. Copyright 1990, Practising Law Institute (New York City).

- Schwartz, A Theory of Loan Priorities, 18 Journal of Legal Studies 209 (1989).

- A Second Look at the Amendments to Article 9 of the UCC, 29 The Business Lawyer 973 (1974).

- Shupack, Solving the Puzzle of Secured Transactions, 41 Rutgers Law Review 1067 (1989).

- Steffen & Starr, A Blueprint for the Certified Check, 13 N.C.L.Rev. 450 (1935).

- Turner, Barnes, Kershen, Noble & Shumm, Agricultural Liens and the U.C.C.: A Report on Present Status and Proposals for Change, 44 Oklahoma Law Review 9 (1991).

- Uniform Commercial Code, 1990 Official Text. Copyright 1990 by The American Law Institute and the National Conference of Commissioners on Uniform State Laws. Reprinted with the permission of the Permanent Editorial Board for the Uniform Commercial Code.

- White & Summers, Uniform Commercial Code Hornbook (3d ed. 1988).

In editing the foregoing works and the principal cases, we have taken the liberty of making minor adjustments to style and deleting footnotes and authorities without indication. For footnotes that remain, we have retained the original footnote numbers. Editorial interpolations, including additional footnotes, have been bracketed.

NOTE ON SOURCES

Unless otherwise indicated, citations to the Uniform Commercial Code are to the 1990 Official Text, except that all citations in cases are to former Articles 3 and 4. In principal cases that involve a pre–1972 version of the Code (or, when material, a pre–1978 version), we have added footnotes to indicate that fact. Citations to the Bankruptcy Code are to Title 11, United States Code, as amended through January 1, 1992.

*

SUMMARY OF CONTENTS

*

DETAILED TABLE OF CONTENTS

PART IV. SECURED TRANSACTIONS

*

TABLE OF STATUTES

TABLE OF STATUTES

TABLE OF STATUTES

TABLE OF STATUTES

TABLE OF STATUTES

TABLE OF STATUTES

TABLE OF STATUTES

TABLE OF CASES

Principal cases are in italic type. Non-principal cases are in roman type. References are to Pages.

1

*

CASES AND MATERIALS

ON

COMMERCIAL LAW

*

GENERAL INTRODUCTION

Scope of the Course. The concept of an integrated course in "commercial law" or "commercial transactions," covering commercial paper, sales, and secured transactions in personal property, is to a large extent the result of the promulgation of the Uniform Commercial Code. The focus of this book is the same as the focus of the Code—legal problems that arise in the distribution of goods. The subject is a challenging one, in part because of the wide variety of the factual settings and the dynamic part they play in modern economic life. Rules of law must be devised or contract provisions drafted for transactions as disparate as trades between hard-bitten mule dealers and sales of automobiles to consumers; face-to-face deals between New York textile merchants and cable transactions for the importation of sugar from Indonesia; sales "cash-on-the-barrelhead" and credit transactions which permit extended delay before payment. The variations are endless and an understanding of the transactions themselves is crucial to the legal engineering which is required to make them move off smoothly and safely. For this, among other reasons, the following materials are organized, for the most part, around typical transactions rather than on conceptual lines.

Part I departs from this transactional emphasis. It deals with the concept of good faith purchase, the most pervasive in the field of commercial law. The efficient distribution of goods requires that transactions be arranged without undue delay. To what extent is a good faith purchaser of goods entitled to protection against a claimant who later asserts rights as the true owner of the goods who was deprived of their possession by theft or fraud? To what extent is the good faith purchaser of rights evidenced by a negotiable instrument, such as a promissory note, or by a document of title, such as a warehouse receipt, entitled to such protection? And to what extent is the good faith purchaser of a right freed from defenses that may be asserted by the obligor with respect to that right? Part I traces the historical development of solutions to such problems and their embodiment in the provisions of the Uniform Commercial Code.

Part II of the book is concerned with payment for the goods and the principal means of payment, the check. This material on the law of negotiable instruments comes early in the course on the assumption that it will fill the largest gap in the student's understanding of the basic principles governing commercial transactions. The student may survive for a time on the sales law learned in the course in contracts but has no similar grounding in the law of negotiable instruments.

1

What, then, are the remedies of a seller who has taken in payment a check drawn on insufficient funds? What power has the buyer, after paying by check, to countermand the check by a stop payment order? What rights has the holder of the check when the bank on which it is drawn obeys such an order and dishonors the check? At what point in time does payment take place? And what rights has the bank if it overlooks the order and pays by mistake? Who bears the risk of loss on forgery and alteration of checks?

In Part III we turn to responsibility for and power over the goods. From the use of the check as a medium of payment we move to the use of its progenitor the draft in the documentary exchange. How can the seller use the documentary exchange to retain control of the goods until payment? If the goods are destroyed, can the seller recover the price from the buyer or must the seller take the loss, and who gets the proceeds if the goods are insured? What quality of goods must the seller supply? And what are the buyer's remedies in the event that seller breaches in this or some other regard? If the seller repudiates or becomes insolvent, can the buyer get the goods or only damages for breach of contract? If the buyer wrongfully rejects the goods, does the seller have the burden of disposing of the goods, with compensation in damages for breach of contract, or can the seller force them on the buyer and recover the price? In addition to the legal rules, we shall consider the relevant commercial practices, unwritten or formalized in documents, and ways in which farsighted counselling may avoid some of these hazards.

Part IV centers on legal arrangements that expand credit by giving the creditor power over assets being used by the debtor. Goods are delivered to the buyer on credit: to meet the danger of buyer's failure to pay, can the seller or bank which is financing the sale keep a hold on the goods which is adequate to recapture them from the buyer or from his creditors? A business needs more working capital: can a loan at a workable interest rate be arranged if the borrower agrees that the lender will have a claim on the borrower's equipment, inventory, accounts receivable and other personal assets that will defeat attack by other creditors? What is the impact of these arrangements on the borrower's suppliers and other creditors? Will courts enforce against borrowers the full range of rights which lenders write into the contract? This last question becomes insistent as legislators and judges become increasingly concerned with the problems of necessitous and ill-informed buyers and borrowers. A fuller introduction to this part of the book may be found at the beginning of Part IV.

DEVELOPMENT OF COMMERCIAL LAW

(1) Historical Background. The following summary traces the development of the tribunals and sources of law that determine commercial disputes. It will serve as a background for later discussion of the development of the law itself.

(a) English Law. The Uniform Commercial Code refers to the law merchant as a source of law. (See UCC 1–103.) Malynes' classic work, *Lex Mercatoria,* first published in England in 1622, included in the law merchant such subjects as banks and bankers, bills of exchange, letters of credit, buying and selling commodities by contract, insurance and admiralty. To Malynes, a seventeenth century merchant, this was a comprehensive body of authority that had been created not by kings or judges but by the customs of merchants, that was international rather than national in character, and that was distinct from the common law of England. How had the law merchant come to have this status in England by 1622?

Soon after the Norman invasion, local courts which became known as piepowder courts [1] were created as incident to the royal charters that authorized medieval fairs. The jurisdiction of these courts included commercial cases. The law was declared by a jury of merchants, the defendant's right to resort to compurgation was limited, and the procedure was summary enabling the participants to move on as their trade demanded.

In 1353 the Statute of the Staples [2] was enacted, regulating dealing in staple commodities, particularly wool which was of great economic and political importance. It created staple courts in certain boroughs with jurisdiction over commercial matters, and provided that the law merchant rather than the common law should govern. A mayor of the staple, who was required to be versed in the law merchant, presided and cases were tried before a merchant jury. With the advent of these courts a decline in the fair courts began and when, in 1477, legislation limited the jurisdiction of the piepowder courts to causes arising out of the fair at which the court sat, merchants began to take their cases in greater numbers to the staple courts, which were not so limited.

In the sixteenth century, control of the staple courts was given to officers of the king's court, and the common law courts began their interference in commercial cases. The merchants, unwilling to submit to the common law, retreated to the courts of admiralty, which then had a substantial commercial jurisdiction and which applied the law merchant. However, by the second half of the seventeenth century the common law courts, led by Lord Coke, had wrenched jurisdiction in all but the most maritime mercantile matters from the admiralty courts. At this point, common law lawyers and judges assumed roles which had previously been played by merchants and civilians. In 1690 Sir Josiah Child in his Discourse About Trade complained of "... his Majesties

---

1. From *pie poudre* (dusty foot) in reference to the shoes of itinerant merchant litigants. See generally Honnold, The Influence of the Law of International Trade on the Development and Character of English and American Commercial Law, in Sources of the Law of International Trade (1964) 70 (C. Schmitthoff ed. 1964); Coquillette, Legal Ideology and Incorporation II:

Sir Thomas Ridley, Charles Molloy, and the Literary Battle for the Law Merchant, 1607–1676, 61 B.U.L.Rev. 315, 346–70 (1981); Trakman, The Evolution of the Law Merchant: Our Commercial Heritage (pts. 1 & 2), 12 J.Mar.L. & Com. 1, 153 (1981).

2. Stat. 27 Edward III, Stat. 2 (1353).

Court of Kings–Bench, where after great expences of Time and Money, it is well if we can make our own Council (being common lawyers) understand one half of our case, we being amongst them as in a foreign country, our Language strange to them, and theirs as strange to us."

The judges at Westminster were not versed in the problems of merchants and common law procedure was not conducive to the prompt adjudication of disputes. Their antipathy toward freedom of assignment was particularly distressing to merchants, many of whom resorted to commercial arbitration to stay out of court. In such cases as did come before the common law courts in the seventeenth century, testimony as to the customs of the law merchant began to be accepted, at first only in controversies where both litigants were merchants and, in the latter half of the seventeenth century, in cases involving nonmerchants. But by the turn of the century the practice changed and the court itself declared the custom which was then deemed to be a part of the common law. This simplified pleading and proof, for it was no longer necessary to establish by evidence the custom of merchants in each case, but it also lessened the influence of merchantile practices upon English courts. Nevertheless, custom played a leading role under Lord Mansfield, a Scot, Chief Justice of the King's Bench from 1756 to 1788, and England's greatest commercial judge.[3] Mansfield familiarized himself with commercial usages, selected a group of merchants that sat as a special jury to advise him on controversies between merchants, and thus translated custom into judicial precedent. Karl Llewellyn attributed the fact that more of the law merchant was absorbed into the law of negotiable instruments than into the law of sales to the accident that the significant mercantile sales cases of this time did not come before Mansfield.[4]

For a century after Mansfield's death the then common law of commercial transactions grew as case law, with relatively few statutory enactments. In 1882, however, the Bills of Exchange Act, drafted by Sir Mackenzie Chalmers, was enacted by Parliament. A decade later, Chalmers performed a similar service for the law of sales, resulting in the enactment of the Sale of Goods Act in 1893. This act, like its predecessor, was intended as a restatement of English law and in turning the case law of sales into statutory form, he followed advice, prompted by the difficulty of getting innovations through Parliament, that he should "reproduce as exactly as possible the existing law."[5] Both statutes are now in effect in England and much of the Commonwealth and are of importance in foreign trade as well as historically.

3. Mansfield's work in commercial law is detailed in C. Fifoot, Lord Mansfield Chapter 4 (1936). For a briefer account see W. Holdsworth, Some Makers of English Law 160–75 (1938). Mansfield's Scottish background is not irrelevant, for it may explain his receptiveness to civil law doctrines prevalent in Scotland.

4. Llewellyn, Across Sales on Horseback, 52 Harv.L.Rev. 725, 742 (1939).

5. M. Chalmers, Sale of Goods Act p. x (13th ed. 1957) (introduction to the First Edition).

(b) American Unification. During the nineteenth century, commercial law in America had developed in part under the influence of England, with variations caused by differing treatment of the problem of reception. Jeremy Bentham argued the case for codification in England, and in 1811 he wrote to President Madison volunteering personally to write a code of law for the new world. In New York, the constitution of 1846 called for the codification of the entire body of law of the state. Under the leadership of David Dudley Field, New York adopted the first Code of Civil Procedure and prepared a code of substantive law which, although rejected in New York, was adopted in California in 1872, and in the Dakotas, Idaho and Moͷtana. But proposals for general codification were, for the most part, rejected.[6]

Maintaining uniformity of commercial law among the settled states of the Eastern seaboard was difficult enough; the problem became wholly unmanageable as new states were carved out of the wilderness. Frontier law was rough and ready, marked by a shortage of law books and legal education, and a cheerful willingness to improvise.[7] The rapidly developing commerce of the new world lacked uniform or even predictable rules of law.

In 1821 Joseph Story, speaking in his home state of Massachusetts, called for codification of aspects of commercial law. This call was not answered, and in 1842 Story wrote the opinion in Swift v. Tyson holding that federal courts, unhampered by divergent state court decisions, could declare uniform rules for "general commercial law." Indeed the opinion opened up wider vistas: Lord Mansfield and Cicero were cited for the proposition that commercial law was "in a great measure, not the law of a single country only, but of the commercial world."[8] The federal courts continued to declare rules of "general commercial law," in a sporadic manner and with decreasing effectiveness, until 1938 when such federal law-making was held unconstitutional in Erie Railroad Co. v. Tompkins.[9]

By 1890 every state had at least one statute on negotiable instruments, seven states led by California had comprehensive codes, and the result was chaotic. There was talk of federal legislation. A year later, under the leadership of New York, the National Conference of Commissioners on Uniform State Laws came into being and in 1895 it appointed John J. Crawford, of the New York bar, to draft a Uniform Negotiable Instruments Law, which it recommended for adoption in 1896.[10] It

6. For materials and further references on the codification movement see J. Honnold, The Life of the Law: Readings on the Growth of Legal Institutions 100–122, 494–496 (1964).

7. R. Pound, The Formative Era of American Law 7–12 (1938).

8. Swift v. Tyson, (41 U.S.) 16 Pet. 1, 18 (1842). See Gilmore, Commercial Law in the United States: Its Codification and Other Misadventures, in Aspects of Comparative Commercial Law, 449, 452–457 (J. Ziegel and W. Foster eds. 1969).

9. Erie Railroad Co. v. Tompkins, 304 U.S. 64 (1938). See Heckman, Uniform Commercial Law in the Nineteenth Century Federal Courts: The Decline and Abuse of the *Swift* Doctrine, 27 Emory L.J. 45 (1978).

10. An expenditure of not more than two thousand dollars was authorized for the project. Report of the Fifth Annual

closely followed the Bills of Exchange Act in many respects. By 1924 every state had enacted it, with occasional variations in a few sections.

In 1902 the Commissioners appointed Professor Samuel Williston to draft a uniform law of sales. The Uniform Sales Act was approved by the Commissioners in 1906 and shows the strong influence of Chalmers' Sale of Goods Act, both in substance and language. It was enacted in over thirty states, the principal exceptions being in the South. There followed the Uniform Warehouse Receipts Act (1906) drafted by Professor Williston and Barry Mohun, the Uniform Bills of Lading Act (1909) drafted by Professor Williston, the Uniform Conditional Sales Act (1918) drafted by Professor George Gleason Bogert, and the Uniform Trust Receipts Act (1933) drafted by Professor Karl Nickerson Llewellyn.

Some legislation came from other sources. In 1916, in the wake of frauds involving bills of lading in the cotton trade,[11] Congress enacted the Federal Bills of Lading or Pomerene Act (49 U.S.C. §§ 81–124) to govern bills of lading in exports and interstate shipments. It followed the wording of the uniform act in most respects and is still in effect. The Bank Collection Code, which was drafted in 1929 under the auspices of the American Bankers Association, supplemented the Negotiable Instruments Law in almost twenty states. Statutes on such subjects as bulk sales and factors' liens were first adopted by a few states on their own initiative and then borrowed by others so that they tended to follow uniform patterns. These uniform laws and related statutes are discussed in the notes in this casebook when an understanding of their provisions is important in solving problems under the Uniform Commercial Code.

(2) **The Uniform Commercial Code.** During the half-century after the first uniform acts, a number of proposals were made for change, and some states passed amendments to certain sections. A federal sales act was proposed in Congress in 1940, but the Commissioners succeeded in having it postponed. Work began in that year on a Uniform Revised Sales Act and in 1945 this project was expanded to concentrate upon a comprehensive Uniform Commercial Code. The American Law Institute joined forces with the National Conference of Commissioners in this effort, with Professor Llewellyn as Chief Reporter and Dean Soia Mentschikoff as Associate Chief Reporter. A final Official Draft with extensive comments was prepared, approved by the two sponsoring organizations in 1952, and promptly enacted by Penn-

---

Conference of Commissioners 14 (1895). Mr. Crawford's fee as draftsman was one thousand dollars. Report of the Sixth Annual Conference of Commissioners 7 (1896). The discussion of the draft at the 1896 Convention of the Commissioners lasted for only three days. 19 A.B.A.Reports 407 (1896).

11. The frauds involved issuance of bills of lading for goods that had been received by the carrier. The uniform act changed the common law rule that exonerated the carrier, but most of the southern states where the frauds occurred had not adopted the uniform act.

sylvania in April 1953, effective July 1, 1954.[12]

The Code is now divided into the following substantive articles: Article 1, General Provisions; Article 2, Sales; Article 2A, Leases; Article 3, Negotiable Instruments; Article 4, Bank Deposits and Collections; Article 4A, Funds Transfers; Article 5, Letters of Credit; Article 6, Bulk Transfers; Article 7, Warehouse Receipts, Bills of Lading and Other Documents of Title; Article 8, Investment Securities; Article 9, Secured Transactions; Sales of Accounts and Chattel Paper.[13] All but Article 8 are dealt with in this book.

In many areas the Code took an entirely new approach to problems. The New York Law Revision Commission began to study it in 1953 and in response to criticism, the sponsors of the Code published in 1955 a number of amendments in Supplement Number 1 to the 1952 Official Draft. The Commission held public hearings and retained consultants to study the draft,[14] and in 1956, after three years, it reported to the state legislature that the Code was not satisfactory and would require comprehensive reexamination and revision. Contemporaneous revision by the Editorial Board produced the 1956 Recommendations for the Uniform Commercial Code and these Recommendations became the 1957 Official Edition, which was published with comments and minor revisions early in 1958.

By late 1961, thirteen states, including Pennsylvania, had adopted the 1958 Official Text of the Code, and the New York Law Revision Commission recommended its adoption in New York. It was enacted in 1962. Adoptions of the Code then proceeded at an accelerating pace and by 1968 the Code had been adopted by all states except Louisiana (which has now adopted Articles 1, 3, 4, 4A, 5, 7, 8 and 9). The Code has also been adopted by Congress for the District of Columbia and by Guam and the Virgin Islands.[15]

New York and California made, as did other states, a number of changes in the 1958 Official Text.[16] In order to curb this tendency away from uniformity, a Permanent Editorial Board for the Uniform Commercial Code was established in 1961 to pass upon amendments

---

12. For further details and references see Honnold's account in New York Law Revision Commission, Study of Uniform Commercial Code, Vol. 1, 348 (1955).

13. Two additional articles deal with effective dates and related matters.

14. The studies fill three volumes and were published in 1955. See fn. 12 supra. The hearings fill two volumes and were published in 1954.

15. Courts have occasionally given the Code an anticipatory impact by applying its principles before their effective date. See, e.g., Williams v. Walker–Thomas Furniture Co., 121 U.S.App.D.C. 315, 350 F.2d 445 (1965) (adoption of UCC 2–302 subsequent to contracts in suit was "persuasive

authority for following the rationale of the cases from which the section is explicitly derived"). For a case giving interpretative effect to the 1972 amendments, see PPG Industries, Inc. v. Hartford Fire Insurance Co., 531 F.2d 58 (2d Cir.1976) (although 1972 amendment of UCC 9–306(1) "has not yet been adopted in New York, it is a persuasive indication of the effect which § 9–306 was originally intended to have"). For a summary of such cases, see In re Sexton, 16 B.R. 240 (Bkrtcy.Tenn.1981).

16. See Penney, New York Revisits the Code: Some Variations in the New York Enactment of the Uniform Commercial Code, 62 Colum.L.Rev. 992 (1962).

made or proposed by the states. For over a decade the sponsors held the line against proposals for change, and only glaring errors were corrected in the Official Texts of 1962 and 1966.[17] Nevertheless, hundreds of changes were made by the various states in enacting the Code. Merely counting the changes grossly exaggerates the divergencies among the various enacted versions of the Code, but it drives home the fact that a careful practicing lawyer must work from statutory materials that embody the version of the Code actually enacted in a particular state.

(3) **Ongoing Revision.** The 1972 Official Text made substantial revisions, centering on Article 9 (Secured Transactions); in 1977 there were important changes centering on Article 8 (Investment Securities). In the 1980's, the Code's sponsors launched a program of major additions and revisions. Two new Articles were added in the late 1980's— Article 2A (Leases) (1987 with 1990 amendments) and Article 4A (Funds Transfers) (1989). In 1988, the sponsors of the Code recommended that states repeal Article 6 (Bulk Sales). For those states reluctant to repeal, the sponsors prepared a substantially revised Article 6.

A major revision of Article 3 (Negotiable Instruments), with related changes in Article 4 (Bank Deposits and Collections), was concluded in 1990.[18] (Because the members of many of the sections were changed in revising Article 3, it is important to use the Table of Disposition of Sections in order to find the revised counterpart of original sections cited in cases.) Meanwhile, a drafting committee to revise Article 8 (Investment Securities) began working in 1991, with the expectation of completing its task in 1993.

The National Conference and the American Law Institute turned next to Article 2 (Sales) and Article 9 (Secured Transactions). In 1991, a drafting committee was authorized to revise Article 2. That step followed the completion of a major report by a study committee on that Article. In 1990 a study committee began reviewing Article 9, and it is safe to predict that Article 9 will be revised substantially in the 1990's.

Students studying commercial law while these important changes are in progress have an obvious problem and a significant opportunity. For parts of the Code, two versions of the text and Comments must be considered;[19] since uniform enactment of revisions and additions takes several years to complete, both the new and old versions of the Code will be in force in different states. Inevitably, some parts of the Code will not be "uniform" for years. For other parts of the Code, students

---

17. Revealing and amusing comments on the making of the Code appear in Symposium: Origins and Evolution: Drafters Reflect Upon the Uniform Commercial Code, 43 Ohio St.L.J. 537 (1982).

18. See Symposium: Revised U.C.C. Articles 3 & 4 and New Article 4A, 42 Ala. L.Rev. 351 (1991).

19. Current statutory supplements of the Code published for student use contain recently superseded versions of the text and Comments in appendices to the most recent Official Text promulgated by the National Conference and the American Law Institute.

can know that changes are forthcoming but cannot know what the new texts and Comments will be. This may be unsettling to someone looking merely to learn what the law "is." But considering a major body of statutory law in flux is a unique opportunity to gain the deeper understanding that comes from evaluating the perceived weaknesses in older texts and considering whether the new or proposed changes will be better.[20]

(4) **Use of the Code and Comments.** The Code makes much less of an attempt than did the earlier legislation in Britain and the United States, to follow existing formulations of the law. Very little of the language of the Negotiable Instruments Law and the Uniform Sales Act is retained, and in some respects the Code takes a drastically new approach to the law. Professor Williston stated that some of the changes in the law of Sales under the Code "are not only iconoclastic but open to criticisms that I regard so fundamental as to preclude the desirability of enacting [the Sales Article] of the proposed Code." Professor Corbin was among those who took a different view.[21] We shall have a chance to consider the soundness of many of the changes made by the Code.

One question in working with the Code is the extent to which recourse is to be had to prior drafts as an aid to interpretation. The 1952 edition of the Code attempted to close the door on such legislative history by providing in UCC 1–102(3)(g): "Prior drafts of text and comments may not be used to ascertain legislative intent." The drafting process had, of course, been in the hands of the sponsors of the Code and not the state legislatures which ultimately enacted it. The explanation given in the Comments for the provision was, however, somewhat different from this: "Frequently matters have been omitted as being implicit without statement and language has been changed or added solely for clarity. The only safe guide to intent lies in the final text and comments."

Subsection (3)(g) was deleted as the result of the revisions leading to the 1957 and 1958 editions of the Code. The Comments to the 1956 Recommendations of the Editorial Board for the Uniform Commercial Code state that "paragraph (3)(g) was deleted because the changes from the text enacted in Pennsylvania in 1953 are clearly legitimate legislative history." Is this intended to suggest that changes made prior to the 1952 edition adopted in Pennsylvania are *not* clearly legitimate legislative history? And to what extent *should* changes made by a drafting group, unconnected to the legislature, be considered as legiti-

---

20. Current students may find that their up-to-date knowledge of the emerging Code is an asset that prospective employers will value, as happened three decades ago when very few practicing lawyers had studied the Code as initially promulgated.

21. Compare Williston, The Law of Sales in the Proposed Uniform Commercial Code, 63 Harv.L.Rev. 561 (1950) with Cor-

bin, The Uniform Commercial Code—Sales; Should it be Enacted? 59 Yale L.J. 821 (1950). See also Mellinkoff, The Language of the Uniform Commercial Code, 77 Yale L.J. 185 (1967), where the author states that "for all its substantive contributions, the UCC is a slipshod job of draftsmanship."

mate legislative history? For an example of the use of legislative history, see *Industrial National Bank v. Leo's Used Car Exchange*, p. 228 infra.

A comparable question is the extent to which, in interpreting the Code, recourse should be had to the Comments that follow each section. A hazard for the lazy mind, and a help for the responsible lawyer, the Comments raise troublesome problems about their place in the Code system which need to be faced at the outset.

The most obvious point about the Comments is the one which, curiously enough, is most often overlooked: The text of the Code was enacted by the legislature; the Comments were not. One is tempted to ignore this point because the Comments, written in an explanatory and non-statutory style, are easier to read. *Facilis est descensus Averno.* But the tempter will whisper: The drafters wrote these Comments, did they not? If they say what the Code does, that is bound to be right, is it not? Why bother then with this prickly statutory language? (You may find it easier to resist these temptations if you put yourself, in your mind's eye, in the role of a judge to whom this argument has been made and then imagine your comments to that hapless attorney.)

The problem of the force of the Comments is sufficiently important to justify some background. The 1952 edition of the Code included as UCC 1–102(3)(f) a significant provision about the Comments: "The Comments of the National Conference of Commissioners on Uniform State Laws and the American Law Institute may be consulted in the construction and application of this Act but, if text and comment conflict, text controls."

The 1956 Recommendations of the Editorial Board for the Uniform Commercial Code deleted UCC 1–102(3)(f), and did not substitute any new provision on the status of the Comments. The question immediately arises: Does this deletion imply the rejection of the idea behind the deleted provision so that reference to the Comments has become illegitimate? An answer appears in the Comments to the 1956 Recommendations. The reasons for this and other changes were only briefly stated; the explanation for this change was as follows: "paragraph (3)(f) was deleted because the old comments were clearly out of date and it was not known when new ones could be prepared." [22] Revised Comments accompanied the 1957 and 1958 versions of the Code, but without any statutory provision referring to them.

Embarrassing questions multiply if one subjects the Comments to the standards often imposed for recourse to legislative history. In some states the revised Comments had not yet been drafted at the time of the Code's adoption. In others it is highly doubtful that the Comments were laid before the legislators in the form of a committee report

---

22. 1956 Recommendations 3. Perhaps we face here an engineering problem: How high can the comments lift themselves by their own boot-straps? See Braucher, The Legislative History of the Uniform Commercial Code, 58 Colum.L.Rev. 798, 808–10 (1958).

explaining the legislation which the legislators were asked to adopt. The practice in recent years has been for the Reporter (i.e., principal drafter) to draft Official Comments after the sponsors have approved the text. These Comments are subject only to the approval of the chair of the drafting committee.

It would be very wrong, however, to conclude that the Comments are without value to lawyers and to courts. Professor Williston's treatise on Sales was given heavy weight by courts in construing the Uniform Sales Act on the ground that it reflected the intent of the drafter, though it was written subsequent to the drafting of the Act; [23] courts have repeatedly quoted the Comments in construing the Code. Surely the Comments may be given at least as much weight as an able article or treatise construing the Code. It is equally clear that the Comments do not approach the weight of legislation; if the statutory provisions adopted by the legislature contradict or fail to support the Comments, the Comments must be rejected.[24] The point is significant, for we shall see instances, easily understood in the light of the Comments' bulk and the many successive revisions of the Code, where the Comments contradict the statute. More frequent are instances of enthusiastic discussion of significant problems on which the statute is silent.

A thorough job of construing the Code calls for using the Comments to make sure one has found the pertinent language of the statute, as a double-check on a tentative construction, and as a secondary aid where the language of the statute is ambiguous. However, the editors warn their students that they sternly reject any reference to Comments until *after* the pertinent statutory language has been carefully examined in the light of the statutory definitions and the statutory structure.

A word of caution is also in order concerning the "Definitional Cross References" which are contained in the Comments. A careful lawyer will not rely on the completeness of these references in the Comments. For a thorough job the lawyer will check Article 1, which contains important provisions applicable to the Code as a whole; Section 1-201 contains the definitions (in alphabetical order) of forty-six terms used throughout the Code. In addition, the lawyer will check the definitions specially applicable to the article involved; in nearly every article there is a helpful section, e.g., UCC 2-103, 3-103, containing an "index of definitions." [25]

---

23. See Braucher, note 22 supra at 809. The Code sponsors criticized this use of Professor Williston's treatise as a "delegation to private persons of essentially legislative power." Id. at note 73. Is this criticism applicable to the use of the Comments to the Code?

24. See also Consolidated Film Industries v. United States, 547 F.2d 533 (10th Cir.1977) (refusing to follow Comment 5 to

UCC 9-302 "in preference to the words of the statute and particularly so in view of the fact that Utah has not chosen to adopt it"); In re Bel Air Carpets, 452 F.2d 1210 (9th Cir.1971) (refusing to follow part of Comment 2 to UCC 2-702).

25. It should be observed, however, that only terms set out in quotation marks are generally included in the definitional cross references. Contrast "receipt" of goods

One recent development necessitates yet another warning. Pursuant to a resolution in 1987, the Permanent Editorial Board for the Uniform Commercial Code (PEB) has issued (and continues to issue) PEB Commentaries. The PEB Commentaries (and the resolution) are set out in full in most statutory supplements published for student use. The PEB Commentaries have necessitated supplemental changes to the Comments. Although the Comments refer to the relevant PEB Commentaries, in some cases portions of the Comments have been deleted and replaced by entirely new language. Because the Comments have been relied upon by legislators, courts, and counsel alike, one hopes that the Code's sponsors would find a way to preserve the Comments intact as *supplemented* by the PEB Commentaries.

(5) General Principles and the Code. You may find it useful to skim through the sections of Article 1 at this time. You should pay particular attention to UCC 1–102, 1–103, and 1–203. If the Code is more than a collection of statutes on separate though related subjects, it should be possible to discern some general principles that run throughout its various articles.[26] The most likely candidate is the principle of good faith. UCC 1–203, which is applicable throughout the Code provides: "Every contract or duty within this Act imposes an obligation of good faith in its performance or enforcement."

The pervasive character of this requirement makes it important to understand the nature of the "obligation of good faith." Article 1 (UCC 1–201(19)) restricts "good faith" to "honesty in fact in the conduct or transaction concerned." Article 2, however, contains a different definition: UCC 2–103(1)(b) provides that " 'Good faith' in the case of a merchant means honesty in fact and the observance of reasonable commercial standards of fair dealing in the trade." For the professional who comes within the definition of merchant in UCC 2–104(1), then, there is a special standard. The revision of Article 3 introduced a similar definition. UCC 3–103(a)(4) provides: " 'Good faith' means honesty in fact and the observance of reasonable standards of fair dealing."

A related provision is UCC 2–302, which deals with "unconscionable" contracts and clauses. The most difficult problem under this section is the lack of any definition in the Code of the key concept of "unconscionability." Comment 1 to UCC 2–302 seeks to meet this gap. At one point, however, it refers to the "basic test" of whether the clause is "onesided"; at another the Comment states that "the principle is one of the prevention of oppression and unfair surprise (cf. Campbell Soup Co. v. Wentz, 172 F.2d 80 (3d Cir.1948)), and not of disturbance of allocation of risks because of superior bargaining power." Can these

---

(which is so set out in UCC 2–103(1)(c) and which is therefore included in the definitional cross references to, e.g., UCC 2–503, 2–509) with "acceptance" of goods (which is not so set out in UCC 2–606 and which is therefore not included in the definitional cross references to, e.g., UCC 2–607, 2–608).

But cf. UCC 2–103(2), where "acceptance" is included in an "index of definitions."

26. On interpretation of codes, see Frier, Interpreting Codes, 89 Mich.L.Rev. 2201 (1989).

two comments be reconciled?[27] The Comment in addition states that "the underlying basis of the section is illustrated by the results in cases such as the following...." It then summarizes the holdings of ten cases. Five of these involved narrow construction of clauses disclaiming implied warranties of quality; the Code deals with this problem specifically in UCC 2–316. The remaining five cases limited the impact of clauses restricting remedies for breach, a problem covered in UCC 2–719. Cf. UCC 2–718 (agreements for unreasonably large liquidated damage are void as a penalty). Thus, even if these Comments are influential in construing the Code, the possible scope of Section 2–302, in areas not duplicated by UCC 2–316, 2–718 and 2–719, is left for case-law development. We shall see the beginnings of this development at various places in this book.

Note, however, that the "unconscionability" rule of UCC 2–302 differs from the "good faith" rule of UCC 1–203 in that it appears in the article on Sales, and not the one on General Provisions. Does this mean that the principle of "unconscionability" would have no relevance to, for example, a contract between a bank and its customer that was governed by Article 4, not Article 2?

The possibilities latent in these two general ideas, "good faith" (including "fair dealing") and "unconscionability" can best be appreciated in the light of rather similar concepts which are important in continental law. One of these bars the "abuse of rights," which in its development in French law seems to be related to the exercise of rights for an improper motive.[28] Broader and more suggestive of the rules of the Code is Section 242 of the German Civil Code: "The obligor is bound to perform the obligation in such a way as is required by the principles of *bona fides* with due regard to existing usage." Another helpful analogy is the famous provision of Article 2 of the Swiss Civil Code that "every person is bound to exercise his rights and fulfill his obligations according to the principles of good faith. The law does not protect the manifest abuse of a right."

Unlike judges in these civil law systems, Anglo–American judges have no generalized principle for the control of abuse of rights, and in dealing with the problem have had to expand limited precedents or categories like "forfeitures" and "penalties." True, civil law judges have difficulty in determining whether any given situation calls for the application of the general rule. But Professor Schlesinger makes the significant observation that in the common law, "When a case arises which does not fit into any of our narrower mental compartments, a common law court must either refuse relief or take the difficult, seemingly revolutionary step of expanding or exploding the existing

---

27. The conflicts in the drafting process that helped produce this ambiguity are exposed in Leff, Unconscionability and the Code—The Emperor's New Clause, 115 U.Pa.L.Rev. 485 (1967). See also Ellinghaus, In Defense of Unconscionability, 78 Yale L.J. 757 (1969).

28. See Gutteridge, Abuse of Rights, 5 Cambr.L.J. 22 (1933); L. Josserand, De l'Abus des Droits (1927); Note, 109 U.Pa. L.Rev. 401, 415–18 (1961).

compartments. In the same situation, a civil law court may find it easier to innovate, because it can rationalize the result as the mere 'application' of an established general principle." [29] The Uniform Commercial Code presents the interesting possibility that general principles have been made available for the control of conduct and of contracts that are not unlike the rules enunciated in the civil law systems. [30]

Is it wise to create different contract rules for contracts that fall within the Code than for other agreements? Is adoption of the Code likely to apply pressure for the drafting of a general code of contract law? Or will the ideas developed in the Code permeate the rest of the law of contracts? In this connection it is of interest that the Restatement (Second) of Contracts contains a section (§ 205) entitled "Duty of Good Faith and Fair Dealing" and one (§ 208) entitled "Unconscionable Contract or Term," both inspired by the comparable Code provision. [31]

(6) Consumer Legislation and Other Federal Incursions. In many of the countries that have a commercial code the code's applicability depends on whether the transaction is classified as "commercial" by criteria derived either from the parties' status as "merchants" or from the nature of the transaction as "mercantile." Lawyers schooled in such a legal setting may be startled to learn that our Uniform Commercial Code extends to transactions among ordinary consumers and that, with only a few exceptions, the rules are the same for both commercial and consumer transactions.

It must quickly be added that these general rules may lead to different results in commercial and in consumer settings. One example is the rule of UCC 2–315 which gives the buyer special protection when he relies "on the seller's skill or judgment"; similar flexibility is inherent in the Code's rules on "good faith" and "unconscionability" that have just been discussed. The point is that the application of

---

29. R. Schlesinger, Comparative Law 530 (3d ed. 1970).

30. See Farnsworth, Good Faith Performance and Commercial Reasonableness Under the Uniform Commercial Code, 30 U.Chi.L.Rev. 666 (1963). On good faith generally, see Burton, Breach of Contract and the Common Law Duty to Perform in Good Faith, 94 Harv.L.Rev. 369 (1980); Burton, Good Faith Performance of a Contract Within Article 2 of the Uniform Commercial Code, 67 Iowa L.Rev. 1 (1981); Burton, More on Good Faith Performance: A Reply to Professor Summers, 69 Iowa L.Rev. 497 (1984); Gillette, Limitations on the Obligation of Good Faith, 1981 Duke L.J. 619; Muris, Opportunistic Behavior and the Law of Contracts, 65 Minn.L.Rev. 521 (1981); Summers, "Good Faith" in General Contract Law and the Sales Provisions of the Uniform Commercial Code, 54 Va.L.Rev. 195 (1968); Summers, The General Duty of Good Faith—Its Recognition and Conceptualization, 67 Cornell L.Rev. 810 (1982).

31. See generally Patterson & Schlesinger, Problems of Codification of Commercial Law, in 1 N.Y.L.Rev.Comm., Study of the Uniform Commercial Code 37 (1955).

Consider also the possible influence on the Code of common law principles pursuant to UCC 1–103. See Hillman, Construction of the Uniform Commercial Code: UCC Section 1–103 and "Code" Methodology, 18 B.C.Ind. & Com.L.Rev. 655 (1977); Nickles, Problems of Sources of Law Relationships Under the Uniform Commercial Code (pts. 1 & 2), 31 Ark.L.Rev. 1, 171 (1977); Summers, General Equitable Principles Under Section 1–103 of the Uniform Commercial Code, 72 Nw.U.L.Rev. 906 (1978).

these rules does not depend on placing the parties or the transaction in a "commercial" or "consumer" category.

One of the striking legal developments of the past several decades has been the enactment of legislation designed to give special protection to "consumers." With respect to general rules of law like those of the Uniform Commercial Code, Congress has traditionally played a subsidiary role. In the field of consumer protection Congress took the lead. Sweeping regulation of seller's warranties in the interests of consumers became effective in 1975 under the federal Magnuson–Moss Warranty Act (15 U.S.C. §§ 2301–2312 (1988)). In 1960 Senator Paul Douglas introduced his first legislative proposal for "Truth in Lending." This proposal stimulated countermeasures for state enactment, including the preparation by the National Conference of Commissioners on Uniform State Laws of a Uniform Consumer Credit Code (the "U3C"). The Uniform Consumer Credit Code, as promulgated in 1968, provided the basis for legislation in a number of states; a revised version was issued in 1974. In the meantime, Congress moved ahead with legislation based on Senator Douglas's early proposals. In 1968 Congress passed the Consumer Credit Protection Act; Title I is the Truth in Lending Act. More recently the Federal Trade Commission has issued important regulations for the protection of consumers.

A particularly far-reaching example of this development came in 1987 with the enactment by Congress of the Expedited Funds Availability Act, intended to decrease the time consumers have to wait before drawing against credits given for checks that they deposit in their bank accounts. The Act broadly delegates to the Federal Reserve Board authority to regulate "any aspect of the payment system, including the receipt, payment, collection, or clearing of checks." The Federal Reserve Board responded to this invitation by issuing Regulation CC, which took effect in 1988. Regulation CC, discussed later in some detail, rewrites in fundamental respects the law of check collections and preempts substantial portions of Article 4 of the Uniform Commercial Code. It casts the long shadow of possible increased federal regulation over this domain of commercial law previously left largely to the states. The possibility of federal incursions into other areas of commercial law previously left to the states should be kept in mind in reading the chapters that follow.

(7) **Uniform Laws for International Transactions.** Important steps have been taken to unify the law applicable to international trade. Trade with the larger part of the world—the continent of Europe, the American republics to the south and much of Asia and Africa—carries the parties to sales contracts and their lawyers into legal systems which stem from unfamiliar roots; the differences in legal concepts are, of course, complicated by linguistic barriers.

Sales. One field for unification is the law applicable to the international sale of goods. As early as 1930 work toward this goal was under way in Europe, and in April 1964 a diplomatic conference at The Hague finalized conventions establishing a Uniform Law on the International Sale of Goods (ULIS) and a Uniform Law on the Formation of Contracts for the International Sale of Goods (ULF). By 1972 sufficient ratifications, primarily by countries of western Europe, had occurred to bring these conventions into force.

These two conventions broke the ground for international unification, but the lack of world-wide collaboration in their preparation stood in the way of general adoption. In 1966 the General Assembly of the United Nations provided for the creation of the United Nations Commission on International Trade Law (UNCITRAL). UNCITRAL's membership, limited to 36 States, is allocated among the regions of the world: Africa, 9; Asia, 7; Eastern Europe, 5; Latin America, 6; Western Europe and Others, 9. This last region (the industrial West) extends to Australia, Canada, and the United States. The United States has been a member from the outset, and has played an active role in UNCITRAL's work.

UNCITRAL promptly created a Working Group (a cross-section of the Commission's world-wide membership) to prepare new international rules that would meet objections to the 1964 conventions on international sales. By 1978 the Working Group and the full Commission had unanimously approved a new draft Convention. In 1980 a diplomatic conference of 62 States, at the end of five weeks of intensive work, approved the United Nations Convention on Contracts for the International Sale of Goods. The Convention went into force on January 1, 1988 following ratification (or similar implementation) by eleven States. The United States was one of those nations. By 1991 the Convention had been ratified by over 30 States, including nations on each continent and with diverse legal and economic systems.

Negotiable Instruments and Credit Transfers. A second field for unification involves the rules governing important instruments used in international payments—bills of exchange, promissory notes, checks. In this field, UNCITRAL developed uniform rules which led in 1988 to the United Nations Convention on International Bills of Exchange and Promissory Notes; an unusual feature of this Convention is that its rules apply only to a special international instrument that states it is issued under the Convention. See G. Herrmann, 10 U.Pa.J.Intl.Bus.L. 517–577 (1988). In 1992, the Commission approved a Model Law on International Credit Transfers, covering electronic and other funds transfers where the sender of a payment order and the bank receiving it are in different countries.

Other Fields. Because of the vital part that sea transport plays in international trade, UNCITRAL decided to examine the rules that govern the responsibility of ocean carriers for cargo. (Problems of risk of loss in this area are examined in Chapter 7). The Commission found that these rules, developed under the strong influence of the carriers, gave inadequate protection to cargo and developed new rules that were submitted in 1978 to diplomatic conference at Hamburg that finalized the United Nations Convention on Carriage of Goods by Sea (the "Hamburg Rules"). In spite of active opposition on behalf of the carriers, in 1991 the Convention received (primarily from developing countries) the twenty ratifications required to bring the Convention into force, which occurs on November 1, 1992. Countries that have indicated interest in the Convention by becoming signatories but have not yet ratified include Brazil, France, Germany, the four Scandinavian nations and the United States.[32]

Other examples of the rapidly growing body of uniform law for international commerce include the 1976 UNCITRAL Arbitration Rules, which become effective by a reference in a contractual arbitration clause, and the 1985 UNCITRAL Model Law on International Commercial Legislation. See A. Broches in ICCA, International Handbook on Commercial Arbitration (Arb.Supp. 11, Jan. 1990); H. Holtzmann & J. Neuhaus, Guide to the UNCITRAL Model Law (1989); A. Redfern & M. Hunter, Law and Practice of International Commercial Arbitration 360–404, 416–430 (text of the UNCITRAL Rules), 435–449 (text of the Model Law) (1986).

(8) Reference Materials. The most useful tool for research on the Code is the Uniform Commercial Code Reporting Service and Case Digest. This service gives local variations of the Code and Comments and brings together with a digest and index all of the cases that cite the Code. Another helpful guide is the Uniform Laws Annotated. Insights into the drafting history of the Code are provided by the 23 volumes of Uniform Commercial Code Drafts (E. Kelly ed. 1984).

On the Code as a whole, see J. White & R. Summers, Uniform Commercial Code (3d ed. 1988); R. Alderman, A Transactional Guide to the Uniform Commercial Code (2d ed. 1983). For an extremely brief treatment, see B. Stone, Uniform Commercial Code in a Nutshell (3d ed. 1989). For descriptions of transactions, including examples of forms, see J. Dolan, Fundamentals of Commercial Activity (1991), adapted for students in J. Dolan, Uniform Commercial Code: Terms and Transactions in Commercial Law (1991); R. Braucher & R. Riegert, Introduction to Commercial Transactions (1977). The myriad intersections of the Code with other laws are developed in R. Hillman, J. McDonnell & S. Nickels, Common Law and Equity Under the UCC (1984 & Supp.1990). On sales see W. Henning & G. Wallach, The Law of Sales Under the Uniform Commercial Code (rev. ed. looseleaf); R. Duesenberg & L. King, Sales and Bulk Transfers Under the Uniform Commercial Code (looseleaf). On negotiable instruments, see C. Weber & R. Speidel, Commercial Paper in a Nutshell (3d ed. 1982); F. Hart & W. Willier, Commercial Paper Under the Uniform Commercial Code (looseleaf). In view of the rapid evolution of consumer protection laws,

---

32. Growing use of large steel containers has stimulated arrangements linking different modes of transport—road, rail, air and sea. Desire for uniform international rules led to the 1980 International Convention on Multimodal Transport, based on the 1978 Hamburg Rules.

loose-leaf services are useful. See Consumer Credit Guide. (References on secured transactions are given at the beginning of Part IV.)

Several commentaries have been published on the International Sales Convention. See C. Bianca & M. Bonell (eds.), Commentary on the International Sales Law (1987); J. Honnold, Uniform Law for International Sales Under the 1980 United Nations Convention (2d ed. 1991); P. Schlechtriem, Uniform Sales Law (1986). For cross reference between the Convention and the Commercial Code, see A. Kritzer, Guide to Practical Applications of the United Nations Convention on Contracts for the International Sale of Goods (1989). Legislative history of the Convention is compiled in J. Honnold, Documentary History of the Uniform Law for International Sales (1989). See also Pfund, International Unification of Private Law: A Report on U.S. Participation—1987–88, 22 Int.Law. 1157 (1988).

Part I

GOOD FAITH PURCHASE

INTRODUCTION

Introduction. This course, like the first-year course in contracts, is primarily concerned with consensual exchange transactions. In contracts, however, the emphasis was on the creation, scope and enforcement of rights to and duties of performance. Here the emphasis is on the transfer of personal property. Part I asks two questions about such transfers. First, to what extent does a good faith purchaser of property take free of conflicting claims of ownership to that property? Second, if the property consists of a right of some kind, to what extent does a good faith purchaser of that right take it free of the obligor's defenses with respect to it? Three types of property will be considered in connection with the first question: goods, rights evidenced by negotiable instruments (promissory notes) and rights evidenced by documents of title (warehouse receipts). The last two of these will be considered again in connection with the second question.

Our objectives are twofold. The first is to examine one of the great doctrines of the common law, the doctrine of good faith purchase. The second is to explore, in connection with that doctrine, the interrelation (or lack of it) of a variety of the articles of the Code.

Chapter 1

FREEDOM FROM CLAIMS OF OWNERSHIP

Prefatory Note. A key problem posed by the transfer of property is the extent to which an innocent transferee, who has given something in exchange for property, takes free of conflicting claims of ownership asserted by persons other than the transferor, e.g., a claim that the property was stolen or obtained by fraud from the rightful owner. In simple terms, can a good faith purchaser keep the property purchased? According to Professor Grant Gilmore: "The triumph of the good faith purchaser has been one of the most dramatic episodes in our legal history. In his several guises, he serves a commercial function: he is protected not because of his praiseworthy character, but to the end that commercial transactions may be engaged in without elaborate investigation of property rights and in reliance on the possession of property by one who offers it for sale...." Gilmore, The Commercial Doctrine of Good Faith Purchase, 63 Yale L.J. 1057 (1954).

The freedom of the "good faith purchaser" from claims of ownership is developed in the following series of problems involving goods and intangibles. The sources suggested for their solution are both contemporary (notably the provisions of the Code) and historical (notably seminal cases from past centuries that fashioned the principles embodied in the Code). (Where Code sections are cited, *read the relevant Comments as well and be sure to find other related sections* including those indexed under the definitional cross references.) As you look through the problems, ask yourself: To what extent would the Code suffice without some understanding of the history behind it, i.e., to what extent did the drafters of the Code assume at least some familiarity of traditional principles?

SECTION 1. GOODS

We begin with goods. Although our principal concern will be with the purchase of goods in typical commercial situations, the doctrine of good faith purchase has important consequences in a more exotic setting: the art market. Thefts of works of art, estimated to total roughly a billion dollars every year, have generated a collection of fascinating cases.[1]

The most celebrated of these arose out of the theft by vandals in the late 1970s of a sixth-century Byzantine mosaic from a church in Kanakaria on Cyprus. In 1988, the Kanakaria mosaics—the original having been split into four parts by the vandals—were sold to Peg Goldberg, an Indianapolis art dealer. She acquired them at the Geneva airport for $1,080,000, borrowed from an Indianapolis bank, which she paid in $100 bills stuffed into two satchels to two persons whom she had met through another Indianapolis art dealer a week before and who purportedly represented the Turkish owner. She had obtained appraisals that valued the mosaics at between $3 and $6 million and had made a cursory inquiry to determine whether the mosaics had been stolen. The conspirators, including the other Indianapolis dealer, split the proceeds, and Goldberg, their innocent victim, took the mosaics back to Indianapolis.

---

1. For discussion of international art thefts, see Bator, An Essay on the International Trade in Art, 34 Stan.L.Rev. 275, 277–82 (1982).

Goldberg's search for a buyer came to the attention of an expert at the Getty Museum in California and through her to a Cypriot official involved in the worldwide search for the mosaics. In 1989, after Goldberg had refused to return the mosaics, the Greek–Orthodox Church of Cyprus brought an action to recover them in the federal district court in Indianapolis.

Goldberg contended that, since the action had not been commenced until ten years after the theft, the action was barred by Indiana's six year statute of limitations for recovering possession of personal property. The court rejected this contention on the ground that Indiana would apply a "discovery rule," under which the statute would not begin to run until the Church, using due diligence, knew or was on reasonable notice of the identity of the possessor of the mosaics. The Church had, the court held, used due diligence. The court then held that the substantive law of Indiana, rather than that of Switzerland, applied because Indiana had the most significant contacts. Under Indiana law, "a thief obtains no title to or right to possession of stolen items and can pass no title or right to possession to a subsequent purchaser." Goldberg therefore did not acquire title to the mosaics, which remained the property of the Church. And even if Swiss law were to apply, under Swiss law "a purchaser of stolen property acquires title superior to that of the original owner only if he purchases the property in good faith." Because of the suspicious circumstances surrounding the sale of the mosaics and Goldberg's failure to make more than a cursory inquiry as to their provenance, she did not purchase the mosaics in good faith. At the end of a 30–page opinion, the court awarded possession of the mosaics to the Church. Autocephalous Greek–Orthodox Church of Cyprus v. Goldberg & Feldman Fine Arts, 717 F.Supp. 1374 (S.D.Ind.1989). After 19 more pages of analysis, beginning with a quotation from Byron, the United States Court of Appeals affirmed. 917 F.2d 278 (7th Cir.1990), cert. denied, 112 S.Ct. 377 (1991). Before the mosaics went home to Cyprus, however, some 40,000 curious visitors thronged the Indianapolis Museum of Art to take a last look. For much more, see Hofstadter, Annals of the Antiquities Trade: The Angel on Her Shoulder (pts. 1 & 2), The New Yorker, July 13, 1992, at 36, July 20, 1992, at 38.

The opinions in this memorable dispute are too lengthy for use here. But, with the exception of choice of law, all of the issues—even under Swiss law—are explored in the materials that follow.

Problem 1. O owned cotton worth $100,000. A stole it and sold it to P, who paid A $100,000 for it, not suspecting that it was stolen. O sued P to replevy the cotton.

(a) What result? When does the statute of limitations begin to run? Does P have a right to be reimbursed by O for the $100,000 P paid for it? See UCC 2–403; Solomon R. Guggenheim Foundation v. Lubell, infra.

(b) Would it make a difference if A is in the cotton business?

(c) Would it make a difference if A had sold it to B who had sold it to P? (As to P's recourse against B, see UCC 2–312.) Can you think of additional facts that would change the result in the case?[2] For a suggestion that O's rights against P might be prejudiced in some circumstances by obtaining an uncollectible judgment against A, see Linwood Harvestore v. Cannon, 427 Pa. 434, 235 A.2d 377 (1967).

SOLOMON R. GUGGENHEIM FOUNDATION v. LUBELL

Court of Appeals of New York, 1991.
77 N.Y.2d 311, 567 N.Y.S.2d 623, 569 N.E.2d 426.

WACHTLER, CHIEF JUDGE. The backdrop for this replevin action ... is the New York City art market, where masterpieces command extraordinary prices at auction and illicit dealing in stolen merchandise is an industry all its own. The Solomon R. Guggenheim Foundation, which operates the Guggenheim Museum in New York City, is seeking to recover a Chagall gouache worth an estimated $200,000. The Guggenheim believes that the gouache was stolen from its premises by a mailroom employee sometime in the late 1960s. The appellant Rachel Lubell and her husband, now deceased, bought the painting from a well-known Madison Avenue gallery in 1967 and have displayed it in their home for more than 20 years. Mrs. Lubell claims that before the Guggenheim's demand for its return in 1986, she had no reason to believe that the painting had been stolen.

On this appeal, we must decide if the museum's failure to take certain steps to locate the gouache is relevant to the appellant's Statute of Limitations defense. In effect, the appellant argues that the museum had a duty to use reasonable diligence to recover the gouache, that it did not do so, and that its cause of action in replevin is consequently barred by the Statute of Limitations. The Appellate Division rejected the appellant's argument. We agree with the Appellate Division that the timing of the museum's demand for the gouache and the appellant's refusal to return it are the only relevant factors in assessing the merits of the Statute of Limitations defense. We see no justification for undermining the clarity and predictability of this rule by carving out an exception where the chattel to be returned is a valuable piece of art. Appellant's affirmative defense of laches remains viable, however, and her claims that the museum did not undertake a reasonably diligent search for the missing painting will enter into the trial court's evaluation of the merits of that defense. Accordingly, the order of the Appellate Division should be affirmed.

---

2. With respect to the availability to P of the defense that O had himself stolen the cotton, see Lieber v. Mohawk Arms, 64 Misc.2d 206, 314 N.Y.S.2d 510 (1970), involving the theft from an ex-GI of Hitler's personal belongings.

The gouache, known alternately as *Menageries* or *Le Marchand de Bestiaux (The Cattle Dealer),* was painted by Marc Chagall in 1912, in preparation for an oil painting also entitled *Le Marchand de Bestiaux.* It was donated to the museum in 1937 by Solomon R. Guggenheim.

The museum keeps track of its collection through the use of "accession cards," which indicate when individual pieces leave the museum on loan, when they are returned and when they are transferred between the museum and storage. The museum lent the painting to a number of other art museums over the years. The last such loan occurred in 1961–62. The accession card for the painting indicates that it was seen in the museum on April 2, 1965. The next notation on the accession card is undated and indicates that the painting could not be located.

Precisely when the museum first learned that the gouache had been stolen is a matter of some dispute. The museum acknowledges that it discovered that the painting was not where it should be sometime in the late 1960s, but claims that it did not know that the painting had in fact been stolen until it undertook a complete inventory of the museum collection beginning in 1969 and ending in 1970. According to the museum, such an inventory was typically taken about once every 10 years. The appellant, on the other hand, argues that the museum knew as early as 1965 that the painting had been stolen. It is undisputed, however, that the Guggenheim did not inform other museums, galleries or artistic organizations of the theft, and additionally, did not notify the New York City Police, the FBI, Interpol or any other law enforcement authorities. The museum asserts that this was a tactical decision based upon its belief that to publicize the theft would succeed only in driving the gouache further underground and greatly diminishing the possibility that it would ever be recovered. In 1974, having concluded that all efforts to recover the gouache had been exhausted, the museum's Board of Trustees voted to "deaccession" the gouache, thereby removing it from the museum's records.

Mr. and Mrs. Lubell had purchased the painting from the Robert Elkon Gallery for $17,000 in May of 1967. The invoice and receipt indicated that the gouache had been in the collection of a named individual, who later turned out to be the museum mailroom employee suspected of the theft. They exhibited the painting twice, in 1967 and in 1981, both times at the Elkon Gallery. In 1985, a private art dealer brought a transparency of the painting to Sotheby's for an auction estimate. The person to whom the dealer showed the transparency had previously worked at the Guggenheim and recognized the gouache as a piece that was missing from the museum. She notified the museum, which traced the painting back to the defendant. On January 9, 1986, Thomas Messer, the museum's director, wrote a letter to the defendant demanding the return of the gouache. Mrs. Lubell refused to return the painting and the instant action for recovery of the painting, or, in the alternative, $200,000, was commenced on September 28, 1987.

In her answer, the appellant raised as affirmative defenses the Statute of Limitations, her status as a good-faith purchaser for value, adverse possession, laches, and the museum's culpable conduct. The museum moved to compel discovery and inspection of the gouache and the defendant cross-moved for summary judgment. In her summary judgment papers, the appellant argued that the replevin action to compel the return of the painting was barred by the three-year Statute of Limitations because the museum had done nothing to locate its property in the 20–year interval between the theft and the museum's fortuitous discovery that the painting was in Mrs. Lubell's possession. The trial court granted the appellant's cross motion for summary judgment, relying on DeWeerth v. Baldinger, 836 F.2d 103, an opinion from the United States Court of Appeals for the Second Circuit. The trial court cited New York cases holding that a cause of action in replevin accrues when demand is made upon the possessor and the possessor refuses to return the chattel. The court reasoned, however, that in order to avoid prejudice to a good-faith purchaser, demand cannot be unreasonably delayed and that a property owner has an obligation to use reasonable efforts to locate its missing property to ensure that demand is not so delayed. Because the museum in this case had done nothing for 20 years but search its own premises, the court found that its conduct was unreasonable as a matter of law. Consequently, the court granted Mrs. Lubell's cross motion for summary judgment on the grounds that the museum's cause of action was time barred.

The Appellate Division modified, dismissing the Statute of Limitations defense and denying the appellant's cross motion for summary judgment. The Appellate Division held that the trial court had erred in concluding that "delay alone can make a replevin action untimely".... The court stated that the appellant's lack of diligence argument was more in the nature of laches than the Statute of Limitations and that as a result, the appellant needed to show that she had been prejudiced by the museum's delay in demanding return of the gouache.... The court also held that summary judgment was inappropriate because several issues of fact existed, including whether the museum's response to the theft was unreasonable, when the museum first realized that the gouache was missing, when the museum should have realized that the gouache had been stolen, whether it was unreasonable for the museum not to have taken certain steps after it realized that the gouache was missing but before it realized that it had been stolen, and when the museum learned of the defendant's possession of the gouache.... The Appellate Division granted leave to this Court, certifying the following question: "Was the order of this Court, which modified the order of the Supreme Court, properly made?" We answer this certified question in the affirmative.

New York case law has long protected the right of the owner whose property has been stolen to recover that property, even if it is in the possession of a good-faith purchaser for value (see, Saltus & Saltus v.

Everett, 20 Wend. 267, 282). There is a three-year Statute of Limitations for recovery of a chattel (CPLR 214[3]). The rule in this State is that a cause of action for replevin against the good-faith purchaser of a stolen chattel accrues when the true owner makes demand for return of the chattel and the person in possession of the chattel refuses to return it.... Until demand is made and refused, possession of the stolen property by the good-faith purchaser for value is not considered wrongful.... Although seemingly anomalous, a different rule applies when the stolen object is in the possession of the thief. In that situation, the Statute of Limitations runs from the time of the theft ..., even if the property owner was unaware of the theft at the time that it occurred....

In *DeWeerth v. Baldinger* (supra), which the trial court in this case relied upon in granting Mrs. Lubell's summary judgment motion, the Second Circuit took note of the fact that New York case law treats thieves and good-faith purchasers differently and looked to that difference as a basis for imposing a reasonable diligence requirement on the owners of stolen art. Although the court acknowledged that the question posed by the case was an open one, it declined to certify it to this Court ..., stating that it did not think that it "[would] recur with sufficient frequency to warrant use of the certification procedure".... Actually, the issue has recurred several times in the three years since *DeWeerth* was decided ... including the case now before us. We have reexamined the relevant New York case law and we conclude that the Second Circuit should not have imposed a duty of reasonable diligence on the owners of stolen art work for purposes of the Statute of Limitations.

While the demand and refusal rule is not the only possible method of measuring the accrual of replevin claims, it does appear to be the rule that affords the most protection to the true owners of stolen property. Less protective measures would include running the three-year statutory period from the time of the theft even where a good-faith purchaser is in possession of the stolen chattel, or, alternatively, calculating the statutory period from the time that the good-faith purchaser obtains possession of the chattel.... Other States that have considered this issue have applied a discovery rule to these cases, with the Statute of Limitations running from the time that the owner discovered or reasonably should have discovered the whereabouts of the work of art that had been stolen (see, e.g., O'Keeffe v. Snyder, 83 N.J. 478, 416 A.2d 862 ...).

New York has already considered—and rejected—adoption of a discovery rule. In 1986, both houses of the New York State Legislature passed Assembly Bill 11462-A (Senate Bill 3274-B), which would have modified the demand and refusal rule and instituted a discovery rule in actions for recovery of art objects brought against certain not-for-profit institutions. This bill provided that the three-year Statute of Limitations would run from the time these institutions gave notice, in a manner specified by the statute, that they were in possession of a particular object. Governor Cuomo vetoed the measure, however, on advice of the United States Department of State, the United States Department of Justice and the United States Information Agency.... In his veto message, the Governor expressed his concern that the statute "[did] not provide a reasonable opportunity for individuals or foreign governments to receive notice of a museum's acquisition and take action to recover it before their rights are extinguished." The Governor also stated that he had been advised by the State Department that the bill, if it went into effect, would have caused New York to become "a haven for cultural property stolen abroad since such objects [would] be immune from recovery under the limited time periods established by the bill."

The history of this bill and the concerns expressed by the Governor in vetoing it, when considered together with the abundant case law spelling out the demand and refusal rule, convince us that that rule remains the law in New York and that there is no reason to obscure its straight-forward protection of true owners by creating a duty of reasonable diligence. Our case law already recognizes that the true owner, having discovered the location of its lost property, cannot unreasonably delay making demand upon the person in possession of that property.... Here, however, where the demand and refusal is a substantive and not a procedural element of the cause of action (... compare, CPLR 206 [where a demand is necessary to entitle a person to commence an action, the time to commence that action is measured from when the right to make demand is complete]), it would not be prudent to extend that case law and impose the additional duty of diligence before the true owner has reason to know where its missing chattel is to be found.

Further, the facts of this case reveal how difficult it would be to specify the type of conduct that would be required for a showing of reasonable diligence. Here, the parties hotly contest whether publicizing the theft would have turned up the gouache. According to the museum, some members of the art community believe that publicizing a theft exposes gaps in security and can lead to more thefts; the museum also argues that publicity often pushes a missing painting further underground. In light of the fact that members of the art community have apparently not reached a consensus on the best way to retrieve stolen art ..., it would be particularly inappropriate for this Court to spell out arbitrary rules of conduct that all true owners of stolen art work would have to follow to the letter if they wanted to preserve their right to pursue a cause of action in replevin. All owners of stolen property should not be expected to behave in the same way and should not be held to a common standard. The value of the property stolen, the manner in which it was stolen, and the type of institution from which it was stolen will all necessarily affect the manner in which a true owner will search for missing property. We conclude that it would be difficult, if not impossible, to craft a reasonable diligence requirement that could take into account all of these variables and that would not unduly burden the true owner.

Further, our decision today is in part influenced by our recognition that New York enjoys a worldwide reputation as a preeminent cultural center. To place the burden of locating stolen artwork on the true owner and to foreclose the rights of that owner to recover its property if the burden is not met would, we believe, encourage illicit trafficking in stolen art. Three years after the theft, any purchaser, good faith or not, would be able to hold onto stolen art work unless the true owner was able to establish that it had undertaken a reasonable search for the missing art. This shifting of the burden onto the wronged owner is inappropriate. In our opinion, the better rule gives the owner relatively greater protection and places the burden of investigating the provenance of a work of art on the potential purchaser.

Despite our conclusion that the imposition of a reasonable diligence requirement on the museum would be inappropriate for purposes of the Statute of Limitations, our holding today should not be seen as either sanctioning the museum's conduct or suggesting that the museum's conduct is no longer an issue in this case. We agree with the Appellate Division that the arguments raised in the appellant's summary judgment papers are directed at the conscience of the court and its ability to bring equitable considerations to bear in the ultimate disposition of the painting. As noted above, although appellant's Statute of Limitations argument fails, her contention that the museum did not exercise reasonable diligence in locating the painting will be considered by the Trial Judge in the context of her laches defense. The conduct of both the appellant and the museum will be relevant to any consideration of this defense at the trial level, and as the Appellate Division noted, prejudice will also need to be shown (153 A.D.2d, at 149, 550 N.Y.S.2d 618). On the limited record before us there is no indication that the equities favor either party. Mr. and Mrs. Lubell investigated the provenance of the gouache before the purchase by contacting the artist and his son-in-law directly. The Lubells displayed the painting in their home for more than 20 years with no reason to suspect that it was not legally theirs. These facts will doubtless have some impact on the final decision regarding appellant's laches defense. Because it is impossible to conclude from the facts of this case that the museum's conduct was unreasonable as a matter of law, however, Mrs. Lubell's cross motion for summary judgment was properly denied.

We agree with the Appellate Division, for the reasons stated by that court, that the burden of proving that the painting was not stolen properly rests with the appellant Mrs. Lubell. We have considered her remaining arguments, and we find them to be without merit. Accordingly, the order of the Appellate Division should be affirmed, with costs, and the certified question answered in the affirmative.

Notes

(1) Nemo Dat v. Possession Vaut Titre. The court cites an 1838 case for the proposition that "New York case law has long protected the right of the owner whose property has been stolen to recover that property, even if it is in the possession of a good faith purchaser for value." Should not the court have cited UCC 2–403(1)? If, under that section, a purchaser "acquires all title that his transferor had," what title does a purchaser get from a thief? It does not appear that the problem troubled either the court or the drafters of the Code enough to elicit a full explanation of the rule favoring the victim of the theft. You should not assume, however, that this is the rule in all legal systems.

"It is necessary in every legal system to reconcile the conflict that arises when a seller purports to transfer title of goods that he does not own, or that are subject to an undisclosed security interest, to a person who buys them in good faith and without notice of the defect in title. The alternative means of resolving this conflict are usually stated in terms of a policy favouring security of ownership, as opposed to a policy that favours the safety of commercial transactions. Few, if indeed any, legal systems have committed themselves fully to the adoption of one or other solution. Between these extremes there lies a range of compromise solutions that depend on the nature of the goods, the persons involved, and the type of transaction." 2 Ontario Law Reform Commission, Report on Sale of Goods 283 (1979).[3]

The common law begins with the principle that a buyer acquires no better title to goods than the seller had, a principle embodied in the maxim *nemo dat quod non habet* (one cannot give what one does not have). To this principle the common law admits a number of exceptions, the most significant of which has been the doctrine of voidable title for cases of fraud, applied in the following case, *Mowrey v. Walsh,* infra.

The civil law, however, begins with a very different principle under which the good faith purchaser of goods is generally protected against the original owner, a principle expressed in the phrase *possession vaut titre* (possession is equivalent to title). Civil law systems have therefore no need for a special rule to protect good faith purchasers in cases of fraud. But most such systems make an exception for cases of theft, allowing the original owner of stolen goods to reclaim them from a good faith purchaser within a statutory period of, in French law, three years. Some of these systems, however, protect the good faith purchaser who has acquired stolen goods at a fair or at a market or from a merchant who deals in similar goods by requiring the purchaser to return the

3. For an economic analysis of the problem, see Weinberg, Sales Law, Economics, and the Negotiability of Goods, 9 J. Legal Stud. 569 (1980).

goods to the original owner only on reimbursement of the purchase price.

For a case in which a Florida court refused to follow its usual choice of law rules and apply the Louisiana version of the *possession vaut titre* rule, on the ground that the rule "contravenes a positive policy of the law of Florida," see Brown & Root, Inc. v. Ring Power Corp., 450 So.2d 1245 (Fla.App.1984).

(2) Market Overt. English law makes an exception to the principle of *nemo dat* by protecting the good faith purchaser of stolen goods where the goods "are sold in market overt according to the usage of the market." Sale of Goods Act § 22(1). A market overt is an open and public market. In Wheelwright v. Depeyster, 1 Johns. 471, 480 (N.Y. 1806), Kent rejected a contention based on the notion of a market overt: "I know of no usage or regulation within this State, no Saxon institution of *market-overt*, which controls or interferes with the application of the common law."

(3) Statute of Limitations. Because UCC 2–403(1) follows the maxim *nemo dat*, a good faith purchaser is usually remitted to the argument that the statute of limitations bars the original owner from reclaiming the goods. In O'Keeffe v. Snyder, 83 N.J. 478, 416 A.2d 862 (1980), cited by the New York Court of Appeals in the preceding opinion, the Supreme Court of New Jersey declined to follow the New York precedents. The case arose when, in 1976, the noted artist Georgia O'Keeffe sought to replevy from a Princeton art gallery three of her pictures that had allegedly been stolen in 1946 from a New York art gallery.

At the outset, the Supreme Court decided that O'Keeffe's claim was governed by the New Jersey statute of limitations, which required that an action for replevin be commenced within six years after the accrual of the cause of action. (O'Keeffe had contended her claim was governed by the New York statute of limitations, since it had been so interpreted that it did not begin to run until after refusal upon demand for the return of the goods.)

The Supreme Court then rejected the conclusion of the Appellate Division, based on New Jersey precedents, "that an action might have accrued more than six years before the date of suit if possession by the defendant or his predecessors satisfied the elements of adverse possession." Instead, it applied a discovery rule, under which "O'Keeffe's cause of action accrued when she first knew, or reasonably should have known through the exercise of due diligence, of the cause of action, including the identity of the possessor of the paintings.... The discovery rule shifts the emphasis from the conduct of the possessor to the conduct of the owner. The focus of the inquiry will no longer be whether the possessor has met the tests of adverse possession, but whether the owner has acted with due diligence in pursuing his or her personal property.... Under the doctrine of adverse possession, the burden is on the possessor to prove the elements of adverse possession.... Under the discovery rule, the burden is on the owner as the one seeking the benefit of the rule to establish facts that would justify deferring the beginning of the period of limitations."

The Supreme Court also concluded that subsequent transfer of the stolen property did not constitute "separate acts of conversion that would start the statute of limitations running anew.... The majority and better view is to permit tacking, the accumulation of consecutive periods of possession by parties in privity with each other." The court recognized, however, that "subsequent transfers ... may affect the degree of difficulty encountered by a diligent owner seeking to recover his goods. To that extent, subsequent transfers and their potential for frustrating diligence are relevant in applying the discovery rule."

A vigorous dissent argued that the majority opinion placed too heavy a burden on the original owner and that "by making it relatively more easy for the receiver or possessor of an artwork with a 'checkered background' to gain security and title than for the artist or true owner to reacquire it, it seems as though the Court surely will stimulate and legitimize art thievery." After remand by the Supreme Court but before trial, the case was settled.

Which is the better rule, New Jersey's or New York's? Is New Jersey's rule justified for stolen art by the circumstance that stolen art, unlike other kinds of stolen property, loses its value if altered or disguised and so may more easily be located by investigation? See Comment, 64 N.Y.U.L.Rev. 909 (1989). On the doctrine of adverse possession as applied to personal property, see Gerstenblith, The Adverse Possession of Personal Property, 37 Buffalo L.Rev. 119 (1988–89).

Problem 2. O owned cotton worth $100,000. A fraudulently induced O to sell it to him. A sold it to P, who paid A $100,000 for it, not suspecting the fraud. O sues P to replevy the cotton.

(a) What result? See UCC 2–403; Mowrey v. Walsh, infra. (A consideration of the effect of UCC 2–702 is best postponed until Chapter 9). What result if O sues P in conversion? Would it make any difference if P is in business? In the cotton business? See UCC 1–201(19), 2–103(1)(b), 2–104(1); Citizens Bank of Clovis v. Runyan, 109 N.M. 672, 789 P.2d 620 (1990) (whether buyer was merchant and therefore subject to merchant's standard of good faith was question of fact and documents detailing buyer's past dealings would be relevant). Would it make any difference if P had notice of the fraud before taking delivery of the cotton? (Compare UCC 2–403(1) with UCC 1–201(20), which requires that a purchaser of a note take possession in order to be a holder.)

(b) What result if P had paid A only $60,000? See Hollis v. Chamberlin, 243 Ark. 201, 419 S.W.2d 116 (1967) (buyer paid $500 for camper unit and did not know seller but "did know that the camper unit looked new and was worth at least $1,000 ... and ... apparently asked no questions concerning [seller's] title"); Liles Brothers & Son v. Wright, 638 S.W.2d 383 (Tenn.1982) (operator of septic tank service, who knew of thefts of equipment in his area, paid $11,000 for new backhoe worth about $20,000, took blank bill of sale, and did not receive usual warranty papers from seller who offered him "a good deal on *any* kind of equipment that he wanted"); cf. Cooper v. Pacific Automobile Insurance Co., 95 Nev. 798, 603 P.2d 281 (1979) (owner of bar bought used Cadillac in sale that "was for cash; was consummated in the nighttime and on a weekend; and, took place at a bar," and buyer "made no effort to verify any of the information given to him"). Would it make any difference if P had promised to pay $100,000, but has not yet paid anything? See UCC 1–201(44).

(c) What result if P, instead of buying the cotton from A, had taken it as security for a loan that P had extended to A six months earlier? See UCC 1–201(32), (33), (44).

(d) What result if P had bought the cotton at a sheriff's execution sale on levy by a judgment creditor? See UCC 1–201(32), (33); Mazer v. Williams Brothers Co., 461 Pa. 587, 337 A.2d 559 (1975).

(e) What result if A had left O in possession of the cotton, and P had then paid A $100,000 for the cotton? (It would be P who would seek to replevy the cotton from O in this situation.) See Ceres Inc. v. ACLI Metal & Ore Co., 451 F.Supp. 921 (N.D.Ill.1978).

MOWREY v. WALSH
Supreme Court of New York, 1828.
8 Cowen 238.

Trover for cotton cloths; tried at the Washington Circuit, November 14th, 1826, before Walworth, C. Judge.

The case at the trial was briefly this: On the 16th of January, 1826, a person calling himself Samuel Stevens, came to the plaintiff's factory in Easton, Washington county, and presented a forged paper, purporting to be signed by Isaac Bishop, mentioning Stevens as a person who wished to purchase cotton goods, as one who might safely be trusted, and assuming to pay whatever amount the plaintiffs might supply him with. The plaintiffs' clerk sold to Stevens the cotton cloths in question, amounting to 172 dollars and 38 cents; and gave him a bill of the goods, which (goods) he took to Lansingburgh the next day, and sold to the defendant, for considerable less than the prices charged at the factory. The defendant's clerk testified, however, that the price was a fair one. The plaintiffs afterwards demanded the goods of the defendant, who refused to surrender them; and the present action was brought.

The judge charged that the goods were obtained fraudulently, but not feloniously; and, that if the defendant purchased them *bona fide,* and without notice of the fraud, (a matter which he left to the jury upon the evidence,) the plaintiffs could not recover.

Verdict for the defendant.

A motion was now made, in behalf of the plaintiffs, for a new trial.

Savage, Ch. J. It seemed to be conceded upon the argument that if the goods were taken feloniously, no title passed from the vendors; and they might pursue and take their goods wherever found. Such is the law in England, unless the stolen goods are sold fairly in market overt.[4] (2 Bl.Com. 449.) And as we have, in this state, no such market, (1 John. 471,) sales here can have no other effect than mere private sales in England. It follows that, in this state, any sale of stolen goods does not divest the title of the owner.

It is proper, therefore, to inquire whether the goods in question were feloniously taken.

Larceny is defined, by East, to be the wrongful, or fraudulent taking or carrying away by any person, of the mere personal goods of another, from any place, with a felonious intent to convert them to his (the taker's) own use, and make them his own property, without the consent of the owner. (2 East's P.C. 553.) It is, therefore, important, in cases of delivery of possession by the owner, to inquire whether he intended to part with the possession or with the property; for if the latter, by whatever fraudulent means he was induced to give the credit, it cannot be felony. (2 East's P.C. 668.) ...

The delivery of the goods in question to Stevens was clearly intended as an absolute sale. It was not, therefore, a case of larceny.

The jury have found that the goods were fairly purchased by the defendant of Stevens, without any notice of the fraud; and in my opinion the testimony fully warrants their finding.

The question then arises, upon a case where the goods are obtained by fraud from the true owner, and fairly purchased of, and the price paid to the fraudulent vendee, without notice, by a stranger, which is to sustain the loss, the owner or the stranger? ...

Parker v. Patrick, (5 T.R. 175), seems to be in point for the defendant. In that case, goods had been fraudulently obtained from the defendant, and pawned, for a valuable consideration, and without notice, to the plaintiff. After conviction of the offender, the defendant obtained possession of his goods, but by what means does not appear. It was contended that the plaintiff, the innocent pawnee, could not recover; as he derived title through a fraud, and was like a person deriving title from a felon. But Lord Kenyon thought the cases distinguishable; and the plaintiff had a verdict. A motion to set aside this verdict was refused; the court saying that the statute of 21 H. 8 ch. 21, did not extend to the case of goods obtained by fraud, but only to a felonious taking of them. By that statute, the owner of stolen goods is entitled to restitution, on conviction of the felon. But as that statute did not apply to a fraudulent obtaining of goods, the owner was not

---

4. See Note 2, p. 29 supra. [Eds.]

entitled to restitution. The question, then, was purely at common law; and the innocent pawnee was allowed to recover against the owner, whose goods had been obtained from him by fraud. According to that decision, had the plaintiffs in this case succeeded in getting their goods in any other way than by voluntary delivery from the defendant, he would be entitled to recover against them. The same principle was adopted by this court in M'Carty v. Vickery, (12 John. 348,) where it was decided, that after a delivery of goods sold, the vendor cannot bring trespass, although the sale was procured by fraud. The court say the property was changed.

Hollingsworth v. Napier, (3 Caines, 182,) was like Parker v. Patrick. The defendant had sold the cotton to Kinworthy, for cash payable on delivery. The defendant, in fact, delivered it by giving an order on the storekeeper without receiving payment. Kinworthy sold it *bona fide* to the plaintiff, though there were some suspicious circumstances. The plaintiff took possession, and the defendant afterwards took and sold it. The plaintiff recovered a verdict; and this court refused to set it aside. Kinworthy's purchase was palpably fraudulent, and so considered by the court.

The plaintiff's counsel relies on a case lately tried in the English common pleas: Tamplin v. Addy, sheriff of Warwickshire. In that case, goods were fraudulently purchased of the plaintiffs by one Staunton. After the delivery of the goods to Staunton, they were levied on by the defendant under an execution, and sold. Best, Ch. J., does indeed lay down the broad proposition, that if the goods were obtained by fraud, the right remained in the original owner, no matter into whose hands they found their way. That proposition was advanced at *nisi prius;* but is certainly at variance with settled principles of law.

It is, no doubt, true, if confined to the parties in the fraud. But it does not extend to an innocent purchaser. Perhaps, too, it may be correct in the particular case. The judgment creditor had not advanced money upon these goods, and his loss placed him in no worse situation than he was in before the fraud. But surely, in point of equity, there is a great difference between the fraudulent purchaser and an innocent one. The case of Noble v. Adams, (7 Taunt. 59,) decides, that between the parties, a fraudulent purchase gives no title; but the case of Parker v. Patrick was admitted to be good law by the counsel for the party defrauded.

The case of Bristol v. Wilsmore, (1 B. & C. 514,) was not cited on the argument; but it is in point to shew the true principle which supports the *nisi prius* decision of Ch. J. Best. The principle is this: that the fraudulent purchaser having no title, and the sheriff having no power to seize and sell any thing but the title of such purchaser, the sheriff's sale did not divest the title of the true owner, the defendant in the execution having no right or title to be sold. (And see Van Cleef v. Fleet, 15 John. 147.)

On the whole, therefore, I am of opinion that the innocent purchaser for valuable consideration must be protected; and the motion for a new trial must be denied.

New trial denied.

Notes

(1) **"Merchants" and "Good Faith."** In the opinion in *Mowrey v. Walsh,* the trial judge is said to have charged "that if the defendant purchased them bona fide, and without notice of the fraud, ... the plaintiffs could not recover." Assuming that the defendant dealt in cotton goods, would the plaintiff have had grounds for objection to this charge under the Code? See UCC 2–103(1)(b), 2–104(1). As to who is a merchant, see Dolan, The Merchant Class of Article 2: Farmers, Doctors, and Others, 1977 Wash.U.L.Q. 1; McDonnell, Purposive Interpretation of the Uniform Commercial Code: Some Implications for Jurisprudence, 126 U.Pa.L.Rev. 795, 801–09 (1978); Newell, The Merchant of Article 2, 7 Valparaiso L.Rev. 307 (1973).

(2) **Voidable Title.** The seminal case in this area is the English case of *Parker v. Patrick,* decided in 1793 and cited and followed in *Mowrey v. Walsh.*[5] In its one sentence per curiam opinion the court gave only the reason mentioned by the New York court for distinguishing fraud and theft—the existence of a statute as to the latter. By the time of White v. Garden, 10 Common Bench, 919, 138 Eng.Rep. 364 (Q.B.1851), however, doctrine had developed to the point that the court could write that where fraud was involved, "the transaction is not absolutely void, except at the option of the seller; that he may elect to treat it as a contract, and he must do the contrary before the buyer has acted as if it were such, and re-sold the goods to a third party."

Professor Gilmore has summarized the historical development: "The initial common law position was that equities of ownership are to be protected at all costs: an owner may never be deprived of his property rights without his consent. That worked well enough against a background of local distribution where seller and buyer met face to face and exchanged goods for cash. But as the marketplace became first regional and then national, a recurrent situation came to be the misappropriation of goods by a faithless agent in fraud of his principal. Classical theory required that the principal be protected and that the risks of agency distribution be cast on the purchaser. The market demanded otherwise.

"The first significant breach in common law property theory was the protection of purchasers from such commercial agents. The reform was carried out through so-called Factor's Acts, which were widely enacted in the early part of the 19th century. Under these Acts any

---

5. For a discussion of *Mowrey v. Walsh* in its historical context, see Weinberg, Markets Overt, Voidable Titles, and Feck- less Agents: Judges and Efficiency in the Antebellum Doctrine of Good Faith Purchase, 56 Tul.L.Rev. 1, 23–32 (1981).

person who entrusted goods to a factor—or agent—for sale took the risk of the factor's selling them beyond his authority; anyone buying from a factor in good faith, relying on his possession of the goods, and without notice of limitations on his authority, took good title against the true owner.　In time the Acts were expanded to protect people, i.e., banks, who took goods from a factor as security for loans made to the factor to be used in operating the factor's own business.　The Factor's Acts, as much in derogation of the common law as it is possible for a statute to be, were restrictively construed and consequently turned out to be considerably less than the full grant of mercantile liberty which they had first appeared to be.　Other developments in the law gradually took the pressure off the Factor's Acts, which came to be confined to the narrow area of sales through commission merchants, mostly in agricultural produce markets.

"Even while they were cutting the heart out of the Factor's Acts, the courts were finding new ways to shift distribution risks.　Their happiest discovery was the concept of 'voidable title'—a vague idea, never defined and perhaps incapable of definition, whose greatest virtue, as a principle of growth, may well have been its shapeless imprecision of outline.　The polar extremes of theory were these: if *B* buys goods from *A,* he gets *A* 's title and can transfer it to any subsequent purchaser; if *B* steals goods from *A,* he gets no title and can transfer none to any subsequent purchaser, no matter how clear the purchaser's good faith.　'Voidable title' in *B* came in as an intermediate term between the two extremes: if *B* gets possession of *A* 's goods by fraud, even though he has no right to retain them against *A,* he does have the power to transfer title to a good faith purchaser.

"The ingenious distinction between 'no title' in *B* (therefore true owner prevails over good faith purchaser) and 'voidable title' in *B* (therefore true owner loses to good faith purchaser) made it possible to throw the risk on the true owner in the typical commercial situation while protecting him in the noncommercial one.　Since the law purported to be a deduction from basic premises, logic prevailed in some details to the detriment of mercantile need, but on the whole voidable title proved a useful touchstone.

"The contrasting treatment given to sales on credit and sales for cash shows the inarticulate development of the commercial principle. When goods are delivered on credit, the seller becomes merely a creditor for the price: on default he has no right against the goods. But when the delivery is induced by buyer's fraud—buyer being unable to pay or having no intention of paying—the seller, if he acts promptly after discovering the facts, may replevy from the buyer or reclaim from buyer's trustee in bankruptcy.　The seller may not, however, move against purchasers from the buyer, and the term 'purchaser' includes lenders who have made advances on the security of the goods.　By his fraudulent acquisition the buyer has obtained voidable title and purchasers from him are protected."　Gilmore, The Commercial Doctrine of Good Faith Purchase, 63 Yale L.J. 1057, 1057–60 (1954).

"The ... rule rests on the premise that it is cheaper for an owner to take precautions against giving title to a defrauder than it is for a purchaser to research the chain of title to every good he purchases. Before the original owner transfers title to someone who, in turn, will become a seller in a transaction of purchase, the original owner has an opportunity to take precautions against fraud, bad credit, and related commercial problems. The buyer may be lying to the owner, or may be using a bad check to pay for the goods. These are things an owner can, at least in theory, take precautions against. If, on the other hand, the person who later becomes a seller breaks into an owner's house and steals the good, or sinks a well and takes oil from the owner's oil and gas estate, the owner cannot take precautions as easily." Welch v. Cayton, 183 W.Va. 252, 395 S.E.2d 496, 501 (1990) (Neely, J.).

Suppose that the defrauded owner discovers the fraud after the fraudulent buyer has disappeared with the goods. How can the owner avoid the passage of title so as to prevail over a subsequent good faith purchaser? Cases on this point are rare. See Car and Universal Finance Co. v. Caldwell, [1965] 1 Q.B. 525.[6]

Problem 3. O owned cotton worth $100,000. A fraudulently induced O to sell it to him for $100,000 payable in 10 days, having obtained 10 days credit by falsely representing that he was B, a responsible dealer in cotton. A sold the cotton to P, who paid A $100,000 for it, not suspecting the fraud. A did not pay for the cotton at the end of 10 days, and O sues P to replevy it. What result? See UCC 2–403; Cundy v. Lindsay, infra.

Problem 4. O owned cotton worth $100,000. A fraudulently induced O to sell it to him by giving O his check in that amount drawn

6. That case was singled out for criticism in both the English and Ontario studies discussed in Note 4, p. 50 infra. Here is the Ontario view. "Under existing law, a rogue who has a 'voidable' title can transfer good title to a *bona fide* third party purchaser for value, unless the sale is avoided prior to the disposition of the goods to the third party. In the *Caldwell* case, the Court held that, where the fraudulent buyer has disappeared, a substitutional form of notice, such as notification of the police or Automobile Association, is sufficient to rescind the sale. The Law Reform Committee drew attention to the hardship that this decision may cause to third parties, and recommended that the rule should be changed to require notice of rescission to the rogue. It is not easy to see how this recommendation will relieve the hardship to the third party since, *ex hypothesi*, he will not know of the rescission. The Committee thought the third party would be sufficiently protected in the great majority of cases, since it will usually be impractical for the original owner to communicate with the rogue. It seems curious that the third party's position should depend on the accessibility of the rogue.

"It appears to us that the Committee failed to come to grips with a more fundamental question: namely, whether it should be necessary that rescission be accompanied by the recovery of possession, and whether, in the meantime, the buyer should retain his power to transfer good title.... [We recommend a] provision to the effect that a purported avoidance of such a contract shall not affect the position of a third party who has purchased the goods in good faith, unless the goods are recovered by the owner before they are delivered to the third party by the person in possession of the goods." 2 Ontario Law Reform Commission, Report on Sale of Goods 287–88 (1979).

on a bank in which he had no account. A sold the cotton to P, who paid A $100,000 for it, not suspecting the fraud. The check was dishonored, and O sues to replevy the cotton. What result? Would it make a difference if O had noted on his check, "This is a cash sale"? See UCC 2–403.

CUNDY v. LINDSAY, 1878 L.R. 3 A.C. 459 (H.L.). Alfred Blenkarn hired a room on the top floor of a house down the street from the firm of W. Blenkiron & Son. He wrote letters appearing to come from "Blenkiron & Co." but giving his address down the street, ordering linen handkerchiefs on credit from Lindsay & Co. Lindsay, who knew of the respectability of W. Blenkiron & Sons, but not the address, sent handkerchiefs to "Blenkiron & Co." at Blenkarn's address. Blenkarn sold some of them to Cundy, a good faith purchaser, who resold them in the course of their business. Blenkarn failed to pay Lindsay and was ultimately prosecuted and convicted. Lindsay then sued Cundy in conversion. From a judgment for Lindsay, Cundy appealed.

"THE LORD CHANCELLOR (LORD *Cairns*): ... Now, my Lords, there are two observations bearing upon the solution of that question which I desire to make. In the first place, if the property in the goods in question passed, it could only pass by way of contract.... The second observation is this, ... the whole history of the whole transaction lies upon paper. The principal parties concerned, the Respondents and *Blenkarn,* never came in contact personally—everything that was done was done by writing. What has to be judged of, and what the jury in the present case had to judge of, was merely the conclusion to be derived from that writing, as applied to the admitted facts of the case.

"Now, my Lords, discharging that duty and answering that inquiry, what the jurors have found ... that by the form of the signatures to the letters which were written by *Blenkarn,* by the mode in which his letters and his applications to the Respondents were made out, and by the way in which he left uncorrected the mode and form in which, in turn, he was addressed by the Respondents; that by all those means he led, and intended to lead, the Respondents to believe, and they did believe, that the person with whom they were communicating was not *Blenkarn,* the dishonest and irresponsible man, but was a well known and solvent house of *Blenkiron & Co.,* doing business in the same street.... Now, my Lords, stating the matter shortly in that way, I ask the question, how is it possible to imagine that in that state of things any contract could have arisen between the Respondents and *Blenkarn,* the dishonest man? Of him they knew nothing, and of him they never thought. With him they never intended to deal. Their minds never, even for an instant of time rested upon him, and as between him and them there was no *consensus* of mind which could lead to any agreement or any contract whatever. As between him and them there was merely the one side to a contract, where, in order to produce a contract, two sides would be required. With the firm of *Blenkiron & Co.* of course there was no contract, for as to them the matter was entirely unknown, and therefore the pretence of a contract was a failure."

[Affirmed.]

Notes

(1) **Imposters.** Four decades after *Cundy v. Lindsay,* the New York Court of Appeals heard a very similar case, Phelps v. McQuade, 220 N.Y. 232, 115 N.E. 441 (1917). Walter J. Gynne falsely represented to Phelps that he was Baldwin J. Gwynne, a man of financial responsibility, and Phelps delivered jewelry to Walter on credit, which Walter sold to McQuade. When the fraud was discovered, Phelps sued McQuade in replevin to recover the jewelry. The Court of Appeals affirmed a judgment for McQuade. It distinguished *Cundy v. Lindsay* on the ground that it involved impersonation by mail rather than face to face impersonation. "The fact that the vendor deals with the person personally rather than by letter is immaterial, except in so far as it bears upon the question of intent. Where the transaction is a personal one, the seller intends to transfer title to a person of credit, and he supposes the one standing before him to be that person. He is deceived. But in spite of that fact his primary intention is to sell his goods to the person with whom he negotiates. Where the transaction is by letter the vendor intends to deal with the person whose name is signed to the letter. He knows no one else. He supposes he is dealing with no one else. And while in both cases other facts may be shown that would alter the rule, yet in their absence, in the first, title passes; in the second, it does not." Does UCC 2–403(1)(a) make an exception for impersonation by mail?[7] Is it as explicit in this regard as UCC 3–404(a)? Is the difference between these two sections significant?

(2) **The "Cash Sale" Doctrine.** UCC 2–403(1)(b) and (c) are intended to stamp out the "cash sale" doctrine, exemplified by Young v. Harris–Cortner Co., 152 Tenn. 15, 268 S.W. 125 (1924). Young, a farmer, sold cotton to McNamee, a middleman, who resold to Harris–Cortner, cotton merchants. McNamee paid by a check drawn on insufficient funds, and when it was dishonored because of lack of funds, Young sued Harris–Cortner to replevy the cotton. Young prevailed. "Looking to the intention of the parties, which is the governing principle, we are satisfied that Young purposed to transfer title to the cotton only upon receiving cash therefor.... We are therefore of the opinion that title to said ten bales of cotton never passed from Young to

---

7. In the study discussed in Note 4, p. 50 infra, the Ontario Law Reform Commission recommended "a provision stating that a purchaser shall be deemed to have a voidable title notwithstanding that the transferor was deceived as to the identity of the purchaser or the presence of some other mistake affecting the validity of the contract of sale." 2 Ontario Law Reform Commission, Report on Sale of Goods 287 (1979).

McNamee.... A farmer brings his cotton, tobacco, or wheat to town for sale and sells same, and, as a general rule, is paid by check, although all of such sales are treated as cash transactions. If, in such a case, the purchaser can immediately resell to an innocent party and convey good title, it would follow that vendors would refuse to accept checks and would require the actual money, which would result in great inconvenience and risk to merchants engaged in buying such produce since it would require them to keep on hand large sums of actual cash." Does the "cash sale" doctrine seem more in keeping with an agricultural or an industrial economy? (The "cash sale" is discussed further in Chapter 9.)

Problem 5. O owned cotton worth $100,000. O placed it in storage with A, who both stores cotton and buys and sells it. A wrongfully sold the cotton to P, who did not suspect A's wrongdoing, for $100,000. O sues P to replevy the cotton.

(a) What result? Does it make a difference whether O knows that A buys and sells cotton? See UCC 2–403, 1–201(9); Porter v. Wertz, infra; Simonds–Shields–Theis Grain Co. v. Far–Mar–Co., 575 F.Supp. 290 (W.D.Mo.1983) (owner entrusted soybeans to independent trucker who also sold soybeans); Canterra Petroleum, Inc. v. Western Drilling & Mining Supply, 418 N.W.2d 267 (N.D.1987) (whether a party is a "merchant" is a question of fact).

(b) What result if P had promised to pay $100,000, but has not yet paid it when O claims the cotton?

(c) What result if P, instead of buying the cotton from A, had taken it as security for a loan that P had extended to A six months earlier? See In re Sitkin Smelting & Refining, Inc., 639 F.2d 1213 (5th Cir.1981). Compare Problem 2(c), supra.

(d) What result if A had wrongfully delivered the cotton to B, who is in the cotton business, as security for a loan that B had extended to A six months earlier and B had sold the cotton to P, who suspected nothing, for $100,000. See Leary & Sperling, The Outer Limits of Entrusting, 35 Ark.L.Rev. 50, 55–60, 66–71 (1981). Cf. Canterra Petroleum, Inc. v. Western Drilling & Mining Supply, supra (policy underlying UCC 2–403(2) "supports application of the entrustment doctrine to a situation where employees of the entrustee transfer the entrusted goods to their sham corporation, which in turn sells the goods to a buyer in ordinary course of business").

PORTER v. WERTZ

New York Supreme Court, Appellate Division, First Department, 1979.
68 A.D.2d 141, 416 N.Y.S.2d 254.

BIRNS, JUSTICE: Plaintiffs-appellants, Samuel Porter and Express Packaging, Inc. (Porter's corporation), owners of a Maurice Utrillo painting entitled "Chateau de Lion-sur-Mer", seek in this action to recover possession of the painting or the value thereof from defendants, participants in a series of transactions which resulted in the shipment of the painting out of the country. The painting is now in Venezuela.

Defendants-respondents Richard Feigen Gallery, Inc., Richard L. Feigen & Co., Inc. and Richard L. Feigen, hereinafter collectively referred to as Feigen, were in the business of buying and selling paintings, drawings and sculpture.

The amended answer to the complaint asserted, *inter alia,* affirmative defenses of statutory estoppel (UCC, § 2–403) and equitable estoppel.[1] The trial court, after a bench trial, found statutory estoppel inapplicable but sustained the defense of equitable estoppel and dismissed the complaint.

On this appeal, we will consider whether those defenses, or either of them, bar recovery against Feigen. We hold neither prevents recovery.[2]

Porter, the owner of a collection of art works, bought the Utrillo in 1969. During 1972 and 1973 he had a number of art transactions with one Harold Von Maker who used, among other names, that of Peter Wertz.[3] One of the transactions was the sale by Porter to Von Maker in the spring of 1973 of a painting by Childe Hassam for $150,000, financed with a $50,000 deposit and 10 notes for $10,000 each. At about that time, Von Maker expressed an interest in the Utrillo. Porter permitted him to have it temporarily with the understanding that Von Maker would hang it in his (Von Maker's) home,[4] pending

1. The defense of equitable estoppel was not contained in the original answer. At the close of the trial, Feigen moved to amend the answer to include that defense. We are not at all certain that amendment of the pleading should have been allowed at that point. In any event, as the defense was raised, we will consider it.

2. We note that the appeal is from the trial court's determination that equitable estoppel constitutes a bar to the action. However, because the enactment of statutory estoppel (UCC, § 2–403) was intended to embrace prior uniform statutory provisions and case law thereunder (so as "to continue unimpaired all rights acquired under the law of agency or of apparent agency or ownership or other estoppel"), and to state a unified and simplified policy on good faith purchase of goods (see Practice Commentary, Alfred A. Berger and William J. O'Connor, Jr., McKinney's Cons.Laws of N.Y., Book 62½, p. 395), we find it necessary to enter into some discussion of section 2–403 of the Uniform Commercial Code.

3. As will be seen, Peter Wertz was a real person, at least an acquaintance of Von Maker; who permitted Von Maker to use his name. Von Maker's true name was Harold Maker, presumably he was born in New Jersey. Apparently Maker added the prefix "Von" to his name to indicate nobility of birth.

4. It is questioned as to where Porter believed Von Maker was living at the time. Respondents claim Porter knew only that Von Maker had a townhouse in Manhattan, whereas Porter testified he was aware Von Maker had two residences, one of them being in Westchester County. There

Von Maker's decision whether to buy the painting. On a visit to Von Maker's home in Westchester in May 1973, Porter saw the painting hanging there. In June 1973, lacking a decision from Von Maker, Porter sought its return, but was unable to reach Von Maker.

The first note in connection with Von Maker's purchase of the Childe Hassam, due early July 1973, was returned dishonored, as were the balance of the notes. Porter commenced an investigation and found that he had not been dealing with Peter Wertz—but with another man named Von Maker. Bishop reports, dated July 10 and July 17, 1973, disclosed that Von Maker was subject to judgments, that he had been sued many times, that he had an arrest record for possession of obscene literature, and for "false pretenses", as well as for "theft of checks", and had been convicted, among other crimes, of transmitting a forged cable in connection with a scheme to defraud the Chase Manhattan Bank and had been placed on probation for three years. Porter notified the FBI about his business transactions concerning the notes. He did not report that Von Maker had defrauded him of any painting, for, as will be shown, Porter did not know at this time that Von Maker had disposed of the Utrillo.

Porter did, however, have his attorney communicate with Von Maker's attorney. As a result, on August 13, 1973, a detailed agreement, drawn by the attorneys for Porter and Von Maker, the latter still using the name Peter Wertz, was executed. Under this agreement the obligations of Von Maker to Porter concerning several paintings delivered by Porter to Von Maker (one of which was the Utrillo) were covered. In paragraph 11, Von Maker acknowledged that he had received the Utrillo from Porter together with a certain book [5] on Utrillo, that both "belong to (Porter)", that the painting was on consignment with a client of Von Maker's, that within 90 days Von Maker would either return the painting and book or pay $30,000 therefor, and that other than the option to purchase within said 90–day period, Von Maker had "no claim whatsoever to the Utrillo painting or Book."

Paragraph 13 provided that in the event Von Maker failed to meet the obligations under paragraph 11, i.e., return the Utrillo and book within 90 days or pay for them, Porter would immediately be entitled to obtain possession of a painting by Cranach held in escrow by Von Maker's attorney, and have the right to sell that painting, apply the proceeds to the amount owing by Von Maker under paragraph 11, and Von Maker would pay any deficiency. Paragraph 13 provided further that "[t]he above is in addition to all [Porter's] other rights and remedies which [Porter] expressly reserved to enforce the performance of [Von Maker's] obligations under this Agreement."

We note that the agreement did not state that receipt of the Cranach by Porter would be in full satisfaction of Porter's claim to the

is no support in the record for the trial court's finding that the painting was to be hung only in the Manhattan townhouse.

5. The book, entitled "Petrides on Utrillo", was purchased by Porter in 1971 in Paris for the sum of $200.00.

Utrillo and book. Title to the Utrillo and book remained in Porter, absent any payment by Von Maker of the agreed purchase price of $30,000. Indeed, no payment for the Utrillo was ever made by Von Maker.

At the very time that Von Maker was deceitfully assuring Porter he would return the Utrillo and book or pay $30,000, Von Maker had already disposed of this painting by using the real Peter Wertz to effect its sale for $20,000 to Feigen. Von Maker, utilizing Sloan and Lipinsky, persons in the art world, had made the availability of the Utrillo known to Feigen. When Wertz, at Von Maker's direction, appeared at the Feigen gallery with the Utrillo, he was met by Feigen's employee, Mrs. Drew–Bear. She found a buyer for the Utrillo in defendant Brenner. In effecting its transfer to him, Feigen made a commission. Through a sale by Brenner the painting is now in Venezuela, S.A.

We agree with the conclusion of the trial court that statutory estoppel does not bar recovery.

The provisions of statutory estoppel are found in section 2–403 of the Uniform Commercial Code. Subsection 2 thereof provides that "any entrusting of possession of goods to a merchant who deals in goods of that kind gives him power to transfer all rights of the entruster to a buyer in the ordinary course of business." Uniform Commercial Code, section 1–201, subdivision 9, defines a "buyer in [the] ordinary course of business" as "a person who in good faith and without knowledge that the sale to him is in violation of the ownership rights or security interest of a third party in the goods buys in ordinary course from a person in the business of selling goods of that kind. . . ."

In order to determine whether the defense of statutory estoppel is available to Feigen, we must begin by ascertaining whether Feigen fits the definition of "[a] buyer in [the] ordinary course of business." (UCC, § 1–201[9].) Feigen does not fit that definition, for two reasons. First, Wertz, from whom Feigen bought the Utrillo, was not an art dealer—he was not "a person in the business of selling goods of that kind." (UCC, § 1–201[9].) If anything, he was a delicatessen employee.[6] Wertz never held himself out as a dealer. Although Feigen testified at trial that before he (Feigen) purchased the Utrillo from Wertz, Sloan, who introduced Wertz to Feigen told him (Feigen) that Wertz was an art dealer, this testimony was questionable. It conflicted with Feigen's testimony at his examination before trial where he stated he did not recall whether Sloan said that to him.[7] Second, Feigen was not "a person . . .

---

6. Wertz is described as a seller of caviar and other luxury food items (because of his association with a Madison Avenue gourmet grocery) and over whom the Trial Term observed, Von Maker "cast his hypnotic spell . . . and usurped his name, his signature and his sacred honor."

7. Feigen's explanation for his changed version was that after his examination before trial and before the trial, his memory was "jogged" by Lipinsky, who had introduced Sloan to Feigen.

In connection with Feigen's claim that Wertz was a dealer, it is observed that on a previous appeal, Porter v. Wertz, et al., defendants, and Richard Feigen Gallery, Inc., et al., appellants, 56 A.D.2d 570, 392 N.Y.S.2d 10, this court unanimously affirmed an order of Special Term denying

in good faith" (UCC, § 1–201[9]) in the transaction with Wertz. Uniform Commercial Code, section 2–103, subdivision (1)(b), defines "good faith" in the case of a merchant as "honesty in fact and the observance of reasonable commercial standards of fair dealing in the trade." Although this definition by its terms embraces the "reasonable commercial standards of fair dealing in the trade", it should not—and cannot—be interpreted to permit, countenance or condone commercial standards of sharp trade practice or indifference as to the "provenance", i.e., history of ownership or the right to possess or sell an object d'art, such as is present in the case before us.

We note that neither Ms. Drew–Bear nor her employer Feigen made any investigation to determine the status of Wertz, i.e., whether he was an art merchant, "a person in the business of selling goods of that kind." (UCC, § 1–201[9].) Had Ms. Drew–Bear done so much as call either of the telephone numbers Wertz had left, she would have learned that Wertz was employed by a delicatessen and was not an art dealer. Nor did Ms. Drew–Bear or Feigen make any effort to verify whether Wertz was the owner or authorized by the owner to sell the painting he was offering. Ms. Drew–Bear had available to her the Petrides volume on Utrillo which included "Chateau de Lion-sur-Mer" in its catalogue of the master's work.[8] Although this knowledge alone might not have been enough to put Feigen on notice that Wertz was not the true owner at the time of the transaction, it could have raised a doubt as to Wertz's right of possession, calling for further verification before the purchase by Feigen was consummated. Thus, it appears that statutory estoppel provided by Uniform Commercial Code, section 2–403(2), was not, as Trial Term correctly concluded, available as a defense to Feigen.

We disagree with the conclusion of the trial court that the defense of equitable estoppel (see Zendman v. Harry Winston, Inc., 305 N.Y. 180, 111 N.E.2d 871) raised by Feigen bars recovery.

We pause to observe that although one may not be a buyer in the ordinary course of business as defined in the Uniform Commercial Code, he may be a good-faith purchaser for value and enjoy the protection of pre-Code estoppel (see Tumber v. Automation Design & Mfg. Corp., 130 N.J.Super. 5, 13, 324 A.2d 602, 616; UCC, § 1–103). We now reach the question whether the defense of equitable estoppel has been established here.

In general terms:

> Equitable estoppel or estoppel in pais is the principle by
> which a party is absolutely precluded, both at law and in

appellants' motion for summary judgment in that there was an issue of fact as to whether Wertz was a dealer or a collector. If a dealer, appellants claimed, as they do now, the applicability of UCC, § 2–403(2).

8. Page 32 of that book clearly contained a reference to the fact that that painting, at least at the time of publication of the book in 1969, was in the collection of Mrs. Donald D. King of New York, supposedly the party from whom Porter obtained it.

equity, from denying, or asserting the contrary of, any material fact which, by his words or conduct, affirmative or negative, intentionally or through culpable negligence, he has induced another, who was excusably ignorant of the true facts and who had a right to rely upon such words or conduct, to believe and act upon them thereby, as a consequence reasonably to be anticipated, changing his position in such a way that he would suffer injury if such denial or contrary assertion were allowed. An estoppel in pais can arise only when a person, either by his declarations or conduct, has induced another person to act in a particular manner. The doctrine prohibits a person, upon principles of honesty and fair and open dealing, from asserting rights the enforcement of which would, through his omissions or commissions, work fraud and injustice. (21 N.Y.Jur., Estoppel, § 15 [citing cases].)

As the Court of Appeals reiterated in Zendman v. Harry Winston, Inc., supra, an " 'owner may be estopped from setting up his own title and the lack of title in the vendor as against a *bona fide* purchaser for value where the owner has clothed the vendor with possession and other indicia of title (46 Am.Jur., Sales, § 463).' " Indeed, "[t]he rightful owner may be estopped by his own acts from asserting his title. If he has invested another with the usual evidence of title, or an apparent authority to dispose of it, he will not be allowed to make claim against an innocent purchaser dealing on the faith of such apparent ownership (Smith v. Clews, 114 N.Y. 190, 194, 21 N.E. 160, 161)."

In Zendman v. Harry Winston, Inc., supra, a diamond merchant in New York City sent a ring to Brand, Inc., a corporation which conducted auctions on the boardwalk in Atlantic City, New Jersey, with a memorandum reciting that the ring was for examination only and that title was not to pass until the auctioneer had made his selection, and had notified the sender of his agreement to pay the indicated price and the sender had indicated acceptance thereof by issuing a bill of sale. The ring was placed in a public show window at the auctioneer's place of business, remaining there for more than a month, before being sold to the plaintiff at a public auction. Under circumstances where it was demonstrated that the defendant had permitted other pieces of jewelry it owned to be exhibited and sold by the auctioneer, it was held that the defendant by his conduct was estopped from recovering the ring from the plaintiff.

In the case at bar, Porter's conduct was not blameworthy. When the first promissory note was dishonored, he retained Bishop's investigative service and informed the FBI of the financial transactions concerning the series of notes. His attorney obtained a comprehensive agreement covering several paintings, within which was the assurance (now proven false) by Von Maker that he still controlled the Utrillo. Although Porter had permitted Von Maker to possess the painting, he conferred upon Von Maker no other indicia of ownership. Possession without more is insufficient to create an estoppel (Zendman v. Harry Winston, Inc., supra, 305 N.Y. at 186–187, 111 N.E.2d 874–875).

We find that the prior art transactions between Porter and Von Maker justified the conclusion of the trial court that Porter knew that Von Maker was a dealer in art. Nevertheless, the testimony remains uncontradicted, that the Utrillo was not consigned to Von Maker for business purposes, but rather for display only in Von Maker's home (compare Zendman v. Harry Winston, Inc., supra). In these circumstances, it cannot be said that Porter's conduct in any way contributed to the deception practiced on Feigen by Von Maker and Wertz.

Finally, we must examine again the position of Feigen to determine whether Feigen was a purchaser in good faith.

In purchasing the Utrillo, Feigen did not rely on any indicia of ownership in Von Maker. Feigen dealt with Wertz, who did not have the legal right to possession of the painting. Even were we to consider Wertz as the agent of Von Maker or merge the identities of Von Maker and Wertz insofar as Feigen was concerned, Feigen was not a purchaser in good faith. As we have commented, neither Ms. Drew–Bear nor Feigen made, or attempted to make, the inquiry which the circumstances demanded.

The Feigen claim that the failure to look into Wertz's authority to sell the painting was consistent with the practice of the trade does not excuse such conduct. This claim merely confirms the observation of the trial court that "in an industry whose transactions cry out for verification of ... title ... it is deemed poor practice to probe...." Indeed, commercial indifference to ownership or the right to sell facilitates traffic in stolen works of art. Commercial indifference diminishes the integrity and increases the culpability of the apathetic merchant. In such posture, Feigen cannot be heard to complain.

In the circumstances outlined, the complaint should not have been dismissed. Moreover, we find (CPLR 4213[b] and 5712[c][2]) that plaintiffs-appellants are the true owners of the Utrillo painting and are entitled to possession thereof, that defendants-respondents wrongfully detained that painting and are obligated to return it or pay for its value at the time of trial (CPLR 7108[a]; 10 Fuchsberg, New York Damages Law, § 934; 7A Weinstein–Korn–Miller, N.Y.Civ.Prac., par. 7108.02 and cases cited).

In view of the inconclusive nature of the evidence at trial as to damages (the painting apparently being irretrievable), that sole issue remains to be determined. Further, plaintiffs-appellants may have obtained the proceeds from a sale of the Cranach (as to which we have no information) and that could be a credit against those damages.

Accordingly, the judgment of the Supreme Court, New York County, entered June 22, 1978, should be reversed and vacated, on the law and the facts, the complaint reinstated, judgment entered in favor of plaintiffs-appellants on liability, and the matter remanded for an assessment of damages, with costs and disbursements to plaintiffs-appellants....

PORTER v. WERTZ

Court of Appeals of New York, 1981.
53 N.Y.2d 696, 439 N.Y.S.2d 105, 421 N.E.2d 500.

MEMORANDUM. The judgment appealed from an order of the Appellate Division brought up for review should be affirmed ... with costs. We agree with the Appellate Division's conclusion that subdivision (2) of section 2–403 of the Uniform Commercial Code does not insulate defendants from plaintiff Porter's lawful claim to the Utrillo painting.... The "entruster provision" of the Uniform Commercial Code is designed to enhance the reliability of commercial sales by merchants (who deal with the kind of goods sold on a regular basis) while shifting the risk of loss through fraudulent transfer to the owner of the goods, who can select the merchant to whom he entrusts his property. It protects only those who purchase from the merchant to whom the property was entrusted in the ordinary course of the merchant's business.

While the Utrillo painting was entrusted to Harold Von Maker, an art merchant, the Feigen Gallery purchased the painting not from Von Maker, but from one Peter Wertz, who turns out to have been a delicatessen employee acquainted with Von Maker. It seems that Von Maker frequented the delicatessen where Peter Wertz was employed and that at some point Von Maker began to identify himself as Peter Wertz in certain art transactions. Indeed, Von Maker identified himself as Peter Wertz in his dealings with Porter.

Defendants argued that Feigen reasonably assumed that the Peter Wertz who offered the Utrillo to him was an art merchant because Feigen had been informed by Henry Sloan that an art dealer named Peter Wertz desired to sell a Utrillo painting. Feigen therefore argues that for purposes of subdivision (2) of section 2–403 of the Uniform Commercial Code it is as though he purchased from a merchant in the ordinary course of business. Alternatively, he claims that he actually purchased the Utrillo from Von Maker, the art dealer to whom it had been entrusted, because Peter Wertz sold the painting on Von Maker's behalf. Neither argument has merit.

Even if Peter Wertz were acting on Von Maker's behalf, unless he disclosed this fact to Feigen, it could hardly be said that Feigen relied upon Von Maker's status as an art merchant. It does not appear that the actual Peter Wertz ever represented that he was acting on behalf of Von Maker in selling the painting.

As to the argument that Feigen reasonably assumed that Peter Wertz was an art merchant, it is apparent from the opinion of the

Appellate Division that the court rejected the fact finding essential to this argument, namely, that Peter Wertz had been introduced to Feigen by Henry Sloan as an art merchant. The court noted that in his examination before trial Richard Feigen had testified that he could not recall whether Henry Sloan had described Peter Wertz as an art dealer and concluded that this substantially weakened the probative force of Feigen's trial testimony on this point. Indeed, Peter Wertz testified that Von Maker had not directed him to the Feigen Gallery but had simply delivered the painting to Wertz and asked him to try to find a buyer for the Utrillo. Wertz had been to several art galleries before he approached the Feigen Gallery. Thus, the Appellate Division's finding has support in the record.

Because Peter Wertz was not an art dealer and the Appellate Division has found Feigen was not duped by Von Maker into believing that Peter Wertz was such a dealer, subdivision (2) of section 2–403 of the Uniform Commercial Code is inapplicable for three distinct reasons: (1) even if Peter Wertz were an art merchant rather than a delicatessen employee, he is not the same merchant to whom Porter entrusted the Utrillo painting; (2) Wertz was not an art merchant; and (3) the sale was not in the ordinary course of Wertz' business because he did not deal in goods of that kind (Uniform Commercial Code, § 1–201, subd. [9]).

Nor can the defendants-appellants rely on the doctrine of equitable estoppel. It has been observed that subdivision (1) of section 2–403 of the Uniform Commercial Code incorporates the doctrines of estoppel, agency and apparent agency because it states that a purchaser acquires not only all title that his transferor had, but also all title that he had power to transfer (White & Summers, Uniform Commercial Code, § 3–11, p. 139).

An estoppel might arise if Porter had clothed Peter Wertz with ownership of or authority to sell the Utrillo painting and the Feigen Gallery had relied upon Wertz' apparent ownership or right to transfer it. But Porter never even delivered the painting to Peter Wertz, much less create apparent ownership in him; he delivered the painting to Von Maker for his own personal use. It is true, as previously noted, that Von Maker used the name Peter Wertz in his dealings with Porter, but the Appellate Division found that the Feigen Gallery purchased from the actual Peter Wertz and that there was insufficient evidence to establish the claim that Peter Wertz had been described as an art dealer by Henry Sloan. Nothing Porter did influenced the Feigen Gallery's decision to purchase from Peter Wertz, a delicatessen employee. Accordingly, the Feigen Gallery cannot protect its defective title by a defense of estoppel.

The Appellate Division opined that even if Von Maker had duped Feigen into believing that Peter Wertz was an art dealer, subdivision (2) of section 2–403 of the Uniform Commercial Code would still not protect his defective title because as a merchant, Feigen failed to

purchase in good faith. Among merchants good faith requires not only
honesty in fact but observance of reasonable commercial standards.
(Uniform Commercial Code, § 2–103, subd. [1], par. [b]). The Appellate
Division concluded that it was a departure from reasonable commercial
standards for the Feigen Gallery to fail to inquire concerning the title
to the Utrillo and to fail to question Peter Wertz' credentials as an art
dealer. On this appeal we have received *amicus* briefs from the New
York State Attorney–General urging that the court hold that good faith
among art merchants requires inquiry as to the ownership of an *object
d'art,* and from the Art Dealers Association of America, Inc., arguing
that the ordinary custom in the art business is not to inquire as to title
and that a duty of inquiry would cripple the art business which is
centered in New York. In view of our disposition we do not reach the
good faith question.[1]

Notes

(1) **Questions.** Would it have made a difference if Feigen had
bought the Utrillo from Von Maker rather than from Wertz? Why?

Does it make a difference under UCC 2–403(2) if the original owner
of the goods does not know that the person to whom the owner entrusts
them is a merchant who deals in goods of that kind? See Atlas Auto
Rental Corp. v. Weisberg, 54 Misc.2d 168, 281 N.Y.S.2d 400 (1967);
Leary & Sperling, The Outer Limits of Entrusting, 35 Ark.L.Rev. 50,
83–85 (1981). But cf. Antigo Co-op Credit Union v. Miller, 86 Wis.2d 90,
271 N.W.2d 642 (1978).

Suppose that Feigen had been duped by Von Maker into believing
that Wertz was an art dealer. Suppose that Feigen had been duped by
Wertz, who held himself out as an art dealer. Compare UCC 2–104(1)
with UCC 2–403(2). In Sea Harvest v. Rig & Crane Equipment Corp.,
181 N.J.Super. 41, 46, 436 A.2d 553, 556 (1981), the court said: "A
buyer's misunderstanding that the seller was in the business of selling
does not improve the former's position." Do you agree with this
reading of the Code?

(2) **"Entrusting" and Buyers in Ordinary Course.** The Code's
sharpest break with the traditional law of good faith purchase is that in
UCC 2–403(2). Suppose an owner leaves a diamond ring for repair with
a jeweler who both repairs and sells jewelry. The jeweler wrongfully
sells the ring to a good faith purchaser. Who has the right to the
ring—the original owner or the good faith purchaser?

The common law favored the original owner. Merely entrusting
possession to a dealer was not sufficient to clothe the dealer with the
authority to sell. "If it were otherwise people would not be secure in

---

1. For a prediction "that the New Jersey Supreme Court would not impose ... a
duty to inquire" as the Appellate Division
did on the Feigen Gallery, see Johnson &
Johnson Products v. Dal International
Trading Co., 798 F.2d 100, 105 (3d Cir.
1986). [Eds.]

sending their watches or articles of jewelry to a jeweler's establishment to be repaired or cloth to a clothing establishment to be made into garments." Levi v. Booth, 58 Md. 305, 315 (1882).

During the nineteenth century, however, many states enacted "factor's acts" under which an owner of goods who entrusted them to an agent (or "factor") for sale took the risk that the agent might sell them beyond his authority. A good faith purchaser from the agent, relying on the agent's possession of the goods and having no notice that he exceeded his authority, took good title against the original owner. (See the discussion by Gilmore at p. 34 supra.) But the factor's acts did not protect the good faith purchaser where, as in the example of the diamond ring, the owner entrusted the goods to another for some purpose other than that of sale. A mere bailee could not pass good title to a good faith purchaser.

Here UCC 2–403(2) goes well beyond the factor's acts, since it applies to "[a]ny entrusting," i.e., "any delivery" under (3), regardless of the purpose. Who is entitled to the diamond ring under the Code? Would it make a difference in the result if the jeweler sold the ring from his home through an advertisement in the newspaper? Contrast the narrow scope of "buyer in ordinary course" under UCC 1–201(9) with the definitions of "purchase" and "purchaser" under UCC 1–201(32) and (33). See Comment 3 to UCC 2–403.[2] See generally Note, 38 Ind.L.J. 675 (1963); Note, 20 Wm. & Mary L.Rev. 513 (1979); Comment, 72 Yale L.J. 1205 (1963).

In a remarkable recantation, Professor Gilmore has expressed doubt about the wisdom of the Code's expansion of the rights of good faith purchasers. "If, in the 1940's, we had paid any attention to what the courts had been doing for fifty or seventy-five years past, we might have come up with something like this: the good faith purchase idea was an intuitive judicial response to economic conditions that ceased to exist after 1850 or thereabouts. During the second half of the nineteenth century, the courts, losing their enthusiasm for the good faith purchase idea, began cutting back instead of further expanding it." Gilmore, The Good Faith Purchase Idea and the Uniform Commercial

---

2. According to Professor Gilmore: "For some reason, the security transferees who were protected in the voidable title subsection by the use of the term 'purchaser' do not qualify for protection under the entrusting subsection. I have no idea why the draftsmen chose thus to narrow the protected class." Gilmore, The Good Faith Purchase Idea and the Uniform Commercial Code: Confessions of a Repentant Draftsman, 15 Ga.L.Rev. 605, 618 (1981).

According to the Ontario Law Reform Commission, which was "attracted to the distinction": "The supporting theory is, presumably, grounded on either of the following premises: namely, that commerce will not be impeded if lenders are required to assume the risk of a merchant-borrower exceeding his actual authority; or, that lenders are in as good a position as are entrusters, or perhaps even better, to protect themselves against a dishonest merchant." 2 Ontario Law Reform Commission, Report on Sale of Goods 314–15 (1979).

It has also been suggested that transfers for security are transfers "in which the price or consideration received for the goods ... is likely to be considerably less than the amount normally received in a sale of the same goods in other transactions." Leary & Sperling, The Outer Limits of Entrusting, 35 Ark.L.Rev. 50, 65 (1981).

Code: Confessions of a Repentant Draftsman, 15 Ga.L.Rev. 605, 615 (1981).

(3) Entrusting of Cars and Certificates of Title. Because of the value and mobility of motor vehicles, state statutes have established certificate of title systems for their transfer. Such certificates were originally developed as a police measure to impede the sale of stolen vehicles. Certificate of title statutes usually provide for the issuance of a certificate describing the vehicle in detail and identifying the owner, and state that transfer of title to the vehicle is to be completed by delivery of the certificate signed by the owner. Thus, if a car is stolen, the original owner who retains the certificate will generally prevail over a good faith purchaser who takes the car without the certificate.[3]

But what if the original owner entrusted the car to a dealer who wrongfully sold it to a buyer in ordinary course? Will retention of the certificate protect the original owner despite the rule of UCC 2–403(2)? Courts that have faced this question have generally held that UCC 2–403(2) prevails over the certificate of title statute. See Atwood Chevrolet–Olds v. Aberdeen Municipal School District, 431 So.2d 926 (Miss. 1983) (buyer in ordinary course who did not get certificate prevailed over owner of bus chassis who entrusted it to dealer after assembly, followed in Cherry Creek Dodge, Inc. v. Carter, 733 P.2d 1024 (Wyo. 1987)); Godfrey v. Gilsdorf, 86 Nev. 714, 476 P.2d 3 (1970) (buyer in ordinary course prevailed over owner who entrusted car but not certificate to used car dealer); Martin v. Nager, 192 N.J.Super. 189, 469 A.2d 519 (Ch.1983) (same). But some courts have held that a buyer who does not get a certificate of title is not a buyer in ordinary course. See Ellsworth v. Worthey, 612 S.W.2d 396 (Mo.App.1981); Kaminsky v. Karmin, __ A.D.2d __, 589 N.Y.S.2d 588 (1992); Mattek v. Malofsky, 42 Wis.2d 16, 165 N.W.2d 406 (1969). Is this justified by the prevailing practice of having the dealer handle the paperwork involved in the transfer of the certificate of title, with the buyer not receiving the certificate until after taking delivery of the car? That UCC 2–403(1) also prevails over the certificate of title statute, see Dartmouth Motor Sales, Inc. v. Wilcox, 128 N.H. 526, 517 A.2d 804 (1986) (good faith purchaser received "facially valid" certificate of title).

(4) Efforts at Reform. Since the drafters of the Code reexamined the doctrine of good faith purchase, there have been three other notable studies of the subject: by the English Law Reform Committee, by the Ontario Law Reform Commission, and by the International Institute for the Unification of Private Law at Rome.

In a 1966 report on good faith purchase, the English Law Reform Committee rejected the idea that courts be given the power to apportion loss in controversies involving good faith purchasers because "it would introduce into a field of law where certainty and clarity are particular-

---

3. Certificate of title statutes also generally provide for perfection of security interests in the vehicle by notation on the certificate itself. Problems arising out of the relationship between such statutes and Article 9 of the Code are of great practical importance and are dealt with in Part IV infra.

ly important that uncertainty which inevitably follows the grant of a wide and virtually unrestrained judicial discretion." The Committee reaffirmed the principle of *nemo dat*, but a majority recommended a major change in the rule on market overt, which the Committee characterized as "capricious in its application." Under the Committee's recommendation, the rule "should be replaced by a provision that a person who buys goods by retail at trade premises or by public auction acquires a good title provided he buys in good faith and without notice of any defect or want of title on the part of the apparent owner.... By 'trade premises' we mean premises open to the public at which goods of the same or a similar description to those sold are normally offered for sale by retail in the course of business carried on at those premises...." There was a strong dissent to this recommendation on the ground that it would encourage trafficking in stolen goods. (English) Law Reform Committee, Twelfth Report (Transfer of Title to Chattels) Cmnd. 2958, par. 9, 31, 33 (1966). The Committee's major recommendations, including the one just described, have not been implemented.

In 1979 the Ontario Law Reform Commission took up the subject of good faith purchase in the course of its report on revision of the Ontario Sale of Goods Act. The Commission reaffirmed the principle of *nemo dat*, as the English Law Reform Committee had done. It found it "a little surprising that the English Law Reform Committee should have voted in favour of extending its modernized *market overt* concept to stolen goods" and rejected that recommendation, noting that "restricting protection to those who purchase at retail premises would create a new set of anomalies." Instead, the Ontario Commission recommended "that the revised Act contain an additional exception to the *nemo dat* rule, along the lines of UCC 2–403(2) and (3), in the case of entrustment to a merchant." 2 Ontario Law Reform Commission, Report on Sale of Goods 312–13 (1979).

The Ontario Commission also considered whether an owner who has been deprived of title to goods because of one of the exceptions to the *nemo dat* rule should be entitled to recover the goods on reimbursing the good faith purchaser for the purchase price (see Note 1, p. 28 supra), "a principle ... recognized in French and Quebec law in the case of lost or stolen goods acquired in a commercial sale.... The argument put to us has been that an owner may have a particular attachment to an article, and that the third party will not ordinarily be prejudiced by being required to surrender the goods, so long as his reliance interests are protected. Once again, what may appear to be a simple proposition is considerably complicated by several factors. First, the goods may have passed through a number of hands. Secondly, the goods may have been altered or improved since leaving the owner's hands. While we have concluded that a right of recovery should be recognized, and so recommend, we are of the view that, in light of the above-mentioned factors, the right of recovery should be subject to the following qualifications. The right of recovery should not apply where the owner originally entrusted the goods to a merchant who sold them in the ordinary course of his business. It should only apply where the court considers it fair to make such an order. Further, the terms of the order should be in the court's discretion, but in making such an order no account should be taken of any expectation losses suffered by the third person in whose hands the goods are located." Id. at 314. The Commission's proposals have not yet been enacted, but they have been incorporated in a Draft Uniform Sale of Goods Act prepared by the Uniform Law Conference of Canada. See Uniform Law Conference of Canada, Proceedings of the Sixty–Third Annual Meeting 185–321 (1981).

The International Institute for the Unification of Private Law published in 1968 a draft proposal for a uniform international law in the form of a multilateral treaty on the protection of good faith purchasers of goods. This draft adopted the principle of *possession vaut titre* in the case of stolen goods that were bought in good faith "under normal conditions from a dealer who usually sells goods of the same kind." International Institute for the Unification of Private Law (Unidroit), Draft Uniform Law on the Protection of the Bona Fide Purchaser of Corporeal Moveables with Explanatory Report art. 10(2) (1968). A committee of governmental experts studied this draft and prepared a revision, which receded from this extreme position because a majority feared that it might encourage trafficking in stolen goods, particularly works of art. The goal of the work then shifted to the preparation of a multilateral treaty on the return of stolen or illegally exported cultural objects. The present draft covers two main subjects: restitution of stolen cultural objects and return of illegally exported cultural objects. See International Institute for the Unification of Private Law (Unidroit), Preliminary Draft Convention on Stolen or Illegally Exported Cultural Objects (1992).

Problem 6. A, who is in the cotton business, sold cotton to O, who paid A $60,000 and promised to pay the balance of $40,000 when O took delivery of the cotton in two weeks. The bill of sale recited: "A hereby sells and conveys to O all right and title to cotton [giving description] and agrees to take good care and custody of said cotton until final delivery." A week later, A sold the same cotton to P, who took delivery without knowing of the sale to O and promised to pay A $90,000 in 30 days. O sues P to replevy the cotton.

(a) What result? See UCC 2–403, 1–201(9). (If P has not yet paid A the $90,000, what would you advise O to do?)

(b) Suppose that P also left A in possession of the cotton and O got wind of the sale and took delivery. P sues O to replevy the cotton. What result? Does P run any risk if he leaves A in possession of the cotton?

Problem 7. A, who is in the cotton business, sold a used cotton gin to O, who paid A $60,000 and promised to pay the balance of $40,000 when O took delivery of the machine in two weeks. The bill of sale recited: "A hereby sells and conveys to O all right and title to cotton gin [giving description] and agrees to take good care and custody of said machine until final delivery." A week later, A sold the same machine to P, who took delivery without knowing of the sale to O. O sues P to replevy the machine. What result? For additional circumstances that might justify a decision for P on the ground of "apparent authority" or "estoppel" under UCC 1–103, see Tumber v. Automation Design & Manufacturing Corp., 130 N.J.Super. 5, 324 A.2d 602 (1974); Farmers Livestock Exchange v. Ulmer, 393 N.W.2d 65 (N.D.1986).

SECTION 2. NEGOTIABLE INSTRUMENTS

Prefatory Note. We turn now from the good faith purchase of goods to the good faith purchase of another kind of property, negotiable instruments. Without the advantage of some business background, the law student is likely to find the law of negotiable instruments, at least at the outset, the most esoteric and intractable area of commercial law. The student is to some extent familiar with the law of sales from a course in contracts, but the forms, the functions, and even the terminology of negotiable instruments remain to be explored. Because they can be fully understood only in the light of some six centuries of development, it is the purpose of this brief introduction to present at least some of the highlights of that development. The Code classifies negotiable instruments under three main headings: "notes," "drafts," and "checks" (a subspecies of drafts). (UCC 3–104).[1] Their origins will be separately discussed.

Origin of the Draft. The draft, or bill of exchange as it is often called,[2] grew out of the practices of fourteenth-century merchants who sought to avoid the hazards and the publicity of transporting money. It thus began as a device for the transmission of funds. If a London merchant received goods on credit from a Venetian merchant, the London merchant would send to the Venetian an acknowledgement of the debt together with his promise to pay it at a fixed date at one of the fairs where trade was centered in medieval Europe.[3] The London merchant then chose a London banker who was going to that fair and

1. The Code also mentions two other types of negotiable instrument: the "traveler's check," a demand instrument drawn on or payable at or through a bank and requiring a countersignature; and the "certificate of deposit," a written acknowledgment by a bank of the receipt of a deposit coupled with a promise to repay it. See UCC 3–104(i), (j).

2. The terms "draft" and "bill of exchange" are synonymous. The latter was used throughout the Negotiable Instruments Law. The Code uses the former.

3. The example which follows is adapted from P. Huvelin, Le Droit des Marchés et des Foires 557–58 (1897), as translated in 8 W. Holdsworth, History of English Law 129–30 (1925).

gave him an authority to pay the debt in the London merchant's name when it fell due. The Venetian merchant chose a Venetian banker going to the same fair and authorized him to receive payment. All of the principal trading cities of Western Europe would be represented at the fair and each banker would have many payments to make and to receive from many other bankers. Probably the debts owed by the Venetian banker to the London banker would not exactly equal those owed by the London banker to the Venetian banker so that they could not be extinguished by set-off. But if the Venetian should still have an adverse balance as against London, the Venetian might well have a favorable balance as against, say, Geneva. To settle his adverse balance to London, he would draw an order (*draft*) upon a debtor from Geneva directing him to pay a specified amount to the London creditor. By this means accounts could be settled with the exchange of a minimum amount of money.

From these orders, the draft developed so that it was no longer necessary for bankers to meet at a fair. If a London buyer wished to pay a Venetian seller for goods, the London buyer would find a London banker who had an account with a correspondent in Venice. The London buyer would then pay the London banker, the sum to be remitted to Venice. The London banker (as *drawer*) would then draw on the Venetian correspondent (as *drawee*), ordering him to pay the sum to the Venetian seller (as *payee*). The letter would then be given to the London buyer (as *remitter*), who would send it to the Venetian seller. The Venetian seller would then present it to the Venetian banker to receive payment. The early development of the concept of negotiability in connection with drafts is discussed in Rogers, The Myth of Negotiability, 31 B.C.L.Rev. 265 (1990).

Origin of the Check. The London "bankers" mentioned in the foregoing examples were probably Lombard or Florentine money changers rather than bankers in the modern sense, for, although private banking had originated in Venice in the fourteenth century, it was not until the seventeenth century that banking began in England. At that time the goldsmiths of Lombard Street in London were experiencing a decline in their trade in gold and silver plate with the dwindling landed class, and sought to augment their business by accepting for safekeeping the valuables of their customers. The merchants of London, however, preferred to deposit their funds at the king's mint in the Tower of London until Charles I, in 1640, forcibly borrowed about £200,000. Thereafter the merchants patronized the goldsmiths in increasing numbers. The latter began to lend the money on deposit, thus becoming true bankers, whose loans were made from the deposits of others, as opposed to moneylenders, whose loans were made from their own capital. The legal relationship between goldsmith and customer changed from bailor-bailee to debtor-creditor, that which exists today between a bank and its depositors.

The merchant looked to the goldsmith banker not only as a depository but also as an intermediary for making payment to his creditors. The draft or bill of exchange provided a pattern. At first the merchant probably addressed a letter to the goldsmith, directing payment to the creditor. Later the form become that of a check. Printed checks came into use in the second half of the eighteenth century. The word "check" itself dates from about the same period and is derived from "the name of the counterfoil of an Exchequer or other bill, the purpose of which was to check forgery or alteration." [4] In the nineteenth century the English adopted the spelling "cheque," while the traditional spelling has been retained in the United States.

Origin of the Note. The draft and the check, at least as they are used in the foregoing examples, are both instruments for the safe and convenient transmission of funds, in place of money. Marius however, mentions another use for the draft, as an instrument of credit rather than for transmission of funds. Two parties only are involved, a debtor and a creditor. Suppose that a buyer buys goods from a seller, who is unable or unwilling to finance the transaction himself until the buyer pays. The seller, as creditor, may draw a draft on the buyer, as debtor, payable to the order of the seller at the end of a fixed time. The seller then presents it to the buyer who accepts it by signing his name across the draft itself, indicating his agreement to pay. Then "the drawer, before the Bill falls due, doth negotiate the parcell, with another man, and so draws in the money at the place where he liveth, and makes only an Assignment on the Bill, payable to him of whom he hath received the value." [5] The buyer has the goods, the seller gets his money immediately upon negotiating the draft, and the new holder of the draft finances the transaction. In modern parlance the seller has "discounted" the draft, receiving its face value less a discount equal to interest from the time of the discount until maturity. Today, however, it might seem simpler for the buyer (as *maker*) merely to execute a promissory note, promising to pay the sum to the seller (as *payee*), and this form of instrument did become popular among the goldsmith bankers in the late seventeenth century. The promissory note could then be transferred by means of the indorsement of the seller, as payee to a third party who would purchase it and finance the transaction. [6]

4. 2 J. Murray, A New English Dictionary 320 (1893).

5. Page 3 of 1655 edition.

6. The fact that the note was transferable at all was only grudgingly conceded. As will be recalled from the study of contracts, the assignability of simple contract rights had at first met with objection. However, by the beginning of the eighteenth century it was well established that a *draft* payable to order was freely transferable and that suit could be brought by the transferee, as indorsee, in his own name. Yet in Buller v. Crips, 6 Mod.Rep. 29, 87 Eng.Rep. 793 (1704) Lord Holt refused to allow the indorsee of a *promissory*

note payable to order to maintain an action against the maker under the custom of merchants, calling "the notes in question . . . only an invention of the goldsmiths in Lombard–Street, who had a mind to make a law to bind all those that did deal with them." But while the courts lagged behind the custom, the legislature was not slow to act, and in 1704, Parliament enacted the Statute of Anne, "An Act for Giving like Remedy upon Promissory Notes, as is now used upon Bills of Exchange. . . ." The act overruled Buller v. Crips, making promissory notes as freely transferable as drafts.

Uses of the Note. "I shall not undertake to explain how or why the commercial system of a century ago lost the use of notes to evidence the credit-price of freshly delivered goods. It is enough here that the practice went into decline, and that between merchants goods are now delivered typically on purely 'open' credit (resulting in a 'book account,' and 'account receivable'), often with the buyer, if he is financially strong, paying within ten days against a large 'cash discount.' The giving of a commercial note between dealers has come to be the gesture with which a stale account, long overdue, is promised *really* to be met next time. Such a note smells." Llewellyn, Meet Negotiable Instruments, 44 Colum.L.Rev. 299, 321–22 (1944). However the note came to have commercial significance in three other important areas.

First, and most important for the purposes of this casebook, is the use of the note in a secured sale. The consumer purchaser of an automobile on credit will be asked by the seller to execute a security agreement, perhaps called a conditional sale contract, under which the purchaser, in return for payment of a financing charge, has the right to make installment payments over a period of time and the seller's rights include that of repossession of the car, which is security for the balance of the purchase price, in the event of the buyer's default. Together with the security agreement the seller may ask the purchaser to execute a negotiable promissory note. The seller's rights under the security agreement will then be assigned and the note negotiated to a finance company or bank which will finance the transaction. Much the same pattern is followed in the installment financing of industrial equipment. The note is also commonly used in secured transactions involving real estate, but the problems thus raised can best be studied in the context of a course in real estate transactions.

A second significant use of the note is in connection with the loan of money, a function that is epitomized by the banker's "collateral note." Here, as in the case of the secured sale, the creditor is intent upon security and the loan may be secured by a pledge of stock or in a variety of other ways. The bank that takes the note may, instead of financing the transaction itself, choose to negotiate the note to a Federal Reserve bank for rediscount.

A third important use of the note is the corporate bond, which is a long-term promissory note. However, the difficulty of dealing with investment paper such as bonds under the general rules for negotiable instruments led the drafters of the Code to treat it separately in Article 8, Investment Securities.

Promissory Note - Commercial

Date: _____, 19___

Note Amount: $ _____

1. Payment of Note Amount.

For value received, the undersigned promise(s) to pay to the order of the Bank the Note Amount:

☐ on _____.

☐ on demand.

☐ in ____ payments, consisting of ____ payments of $ _____ each, followed by a payment of

$ _____. Payments will be due on the same day of each _____

(If other than each month, specify names of months)

beginning _____.

2. Payment of Interest.

a. The undersigned will pay interest on the unpaid portion of the Note Amount for each day from the date of this Note until the Note Amount is paid in full at a rate per annum equal to:

☐ ____ %.

☐ the rate of interest publicly announced (or if not publicly announced, established and available for quotation) from time to time by the Bank as its prime rate, as in effect on such day, plus ____ %. The applicable interest rate shall be adjusted automatically as of the opening of business on the effective date of each change in such prime rate.

☐ _____

_____

If no box is checked this Note has been discounted and the Note Amount includes interest computed at the rate of ____ % per annum.

b. Interest shall be payable on the same day of each _____, beginning

(If other than each month, specify names of months)

_____, and when the Note Amount is due.

c. Overdue portions of the Note Amount shall bear interest for each day from the due date thereof until paid in full at a rate per annum equal to the rate of interest otherwise payable thereon, plus 2%, such interest to be payable on demand.

d. Interest shall be computed on the basis of a 360 day year, but shall be charged for the actual number of days elapsed in the year.

3. Payment of Costs and Expenses.

The undersigned will pay all costs and expenses, including attorneys' fees and disbursements, incurred by the Bank in connection with the administration, enforcement or attempted enforcement of this Note.

4. Place and Means of Payment; Holidays.

Payment of the Note Amount and interest shall be made at the Bank's office specified above in lawful money of the United States of America and in immediately available funds. Whenever any payment to be made pursuant to this Note shall be due on a Saturday, Sunday or other day on which banks are authorized to close under the laws of the State of New York, such payment may be made on the next succeeding business day and any extension of time shall be included in computing interest, if any, with respect to such payment.

5. Acceleration.

a. The Bank may without notice to or demand upon the undersigned declare all amounts payable pursuant to this Note immediately due and payable, whereupon the same shall become so due and payable, if:

(i) The undersigned (or, if more than one, any of the undersigned) or any guarantor or endorser of this Note (A) defaults in the payment when due of, or otherwise defaults in the performance of, any obligation to the Bank; (B) has made or makes to the Bank any representation or warranty that proves to have been incorrect or misleading in any material respect when made; (C) fails to pay when due any other indebtedness for borrowed money, the maturity of any such indebtedness is accelerated or an event occurs which, with notice or lapse of time or both, would permit acceleration of such indebtedness; (D) if an individual, dies or becomes incompetent; (E) if not an individual, is dissolved or is a party to any merger or consolidation or sells or otherwise disposes of all or substantially all of its assets without the written consent of the Bank; (F) challenges, or institutes any proceedings, or any proceedings are instituted, to challenge, the validity, binding effect or enforceability of this Note, any guaranty or endorsement of this Note or any other obligation to the Bank; (G) makes any payment on account of any indebtedness subordinated to this Note in contravention of the terms of such subordination; (H) fails to furnish information upon request of, or permit inspection of its books and records by, the Bank; (I) creates, without the written consent of the Bank, a security interest in or lien upon, or an attachment or levy is made upon, any of its assets, or a judgment is rendered against it; or (J) is, or is a member of any co-partnership which is, expelled from or suspended by any stock or securities exchange or other exchange; or

(ii) The Bank at any time and for any reason in good faith deems itself to be insecure or the risk of nonpayment or nonperformance of this Note or any guaranty or endorsement of this Note to be increased.

b. All amounts payable pursuant to this Note shall be immediately due and payable, without presentment, demand, protest or notice of any kind, if the undersigned (or, if more than one, any of the undersigned) or any guarantor or endorser of this Note (i) becomes insolvent or unable to meet its debts as they mature or is generally not paying its debts as they become due, or suspends or ceases its present business, or a custodian, as defined in Title 11 of the United States Code, of substantially all of its property shall have been appointed or taken possession, or (ii) commences, or has commenced against it, a case under such Title 11, or any proceeding under any other federal or state bankruptcy, insolvency or other law relating to the relief of debtors, the readjustment, composition or ex-

Demand for payment may be made whether or not any of the foregoing events shall have occurred if the Note Amount is payable on demand.

6. General.
If the undersigned are more than one, they shall be jointly and severally liable hereunder. The words "it" or "its" as used herein shall be deemed to refer to individuals and to business entities.

7. Waivers; Governing Law.
The undersigned waive(s) presentment, protest, notice of dishonor and the right to assert in any action or proceeding with regard to this Note any offsets or counterclaims which the undersigned may have. No failure or delay by the Bank in exercising any right hereunder shall operate as a waiver thereof, nor shall any single or partial exercise of any right preclude other or further exercises thereof or the exercise of any other right. This Note shall be governed by and interpreted and enforced in accordance with the laws of the State of New York.

_____
(Name of Company)

By: _____
Title:

By: _____
Title:

_____
(Name of Company)

By: _____
Title:

By: _____
Title:

C6064/00 (8-81) Rev. 8-82

PROMISSORY NOTE (COMMERCIAL)

[Front]

[D616]

Guaranty of Payment

The undersigned (if more than one, jointly and severally) (a) unconditionally guarantee(s) the payment when due, without any setoff or other deduction, of all amounts payable pursuant to the Note on the reverse side, (b) waive(s) all acts and other things upon which, but for such waiver, this guaranty would or might be conditioned, including, but not limited to, any presentment, demand for payment, protest, notice of dishonor, and exercise of any right or remedy, and (c) consent(s), without notice to the undersigned, to all acts, omissions and other things that would or might, but for such consent, impair or otherwise affect this guaranty, including, but not limited to, any extension, regardless of length and whether preceded by another or others, any renewal, modification or acceleration, any substitution or release of any collateral or party liable for payment, any failure to call for, take, hold, protect or perfect, continue the perfection of or enforce any security interest in or other lien upon, any collateral and any failure to exercise, delay in the exercise, exercise or waiver of, or forbearance or other indulgence with respect to, any right or remedy.

PROMISSORY NOTE (COMMERCIAL)

[Reverse]

Problem 8. O owned $100,000 in $100 bills. A stole it and gave it to P, who did not suspect the theft, in payment for cotton. O sues P to replevy the money. What result? Does Article 2 or 3 of the Code apply? See UCC 2–105(1), 3–102(a); *Miller v. Race,* infra; In re Koreag, Controle et Revision S.A., 961 F.2d 341 (2d Cir.1992) (in currency exchange contract "money is not the *medium* of exchange, but rather the *object* of exchange" and "currency thus constitutes 'goods'" under Article 2), cert. denied, 113 S.Ct. 188 (1992); City of Portland v. Berry, 86 Or.App. 376, 739 P.2d 1041 (1987) ("money rule" applied to $500 and $1,000 bills though Treasury has not printed them since 1945 and "has been systematically taking them out of circulation and destroying them since 1969").

Problem 9. O was the owner of a negotiable promissory note, made by M, who promised "to pay on demand to bearer $100,000." A stole it from O and gave it to P, who did not suspect the theft, in return for $100,000. O sues P to replevy the note.

(a) What result? See UCC 3–306, 3–302, 1–201(20), 3–201, 3–109; Miller v. Race, infra.

(b) What result if P had paid only $60,000 for the note? See UCC 3–103(a)(4), 3–303; Stewart v. Thornton, 116 Ariz. 107, 568 P.2d 414 (1977) (note "was discounted one-third").

(c) What result if P had promised to pay $100,000 but has not yet paid it?

(d) What result if P had given a check for $100,000, which is still in the hands of A?

(e) To what extent would P be a holder in due course if P had promised to pay $90,000 and had paid only $80,000 before learning of the theft? See 3–302(d). Would it make a difference if P had then paid the remaining $10,000? (Where does the Code deal with the effect of value given after notice?)

Problem 10. O was the owner of a negotiable promissory note, made by M, who promised "to pay on demand to the order of O $100,000." A stole it from O, forged O's indorsement,[7] and sold it to P, who did not suspect the theft, for $100,000. O sues P to replevy the note.

(a) What result? See UCC 3–306, 3–302, 1–201(20), 3–201, 3–109, 3–403. (As to A's liability to P, see UCC 3–415(a), 3–416(a)(2).)

(b) What result if, before the theft, O had indorsed the note on the back by signing "O"? See UCC 3–205.

---

7. Those curious about the spelling of this word may find the following helpful. "The P.E.G. stamp employed by banks stands for 'Prior endorsements guaranteed.' While the Uniform Commercial Code, as will be seen, frequently fails to provide clear answers to questions in the area of negotiable instruments, it is unequivocal in its insistence that indorsement is to be spelled with the letter 'i'. Bankers, who claim to know much of such weighty matters, may insist on beginning with 'e', but this practice could be attributed to the bankers' understandable reluctance to stamp 'Pay any Bank PIG' on the backs of the checks they handle." Perini Corp. v. First National Bank of Habersham County, 553 F.2d 398, 401 n. 1 (5th Cir. 1977).

(c) What result if, before the theft, O had indorsed the note on the back by writing "Pay to the order of B, (signed) O."? [8]

Problem 11. O was the owner of a promissory note made by M, who promised "to pay to the order of O $100,000." A fraudulently obtained it from O, who did not indorse the note. A gave it to P, who did not suspect the fraud, in payment for cotton delivered by P to A. O sues P to replevy the note. What result? See UCC 3–306; Note 4, p. 69 infra. Would the result be different if P had promised to deliver cotton to A but has not yet done so?

————

MILLER v. RACE

Court of King's Bench 1758.
1 Burr. 452, 97 Eng.Rep. 398.

It was an action of trover against the defendant, upon a bank note,[9] for the payment of twenty-one pounds ten shillings to one William Finney or bearer, on demand.

The cause came on to be tried before Lord Mansfield at the sittings in Trinity term last at Guildhall, London: and upon the trial it appeared that William Finney, being possessed of this bank note on the 11th of December 1756, sent it by the general post, under cover, directed to one Bernard Odenharty, at Chipping Norton in Oxfordshire; that on the same night the mail was robbed, and the bank note in question (amongst other notes) taken and carried away by the robber; that this bank note, on the 12th of the same December, came into the hands and possession of the plaintiff, for a full and valuable consideration, and in the usual course and way of his business, and without any notice or knowledge of this bank note being taken out of the mail.

It was admitted and agreed, that, in the common and known course of trade, bank notes are paid by and received of the holder or possessor of them, as cash; and that in the usual way of negotiating bank notes, they pass from one person to another as cash, by delivery only and without any further inquiry or evidence of title, than what arises from the possession. It appeared that Mr. Finney, having notice of this

---

8. Those with a penchant for the daedal may wonder at this point about the case in which a note made by M to the order of O is stolen by A, who forges O's name on a special indorsement to B and delivers it to B, who specially indorses and delivers it to C, who does the same to D. If the note is dishonored, what are D's rights against B? Some may be satisfied with the answer that the practical importance of the problem is negligible because both forgery and such multiple negotiation are rare. Others may wish to pursue the implications of the "new bill" doctrine, according to which, as

Lord Holt put it in 1704, "the indorsement may be said to be tantamount to the drawing of a new bill." Buller v. Crips, 6 Mod. Rep. 29, 30, 87 Eng.Rep. 793, 794 (1704). Cf. Cormack and Browne, Indorsements After Maturity and the "New Bill" Doctrine, 30 Ill.L.Rev. 46 (1935). As to whether the "new bill" doctrine survived enactment of the Code, see UCC 1–103.

9. Bank of England notes did not become legal tender until 1833. 3 & 4 Wm. IV, c. 98, § 6. [Eds.]

robbery, on the 13th December, applied to the Bank of England, "to stop the payment of this note:" which was ordered accordingly, upon Mr. Finney's entering into proper security "to indemnify the bank."

Some little time after this, the plaintiff applied to the bank for the payment of this note; and for that purpose delivered the note to the defendant, who is a clerk in the bank: but the defendant refused either to pay the note, or to re-deliver it to the plaintiff. Upon which this action was brought against the defendant.

The jury found a verdict for the plaintiff, and the sum of 21*l*. 10s. damages, subject nevertheless to the opinion of this Court upon this question—"Whether under the circumstances of this case, the plaintiff had a sufficient property in this bank note, to entitle him to recover in the present action?" ...

LORD MANSFIELD now delivered the resolution of the Court.

After stating the case at large, he declared that at the trial, he had no sort of doubt, but this action was well brought, and would lie against the defendant in the present case; upon the general course of business, and from the consequences to trade and commerce: which would be much incommoded by a contrary determination.

It has been very ingeniously argued by Sir Richard Lloyd for the defendant. But the whole fallacy of the argument turns upon comparing bank notes to what they do not resemble, and what they ought not to be compared to, viz. to goods, or to securities, or documents for debts.

Now they are not goods, not securities, nor documents for debts, nor are so esteemed: but are treated as money, as cash, in the ordinary course and transaction of business, by the general consent of mankind; which gives them the credit and currency of money, to all intents and purposes. They are as much money, as guineas themselves are; or any other current coin, that is used in common payments, as money or cash.

They pass by a will, which bequeaths all the testator's money or cash; and are never considered as securities for money, but as money itself. Upon Ld. Ailesbury's will, 900*l*. in bank-notes was considered as cash. On payment of them, whenever a receipt is required, the receipts are always given as for money; not as for securities or notes.

So on bankruptcies, they cannot be followed as identical and distinguishable from money: but are always considered as money or cash.

It is a pity that reporters sometimes catch at quaint expressions that may happen to be dropped at the Bar or Bench; and mistake their meaning. It has been quaintly said, "that the reason why money can not be followed is, because it has no ear-mark:" but this is not true. The true reason is, upon account of the currency of it: it can not be recovered after it has passed in currency. So, in case of money stolen, the true owner can not recover it, after it has been paid away fairly and honestly upon a valuable and bona fide consideration: but before money has passed in currency, an action may be brought for the money itself. There was a case in 1 G. 1, at the sittings, Thomas v. Whip, before Ld. Macclesfield: which was an action upon assumpsit, by an administrator against the defendant, for money had and received to his use. The defendant was nurse to the intestate during his sickness; and, being alone, conveyed away the money. And Ld. Macclesfield held that the action lay. Now this must be esteemed a finding at least.

Apply this to the case of a bank-note. An action may lie against the finder, it is true; (and it is not at all denied:) but not after it has been paid away in currency. And this point has been determined, even in the infancy of bank-notes; for 1 Salk. 126, M. 10 W. 3, at Nisi Prius, is in point. And Ld. Ch. J. Holt there says that it is "by reason of the course of trade; which creates a property in the assignee or bearer." (And "the bearer" is a more proper expression than assignee.)

Here, an inn-keeper took it, bona fide, in his business from a person who made an appearance of a gentleman. Here is no pretence or suspicion of collusion with the robber: for this matter was strictly inquired and examined into at the trial; and is so stated in the case, "that he took it for a full and valuable consideration, in the usual course of business." Indeed if there had been any collusion, or any circumstances of unfair dealing, the case had been much otherwise. If it had been a note for 1000*l*. it might have been suspicious: but this was a small note for 21*l*. 10s. only: and money given in exchange for it.

Another case cited was a loose note in 1 Ld.Raym. 738, ruled by Ld. Ch. J. Holt at Guildhall, in 1698; which proves nothing for the defendant's side of the question: but it is exactly agreeable to what is laid down by my Ld. Ch. J. Holt, in the case I have just mentioned. The action did not lie against the assignee of the bank-bill; because he had it for valuable consideration.

In that case, he had it from the person who found it: but the action did not lie against him, because he took it in the course of currency; and therefore it could not be followed in his hands. It never shall be followed into the hands of a person who bona fide took it in the course of currency, and in the way of his business.

The case of Ford v. Hopkins, was also cited: which was in Hil. 12 W. 3, coram Holt Ch. J. at Nisi Prius, at Guildhall; and was an action of trover for million-lottery tickets. But this must be a very incorrect report of that case: it is impossible that it can be a true representation of what Ld. Ch. J. Holt said. It represents him as speaking of bank-notes, Exchequer-notes, and million lottery tickets, as like to each other. Now no two things can be more unlike to each other than a lottery-ticket, and a bank-note. Lottery tickets are identical and specific: specific actions lie for them. They may prove extremely unequal in value: one may be a prize; another, a blank. Land is not more specific than lottery-tickets are. It is there said, "that the delivery of the plaintiff's tickets to the defendant, as that case was, was no change of property." And most clearly it was no change of the property; so far, the case is right. But it is here urged as a proof "that the true owner may follow a stolen bank-note, into what hands soever it shall come."

Now the whole of that case turns upon the throwing in banknotes, as being like to lottery-tickets.

But Ld. Ch. J. Holt could never say "that an action would lie against the person who, for a valuable consideration, had received a bank note which had been stolen or lost, and bona fide paid to him:" even though the action was brought by the true owner: because he had determined otherwise, but two years before; and because banknotes are not like lottery-tickets, but money.

The person who took down this case, certainly misunderstood Lord Ch. J. Holt, or mistook his reasons. For this reasoning would prove, (if it was true, as the reporter represents it,) that if a man paid to a goldsmith 500*l*. in bank-notes, the goldsmith could never pay them away.

A bank-note is constantly and universally, both at home and abroad, treated as money, as cash; and paid and received, as cash; and it is necessary, for the purposes of commerce, that their currency should be established and secured.

Lord Mansfield declared that the Court were all of the same opinion, for the plaintiff; and that Mr. Just. Wilmot concurred.

Rule—That the postea be delivered to the plaintiff.

Notes

(1) **Good Faith.** It is tautological that a good faith purchaser must take in good faith. But what is "good faith"? UCC 1–201(19) says that it means "honesty in fact in the conduct or transaction concerned," the traditional subjective definition that is sometimes characterized as that of the "pure heart and empty head." However, the merchant who claims to be a good faith purchaser under UCC 2–403 must also meet an objective standard. For the purposes of Article 2, "Good faith in the case of a merchant means honesty in fact and the observance of reasonable commercial standards of fair dealing in the trade" (UCC 2–103(1)(b)).

The standard of good faith applicable to commercial paper has had a checkered career. In *Miller v. Race,* Lord Mansfield observed that Miller had taken the note "bona fide ... 'in the usual course of business.'" In Gill v. Cubitt, 3 B. & C. 466, 107 Eng.Rep. 806 (K.B. 1824), Bayley, J. of the Court of King's Bench concluded that "the course of business must require ... a proper and reasonable degree of caution necessary to preserve the interest of trade." It thus appeared that the absence of simple negligence was required. But in Crook v. Jadis, 5 B. & Ad. 909, 110 Eng.Rep. 1028 (K.B.1834), decided only a decade after *Gill v. Cubitt,* the same court decided that the absence of gross negligence was enough. Two years later, in Goodman v. Harvey,

4 A. & E. 870, 111 Eng.Rep. 1011 (1836), Lord Denman declared: "I believe we are all of opinion that gross negligence only would not be a sufficient answer, where the party has given consideration for the bill. Gross negligence may be evidence of mala fides, but is not the same thing. We have shaken off the last remnant of the contrary doctrine." The result in the United States was confusion; some courts following *Gill v. Cubitt,* others adopting *Goodman v. Harvey.* In Goodman v. Simonds, 61 U.S. (20 How.) 343, 15 L.Ed. 934 (1857), the Supreme Court of the United States determined to follow *Goodman v. Harvey,* repudiating *Gill v. Cubitt,* and nearly all American jurisdictions were in accord by the time of the enactment of the Negotiable Instruments Law. The Negotiable Instruments Law did not define good faith, so that the earlier cases such as *Goodman v. Simonds,* remained authoritative under it.

The drafters of Article 3 originally laid down a standard of good faith that was not unlike the merchant's standard of good faith in Article 2. In the 1952 edition of the Code, UCC 3–302(1)(b) read: "(b) in good faith including observance of the reasonable commercial standards of any business in which the holder may be engaged...."

The comment to this section explained: "... The 'reasonable commercial standards' language added here and in comparable provisions elsewhere in the Act, e.g., Section 2–103, merely makes explicit what has long been implicit in case-law handling of the 'good faith' concept. A business man engaging in a commercial transaction is not entitled to claim the peculiar advantages which the law accords to the good faith purchaser—called in this context holder in due course—on a bare showing of 'honesty in fact' when his actions fail to meet the generally accepted standards current in his business, trade or profession. The cases so hold; this section so declares the law."

The present version of UCC 1–201(19) was adopted in the 1957 edition of the Code. The reason given for the change was: "... to make clear that the doctrine of an objective standard of good faith, exemplified by the case of Gill v. Cubitt, 3 B. & C. 446 (1824), is not intended to be incorporated...." 1956 Recommendations of the Editorial Board for the Uniform Commercial Code.

Revised Article 3, however, adopts a definition of good faith for both Article 3 and Article 4 that is similar to the merchant's definition in Article 2 and is redolent of the standard in *Gill v. Cubitt.* UCC 3–103(a)(4) defines "good faith" as meaning "honesty in fact and the observance of reasonable commercial standards of fair dealing." Comment 4 cautions: "Although fair dealing is a broad term that must be defined in context, it is clear that it is concerned with the fairness of conduct rather than the care with which an act is performed. Failure to exercise ordinary care in conducting a transaction is an entirely different concept than failure to deal fairly in conducting the transaction. Both fair dealing and ordinary care, which is defined in Section 3–103(a)(7), are to be judged in the light of reasonable commercial standards, but those standards in each case are directed to different aspects of commercial conduct."

(2) Notice. UCC 3–302(a)(2) requires that the purchaser of commercial paper take not only "in good faith" but "without notice" that it is overdue or has been dishonored or of any defense or claim. Although it is traditional to state the requirement of lack of notice separately in the case of commercial paper, it is frequently not separately stated for the purchaser of goods. See UCC 2–403(1).

"Notice" is defined by the Code in UCC 1–201(25). The last three sentences were added by the 1957 edition. Note the objective standard in UCC 1–201(25).[10] Often the same facts may be used both to show lack of good faith and to show notice, but good faith and notice do not always overlap in this way. For a case in which notice but not good faith was involved, see *First National Bank of Odessa v. Fazzari,* p. 86 infra. See generally Blum, Notice to Holders in Due Course and Other Bona Fide Purchasers Under the Uniform Commercial Code, 22 B.C.L.Rev. 203 (1981).

(3) Value. In order to show that he is a good faith purchaser, not merely a donee, the person in possession of personal property must show that he gave value. See, e.g., UCC 2–403(1), 3–302(a)(2). A general definition of "value" appears in UCC 1–201(44), subparagraph (d) of which makes it clear that one gives "value" if one gives "any consideration sufficient to support a simple contract." But under subparagraphs (b) and (c), "value" is a broader concept than "consideration," for one can also give value by giving something that would not, because of the pre-existing duty rule, be consideration. The argument for this view was stated by Mr. Justice Story, in connection with the good faith purchase of commercial paper, in Swift v. Tyson, 41 U.S. (16 Pet.) 1, 20 (1842)[11]:

> ... And why upon principle should not a pre-existing debt be deemed such a valuable consideration? It is for the benefit and convenience of the commercial world to give as wide an extent as practicable to the credit and circulation of negotiable paper, that it may pass not only as security for new purchases and advances, made upon the transfer thereof, but also in payment of and as security for pre-existing debts. The creditor is thereby enabled to realize or to secure his debt, and thus

---

10. The Negotiable Instruments Law defined notice in a purely subjective manner, as "actual knowledge ... or knowledge of such facts that his action in taking the instrument amounted to bad faith." NIL 56.

11. Ironically, *Swift v. Tyson* is better known today for the rule of choice of law that was given its quietus in Erie Railroad Co. v. Tompkins, 304 U.S. 64, 58 S.Ct. 817, 82 L.Ed. 1188 (1938), than for the rule of commercial paper that survived. Devotees of the "federal common law" will recall

Clearfield Trust Co. v. United States, 318 U.S. 363, 63 S.Ct. 573, 87 L.Ed. 838 (1943), in which it was concluded that "the rights and duties of the United States on commercial paper which it issues are governed by federal rather than local law." For later applications of the *Clearfield* doctrine, see Note, 66 Iowa L.Rev. 391 (1981). That the Code is a source of federal common law, see United States v. Conrad Pub. Co., 589 F.2d 949, 953 (8th Cir.1978); Note, 20 B.C.L.Rev. 680, 680–81 (1979).

may safely give a prolonged credit or forbear from taking any legal steps to enforce his rights. The debtor also has the advantage of making his negotiable securities of equivalent value to cash. But establish the opposite conclusion, that negotiable paper cannot be applied in payment of or as security for pre-existing debts, without letting in all the equities between the original and antecedent parties, and the value and circulation of such securities must be essentially diminished, and the debtor driven to the embarrassment of making a sale thereof, often at a ruinous discount to some third person, and then by circuity to apply the proceeds to the payment of his debts. What, indeed, upon such a doctrine would become of that large class of cases, where new notes are given by the same or by other parties, by way of renewal or security to banks, in lieu of old securities discounted by them, which have arrived at maturity? Probably more than one-half of all bank transactions in our country, as well as those of other countries, are of this nature. The doctrine would strike a fatal blow at all discounts of negotiable securities for pre-existing debts.

But, for the purposes of Articles 3 and 4, the general definition of "value" in UCC 1–201(44) is subject to the modifications imposed by UCC 3–303, 4–210 and 4–211.

UCC 3–303(a)(3) preserves the departure from the pre-existing debt rule justified by Mr. Justice Story. Indeed, UCC 3–303(b) goes on to say that an instrument issued for value is supported by consideration even if this would not be so under contract law, as in the case of a note issued for an antecedent debt. (See Case # 1 in Comment 1 to UCC 3–303.) But subparagraph (a)(1) substantially narrows the definition of "value" for the purposes of Article 3 by providing that a purchaser that gives a promise only "takes the instrument for value ... to the extent that the promise has been performed." As Comment 2 explains it: "The policy basis for subsection (a)(1) is that the holder who gives an executory promise of performance will not suffer an out-of-pocket loss to the extent the executory promise is unperformed at the time the holder learns of dishonor of the instrument." In terms familiar to the law of contracts, the *expectation* to which an executory promise gives rise is not enough; there must be actual *reliance* in the form of performance of that promise. Subparagraphs (a)(4) and (5) make a limited exception to this, notably in the case where the executory promise is embodied in a negotiable instrument. (A further exception made in UCC 4–210(a)(2) will be considered later.)

Dean Frederick Beutel criticized the Code for its various definitions of "value," Beutel, The Proposed Uniform [?] Commercial Code Should Not Be Adopted, 61 Yale L.J. 334, 339–41 (1952). Professor Gilmore replied: "In effect the Code says that value is any consideration sufficient to support a simple contract (including extension of credit) except that for the purpose of determining when a person ... is a holder in due course of a negotiable instrument, the extension of credit is not enough: the consideration must be executed. Is the exception necessary? There was considerable sentiment among members of the drafting staff in favor of abolishing the exception and thereby achieving a uniformity in this important concept which the earlier Acts had failed to do. This proposal met the massed opposition of the legal profession as represented in the Conference and the Institute." Gilmore, The Uniform Commercial Code: A Reply to Professor Beutel, 61 Yale L.J. 364, 369 (1952). See also Lawrence, Misconceptions About Article 3 of the Uniform Commercial Code: A Suggested Methodology and Proposed Revisions, 62 N.C.L.Rev. 115, 134–136 (1984). Revised Article 3 makes no change in this respect.

(4) Contract Rights. In a case involving a good faith purchaser of a bill of exchange that had been stolen after the payee had indorsed it in blank, Lord Mansfield distinguished negotiable instruments from ordinary contract rights. "The holder of a bill of exchange, or promissory note, is not to be considered in the light of an assignee of the payee. An assignee must take the thing assigned, subject to all the equity to which the original party was subject. If this rule applied to bills and promissory notes, it would stop their currency." Peacock v. Rhodes, 2 Dougl. 633, 99 Eng.Rep. 402 (K.B. 1781). But should not the assignee of a contract right who has purchased it in good faith have at least the protection accorded by the doctrine of voidable title in the case of fraud?

The modern rule applicable to such an assignee is set out in the Restatement (Second) of Contracts § 343, entitled "Latent Equities."

> If an assignor's right against the obligor is held in trust or constructive trust for or subject to a right of avoidance or equitable lien of another than the obligor, an assignee does not so hold it if he gives value and becomes an assignee in good faith and without notice of the right of the other.

Comment *c* to that section includes an interesting comparison to the Code rules on the same subject.

> The rule of this Section is negated with respect to negotiable instruments and documents of title which are transferred but not duly negotiated by Uniform Commercial Code §§ 3–306,[12] 7–504, 8–301. But compare § 9–308 (chattel paper).

What does § 343 mean by "value"? Comment *d* to § 338, after reviewing the various definitions of "value" found in the Code, concludes:

> The extent to which by analogy this statutory rule [of UCC 1–201(44)] may be applicable to purchases of contractual rights

12. Former UCC 3–306, the version referred to, read: "Unless he has the rights of a holder in due course any person takes the instrument subject to ... all valid claims to it on the part of any person...."

not subject to the statutory provisions is beyond the scope of this Restatement.

———

BOARD OF INLAND REVENUE v. HADDOCK
(THE NEGOTIABLE COW)

A.P. Herbert, The Uncommon Law 112–117 (1936).

"Was the cow crossed?"

"No, your worship, it was an open cow."

These and similar passages provoked laughter at Bow Street today when the Negotiable Cow case was concluded.

Sir Joshua Hoot, K.C. (appearing for the Public Prosecutor): [Sir Joshua stated, for Sir Basil String, the justice sitting, the history of Mr. Albert Haddock's dispute with the Collector of Taxes.] On the 31st of May the Collector was diverted from his respectable labours by the apparition of a noisy crowd outside his windows. The crowd, Sir Basil, had been attracted by Mr. Haddock, who was leading a large white cow of malevolent aspect. On the back and sides of the cow were clearly stencilled in red ink the following words:

"*To the London and Literary Bank, Ltd.*

"Pay the Collector of Taxes, who is nc gentlemen, or Order, the sum of fifty-seven pounds (and may he rot!).

£57/0/0   "Albert Haddock."

Mr. Haddock conducted the cow into the Collector's office, tendered it to the Collector in payment of income-tax and demanded a receipt.... The Collector then endeavoured to endorse the cheque—

Sir Basil String: Where?

Sir Joshua: On the back of the cheque, Sir Basil, that is to say on the abdomen of the cow. The cow, however, appeared to resent endorsement and adopted a menacing posture. The Collector, abandoning the attempt, declined finally to take the cheque....

Mr. Haddock, in the witness-box, said that he had tendered a cheque in payment of income-tax, and if the Commissioners did not like his cheque they could do the other thing. A cheque was only an order to a bank to pay money to the person in possession of the cheque or a person named on the cheque. There was nothing in statute or customary law to say that that order must be written on a piece of paper of specified dimensions. A cheque, it was well known, could be written on a piece of notepaper. He himself had drawn cheques on the backs of menus, on napkins, on handkerchiefs, on the labels of wine-bottles; all these cheques had been duly honoured by his bank and passed through the Bankers' Clearing House. He could see no distinction in law between a cheque written on a napkin and a cheque written on a cow. The essence of each document was a written order to pay money, made in the customary form.... There were funds in his bank sufficient to meet the cow; the Commissioners might not like the cow, but, the cow having been tendered, they were estopped from charging him with failure to pay....

Sir Basil String (after hearing of further evidence):

[The court's discussion of the law is omitted.]

In my judgment, Mr. Haddock has behaved throughout in the manner of a perfect knight, citizen, and taxpayer. The charge brought by the Crown is dismissed.... What is the next case, please?

SECTION 3. DOCUMENTS OF TITLE

Prefatory Note. We now turn to the good faith purchase of yet another kind of property, documents of title (UCC 1–201(15)). We focus on warehouse receipts (UCC 1–201(45)) in particular. Bills of lading (UCC 1–201(6)), the other major type of document of title, will be considered in Chapter 6, infra.

Nature delivers crops at annual harvests, while consumption is gradual throughout the year. Consequently, commodities of enormous value must be kept in storage pending processing, distribution and use. Other commodities—like fuel oil—are stored in large quantities because their use is seasonal. In still other instances, storage is a significant part of preparation for use. Seasoning for years in charred oak barrels is of the essence in making good whiskey. According to UCC 1–201(45), "a receipt issued by a person engaged in the business of storing goods for hire" is a "warehouse receipt." Warehouse receipts may be employed as a means for traders to deal in these goods without the inconvenience of physical delivery. A slightly different use arises when a concern, such as a brewer or a mill, needs to hold commodities which tie up more capital than it can spare. Using warehouse receipts as collateral may facilitate a low-interest loan that otherwise would not be available.

Plainly, the rights of such transferees of such documents are an important factor in such transactions. A transferee of a warehouse receipt wants to be sure of taking both the document and the goods free from claims of third parties. To what extent, since a warehouse receipt embodying the obligation of the bailee to deliver goods has some similarity to a promissory note embodying the obligation of the maker to pay money, are the rules applicable to the transfer of warehouse receipts similar to those applicable to the transfer of commercial paper?

And to what extent are they similar to those applicable to the transfer of the goods themselves?

Confusion in the early case-law concerning these problems was largely dissipated by the detailed provisions of the Uniform Sales Act and the Uniform Bills of Lading and Warehouse Receipts Acts. These provisions have been reorganized and strengthened in the Code's Article 7—Warehouse Receipts, Bills of Lading and other Documents of Title. In this section especially close attention must be given to the structure and language of these statutory rules.

References. For discussions of the statutory rules under consideration in this Section, see R. Henson, Documents of Title Under the Uniform Commercial Code (2d ed. 1990); Dolan, Good Faith Purchase and Warehouse Receipts: Thoughts on the Interplay of Articles 2, 7, and 9 of the UCC, 30 Hastings L.J. 1 (1978).

AMERICAN WAREHOUSE COMPANY
A PUBLIC WAREHOUSE
2121 AMERICAN AVENUE ● AMERICA

Seal of Security

Date of Issue___July 30, 1993___　　Consecutive No.___432___

THIS IS TO CERTIFY that we have received in Storage Warehouse_____

situated at ___2121 American Avenue___

for the account of ___O Company, Inc.___

in apparent good order, except as noted hereon (contents, condition and quality unknown) the following described property, subject to all the terms and conditions contained herein and on the reverse hereof, such property to be delivered to (His) (Their) (Its) order, upon payment of all storage, handling and other charges and the surrender of this Warehouse Receipt properly endorsed,

LOT NO.	QUANTITY	SAID TO BE OR CONTAIN	STORAGE PER MONTH		HANDLING IN AND OUT	
			RATE	PER	RATE	PER
3628	250 bales	cotton	___¢	bale	___¢	bale

NEGOTIABLE

Quantities subject to deliveries noted below.

Advances have been made and liability incurred on such goods, as follows:

_____

_____

The property covered by this receipt has NOT been insured by this company for the benefit of the depositor against fire or any other casualty.

(This clause to be omitted from forms used in those states where warehousemen are required by law to insure goods.)

American Warehouse Company claims a lien for all lawful charges for storage and preservation of the goods; also for all lawful claims for money advanced, interest, insurance, transportation, labor, weighing, coopering and other charges and expenses in relation to such goods.

AMERICAN WAREHOUSE COMPANY

By___*K. L. Bailey*___

THE GOODS MENTIONED BELOW ARE HEREBY RELEASED FROM THIS RECEIPT FOR DELIVERY FROM WAREHOUSE. ANY UNRELEASED BALANCE OF THE GOODS IS SUBJECT TO A LIEN FOR UNPAID CHARGES AND ADVANCES ON THE RELEASED PORTION.

DELIVERIES

DATE	LOT NUMBER	QUANTITY RELEASED		SIGNATURE	QUANTITY DUE ON RECEIPT
8/19/93	3628	50	bales	*J. T. Bailer*	200 bales

This Receipt Is Valid Only When Signed by an Officer of the Company.

NEGOTIABLE WAREHOUSE RECEIPT [1]

[Front—Printed on Green Paper—Reduced in Size]

1. Forms of Warehouse Receipts reproduced by courtesy of the American Warehousemen's Association, Merchandise Division. The backs of the two types of receipts are identical except for color.

The property described on this receipt is stored and handled in accordance with the terms and conditions of the Contract and Rate Quotation approved by the American Warehousemen's Association. These Contract and Rate Quotation terms and conditions are repeated below for the convenience of the storer and others having an interest in the property.

STANDARD CONTRACT TERMS AND CONDITIONS FOR MERCHANDISE WAREHOUSEMEN

(APPROVED AND PROMULGATED BY THE AMERICAN WAREHOUSEMEN'S ASSOCIATION, OCTOBER 1968)

ACCEPTANCE — Sec. 1

(a) This contract and rate quotation including accessorial charges endorsed on or attached hereto must be accepted within 30 days from the proposal date by signature of depositor on the reverse side of the contract. In the absence of written acceptance, the act of tendering goods described herein for storage or other services by warehouseman within 30 days from the proposal date shall constitute such acceptance by depositor.

(b) In the event that goods tendered for storage or other services do not conform to the description contained herein, or conforming goods are tendered after 30 days from the proposal date without prior written acceptance by depositor as provided in paragraph (a) of this section, warehouseman may refuse to accept such goods. If warehouseman accepts such goods, depositor agrees to rates and charges as may be assigned and invoiced by warehouseman and to all terms of this contract.

(c) This contract may be cancelled by either party upon 30 days written notice and is cancelled if no storage or other services are performed under this contract for a period of 180 days.

SHIPPING — Sec. 2

Depositor agrees not to ship goods to warehouseman as the named consignee. If, in violation of this agreement, goods are shipped to warehouseman as named consignee, depositor agrees to notify carrier in writing prior to such shipment, with copy of such notice to the warehouseman, that warehouseman named as consignee is a warehouseman and has no beneficial title or interest in such property and depositor further agrees to indemnify and hold harmless warehouseman from any and all claims for unpaid transportation charges, including undercharges, demurrage, detention or charges of any nature, in connection with goods so shipped. Depositor further agrees that, if it fails to notify carrier as required by the next preceding sentence, warehouseman shall have the right to refuse such goods and shall not be liable or responsible for any loss, injury or damage of any nature to, or related to, such goods. Depositor agrees that all promises contained in this section will be binding on depositor's heirs, successors and assigns.

TENDER FOR STORAGE — Sec. 3

All goods for storage shall be delivered at the warehouse properly marked and packaged for handling. The depositor shall furnish at or prior to such delivery, a manifest showing marks, brands, or sizes to be kept and accounted for separately, and the class of storage and other services desired.

STORAGE PERIOD AND CHARGES — Sec. 4

(a) All charges for storage are per package or other agreed unit per month.

(b) Storage charges become applicable upon the date that warehouseman accepts care, custody and control of the goods, regardless of unloading date or date of issue of warehouse receipt.

(c) Except as provided in paragraph (d) of this section, a full month's storage charge will apply on all goods received between the first and the 15th, inclusive, of a calendar month; one-half month's storage charge will apply on all goods received between the 16th and last day, inclusive, of a calendar month, and a full month's storage charge will apply to all goods in storage on the first day of the next and succeeding calendar months. All storage charges are due and payable on the first day of storage for the initial month and thereafter on the first day of the calendar month.

(d) When mutually agreed by the warehouseman and the depositor, a storage month shall extend from a date in one calendar month to, but not including, the same date of the next and all succeeding months. All storage charges are due and payable on the first day of the storage month.

TRANSFER, TERMINATION OF STORAGE, REMOVAL OF GOODS — Sec. 5

(a) Instructions to transfer goods on the books of the warehouseman are not effective until delivered to and accepted by warehouseman, and all charges up to the time transfer is made are chargeable to the depositor of record. If a transfer involves rehandling the goods, such will be subject to a charge. When goods in storage are transferred from one party to another through issuance of a new warehouse receipt, a new storage date is established on the date of transfer.

(b) The warehouseman reserves the right to move, at his expense, 14 days after notice is sent by certified or registered mail to the depositor of record or to the last known holder of the negotiable warehouse receipt, any goods in storage from the warehouse in which they may be stored to any other of his warehouses; but if such depositor or holder takes delivery of his goods in lieu of transfer, no storage charge shall be made for the current storage month. The warehouseman may, without notice, move goods within the warehouse in which they are stored.

(c) The warehouseman may, upon written notice to the depositor of record and any other person known by the warehouseman to claim an interest in the goods, require the removal of any goods by the end of the next succeeding storage month. Such notice shall be given to the last known place of business or abode of the person to be notified. If goods are not removed before the end of the next succeeding storage month, the warehouseman may sell them in accordance with applicable law.

(d) If warehouseman in good faith believes that the goods are about to deteriorate or decline in value to less than the amount of warehouseman's lien before the end of the next succeeding storage month, the warehouseman may specify in the notification any reasonable shorter time for removal of the goods and in the event goods are not removed, may sell them at public sale held one week after a single advertisement or posting as provided by law.

(e) If as a result of a quality or condition of the goods of which the warehouseman had no notice at the time of deposit the goods are a hazard to other property or to the warehouse or to persons, the warehouseman may sell the goods at public or private sale without advertisement on reasonable notification to all persons known to claim an interest in the goods. If the warehouseman after a reasonable effort is unable to sell the goods he may dispose of them in any lawful manner and shall incur no liability by reason of such disposition. Pending such disposition, sale or return of the goods, the warehouseman may remove the goods from the warehouse and shall incur no liability by reason of such removal.

HANDLING — Sec. 6

(a) The handling charge covers the ordinary labor involved in receiving goods at warehouse door, placing goods in storage, and returning goods to warehouse door. Handling charges are due and payable on receipt of goods.

(b) Unless otherwise agreed, labor for unloading and loading goods will be subject to a charge. Additional expenses incurred by the warehouseman in receiving and handling damaged goods, and additional expense in unloading from or loading into cars or other vehicles not at warehouse door will be charged to the depositor.

(c) Labor and materials used in loading rail cars or other vehicles are chargeable to the depositor.

(d) When goods are ordered out in quantities less than in which received, the warehouseman may make an additional charge for each order or each item of an order.

(e) The warehouseman shall not be liable for demurrage, delays in unloading inbound cars, or delays in obtaining and loading cars for outbound shipment unless warehouseman has failed to exercise reasonable care.

DELIVERY REQUIREMENTS — Sec. 7

(a) No goods shall be delivered or transferred except upon receipt by the warehouseman of complete instructions properly signed by the depositor. However, when no negotiable receipt is outstanding, goods may be delivered upon instructions by telephone in accordance with a prior written authorization, but the warehouseman shall not be responsible for loss or error occasioned thereby.

(b) When a negotiable receipt has been issued no goods covered by that receipt shall be delivered, or transferred on the books of the warehouseman, unless the receipt, properly indorsed, is surrendered for cancellation, or for indorsement of partial delivery thereon. If a negotiable receipt is lost or destroyed, delivery of goods may be made only upon order of a court of competent jurisdiction and the posting of security approved by the court as provided by law.

(c) When goods are ordered out a reasonable time shall be given the warehouseman to carry out instructions, and if he is unable because of acts of God, war, public enemies, seizure under legal process, strikes, lockouts, riots and civil commotions, or any reason beyond the warehouseman's control, or because of loss or destruction of goods for which warehouseman is not liable, or because of any other excuse provided by law, the warehouseman shall not be liable for failure to carry out such instructions and goods remaining in storage will continue to be subject to regular storage charges.

EXTRA SERVICES (SPECIAL SERVICES) — Sec. 8

(a) Warehouse labor required for services other than ordinary handling and storage will be charged to the depositor.

(b) Special services requested by depositor including but not limited to compiling of special stock statements; reporting marked weights, serial numbers or other data from packages; physical check of goods; and handling transit billing will be subject to a charge.

(c) Dunnage, bracing, packing materials or other special supplies, may be provided for the depositor at a charge.

(d) By prior arrangement, goods may be received or delivered during other than usual business hours, subject to a charge.

(e) Communication expense including postage, teletype, telegram, or telephone, will be charged to the depositor if such concern more than normal inventory reporting or if, at the request of the depositor, communications are made by other than regular United States Mail.

BONDED STORAGE — Sec. 9

(a) A charge in addition to regular rates will be made for merchandise in bond.

(b) Where a negotiable receipt covers goods in U. S. Customs bond, such receipt shall be void upon the termination of the storage period fixed by law.

MINIMUM CHARGES — Sec. 10

(a) A minimum handling charge per lot and a minimum storage charge per lot per month will be made. When a warehouse receipt covers more than one lot or when a lot is in assortment, a minimum charge per mark, brand or variety will be made.

(b) A minimum monthly charge to one account for storage and/or handling will be made. This charge will apply also to each account when one customer has several accounts, each requiring separate records and billing.

LIABILITY AND LIMITATION OF DAMAGES — Sec. 11

(A) THE WAREHOUSEMAN SHALL NOT BE LIABLE FOR ANY LOSS OR INJURY TO GOODS STORED HOWEVER CAUSED UNLESS SUCH LOSS OR INJURY RESULTED FROM THE FAILURE BY THE WAREHOUSEMAN TO EXERCISE SUCH CARE IN REGARD TO THEM AS A REASONABLY CAREFUL MAN WOULD EXERCISE UNDER LIKE CIRCUMSTANCES AND WAREHOUSEMAN IS NOT LIABLE FOR DAMAGES WHICH COULD NOT HAVE BEEN AVOIDED BY THE EXERCISE OF SUCH CARE.

(B) GOODS ARE NOT INSURED BY WAREHOUSEMAN AGAINST LOSS OR INJURY HOWEVER CAUSED.

(C) THE DEPOSITOR DECLARES THAT DAMAGES ARE LIMITED TO _____ PROVIDED, HOWEVER, THAT SUCH LIABILITY MAY AT THE TIME OF ACCEPTANCE OF THIS CONTRACT AS PROVIDED IN SECTION I BE INCREASED ON PART OR ALL OF THE GOODS HEREUNDER IN WHICH EVENT A MONTHLY STORAGE CHARGE OF _____ WILL BE MADE IN ADDITION TO THE REGULAR MONTHLY STORAGE CHARGE.

NOTICE OF CLAIM AND FILING OF SUIT — Sec. 12

(a) Claims by the depositor and all other persons must be presented in writing to the warehouseman within a reasonable time, and in no event longer than either 60 days after delivery of the goods by the warehouseman or 60 days after depositor of record or the last known holder of a negotiable warehouse receipt is notified by the warehouseman that loss or injury to part or all of the goods has occurred, whichever time is shorter.

(b) No action may be maintained by the depositor or others, against the warehouseman for loss or injury to the goods stored unless timely written claim has been given as provided in paragraph (a) of this section and unless such action is commenced either within nine months after date of delivery by warehouseman or within nine months after depositor of record or the last known holder of a negotiable warehouse receipt is notified that loss or injury to part or all of the goods has occurred, whichever time is shorter.

(c) When goods have not been delivered, notice may be given of known loss or injury to the goods by mailing of a registered or certified letter to the depositor of record or to the last known holder of a negotiable warehouse receipt. Time limitations for presentation of claim in writing and maintaining of action after date of mailing of such notice by warehouseman.

NEGOTIABLE OR NON-NEGOTIABLE WAREHOUSE RECEIPT

[Back—Printed on Same Color Paper as Front]

AMERICAN WAREHOUSE COMPANY STREET ADDRESS ● CITY & AMERICA 00000 TELEPHONE: (312) – 123-4567	ORIGINAL NON-NEGOTIABLE WAREHOUSE RECEIPT	DOCUMENT NUMBER 1046

ORIGINAL

NON-NEGOTIABLE WAREHOUSE RECEIPT

AMERICAN WAREHOUSE COMPANY claims a lien for all lawful charges for storage and preservation of the goods; also for: all lawful claims for money advanced, interest, insurance, transportation, labor, weighing, coopering and other charges and expenses in relation to such goods, and for the balance on any other accounts that may be due. The property covered by this receipt has NOT been insured by this Company for the benefit of the depositor against fire or any other casualty.

DOCUMENT NUMBER: 1046

DATE: July 30, 1993

RECEIVED FROM: O Company, Inc. / 200 State Street / Statesville, New York

CUSTOMER NUMBER: 8919

CUSTOMER ORDER NO.

THIS IS TO CERTIFY THAT WE HAVE RECEIVED the goods listed hereon in apparent good order, except as noted herein (contents, condition and quality unknown), SUBJECT TO ALL TERMS AND CONDITIONS INCLUDING LIMITATION OF LIABILITY HEREIN AND ON THE REVERSE HEREOF. Such property to be delivered to THE DEPOSITOR upon the payment of all storage, handling and other charges. Advances have been made and liability incurred on these goods as follows:

FOR ACCOUNT OF: O Company, Inc. / 200 State Street / Statesville, New York

WAREHOUSE NO.: 1046

DELIVERING CARRIER	CARRIER NUMBER	PREPAID/COLLECT	SHIPPERS NUMBER
PC	PC 458632	Prepaid	

QUANTITY	SAID TO BE OR CONTAIN (CUSTOMER ITEM NO., WAREHOUSE ITEM NO., LOT NUMBER, DESCRIPTION, ETC.)	WEIGHT	R C A O T D E E	STORAGE RATE / HANDLING RATE	DAMAGE & EXCEPTIONS
				¢cs	None
250	bales cotton　　　　500 lbs.	125,000		¢cs	
	TOTALS				

NO DELIVERY WILL BE MADE ON THIS RECEIPT EXCEPT ON WRITTEN ORDER.

AMERICAN WAREHOUSE COMPANY

BY *K. L. Bailey*

AUTHORIZED SIGNATURE

FORM 2 3/70

NON–NEGOTIABLE WAREHOUSE RECEIPT

[Front—Printed on White Paper—Reduced in Size]

Problem 12. O owned cotton worth $100,000. A, who is in the cotton business, stole it from O and stored it in the W warehouse, which issued a negotiable warehouse receipt to A's order. A negotiated the receipt to P, who did not suspect the theft, for $100,000. Who gets the cotton? See UCC 7–501, 7–502, 7–503, 7–504; *Lineburger v. Hodge,* infra. (As to A's liability to P, see UCC 7–507.)

Problem 13. O owned cotton worth $100,000. O stored the cotton in the W warehouse which issued a negotiable warehouse receipt to O's order, which O placed in a safe. A, O's bookkeeper, stole the receipt and indorsed it in the name of "O" and sold it to P, who did not suspect the theft, for $100,000. Who gets the cotton?

Problem 14. O owned cotton worth $100,000. O stored the cotton in the W warehouse which issued a negotiable warehouse receipt to O's order. O in preparation for a proposed sale, indorsed the receipt by signing "O," and placed it in a safe. A, O's bookkeeper, stole the receipt and sold it to P for $100,000.

(a) Who gets the cotton? See Cleveland v. McNabb, 312 F.Supp. 155 (W.D.Tenn.1970).

(b) What result if A had negotiated the receipt to a friend B, who is in the cotton business, who had sold it to P?

(c) What result if P had promised to pay $100,000 for the receipt but had not yet paid it?

Problem 15. O owned cotton worth $100,000. O stored the cotton in the W warehouse, which issued a negotiable warehouse receipt to O's order. A fraudulently obtained it from O, who indorsed it by signing "O." A, who is in the cotton business, negotiated it to P, who did not suspect the fraud, for $100,000.

(a) Who gets the cotton?

(b) What result if O had not indorsed the receipt? See UCC 7–504(1) and Comment 1.

(c) What result if the receipt were a non-negotiable one, which was transferred (not negotiated) to P? Would P's position be improved if P had notified W of the transfer before O claimed the cotton? See UCC 7–504(2).

Problem 16. O owned cotton worth $100,000. O gave the cotton to A, one of its truck drivers, with instructions to haul it to the ginhouse. A stole the cotton and stored it in the W warehouse, which issued a negotiable receipt to "A or order." A sold the receipt to P, who did not suspect the theft, for $100,000, indorsing it by signing his name "A."

(a) Who gets the cotton?

(b) What result if A had negotiated the receipt to a friend B, who is in the cotton business, who had negotiated it to P?[1]

1. The demise of the course in agency at many law schools makes it desirable to underline the limited applicability of the words "apparent authority" in UCC 7–503(1)(a). According to Comment *a* to § 8 of the Restatement Second of Agency, "Ap-

parent authority results from a manifestation by a person that another is his agent, the manifestation being made to a third person and not, as when authority is created, to the agent." The illustrations to that section give this example:

Problem 17. O owned cotton worth $100,000. O placed it in storage with A, who both stores cotton and buys and sells it. A wrongfully delivered the cotton to the W warehouse, which issued a negotiable warehouse receipt to "A or order." A sold the receipt to P, who did not suspect A's wrongdoing, for $100,000, indorsing it by signing "A." Who gets the cotton? Compare Problem 5 supra.

LINEBURGER BROTHERS v. HODGE

Supreme Court of Mississippi, 1951.
212 Miss. 204, 54 So.2d 268.

ALEXANDER, JUSTICE. Separate bills were filed against the Federal Compress & Warehouse Company, a corporation, by E.S. Vancleve, J.R. Hodge, and E.A. Bates & Company, a partnership, each praying for a mandatory injunction against the defendant to compel delivery of cotton held by the defendant to them as purchasers and holders of the warehouse receipts covering the number of bales of cotton held respectively by each of the complainants, or in the alternative for the value of the cotton thereby represented. The total number of bales is twenty-four, Vancleve claiming nine, Hodge six, and E.A. Bates & Company nine.

It is adequately shown that all of the cotton was grown and ginned by Lineburger Brothers, B.C. Lineburger, J.G. Outlaw and F.A. Little, and stolen by one J.V. Carr from a gin where the cotton had been processed and tagged. This asportation occurred at night and was conducted with the aid of a truck driver who was not a regular employee of Carr. Early the next morning Carr carried the cotton to the defendant warehouse, and, after weighing, had the receipts issued in three fictitious names and delivered to him. Carr took the receipts to nearby towns and sold the cotton, so identified, to the three complainants in separate lots. The purchasers gave their separate checks to Carr who procured payment by endorsing them respectively in the names of the three fictitious persons. He then disappeared and has not since been located.

As stated, the three buyers filed their separate bills against the warehouse. The gin company was not made a party. Upon application of the planters or owners, they were allowed to intervene and claim the cotton. From a decree dismissing the petition of the intervenors, absolving the warehouse of negligence in the issuance of the receipts,

P writes to A directing him to act as his agent for the sale of Blackacre. P sends a copy of this letter to T, a prospective purchaser.... [I]n the letter to A, P adds a postscript, not included in the copy to T, telling A to make no sale until after communication with P. A has no authority to sell Blackacre but, as to T, he has apparent authority.

The notion of "apparent authority" does not, for example, extend to the situations covered by the "entrusting" provision of UCC 2–403(2). See Note 2, p. 48 supra.

and awarding title to the respective warehouse receipts to the purchasers with full rights to claim the cotton thereby represented, after paying storage charges to the warehouse, the planters, or owners, appeal. A cross-appeal is filed by the complainants which urges that in event of a reversal of the decree, they be awarded a decree against the warehouse for the value of the cotton.

We deal first with the cross-appeal. It is grounded chiefly upon the alleged negligence of the warehouse in issuing the receipts to Carr in the names given by him....

Regardless of the plausibility of the contention of the appellees, there was an issue of fact in the matter of negligence of the warehouse, and we find no basis for overturning the finding of the chancellor, whose acquittance of the warehouse must of necessity have been upon such absence of negligence.

We approach, then, the rights of the appellants, the planters and owners. As heretofore stated, they had given Carr no authority to take and haul away any of this cotton. Specific instructions, including the time and identity of cotton to be so hauled, were always given, and Carr knew this. It is immaterial whether the warehouse knew of this limitation upon Carr's authority. It is sufficient that this limitation was understood between Carr and appellants. Here there was no dispute, and it is without question that the taking by Carr, under all the circumstances, was larceny, and that the receipts were fraudulently obtained. The next morning Carr was seen and made two different and untrue statements as to where the receipts were. One of these reports was to one of the owners who had discovered that the cotton was missing and was seeking to locate the receipts. There was no one at the gin when the cotton was abstracted, except Carr, his driver, and Mrs. Carr and her small son. The manager of the gin was not present, and he later testified that he had instructions that Carr was not to haul the Lineburger cotton except upon specific instructions. We repeat that the gin is not a party here and the test of the right of the owners must depend on whether this cotton was under any circumstances entrusted to Carr by permission and knowledge of the owners.

We find that the cotton was not so entrusted to Carr, and since the cotton was in fact stolen and the receipts fraudulently obtained, the defense of apparent authority, although available to the warehouse, does not aid the claim of the purchasers of the receipts.

It was held in Unger v. Abbott, 92 Miss. 563, 46 So. 68, that the rule caveat emptor applies against the claim of an innocent purchaser of warehouse receipts who purchased them from the owner's servant who had been sent with cotton to a compress company with instructions to have it weighed and to bring the receipts back to the owner, but who, contrary to his authority and instructions, took the receipts in his own name and sold them.

If it be observed that this case was decided prior to our statutes upon Warehouse Receipts, Chap. 16, Vol. 4, Code 1942 [the Uniform

Warehouse Receipts Act], attention is directed to Section 5051 [UWRA 40], which is as follows: "A negotiable receipt may be negotiated: ...

"(b) By any person to whom the possession or custody of the receipt has been entrusted by the owner, if, by the terms of the receipt, the warehouseman undertakes to deliver the goods to the order of the person to whom the possession or custody of the receipt has been entrusted, or if at the time of such entrusting the receipt is in such form that it may be negotiated by delivery."

We look next at Section 5052 [UWRA 41]: "A person to whom a negotiable receipt has been duly negotiated acquires thereby:

"(a) Such title to the goods as the person negotiating the receipt to him had or had ability to convey to a purchaser in good faith for value, and also such title to the goods as the depositor or person to whose order the goods were to be delivered by the terms of the receipt had or had ability to convey to a purchaser in good faith for value, and...."

Section 5058 [UWRA 47] is also in point. It is as follows: "The validity of the negotiation of a receipt is not impaired by the fact that such negotiation was a breach of duty on the part of the person making the negotiation, or by the fact that the owner of the receipt was induced by fraud, mistake, or duress to entrust the possession or custody of the receipt to such person, if the person to whom the receipt was negotiated, paid or a person to whom the receipt was subsequently negotiated, paid value therefor, without notice of the breach of duty, or fraud, or mistake or duress."

Appellees cite for support Weil Bros., Inc. v. Keenan, 180 Miss. 697, 178 So. 90. Here there was an interpleader suit filed by the warehouse. The testimony disclosed that the receipts had been entrusted to one Spencer by the owner, and were misappropriated by the former. After recognizing that one, especially a trespasser, can not convey a better title than he has, the Court found that the receipts had been entrusted to the thief and an innocent purchaser was protected. To the same effect is Lundy v. Greenville Bank & Tr. Co., 179 Miss. 282, 174 So. 802, and other cases cited by appellees. See also 56 Am.Jur., Warehouses, Sec. 62.

Our statutes do not go so far as those of some other states in protecting a bona fide purchaser of negotiable receipts in cases where the receipts had been stolen. See 56 Am.Jur., Warehouses, Sec. 53. Since such receipts were not negotiable at common law, their negotiability is to be measured by our statutes.

We hold, therefore, that neither the cotton nor the receipts had been entrusted to Carr by the owners and that the latter are not estopped to set up their claim to the cotton as against the several appellees who purchased the receipts....

The assertion wants no support that the statutes referred to were designed to insure the negotiability of warehouse receipts and to facilitate commerce in the market places where cotton is bought and sold. The innocent purchaser of a negotiable receipt is guaranteed an assurance without which the traffic could not be conducted. Yet, such assurance must take into account the older principle that an owner of cotton may not be divested of title by a trespasser or a thief. In order to strike a just balance between these two concepts the statutes were enacted. The buyer must still beware lest he is buying receipts which have been fraudulently obtained or cotton which has been stolen. We need not analyze the statutes to divine whether the owner, who has voluntarily clothed another with indicia of ownership or entrusted him with possession of receipts, is barred of recovery from an innocent purchaser by principles of estoppel or pursuant to the rule that where two innocent persons must suffer from a fraud, he who reposes confidence in the fraudulent agent must suffer. It is enough that the statute recognizes title in the innocent purchaser who has bought receipts from one to whom they have been entrusted by the owner.

Here, as in all such cases, one of two innocent persons must suffer the loss. The thief has stolen or fraudulently obtained property from someone. We hold that the unlawful act was committed against the owners and that the title to the cotton remains in them. As stated in Unger v. Abbott, supra, "(The appellees) are to be condoled with for their loss by this swindle; but their misfortune can not affect the right of (the appellants) to have (their) cotton.... 'Caveat emptor' applies." [92 Miss. 563, 46 So. 68.]

The cause will be reversed and decree awarded to the appellants for the cotton, and the Federal Compress & Warehouse Company is directed to hold the same to the order of appellants, but without storage charges thereon. The cross-appeal is thereby decided adversely.

Reversed and decree here for appellants.

Notes

(1) **"Regular Course."** UCC 7–502(1) requires that the document have been "duly negotiated" and UCC 7–501(4) provides that due negotiation may be negated by showing "that the negotiation is not in the regular course of business or financing." Why do not UCC 3–302 and 3–305 impose a similar requirement in the case of commercial paper? Consider Comment 1 to UCC 7–501. (Does it strike you as a legitimate use of commentary?)

"In general this section is intended to clarify the language of the old acts and to restate the effect of the better decisions thereunder. An important new concept is added, however, in the requirement of 'regular course of business or financing' to effect the 'due negotiation' which will transfer greater rights than those held by the person negotiating. The foundation of the mercantile doctrine of good faith purchase for value has always been, as shown by the case situations, the furtherance and protection of the regular course of trade. The reason for allowing a person, in bad faith or in error, to convey away rights which are not his own has from the beginning been to make possible the speedy handling of that great run of commercial transactions which are patently usual and normal.

"There are two aspects to the usual and normal course of mercantile dealings, namely, the person making the transfer and the nature of the transaction itself. The first question which arises is: Is the transferor a person with whom it is reasonable to deal as having full powers? In regard to documents of title the only holder whose possession appears, commercially, to be in order is almost invariably a person in the trade. No commercial purpose is served by allowing a tramp or a professor to 'duly negotiate' an order bill of lading for hides or cotton not his own, and since such a transfer is obviously not in the regular course of business, it is excluded from the scope of the protection of subsection (4).

"The second question posed by the 'regular course' qualification is: Is the transaction one which is normally proper to pass full rights without inquiry, even though the transferor himself may not have such rights to pass, and even though he may be acting in breach of duty? In raising this question the 'regular course' criterion has the further advantage of limiting the effective wrongful disposition to transactions whose protection will really further trade. Obviously, the snapping up of goods for quick resale at a price suspiciously below the market deserves no protection as a matter of policy: it is also clearly outside the range of regular course.

"Any notice from the face of the document sufficient to put a merchant on inquiry as to the 'regular course' quality of the transaction will frustrate a 'due negotiation'. Thus irregularity of the document on its face or unexplained staleness of a bill of lading may appropriately be recognized as negating a negotiation in 'regular' course.

"A pre-existing claim constitutes value, and 'due negotiation' does not require 'new value.' A usual and ordinary transaction in which documents are received as security for credit previously extended may be in 'regular' course, even though there is a demand for additional collateral because the creditor 'deems himself insecure.' But the matter has moved out of the regular course of financing if the debtor is thought to be insolvent, the credit previously extended is in effect cancelled, and the creditor snatches a plank in the shipwreck under the guise of a demand for additional collateral. Where a money debt is 'paid' in commodity paper, any question of 'regular' course disappears, as the case is explicitly excepted from 'due negotiation'."

(2) **Consistency.** Before proceeding to the next chapter, review your answers to the problems in this chapter to see if the rules relating to good faith purchase of goods, negotiable instruments, and documents of title are consistent. Is the treatment of "value" consistent? Compare Problem 2, Problem 5, Problem 9, Problem 11, and Problem 15. Is the treatment of "good faith" (and "regular course") consistent? Com-

pare Problem 2, Problem 5, Problem 9, and Problem 15. Can you think of adequate explanations for the variations that you find?

Do the differences in treatment of transactions in goods, negotiable documents of title, and non-negotiable documents of title make sense? Professor Gilmore wrote of the "odd result" of the "forked development" of negotiable and non-negotiable documents, in that "although goods covered by a negotiable document become for all intents themselves negotiable, the same goods, covered by a non-negotiable document, revert to the status of a common law chose, less susceptible to the operation of the good faith purchase concept than before they were covered by the document." Gilmore, The Commercial Doctrine of Good Faith Purchase, 63 Yale L.J. 1057, 1078 (1954). Compare Problem 15 with Problem 11. For criticism of the proposition "that a mere transferee of a document of title (a transferee who is not a holder by due negotiation) acquires no greater rights than those of his transferor," see Riegert, The Rights of a Transferee of a Document of Title Who Is Not a Holder by Due Negotiation, 9 Cum.L.Rev. 27 (1978).

Do the provisions that you have studied on good faith purchase (UCC 2–403(1), 3–306, 7–502(1)) have helpful similarities in format and style that encourage you in the notion that the Code is a "code" rather than a collection of related statutes? (Although Article 8, Investment Securities, is beyond the scope of this book, the same question can also be asked with respect to UCC 8–301.) See Gilmore, The Good Faith Purchase Idea and the Uniform Commercial Code: Confessions of a Repentant Draftsman, 15 Ga.L.Rev. 605 (1981) ("One of the sad truths about the Code is that its several articles were never coordinated as they should have been.").

Chapter 2

FREEDOM FROM DEFENSES;
OTHER CONSEQUENCES

Introduction. The preceding chapter was concerned with the purchaser's freedom from conflicting *claims* of ownership with respect to the property. (Can a good faith purchaser keep the property purchased?) Where the property consists of an obligation of some kind, further questions arise concerning the purchaser's freedom from *defenses* of the obligor with respect to that obligation. Can a good faith purchaser enforce the obligation purchased? The simplest questions are those arising out of the assignment of an ordinary contract right. The familiar rule is stated by the Code in UCC 9–318(1) and by the Restatement (Second) of Contracts in § 336(1).

> By an assignment the assignee acquires a right against the obligor only to the extent that the obligor is under a duty to the assignor; and if the right of the assignor would be voidable by the obligor or unenforceable against him if no assignment had been made, the right of the assignee is subject to the infirmity.

This chapter explores analogous questions arising out of the transfer of negotiable instruments and documents of title.

SECTION 1. NEGOTIABLE INSTRUMENTS

(A) IN GENERAL

Problem 1. By fraudulent representations B sold A a defective machine for A's factory for $100,000, payable in 30 days. B assigned the right to payment to the C finance company, which did not know of the fraud and paid B $100,000 less a discount. On discovery of the fraud, A tendered the machine back to C and refused to pay anything.

(a) Can C recover the $100,000 from A? See UCC 9–318(1); Restatement (Second) of Contracts § 336(1), supra.[1]

(b) What result if the contract between A and B contained a waiver-of-defense clause—an agreement that A will not assert against an assignee any claim or defense that A may have against B? See UCC 9–206, 3–305. (Would a *promise* by C to pay B $100,000 less a discount be value under UCC 9–206(1)? See Note 3, p. 67 supra.)

Problem 2. By fraudulent representations, B sold A a defective machine for A's factory for $100,000, payable in 30 days. In connection with the sale, A executed a negotiable promissory note, promising "to pay to the order of B, $100,000" in 30 days. B assigned the right to payment and negotiated the note to the C finance company, by indorsing it "Pay to the order of C, (signed) B." C did not suspect the fraud and paid B $100,000 less a discount.

(a) On discovery of the fraud, A tendered the machine back to C and refused to pay anything. Can C recover the $100,000 from A? See UCC 3–305; First National Bank of *Odessa v. Fazzari,* infra; *Universal C.I.T. Credit Corp. v. Ingel,* infra.

(b) On discovery of the fraud, A kept the machine, but because of its defects made $30,000 in repairs, and refused to pay more than $70,000. Can C recover the full $100,000 from A? See Note 2, p. 89 infra.

Problem 3. Would the answer to the preceding problem be different if the body of the promissory note read as follows:

For value received, I promise to pay to the order of B, $100,000, payable $50,000 in six months after date and $50,000 in twelve months after date, with interest payable monthly at three per cent over Chase Manhattan Prime to be adjusted monthly, with the privilege of discharging this note by payment of principal less a discount of five per cent within thirty days from the date hereof. The entire principal of this note shall become due and payable on demand should the holder at any time deem itself insecure. This note is secured by a security agreement of the same date to which reference is made as to rights in collateral.

See UCC 3–104, 3–106, 3–108, 3–109, 3–112.

———

1. As to B's liability to C, Restatement (Second) of Contracts § 333(1) provides: "Unless a contrary intention is manifested, one who assigns ... a right by assignment ... for value warrants to the assignee ... that the right, as assigned, actually exists and is subject to no limitations or defenses good against the assignor other than those stated or apparent at the time of the assignment...."

FIRST NATIONAL BANK OF ODESSA v. FAZZARI

Court of Appeals of New York, 1961.
10 N.Y.2d 394, 223 N.Y.S.2d 483, 179 N.E.2d 493.

FOSTER, JUDGE. On December 16, 1957 defendant executed a six-month promissory note to the order of John Wade, Jr. The instrument was payable at the Glen National Bank, Watkins Glen, N.Y., in the amount of $400, with interest. Apparently defendant was unable to read or write English. It was found below that the payee, Wade, prepared the note and induced defendant to sign it upon the misrepresentation that it was a statement of wages earned by Wade while working for defendant, and that it was necessary for income tax purposes. Defendant was not in debt to Wade, and there was no consideration given for the note. The note was signed at the home of defendant in Watkins Glen. At the time, his wife and daughter were present in the house, and his wife, who was able to read, was in an adjoining room. Defendant did not request his wife to read the instrument.

Subsequently defendant learned that the instrument he had signed might have been a note. He consulted his attorney who advised him to notify all of the banks in Schuyler County, and to advise them not to accept the note. In January of 1958, defendant orally informed the cashier of the plaintiff bank in Odessa that he "had been tricked" and that he did not intend to sign a note. He instructed the cashier not to "cash a note" for John Wade, and "not to give him any money under my name". The cashier told him "not to worry" and defendant departed. The cashier, Gilbert, recalled the incident, and testified that defendant told him not to give any money to anyone under Fazzari's name. Gilbert acknowledged that he probably did tell defendant "not to worry", but testified that at the time the note was presented to him for discount he had forgotten the incident.

We thus have an element presented in this case not present in any of the "forgotten notice" cases so far as we have been able to discover. Not only was notice given to the very cashier who subsequently discounted the note, but the defendant was assured that he had no cause to be concerned about the bank's discounting the note. The phrase "not to worry" would present no other realistic meaning to the average person.

On April 10, 1958 the note was presented to the First National Bank of Odessa by Wellington R. Doane, a customer of the bank and an indorsee of the payee, Wade. Doane indorsed the instrument in blank, and the plaintiff bank, by its cashier, Gilbert, accepted it for value, paying $400 by cashier's check. It was found by the trial court that the cashier, at the time of the negotiation of the note to the bank, had forgotten defendant's prior visit to the bank and the oral notice he had given.

After nonpayment and protest, the plaintiff bank brought this action against defendant. At the close of the evidence the trial court awarded judgment to the plaintiff, holding that the bank was a holder in due course under section 91, Consol.Laws, c. 38, of the Negotiable Instruments Law [NIL 52], since its agent had forgotten the prior notice and had acted in good faith in accepting the note. The Appellate Division reversed, holding that the notice, once given, was binding on the bank (Negotiable Instruments Law, § 91, subd. 4) [NIL 52(4)]; that the bank was not a holder in due course; and that the maker's defense, therefore, was valid.

Thus the status of the bank is determinative here. The courts below found fraud in the factum; that is, defendant was induced to sign something entirely different than what he thought he was signing. *In the absence of negligence on the part of the maker,* such fraud constitutes a real defense and is sufficient against a holder in due course [citations omitted]. But the courts below have determined as a fact that defendant was negligent in not asking his wife to read over the instrument prior to signing. We cannot say this finding was erroneous as a matter of law, particularly since defendant, an experienced business man, on prior occasions, asked that documents of obvious legal import be read to him before signing. Defendant also knew that he had paid Wade $500 in wages, and yet signed a purported statement of wages in the amount of $400.

The facts as determined by the trial court have been affirmed. The sole question presented is this: Did the bank, the purchaser of a negotiable promissory note, qualify as a holder in due course, and defeat the effect of a prior oral notice of infirmity in the note, by showing that it had forgotten the notice at the time of purchase?

Section 91 of the Negotiable Instruments Law [NIL 52] provides:

"A holder in due course is a holder who has taken the instrument under the following conditions:

"1.   That it is complete and regular upon its face;

"2.   That he became the holder of it before it was overdue, and without notice that it had been previously dishonored, if such was the fact;

"3.   That he took it in good faith and for value;

"4.   That at the time it was negotiated to him he had no notice of any infirmity in the instrument or defect in the title of the person negotiating it."

Section 95 [NIL 56] provides: "To constitute notice of an infirmity in the instrument or defect in the title of the person negotiating the same, the person to whom it is negotiated must have had actual knowledge of the infirmity or defect, or knowledge of such facts that his action in taking the instrument amounted to bad faith."

The bank contends that the cashier did not have notice of the infirmity *at the time of the negotiation,* and thus the bank met each of the conditions of sections 91 and 95 [NIL 52, 56], and we are asked to apply the doctrine of forgotten notice. This doctrine was first enunciated in Raphael v. Bank of England (17 C.B. 161, 84 Eng.Com.Law 160) cited with approval by this court in Magee v. Badger (34 N.Y. 247, 249). In the Raphael case notice of a robbery of a certain note was given to a bank, but thereafter the bank accepted the note for value and contended that it had forgotten the notice. It was held that a jury question existed as to whether the bank had forgotten the notice or omitted inadvertently to look for the notice, and that such a lapse of memory and omission to look for the notice, if established, would constitute mere negligence, not *mala fides*. Mere negligence, it was held, would not destroy the bank's status as a holder in due course. In Lord v. Wilkinson (56 Barb. 593 [Sup.Ct., Broome County, 1870]) the doctrine of forgotten notice was adopted by a court of this State, and Raphael v. Bank of England specifically was followed. In the Lord case the facts again were strikingly similar to those herein involved. In Graham v. White–Phillips Co., 296 U.S. 27, 56 S.Ct. 21, 80 L.Ed. 20, the United States Supreme Court, construing the Illinois Negotiable Instruments Law (containing the same provisions as the New York law), followed the Lord and Raphael cases, and referred specifically thereto. That case involved forgotten notice of stolen bonds, and it was held that the negligent omission to look for the notice, or to recall it, did not destroy the status of the defendant as a holder in due course.

The rule was followed in Merchants Nat. Bank v. Detroit Trust Co. (258 Mich. 526, 242 N.W. 739, 85 A.L.R. 350, cited with approval in Graham v. White–Phillips Co., supra) and in State Bank of Benkelman v. Iowa–Des Moines Nat. Bank & Trust Co. (223 Iowa 596, 273 N.W. 160; see, also, Seybel v. National Currency Bank, 54 N.Y. 288, wherein this court virtually approved the doctrine; contra, Northwestern Nat. Bank v. Madison & Kedzie State Bank, 242 Ill.App. 22, holding notice, once given, is binding on the bank). The doctrine is not without its critics, who favor an objective test of notice. Thus, it is said, notice once given should bind the purchaser, for such a rule would impose upon the banks no more difficult administrative responsibility than they are under in many analogous situations (see e.g., Britton, Bills and Notes [1943], p. 449; Merrill, The Wages of Indifference, 10 Temp.L.Q. 147; Unforgettable Knowledge, 34 Mich.L.Rev. 474; The Anatomy of Notice, 3 U. of Chi.L.Rev. 416; 10 Tul.L.Rev. 302; cf. 40 Harv.L.Rev. 315; 45 Yale L.J. 539).

Perhaps the doctrine is in accord with the general rule in New York, that "The rights of the holder [of a negotiable instrument] are to be determined by the simple test of honesty and good faith, and not by speculations in regard to the purchaser's diligence or negligence" (Manufacturers & Traders Trust Co. v. Sapowitch, 296 N.Y. 226, 230, 72 N.E.2d 166; Magee v. Badger, 34 N.Y. 247, 249). "The requirement of the statute is good faith, and bad faith is not mere carelessness. It is nothing less than guilty knowledge or willful ignorance" (Manufacturers & Traders Trust Co. v. Sapowitch, supra, 296 N.Y. p. 229, 72 N.E.2d

p. 168 ...). The doctrine, of course, is based on a policy of freedom of negotiability.

The Appellate Division was of the opinion that since the doctrine was adopted prior to the enactment of the Negotiable Instruments Law (Lord v. Wilkinson, supra) its rationale should be rejected. We are not prepared to reject the doctrine summarily and to hold that once notice is given it is fixed and immutable for all time as to negotiable instruments, particularly in the case where a blanket notice is broadcast with relation to stolen bonds and other securities (Kentucky Rock Asphalt Co. v. Mazza's Adm'r, 264 Ky. 158, 165, 94 S.W.2d 316). But we also think that the doctrine should be applied with great caution in the case where a simple promissory note is involved. A lapse of memory is too easily pleaded and too difficult to controvert to permit the doctrine to be applied automatically irrespective of the circumstances surrounding each transaction and the relationship of the parties. Under the peculiar facts of this case a strict application of the doctrine would be unrealistic and not in the interests of substantial justice. As we have heretofore said, something more than the naked fact of notice is involved here. The defendant was practically assured that his notice would be honored and that the note would not be discounted by the plaintiff bank. Under such circumstances, the bank should be precluded from invoking the doctrine of "forgotten notice."

Holding

The judgment should be affirmed.

Notes

(1) Defenses Under the Code. What result in the *Fazzari* case under the Code? See UCC 1–201(25), 3–302, 3–305. Note that there was no conflicting *claim* of a property right under UCC 3–304 since it was not argued that the bank was not the owner of the instrument. Rather there was a *defense* of fraud under UCC 3–305 asserted by the maker of the note. In order to be free from that defense under the Code the bank would have to establish four things. First, the bank would have to show that the note was negotiable, that is that it met the requisites of negotiability laid down by UCC 3–104. Second, it would have to show that it took the note by negotiation so as to become a holder of it under UCC 1–201(20), 3–201(a). Third, it would have to show that it complied with the requirements for holding in due course under UCC 3–302. And fourth, it would have to show that the maker's defense was one of those defenses known as *personal* defenses, to which the holder in due course is immune rather than one of those exceptional defenses known as real defenses, to which the holder in due course is subject under UCC 3–305(a)(1). As to which of these four was there a good faith controversy in the *Fazzari* case? Which would be the bank's weakest point under the Code?

(2) Claims in Recoupment Under the Code. Former Article 3 afforded the holder in due course protection from "defenses" and from "claims," meaning what revised Article 3 refers to as "claims to the instrument." Revised Article 3 introduces a third concept, somewhat confusingly styled "claims in recoupment." These "claims" are more like defenses than like claims to the instrument, and are dealt with along with defenses in UCC 3–305, while claims to the instrument are left for UCC 3–306. Comment 3 to UCC 3–305 explains what claims in recoupment are.

"Subsection (a)(3) is concerned with claims in recoupment which can be illustrated by the following example. Buyer issues a note to the order of Seller in exchange for a promise of Seller to deliver specified equipment. If Seller fails to deliver the equipment or delivers equipment that is rightfully rejected, Buyer has a defense to the note because the performance that was the consideration for the note was not rendered. Section 3–303(b). This defense is included in Section 3–305(a)(2). That defense can always be asserted against Seller. This result is the same as that reached under former Section 3–408.

"But suppose Seller delivered the promised equipment and it was accepted by Buyer. The equipment, however, was defective. Buyer retained the equipment and incurred expenses with respect to its repair. In this case, Buyer does not have a defense under Section 3–303(b). Seller delivered the equipment and the equipment was accepted. Under Article 2, Buyer is obliged to pay the price of the equipment which is represented by the note. But Buyer may have a claim against Seller for breach of warranty. If Buyer has a warranty claim, the claim may be asserted against Seller as a counterclaim or as a claim in recoupment to reduce the amount owing on the note. It is not relevant whether Seller is or is not a holder in due course of the note or whether Seller knew or had notice that Buyer had the warranty claim. It is obvious that holder-in-due-course doctrine cannot be used to allow Seller to cut off a warranty claim that Buyer has against Seller. Subsection (b) specifically covers this point by stating that a holder in due course is not subject to a "claim in recoupment * * * against a person other than the holder."

"Suppose Seller negotiates the note to Holder. If Holder had notice of Buyer's warranty claim at the time the note was negotiated to Holder, Holder is not a holder in due course (Section 3–302(a)(2)(iv)) and Buyer may assert the claim against Holder (Section 3–305(a)(3)) but only as a claim in recoupment, i.e. to reduce the amount owed on the note. If the warranty claim is $1,000 and the unpaid note is $10,000, Buyer owes $9,000 to Holder. If the warranty claim is more than the unpaid amount of the note, Buyer owes nothing to Holder, but Buyer cannot recover the unpaid amount of the warranty claim from Holder. If Buyer had already partially paid the note, Buyer is not entitled to recover the amounts paid. The claim can be used only as an offset to amounts owing on the note. If Holder had no notice of Buyer's claim and otherwise qualifies as a holder in due course, Buyer may not assert the claim against Holder. Section 3–305(b)."

The comment goes on to discuss how such claims were treated under former Article 3.

(3) **Who Benefits From Negotiability?** Take the simple situation in which a buyer, as maker, executes a negotiable promissory note for the price of goods to the order of the seller, as payee, who then indorses it to a financing agency, as holder in due course. In considering who benefits from the negotiability of the note, it is best to concentrate on the normal case, in which the buyer asserts no defense on the note, rather than the abnormal case (popular with editors of casebooks), such as the *Fazzari* case, in which the buyer does assert a defense. Obviously the financing agency benefits by being freed from most defenses in the abnormal case. But in the normal case, the seller and the buyer benefit as well because of the resulting expansion of the "market" for negotiable instruments. The seller, who dealt with the buyer, would not have been protected as the payee if the seller had retained the note. However, the seller benefits indirectly from the protection that that section affords the financing agency to which the seller negotiates it because such financing agencies, freed from most of the buyer's defenses, are more willing to finance such transactions and to do so on more favorable terms. This, in turn, enables the seller to sell to more buyers on credit and to offer them more favorable terms. And this benefits the buyer since it increases the opportunity to buy on credit and to obtain more favorable terms. On this reasoning, a buyer's ability to relinquish most defenses as against a financing agency by signing a negotiable promissory note, may make credit available when it would otherwise be denied or may make credit available to the buyer at more favorable terms than would otherwise be available. Are there instances in which society should restrict a buyer's freedom to obtain these advantages in return for the relinquishment of most defenses?

(4) **Rights of FDIC.** Troubled times in the banking industry have highlighted the special rights of the Federal Deposit Insurance Corporation when it acquires negotiable instruments by taking over the assets of a failed bank. In 1942 the United States Supreme Court announced that, under federal common law, the maker of a note cannot assert against the FDIC defenses based upon "secret agreements" with the failed bank designed to deceive creditors or the public authority or tending to do so. D'Oench, Duhme & Co. v. FDIC, 315 U.S. 447 (1942). In 1950 Congress enacted a statutory version of the *D'Oench, Duhme* doctrine, found in 12 U.S.C. § 1823(e).

Both the common law and the statutory versions of the doctrine have generated an enormous amount of litigation and both have been broadly applied by the courts "to develop the body of law that now instructs that one who has dealt with a failed FDIC-insured institution may not assert a claim or defense against the FDIC that depends on some understanding that is not reflected in the insolvent bank's records." Texas Refrigeration Supply v. FDIC, 953 F.2d 975, 979 (5th Cir.1992). In other words, as one court put it, "transactions not reflected on the bank's books do not appear on the judicial radar screen either." Bowen v. FDIC, 915 F.2d 1013, 1016 (5th Cir.1990).

In addition, courts have been held that even when the FDIC acquires notes in bulk as receiver of a failed bank, so that it would not be a holder in due course under UCC 3–302(c)(ii), it nevertheless enjoys the status of holder in due course under federal common law. FDIC v. Wood, 758 F.2d 156 (6th Cir.), cert. denied, 474 U.S. 944 (1985). See generally Flint, Why *D'Oench, Duhme*? An Economic, Legal and Philosophical Study of a Failed Bank Policy, 26 Valparaiso L.Rev. 465 (1992); Gray, Limitations on the FDIC's *D'Oench* Doctrine of Federal Common–Law Estoppel: Congressional Preemption and Authoritative Statutory Construction, 31 S.Tex.L.Rev. 245 (1990); Reilly, The FDIC as Holder in Due Course: Some Law and Economics, 1992 Colum.Bus.L.Rev. 165.

UNIVERSAL C.I.T. CREDIT CORP. v. INGEL

Supreme Judicial Court of Massachusetts, 1964.
347 Mass. 119, 196 N.E.2d 847.

SPIEGEL, JUSTICE. This is an action of contract on a promissory note by the assignee of the payee against the maker. The case was first tried in the District Court of Fitchburg, to which it had been remanded by the Superior Court. There was a finding for the plaintiff in the sum of $1,630.12. At the request of the defendants, the case was retransferred to the Superior Court for trial by jury. Upon conclusion of the evidence the court allowed a motion by the plaintiff for a directed verdict to which the defendants excepted. They also excepted to the exclusion of certain evidence.

At the trial the plaintiff introduced in evidence the note,[1] a completion certificate signed by the defendants, and the District Court's

---

1.

"This Is A Negotiable Promissory Note
$1890.00
(Total Amount of Note)

      Fitchburg, Mass., 6/22, 1959
      (City, State)   (Date)

I/WE JOINTLY AND SEVERALLY PROMISE TO PAY TO ALLIED ALUMINUM ASSOCIATES, INC. OR ORDER THE SUM OF EIGHTEEN HUNDRED NINETY DOLLARS IN 60 SUCCESSIVE MONTHLY INSTALMENTS OF $31.50 EACH, EXCEPT THAT THE FINAL INSTALMENT SHALL BE THE BALANCE THEN DUE ON THIS NOTE. COMMENCING THE 25 DAY OF JULY, 1959, AND THE SAME DATE OF EACH MONTH THEREAFTER UNTIL PAID, with interest after maturity at the highest lawful rate, and a reasonable sum (15% if permitted by law) as attorney's fees, if this note is placed in the hands of any attorney for collection after maturity. Upon non-payment of any instalment at its maturity, all remaining instalments shall at the option of the holder become due and payable forthwith. Charges for handling late payments, of 5¢ per $1 (maximum $5), are payable on any instalment more than 10 days in arrears.... *Notice of Proposed Credit Life Insurance:* Group credit life insurance will be obtained by the holder of this instrument, without additional charge to customer, subject to acceptance by the insurer, Old Republic Life Insurance Company, Chicago, Illinois. Such insurance

finding for the plaintiff. The defendants admitted the authenticity of the signatures on the note and the completion certificate. As a witness for the defendants, one Charles D. Fahey testified that he was the plaintiff's Boston branch manager at the time the defendants' note was purchased, and that the plaintiff purchases instalment contracts regarding automobile and property improvement purchases. He described the procedures by which purchases of commercial paper are arranged by the plaintiff; these procedures included a credit check on the "customer," i.e., the maker of the note which the plaintiff is planning to purchase. The defendants attempted to introduce through Fahey a credit report obtained by the plaintiff on Allied Aluminum Associates, Inc. (Allied), the payee of the note. The defendants excepted to the exclusion of this evidence. They offered to prove that the excluded report, which was dated "3–31–59," contained the following statement: "The subject firm is engaged in the sale of storm windows, doors, roofing, siding, and bathroom and kitchen remodeling work. The firm engages a crew of commission salesmen and it is reported they have been doing a good volume of business. They are reported to employ high pressure sales methods for the most part. They have done considerable advertising in newspapers, on radio, and have done soliciting by telephone. They have been criticized for their advertising methods, and have been accused of using bait advertising, and using false and misleading statements. The Boston Better Business Bureau has had numerous complaints regarding their advertising methods, and have reported same to the Attorney General. *FHA has had no complaints other than report of this from Better Business Bureau and have warned the firm to stop their practice.*"

The defendants excepted to the exclusion of testimony by the defendant Dora Ingel concerning certain of her negotiations with Allied. An offer of proof was made which indicates that this testimony might have been evidence of fraud or breach of warranty on the part of

will cover only the individual designated and signing below as the person to be insured (who must be an officer if customer is a corporation, a partner if partnership), except that no individual 65 years of age or older on the date the indebtedness is incurred will be eligible for such insurance. Such insurance will become effective, upon acceptance by the insurer, as of the date the indebtedness is incurred, and will terminate when the indebtedness terminates or upon such default or other event as terminates the insurance under the terms of the group policy. The amount of such insurance will be equal to the amount of customer's indebtedness hereunder at any time but not to exceed $10,000; proceeds will be applicable to reduction or discharge of the indebtedness. The provisions of this paragraph are subject to the terms of the group policy and the certificate to be issued.

PLEASE PRINT MAILING ADDRESS

Customer acknowledges receipt of a completed copy of this promissory note, including above Notice.

ALBERT T. INGEL

Customer (Person on whose life group credit life insurance will be obtained, if applicable.)

DORA INGEL

(Additional Customer, if any)

ORIGINAL"

Allied. They also excepted to the exclusion of a letter [2] from the plaintiff to the defendant Albert.

I.

The defendants contend that the note was nonnegotiable as a matter of law and, therefore, any defence which could be raised against Allied may also be raised against the plaintiff. They argue that the note contained a promise other than the promise to pay, failed to state a sum certain, and had been materially altered.

It appears that the note was a form note drafted by the plaintiff. The meaning of Fahey's general testimony that the note and the completion certificate were "together" when given by the plaintiff to Allied is unclear. However, we see nothing in this testimony to justify the inference urged upon us by the defendants that in this case the note and completion certificate were "part of the same instrument" and that an additional obligation in the completion certificate rendered the note nonnegotiable under G.L. c. 106, § 3–104(1)(b).[3] Similarly, we are not concerned with any variance between the written contract (entered into by Allied and the defendants) and the note, since there is nothing in the note to indicate that it is subject to the terms of the contract. We are equally satisfied that the insurance clause in the note does not affect negotiability under § 3–104(1)(b) since it is clear that the "no other promise" provision refers only to promises by the maker.

The provision in the note for "interest after maturity at the highest lawful" rate does not render the note nonnegotiable for failure to state a sum certain as required by § 3–104(1)(b). We are of opinion that after maturity the interest rate is that indicated in G.L. c. 107, § 3,[4] since in this case there is no agreement in writing for any other rate

2.

"October 27, 1959
Identification
'B'

Mr. Albert Ingel
115 Belmont
Fitchburg, Massachusetts
　Re: 200–12–51767

Dear Sir,

We are sorry to learn that the Aluminum Siding on which we hold your promissory note, is giving you cause for complaint. Our part in the transactions consisted of extending the credit which you desired, and arranging to accept prepayment of the advance on terms convenient to you. We did not perform any of the work, and any questions in connection with materials and workmanship should be adjusted with the dealer from whom you made your purchase. Therefore, we have passed your report along to Allied Aluminum and we are confident that everything reasonably possible will be done to correct any faulty conditions which may exist.

In the meantime, we shall appreciate your continuing to make payments on your note as they fall due so that your account may be kept in current condition.

Very truly yours,

UNIVERSAL C.I.T. CREDIT

CORPORATION

C. KEVENY

Collection Man"

3. "Any writing to be a negotiable instrument within this Article must * * * contain an unconditional promise or order to pay a sum certain in money and no other promise, order, obligation or power given by the maker or drawer except as authorized by this Article."

4. "If there is no agreement or provision of law for a different rate, the interest of money shall be at the rate of six dollars on each hundred for a year, but, except as provided in sections seventy-eight, ninety, ninety-two, ninety-six and one hundred of chapter one hundred and forty, it shall be lawful to pay, reserve or contract for any rate of interest or discount. No greater rate than that before mentioned shall be recovered in a suit unless the agreement to pay it is in writing."

after default. This being the case, we do not treat this note differently from one payable "with interest." The latter note would clearly be negotiable under G.L. c. 106, § 3–118(d).[5]

The note in question provides that payment shall be made "commencing the 25 day of July, 1959." It appears that there is an alteration on the face of the note in that "July" was substituted for "June," the "ly" in the former word being written over the "ne" in the latter. The alteration has no effect in this case, where the defendants admitted that they had paid a particular sum on the note and where the sum still owing (assuming the note to be enforceable on its face) is not in dispute. See Mindell v. Goldman, 309 Mass. 472, 473–474, 35 N.E.2d 669.

We thus conclude that the note in question is a negotiable instrument.[6]

II.

The finding of the District Court which the plaintiff offered in evidence is, under G.L. c. 231, § 102C, prima facie evidence upon such matters as are put in issue by the pleading at the trial in the Superior Court. Lubell v. First Nat. Stores, Inc., 342 Mass. 161, 164, 172 N.E.2d 689. The defendants' answer denies that the plaintiff is "a holder in due course" of the note on which the action is brought; accordingly, this must be regarded as a matter "put in issue by the pleadings." We are satisfied that the finding of the District Court was prima facie evidence that the plaintiff took the note for value and without notice, and notwithstanding the provisions of G.L. c. 106, § 3–307(3),[7] the burden was on the defendants to rebut the plaintiff's prima facie case. See Cook v. Farm Service Stores, Inc., 301 Mass. 564, 566, 17 N.E.2d 890.

III.

The trial judge correctly excluded the evidence offered by the defendants to show that the plaintiff and Allied had worked together on various aspects of the financing and that the plaintiff was aware of complaints against Allied by previous customers. We are of opinion that there was nothing in the evidence by which the plaintiff had "reason to know" of any fraud. The letter of October 27, 1959, from the plaintiff to the defendant Albert was also properly excluded; it is immaterial that the plaintiff may have found out about Allied's allegedly fraudulent representations after the note had been purchased.

Exceptions overruled.

5. "Unless otherwise specified a provision for interest means interest at the judgment rate at the place of payment from the date of the instrument, or if it is undated from the date of issue."

6. By G.L. c. 255, § 12C, inserted by St.1961, c. 595, certain notes given in connection with the sale of consumer goods were made nonnegotiable.

7. "After it is shown that a defense exists a person claiming the rights of a holder in due course has the burden of establishing that he or some person under whom he claims is in all respects a holder in due course."

Notes

(1) **Requisites of Negotiability.** Promissory notes, which are often relatively elaborate and may contain hand tailored provisions to suit the particular transaction, are more likely to run afoul of the requisites of negotiability than are checks and other drafts, which are usually relatively simple in form. The creditor who is the payee of a note will want to bind the debtor with numerous obligations in addition to the clean-cut promise to pay money. The creditor wants to be able to declare the entire debt due if the debtor defaults on any obligation or if the debtor's financial position becomes shaky. The creditor who takes a security interest in personal property wants to bind the debtor not to make off with the collateral and also to keep it insured, undamaged, and free from liens.

This need to secure a wide assortment of promises from the debtor came into collision with the traditional rules on the proper scope of negotiability—a tradition epitomized by Chief Justice Gibson's famous dictum that a negotiable instrument must be "a courier without luggage." [1] The fences that were erected to confine the doctrine of negotiability took the form of the "formal requisites" for negotiable instruments set forth in painful detail in the Negotiable Instruments Law and carried forward, with significant relaxations, in Article 3 of the Code. See UCC 3–104 through 3–113.

Why have such complex "formal requisites"? Why not permit the parties to a contract to make it a negotiable instrument simply by so stating in the contract itself? Professor Chafee advanced the following explanation: "Although the law usually cares little about the form of a contract and looks to the actual understanding of the parties who made it, the form of a negotiable instrument is essential for the security of mercantile transactions. The courts ought to enforce these requisites of commercial paper at the risk of hardship in particular cases. A businessman must be able to tell at a glance whether he is taking commercial paper or not. There must be no twilight zone between negotiable instruments and simple contracts. If doubtful instruments are sometimes held to be negotiable, prospective purchasers of queer paper will be encouraged to take a chance with the hope that an indulgent judge will call it negotiable. On the same principle, if trains habitually left late, more people would miss trains than under a system of rigid punctuality." Chafee, Acceleration Provisions in Time Paper, 32 Harv.L.Rev. 747, 750 (1919). Is this the only reason for confining the attributes of negotiability to a limited class of paper? If the "security of mercantile transactions" is the only object, why have such complex requisites?

---

1. Overton v. Tyler, 3 Pa. 346, 45 Am. Dec. 645 (1846).

Contrast with Chafee's remarks the following comment by Professor Gilmore: "Few generalizations have been more fully repeated, or by generations of lawyers more devoutly believed, than this: negotiability is a matter rather of form than substance. It is bred in the bone of every lawyer that an instrument to be negotiable must be 'a courier without luggage.' It must conform to a set of admirably abstract specifications which, for our generation, have been codified in Section 1 of the Negotiable Instruments Law and spelled out in the nine following sections. These rules are fixed, external and immutable. No other branch of law is so clear, so logical, so inherently satisfying as the law of formal requisites of negotiability. To determine the negotiability of any instrument, all that need be done is to lay it against the yardstick of NIL sections 1–10: if it is an exact fit it is negotiable; a hair's breadth over or under and it is not.

"Few generalizations, legal or otherwise, have been less true; the truth is, in this as in every other field of commercial law, substance has always prevailed over form. 'The law' has always been in a constant state of flux as it struggles to adjust itself to changing methods of business practice; what purport to be formal rules of abstract logic are merely *ad hoc* responses to particular situations.

"Nevertheless, the cherished belief in the sacrosanct nature of formal requisites serves, as do most legal principles, a useful function. The problem is what types of paper shall be declared negotiable so that purchasers may put on the nearly invincible armor of the holder in due course. The policy in favor of protecting the good faith purchaser does not run beyond the frontiers of commercial usage. Beyond those confines every reason of policy dictates the opposite approach. The formal requisites are the professional rules with which professionals are or ought to be familiar. As to instruments which are amateur productions outside any concept of the ordinary course of business, or new types which are just coming into professional use, it is wiser to err by being unduly restrictive than by being over liberal. The formal requisites serve as a useful exclusionary device and as a brake on a too rapid acceptance of emerging trends. . . .

"As long as the law distinguishes between commercial and non-commercial property on the basis of form, there will have to be borderline or fringe litigation. On the whole a continuing trickle of such litigation is not obnoxious; it produces a clearer state of the law than does the law of sales where the doctrines say one thing and mean another, a situation not productive of certainty and predictability." Gilmore, The Commercial Doctrine of Good Faith Purchase, 63 Yale L.J. 1057, 1068–69, 1072 (1954).

According to Dean Mentschikoff, the Associate Chief Reporter for the Code, "the classification of these pieces of paper [bills of exchange, notes, checks] as negotiable instruments should be dependent on commercial use and the nature of the current markets to be protected." Mentschikoff, Highlights of the Uniform Commercial Code, 27 Mod.

L.Rev. 167, 176 (1964). Do the Code provisions seem to take "commercial usage" and current markets into account?

(2) **Variable Interest Rates.** Mentschikoff's suggestion that negotiability "should be dependent on commercial use and the nature of current markets to be protected" was severely tested when, after the enactment of former Article 3, variable rate notes came into widespread use during the double-digit inflation of the 1970s. Under former UCC 3–104, the sum payable was a sum certain even though payable "with stated interest," but there was no provision for a variable rate of interest.

In Taylor v. Roeder, 234 Va. 99, 360 S.E.2d 191 (1987), the court concluded that a note providing for interest at "Three percent (3.00%) over Chase Manhattan Prime to be adjusted monthly" could not be negotiable because this was not a *stated* rate. Although most courts reached the same conclusion, there were occasional contrary decisions. Thus in Amberboy v. Societe de Banque Privee, 831 S.W.2d 793 (Tex. 1992), the court held that a clause providing for interest at a rate that was tied to a bank's published prime rate did not impair negotiability. The court stated that the "Code's fundamental purpose ... is to 'simplify, clarify and modernize the law governing commercial transactions' " (UCC 1–102(2)(a)) and that the drafters "expressly contemplated that the courts would advance the basic purpose of the Code by construing the U.C.C.'s provisions 'in the light of unforeseen and new circumstances and practices' " (UCC 1–102, Comment 1) in order to "permit the continued expansion of commercial practices through custom, usage and agreement of the parties" (UCC 1–102(2)(b)). "Widespread use and acceptance of VRNs in the 1980s is precisely the type of new circumstances contemplated by the drafters...."

Many states enacted statutes allowing variable rate notes to be negotiable. See, e.g., N.Y.U.C.C. § 3–106(2). These statutes are replaced by UCC 3–112(b), which provides that a variable rate of interest does not impair negotiability and adds that the rate "may require reference to information not contained in the instrument."

The United Nations Convention on International Bills of Exchange and International Promissory notes contains a comparable provision. Under article 8(6), any rate referred to "must be published or otherwise available to the public and not be subject, directly or indirectly, to unilateral determination by a person who is named in the instrument at the time the bill is drawn or the note is made, unless the person is named only in the reference rate provisions." Does the absence of such language in UCC 3–112(b) suggest a different rule?

(3) **Acceleration Clauses.** Under UCC 3–108(b), negotiability is not impaired by the fact that the instrument is subject to rights of acceleration. It may seem surprising that such a provision was thought to be necessary since a note payable at a definite time but subject to acceleration is no less certain as to time of payment than a note payable on demand. Nevertheless, under the Negotiable Instruments

Law courts generally held that at least some types of acceleration clauses impaired negotiability. Typical of the clauses condemned by this argument were those giving the holder the power to accelerate "at will" or "when he deems himself insecure."

The comments to an early draft of Article 3 of the Code gave the following explanation for this line of decisions: "It seems evident that the courts which give uncertainty of time of payment as a reason for denying negotiability are in reality objecting to the acceleration clause itself. This objection may be founded on abuses of the clause. The signer of an acceleration note, unlike the signer of a demand note, does not expect to be called upon to pay before the ultimate date. Normally he understands the acceleration clause to be for the protection of the holder against his own insolvency or similar contingencies, and he expects that the note will not be accelerated without good reason. An unscrupulous creditor can accelerate it without reason, and a note prematurely called may ruin the debtor. . . . Inquiry among banks has led to the conclusion that the privilege of acceleration at the option of the holder has real advantage to the creditor, who frequently must act on the basis of confidential information or evidence as to the condition of the debtor which does not amount to definite proof. The effect of denying negotiability to acceleration paper is not to remedy any abuses arising in connection with the acceleration clause, which remains in effect even if the instrument be treated as a simple contract. It is merely to open the paper to defenses which have nothing to do with acceleration." Commercial Code, Comments and Notes to Article III 43–44 (Tent.Draft No. 1, 1946).

The Code, therefore, makes the power to accelerate irrelevant to the issue of negotiability. But UCC 1–208 limits the holder's power to accelerate "at will" or "when he deems himself insecure" by requiring "good faith." What does good faith mean in this sense? See UCC 1–201(19). How easy would it be for the maker to prove lack of good faith? Does UCC 1–208 limit the power of the holder of a note payable on demand to demand payment? Why? See Comment to UCC 1–208. Does it limit the power of the holder of a note that permits acceleration at the holder's option on the maker's default? See Greenberg v. Service Business Forms Industries, 882 F.2d 1538 (10th Cir.1989), cert. denied, 493 U.S. 1045 (1990).

One reason for including a clause permitting acceleration "should the holder of this note deem the debt insecure" is suggested by State National Bank of Decatur v. Towns, 36 Ala.App. 677, 62 So.2d 606 (1952). In that case the bank which held such a note as payee was served, before the maturity date of the note, with a writ of garnishment by which a judgment creditor of the maker sought satisfaction from the maker's bank account. However the bank was held to be entitled to accelerate the maturity date under the clause and set off its debt ahead of the judgment creditor. "By the garnishment the judgment plaintiff acquired only the rights to the judgment defendant. As to the judgment defendant the bank, as a result of the acceleration clause in the note, had a right of set off against any claim of the judgment defendant in a suit against it." The note held by the bank also contained a clause purporting to give the bank a "lien" on the maker's account, but the court did not rely on this, pointing out that a bank has a right to set off a general deposit against a debt of the depositor if the debt is matured. See Note 2, p. 159 infra.

(4) **Reference to Other Documents.** The effects of other documents upon negotiability are dealt with in UCC 3–106(b) and 3–117. The references to "prepayment" and "acceleration" were added in 1962. "This change was made to meet a criticism of the [New York Clearing House Association] that the 1958 Official Text appears to preclude a very common provision in notes that allows acceleration or prepayment in accordance with the terms of a loan agreement or mortgage of a particular date. This provision is of primary concern to banks who wish to discount or pledge commercial paper with Federal Reserve Banks or other large banking institutions. [Footnote:] Although negotiability is not required in specific terms by the Federal Reserve Act ... or the Federal Reserve Board's regulations, the definitions of promissory notes, drafts, and bills of exchange contained in Regulation A have been so interpreted. See 9 Fed.Reserve Bull. 559 (1923)." Penney, New York Revisits the Code: Some Variations in the New York Enactment of the Uniform Commercial Code, 62 Colum.L.Rev. 992, 994–95 (1962).

(5) **Negotiability Revisited.** A quarter of a century after expressing the thoughts in Note 1 supra, Professor Gilmore had these harsh words for former Article 3. "As a general rule, anything—including negotiability—which was good enough for Lord Mansfield was good enough for Llewellyn. That attitude, unfortunately, carried through to the drafting of Article 3 of the Code, which can be described as the N.I.L. doubled in spades or negotiability *in excelsis*. Article 3 gravely takes up each of the pressure points which developed in the N.I.L. case law and resolves the issue in favor of negotiability. [In a footnote he gives examples including the provisions of former UCC 3–109 on acceleration clauses and of former UCC 3–105 on notes with security agreements, discussed in Notes 2 and 3 supra.] ... What Article 3 really is is a museum of antiquities—a treasure house crammed full of ancient artifacts whose use and function have long since been forgotten. Another function of codification, we may note, is to preserve the past, like a fly in amber." Gilmore, Formalism and the Law of Negotiable Instruments, 13 Creighton L.Rev. 441 (1979).

(6) **Non-negotiable Instruments and Magic Words.** Under the Negotiable Instruments Law, unless the instrument complied with the requisites of negotiability, none of the statutory provisions was applicable. In many instances the rules were the same for instruments that were not negotiable, but this was not because the statute controlled but because the statute was, in part, a codification of common law rules, some of which applied to non-negotiable instruments as well. In addition, in a few instances, courts applied the statutory provisions to

non-negotiable instruments by analogy. Former Article 3 departed from the Negotiable Instruments Law in two significant respects. First, while NIL 1 provided that an instrument had to comply with the stated requisites "to be negotiable" former UCC 3–104 said only that it must comply "to be a negotiable instrument within this Article." According to Comment 1 to that section this language left "open the possibility that some writings may be made negotiable by other statutes or by judicial decision." Second, former UCC 3–805, which had no counterpart in the Negotiable Instruments Law, created a special class of non-negotiable instrument to which all of former Article 3 applied with the very important exception that "there can be no holder in due course of such an instrument." Because it covered non-negotiable as well as negotiable instruments, former Article 3 was styled "Commercial Paper."

Revised Article 3, like the Negotiable Instruments Law, "applies to negotiable instruments" (UCC 3–102(a)) and is styled "Negotiable Instruments" to reflect its more limited scope (UCC 3–101). Its provisions might, of course, be applied by analogy to what would have been non-negotiable instruments under former Article 3, but such instruments seem rarely to produce litigation.

To come under revised Article 3, then, an instrument must contain the words "order" of "bearer," since UCC 3–104(a)(1) insists on these "magic words." However, UCC 3–104(c) makes a significant exception in this respect for checks, as to which magic words are not necessary for negotiability. As Comment 2 to UCC 3–104 explains, the absence of such words on a check "can easily be overlooked and should not affect the rights of holders who may pay money or give credit for a check without being aware that it is not in conventional form." While a check that does not contain magic words would have been a non-negotiable instrument under former Article 3, it is a negotiable instrument under revised Article 3.

(B) In Consumer Transactions

The Nature of the Problem. The situation in which Albert and Dora Ingel found themselves was a common one in which a consumer buyer purchases goods from a retail seller and signs documents that the seller transfers to a financing agency, usually a finance company or a bank. See the Prototype Transaction at p. 769 infra. The goods prove to be defective. If it were the seller who claimed payment from the buyer, the buyer would have a defense, either by rejecting (UCC 2–601) them if they have not already been accepted, or by revoking acceptance (UCC 2–608) or setting off damages for breach of warranty against the price (UCC 2–714, 2–717) if they have been accepted. But are these remedies still available when the claim against the buyer is made by the financing agency to whom the seller's rights have been transferred?

Of course, even if the buyer must pay the price to the financing agency, the buyer still has a claim against the seller. The buyer's interest in asserting a claim against the one who demands the price grows out of the following considerations, which are particularly strong in consumer transactions. (1) *The inertia of litigation.* Setting up a defense as a defendant is easier than starting an action, even though the "burden of proof" with regard to the seller's breach may fall on the buyer in either case. In practice, this consideration has its greatest impact on the settlement value of the buyer's claim, since a reduction in price is much easier to negotiate than a cash refund. (2) *The strain of current cash outlay.* The buyer may not have the resources to pay the full amount for defective goods and wait until a legal action against the seller can reach trial, which in many jurisdictions may take years, and finally be converted into a judgment. (3) *The risk of the seller's insolvency.* The seller may be insolvent or judgment proof. The seller may have been a fly-by-night operator, or driven into sharp practice by financial pressure, or forced to the wall by keen competition, poor management or a business recession.

Conversely, these advantages to the buyer in preserving defenses against the financing agency, suggest the importance to it of freeing itself from these defenses. In addition, its interest is magnified to the extent that buyers interpose spurious defenses in an attempt to scale down or avoid their obligation to pay for what they buy.

For several decades, opposing interests struggled over whether a financing agency should be permitted to insulate itself from defenses that a *consumer* buyer, as distinguished from a *commercial* buyer, would have had against the seller, either by using a negotiable instrument (as in the *Ingel* case) or a waiver-of-defense clause (as in Problem 1(b), supra). The result was a substantial revision of the traditional concept of good faith purchase as applied to consumer transactions. For recognition of this by the Code, see UCC 3–302(g) and Comment 7.

Judicial Intervention. The first victories for the consumer oriented view came in the courts, which began to hold by the early 1950s that a financing agency that was closely connected with a retailer could not be a holder in due course and was not protected by a waiver-of-defense clause. In the teeth of statutory language designed to protect the negotiability of notes, a substantial number of courts found legal grounds to place the burden of adjustment for the seller's default upon the financing agency. These courts twisted traditional notions of good faith and notice to reach what they regarded as a just result. According to the Supreme Court of Arkansas, in an early seminal case, the finance company "was so closely connected ... with the deal that it can not be heard to say that it, in good faith, was an innocent purchaser" of a note given by a buyer for a car. Commercial Credit Co. v. Childs, 199

Ark. 1073, 1077, 137 S.W.2d 260, 262 (1940). According to the Supreme Court of Florida, where a finance company had been involved in the transaction it "had such notice of . . . infirmity" in a note given by a grocer for a freezer. The court also stated the policy behind such decisions. "We believe the finance company is better able to bear the risk of the dealer's insolvency than the buyer and in a far better position to protect his interests against unscrupulous and insolvent dealers." Mutual Finance Co. v. Martin, 63 So.2d 649, 653 (Fla.1953). The nature of the transaction made it difficult for the financing agency to divorce itself from the seller sufficiently to avoid being characterized as "closely connected." Since the relationship is ordinarily a continuing one, there is typically a master agreement and some arrangement for a fund to be retained by the financing agency to secure its right of recourse against the seller.[1] In addition, the financing agency will insist that the standard forms for contracts with buyers as well as for assignments be its own.

The rapid growth and varying contours of this development are described in Hudak & Carter, The Erosion of the Holder in Due Course Doctrine, 9 UCC L.J. 165, 179–83 (1976). See also Countryman, The Holder in Due Course and Other Anachronisms in Consumer Credit, 52 Tex.L.Rev. 1 (1973); Rogers, The Myth of Negotiability, 31 B.C.L.Rev. 265 (1990); Rosenthal, Negotiability—Who Needs It?, 71 Colum.L.Rev. 375 (1971).

Legislative Intervention. Inasmuch as buyers had to show a sufficiently close connection between the seller and the financing agency in each case, judicial decisions fell short of giving the buyer optimum protection. By the early 1970's, however, most states had enacted statutes applicable to consumer transactions[2] prohibiting negotiable instruments and waiver-of-defense clauses, limiting their effectiveness, or depriving them of effect altogether. Thus the Uniform Consumer Credit Code, as promulgated in 1974, generally prohibits taking a

---

1. Under recourse financing, the dealer is liable to the financing agency in the event of the buyer's default. But the assignment of a simple contract right does not of itself operate as a warranty that the obligor is solvent or will perform his obligation. See Restatement (Second) of Contracts § 333(2). Therefore, if recourse financing is intended, an express provision to that effect must be added to the language of assignment or to the master agreement under which the assignment is made. An indorser of commercial paper, however, engages that if the obligor refuses to pay, he, the indorser, will pay the instrument to his indorsee (UCC 3–415(a)), if the indorsee takes prescribed steps such as giving prompt notice of dishonor. (These steps will be studied in Chapter 3.) If a promissory note is used, nothing further need be said if recourse financing is intended. If non-recourse financing is intended,

language such as "without recourse" must be added to the indorsement (UCC 3–415(b)).

2. Definitions of "consumer" differ, but Uniform Consumer Credit Code § 1.301 is typical. Its definition of "consumer credit sale" requires: that the buyer be a person other than an organization; that the credit be granted pursuant to a seller credit card or by a seller who regularly engages in credit transactions of the same kind; that the goods, services, or interest in land sold be purchased primarily for a personal, family, household or agricultural purpose; that the debt be payable in installments or a finance charge is made; and that, with respect to a sale of goods or services, the amount financed not exceed $25,000. Furthermore, the sections quoted here do not apply to transactions primarily for an agricultural purpose.

negotiable promissory note in connection with a consumer credit sale or consumer lease (U3C 3.307). It goes on to provide that "an assignee of the rights of the seller or lessor is subject to all claims and defenses of the consumer against the seller or lessor arising from the sale or lease of property or services, notwithstanding that the assignee is a holder in due course of a negotiable instrument issued in violation of the provisions prohibiting certain negotiable instruments." But a consumer can assert a claim or defense "only to the extent of the amount owing to the assignee with respect to the sale or lease of the property or services as to which the claim or defense arose at the time the assignee has notice of the claim or defense." (U3C 3.404). Note that under such statutes it is no longer necessary to show that the financing agency and the seller were closely connected.

For discussion of the justification for such legislation, see Banta, Negotiability in Consumer Sales: The Need for Further Study, 53 Neb.L.Rev. 195 (1974); Rohner, Holder in Due Course in Consumer Transactions: Requiem, Revival or Reformation?, 60 Cornell L.Rev. 503 (1975); Schwartz, Optimality and the Cutoff of Defenses Against Financers of Consumer Sales, 15 B.C.Ind. & Com.L.Rev. 499 (1974); Note, 78 Yale L.J. 618 (1969).

Direct Loans. Neither the judicial decisions nor the statutes described above deal with a developing practice in which the seller refers the buyer to a financing agency that makes a direct loan to the buyer.[3] The loan is secured by an interest in the goods purchased by the buyer and the financing agency makes sure that the loan is applied to purchase the goods by making its check payable jointly to the buyer and the seller. Should the buyer refuse payment of the loan on the ground of a defense against the seller, the financing agency's response is that its contract with the buyer is entirely separate from the seller's contract with the buyer and was fully performed when it gave the buyer the money. Statutes protecting consumers in the case of direct loans are newer and less common than those described above.

The Uniform Consumer Credit Code contains an example. U3C 3.405 provides that, issuers of credit cards excepted, one who makes a consumer loan to enable a consumer to buy or lease from a particular seller or lessor "is subject to all claims and defenses of the consumer against the seller or lessor arising from that sale or lease of the property or services if:

(a) the lender knows that the seller or lessor arranged for the extension of credit by the lender for a commission, brokerage, or referral fee;

(b) the lender is a person related to the seller or lessor, unless the relationship is remote or is not a factor in the transaction;

---

3. This practice is known, picturesquely as "dragging the body" to suggest that the seller "drags" the buyer to the financing agency's office.

(c) the seller or lessor guarantees the loan or otherwise assumes the risk of loss by the lender upon the loan;

(d) the lender directly supplies the seller or lessor with the contract document used by the consumer to evidence the loan, and the seller or lessor has knowledge of the credit terms and participates in preparation of the document;

(e) the loan is conditioned upon the consumer's purchase or lease of the property or services from the particular seller or lessor, but the lender's payment of proceeds of the loan to the seller or lessor does not in itself establish that the loan was so conditioned; or

(f) the lender, before he makes the consumer loan, has knowledge or, from his course of dealing with the particular seller or lessor or his records, notice of substantial complaints by other buyers or lessees of the particular seller's or lessor's failure or refusal to perform his contracts with them and of the particular seller's or lessor's failure to remedy his defaults within a reasonable time after notice to him of the complaints."

But a consumer can assert a claim or defense "only to the extent of the amount owing to the lender with respect to the sale or lease of the property or services as to which the claim or defense arose at the time the lender has notice of the claim or defense."

Note the complexity introduced by the requirement that the lender be closely connected with the seller. Would it be practicable to allow consumers to assert defenses against the lender in all cases? What of the consumer who obtains a loan from his savings bank, giving a passbook as security?

FTC Initiative. In 1976, Federal Trade Commission rule 433 took effect. Its stated purpose is to deny protection to financing agencies in transactions involving consumer goods and services.[4] But because the FTC has no jurisdiction over banks and it was thought undesirable to regulate some financing agencies but not others, the rule was not made applicable to financing agencies. Instead the rule makes it an unfair and deceptive trade practice for the *seller* to fail to incorporate in a contract of sale a legend that will preserve the buyer's defenses against the financing agency.

If the transaction is one in which the seller assigns the contract with the buyer to a financing agency, the contract must include the following legend in ten-point type:

---

4. The rule defines a consumer as: "A natural person who seeks or acquires goods or services for personal, family, or household use."

NOTICE

ANY HOLDER OF THIS CONSUMER CREDIT CONTRACT IS SUBJECT TO ALL CLAIMS AND DEFENSES WHICH THE DEBTOR COULD ASSERT AGAINST THE SELLER OF GOODS OR SERVICES OBTAINED PURSUANT HERETO OR WITH THE PROCEEDS HEREOF. RECOVERY HEREUNDER BY THE DEBTOR SHALL NOT EXCEED AMOUNTS PAID BY THE DEBTOR HEREUNDER.

If the seller receives the proceeds from a direct loan made to the buyer by a financing agency to which the seller "refers consumers" or with whom the seller "is affiliated ... by common control, contract, or business arrangement," the loan contract must include a similar legend. 16 C.F.R. 433.1(d); 433.2 (1991). Placing the required legend on a note does not of itself destroy the note's negotiability; however, there cannot be a holder in due course of the note, even if the note otherwise is negotiable. UCC 3–106(d).

Suppose that sellers and lenders are not inclined to obey the FTC Regulation and fail to use the prescribed provision. How effective are the FTC's tools to compel compliance? Staggering numbers of sellers and lenders, large and small, fall within the terms of the FTC Regulation. The slow and cumbersome course of administrative proceedings leading to the issuance by the FTC of cease and desist orders has produced notorious delays in securing compliance with the Federal Trade Commission Act, even in fields where the numbers of businesses are small in comparison with those affected by the holder in due course regulation. See Cox et al., The Nader Report on the Federal Trade Commission (1969); Gard, Purpose and Promise Unfulfilled: A Different View of Private Enforcement Under the Federal Trade Commission Act, 70 Nw.U.L.Rev. 274, 279–80 (1975). To provide improved sanctions for enforcement, in 1975 Congress authorized the FTC to bring civil actions against persons who violate FTC cease and desist orders and (more importantly) against persons who violate FTC rules respecting "unfair or deceptive acts or practices." See 15 U.S.C. § 57(b) (1988).

Suppose the seller or lender nevertheless fails to include the prescribed formula in a contract and that, under state law, negotiable notes and waiver-of-defense clauses are effective to bar buyers from asserting defenses against transferees. Will the FTC Regulation override state law and allow the buyer to assert a defense or claim a refund? A substantial body of case law holds that FTC regulations do not ipso facto modify private rights or confer private rights of action. See, e.g., Holloway v. Bristol–Myers Corp., 485 F.2d 986 (D.C.Cir.1973); Comment, 69 Nw.U.L.Rev. 462 (1974), Gard, supra, 70 Nw.U.L.Rev. at 276–77 (deploring the cases withholding private enforcement). Cf. Guernsey v. Rich Plan of the Midwest, 408 F.Supp. 582 (N.D.Ind.1976); Middlesex County Sewerage Authority v. National Sea Clammers Association, 453 U.S. 1, 101 S.Ct. 2615, 69 L.Ed.2d 435 (1981). Even so, it may not follow that a state court would give no effect to the FTC Regulation. For a well-reasoned argument that a court should not protect the holder of a contract that violates the FTC Regulation, see Comment, Implied Consumer Remedy, 125 U.Pa.L.Rev. 876, 904–16 (1977). For a more pessimistic view (from the buyer's perspective), see

Banks, The FTC Holder in Due Course Rule: A Rule Without a Private Remedy, 44 Mont.L.Rev. 113 (1983).

Claims Against Financing Agency. We have thus far been concerned with the buyer's right to assert a defense against the financing agency in order to reduce the buyer's obligation to pay that agency. What of claims by the buyer against the financing agency to recover payments already made in ignorance of such a defense?

Even in the case of an assignee of a simple contract right, the question is not free from dispute. But there is authority that if, after a defense or claim has arisen but before learning of it, the buyer mistakenly and even negligently renders performance to the assignee when not required to do so, the buyer may have restitution if the assignee has not changed position in reliance on the performance. Compare Farmers Acceptance Corp. v. DeLozier, 178 Colo. 291, 496 P.2d 1016 (1972) (where contractor's progress payments to assignee exceeded amount to which subcontractor was entitled because of breach, contractor could recover excess from assignee where there was no showing of reliance by further loans), with Michelin Tires (Canada), Limited v. First National Bank of Boston, 666 F.2d 673 (1st Cir.1981) (where owner's progress payments to assignee were based on fraudulent invoices, owner could not recover from innocent assignee). Statutes such as the Uniform Consumer Credit Code do not appear to be dispositive on this issue, though by preserving a buyer's defense against the financing agency they open the door to a claim to restitution of payments made in ignorance of that defense.

The legend required by FTC rule 433, however, states that the financing agency is subject to all "claims and defenses which the debtor could assert against the seller" and provides, that "recovery hereunder by the debtor shall not exceed amounts paid by the debtor hereunder." See Home Savings Association v. Guerra, 733 S.W.2d 134 (Tex.1987). Does this give the buyer a right to restitution of payments made in ignorance of a defense in any of the situations covered by the rule? For an affirmative answer, see Eachen v. Scott Housing Systems, Inc., 630 F.Supp. 162 (M.D.Ala.1986).

Credit Cards. Suppose that a buyer uses a credit card to pay for goods that turn out to be defective. Can the buyer, when billed by the issuing bank, set up defenses that would be good against the seller? Is it significant that a credit card system is not entirely lacking in control over the merchants that are allowed to put its decal on the door?

Congress dealt with this problem in Truth in Lending Act § 170, as added by the Fair Credit Billing Act of 1974 (15 U.S.C. § 1666i). That section generally subjects a card issuer "to all claims (other than tort claims) and defenses arising out of any transaction in which the credit card is used" up to "the amount of credit outstanding with respect to such transaction" at the time the cardholder first gives notice of the claim of defense.[5] There are, however, three limitations.

First, the cardholder must have made "a good faith attempt to obtain satisfactory resolution of a disagreement or problem relative to the transaction from the person honoring the credit card." Second, the amount of the initial transaction must exceed $50. Third, the place where the initial transaction occurred must be in the same state as the mailing address previously provided by the cardholder or within 100 miles from that address.[6] What are the justifications for these limitations?

SECTION 2. DOCUMENTS OF TITLE

Problem 4. B fraudulently induced the A warehouse to issue a negotiable warehouse receipt for $100,000 worth of cotton that was not delivered to it. B duly negotiated the receipt to C, who did not suspect the fraud and paid B $100,000.

(a) What are C's rights against A? See UCC 7–203. (As to C's recourse against B, see UCC 7–507.) Would it make a difference if the warehouse receipt had not been indorsed? If it had not been negotiable?

(b) What result if the receipt had covered barrels of whiskey instead of bales of cotton and the barrels had contained water? (Is the answer affected by any of the language of the forms supra?)

(c) What result if A had received the cotton from B but had lost it in some way? See UCC 7–204; I.C.C. Metals v. Municipal Warehouse Co., infra. (Is the answer affected by any of the language of the forms supra?)

I.C.C. METALS, INC. v. MUNICIPAL WAREHOUSE CO.
New York Court of Appeals, 1980.
50 N.Y.2d 657, 431 N.Y.S.2d 372, 409 N.E.2d 849.

GABRIELLI, JUDGE. At issue on this appeal is whether a warehouse which provides no adequate explanation for its failure to return stored property upon a proper demand is entitled to the benefit of a contractu-

---

5. The amount of claims or defenses may not exceed the amount of credit outstanding with respect to the transaction at the time the cardholder first gives notice of the claim or defense.

6. The second and third limitations do not apply in a few limited situations.

al limitation upon its liability. For the reasons discussed below, we conclude that proof of delivery of the stored property to the warehouse and its failure to return that property upon proper demand suffices to establish a prima facie case of conversion and thereby renders inapplicable the liability-limiting provision, unless the warehouse comes forward with evidence sufficient to prove that its failure to return the property is not the result of its conversion of that property to its own use. If the warehouse does proffer such evidence and is able to persuade the trier of facts of the truth of its explanation, then the limitation of liability will be given effect and the bailor will be required to prove the warehouse to be at fault if it is to recover even those limited damages allowed by the provision.

The facts relevant to this appeal are undisputed and may be simply stated. In the autumn of 1974, plaintiff, an international metals trader, delivered three separate lots of an industrial metal called indium to defendant commercial warehouse for safekeeping. The parties have stipulated that the three lots of indium, which had an aggregate weight of some 845 pounds, were worth $100,000. When the metal was delivered to defendant, it supplied plaintiff with warehouse receipts for each lot. Printed on the back of each receipt were the terms and conditions of the bailment, as proposed by defendant. Section 11 of those terms and conditions provided as follows: "Limitation of Liability—Sec. 11. The Liability of the warehouseman as to all articles and items listed on the face of this warehouse receipt is limited to the actual value of each article and item, but the total liability of the warehouseman shall not exceed in any event for damage to any or all the items or articles listed on this warehouse receipt the sum of fifty ($50.00) dollars; provided, however, that such liability may, on written request of the bailor at the time of signing this warehouse receipt or within twenty (20) days after receipt of this warehouse receipt, be increased on part or all of the articles and items hereunder, in which event, increased rates shall be charged based upon such increased valuation, but the warehousemen's maximum liability shall in no event exceed the actual value of any or all of the articles and items in question. In no case shall the liability be extended to include any loss of profit." [1] Plaintiff did not request any increase in defendant's contractual liability, nor did it inform defendant of the value of the metal.

For almost two years, defendant billed plaintiff for storage of each of the three lots by means of monthly invoices that specifically identified the stored metal, and plaintiff duly paid each invoice. Finally, in May of 1976, plaintiff requested the return of one of the three lots of indium. At that point defendant for the first time informed plaintiff that it was unable to locate any of the indium. Plaintiff then commenced this action in conversion, seeking to recover the full value of

1. In light of our disposition of the main issue presented by this case we need not and accordingly do not determine whether this limitation applies to loss of bailed property as well as damage to that property.

the indium. In response, defendant contended that the metal had been stolen through no fault of defendant's and that, at any rate, section 11 of the terms printed on each warehouse receipt limited plaintiff's potential recovery to a maximum of $50 per lot of indium.

Special Term granted summary judgment to plaintiff for the full value of the indium. The court found that plaintiff had made out a prima facie case of conversion by proffering undisputed proof that the indium had been delivered to defendant and that defendant had failed to return it upon a proper demand. As to defendant's contention that the metal had been stolen, the court concluded that this allegation was completely speculative and that defendant had failed to raise any question of fact sufficient to warrant a trial on the issue. Finally, Special Term held that the contractual limitation upon defendant's liability was inapplicable to an action in conversion. The Appellate Division, 67 A.D.2d 640, 412 N.Y.S.2d 531, affirmed the judgment in favor of plaintiff and we granted defendant leave to appeal to this court. We now affirm the order appealed from.

Absent an agreement to the contrary, a warehouse is not an insurer of goods and may not be held liable for any injury to or loss of stored property not due to some fault upon its part (Uniform Commercial Code, § 7–204, subd. [1]). As a bailee, however, a warehouse is required both to exercise reasonable care so as to prevent loss of or damage to the property ... and, a fortiori, to refrain from itself converting materials left in its care.... If a warehouse does not convert the goods to its own use and does exercise reasonable care, it may not be held liable for any loss of or damage to the property unless it specifically agrees to accept a higher burden. If, however, the property is lost or damaged as a result of negligence upon the part of the warehouse, it will be liable in negligence. Similarly, should a warehouse actually convert stored property to its own use, it will be liable in conversion. Hence, a warehouse which fails to redeliver goods to the person entitled to their return upon a proper demand, may be liable for either negligence or conversion, depending upon the circumstances....

A warehouse unable to return bailed property either because it has lost the property as a result of its negligence or because it has converted the property will be liable for the full value of the goods at the time of the loss or conversion (Procter & Gamble Distr. Co. v. Lawrence Amer. Field Warehousing Corp., 16 N.Y.2d 344, 266 N.Y.S.2d 785, 213 N.E.2d 873; 1 Harper and James, Torts, § 2.36), unless the parties have agreed to limit the warehouse's potential liability. It has long been the law in this State that a warehouse, like a common carrier, may limit its liability for loss of or damage to stored goods even if the injury or loss is the result of the warehouse's negligence, so long as it provides the bailor with an opportunity to increase that potential liability by payment of a higher storage fee. ... If the warehouse converts the goods, however, strong policy considerations bar enforcement of any such limitation upon its liability.... This rule, which has now been codified in subdivision (2) of section 7–204 of the Uniform Commercial Code,[2] is premised on the distinction between an intentional and an unintentional tort. Although public policy will in many situations countenance voluntary prior limitations upon that liability which the law would otherwise impose upon one who acts carelessly ... such prior limitations may not properly be applied so as to diminish one's liability for injuries resulting from an affirmative and intentional act of misconduct (see, generally, Restatement, Torts 2d, § 500; Restatement, Contracts 2d, Tent. Draft No. 12, § 337), such as a conversion. Any other rule would encourage wrongdoing by allowing the converter to retain the difference between the value of the converted property and the limited amount of liability provided in the agreement of storage. That result would be absurd. To avoid such an anomaly, the law provides that when a warehouse converts bailed property, it thereby ceases to function as a warehouse and thus loses its entitlement to the protections afforded by the agreement of storage. In short, although the merely careless bailee remains a bailee and is entitled to whatever limitations of liability the bailor has agreed to, the converter forsakes his status as bailee completely and accordingly forfeits the protections of such limitations. Hence, in the instant case, whether defendant is entitled to the benefit of the liability-limiting provision of the warehouse receipt turns upon whether plaintiff has proven conversion or merely negligence.

Plaintiff has proffered uncontroverted proof of delivery of the indium to defendant, of a proper demand for its return, and of defendant's failure to honor that demand. Defendant has failed to make a sufficient showing in support of its suggested explanation of the loss to defeat plaintiff's motion for summary judgment. Its unsupported claim that the metal was stolen does not suffice to raise any issue of fact on this point.[3] Upon this record, it is beyond cavil that plaintiff would be

---

2. We find no merit to defendant's suggestion that the term "conversion to his own use" as used in subdivision (2) of section 7–204 means something more than a simple conversion (see Lipman v. Petersen, 223 Kan. 483, 575 P.2d 19).

3. The explanation proffered by the warehouse in such a case must be supported by sufficient evidence and cannot be merely the product of speculation and conjecture. "The explanation must show with reasonable certainty how the loss occurred, as, by theft or fire ... It is not enough to show that defendant-bailee used reasonable care in its system of custody if mysterious disappearance is the only 'explanation' given" (PJI 4:93, at pp. 1090–1091; see Dalton v. Hamilton Hotel Operating Co., 242 N.Y. 481, 488–489, 152 N.E. 268). In the instant case, defendant offered proof of the following facts in support of its claim that the indium had been stolen: "(1) the storage of the indium in three different locations in two different buildings, and the absence of any indication in [defendant] Municipal's records that the indium was moved, negate the possibility of misdelivery; (2) the storage of the indium without special precautions, because [plaintiff] ICC failed to advise Municipal of its true value, supports the likelihood of theft; (3) the form of the indium (small bars) would have facilitated removal without detection; (4) a recently discharged employee was experienced in 'weighing and sampling' and thus presumably was aware of the value of indium; (5) there was a series of alarms, any one of which could have been caused by a theft; (6) Municipal promptly reported the loss to the police; and (7) ICC reported the loss to its insurers as a theft and continued to employ Municipal's services, thus negating any suspicion that Municipal had misappropriated the indium or had been grossly negligent in its care." Viewed most favorably to defen-

entitled to judgment had it elected to sue defendant in negligence.... We now hold that such a record also suffices to sustain plaintiff's action in conversion, thereby rendering inapplicable the contractual limitation upon defendant's liability.[4]

The rule requiring a warehouse to come forward with an explanation for its failure to return bailed goods or be cast in damages in negligence is based upon practical necessity.... Since bailed property is in the possession of and under the sole control of the warehouse at the time of injury or loss, however, it is the warehouse which is in the best, if not the only, position to explain the loss of or damage to the property. Indeed, such information normally will be exclusively in the possession of the warehouse and will not be readily accessible to the bailor. Because of this, the law properly refuses to allow a warehouse, which has undertaken for a fee to securely store goods belonging to another, to avoid liability by simply pleading ignorance of the fate of the stored merchandise. To allow the warehouse to so easily escape its responsibilities would be to place the bailor in an untenable position and would serve to encourage both dishonesty and carelessness. Clearly, the temptation to convert stored property would be significantly increased could the warehouse then avoid all civil liability by simply denying all knowledge of the circumstances of the loss and placing upon the bailor the well nigh impossible burden of determining and proving what happened to his property while it was hidden from sight in the depths of the defendant's warehouse. Similarly, such a rule would reward those warehouses with the least efficient inventory control procedures, since they would be most able to honestly plead ignorance of the fate of goods entrusted to their care.

This does not mean that the warehouse is required to prove that it acted properly, nor does this doctrine shift the burden of proof to the warehouse. Rather, the warehouse must come forward and explain the circumstances of the loss of or damage to the bailed goods upon pain of being held liable for negligence. If the warehouse does provide an explanation for the loss or damage, the plaintiff then must prove that the warehouse was at fault if he is to recover.... [W]here the warehouse does suggest an explanation for the loss but is unable to proffer sufficient evidentiary support for that explanation to create a

---

dant, this evidence would indicate at most that theft by a third party was one possible explanation for the defendant's failure to redeliver the indium to plaintiff. This is simply insufficient, since the warehouse is required to show not merely what might conceivably have happened to the goods, but rather what actually happened to the goods. Defendant proved only that theft was possible, and presented no proof of an actual theft. Hence, the proffered explanation was inadequate as a matter of law.

4. We emphasize at this point that we do not suggest by our holding in this case that proof of negligence will support a re-

covery in conversion. Rather, our holding is limited to those situations in which the warehouse fails to provide an adequate explanation for its failure to return stored goods. If the warehouse comes forward with an explanation supported by evidentiary proof in admissible form, the plaintiff will then be required to prove that the loss was due to either negligence or conversion, depending on the circumstances. For plaintiff to recover in conversion after the warehouse has established a prima facie explanation for its failure to deliver, the trier of facts must find all the traditional elements of conversion.

question of fact, as in this case, the plaintiff will be entitled to recover without more. Where, however, the warehouse proffers sufficient evidence supporting its explanation to create a question of fact, the jury must be instructed that if it believes that explanation, the plaintiff must be denied any recovery unless he has proven that the warehouse was at fault (Uniform Commercial Code, § 7–403, subd. [1], par. [b]). In other words, if the jury is persuaded that the goods were accidentally mislaid or destroyed in a fire or accident or stolen by a third party, the plaintiff cannot recover unless he has proven that the loss or the fire or the accident or the theft were the proximate result of either a purposive act or a negligent commission or omission by the warehouse.

Although it has long been settled that this is the rule in an action in negligence, there has been considerable inconsistency and uncertainty as to the application of this principle to an action in conversion. Thus, although we have on occasion declared that a bailor establishes a prima facie case of conversion by simply proving delivery to the bailee and an unexplained failure to return the stored goods upon demand ..., we have at other times indicated that something more is needed to maintain an action in conversion and that a plaintiff will be required to provide positive evidence of an intentional act by the warehouse inconsistent with the plaintiff's interest in the property.... [W]e have decided to take this opportunity to re-examine the matter and to determine the most appropriate resolution of this controversy.

We now conclude that there exists no sound reason to apply a different rule to the two types of action where, as here, the bailee comes forward with insufficient proof of its explanation for the loss of the bailed goods. The same policy considerations which prevent a warehouse from avoiding liability in negligence by a declaration of ignorance appear equally applicable to an action in conversion. Indeed, as a practical matter, a bailor will be even less able to prove conversion by a warehouse than he would negligence, since a warehouseman who actually converts stored property will generally strive mightily to prevent knowledge of his malfeasance from coming to light. The possibility of fraud is obvious, for a dishonest warehouseman might well be encouraged to convert bailed property if he could then obtain the benefit of a contractual limitation of liability by the simple expedient of professing ignorance as to the fate of the goods. The rule requiring a warehouse to explain the loss of or damage to the goods lest it be held liable would be severely undermined could a warehouse avoid the bulk of potential liability in such a case by means of a contractual provision.

Quite simply, plaintiff proved delivery of the indium to defendant warehouse and defendant's subsequent failure to return the metal, whereas defendant has not come forward with adequate evidentiary proof in admissible form to support its suggested explanation of that failure. That being so, the limitation on liability was inapplicable, and plaintiff was entitled to recover the actual value of the missing indium.

Accordingly, the order appealed from should be affirmed, with costs.

JASEN, JUDGE (dissenting). My disagreement with the majority stems from their conclusion that plaintiff is entitled to summary judgment on the theory of conversion absent any proof whatsoever that defendant converted the indium metal to its own use or the use of another.... I cannot subscribe ... to the majority's conclusion that conversion, rather than negligence, can be presumed where the bailee is unable, for whatever reason, to explain the absence of stored property. Such a holding, in my opinion, erases the critical distinction between negligence and conversion....

First, I would consider the law in this commercial area well settled and in accordance with the basic principle that a cause of action sounding in conversion will not be maintainable absent proof of intentional wrongdoing by the bailee.... Here, plaintiff has presented no proof whatsoever of an intentional wrongdoing by defendant, and the majority's conclusion that this "record ... suffices to sustain plaintiff's action in conversion" flies in the face of this established rule that an action for conversion requires an evidentiary showing that defendant bailee intentionally acted in a manner so as to deprive plaintiff of its property.

Second, I take issue with the policy reasons cited by the majority to support their obliteration of the distinction between negligence and conversion—that the bailee is in the better position to explain what happened to the goods and, thus, should be required to come forth with such explanation; and that instances of fraud would proliferate if a bailee could merely profess ignorance as to the goods' disappearance and, then, claim as a sanctuary the contractual limitation of liability.... There is simply no rational reason, under the guise of policy considerations, to shift the burden of coming forward with evidence of what "actually happened"[1] to the goods when a cause of action is framed in conversion....

This, it seems to me, is fundamentally unfair, especially when one considers that plaintiff voluntarily signed as a condition of bailment a contractual limitation of liability ($50) as to each article and item stored, although the true value of the three lots of indium was $100,-000. The limitation of liability and the actual value of the stored property were known to plaintiff, and yet it chose not to avail itself of

---

1. The majority stresses that their holding is limited to only requiring a warehouseman to establish, in the first instance, "a prima facie explanation for its failure to deliver" the goods (p. 655, n. 4, 431 N.Y.S.2d p. 377, n. 4, 409 N.E.2d p. 854, n. 4). However, I derive little solace from this qualification, inasmuch as a bailee "is required to show not merely what might conceivably have happened to the goods, but rather what *actually* happened to the goods" (p. 664, n. 3, 431 N.Y.S.2d p. 377, n. 3, 409 N.E.2d p. 853, n. 3 [emphasis added]). Since we are concerned with cases involving unexplained losses, the majority opinion sanctions, for all practical purposes, the imposition of full liability for the value of the goods stored whenever the bailee is unable to deliver the stored goods or explain "what actually happened to the goods." This, I suggest, is an onerous burden upon the warehouseman.

the opportunity to declare the full value of the goods to insure that it would be made whole in case of loss. Plaintiff had only to be candid about the true value of the goods entrusted to defendant and pay a storage rate commensurate with the risk in order to protect itself from any and all loss, whether such loss be precipitated by fraud, conversion, negligence, or otherwise. Having not exercised this option and, thus, having paid a much lower storage fee than what would have been charged had the bailee known the true value of the goods and been responsible for the same, the bailor should be held to the terms of the bailment absent an affirmative evidentiary showing of intentional wrongdoing by the bailee. In this commercial setting, dealing as we are with sophisticated businessmen, we should not reach out and relieve the plaintiff of its failure to protect itself contractually. I can only read the majority's opinion as doing violence to the law, without rhyme or reason. . . .

Notes

(1) **The Scope of the Warehouseman's Responsibility When Goods Disappear.** In practical effect, how far removed is the approach in the *I.C.C. Metals* case from the imposition of absolute liability on the warehouseman? Is this result consistent with the standard of "care" in UCC 7–204(1)?

Goods continue to vanish from warehouses, and judicial response to the *I.C.C. Metals* decision has been mixed. Contrast Joseph H. Reinfeld v. Griswold & B. Warehouse Co., 189 N.J.Super. 141, 458 A.2d 1341 (1983), (misdelivery by negligence is conversion barring limits on liability), with International Nickel Co. v. Trammel Crow Distribution Corp., 803 F.2d 150 (5th Cir.1986) (Texas court would not "make the leap to a presumption of conversion").

Questions of warehouse responsibility *in excelsis* arose in connection with the 1963 disappearance from field warehouse tanks in Bayonne, New Jersey, of over a billion pounds of vegetable oils—perhaps the greatest swindle since the days of Ivar Kreuger. Leading banks in the United States and Britain had made loans totalling $150 million "secured" by the pledge for warehouse receipts for non-existent oil. See Procter & Gamble Distributing v. Lawrence American Field Warehousing Corp., 16 N.Y.2d 344, 266 N.Y.S.2d 785, 213 N.E.2d 873 (1965); Miller, The Great Salad Oil Swindle (1965), The New Yorker, Nov. 14, 1964.

Warehouses and Carriers. An interesting (and puzzling) contrast is presented by the Code's language on the responsibility of warehouses (UCC 7–204) and the provision on the responsibility of carriers (UCC 7–309). Subsection 4 of UCC 7–204 states: "This section does not impair or repeal . . ." and leaves a blank for the preservation of *named* statutes that may impose a higher responsibility on the warehouse. On the other hand, UCC 7–309(1) on the responsibility of carriers, after articulating the "reasonably careful man" test, adds: "This subsection does not repeal or change any law *or rule of law* which imposes liability upon a common carrier for damages not caused by its negligence" (emphasis added). The phrase "rule of law" (as contrasted with the reference to specific statutes in UCC 7–204) provides access to (and possibly development of) the broad common law liability of carriers as insurers of goods. Do the reasons that led to the liability of carriers apply to warehouses? Does the difference between the approaches of these two sections of the Code bar the extension by analogy of absolute liability to warehouses? Would the failure of a warehouse to carry insurance protecting both itself and the owner constitute a default in the "reasonable care" standard? If so, should the net result be simplified by change in the language of the Code? In the drafting of statutory provisions like those of Article 7, who are likely to be more vocal—warehouses or those who may store goods with warehouses? Over a dozen states have enacted bracketed language in UCC 7–403(1)(b) placing "the burden of establishing negligence ... on the person entitled under the document." Does this reflect a fair allocation of the burden of proof?

(2) **Misdelivery.** Under the Code a bailee is, in general, absolutely liable if it delivers goods to a person not "entitled under the document" (UCC 7–403(1)). If stored goods are stolen with the connivance of an employee of the warehouse company, would the warehouse be absolutely liable? See: Boshkoff, The Irregular Issuance of Warehouse Receipts and Article 7 of the UCC, 65 Mich.L.Rev. 1361 (1967); Murray, The Warehouseman's and Carrier's Liability for Theft by Their Employees in England and the United States, 39 U.Pitt.L.Rev. 707 (1978).

When stored goods disappear, what suggestions do the above materials offer for drafting the owner's complaint and preparation for trial?

(3) **Analogies From Other Fields; Maritime "Deviation."** The approach of the *I.C.C. Metals* case is reminiscent of maritime case law that "deviation" by the carrier "ousted" or nullified bill of lading clauses limiting the carrier's liability. See Mills, The Future of Deviation in the Law of the Carriage of Goods, 1983 Lloyd's Mar. & Comm.L. 587. Cf. UCC 2–719(2) (failure of "essential purpose").

(4) **Consistency.** Compare the rules relating to the freedom of a good faith purchaser from defenses in the case of: (1) a simple contract right; (2) a negotiable warehouse receipt; and (3) a negotiable promissory note. Do the differences make sense?

SECTION 3. OTHER CONSEQUENCES

Introduction. The most dramatic consequence of the negotiability of commercial paper or documents of title is the protection that may be afforded the good faith purchaser against claims and defenses, illustrated by the preceding materials in the first two chapters. This protection is not, however, the only consequence.

Another consequence of the negotiability of commercial paper is that the party seeking to enforce such an instrument has advantages of pleading and proof. For example, every negotiable instrument is presumed to have been issued for consideration, so that even when the instrument remains in the hands of the original payee, the burden is shifted to the obligor on the instrument to show that there was no consideration.[1] See UCC 3–308(b), 3–303(b). Two additional consequences are considered in the following two subsections.

(A) DISCHARGE

Prefatory Note. To what extent, in performing an obligation, must the obligor pay attention to the whereabouts of the writing that evidences it? An obligor on an ordinary contract right can safely deal with the original obligee in discharging the obligation, even if the right is evidenced by a writing, unless the obligor has received notice of an assignment. The Code so provides in UCC 9–318(3). The Restatement (Second) of Contracts § 338(1) puts it as follows:

> ... notwithstanding an assignment, the assignor retains his power to discharge or modify the duty of the obligor to the extent that the obligor performs or otherwise gives value until but not after the obligor receives notification that the right has been assigned and that performance is to be rendered to the assignee.

The obligor on a negotiable instrument or document of title, however, cannot safely deal with the original obligee without paying attention to the writing that embodies the obligation.[2]

---

1. By the beginning of the eighteenth century, it had been established that in an action upon the custom of merchants on a *draft* payable to order, the plaintiff need not prove consideration. Yet in Clerke v. Martin, 2 Ld.Raym. 757, 1 Salk. 129, 92 Eng.Rep. 6 (1702), Lord Holt, Chief Justice of the Queen's Bench, refused to apply this rule in favor of the payee of a *promissory note* payable to order who sought recovery from the maker, describing "such notes [as] innovations ... unknown to the common law, and invented in Lombard–Street,

which attempted in these matters of bills of exchange to give laws to Westminster–Hall." Clerke v. Martin was overruled two years later by the Statute of Anne, which provided that the holder of a note could maintain an action just as could the holder of a draft. See footnote 6, p. 55 supra.

2. Note also that under UCC 3–604 the obligee on a negotiable instrument can, even without consideration, discharge an obligor on the instrument simply by cancelling, destroying, or mutilating it or by striking out the obligor's signature.

Problem 5. B sold A a machine for A's factory for $100,000, payable in 30 days. B assigned the right to payment to the C finance company, which paid B $100,000 less a discount. At the end of the 30 days, A, who did not know of the assignment, paid B $100,000. Can C recover the $100,000 from A? See UCC 9–318(3); Restatement (Second) of Contracts § 338(1), supra.[3]

Problem 6. B sold A a machine for A's factory for $100,000, payable in 30 days. In connection with the sale, A executed a negotiable promissory note, promising to "pay to the order of B, $100,000" in 30 days. B assigned the right to payment and negotiated the note to the C finance company by indorsing it "Pay to the order of C, (signed) B." At the end of the 30 days, A, who did not know of the assignment and negotiation, paid B $100,000. Can C recover the $100,000 from A? See UCC 3–602, 3–301.

Problem 7. B, a dealer in cotton, deposited $100,000 worth of cotton with the A warehouse, which issued a negotiable warehouse receipt to B's order. B negotiated the receipt to C, who paid B $100,000. Later, on demand by B, A redelivered the cotton to B.

(a) Is A liable to C? See UCC 7–403, 7–404, 7–502.

(b) What result if the warehouse receipt had been a non-negotiable one, which was transferred (not negotiated) to C? Would it make a difference if C had notified A of the transfer before A's redelivery to B? See UCC 7–504.

Note

Modification by Contract. Would it be possible, by an appropriate provision, to make the rule of UCC 3–602 applicable to the discharge of a debt under an ordinary contract? See UCC 3–805. Might there be disadvantages as well as advantages to doing this?

Consider the financing agency that finances retail instalment sales without the use of a negotiable note. (The financing agency might then use a clause like that mentioned in Problem 1(b) supra.) Buyers change their addresses and employees of financing agencies occasionally make mistakes. If a negotiable note were used, the rule of UCC 3–602 would protect the financing agency if it failed to notify the buyer of the transfer to it of the buyer's obligation. But what precautions would the cautious buyer then have to insist upon before paying each instalment?[4]

Is there a better way to protect the financing agency if it fails to notify the buyer? Forms furnished to dealers by financing agencies

---

3. As to B's liability to C, Restatement (Second) of Contracts § 333(1)(a) provides: "... one who assigns ... a right ... for value warrants to the assignee ... that he will do nothing to defeat or impair the value of the assignment...."

4. A comparable problem arises in connection with the use of warehouse receipts in field warehousing and is solved by the use of non-negotiable receipts.

frequently provide that instalments are to be payable at the office of the financing agency. Will such a clause adequately protect the financing agency if it fails to notify the buyer of the fact of assignment? Would the following clause be preferable: "I acknowledge, this day, receipt of a duplicate of this contract and admit notice of the intended assignment of this contract to Friendly Finance Company"?

(B) "Spent" Instruments and Documents

Prefatory Note. To what extent, after performing an obligation, does the obligor run a risk by leaving outstanding (without cancellation or some appropriate notation of performance) the writing that evidences it? In other words, to what extent can the good faith purchaser of the right to performance safely rely on the writing as an indication that the obligation has not already been discharged? The obligor on an ordinary contract right runs no risk by leaving the writing that evidences it outstanding, or to put it differently, the good faith purchaser who takes that right by assignment cannot safely rely on the writing as an indication that the obligation has not already been discharged. This is clear from Restatement (Second) of Contracts § 336(1):

> By an assignment the assignee acquires a right against the obligor only to the extent that the obligor is under a duty to the assignor; and if the right of the assignor would be voidable against the obligor or unenforceable against him if no assignment had been made, the right of the assignee is subject to the infirmity.

As might be expected, the rule is different for a negotiable instrument or document of title.

Problem 8. B sold A a machine for A's factory for $100,000, payable in 30 days. Before the 30 days were up, A paid B $100,000, but left the written contract of sale in B's hands without any notation on it. B then assigned the right to payment and delivered the written contract to the C finance company, which paid B $100,000 less a discount without knowing of A's payment to B. At the end of the 30 days, A refused to pay C. Can C recover the $100,000 from A? See UCC 9–318(1); Restatement (Second) of Contracts § 336(1), supra.[5]

Problem 9. B sold A a machine for A's factory for $100,000, payable in 30 days. In connection with the sale, A executed a negotiable promissory note, promising "to pay to the order of B $100,000" in 30 days. Before the 30 days were up, A paid B $100,000 but left the written contract of sale and the promissory note in B's hands without

---

5. As to B's liability to C, see footnote 3, p. 116 supra.

any notation on them. B then assigned the right to payment, negotiated the note, and delivered both the written contract and the note to the C finance company, which paid B $100,000 less a discount without knowing of A's payment to B. At the end of the 30 days, A refused to pay C. Can C recover the $100,000 from A? See UCC 3–601, 3–602, 3–305.

Problem 10. B, a dealer in cotton, deposited $100,000 worth of cotton with the A warehouse, which issued a negotiable warehouse receipt to B's order. On demand by B, A redelivered the cotton to B but left the "spent" warehouse receipt in B's hands without any notation on it. (See the notations on the form supra.) B negotiated the receipt to C, who paid B $100,000 without knowing of the redelivery of the cotton to B.

(a) Is A liable to C? See UCC 7–403, 7–502.

(b) What result if the receipt had been a non-negotiable one, which was transferred (not negotiated) to C? See UCC 7–504.

Note

"Spent" Bills of Lading. A railroad delivered goods without requiring surrender of the negotiable bill of lading. Months later the holder of the bill of lading changed the dates to reflect a current transaction and negotiated it to a bank as security for a loan. The bank was denied recovery against the railroad on the ground that, in view of the intervening "forgery," the railroad's default was not the "proximate cause" of the bank's loss. Saugerties Bank v. Delaware & Hudson Co., 236 N.Y. 425, 141 N.E. 904 (1923) (4–3 decision). The result has been sharply criticized. See Fulda, Surrender of Documents of Title on Delivery of the Property, 25 Cornell L.Q. 203 (1940). The Code seems not to have dealt with this problem. See UCC 7–306, 7–403(3), 7–501(4), 7–502 and Comment 3. Could a warehouseman make an equally strong argument for freedom of liability on a "spent" warehouse receipt? Cf. American Cotton Cooperative Association v. Union Compress & Warehouse Co., 193 Miss. 43, 7 So.2d 537, 139 A.L.R. 1483 (1942).

Part II

PAYMENT TRANSACTIONS: THE CHECK AND ITS SUBSTITUTES

INTRODUCTION

Of the three main types of negotiable instruments (notes, drafts and checks), the note has already been discussed in Chapters 1 and 2, the draft will be encountered in Chapter 6, and the check is the subject of the three chapters that follow.

Although the check has undergone the most dramatic growth of any negotiable instrument and has been most subjected to modern techniques of bulk handling and automation, both its form and its function remain remarkably close to those of the first checks over three centuries ago. See the typical example of a personal check (Form 2 infra). When is it payable? (See UCC 3–108(a)). To whom is it payable? (See UCC 3–109.)

The primary function of the check also remains essentially the same—it is ordinarily an instrument for the payment of the drawer's own debts. Today, if a buyer owes a seller for goods, the buyer will in most instances pay by a personal check made payable to the order of the seller as payee. The seller will take the check to the seller's bank and deposit the check for collection. The check will then be sent by the seller's bank, often through a chain of collecting banks, to the buyer's bank upon which it was drawn, the payor bank. For a more detailed description of the check collection process, see the Prototype infra. Sometimes the payee will "cash" the check, that is transfer it for value, at a store or bank instead of depositing it in the payee's bank, but particularly in a commercial setting this is the exception rather than the rule.

Payment of the drawer's own debt is not, however, the only function of the check, for checks today may take a number of forms and have a variety of purposes. You will recall the draft, described earlier (p. 53 supra), that was used by a London buyer to pay a Venetian seller. Its modern counterpart would be a teller's check (UCC 3–104(h)), which might be used by a New York buyer, as remitter, to pay a San Francisco seller, drawn by the buyer's New York bank as drawer, upon its correspondent bank in San Francisco, as payor bank. When it is

121

received the San Francisco seller will probably deposit it in the seller's own bank for collection, just as the seller would deposit the buyer's personal check. Note that this instrument is a type of check (UCC 3–104(f)). Can you think of any reasons why the seller might prefer it to the buyer's personal check? If the payor bank in San Francisco should refuse to pay, would the seller, the payee, have recourse against the buyer, the remitter (UCC 3–310)? Against the New York drawer (UCC 3–414)? Against the San Francisco payor bank (UCC 3–408)?

Still another variety of check that the buyer might use to pay the seller is what is known as a cashier's or official check, a check drawn by a bank as drawer upon itself as payor bank.

The great majority of the more than one billion checks drawn each week are properly honored upon presentment to the payor bank and give rise to no legal problems. Well under one per cent are dishonored, although in absolute terms this amounts to hundreds of millions of checks a year. The most frequent reasons for dishonor are "insufficient funds" and "uncollected funds." Other reasons appear on the return item stamp which the payor bank usually places on dishonored checks when they are returned (see p. 143 infra). In an even smaller number of instances checks are paid by the payor bank by mistake—perhaps in violation of a stop order or in spite of a forgery or alteration.

Nevertheless, most of the reported cases involving checks arise out of these unusual situations in which a payor bank has either refused to pay a check, or has paid a check by mistake. These cases make up the bulk of Part II of this book. Llewellyn put it this way: "A course in Negotiable Instruments is in this like so many hours a week spent in an operating room, as giving light on the normal functioning of the human body. In the course the student meets only wrecked transactions. Yet the rules that govern the lawsuits are modelled upon the normal, natural *unwrecked* transaction; the rules seek as best may be to approximate the result which should have been, and which *would* have been, except for the wreck." Llewellyn, Meet Negotiable Instruments, 44 Colum.L.Rev. 299, 321 (1944).

Each of the three chapters in Part II deals with a general risk inherent in the use of checks. Chapter 3 is concerned with the risk of checks drawn on insufficient funds. Chapter 4 deals with the risk of attempts to countermand checks. Chapter 5 explores the risk of forgery and alteration. But first, a brief description of the check system is in order.

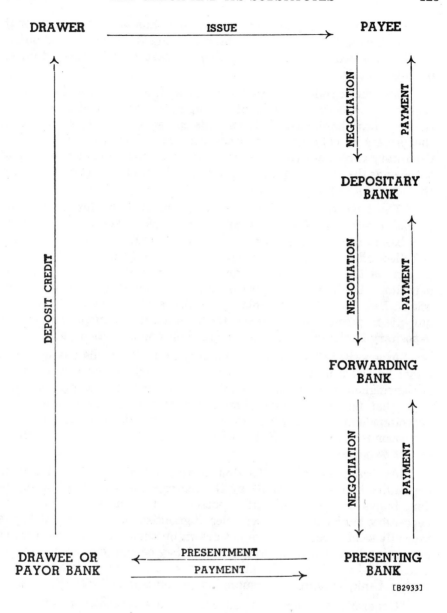

"The check collection process involves the movement of checks from the depositary bank to the paying bank and the corresponding movement of the funds represented by the check from the paying bank to the depositary bank. The check collection system, which is composed of depositary banks, intermediary collecting banks (including correspondent banks and Federal Reserve Banks), and paying banks, makes use of automated equipment to sort checks, extensive ground and air transportation to move checks, and bank accounting systems.

"Approximately 56 billion checks are written annually in the United States. An estimated 30 percent of these checks are deposited

in the bank on which they are drawn, and thus are not sent through
the check collection system. Of the remaining 70 percent, or 39 billion
checks, it is estimated that more than 85 percent are collected on an
overnight basis.

"The check collection process begins at the depositary bank where
checks are deposited by the bank's customers. At the end of each day,
the depositary bank posts deposits to its customers' accounts and begins
the process of collecting the funds represented by the checks. The
depositary bank outsorts the checks drawn on itself (on-us checks) and
then sends the remaining checks through the check collection system to
the appropriate paying bank.

"The depositary bank has several options available for clearing the
checks it receives. The check collection paths chosen by each depositary bank are influenced by many factors, including the cost and speed
of collection alternatives, the location of the paying bank, the dollar
amount of the check, the size and check processing capability of the
depositary bank, and the correspondent relationships the bank has
established. Depositary banks generally seek to collect checks as
quickly as possible to maximize the availability of funds, and larger
depositary banks frequently use more than one collection path.

"A depositary bank may send a check directly to the paying bank,
either by direct presentment or through a clearinghouse arrangement.
A clearinghouse is a group of banks, usually in a city or metropolitan
area, that has agreed to exchange checks among themselves.[1] The
depositary bank may also use an intermediary collecting bank, either a
correspondent bank or a Federal Reserve Bank, to complete the check
collection process.

"A portion of the checks that correspondent banks receive from
depositary banks are payable by the correspondent bank. Correspondent banks may also present a portion of the checks received from
depositary banks through local clearinghouses. Correspondent banks
typically send checks that are not drawn on themselves or that cannot
be presented at clearinghouses to which they belong to other correspondent banks or to Federal Reserve Banks for collection or directly to the
paying bank, generally pursuant to an agreement with that bank.

"Generally, settlement for checks that are presented directly by a
private-sector collecting bank will occur by a credit to the account of
the collecting bank on the books of the paying bank, or the settlement
may occur through the accounts of the collecting and paying banks on
the books of the Federal Reserve Banks. Settlement for presentments
made through clearinghouse arrangements typically occurs on a net

---

1. When checks first became common
in London, bank clerks presented city
items by making daily trips to each of the
other banks. Soon they arranged meetings
and exchanged checks on street corners,
and later chose a public house when they
transacted their business. In about 1773
the bankers of London rented a room in
Lombard Street for the settlement of their
accounts, thus establishing the London
Clearing House. The New York Clearing
House Association was organized in 1853
and similar institutions now exist in many
cities. [Eds.]

basis through accounts of the participating banks maintained at the Federal Reserve. With respect to checks collected through the Federal Reserve, the Federal Reserve credits the account of the collecting bank on the books of the Reserve Bank; the paying bank's account held at the Reserve Bank is debited in accordance with an automatic-charge agreement.

"The Federal Reserve Banks collected about 18.5 billion checks in 1990. Approximately 64 percent of the checks they handle are received from local depositors—banks located in the region served by the particular Federal Reserve office. Nearly ten percent of the checks received by Federal Reserve offices were previously processed by another Federal Reserve office. Another five percent of the checks were deposited initially at another Federal Reserve office under the 'consolidated' deposit program. The remaining approximately 21 percent of the checks received by a Federal Reserve office are deposited directly by nonlocal banks without being handled by the depositor's local Federal Reserve office—'direct send' checks.

"About 25 percent of all checks handled by the Federal Reserve are deposited in 'fine-sort' packages. Approximately 26 percent of the fine-sorted checks are drawn on city banks, 70 percent on regional banks, and 4 percent on country banks.

"The Federal Reserve maintains an Interdistrict Transportation System (ITS) that utilizes contracted air and ground transportation to transport checks among Federal Reserve check processing offices. All Federal Reserve offices are interconnected through a 'hub and spoke' transportation network that provides each Federal Reserve office a convenient and reliable means to transport checks nationwide. In addition, each Federal Reserve office has a local transportation network to deliver checks from the Federal Reserve office to the paying bank." Federal Reserve System, Supplementary Information for Proposed Rule, 56 Fed.Reg. 4744–45 (1991).

The law relating to checks is discussed in H. Bailey, Brady on Bank Checks (6th ed. 1987); B. Clark, The Law of Bank Deposits, Collections and Credit Cards (3d ed. 1990). See also Rogers, The Irrelevance of Negotiable Instruments Concepts in the Law of the Check–Based Payment System, 65 Tex.L.Rev. 929 (1987).

Impact of Regulation CC. Federal Reserve Board Regulation CC (12 C.F.R. 229), promulgated in 1988 pursuant to the Expedited Funds Availability Act of 1987 (12 U.S.C. § 4001 et seq.), made major changes in the check collection process. Congress passed the Act in response to consumer dissatisfaction with long holding periods placed on checks by some banks, during which depositors could not draw against credits given for checks deposited for collection. UCC 4–213(4)(a) allowed a depositary bank to place a hold on such checks in order to give it a "reasonable time" to learn that they had been paid. This laissez-faire attitude permitted holding periods in some cases of six business days for local checks and fifteen business days for nonlocal checks. See Rapp v. Dime Savings Bank, 48 N.Y.2d 658, 421 N.Y.S.2d 347, 396 N.E.2d 740 (1979).

Depositary banks justified such long holds by citing the Code's slow scheme for return of unpaid checks. If the payor bank paid the item, each of these provisional credits along the collection chain automatically "firmed up," becoming a final credit. Under this system, no news was good news, and the depositary bank, after a time, simply assumed that the check had been paid. If, however, the payor bank refused to pay the check, the presenting bank would return the check to the collecting bank from which it had received it, revoking the provisional credit previously given. Each prior bank in the collection chain then did the same. Because the return of a check retraced the forward collection path, the return process was often slow and cumbersome. Hence, long holds seemed necessary for depositary bank protection.

Regulation CC addresses concerns of both consumers and banks. First, it requires banks to make deposited funds available to customers within the periods fixed by a mandatory availability schedule. Generally, the regulation requires a depositary bank to make local checks available for withdrawal "not later than the second business day following the banking day on which funds are deposited." Reg CC 229.12(b). Nonlocal checks must be made available "not later than the fifth business day following the banking day on which funds are deposited." Reg CC 229.12(c). In addition, up to $100 of the aggregate amount of ordinary checks deposited on any one banking day must be given next-day availability. Reg CC 229.10(c). Cash deposits made in person to an employee of the depositary bank and certain low risk check deposits, e.g., cashier's, certified, and on-us checks, must be made available for withdrawal "not later than the business day after the banking day on which the funds are deposited." Reg CC 229.10(c).

Second, Regulation CC attempts to protect depositary banks saddled with early availability by speeding up the return of unpaid checks. It eliminates the practice of giving provisional credit between banks and thereby eliminates the need to revoke provisional credits by retracing the forward collection path. Instead, the Regulation authorizes direct return of a dishonored item to the depositary bank and requires that returns be expeditious. Thus, at least in a well-ordered world, a depositary bank will know that the payor bank has refused to pay a check before the depositary bank must allow the customer to draw against that check. A brief description of the expeditious return test of Regulation CC is given later. For a more detailed discussion of Regulation CC, see B. Clark & B. Clark, Regulation CC Funds Availability and Check Collection (1988), reprinted as chapters 6 and 7 of B. Clark, The Law of Bank Deposits, Collections, and Credit Cards (3d ed. 1990).

THE MECHANICS OF CHECK COLLECTIONS:
A PROTOTYPE [1]

Quaker Manufacturing Co., a Philadelphia manufacturer of containers, sells large quantities of cans to Empire Enterprises Co., a New York firm. Quaker sells on open credit, under the terms shown on its Acknowledgement (Form 1), and receives payment by check. On Monday, January 25, Empire mails its check (Form 2) for $22,178.50 drawn on The Bank of New York, its New York bank, to Quaker in payment for April purchases. Quaker receives the check on Tuesday, January 26, and enters this payment in its books as part of its daily receipts. On the same day it stamps its indorsement on the back of the check (Form 2B), lists the check on a deposit slip (Form 3) along with other checks received the same day, and takes the check with the deposit slip to its bank, Philadelphia National Bank, for deposit.

Collection. Philadelphia National Bank, the depositary bank, returns a receipted copy of the deposit slip to Quaker. Check collection is a highly automated procedure in which reader-sorter machines process checks on the basis of information encoded on the check in machine-readable form on a Magnetic Ink Character Recognition (MICR) line. Philadelphia National Bank encodes the amount on the MICR line (compare Form 2A with Form 2). It handles Empire's check, along with other checks received for deposit, in bulk rather than individually, on the assumption that in all probability it will be paid when it is presented to The Bank of New York. Quaker's deposit is proved, that is the depositor's addition is checked by the bank, and the amount is then credited to its account. (From this point until the check is paid by the payor bank, the check is not usually examined by anyone unless the amount of the check or a random security program triggers sight review by the payor bank.) Since it is not certain that the check will be paid by The Bank of New York, the credit is provisional, with the understanding that Quaker has no right to draw checks against the credit as long as it is provisional. The provisional credit will become final without any further entry at a time fixed by Federal Reserve Regulation CC 229.12, unless Philadelphia National Bank sooner learns that the item has been dishonored, in which case it will reverse the provisional credit previously given for the item. The Empire check, along with all other deposited checks drawn on out-of-town banks, is handled by Philadelphia National Bank's transit department, which sorts the checks mechanically according to place of payment. Transit items, such as the Empire check, are sent along with other checks drawn on banks in the New York City area to its New York correspondent, Citibank. During the sorting process, each check is indorsed by Philadelphia National Bank on the back (Form 2B). Along with the

1. Thanks are due to Mr. Arsenio Calle of The Bank of New York and to Richard L. Krzyzanowski, Esq. of Crown Cork and Seal Company for their help in assembling and preparing the sample forms, and also to Philadelphia National Bank for its forms.

checks goes a transmittal form called a "cash letter" with a machine listing of the amounts of the items sent.

When the cash letter and checks are received by Citibank, the total is credited, again provisionally, awaiting final payment of the checks, to the account of Philadelphia National Bank. The total is proved and the checks are sorted by Citibank, which adds its indorsement to the back of the check (Form 2B). Checks drawn on banks which are members of the New York Clearing House Association are sorted into packages for each payor bank, and the Empire check is therefore placed with other checks received by Citibank that are drawn on The Bank of New York. The package containing the Empire check is then presented to The Bank of New York at the New York Clearing House at the clearing on the morning of Wednesday, January 27. By this procedure The Bank of New York, the payor bank, has received the check drawn on it by Empire, the drawer, mailed by Empire to Quaker, the payee, in Philadelphia, deposited by Quaker in Philadelphia National Bank, the depositary bank, forwarded by it to Citibank, the presenting bank, and presented by Citibank to The Bank of New York.

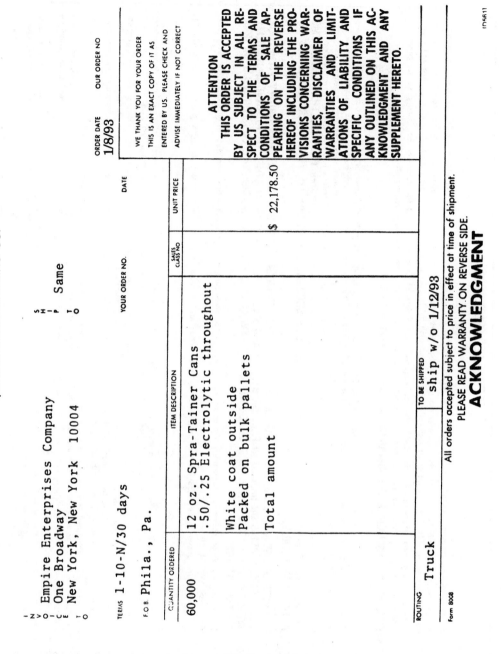

FORM 1

SELLER'S ACKNOWLEDGEMENT

[Front]

TERMS AND CONDITIONS

1. Prices for the goods sold hereunder will be Seller's list prices in effect on the date of shipment plus applicable taxes and governmental charges.

2. On all orders for private decorated or other specially manufactured products an under or over run of 10% of the quantity ordered will be considered as fulfillment of the order. The amount of all such orders must be accepted by the Purchaser within ninety days from first shipment against each order.

3. Seller will use its best efforts to make delivery of the goods ordered on the date or dates specified by the Purchaser, but Seller does not guarantee delivery on any date or dates so specified and shall be subject to no liability for any damage caused by delayed delivery.

4. **WARRANTIES, DISCLAIMER OF WARRANTIES AND LIMITATIONS OF LIABILITY.**

   (a) CONTAINERS

   Seller warrants that containers sold by it shall be free from defects in workmanship and materials. However, in no event shall Seller incur any liability under this warranty, where the containers are not packed, stored and distributed in accordance with good business practice, or where the alleged damage results from rust or outside corrosion occurring after receipt of containers by Purchaser, or from improper capping, closing, crimping, filling and gassing operations by Purchaser, or from the use of parts other than those supplied by Seller. Seller's liability under this warranty whether based on tort or contract is limited exclusively to the repayment of the purchase price of the defective containers. **PROVIDED THAT ANY CLAIMS OR ANY COURT ACTION ARISING UNDER THIS WARRANTY IS BROUGHT WITHIN ONE (1) YEAR AFTER SUCH CAUSE OF ACTION HAS ACCRUED.**

   IN VIEW OF THE ABOVE WARRANTY, SELLER MAKES NO OTHER WARRANTY, WHETHER OF MERCHANTABILITY, FITNESS OR OTHERWISE, EXPRESS OR IMPLIED IN FACT OR BY LAW AND SELLER SHALL HAVE NO FURTHER OBLIGATION OR LIABILITY WITH RESPECT TO THE CONTAINERS. SELLER SHALL IN NO EVENT BE LIABLE FOR ANY GENERAL, CONSEQUENTIAL OR INCI-DENTAL DAMAGES.

   Purchaser waives all claims for shortages in the containers ordered and received hereunder unless they are submitted, in writing, within thirty (30) days after delivery.

   Subject to the above provisions, Seller shall not bring any other action arising under this agreement unless such action is brought within two (2) years after such cause of action has accrued.

   (b) OTHER PRODUCTS

5. Seller shall in no event be liable for damages arising directly or indirectly from the use of goods sold hereunder. Seller's liability, in any event, shall be limited to the invoice price of goods sold, and in this respect, no claim will be allowed after 30 days from billing date.

6. Fires, strikes, differences with workmen, accidents, failure of usual sources of supply, priorities, or other Governmental regulations, or any contingencies beyond the control of Seller, whether related or unrelated to any of the foregoing, shall excuse any failure of performance on the part of the Seller, and similar causes unavoidable by Purchaser shall be sufficient excuse for failure to take goods ordered, beyond those in transit, or manufactured or in process of manufacture, until such contingencies are removed.

7. The Seller shall be entitled to refuse to honor any order or to ship any part of the goods sold if any indebtedness or liability of the Purchaser to the Seller under this or any other contract shall at that time be overdue. Seller may fix or change from time to time the terms of credit under which the goods ordered shall be shipped, and may decline to ship all or any part thereof until such credit terms are met. The interest is changeable on post due accounts.

8. The terms and conditions set forth herein and in any written supplement hereto represent the entire agreement between Purchaser and Seller with respect to the goods mentioned in Purchaser's order and supersede all prior agreements, oral or written in respect of the subject matter of said order.

9. This agreement shall be governed by the law of the State of Pennsylvania.

[B2878?]

[*Reverse*]

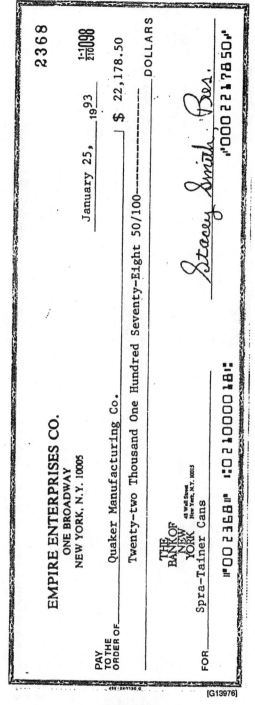

FORM 2

CHECK

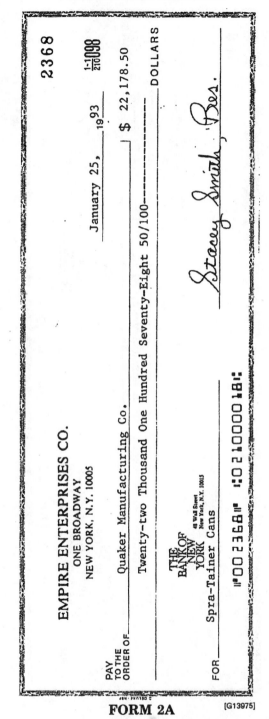

FORM 2A   [G13975]

FRONT OF PAID CHECK

ENDORSE HERE

FOR DEPOSIT. ONLY.

QUAKER MFG. CO.

DO NOT WRITE, STAMP OR SIGN BELOW THIS LINE
RESERVED FOR FINANCIAL INSTITUTION USE

★FEDERAL RESERVE BOARD OF GOVERNORS REG. CC

[G14746]

FORM 2B

BACK OF PAID CHECK

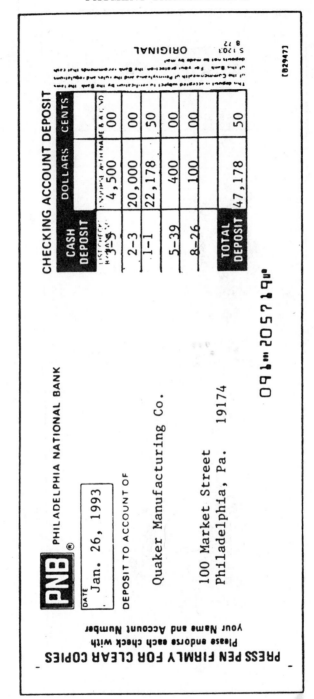

FORM 3

DEPOSIT SLIP

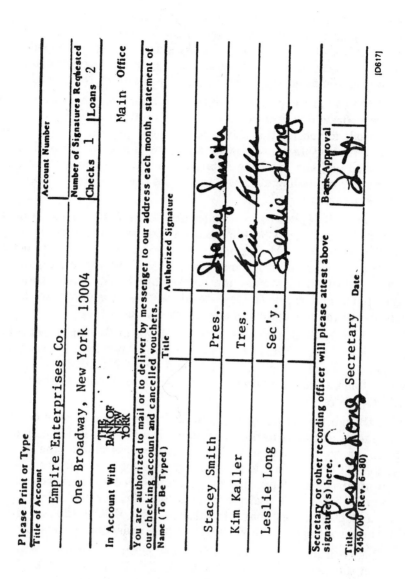

FORM 4

SIGNATURE CARD

Payment. On Wednesday, January 27, the Empire check, along with other checks received by The Bank of New York for payment, is sorted, proved, examined for date, alteration and missing indorsements, checked for sufficiency of funds, stop orders, and attachment or garnishment of Empire's account. The drawer's signature is checked against that on the signature card (Form 4) which Empire filled out when it opened its account at The Bank of New York. The check is then posted, that is, charged to Empire's account, and stamped "Paid" (Form 2B). (The order of these steps may vary depending upon the degree of automation employed by the The Bank of New York.)

At the end of the periodic banking cycle for Empire's account, all of the checks drawn by Empire and paid by The Bank of New York during this period, including the check payable to Quaker, are returned to Empire with a statement showing all deposits and withdrawals during that period and the resulting balance. Empire compares these checks and the corresponding entries against its own records to verify the bank's statement.

Check–Like Instruments Drawn on Thrift Institutions. Congress enacted the Consumer Checking Account Equity Act of 1980, Pub.L. No. 96–221, §§ 301–313, 94 Stat. 132, to resolve a controversy between commercial banks and thrift institutions. The controversy involved the power of thrift institutions—mutual savings banks, savings and loan associations, and credit unions—to allow their customers to draw on such institutions instruments similar to checks.

The Act resolved the controversy in favor of the thrift institutions. It permits mutual savings banks and savings and loan associations to furnish negotiable orders of withdrawal (NOWs) to their noncommercial customers, and it permits credit unions to furnish share drafts to their members.

Although the power of thrift institutions to make these check-like instruments available to their customers is no longer in issue, questions remain as to the status of these instruments under the Uniform Commercial Code. This is particularly true for share drafts. Because credit unions do not have direct access to the Federal Reserve collection system, a share draft indicates on its face the name of a commercial bank that the draft is "payable through" (see UCC 3–120), in order to gain the advantage of the Federal Reserve collection system.

This book does not discuss these new check-like instruments. For more on the subject, see Leary, Is the U.C.C. Prepared for the Thrifts' NOWs, NINOWs, and Share Drafts?, 30 Cath.U.L.Rev. 159 (1981); Wilson, The "New Checks": Thrift Institution Check–Like Instruments and the Uniform Commercial Code, 45 Mo.L.Rev. 199 (1980).

CREDIT CARDS

The introduction of electronic fund transfer systems has been aided by the growing use of credit cards.[1] Although this book does not offer a detailed treatment of credit cards, a little background will be helpful.

1. A credit card is to be distinguished from a debit card, an access device that enables the holder to transfer funds from an account. Sometimes, however, a credit card doubles as a debit card, enabling the holder to transfer funds from an account to that of a merchant. For the applicability of federal legislation to such cards, see B. Clark, The Law of Bank Deposits, Collec-

Extensive use of the credit card goes back to the 1950s, when Diner's Club, American Express, and Carte Blanche cards were introduced. By the beginning of the 1960s the banks had entered the field. In 1966 the Bank of America enlarged its credit card program by offering to license the operation of its card to other banks, giving rise to the system now known as VISA. In 1969 Interbank Card Association launched a competing nationwide program that resulted in the system now known as MasterCard. Since 1976, most banks have been members of both systems, providing merchants with services for both cards. Many banks offer both cards to their customers.

Although the volume of credit card charges is still dwarfed by the amount of payments by check in the same year, for many consumers, the bank card has become an indispensable device for access to a payment system.

A typical bank card transaction involves four parties: the cardholder, the issuing bank, the merchant, and the depositary bank. A consumer obtains a card by applying to a local bank. The cardholder's agreement with the issuing bank establishes a line of credit for the cardholder and states conditions for the use of the card. The cardholder agrees to pay the issuing bank for purchases made with the card prior to its surrender to the bank or the receipt by the bank of notice of its loss. The issuing bank is connected, through an interchange system, with thousands of other banks. Banks in the system solicit merchants to participate in the system. After joining the system, a merchant deals with the soliciting bank, which becomes the merchant's depositary bank. In its agreement with the merchant, the bank agrees to exchange credit available for withdrawal at a discounted rate for sales slips generated by cardholders using their cards.

When a cardholder uses a card the merchant may, depending on the size of the transaction, be required to seek credit authorization by a telephone connected with a computer to make sure, for example, that the card has not been lost and that the cardholder's credit limit will not be exceeded. The merchant then fills out and the cardholder signs a sales slip, which authorizes the issuing bank to pay the amount indicated and which restates the cardholder's promise to pay that total. The merchant imprints on the slip the information on the face of the card, identifying the cardholder and the issuing bank, and enters a description of the goods or services and the price. The merchant gives the cardholder a copy and deposits the slip with the depositary bank. The bank credits the merchant's account with the discounted amount and the information is then transmitted electronically to the issuing bank. The issuing bank enters this information on the cardholder's monthly bill. On receipt of the bill, the cardholder typically has the option of paying with a "free period" without any additional cost or deferring payment and paying a finance charge.

tions and Credit Cards ¶ 11.03[2][c] (3d ed. 1990).

The relationship between the cardholder and the issuing bank that results from the use of the card is one of debtor and creditor. These transactions are subject to federal legislation, now found in the Consumer Protection Act, 15 U.S.C. § 1601 et seq. Of special importance are §§ 132–135 and §§ 161–171 (as added by the Fair Credit Billing Act of 1974). Some aspects of the legislation will be considered later.

ELECTRONIC FUND TRANSFERS

Recent years have at last begun to bear out the promise of electronic fund transfer (EFT) as a common means of payment. This long-heralded development has many advantages, including cutting the enormous cost of our present paper-based system of payment by check and reducing the "float" of items in the process of collection. It is not expected, however, that EFT will completely replace the use of checks, at least not in the near future. A lawyer must therefore be prepared to cope with the legal problems presented by a variety of different systems of payment.

The following materials emphasize problems arising out of the use of the check, a means of payment on which courts, legislatures, and scholars have lavished attention over the past century. The materials also consider those problems in the context of other payment systems. Thus, for example, the discussions of wrongful dishonor and of stopping payment refer to other payment systems as well as to checks. The materials do not, however, deal with problems that are largely peculiar to other payment systems, such as the provision of receipts and the resolution of errors in an EFT system.

Draw Orders. A check is the most common example of what has been called a "draw order." It is initiated by the transferor (Empire) and transmitted to the transferee (Quaker), and directs the transferor's bank (The Bank of New York) to pay the transferee. The transferee obtains the money by instructing its bank (PNB) by means of a deposit slip to collect the money from the payor bank, which pays the sum and debits the transferor's account. A draw order *pulls* funds back from the transferor's bank back to the transferee's bank.

The check collection process does not easily lend itself to EFT procedures. One possibility is what is called "check truncation." Instead of hauling billions of checks all over the country for collection every year in trucks and airplanes, the information on the checks would be fed by the transferee's bank into an electronic system and transmitted to the transferor's bank, which would pay the check and remit the funds electronically to the transferee's bank. The check, or an electronic image of it, would be stored at the point of transmission. The transferor would receive a statement describing the transaction (much as the holder of a credit card now does [1]) and could obtain a copy

1. Truncation occurred in connection with bank credit cards, when a shift was made from "country club" to "descriptive" billing. Although the sales slips formerly cleared through the system and were returned to the customer like checks, the

of the check if the need arose. One problem with such a system of truncation, or collecting bank check retention, is that of verifying the transferor's signature as drawer of the check. This problem is avoided in a less ambitious system of payor bank check retention, in which the check is sent to the transferor's bank but is not returned by that bank to the transferor, its customer. The facilitation of truncation was a major goal in the revision of Articles 3 and 4.

A more efficient system of draw orders can be devised, however, for a debtor's recurring payments to a single creditor, such as mortgage payments, insurance premiums, and loan payments. The debtor first gives the creditor authority to initiate periodic transfers. The creditor, as transferee then initiates these pre-authorized transfers by periodically sending the billing information to its bank. The bank will arrange the transfer of funds from the bank of the debtor, as transferee, through an Automated Clearing House (ACH), a computerized clearing facility that effects the paperless exchange of funds between banks. Instructions to transfer funds are on magnetic tape or in some other form that can be read by a computer. As will be pointed out shortly, ACHs perform other functions than those connected with such pre-authorized recurring payments.

Payment Orders. A more promising type of transaction for an EFTS involves what has been called a "payment order." Such an order is initiated by the transferor and is transmitted by the transferor to the payor bank, directing the payor bank to pay or to arrange payment to the transferee. Under a payment order, the transferor (Empire) instead of giving the transferee (Quaker) an order addressed to the payor bank (The Bank of New York), would instruct the payor bank directly to arrange to have payment made to the transferee. A payment order *pushes* funds from the transferor's bank to the transferee's bank. Such a system, known as a "giro system," has long been in existence in a number of European countries, sometimes through the postal system.

Payment orders in electronic form are well-established in this country for large transfers between banks. Two major domestic electronic fund transfer systems carry out or facilitate such transactions: Fedwire, the national Federal Reserve Wire Network, and the Clearing House Interbank Payment System (CHIPS), a private system operated by the New York Clearing House that serves a large number of foreign and domestic banks. The daily clearings of each system are in the neighborhood of a trillion dollars.

Furthermore, the great bulk of ACH EFT volume consists of preauthorized recurring payment orders under direct deposit programs of both the federal government and the private sector. Most of the government transfers involve Social Security benefits and most of the private transfers involve payrolls. EFTS for payment orders by consumers are also available for such recurring bills as insurance premiums and mortgage payments. The consumer's bank pays the creditor

transaction is now truncated and the slips
remain with the merchant bank.

by an ACH transfer and debits the consumer's account as payments come due.

Some payment orders may be available to a consumer through an automated teller machine (ATM), an EFT terminal that is available twenty-four hours a day and may be placed at such off-premises locations as a supermarket or a shopping mall. The consumer activates the ATM by inserting a plastic debit card and entering a personal identification number (PIN). ATMs generally permit not only deposits and withdrawals, but also transfers between the customer's checking and savings accounts and at least some transfers to pay mortgages, credit cards, utility bills, and the like.

A more sophisticated system for consumer payment orders uses a point-of-sale (POS) terminal, located on a merchant's premises to enable consumers to pay for purchases from the merchant. The customer activates the POS terminal by a plastic debit card and PIN, just as in the case of an ATM. The customer's account is debited and the merchant's account is credited at the same time.

In addition, some banks have instituted bill paying by telephone. And home electronic banking, in which a customer may order a bank to pay bills by using a computer terminal in the home, is under development.

Legislation. In 1974, Congress established the National Commission on Electronic Fund Transfers to make a study and to recommend legislation "in connection with the possible development of public or private electronic fund transfer systems." 12 U.S.C. § 2401 et seq. In 1977, the Commission presented its report, EFT in the United States: Policy Recommendations and the Public Interest (The Final Report of the National Commission on Electronic Fund Transfers 1977). In 1978, Congress passed the Electronic Fund Transfer Act (EFT Act), 15 U.S.C. § 1693 et seq., as Title IX of the Consumer Credit Protection Act. Many, though not all, of the provisions of the EFT Act have been amplified by Regulation E of the Federal Reserve Board, 12 C.F.R. Part 205. There is also some state legislation on the subject.

According to Regulation E, "The Act establishes the basic rights, liabilities, and responsibilities of consumers who use electronic money transfer services and of financial institutions that offer these services." 12 C.F.R. § 205.1(b). Its scope is thus limited in two important respects. First, the Act applies only to services used by or offered to *consumers,* and a "consumer" is defined as "a natural person." 12 C.F.R. § 205.2(e). The Act does not cover the large volume of electronic fund transfers initiated by businesses and banks. Second, the Act applies only to electronic money transfer services. An "electronic fund transfer" is defined to include "any transfer of funds ... that is initiated through an electronic terminal, telephone, or computer or magnetic tape for the purpose of ordering, instructing, or authorizing a financial institution to debit or credit an account," including "point-of-sale transfers, automated teller machine transfers, direct deposits or withdrawals of funds, and transfers initiated by telephone." It does not, however, include transfer of funds by paper instruments such as checks. 12 C.F.R. § 205.2(g).

A much more ambitious project was mounted in 1977 by the Permanent Editorial Board of the Uniform Commercial Code—the drafting of a Uniform New Payments Code. It was to apply to transactions by consumers as well as by businesses and banks and to all payments, except cash, including those by check and credit card as well as by electronic fund transfers. It would thus have replaced Articles 3 and 4 as far as checks were concerned. Because of its ambitious scope and some of its consumer-oriented provisions, however, the project provoked intense controversy and was abandoned.

Instead the Permanent Editorial Board decided to revise Articles 3 and 4 and to draft a new Article 4A limited to electronic funds transfers. Article 4A, Funds Transfers was approved and recommended for adoption in 1989. It excludes consumer transactions. According to UCC 4A–108, Exclusion of Consumer Transactions Governed by Federal Law, Article 4A "does not apply to a funds transfer any part of which is governed by the Electronic Fund Transfer Act of 1978." [2] Here is a description of how a funds transfer works under Article 4A.

"The transaction governed by Article 4A is called a 'funds transfer' and comprises the series of transactions by which a person called the 'originator' makes payment to a person called the 'beneficiary.' The funds transfer is made by one or more 'payment orders' beginning with that of the originator. A payment order is always given directly to a bank and it instructs the bank to pay money to the beneficiary or to cause (by means of a payment order) another bank to make the payment. In a large percentage of cases, payment orders are transmitted electronically, and this is the derivation of the term 'wire transfer,' but a payment order can also be given in writing or orally. Payment to the beneficiary is normally made by credit to an account of the beneficiary in the beneficiary's bank. The terms 'payment order' [UCC 4A–103(a)(1)] and 'funds transfer' [UCC 4A–104(2)] determine the scope of Article 4A and they are discussed in detail in the official comment to section 4A–104.

"Rights and obligations under Article 4A arise as the result of 'acceptance' [UCC 4A–209] of a payment order by the bank to which the order is sent (the 'receiving bank' [UCC 4A–103(a)(4)]). A receiving bank is not required to carry out a funds transfer for its customer, the sender [UCC 4A–103(a)(5)] of the payment order, unless it has agreed to do so. Substantial risk is involved in funds transfers and a bank may not be willing to give this service to all its customers, and may not be willing to offer it to any customer unless certain safeguards against loss such as security procedures are in effect. Moreover, funds transfers

2. In 1990, the Federal Reserve Board made Article 4A applicable to Fedwire transfers by incorporating Article 4A in Regulation J. 12 C.F.R. §§ 210.25–210.32.

often involve the giving of credit by the receiving bank to the customer, and that also is based on agreement. These considerations are reflected in Article 4A by the principle that, in the absence of a contrary agreement, a receiving bank does not incur liability with respect to a payment order until it accepts it [UCC 4A–212]. In the case of a payment order sent to a receiving bank other than the beneficiary's bank, acceptance occurs when the receiving bank 'executes' the payment order of the sender by sending a payment order to some other bank intended to carry out the payment order received by the receiving bank [UCC 4A–209(a), 4A–301(a)]. In the case of a payment order to the beneficiary's bank, acceptance usually occurs when that bank receives payment of the sender's payment order or when that bank pays the beneficiary or notifies the beneficiary of receipt of the payment order [UCC 4A–209(b)(1), (2)]. When a payment order is accepted, the sender of the order is obliged to pay the amount of the order to the receiving bank [UCC 4A–402(b), (c)]. If a payment order is accepted by the beneficiary's bank, that bank is obliged to pay the amount of the order to the beneficiary [UCC 4A–404(a)]. Acceptance by the beneficiary's bank also means that the funds transfer has been completed (payment by the originator of the funds transfer to the beneficiary occurs when the acceptance occurs) [UCC 4A–406(a)]. Thus, under Article 4A, if a funds transfer is made to pay an obligation, the obligation is paid by the originator at the time the beneficiary's bank incurs an obligation to pay the beneficiary and in the amount of the payment order accepted by that bank [UCC 4A–406(b)]." Jordan & Warren, Introduction to Symposium: Revised U.C.C. Articles 3 & 4 and New Article 4A, 42 Ala.L.Rev. 373, 378–79 (1991).

For a general discussion of EFT, see D. Baker & R. Brandel, The Law of Electronic Fund Transfer Systems (2d ed. 1988); B. Geva, The Law of Electronic Funds Transfers (looseleaf).

Chapter 3

CHECKS DRAWN ON INSUFFICIENT FUNDS

INTRODUCTION

It has already been pointed out that the most common cause of dishonor is insufficient funds. What happens when a "bad" check "bounces"? Most commonly the cause is a mistake by the drawer in calculating its bank balance or in drawing against uncollected checks, checks that it has already deposited in its account but on which it is not yet entitled to draw. The payor bank will return the check with a return item ticket marked with the appropriate reason. If the check is presented a second time it will be paid by the payor bank, or if the drawer is asked for payment it will be paid by the drawer. But not all bad checks are so simply collected. This chapter is concerned in large part with the holder's recourse in such cases. (It will be assumed that the drawer does not assert that it is not liable on the check because of some defense; problems involving defenses are discussed in Chapter 4.) The final section of the chapter deals with the situation where the payor bank has paid by mistake a check drawn on insufficient funds. See generally Zaretsky, Contract Liability of Parties to Negotiable Instruments, 42 Ala.L.Rev. 627 (1991).

	TO:	THE BANK OF NEW YORK 1-1
RETURNED UNPAID	For Reason Indicated	☐ Date
	☒ Insufficient Funds	☐ Signature
	☐ Uncollected Funds	☐ Endorsement
	☐ Account Closed	☐ Other_____
	☐ Payment Stopped	

[G13977]

RETURN ITEM STAMP

SECTION 1. LIABILITY ON DISHONOR

(A) LIABILITY OF PAYOR BANK TO DRAWER

Prefatory Note. Before inquiring into the holder's recourse, we take a brief look at the problem of the dishonored check from the drawer's standpoint. Suppose that a check was drawn on sufficient funds and should have been honored, but was instead returned to the holder as a bad check. What recourse has the drawer against the payor bank? Or, to put the question differently, what legal sanctions stand behind the natural incentive of banks as competing businesses to keep the good will of their customers by honoring their properly drawn orders? What does the signature card (Form 4 supra) have to say about this?

Problem 1.[1] After drawing the Empire check, Stacey Smith stops payment on it, using the form on p. 222 infra, at a time when Empire has a balance of $40,000, and withdraws all but $10,000 from the account. When Quaker presents the check, The Bank of New York dishonors it, indicating on the return item stamp "insufficient funds." A criminal proceeding is instituted against Smith under a penal statute making it a crime to draw a check with knowledge that sufficient funds are not on deposit. After Smith's arrest and release on bail, the information is dismissed. Smith sues The Bank of New York alleging the above facts and claiming damages for harm to business reputation and credit and for legal expenses in connection with the criminal charges. On The Bank of New York's demurrer to the complaint, what decision? See UCC 4–402, 4–403, 4–104(a)(5), 1–103, 1–109; *Parrett v. Platte Valley State Bank & Trust Co.*, infra. Consider, in formulating your answer, whether Smith was a "customer" and whether there was a "wrongful dishonor." Would it be advisable for The Bank of New York to check "refer to maker" on all checks dishonored?[2] See UCC 3–505(a)(2). Can you think of any practical disadvantage of such a step?

Problem 2. Along with the Empire check for $22,178.50, three other checks drawn by Empire, for $2,000, $5,000, and $10,000, are presented in the same bundle at the Clearing House. Empire has only $24,000 in its account. What may The Bank of New York do without risking liability under UCC 4–402? Refuse to pay all of them? Refuse to pay some of them? If the payor bank processes checks by a computer that automatically rejects overdrafts, would the order in

---

1. The facts in most of the problems in Part II are those in the Prototype Transaction, except as varied in the problem itself. Such variations in the facts in one problem are not to be made in the next problem unless so indicated.

2. Regulation CC 229.30(d) requires a payor bank to "clearly indicate on the face of the check ... the reason for return." Comment 30(d) says that a "reason such as 'Refer to Maker' is permissible in appropriate cases."

which the computer processes checks be important? Is it important for the payor bank to make sure that additional deposits have not been received before any checks are returned as dishonored? If the payor bank imposes on the drawer a fee for dishonored checks that exceeds its costs, is it free to dishonor many small checks rather than one large check? See UCC 4–303(b), 4–402(c); Hillebrand, Revised Articles 3 and 4 of the Uniform Commercial Code: A Consumer Perspective, 42 Ala.L.Rev. 679, 684–85 (1991); Rubin, Efficiency, Equity and the Proposed Revisions of Articles 3 and 4, 42 Ala.L.Rev. 551, 572 (1991). Is UCC 1–203 relevant?

PARRETT v. PLATTE VALLEY STATE BANK & TRUST CO.

Supreme Court of Nebraska, 1990.
236 Neb. 139, 459 N.W.2d 371.

PER CURIAM. Robert Parrett appeals from the judgment of the district court for Buffalo County which sustained the demurrer of Platte Valley State Bank & Trust Co. and dismissed Parrett's suit....

Parrett was the principal shareholder, president, and chief operating officer of P & P Machinery, Inc., a Nebraska corporation engaged in the business of buying and selling farm machinery. P & P Machinery had its principal place of business in Kearney, Nebraska, where the bank was located.

For several years before March 1984, the bank provided operating loans and financing to P & P Machinery, which had its checking account at the bank. Parrett personally participated in the business relationship between P & P Machinery and the bank, including Parrett's personal guaranty to the bank for all obligations owed by P & P Machinery to the bank. Also, Parrett was authorized to sign checks drawn on P & P Machinery's account at the bank.

On March 1, 1984, Parrett signed and delivered a check from P & P Machinery to Nelson Farm Equipment at Madison, South Dakota, for the purchase of farm machinery and equipment. Later, on March 7, the bank dishonored the check to Nelson Farm Equipment and returned the check without payment, although, when the check was presented for payment, P & P Machinery had sufficient funds in its account with the bank to pay the check. As a result of the dishonored check, Parrett was charged with felony theft in South Dakota and was extradited from Nebraska to stand trial in Lake County, South Dakota. Parrett went to trial on the charge in South Dakota. However, at trial the court dismissed the charge against Parrett.

Parrett sued the bank for damages proximately caused by the bank's dishonor of the P & P Machinery check signed by Parrett and alleged three causes of action: (1) the bank's negligence in failing to pay the check to Nelson Farm Equipment; (2) the bank's wrongful dishonor of the check, which, pursuant to Neb.U.C.C. § 4–402 (Reissue 1980), resulted in the bank's liability to Parrett for damages; and (3) the bank's breach of its duty of good faith performance under Neb. U.C.C. § 1–203 (Reissue 1980)....

In Parrett's appeal, the sole issue is whether Parrett, as president and principal shareholder of P & P Machinery, is the bank's "customer" under § 4–402, which provides in part: "A payor bank is liable to its customer for damages proximately caused by the wrongful dishonor of an item." "Customer" is defined as "any person having an account with a bank or for whom a bank has agreed to collect items...." Neb.U.C.C. § 4–104(1)(e) (Reissue 1980).

In Loucks v. Albuquerque National Bank, 76 N.M. 735, 418 P.2d 191 (1966), Loucks and Martinez, as partners, had a partnership checking account at Albuquerque National. The bank dishonored the partnership's check after it had improperly charged the partnership account with a payment on a debt owed by Martinez. Loucks and Martinez individually sued the bank for wrongful dishonor of the partnership check. Under New Mexico law, a partnership was a legal entity distinct from the partners and was entitled to sue in the partnership name. New Mexico, which had adopted the Uniform Commercial Code, had statutes containing the same language as Neb. U.C.C. §§ 4–402 and 4–104(1)(e). In determining that Loucks and Martinez, as individuals, had no cause of action against the bank for the alleged wrongful dishonor, the court stated:

> It would seem that logically the "customer" in this case to whom the bank was required to respond in damages for any wrongful dishonor was the partnership....

> The question of whether a wrongful dishonor is to be considered as a breach of contract or as a breach of a tort duty was apparently avoided by the drafters of the Uniform Commercial Code by using the words "wrongful dishonor." ...

> We have not overlooked the fact that tortious conduct may be tortious as to two or more persons, and that these persons may be the partnership and one or more of the individual partners. [Citation omitted.]

> The relationship, in connection with which the wrongful conduct of the bank arose, was the relationship between the bank and the partnership. The partnership was the customer, and any damages arising from the dishonor belonged to the partnership and not to the partners individually.

> ... No duty was owed to [Loucks] personally by reason of the debtor-creditor relationship between the bank and the partnership.

76 N.M. at 742, 744, 418 P.2d at 196–97.

A cause of action for a bank's wrongful dishonor of checks was presented in Kendall Yacht Corp. v. United California Bank, 50 Cal.

App.3d 949, 123 Cal.Rptr. 848 (1975). Lawrence and Linda Kendall were officers and prospective principal shareholders of Kendall Yacht Corporation, which maintained its checking accounts at United California Bank. The corporation never issued stock. Both Kendalls executed their personal guaranties for the bank's loans to the corporation. Under the financing arrangements approved by one Ron Lamperts, a bank loan officer, the bank honored the corporation's checks, although there were sometimes insufficient funds in the corporation's account to pay the checks. The bank dishonored checks from the corporation. After the corporation collapsed, criminal charges were brought against Linda Kendall, but the charges were dismissed before trial. Kendalls sued the bank for its wrongful dishonor of the corporation's checks and were awarded a judgment for damages. The bank appealed. In affirming the judgment for the Kendalls, the court stated:

> The Bank contends first that under Commercial Code section 4402 the wrongful dishonor of a check of a *corporation* does not give a cause of action for damages to individual officers and shareholders of the corporation. California Uniform Commercial Code section 4402, which represents section 4–402 of the Uniform Commercial Code, reads as follows: "A payor bank is liable to its customer for damages proximately caused by the wrongful dishonor of an item. When the dishonor occurs through mistake liability is limited to actual damages proved." The Bank relies on Loucks v. Albuquerque National Bank, 76 N.M. 735 [418 P.2d 191], where it was held that under Uniform Commercial Code section 4–402 individuals doing business as partners could not recover for damages to their personal credit, good reputation, and business standing which resulted from the wrongful dishonor of checks written on the partnership account....

> It is not clear whether the New Mexico court meant to say that in every case where an account stands in the name of a partnership or a corporation, only the business entity may recover under section 4–402, regardless of the circumstances. Such a narrow and technical reading of the statute and the term "customer" does not seem warranted. The purpose of the statute—to hold banks accountable for damages proximately caused by wrongful dishonors—is more readily served by allowing a flexible and reasonable interpretation of the word "customer."

> We would certainly not hold as a general proposition that the shareholders or officers of a corporation could recover under section 4402 for the wrongful dishonor of a corporation check. Here, however, it is difficult to avoid the conclusion that Mr. and Mrs. Kendall were as much "customers" of the Bank within the contemplation of the statute as was the Corporation. Lamperts and the Bank looked directly to the Kendalls to satisfy the obligations of the Corporation. They

were required to execute a personal guarantee of the initial $14,000 loan, and later they were required to increase that guarantee to $20,000 to cover the additional credit the Bank was extending to the Corporation in the form of honoring its overdrafts. The reason the Bank required the guarantees is obvious. The Corporation had never issued shares and was undercapitalized; it was, in effect, nothing but a transparent shell, having no viability as a separate and distinct legal entity. The Kendalls alone were controlling its financial affairs and were personally vouching for its fiscal responsibility. Not only the Bank, but also the suppliers and employees of the Corporation knew that this was the situation.... Thus it was entirely foreseeable that the dishonoring of the Corporation's checks would reflect directly on the personal credit and reputation of the Kendalls and that they would suffer the adverse personal consequences which resulted when the Bank [dishonored the checks]. Under these circumstances we would elevate form over substance if we were to hold that the wrong defined by section 4402 was done only to the Corporation and that the Kendalls as individuals could not recover.

(Emphasis in original.) 50 Cal.App.3d at 955–56, 123 Cal.Rptr. at 852–53.

[The court discussed several other cases at length.]

After considering the preceding cases, we find the reasoning expressed in Kendall Yacht Corp. v. United California Bank, 50 Cal. App.3d 949, 123 Cal.Rptr. 848 (1975), to be persuasive. Directing the Kendall rationale to Parrett's case, and accepting Parrett's alleged facts to be true with reasonable inferences drawn therefrom, see Security Inv. Co. v. State, 231 Neb. 536, 437 N.W.2d 439 (1989), we find that Parrett was a "customer" of the bank within the meaning of § 4–402 and that Parrett's petition does state a cause of action for the bank's wrongful dishonor of the P & P Machinery check signed by Parrett. As reflected by Parrett's petition, the parties' business relationship, which included Parrett's personal guaranty for P & P Machinery's obligations to the bank, was such that it was foreseeable that dishonoring the corporation's check would reflect directly on Parrett. This is borne out by the fact that a criminal charge based on the dishonored check was brought against Parrett, but was dismissed during Parrett's trial. Since the consequences of the wrongful dishonor fell upon Parrett, it would elevate form over substance to say that he was not the bank's "customer" within the meaning of § 4–402. This is not to say that in every case a corporate officer has a wrongful dishonor action against the depository bank on which the corporation's check has been drawn and later dishonored. However, in view of the facts of this case alleged in Parrett's petition, Parrett has a cause of action against the bank.

The bank argues that it owed no special duty to Parrett, who has based his suit on a transaction which occurred by reason of Parrett's being the principal shareholder of P & P Machinery and an officer who signed the corporate check which was dishonored by the bank.

Recently, in Meyerson v. Coopers & Lybrand, 233 Neb. 758, 762, 448 N.W.2d 129, 133 (1989), we stated:

> As a general rule a shareholder may not bring an action in his or her own name to recover for wrongs done to the corporation or its property. Such a cause of action is in the corporation and not the shareholders. The right of a shareholder to sue is derivative in nature and normally can be brought only in a representative capacity for the corporation. [Citations omitted.]

> There is a well-recognized exception to the general rule: If the shareholder properly establishes an individual cause of action because the harm to the corporation also damaged the shareholder in his or her individual capacity, rather than as a shareholder, such individual action may be maintained. [Citations omitted.]

> The courts generally are in agreement that to come within this exception, the shareholder must demonstrate that there is a special duty, such as a contractual duty, between the wrongdoer and the shareholder or that the shareholder suffered an injury separate and distinct from that suffered by other shareholders. [Citations omitted.]

If the facts alleged in Parrett's petition are true, which we must assume for the purposes of our review in this case, Parrett, as a shareholder of P & P Machinery, has established an individual cause of action because any harm to P & P Machinery also damaged Parrett in his individual capacity, rather than as a shareholder. See Meyerson v. Coopers & Lybrand, supra. The history of the business relationship between the bank and P & P Machinery, which included Parrett's personal guaranty for P & P Machinery's obligations to the bank, provides special circumstances and, therefore, a special duty owed by the bank to Parrett as the principal shareholder of P & P Machinery. Thus, according to Parrett's petition, Parrett is not only a customer of Platte Valley State Bank & Trust Co., but has an individual cause of action based on the bank's special duty to Parrett under the circumstances.

Therefore, we reverse the judgment of the district court and remand this matter to the district court for further proceedings.

SHANAHAN, JUSTICE, dissenting. Although I agree with the general proposition of law that a corporate officer, as a signatory for a check drawn on the corporation's account, may, under certain circumstances, be a "customer" within Neb.U.C.C. § 4-402 (Reissue 1980) for the purpose of a depository bank's liability for wrongful dishonor of the corporation's check, the facts alleged by Parrett fail to provide the circumstances necessary for application of that general proposition of law.

The allegations of Parrett's amended petition supply the following facts: Parrett was an authorized signatory on the checking account of P & P Machinery; there was a history of credit transactions between P & P Machinery and the bank; Parrett had given the bank his personal guaranty for obligations of P & P Machinery; and Parrett was a corporate officer and the principal shareholder of P & P Machinery.

What is not supplied in Parrett's petition, and cannot be reasonably inferred from the allegations, are those facts which permit application of the general proposition of law regarding a corporate officer as a "customer" of a bank in reference to the bank's wrongful dishonor of a corporate check signed by the officer.

Although Kendall Yacht Corp. v. United California Bank, 50 Cal. App.3d 949, 123 Cal.Rptr. 848 (1975), seems to be the basis for determining whether Parrett was the bank's customer, the salient facts found in *Kendall* are absent from Parrett's case. The checking account stood in the name of P & P Machinery, an existing corporation with a long history of credit transactions with the bank. However, in those transactions nothing indicates that the bank ever disregarded the corporate existence of P & P Machinery and treated Parrett as the principal or otherwise identified Parrett as the individual responsible for satisfaction of the corporation's obligations to the bank. Actually, the facts alleged and inferences therefrom are to the contrary. Although Parrett gave his guaranty for P & P Machinery's obligations to the bank, on no occasion did the bank enforce, or threaten to enforce, Parrett's guaranty. Mere existence of the guaranty is neutral in Parrett's case. Moreover, Parrett did not, either voluntarily or in response to the bank's request or demand, use his funds or property to pay P & P Machinery's indebtedness to the bank. Regarding P & P Machinery, there is no allegation or justifiable inference that the corporation was "undercapitalized," a "transparent shell" as a corporation in name only without the issuance of stock, or lacked "viability as a separate and distinct legal entity." *Kendall*, supra. None of those *Kendall* conditions exist in Parrett's situation. Hence, there is no basis to conclude that Parrett was the bank's customer at the time the check was dishonored. The district court was correct in sustaining the bank's demurrer and dismissing Parrett's action.

Since Parrett was not the bank's customer in the subject transaction, there is no need to consider the question about special duty in relation to a shareholder's cause of action. Consequently, the judgment of the district court should have been affirmed.

Notes

(1) **Recovery by Non-customer.** There was authority prior to the Code that allowed a non-customer to recover for wrongful dishonor.

In Macrum v. Security Trust & Savings Co., 221 Ala. 419, 129 So. 74 (1930), it was held that the manager of a corporation could recover damages that he suffered as the result of the wrongful dishonor of a check that he had drawn on behalf of the corporation on its account. Would the "principles of law" that allowed recovery in that case be "displaced" by UCC 4–402, or would they be "supplementary general principles of law" under UCC 1–103? Note that Comment 5 to UCC 4–402, citing *Macrum,* explains that "the issue is whether the statutory cause of action in section 4–402 displaces, in accordance with section 1–103, any cause of action that existed at common law in a person who is not the customer whose reputation is damaged." What does the section caption to UCC 4–402 suggest concerning its intended coverage? Are section captions part of the Code? See UCC 1–109. Are there any dangers in codifying an area such as this?

(2) **Scope of Damages.** Former UCC 4–402 provided, "When the dishonor occurs through mistake liability is limited to actual damages proved." Revised UCC 4–402(b) deletes the first six words. Comment 1 explains that this is intended to make clear the rejection of "the so-called 'trader' rule ... that allowed a 'merchant or trader' to recover substantial damages for wrongful dishonor without proof of damages actually suffered." (Some courts had held that the "trader" rule survived where dishonor occurred for a reason other than mistake.) Would revised UCC 4–402 change the result in American Bank of Waco v. Waco Airmotive, 818 S.W.2d 163 (Tex.App.1991), in which punitive damages were upheld where the jury found that the bank that dishonored checks "acted willfully, wantonly, or maliciously"? Would it change the result in Twin City Bank v. Isaacs, 283 Ark. 127, 672 S.W.2d 651 (1984), in which damages for mental suffering, as well as punitive damages, were upheld where there was evidence of "the loss of two vehicles, credit loss through loan denials, loss of the use of their money for four years, the suffering occasioned by marital difficulties, the inability to acquire a home they wanted, and the general anxieties which accompanied the financial strain"? For the background of UCC 4–402, see Dow, Damages and Proof in Cases of Wrongful Dishonor: The Unsettled Issues Under U.C.C. Section 4–402, 63 Wash.U.L.Q. 237 (1985).

(3) **Consumer Complaints.** Although most checks are deposited for collection in the payee's bank, occasionally a payee—usually a consumer—will take a check directly to the payor bank for payment. The experience may be an irritating and time-consuming one for the payee. Unless the payee happens to have an account at the payor bank, that bank may be uneasy about paying a stranger in possession of the check and reluctant to take the risk of paying the wrong person.

What is the payor bank entitled to do in order to satisfy itself that the person in possession of the check is actually the payee? UCC 3–501(b)(2) allows it to demand "reasonable identification". How long can the payor bank take to satisfy itself? UCC 3–502(b)(2) says that the check is dishonored if it "is not paid on the day of presentment." But

UCC 3–501(b)(4) allows the payor bank to fix a "cutoff hour not earlier than 2 P.M." and treat presentment as occurring on the following day if presentment is made after that hour. Does this mean that the payee must come back the following day? Do these Code provisions give the payee an action against the payor bank if it does not observe the provision?

(4) Failure to Execute Payment Order. Suppose that a bank receives a payment order from a depositor ordering it to transfer a sum of money to a transferee's account, but the bank negligently fails to make the transfer. As a result, the transferee cancels its contract with the depositor. Is the bank liable to the depositor for the resulting loss? Under UCC 4A–305, a receiving bank is not liable for consequential damages for failure to execute a payment order except "to the extent provided in an express written agreement of the receiving bank." [1] The evolution of this restriction is described in detail in Comment 2.

"Subsection (b) applies to cases of breach of Section 4A–302 involving more than mere delay. In those cases the bank is liable for damages for improper execution but they are limited to compensation for interest losses and incidental expenses of the sender resulting from the breach, the expenses of the sender in the funds transfer and attorney's fees. This subsection reflects the judgment that imposition of consequential damages on a bank for commission of an error is not justified.

"The leading common law case on the subject of consequential damages is Evra Corp. v. Swiss Bank Corp., 673 F.2d 951 (7th Cir.1982), in which Swiss Bank, an intermediary bank, failed to execute a payment order. Because the beneficiary did not receive timely payment the originator lost a valuable ship charter. The lower court awarded the originator $2.1 million for lost profits even though the amount of the payment order was only $27,000. The Seventh Circuit reversed, in part on the basis of the common law rule of Hadley v. Baxendale that consequential damages may not be awarded unless the defendant is put on notice of the special circumstances giving rise to them. Swiss Bank may have known that the originator was paying the shipowner for the hire of a vessel but did not know that a favorable charter would be lost if the payment was delayed. 'Electronic payments are not so unusual as to automatically place a bank on notice of extraordinary consequences if such a transfer goes awry. Swiss Bank did not have enough information to infer that if it lost a $27,000 payment order it would face liability in excess of $2 million.' 673 F.2d at 956.

"If *Evra* means that consequential damages can be imposed if the culpable bank has notice of particular circumstances giving rise to the damages, it does not provide an acceptable solution to the problem of bank liability for consequential damages. In the typical case transmission of the payment order is made electronically. Personnel of the receiving bank that process payment orders are not the appropriate

---

1. Note, however, the "money-back guarantee" in UCC 4A–402(d).

people to evaluate the risk of liability for consequential damages in relation to the price charged for the wire transfer service. Even if notice is received by higher level management personnel who could make an appropriate decision whether the risk is justified by the price, liability based on notice would require evaluation of payment orders on an individual basis. This kind of evaluation is inconsistent with the high-speed, low-price, mechanical nature of the processing system that characterizes wire transfers. Moreover, in *Evra* the culpable bank was an intermediary bank with which the originator did not deal. Notice to the originator's bank would not bind the intermediary bank, and it seems impractical for the originator's bank to convey notice of this kind to intermediary banks in the funds transfer. The success of the wholesale wire transfer industry has largely been based on its ability to effect payment at low cost and great speed. Both of these essential aspects of the modern wire transfer system would be adversely affected by a rule that imposed on banks liability for consequential damages. A banking industry amicus brief in *Evra* stated: 'Whether banks can continue to make EFT services available on a widespread basis, by charging reasonable rates, depends on whether they can do so without incurring unlimited consequential risks. Certainly, no bank would handle for $3.25 a transaction entailing potential liability in the millions of dollars.'

"As the court in *Evra* also noted, the originator of the funds transfer is in the best position to evaluate the risk that a funds transfer will not be made on time and to manage that risk by issuing a payment order in time to allow monitoring of the transaction. The originator, by asking the beneficiary, can quickly determine if the funds transfer has been completed. If the originator has sent the payment order at a time that allows a reasonable margin for correcting error, no loss is likely to result if the transaction is monitored. The other published cases on this issue reach the *Evra* result. Central Coordinates, Inc. v. Morgan Guaranty Trust Co., 40 U.C.C.Rep.Serv. 1340 (N.Y.Sup.Ct.1985), and Gatoil (U.S.A.), Inc. v. Forest Hill State Bank, 1 U.C.C.Rep.Serv.2d 171 (D.Md.1986).

"Subsection (c) allows the measure of damages in subsection (b) to be increased by an express written agreement of the receiving bank. An originator's bank might be willing to assume additional responsibilities and incur additional liability in exchange for a higher fee."

(5) Other Failures to Pay. Suppose that a cardholder tries to use a credit card to purchase goods in an amount for which telephonic authorization is required, but authorization is mistakenly denied on the erroneous ground that the cardholder's dollar limit has been exceeded, and the cardholder is unable to make the purchase. Is the issuing bank liable to the cardholder for damages? Would it make a difference if the agreement between the cardholder and the issuing bank provided that the bank could cancel the credit privileges at any time without notice? See Smith v. Federated Department Stores, 165 Ga.App. 459, 301 S.E.2d

652 (1983). As to the impact of the Fair Credit Reporting Act, see Wood v. Holiday Inns, 508 F.2d 167 (5th Cir.1975).

Suppose that instead of using a credit card, a consumer attempts to pay for the goods using a point of sale system, but the consumer's order is wrongfully dishonored. Is the financial institution liable to the consumer for damages? EFT Act § 1693(h) lays down as a general rule that a financial institution is liable to a consumer "for all damages proximately caused" by its wrongful failure to observe the consumer's instruction to make an electronic funds transfer. The institution is not liable, however, if it "shows by a preponderance of the evidence": (1) that its failure resulted from a "circumstance beyond its control, that it exercised reasonable care to prevent such an occurrence, and that it exercised such diligence as the circumstances required," or (2) that its failure resulted from "a technical malfunction which was known to the consumer at the time he attempted to initiate an electronic fund transfer or, in the case of a preauthorized transfer, at the time such transfer should have occurred." Furthermore, if the failure "was not intentional and ... resulted from a bona fide error, notwithstanding the maintenance of procedures reasonably adapted to avoid any such error, the financial institution shall be liable for actual damages proved."

Finally, suppose that a commercial buyer attempts to pay for goods by sending a payment order to its own bank, in which the buyer has a sufficient credit balance. What is that bank's liability if it fails to accept the order and execute it by issuing its own payment order to the seller's bank? According to UCC 4A–212, if the receiving bank's failure amounts to a breach of an "express agreement" with the buyer to accept the order, the bank may be liable for breach of that agreement, but not otherwise. The receiving bank's liability for its failure is limited by UCC 4A–305(d) to compensation of the buyer "for its expenses in the transaction and for incidental expenses and interest losses resulting from the failure." The buyer can recover additional damages, including consequential damages, only "to the extent provided in an express written agreement of the receiving bank." See Note 4, supra. As to attorney's fees, see UCC 4A–305(c). As to interest if the receiving bank fails to notify the buyer of its rejection of the order, see UCC 4A–210(b).

(6) Dishonor of Stale Checks. Before the enactment of the Code, most states had adopted special statutes which relieved the payor bank from liability for wrongful dishonor of a check presented more than a fixed period, six months or a year, after its date. The comparable provision of the Code is UCC 4–404, which uses a six month period.

Like its predecessors, UCC 4–404 is designed to save the payor bank from the horns of a dilemma that it faces when a check is presented long after its date. At some point in time the check may be regarded as having become so stale that if the bank paid it, the drawer could resist a charge to his account, assuming, of course, that the drawer has not received the benefit of it. But in a doubtful case how is the bank to tell whether the check is so stale that it should dishonor the check to avoid this risk, or not so stale so that the bank should pay the check to avoid risk of liability to the drawer for wrongful dishonor? UCC 4–404 solves the problem by amputating one of the horns of the dilemma, that is, by relieving the payor bank of liability for wrongful dishonor in any doubtful case. What practice would you expect a payor bank to follow with respect to ten month old checks presented to it? See Comment to UCC 4–404.

(B) Liability of Payor Bank to Holder

Prefatory Note. The inquiry turns now to the problem of the dishonored check from the holder's standpoint, and first to the holder's rights against the payor bank. What recourse has the holder of a check against a payor bank that has dishonored the check?

Before the Negotiable Instruments Law there was authority for the proposition that a check operated as an assignment to the payee of a part of the claim which the drawer, as depositor, had against the payor bank. The result was, of course, to give the holder a right of action against the drawee bank on the assigned claim. This did not appeal to bankers who feared that banking practices in dealing with checks could not survive if checks were regarded as assignments. Take, for example, the rule that an obligor is not discharged by payment to one assignee if the obligor has notice of a prior irrevocable assignment to another assignee. How would this affect a bank in the position of the payor bank in Problem 2, supra? Would it then be liable to the holders of earlier checks if it had first paid the holders of later checks? If the numbers on the checks were not consistent with the dates on the checks, which should the bank follow?

Happily for the bankers, the Negotiable Instruments Law laid to rest the argument that a check is, of itself, an assignment and the Code follows the Negotiable Instruments Law on this point. See UCC 3–408. Note, however, the words "of itself" in UCC 3–408. And see Comment 1, which suggests that "a bank that has not certified a check may engage in other conduct that might make it liable to a holder" and that "Section 1–103 is adequate to cover those cases."

Two questions remain: (1) What difference does it make that a check is not, of itself, an assignment? (2) What additional facts may cause a check to operate as an assignment or otherwise make the payor bank liable to the holder?

Problem 3. At the time that Empire draws the check at page 131 supra, it has $40,000 in its account in The Bank of New York. The Bank of New York has not yet paid the check.

(a) If Empire discovers that the cans are defective, orders The Bank of New York not to pay, and The Bank of New York refuses to pay, what are Quaker's rights against The Bank of New York?

(b) Can a judgment creditor of Empire attach any part of the $40,000 debt owed by The Bank of New York? How much?

(c) Can a judgment creditor of Quaker attach any part of the $40,000 debt owed by The Bank of New York? How much? See *State Bank of Southern Utah v. Stallings,* infra.

(d) If Empire goes into bankruptcy, can its trustee in bankruptcy claim any part of the $40,000 as an asset of Empire? How much?

Note

Time of "Transfer" in Bankruptcy. Problem 3(d) asks whether Empire's trustee in bankruptcy could claim any part of the $40,000 if the check had not been paid. What if the check *had* been paid? Under Bankruptcy Code § 547, the trustee is permitted, with some exceptions, to recover a transfer of property made by the bankrupt debtor to an unsecured creditor within 90 days before the filing of the bankruptcy petition. Such a transfer is termed "preferential" because its effect is to prefer one creditor, the transferee, over others.

Suppose that the check was delivered to Quaker more than 90 days before filing but was paid by Bank of New York less than 90 days before filing. When would the transfer have been made for the purposes of § 547? Federal courts of appeal split and the issue was settled in favor of the time of payment by the United States Supreme Court in Barnhill v. Johnson, 112 S.Ct. 1386 (1992). Chief Justice Rehnquist wrote for a seven-justice majority, with two justices dissenting.

"We begin by noting that there can be no assertion that an unconditional transfer of the debtor's interest in property had occurred [before the check was paid]. This is because, as just noted above, receipt of a check gives the recipient no right in the funds held by the bank on the drawer's account. Myriad events can intervene between delivery and presentment of the check that would result in the check being dishonored. The drawer could choose to close the account. A third party could obtain a lien against the account by garnishment or other proceedings. The bank might mistakenly refuse to honor the check.[1]

"The import of the preceding discussion for the instant case is that no transfer of any part of the debtor's claim against the bank occurred until the bank honored the check.... At that time, the bank had a right to 'charge' the debtor's account, U.C.C. § 4–401 ...—i.e., the

---

1. Admittedly, such behavior might create a cause of action for the debtor-drawer, see U.C.C. § 4–402, 2B U.L.A. 59 (1991), but the recipient would not have any claim against the bank.

debtor's claim against the bank was reduced by the amount of the check—and petitioner no longer had a claim against the debtor. Honoring the check, in short, left the debtor in the position that it would have occupied if it had withdrawn cash from its account and handed it over to petitioner. We thus believe that when the debtor has directed the drawee bank to honor the check *and* the bank has done so, the debtor has implemented a 'mode, direct or *indirect* ... of disposing of property or an interest in property.' 11 U.S.C. § 101(54) (emphasis added). For the purposes of payment by ordinary check, therefore, a 'transfer' as defined by § 101(54) occurs on the date of honor, and not before. And since it is undisputed that honor occurred within the 90–day preference period, the trustee presumptively may avoid this transfer."

STATE BANK OF SOUTHERN UTAH v. STALLINGS

Supreme Court of Utah, 1967.

19 Utah 2d 146, 427 P.2d 744.

ELLETT, JUSTICE: The appellants [Kaze & Gammon Construction Co.] as general contractors constructed a public school building. The defendant, Thomas A. Stallings was the electrical subcontractor and bought his merchandise from Westinghouse Supply Company. He owed Westinghouse some $8,000, $2,200 of which was past due.

Appellants made out a check to Stallings in the amount of $2,250 and requested Stallings to endorse it so the appellants could take it to Westinghouse and apply it on the delinquent account. Stallings claimed that Westinghouse had requested only $2,200 and refused to endorse the check, whereupon appellants gave their check to Stallings to be deposited in Stallings' checking account in the Hurricane Branch of the Bank of St. George, Stallings then gave his own check made payable to Westinghouse in the amount of $2,200 to the appellants to deliver to Westinghouse.

The respondent, State Bank of Southern Utah, had a couple of judgments against Stallings, and before the Westinghouse check could pass through the clearing house, the respondent had placed two garnishments against the Stallings account in the Hurricane Branch Bank.

The appellants intervened by some means not here questioned in the two cases from which the garnishments were issued and now claim that the check from Stallings was an assignment of $2,200 of the bank account when and if the $2,250 check from the appellants was deposited.

The trial court allowed the intervention and then gave a summary judgment against the intervenor and a garnishee judgment against the Hurricane Branch Bank of St. George. The appellants do not contend that the assignment of the $2,200 was made to them. They say it was an assignment out of the $2,250 given by them and was assigned to Westinghouse. They claim an interest by reason of the fact that unless Stallings pays Westinghouse, they as general contractors will have to pay the bill themselves.

If appellants are correct in their contention, then the trial court was in error in giving a garnishee judgment, and Westinghouse should be here doing the appealing in order to protect its rights. However, Westinghouse has made no intervention and is not a party to the proceedings in this court.

We do not think the giving of the check operated as an assignment in this case. Section 3–409 in Chapter 154 of Laws of Utah 1965 provides as follows:

> (1) A check or other draft does not of itself operate as an assignment of any funds in the hands of the drawee available for its payment, and the drawee is not liable on the instrument until he accepts it. . . .

In the Idaho case of Kaesemeyer v. Smith, 22 Idaho 1, 123 P. 943, at page 947, 43 L.R.A., N.S., 100, the court in speaking of a situation like the one before us said:

> The check given to Carscallen was a mere direction to the bank to pay a certain sum of money to the person named therein. By the giving of such check the amount of the same did not become the property of the payee of the check nor place such fund beyond the control of Smith. Until the check was presented to the bank, Smith could have countermanded its payment and could have given different directions for the disposition of the money remaining in the bank to his credit, and could even have personally demanded payment, and the bank could have been required to pay the same, and by so doing its indebtedness to Smith would have been discharged.

This court has heretofore spoken concerning what constituted an assignment. In the case of Milford State Bank v. Parrish et al., 88 Utah 235, 53 P.2d 72, the court said at page 238 of the Utah Reports, 53 P.2d at page 73:

> The evidence relating to this primary and controlling question is brief and free from conflict. The law as to what constitutes an equitable assignment is well settled. The application of the law and the facts is sometimes difficult.

In the case of Nickerson v. Hollet (National Bank of Goldendale, Intervener) 149 Wash. 646, 272 P. 53, Tolman, J., quotes the law and cites authority as follows:

> In order to work an equitable assignment there must be an absolute appropriation by the assignor of the debt or fund sought to be assigned to the use of the assignee. The intention of the assignor must be to transfer a present interest in the

debt or fund or subject matter; if this is done the transaction is an assignment; otherwise not. 5 C.J. 909.

The assignor of a chose in action must part with the power of control over the thing assigned; if he retains control it is fatal to the claim of the assignee, 5 C.J. 912. See, also, Hossack v. Graham, 20 Wash. 184, 55 P. 36.

In this case there can be no question but that Stallings had the power to stop payment on the check.

Of course, the assignor and the assignee may by agreement make an assignment by means of a check. See Merchants' National Bank of St. Paul v. State Bank, 172 Minn. 24, 214 N.W. 750; Slaughter v. First National Bank, Tex.Civ.App., 18 S.W.2d 754. However, no such agreement was ever made by the parties to the alleged assignment. Stallings and Westinghouse never spoke to each other about the check. The appellants planned the transactions but did not foresee the consequences. Had they wished an assignment, they could have taken the Stallings check to the bank and had it certified.

We feel sorry for appellants, but the law, like the north wind, cannot be altered to suit the needs of the mangy fleece. We hold that there was no assignment of the $2,200 represented by the Stallings check and that the garnishment being served before the check was presented for payment gives priority to the garnishment. See Commercial Bank of Tacoma v. Chilberg et al., 14 Wash. 247, 44 P. 264.

The judgment of the lower court is affirmed with costs to the respondent. [Dissenting opinion omitted.]

Notes

(1) **Counselling.** Could Kaze & Gammon have protected themselves by having Stallings write appropriate language on his check? What language would you suggest? Would it be enough if he wrote: "The above amount is on deposit and will be kept there subject to this check"? For an exhaustive discussion of the history of payees' claims against payor banks, see Sabbath, Drawee Bank's Liability for Wrongful Dishonor; A Proposed Checkholder Cause of Action, 58 St. John's L.Rev. 318 (1984).

(2) **Agricultural Marketing Finance.** Considerable litigation has arisen in agricultural regions from variations on the following typical fact situation. Dealer purchases commodities from farmers and resells them to commission houses. To finance its business Dealer makes an agreement with Bank whereby Bank promises Dealer to honor Dealer's checks drawn in payment for such purchases and Dealer agrees to deposit immediately the proceeds from his resale. Dealer's turnover is rapid and normally the proceeds are deposited before the checks are presented. However, should checks arrive before the deposit of proceeds to cover them, Bank agrees to honor these overdrafts.

After the agreement, Farmer presents one of Dealer's checks given in payment for goods, but Bank refuses to pay it and applies Dealer's balance to outstanding debts owed to Bank, under the general rule that where a bank holds the matured debt of its depositor it may apply the deposit in payment of it. Farmer sues Bank. On what theories might Farmer recover? Would it be sufficient for Farmer to show that the check was an assignment of Dealer's rights against Bank? Might he claim rights as a third party beneficiary? As the beneficiary of a trust? Is it arguable that this was a "special deposit" not subject to set-off? Compare Bradley Grain Co. v. Farmers & Merchants National Bank, 274 S.W.2d 178 (Tex.Civ.App.1954), with Ballard v. Home National Bank, 91 Kan. 91, 136 P. 935 (1913). For a case raising similar questions in the context of a construction contract, see Mid–Continent Casualty Co. v. Jenkins, 431 P.2d 349 (Okl.1967).

In answering these questions, it may be useful to know a little about the bank's right of setoff, "the common law, equitable right of a bank to apply the general deposits of a depositor against the matured debts of the depositor. This right grows out of the contractual debtor-creditor relationship created between the depositor and the bank at the time the account is opened, and it rests on the principle that it would be inequitable to permit the debtor-depositor to carry an open account that induces the bank to extend credit, and then allow the debtor to apply the funds to other purposes because he had not expressly agreed to apply them to the debt." TeSelle, Banker's Right of Setoff—Banker Beware, 34 Okla.L.Rev. 40, 40 (1981).

The right is often misleadingly termed a "banker's lien." "The so-called 'lien' of the bank on the depositor's account or funds on deposit is not technically a lien, for the bank is the owner of the funds and the debtor of the depositor, and the bank cannot have a lien on its own property. The right of the bank to charge the depositor's fund with his matured indebtedness is more correctly termed a right of setoff, based on general principles of equity." Gonsalves v. Bank of America, 16 Cal.2d 169, 173, 105 P.2d 118, 121 (1940).

It has been held that "the act of setoff is not complete until three steps have been taken: (1) the decision to exercise the right, (2) some action which accomplishes the setoff and (3) some record which evidences that the right of setoff has been exercised." Baker v. National City Bank of Cleveland, 511 F.2d 1016 (6th Cir.1975).

This right of set-off exists, however, only where the deposit is "general," not "special." "From the special deposit approach, stated broadly, funds deposited for a special purpose known to the bank, or under special agreement, cannot be set off by the bank.... A deposit is special rather than general when there is specific direction, or agreement express or implied, that it be special or where there are circumstances sufficient to create a trust by operation of law." Kaufman v. First National Bank of Opp, 493 F.2d 1070, 1072 (5th Cir.1974).

Problem 4. A gave the First Bank B's personal check for $500 payable to First Bank plus a small fee and received a "Personal Money Order" like that shown with the amount "five hundred dollars" imprinted on it by machine. A filled in A's own name as payee and indorsed it to Dealer in payment for a stereo. When Dealer presented it for payment, First Bank refused to pay it because B's check had been dishonored for insufficient funds. Is First Bank liable to Dealer? See UCC 3–104(f), 3–401; *Sequoyah State Bank v. Union National Bank of Little Rock,* infra. What is the answer to "the question of whether the purchaser may stop payment"? See Comment 4 to UCC 3–104. Would your answers be affected if banks' advertisements suggested that personal money orders were more reliable than personal checks?

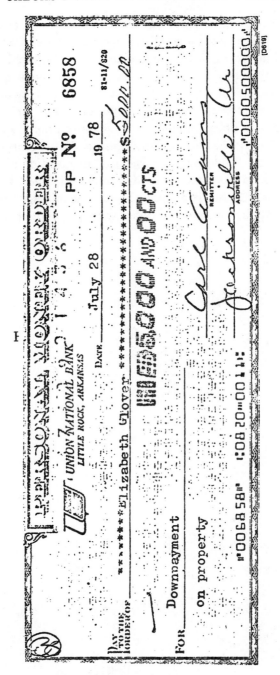

PERSONAL MONEY ORDER

[A copy is retained by the bank and a record copy is given to the customer. The latter contains a space to enter the date and the name of the payee. It may also contain a provision such as: "Purchaser agrees that no request for refund or to stop payment or otherwise will be made

*to this Bank with respect to the said Money Order unless the customer's
RECORD is submitted therewith."*]

————

SEQUOYAH STATE BANK v. UNION NATIONAL BANK

Supreme Court of Arkansas, 1981.
274 Ark. 1, 621 S.W.2d 683.

ADKISSON, CHIEF JUSTICE. The only issue in this case is whether
Union Bank by its own initiative can stop payment on a personal
money order it had issued in exchange for a hot check and, thereby,
cause Sequoyah Bank, a holder in due course, to bear the loss. Under
these circumstances the loss must be borne by Union Bank which
issued the negotiable instrument to be circulated in commerce.

We do not decide the question of whether the purchaser may stop
payment, but we do hold that after the sale of a personal money order,
the issuing bank cannot stop payment on the instrument.

A personal money order is issued with unfilled blanks for the name
of the payee, the date, and the signature of the purchaser. Only the
amount is filled out at the time of issue, usually by checkwriter
impression as was done in this case.

The Uniform Commercial Code apparently did not directly contemplate the use of money orders and made no specific provision for them.
Mirabile v. Udoh, 92 Misc.2d 168, 399 N.Y.S.2d 869 (1977). It was
recognized in Mirabile that it is the custom and practice of the business
community to accept personal money orders as a pledge of the issuing
bank's credit. We may consider this custom and practice in construing
the legal effect of such instruments. See Ark.Stat.Ann. § 85–1–103
(Add.1961).

Appellee relies on the cases of Garden Check Cashing Service, Inc.
v. First National City Bank, 25 A.D.2d 137, 267 N.Y.S.2d 698 (1966),
aff'd. 18 N.Y.2d 941, 223 N.E.2d 566, 277 N.Y.S.2d 141 (1966) and Krom
v. Chemical Bank New York Trust Co., 63 Misc.2d 1060, 313 N.Y.S.2d
810 (1970), rev'd. 38 A.D.2d 871, 329 N.Y.S.2d 91 (A.D.1972) which held
that a purchaser of a personal money order may stop payment on it.
However, the only cited case to specifically address the issue of whether
the issuing bank, on its own initiative, may stop payment on a personal
money order is Rose Check Cashing Service, Inc. v. Chemical Bank N.Y.
Trust Co., 40 Misc.2d 995, 244 N.Y.S.2d 474, 477 (1963). In holding that
the issuing bank could not stop payment and therefore must suffer the
loss the court stated:

All of these differences between the instrument at issue and an
ordinary check would seem to indicate that the bank would
honor the order to pay no matter who signed the face of the

instrument, assuming of course an otherwise valid negotiation of the instrument. . . .

In the instrument in suit, the drawer *purchases* the instrument from the bank. The transaction is in the nature of a sale. No deposit is created. The funds to pay the instrument, immediately come within the bank's exclusive control and ownership. . . .

The bank's contention that the instrument is a check is inconsistent with its own acts. The bank (drawee) stamped "Stop Payment" on the instrument in suit on its own order. Nowhere in the Negotiable Instruments Law is there any provision that a drawee [bank] may "Stop Payment" of a check unless ordered to do so by the drawer.

Appellee also denies liability on the instrument based upon Ark. Stat.Ann. § 85–3–401(1) which states that "No person is liable on an instrument unless his signature appears thereon." Subdivision (2) of this same section provides that a signature may be "any word or mark used in lieu of a written signature." The authenticity of the instrument involved here is not in question. The issuance of the money order with the bank's printed name evidences the appellee's intent to be bound thereby. *Mirabile,* supra.

Appellee also relies on Ark.Stat.Ann. § 85–3–409 for the proposition that it is not liable on the personal money order since it did not accept it. In our opinion, however, the appellee accepted the instrument in advance by the act of its issuance. Rose Check Cashing Service Inc. v. Chemical Bank New York Trust Co., 43 Misc.2d 679, 252 N.Y.S.2d 100 (1964).

The personal money order constituted an obligation of Union from the moment of its sale and issuance. The fact that Union was frustrated in retaining the funds because instead of cash it accepted a check drawn on insufficient funds is no reason to hold otherwise. We note by analogy that the Uniform Commercial Code on sales Ark.Stat.Ann. § 85–2–403(1)(b) provides that a purchaser of goods, who takes delivery in exchange for a check which is later dishonored, transfers good title to the goods.

Union placed the personal money order in commerce for a consideration it accepted as adequate and was, thereafter, liable on it. Banks are not allowed to stop payment on their depositor's checks and certainly should not be allowed to stop payment on personal money orders. See Note, Personal Money Orders and Teller's Checks: Mavericks Under the UCC, 67 Colum.L.Rev. 524 (1967).

Reversed.

DUDLEY, JUSTICE, dissenting. This case involves a personal money order, not a bank money order, not a certificate of deposit and not a certified check. A personal money order is for the convenience of anyone who does not have an ordinary checking account and needs a safe, inexpensive and readily acceptable means of transferring funds. The bank simply sells to the individual a check-sized form which has the amount impressed into the face of the paper, an identification number and the name of the issuing bank. No authorized representative of the bank signs the instrument. When the purchaser of the instrument decides to pass it, he dates it, enters the name of the payee and signs the instrument.

Ark.Stat.Ann. § 85–3–104(1)(a) (Add.1961) requires that a writing be signed by the drawer or maker in order to be negotiable. Any item which is an order to pay is considered a "draft" and any draft drawn on a bank and payable on demand is a "check." § 85–3–104(2)(a), (b). Since the only signature on a personal money order is that of the purchaser, since the instrument takes the form of an order to pay, and since it is drawn on a bank and payable on demand, it is clearly within the classification of a check. The absence of the bank's signature as a "maker" and the absence of any express "undertaking" to pay by the bank, § 85–3–102(1)(c) and § 85–3–104(2)(d) preclude a finding that the instrument is a note. Aside from "draft," "check" and "note" the only other form of negotiable instrument recognized by the Uniform Commercial Code is a "certificate of deposit" and that requires an acknowledgment that the bank will repay it. § 85–3–104(2)(c). Under these code provisions a personal money order must be classified as a check. There is no other code classification of negotiable commercial paper. § 85–3–104. For the sake of clarity in the law of commercial paper this personal money order should be classified as a check.

However, the matter of classification is not nearly as important as the issue of liability. No authorized representative of appellee bank signed this check. Section 85–3–401 states: "*No person is liable on an instrument unless his signature appears thereon.*" Section 85–3–409(1) states that a check or other draft is not an assignment of funds held by the drawee (appellee Union Bank) and *the drawee is not liable until it accepts the check or draft.* Appellee did not accept this instrument. It stopped payment. The language of these statutes, a part of the Uniform Commercial Code, is unmistakable.

The majority opinion holds:

> The personal money order constituted an obligation of Union from the moment of its sale and issuance.

I respectfully submit that statement is supported by absolutely no authority and it creates an unnecessary legal quagmire. Assume that a purchaser of a personal money order has not filled in the name of the payee or has not signed the check and it is lost or stolen. The purchaser then wants to stop payment before it is negotiated to a third party. The majority has stated that it was an obligation of the bank from the moment of sale and issuance. Fairness and logic dictate that the purchaser should not be allowed to stop payment and leave the bank liable. Yet, § 85–4–403(1) provides:

Customer's right to stop payment—Burden of proof of loss. A customer may by order to his bank stop payment of any item payable for his account but the order must be received at such time and in such manner as to afford the bank a reasonable opportunity to act on it prior to any action by the bank with respect to the item described in Section 4–303.

Comment 4 to this statute makes it abundantly clear that personal money orders are intended to be covered by this broad language.

One of the three explanations given for the holding is:

The issuance of the money order with the bank's printed name evidences the appellee's intent to be bound thereby.

That notion will echo because the name of the drawee bank is printed on every ordinary check in circulation.

The other two explanations are that banks should not be allowed to stop payment and business custom. Both explanations are dead letters. Assume, for the sake of argument only, that banks should not be allowed to stop payment. That occurrence takes place after the sale and issuance of the instrument. The majority has held that liability attached upon issuance. Therefore this subsequent event logically cannot have any effect on liability. It very simply is not a reason for a decision that liability attached at the time of issuance. Business custom is not proven. There is not one single word in the transcript or abstract about business custom. Even if this defense had been proven it would be an estoppel defense, or a defense which accrues after the sale and, once again, it would not be a reason for a decision that liability attached at the time of issuance.

The master purpose of the Uniform Commercial Code is to clarify the law governing commercial transactions. The tragedy of this case is that both the purpose and the Code are emaciated [sic] for no reason.

Notes

(1) **Personal Money Orders.** "Personal money orders were first issued in 1937 and have grown steadily in popularity since 1944, when the price of the competing Post Office Money Order was raised. Personal money orders are attractive to people who have no ordinary checking account, for they offer a safe, inexpensive, and readily acceptable means of transferring funds, in a form that has the prestigious appearance of a personal check. Moreover, banks favor the instruments because they are simpler, faster, and less expensive to issue than cashier's checks and bank money orders; because they attract potential customers for other bank services; and because they can create a substantial deposit balance for the bank's use." Note, 67 Colum.L.Rev. 524, 525–26 (1967). The second sentence of UCC 3–104(f) had no counterpart in former Article 3. Would it change the result in the Sequoyah State Bank case in view of the "custom and practice" consid-

ered by the majority? See UCC 1–205(2). Might the issuing bank be regarded as representing at least that it had funds to cover the instrument?

(2) Remitters. Buyer, who wishes to make payment to Seller by a cashier's check or teller's check, may have it made payable to Buyer's own order and later indorse it to Seller, or may have it made payable to Seller's order. In this latter case Buyer is known as a "remitter," a term defined in UCC 3–103(a)(11). Although not a holder or a transferee from the payee without indorsement, Buyer has purchased the instrument from the bank and is the owner until its delivery to the payee. Suppose that Seller refuses to take the instrument or that Buyer decides not to give it to Seller. What are Buyer's rights against the bank from which Buyer bought it? Remitters have been allowed recovery in such situations, but there may be a dispute as to whether the action is one on the instrument or one to recover the amount paid for the instrument. The difference is particularly important in foreign remittance transactions, where the remitter arranges with a domestic bank to have its foreign correspondent pay in foreign currency to the remitter's foreign creditor. If the remitter's action is on the instrument, the remitter will bear the risk of depreciation of the foreign currency. If the remitter can recover the amount paid for the instrument, the bank must bear this risk. On this problem see Kerr Steamship Co. v. Chartered Bank of India, Australia & China, 292 N.Y. 253, 54 N.E.2d 813 (1944); Note, 57 Yale L.J. 1426 (1948); cf. Bunge Corp. v. Manufacturers Hanover Trust Co., 31 N.Y.2d 223, 335 N.Y.S.2d 412, 286 N.E.2d 903 (1972).[1]

ACCEPTANCE AND CERTIFICATION

UCC 3–408 provides: "A check or other draft does not of itself operate as an assignment ..., and the drawee is not liable on the instrument until the drawee accepts it." Acceptance is defined in UCC 3–409 as "the drawee's signed undertaking to pay a draft as presented." The acceptor's contract is set out in UCC 3–413(a). Acceptance has always been commonly written on the instrument itself and the drawee's signature alone, on the face of the bill, has been considered sufficient. Under UCC 3–409 the acceptance "must be written on the draft." The problem of the acceptance that varies the terms of the draft is dealt with in UCC 3–410.

In the case of a check, the counterpart of acceptance is commonly certification by a stamp. Under UCC 3–409(d), " 'Certified check' means a check accepted by the bank on which it is drawn." Upon certification the payor bank charges the amount of the check to the drawer's account and transfers it to the "certified check" account on its

---

1. Note the loose use of the term "remitter" on the Personal Money Order form   to refer to the drawer.

books. It therefore will not certify a postdated check before its date. The practice of certifying checks does not exist in England and has been common in this country for only a century. On the history of the certified check, see Steffen & Starr, A Blue Print for the Certified Check, 13 N.C.L.Rev. 450, 463–67 (1935).

(C) Liability of Drawer and Indorsers to Holder

DISHONOR AND NOTICE

Rights on Dishonor. Buyer's obligation under a contract of sale is usually to pay money, but the medium of payment is not commonly specified. In the absence of such a specification, Buyer must pay in "legal tender." Since a check is not legal tender, Seller has the right to refuse a check. However, if Buyer tenders a check, drawn upon ample funds in a solvent bank, Seller is deemed to have waived this right unless Seller objects on the specific ground that the check is not legal tender. Were Seller to so object, Buyer could probably make a conforming tender. See UCC 2–511(2); Restatement (Second) of Contracts § 249.

Usually Seller will take Buyer's check. Because, as was seen in the preceding section, the holder of an uncertified check generally has no rights against the payor bank, it becomes especially important to ask what rights the holder has against the drawer and any indorsers in the event that the check is dishonored. First, what are the holder's rights on the underlying obligation for which the instrument was given? Second, what are the holder's rights on the instrument itself? The first question is dealt with in UCC 3–310, where the usual rule that a check is conditional payment is restated in more helpful terms of suspension of the underlying obligation. The second question is dealt with in UCC 3–414, which sets out the drawer's contract, and in UCC 3–415, which sets out the indorser's contract.[1] (See also UCC 4–207(b) for the similar obligation imposed on a customer or collecting bank transferring an item for collection.) These contracts of the drawer and indorser are similar in that each is conditional upon dishonor.[2] Their liability thus

---

1. UCC 3–402 deals with questions that arise when an agent signs on behalf of a principal. Suppose, for example, that the president of Empire had signed the check on page 131 "Stacey Smith" instead of "Stacey Smith, Pres." Would Smith be personally liable as drawer if the check were dishonored? Suppose Smith had signed "By Stacey Smith"? Would parol evidence be admissible to resolve these questions? Compare Colonial Baking Co. of Des Moines v. Dowie, 330 N.W.2d 279 (Iowa 1983), with Valley National Bank v. Cook, 136 Ariz. 232, 665 P.2d 576 (App. 1983).

2. Protest, which was occasionally a condition under former Article 3, is no longer required. See UCC 3–505 and Comment. Protest is usually made by a notary public, who executes a certificate of protest. In most civil law countries, protest is generally required in the case of any dishonor of a negotiable instrument.

differs from that of the maker of a note and acceptor of a bill whose contracts are not so conditioned under UCC 3–412 and 3–413. (Under former UCC 3–102(1)(d), a drawer or indorser was called a "secondary" party, a term not used in revised Article 3. See Comment 2 to UCC 3–414.)

Dishonor. Dishonor is dealt with in UCC 3–502. It usually consists of the maker's or drawee's refusal to pay when the instrument is presented for payment.[3] Thus a check is dishonored if, on presentment, the payor bank refuses to pay it for reasons other than those in UCC 3–501(b)(3). However, presentment is excused in the situations described in UCC 3–504, as where the drawer of a check has stopped payment or has no right to expect payment of an overdraft. Evidence of dishonor is dealt with in UCC 3–505.

If the holder of a check takes it directly to the payor bank for immediate payment over the counter, the bank must decide on the day of presentment whether to pay it, but UCC 3–501(b)(4) allows the bank to set a cut-off hour for receipt of checks presented. Most checks, however, are deposited for collection in a depositary bank and are presented as part of the check collection process in accordance with rules described later in this chapter.

To facilitate truncation, UCC 3–501(b)(1) authorizes electronic presentment. As the comment to UCC 3–501 notes, "Subsection (b)(2)(i) allows the person to whom presentment is made to require exhibition of the instrument, unless the parties have agreed otherwise as in an electronic presentment agreement." UCC 4–110(a) defines an "agreement for electronic presentment" as one "providing that presentment of an item may be made by transmission of an image of an item or information describing the item ('presentment notice') rather than delivery of the item itself."

Notice of Dishonor. "Notice of dishonor," a second condition of importance to indorsers, is treated in UCC 3–503 and 3–504.[4] The purpose of requiring that notice be given to indorsers is to enable them promptly to seek recourse against prior parties and others who may in turn be liable in the event of dishonor. The penalty for failure to give the required notice is generally discharge of the indorser. However, notice of dishonor can be waived under UCC 3–504(b). Under UCC 3–503(c), notice of dishonor must be given within 30 days, but a depositary bank must give notice to its depositor within the bank's midnight deadline.

Notice of Nonpayment. Regulation CC requires a payor bank to send a depositary bank direct notice of nonpayment of any check of $2,500 or more. This notice requirement is in addition to the payor's

---

3. In the case of a draft, dishonor sometimes consists of the drawee's refusal to accept the draft (UCC 3–502(b)(3) and (4)), but this is not the case for refusal to certify a check (UCC 3–409(d)).

4. It is almost never required for drawers. See UCC 3–503(a) and Comment 1.

duty of expeditious return. The depository bank must receive notice of nonpayment by 4:00 p.m. on the second business day following presentment. Upon receiving notice of nonpayment, the depository bank must notify its customer before the Code's midnight deadline or within a longer reasonable time.

Notice may be provided by any reasonable means, including the check itself, a writing, telephone, or wire. Notice must include the (1) name and routing number of the payor bank; (2) name of payee; (3) amount; (4) date of depository bank's indorsement; (5) depositor's account number; (6) depository bank's branch name or number from its indorsement; (7) trace number associated with depository bank's indorsement; and (8) reason for nonpayment. If written notice is sent, it also must include the depository bank's name and routing number from its indorsement. Reg CC 229.33.

This requirement of direct notice of nonpayment is new. It replaces Regulation J, which required wire notice of nonpayment of checks of $2,500 or more, but only if they were collected through Federal Reserve banks.

UCC 4–301(a)(2) requires notice of nonpayment only where the check itself is unavailable for return. The notice requirement, like other Code provisions, may be varied by agreements to which the parties did not specifically assent, such as Federal Reserve regulations and operating circulars. See UCC 4–103(b); Wells Fargo Bank v. Hartford National Bank & Trust Co., 484 F.Supp. 817 (D.Conn.1980). The notice requirements of Regulation CC cannot be varied so easily because the Regulation rejects the Code's position that parties can be bound by agreements to which they have not assented. Reg CC 229.37 and commentary.

CONSEQUENCES OF DELAY IN PRESENTMENT

Discharge of Drawer. The check has traditionally been regarded as an instrument that contemplates prompt presentment for payment. Take the case of a check for $1,000 drawn on an account with sufficient funds. If promptly presented, it will be paid and the amount charged to the drawer's account. Suppose the holder delays presentment, however, and during the delay the payor bank becomes insolvent. When the check is then presented, it will be dishonored, leaving the drawer with a claim against an insolvent bank that is $1,000 greater than it would have been had the check been paid. In that circumstance, it would be unjust to require the drawer to pay the full amount of the check to the holder, and seek reimbursement from the insolvent bank.

UCC 3–414(f) therefore provides that if the delay exceeds 30 days and the payor bank then suspends payment, "the drawer to the extent deprived of funds may discharge its obligation to pay the check by assigning to the person entitled to enforce the check the rights of the drawer against the drawee with respect to the funds."

The likelihood of discharge of the drawer by delay in presentment is therefore remote. Furthermore, if the drawer's account is fully insured by the Federal Deposit Insurance Corporation the drawer will not lose any of his deposit and this problem will presumably not arise. See Comment 6 to UCC 3–414.

The Federal Deposit Insurance Corporation was established by Congress in 1933 and now finds its authority in the Federal Deposit Insurance Corporation Act of 1950, 12 U.S.C. §§ 1811–1832. It has not only afforded protection to depositors of failed banks, but has contributed to the striking reduction in bank failures. During the three years 1930–32, more than 5,100 banks suspended business. The number fell to about 100, all of which were insured, during the first three years of the 1980s, but rose to well over 500 by the last three years of that decade. Deposits in virtually all commercial banks are insured by the FDIC. Each depositor is insured up to $100,000 which may be paid in cash or by making available a deposit in a new bank or in another insured bank. Holders of certified checks, cashiers' checks, and remittance drafts are treated as depositors. 12 Code Fed.Reg. § 330. However, the holder of an uncertified check is not protected and the deposit of the check for collection does not result in an insured deposit in the depositary bank until the item has been collected.

Discharge of Indorser. Under UCC 3–415(e), an indorser is discharged by a 30–day delay in presentment, regardless of whether the delay has caused any loss to the indorser. Under UCC 3–503, the same result follows from failure to give timely notice of dishonor. Delay is therefore much more likely to result in the discharge of an indorser than in the discharge of a drawer.

OTHER BASES OF LIABILITY

Liability on the Underlying Obligation. Under UCC 3–310(b), a check is ordinarily taken as conditional rather than absolute payment, suspending the obligation rather than discharging it. The question then arises whether an action can be brought on the underlying obligation for which the check was given even though liability on the instrument has been lost by delay. In the unlikely event that a drawer, having given a check in payment of an obligation, is deprived of funds by delay in presentment and discharges its obligation to pay the check by an assignment under UCC 3–414(f), payment of the check discharges the underlying obligation under UCC 3–310(b)(1). If a payee, having indorsed a check in payment of an obligation, is discharged by delay in presentment or notice of dishonor, the underlying obligation is also thereby discharged under UCC 3–310(b)(3).

Liability on Warranties. The sale of a negotiable instrument, like the sale of goods, also gives rise to implied warranties. These warranties are found in UCC 3–416, 4–207. Although the holder will usually prefer to sue the transferor on the more extensive engagement

of the indorser spelled out in UCC 3–415(a), the warranties are important in at least four situations. (1) Where an instrument payable to
bearer is negotiated by delivery without indorsement, the transferor
does not make the indorser's engagement but does make implied
warranties to his immediate transferee. (2) Where an instrument is
negotiated by indorsement that includes such words as "without recourse" the transferor does not make the indorser's engagement, but
does make implied warranties to the transferee and subsequent holders.
(3) Where an instrument is negotiated by the usual indorsement, but
the transferor is discharged from the indorser's engagement because of
delay in presentment or notice, the transferor may still be liable to the
transferee or subsequent holders on warranties that are not so conditioned. (4) Where an instrument is negotiated by the usual indorsement, but payment is refused for a reason not consistent with dishonor,
such as a forged indorsement, the transferor may be liable on the
warranties though not on the indorser's engagement. But note the
scope of the warranties. Do they cover the common case where a check
is dishonored because of insufficient funds? Note the analogy to
warranties in the sale of goods. Do the warranties of Articles 3 and 4
apply only to "sales" of negotiable instruments or to gifts as well? Is
privity of contract required for an action for their breach?

Right of Charge–Back or Refund. A bank, such as Philadelphia
National, that takes a check from a depositor, such as Quaker, for
collection, giving it a provisional credit, has yet another ground on
which to proceed against its depositor should the check be dishonored.
UCC 4–214(a) gives the collecting bank a right to "revoke the settlement given by it" and "charge back the amount of any credit given for
the item to its customer's account, or obtain refund from its customer."
In order to preserve this right, however, it must either return the item
or send notification of the facts to its customer "by its midnight
deadline or within a longer reasonable time after it learns the facts."
See UCC 4–104(a)(10).

Although the quoted language is unchanged from former Article 4,
the second sentence of UCC 4–214(a) is new. As Comment 3 explains, it
"adopts the view of Appliance Buyers Credit Corp. v. Prospect National
Bank, 708 F.2d 290 (7th Cir.1983), that if the midnight deadline for
returning an item or giving notice is not met, a collecting bank loses its
rights only to the extent of damages for any loss resulting from the
delay." Compare this consequence with that of delay in giving notice of
dishonor under UCC 3–503.

Statute of Limitations. The liability of a party to a check may, of
course, be affected by the running of the statute of limitations, as well
as in the ways mentioned above. The Code deals with this subject in
UCC 3–118.

Problem 5. A grocer delivers groceries, and occasionally cash, to
customers, taking in return personal checks drawn by them. What
risks, if any, does the grocer run by failing to deposit these checks for

collection for two weeks? For two months? See UCC 3–310, 3–414, 3–501, 3–502, 3–504, 3–416.

Problem 6. A grocer delivers groceries, and occasionally cash, to customers, taking in return their pay checks, drawn by their employers to their order, and specially indorsed by them to him. What risks, if any, does he run by failing to deposit these checks for collection for two weeks? For two months? See UCC 3–415. Are there any circumstances in which the grocer may end up in a worse position, as a result of having taken a negotiable instrument, than by selling on open credit? If so, can you think of an explanation?

CERTIFICATION

Effect of Certification on Liability of Drawer and Indorsers. Ordinarily, the drawee's acceptance of a draft merely adds the drawee's liability to that of the drawer and any indorsers. Under UCC 3–414(c), however, when "a draft is accepted by a bank, the drawer is discharged." If a creditor insists on payment by a certified check, the creditor has no recourse against the drawer in the event of bank insolvency unless the creditor requires "a specific guaranty of payment by the drawer or ... an indorsement by the drawer." Comment 3 to UCC 3–414. If a holder of an uncertified check has it certified, the result is a novation in which the liability of the bank is substituted for that of the drawer. Usually, the holder will prefer payment to certification anyway, but there are, for example, instances in which the holder's agent, who is in possession of a check but is not authorized to indorse it, has it certified on behalf of the holder before remitting it.

Refusal to Certify as a Dishonor. Furthermore, under UCC 3–409(d) the payor bank's "refusal to certify is not dishonor." The drawer is therefore not liable to the holder under UCC 3–414 if the bank refuses to certify the check. (What would you advise the holder to do in that situation?)

More important to bankers is the corollary found in UCC 3–409(d) that the "drawee of a check has no obligation to certify the check." The payor bank therefore runs no risk of liability for wrongful dishonor under UCC 4–402 if it refuses to certify. Why would such a rule appeal to bankers? Consider the fact that banks often charge the holder a fee for certifying. Does the rule of UCC 3–409(d) affect the advisability of this practice?

Automation and Certification. In automated systems, processing certified checks becomes an expensive procedure because cashier's checks seem to provide an entirely satisfactory substitute for them. Certified checks are demanded because they signify that funds are on hand at the bank. However, if such checks were processed by computers in the normal manner, when presented for payment, they would make double deductions from the depositors' accounts. Some banks have discontinued the practice of certifying checks and issue cashier's checks instead. Others mutilate the customer's MICR number when making the certification to cause a computer rejection. Still others paste a computer-readable label over part of the MICR line. In sharp contrast, cashier's checks flow smoothly and normally through computerized systems. Does the rule of UCC 3–409(d) have any bearing upon this problem?

Problem 7. Assume that Empire, instead of mailing its check to Quaker, delivers it in New York to Quaker's sales representative. If the representative, who is not authorized to indorse the check, takes the precaution of having The Bank of New York certify it before forwarding it to Philadelphia, how does this affect Quaker's recourse on the instrument should it ultimately be dishonored? See UCC 3–414(c).

Problem 8. If, under the facts in Problem 7, The Bank of New York had refused to certify the check, would it thereby have become liable to Empire under UCC 4–402 for wrongful dishonor? Would Empire thereby have become liable to Quaker under UCC 3–414(b)? See UCC 3–409(d).

SECTION 2. PAYOR BANK'S RECOURSE AFTER PAYMENT BY MISTAKE

(A) BASIC RULES

Prefatory Note. In the absence of a contrary agreement with the depositor, American banks do not make a practice of paying overdrafts. But if the payor bank should, either intentionally or by mistake, pay an overdraft it is clear that it can recover the amount from the drawer. According to UCC 4–401(a), a bank may charge any properly payable item to its customer's account "even though the charge creates an overdraft." The provision restates what was a rule of case law before the Code, since the check, being an unconditional order, authorizes payment for the drawer's account even if the account is overdrawn and carries an implied promise to reimburse the payor bank. Comment 1 to UCC 4–401; see also UCC 3–106(b)(ii).

But what if the overdrawn drawer is judgment proof so that recourse against him is of no avail? What alternatives are open to the payor bank? Where does the loss ultimately fall?

Problem 9. When the Empire check is presented, Empire has only $10,000 in its account at The Bank of New York. If The Bank of New York nevertheless pays the check as a courtesy to Empire, can it recover the balance of $12,178.50 from Empire? From Quaker? Would your answer be different if The Bank of New York pays the check by mistake, without realizing that it was an overdraft? See UCC 4–401, 3–418 and Comment 3, 3–417; *Kirby v. First & Merchants National Bank,* infra. If, instead of *paying* an overdraft by mistake, The Bank of New York had *certified* an overdraft by mistake, would its mistake justify it in refusing to pay Quaker?

KIRBY v. FIRST & MERCHANTS NATIONAL BANK

Supreme Court of Virginia, 1969.
210 Va. 88, 168 S.E.2d 273.

GORDON, JUSTICE. On December 30, 1966, defendant Margaret Kirby handed the following check to a teller at a branch of plaintiff First & Merchants National Bank:

NEUSE ENG. AND DREDGING CO.

Check
Number _____

68–728
514

12–29–1966

Pay to the
order of ____ William J. Kirby & Margaret Kirby ____ $ 2,500.00

Twenty–Five Hundred ------------------------------ Dollars

FIRST & MERCHANTS
NATIONAL BANK
Virginia Beach, Virginia
. . . 0514 . . . 0728

NEUSE ENG. & DREDGING CO.
/s/ W.R. Wood

The back of the check bore the signatures of the payees, Mr. and Mrs. Kirby.

Mrs. Kirby, who also had an account with the Bank, gave the teller the following deposit ticket: [1]

1. The handwriting in the upper-left portion of the deposit ticket corresponds with Mrs. Kirby's handwriting on the back of the check. The record does not indicate what persons added the other handwritten information on the ticket.

The symbol "68–728–514" designates a check drawn on First & Merchants by a depositor who has an account with a branch of that Bank in the Norfolk–Virginia Beach area. The word following the symbol is "partial".

The teller handed $200 in cash to Mrs. Kirby, and the Bank credited her account with $2,300 on the next business day, January 3, 1967. The teller or another Bank employee made the notation "Cash for Dep." under Mr. and Mrs. Kirby's signatures on the back of the Neuse check.

On January 4 the Bank discovered that the Neuse check was drawn against insufficient funds. Instead of giving written notice, a Bank officer called Mr. and Mrs. Kirby on January 5 to advise that the Bank had dishonored the check and to request reimbursement. Mr. and Mrs. Kirby said they would come to the Bank to cover the check, but they did not. On January 10 the Bank charged Mrs. Kirby's account with $2,500, creating an overdraft of $543.47.

On January 18 the Bank instituted this action to recover $543.47 from Mr. and Mrs. Kirby. At the trial a Bank officer, the only witness in the case, testified:

"Q. Did you cash the check [the Neuse check for $2,500] before you credited this deposit [the deposit of $2,300 to Mrs. Kirby's account]?

"A. Yes, sir.

"Q. So the bank, in effect, cashed the check for $2,500.00 and then gave the defendant a credit of $2,300.00 to their [sic] account and gave them [sic] $200.00 in cash?

"A. Correct.

". . .

"Q. So you cashed the check for $2,500.00?

"A. Yes, sir."

The trial court, sitting without a jury, entered judgment for the plaintiff First & Merchants, and the defendants Mr. and Mrs. Kirby appeal. The question is whether the Bank had the right to charge Mrs. Kirby's account with $2,500 on January 10 and to recover from Mr. and Mrs. Kirby the overdraft created by that charge ($543.47).

U.C.C. § 4–213 [2] provides:

"(1) An item [3] is finally paid by a payor bank when the bank has done any of the following, whichever happens first:

"(a) paid the item in cash;".

So if First & Merchants paid the Neuse check in cash on December 30, it then made final payment and could not sue Mr. or Mrs. Kirby on the check except for breach of warranty. [4]

When Mrs. Kirby presented the $2,500 Neuse check to the Bank on December 30, the Bank paid her $200 in cash and accepted a deposit of $2,300. The Bank officer said that the Bank cashed the check for $2,500, which could mean only that Mrs. Kirby deposited $2,300 in cash.

And the documentary evidence shows that cash was deposited. The deposit of cash is evidenced by the word "currency" before "2,300.-00" on the deposit ticket and by the words "Cash for Dep." on the back of the check. [5] The Bank's ledger, which shows a credit of $2,300 to Mrs. Kirby's account rather than a credit of $2,500 and a debit of $200, is consistent with a cashing of the Neuse check and a depositing of part of the proceeds. We must conclude that First & Merchants paid the Neuse check ʾ ı cash on December 30 and, therefore, had no right thereafter to cɩarge Mrs. Kirby's account with the amount of the check.

The trial court apparently decided that Mr. and Mrs. Kirby were liable to the Bank because they had indorsed the Neuse check. But under U.C.C. § 3–414(1) an indorser contracts to pay an instrument only if the instrument is dishonored. And, as we have pointed out, the

---

2. The Uniform Commercial Code ("U.C.C.") has been codified as Titles 8.1 through 8.10 of the Code of Virginia. References to the U.C.C. are to that Code as adopted in Virginia, but citations will omit the title number 8. E.g., U.C.C. § 4–213 means Va.Code Ann. § 8.4–213.

3. The Uniform Commercial Code gives "item" its generally accepted meaning: " 'Item' means any instrument for the payment of money even though it is not negotiable but does not include money." U.C.C. § 4–104(1)(g).

4. As shown by the quotation in the text, U.C.C. § 4–213, which deals with bank deposits and collections, provides without qualification that a payor bank's payment of an item in cash is final. The Code recognizes, however, that a bank may recover a payment when a presenter's warranty is breached, e.g., when an indorsement is forged. U.C.C. §§ 3–417(1), 4–207(1). And under the established law before adoption of the Uniform Commercial Code, a bank could also recover a payment in case of fraud or bad faith on the part of the person receiving the payment. 3 Pa-

ton's Digest of Legal Opinions, Overdrafts § 4:1 (1944). In this case there is no evidence of breach of a presenter's warranties or of fraud or bad faith.

Unlike U.C.C. § 4–213, U.C.C. § 3–418, which deals with commercial paper generally, implies that payment of an instrument is final only in favor of a holder in due course or a person who has changed his position in reliance on the payment. First & Merchants neither relied on U.C.C. § 3–418, nor based its right to recover on an assertion that Mr. and Mrs. Kirby were not holders in due course and did not change their position. See U.C.C. § 3–307 and comment. Moreover, insofar as U.C.C. §§ 3–418 and 4–213 conflict, U.C.C. § 4–213 prevails. U.C.C. § 4–102(1).

5. Since no dollar amount was inserted after "checks" on the deposit ticket, the notation "6–28–728–514 partial" was apparently inserted to identify the source of the currency being deposited. See n. 1 supra.

Bank did not dishonor the Neuse check, but paid the check in cash when Mrs. Kirby presented it.

As a practical matter, the contract of an indorser under U.C.C. § 3–414(1) does not run to a drawee bank. That contract can be enforced by a drawee bank only if it dishonors a check; and if the bank dishonors the check, it has suffered no loss.

The warranties that are applicable in this case are set forth in U.C.C. §§ 3–417(1) and 4–207(1): warranties made to a drawee bank by a presenter and prior transferors of a check. Those warranties are applicable because Mrs. Kirby presented the Neuse check to the Bank for payment. U.C.C. § 3–504(1); Bunn, Snead & Speidel, An Introduction to the Uniform Commercial Code § 3.4(B) (1964). And those warranties do not include a warranty that the drawer of a check has sufficient funds on deposit to cover the check.

The rule that a drawee who mistakenly pays a check has recourse only against the drawer was firmly established before adoption of the Uniform Commercial Code:

> "The drawer of a check, and not the holder who receives payment, is primarily responsible for the drawing out of funds from a bank. An overdraft is an act by reason of which the drawer and not the holder obtains money from the bank on his check. The holder therefore in the absence of fraud or express understanding for repayment, has no concern with the question whether the drawer has funds in the bank to meet the check. The bank is estopped, as against him, from claiming that by its acceptance an overdraft occurred. A mere mistake is not sufficient to enable it to recover from him. Banks cannot always guard against fraud, but can guard against mistakes.

> "It is therefore the general rule, sustained by almost universal authority, that a payment in the ordinary course of business of a check by a bank on which it is drawn under the mistaken belief that the drawer has funds in the bank subject to check is not such a payment under a mistake of fact as will permit the bank to recover the money so paid from the recipient of such payment. To permit the bank to repudiate the payment would destroy the certainty which must pertain to commercial transactions if they are to remain useful to the business public. Otherwise no one would ever know when he can safely receive payment of a check."

7 Zollman, The Law of Banks and Banking § 5062 (1936). See generally 3 Paton's Digest of Legal Opinions, Overdrafts § 4 (1944).

Virginia followed the same rule. Citizens Bank of Norfolk v. Schwarzchild & Sultzberger Co., 109 Va. 539, 64 S.E. 954, 23 L.R.A., N.S. 1092 (1901); Bank of Virginia v. Craig, 33 Va. (6 Leigh) 399, 431 (1835); see Va.Code Ann. § 8.3–417, Virginia Comment at 220 (1965 added vol.); Va.Code Ann. § 8.4–207, Virginia Comment at 271 (1965 added vol.)

Nevertheless, First & Merchants contends that under the terms of its deposit contract with Mrs. Kirby, the settlement was provisional and therefore subject to revocation whether or not the Neuse check was paid in cash on December 30.[6] It contends that in this regard the deposit contract changes the rule set forth in the Uniform Commercial Code. But in providing that "all items are credited subject to final payment", the contract recognizes that settlement for an item is provisional only until the item is finally paid. Since the deposit contract does not change the applicable rule as set forth in the Uniform Commercial Code, we do not decide whether a bank can provide by deposit contract that payment of a check in cash is provisional.

Even if the Bank's settlement for the Neuse check had been provisional, the Bank had the right to charge that item back to Mrs. Kirby's account only if it complied with U.C.C. §§ 4–212(3) and 4–301. Those sections authorize the revocation of a settlement if, before the "midnight deadline",[7] the bank

"(a) returns the item; or

"(b) sends written notice of dishonor or nonpayment if the item is held for protest or is otherwise unavailable for return". U.C.C. § 4–301.

The Bank concedes that it neither sent written notice of dishonor nor returned the Neuse check before the "midnight deadline". So the Bank had no right to charge the item back to Mrs. Kirby's account.

For the reasons set forth, the trial court erred in entering judgment for First & Merchants against Mr. and Mrs. Kirby.

Reversed and final judgment.

---

6. The depositor's contract provides:

"Items received from deposit or collection are accepted on the following terms and conditions. *This bank acts only as depositor's collecting agent and assumes no responsibility beyond its exercise of due care. All items are credited subject to final payment and to receipt of proceeds of final payment in cash or solvent credits by this bank at its own office.* This bank may forward items to correspondents and shall not be liable for default or negligence of correspondents selected with due care nor for losses in transit, and each correspondent shall not be liable except for its own negligence. Items and their proceeds may be handled by any Federal Reserve bank in accordance with applicable Federal Reserve rules, and by this bank or any correspondent, in accordance with any common bank usage, with any practice or procedure that a Federal Reserve bank may use or permit another bank to use, or with any other lawful means. *This bank may charge back, at any time prior to midnight on its business day next following the day of receipt, any item drawn on this bank which is ascertained to be drawn against insufficient funds or otherwise not good or payable. An item received after this bank's regular afternoon closing hour shall be deemed received the next business day.*

"This bank reserves the right to post all deposits, including deposits of cash and of items drawn on it, not later than midnight of its next business day after their receipt at this office during regular banking hours, and shall not be liable for damages for nonpayment of any presented item resulting from the exercise of this right.

" * * * * " (Italicized language is quoted in First & Merchants brief.)

7. "Midnight deadline" is defined in U.C.C. § 4–104(1)(h). See also the Bank's deposit contract, supra n. 6.

HARRISON, JUSTICE (dissenting). I dissent from the holding of the majority that the check involved here was "cashed". It is apparent that the check of Neuse Engineering and Dredging Company was "deposited" in normal course by Mrs. Kirby, and received and accepted for deposit by the Princess Anne Plaza Branch of the First and Merchants National Bank. The same bank official, quoted by the majority, also testified:

Q. "Did Margaret Kirby or William Kirby bring you a check to deposit on December 29, 1966?

A. "Yes, sir, they did.

Q. "Tell what happened to this particular check.

A. "We received it for deposit on Friday night, the 29th. We deposited $2,300 and gave back cash, $200. . . ."

(Admittedly the correct date of the deposit was Friday, December 30, 1966.)

This witness, the only one who testified in the case, was Mr. Floyd E. Waterfield, Vice President of the bank. From his testimony we learn that late in the afternoon of December 30, 1966, Mrs. Kirby, a customer of the bank with an active checking account, came into the bank with the Neuse check. Apparently she desired $200 in cash. In making out the deposit slip, $2300 was erroneously written opposite the currency line instead of opposite the check line. However, indicated in writing on the face of the deposit slip is a notation that the deposit was evidenced by a check drawn on another of the bank's branches in the Norfolk–Virginia Beach area. Also on the face of the deposit slip is shown the manner in which Mrs. Kirby obtained the $200 she wanted, i.e. by deducting $200 from the $2500 check.

This was a perfectly normal and customary banking transaction. Mrs. Kirby, as a customer of that particular branch bank, presumably could have obtained $200 by writing her personal check, or by having the bank issue and she initial a debit memorandum or charge on her account, or by having the transaction reflected on the face of the deposit slip. She and the bank teller obviously pursued the latter course, and this was entirely in order. When the books of the bank were balanced for the day's operations, the bank had a $2500 check of Neuse, which was offset or balanced against a cash withdrawal of $200, plus a tentative or provisional credit of $2300 in the Kirby checking account.

There is nothing in this record from which it could possibly be deduced that Mrs. Kirby walked into the bank and cashed the Neuse check for $2500. That is, she presented the check and demanded and received $2500 in cash, and afterwards redeposited $2300 of it in currency. This simply did not occur, and the evidence does not reflect it. While the bank officer does refer to "cashing the check", the evidence and the records of the bank show that it was not cashed, but was accepted for deposit and clearance as any other check.

The fact that the bank permitted Mrs. Kirby to withdraw $200 is of no significance. She was a customer of the bank, with a checking account. Had the withdrawal, absent the Neuse deposit, caused an overdraft, this would not have been unusual for banks permit customers to overdraw from time to time in reasonable amounts. Furthermore, at that time neither Mrs. Kirby nor the bank had reason to anticipate that the Neuse check would be dishonored because of insufficient funds. . . .

Note

When "Final Payment" is Final. As the court suggested in footnote 4, it was argued that former UCC 4–213(1) and 3–418 dealt with the same question and that former UCC 4–213(1) differed from former UCC 3–418 in imposing no requirement of holding in due course or reliance. Comment 4 to UCC 3–418 disposes of this argument. "The right of a drawee to recover a payment or to revoke an acceptance under Section 3–418 is not affected by the rules under Article 4 that determine when an item is paid. Even though a payor bank may have paid an item under UCC 4–215, it may have a right to recover the payment under Section 3–418." Unlike former UCC 3–418, revised UCC 3–418 does not speak of payment being "final" but instead speaks of the right to recover a payment made by mistake.

Note that under former UCC 3–418, unless the Kirbys were prepared to show that they had "in good faith changed [their] position in reliance on the payment," they had to show that they were holders in due course. Since most checks are not negotiated but are presented for payment by their payees, UCC 3–418 is most likely to be invoked by a payee, just as it was in the *Kirby* case. The scheme employed by the drafters of the Code in former UCC 3–418 and 3–417, to replace the common law analysis based on restitution, made it essential, therefore, that payees such as the Kirbys were able to qualify as holders in due course. Former UCC 3–302(2), which stated that "A payee may be a holder in due course" was intended to accomplish this. UCC 3–418(c) eliminates the reference to holding in due course and speaks instead of "a person who took the instrument in good faith and for value." Former UCC 3–302(2) is also eliminated. See Comment 4 to UCC 3–302 and the discussion at p. 252 infra.

———————

(B) What Amounts To Payment

———————

Prefatory Note. In *Kirby v. First & Merchants National Bank,* the court concluded that the transaction at the counter on December 30 was "consistent with a cashing of the Neuse check" and that therefore "First & Merchants paid the Neuse check in cash on December 30 and ... had no right thereafter to charge Mrs. Kirby's account with the amount of the check." As UCC 4–215(a) expresses it: "An item is finally paid by a payor bank when the bank has ... paid the item in cash...." [1]

Suppose, however, that the bank had not paid $200 in cash to Mrs. Kirby; that nothing had been entered on the deposit slip under "currency"; and that "$2,500" had been entered under "checks" and under "Total." Would the check then have been paid at the time that the teller took the check and the deposit slip at the counter or at some other time?

A leading pre-Code case on this point was White Brokerage Co. v. Cooperman, 207 Minn. 239, 290 N.W. 790 (1940), which held that a check presented over the counter was paid when the bank completed the transaction at its counter. This rule was not calculated to please banks whose tellers were too busy to look up each "on us" item as it came over the counter, nor perhaps the depositors who would be required to wait at the window while this was done. The simplest answer was a properly drafted clause in the deposit slip, making the settlement provisional, subject to revocation. Bank Collection Code § 3 made it provisional, even in the absence of such a clause at least until the end of the day of deposit. The Code deals with the problem in UCC 4–215(a).

Problem 10. Quaker and Empire both bank at The Bank of New York. Empire's account has only $10,000 in it. Quaker deposits the Empire check along with the other checks in The Bank of New York, using a deposit slip similar to that furnished by Philadelphia National. Later on the same day, when the check is put through the regular computer run, it is rejected as drawn on insufficient funds. What are The Bank of New York's rights against Quaker? See UCC 4–214 215, 4–301, 4–302; *Douglas v. Citizens Bank of Jonesboro*, infra.

DOUGLAS v. CITIZENS BANK OF JONESBORO

Supreme Court of Arkansas, 1968.
244 Ark. 168, 424 S.W.2d 532.

HARRIS, CHIEF JUSTICE. This litigation involves two separate causes of action, which however, by agreement, were set forth in one set of pleadings, and disposed of at one hearing. Appellants, Weldon Doug-

1. In the *Kirby* case, the check was apparently drawn on a different branch of First & Merchants than the one to which Mrs. Kirby took it. (The dissenting opinion says it was deposited in the Princess Anne Plaza Branch. See footnote 1 to the court's opinion.) Does UCC 4–107 call into question the applicability of UCC 4–215(a)(1) in such a case? (Was the bank that paid cash the "payor bank" or a different bank under UCC 4–107?)

las, and Janie Chandler, each maintained a checking account in the Citizens Bank of Jonesboro. Rees Plumbing Company, Inc. (which is not presently a party to this proceeding), was a customer of the bank, and maintained checking accounts. On August 19, 1966, the plumbing company delivered its check in the amount of $1,000.00 to Douglas. On that same day Douglas presented the check to the bank for deposit to his own checking account; an employee at the teller's window prepared a deposit slip, dated as of that day, reflecting that the check was being deposited to Douglas' account. He was given a duplicate of the deposit slip, and an employee of the bank thereafter affixed to the back of the check a stamp in red ink, denoting the August 19th date, and stating, "Pay to any bank—P.E.G., Citizens Bank of Jonesboro, Jonesboro, Arkansas." Under date of August 20, 1966, the bank dishonored the check because of insufficient funds, and charged the amount back to the account of Douglas. This same statement of facts applies to Mrs. Chandler, except that the check she presented was originally made payable to a Richard R. Washburn (in the amount of $1,600.00) by the same Rees Company, and this check had been properly endorsed by Washburn before coming into the hands of Mrs. Chandler.[1]

Rees Plumbing Company filed an unverified complaint against the bank, alleging that it had issued the aforementioned checks to the parties, and that it had sufficient funds in the accounts to honor these checks. It was alleged that the checks were wrongfully dishonored, and Rees sought damages due to the alleged willful and wanton negligence of the bank in handling its checks. Subsequently, the complaint was amended to join appellants as parties plaintiff (together with another party which later took a non-suit). Thereafter, on motion of appellee, Rees Plumbing Company was stricken as a party plaintiff. After first demurring, and moving to make the complaint more definite and certain, the bank filed an answer setting out that the accounts of Rees were insufficient on August 19 to honor the checks, and further, that both were charged back to the accounts of the respective appellants on August 20, and the appellants so notified. The bank further denied that the endorsement stamp, heretofore mentioned, constituted an acceptance stamp. The bank asserted that the stamp was no more than a method of identification. Both appellants and the bank, appellee herein, filed verified motions for summary judgment. Appellants' motion was supported by the checks and the deposit slips, which had already been filed, and appellee's motion was supported by the affidavit of Major Griffin, Vice–President of the Citizens Bank, filed with the motion for summary judgment. The affidavit reflects that Griffin had been engaged in banking with the Citizens Bank for 20 years, and it asserted that he was familiar with the processing of items in the Citizens Bank, as well as the normal procedures of other banks, and particularly familiar with the stamps and symbols used by banks in the

---

1. The check presented to the bank by Mrs. Chandler was dated on August 18, instead of 19, and was drawn by Rees on another account, which it had in the Citizens Bank.

area. He then explained the procedure used by appellee, and stated that the stamp served only to identify the depository bank, and that the endorsement appeared on all checks received by appellee which are not received from other banking institutions. He then stated:

"Any item for any reason can be returned by the Citizens Bank or any other banking institution (except those cashed over the counter) if rejected before midnight of the next banking day following the banking day on which the item is received, and prior to the bank stamping its 'paid' stamp thereon and filing in the customer's file.

"I have examined the Citizens Bank records with reference to a $1,600.00 check drawn on Rees Plumbing Company, Inc. account number 810 657 payable to Richard R. Washburn and find that it was deposited to the account of Mrs. Janie Chandler, a customer of the Citizens Bank in account number 301 191 on August 19, 1966. This deposit was posted to the Citizens Bank Journal to the credit of Mrs. Janie Chandler's account on August 19, 1966, but the check was not posted to Citizens Bank Journal as a charge to the Rees Plumbing Company account on which it was drawn because there was no balance in the Rees Plumbing Company Account at close of business on the date of August 19, 1966. The account of Mrs. Janie Chandler was debited for the insufficiency under date of August 20, 1966, and was returned to Mrs. Chandler."

He stated that the same procedure was followed with the Douglas check. The court denied the motion of the appellants, but granted that of the bank.

Thereafter, appellants petitioned the court to reopen the case for the purpose of receiving additional evidence on the question of what weight, if any, might be given to a statement printed on the backs of the deposit slips which had been introduced into evidence by agreement. The language on the bank of the deposit slips provides, *inter alia,* that "items drawn on this bank not good at close of business day on which they have been deposited may be charged back to depositor." Appellants desired to introduce evidence to show that they did not know of the language on the back of the slips. The court refused to reopen the case, but the trial judge did state that, in reaching his conclusions, he gave no consideration at all to this language; nor do we consider same in the present instance, it-being immaterial to the disposition of the litigation. From the judgment denying the motion to reopen the case; denying the motion for summary judgment filed on behalf of appellants, and granting the motion for summary judgment on behalf of appellee, comes this appeal.

The principal question at issue is, "Did the bank, by stamping the endorsement upon the checks deposited by appellants, and by delivering to appellants the deposit slips, accept both of said checks for payment?" The answer is, "No," and it might be stated at the outset that cases decided prior to the passage of the Uniform Commercial Code are not controlling. This case is controlled by the following sections of the Code: Ark.Stat.Ann. § 85–4–212(3), § 85–4–213, and § 85–4–301(1) (Add.1961).

Subsection (3) of Section 85–4–212 reads as follows:

"A depositary bank which is also the payor may charge back the amount of an item to its customer's account or obtain refund in accordance with the section governing return of an item received by a payor bank for credit on its books (Section 4–301 [§ 85–4–301])."

Subsection (1) of Section 85–4–301 provides:

"Where an authorized settlement for a demand item (other than a documentary draft) received by a payor bank otherwise than for immediate payment over the counter has been made before midnight of the banking day [2] of receipt the payor bank may revoke the settlement and recover any payment if before it has made final payment (subsection (1) of Section 4–213 [§ 85–4–213]) and before its midnight deadline it

(a) returns the item; or

(b) sends written notice of dishonor or nonpayment if the item is held for protest or is otherwise unavailable for return."

Section 85–4–213 simply sets out the time that a payment becomes final, not applicable in this instance.

When we consider the statutes above referred to, it is clear that appellants cannot prevail.[3] Clark, Bailey and Young, in their American Law Institute pamphlet on bank deposits and collections under the Uniform Commercial Code (January, 1959), p. 2, comment as follows:

"If the buyer-drawer and the seller-payee have their accounts in the same bank, and if the seller-payee deposits the check to the credit of his account, his account will be credited provisionally with the amount of the check. In the absence of special arrangement with the bank, he may not draw against this credit until it becomes final, that is to say, until after the check has reached the bank's bookkeeper and, as a result of bookkeeping operations, has been charged to the account of the buyer-drawer. (The seller-payee could, of course, present the check at a teller's window and request immediate payment in cash, but that course is not usually followed.) If the buyer-drawer's account does not have a sufficient balance, or he has stopped payment on the check, or if for any other reason the bank does not pay the check, the provisional credit given in the account of the seller-payee is reversed. If the seller-payee had been permitted to draw against that provisional credit, the

---

2. According to Section 85–4–104, "'midnight deadline' with respect to a bank is midnight on its next banking day following the banking day on which it receives the relevant item or notice or from which the time for taking action commences to run, whichever is later."

3. An order denying a motion for summary judgment is merely interlocutory, leaving the case pending for trial, and is not appealable; however, in holding that the court did not err in granting the summary judgment to the bank, the question of whether appellants were entitled to summary judgment is necessarily answered in the negative.

bank would recoup the amount of the drawing by debit to his account or by other means."

The comment of the commissioners is also enlightening. Comment 4, under Section 85–4–213, states:

"A primary example of a statutory right on the part of the payor bank to revoke a settlement is the right to revoke conferred by Section 4–301. The underlying theory and reason for deferred posting statutes (Section 4–301) is to require a settlement on the date of receipt of an item but to keep that settlement provisional with the right to revoke prior to the midnight deadline. In any case where Section 4–301 is applicable, any settlement by the payor bank is provisional solely by virtue of the statute, subsection (1)(b) of Section 4–213 does not operate and such provisional settlement does not constitute final payment of the item." ...

Affirmed.

Notes

(1) **Need for a Clause.** Did the court in the *Douglas* case read the Code correctly in deciding that it is now unnecessary for a bank to provide on its deposit slip that the credit given is provisional in order to avoid the rule of the *White Brokerage* case? Comment 3 to former UCC 4–303 explained that "In this Section as in Section 4–213 reasoning such as appears in ... White Brokerage Co. v. Cooperman, 207 Minn. 239, 290 N.W. 790 (1940) ... is rejected." But what language in the Code rejects it?

Read with care UCC 4–301(a) and its predecessor, former UCC 4–301(1) on which the court relies. In view of the words "before it has made final payment," is the court in the *Douglas* case correct in its claim that former UCC 4–213 "is not applicable in this instance"? Where does the Code say that, in the absence of appropriate language on the deposit slip, the transaction at the counter is one in which the bank has "made a provisional settlement for the item" under UCC 4–215(a)(3), rather than having "settled for the item without reserving a right to revoke the settlement and without having such right under statute, clearing house rule or agreement" under (a)(2)? See UCC 4–104(a)(11). Are UCC 4–215(a) and 4–301(a) circular in this respect? A portion of Comment 4 to former UCC 4–213, following that quoted by the court, is revealing:

"An example of a reservation of a right to revoke a settlement is where the payor bank is also the depositary bank and has signed a receipt or duplicate deposit ticket or has made an entry in a passbook acknowledging receipt, for credit to the account of A, of a check drawn on it by B. If the receipt, deposit ticket, passbook or other agreement with A is to the effect that any credit so entered is provisional and may be revoked pending the time required by the payor bank to process the item to determine if it is in good form and there are funds to cover it, such reservation or agreement keeps the receipt or credit provisional and avoids it being either final settlement or final payment.

"In other ways the payor bank may keep settlements provisional: by general or special agreement with the presenting party or bank; by simple reservation at the time the settlement is made; or otherwise. Thus a payor bank (except in the case of statutory provisions) has control whether a settlement made by it is provisional or final, by participating in general agreements or clearing house rules or by special agreement or reservation. If it fails to keep a settlement provisional and if no applicable statute keeps the settlement provisional, its settlement is final and, unless the item had previously been paid by one of the other methods prescribed in subsection (1), such final settlement constitutes final payment. In this manner payor banks may without difficulty avoid the effect of such cases as ... White Brokerage Co. v. Cooperman, 207 Minn. 239, 290 N.W. 790 (1940)...."

When former UCC 4–213 was revised as UCC 4–215, the following was added as part of Comment 4 to the new section:

"An example of an agreement allowing the payor bank to revoke a settlement is a case in which the payor bank is also the depositary bank and has signed a receipt or duplicate deposit ticket or has made an entry in a passbook acknowledging receipt, for credit to the account of A, of a check drawn on it by B. If the receipt, deposit ticket, passbook or other agreement with A is to the effect that any credit so entered is provisional and may be revoked pending the time required by the payor bank to process the item to determine if it is in good form and there are funds to cover it, the agreement keeps the receipt or credit provisional and avoids its being either final settlement or final payment.

"The most important application of subsection (a)(2) is that in which presentment of an item has been made over the counter for immediate payment. In this case Section 4–301(a) does not apply to make the settlement provisional, and final payment has occurred unless a rule or agreement provides otherwise."

(2) **Split Deposits.** What instructions should a bank issue to its tellers with respect to the common situation in which a customer wishes, as Kirby did, to make a "split deposit" of a check, i.e., to deposit only part of the amount of the check and to take the rest in cash?

(C) EFFECT OF THE MIDNIGHT DEADLINE

Prefatory Note. In *Kirby v. First & Merchants National Bank,* the court stated, as an alternative ground for its decision, that since the bank "neither sent written notice of dishonor nor returned the Neuse check before the 'midnight deadline,' ... the Bank had no right to charge the item back to Mrs. Kirby's account." To understand the effect of a bank's midnight deadline on the question of payment, it is useful to know a little history.

History of Check Collections. For an appreciation of the forces and events that shaped the check collection process and led to the midnight deadline, we turn back to the late nineteenth and early twentieth centuries. The critical periods were those of bank failures.

Suppose that a Seller received in the mail a check from Buyer in a distant city in payment for goods. Seller would deposit the check for collection in Seller's bank, Sellersville Bank. Most such nonlocal items were collected through correspondents. Thus Sellersville Bank might forward the check to Correspondent Bank in a nearby large city, which would undertake to present it to Buyersville Bank, the payor bank. This system raised several questions.

First, what was the relationship of Sellersville Bank, the depositary bank, to Seller, the depositor? Did the bank become an owner of the check? Bankers, conscious of the risk of bank failure, feared that if the depositary bank took the check as owner it would bear the loss if the check were paid and the proceeds then lost due to the failure of a subsequent bank in the chain of collection. (There could be no recourse against the depositor on the depositor's indorsement because the check would not have been dishonored.) If, however, the bank were an agent, the loss would fall on its principal, the depositor. Therefore clauses were added to deposit slips to make it clear that a collecting bank was only an agent and not an owner of the check.

Second, assuming that Sellersville Bank, the depositary bank, was the agent of Seller, the depositor, what was the relationship between the depositor and subsequent collecting banks such as Correspondent Bank? There were two schools of thought. Under the "Massachusetts collection rule," such banks were regarded as sub-agents of the depositor, responsible directly to the depositor; the authority of the depositary bank to employ such sub-agents was inferred from the deposit of the check for collection; the depositary bank discharged its duty to its principal if it selected sub-agents with care. Under the "New York collection rule," the depositary bank appointed its own agents and not those of the depositor; the deposit of the check did not authorize the depositary bank to appoint agents on behalf of its depositor; the depositary bank, rather than the subsequent bank, was liable to the depositor for the defaults of the subsequent bank. Where the depositor had been caused loss by the fault of a distant collecting bank, the Massachusetts rule often left the depositor with recourse only against that bank and not against the bank with which the depositor had dealt.[1] Clauses were added to deposit slips invoking the Massachusetts rule.

1. It is interesting that when payor banks were faced with a similar inconvenience in the case of checks bearing forged indorsements, their situation was quickly

A third question caused bankers more trouble than the first two. How was presentment of the check to be made? A simple way to present the check was by direct sending, in which Correspondent Bank mailed the check, along with any others drawn on Buyersville Bank, directly to that bank. Buyersville Bank would then make payment for all of these checks by mailing its remittance draft, its own check on yet another bank, to Correspondent Bank.

Before the First World War, however, there was a practical obstacle to direct sending. At that time many banks refused to remit at par, or face value, exacting an exchange charge when paying checks by remittance draft. They argued that their contract with the drawer called for no more than payment at par over the counter; for remitting to a distant point they should be allowed a fee. Because of the competition for accounts, depositary banks were reluctant to pass on such fees to the depositor of the check, and to avoid exchange charges the practice of circuitous routing developed. Banks made reciprocal agreements to remit at par, and checks were shunted about the country over devious routes, in order to take advantage of these agreements and avoid paying exchange fees.[2]

Aside from the obvious disadvantages of delay and expense, circuitous routing compounded another evil—paper reserves. It was then the practice of banks to give the depositor immediate credit, subject to drawing, for out of town checks. The depositary bank was frequently also given immediate credit when it forwarded the check to its correspondent, and this counted as part of its reserves. The dangers of this practice were demonstrated during the panic of 1907 when many checks were dishonored and banks were unable to realize on much of their paper reserves. The delay due to circuitous routing increased the amount of such reserves created by the "float" of items in the process of collection.

ameliorated by the use of "prior indorsements guaranteed." See p. 299 infra.

When shippers of goods were in a somewhat analogous situation with respect to the liability of a connecting carrier for loss, their situation was ameliorated by enactment of the Carmack Amendment, now recodified in 49 U.S.C. § 11707(a)(1). The amendment allowed a shipper to hold the carrier that received the goods from the shipper, and that carrier could, if the loss had occurred while the goods were in the hands of a later carrier, recover over against the later carrier. Prior to the amendment, "the shipper could look only to the initial carrier for recompense for loss, damage or delay occurring on its part of the route. If such primary carrier was able to show a delivery to the rails of the next succeeding carrier, although the packages might and usually did continue the journey in the same car in which they had been originally loaded, the shipper must fail in his suit. He might, it is true, then bring his action against the carrier so shown to have next received the shipment. But here, in turn he might be met by proof of safe delivery to a third separate carrier." Atlantic Coast Line Railroad Co. v. Riverside Mills, 219 U.S. 186, 200, 31 S.Ct. 164, 168, 55 L.Ed. 167 (1911).

2. In one notorious instance a check drawn on a Sag Harbor, Long Island bank was deposited in a bank in Hoboken, New Jersey, one hundred miles distant, and traveled 1,500 miles in eleven days, passing through banks in New York City, Boston, Tonawanda, Albany, Port Jefferson, Far Rockaway, New York City, Riverhead and Brooklyn before reaching Sag Harbor. Spahr, The Clearing and Collection of Checks 106 (1926).

The Federal Reserve System, established by the Federal Reserve Act of 1913, undertook corrective action and in 1916 issued Regulation J requiring Federal Reserve banks to establish a clearing and collection system. Among the objectives of the System was the elimination of three evils: (1) exchange charges; (2) paper reserves; and (3) circuitous routing. The attack on the first resulted in the stormy par clearance controversy, in which the System scored an incomplete victory. The second evil was substantially eliminated by setting up availability schedules using estimated times for collection based on the location of the bank. A bank using the collection facilities of the Federal Reserve System is not given absolute credit, subject to drawing, until the available date determined from the schedule.

The third evil, circuitous routing, was reduced by granting to member and certain other banks the privilege of forwarding out of town checks through the Federal Reserve bank in the depositary bank's district.[3] Thus a bank in Sacramento, California, which received from a depositor a check drawn upon a bank in Albany, New York, might mail it to the Federal Reserve Bank of San Francisco, which would forward it to the Federal Reserve Bank of New York, which would in turn mail it to the drawee bank in Albany.[4]

The practice of direct sending, however, posed legal problems. Suppose that Buyersville Bank delayed before sending its remittance draft and then became insolvent, so that its remittance draft, which would have been paid had there been no delay, was dishonored. Might not Seller hold Sellersville Bank for negligence? Mailing the check to the drawee, Buyersville Bank, placed Seller's check in the hands of an adversary in whose interest it would be to procrastinate. A bank is not a suitable agent to collect from itself. Had the check been presented by a proper third party and prompt payment demanded, even the use of a remittance draft would not have caused loss. So it was held in cases such as Minneapolis Sash & Door Co. v. Metropolitan Bank, 76 Minn. 136, 78 N.W. 980 (1899).

3. There are twelve numbered districts with Federal Reserve banks in (1) Boston, (2) New York City, (3) Philadelphia, (4) Cleveland, (5) Richmond, (6) Atlanta, (7) Chicago, (8) St. Louis, (9) Minneapolis, (10) Kansas City, (11) Dallas, and (12) San Francisco. Most of these banks have branches in the same district. The numerator (1-1) of the fraction on the check (Form 2 supra) is the bank transit number of the payor bank. The number 1 indicates New York City, and 1 is the number, in that city, of The Bank of New York. (It is New York's oldest bank, founded by Alexander Hamilton in 1784, only a decade after his matriculation at Columbia (then King's College.) The denominator (210) is the routing symbol. The first digit, 2, indi-

cates that the payor bank is in District Number 2. The second digit, 1, indicates that the payor bank is served by the Reserve bank head office rather than a branch. The third digit, 0, indicates that credit for the check will be available immediately upon its receipt by that office of the Reserve bank. If the digit is other than zero, the item is receivable for deferred credit. The bank transit number and the routing symbol also appear in the magnetized symbols in the lower left-hand corner of the check.

4. The Sacramento bank might have the privilege of direct sending, in which case it could mail the check directly to the Federal Reserve Bank of New York.

To avoid the result of such cases and encourage direct sending, the Federal Reserve Board included in its Regulation J a provision that banks using the System authorized Federal Reserve Banks to send checks directly to the payor bank. But was this sufficient? Might not Seller, the depositor, hold Sellersville Bank, the depositary bank, for negligence since Seller had not consented to direct sending? This was clearly a problem under states that applied the New York collection rule. Even under the Massachusetts collection rule, was it due care for a depositary bank to select a Federal Reserve Bank if that bank was expected to mail the check to the payor bank? To protect themselves, banks put clauses on their deposit slips granting themselves permission to use direct sending and invoking the Massachusetts collection rule. In 1918 the American Bankers Association proposed a statute authorizing direct routing and many states adopted this or a similar statute. Thus armed, the banks were ready for the next round.

That round was fought and lost by the banks in the Supreme Court of the United States in Federal Reserve Bank v. Malloy, 264 U.S. 160, 44 S.Ct. 296, 68 L.Ed. 617 (1924). That case involved the familiar situation of a remittance draft that had been dishonored because the drawer of the remittance draft (the payor bank on the check) had become insolvent after issuing it. The payee of the check sued the Federal Reserve Bank that had presented it, alleging negligence in collection of the check. The Supreme Court affirmed a judgment for the plaintiff, holding that the Federal Reserve Bank was liable for its negligence in taking in payment a remittance draft instead of cash. The Court did not quarrel with the proposition that under Regulation J the Federal Reserve Bank was authorized to send the check directly to the payor bank. But the Court pointed out that "a collecting agent is without authority to accept for the debt of his principal anything but 'that which the law declares to be a legal tender, or which is by common consent considered and treated as money, and passes as such at par.' ... This regulation, while it contemplates the sending of checks for collection to the drawee banks, does not expressly permit the acceptance of payment other than in money." Nor would the Court read in that authority by implication or from custom.

However, it was simple enough to deprive the depositor of the right upheld in the *Malloy* case. Regulation J was amended to allow Federal Reserve banks to accept remittance drafts, and a new crop of clauses appeared on deposit slips permitting collecting banks to take remittance drafts.

Now that Seller, as depositor, was deprived of any right against either Sellersville Bank or Correspondent Bank, the collecting banks, it was important to ask whether Seller had any action on the check against Buyer, as drawer. Logically it followed from decisions like that in the *Malloy* case that the check had been paid and Buyer was no longer liable to Seller. For if Seller could still sue Buyer, Seller would have sustained no loss as the result of Correspondent Bank's taking a remittance draft. There was dictum to this effect in the *Malloy* opinion and it was borne out in other cases. The result was that the Seller's rights against the collecting banks were Seller's sole recourse, and this recourse had been effectively cut off. It could be argued that when Regulation J and deposit slips were amended to avoid the result in the *Malloy* case, this had the incidental effect of imposing liability on the Buyer as drawer of the check. But most courts found it hard to see any reason why Buyer, as drawer, should be adversely affected by such a contract between Seller, as depositor, and the collecting banks. Therefore Buyer was still discharged because the check had been paid.

The erosion of Seller's rights as depositor was now nearly complete. Seller had lost the right to hold Sellersville Bank, the depositary bank, and was left to an action against a remote collecting bank when the banks invoked the Massachusetts collection rule. Seller had lost the right to hold even that bank for loss caused by direct routing when deposit slips and Federal Reserve Board Regulation J were amended and statutes were enacted to permit direct sending. Seller had lost the right to hold that bank for loss caused by accepting payment by remittance draft when there was a similar response to the *Malloy* case. Seller had, at least in most states, no recourse against Buyer, the drawer of the check, because the check had been paid. So Seller was left with what he had received in payment, a bank draft on which only Buyersville Bank, the payor bank on the check, was liable, and that bank was insolvent. Seller would have to stand in line for the money with its general depositors.

There was one hope left for Seller as depositor of the check. If Seller came ahead of the general depositors of the insolvent bank on the ground that Seller had a preferred claim, Seller stood a chance of being paid in full. This was the tack followed by ingenious counsel and in a number of states they succeeded. An example is People ex rel. Nelson v. People's Bank & Trust Co., 353 Ill. 479, 187 N.E. 522, 89 A.L.R. 1328 (1933), where the court concluded that the payor bank on the check, the insolvent drawer of the remittance draft, was the agent of the depositor, that the agent bank's assets had been augmented by the transaction, that the depositor could trace the funds into the hands of the receiver, and that therefore the depositor had a preferred claim in the assets of the insolvent bank based on trust doctrines. Other courts rejected this argument and left the depositor to share with general depositors.

The Bank Collection Code. In 1929 the American Bankers Association proposed for adoption the Bank Collection Code. By 1932 eighteen states had adopted it. Because of the statute's origin, it is hardly surprising that it was bank-oriented. It made collecting banks agents rather than owners, adopted the Massachusetts collection rule, sanctioned direct routing, authorized the acceptance of remittance drafts, and gave the depositor a preferred claim.

For a discussion of the history of check collections up to this point, see Scott, The Risk Fixers, 91 Harv.L.Rev. 737 (1978).

The Code. The Code carries over many of the provisions of the Bank Collection Code into the comparable provisions of the Code. The Code also makes banks agents rather than owners (UCC 4–201(a)), and adopts the Massachusetts collection rule (UCC 4–202(c)). The Code authorizes direct sending (UCC 4–204(b)(1)) and gives a preferred claim on insolvency (UCC 4–216 and Comment 3).

The Federal Reserve System and Remittance Drafts. Member banks of the Federal Reserve System commonly rely on its facilities. Settlement between member banks in the same district can be effected through the account that they are required to maintain in the Federal Reserve bank. Settlements between member banks in different districts are made through their respective Federal Reserve banks by means of the Interdistrict Settlement Fund in Washington, in which each Reserve bank has a share.

In 1972, the Federal Reserve Board amended Regulation J so that payor banks no longer had the right to use remittance drafts to pay for checks presented by Federal Reserve Banks. Payment was instead to be by debit "to an account on the Reserve Bank's books." 12 C.F.R. § 210.9. The purpose was to reduce the "float" of checks in the process of collection. The requirement of "expeditious return" under Regulation CC has given the quietus to the remittance draft as an instrument to be used in the normal check collection process.

The Federal Reserve System and the Midnight Deadline. In amending Regulation J in 1972, the Federal Reserve Board also tightened up on the midnight deadline. The history of the midnight deadline goes back to a problem that arose well before the advent of the Code.

Before the Second World War banks generally exchanged checks at the clearing house by eleven in the morning and the return item clearing took place at two or three in the afternoon of the same day. The heavy workload, combined with the wartime labor shortage, put a severe strain on the system and banks began deferred posting. Clearing house rules were changed to allow until afternoon of the day following receipt of the item for the return of "not good" items. But bankers worried about Negotiable Instruments Law § 137, which provided that "where a drawee to whom a bill is delivered for acceptance ... refuses within twenty-four hours ... to return the bill," he was deemed to have accepted it. Could a payor bank safely retain a check for more than twenty-four hours? The law on such a "constructive acceptance" was unclear.

To eliminate the risk that deferred posting might result in constructive acceptance, committees appointed by the Federal Reserve Banks and the American Bankers Association met and agreed upon a Model Deferred Posting Statute. In order to reduce the "float," the Federal Reserve Banks insisted that the privilege of making delayed returns be limited to banks that settled by giving credit on the day of receipt. Under the model statute, therefore, only if a payor bank settled before midnight on the day of receipt, did it have until midnight of its next banking day to revoke the credit and refuse to pay the check. All states adopted deferred posting legislation, most of them substantially in the form recommended by the Association in 1948. Regulation J of the Board of Governors of the Federal Reserve System was amended, effective in 1949, to permit deferred posting."

The Code abolishes the constructive acceptance in UCC 3–409(a). The Code adopts deferred posting in UCC 4–301, 4–302.

Note that under UCC 4–302, if the payor bank "is also the depositary bank," the payor bank has until its midnight deadline—"midnight on its next banking day following the banking day on which it receives the relevant item" (UCC 4–104(a)(10))—to revoke any settlement if it has not already made final payment. See also UCC 4–301(a). Thus in *Douglas v. Citizens Bank of Jonesboro,* supra, the bank would have been "accountable" for the checks under UCC 4–302 if it did not "pay or return the item or send notice of dishonor until after its midnight deadline." Since the checks were received by the bank on August 19, the bank's midnight deadline under UCC 4–104(a)(10) was midnight on the next banking day, August 20.[5] But because both checks "were charged back to the accounts of the respective [drawers] on August 20, and the [drawers] so notified," the bank acted before its midnight deadline and so did not become accountable under UCC 4–302.

Note, however, that under UCC 4–301, if the payor bank "is not also the depositary bank," the payor bank has until its midnight deadline only if it "settles ... before midnight of the banking day of receipt."[6] This requirement is intended to reduce the "float" and, in effect, codifies the compromise reached between the Federal Reserve Banks and the American Bankers Association in the Model Deferred Posting Statute.

When the Federal Reserve Board amended Regulation J in 1972, it required that the "proceeds of any payment shall be available to the Reserve Bank by the close of the Reserve Bank's banking day on the banking day of receipt of the item by the paying bank." If the payor bank did not do this, it lost the benefit of its midnight deadline and became accountable for the amount of the check "at the close of the paying bank's banking day" on which it received the item. 12 C.F.R. § 210.9; see also § 210.12. Thus the Board, in an effort further to reduce the "float," required that the payor bank settle before the end of the banking day of receipt and not merely before midnight on the day of receipt as required by the Code.

Expeditious Return Under Regulation CC. The Code's emphasis on timely dispatch of unpaid items did nothing to encourage expedi-

---

5. Purists may question whether a "banking day," as UCC 4–104(a)(3) defines that term, will commonly have a "midnight," as UCC 4–104(a)(10) suggests that it must. Would it be better if UCC 4– 104(a)(10) said "midnight on the date of its next banking day"? See Mellinkoff, The Language of the Uniform Commercial Code, 77 Yale L.J. 185, 188 (1967).

tious return. The bank's job was to rid itself of an item before its midnight deadline, rather than to choose an efficient method of return. As a consequence, the return of a check often involved a slow retracing of the forward collection path until the check finally reached the depositary bank.

Regulation CC changes this. It retains the midnight deadline rule in most cases, but also requires expeditious return of an unpaid check. A bank that fails in its duty of expeditious return may be liable for damages caused to a depositary bank or its customer.

Payor Banks. A payor bank may satisfy its duty of expeditious return under either the two-day/four-day test or the forward collection test. Reg CC 229.30(a)(1), (2).

A payor bank returns a check expeditiously if it returns it in such a way that it normally would be received by a depositary bank within two days if the banks are in the same check-processing region and within four days if they are in different regions. These periods reflect average collection times for local and nonlocal checks. If the banks are in the same region, a check is returned expeditiously if it is received by the depositary bank by 4:00 p.m. (local time of the depositary bank) of the second business day after the banking day on which the check was presented to the payor bank. For example, if a payor bank decides to dishonor a check presented on Monday, it returns the check expeditiously if it is received by a depositary bank in the same check-processing region by 4:00 p.m. on Wednesday. If the banks are not in the same region, the check is returned expeditiously if it is returned to the depositary bank by 4:00 p.m. of the fourth business day after the banking day on which the check was presented to the payor bank. The payor bank need not establish that the depositary bank actually received the check within the specified time. It need show only that it dispatched the check in such a way that the payor bank normally would have received the check within that time.

A payor bank satisfies the forward collection test if it returns a check as quickly as a similarly situated bank would collect a forward-collection check (1) of similar amount, (2) drawn on the same depositary bank, and (3) received for deposit by a similarly situated bank by noon on the banking day following the banking day on which the check was presented to the payor bank. Underlying this test is the assumption that since forward collection is usually swift, the return process will be expeditious if it approximates the speed of forward collection. The expeditiousness of a payor bank's return is measured against community standards established for forward collection. For example, if a payor bank generally mails its forward collection checks to a Federal Reserve bank, but similarly situated banks use a courier to forward checks to a Federal Reserve bank, the payor bank must return checks by courier. A bank is similarly situated if it is of similar asset size, in the same community, and with similar check-handling activity.

Regulation CC allows a payor bank to convert a check to a qualified return check by encoding the check in magnetic ink with the routing number of the depositary bank, the amount of the check, and a return identifier. Conversion of a check to a qualified return check may expedite handling by returning banks. The Regulation does not, however, encourage such conversion by relaxing the return timetable for a payor bank that elects to qualify a check.

Under either the two-day/four-day test or the forward collection test, the payor bank may return a check directly to the depositary bank. The provision is significant, because direct return was not authorized by the Code in every state. Alternatively, the payor bank may route the check to a Federal Reserve bank or any returning bank that agrees to handle the check expeditiously, whether or not that bank participated in forward collection of the check. The ability to return a check through a non-collecting bank is an important departure from the Code, which required return of a check through the chain of forward collection.

If a payor bank, through no fault of its own, cannot identify the depositary bank, the expeditious return requirements do not apply. The payor bank may send the check to any bank that handled it for forward collection, whether or not that bank agrees to return the check expeditiously. In such cases, the payor bank is still required to meet its midnight deadline under the Code. This scenario should occur only rarely since Regulation CC imposes strict indorsement standards designed to ensure easy identification of the depositary bank.

In addition to its duty of expeditious return, the payor bank generally must meet its midnight deadline under the Code. However, the Regulation removes the midnight-deadline constraint where doing so will further the Regulation's paramount goal of expeditious return. The payor bank is not bound by its midnight deadline if, in an effort to expedite return, it dispatches the check so that ordinarily it would be received by the receiving bank's next banking day following the midnight deadline. The payor bank's midnight deadline is extended further if it uses a "highly expeditious means of transportation."

In all cases, the payor bank must indicate clearly on the face of the check the reason for return, a practice that has been traditional among banks, though not required by the Code. If neither the check nor a copy of the check is available, the payor bank may send a written notice of nonpayment in lieu of return. This notice is subject to the same standard of expeditious return as the check itself.

Returning Banks. Regulation CC also imposes a duty of expeditious return on a returning bank that has agreed to handle a check for expeditious return (probably for a fee). Reg CC 229.31(a). Unlike the Code, which authorizes return through all banks in the forward collection chain, the Regulation authorizes return only through banks that have agreed to handle the check for expeditious return. Participation in forward collection does not constitute such an agreement.

If a bank does agree to return a check it must satisfy either the two-day/four-day test or the forward collection test. The two-day/four-day test employs the same standard applied to payor banks.

The forward collection test, while similar to the forward collection test for payor banks, allows a returning bank to set a cut-off hour for receipt of returned checks that is earlier than a similarity situated bank's cut-off hour for checks received for forward collection, but no earlier than 2:00 p.m. In addition, the timetable under the forward collection test is extended by one business day if the returning bank elects to convert a returned check to a qualified returned check. The returning bank may return a check directly to the depositary bank or through a returning bank, including a Federal Reserve bank that has agreed to handle the check expeditiously.

Liability. Banks must exercise ordinary care and act in good faith in complying with the duty of expeditious return. A bank failing to satisfy this standard of care may be liable to the depositary bank, the depositary bank's customer, the owner of the check, or another party to the check. The measure of damages is the amount of actual loss, i.e., the amount of loss incurred, up to the amount of the check, less the amount of loss that would have been incurred had the bank exercised ordinary care. If a bank fails to act in good faith it also may be liable for other damages proximately caused by its failure. Reg CC 229.38.

In cases involving lack of due care by more than one bank, Regulation CC applies a "pure" comparative negligence rule. Reg CC 229.38(c) and Comment 38(c). Damages for which a person, including a bank, is liable are reduced in proportion to the negligence or bad faith of another person.

Problem 11. Empire's account has only $10,000 in it. On Wednesday, The Bank of New York receives the check payable to Quaker directly from the Federal Reserve Bank in Philadelphia, to which Philadelphia National had sent it. The Bank of New York mislays the check for two days and on Friday, when the check is put through the regular computer run, it is rejected as drawn on insufficient funds. What are The Bank of New York's rights against Quaker? See UCC 4–215, 4–301, 4–302; *First Wyoming Bank v. Cabinet Craft Distributors,* infra. (How would it affect your answer if the check were presented through the Clearing House?) Would your answer be the same if the check had already been presented and dishonored by insufficient funds and was being represented when it was mislaid? See *David Graubart v. Bank Leumi Trust Co.,* infra.

———

FIRST WYOMING BANK v. CABINET CRAFT DISTRIBUTORS, INC.

Supreme Court of Wyoming, 1981.
624 P.2d 227.

ROSE, CHIEF JUSTICE. The Uniform Commercial Code provides that except in certain circumstances a bank is liable for the amount of a check which it fails to timely dishonor. Section 34–21–451, W.S.1977 (U.C.C. § 4–302). In this case, the appellee presented a check payable to itself to the appellant bank. The payor had insufficient funds on deposit with the bank to cover the check. The bank dishonored the check but failed to do so within the time mandated by the Uniform Commercial Code.

Appellee then sued in district court for the face amount of the check, interest and costs. The district court agreed with the appellee that the bank was liable under the Code and gave judgment accordingly. The bank has appealed and argues that its "excuse" for failing to timely dishonor the check is sufficient under the Code to enable it to escape liability. Section 34–21–408(b), W.S.1977 (U.C.C. § 4–108(2))....
In arguing that the delay in dishonoring the check was excusable, appellant bank also relies on 12 Code of Federal Regulations 210.14 which provides:

"If, because of interruption of communication facilities, suspension of payments by another bank, war, emergency conditions or other circumstances beyond its control, any bank (including a Federal Reserve bank) shall be delayed beyond the time limits provided in this part or the operating letters of the Federal Reserve banks, or prescribed by the applicable law of any State in taking any action with respect to a cash item or a noncash item, including forwarding such item, presenting it or sending it for presentment and payment, paying or remitting for it, returning it or sending notice of dishonor or nonpayment or making or providing for any necessary protest, the time of such bank, as limited by this part or the operating letters of the Federal Reserve banks, or by the applicable law of any State, for taking or completing the action thereby delayed shall be extended for such time after the cause of the delay ceases to operate as shall be necessary to take or complete the action, provided the bank exercises such diligence as the circumstances require."

The bank points out that under § 34–21–403, W.S.1977 (U.C.C. § 4–103), if not under the supremacy clause of the Federal Constitution, the above regulation is controlling law in Wyoming. We agree that the regulation controls but fail to see how it adds anything to § 34–21–408(b) (U.C.C. § 4–108(2)), supra. In light of the stipulated facts to be presented immediately below, it appears that either under the statute or the regulation the bank must show that its delay in dishonoring the check was due to circumstances beyond its control and that the bank exercised such diligence as the circumstances required....

As we understand the facts, both parties to this suit have acted in good faith and the plaintiff-appellee has made no showing that it was prejudiced by the untimely dishonor of the check. The untimely dishonor of the check was due to delay in delivering checks from a computer center in Billings, Montana, to the bank in Sheridan. Normally, the same courier delivering the checks to the Montana computer center from Sheridan would have driven them back to Sheridan after the center had processed them. However, after the check in issue had been taken to Billings, the main road between Billings and Sheridan became flooded. Although the courier could have taken an alternate route back to Sheridan, the check was instead given to Western Airlines by the computer center to be placed on the next morning's flight to Sheridan. For unknown reasons Western Airlines failed to deliver the check to Sheridan although it made its usual flight. Western Airline's failure to deliver the check to Sheridan as planned caused the bank to miss its Uniform Commercial Code deadline for dishonoring the check.... [1]

Liability Under U.C.C. § 4–302

Courts generally interpret U.C.C. § 4–302 (our § 34–21–451), supra, as imposing strict liability upon a bank which fails to dishonor a check in time unless the bank meets its burden of proving a valid defense. In Sun River Cattle Co., Inc. v. Miners Bank of Mont. N.A., 164 Mont. 237, 521 P.2d 679, 684 (1974), reh. den., the Montana Supreme Court spoke of U.C.C. § 4–302 as imposing a "standard of strict accountability" and cited the Official Code Comment for the proposition that the bank has the burden of proving an excuse under U.C.C. § 4–108(2) (our § 34–21–408(b)), supra. *Sun River Cattle Co.*, supra, 521 P.2d at 685 and also citing 3 Anderson, Uniform Commercial Code 191. The United States Tenth Circuit Court of Appeals has said that if it is shown that a check has not been dishonored within the Code time limit, a prima facie case is established for imposing liability on the bank and the bank has the obligation of proving an excuse for untimely dishonor under U.C.C. § 4–108(2) (our § 34–21–408(b)), supra. Port City State Bank v. American

---

1. The briefs on appeal reveal that the check was for $10,000 and was drawn by Quality Kitchens to the order of Cabinet Craft as partial payment for cabinets and related kitchenware. Cabinet Craft deposited the check in its account in the Security Bank of Billings, which sent it on for collection. On Saturday, May 20, 1978, the Federal Reserve Bank of Denver mailed the check to the First Wyoming Bank of Sheridan, which received it before three in the afternoon on Monday, May 22 and sent it at six that evening to a computer center in Billings run by Data Share, Inc. The computer center's printout showed "insufficient funds."

The checks that ordinarily would have been returned to the First Wyoming Bank late on Monday night were put on an early morning Western Airlines flight and arrived in Sheridan shortly after eight on Tuesday morning. Counsel for Cabinet Craft writes that, apparently because First Wyoming Bank did not meet the plane, the checks were not taken off the plane at Sheridan. On Thursday, the bank was notified by First Wyoming Bank in Casper that the checks had been received there. Counsel for First Wyoming Bank writes that the bank ultimately recovered from Western Airlines for negligence. (The facts in the court's opinion are taken from a brief stipulation entered into by the parties in order to reduce expenses.) [Eds.]

National Bank, Lawton, Okl., 10 Cir., 486 F.2d 196, 198 (1973). The United States Fifth Circuit Court of Appeals recently said, "Failure ... to perform these duties within the time limits prescribed [by U.C.C. § 4–302] mandates the imposition of strict liability for the face amount of any late instrument...." Union Bank of Benton v. First Nat. Bank, 5 Cir., 621 F.2d 790, 795 (1980). The Supreme Court of New Mexico has said, "The liability created by [U.C.C. § 4–302 (our § 34–21–451), supra] is independent of negligence and is an absolute or strict liability for the full amount of the items which it fails to return, ..." Engine Parts v. Citizens Bank of Clovis, 92 N.M. 37, 582 P.2d 809, 815 (1978).

Both the Illinois Supreme Court and the Kentucky Court of Appeals have rejected arguments that a bank which fails to timely dishonor a check under U.C.C. § 4–302 (our § 34–21–451), supra, is only liable if the delay in the dishonoring of the check injured the check's payee. Rock Island Auction Sales v. Empire Packing Co., 32 Ill.2d 269, 204 N.E.2d 721, 723–724 (1965); and Farmers Coop. Livestock Mkt. v. Second Nat. Bank, Ky., 427 S.W.2d 247, 250 (1968).

Other cases which have come to similar conclusions concerning the relevant Code provision include: Pecos County State Bank v. El Paso Livestock, Tex.Civ.App., 586 S.W.2d 183, 187 (1979), reh. den.; and Templeton v. First Nat. Bank of Nashville, 47 Ill.App.3d 443, 5 Ill.Dec. 720, 362 N.E.2d 33, 37 (1977).

Thus, since there is no issue of bad faith, our examination of appellant bank's claim of a valid excuse under U.C.C. § 4–108(2) (our § 34–21–408(b)), supra, does not entail a consideration of the equities involved. Rather our task is simply to determine whether the record demonstrates a sufficient excuse under the above statute....

Excuses Under U.C.C. § 4–108(2)

It is obvious that the flooded road between Billings and Sheridan which disrupted the normal procedure for delivery of the check was a "circumstance beyond the control of the bank" as contemplated by § 34–21–408(b) (U.C.C. § 4–108(2)), supra. Our inquiry is whether the bank used "such diligence as the circumstances required," in allowing the Montana computer center to give the check to Western Airlines for delivery and in not following up the failure of the airline to deliver the packet on schedule. In answering this question we must consider that the stipulated facts show that the bank had an alternative to using Western Airlines: its courier could have taken a different route. We are also somewhat handicapped by a lack of information. For example, although we know that the bank had previously used the airline's delivery service, we do not know what the airline's previous record for timely deliveries had been. We do not know if the computer center in turning the check over to the airline emphasized the need for a timely delivery. We do not know if the bank could have traced the checks which failed to arrive on the Western Airlines flight and gotten them sooner.

We have found no case involving a claimed U.C.C. § 4–108(2) (our § 34–21–408(b)), supra, excuse identical to the one involved here and only a few cases involving somewhat similar excuses. Surveying the area in 1977 the Kentucky Court of Appeals found "only two cases involving the application of U.C.C. § 4–108 to a payor bank's midnight deadline." Blake v. Woodford Bank & Trust Co., Ky.App., 555 S.W.2d 589, 594 (1977). The two cases found by the Kentucky court are *Sun River Cattle Co.,* supra, and *Port City State Bank,* supra. We have not been able to discover any cases in addition to the Kentucky, Montana and Tenth Circuit decisions.

The Montana case is, perhaps, most in point. A bank in Butte, Montana, had its checks processed at a computer center in Great Falls, Montana. In the usual course of business the Butte bank's checks were sent by armored car to Great Falls for processing. Ordinarily, the checks would leave Butte at 5:00 or 6:00 p.m. on the day of receipt, arrive at Great Falls about 10:30 p.m., be processed by 11:30 p.m., be loaded back onto the armored car headed for Butte at 4:00 a.m. and arrive back in Butte at 7:00 a.m. *Sun River Cattle Co.,* supra, 521 P.2d at 684.

Unfortunately for the Butte bank, it received some checks on May 11, 1970. That day the armored car broke down and did not reach Great Falls until 1:30 a.m., May 12. Moreover, the computer in Great Falls malfunctioned with the result that the checks were not returned to Butte until 2:30 p.m. on May 12, rather than at 7:00 a.m. on that date. The Butte bank's "midnight deadline" for dishonoring the checks was midnight of May 12. Id. and U.C.C. § 4–104(1)(h) (our § 34–21–404(a)(viii)), supra. Thus, even though the armored car and computer breakdowns threw the bank off its normal schedule, it would have been physically possible for the bank to have dishonored the checks by midnight of May 12. The bank was unable to offer an explanation for failing to dishonor the checks by midnight of May 12.

The Montana court said:

> "Under the exception of section 4–108(2) the bank must show: (1) A cause for the delay; (2) that the cause was beyond the control of the bank; and (3) that under the circumstances the bank exercised such diligence as required. *In the absence of any one of these showings, the excuse for the delay will not apply,* and the bank will be held liable under the provisions of section 4–302...." (Emphasis added.) 521 P.2d at 686.

Along these lines our appellee urges that we note that there is no evidence in the record that the appellant bank made any efforts to trace the checks when they did not arrive in Sheridan aboard the Western Airlines flight as scheduled. Perhaps a trace started on the missing checks that morning would have enabled the bank to obtain the checks that day and meet the midnight deadline for dishonoring the insufficient-funds check which is the focus of this appeal.

However, although the appellant does not discuss this case, there is a distinguishing feature about *Sun River Cattle* which favors the appellant's cause. In the Montana case the checks in question were drawn on a business greatly indebted to the Butte bank and in precarious financial shape. The Montana court stated that it was holding the Butte bank to a stricter standard of proof under U.C.C. § 4–108(2) (our § 34–21–408(b)), supra, than would ordinarily be required. *Sun River Cattle*, supra, 521 P.2d at 685.

Our appellant bank relies almost solely on the Tenth Circuit case. *Port City State Bank*, supra. In this case the defendant, American National Bank, failed to timely dishonor two checks submitted to it by Port City State Bank. It was stipulated that the midnight deadlines for the two checks were December 1, and December 3. On December 1, American National computerized its operations and the computer broke down on its inauguration day. Despite assurances from the manufacturer that it could be repaired quickly, the computer was not repaired until late at night. When it became apparent that the computer could not be rapidly repaired, American National decided to use an identical computer in a bank some two and a half hours away, under a previous backup arrangement. Processing of checks was begun at 11:30 p.m. on December 1 on the backup bank's computer. Work was proceeding nicely on the backup computer when American National was notified by the computer manufacturer that its own computer was ready. The American National employees returned to their own bank. American National's computer worked for awhile and then broke down on December 2 and was rendered inoperable until a replacement part was installed on December 4. Because of the second failure of its new computer, American National Bank was again forced to utilize its backup arrangement. However, because of the distance between the American Bank and its backup computer, and the need of American to work around the schedule of the bank which owned the backup computer, American got behind in its processing.

The district court held that the cause of the delay in dishonoring the checks was the computer breakdowns, and the Tenth Circuit, applying its usual appellate rules, concluded that the holding was "not clearly erroneous." *Port City State Bank*, supra, 486 F.2d at 199. The Tenth Circuit also found that American reasonably relied on the assurance of the computer manufacturer that the initial malfunction could be repaired quickly; thus, the Tenth Circuit held that the bank was justified in not using the backup computer earlier. Id. at 200. Also, the Tenth Circuit accepted the argument that the bank's duty when the emergency became apparent was to remain open and serve its customers as best it could. "To abandon the orderly day by day process of bookkeeping to adopt radical emergency measures would have likely prolonged the delay in returning the bank to normal operations," the court said. Id. at 200.

As pointed out earlier, the Tenth Circuit stated in this case that it was the defendant bank's burden to prove an excuse under U.C.C. § 4–

108(2) (our § 34–21–408(b)), supra. We agree with our appellee in this case that the Tenth Circuit case is readily distinguishable from the case before us. The defendant bank in the Tenth Circuit case proved to the satisfaction of the trial court that it used the diligence required by the above statute and that its failure to timely dishonor the checks was due to circumstances beyond its control—computer breakdowns. The showing of diligence included proof of utilization of a backup system. In the case before us, there is no showing that defendant-appellant bank used any diligence when the packet of checks failed to arrive as scheduled on the flight from Montana.

The Kentucky case involved a failure to timely dishonor two checks. *Blake,* supra. The two checks in this case were presented for payment to the defendant bank on December 24, 1973, so that under the midnight-deadline rule the bank was responsible for dishonoring the checks by midnight of December 26, December 25, of course, being a bank holiday. *Blake,* supra, 555 S.W.2d at 591. Unfortunately for the bank, it did not send notice that it was dishonoring the checks until December 27. In the trial court the bank sought to justify the delay for several reasons. The bank presented evidence that while it normally processes only 4,200 to 4,600 checks a day, it had 6,995 to process on December 26. The bank had four posting machines but two broke down on December 26, one for two and a half hours and one for one and a half hours. Also, one of the four regular bookkeepers was absent on December 26 and had to be replaced by a less proficient substitute. The bank regularly employed a Purolator courier to pick up checks at 4:00 p.m. and take them to the Federal Reserve bank. Because of the above-described problems, the bank did not have the two checks in question processed on December 26 in time for the Purolator courier. Id. at 595–596.

The trial court found these excuses sufficient under U.C.C. § 4–108(2) (our § 34–21–408(b)), supra, to relieve the bank of liability under U.C.C. § 4–302 (our § 34–21–451), supra. The Kentucky appellate court reversed. The appellate court focused on additional facts. One of the bookkeepers had in fact discovered that there were insufficient funds to pay the two checks on December 26 after the Purolator courier left. However, because of "the lateness of the hour" there was no responsible bank official on the premises and the bookkeeper merely left the two checks on the desk of the bank official who was supposed to handle insufficient funds checks. Id. at 596. Thus, the bank did not send out notice that it was dishonoring the check until the next day.

The Kentucky appellate court concluded:

> "Even though the bank missed returning the two checks by the Purolator courier, it was still possible for the bank to have returned the checks by its midnight deadline. Under U.C.C. § 4–301(4)(b) [footnote] an item is returned when it is 'sent' to the bank's transferor, in this case the Federal Reserve Bank. Under U.C.C. § 1–201(38) [footnote] an item is 'sent'

when it is deposited in the mail. 1 R. Anderson, Uniform Commercial Code § 1–201 pp. 118–119 (2d ed. 1970). Thus, the bank could have returned the two checks before the midnight deadline by the simple procedure of depositing the two checks in the mail, properly addressed to the Cincinnati branch of the Federal Reserve Bank.

"This court concludes that circumstances beyond the control of the bank did not prevent it from returning the two checks in question before its midnight deadline on December 26. The circumstances causing the delay in the bookkeeping department were foreseeable. On December 26, the bank actually discovered that the checks were 'bad,' but the responsible employees and officers had left the bank without leaving any instructions to the bookkeepers. The circuit court erred in holding that the bank was excused under § 4–108 from meeting its midnight deadline. The facts found by the circuit court do not support its conclusion that the circumstances in the case were beyond the control of the bank." 555 S.W.2d 596–597.

The cases discussed above persuade us that the appellant bank has failed to prove an excuse sufficient under § 34–21–408(b) (U.C.C. § 4–108(2)), supra, to enable it to escape liability under § 34–21–451 (U.C.C. § 4–302), supra, for its failure to dishonor the check in question by the midnight deadline imposed by the U.C.C.

The judgment of the district court is affirmed.

Notes

(1) **Expeditious Return and Midnight Deadline.** Under Regulation CC 229.38(b), a bank that fails both to comply with its obligation of expeditious return under Section 229.30(a) and to comply with the deadline for return under UCC 4–302 is liable under either Section 229.30(a) or UCC 4–302, but not both. Which basis of liability would be more advantageous for the claimant?

Regulation CC 229.38(c), which details the excuses available to a payor bank for noncompliance with its obligation of expeditious return, resembles UCC 4–108, which details the excuses available to a payor bank for failure to meet its midnight deadline under UCC 4–302. Regulation CC lists two excuses not listed by former UCC 4–108: "interruption of . . . computer facilities" and "failure of equipment." Both have now been added to UCC 4–108.

(2) **When the Midnight Deadline Begins to Run.** According to UCC 4–104(a)(10), the payor bank's midnight deadline begins to run on "the banking day on which it receives the relevant item." But UCC 4–108 allows the bank to "fix an afternoon hour of 2 P.M. or later as a cutoff hour for the handling of . . . items," and an item "received on any day after a cutoff hour so fixed . . . may be treated as being received at the opening of the next banking day."

Comment 1 to UCC 4–108 explains: "Each of the huge volume of checks processed each day must go through a series of accounting procedures that consume time. Many banks have found it necessary to establish a cutoff hour to allow time for these procedures to be completed within the time limits imposed by Article 4. Subsection (a) approves a cutoff hour of this type provided it is not earlier than 2 P.M. Subsection (b) provides that if such a cutoff hour is fixed, items received after the cutoff hour may be treated as being received at the opening of the next banking day. If the number of items received either through the mail or over the counter tends to taper off radically as the afternoon hours progress, a 2 P.M. cutoff hour does not involve a large portion of the items received but at the same time permits a bank using such a cutoff hour to leave its doors open later in the afternoon without forcing into the evening completion of its settling and proving process."

(3) Branches and the Midnight Deadline. If a check drawn on one branch of a bank is deposited in another branch of the same bank, is the midnight deadline determined by the time that the check is received by the branch in which it is deposited or the branch on which it is drawn? See UCC 4–107. When was the check in the *Kirby* case received by the payor bank for this purpose? See footnote 1, p. 182 supra.

(4) Automation and the Midnight Deadline. Suppose that a bank has a data processing center that serves all the bank's branches. Is the running of the period that determines the midnight deadline under UCC 4–302 triggered by the receipt of the check at the data processing center or by the subsequent receipt of the check by the payor bank?

Courts gave conflicting answers under the Code. Thus in Idah–Best v. First Security Bank, 99 Idaho 517, 584 P.2d 1242 (1978), the court held that the period was not triggered until receipt by the payor bank. But in Central Bank of Alabama v. Peoples National Bank, 401 So.2d 14 (Ala.1981), the Supreme Court of Alabama declined to apply *Idah–Best*, concluding that the computer was "an integral part" of the bank. To postpone the running of the period until receipt by the payor bank, the court reasoned, would "thwart the very purpose of the midnight deadline: to encourage prompt return of dishonored checks" and "would have the effect of allowing the payor bank to unilaterally decide when the midnight deadline would begin to run by the simple device of choosing the time to forward the check to the branch."

Regulation CC 229.36(b)(1) takes this latter position adopting, as Comment 36(b) puts it, "the common-law rule of a number of legal decisions that the processing center acts as the agent of the paying bank to accept presentment and to begin the time for processing of the check."

(5) Liability not "Absolute". The payor bank's liability under UCC 4–302 is not based on fault. Nonetheless, subsection (b) gives a payor bank the defense "that the person seeking enforcement of the liability presented or transferred the item for the purpose of defrauding the payor bank." Comment 3 explains: "Decisions that hold an accountable bank's liability to be 'absolute' are rejected. A payor bank that makes a late return of an item should not be liable to a defrauder operating a check kiting scheme. In Bank Leumi Trust Co. v. Bally's Park Place, Inc., 528 F.Supp. 349 (S.D.N.Y.1981), and American National Bank v. Foodbasket, 497 P.2d 546 (Wyo.1972), banks that were accountable under Section 4–302 for missing their midnight deadline were successful in defending against parties who initiated collection knowing that the check would not be paid."

(6) **Underencoded Checks.** Suppose that a bank receives for deposit a $255,000 check drawn on it, erroneously encodes the amount as $25,000, and credits the payee and charges the drawer in that amount. Months later, when the error is discovered, the drawer has closed its account and gone out of business. Is the bank liable to the payee for $230,000? That is what happened in SOS Oil Corp. v. Norstar Bank of Long Island, 76 N.Y.2d 561, 561 N.Y.S.2d 887, 563 N.E.2d 258 (1990). In an opinion by Judge Kaye, the court held for the payee.

"The Uniform Commercial Code imposes distinct accountability on payor banks, providing in section 4–302 that: 'In the absence of a valid defense such as breach of a presentment warranty (subsection [1] of Section 4–207), settlement effected or the like, if an item is presented on and received by a payor bank the bank is accountable for the amount of * * * a demand item other than a documentary draft whether properly payable or not if the bank, in any case where it is not also the depositary bank, retains the item beyond midnight of the banking day of receipt without settling for it or, regardless of whether it is also the depositary bank, does not pay or return the item or send notice of dishonor until after its midnight deadline'.

"Absent certain defenses, a payor bank, even when also functioning as a depositary bank, may by the operation of UCC 4–302 be held accountable to a payee for the amount of a check presented for immediate payment when it fails to pay, return or send notice of dishonor before the midnight deadline—that is, midnight of the next banking day following the banking day on which the bank receives the check.... A payor bank's delay is thus tantamount to final payment of the item according to its tenor.... The statute makes the bank fully accountable whether it has paid nothing or—as here—something less than the face amount of the instrument....

"The midnight deadline rule of UCC 4–302 places a heavy burden on payor banks—one that exceeds that of depositary or collecting banks, which can reduce their obligation by the amount that could not have been recovered had ordinary care been used.... The heavy burden imposed by UCC 4–302 serves important commercial purposes: it expedites the collection process by motivating banks to process instruments quickly, and it firms up the provisional credits received by each bank in the collection chain, thereby supplying a key element of certainty in commercial paper transactions.... By requiring that deficiencies in a drawer's account be determined swiftly, the midnight deadline rule is a vital part of the payor bank's role in assuring the integrity of commercial paper....

"In the present case, it is undisputed that [the payee's] check and deposit slip were in all respects regular and accurate, that the only actual mistake was [the bank's], and that [the bank] retained the check past its midnight deadline. Under UCC 4–302, [the bank] is therefore accountable for the face amount of the check."

Suppose that the check had not been an on-us item and that it was the depositary bank that made the encoding error before forwarding it to the payor bank. Is the payor bank liable to the payee for $230,000? If so, has the payor bank a claim against the depositary bank? See UCC 4–209.

What difference would it make in either case if the drawer had over $230,000 in its account? See Comment 2 to UCC 4–209.

DAVID GRAUBART, INC. v. BANK LEUMI TRUST CO.

Court of Appeals of New York, 1979.
48 N.Y.2d 554, 423 N.Y.S.2d 899, 399 N.E.2d 930.

FUCHSBERG, JUDGE. On this appeal, here on a question certified by the Appellate Division pursuant to CPLR 5602 (subd. [b], par. 1), we are called upon to determine the role played by article 4 of the Uniform Commercial Code in fixing rights and obligations arising out of a second presentment of a check previously returned for insufficient funds. The heart issue is whether a payor bank is relieved of liability for retaining such an instrument beyond its "midnight deadline" (see Uniform Commercial Code, § 4–302) when it does so pursuant to an agreement concordant with a practice among banks for a payor to hold a previously dishonored item long enough to provide an opportunity for sufficient funds to be deposited by the drawer to meet the check.

The operative facts are uncomplicated. Plaintiff David Graubart, Inc. (payee), was issued a check for $13,000 drawn by the Prins Diamond Company on the latter's account with the defendant Bank Leumi Trust Company (payor bank). Graubart then deposited the check in its own account with the National Bank of North America (depositary bank), which, pursuing normal collection channels, routed it to the payor bank via the New York Clearing House.[1] When the payor bank found that the Prins account had been overdrawn, it marked the item "insufficient funds" and promptly returned it to the depositary

---

1. A clearing house, of course, is a facility for transferring checks and other items to and from depositary banks and payor banks and for settling the balances due among them as a result of such transactions (see 8 Michie, Banks and Banking, ch. 18, § 1, p. 331, and n. 1).

bank, again through clearing house channels. Notified of the dishonor, the payee redeposited the check with its bank, which this time apparently chose to forward it directly to Leumi on a collection basis, thus bypassing the clearing house (see Uniform Commercial Code, § 4–204, subd. [2], par. [a]). The item was accompanied by an "advice to customer" slip—a copy of which was also delivered to Graubart—indicating, as with collection items generally, that credit would only be given on payment. In addition, in a space bearing the printed legend "Special Instruction: (Return immediately if not paid unless otherwise instructed)", the slip contained a typed direction that the payor bank was to "remit [its] cashiers' [sic] check when paid" (cf. Uniform Commercial Code, § 4–211, subd. [1], par. [b]). But when, after no more than seven banking days, the drawer's account remained bare of funds to permit the check to clear, Leumi again returned the check to the depositary bank. Sometime during the course of these transactions the drawer made an assignment for the benefit of creditors.

The gravamen of the fourth cause of action[2] in the suit the payee thereafter commenced against Leumi, as well as of its subsequent motion for summary judgment, was that the latter's failure to return the resubmitted check to the depositary bank before its "midnight deadline"—defined as midnight of the next banking day following that on which the item was received (Uniform Commercial Code, § 4–104, subd. [1], par. [h])—without more, rendered it liable to the payee for the face amount of the check under subdivision (a) of section 4–302 of the Uniform Commercial Code. This section, with seeming finality, provides, in pertinent part, that "if an item is presented on and received by a payor bank the bank is accountable[3] for the amount of . . . a demand item . . . if the bank . . . retains the item beyond midnight of the bank day of receipt without settling for it or . . . does not pay or return the item or send notice of dishonor until after its midnight deadline."

In opposition, and in support of its own cross motion, the payor bank submitted an affidavit by its assistant vice-president, who, after setting out his knowledge of banking practice, asserted that the "advice to customer" slip constituted a memorandum of an agreement requiring it to process the instrument in question in accordance with a common banking practice whereunder previously dishonored checks were to be held for such time as is reasonable under all the circumstances, even beyond the midnight deadline if necessary, to enable funds from which to pay them to come into the account. To this the payee's only reply was in the form of counsel's affirmation. Aside from a bald assertion, for which no foundation was supplied, challenging the existence of the custom, the affirmation merely interjected, for the first time, unsupported allegations of bad faith and collusion on Leumi's

---

2. The other causes of action in the payee's complaint challenged the timeliness of the payor bank's action in processing the check upon its initial deposit. These claims have been dismissed and are not before us on this appeal.

3. (I.e., liable, Rock Is. Auction Sales v. Empire Packing Co., 32 Ill.2d 269, 204 N.E.2d 721; Sun Riv. Cattle Co. v. Miners Bank, 164 Mont. 237, 521 P.2d 679.)

part. Though it stated that the drawer was indebted to Leumi at the time of the assignment for the benefit of creditors, it made no showing of any unfair conduct on the part of the payor bank whatsoever.

Special Term denied both motions, holding that triable issues existed, and the Appellate Division, over a vigorous dissent by Mr. Justice Joseph P. Sullivan, has since affirmed. In thereafter granting leave to appeal to this court, it posed the very broad question: "Was the order of the Supreme Court, as affirmed by this Court, properly made?" For the reasons that follow, we conclude a negative response is mandated.

The payor bank's assault on the conclusion of the courts below is grounded on the contention that there were no factual issues precluding summary judgment and that, on the undisputed facts, its actions were proper as a matter of law for two reasons: (1) on the authority of Leaderbrand v. Central State Bank, 202 Kan. 450, 450 P.2d 1, it need not have given the payee notice of dishonor upon representment of the previously dishonored item, and (2) its conduct in varying the code's midnight deadline pursuant to a valid agreement which accords with custom and usage in the banking community relieves it of the effect of the provisions of article 4 (citing, *inter alia*, Uniform Commercial Code, § 4–103).

The preliminary dispute as to the existence of unresolved questions of fact need not detain us. The date of the contested transactions and the nonadherence to the midnight deadline, if applicable, were conceded for the purposes of the motion. The payor bank's officer established the custom as to collection of previously dishonored checks, and the payee's own submission of the "advice to customer" slip confirmed that the agreement had been made in contemplation of the custom. And, since Graubart's counsel's affirmation was made without personal knowledge of the facts, it was not competent to defeat the motion for summary judgment (Rotuba Extruders v. Ceppos, 46 N.Y.2d 223, 229, n. 4, 413 N.Y.S.2d 141, 144, 385 N.E.2d 1068, 1071; Columbia Ribbon & Carbon Mfg. Co. v. A–1–A Corp., 42 N.Y.2d 496, 500, 398 N.Y.S.2d 1004, 1007, 369 N.E.2d 4, 7; CPLR 3212, subd. [b]; see, generally, Mallad Constr. Corp. v. County Fed. Sav. & Loan Assn., 32 N.Y.2d 285, 292–293, 344 N.Y.S.2d 925, 931–932, 298 N.E.2d 96, 100–101). Leumi's recitations therefore went undisputed.

Turning to the legal merits, we conclude first that Leumi's reliance on Leaderbrand v. Central State Bank, 202 Kan. 450, 450 P.2d 1, supra, which held that no notice of dishonor need be given as to an item previously returned for insufficient funds, is unavailing. The *Leaderbrand* court reasoned that subdivision (4) of section 3–511 of the code, in excusing further notice of dishonor with respect to "drafts" once dishonored by "nonacceptance", necessarily encompassed dishonor of "checks" by "nonpayment". But, while a check is a kind of draft (Uniform Commercial Code, § 3–104, subd. [2], par. [b]), "nonpayment" and "nonacceptance" are distinctly different concepts, the latter referring specifically to a payor's refusal to certify that it will honor a *time* instrument when later presented for payment (Uniform Commercial Code, § 3–410, subd. 1; see Wiley v. Peoples Bank & Trust Co., 438 F.2d 513, 516–517 (5th Cir.); Comment, 18 Kan.L.Rev. 679, 682–684, n. 48). Since it would be futile to present for payment a draft that has been dishonored by nonacceptance (when the obligation is conditioned on acceptance [see Uniform Commercial Code, § 3–501, subd. (1), par. (a)]), such presentment and further notice are excused as superfluous. In contrast, a *demand* item such as a check may eventually be paid if resubmitted at a time when the drawer's account has an adequate balance. This possibility makes it entirely reasonable to afford rede-posited checks the full panoply of article 4 protections. (See, generally, Clark & Squillante, Law of Bank Deposits, Collections and Credit Cards [1970], pp. 71–72.)

Though its *Leaderbrand* point is, therefore, without merit, Leumi's argument that its retention of the check beyond its midnight deadline was consonant with its agreement with the depositary bank is another matter. In this connection, initially we note that section 4–301 of the code, which establishes the procedural rules enforced by section 4–302, nowhere suggests that the deadline does not apply to previously dishon-ored items. But, it is well recognized that the code's requirements can be modified by agreement to conform them with commercial usage, in or out of banking circles, so that parties may advantage themselves of the "wisdom born of accumulated experience" (Bankers Trust Co. v. Dowler & Co., 47 N.Y.2d 128, 134, 417 N.Y.S.2d 47, 50–51, 390 N.E.2d 766, 769).[4] [The court quoted UCC 4–103(1), (4).]

The concept of an "agreement" under the code is, as with contract law generally, broad enough to permit the written terms of a memoran-dum to be supplemented and clarified by reference to customs and usages in the commercial milieu in which it is to be performed (e.g., Uniform Commercial Code, § 1–201, subd. [3]; § 1–205; 3 Corbin, Contracts [1960 ed.], § 556; Walls v. Bailey, 49 N.Y. 464). But the bare fact that the payor bank acted in accordance with its agreement with the depositary bank does not, in and by itself, relieve the former of liability (Official Comment, McKinney's Cons.Laws of N.Y., Book 62½, part 2, Uniform Commercial Code, § 4–203, p. 555). Section 4–103 demands that every party sought to be bound—here the payee—have assented to the agreement's terms (Official Comment 2, op. cit., Uni-form Commercial Code, § 4–103, pp. 519–520). However, we hold that here there was such consent.

4. As the Official Comments explain: "In view of the technical complexity of the field of bank collections, the enormous number of items handled by banks, the certainty that there will be variations from the normal in each day's work in each bank, the certainty of changing conditions and the possibility of developing improved methods of collection to speed the process, it would be unwise to freeze present meth-ods of operation by mandatory statutory rules" (Official Comment 1, McKinney's Cons. Laws of N.Y., Book 62½, part 2, Uniform Commercial Code, § 4–103, p. 519).

Under section 4–201 of the code, a payee's presentment of an item to a depositary bank for collection creates a principal-agent relationship between the two, a status that persists until final settlement (see Official Comment 4, op. cit., Uniform Commercial Code, § 4–201, pp. 544–545). Graubart's voluntary establishment of its bank's authority constitutes an assent to the latter's dealing with the check in the manner customary in the banking industry (see Restatement, Agency 2d, § 36).[5] To the extent that a payee deems itself aggrieved by a depositary bank's ignoring of limitations on its authority, of which none are claimed here, the law provides recourse against it, but not against a third party who relies on the agent's apparent authority. . . .

As to good faith and ordinary care, neither of these is a serious obstacle in the circumstances of this case. The payee's complaint alleges no bad faith or favoritism on the part of the payor bank, and the mere fact that the drawer was indebted to Leumi when it assigned for the benefit of creditors does not permit us to presume collusion in the absence of specific evidence. Moreover, beyond the superficial sense in which ordinary care is relevant to virtually every step in the collection process (see Uniform Commercial Code, § 4–202, subd. [1]), this standard was not intended to prohibit banking procedures that themselves are reasonable and carried out with care. . . .

Further, in this case the reasonableness of the suspension of the midnight deadline is demonstrated by an examination of the underlying purpose of the rule. Far from merely encouraging banks to process deposited instruments promptly, the deadline plays the central role in "firming up" the provisional credit received by each transferor in the payee—depositary bank—intermediary bank[6] chain. Under section 4–213 of the code, provisional credits become final as soon as the payor bank settles for the item and the time for revocation under the midnight deadline passes. This point is particularly critical for banks that funnel hundreds or thousands of checks per day into the collection stream because it enables them to assume that payment has been effectuated after a certain period of time unless there is a prompt return. (See, generally, Blake v. Woodford Bank & Trust Co., 555 S.W.2d 589, 600–601 [Ky.App.]; Official Comments 7–11, op. cit., Uniform Commercial Code, § 4–213, pp. 591–593.)

These concerns, however, are irrelevant to any evaluation of the custom followed under the agreement between the banks here. It creates no provisional credits that must be firmed up, and the payee can only collect when the payor bank remits its cashier's check, thus signifying that the drawer's account received sufficient funds to cover the check. By its nature, the procedure singles out the item as an

---

5. The payee's second presentment of the check for payment was with full knowledge that its previous rejection was for insufficiency of the drawer's balance.

6. In some collection transactions convenience dictates that checks pass through so-called "intermediary banks" in addition to or instead of a clearing house before being forwarded to the payor bank (see Uniform Commercial Code, § 4–105, subd. [c]).

exceptional one; no transferor will assume it has been paid until specific notice is received.

Moreover, the concept of a midnight deadline is not compatible with any approach under which the payor bank seeks to wait for the deposit of funds in the drawer's account. The reasonableness of such a banking custom must, therefore, be measured on its own terms. We conclude that this criterion is met when a depositary bank takes a possibly worthless instrument and directs the payor bank to adopt a technique that may provide the only chance for collection.[7]

There is nothing unfair about this procedure. It is calculated to produce satisfied obligations in many instances where legal recourse, with all its attendant expense, inconvenience and uncertainty, would otherwise be necessary. Furthermore, the payee here cannot claim it was injured by its reliance on the payor bank's silence after receipt of the item; the prior dishonor provided adequate warning of the questionable safety of the instrument. In any event, the payee's right to sue the drawer on the underlying obligation was revived upon the first dishonor, and representment in no way cut short that prerogative (Uniform Commercial Code, § 3–802, subd. [1], par. [b]; § 4–301, subd. [3]; Blake v. Woodford Bank & Trust Co., supra, pp. 598–599).

We therefore hold that the payor bank's adherence to the depositary bank's instructions for processing the drawer's check does not render it liable to the payee under section 4–302. Accordingly, the certified question should be answered in the negative, the order of the Appellate Division reversed, and summary judgment granted in the defendant's favor on the fourth cause of action.[8]

Notes

(1) **Conflicting Views.** The *Leaderbrand case*, discussed and rejected in *David Graubart*, represents a minority view. The counterpart of former UCC 3–511(4), relied on in *Leaderbrand*, is UCC 3–502(f).

(2) **Variation by Agreement.** In Idaho Forest Industries v. Minden Exchange Bank & Trust Co., 212 Neb. 820, 326 N.W.2d 176 (1982), the depositary bank represented checks by mailing them directly to the payor bank with a transmittal letter that stated "Hold 10 days if necessary." The court followed the *Graubart* case on the ground that the midnight deadline had been varied by an agreement "that the checks were to be held for collection by the defendant for a reasonable time until funds became available."

---

7. Other than that the payor bank, permissibly, as we have demonstrated, did not feel bound by the deadline, the payee pointed to no facts indicating that the check was held for an unreasonable length of time.

8. Regulation CC Section 229.13(c) makes an explicit exception to the availability rules in the case of redeposited checks. The depositary bank may have an additional reasonable period of time of at least four days if it gives its depositor written notice of the extended hold. See Section 229.13(g), (h) [Eds.]

Is there any limit on the power of banks to vary the midnight deadline by agreement? Is the power limited to the situation of representment? Could banks by a clearinghouse rule agree that checks could be returned after the midnight deadline? See UCC 4–302 and 4–103(a) and (b), and recall the history of the midnight deadline recounted at p. 193 supra. Cf. Catalina Yachts v. Old Colony Bank & Trust Co., 497 F.Supp. 1227 (D.Mass.1980) (agreement that "receipt" occurred when payor bank had actual receipt of check and not when check was received by off-premises processing center was "mere definition of what action constitutes receipt").[1]

DEMISE OF "THE PROCESS OF POSTING"

Suppose that the payor bank has completed the usual procedure that it follows in determining to pay a check, including signature verification and determination that sufficient funds are available and that payment has not been stopped, and has stamped the check "paid" and charged it to the drawer's account. Is the check nevertheless not paid until the payor bank's midnight deadline has passed?

The drafters of former Article 4 provided that a check was paid when the payor bank had "completed the process of posting the item to the indicated account of the drawer" (former UCC 4–213(1)(c)). Bankers became concerned about how this language would be applied to an automated processing system in which checks were first run through a computer and automatically charged to the drawer's account. After subsequent human examination, checks that the payor bank decided to dishonor were then sent back through the computer and charges to the appropriate accounts reversed. Might a court conclude that "the process of posting" had been completed after the initial computer run?

Two important commercial states reached contrasting solutions. California simply deleted the offending language. But New York retained the language and added a definition of "the process of posting." The Code's Permanent Editorial board chose the New York solution and added the New York definition as former UCC 4–109. The comment to that section gave three illustrations of what was meant.

The New York solution was not, however, pellucid, and after several decades of confused litigation, the drafters of revised Article 4 opted for the California solution. Comment 5 to UCC 4–215 explains:

---

1. The Code's provisions on variation by agreement have a counterpart in Regulation CC 229.37. The commentary explains that, "as stated in official comment 2 to section 4–103, owners of items and other interested parties are not affected by agreements under this section unless they are parties to the agreement or are bound by adoption, ratification, estoppel, or the like. In particular, agreements varying this subpart that delay the return of a check beyond the times required by this subpart may result in liability under section 229.38 to entities not party to the agreement." The commentary goes on to note that, unlike the Code, Regulation CC does not treat Federal Reserve regulations and operating letters, clearinghouse agreements, and the like as agreements that may apply to parties that have not specifically assented.

"In the present Article, Section 4–109 has been deleted and the process-of-posting test has been abandoned in Section 4–215(a) for determining when final payment is made. Difficulties in determining when the events described in former Section 4–109 take place make the process-of-posting test unsuitable for a system of automated check collection or electronic presentment." The case that follows suggests some of the considerations that led to this decision.

- - -

MERRILL LYNCH, PIERCE, FENNER & SMITH, INC. v. DEVON BANK

United States Court of Appeals, Seventh Circuit, 1987.
832 F.2d 1005.

EASTERBROOK, CIRCUIT JUDGE. Manus, Inc., gave the Los Angeles office of Merrill Lynch, Pierce, Fenner & Smith, Inc., a check for $647,250 payable to Merrill Lynch's order. The check was drawn on Devon Bank in Chicago. Merrill Lynch immediately deposited the check with Crocker National Bank in Los Angeles; a clearing house presented the check to Devon for payment at 9:30 a.m. on Wednesday, August 1, 1979. The clearing house and Devon provisionally settled for the check immediately. Under § 4–301(1) of the Uniform Commercial Code, Devon had to decide no later than midnight of the next banking day whether to make final payment. See Ill.Rev.Stat. ch. 26 ¶ 4–301(1). Devon gave notice of dishonor at 4:22 p.m. on August 3. If this is too late, Devon is liable on the check even though Manus cannot cover the instrument. The district court thought the dishonor timely, 654 F.Supp. 506 (N.D.Ill.1987), and granted summary judgment to Devon in this diversity litigation.

I

The initial question is whether Devon gave notice of dishonor before the deadline on midnight of the "banking day" after it received the instrument. Under § 4–104(1)(c) of the UCC, a " 'banking day' means that part of any day on which a bank is open to the public for carrying on substantially all of its banking functions". On Wednesday, August 1, 1979, Devon's lobby was closed to the public. It offered services, essentially limited to deposits and withdrawals, at a walk-up window. No one could open an account or arrange for a loan; so far as the record reveals, no one could draw down a line of credit previously arranged. Merrill Lynch observes that on Wednesdays Devon processed checks and made inter-bank loans, but neither these nor related activities made it "open to the public" for "substantially all of its banking functions"....

Devon, which was open to the public for only the deposit side of the banking business on August 1, 1979, was not open for "substantially all" of the services of a bank.... The district court properly resolved this question by summary judgment. It would unacceptably disrupt commercial relations to put to a jury, case-by-case, the question whether a given day was a "banking day". Billions of dollars in transactions must be processed by every midnight deadline, and everyone has an interest in having this time defined with precision. The record supplies enough information to make decision possible. Devon's midnight deadline was 11:59 p.m. on Friday, August 3, 1979.

II

The midnight deadline is only the outside limit, however. Section 4–301(1) allows a bank to return an item if it acts "before it has made final payment (subsection (1) of Section 4–213) *and* before its midnight deadline" (emphasis added). Section 4–213(1) says that a settlement becomes final "when the bank has done any of the following, whichever happens first". The only subsection we need consider is § 4–213(1)(c), which provides that payment becomes final when the bank has "completed the process of posting the item to the indicated account of the drawer, maker, or other person to be charged therewith". Section 4–109 defines the process of posting, to which we return after stating some undisputed facts.

Manus, the maker of the check, had a subsidiary, Cash Reserve Management, Inc. Cash Management maintained an account in Boston. Manus gave its check to Merrill Lynch on July 26; on July 27 Manus deposited in Devon a check for an identical sum of which Cash Management was the maker. Devon promptly submitted that check for payment. Devon places a "hold" of three or four business days on uncollected funds. The Manus check was presented for payment on August 1, the fourth business day (the fifth if Devon counted Saturday, July 28).

When Devon receives a bundle of checks from its clearing house, its computers tally the checks to ensure that the clearing house has debited Devon the correct amount. During the evening, reader/sorter machines read the account code on each check and compute the balance in each active account; a computer compares the balance and activity information with information the bank maintains to facilitate the decision whether to pay checks. The computer prepares, by the morning of the next business day, several reports for the bank's staff. One report lists checks that have caused overdrafts in the account; another report lists checks that are subject to stop payment orders; a third report lists accounts in which uncollected funds are essential to cover the latest checks; there are more. The morning of the second business day, Devon returns most of the checks that appear on these lists— though its staff may elect to pay some of them. The bookkeeping department stamps checks "paid" and photographs them. Devon then examines the signatures on substantial checks. If the signature appears genuine (or if the bank elects not to examine the signature), Devon places the check in the customer's file. This process usually is completed in the afternoon.

Manus's check was processed in the ordinary course. The account contained about $1.2 million, more than enough to cover the check. About $650,000 of this represented the Cash Management check deposited on July 27. Devon's computer treated these as "collected" funds because the check had been deposited four or more business days ago. The uncollected funds reports of August 1 and 2 do not flag the Manus check. Devon verified the signature and placed the Manus check in the file during the afternoon of August 2. There it remained until 4:10 p.m. on August 3, when Continental Illinois National Bank told Devon by telephone that Cash Management's bank in Boston had dishonored the check of July 27. At 4:22 p.m. Devon gave telephonic notice of dishonor of the Manus check. Crocker Bank resubmitted the Manus check, which was dishonored a second time; Manus was placed in receivership on August 28.

Merrill Lynch, which prefers collecting from a solvent Devon Bank to standing in line as one of Manus's creditors, maintains that Devon "completed the process of posting the item" within the meaning of § 4–213(1)(c) during the afternoon of August 2, when it placed the check in the file. Devon had carried out all the steps in its ordinary process and planned to do nothing further. The process was free from operational error; no steps had been omitted, no judgmental blunders made along the way. Devon replies that it does not intentionally pay checks written against uncollected funds, to which Merrill Lynch responds that Devon made a business judgment to pay checks written against instruments that had been on deposit for four business days. Devon applied that rule to Manus's check, and the belated return of the item may show that four days was too short but does not undermine the conclusion that "the process of posting" had come to an end.

The district court sided with Devon, 654 F.Supp. at 509–10, relying on § 4–109, which provides:

> The "process of posting" means the usual procedure followed by a payor bank in determining to pay an item and in recording the payment including one or more of the following or other steps as determined by the bank:
>
> (a) verification of any signature;
>
> (b) ascertaining that sufficient funds are available;
>
> (c) affixing a "paid" or other stamp;
>
> (d) entering a charge or entry to a customer's account;
>
> (e) correcting or reversing an entry or erroneous action with respect to the item.

Devon completed its ordinary steps, including each of (a) through (d), but the court concluded that § 4–109(e) gives a bank the privilege to dishonor a check until the midnight deadline. To return the item is to "reverse" the entry. As the court put it, "Devon's returning the check ... demonstrated that the posting process was not completed" (654 F.Supp. at 510).

This reading of § 4–109(e) rips § 4–213(1)(c) out of the Uniform Commercial Code. Section 4–301(1) sets the midnight deadline as the last instant at which a check may be returned; § 4–213(1) lists four events that terminate the return privilege sooner. If the return of an item establishes that the "process of posting" was not completed, then § 4–213(1)(c) is meaningless. It is not beyond belief that statutes contain meaningless provisions, but a court should treat statutory words as dross only when there is no alternative. The Uniform Commercial Code is an uncommonly well drafted statute, with links among its provisions. Section 4–213(1) is there for a reason—to expedite the final settlement on checks, so that banks such as Devon Bank may make funds available to customers faster. The "midnight deadline", and "deferred posting" in general, is a concession to the flux of paper with which any bank must contend. See Official Comment 1 to § 4–301. Section 4–213(1)(c) provides that final payment should not take any longer than the bank actually requires to process each item. That function would be defeated if the bank could reverse any posting under § 4–109(e) until the midnight deadline.

Perhaps § 4–213(1)(c) causes more trouble than it is worth. It potentially calls for a case-by-case inquiry into the details of posting; a bank may defeat its function by dragging out its normal processes so that they consume the entire period allotted by § 4–301(1); the drawee's bank cannot rely on § 4–213(1)(c) to credit a customer's account, because it does not know how long the drawer's bank takes to post any given item. Considerations of this sort led the UCC's Permanent Editorial Board, now at work on a Uniform New Payments Code, to propose the repeal of § 4–213(1)(c). See Uniform New Payments Code P.E.B. Draft No. 3 at 267–68 (1983) (calling the criteria of § 4–109 "unworkable in locating the precise time of payment"). Draft No. 3 was not adopted, though for reasons unrelated to §§ 4–109 and 4–213(1)(c); the Board continues to contemplate the problem. See Fred H. Miller et al., Commercial Paper, Bank Deposits and Collections, and Commercial Electronic Fund Transfers, 42 Bus.Law. 1269, 1288 (1987). Until the Board makes a final revision in the model UCC and states delete § 4–213(1)(c)—if that should occur—our job is to enforce the statute.

That § 4–213(1)(c) has meaning is reinforced by Official Example 3 to § 4–109:

> A payor bank receives in the mail on Monday an item drawn upon it. The item is sorted and otherwise processed on Monday and during Monday night is provisionally recorded on tape by an electronic computer as charged to the customer's account. On Tuesday a clerk examines the signature of the item and makes other checks to determine finally whether the item should be paid. If the clerk determines the signature is valid and makes a decision to pay and all processing of this item is complete, e.g., at 12 noon on Tuesday, the "process of posting" is completed at that time. If, however, the clerk determines

that the signature is not valid or that the item should not be paid for some other reason, the item is returned to the presenting bank and in the regular Tuesday night run of the computer the debit to the customer's account for the item is reversed or an offsetting credit entry is made. In this case ... there has been no determination to pay the item, no completion of the process of posting and no payment of the item.

This puts the "payment" of the check at the completion of the bank's ordinary process, whatever that process may be. The check that passes the bank's internal controls and is posted to the account is "paid". None of the official comments suggests that a check that has been accurately handled in accordance with the bank's ordinary procedure nonetheless may be dishonored any time before the midnight deadline.

Doubtless we must give § 4–109(e) meaning, just as we must leave some function for § 4–213(1)(c). The Supreme Court of Wisconsin thought the language of § 4–109(e) so "plain" that it overrode § 4–213(1)(c). West Side Bank v. Marine National Exchange Bank, 37 Wis.2d 661, 669–72, 155 N.W.2d 587 (1968). That court read the language with this emphasis: "correcting or *reversing an entry* or erroneous action with respect to the item." The "reversing an entry" language, the court thought, allowed the bank to dishonor a check at any time before the midnight deadline, whether or not the processing had been completed without error. This reading is inconsistent with the official comments to § 4–109 and any plausible reason for making payment final on posting. As a result, the courts that have addressed the problem since 1968 have rejected *West Side*. Nelson v. Platte Valley State Bank & Trust Co., 805 F.2d 332 (8th Cir.1986); North Carolina National Bank v. South Carolina National Bank, 449 F.Supp. 616, 620 (D.S.C.1976); H. Schultz & Sons, Inc. v. Bank of Suffolk County, 439 F.Supp. 1137 (E.D.N.Y.1977); R. Hoag v. Valley National Bank, 147 Ariz. 137, 708 P.2d 1328 (1985). Students of the subject likewise disagree with the reading of § 4–109(e) proposed by *West Side,* although they are not entirely in accord on the meaning the section should take. E.g., William D. Hawkland & Lary Lawrence, 5 Uniform Commercial Code Series 323, 339–40, 345–46 (1984); James J. White & Robert S. Summers, Uniform Commercial Code § 16–4 & n. 38 (1980); Walter Malcolm, Reflections on *West Side Bank*: A Draftsman's View, 18 Catholic U.L.Rev. 23 (1968); Note, Bad Checks and the U.C.C.— When is a Check Finally Paid?, 9 B.C.Ind. & Com.L.Rev. 957 (1968). We think it likely that the Supreme Court of Illinois would follow *Nelson* and *Schultz* rather than *West Side.*

Section 4–109(e) does not simply say that a bank may reverse an entry; the full text of the section says that it may correct or reverse an entry or erroneous action. It is not possible to divorce the "reversing an entry" language from the words immediately before and after. If we group the words this way—"(correcting or reversing) an (entry or erroneous action)"—the statute makes sense. The bank may correct (alter) or reverse (set aside completely) an entry that should not have been made or an "erroneous action" that does not involve an "entry". This reading leaves a role for both § 4–109(e) and § 4–213(1)(c), and it also makes sense of the official comment to § 4–109, which states that when the bank's ordinary process is completed before the midnight deadline, the check has been paid.

Nelson, Schultz, and the commentators on the payments process have stressed that the decision to pay a check has both mechanical and judgmental components. The examination of the signature and the determination that an account has sufficient funds are mechanical; the decision whether to permit an overdraft in the account is judgmental. Section 4–109 allows a bank to follow its *ordinary* processes for dealing with both of these. There is nothing magical about putting the instrument in the customer's file. Suppose, for example, the bank mechanically puts all checks in customers' files and then makes random spot checks to verify signatures; that an item with a forged signature had to be pulled from the file to be returned would not prevent its dishonor. Or suppose the bank verifies signatures and puts the checks (stamped "paid") in customers' files before examining the computer printouts for stop payment orders. Again it would not be important that the bank had to remove the stopped check from the customer's file. The alternative—holding all checks in stasis until each of the bank's steps had been completed—would delay "final payment" for the checks as a group even longer, contrary to the purpose of § 4–213(1)(c). *West Side* may have been a case of this sort; if it was, we do not question its result even though its language was unduly broad. But none of this assists Devon. Its process—as Devon defines its process—had been completed by the afternoon of August 2. All of the check-specific steps, mechanical and judgmental, had been finished to the Bank's satisfaction. The system functioned as it was supposed to. True, Devon may wish that it had told its computer to assume that checks take five rather than four business days to clear, but regret over a managerial judgment in the design of the check processing system is not a reason to dishonor a check after it has been posted to the account and finally paid....

Reversed.

Problem 12. Philadelphia National, after giving Quaker a provisional credit, negligently mislays the check and does not forward it for three days. It is dishonored because Empire has become insolvent. Philadelphia National returns the check to Quaker and revokes the credit. Quaker disputes Philadelphia National's right to do this, arguing that the Empire check would have been paid if Philadelphia National had used due care. Quaker draws checks against the disputed $22,178.50 credit which Philadelphia National marks "N.S.F." and dishonors. Quaker sues Philadelphia National for wrongful dishonor. What result? See UCC 4–103(e), 4–202, 4–214(d) and Comment 5.

Problem 13. Philadelphia National and The Bank of New York use a system of electronic processing of checks in which the depositary bank "encodes" the amount of the check in a third "field" on the bottom right hand corner of the check, so that it can be "read" by a machine at the payor bank. (Compare Forms 2 and 2A pp. 131, 132 supra.) Philadelphia National mistakenly encodes the Empire check as a $32,178.50 check, and it is paid in that amount by The Bank of New York. Shortly thereafter, The Bank of New York dishonors several other checks drawn by Empire which would have been honored had the mistaken overpayment not been made. What are the rights of Empire and The Bank of New York? See UCC 4–209 and Comment 2. In J. Clarke, H. Bailey and R. Young, Bank Deposits and Collections 147–49 (4th ed. 1972) the authors state: "It would seem unlikely that the payor bank that had dishonored an over-encoded item, which if correctly encoded would have been paid, could recover damages arising out of the wrongful dishonor from the encoding bank in such circumstances, for presumably the payor bank would have had the 'last clear chance' to examine the item about to be returned and to discover the error." Does the doctrine of "last clear chance" apply to our problem? Could the banks involved allocate the risk by contract? See also H. Bailey, Brady on Bank Checks § 15.26 (5th ed. 1979).

Problem 14. On Friday, January 29, after The Bank of New York has paid the Empire check, a $15,000 check drawn by Quaker is presented to Philadelphia National for payment. Quaker has in its account, exclusive of the $22,178.50 credit from the Empire check, only $10,000. Philadelphia National dishonors the $15,000 check and returns it to the payee with a return item ticket marked "uncollected funds." Can Quaker recover from Philadelphia National for wrongful dishonor? Would the answer be different if the Empire check had been drawn on Penn Bank, another bank in Philadelphia? See Reg CC 229.12, 229.13(b).

Chapter 4

COUNTERMANDED CHECKS

Introduction. Some of the most troublesome problems concerning checks result from attempts by drawers to stop payment. Suppose, for example, that Buyer as drawer has issued a check to Seller as payee in payment for goods, and then discovers that Seller has breached a warranty and the goods are defective. As has already been observed, since a check is not of itself an assignment, Buyer as drawer retains the power to countermand the order to the payor bank. But if the check is dishonored as a result of a stop payment order, Buyer will still be subject to suit as drawer of the instrument.[1] Buyer may, however, set up by way of defense the breach of warranty that prompted the stop payment order. Should the check still be in the hands of Seller, the payee, this defense is, of course, good against Seller (UCC 3–305(a)(2)). Should the check have come into the hands of another, however, Buyer may be met with the claim that the instrument has been negotiated to a holder in due course against whom the defense is unavailable. The first section of this chapter takes up three aspects of this problem: first, when is there a negotiation; second, what are the requirements of holding in due course; and third, which are the real defenses, good even as against a holder in due course, and which the personal defenses, no good against a holder in due course? The second section considers the problems that arise when a bank mistakenly pays a check in violation of a stop payment order, including fixing the points in time at which it is too late for the drawer to stop payment. The third section considers the assertion of an adverse claim as an alternative to stopping payment.

SECTION 1. LIABILITY OF DRAWER
TO HOLDER ON DISHONOR

(A) NEGOTIATION

Prefatory Note. The Code, in UCC 3–201 and 3–203, distinguishes between transfer and negotiation. Although the transferee

---

1. Recall that, under UCC 3–504(a)(v), presentment of a check is excused if "the drawer instructed the drawee not to pay or accept" it.

221

acquires "any right of the transferor to enforce the instrument," a mere transferee cannot qualify as a holder in due course. According to UCC 3–201(b), "if an instrument is payable to an identified person, negotiation requires transfer of possession of the instrument and its indorsement by the holder," while if it "is payable to bearer it may be negotiated by transfer of possession alone." Most of the difficulties arise in connection with negotiation that requires indorsement.

THE BANK OF NEW YORK

STOP PAYMENT ORDER

STOP PAYMENT IS EFFECTIVE FOR SIX MONTHS

Date: January 26, 1993　Account No.: 5330858　Account Title: Empire Enterprises Co.

A stop payment has been placed on the item described below.

Check No.:	Check Date:	Payee/Description:	Amount:
2368	1/26/93	Quaker Manufacturing Co.	$22,178.50

The bank shall have reasonable time to process this Stop Payment order.

A Stop Payment fee will be posted directly to your account. Please adjust your records to reflect the charge to your account in the amount of $15.00.

[G14747]

Problem 1. Instead of depositing the Empire check in its account for collection, Quaker asks Philadelphia National to "cash" it, and Philadelphia National pays Quaker $22,178.50 in cash. Quaker, however, neglects to indorse the check and the Philadelphia National does not notice this. The check is then dishonored by The Bank of New York because Empire has stopped payment. Empire stopped payment on discovering that the cans are defective and on justifiably refusing to take and pay for them. Quaker is now insolvent. Can Philadelphia National recover the $22,178.50 from Empire? See UCC 3–201, 3–203, 4–205; *Bowling Green v. State Street Bank & Trust*, infra.

Problem 2. Instead of depositing the Empire check in its account for collection, Quaker asks Philadelphia National to "cash" it. Philadelphia National is willing to do so, but notices that Empire, evidently by an oversight, has made it payable to "Quaker Supply Co." How should Philadelphia National have Quaker indorse it if it cashes it? See UCC 3–204(d). Does it take any risk if Quaker so indorses it? See UCC 3–110(a).

BOWLING GREEN, INC. v. STATE STREET BANK AND TRUST CO.

United States Court of Appeals, First Circuit, 1970.
425 F.2d 81.

COFFIN, CIRCUIT JUDGE. On September 26, 1966, plaintiff Bowling Green, Inc., the operator of a bowling alley, negotiated a United States government check for $15,306 to Bowl–Mor, Inc., a manufacturer of bowling alley equipment. The check, which plaintiff had acquired through a Small Business Administration loan, represented the first installment on a conditional sales contract for the purchase of candle-pin setting machines. On the following day, September 27, a representative of Bowl–Mor deposited the check in defendant State Street Bank and Trust Co. The Bank immediately credited $5,024.85 of the check against an overdraft in Bowl–Mor's account. Later that day, when the Bank learned that Bowl–Mor had filed a petition for reorganization under Chapter X of the Bankruptcy Act, it transferred $233.61 of Bowl–Mor's funds to another account and applied the remaining $10,047.54 against debts which Bowl–Mor owed the Bank. Shortly thereafter, Bowl–Mor's petition for reorganization was dismissed and the firm was adjudicated a bankrupt. Plaintiff has never received the pin-setting machines for which it contracted. Its part payment remains in the hands of defendant Bank.

Plaintiff brought this diversity action to recover its payment from defendant Bank on the grounds that the Bank is constructive trustee of the funds deposited by Bowl–Mor. In the court below, plaintiff argued that Bowl–Mor knew it could not perform at the time it accepted payment, that the Bank was aware of this fraudulent conduct, and that the Bank therefore received Bowl–Mor's deposit impressed with a constructive trust in plaintiff's favor. The district court rejected plaintiff's view of the evidence, concluding instead that the Bank was a holder in due course within the meaning of Mass.Gen.Laws Ann. c. 106 §§ 4–209 and 3–302, and was therefore entitled to take the item in question free of all personal defenses. Bowling Green, Inc., etc. v. State Street Bank and Trust Co., 307 F.Supp. 648 (D.Mass.1969).

Plaintiff's appeal challenges the conclusion of the district court in three respects. First, plaintiff maintains that the Bank has not met its burden of establishing that it was "holder" of the item within the meaning of Mass.Gen.Laws Ann. c. 106 § 1–201(20), and thus cannot be a "holder in due course" within the meaning of § 4–209 and § 3–302.[1] Second, plaintiff argues that the Bank's close working relation with Bowl–Mor prevented it from becoming a holder in good faith. Finally, plaintiff denies that defendant gave value within the meaning of § 4–209 for the $10,047.54 which it set off against Bowl–Mor's loan account.

Plaintiff's first objection arises from a technical failure of proof. The district court found that plaintiff had endorsed the item in question to Bowl–Mor, but there was no evidence that Bowl–Mor supplied its own endorsement before depositing the item in the Bank. Thus we cannot tell whether the Bank is a holder within the meaning of § 1–201(20), which defines holder as one who takes an instrument endorsed to him, or to bearer, or in blank. But, argues plaintiff, once it is shown that a defense to an instrument exists, the Bank has the burden of showing that it is in all respects a holder in due course. This failure of proof, in plaintiff's eyes, is fatal to the Bank's case.

We readily agree with plaintiff that the Bank has the burden of establishing its status in all respects. Mass.Gen.Laws Ann. c. 106 § 3–307(3),[2] on which plaintiff relies to establish the defendant's burden, seems addressed primarily to cases in which a holder seeks to enforce an instrument, but Massachusetts courts have indicated that the policy of § 3–307(3) applies whenever a party invokes the rights of a holder in due course either offensively or defensively. Cf. Elbar Realty Inc. v.

---

1. Mass.Gen.Laws Ann. c. 106 § 4–209.

"When Bank gives Value for Purposes of Holder in Due Course. For purposes of determining its status as a holder in due course, the bank has given value to the extent that it has a security interest in an item provided that the bank otherwise complies with the requirements of section 3–302 on what constitutes a holder in due course."

Mass.Gen.Laws Ann. c. 106 § 3–302.

"Holder in Due Course.

(1) A holder in due course is a holder who takes the instrument

(a) for value; and

(b) in good faith; and

(c) without notice that it is overdue or has been dishonored or of any defense against or claim to it on the part of any person. ..."

2. Mass.Gen.Laws Ann. c. 106 § 3–307. "Burden of Establishing Signatures, Defenses and Due Course. ...

(3) After it is shown that a defense exists a person claiming the rights of a holder in due course has the burden of establishing that he or some person under whom he claims is in all respects a holder in due course."

City Bank & Trust Co., 342 Mass. 262, 267–268, 173 N.E.2d 256 (1961). The issue, however, is not whether the Bank bears the burden of proof, but whether it must establish that it took the item in question by endorsement in order to meet its burden. We think not. The evidence in this case indicates that the Bank's transferor, Bowl–Mor, was a holder. Under Mass.Gen.Laws Ann. c. 106, § 3–201(1), transfer of an instrument vests in the transferee all the rights of the transferor. As the Official Comment to § 3–201 indicates, one who is not a holder must first establish the transaction by which he acquired the instrument before enforcing it, but the Bank has met this burden here.

We doubt, moreover, whether the concept of "holder" as defined in § 1–201(20) applies with full force to Article 4. Article 4 establishes a comprehensive scheme for simplifying and expediting bank collections. Its provisions govern the more general rules of Article 3 wherever inconsistent. Mass.Gen.Laws Ann. c. 106 § 4–102(1). As part of this expediting process, Article 4 recognizes the common bank practice of accepting unendorsed checks for deposit. *See* Funk, Banks and the UCC 133 (1964). § 4–201(1) provides that the lack of an endorsement shall not affect the bank's status as agent for collection, and § 4–205(1) authorizes the collecting bank to supply the missing endorsements as a matter of course.[3] In practice, banks comply with § 4–205 by stamping the item "deposited to the account of the named payee" or some similar formula. Funk, supra at 133. We doubt whether the bank's status should turn on proof of whether a clerk employed the appropriate stamp, and we hesitate to penalize a bank which accepted unendorsed checks for deposit in reliance on the Code, at least when, as here, the customer himself clearly satisfies the definition of "holder". Section 4–209 does provide that a bank must comply "with the requirements of section 3–302 on what constitutes a holder in due course," but we think this language refers to the enumerated requirements of good faith and lack of notice rather than to the status of holder, a status which § 3–302 assumes rather than requires. We therefore hold that a bank which takes an item for collection from a customer who was himself a holder need not establish that it took the item by negotiation in order to satisfy § 4–209.

[The rest of the opinion in this case, dealing with plaintiff's remaining two objections, is at p. 233 infra.]

Notes

(1) Criticism of *Bowling Green* Case. Reaction to the *Bowling Green* case, on the indorsement issue, was largely negative. With respect to the reading of UCC 4–205(1), one court wrote: "Nothing in

---

3. See also § 4–105(2), which defines "depositary bank" in terms of transfer rather than negotiation, and § 4–206, which speaks of transfer between banks. For the difference between transfer and negotiation, compare § 3–201 with § 3–203.

this section or the comments indicates that a depository bank need not comply with endorsement requirements incident to the negotiation of 'order' paper if it seeks to be a holder. The purpose of the section is to permit the bank, in the interest of expediency ..., to supply what the bank could have required the customer to supply initially. Had § 4–205(1) been intended to eliminate the need for an endorsement ..., it would have been a simple matter for the drafters of the code to have [so] provided ...." United Overseas Bank v. Veneers, Inc., 375 F.Supp. 596 (D.Md.1973). With respect to the reading of UCC 3–201(1), another court wrote: "If the *Bowling Green* court intended to say that a transfer by a holder without indorsement gives the transferee the status of a holder, that statement is irreconcilable with the language of section 3201 ...." Security Pacific National Bank v. Chess, 58 Cal. App.3d 555, 129 Cal.Rptr. 852 (1976).

(2) **Utility of Indorsements and Revised Article 4.** In 1957 Parliament enacted the Cheques Act, which had as its principal objective elimination of the necessity for British banks to examine indorsements. It was found that over ninety-five per cent of the 800 million checks processed by British banks each year were deposited to the payees' accounts for collection through banking channels. Banks and commercial customers objected to the expense and inconvenience in indorsing and examining these checks. For a discussion of the British legislation see 71 Harv.L.Rev. 1374 (1958), and for its effect, see Perry, The Cheques Act 1957—The Experience of the Banks, 1967 J.Bus.Law 107.

Revised Article 4 takes the same approach in UCC 4–205. The comment to that section explains: "Section 3–201(b) provides that negotiation of an instrument payable to order requires indorsement by the holder. The rule of former Section 4–205(1) was that the depositary bank may supply a missing indorsement of its customer unless the item contains the words 'payee's indorsement required' or the like. The cases have differed on the status of the depositary bank as a holder if it fails to supply its customer's indorsement. Marine Midland Bank, N.A. v. Price, Miller, Evans & Flowers, 446 N.Y.S.2d 797 (N.Y.App.Div. 4th Dept.1981), *rev'd*, 455 N.Y.S.2d 565 (N.Y.1982). It is common practice for depositary banks to receive unindorsed checks under so-called 'lockbox' agreements from customers who receive a high volume of checks. No function would be served by requiring a depositary bank to run these items through a machine that would supply the customer's indorsement except to afford the drawer and the subsequent banks evidence that the proceeds of the item reached the customer's account. Paragraph (1) provides that the depositary bank becomes a holder when it takes the item for deposit if the depositor is a holder. Whether it supplies the customer's indorsement is immaterial. Paragraph (2) satisfies the need for a receipt of funds by the depositary bank by imposing on that bank a warranty that it paid the customer or deposited the item to the customer's account. This warranty runs not only to collecting banks and to the payor bank or nonbank drawee but also to the drawer, affording protection to these parties that the depositary bank received the item and applied it to the benefit of the holder."

How would the *Bowling Green* case have been decided under UCC 4–205?

(3) Special Indorsement of Bearer Paper. The Code made a major change with respect to the effect of a special indorsement on bearer paper. The rule at common law was "once bearer paper always bearer paper." This rule was applied when a special indorsement was put on an instrument that was either (1) issued payable to bearer or (2) issued payable to order and later indorsed in blank. The subsequent special indorsement did not convert the instrument to an order instrument in either case.

It was commonly supposed that the Negotiable Instruments Law had the effect of changing the result in the second case but not the first case. In other words, a special indorsement still had no effect on an instrument issued payable to bearer.

The Code reverses the common law rule in both cases. Under UCC 3–109(c), "An instrument payable to bearer may become payable to an identified person if it is specially indorsed pursuant to Section 3–205(a)." Under UCC 3–205(a), an indorsement is a "special indorsement" if it "identifies a person to whom it makes the instrument payable," even if the instrument is payable to bearer, and when so indorsed it "becomes payable to the identified person and may be negotiated only by the indorsement of that person."

(B) Holding in Due Course

Prefatory Note. In order to qualify as a holder in due course, a holder must satisfy the tests of UCC 3–302. The holder must have taken "in good faith," "without notice," and "for value." The following materials examine these requirements, in relation to checks.

Problem 3. If in Problem 1, supra, Quaker indorses the check in such a way that Philadelphia National is a holder and has Philadelphia National cash it, can Philadelphia National recover the $22,178.50 from Empire? See UCC 3–302, 3–103(a)(4). Would it make a difference if Empire can prove that it is highly unusual for banks in the Philadelphia area to cash a check for such a large amount? Would it make a difference if the assistant cashier of the Philadelphia National telephones a vice president of The Bank of New York before cashing the Empire check and is assured that the check is "good" and that The Bank of New York has had no problems with Empire's checks in the past? Would it make a difference if the assistant cashier is told that Empire's balance in The Bank of New York is too low to cover the check? See *Industrial National Bank v. Leo's Used Car Exchange,* infra. Who has the burden of proof on the issue of "good faith"? See UCC 3–308(b), 1–201(8).

Problem 4. Assuming that the facts in the preceding problem are such that Philadelphia National takes in good faith, would it make any difference if Quaker does not have Philadelphia National cash the check until six months after its issue? See UCC 3–302, 3–304(a).

INDUSTRIAL NATIONAL BANK v. LEO'S USED CAR EXCHANGE

Supreme Judicial Court of Massachusetts, 1973.
362 Mass. 797, 291 N.E.2d 603.

HENNESSEY, JUSTICE. This is an action in contract in which the plaintiff seeks to recover on two checks drawn by the defendant on the Security National Bank, one in the amount of $9,650 payable to Villa's Auto Sales, Inc., and the other in the amount of $5,500 payable to Villa's Auto Sales. The District Court judge found for the defendant, and the report to the Appellate Division was dismissed. The case is before us on appeal by the plaintiff.

We summarize the relevant evidence. On October 9, 1968, an agent of the defendant attended a car auction in the State of Connecticut, and purchased three cars from Frederick Villa, for which he gave the two checks described above. The defendant subsequently resold the cars at a profit.

Frederick Villa was a customer of the plaintiff bank and had a corporate account there under the name of Villa Auto Sales, Inc. The manager of the Centerville Branch of the plaintiff bank in Providence, Rhode Island, was personally acquainted with Frederick Villa. Corporate authority stating that Frederick Villa was the president and treasurer of Villa Auto Sales, Inc., and that he was authorized to sign or indorse any check held by the corporation, was on file with the bank.[1]

---

1. The material provisions of this authority are as follows:

"Voted: That the President–Vice President–Treasurer or Secretary of this Corporation, signing singly and their successors in office, be and they hereby are authorized to sign, endorse or deposit on behalf of this Corporation, any and all checks drawn or held by this Corporation, and the use is hereby authorized of a rubber stamp endorsement on any check the proceeds of which are credited to any account of this Corporation with the Bank.

"Voted: That the Bank is hereby directed to pay or apply without limit as to amount, without inquiry and without regard to the application of the proceeds thereof, any or all checks of this Corporation when signed by the personnel set forth in the preceding vote and in the manner specified therein, including any such check drawn to the individual order of any person whose signature appears thereon or of any officer or officers,

Frederick Villa presented both checks to the plaintiff bank on October 10, 1968, and as was his practice, asked the teller to cash them and give him the cash since he was going to another auction and needed it. The checks were cashed and sent through the bank collection process. Meanwhile, the defendant stopped payment on the checks at the Security National Bank in Springfield, Massachusetts, following a telephone call from an officer of the Rhode Island Hospital Trust Company which claimed to hold security interests in the cars he purchased. Consequently, the checks were not honored when presented, and were returned to the plaintiff bank.

There was also evidence of a rule at the plaintiff bank that any corporate checks drawn on another bank must be approved by the manager before being cashed by a teller. In this case, the teller did not obtain the manager's approval before he cashed both checks. However, the manager would cash a check for a corporation if he knew the person cashing the check and knew his business.

The plaintiff requested, among others, a ruling that there was no evidence that in cashing both checks it did not act in good faith. While the District Court judge found that the plaintiff met all the other requirements to qualify as a holder in due course, he denied this request and therefore found that the plaintiff was not a holder in due course of either check. The report to the Appellate Division was dismissed. The plaintiff claims an appeal on the basis that there was no evidence to support the District Court judge's finding of lack of good faith.

1. We first determine which State's law applies. The Appellate Division held that since the checks were negotiated in Rhode Island, its law should apply. See Restatement 2d: Conflict of Laws, § 216(2). This was erroneous. Conflict of law problems arising under the Uniform Commercial Code are resolved by the Code. The rule is stated in G.L. c. 106, § 1–105.[2] Since no special provision for Article three—Commercial Paper—is contained in paragraph (2) of § 1–105, paragraph (1) applies to this case. G.L. c. 106, § 3–102(4). Since there is no evidence that the parties agreed that a particular State's[3] law would

agent or agents, of this Corporation, which may be deposited with, or delivered or transferred to, the Bank, or any other individual, firm or corporation for the personal credit or account of any such person, officer or agent; and the Bank shall not be liable for any disposition which any such person, officer or agent shall make of all or any part of the proceeds of any such check, notwithstanding that such disposition may be for the personal account or benefit or in payment of the individual obligation to the Bank of any such person, officer or agent."

2. Section 1–105, inserted by St.1957, c. 765, § 1, reads in part: "(1) Except as

provided hereafter in this section, when a transaction bears a reasonable relation to this state and also to another state or nation the parties may agree that the law either of this state or of such other state or nation shall govern their rights and duties. Failing such agreement this chapter applies to transactions bearing an appropriate relation to this state."

3. Since the parties could have selected any State to which the transaction bore a reasonable relation, Rhode Island, Connecticut or Massachusetts could have been eligible. G.L. c. 106, § 1–105(1). Since all three States have adopted the Uniform Commercial Code, § 3–302, any choice may have had little consequence. See G.L. (R.I.

apply, and since the transaction bears an appropriate relation to this State, Massachusetts law applies. G.L. c. 106, § 1–105(1).

2. A holder in due course is a holder who takes the instrument for value, in good faith, and without notice that it is overdue or has been dishonored or of any defense against or claim to it on the part of any person. G.L. c. 106, § 3–302(1). To the extent that a holder is a holder in due course he takes the instrument free from all claims to it on the part of any person, and all defences of any party to the instrument with whom the holder has not dealt (personal defences) except specifically enumerated "real defences," G.L. c. 106, § 3–305.

The District Court judge found that the plaintiff was a holder who took the checks for value, and without notice that they had been dishonored or of any defence against or claim to the checks on the part of any person. However, the judge found that the checks were not taken in good faith, and therefore the plaintiff was not a holder in due course. Since the judge also found that a defence existed, he found for the defendant. See G.L. c. 106, § 3–306. The only substantive issue before us is whether or not the evidence supports the finding of the judge that the plaintiff did not take the checks in good faith. If it is found that the plaintiff did take the checks in good faith, it is clear that it is entitled to judgment in its favor in the absence of real defences. G.L. c. 106, § 3–305. No evidence of any real defence appears in the report.

The defendant argues that the plaintiff failed to exercise ordinary care in this transaction by violating the plaintiff's own rule of management when its teller cashed these checks without managerial approval. The defendant points to this as evidence of lack of good faith, which would support the judge's finding. Since there is no other evidence in the report which even arguably goes to the issue of good faith, we conclude that there was no evidence to support a finding of lack of good faith, and therefore both the District Court judge and the Appellate Division were in error.

"Good faith" as used in G.L. c. 106, § 3–302(1)(b), is defined in G.L. c. 106, § 1–201(19), as "honesty in fact in the conduct or transaction concerned." G.L. c. 106, § 3–102(4). Nothing in the definition suggests that in addition to being honest, the holder must exercise due care to be in good faith. Where the Uniform Commercial Code has required more than "honesty in fact" it has explicitly so stated: as in the case of a payor in Article 3—Commercial Paper—who pays on an instrument which has been altered or has an unauthorized signature (good faith and in accordance with the reasonable commercial standards of his business) § 3–406; as in the case of a merchant in Article 2—Sales (honesty in fact and the observance of reasonable commercial standards of fair dealing in the trade) § 2–103(1)(b); as in the case of a bailee in Article 7—Documents of Title (good faith including observance of reasonable commercial standards) § 7–404; and as in the case of an

1956), § 6A–3–302, and Conn.Gen.Sts.Ann. § 42a–3–302 (1962).

agent or bailee in Article 8—Investment Securities (good faith, including observance of reasonable commercial standards if he is in the business of buying, selling or otherwise dealing with securities) § 8–318. Each word of a statute is presumed to be necessary. Hence, if good faith as defined by § 1–201(19) and applicable to § 3–302(1)(b) included the observance of due care or reasonable commercial standards, the additional words used in the articles cited above would be surplusage.

This conclusion which is so clear from the Uniform Commercial Code itself, is supported by the legislative history of § 3–302(1)(b). Reference to "reasonable commercial standards" in the definition of a holder in due course of a negotiable instrument in the 1951 Final Text Edition [4] was deleted by the Editorial Board for the Uniform Commercial Code. Section 3–302(1)(b) of the 1956 Recommendations and text [5] reads as follows: "in good faith [including observance of the reasonable commercial standards of any business in which the holder may be engaged]." (P. 102) As the comment states: "The omission [of the bracketed material] is intended to make clear that the doctrine of an objective standard of good faith, exemplified by the case of Gill v. Cubitt, 3 B. & C. 466 (1824), is not intended to be incorporated in Article 3." (P. 103) Our conclusion is also supported by the pre-code case of Macklin v. Macklin, 315 Mass. 451, 455, 53 N.E.2d 86, 88, where we said, "The rights of a holder of a negotiable instrument are to be determined by the simple test of honesty and good faith, and not by a speculative issue as to his diligence or negligence."

This is not to say that negligence has no role in the determination of a holder's status as a holder in due course under § 3–302.[6] But negligence goes to the notice requirement of § 3–302(1)(c), as defined by § 3–304, and § 1–201(25). See also § 3–406. Since the District Court judge found that the plaintiff had no notice of dishonor, defence or claim, and the evidence supports this finding, the defendant's argument that the plaintiff failed to exercise due care is inapposite.

Since the evidence discloses no dishonesty, it does not support the District Court judge's finding that the plaintiff did not act in good faith. The order of the Appellate Division dismissing the report is reversed, the finding on each count for the defendant is vacated, and judgments are to be entered for the plaintiff.

So ordered.

Notes

(1) **New Definition of "Good Faith."** Recall that a new definition of "good faith" appears in UCC 3–103(a)(4). See Note 1, p. 65 supra. How would *Leo's Used Car Exchange* be decided under Revised Article 3?

---

4. Am.Law Inst.Uniform Commercial Code, 1951 Final Text Edition.

5. Am.Law Inst.Uniform Commercial Code, 1956 Recommendations.

6. Indeed, conduct which is outrageous may provide evidence relevant to the issue of honesty, and therefore, good faith.

(2) Burden of Proof. Since the questions of good faith and lack of notice are usually for the trier of the facts, the burden of proof can be of controlling importance, a point that might well cause concern to an out-of-state bank if its case went to a jury. Where would that burden fall in the preceding case under UCC 3–308(b), 1–201(8)?

(3) Check Kiting and the Requirements of Good Faith and Lack of Notice. Interesting questions of good faith and lack of notice may arise as a result of check-kiting schemes. Check kiting is a type of fraud in which the kiter creates a continuous exchange of overdrafts between accounts in at least two banks. Kiting depends on the combination of two circumstances: first, the willingness of depositary banks to allow the kiter immediate credit when he deposits checks drawn on other banks and, second, the period of time between the deposit of those checks and their presentment to the payor banks.

The simplest form of check kiting involves only two banks, preferably some distance apart. For example, the kiter opens accounts in X Bank and in Y Bank by depositing $1,000 in each. The kiter then draws on X Bank a $5,000 check in payment for goods or in exchange for cash. But before this overdraft is presented to X Bank, the kiter covers it by depositing in X Bank a $5,000 check drawn on Y Bank. And before this second overdraft is presented to Y Bank, the kiter covers it with a $5,000 check drawn on X Bank. The process is then repeated, escalating the amounts of which the banks have been defrauded.

In practice, kiting schemes are more complex than this and often involve several banks, for if one of the banks notices the pattern of deposits and withdrawals, the kite will be discovered. The bank that discovers the kite can maneuver to avoid loss by waiting for an opportune moment in the kite, presenting checks deposited in it, and then dishonoring at the last possible moment checks drawn on it.[1]

The questions with which we are concerned arise when a kiter exchanges a check drawn on a kited account for a check of an innocent drawer and then deposits the innocent drawer's check in a kited account. If the innocent drawer stops payment on the check, the drawer can set up against the kiter the defenses of fraud and failure of performance. Is the bank in which the kiter has deposited the innocent drawer's check a holder in due course that takes free of these defenses? Or does its involvement in the kiting scheme prevent its taking in good faith and without notice?

---

1. It has been held that this is not a breach of any duty owed to other banks involved in the kite. Citizens National Bank v. First National Bank, 347 So.2d 964 (Miss.1977) ("these two banks were competitors in the banking field and ordinarily banks deal with each other at arm's length"); cf. Mid–Cal National Bank v. Federal Reserve Bank of San Francisco, 590 F.2d 761 (9th Cir.1979) ("if a bank in such a situation cannot be held liable for failing to notify even when it knows of kiting activity, a bank should not be called to account for failing to discover information that, in any event, it was not required to convey").

In First State Bank & Trust Co. of Edinburg v. George, 519 S.W.2d 198 (Tex.Civ.App.1974), the court affirmed a judgment for the innocent drawer based on a jury verdict. The court held that the jury was justified in finding that the bank did not take in good faith because there was testimony that the bank should have known of the kite and that "by looking at the accounts involved, any banker could see that check kiting was going on." The jury was also justified in finding that the bank had notice since UCC 1–201(25) provides that a person has notice of a fact when "from all the facts and circumstances known to him at the time in question he had reason to know that it exists." Would the Article 3 revisions affect such a case? See UCC 3–103(a)(4); see also Comment 3 to UCC 3–418.

(4) Status of Collecting Bank. As was pointed out earlier, a depositary bank that takes a check for collection acts as agent for the depositor and does not take the check as owner. See p. 188 supra. This rule reflects the banker's fear that if the bank were owner it would bear the loss if the check were paid and the proceeds then lost due to the insolvency of a subsequent bank in the chain of collection. But situations also arose where the banker found it advantageous to claim at least some of the attributes of an owner. Compare UCC 4–201 with 4–210 and 4–211.

Comment 1 to UCC 4–201 states: "The general approach of Article 4, similar to that of other articles, is to provide, within reasonable limits, rules or answers to major problems known to exist in the bank collection process without regard to questions of status and ownership but to keep general principles such as status and ownership available to cover residual areas not covered by specific rules." Comment 6 goes on to explain: "It is unrealistic ... to base rights and duties on status of agent or owner. Thus Section 4–201 makes the pertinent provisions of Article 4 applicable to substantially all items handled by banks for presentment, payment or collection, recognizes the prima facie status of most banks as agents, and then seeks to state appropriate limits and some attributes to the general rules and presumptions so expressed."

BOWLING GREEN, INC. v. STATE STREET BANK AND TRUST CO.

United States Court of Appeals, First Circuit, 1970.
425 F.2d 81.

[The facts and the first part of the opinion in this case are at p. 223 supra. The court there rejected plaintiff's contention that the absence of an endorsement by Bowl–Mor was fatal to the Bank's case.]

COFFIN, CIRCUIT JUDGE.... Plaintiff's second objection arises from the intimate relationship between Bowl–Mor and the Bank, a relationship which plaintiff maintains precludes a finding of good faith. The record shows that the Bank was one of Bowl–Mor's three major creditors, and that it regularly provided short term financing for Bowl–Mor against the security of Bowl–Mor's inventory and unperformed contracts. The loan officer in charge of Bowl–Mor's account, Francis Haydock, was also a director of Bowl–Mor until August 1966. Haydock knew of Bowl–Mor's poor financial health and of its inability to satisfy all its creditors during 1966. In the five months before the transaction in question, the Bank charged $1,000,000 of Bowl–Mor's debt to the Bank's reserve for bad debts. However, the record also shows that the Bank continued to make loans to Bowl–Mor until September 12.

The Bank was also aware of the underlying transaction between Bowl–Mor and the plaintiff which led to the deposit on September 26. During the week prior to this transaction, Bowl–Mor had overdrawn its checking account with the Bank to meet a payroll. In order to persuade the Bank to honor the overdraft, officials of Bowl–Mor contacted Haydock and informed him that a check for $15,000 would be deposited as soon as plaintiff could obtain the funds from the Small Business Administration. The district court found, however, that the Bank was not aware that the directors of Bowl–Mor had authorized a Chapter X petition or that Bowl–Mor officials planned to file the petition on September 27.

On the basis of this record, the district court found that the Bank acted in good faith and without notice of any defense to the instrument.... The findings of the district court are not ... clearly erroneous....

This brings us to plaintiff's final argument, that the Bank gave value only to the extent of the $5,024.85 overdraft, and thus cannot be a holder in due course with respect to the remaining $10,047.54 which the Bank credited against Bowl–Mor's loan account. Our consideration of this argument is confined by the narrow scope of the district court's findings. The Bank may well have given value under § 4–208(1)(a) when it credited the balance of Bowl–Mor's checking account against its outstanding indebtedness. See Banco Espanol de Credito v. State Street Bank & Trust Co., 409 F.2d 711 (1st Cir.1969). But by that time the Bank knew of Bowl–Mor's petition for reorganization, additional information which the district court did not consider in finding that the Bank acted in good faith and without notice at the time it received the item. We must therefore decide whether the Bank gave value for the additional $10,047.54 at the time the item was deposited.[4]

---

4. Defendant suggests that we can avoid the analytical problems of § 4–209 by simply holding that the Bank's inchoate right to set off Bowl–Mor's outstanding indebtedness against deposits, as they were made constituted a giving of value. See Wood v. Boylston National Bank, 129 Mass. 358 (1880). There are, however, some pitfalls in this theory. First, under prior law a secured creditor could not exercise its right of set-off without first showing that its security was inadequate. Forastiere v. Springfield Institution for Savings, 303 Mass. 101, 104, 20 N.E.2d 950 (1939). Second, although the Uniform Commercial Code forswears any intent to change a banker's right of set-off, § 4–201 does change the presumption that a bank owns items deposited with it. This presumption played a role under prior law in

Resolution of this issue depends on the proper interpretation of § 4–209, which provides that a collecting bank has given value to the extent that it has acquired a "security interest" in an item. In plaintiff's view, a collecting bank can satisfy § 4–209 only by extending credit against an item in compliance with § 4–208(1).[5] The district court, on the other hand, adopted the view that a security interest is a security interest, however acquired. The court then found that defendant and Bowl–Mor had entered a security agreement which gave defendant a floating lien on Bowl–Mor's chattel paper. Since the item in question was part of the proceeds of a Bowl–Mor contract, the court concluded that defendant had given value for the full $15,306.00 at the time it received the deposit.

With this conclusion we agree. Section 1–201(37) defines "security interest" as an interest in personal property which secures payment or performance of an obligation. There is no indication in § 4–209 that the term is used in a more narrow or specialized sense. Moreover, as the official comment to § 4–209 observes, this provision is in accord with prior law and with § 3–303, both of which provide that a holder gives value when he accepts an instrument as security for an antecedent debt. Reynolds v. Park Trust Co., 245 Mass. 440, 444–445, 139 N.E. 785 (1923). Finally, we note that if one of the Bank's prior loans to Bowl–Mor had been made in the expectation that this particular instrument would be deposited, the terms of § 4–208(1)(c) would have been literally satisfied. We do not think the case is significantly different when the Bank advances credit on the strength of a continuing flow of items of this kind. We therefore conclude that the Bank gave value for the full $15,306.00 at the time it accepted the deposit.

We see no discrepancy between this result and the realities of commercial life. Each party, of course, chose to do business with an eventually irresponsible third party. The Bank, though perhaps unwise in prolonging its hopes for a prospering customer, nevertheless protected itself through security arrangements as far as possible without hobbling each deposit and withdrawal. Plaintiff, on the other hand, not only placed its initial faith in Bowl–Mor, but later became

---

assessing the bank's rights against uncollected commercial paper. Compare Wood v. Boylston National Bank, supra, with Boston–Continental National Bank v. Hub Fruit Co., 285 Mass. 187, 190, 189 N.E. 89 (1934) and American Barrel Co. v. Commissioner of Banks, 290 Mass. 174, 179–181, 195 N.E. 335 (1935). [This thought is pursued in the later case of Rockland Trust Co. v. South Shore National Bank, 314 N.E.2d 438 (Mass.1974). [Eds.]]

5. Mass.Gen.Laws Ann. c. 106, § 4–208.

"Security Interest of Collecting Bank in Items, Accompanying Documents and Proceeds. (1) A bank has a security interest in an item and any accompanying documents or the proceeds of either

(a) in case of an item deposited in an account to the extent to which credit given for the item has been withdrawn or applied;

(b) in case of an item for which it has given credit available for withdrawal as of right, to the extent of the credit given whether or not the credit is drawn upon and whether or not there is a right of charge-back; or

(c) if it makes an advance on or against the item. . . ."

aware that Bowl–Mor was having difficulties in meeting its payroll. It seems not too unjust that this vestige of caveat emptor survives.

Affirmed.

Notes

(1) **Revisions.** Former UCC 4–208(1) is now UCC 4–210(a), and former UCC 4–209 is now UCC 4–211. Would the result in *Bowling Green* be affected?

(2) **Stale Checks.** To be a holder in due course, a holder must take the instrument "without notice that the instrument is overdue" (UCC 3–303(a)(2)). Although a check, as a demand instrument, has no due date, the rule grew up that after the passage of time a check became "stale" and should be treated as overdue. UCC 3–304(a)(2) provides that a check becomes overdue after 90 days. What is the difference between this and the 30–day period of UCC 3–414(f)?

(3) **Rights of Purchasers After Maturity and Other Holders Not in Due Course.** Chafee, in Rights in Overdue Paper, 31 Harv. L.Rev. 1104, 1122 (1918), distinguished between "equitable defenses" and "equitable claims to ownership" and argued that one who took a negotiable instrument in good faith and for value after maturity should not be subject to the latter. "Maturity indicates nothing about them. Instead of being a red flag to give warning of all hidden dangers, it resembles more closely a printed placard calling attention to one special peril. A person approaching a grade-crossing and seeing the sign 'Stop, Look, and Listen' is bound to watch for trains, but he does not assume the risk of a savage bull-dog maintained on the railroad right of way to scare off track-walkers." The Code rejects Chafee's views in UCC 3–306. See Warren, Cutting Off Claims of Ownership Under the Uniform Commercial Code, 30 U.Chi.L.Rev. 469, 478–82 (1963).

But note that under the "shelter" provision of UCC 3–203(b) a transferee from a holder in due course ordinarily has all the rights of the holder in due course. This preserves for a holder in due course the market for the instrument should knowledge of a defense or claim of ownership become widespread.

(4) **Fiduciaries.** The law relating to transfers by a fiduciary, except as it concerns negotiable instruments, is beyond the scope of this course. Generally, a good faith purchaser for value of trust property from a trustee may retain the property and is under no liability to the beneficiary, even though the transfer may have been in breach of trust. But if the transferee has notice of the breach of trust the transfer will not cut off the beneficiary's interest and the transferee will take subject to the trust. This principle applies to transfers of negotiable instruments which are held in trust, where the paramount question is what amounts to notice of the breach of trust. See UCC 3–307. The Prefatory Note to revised Article 3 states: "Section 3–307 protects

drawers and persons owed a fiduciary responsibility by imposing stricter standards for obtaining holder in due course rights by a person dealing with the defaulting agent or fiduciary. It also spells out the circumstances under which a person receiving funds has notice of a breach of fiduciary duty, and resulting liability."

Problem 5. In indorsing the Empire check, Quaker omits the words "For deposit only." A few hours after giving Quaker a provisional credit for the Empire check, Philadelphia National allows Quaker to draw upon that credit to the extent of $10,000. The check is then dishonored because Empire has stopped payment. Empire stopped payment on discovering that the cans are defective and on justifiably refusing to take and pay for them. Quaker is now insolvent. Can Philadelphia National recover any part of the $22,178.50 from Empire? (It may help to assume first that the Empire check was deposited by itself.) Does the answer depend on whether the other checks deposited at the same time are paid? See the deposit slip (Form 3 supra.) See UCC 3–303, 4–210(a), 4–211; *Citizen's National Bank of Englewood v. Fort Lee Savings & Loan Association,* infra; *Bowling Green v. State Street Bank and Trust,* supra.

Note that under Regulation CC Philadelphia National is required to make the $22,178.50 available for withdrawal by Empire at a time determined by Section 229.12, 229.13(b). At that time, under UCC 4–210(a)(2), Philadelphia National acquires a security interest in the Empire check, assuming that it has not been paid. If the check is later returned unpaid to Philadelphia National, might Philadelphia National have a claim against The Bank of New York in some circumstances? What circumstances? See Reg CC 229.30, 229.38.

Problem 6. How can one tell whether a provisional credit has been "withdrawn or applied" under UCC 4–210(a)(1)? Assume that Quaker had a balance of $10,000 before making the deposit and that a few hours after the deposit the Philadelphia National allowed Quaker to withdraw $15,000 in cash and certified a check drawn by Quaker in the amount of $20,000. To what extent, if any, would the $22,178.50 provisional credit be "withdrawn or applied"? See UCC 4–210(b). Would it make any difference if Quaker deposited $25,000 in cash immediately after the $22,178.50 deposit and before the withdrawal and certification?

Problem 7. Assume that before Quaker deposited the Empire check, Quaker's account was overdrawn in the amount of $25,000, and that after the deposit the account showed a balance of $22,178.50. To what extent, if any, has Philadelphia National taken the check for value? See UCC 3–303 and Comment 3, 4–210, 4–211; and compare *Bowling Green v. State Street Bank & Trust,* supra, with Marine Midland Bank New York v. Graybar Electric Co., 41 N.Y.2d 703, 395 N.Y.S.2d 403, 363 N.E.2d 1139 (1977).[1]

---

1. As to the depositary bank's power to affect the answer to this problem by a dragnet security clause in its agreement with its customer, see Rosenthal, Negotia-

CITIZENS NATIONAL BANK OF ENGLEWOOD v. FORT LEE SAVINGS AND LOAN ASSOCIATION

Superior Court of New Jersey, 1965.
89 N.J.Super. 43, 213 A.2d 315.

BOTTER, J.S.C. Citizens National Bank of Englewood has moved for summary judgment to recover monies advanced against a check which was deposited with the bank for collection but was later dishonored. The issue is whether the bank should be protected for advances made to its depositor before the check cleared. The summary judgment is sought against the drawer and payee-indorser who stopped payment on the check.

On August 27, 1963, George P. Winter agreed to sell a house in Fort Lee, New Jersey to defendant Jean Amoroso and her husband. On the same day Amoroso requested her bank, Fort Lee Savings and Loan Association (Fort Lee Savings), to issue the bank's check to her order for $3,100 to be used as a deposit on the contract for sale. Fort Lee Savings complied by drawing the check against its account with the Fort Lee Trust Company. Later that day Amoroso indorsed and delivered the check to Winter, and he deposited the check in his account at the plaintiff bank. At that time he had a balance of $225.33. After the $3,100 check was deposited the bank cashed a $1,000 check for him against his account. In addition, on August 27 or August 28, the bank cleared and charged Winter's account with four other checks totaling $291.76.

The next day Amoroso discovered that Winter had previously sold the property to a third party by agreement which had been recorded in the Bergen County Clerk's Office. Amoroso immediately asked Winter to return her money. She claims that he admitted the fraud and agreed to return the deposit. But when Mrs. Amoroso and her husband reached Winter's office they learned that he had attempted suicide. He died shortly thereafter.

Upon making this discovery, in the afternoon of August 28, the Amorosos went to Fort Lee Savings to advise it of the fraud and request it to stop payment on the check. The bank issued a written stop payment order which was received by the Fort Lee Trust Company, the drawee, on the following day, August 29. In the meantime the $3,100 check was sent by plaintiff through the Bergen County Clearing House to the Fort Lee Trust Company. By then the stop payment order had been received. Notice of nonpayment was thereafter transmitted to plaintiff.

Plaintiff contends that, under the Uniform Commercial Code, N.J.S. 12A:1–101 et seq., N.J.S.A., it is a holder in due course to the

bility—Who Needs It?, 71 Colum.L.Rev. 375, 391–92 (1971).

extent of the advances made on Winter's account and is entitled to recover these moneys from the drawer and payee-indorser of the check. Plaintiff's claim against the drawee, Fort Lee Trust Company, was voluntarily dismissed by plaintiff at the pretrial conference.

The central issue is whether plaintiff bank is a holder in due course, since a holder in due course will prevail against those liable on the instrument in the absence of a real defense. Of course, it must first be determined that plaintiff is a "holder" if plaintiff is to be declared a holder in due course. Amoroso contends that plaintiff bank does not own the check because it is only an agent of its depositor Winter for collection purposes and, consequently, plaintiff is not a "holder." It is true that a collecting bank is presumed to be an agent of the owner of the item unless a contrary intention appears, or until final settlement. N.J.S. 12A:4–201(1), N.J.S.A. Assuming that the bank was at all times an agent in this case, it does not follow that the bank cannot also be a holder. On the contrary, a collecting bank may be a holder whether or not it owns the item. N.J.S. 12A:4–201(1) and 12A:3–301, N.J.S.A. Pazol v. Citizens Nat'l Bank of Sandy Springs, 110 Ga.App. 319, 138 S.E.2d 442 (Ct.App.1964); and see generally Bunn, "Bank Collections under the Uniform Commercial Code," Wis.L.Rev. 278 (1964). The definition of "holder" includes a person who is in possession of an instrument indorsed to his order or in blank. N.J.S. 12A:1–201(20), N.J.S.A. It is clear that the bank is a holder of the check notwithstanding that it may have taken the check solely for collection and with the right to charge back against the depositor's account in the event the check is later dishonored. Pazol v. Citizens Nat'l Bank of Sandy Springs, supra; accord, Citizens Bank of Booneville v. Nat'l Bank of Commerce, 334 F.2d 257 (10 Cir.1964).

To be a holder in due course one must take a negotiable instrument for value, in good faith and without notice of any defect or defense. N.J.S. 12A:3–302(1), N.J.S.A. Amoroso contends that plaintiff did not act in good faith or is chargeable with notice because it allowed Winter to draw against uncollected funds at a time when his account was either very low or overdrawn. Winter's account was low in funds. However, this fact, or the fact that Winter's account was overdrawn, currently or in the past, if true, would not constitute notice to the collecting bank of an infirmity in the underlying transaction or instrument and is not evidence of bad faith chargeable to the bank at the time it allowed withdrawal against the deposited check. N.J.S. 12A:1–201(19) and (25); N.J.S. 12A:3–304, N.J.S.A. See United States Cold Storage Corp. v. First Nat'l Bank of Fort Worth, 350 S.W.2d 856 (Tex.Civ.App.1961), declaring the bank a holder in due course where it applied a deposited check against a large overdraft of its depositor, the court specifically holding that lack of good faith was not shown merely by the fact that the bank knew the depositor was considerably overdrawn in his account.... Moreover a depositary bank may properly charge an account by honoring a check drawn by a depositor even though it creates an overdraft. N.J.S. 12A:4–401(1), N.J.S.A. It would be anomalous for a bank to lose its status as a holder in due course merely because it has notice that the account of its depositor is overdrawn.

Lacking bad faith or notice of a defect or defense, plaintiff will be deemed a holder in due course if one additional element is satisfied, namely, the giving of value for the instrument. Prior to the adoption of the Uniform Commercial Code the general rule was that a bank does give value and is a holder in due course to the extent that it allows a depositor to draw against a check given for collection notwithstanding that the check is later dishonored.... The cases clearly hold that this rule applies even though the item is received for collection only under an agreement with the bank that gives the bank the right to charge back against the depositor's account the amount of any item which is not collected. It is sometimes said that the contract of conditional credit is changed when the bank honors the deposit by allowing a withdrawal, and the bank then becomes the owner of or holder of a lien on the item to the extent of value given....

This result is continued by provisions of the Uniform Commercial Code which give plaintiff a security interest in the check and the monies represented by the check to the extent that credit given for the check has been withdrawn or applied. N.J.S. 12A:4–208 and 209, N.J.S.A. See also N.J.S. 12A:4–201, N.J.S.A. and U.C.C. Comment 5 thereunder.

N.J.S.A. 12A:4–208, N.J.S.A., provides in part as follows:

"(1) A bank has a security interest in an item and any accompanying documents or the proceeds of either

(a) in case of an item deposited in an account to the extent to which credit given for the item has been withdrawn or applied;

(b) in case of an item for which it has given credit available for withdrawal as of right, to the extent of the credit given whether or not the credit is drawn upon and whether or not there is a right of charge-back; or

(c) if it makes an advance on or against the item."

N.J.S. 12A:4–209, N.J.S.A., is as follows:

"For purposes of determining its status as a holder in due course, the bank has given value to the extent that it has a security interest in an item provided that the bank otherwise complies with the requirements of 12A:3–302 on what constitutes a holder in due course."

The New Jersey Study Comment under N.J.S. 12A:4–209, N.J.S.A., includes the following: "Because the bank is a holder of the item in most cases, it is possible for it to be a holder in due course if it otherwise qualifies by its good faith taking, prior to maturity, for value. See, U.C.C. sec. 3–302; NIL sec. 52 (N.J.S.A. 7:2–52). It is important for a bank to be a holder in due course when the depositor fails, for this status enables it to prevail over the obligor (drawer or maker) of the instrument even though the obligor has some personal defense against the payee (depositor)."

It would hinder commercial transactions if depositary banks refused to permit withdrawal prior to clearance of checks. Apparently banking practice is to the contrary. It is clear that the Uniform Commercial Code was intended to permit the continuation of this practice and to protect banks who have given credit on deposited items prior to notice of a stop payment order or other notice of dishonor. N.J.S. 12A:4–208 and 209, N.J.S.A., supra; Pazol v. Citizens Nat'l Bank of Sandy Springs, supra; Citizens Bank of Booneville v. Nat'l Bank of Commerce, supra; see also Universal C.I.T. Credit Corp. v. Guaranty Bank & Trust Co., 161 F.Supp. 790 (D.C.Mass.1958); Trumbull, "Bank Deposits and Collections in Illinois Under the Proposed Uniform Commercial Code," 55 Nw.U.L.Rev. 253, 270–272 (1960); Penney, "Uniform Commercial Code: Symposium—A Summary of Articles 3 and 4 and Their Impact in New York," 48 Cornell L.Q. 47, 58–59 (1962).

It is also contended that liability on the check is excused because N.J.S. 12A:4–403, N.J.S.A. gives Fort Lee Savings the right to order Fort Lee Trust Company to stop payment on the check. However, U.C.C. comment 8 under this section makes it clear that the stop payment order cannot avoid liability to a holder in due course. "The payment can be stopped but the drawer remains liable on the instrument to the holder in due course...." See Carhart v. Second Nat'l Bank, 98 N.J.L. 373, 120 A. 636 (Sup.Ct.1923).

Finally, Amoroso attempts to raise the fraud perpetrated by Winter against Amoroso as a defense to plaintiff's claim. Plaintiff's status as a holder in due course insulates it from all personal defenses of any party to the instrument with whom it has not dealt, although real defenses may still be asserted. N.J.S. 12A:3–305, N.J.S.A. The defense raised here is fraud in inducing Amoroso to enter into the contract. There is no suggestion that either defendant signed the check without knowledge of "its character or its essential terms." N.J.S. 12A:3–305(2)(c), N.J.S.A. Therefore the fraud is a personal defense available only against Winter and cannot be asserted against plaintiff. See Bancredit, Inc. v. Bethea, 65 N.J.Super. 538, 168 A.2d 250 (App.Div.1961); Meadow Brook Nat'l Bank v. Rogers, 44 Misc.2d 250, 253 N.Y.S.2d 501 (D.Ct. 1964).

Accordingly both Fort Lee Savings as drawer and Amoroso as indorser of the check are liable to plaintiff. N.J.S. 12A:3–413(2) and 12A:3–414(1), N.J.S.A., defining the liability of a drawer and indorser of a negotiable instrument to a holder in due course.

The motion for summary judgment will be granted in the sum of $1,066.43, plus interest. The amount of the judgment represents advances made on Winter's account before notice of dishonor, $1,291.76, less the existing balance of $225.33 in Winter's account. This opinion will not deal with the disposition of claims between Amoroso and Fort Lee Savings. By reason of the stop payment order Fort Lee Savings has on hand sufficient funds which were charged against Amoroso's account to meet plaintiff's judgment, and part of these funds, representing the difference between the potential judgment and the $3,100 retained, has been refunded to Amoroso pursuant to the pretrial order.

Notes

(1) **Negotiability of Checks.** Dean Albert Rosenthal pointed out that there is likely to be an increase in the number of instances in which withdrawals are permitted against unpaid checks, both because of the increased use of automation and the growing practice of banks to agree to let their customers overdraw subject to interest charges. He believed that the Code "sometimes gives a bank a windfall at the expense of drawers, who lose the right to assert legitimate defenses" under "a thoroughly irrational rule as applied in most check deposit situations." As an alternative, he suggested that "the right of a depositary bank, as a holder in due course, to cut off defenses of a drawer ought to be limited to cases in which the bank can prove that, in allowing withdrawals against the check before collection, it had relied at least in part on the credit of the drawer." Rosenthal, Negotiability—Who Needs It?, 71 Colum.L.Rev. 375, 381–94 (1971).

Would the practices of depositary banks be affected by such proposals? Consider the following: "With the high percentage of good checks, and the high cost of maintaining any record of the journeys of a particular check, obviously banks do not keep track on an individual item basis. The availability of deposited tentative credits to a depositing customer depends on two factors, the credit rating of the customer and schedules of normal availability. The accounts of customers with a high credit rating are not normally monitored for drawing against uncollected funds, as the chance of not having a balance against which to charge back a returned item is negligible. In the case of the monitored accounts, the availability schedules also reflect average times. Hence, there always will be cases in which checks will come back unpaid with no balance in the depositor's account to cover the charge-back. The holder in due course status of depositary banks in this situation gives the bank an added chance of recovery if the reason for the return is not the insolvency or permanent inability to pay of the drawer." Leary and Tarlow, reflections on Articles 3 and 4 for a Review Committee, 48 Temple L.Q. 919, 923 (1975).

The great majority of all checks are deposited by the payees for collection and never come into the hands of a holder in due course. Would there be any serious adverse effects if checks were not negotiable instruments? Would there be any advantages? Compare the significance of negotiability of checks with that of the negotiability of credit instruments such as time drafts and notes.

Regulation CC increases the likelihood that a depositary bank will allow a customer to draw against uncollected funds, thereby increasing the depositary bank's need to establish status as a holder in due course. (Proof of value should be simple in such cases, because as soon as the depositary bank is required to make funds available to its depositor under Regulation CC, the depositor acquires a right to withdraw those funds that satisfies UCC 4–210(a)(2)). On the other hand, Regulation CC may decrease the depositary bank's need to establish status as a holder in due course, since the rules on direct notice and expeditious return should reduce the possibility that a depositary bank will allow a customer to draw against a check that ultimately is returned.

(2) **Negotiability Under the Uniform New Payments Code.** The Uniform New Payments Code would have made a dramatic change in the rights of depositary banks and others who claim to be holders in due course of checks. Under UNPC 103, the rights of a claimant on an order that is "drawn on a consumer account" would have been subject to claims and defenses arising out of the underlying transaction until the order was finally paid. After discussing the abolition of the holder-in-due-course doctrine in connection with promissory notes, the commentary concluded that the same "concerns also apply to checks and other orders drawn by consumers ... If a bank takes a check from a payee, it is relying on that person's credit if it allows withdrawal against uncollected funds, not the credit standing of a drawer with whom it is unfamiliar. The bank in the case of checks, just as the merchant in the case of notes, is in a better position to appraise and take the risk of insolvency of the party with which it deals in the event the check is unpaid. If the 'purchaser' of the check can cut-off the defenses of the buyer-drawer, the drawer is remitted to a second action against the seller-payee, thus incurring litigation costs and current outlay of funds."

(3) **Negotiability Under Revised Article 3.** Revised Article 3 takes a different tack than that suggested in the two preceding notes by increasing the chance of a depositary bank becoming the holder in due course of a check. Under UCC 3–104(c), a check that meets all of the requisites of negotiability except that it is not payable to order or to bearer is nevertheless negotiable. A bank or other transferee of such a check may therefore qualify as a holder in due course.

Comment 2 to UCC 3–104 explains: "Unless subsection (c) applies, the effect of subsection (a)(1) and Section 3–102(a) is to exclude from Article 3 any promise or order that is not payable to bearer or to order. There is no provision in revised Article 3 that is comparable to former Section 3–805. The comment to former Section 3–805 states that the typical example of a writing covered by that section is a check reading 'Pay John Doe.' Such a check was governed by former Article 3 but there could not be a holder in due course of the check. Under Section 3–104(c) such a check is governed by revised Article 3 and there can be a holder in due course of the check. But subsection (c) applies only to checks. The comment to former Section 3–805 does not state any example other than the check to illustrate that section.   Subsection (c) is based on the belief that it is good policy to treat checks, which are payment instruments, as negotiable instruments whether or not they contain the words 'to the order of'.   These words are almost always preprinted on the check form.   Occasionally the drawer of a check may strike out these words before issuing the check.   In the past some credit unions used check forms that did not contain the quoted words.   Such check forms may still be in use but they are no longer common. Absence of the quoted words can easily be overlooked and should not affect the rights of holders who may pay money or give credit for a check without being aware that it is not in the conventional form."

Is such a check payable to order or to bearer?   See UCC 3–109. Would a supermarket need an indorsement to be a holder in due course of such a check?   See UCC 3–201(b).   Would a bank?   See UCC 4–205.

RESTRICTIVE INDORSEMENTS

In the *Citizens National Bank* case, the court began its opinion by mentioning that the check "was deposited with the bank for collection." The holder of a check deposits it for collection by using the kind of restrictive indorsement described in UCC 3–206(c)—an indorsement "using the words 'for deposit,' 'for collection,' or other words indicating a purpose of having the instrument collected by a bank."   (The other kinds of restrictive indorsements dealt with in UCC 3–206 are not of great practical importance.)

In understanding the Code provisions on restrictive indorsements, it is helpful to realize that prior to the Code there was a substantial body of authority for the view that if a depositor restrictively indorsed a check, the depositary bank could not become a holder in due course of it.   This was based on a restrictive reading of Negotiable Instruments Law §§ 37 and 47.   Other courts rejected this view.   All courts, however, agreed that if the depositary bank had not given value, no intermediary collecting bank could, by giving value itself, rise above the depositary bank and become a holder in due course of such a check.

Impact of Regulation CC.   Regulation CC abandons the Code's lackadaisical attitude toward indorsements and imposes strict indorsement standards.   These standards are designed to facilitate easy identification of the depositary bank and thus the rapid return of checks. The standards apply to all banks except the payor bank.   The Regulation prescribes the content, location, and ink color of indorsements.

The indorsement of the depositary bank must contain the bank's routing number, its name and location, and the indorsement date.   It may also include a branch identifier, trace/sequence number, phone number for receipt of notice of nonpayment, and other optional information if it does not interfere with readability of the indorsement.   The Regulation permits a depositary bank to arrange with another bank to indorse its checks.   The indorsement of each subsequent collecting bank must contain only that bank's routing number, the indorsement date, and an optional trace/sequence number. The content of a returning bank's indorsement is not specified.

These strict indorsement standards have an impact on restrictive indorsements by collecting banks. Prior to Regulation CC, banks forwarding checks for collection added language such as "pay any bank" to their indorsements. This made the indorsement restrictive so that only a bank could acquire the rights of a holder. See UCC 4–201(b). In order to remove clutter from the backs of checks, Appendix D to Regulation CC discourages the addition of such language by depositary banks and prohibits it by subsequent collecting banks. Under Section 229.35(c), after indorsement by a bank, without any additional words, only a bank can acquire the rights of a holder.

Problem 8. Would it make any difference in Problem 5 if Quaker included the words "For deposit only" in its indorsement? See UCC 3–206.

Problem 9. After the Empire check is indorsed "For deposit only, Quaker Manufacturing Co.," but before it is deposited in Philadelphia National, it is stolen by a thief who deposits it in the thief's own account in Philadelphia National. Philadelphia National then sends the check to Citibank, which obtains payment from The Bank of New York, and the $22,178.50 is ultimately withdrawn by the thief. What rights has Quaker against Philadelphia National, Citibank and The Bank of New York? See UCC 3–206, 3–420. What advantages, if any, does this indorsement have over "Quaker Manufacturing Co."? Over "To Philadelphia National Bank, Quaker Manufacturing Co."? Would Quaker be better protected if it indorsed "For deposit in Philadelphia National Bank, Quaker Manufacturing Co."? See *Rutherford v. Darwin,* infra.

RUTHERFORD v. DARWIN

Court of Appeals of New Mexico, 1980.
95 N.M. 340, 622 P.2d 245.

ANDREWS, JUDGE. Tom Darwin was a general partner of both Rancho Village Partners and The Settlement, Ltd., which are New Mexico limited partnerships. He had full authority to manage the funds of both entities with his signature alone.

On May 17, 1977, Darwin made a $300,000 draw against a construction loan made by Albuquerque National Bank (ANB) to Rancho Village Partners. He received the money in the form of a money order payable to "Rancho Village Partnership, Ltd." He endorsed the money order with "Deposit to the account of Rancho Village Partners, Ltd.", and took it to the First National Bank in Albuquerque (FNBIA), where both Rancho Village Partners and The Settlement had accounts. Darwin gave the money order to the teller with a preprinted deposit slip for the account of The Settlement, and the teller wrote out the account number of The Settlement on the reverse side of the money order, below the endorsement. The teller then deposited the money order to the account of The Settlement, notwithstanding the endorsement, which directed otherwise.

Darwin intended that the deposit be made into The Settlement account. He then withdrew the bulk of the $300,000 within two weeks of the deposit of the money order, and the account was almost entirely depleted before any of the other members of the Rancho Village partnership learned of the draw seven months later. The embezzlement of Darwin was not earlier discovered because the construction loan on which the draw was made was not monitored by monthly statements which would normally be sent in conjunction with monthly billings of interest. It was unusual for a loan of that size not to be so monitored and was a deviation from the usual ANB practice with regard to such loans. Rancho Village Partners acted promptly to notify FNBIA and to protect its interest after the other members of the partnership learned of Darwin's action.

Rancho Village Partners brought suit against Darwin, The Settlement, and FNBIA to recover the $300,000. A stipulated judgment was entered against Darwin and The Settlement, and the trial court entered summary judgment against the bank. FNBIA appeals from this summary judgment.

The words "Deposit to the account of Rancho Village Partnership, Ltd." clearly constitute a restrictive endorsement under § 55–3–205, N.M.S.A.1978. Section 55–3–206 imposes upon FNBIA the duty to pay consistently with the restrictive endorsement, and this duty gives rise to liability for the bank if it fails to do so. Underpinning & Foundation Constructors, Inc. v. Chase Manhattan, 46 N.Y.2d 459, 386 N.E.2d 1319, 414 N.Y.S.2d 298 (1979).

FNBIA contends that Darwin "waived" the restrictive endorsement, and thus released it from its duty to pay as directed by the endorsement. We conclude, however, that New Mexico does not recognize any doctrine of the waiver of restrictive endorsements, and thus we cannot accept FNBIA's theory.

There has never been a case recognizing a doctrine of waiver of restrictive endorsements in New Mexico, but several cases decided in other jurisdictions under the Uniform Negotiable Instruments Law (NIL) suggest that the doctrine was once generally recognized. See, e.g., Glens Falls Indemnity Co. v. Palmetto Bank, 104 F.2d 671 (4th Cir.1939). We are aware of no cases decided since the Uniform Commercial Code (UCC) superseding the NIL as the law governing negotiable instruments which has recognized the doctrine, and thus the dispositive issue is whether the doctrine survives as part of the common law under the UCC.

The NIL was silent on the key issue of this case; both the bank's duty to pay as directed by a restrictive endorsement and the waiver exception to that rule were matters of common law under the NIL. With the adoption of the UCC, the rule as to the duty of the bank was codified in § 55–3–206.

Courts have frequently given effect to common law limitations and exceptions to newly codified common law rules. For example, many jurisdictions have held that a murderer may not take from the estate of his victim even where the general law of descent and distribution of the jurisdiction has been codified without the inclusion of that sensible and time honored common law limitation. See, e.g., Budwit v. Herr, 339 Mich. 265, 63 N.W.2d 841 (1954). However, the general rule is that:

> general and comprehensive legislation prescribing minutely a course of conduct to be pursued and the parties and things affected, and specifically describing limitations and exceptions, is indicative of a legislative intent that the statute should totally supersede and replace the common law dealing with the subject matter.

2A Sutherland, Statutory Construction § 50.05 (Rev.3d Ed.1972).

This idea was applied in Tietzel v. Southwestern Const. Co., 43 N.M. 435, 94 P.2d 972 (1939), where it was held that a statute empowering a trial judge to refer certain enumerated sorts of cases to a special master over the objection of the parties abrogated his common law power to do so in any other kind of case which sounded in equity.

We hold that the codification of the law of restrictive endorsements contained in the UCC is sufficiently comprehensive and detailed to exclude common law exceptions which are not mentioned. Section 55–3–206, which is entitled "Effect of restrictive endorsement", sets forth with particularity when and by whom restrictive endorsements must be observed; it must be inferred that if the legislature had intended that restrictive endorsements would become ineffective for some other reason, such a direction would have been included in this section or elsewhere in the UCC.

The official comment to this section, which is persuasive authority of the meaning of the section even though it is not binding on this Court, First State Bank v. Clark, 91 N.M. 117, 570 P.2d 1144 (1977), gives a further indication that the section was not to be encumbered with the common law accessories of the NIL. The comment describes the changes made by the new section as "completely revised" from the prior provision under the NIL. FNBIA argues that waiver of a restrictive endorsement as recognized prior to the UCC should be allowed because § 55–1–103 of the UCC provides for the continued effect of common law principles unless displaced by particular provisions of the UCC. However, as discussed above, we believe that § 55–3–206 displaces the preexisting law in the entire area of the effect of restrictive endorsements. Section 55–1–103 does not preserve common law principles in an area which is thoroughly covered by the UCC simply because they are not expressly excluded. Alaska Airlines, Inc. v. Lockheed Aircraft Corp., 430 F.Supp. 134 (D.Alaska 1977).

FNBIA further argues the endorser of an instrument should be allowed to waive the endorsement by analogy to § 55–3–208, which states that one who reacquires an instrument may cancel any endorsement which is not necessary to his title. While the presence of this section cuts against any notion of the "sanctity" of restrictive endorsements, it very specifically suggests that it was not the intention of its drafters to make such endorsements freely negatable. The section is not applicable because the instrument was not reacquired and because Darwin did not strike the restrictive endorsement.

This second distinction is particularly important. The presence of an uncancelled restrictive endorsement on a negotiable instrument creates the legitimate expectation that it was negotiated in accordance with the restriction, and thus it would, at least in some cases, tend to conceal embezzlement or misappropriation to allow such endorsements to be waived without being physically struck from the instrument.

FNBIA also argues that Rancho Village Partners is estopped from recovering from the bank for its wrongful disregard of the restrictive endorsement because it did not use ordinary care in structuring its affairs so that Darwin's actions should have been discovered sooner. In particular, FNBIA would have us rule that Rancho Village Partners should have arranged to receive a monthly statement showing any draws on the construction loan account at the Albuquerque National Bank, as would have been the usual practice with a loan of that size. [The court discussed and rejected this argument. Even if we were willing to impose upon the customer the obligation to structure his relationship with a third party so as to discover the improper payment the trial court would have had to believe FNBIA exercised ordinary care in its handling of the money order. The trial court did not so find.

The circumstances of the transaction cry out for attention on the part of the bank. We hold, as a matter of law, that the bank had a duty to refuse to deposit the money to the account of The Settlement. The money order was restrictively endorsed to the account of an entity entirely different from that named, on the accompanying deposit slip. The trial court observed that, particularly in light of the sum involved, the bank had an obligation to be sure that the money went into the proper account.

We adopt the reasoning of the New York Court of Appeals in Underpinning & Foundation Constructors, Inc. v. Chase Manhattan, supra:

> The presence of a restriction imposes upon the depository bank an obligation not to accept that item other than in accord with the restriction. By disregarding the restriction, it not only subjects itself to liability for any losses resulting from its actions, but it also passes up what may well be the best opportunity to prevent the fraud. The presentation of a check in violation of a restrictive endorsement is an obvious warning sign, and the depositary bank is required to investigate the

situation rather than blindly accept the check. Based on such a failure to follow the mandates of due care and commercially reasonable behavior, it is appropriate to shift ultimate responsibility from the drawer to the depository bank.

46 N.Y.2d at 469, 386 N.E.2d at 1324, 414 N.Y.S.2d at 303.

FNBIA also suggests that the endorsement on the money order was not restrictive or that it was deposited in accord with the restriction. These arguments are entirely without merit.

The decision of the trial court is affirmed.

SUTIN, JUDGE (dissenting).... A waiver is the intentional relinquishment of a known right. The Bank had to establish (1) that Darwin knew of the restrictive endorsement on the money order—that which he himself wrote, and (2) that Darwin intended to give up the Rancho Village's right to the deposit of the money. These facts were established beyond dispute. Regardless of what endorsement he, himself, wrote on the ANB money order, Darwin had the exclusive right to change the endorsement at anytime before or at the time of deposit. When Darwin obtained the money order he wrote in the restrictive endorsement. He intended to deposit it to the account of Rancho Village. Thereafter, he wrote up a Settlement deposit slip, either to carry out the order of Rutherford or on his own, effect a transfer of the money order from Rancho Village to Settlement.

"No restrictive endorsement prevents further transfer or negotiation of the instrument." Section 55–3–206(1), N.M.S.A.1978. Darwin negotiated the restrictive endorsement to FNB. After any transfer or negotiation with the Bank, the Bank must act consistently with the type of endorsement that appears. Section 55–3–206(2). It logically follows that when the general partner of payee, Rancho Village, acts as endorser of the money order and presents the money order with The Settlement slip to the bank teller, and the bank teller writes The Settlement account number thereon, the deposit slip was equivalent to a line drawn through the restrictive endorsement. The restrictive endorsement was cancelled.

When FNB accepted the money order and deposited it to the account of Settlement, FNB became a holder in due course. It owed no duty of inquiry to Rancho Village, the payee. Handley v. Horak, 82 Misc.2d 692, 370 N.Y.S.2d 313 (1975)....

In Cooper v. Albuquerque National Bank, 75 N.M. 295, 404 P.2d 125 (1965), Peke was administrator of a trust fund and general manager of an association of contractors. He received checks payable to the trust fund. He stamped the endorsement of the trust fund and immediately followed it by another stamp endorsement in sum:

Pay to the Order of

Albuquerque National Bank
For Deposit Only

All prior endorsements guaranteed
Associated Contractors.

The trust fund sued the Bank to recover the amount of the trust fund checks paid by ANB on forged, unauthorized, unlawful, fraudulent, or irregular endorsements. The court held that since Peke had authority to make the deposits, there being no evidence that the Bank acted in bad faith, the Bank was not put upon inquiry as to the amount Peke was authorized to deposit.

In the instant case, Darwin acted under authority and there was no evidence of bad faith on the part of FNB. The only person to whom the FNB teller could inquire as to propriety and priority of the restrictive endorsement was Darwin. No duty existed to inquire of a general partner, who acted for the payee as endorser, whether he was violating his duty to Rancho Village. It would have been a useless gesture. The teller's duty was to deposit the money order to The Settlement account. She did. In good faith, she accepted the deposit slip and the money order and wrote The Settlement account number under the restrictive endorsement and credited The Settlement account. She knew the account numbers of both limited partnerships. A reasonable inference can be drawn that she may have known of Darwin's relationship with Rancho Village and Settlement. We can arrive at no other conclusion but that Darwin waived the Rancho Village restrictive endorsement as a matter of law. The "contradiction" in the two endorsements is irrelevant.

The majority opinion concluded that "New Mexico does not recognize any doctrine of the waiver of restrictive endorsements, and thus we cannot accept FNBIA's theory." This issue is a matter of first impression.... Section 55–1–103 reads in pertinent part:

> Unless displaced by the particular provisions of this act [this chapter], the principles of law and equity ... shall supplement its provisions.

Inasmuch as there is nothing in the Code to take the place of "waiver" of restrictive covenants, "waiver" in its pre-code law is a supplement of the Uniform Commercial Code....

Section 48 of the former Negotiable Instruments Law (Section 50–1–48, N.M.S.A.1953) repealed by the Uniform Commercial Code reads:

> The holder may at any time strike out any endorsement which is not necessary to his title. The endorser whose endorsement is struck out, and all endorsers subsequent to him are thereby relieved from liability on the instrument.

Under official Comment of § 55–3–208 it is stated with reference to § 48 of the Negotiable Instruments Law, "No change in the substance of the law is intended."

Glens Falls Indemnity Co. v. Palmetto Bank, 104 F.2d 671 (4th Cir.1939), quoted at length in *Cooper*, supra, established the right of Darwin to waive a "for deposit" endorsement on the Rancho Village money order under § 48 of the Negotiable Instruments Law. The court said:

> ... If he had authority to indorse the checks in the name of the mill and collect the cash on them, as is admitted, it necessarily follows that he had authority to waive the restrictive character of a special indorsement which he himself had placed on them and to collect them as though they had been generally indorsed.... [Id. 674.]

Glens Falls was not only followed in New Mexico, it was followed in other jurisdictions....

New Mexico via *Glens Falls* does recognize the doctrine of waiver of restrictive endorsements. It is undisputed that Darwin waived the restrictive endorsement and absolved FNB of any liability.

[W]e turn to the case relied on in the majority opinion which held that a claim based upon an effective forged restrictive endorsement, stated a claim for relief. Underpinning, etc. v. Chase Manhattan, 46 N.Y.2d 459, 386 N.E.2d 1319, 414 N.Y.S.2d 298 (1979). The court was "called upon to determine when, if ever, the drawer of a check may sue a depositary bank which accepts the check and pays out the proceeds in violation of a forged restrictive endorsement." In this case, "[a]n employee of plaintiff ... falsified invoices from plaintiff's suppliers, stole the checks written to pay these false invoices, *restrictively indorsed them to the named payees and then deposited them to his own or confederate's accounts,* maintained with, among others the defendant Bank of New York (BNY). When these checks were presented BNY, despite the restrictive indorsements, accepted them and applied the proceeds thereof to the credit of accounts other than those indicated in the indorsements." [Emphasis added.] None of the named payees kept accounts there, 403 N.Y.S.2d 501–2, 61 A.D.2d 628 (1978). The Court of Appeals affirmed the lower court. It held that the complaint stated a claim upon which relief could be granted. The court said:

> In summary, we hold today that a drawer may directly sue a depositary bank which has honored a check in violation of a forged restrictive indorsement in situations in which the forgery is effective ... It is basic to the law of commercial paper that as between innocent parties any loss should ultimately be placed on the party which could most easily have prevented that loss.... [386 N.E.2d 1323, 414 N.Y.S.2d 302.]

Underpinning stands for the proposition that a depositary bank like FNB can be held liable if it and Rancho Village were innocent parties and FNB could most easily have prevented the loss. FNB was an innocent party. It cannot be said with impunity that Rancho Village was an innocent party. It put the conduct of its business solely in the hands of its general partner. Its general partner, acting within the scope of his authority, set this transaction in motion and directly caused the loss of Rancho Village. In effect, Rancho Village promoted the loss by making Darwin its general manager. The loss must fall on

Rancho Village. Continental Bank v. Wa–Ho Truck Brokerage, 122 Ariz. 414, 595 P.2d 206 (1979).

Note

The Bank's Own Petard. Marine Midland Bank v. Price, Miller, Evans & Flowers, 57 N.Y.2d 220, 455 N.Y.S.2d 565, 441 N.E.2d 1083 (1982), involved two checks totalling $36,906.54, given to a building contractor as progress payments on a construction job. Marine Midland Bank, as it had done with several previous progress payments, cashed the checks, wired the amount to another bank, and then forwarded the checks for collection. Since the checks had not been indorsed, Marine Midland stamped them "credited to the account of the payee herein named," though the payee had no account at the bank. The building contractor defaulted on the construction contract, the drawer stopped payment, and Marine Midland sued the drawer claiming to be a holder in due course, free of the drawer's defenses. Marine Midland lost.

The court noted that under former UCC 4–205(1), "a statement placed on the item by the depositary bank to the effect that the item was deposited by a customer or credited to his account is effective as the customer's indorsement." The court thought this provision applicable though the payee had no account capable of being credited. However, the court went on to conclude that the bank's stamp had the effect of a restrictive indorsement, and, since "the bank did not comply with the conditions of the indorsement which it supplied, it cannot be said to have given value within the contemplation of the code and therefore was not a holder in due course." What result under UCC 4–205 as amended?

PAYEE AS HOLDER IN DUE COURSE

Can a payee be a holder in due course? Former Article 3 answered with a resounding "yes." Under former UCC 3–302(2), "A payee may be a holder in due course."

It might seem that this rule would be infrequently relevant. The principal reason for wanting to be a holder in due course is to be free from personal defenses, and if, for example, the drawer of a check has a personal defense such as fraud or lack of consideration against the payee, the payee will not ordinarily meet the requirements for holding in due course.

There are, however, a few unusual situations in which a payee should take free of personal defenses. Here is one from Comment 2 to former UCC 3–302: "A remitter, purchasing goods from P, obtains a bank draft [teller's check] payable to P and forwards it to P, who takes it for value, in good faith and without notice as required by this section." Had the buyer been not a remitter but the payee, who had indorsed the instrument to P, P would plainly have been a holder in due course, free of the drawer bank's personal defenses against the buyer. The same result followed in the illustration.

But under former Article 3 there was a much more important reason for proclaiming that a payee could be a holder in due course, for holder-in-due-course status could be vital to a payee even though no defense was involved. As mentioned in the preceding chapter after the *Kirby* case (p. 175 supra), under former Article 3 the concept of holder in due course did double duty. Thus a holder in due course had not only the advantage of freedom from defenses but also the advantage of finality in the case of a payor bank's mistaken payment of an overdraft. Had the Kirby's—payees—not been holders in due course, they would not have had the benefit of this rule. And their situation is an oft occurring one for payees, which made it desirable to confer the status of holder in due course generously among payees.

As we saw in connection with the *Kirby* case, however, revised Article 3 abandons the holder in due course requirement in UCC 3–418. It is therefore now true, as stated in Comment 4 to Section 3–302, that the "primary importance of the concept of holder in due course is with respect to assertion of defenses or claims in recoupment ... and of claims to the instrument." Former Section 3–302(2) has therefore "been omitted in revised Article 3 because it is surplusage and may be misleading. The payee of an instrument can be a holder in due course, but use of the holder-in-due-course doctrine by the payee of an instrument is not the normal situation."

How would Eldon's Super Fresh Stores v. Merrill Lynch, Pierce, Fenner & Smith, 296 Minn. 130, 207 N.W.2d 282 (1973), be decided under revised Article 3? In that case, Merrill Lynch, a stock brokerage firm, took as payee a $4,150 check drawn by Eldon Prinzing as president of Eldon's Super Fresh Stores. The check was delivered to Merrill Lynch by William Drexler, who was lawyer for both Eldon's and Prinzing, in payment for stock that he had bought for himself. Drexler, who was later disbarred, claimed that the check was given to him in payment for legal services. Prinzing, however, claimed that the check was given to Drexler as agent for Eldon's to buy the stock for Eldon's.

The court decided that it was not necessary to resolve this dispute. Merrill Lynch, though a payee, was a holder in due course who had not dealt with Eldon's, so Merrill Lynch took the check free of any defenses that Eldon's might have against Drexler. As to whether Merrill Lynch had taken in good faith, the court noted that Drexler had an account at Merrill Lynch, but Eldon's did not. "Merrill Lynch was entitled to conclude that Drexler, known to be an attorney, had lawfully obtained and was delivering the instrument to discharge the debt incurred by his own stock purchase."[1]

---

1. Suppose that both Drexler and Eldon's had had accounts with Merrill Lynch. Or suppose that neither had had an account with Merrill Lynch. Would

(C) Defenses and Claims in Recoupment

Prefatory Note. A holder that qualifies as a holder in due course of an instrument takes it free from all defenses of any obligor on the instrument except for a small number of defenses that are known as *real* defenses. See UCC 3–305. Those defenses that are cut off as against a holder in due course are commonly called *personal* defenses. These include such common defenses as want or failure of consideration, breach of warranty in the sale of goods, non-performance of a condition precedent, fraud in the inducement to undertake the obligation, and most cases of illegality. Note that the list includes those defenses which are most commonly asserted in commercial transactions. Real defenses include such less common defenses as infancy and some other types of incapacity, some instances of duress and illegality, fraud in the execution of the instrument, and discharge in insolvency proceedings.

The most common instances of illegality that nullify the obligation of an obligor and thus come within UCC 3–305(a)(1) are violations of the gambling and usury laws, which expressly make contracts that violate them "void." In Farmers' State Bank v. Clayton National Bank, 31 N.M. 344, 245 P. 543, 46 A.L.R. 952 (1925), the court said: "The consideration of an instrument won at gambling may, of course, be said to be 'illegal,' but that is not all. The instrument itself is void.... Giving the term 'illegal consideration' the interpretation placed upon it at the common law, no change took place in the law of this state when we adopted ... the Negotiable Instruments Law. If the Legislature did not change, nor intend to change even the law of negotiable instruments, it, of course, did not intend to change the gaming law."

Other kinds of illegality have generally not been held to be real defenses. Commercial bribery was held to be only a personal defense in Bankers Trust Co. v. Litton Systems, 599 F.2d 488 (2d Cir.1979). The court said: "Bribery which induces the making of a contract is much like a fraud which has the same result. The bribery of a contracting party's agent or employee is, in effect, a fraud on that party. ... Inasmuch as the New York Uniform Commercial Code allows a holder

---

Merrill Lynch then have been "required to surmise that the check, rather than being a payment for Drexler's legal services, was being misused"? See Saka v. Sahara–Nevada Corp., 92 Nev. 703, 558 P.2d 535 (1976), rejecting the argument that a hotel had "a duty to make further inquiries" when it took as payee a third person's check in payment for a $3,046.03 hotel bill. But cf. Key Appliance v. National Bank of North America, 75 A.D.2d 92, 428 N.Y.S.2d 238 (1980), holding that a bank that cashed for the drawer's comptroller checks drawn on the bank and payable to its order "had a duty to inquire as to the disposition of the funds" since though "cashing checks in small amounts without inquiry may not be unusual, cashing 26 checks in odd and large amounts so as to total $363,489.50 is plainly not ordinary banking practice." Would revised Article 3 make a difference as to this?

in due course to enforce a contract induced by fraud, § 3–305(2) [revised as § 3–305(a)(1)], the same treatment should be given to a contract induced by bribery. The result ought not be changed by the additional fact that commercial bribery is a criminal offense in New York. Finally, it would be poor policy for courts to transform banks and other finance companies into policing agents charged with the responsibility of searching out commercial bribery committed by their assignors. We doubt that denying recovery to holders in due course would have an appreciable effect on the frequency of commercial bribery."

For what amounts to fraud in the execution of the instrument under UCC 3–305(a)(1), see *First National Bank of Odessa v. Fazzari,* p. 86 supra. UCC 3–305 does not list unconscionability in violation of UCC 2–302 as a real defense. How strong an argument can be made that it is nevertheless a real defense? (Remember that fraud in the inducement to undertake the obligation is only a personal defense.)

Claims in recoupment (see Note 2, p. 89 supra) are treated much like personal defenses and are cut off as against a holder in due course. See UCC 3–305(b).

Problem 10. Would it make any difference in Problem 5, p. 237 supra, if Empire discovered not only that the cans are defective, but also that Quaker had fraudulently misrepresented their quality before the contract was made? See UCC 3–305.

SECTION 2. PAYOR BANK'S RECOURSE AFTER PAYMENT BY MISTAKE

Prefatory Note. What is the legal position of a payor bank that overlooks its depositor's stop order and pays the check by mistake? The case law in New York prior to the Code affords an interesting contrast with the law under the Code.

New York law began with the rule that the bank was not entitled to charge the amount of the check to its depositor's account as long as the depositor had not ratified the wrongful payment by, for example, taking and keeping goods for which the check had been given.[1] The bank, therefore, had to bear the loss, as against its depositor, even though the depositor may have issued the stop payment order without justification.

Banks counterattacked by putting on stop payment order forms clauses disclaiming any liability to the depositor for ignoring a stop

---

1. American Defense Society v. Sherman National Bank, 225 N.Y. 506, 122   N.E. 695 (1919).

order. Courts in some states had held such clauses invalid, sometimes on the ground of public policy and sometimes on the ground of lack of consideration. See Note 2, p. 258 infra. But the New York Court of Appeals, mindful of having already fastened liability on the bank without regard to the depositor's justification for stopping payment, sustained such a clause.[2]

The use of such a clause generally gave the bank adequate protection by allowing it to charge the check to its depositor, whether justified or not in stopping payment. Could it, in the alternative, recover the amount paid by mistake from the payee to whom it had paid it? The Court of Appeals concluded that, in the usual case, the bank's recourse against its depositor was exclusive, so that "when a bank pays a check after and despite receiving a stop-payment order from its depositor it cannot recover on the check from the payee of the check."[3]

The Code deals with the problem in a very different way. UCC 3–418 generally makes the bank's payment final. But UCC 4–407 gives the bank rights of subrogation that may allow it to recover against either its depositor or the payee, depending on the facts relating to the transaction between the two of them.[4] This is in sharp contrast to the prior New York law under which "Our courts have never permitted a bank ..., after breaching its depositor's instructions, to involve him against his will in litigation with a third party in order that the bank may recoup a potential loss resulting from its own error. The doctrine of subrogation ... is not properly applicable under such circumstances."[5] If the bank has already charged the amount of the check to its depositor's account and refuses to recredit it, the depositor presumably has an action against the bank to the extent that its payment caused loss. Where is there an express provision to this effect? Can such a rule fairly be read into the Code by inference from UCC 4–403(c) or by analogy to UCC 4–407(1)?[6]

2. Gaita v. Windsor Bank, 251 N.Y. 152, 167 N.E. 203 (1929).

3. Rosenbaum v. First National City Bank, 11 N.Y.2d 845, 227 N.Y.S.2d 670, 182 N.E.2d 280 (1962). An exception was made, however, "if at the time of presentation and payment the payee has notice that payment has been stopped; then the payee has no right to retain the proceeds of the check mistakenly paid by the bank." National Boulevard Bank v. Schwartz, 175 F.Supp. 74 (S.D.N.Y.1959). See also Chase National Bank v. Battat, 105 N.Y.S.2d 13 (Sup.Ct.1951).

4. For the reader who has not studied the concept of subrogation in another course, it may be helpful to know that subrogation is often referred to as an "equitable assignment." When, to prevent unjust enrichment, one person is subrogated to another's rights with respect to an obligation, the result is essentially the same as if the latter had assigned those rights to the former. Thus if A owes B $100, and C, believing that C owes this debt to B, pays B $100, then C is entitled to be subrogated to B's claim against A in the amount of $100.

5. Chase National Bank v. Battat, 297 N.Y. 185, 78 N.E.2d 465 (1948).

6. It is worthy of note at this point that in the 1952 edition of the Code a person who obtained payment or certification warranted that he had "no knowledge of any effective direction to stop payment" (UCC 3–417(1)(b) (1952 ed.); see also UCC 4–207(1)(d) (1952 ed.)). At the 1954 hearings on the Code in New York, the New York Clearing House Association objected to this rule. "The holder who is told that the drawer intends to stop payment who thereafter collect[s] the check takes the risk that, if it is paid over an effective order, he may have to repay the payor at some fu-

Problem 11. Before the Empire check has been presented to The Bank of New York, Empire offers to return the cans to Quaker and stops payment on the check, in the belief that they are defective and that it is entitled to refuse to pay for them. The Bank of New York mislays the stop payment order, pays the check, and charges Empire's account.

(a) What are the rights of The Bank of New York, Empire and Quaker? Does it make any difference whether Empire is correct in its belief? See UCC 4–403, 4–407.

(b) Would it make any difference if the stop payment order contained the following clause:

Should you pay this check through inadvertence or oversight, it is expressly understood that you will in no way be held responsible.

(c) Suppose that Empire is correct in its belief that it is entitled to refuse to pay for the cans. Assume that Quaker had a balance of $10,000 before making the deposit and that on that afternoon the Philadelphia National allowed Quaker to withdraw $15,000 in cash and certified a check drawn by Quaker in the amount of $20,000. What would be the rights of Empire, Quaker, the Philadelphia National and The Bank of New York? Would it make any difference if Quaker had included the words "for deposit" in its indorsement? Does the answer depend on whether the other checks deposited at the same time are paid? (See the deposit slip at p. 134 supra.) See Problems 5 and 6 supra.

(d) Suppose that the facts are otherwise the same as in (d) but that the withdrawal from and certification by the Philadelphia National do not occur until after The Bank of New York has paid the check. Will the result be the same? (Can a holder become a holder in due course of a check after it has been paid?)

---

ture time when he may have changed his position. It has been suggested that the holder should advise the payor bank of his information after which the payor bank may not, it is suggested, hold him on his warranty. This is not practical in most cases because any such notice would require that the item be given special handling; and it is unrealistic in all cases. The only practical alternative is to suggest that the holder disclaim the warranty in his indorsement. But how many holders are sufficiently learned in the law to do so? And if this is what the holder should do, why propose the rule at all?" Record of Hearings on the Uniform Commercial Code (N.Y.Leg.Doc. (1954) No. 65) 445–46.

The warranty was dropped out of the 1957 edition of the Code. The Editorial Board gave the following reason: "This warranty was consistent with some case law but has been extensively criticized and appears to be productive of more trouble than benefit. Further, the protection afforded payors by this statutory warranty becomes less necessary in view of the provisions of Section 4–407. However, deletion of the warranty evidences no intent to change the common law, insofar as there are common law decisions on the question." 1956 Recommendations of the Editorial Board for the Uniform Commercial Code 146. What, then, is the rule under the Code in New York? See footnote 3, supra.

Notes

(1) **Validity of Stop Payment Orders and Automation.** The order, to be effective must, of course, sufficiently identify the check. At common law a stop payment order could be oral and in the absence of agreement was valid indefinitely. However, a majority of states enacted statutes limiting the period of effectiveness. Statutory periods ranged from 30 days to one year with similar variations as to renewals. Under UCC 4–403(b) an oral order is effective for fourteen days, a written order for six months.

In a computerized bank, stop payment orders may be handled by having the computer reject all checks of the amount of the stopped check until the stopped check is selected manually from among those rejected. Would the payor bank be responsible if the computer failed to reject a stopped check for $4,999.99 because the stop payment order had incorrectly described it as a check for $4,999.98? See UCC 4–403(a). Would the depositary bank be responsible if the computer failed to reject a stopped check for $4,999.99 because it had incorrectly encoded it as one for $4,999.98? See UCC 4–209.

In FJS Electronics v. Fidelity Bank, 288 Pa.Super. 138, 431 A.2d 326 (1981), the court said that the payor bank "made a choice when it elected to employ a technique which searched for stopped checks by amount alone. . . . A bank's decision to reduce operating costs by using a system which increases the risk that checks as to which there is an outstanding stop payment order will be paid invites liability when such items are paid. An error of fifty cents ['$1,844.48' for $1,844.98 check] in the amount of a stop payment order does not deprive the bank of a reasonable opportunity to act on the order."

UCC 4–403 as amended rejects this view by requiring that the stop payment order describe the item "with reasonable certainty." Comment 5 explains: "In describing the item, the customer, in the absence of a contrary agreement, must meet the standard of what information allows the bank under the technology then existing to identify the item with reasonable certainty." Would it make a difference if a customer erred in describing the number of the check as "292" rather than 280, as long as the amount was correct? See *Hughes v. Marine Midland Bank, infra.*

(2) **Validity of Stipulations.** Prior to the Code banks frequently printed on their stop payment order forms clauses like that in Problem 11 supra. There was a conflict of authority on the validity of such clauses. Some courts held them invalid on the ground of public policy, at least in so far as they purported to relieve the bank of liability for its negligence. Other courts held them invalid on the basis of lack of consideration, since a bank was bound to observe a stop payment order and gave up nothing in exchange for the clause.

The Code, in UCC 4–103(a), prohibits disclaimer of the bank's responsibility for "failure to exercise ordinary care." Does this mean that an exculpatory clause on a stop payment order is of *no* effect under the Code? What would be the effect under the Code of a clause on the signature card requiring stop payment orders to be in writing and on a form provided by the bank? What risk inherent in an oral stop payment order might a bank seek to avoid by such a clause?

Even where it is against public policy for a bank to limit its liability for negligent payment, might it not be advantageous to a bank to put such a clause on its stop payment order form? Would the inclusion of such a clause come within Rule 1.2(d) of the American Bar Association's Model Rules of Professional Conduct (1983), which states: "A lawyer shall not counsel a client to engage, or assist a client, in conduct that the lawyer knows is criminal or fraudulent ...."? The final draft of that rule contained additional language that was deleted: " ... or in the preparation of a written instrument containing terms the lawyer knows are expressly prohibited by law...." The following comment was also deleted: "Law in many jurisdictions expressly prohibits various provisions in contracts and other written instruments. Such proscriptions may include usury laws, statutes prohibiting provisions that purport to waive certain legally conferred rights and contract provisions that have been held to be prohibited as a matter of law in the controlling jurisdiction. A lawyer may not employ expressly prohibited terms. On the other hand, there are legal rules that simply make certain contractual provisions unenforceable, allowing one or both parties to avoid the obligation. Inclusion of the latter kind of provision in a contract may be unwise but it is not a violation of this Rule, nor is it improper to include a provision whose legality is subject to reasonable argument."

Can you draft a clause that would meet this standard under UCC 4–103(a)? Would the same reasoning apply to a clause which was unenforceable because of lack of consideration?

In the *FJS Electronics* case, discussed in the preceding note, the bank's notice confirming the stop payment order said "PLEASE ENSURE AMOUNT IS CORRECT." Would it be to a bank's advantage to be more specific in explaining the importance of the amount? Would it be to a bank's advantage to put the following clause in its agreements with customers?

> The bank is not responsible for payment over a stop payment order unless the order gives your account number and the number and exact amount of the check. Otherwise our computer may not be able to execute your order.

See UCC 4–103(a) and Comment 1 to UCC 4–403.

(3) Consumer Complaints. Consumer advocates, who regard the stop payment order as an important weapon in the consumer's modest arsenal, have criticized the Code's subrogation rules as eroding that right. "If a merchant-payee delivered a defective refrigerator, he should not receive full payment simply because the financial institution mistakenly paid the check. On the other hand, subrogating the financial institution to the payee's claims against the consumer, and requiring the consumer to overcome that claim to receive compensation for a mistaken payment, completely vitiates the original purpose of the countermand, which is to reduce underenforcement of consumer rights. Instead ... the institution should be liable for the face amount of the instrument." Cooter & Rubin, A Theory of Loss Allocation for Consumer Payments, 66 Tex.L.Rev. 63, 123 (1987). How does this suggestion differ from the pre-Code New York law described in the Prefatory Note, supra?

For an argument that a stop payment order should not be subject to a fee, see Hillerbrand, Revised Articles 3 and 4 of the Uniform Commercial Code: A Consumer Perspective, 42 Ala.L.Rev. 679, 715–16 (1991). Is this argument supported by the statement in Comment 1 to UCC 4–403 that "stopping payment ... is a service which depositors expect and are entitled to receive from banks notwithstanding its difficulty, inconvenience and expense"?

(4) **More Consumer Complaints.** Drawers sometimes postdate checks on the assumption that a postdated check is not payable until the stated date and so cannot be properly paid and charged to the drawer's account before that date. While the practice of postdating checks is by no means limited to consumers, the postdated check is regarded by consumer advocates as being, like the stop payment order, an important weapon in the consumer's modest arsenal. A consumer who arranges to give a seller a postdated check has, in effect, bargained for a window of time in which the consumer can back out of the transaction, stop payment on the check, and resist having to pay instead of trying to recover from the seller.

Under former UCC 3–114(2), drawers were correct in assuming that "the time when [a postdated check] is payable is determined by the stated date." (Under former UCC 4–407, however, the payor bank that mistakenly paid a postdated check was, like the payor bank that mistakenly paid over a stop payment order, subrogated to the seller's rights against the buyer. A postdated check did not, therefore, avoid the sorts of consumer complaints described in the preceding note.)

All this is changed by revised Articles 3 and 4. Since the date of the check does not appear on the MICR line, a postdated check cannot be identified by a payor bank's automated system. UCC 4–401(c) therefore allows the payor bank to charge a check to a customer's account "even though payment was made before the date of the check, unless the customer has given notice to the bank of the postdating describing the check with reasonable certainty." The rules for stop payment orders are made applicable to such notices, and a bank that overlooks such a notice "is liable for damages for the loss resulting from its act," and these "may include damages for dishonor of subsequent items." May a bank charge the customer that gives such a notice a fee? How will customers find out about the change in the law? See Hillebrand, Revised Articles 3 and 4 of the Uniform Commercial Code: A Consumer Perspective, 42 Ala.L.Rev. 679, 704–06 (1991).[1]

Prefatory Note. As Problem 11(a) shows, if a payor bank pays a check over a stop payment order, the rights of the parties may depend on the rights of the drawer and the payee on the underlying transaction between them. Suppose that those rights are unclear, because of unresolved questions of either law or fact. May the payor bank maintain the charge to its customer's account until those questions are resolved? Or must it recredit its customer's account until they are resolved?

UCC 4–403(c) puts on the customer the "burden of establishing the fact and amount of the loss resulting from the payment" of a check over a stop payment order. What does this language mean? (The quoted words were the same in former UCC 4–303(3).) Even the drafters of former Article 4 seem to have been uncertain about the answer to this question.

The 1952 edition of the Code contained a Comment 9 to U.C.C. § 4–403: "When a bank pays an item over a stop payment order, such payment automatically involves a charge to the customer's account. Subsection (3) imposes upon the customer the burden of establishing the fact and amount of loss resulting from the payment. Consequently until such burden is maintained either in a court action or to the satisfaction of the bank, the bank is not obligated to recredit the amount of the item to the customer's account and, therefore, is not liable for the dishonor of other items due to insufficient funds caused by the payment contrary to the stop payment order."

The Study of the Uniform Commercial Code made by the New York Law Revision Commission in 1955 had this to say about Comment 9: "Subrogation to a right to enforce is not the same thing as a right to charge the customer's account. However, Section 4–403, providing for the right to stop-payment, provides that the burden is on the customer to establish the fact and amount of loss resulting from payment contrary to a binding stop-payment order, and Comment 9 to that section states that until such burden is maintained the bank is not obligated to recredit the customer's account. It is not clear that the rule indicated in this Comment 9 does result from the text of Section 4–403(3)." N.Y.L.Rev.Comm.Study of UCC, Vol. 2, p. 339 (1955).

---

1. "Consideration was given to the matter of how banks should deal with checks bearing legends such as 'not valid for more than $50,' or 'not good after 60 days.' There are obvious difficulties in requiring banks to respect these legends in an automated or truncated check collection system. Thus, throughout most of the project a section was included in revised Article 4 that authorized the banking system to disregard nonessential terms written on checks. Toward the end of the project opposition was raised to the inclusion of the section by users who urged the importance to drawers of being able to rely on the two legends quoted above. In the rush of activities at the end of the project, no resolution of these problems was reached, and the draft approved by the NCCUSL and the ALI does not include such a section." Jordan & Warren, Introduction to Symposium: Revised U.C.C. Articles 3 & 4 and New Article 4A, 42 Ala.L.Rev. 373, 395 n. 26 (1991).

In 1955 the Code's Enlarged Editorial Board stated, "We ... believe that Comment 9 is consistent with Section 4–403(3) and should stand." Supplement November 1 to the 1952 Official Draft 145 (1955). The text of UCC 4–403(3) remained the same but when the revised Comments to the Code appeared early in 1958, Comment 9 had been dropped without explanation.

As shown by the next case and the notes following it, subsequent judicial opinions had no greater success in interpreting the troublesome language of UCC 4–303. Revised Article 4 makes no significant change. "In the initial revisions of Article 4, section 4–403 was modified. The reporters provided that the bank must recredit the customer's account and would then have the burden of proving that no loss to the customer had resulted from its error. Since the bank is subrogated to the customer's rights against the merchant-payee in this situation, by virtue of existing section 4–407, it would not necessarily absorb the loss. If the customer was justified, and the bank was required to reimburse her, it could assert her rights in a suit against the payee. The customer was required to cooperate with the bank in such a suit by providing an affidavit about the reasons for stopping payment of the check, and that doing so would be a precondition to obtaining the recredit. But the banks objected to this revision; they argued that they usually recredit a customer's account anyway, so no legal requirement was necessary. This position prevailed and the revision now continues subsection 4–403(3) essentially unchanged." Rubin, Efficiency, Equity and the Proposed Revision of Articles 3 and 4, 42 Ala.L.Rev. 551, 578 (1991).

Problem 12. Suppose, in Problem 11(a) that Empire insists that the cans are defective and Quaker insists that they are not. Before The Bank of New York has a chance to investigate, a second check drawn by Empire is presented for payment. Empire's balance is insufficient to pay it, but it would be sufficient if the amount of the check payable to Quaker had not been charged to Empire's account. Advise The Bank of New York whether or not to pay the second check. See UCC 4–403, 4–407; *Hughes v. Marine Midland Bank*, infra.

HUGHES v. MARINE MIDLAND BANK

Civil Court of Rochester, Civil Branch, Monroe County, 1985.
127 Misc.2d 209, 484 N.Y.S.2d 1000.

JOHN MANNING REGAN, JUDGE. ... Plaintiffs, Dr. and Mrs. Frederick Hughes are depositors in the defendant, Marine Midland's bank. They have transacted banking with the defendant at its office on East Avenue in Rochester, New York, for some years.

In February, 1983, the plaintiffs were on vacation in Sarasota, Florida. In Sarasota, they leased a resort cottage from Diane Barth, a real estate agent. Ms. Barth insisted, prior to granting possession of the cottage, that the plaintiffs pay the full month's rental of the property in the sum of $1,470.00. Mrs. Hughes tendered her personal check, dated February 1, 1983, for the sum of $1,470.00 to Ms. Barth in compliance with her preconditions. The check was drawn on defendant bank's East Avenue, Rochester, New York, office from the Hughes' personal joint account. Ms. Barth deposited the check in the First Presidential Savings & Loan of Sarasota the very next day, February 2, 1983, for collection.

On February 4, 1983, a Friday, Dr. Hughes telephoned the defendant bank and spoke with Gail Stevens, a bank employee whose duties as an operations supervisor included the processing of telephoned stop payment orders. Dr. Hughes told Ms. Stevens the correct account number, the correct name of the payee, the correct date of the check, and the correct amount of money for which the check was drawn. He did not give her the correct check number, however, describing the number as 292 instead of 280.

Moreover, Dr. Hughes amplified his stop payment telephone call with his reasons for stopping payment. He advised that the payee, Ms. Barth, had misrepresented the quality of the accommodations for which the check had been delivered to her, where-upon Ms. Stevens duly recorded "misrepresentation" as the reason for the stop order.

This telephone call was placed at 8:55 a.m. on Friday, the 4th day of February, 1983. On Monday, February 7, 1983, the Barth check was posted as a debit to the Hughes' account, and the full sum of $1,470.00 was deducted.

In reliance on the conversation with Ms. Stevens, Dr. Hughes notified Ms. Barth that he and his wife were leaving the premises. After contentious arguments had ended, the Hughes paid Ms. Barth the sum of $350.00 later that same Friday afternoon, February 4, 1983, in full settlement of all claims between them.

The bank sent the Hughes a form for written confirmation of the stop-payment order and Dr. Hughes returned it, duly signed, to the bank on February 18, 1983. On February 22, 1983, the bank mailed the plaintiffs their monthly statement which showed the $1,470.00 deduction for the Barth check on February 7, 1983. When they received the statement some three days later, they learned, for the first time, that the bank had not honored their stop-payment order.

The Hughes' cause of action asserts that the bank is liable to them for this loss of $1,470.00 under the provisions of Article 4, Section 4–403 of the Uniform Commercial Code, which reads as follows:

"(1) A customer may by order to his bank stop payment of any item payable for his account but the order must be received at such time and in such manner as to afford the bank a reasonable opportunity to act on it prior to any action by the bank with respect to the item described in Section 4–303.

(2) An oral order is binding upon the bank only for fourteen calendar days unless confirmed in writing within that period.

A written order is effective for only six months unless renewed
in writing.

(3) The burden of establishing the fact and amount of loss
resulting from the payment of an item contrary to a binding
stop payment order is on the customer." ...

The bank's principal defenses to plaintiffs' assertion of liability is
that the bank's actions did not cause the loss, but, rather, the plaintiffs'
error did, for when plaintiffs gave Ms. Stevens the wrong check number, the bank's computer correctly reported that check number 292 had
not been negotiated, and thereafter payment of check number 292 was,
in fact, stopped. But, of course, payment of check number 280 was not
stopped....

Because the bank received the stop payment order in plenty of time
to act on it,[1] the only flaw in the plaintiffs' case is the error they made
in providing Ms. Stevens with an incorrect check number. Ms. Stevens'
affidavit states that the bank's central computer in Syracuse, New
York, "can be directed to identify: (1) a specific check by number; (2)
all checks for a specific amount; (3) a specific check having a stated
number and amount." Ms. Piper, a bank employee who actually works
at the computer center in Syracuse, and whose affidavit states that the
center processes almost a million items a day, reports that any stop
payment order can be processed in any of three ways: "(1) by check
number and dollar amount (2) by check number, or (3) by dollar
amount."

From these circumstances, it is evident that the bank's intraoffice
memorandum, which Ms. Stevens made from her conversation with Dr.
Hughes over the telephone on February 4, 1983, contained enough
information—the account number, and the amount of the check—to
process the stop payment order at the computer center in Syracuse.

The legal question then becomes whether these facts meet the
standards of legal sufficiency set out in U.C.C. § 4–403(1) which are
that: "the order must be received at such time and in such manner as
to afford the bank a reasonable opportunity to act." The case law is
not easily reconciled. In Mitchell v. Security Bank, 85 Misc. 360, 147
N.Y.S. 470 (App.Term 1st Dept1914) a wrong date, and a single digit
error in the amount of the check was held insufficient. Yet in Thomas
v. Marine Midland Tinkers Natl. Bank, 86 Misc.2d 284, 287, 381
N.Y.S.2d 797 (Civ.Ct.N.Y.Co.1976), a digit error in the check number
was deemed "trivial and insignificant", and the check description held
to be adequate.

In view of the *Thomas* decision in 1976, and recognizing the
capabilities of modern computers to respond to programmed software,
the Court concludes that New York banks have had ample time to

---

1. A full banking day, a full weekend, and a portion of the next banking day elapsed before payment. This is time enough to act as a matter of law. Dunbar v. First National Bank, 63 A.D.2d 755, 404 N.Y.S.2d 722 (3rd Dept1978). See also Chute v. Bank One of Akron, 10 Ohio App.3d 122, 460 N.E.2d 720 (1983).

design software to identify and stop payment on checks from a specific account simply by account number and dollar amount. In fact, Ms. Piper's affidavit admits that Marine's computers now have that capability. Accordingly, in the interests of commercial stability and predictability, and in furtherance of the doctrine of *stare decisis*,[2] this Court will follow the rule in *Thomas* and hold that the information provided met the statutory standards of reasonable accuracy, and did therefore provide a reasonable opportunity for the bank to act.

Subdivision (3) of § 4–403 of the U.C.C. puts the burden of establishing the fact and amount of loss occurring upon payment over a valid stop order on the customer. At first glance, most would infer that this loss would always be equal to the face amount of the check, and that deducting that face sum from the customer's account would establish that sum as "the amount of the loss". For example, the Complaint in this case makes that assumption and demands judgment for $1,470.00, the sum defendant deducted from the account.

Prior to enactment of the U.C.C., this was the law in New York. Unless a customer ratified, and adopted as correct, the bank's wrongful payment over a valid stop order, the bank was liable for the full sum deducted from a customer's account. Chase Natl. Bank v. Battat, 297 N.Y. 185, 78 N.E.2d 465 (1948). Moreover, the Court specifically held in *Battat* that the validity or invalidity of the underlying transaction was *no defense* to the customer's cause of action:

"*In the absence of ratification the bank [is] liable to the depositor,* as [a bank cannot] justify paying out the depositor's money without authority by showing *that the recipient* [payee] *was justly entitled to it.*" 297 N.Y. at p. 190, 78 N.E.2d 465. Citing American Defense Society v. Sherman National Bank, 225 N.Y. 506, 122 N.E. 695 (1919).

In post-Code cases in New York, particularly in *Thomas v. Marine Midland,* supra, and, obliquely, in Sunshine v. Bankers Trust Co., 34 N.Y.2d 404, 358 N.Y.S.2d 113, 314 N.E.2d 860 (1974), that issue has become muddled.[3]

Thomas regards the problem as a conflict between § 4–403(3) and § 4–407 (the subrogation provisions) and holds, under the authority of *Sunshine,* that the plaintiff must prove, as part of his case, that the

---

2. Other state courts have agreed with the decision in *Thomas.* See Parr v. Security National Bank, 680 P.2d 648, 38 U.C.C. Reporting Service 275 (1984) reporting a Court of Appeals case from Oklahoma, which held that a digit error in the check number did not vitiate the sufficiency of the stop order.

3. Under the official comments to U.C.C. § 4–407, at McKinney's Consolidated Laws of N.Y., Book 62½, at page 631, the author informs us that the code drafters were aware that a routine defense to a valid stop order action was that the under-

lying debt was due in any event. While this defense was available in some states, it was *not in New York.* See Chase Natl. v. Battat, supra. The New York Annotations in McKinney's Consolidated Laws of N.Y., Book 62½, U.C.C. § 4–403, at page 613, meekly suggest that subdivision (3) of U.C.C. § 4–403 appears to be "contra" the rule, but they cite no authority for that interpretation, and this court can find none. Certainly, the language itself creates no categorical imperative for such an interpretation.

underlying transaction caused a loss so long as the bank's answer raises that issue; and the bank adduces some evidence of that fact. Much of this rationale is dicta, however, because the bank in *Thomas* did not plead, nor prove, any affirmative defense as to non-loss. See 86 Misc.2d at page 291, 381 N.Y.S.2d 797.

In the instant case, the bank has pleaded forum non conveniens both as a procedural and affirmative defense. In its affidavits and briefs, it has argued that the underlying transaction with Barth raises factual questions about whether the plaintiffs truly sustained a loss, and, if so, what the amount of that loss was.

This Court agrees with the bank to this extent: if the underlying transaction is part of the plaintiff's case—as *Thomas* says it is—then the bank has raised a factual issue in this case, and summary judgment should be denied. However, *Thomas* cannot bind this Court in the face of both common sense and the holding of the Court of Appeals in both *American Defense Society* and the *Battat* cases. *Sunshine* did not overrule either *American Defense Society*, or *Battat*, explicitly or implicitly, and, moreover, unequivocally, *Sunshine* still held that: "a stop-payment order need not be supported by a sound legal basis". See 34 N.Y.2d at p. 413, footnote 5, 358 N.Y.S.2d 113, 314 N.E.2d 860.

Therefore, in this Court's judgment, *Battat* is still good law in New York; and a bank may not defend a U.C.C. § 4–403 violation by pleading that the payee of the check, which was the subject of a valid stop order, was justly entitled to the money. Further, the payee, Ms. Barth's, entitlements, if any, are not a part of the plaintiffs' *prima facie* case. This Court now holds that the plaintiffs meet their burden to prove loss both under the common law, and under the code, if they show that the bank has paid out from the depositor's account a sum of money over a valid stop order, and the loss, both *prima facie*, and at trial, is that sum so paid out.[4]

---

4. The Court must here acknowledge that decisions in other states, particularly Florida, are to the contrary. See Southeast First National Bank v. Atlantic Telec, Inc., 389 So.2d 1032 (Fla.App.1980), which follows the rules set out in *Thomas v. Marine Midland Bank.*

Contrary judicial interpretations of U.C.C. § 4–403, subdivision (3) are the rule, however, not the exception; and Florida and New York are merely examples....

Georgia courts have ruled that the underlying transaction between a depositor and a third party is wholly irrelevant in a U.C.C. § 4–403 action between the bank and its depositor based on an improper payment over a valid stop order. See Whitmire v. Woodbury, 154 Ga.App. 159, 267 S.E.2d 783 (1980).

Massachusetts courts, on the contrary, have espoused the rule enunciated in *Thomas v. Marine Midland Bank*, supra.

See Siegel v. Northeast Merchants Nat'l Bank, 386 Mass. 672, 437 N.E.2d 218 (1982), which allows the bank to introduce proof of the underlying transaction on the question of plaintiff's damages.

This Court's decision, in the instant case, does not stem from any animadversions to North Carolina, Massachusetts, or Florida courts. The predicates for the instant holding are two-fold: (1) *Battat, American Defense Society*, and *Sunshine*, all eschew involvement with the underlying transaction either as part of plaintiff's damages, or as an affirmative defense, and all three cases bind this Court; and (2) absolutely nothing in the official comments to U.C.C. § 4–403, nor in the language of subdivision (3), itself, constrains so bizarre and cumbersome an interpretation.

Finally, the law of damages has always been to *confine* economic losses, not expand

Common sense precludes involving banking institutions in litigation among their customers and those with whom their customers deal. The bank's contract obligations with their customers are separate and distinct from the commercial transactions which the customers may have with others. In granting subrogation rights to any bank which has sustained a loss due to a wrongful payment over a valid stop order, the Legislature in U.C.C. § 4–407, gave a method of mitigating such losses, if a bank chose to exercise such rights. The analogy to an insurance subrogation—where the carrier must pay the insured upon the event of loss—is apposite and comparable. The carrier can sue the guilty party—and it frequently does; but that option bears no relationship to the carrier's duty to pay its insured under its insurance contract on a proper proof of loss.[5] Here the debtor-creditor contract between the Hughes and the bank governs the bank's liability. The bank's subrogation rights, after it has experienced a liability for its breach of that debtor-creditor contract, are irrelevant.

Sunshine is not contrary to this holding. That case holds that regardless of whether the underlying transaction between the bank's customer and a third party is valid or invalid, and regardless of whether the *depositor* himself has sustained a loss, subrogation (the equitable transfer of legal rights from one person to another) occurs when the bank has sustained a loss.

If the underlying transaction were an ingredient of the § 4–403 claim, then the § 4–403 action would subsume the underlying transaction and subdivisions (b) and (c) of § 4–407, the subrogation statute, would become superfluous since the underlying transaction would always be litigated in the § 4–403 suit, because the parties in the underlying transaction would be necessary (C.P.L.R. § 1001) to any depositor's *prima facie* case. The effect of any such rule would be to merge these statutes into a single cause of action.

Sunshine (34 N.Y.2d 404, 358 N.Y.S.2d 113, 314 N.E.2d 860, supra), however, recognizes separate causes of action: One by the customer against the bank under § 4–403, and one by the bank, as subrogee, against the payee under § 4–407(c). In footnote 5 on page 413 of 34 N.Y.2d, 358 N.Y.S.2d 113, 314 N.E.2d 860, the Court of Appeals candidly admits that the finality of the trial court's order precluded their consideration of the cause of action under subdivision (b) of § 4–407 against the depositor-maker, but their implication is that such a cause of action, as that statute gives, does exist.

them. The direct damages from the breach of the depositor's contract is the sum wrongfully deducted. The underlying transaction introduces, at least, the issue of consequential damages. Opening that issue may expand a bank's liability beyond immediate reckoning, and allow plaintiffs to prove that wrongful payment of the stopped item caused a whole series of events far more damaging, financially, than the amount paid out. Excursions of this kind are at war with the conservative history of commercial law and the law of contracts generally.

5. While large banks may be self-insurers, many smaller banks insure themselves against both forgeries and collection losses. In those cases, the insurance subrogation process is more than an analogy, it is a fact, as the carrier who pays eventually winds up as the subrogee under § 4–407.

Moreover, the cases contain two persuasive reasons for recognizing this sequential separateness of these causes of action: (1) The "innocent" party who has issued a timely stop-payment order is entitled to the use of his funds pending the determination of his legal obligations in the underlying transaction; and (2) the cost of prosecuting the suit on the underlying transaction may exceed the maximum possible recovery, and it may never be brought. In such event, the bank must bear the loss as a cost of doing business. See 34 N.Y.2d at page 413, footnote 5, 358 N.Y.S.2d 113, 314 N.E.2d 860.

This Court understands that this holding allows a depositor-plaintiff possibly to become a third-party defendant in his own § 4–403 action. In such an action, the defendant bank can, and sometimes surely will, prosecute its subrogation claims under U.C.C. § 4–407(b) and (c) in a third-party suit against both its depositor and the person with whom the depositor has had an underlying transaction. But that possible procedural posture should not, and does not, affect or alter the substantive legal relationships among all these parties, nor ought it to confuse and merge the sequential separateness of the causes of action each of these statutes has created. . . .

In view of the foregoing, the Court grants the plaintiffs' motion for Summary Judgment, and directs entry of a judgment for plaintiffs in the sum of $1,470.00, with interest at 9% from February 7, 1983, together with the costs and disbursements of this action.

Notes

(1) **Another Scenario.** Would the result in *Hughes* have been different if Ms. Barth's cottage had been as represented by her, if the Hughes had moved out because they had found a condo that they preferred because of a Gulf view, if the Hughes had not attempted any settlement with Ms. Barth, and if Dr. Hughes had lied to Ms. Stevens about the supposed "misrepresentation"?

(2) **The Effect of Sunshine.** Do you agree, with Judge Regan's reading of the Code? In a footnote he acknowledges "that decisions in other states . . . are to the contrary." Consider also his analysis of decisions in New York. Is he right to rely on pre-Code decisions? He refers to the opinion of the New York Court of Appeals in Sunshine v. Bankers Trust Co., 34 N.Y.2d 404, 358 N.Y.S.2d 113, 314 N.E.2d 860 (1974). Here is what that court said.

"Banks are in the unique position of holding the very stakes for which they are contending. Respondent asserts that if we send this case back for trial, we would in effect, allow the Bank to be the arbiter of a dispute between two outside parties. We are not unmindful that banks may, perhaps even under a colorable claim of right, charge back a depositor's account even when no such right exists. The burden on a depositor of then going forward to bring a suit is a heavy one, and, indeed, an impossible one to bear where the amount involved is small.

Our decision should not be interpreted to permit this result. Before payment becomes final, or the midnight deadline has passed, a bank may charge back an account when it has received a timely stop order precisely so the Bank can avoid taking part in the dispute at all. However, once the Bank loses its right to charge back, the item becomes comingled with the general funds of the depositor.... When the Bank is suing as subrogee, it may not at the same time make a preliminary determination of the merits of the case by charging back on the depositor's account.... When the Bank is acting as subrogee, it has the burden of going forward."

Judge Regan also refers to Thomas v. Marine Midland Tinkers National Bank, 86 Misc.2d 284, 381 N.Y.S.2d 797 (1976). In that case a buyer of rugs, who had given the seller a $2,500 check as a deposit, stopped payment on the check. When the payor bank mistakenly paid the check, the buyer sued the bank. The bank "chose to try its case against the plaintiff alone without asserting any affirmative defense as to non loss, or adducing any evidence to negate the claimed loss at trial. No attempt was made to implead any other party from whom the defendant might acquire subrogated rights, to vouch any such party into the action, or to commence its own action against such party and thereafter move for a single consolidated trial. The defendant bank chose rather to maintain a position that plaintiff was required to come forward with evidence as to the underlying transaction to negate any inference of non loss or lesser loss in order to prove plaintiff's prima facie case."

The court awarded the buyer a $2,500 judgment against the bank. "The Court of Appeals in Sunshine clearly states that a defendant bank exercising its subrogation rights created by UCC § 4–407 has the burden of coming forward and presenting evidence which would show an absence of actual loss sustained by a plaintiff depositor suing it for damages arising from an improper payment over a stop payment order. In so stating, the Court of Appeals has not negated plaintiff's ultimate burden of proof upon the issue of loss if the defendant comes forward with proof. The Court of Appeals has thereby provided a means of harmoniously construing §§ 4–403(1), 4–403(3) and 4–407 of the Uniform Commercial Code to effectuate the statutory intent and design. This distinction between burden of proof and burden of coming forward is not uncommon.... [I]f the bank fails to meet its burden with legally sufficient proof of non loss, the customer has proven a prima facie case and is entitled to judgment. Where the burden of going forward is met by the bank, the customer must sustain the ultimate burden of proof on the issue of loss."

(3) Another Analysis. In Siegel v. New England Merchants National Bank, 386 Mass. 672, 437 N.E.2d 218 (1982), the Supreme Judicial Court of Massachusetts gave a different reading to UCC 4–401, 4–403, and 4–407.[1] The court began with UCC 4–401 and 4–407.

---

1. The check in Siegel was postdated, not stopped, when paid. Under former Article 4, however, the rules for stopped checks applied. See Note 4, p. 258 supra.

"The depositor has a claim against the bank for the amount improperly debited from its account, and the bank has a claim against the depositor based on subrogation to the rights of the payee and other holders. The bank may assert its subrogation rights defensively when its depositor brings an action for wrongful debit.... The rule of § 4–403(3), that a depositor must prove his loss, may at first seem at odds with our conclusion that § 4–401(1) provides the depositor with a claim against the bank in the amount of the check, leaving the bank with recourse through subrogation under § 4–407.... We believe, however, that § 4–403(3) was intended to operate within the process of credit and subrogation established by §§ 4–401(1) and 4–407.... Section 4–403(3) simply protects the bank against the need to prove events familiar to the depositor, and far removed from the bank, before it can realize its subrogation rights. The depositor, who participated in the initial transaction, knows whether the payee was entitled to eventual payment and whether any defenses arose. Therefore, § 4–403(3) requires that he, rather than the bank, prove these matters.

"This view of the three relevant sections of the code suggests a fair allocation of the burden of proof. The bank, which has departed from authorized bookkeeping, must acknowledge a credit to the depositor's account. It must then assert its subrogation rights, and in doing so must identify the status of the parties in whose place it claims. If the bank's subrogation claims are based on the check, this would entail proof that the third party subrogor was a holder, or perhaps a holder in due course. This responsibility falls reasonably upon the bank, because it has received the check from the most recent holder and is in at least as good a position as the depositor to trace its history.

"The depositor must then prove any facts that might demonstrate a loss. He must establish defenses good against a holder or holder in due course, as the case may be. See G.L. c. 106, § 3–305, 3–306. If the initial transaction is at issue, he must prove either that he did not incur a liability to the other party, or that he has a defense to liability. Thus the bank, if it asserts rights based on the transaction, need not make out a claim on the part of its subrogor against the depositor. Responsibility in this area rests entirely with the depositor, who participated in the transaction and is aware of its details. Further, the depositor must establish any consequential loss."

Among other cases, the court cited *Thomas v. Marine Midland Tinkers National Bank,* Note 2 supra, and said by way of comparison: "Although our analysis will often have the same result ... it may in some cases give greater force to § 4–403(3)." Which is the better analysis?

(4) **Right to Restitution.** Former UCC 3–418 determined when payment was final without mentioning the possibility of restitution. Comment 1 to revised UCC 3–418 explains: "Under former Article 3, the remedy of a drawee that paid or accepted a draft by mistake was

based on the law of mistake and restitution, but that remedy was not specifically stated. It was provided by Section 1–103. Former Section 3–418 was simply a limitation on the unstated remedy under the law of mistake and restitution. Under revised Article 3, Section 3–418 specifically states the right of restitution in subsections (a) and (b).... But ..., by virtue of subsection (c), the drawee loses the remedy if the person receiving payment ... was a person who took the check in good faith and for value or who in good faith changed position in reliance on the payment...."

(5) **Death of a Customer.** Since a check operates as the drawer's order on the payor bank and not as an assignment, in principle the drawer's death revokes the drawer's order just as would a stop payment order. This means that if the drawer has attempted to use a check in place of a will, and then dies before it is paid, the payee, as donee, not only has no right to payment against the payor bank, but has none against the drawer's estate. Occasionally, however, a sympathetic court has allowed recovery against the estate. See Burks v. Burks, 222 Ark. 97, 257 S.W.2d 369, 38 A.L.R.2d 589 (1953). But see Burrows v. Burrows, 240 Mass. 485, 137 N.E. 923, 20 A.L.R. 174 (1922).

A more important consequence of the rule that death revokes the drawer's order, and one that is by no means limited to checks issued as gifts, is that it puts the bank in a precarious position if it pays after the drawer's death. Case law generally relieved the bank where it paid without knowledge of the death. In a few states special statutes were enacted permitting the payor bank to pay a depositor's checks after death, even with knowledge.

For the Code provisions, see UCC 4–405. Comment 2 states that, "The purpose of the provision, as of the existing statutes, is to permit holders of checks drawn and issued shortly before death to cash them without the necessity of filing a claim in probate. The justification is that such checks normally are given in immediate payment of an obligation, that there is almost never any reason why they should not be paid, and that filing in probate is a useless formality, burdensome to the holder, the executor, the court and the bank. [What of other creditors if the estate has insufficient assets?] The section does not prevent an executor or administrator from recovering the payment from the holder of the check. It is not intended to affect the validity of any gift causa mortis or other transfer in contemplation of death, but merely to relieve the bank of liability for the payment." In what circumstances might a payor bank be entitled to restitution of a mistaken payment made after the 10–day period with knowledge of the death?

(6) **Bankruptcy of a Customer.** A problem analogous to that posed by the drawer's death is posed by the drawer's bankruptcy. Suppose that a drawer issues a check and then files a voluntary petition in bankruptcy, but the bank subsequently pays the check in

ignorance of the petition. Is the bank liable to the trustee in bankruptcy?

In Bank of Marin v. England, 385 U.S. 99 (1966), the Supreme Court read the old Bankruptcy Act to protect the bank. The new Bankruptcy Code § 542(c) codifies the rule of that case, protecting the bank if it pays "in good faith" and with "neither actual notice nor actual knowledge of the commencement of the case concerning the debtor." (However, the recipient of such a postpetition payment may not be protected against the trustee in bankruptcy. See § 549(b).) In what circumstances might a payor bank be entitled to restitution of a mistaken payment made with knowledge of the bankruptcy?

(7) **Electronic Fund Transfers Act.** The Electronic Fund Transfers Act and Regulation E deals with countermanding payment only in connection with preauthorized transfers. Under Regulation E:

> A consumer may stop payment of a preauthorized electronic fund transfer from the consumer's account by notifying the financial institution orally or in writing at any time up to three business days before the scheduled date of the transfer. The financial institution may require written confirmation of the stop-payment order to be made within 14 days of an oral notification if, when the oral notification is made, the requirement is disclosed to the consumer together with the address to which confirmation should be sent. If written confirmation has been required by the financial institution, the oral stop-payment order shall cease to be binding 14 days after it has been made.

12 C.F.R. § 205.10(c).

(8) **Article 4A.** Suppose that a commercial buyer, after sending a payment order to its bank to pay for goods, wishes to countermand the order. Can it do so? UCC 4A–211(a) allows a communication "canceling or amending the order" to be sent "orally, electronically, or in writing." Under subsection (b), such a communication "is effective to cancel or amend the order if notice of the communication is received at a time and in a manner affording the receiving bank a reasonable opportunity to act on the communication before the bank accepts the payment order" by executing it, that is, by issuing its own payment order to the seller's bank. As to contrary agreement, see UCC 4A–211(c).

If the buyer's bank overlooks the buyer's countermand and executes the buyer's payment order by mistake, is the buyer's bank entitled to restitution? In Banque Worms v. BankAmerica International, 77 N.Y.2d 362, 568 N.Y.S.2d 541, 570 N.E.2d 189 (1991), the question was whether a receiving bank's right to restitution in such a situation, involving a payment order of nearly $2 million, was governed by the "discharge for value" rule. Under that rule, an innocent creditor (here the seller) who has mistakenly been paid a debt by a third person (here the buyer's bank) is under no duty to make restitution even if the creditor has not changed position in reliance on the payment. (Note the analogy to UCC 3–418(c), under which an innocent creditor who had not changed position in reliance on a payment would be under no duty to make restitution because the creditor would have given value under the "antecedent claim" rule of UCC 3–303(a)(3).)

The court looked to Article 4A, even though the transaction had occurred before that article's effective date in New York. After observing that the "concern for finality has long been a significant policy consideration in this State" and that the " 'discharge for value' rule is consistent with and furthers the policy goal of finality in business transactions," the court quoted UCC 4A–303(c), which provides that if "a receiving bank executes the payment order of the sender by issuing a payment order to a beneficiary different from the beneficiary of the sender's order and the funds transfer is completed on the basis of that error, ... [t]he issuer of the erroneous order is entitled to recover from the beneficiary ... to the extent allowed by the law governing mistake and restitution." The court then looked to the example in Comment 2 to UCC 4A–303, under which a beneficiary that had mistakenly been paid $2,000,000 on a payment order of $1,000,000 might be allowed to keep the extra $1,000,000 "if Originator owed $2,000,000 to Beneficiary and Beneficiary received the extra $1,000,000 in good faith in discharge of the debt." The court concluded that "it seems clear ... that the drafters of UCC article 4A contemplated that the 'discharge for value' rule could appropriately be applied in respect to electronic fund transfers."

WHEN STOP PAYMENT ORDER COMES TOO LATE

If "a payor bank has *paid* an item" over the drawer's stop payment order, the bank is subrogated as provided in UCC 4–407. UCC 4–215(a) determines when payment has occurred. We have already seen (Chapter 3, Section 2(B)) that a bank generally has until its midnight deadline to decide whether to dishonor a check for insufficient funds. During that time it can also make sure that the check has not been stopped.

The bank will usually take steps to pay the check well before its midnight deadline, however, and may not always find it convenient to reverse those steps and stop payment on the check even though the check has not yet been paid under UCC 4–215. Therefore a separate section, UCC 4–303, fixes the time at which a stop payment order "comes too late" to terminate the payor bank's right to charge its customer's account for the check. After the time fixed in UCC 4–303, even if the check has not been paid, the payor bank is free to ignore the stop payment order and pay the check. (Although we are concerned only with stop payment orders, UCC 4–303 applies not only to stop payment orders but to all of what are known as the "four legals."[1])

As a comparison of the two lists in UCC 4–303(a) with that in UCC 4–215(a) will show, most of the items in the first list are simply times of payment in the second list and so do not give the payor bank a period before payment during which it is free to ignore a stop payment order. But UCC 4–303(a)(5) permits a bank to set "a cutoff hour no earlier than one hour after the opening of the next banking day after the banking day on which the bank received the check." After that hour, a stop payment order comes too late. Comment 4 explains: "Since the process-of-posting test has been abandoned as inappropriate for automated check collection, the determining event for priorities is a given hour on the day after the item is received."

Problem 13. Assume that The Bank of New York has fixed a cutoff hour of 11 a.m. under UCC 4–303(a)(2), (5). At noon on Thursday it receives a stop payment order from Empire. Advise The Bank of New York as to its legal position if it: (a) ignores the stop payment order and takes no further action with respect to the check; (b) promptly reverses the steps that it has just taken, stamps the check "cancelled in error" and returns it through the Clearing House to the First National City with a return item stamp like that on page 143 with "payment stopped" checked; (c) waits until Friday and then takes the steps described in (b). Would your advice be different if The Bank of New York had not received the check until 3 p.m. on Wednesday and had fixed a cutoff hour of 2 p.m. under UCC 4–108?

1. "Bankers call the matters handled by section 4–303(1) [revised as 4–303(a)] 'the four legals' because four legal questions are answered by determining the exact point of time at which the drawer loses control of the funds against which he has drawn his checks: (1) If the drawee (payor) bank becomes insolvent, who takes the loss, the drawer of the check or its holder?; (2) At what point does the drawer lose his right to stop payment?; (3) For how long may creditors attach the funds against which a check is drawn?; and (4) For how long may the bank set off against the drawer's account the various claims it holds against him?" 1 W. Hawkland, A Transactional Guide to the Uniform Commercial Code 399 (1964).

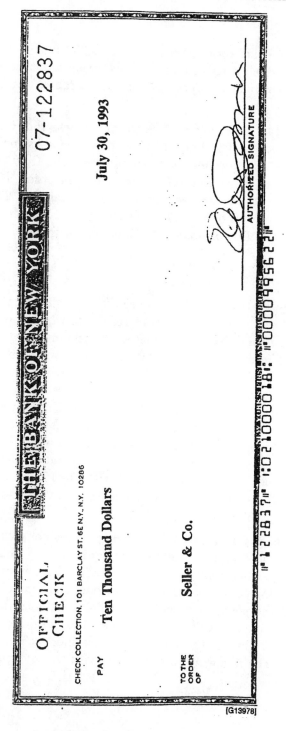

CASHIER'S OR OFFICIAL CHECK

Note

Period of Discretion. Do not UCC 4–303 and 4–215 create a period during which a payor bank has discretion to either honor or to ignore a stop payment order? Is this undesirable? Is UCC 1–203 relevant?

Problem 14. In Problem 11(a), supra, suppose that Quaker takes the Empire check to The Bank of New York and asks for a cashier's check for $22,178.50 payable to Quaker's order, and that The Bank of New York, having mislaid Empire's stop payment order, issues such a cashier's check. What are the rights of Quaker against The Bank of New York if it refuses to pay the cashier's check? See *Travi Construction Corp. v. First Bristol County National Bank*, infra.

————

Prefatory Note. A cashier's check is a troublesome instrument. " 'Cashier's check' means a draft with respect to which the drawer and drawee are the same bank or branches of the same bank."[1] UCC 3–104(g). Under former Article 3, a cashier's check was treated as a note since, under former UCC 3–118(a), "A draft drawn on the drawer is effective as a note." Now, however, a cashier's check is classified not only as a "draft" under UCC 3–104(g) but as a "check" under UCC so that it is generally subject to the rules laid down for drafts and checks. But UCC 3–414, which governs the liability of drawers of drafts states that it "does not apply to cashier's checks." Instead, the liability of the issuer of a cashier's check is governed by UCC 3–412, and it is identical with the liability of the issuer of a note—a throwback to the rule of former UCC 3–118(a).

Because of the issuing bank's liability, a cashier's check is often said to be "as good as cash" or "a cash equivalent". This notion has confused courts when confronted with cases in which a payor bank has overlooked a stop payment order on a personal check and has issued to the holder of the personal check a cashier's check with that holder as payee. If the payor bank refuses to pay the cashier's check, what should be the rights of the payee of the cashier's check against the payor bank? The following case wrestles with this question.

————

[1]. Where the issuing bank is a state chartered bank, which unlike a federally chartered bank does not have an officer known as a "cashier," the check may be called an "official check" rather than a "cashier's check."

TRAVI CONSTRUCTION CORP. v. FIRST BRISTOL COUNTY NATIONAL BANK

Court of Appeals of Massachusetts, 1980.
10 Mass.App.Ct. 32, 405 N.E.2d 666.

PERRETTA, JUSTICE. This appeal is from a summary judgment granted in favor of the plaintiff Travi Construction Corporation against the defendant First Bristol County National Bank. Mass.R.Civ.P. 56, 365 Mass. 824 (1974). In its action Travi sought to recover the sum of $7,500, representing the face amount of a cashier's check issued by the Bank to Travi as payee. The Bank stopped payment on this check because Travi purchased it with a personal check it had received from the third-party defendant Lesser. Lesser's check was drawn on the Bank, but he placed a stop-payment order on his check prior to Travi's presentment of it at the Bank in exchange of the cashier's check. Due to an error on its part, the Bank accepted Lesser's check and issued its cashier's check to Travi. When the cashier's check was subsequently presented to the Bank by Travi's bank, the Bank refused to honor it, and Travi brought suit. The Bank argues that it can refuse to honor its cashier's check for a failure of consideration when it is presented by a party to the instrument with whom the Bank has dealt. We agree, and we reverse the judgment.

There are two conflicting lines of authority on the question whether a bank can dishonor its cashier's check. Those jurisdictions which apply a flat prohibition against dishonor of a cashier's check by the issuing bank do so on the reasoning that a cashier's check is a bill of exchange or draft drawn by a bank upon itself and accepted in advance by the act of its issuance. Because a stop-payment order must be made prior to acceptance of the instrument, Uniform Commercial Code, § 4–303(a), a cashier's check cannot be dishonored.[1] Some jurisdictions refuse to recognize such an ironclad rule, and they allow a bank to dishonor its cashier's check in certain situations, primarily a failure of consideration. In such a case the bank may assert its own defenses against one who is not a holder in due course.[2]

1. See Swiss Credit Bank v. Virginia Natl. Bank–Fairfax, 538 F.2d 587 (4th Cir. 1976); State v. Curtiss Natl. Bank, 427 F.2d 395 (5th Cir.1970); Munson v. American Natl. Bank & Trust Co., 484 F.2d 620 (7th Cir.1973); Texaco, Inc. v. Liberty Natl. Bank & Trust Co., 464 F.2d 389 (10th Cir. 1972); Kaufman v. Chase Manhattan Bank Natl. Assn., 370 F.Supp. 276 (S.D.N.Y. 1973); Able & Associates, Inc. v. Orchard Hill Farms, 77 Ill.App.3d 375, 32 Ill.Dec. 757, 395 N.E.2d 1138 (1979), overruling Bank of Niles v. American State Bank, 14 Ill.App.3d 729, 303 N.E.2d 186 (1973); Meador v. Ranchmart State Bank, 213 Kan. 372, 517 P.2d 123 (1973); State ex rel. Chan Siew Lai v. Powell, 536 S.W.2d 14 (Mo.1976); National Newark & Essex Bank v. Giordano, 111 N.J.Super. 347, 268 A.2d 327 (1970); Moon Over the Mountain, Ltd. v. Marine Midland Bank, 87 Misc.2d 918, 386 N.Y.S.2d 974 (N.Y.Civ.Ct.1976); Wertz v. Richardson Heights Bank & Trust, 495 S.W.2d 572 (Tex.1973).

2. See TPO, Inc. v. Federal Deposit Ins. Corp., 487 F.2d 131 (3rd Cir.1973); Wilmington Trust Co. v. Delaware Auto Sales, 271 A.2d 41 (Del.1970); Tropicana Pools, Inc. v. First Natl. Bank, 206 So.2d 48 (Fla. App.1968); Wright v. Trust Co. of Georgia, 108 Ga.App. 783, 134 S.E.2d 457 (1963); State Bank v. American Natl. Bank, 266 N.W.2d 496 (Minn.1978); Dakota Transfer & Storage Co. v. Merchants Natl. Bank & Trust Co., 86 N.W.2d 639 (N.Dak.1957).

This conflict among jurisdictions is treated by Brady on Bank Checks, wherein it is concluded, at § 20.12, at 20–30—20–31 (5th ed. 1979), "While courts have not set forth a clear rule on this matter, it would seem that courts which hold flatly that payment may not be stopped are in error. . . . In short, the rule that payment may not be stopped on a cashier's check should not be regarded as an immutable principle; under some situations, it would seem that the issuing bank ought to be able to resist payment." To each dispute Brady would apply the "finality of payment" rule found in § 3–418 of the Uniform Commercial Code.[3] Jurisdictions eschewing the flat-prohibition against dishonor take notice of the fact that the analysis of the question employed by conflicting courts depends upon the premise that a cashier's check is a draft. For example, in TPO, Inc. v. Federal Deposit Ins. Corp., 487 F.2d 131, 135–136 (3rd Cir.1973), the court observed that the "acceptance upon issuance" reasoning fails when § 3–118(a) of the Uniform Commercial Code is applied to a cashier's check. That section of the Code states: "Where there is doubt whether the instrument is a draft or a note the holder may treat it as either. A draft drawn on the drawer is effective as a note." The observation that a cashier's check is a negotiable promissory note and not a draft is, however, by no means central to the rule that a bank may, in certain circumstances, dishonor its cashier's check. These cases turn on whether the holder of the check is a holder in due course because "whether a bank is considered to have accepted a cashier's check, as a draft, by the act of its issuance, or is considered to be the maker of a note, it is primarily obligated upon the instrument." Banco Ganadero y Agricola, S.A. Agua Prieta, Sonora, Mexico v. Society Natl. Bank, 418 F.Supp. 520, 523 (N.D.Ohio 1976). See also 6 E. Bender's Uniform Commercial Code Service, Reporter—Digest § 2–1194 (Willier and Hart, 1980) ("This difference alone would not alter the result, however, since the liability of an acceptor is precisely the same as that of a maker. See Section 3–413[1].").

We are persuaded that an issuing bank may refuse to honor its cashier's check because of a failure of consideration when the check is held by a party to the instrument with whom it has dealt. We do not look to either G.L. c. 106, § 3–118(a) or § 3–418, in reaching this conclusion. Instead, we rely upon the fact that in this limited situation the policy concerns which justify a rule against dishonor do not exist, and there is overwhelming reason for an exception to the rule. As stated in TPO, Inc., 487 F.2d at 135, "There are no third parties, or customers of the Bank, or holders in due course whose rights are involved . . . Hence, the strong considerations of public policy favoring

---

3. General Laws c. 106, § 3–418, inserted by St.1957, c. 765, § 1, provides: "Except for recovery of bank payments as provided in the Article on Bank Deposits and Collections (Article 4) and except for liability for breach of warranty on presentment under section 3–417, payment or acceptance of any instrument is final in favor of a holder in due course, or a person who has in good faith changed his position in reliance on the payment." Brady suggests that because in Rockland Trust Co. v. South Shore Natl. Bank, 366 Mass. 74, 78, 314 N.E.2d 438 (1976), the court hinted that the rule applied to certified checks, it would also be applicable to cashier's checks.

negotiability and reliability of cashier's checks are not germane."
Compare Dziurak v. Chase Manhattan Bank, 58 App.Div.2d 103, 107,
396 N.Y.S.2d 414 (1977). Moreover, where the bank, and not its
customer, stops payment on a cashier's check the bank's reputation and
credit are not exposed to third party reprobation. See 6 Michie, Banks
and Banking 371 (1975). Compare White & Summers, Uniform Commercial Code 579, n. 91 (1972) (concern for a bank's reputation and
credit may be legitimate where a customer can demand that its bank
stop payment on a cashier's check).

These policy concerns are not at issue in the present case. The
Bank received Lesser's stop-payment order on March 30, 1978, at 5:15
P.M. Travi presented Lesser's check at the Bank's branch office on
Friday, March 31, sometime between 12:00 P.M. and 1:00 P.M. The
cashier's check was presented to the Bank for payment by Travi's bank
on or about April 4. Lesser's account cannot be charged; the Bank
admits his stop-payment order was timely made.[4] Travi has received
no funds on account of the cashier's check which bears the stamped
legend "Payment Stopped." The check cannot fall into the hands of an
innocent third party. In this situation, we perceive no policy need for
application of a stringent rule prohibiting the Bank's dishonor of its
cashier's check.

The issue for resolution is whether the Bank has a defense which it
can assert against Travi's presentment of the check for payment. Travi
argues that it does not. It claims that the pleadings, the affidavits, and
the Bank's responses to interrogatories demonstrate that there is no
dispute that Travi took the cashier's check in good faith and without
notice of the fact that Lesser had stopped payment on his check. We
reject Travi's assessment of the affidavits,[5] but even were we to agree
that Travi holds the check as a holder in due course, Travi would not be
sheltered from the Bank's defense to payment.

The Bank received Lesser's order before it issued its check to Travi,
and it has no right to charge Lesser's account with the amount of his

---

4. Lesser's order, although timely under G.L. c. 106, § 4–303, was received by
the Bank after the "cut-off" time of 4:30
P.M. for its computer center to process the
work for that day. The order was then
posted at the close of business on March
31. The Bank's mistake occurred when,
for some reason not revealed on the record
before us, Lesser's order was not manually
brought forward on his account on the
morning of March 31.

5. Lesser alleged in his affidavit that he
notified Travi's bookkeeper and president
by telephone and "explained that I was
stopping payment on my check" to Travi.
Travi's bookkeeper and president denied
any such notice from Lesser in their affidavits. Travi claims that a factual dispute as
to its status as a holder in due course does
not exist because the Bank's answers to

interrogatories demonstrate that Lesser
stopped payment on his check at 5:15 P.M.
on March 30, after his alleged notice to
Travi's employees. Travi concludes that
even if Lesser's affidavit is accepted, it
shows only a threat or indication that payment on his check might be stopped, and
Travi could not have had knowledge of the
order when it presented Lesser's check.
Lesser's affidavit was sufficient to dispute
Travi's status as a holder in due course on
the elements of good faith and notice. G.L.
c. 106, §§ 1–201(19) and (25). See Industrial Natl. Bank v. Leo's Used Car Exchange,
Inc., 362 Mass. 797, 800–802, 291 N.E.2d
603 (1973). See also Bowling Green, Inc. v.
State Street Bank & Trust Co., 425 F.2d 81,
85 (1st Cir.1970).

check. "A complete failure of consideration for the [cashier's] check resulted and the bank had the right to refuse to honor it when presented by the payee." Wilmington Trust Co., supra, 271 A.2d at 42. While the defense of a failure of consideration cannot be asserted against a holder in due course, compare G.L. c. 106, § 3–305(2) with §§ 3–306 and 3–408, even a holder in due course takes an instrument subject to the defenses of any party to the instrument with whom the holder has dealt, G.L. c. 106, § 3–305(2). See Waltham Citizens Natl. Bank v. Flett, 353 Mass. 696, 699, 234 N.E.2d 739 (1968). See also Wilmington Trust, supra, 271 A.2d at 42; Brotherton v. McWaters, 438 P.2d 1, 4 (Okl.1968); Brady on Bank Checks, supra, at 9–7—9–8, 15–3; Quinn, UCC Commentary and Law Digest par. 3–305(A)(5) (1978).

The Bank had a right to refuse to honor its cashier's check because of a failure of consideration when the check was presented by Travi, a party to that instrument with whom the Bank had dealt. The foregoing analysis obviates the need to consider the Bank's remaining contention[6] because it establishes that summary judgment against Travi is appropriate under Mass.R.Civ.P. 56(c), 365 Mass. 824 (1974).

The order allowing Travi's motion for summary judgment and the judgment are reversed. The Superior Court is to enter a new judgment dismissing the action.

Notes

(1) **The "Iron–Clad Rule."** A case recognizing what the Massachusetts court called the "iron-clad rule" that a bank cannot refuse to pay its cashier's check, even when the cashier's check is still in the payee's hands, is *Able & Associates v. Orchard Hill Farms of Illinois,* cited in the Massachusetts court's first footnote. There the Illinois court asserted that "policy considerations require a rule which prohibits a bank from refusing to honor its cashier's checks." But it concluded that the payee of the cashier's check would be "nonetheless liable to the bank on an offset claim ... based on the underlying contract obligations for the purchase of the cashier's checks." The court remanded the case to permit the bank "to amend its answer to include as an affirmative defense its claim of a breach of the underlying contractual obligation." How does this "iron-clad rule" as applied by the Illinois court differ in practice from the rule laid down by the Massachusetts court?

Is the "iron-clad rule" consistent with revised Article 3? As the Massachusetts court explains, that rule was justified "on the reasoning that a cashier's check is ... a draft ... accepted in advance." Is this

---

6. The Bank also complains of the order denying its motion to amend its answer to include a compulsory counterclaim against Travi. Mass.R.Civ.P. 13(a), 365 Mass. 758 (1974). The basis for the counterclaim was that when Travi endorsed Lesser's check, it engaged that upon dishonor it would pay the instrument according to the tenor at the time of its endorsement. G.L. c. 106, § 3–414(1). See Community Natl. Bank v. Dawes, 369 Mass. 550, 561, 340 N.E.2d 877 (1976).

consistent with UCC 3–412? See Davis, The Future of Cashier's Checks Under Revised Article 3 of the Uniform Commercial Code, 27 Wake Forest L.Rev. 613, 630–32, 645–52 (1992). Is UCC 3–411 relevant? Is UCC 3–418? Is UCC 4–407?

(2) **Wrongful Refusal to Pay a Cashier's Check.** What is the scope of the damages for which the bank may be liable to the holder of a cashier's check if it wrongfully refuses to pay the check? UCC 3–411(b) provides for "compensation for expenses and loss of interest resulting from the nonpayment" and for consequential damages if the "bank refuses to pay after receiving notice of particular circumstances giving rise to the damages." Under subsection (c), however, expenses or consequential damages are not recoverable if the reason for the refusal to pay is one of those stated. Would this provision have protected the bank in the *Travi* case if it turned out that Lesser owed the money to Travi? According to Comment 3, the purpose is to limit recovery "to cases in which the bank refuses to pay even though its obligation to pay is clear and it is able to pay."

SECTION 3. ADVERSE CLAIM

Prefatory Note. Thus far we have considered the power to countermand only in the case of the drawer's personal uncertified check. Can the drawer ever countermand a cashier's check or a certified check? UCC 4–403(a) answers this question in the negative for cashier's checks by restricting the power to stop payment to items "drawn on the customer's account" (see Comment 4), and UCC 4–303(a)(1) answers it in the negative for certified checks by providing that once a check is certified a stop payment order "comes too late" (see Comment 3). There is, however, another means by which the drawer might attempt to accomplish the same result—by assertion of an adverse claim to the property represented by the cashier's check or the certified check, i.e., to the debt owed by the payor bank on that check.

At common law, when ownership of a deposit in a bank was claimed by a person other than the depositor, the adverse claimant might, by giving the bank adequate notice of the claim, require it to hold the deposit for a reasonable length of time to afford the claimant an opportunity to assert the claim in court. Thus if a person who had paid by a cashier's check or a certified check were to assert an adverse claim to the deposit represented by the check, the court might properly require the bank to refuse payment on the check, for at least a reasonable time. (What was a reasonable time in such a case was not entirely clear.) Note, however, that in order for there to be an adverse claim, there must be a claim of ownership of the deposit, as where it is asserted that the instrument representing the deposit was procured by theft or by fraud;[1] it is not enough for the person who had paid by the instrument to assert that there has been a want or failure of consideration. Note too that the payor bank must be given adequate notice of the facts in support of the claim to justify it in acting upon it; it is not enough for the claimant merely to countermand payment.

In order to afford banks some protection from the risk of adverse claims, over half of the states adopted adverse claim statutes usually in the form recommended by the American Bankers Association. These statutes provided that a notice of an adverse claim was not effective unless it was accompanied by a court order restraining payment of the deposit or a bond indemnifying the bank against loss.

The Code's version of an adverse claim statute is set out in UCC 3–602, which requires a court order in most cases of adverse claim to a deposit represented by a negotiable instrument. When and how can a person who has paid by a cashier's check or a certified check take advantage of the doctrine of adverse claim under the Code? The Comment to UCC 3–602 explains that revised Article 3 changes the rule of former Section 3–603(1) by allowing the bank to discharge its obligation "to both the holder and the claimant even though indemnity has been given by the person asserting the claim." But UCC 3–602 "continues the rule that the obligor is not discharged on the instrument if payment is made in violation of an injunction against payment."

The discussion so far has centered on whether the adverse claimant can require the bank to recognize a claim. But suppose that the bank is willing to recognize it. Then the question arises whether the bank can set up the adverse claim when it is sued by the holder of the instrument. Whether a party to a negotiable instrument can set up in defense the *jus tertii*, a claim of ownership of a third party, has been the subject of considerable controversy. Although the Negotiable Instruments Law was not explicit on the matter, its implication was that a party to the instrument could set up a third party's claim of ownership, at least in defense against one who was not a holder in due course. Perhaps if, under the common law rules relating to adverse claims, voluntary payment made following notice of an adverse claim might have left the payor liable to the adverse claimant, it was only reasonable to allow the payor to set up the adverse claim against the holder, even in an action to which the adverse claimant is not a party. On the other hand, might not such a rule have made possible inconsistent findings of fact in separate actions, and consequent double liability or unjust enrichment?

The Code, in UCC 3–305(c) provides that in an action to enforce a party's obligation, "the obligor may not assert against the person entitled to enforce the instrument a defense, claim in recoupment, or

---

1. Even where there has been fraud, so that the transaction is voidable, the adverse claimant may be required to rescind before the bank must recognize his claim. See Note, 21 U.Chi.L.Rev. 135, 141 (1953).

claim to the instrument (Section 3–306) of another person, but the other person's claim to the instrument may be asserted by the obligor if the other person is joined in the action and personally asserts the claim." Comment 4 gives an example.

"For example, Buyer buys goods from Seller and negotiates to Seller a cashier's check issued by Bank in payment of the price. Shortly after delivering the check to Seller, Buyer learns that Seller had defrauded Buyer in the sale transaction. Seller may enforce the check against Bank even though Seller is not a holder in due course. Bank has no defense to its obligation to pay the check and it may not assert defenses, claims in recoupment, or claims to the instrument of Buyer, except to the extent permitted by the but clause of the first sentence of subsection (c). Buyer may have a claim to the instrument under Section 3–306 based on a right to rescind the negotiation to Seller because of Seller's fraud. Section 3–202(b) and Comment 2 to Section 3–201. Bank cannot assert that claim unless Buyer is joined in the action in which Seller is trying to enforce payment of the check. In that case Bank may pay the amount of the check into court and the court will decide whether that amount belongs to Buyer or Seller."

Note, however, that the rule is different if "the obligor proves that the instrument is a lost or stolen instrument." What is the reason for this difference?

Would the greater certainty that is usually possible in establishing the fact of theft as opposed, for example, to the fact of fraud help to explain it? See generally Davis, The Future of Cashier's Checks Under Revised Article 3 of the Uniform Commercial Code, 27 Wake Forest L.Rev. 613, 632–39, 642–44 (1992).

Problem 15. Seller fraudulently induced Buyer to give a certified check on X Bank in payment for worthless goods. Upon discovery of the fraud, Buyer rescinded the sale, tendered the goods back to Seller, notified X Bank of these circumstances, and instructed it not to pay the check.

(a) If X Bank refuses to pay, can it successfully resist an action brought by Seller by setting up the right of a third party (the *jus tertii*), the Buyer, even though the Buyer is not a party? If X Bank were to be allowed to set up Seller's fraud, but lost because of a finding of fact that there was no fraud, would X Bank then be protected against a subsequent recovery by Buyer?

(b) Could X Bank have safely paid Seller after having received notice of the fraud?

(c) What answers if Seller were instead a thief who had stolen from Buyer a certified check payable to the order of "Cash"?

See UCC 3–305, 3–602; Dziurak v. Chase Manhattan Bank, infra.

———

DZIURAK v. CHASE MANHATTAN BANK

Supreme Court of New York, Appellate Division, Second Department, 1977.
58 A.D.2d 103, 396 N.Y.S.2d 414.

COHALAN, JUSTICE PRESIDING. The sole question on this appeal is whether a bank depositor to whom an "official bank check" has been issued (and by him endorsed to the order of a third party), can legally stop payment thereon, in the absence of a court order or an indemnification bond. An official bank check is commonly referred to as a "cashier's check". Trial Term held it could be stopped. We disagree.

A recitation of the facts is necessary to place the problem in proper focus.

The plaintiff currently holds a judgment against the defendant Chase Manhattan Bank (Bank) in the amount of $17,000, plus interest and costs.

During the year 1973 Dziurak maintained a savings account with "Branch # 40" of the Bank in the sum of $18,000. He was cozened by an acquaintance named Staveris into a proposal whereby, for $22,000 cash, he could acquire a one-third interest in a corporation whose sole asset was a going restaurant. There was nothing in writing to bind the bargain. Dziurak paid Staveris $5,000 down. He then went to the Bank and, through the assistant manager, arranged for the proper withdrawal. He asked for a "check" to be drawn to the order of Staveris. Monaco, the assistant manager, advised him to have the check drawn to himself as payee. A further bit of advice by Monaco was for Dziurak to go to his attorney, who would instruct him how to endorse the check.

The $17,000 was transferred to the Bank's coffers and Dziurak's savings account was debited accordingly. A cashier's check was then issued to the order of "Francis A. Dziurak".

Plaintiff ignored the suggestion that he consult with his attorney. Instead he wrote on the back of the instrument "Francis Dziurak. Pay to order Mario Staveris" and delivered the item to Staveris. The latter, instead of depositing the check into the corporate restaurant account, deposited it in his own savings account.

Before he learned of Staveris' perfidy and before the cashier's check had cleared, Dziurak belatedly sought the advice of a local attorney. Very properly, the attorney advised him to try to stop payment on the cashier's check.

Back went Dziurak to the Bank. He saw Monaco and asked him if the check had cleared. It had not, but had arrived at the Bank that morning.

While plaintiff was with him, Monaco telephoned the Bank's attorneys and was advised that the check could not be stopped, absent a court order. He so advised the plaintiff and while Dziurak was still with him he telephoned the plaintiff's attorney to advise him to the same effect. The attorney said he was aware that a court order could effectively produce a stop of the payment.

This action was started against the Bank after judgment was first taken against Staveris, and after execution was returned unsatisfied.

As to the law, the controlling statutes are contained in several sections of the Uniform Commercial Code (hereafter UCC) which, in turn, are fleshed out in reported decisions of nisi prius and appellate courts.

We begin with subdivision (1) of section 4–403 of the UCC ("Customer's Right to Stop Payment; Burden of Proof of Loss"):

> "A customer may by order to his bank stop payment of *any item payable for his account* but the order must be received at such time and in such manner as to afford the bank a reasonable opportunity to act on it prior to any action by the bank with respect to the item described in Section 4–303" (emphasis supplied).

As to this section (4–403) we part company with Trial Term, which held that the $17,000 represented by the cashier's check was actually Dziurak's money and not that of the Bank. As noted in Wertz v. Richardson Hgts. Bank & Trust, 495 S.W.2d 572, 574 [Tex.]:

> "A cashier's check is not one payable for the customer's account but rather for the bank's account. It is the bank which is obligated on the check".

The reference in section 4–403 more properly fits the situation where the depositor, as drawer, issues his own check on his own bank, as drawee. Such a check can be stopped if reasonable notice is given.

> "A cashier's check is of a very different character. It is the primary obligation of the bank which issues it (citation omitted) and constitutes its written promise to pay upon demand (citation omitted). It has been said that a cashier's check is a bill of exchange drawn by a bank upon itself, accepted in advance by the very act of issuance" (Matter of Bank of United States [O'Neill], 243 App.Div. 287, 291, 277 N.Y.S. 96, 100).

This exposition of the law has been followed consistently. (See Garden Check Cashing Serv. v. First Nat. City Bank, 25 A.D.2d 137, 267 N.Y.S.2d 698; Rose Check Cashing Serv. v. Chemical Bank N.Y. Trust Co., 43 Misc.2d 679, 252 N.Y.S.2d 100; Tinker Nat. Bank v. Grassi, 57 Misc.2d 886, 889, 293 N.Y.S.2d 847, 850; Garden Check Cashing Serv. v.

Chase Manhattan Bank, 46 Misc.2d 163, 165, 258 N.Y.S.2d 918, 920; Moon Over Mountain Bank v. Marine Midland Bank, 87 Misc.2d 918, 386 N.Y.S.2d 974).

No decisions holding to the contrary have been unearthed.

But to go on. Subdivision (1) of section 4–303 of the UCC ("When Items Subject to . . . Stop–Order") states, in part:

"Any . . . stop-order received by . . . a payor bank, whether or not effective under other rules of law to terminate . . . the bank's right or duty to pay an item . . . comes too late to so terminate . . . if the . . . stop-order . . . is received . . . and a reasonable time for the bank to act thereon expires . . . after the bank has done any one of the following:

"(a) accepted or certified the item".

The next section to consider is 3–410 ("Definition and Operation of Acceptance"):

"(1) Acceptance is the drawee's signed engagement to honor the draft as presented. It must be written on the draft, and may consist of his signature alone. It becomes operative when completed by delivery or notification."

At this point we can refer back to annotation 5 in the Official Comment under section 4–403 of the UCC (McKinney's Cons.Laws of N.Y., Book 62½, Part 2, p. 611):

"There is no right to stop payment after certification of a check or other acceptance of a draft, and this is true no matter who procures the certification. See Sections 3–411 and 4–303. The acceptance is the drawee's own engagement to pay, and he is not required to impair his credit by refusing payment for the convenience of the drawer."

Thus, the Bank's one signature on the instrument constitutes both a drawing and an acceptance and makes the Bank a drawer and a drawee. (See Matter of Bank of United States [O'Neill] supra).

In the recitation of the facts, mention was made that the local attorney for the plaintiff remarked to Monaco that he was aware that a court order (presumably one of a court of competent jurisdiction) could have acted as a "stop payment" order. The statute providing for such an order is section 3–603 of the UCC. It is headnoted "Payment or Satisfaction" and, pertinently, reads:

"(1) The liability of any party is discharged to the extent of his payments . . . to the holder even though it is made with knowledge of a claim of another person to the instrument unless prior to such payment . . . *the person making the claim either supplies indemnity deemed adequate by the party seeking the discharge* or enjoins payment or satisfaction by order of a court of competent jurisdiction in an action in which the adverse claimant and the holder are parties" (emphasis supplied).

The fact that the attorney for the plaintiff was aware that a court order could effect a stop payment presupposes that he also knew he could file an indemnity bond to protect the Bank, since both options are included in subdivision (1) of section 3–603 of the UCC.

Viewed in retrospect, the Bank, as a practical matter, could quite safely have stopped payment on its cashier's check and, by interpleader, have paid the money into court. Staveris could not have established himself as a holder in due course (see UCC, § 3–302). But, if the Legislature laid upon a bank the onus of questioning the reason for the issuance of all cashier's checks it would destroy the efficacy of such instruments, which, for all practical purposes, are treated as the equivalent of cash (Goshen Nat. Bank v. State of New York, 141 N.Y. 379, 387, 36 N.E. 316, 317).

To do justice to the Bank, it is only fair to observe the the entire brouhaha was occasioned by the intransigence of Dziurak. Had he followed the advice of Monaco to consult his own attorney, the situation in which the parties are now involved would have been averted. It was well said in National Safe Deposit, Sav. & Trust Co. v. Hibbs, 229 U.S. 391, 394, 33 S.Ct. 818, 57 L.Ed. 1241, wherein the doctrine of equitable estoppel was invoked for dismissing the complaint and cited with approval in Bunge Corp. v. Manufacturers Hanover Trust Co., 31 N.Y.2d 223, 228, 335 N.Y.S.2d 412, 415, 286 N.E.2d 903, 905:

"That where one of two innocent persons must suffer by the acts of a third, he who has enabled such third person to occasion the loss must sustain it."

Dziurak provoked the issue; Dziurak should shoulder the blame.

There is a profusion of cases to the effect that a cashier's check, once issued and in the possession of a third party, cannot legally be stopped except as provided by statute (see UCC, § 3–603). One of the leading cases of recent vintage is Kaufman v. Chase Manhattan Bank, Nat. Ass'n, D.C., 370 F.Supp. 276.

There, in an opinion by Chief Judge Edelstein, plaintiff Kaufman was granted summary judgment. In that case the bank, at the request of a depositor, drew a cashier's check to plaintiff as payee. When it was presented for payment the bank refused to honor it. Chief Judge Edelstein wrote that (p. 278):

"A cashier's check ... is a check drawn by the bank upon itself, payable to another person, and issued by an authorized officer of the bank. The bank, therefore, becomes both the drawer and drawee; and the check becomes a promise by the bank to draw the amount of the check from its own resources and to pay the check upon demand. Thus, the issuance of the cashier's check constitutes an acceptance by the issuing bank; and the cashier's check becomes the primary obligation of the bank."

A reference to subdivision (1) of section 3–410 of the UCC was contained in a footnote to the opinion with respect to acceptance upon issuance.

Contrary to Trial Term's opinion, the statute makes no distinction between a cashier's check presented for payment by a payee or one presented by an endorsee of the payee. (See Moon Over Mountain Bank v. Marine Midland, 87 Misc.2d 918, 386 N.Y.S.2d 974, supra, and the cases therein cited.) It engages to pay on demand to the person who presents the check unless he falls within either of the categories listed in subdivision (1) of section 3–603 of the UCC (theft or restrictive endorsement).

From all that has been stated, and harsh as it may appear, it follows that the judgment must be reversed and the complaint dismissed, with costs.

Whether future remedies are available to persons situated as is the plaintiff at bar must be left to the discretion of the State Legislature.

Judgment of the Supreme Court, Kings County, entered September 24, 1976, reversed, on the law, with costs to appellant payable by respondent, and complaint dismissed.

————

DZIURAK v. CHASE MANHATTAN BANK

Court of Appeals of New York, 1978.
44 N.Y.2d 776, 406 N.Y.S.2d 30, 377 N.E.2d 474.

MEMORANDUM. The order of the Appellate Division should be affirmed, with costs.

A cashier's check is the primary obligation of the issuing bank which, acting as both drawer and drawee, accepts the check upon its issuance. (Matter of Bank of United States, 243 App.Div. 287, 291, 277 N.Y.S. 96, 100; Moon Over the Mountain v. Marine Midland Bank, 87 Misc.2d 918, 920, 386 N.Y.S.2d 974, 975.) As such, a cashier's check does not constitute an item payable for a customer's account within the meaning of subdivision 1 of section 4–403 of the Uniform Commercial Code. (White and Summers, Uniform Commercial Code, § 17–5, p. 579, n. 91.) Consequently, respondent was under no legal obligation to honor appellant's order to stop payment.

Note

Relation to "Iron–Clad Rule." Recall that the Massachusetts court in the *Travi* case, supra, asks the reader to "Compare Dziurak...." What do you make of this comparison? Would Dziurak's right to assert against Chase a claim adverse to Staveris's depend on whether the court followed the "iron-clad rule"?

Prefatory Note. A teller's check, like a cashier's check and a certified check, carries a bank's obligation. According to UCC 3–104(h), "a draft drawn by a bank ... on another bank" is a teller's check. A teller's check is sometimes called a "bank draft." (Recall the draft drawn by a London banker on his Venetian correspondent, described at p. ___ supra.) The only bank that is obligated, however, is the one that is the drawer. This means that any *jus tertii* would be asserted by the drawer and any adverse claim would be made against the drawer. The following case involves such a situation.

Problem 16. Buyer bought a used car from Seller, giving Seller a teller's check drawn by Savings Bank on Commercial Bank. Almost immediately, Buyer discovered that the car is seriously defective. Advise Buyer. See UCC 3–305, 3–602; *Fulton National Bank v. Delco*, infra.[1]

FULTON NATIONAL BANK v. DELCO CORP.

Court of Appeals of Georgia, 1973.
128 Ga.App. 16, 195 S.E.2d 455.

Delco Corporation sued the Fulton National Bank and Maslia jointly for $2,500 alleging the following: Maslia is indebted to the plaintiff in the sum of $2,500 for payment of a franchise fee, and delivered to plaintiff a check of the Fulton National Bank drawn on its account in a Federal Reserve Bank, showing Maslia as remitter; upon receipt of the check and in reliance thereof plaintiff expended money in setting Maslia up as a franchisee of the corporation; before the check was cashed, the bank stopped payment on it at Maslia's request, and is therefore liable on the instrument. Maslia undertook to defend on behalf of the bank. Delco then moved for summary judgment against the bank based on its liability as drawer, and Maslia in opposition submitted an affidavit stating in substance that the check was delivered to the plaintiff in the course of negotiation for a contemplated agreement which was never consummated; that in the negotiations it was understood that the proposed transaction was contingent on Maslia's ability to borrow the remainder of the money necessary for the franchise down payment, which he was unable to do; that plaintiff represented to him that he was at liberty to withdraw from the negotiations

---

1. Note that Regulation CC 229.10(c)(v) requires next day availability in the case of teller's checks. How might this rule affect Buyer?

at any time and receive a refund in full of any money paid; that the down payment required before the contemplated contract could be consummated was an undetermined sum between $4,000 and $10,000, and that prior to the presentation of the bank check "affiant advised plaintiff that affiant had decided not to go through with the transaction, that affiant was unable to borrow additional money for the down payment, and requested the return of the check." The motion for summary judgment was granted and defendant appeals.

DEEN, JUDGE. 1. The instrument in question is a bank draft and does not operate as an assignment of funds, as does a certified check (Code Ann. §§ 109A–4–303(1)(a) and 109A–3–411(1), certification constituting a legal acceptance) or a cashier's check or bank money order, which are considered to be notes carrying unconditional promises to pay. 67 Columbia Law Review, Money Orders & Teller's Checks, pp. 524, 527. The plaintiff, being the named payee, is not a holder in due course. Under Code Ann. § 109A–4–403 any *customer* may by order to his bank stop payment on his check prior to action by the drawee, and specifically under Code Ann. § 109A–4–104(1)(e) a bank carrying an account with another bank is included as a customer. The defendant bank therefore had a right to stop payment on its check, which would, however, still leave it liable for the value of the item unless some legal and valid defense is available to it.

2. Code Ann. § 109A–3–306 provides: "Unless he has the rights of a holder in due course any person takes the instrument subject to (a) all valid claims to it on the part of any person" but "(d) The claim of any third person to the instrument is not otherwise available as a defense to any party liable thereon unless the third person himself defends the action for such party." The defendant bank has of course no defense against the check, having voluntarily stopped payment on it at Maslia's request and refunded Maslia's money to him, unless Maslia's own defense is both good and available to the bank. Maslia himself cannot defend on the instrument, not being a party to it, but he can, under the above quoted code section, defend in behalf of the bank provided he has a "valid claim." A "claim" is more than a mere "defense" as indicated by Code Ann. § 109A–3–305. The word descends from the law merchant and indicates certain rights in the instrument on which the suit is based rather than mere reasons why the alleged debtor is not liable for the fund. It is, however, to some extent broader than the concept of legal title to the instrument. Note 2 of the Official Comment to UCC 3–306 states: " 'All valid claims to it on the part of any person' includes not only claims of legal title, but all liens, equities, or other claims of right against *the instrument or its proceeds.* It includes claims to *rescind a prior negotiation and to recover the instrument or its proceeds.*" (Emphasis supplied). The affidavit opposing the motion for

summary judgment states that the underlying transaction consisted of a prior negotiation which was rescinded; that it was understood during such negotiations that Maslia was at liberty to withdraw at any time before they were concluded and receive a refund of any down payment, and that he has requested the return of the check. Since the bank, being the party opposing the motion for summary judgment, is entitled to all reasonable inference in its favor, we take this to mean a claim of ownership in the uncashed check as well as ownership of the fund represented by it, and it is therefore such a third party claim as is available to the defendant bank, the party prima facie liable, since Maslia is himself defending the action on its behalf. The validity of the claim is thus the only real issue in the case; it is controverted, and the bank's ultimate liability must depend upon its outcome. It was accordingly error to grant the motion for summary judgment.

Nothing in Wright v. Trust Co. of Ga., 108 Ga.App. 783, 134 S.E.2d 457, is contradictory of what is said here. The appellee further cites State of Pa. v. Curtiss Nat. Bank of Miami Springs, Fla., 5 Cir., 427 F.2d 395 involving a cashier's check and Krom v. Chemical Bank New York Trust Co., 329 N.Y.S.2d 91 involving a bank money order, both of which differ from a bank draft, as observed above, because they are considered unconditional promises to pay. This leaves two New York cases, Malphrus v. Home Savings Bank of City of Albany, 44 Misc.2d 705, 254 N.Y.S.2d 980 and Ruskin v. Central Fed. Savings & Loan Assn. of Nassau County, 3 UCC Rep.Serv. 150 (N.Y.Sup.Ct., 1966), which reached a conclusion that the bank would be unconditionally liable to the plaintiff and could seek reimbursement in a separate action against the remitter at whose request payment was stopped. These cases are not binding upon us and have been severely criticized in 67 Columbia Law Review p. 524, supra, and denominated erroneous in 71 Columbia Law Review, "Negotiability—Who Needs it?", pp. 375, 388. With all parties before the court, it is obviously the better procedure, where possible, to allow the issues to be tried out here, rather than require a possible second lawsuit by the bank against Maslia and a possible third lawsuit by Maslia against Delco.

Judgment reversed.

Note

Teller's Checks. The Malphrus case, criticized by the court, involved the common situation in which a buyer, in order to pay for goods, makes a withdrawal from a savings bank, taking a teller's check drawn by the savings bank on a commercial bank payable to the seller's order. If the buyer, after giving the seller the teller's check, claims that the goods are defective and induces the savings bank to stop payment on the check, what are the rights of the seller on the

dishonored check against the savings bank? See UCC 3–305(c), 3–411.
Why is the exception in the first sentence of UCC 3–305(c) limited to a
"claim to the instrument"?

Chapter 5

FORGERY AND ALTERATION

SECTION 1. BASIC RULES FOR ALLOCATION OF LOSS

Prefatory Note. Although forgery and alteration of negotiable instruments are far from common, they give rise to a surprisingly large number of litigated cases, and the risk of loss due to forgery and alteration is not to be ignored by one who deals in negotiable paper. This is particularly true since the wrongdoer is often not caught until after having disposed of part or all of the gains, with the consequence that one of several innocent parties must be selected to bear the loss. What policies should govern the allocation of that loss? Which party should be selected? What remedies should be available to shift the loss to that party? The materials which follow are directed to answering these questions.

COOTER & RUBIN, A THEORY OF LOSS ALLOCATION FOR CONSUMER PAYMENTS
66 Tex.L.Rev. 63, 70–75, 78–79 (1987).

[A system of legal rules governing the] allocation of fraud, forgery, and error losses between consumers and financial institutions ... can increase the efficiency of the payment system if those rules are properly designed. This Part identifies three major principles of economic efficiency for the design of such rules: loss spreading, loss reduction, and loss imposition.

A. The Loss Spreading Principle

A basic characteristic of economic actors is their attitude toward risk. Most people are risk averse: when facing a possible loss, they will pay more than the loss's average value to eliminate the risk of it. In contrast, a risk neutral person places a value on risk equal to the loss's average value....

Two conditions affecting a party's ability to achieve risk neutrality are the relative size of the loss and the party's ability to spread it.

293

Most decision makers are risk neutral toward losses that are small in
proportion to their wealth, and risk averse toward losses that are
relatively large. In addition, financial institutions, unlike consumers,
can achieve complete risk neutrality by spreading the resulting losses
across their entire group of customers. To be spread, the losses must be
sufficiently small and occur frequently enough to be predictable. For
example, a financial institution often cannot know whether specific
payment instruments are forged, but because it engages in a large
number of transactions, it can accurately predict the number of forgeries that will occur in a given year. Once the institution makes that
prediction, it can pass on the cost to its customers as a charge for its
service, just as it passes on the cost of paying tellers or encoding checks.

These considerations suggest the first principle of efficient payment
law, which is frequently called the loss spreading principle: assign
liability for a loss to the party that can achieve risk neutrality at the
lowest cost. In general, the party that can achieve risk neutrality at
the lowest cost is the one that has greater economic resources and is in
a position to spread the loss most effectively. This principle, therefore,
suggests that liability for losses should fall on financial institutions
rather than on individual consumers. The forgery or alteration of a
single payment item, like a check, can involve a significant proportion
of an individual's wealth, but will typically constitute an insignificant
loss for a financial institution. Moreover, the institution can predict
the total volume of its losses and spread them over a large group of
consumers, whereas consumers will generally end up bearing the entire
loss themselves. . . .

B.   The Loss Reduction Principle

Independent of their ability to spread payment losses, consumers
and financial institutions often have the ability to reduce these losses,
and one of them can often do so at less cost than the other. Efficiency
requires that the legal rules create incentives for such loss reduction.
The standard means for creating legal incentives is the assignment of
liability, which suggests the loss reduction principle: an efficient legal
system assigns liability to the party that can reduce losses at the lowest
cost. . . .

Consumers and financial institutions often can reduce payment
losses by taking the precautions that are presently available to them.
Consumers can do so through ordinary prudence and care in making
payments, and financial institutions can reduce losses through internal
measures similar to quality control in manufacturing. Precautions,
however, entail costs in money, time, and effort, which discourage
consumers and financial institutions from undertaking them. Legal
rules that impose liability on consumers or financial institutions force
them to include this potential liability in their calculus of costs, and
thus weigh it against the cost of precaution. In economic terms, the
liable party internalizes the social value of the precaution. To achieve
internalization at the most efficient level, payment rules must assign

liability to the party who, on the basis of its position in the process, is able to take precaution against the loss at the lowest cost....

This conclusion, which is valid when means of precaution are presently available at relatively low cost, must be tempered by dynamic considerations. Recent technological innovations, such as automated check processing, have altered the cost of precaution and will continue to do so in the future. The imposition of liability can create an incentive for the development of innovations that reduce both the cost of precaution and the frequency of losses. Thus, the innovation element, which interacts with the precaution element in a dynamic context, suggests payment rules that assign liability to the party most likely to develop innovative methods of precaution over time.

Liability, however, is a useful incentive, whether for precaution or innovation, only to the extent that behavior responds to it; a particular assignment of liability that does not influence behavior has no economic justification. Moreover, if it influences behavior only to a limited extent, then its effectiveness must be discounted by that limitation....

C. *The Loss Imposition Principle*

The loss spreading and loss reduction principles indicate the party to which payment rules can most efficiently assign liability. The third principle in establishing an efficient payment law, the loss imposition principle, concerns the enforcement of this assigned liability. The enforcement process turns the law from a set of legal rules into a series of actual monetary transfers. Liability may be enforced through civil suits, criminal trials, or administrative proceedings, as well as through the many informal devices for settling disputes. One feature that all these mechanisms share is that they are costly; they represent a deadweight loss to the participants in the payment system. To achieve efficiency, therefore, the enforcement process should be as inexpensive as possible....

If reallocating the loss is required for increased efficiency, then the most desirable enforcement process is the one that will shift liability as cheaply as possible from the creditor to the party that should suffer the final loss. This goal can be achieved by fashioning simple, clear, and decisive liability rules. Such rules discourage people from bringing meritless lawsuits by decreasing the law's level of ambiguity. In addition, they simplify court proceedings and lower litigation costs by decreasing the number of issues, the amount of relevant evidence, the number of required court appearances, and the amount of prelitigation legal counseling. The mechanisms that will generate simple, clear, and decisive liability rules, and thus achieve these advantages, are familiar: strict liability rather than fault-based liability, single factor standards rather than multiple factor standards, objective rather than subjective tests, and statutory liquidated damages rather than damages based on individualized determinations of loss.

Of course, structuring the enforcement process in this way may deprive it of the flexibility necessary for loss spreading and loss reduction, because it represents a fairly rough allocation of liability, rather than the precise allocation that these principles would recommend. The choice ultimately depends on the relative economic impact of all three principles of efficient loss allocation. In weighing the impact of these three principles, loss imposition factors will tend to be extremely significant, much more so than the precaution-oriented rules of the UCC would suggest. The cost of making even a single factual determination would quickly surpass all but the most catastrophic losses on a consumer account. . . .

Note

Availability of Insurance. Since nearly all of the bank's share of loss due to forgery and alteration, as well as some of the rest, is covered by insurance, no contemporary discussion of the allocation of risk of loss is complete without reference to available insurance. Three principal types of coverage are available: fidelity bonds, depositors' forgery bonds, and forgery insurance under bankers' blanket bonds.

The fidelity bond protects an employer against losses sustained through forgeries by employees who are covered by the bond. Such bonds were originally written on an individual basis by a bonding company as surety, on behalf of a named employee as principal, and in favor of a named employer. When the number of employees in a single concern made this cumbersome, surety companies drafted schedule bonds to cover two or more employees, who may be designated by name in a name schedule bond or by position in a position schedule bond. More recently, blanket fidelity bonds have been made available, covering all officers and employees collectively. Nevertheless, many businesses eligible for fidelity coverage carry none at all.

The depositor's forgery bond, which is available to all persons and commercial enterprises other than financial institutions, insures against loss due to forgery or alteration in connection with checks, drafts or notes made or purporting to have been made by the insured or its agent. In order to prevent litigation between the insured and its bank, the insured is permitted to include loss suffered by the depositary bank in its proof of loss. The bond covers only outgoing checks. An incoming check rider is also available to cover 75% of the insured's interest in checks received in payment for services or property, other than property sold on credit. Coverage under the depositor's forgery bond has not, however, become as popular as that under the fidelity bond.

Bankers' blanket bonds have been issued by domestic underwriters since 1916 and are carried by all banks. They cover losses due to such hazards as robbery, burglary, larceny, misplacement, employee dishonesty. Although forgery insurance is optional for commercial banks under such a bond, most banks have clause D, which covers forgery and alteration. In the case of commercial banks, premiums on clause D are computed on the basis of a standard rate which takes into account the size of the bank, as indicated by total deposits, the number of accounts, and the limit of liability. The blanket bond premium may be substantially reduced on the basis of the experience under the bond during the preceding five years. Where the experience has been unsatisfactory, the underwriter may review the insured's procedures, a deductible policy may be issued or a surcharge may be requested.

Is insurance available to the parties who must bear the risk of loss under the Code? To what extent do those parties in fact insure? Should the answers to these questions affect the allocation of the risk? For a discussion of these questions, see Farnsworth, Insurance Against Check Forgery, 60 Colum.L.Rev. 284 (1960). For a general survey of the field of forgery and fraud under revised Articles 3 and 4, see Rapson, Loss Allocation in Forgery and Fraud Cases: significant changes under Revised Articles 3 and 4, 42 Ala.L.Rev. 435 (1991).

Problem 1. Y Bank presented to X Bank a check which appeared to have been drawn on X Bank by A for $10,000 payable to the order of B, then indorsed by B to C, and then indorsed by C and deposited in Y Bank. Who bears the loss under the Code in each of the following situations, assuming that the forger cannot be held responsible[1] and that none of the parties is at fault? Are the results in any way consistent?

(a) A's signature was forged by F, who gave it for value to B, who cashed it with C; X Bank discovered the forgery and refused to pay the check.

(b) Same as in (a), but X Bank did not discover the forgery and paid the check by mistake.

(c) S, A's secretary, who had been told to mail the check to B, stole it from A, forged B's indorsement and cashed it with C; A discovered the theft and notified X Bank, which refused to pay the check.

(d) Same as in (c), but A did not discover the theft and X Bank paid the check by mistake. (Would it make a difference if A had discovered the theft and notified X Bank?)

(e) B, to whom A had made out the check for $1,000, raised the amount to $10,000 and cashed it with C; X Bank discovered the alteration and refused to pay the check.

(f) Same as in (e), but X Bank did not discover the alteration and paid the check by mistake.

SOME FUNDAMENTAL RULES

Basic Situations. Consider, at the outset, three basic situations. Suppose that an innocent party has purchased: (1) a check on which

---

1. Because Regulation CC decreases the length of the hold that a depositary bank can place on a deposited check, the regulation increases the likelihood that this assumption is in fact the case.

the drawer's signature has been forged (a "forged check"); (2) a check on which a necessary indorsement has been forged; (3) a check that has been altered by raising the amount. If the check is not paid, what recourse does that party have against prior parties? If the check is paid by mistake, what recourse does the payor bank have, against either its depositor or the person whom it paid? (We shall assume, realistically, that recourse against the forger is not a practicable solution.)

Forged checks. If a forged check is not paid, the innocent purchaser can turn to a prior party, if there is one other than the forger, for recourse. UCC 3–416(a)(2), 4–207(a)(2). If it is paid by mistake, the bank that pays it has no recourse against either its depositor or the person whom it paid. That it has no recourse against its depositor is clear from UCC 3–403(a) and 4–401(a). That it has no recourse against the person whom it paid follows from the provision on finality of payment in UCC 3–418 coupled with the absence of any right to recover for breach of warranty under UCC 3–417(a)(3) and 4–208(a)(3) as long as the person whom it paid had "no knowledge" of the forgery. This rule denying the bank recovery against the person paid is popularly known as "rule in *Price v. Neal,*" after the great case of that name. Lord Mansfield there reasoned that "If there was no neglect in the [drawee], yet there is no reason to throw off the loss from one innocent man upon another innocent man; but in this case, if there was any fault or negligence in any one, it certainly was in the [drawee] and not in the [person paid]." Price v. Neal, 3 Burr. 1354, 97 Eng.Rep. 871 (K.B.1762).

Forged indorsements. If a check on which a necessary indorsement has been forged is not paid, the innocent purchaser can also turn to a prior party, if there is one other than the forger, for recourse. UCC 3–416(a)(1), 4–207(a)(1). Furthermore, as in the case of the forged check, if the payor bank pays a check by mistake over a forged indorsement, it has no recourse against its depositor.[2] UCC 3–403(a), 4–401(a). (Remember that the drawer's order is to pay only to "the order of" the payee.) In contrast to the case of the forged check, however, the bank that pays a check by mistake on a forged indorsement can recover from the person paid, including a collecting bank, on the warranties of UCC 3–417(a)(1) and 4–208(a)(1). In an early leading case, the court justified recovery on the "reason that the parties were equally innocent," and

2. This general statement assumes that payment has in fact been made to the wrong person (or to the right person but in payment of the wrong debt). If, in spite of a forged indorsement or the lack of any indorsement, payment is in fact made as the drawer intended it, the drawee should be entitled to charge the drawer's account. As one court put it, "The drawer is not damaged by the application of the rule, for no person not intended by him to take an interest has done so as a consequence of the forged indorsement...." Gordon v. State Street Bank and Trust Co., 361 Mass. 258, 280 N.E.2d 152 (1972). That case, like most in which this exception has been applied, involved a check made jointly to two payees, one of whom was intended to receive the proceeds to the exclusion of the other, although the indorsements of both were required for negotiation. If the payor bank pays the check to the payee intended to receive the proceeds, it can charge the drawer's account even though that payee has signed the other payee's indorsement without authorization, assuming, of course, that the drawer has not been otherwise adversely affected. Cf. UCC 3–110(d).

said, by way of disposing of the rule of *Price v. Neal*, that "it is sufficient to distinguish the case, that it goes on the superior negligence of the party paying." Canal Bank v. Bank of Albany, 1 Hill 287 (N.Y.1841).

Prior to the adoption of the Code, the theory on which the payor bank was generally allowed to recover was one of restitution of money paid by mistake of fact, rather than one of warranty. Under this theory, if an agent collecting bank had already paid over the proceeds to its principal, it might no longer be liable to the payor bank. To avoid this result, banks voluntarily adopted the practice of adding to their indorsement stamp the words "prior indorsements guaranteed" so that an agent collecting bank could be held on this engagement even though it had paid over the proceeds.

The Code changed the underlying theory of recovery from one of restitution to one of implied warranty under UCC 3–417(a) and 4–208(a). Comment 2 to former UCC 4–207 (the predecessor of UCC 4–208) said that that section was "intended to give the effect presently obtained in bank collections by the words 'prior indorsements guaranteed' in collection transfers and presentments between banks" and "to make it clear that the so-called equitable defense of 'payment over' does not apply to a collecting bank.... Consequently, if for purposes of simplification or the speeding up of the bank collection process, banks desire to cut down the length or size of indorsements ..., they may do so and the standard warranties and engagements to honor still apply."[3]

Banks did not take the authors of the Comment up on their invitation, however, and continued to add the words "prior indorsements guaranteed." But Regulation CC, Appendix D, in order to avoid unnecessary clutter, discourages the depositary bank and prohibits subsequent collecting banks from following this practice.

Altered checks. If a raised check is not paid, an innocent purchaser can enforce the instrument for its original amount even against the drawer. UCC 3–407(c). In addition, the purchaser can turn to a prior party, if there is one other than the forger, for recourse in the raised amount. UCC 3–416(a)(3), 4–207(a)(3). The bank that pays a raised check by mistake can charge its depositor's account for the original amount only. UCC 4–401(d)(1). The balance it can recover from the person paid, on the warranties of UCC 3–417(a)(2) and 4–208(a)(2).

Rationale of Rule in Price v. Neal. Suppose that a merchant cashes for the forger a check bearing a forged drawer's signature. If the payor bank detects the forgery and refuses to pay the check, who bears the loss? If the payor bank fails to detect the forgery and pays the check, who bears the loss? Why the difference in result? Although nearly all states recognized the rule of *Price v. Neal* under the Negotiable Instruments Law, there was no uniformity of reasoning. Is any of the following statements convincing?

---

3. Note that UCC 4–302, which deals with a payor bank's liability if it returns a check after the midnight deadline, is subject to defenses based on UCC 4–208.

(a) "The justification for the distinction between forgery of the signature of the drawer and forgery of an indorsement is that the drawee is in a position to verify the drawer's signature by comparison with one in his hands, but has ordinarily no opportunity to verify an indorsement." Comment 3 to former UCC 3–417. But note that the rule of *Price v. Neal* does not depend on the payor bank's negligence.

(b) "The traditional justification for the result is that the drawee is in a superior position to detect a forgery because he has the maker's [sic] signature and is expected to know and compare it; a less fictional rationalization is that it is highly desirable to end the transaction of an instrument when it is paid rather than reopen and upset a series of commercial transactions at a later date when the forgery is discovered." Comment 1 to former UCC 3–418.

(c) "The rule stated in this Section [that of Price v. Neal] is in accord with mercantile convenience, supporting the finality of transactions with mercantile instruments in situations where ordinarily it is reasonably possible for the payor to ascertain the fraud. Furthermore, the payee has surrendered the instrument." Restatement, Restitution § 30, Comment a (1937).

(d) "Of the variety of justifications that have been advanced over the years, [two] are most convincing. The first is that the rule has a healthy cautionary effect on banks by encouraging care in the comparison of the signatures on 'on us' items against those on the signature cards that they have on file. Prompt detection of the forgery and return of the dishonored check will often prevent loss, especially where the check has been taken from the forger for collection only, and although a detailed examination of every check may not be practicable for a bank that may pay as many as several hundred thousand checks a day, the rule of Price v. Neal ensures that the bank has a lively interest not only in the rapid processing of checks but also in the detection of forgery and the reduction of forgery losses. Although this risk is covered by Clause D of the bankers blanket bond, experience rating retains the cautionary effect of the rule. The second justification is that this very opportunity of the drawee to insure and to distribute the cost among its customers who use checks makes the drawee an ideal party to spread the risk through insurance. This argument, to be sure, is junior to the rule, since forgery insurance is a century and a half younger than Price v. Neal. Nevertheless, there is no question today that forgery bonds are adequate to cover loss due to the mistaken payment of forged checks." Farnsworth, Insurance Against Check Forgery, 60 Colum.L.Rev. 284, 302–03 (1960).

(e) "The traditional reason given for this differential treatment of forged drawers' signatures and forged indorsements is essentially a precaution rationale. The drawee bank is assigned the loss from a forged drawer's signature because it has the consumer's signature on file and can determine whether the signature on the instrument is genuine.... *Price v. Neal* has been criticized as outmoded in the modern era because financial institutions do not visually examine each signature on the forty billion or so checks that they process annually. This criticism, however, ignores the innovation element of loss reduction. If the financial institution is subject to liability, it will be motivated to develop new technology, such as signature reading machines. Whether such devices prove to be economically feasible is a decision that financial institutions must make, but it is precisely this ability to balance the cost of new technology against its benefits that makes them the most efficient bearers of the loss. From an efficiency perspective, however, the problem of allocating forgery losses among the various parties is less significant than its long history suggests. Neither checks nor other payment instruments now pass from one person to another the way they did in eighteenth century mercantile practice.... The result is that the first taker of a check with a forged indorsement is almost always a merchant or a bank, and with increasing frequency it is a bank. Between the merchant, the depositary bank, and the drawee bank, the allocation of liability can be left to the market, at least on a presumptive basis, because no market failure exists.... The rule of *Price v. Neal* need only be retained as a presumptive allocation among merchants and financial institutions." Cooter & Rubin, A Theory of Loss Allocation for Consumer Payments, 66 Tex.L.Rev. 63, 105–07 (1987).

A Contrary View. In a major departure from present law, the ill-fated Uniform New Payments Code provided: "Each customer, transmitting account institution or transferor of an unauthorized draw order is liable to all parties to whom the draw order is subsequently transmitted and who pay, accept or give value in exchange for the order in good faith, if it has transmitted an unauthorized order...." UNPC 204. The commentary gave the following explanation:

"[This provision] marks the death knell for Lord Mansfield's famous opinion in Price v. Neal ..., which held that no warranty of the genuineness of a forged drawer's signature is given to the payor bank by a person transmitting a check for collection....

"The rationale for the rule is not convincing. First, the traditional justification that the drawee is in a superior position to detect the forgery seems dubious today. Given the computerized payment of checks, necessitated by the high volume of items submitted for payment, it is uneconomical for an account institution to check the validity of all signatures. This is reflected by the reality that banks do not check signatures under a certain dollar amount even though they will be liable. It is cheaper to bear the liability than to avoid it....

"The second rationale for the rule is finality—the need for repose on transactions.... It must be recognized, however, that there is no such repose in cases of forged endorsements where warranties are now given to the payor bank....

"Not only is the rationale for the rule questionable, but the rule can be thought of as not giving adequate incentives to payees to check on the bona fides of people drawing checks to them. Under existing law, a merchant cashing a check need not be concerned with whether a person paying by check is actually the owner of the account on which the check is drawn. If Price v. Neal is abolished such incentives would exist. Check cashing outside the banking system is much less computerized thus allowing better opportunities for verifying the identity of a check cashier.... Absent Price v. Neal ..., loss would ultimately lie with the payee, the taker from the thief.... Account institutions should generally support abolishing Price v. Neal because risks now borne by them could be shifted to their customers.

"In addition, application of Price v. Neal makes no sense in cases of check truncation, where the drawer's signature is not available for inspection by the payor account institution—assuming technology could not capture the signature at a reasonable cost. Since, on balance, the rule has no convincing justification and some significant costs in today's high speed check processing environment, it is abolished. The Code rejects the possibility of allowing the collector of a check to avoid liability by showing that the payor account institution was negligent, e.g., failed to detect an obvious forgery on a $1 million check. While such a rule might be justified in theory, importing the issue of negligence into liabilities among account institutions would probably cause more confusion for operations personnel and litigation than it is worth...." [4]

Retention of Rule. Comment 3 to UCC 3–417 says only that "subsection (a)(3) retains the rule in Price v. Neal ... that the drawee takes the risk that the drawer's signature is unauthorized unless the person presenting the draft has knowledge that the drawer's signature is unauthorized." No rationale for the rule is offered.

What is the position under the Code of a holder who takes a check in due course and then discovers that the drawer's signature has been forged? If the holder says nothing and is paid by the payor bank, can the payor bank recover the payment? Which answer accords with the reason behind the rule of *Price v. Neal*? Comment 4 to former UCC 3–417 explained that the warranty of no knowledge of a forged drawer's signature "is pertinent in the case of a holder in due course only in the relatively few cases where he acquires knowledge of the forgery after the taking but before the presentment. In this situation the holder in due course must continue to act in good faith to be exempted from the basic warranty." How is it possible for the holder to act in good faith with knowledge of the forgery?

---

4. The New York Clearing House criticized this proposal to abolish the doctrine of *Price v. Neal* on the ground that it might reduce the willingness of merchants to take checks instead of cash. "Currently, merchants do bear a relatively short-term risk that a check may not be paid during the process of collection. Under the revised rule, however, they would remain liable for the length of the applicable statute of limitations, under UCC § 4–406 now one year." Statement of the New York Clearing House on the Proposed Uniform New Payments Code 13–14 (1983).

COMPARATIVE NOTE

Geneva Convention. The solution of civil law countries to the problem of forged indorsements offers an interesting comparison with our own. Under the Geneva Convention on Cheques, which was promulgated in 1931 and has been adopted in much of the civil law world, a person acquiring a check in good faith and without gross negligence by an interrupted series of indorsements has good title even if the instrument was stolen from the true owner and the true owner's indorsement forged. Similarly, a payor bank that pays a check need only examine the apparent regularity of the chain of indorsements and is discharged if it pays in good faith to a person who takes by virtue of an apparently regular chain. See Kessler, Forged Indorsements, 47 Yale L.J. 863, 863–64 (1938).

Consider the situation illustrated by Problem 1(d) supra, in which a thief steals a check before it is received by the payee, forges the payee's indorsement, and cashes it with an innocent merchant. The merchant deposits the check in a bank, which presents it to the payor bank and obtains payment. In this situation the Code puts the loss on the merchant who, having taken the check from the forger, is left to pursue the forger.

The Geneva Convention, however, puts the loss on the drawer. Since the indorsements appeared on their face to be regular, the payor bank can charge the drawer's account in spite of the forged indorsement.

Under the Geneva Convention, however, the drawer can, by crossing the check, gain protection from the risk that the check will be stolen. Two types of crossing are possible, general and special. A general crossing is made by drawing two parallel lines across the face of the instrument. A special crossing is made in the same way, but the name of the payee's bank is added between the lines. Any bank that fails to observe the crossing is liable for any loss caused by its failure. A bank may not take a crossed check except from its customer or from another bank, and such a check is payable only to a bank or a customer of the payor bank. Thus a general crossing in the example above would have prevented the thief from presenting the check directly to the payor bank but not from cashing it with a merchant or from depositing it in the merchant's own bank for collection. If the crossing is special, however, the payor bank may pay it only to the bank named in the crossing or, if it is the named bank, to a customer.[5] Thus a special crossing in the example above would not only have prevented the thief from presenting the check directly to the payor bank but also from cashing it with a merchant or depositing it in a bank for collection.[6]

---

5. In order to prevent the thief from opening a bank account for the purpose of collecting crossed checks bearing forged indorsements, courts have generally required an "anterior and permanent" relationship between customer and bank.

6. A payee who has received a check may also cross it or may convert a general

Obviously this system will not work unless the drawer has an incentive to cross checks—unless the drawer has an appreciable risk that can be avoided by crossing them. Furthermore, since only a special crossing affords substantial protection, the system will not work unless most payees have bank accounts and most drawers know where their payees bank.[7] See Farnsworth, The Check in France and the United States, 36 Tul.L.Rev. 245, 266–68 (1962).

Problem 2. A drew a $1,000 check on the X Bank, which B the payee raised to $10,000. B negotiated it to C, a holder in due course, who procured its certification and then negotiated it to D, a holder in due course. Must the X Bank pay D $10,000? If it does, has it any recourse against A or C? What answers if the certification were "payable only as originally drawn"? See UCC 3–413(a), 3–417(a), 3–418, 4–208(a).

Problem 3. Suppose that in Problem 2 D had presented the check to X Bank and had been paid $10,000. Could X Bank recover any part of that sum from D? Would it make any difference if D had discovered the alteration between the time that D took the check and the time that D obtained payment from X Bank? See UCC 3–417(d), 4–208(d).

THE CERTIFICATION PUZZLE

The two preceding problems deal with a puzzling question as to which the law before the Code was both uncertain and unsatisfactory. How should the loss be allocated when a check that was raised *before* certification was taken by a holder in due course *after* certification? The holder in due course could, of course, proceed against a prior indorser, if there was one other than the forger, but this would not give the holder the supposed security of a certified check. Could the holder hold the certifying bank on its certification for the *raised* amount of the check? Common sense said that the holder should be able to, if certification was to be meaningful. The Negotiable Instruments Law was ambiguous. Courts disagreed, with decisions in California and Illinois holding the bank liable for the raised amount. See Wells Fargo Bank & Union Trust Co. v. Bank of Italy, 214 Cal. 156, 4 P.2d 781 (1931). In practice, however, it made little difference what courts decided. Banks found a sufficient answer by including on their certification stamps some such phrase as "payable only as originally drawn," which resolved the issue in their favor by making certification less meaningful. (Did they run any risk in refusing certification absent

crossing into a special crossing adding the name of the payee's bank. If an uncrossed check is stolen and paid over the payee's forged indorsement, the payee must bear the loss since the amount will be charged to the drawer, who cannot be required to issue a second check to the payee. By crossing the check, the payee will have a right against the drawer or depositary bank if it has acted inconsistently with the crossing.

7. This information is often given on letterheads, bills, and invoices.

such a qualification? See Refusal to Certify as a Dishonor, p. 173 supra.)

Here is a perceptive analysis of the situation. "At the core of the banker's present discomfiture, insofar as certification matters trouble him at all, is the action of the Illinois and California courts in putting all loss upon the bank where altered paper is certified. To those who see negotiable instruments questions only through the eyes of a bona fide purchaser, without counting costs, those decisions should be codified without qualification. If the bank must take a dead loss, since recourse against the forger is not promising, it can of course insure. Why not? The court in the Wells Fargo case, in fact, went out of its way to deny the bank any other recourse by saying that the holder makes no warranties to the drawee. . . . But while there is reason apparent for charging the drawee with responsibility for the regularity of its drawer's signature and for the adequacy of his account—both matters peculiarly within the bank's knowledge—the same cannot be said for alterations in the body of the paper. On generally accepted risk analysis principles it is the person who takes the paper from the forger, often at a substantial discount, often with more than a suspicion of the fraud, who should take this risk.

"The first suggestion, therefore, is to provide that the person who presents a check for certification warrants to the bank not only that he has title to the item but that it has not been materially altered. The purchaser *after* certification, however, should be deemed to make no warranty to the drawee, either by indorsement or presentment for payment, except of course that his title to the item *as certified* is good. This suggestion proceeds upon the theory that upon certification for the holder, the check is in effect paid . . . and the bank is put in much the same position as if it had taken up the check and issued its cashier's check instead, as is often done. The bank in so doing runs only the usual business risks involved in paying items generally. The purchaser in good faith of the certified item, on his part, takes the instrument in confidence and at its face value. There would thus be no need for the banker either to abandon the practice of certifying checks for the holder or to qualify his undertaking so scrupulously." Steffen and Starr, A Blueprint for the Certified Check, 13 N.C.L.Rev. 450, 477–79 (1935).

Such a complete solution, affecting the rights and duties of several parties, had to await legislative intervention. (Compare the situation involving mistaken payment over a stop order, in which bank disclaimers were followed by Code revision. See Prefatory Note, p. 255 supra.) To the drafters of the Code, the solution suggested was an attractive one in view of their adoption of a theory of liability in warranty to replace that of liability in restitution. It is now implemented in UCC 3–413(a), 3–417(a), (d) and 4–208(a), (d), which greatly simplify the comparable sections of former Article 3 (see Comment 4 to UCC 3–417). Furthermore, once the certifying bank was given recourse for breach of warranty by the person who presented the check for certification, there was scant justification in allowing it to qualify its certification, and UCC 3–413(a) deprives such phrases as "payable as originally drawn" of their effectiveness. (As to the effect of alteration *after* certification, see Problem 9 infra.)

SECTION 2. RIGHTS OF ONE WHOSE INDORSEMENT HAS BEEN FORGED

Prefatory Note. If a check was stolen from the *drawer* and paid on a forged indorsement, the rights of the parties were reasonably clear under former Article 3. If, however, the check was stolen from the *payee* and paid on a forged indorsement, the rights of the parties were far from clear. Prior to the Code, most courts held that the payee could recover from the payor bank in conversion. "It is the conversion by the bank of the payee's property, the check, which gives rise to the action." State v. First National Bank of Albuquerque, 38 N.M. 225, 30 P.2d 728 (1934). At least former Article 3 made it clear that the payor bank was liable on this theory. See former UCC 3–419. (It is not, of course, liable to the payee in contract because of the rule that a check is not an assignment.)

The payee whose check has been paid on a forged indorsement will, however, usually find it more convenient to ask the drawer for a second check to replace the first than to demand payment from the payor bank, ordinarily a stranger to it. Is the drawer liable to the payee if it does not comply with such a request? There was authority before the Code that it was not, a logical view if the payor bank was liable to the payee in conversion. "Under these same circumstances, the liability of the drawer of the check upon the original account, to pay which the check is drawn, should be held discharged, having regard to the general rules of law governing the correlated duties and rights of the parties and to commercial usage and custom." McFadden v. Follrath, 114 Minn. 85, 130 N.W. 542 (1911). The same result follows under the Code. Under UCC 3–310(b)(4), the obligation for which the check was taken "may not be enforced to the extent of the amount payable on the instrument, and to that extent the obligee's rights against the obligor are limited to enforcement of the instrument." As Comment 1 to UCC 3–420 explains: "The payee's rights are restricted to enforcement of the payee's rights in the instrument. In this event the payee is injured by the theft and has a cause of action for conversion." As to how the payee might enforce the instrument against the drawer, see UCC 3–409.

Problem 4. A thief steals Empire's check from Quaker after it has been received in the mail, forges Quaker's indorsement, and obtains payment directly from The Bank of New York. Quaker asks Empire for another check to replace the stolen one. Advise Empire of its legal position if it refuses to give Quaker a second check. Advise Empire of its legal position if it gives Quaker a second check. Compare this situation with that in Problem 1(d), p. 297 supra. See UCC 3–301, 3–309, 3–310(b), 3–420, 3–602(a).

Note

Indemnification. Suppose that a payee loses a check and requests that the drawer send a substitute check. The drawer who does so risks having to pay twice if the first check had already been indorsed by the payee and comes into the hands of a holder in due course. To protect against this risk, the drawer might under former UCC 3–309 require that the payee supply security indemnifying the drawer "against loss by reason of further claims on the instrument." Santos v. First National State Bank of New Jersey, 186 N.J.Super. 52, 451 A.2d 401 (1982), arose out of such a demand for security in the case of a lost cashier's check.

In 1978, Santos, who was preparing to return to Puerto Rico, withdrew the entire balance of $15,514.46 from his savings account and took a cashier's check payable to his own order, which he then mailed to his father in Puerto Rico. Eleven days later, he told the bank that the check had been lost in the mail and asked for a substitute check. The bank insisted on security, but Santos could not, even with the bank's assistance, get a bond because he was unemployed and had no other assets.

In 1980, Santos sued the bank to compel it: (1) to issue a duplicate check or credit him with $15,514.46 without security; or (2) to establish an interest-bearing account in trust, paying him interest periodically, with the principal to be paid six years from the date the check was issued or at another date fixed by the court.

The court concluded that under former UCC 3–122 the six-year statute of limitations began to run when the check was issued and that, though it was "highly improbable" that the check would reappear during that time, "to require payment now without security for indemnification would expose defendant to risk of loss through no fault of its own." The court therefore ordered the bank "to issue at this time a certificate of deposit in plaintiff's name for $15,514.46 bearing the highest prevailing interest rate for such an instrument." Subject to any further order of the court, the bank was to hold the certificate as security for its obligation until the six-year statute ran in 1984, unless the check sooner reappeared, and during this period was to pay Santos quarterly interest.

Cases like *Santos* prompted the insertion of UCC 3–312, which had no counterpart in former Article 3. Under that section a claimant in the situation of Santos can assert a claim effective 90 days after the date of the cashier's check that obligates the bank to pay the claimant rather than a holder, assuming that the cashier's check has not already been paid. Comment 3 explains: "Thus if a lost check is presented for payment within the 90–day period, the bank may pay a person entitled to enforce the check without regard to the claim and is discharged from all liability with respect to the check. This ensures the continued utility of cashier's checks ... as cash equivalents. Virtually all such checks are presented for payment within 90 days. If payment of the check within the 90–day period was not made to a person entitled to enforce the check, the obligated bank is obliged to pay the amount of the check to the claimant. Payment to the claimant discharges all liability of the bank with respect to the checks."

Suit by Drawer Against Depositary Bank. A vexing question under former Article 3 went to the drawer's right to recover from a depositary bank that had handled a check for a thief who had stolen the check from the drawer, forged the payee's indorsement, and gotten the check paid.

As a practical matter, one might wonder why a drawer would want to assert such a right against a depositary bank instead of insisting that the payor bank recredit the drawer's account. See Problem 1(d) supra. The payor bank, which has the drawer's account, would seem more convenient than the depositary bank, which probably has no relationship with the drawer and may be in another jurisdiction. (Might the payor bank put pressure on the drawer, for example by threatening to call in a demand loan, to encourage the drawer to press a claim against the depositary bank instead?)

As a matter of principle, how could a drawer, who has not been harmed by the depositary bank's handling the check for the thief, assert a claim based on conversion by that bank? (Might the drawer argue that since the drawer has a claim against the payor bank and the payor bank has a claim against the depositary bank, allowing the drawer a direct claim against the depositary bank will avoid circuity of action?)

The case that follows was a leading case under former Article 3.

Problem 5. A thief steals Empire's check from Empire before it has been mailed to Quaker, forges Quaker's indorsement, and deposits it in the Penn Bank, which forwards it to The Bank of New York, which pays it. The thief then withdraws the amount of the check from the Penn Bank. Advise Empire of its legal position with respect to Quaker, The Bank of New York, and the Penn Bank. See UCC 3–420; *Stone & Webster Engineering v. First National Bank,* infra.

STONE & WEBSTER ENGINEERING CORP. v.
FIRST NATIONAL BANK & TRUST CO.

Supreme Judicial Court of Massachusetts, 1962.
345 Mass. 1, 184 N.E.2d 358, 99 A.L.R.2d 628.

WILKINS, CHIEF JUSTICE. In this action of contract or tort in four counts for the same cause of action a demurrer to the declaration was sustained, and the plaintiff, described in the writ as having a usual place of business in Boston, appealed. G.L. (Ter.Ed.) c. 231, § 96. The questions argued concern the rights of the drawer against a collecting bank which "cashed" checks for an individual who had forged the payee's indorsement on the checks, which were never delivered to the payee.

In the first count, which is in contract, the plaintiff alleges that between January 1, 1960, and May 15, 1960, it was indebted at various times to Westinghouse Electric Corporation (Westinghouse) for goods and services furnished to it by Westinghouse; that in order to pay the indebtedness the plaintiff drew three checks within that period on its checking account in The First National Bank of Boston (First National) payable to Westinghouse in the total amount of $64,755.44; that before delivery of the checks to Westinghouse an employee of the plaintiff in possession of the checks forged the indorsement of Westinghouse and presented the checks to the defendant; that the defendant "cashed" the checks and delivered the proceeds to the plaintiff's employee who devoted the proceeds to his own use; that the defendant forwarded the checks to First National and received from First National the full amounts thereof; and that First National charged the account of the plaintiff with the full amounts of the checks and has refused to recredit the plaintiff's checking account; wherefore the defendant owes the plaintiff $64,755.44 with interest.

By order, copies of the three checks were filed in court. The checks are respectively dated at Rowe in this Commonwealth on January 5, March 8, and May 9, 1960. Their respective amounts are $36,982.86, $10,416.58, and $17,355. They are payable to the order of "Westinghouse Electric Corporation, 10 High Street, Boston." The first two checks are indorsed in typewriting, "for Deposit Only: Westinghouse Electric Corporation By: Mr. O.D. Costine, Treasury Representative" followed by an ink signature "O.D. Costine." The third check is indorsed in typewriting, "Westinghouse Electric Corporation By: [Sgd.] O.D. Costine Treasury Representative." All three checks also bear the indorsement by rubber stamp, "Pay to the order of any bank, banker or trust co. prior indorsements guaranteed ... [date][1] The First National Bank & Trust Co. Greenfield, Mass."

The demurrer, in so far as it has been argued, is to each count for failure to state a cause of action. . . .

---

1. The respective dates are January 13, March 9, and May 11, 1960. Each check bears the stamped indorsement of the Federal Reserve Bank of Boston and on its face the paid stamp of The First National Bank of Boston.

1. Count 1, the plaintiff contends, is for money had and received. We shall so regard it. "An action for money had and received lies to recover money which should not in justice be retained by the defendant, and which in equity and good conscience should be paid to the plaintiff." ...

The defendant has no money in its hands which belongs to the plaintiff. The latter had no right in the proceeds of its own check payable to Westinghouse. Not being a holder or an agent for a holder, it could not have presented the check to the drawee for payment. Uniform Commercial Code, enacted by St.1957, c. 765, § 1, G.L. c. 106, §§ 3–504(1), 1–201(20). See Am.Law Inst.Uniform Commercial Code, 1958 Official Text with comments, § 3–419, comment 2: "A negotiable instrument is the property of the holder." See also Restatement 2d: Torts, Tent. draft no. 3, 1958, § 241A. The plaintiff contends that "First National paid or credited the proceeds of the checks to the defendant and charged the account of the plaintiff, and consequently, the plaintiff was deprived of a credit, and the defendant received funds or a credit which 'in equity and good conscience' belonged to the plaintiff."

In our opinion this argument is a non sequitur. The plaintiff as a depositor in First National was merely in a contractual relationship of creditor and debtor. Forastiere v. Springfield Inst. for Sav., 303 Mass. 101, 103, 20 N.E.2d 950; Krinsky v. Pilgrim Trust Co., 337 Mass. 401, 405, 149 N.E.2d 665. The amounts the defendant received from First National to cover the checks "cashed" were the bank's funds and not the plaintiff's. The Uniform Commercial Code does not purport to change the relationship. See G.L. c. 106, §§ 1–103, 4–401 to 4–407. Section 3–409(1) provides: "A check or other draft does not of itself operate as an assignment of any funds in the hands of the drawee available for its payment, and the drawee is not liable on the instrument until he accepts it." This is the same as our prior law, which the Code repealed. See, formerly, G.L. c. 107, §§ 150, 212. Whether the plaintiff was rightfully deprived of a credit is a matter between it and the drawee, First National.

If we treat the first count as seeking to base a cause of action for money had and received upon a waiver of the tort of conversion—a matter which it is not clear is argued—the result will be the same. In this aspect the question presented is whether a drawer has a right of action for conversion against a collecting bank which handles its checks in the bank collection process. Unless there be such a right, there is no tort which can be waived.

The plaintiff relies upon the Uniform Commercial Code, G.L. c. 106, § 3–419, which provides, "(1) An instrument is converted when ... (c) it is paid on a forged indorsement." This, however, could not apply to the defendant, which is not a "payor bank," defined in the Code, § 4–105(b), as "a bank by which an item is payable as drawn or accepted." See

Am.Law Inst. Uniform Commercial Code, 1958 Official Text with comments, § 4–105, comments 1–3; G.L. c. 106, §§ 4–401, 4–213, 3–102(b).

A conversion provision of the Uniform Commercial Code which might have some bearing on this case is § 3–419(3).[2] This section implicitly recognizes that, subject to defences, including the one stated in it, a collecting bank, defined in the Code, § 4–105(d), may be liable in conversion. In the case at bar the forged indorsements were "wholly inoperative" as the signatures of the payee, Code §§ 3–404(1), 1–201(43), and equally so both as to the restrictive indorsements for deposits, see § 3–205(c), and as to the indorsement in blank, see § 3–204(2). When the forger transferred the checks to the collecting bank, no negotiation under § 3–202(1) occurred, because there was lacking the necessary indorsement of the payee. For the same reason, the collecting bank could not become a "holder" as defined in § 1–201(20), and so could not become a holder in due course under § 3–302(1). Accordingly, we assume that the collecting bank may be liable in conversion to a proper party, subject to defences, including that in § 3–419(3). See A. Blum Jr.'s Sons v. Whipple, 194 Mass. 253, 255, 80 N.E. 501, 13 L.R.A., N.S., 211. But there is no explicit provision in the Code purporting to determine to whom the collecting bank may be liable, and consequently, the drawer's right to enforce such a liability must be found elsewhere. Therefore, we conclude that the case must be decided on our own law, which, on the issue we are discussing, has been left untouched by the Uniform Commercial Code in any specific section.

In this Commonwealth there are two cases (decided in 1913 and 1914) the results in which embrace a ruling that there was a conversion, but in neither was the question discussed and, for aught that appears, in each the ruling seems to have been assumed without conscious appreciation of the issue here considered. Franklin Sav. Bank v. International Trust Co., 215 Mass. 231, 102 N.E. 363; Quincy Mut. Fire Ins. Co. v. International Trust Co., 217 Mass. 370, 140 N.E. 845, L.R.A.1915B, 725.... The Franklin Sav. Bank case cannot be distinguished on the ground of the limited powers of a city treasurer. That issue was important as charging the bank with notice of the treasurer's lack of authority to indorse but, that fact established there was this further question as to whether there was a remedy in tort for conversion.

The authorities are hopelessly divided. We think that the preferable view is that there is no right of action.... We state what appears to us to be the proper analysis. Had the checks been delivered to the payee Westinghouse, the defendant might have been liable for conversion to the payee. The checks, if delivered, in the hands of the payee

---

2. "Subject to the provisions of this chapter concerning restrictive indorsements a representative, including a depositary or collecting bank, who has in good faith and in accordance with the reasonable commercial standards applicable to the business of such representative dealt with an instrument or its proceeds on behalf of one who was not the true owner is not liable in conversion or otherwise to the true owner beyond the amount of any proceeds remaining in his hands." See Code §§ 1–201(35); 4–201(1).

would have been valuable property which could have been transferred for value or presented for payment; and, had a check been dishonored, the payee would have had a right of recourse against the drawer on the instrument under § 3–413(2). Here the plaintiff drawer of the checks, which were never delivered to the payee (see Gallup v. Barton, 313 Mass. 379, 381, 47 N.E.2d 921), had no valuable rights in them. Since, as we have seen, it did not have the right of a payee or subsequent holder to present them to the drawee for payment, the value of its rights was limited to the physical paper on which they were written, and was not measured by their payable amounts.

The enactment of the Uniform Commercial Code opens the road for the adoption of what seems the preferable view. An action by the drawer against the collecting bank might have some theoretical appeal as avoiding circuity of action. See Home Indem. Co. v. State Bank, 233 Iowa 103, 135–140, 8 N.W.2d 757. Compare 36 Harv.L.Rev. 879. It would have been in the interest of speedy and complete justice had the case been tried with the action by the drawer against the drawee and with an action by the drawee against the collecting bank. See Nichols v. Somerville Sav. Bank, 333 Mass. 488, 490, 132 N.E.2d 158. So one might ask: If the drawee is liable to the drawer and the collecting bank is liable to the drawee, why not let the drawer sue the collecting bank direct? We believe that the answer lies in the applicable defenses set up in the Code.[3]

The drawer can insist that the drawee recredit his account with the amount of any unauthorized payment. Such was our common law.... This is, in effect, retained by the Code §§ 4–401(1),[4] 4–406(4). But the drawee has defences based upon the drawer's substantial negligence, if "contributing," or upon his duty to discover and report unauthorized signatures and alterations. §§ 3–406, 4–406. As to unauthorized indorsements, see § 4–406(4).[5] Then, if the drawee has a valid defence which it waives or fails upon request to assert, the drawee may not assert against the collecting bank or other prior party presenting or transferring the check a claim which is based on the forged indorsement. § 4–406(5).[6] See Am.Law Inst.Uniform Commercial Code, Official Text with comments, § 4–406, comment 6, which shows that there

3. Cases where a payee has acquired rights in an instrument may stand on a different footing.

4. "As against its customer, a bank may charge against his account any item which is otherwise properly payable from that account...."

5. "Without regard to care or lack of care of either the customer or the bank a customer who does not within one year from the time the statement and items are made available to the customer (subsection [1]) discover and report his unauthorized signature or any alteration on the face or back of the item or does not within three years from that time discover and report

any unauthorized indorsement is precluded from asserting against the bank such unauthorized signature or indorsement or such alteration."

6. "If under this section a payor bank has a valid defense against a claim of a customer upon or resulting from payment of an item and waives or fails upon request to assert the defense the [drawee] may not assert against ... [a] collecting bank or other prior party presenting or transferring the item a claim based upon the unauthorized signature or alteration giving rise to the customer's claim."

was no intent to change the prior law as to negligence of a customer.... If the drawee recredits the drawer's account and is not precluded by § 4–406(5), it may claim against the presenting bank on the relevant warranties in §§ 3–417 and 4–207, and each transferee has rights against his transferor under those sections.

If the drawer's rights are limited to requiring the drawee to recredit his account, the drawee will have the defences noted above and perhaps others; and the collecting bank or banks will have the defences in § 4–207(4) [7] and § 4–406(5), and perhaps others. If the drawer is allowed in the present case to sue the collecting bank, the assertion of the defences, for all practical purposes, would be difficult. The possibilities of such a result would tend to compel resort to litigation in every case involving a forgery of commercial paper. It is a result to be avoided.

The demurrer to count 1 was rightly sustained. [The court's discussion of the remaining three counts is omitted.]

Order sustaining demurrer affirmed.

Note

(1) Contrary Authority. The Massachusetts court noted that allowing recovery "by the drawer against the collecting bank might have some theoretical appeal as avoiding circuity of action." In Sun 'N Sand, Inc. v. United California Bank, 21 Cal.3d 671, 148 Cal.Rptr. 329, 582 P.2d 920 (1978), the Supreme Court of California found appeal in such reasoning. Eloise Morales, an employee of Sun 'n Sand, made out nine checks for small amounts payable to United California Bank (UCB), had them signed by her employer, raised the amount of each check by several thousand dollars, and deposited them in her account with UCB. They were paid by the payor bank, Union Bank, which charged them to Sun 'n Sand. Sun 'n Sand sued both Union Bank and UCB. The trial court sustained a demurrer by UCB and ordered the case against it dismissed, and Sun 'n Sand appealed. The Supreme Court of California reversed, holding that Sun 'n Sand had stated a cause of action against UCB for breach of its warranties against material alteration.

"Courts in other jurisdictions that have denied to drawers a direct right of action have apparently been concerned that collecting banks would not always be able to assert defenses available to drawee banks. They have assumed that direct suits by drawers would not merely avoid circuity of action, but would alter substantive rights. (See, e.g., Stone & Webster Eng. Corp. v. First National B. & T. Co. ...) We find nothing to prevent collecting banks (and payees) from asserting the same defenses as drawee banks."

---

7. "Unless a claim for breach of warranty under this section is made within a reasonable time after the person claiming learns of the breach, the person liable is discharged to the extent of any loss caused by the delay in making claim."

(2) Revised Article 3. UCC 3–420 resolves the dispute in favor of Stone & Webster. Comment 1 to that section explains: "Under former Article 3, the cases were divided on the issue of whether the drawer of a check with a forged indorsement can assert rights against a depositary bank that took the check. The last sentence of Section 3–420(a) resolves the conflict by following the rule stated in Stone & Webster Engineering Corp. v. First National Bank & Trust Co. ... There is no reason why a drawer should have an action in conversion. The check represents an obligation of the drawer rather than property of the drawer. The drawer has an adequate remedy against the payor bank for recredit of the drawer's account for unauthorized payment of the check."

Comment 2 to UCC 3–417 addresses *Sun 'n Sand:* "Warranty to the drawer is governed by subsection (d) and that applies only when presentment for payment is made to the drawer with respect to a dishonored draft. In Sun 'N Sand, Inc. v. United California Bank ..., the court held that under former Section 3–417(1) a warranty was made to the drawer of a check when the check was presented to the drawee for payment. The result in that case is rejected."

For a dissenting voice, see Cooter & Rubin, A Theory of Loss Allocation for Consumer Payments, 66 Tex.L.Rev. 63, 109 (1987). After noting that "the revision precludes a suit by the drawer against the depositary bank, apparently on the ground that a suit against a distant party should not be authorized just to satisfy the drawer's commercial sensibilities," the authors argue that "economic analysis suggests a more comprehensive revision: a consumer, either payee or drawer, should be allowed to sue any financial institution that has handled the check. Consumers can be expected to select the most convenient defendant, and financial institutions can be expected to allocate the loss among themselves in an efficient manner."

Problem 6. A thief steals Empire's check from Quaker after it has been received in the mail, forges Quaker's indorsement, and deposits it in the Penn Bank, which forwards it to The Bank of New York, which pays it. The thief then withdraws the amount of the check from the Penn Bank. Advise Quaker of its legal position with respect to Empire, The Bank of New York, and the Penn Bank. See UCC 3–420; *Knesz v. Central Jersey Bank & Trust Co.,* infra. Would it make a difference if the thief had cashed the check at the Penn Bank?

Suit by Payee Against Depositary Bank. The right of a payee to sue the depositary bank stands on a very different footing than the right of a drawer to sue the same bank.

As a practical matter, the payee will often have good reason to prefer an action against the depositary bank over an action against the payee bank. Significant conversion claims typically involve a series of forged indorsements on many checks by the same thief, usually an employee of the payee. While various distant payor banks will be involved, the thief may have used a single depositary bank.

For example, in Sales Promotion Executives Association v. Schlinger & Weiss, Inc., 234 N.Y.S.2d 785 (City Civ.Ct.1962), a thief employed by the payee had forged the payee's indorsement on 49 checks over a nine-month period and cashed them at a supermarket. To recover from the payor banks, the payee would have had to sue 49 different banks scattered throughout the country on checks ranging from $20 to $85. By suing the supermarket in conversion, the payee recovered the entire $1,760 in a single action.

Had the thief taken the checks directly to a depositary bank rather than to a supermarket, the payee's right to recover from the depositary bank would have been more questionable. Former UCC 3–419(3) contained the following perplexing language:

> a representative, including a depositary or collecting bank, who has in good faith and in accordance with the reasonable commercial standards applicable to the business of such representative dealt with an instrument or its proceeds on behalf of one who was not the true owner is not liable in conversion or otherwise to the true owner beyond the amount of any proceeds remaining in his hands.

Could this mean that the depositary bank was not liable to the payee if the thief had withdrawn the proceeds? While the quoted language seemed to compel this senseless conclusion, some courts displayed remarkable creativity in holding that the quoted language did not mean what it seemed to say. But other courts, as in the opinion that follows, opted for fidelity to the Code language.

KNESZ v. CENTRAL JERSEY BANK & TRUST CO.

Supreme Court of New Jersey, 1984.
97 N.J. 1, 477 A.2d 806.

HANDLER, J. [Thomas G. Moringiello, a since-disbarred New York lawyer, arranged the sale to Lois Gartlir of a cooperative apartment in New York City owned by Steve Knesz, a Pennsylvania resident. Moringiello received two checks in part payment. One was a cashier's check for $16,974.24 drawn by Citibank to the order of Knesz. The other was a personal check for $5,000 drawn by Hofheimer, Gartlir, Gottlieb & Gross on Morgan Guaranty, payable to Lois Gartlir and indorsed by her "to the order of Steve Knesz." Moringiello forged Knesz's indorsement on both checks, added his own indorsement, and gave them to James E. Collins, a New Jersey lawyer, in connection with another real estate transaction. Collins indorsed the two checks in his own name, added the stamp of his law firm, and deposited the checks in the firm's trust account in Central Jersey Bank & Trust. Knesz did not discover Moringiello's duplicity until some months after the checks had been paid, and by that time disbursements by Collins' law firm had depleted the entire amount represented by the two checks in its account in Central Jersey.

Knesz sued Central Jersey for the $21,974.24 represented by the two checks. The trial court granted summary judgment for Central Jersey on the ground that it was not liable under former UCC 3–419(3). The Appellate Division reversed and remanded the case to the trial court, and the Supreme Court of New Jersey granted Central Jersey's petition for certification.]

I

N.J.S.A. 12A:3–419(3) by its general terms purports to provide that a depositary or collecting bank that acts in a representative capacity in the negotiation of a forged check, doing so in good faith and in conformity to applicable commercial standards, is not liable to the instrument's true owner except to the extent of any proceeds still remaining with it.[1] Specifically, subsection (3) of N.J.S.A. 12A:3–419 states that these banks may be insulated from liability to the payee or true owner of a forged check when the following circumstances converge: (1) the bank was acting as a "representative;" (2) it honored the forged check in good faith and in accordance with the applicable reasonable commercial standards; and (3) it retained no "proceeds" of the check.

This section of the UCC purports sharply to restrict the causes of action available to the true owner or payee of a check whose endorsement has been forged. Under N.J.S.A. 12A:3–419(1)(c), the owner-payee may bring an action against a drawee or payor bank that transmits final payment on the forged indorsement, the payor bank being defined as "a bank by which an item is payable as drawn or accepted," N.J.S.A. 12A:4–105(b). However, the UCC by the application of the terms § 3–419(3) does not extend this liability to a "depositary" or "collecting" bank that in the chain of collection has handled the check with the forged endorsement, a depositary bank being "the first bank to which an item is transferred for collection" (N.J.S.A. 12A:4–105(a)), and a collecting bank being "any bank handling the item for collection except the payor bank" (N.J.S.A. 12A:4–105(d)).

In concluding that defendant, Central Jersey, was liable to the plaintiff and not entitled to the immunity accorded by § 3–419(3), the Appellate Division did not base its determination on any asserted failure on the part of the bank to adhere to the standards of good faith and commercial reasonableness applicable to such transactions.

---

1. The exact language of N.J.S.A. 12A:3–419(3) is:

Subject to the provisions of this Act concerning restrictive indorsements a representative, including a depositary or collecting bank, who has in good faith and in accordance with the reasonable commercial standards applicable to the business of such representative dealt with an instrument or its proceeds on behalf of one who was not the true owner is not liable in conversion or otherwise to the true owner beyond the amount of any proceeds remaining in his hands.

We note that in this case UCC provisions governing restrictive endorsement are in no way implicated.

N.J.S.A. 12A:3–419(3). Conduct falling short of the standards of good faith and commercial reasonableness includes such matters as the failure to make inquiries about facial irregularities on a check or into the endorsing agent's authority....

Here, the trial court expressly found, and the Appellate Division concurred, that Central Jersey acted in a reasonable manner in accepting the instrument with a forged endorsement, having not dealt with the forger, but with its regular customer, James E. Collins, Esq., an attorney whose law firm maintained an account with the bank.... We agree with both courts below that a claim based on lack of good faith or a departure from commercially reasonable practice under § 12A:3–419(3) is unavailable to the plaintiff under these facts.

II

The immunity of § 3–419(3) is expressly granted to "a representative ... who has ... dealt with an instrument or its proceeds on behalf of one who was not the true owner...." The section explicitly and unmistakably provides that "a representative" shall include "a depositary or collecting bank." Yet, despite the specific designation of depositary or collecting banks as a "representative," the Appellate Division ruled that the term "representative" in § 3–419(3) does not include a depositary bank that accepts for collection a check with a forged indorsement. 188 N.J.Super. 408–10, 457 A.2d 1162.

The Appellate Division equated the bank's "representative" status under § 3–419(3) with that of a bank acting as an agent of the owner of an item submitted for collection under N.J.S.A. 12A:4–201. Id. This statute reads in pertinent part:

> Unless a contrary intent clearly appears and prior to the time that a settlement given by a collecting bank for an item is or becomes final ... the bank is an agent or sub-agent of the owner of the item and any settlement given for the item is provisional.

The Appellate Division reasoned that since the forger can never pass good title if an instrument requires endorsement by the owner, the bank cannot be an agent for the owner when it accepts the check for collection from the forger or his transferee. 188 N.J.Super. at 409, 457 A.2d 1162. Consequently, the bank cannot qualify for the immunity provided for in § 3–419(3) since it has not achieved representative or agent status.

We conclude that the Appellate Division's definition of "representative" is unjustifiably restrictive. The bank's agency status under § 4–201 is based upon its acceptance of a check from "an owner," who by definition cannot be the forger or his transferee. However, § 3–419(3) protects a "representative, including a depositary or collecting bank, who has ... dealt with an instrument or its proceeds *on behalf of one who was not the true owner...*." (Emphasis added). Consequently, "representation" under § 3–419(3) contemplates dealing with a party who is not the true owner of an instrument, whereas "agency" under § 4–201 envisages actions on behalf of a true owner. Thus, the Appellate Division interpretation unreasonably removes the protection of § 3–419(3) from the check-collection process, which, arguably, would provide the most likely occasion for a bank to honor a check with a forged endorsement.

The Appellate Division also stressed that if "agency status" were intended to apply to a bank's handling of a forged check, other language would have accomplished this, "such as use of the word 'customer,' defined by § 4–104(e) to include any person for whom a bank has agreed to collect an item." 188 N.J.Super. at 409, 457 A.2d 1162. However, New Jersey Study Comment 1 to § 4–201, which the Appellate Division relies on, expressly refers to the depositary bank as the agent of "the *customer* initiating collection," (emphasis added), which could be either the owner-payee or the forger or his transferee.

The Appellate Division further observed that agency status provided under § 4–201 was intended to deal with bank insolvency during the collection process, citing New Jersey Study Comment 1 to N.J.S.A. 12A:4–201. Id. This purpose, however, implies that the definition of "representative" under § 3–419(3) is more appropriately related to the broad definition of representative under N.J.S.A. 12A:1–201(35). This section of the UCC provides an expansive definition of the term "representative," namely, "an agent, an officer of a corporation or association, and a trustee, executor or administrator of an estate, or any other person empowered to act for another." The depositary bank must in some sense be "empowered to act for" the third party who presents the check bearing the payee's forged indorsement. Under § 1–201(35), a depositary or collecting bank acts as its customer's representative in the entire check-collection process.[2] In this process the instrument is accepted and presented to the drawee bank and funds are collected and credited to the customer, whether that customer be the owner-payee or the forger or his transferee. As such, the bank meets the requirement for immunity by acting in a representative capacity "on behalf of one who was not the true owner" under § 3–419(3).

The Appellate Division further reasoned that a bank in this context is not a representative because a check can have only one owner at a time; therefore, the depositary bank processing a forged check presented by a depositor is not acting on behalf of the item's true owner since the forger or his transferee cannot take title. 188 N.J.Super. at 410, 457 A.2d 1162. However, the bank can also function as agent for the customer or depositor. The New Jersey Study Comment 1 to § 4–201,

___

2. In some situations extraneous to this case, a bank may immediately give cash to the forger or his transferee, or else provide non-provisional credit to the customer's account, which is then drawn upon. The Court recognizes the existence of authority that finds that a bank under these circumstances does not act in a "representative" capacity for its customer and thus is ineligible for immunity under § 3–419(3). Since the bank in effect has purchased the check, the forger or his transferee, cash already in hand, has no need for the representative services of the depositary bank in the ensuing process of check collection....

as already noted, alludes to the depositary bank as the agent of "the customer initiating collection." If the customer initiating collection were also the owner-payee of the check, the bank would be in that instance a representative of a single party. However, in a case such as this, where the customer initiating collection is not the true owner but the transferee of a forger, the possibility of dual representation is implicated. Thus, a depositary bank can be the "representative" of the customer or depositor in processing the forged check for collection, even if that party is not the true owner of the check.

The strongest argument advanced in favor of the non-representative status of depositary or collecting banks in check collection—the argument that was adopted by the Appellate Division—is extrapolated from the UCC's historical background. The Appellate Division stressed that the singular advantage of the pre–UCC common-law rule of strict and direct liability of a depositary or collecting bank to the owner-payee of a forged check that the bank had honored was the avoidance of prolonged, complicated, and circuitous litigation that would otherwise be set in motion in the absence of such liability. 188 N.J.Super. at 398–99, 457 A.2d 1162. A literal application of § 3–419(3), blocking a direct action against the depositary-collecting bank, would result in a chain of litigation. First, the owner of a check may bring an action against the drawer for fulfillment of the underlying obligation in satisfaction of which the check was originally written, under N.J.S.A. 12A:3–804 (providing recovery for check that has been lost, destroyed, or stolen), or, alternatively, sue the drawee bank for conversion under § 3–419(1)(c). The drawer will sue the drawee or payor bank for wrongfully debiting his or her account for payment to the forger under § 4–401. The drawee or payor bank will be required to proceed against its transferor. Suit will proceed successively up the collection stream on the basis of strict warranties of presentment and transfer under the UCC until the depositary bank, ultimately liable for honoring the forged instrument, is reached.

The Appellate Division agreed—as does the overwhelming body of decisional and scholarly authority—that the policy of a single direct action against the depositary or collecting bank by the owner-payee, and the avoidance of lengthy, circuitous, or chain litigation served by the common-law rule is a powerful reason against the imputation of an intent by the drafters of the Code to abrogate the common-law rule by the enactment of § 3–419(3). In support of its position, the court below pointed to the New Jersey Study Comment 5 on that section indicating that the provisions are new and not founded on past state law, as well as to Official Comment 5 to N.J.S.A. 12A:3–419, which stated:

> Subsection (3), which is new, *is intended to adopt the rule of decisions* which has held that a representative, such as a broker or depositary bank, who deals with a negotiable instrument for his principal in good faith is not liable to the true owner for conversion of the instrument or otherwise, except that he may be compelled to turn over to the true owner the

instrument itself or any proceeds of the instrument remaining in his hands. ... [UCC Comment 5 to § 3–419 (emphasis added).]

The irony of the emphasized reference in Comment 5, however, is that the common law "rule of decisions" governing the liability of such banks is almost diametrically opposite to what is stated by the plain language of § 3–419(3), which provides a near-absolute immunity to these banks in handling forged checks. The common-law decisional rule was that a party that honored a check bearing a forged indorsement was liable—not immune—to the payee who was the instrument's "true owner." [3] ...

Prior to the adoption of the UCC, New Jersey followed the prevailing common-law rule.... The common-law rule of liability was imposed strictly, even when the depositary bank was unaware of the unauthorized indorsement and not in privity with the rightful payee; a bank paying on such a check "did so at its peril and became liable to the payee ... for the proceeds." [4] ...

The Appellate Division did not believe that the Code drafters intended to abrogate this well-settled common-law doctrine, at least in the absence of an express announcement of such a purpose. The court emphasized, as we noted earlier, that the New Jersey Study Comment mentioned that § 3–419(3) and § 3–419(4) " 'are new provisions on which no New Jersey law has been found,' " 188 N.J.Super. at 404–05, 457 A.2d 1162. It therefore surmised that "the section impacted upon some other legal principle or problem which had not been theretofore addressed in this jurisdiction." Id. at 405, 457 A.2d 1162. The court determined that this new legal principle adopting the rule of decisions related to "the liability of persons acting as brokers in negotiating the sale of securities," as distinguished from granting a new immunity to banks in the collection process. Id. Because brokers dealing in negotiable instruments were immune from liability in conversion at common law, the court concluded that § 3–419(3) was intended to codify this immunity for brokers, including banks acting as brokers, but was not intended to extend such immunity to depositary or collecting banks engaged in routine check collection. Id. at 406–07, 457 A.2d 1162.

We disagree with the conclusion of the court below, while acknowledging, as we must, respectable decisional and scholarly support for its result.... We are persuaded by other cases and authority that have recognized that § 3–419(3) is phrased in clear and plain language, that applying this provision in accordance with its unambiguous meaning constitutes a reasonable—not an absurd—policy choice by the Legisla-

3. The defrauded payee generally could avail itself of two common-law forms of action against the depositary bank. One was a suit in assumpsit, for "moneys had and received." ... Alternatively, the payee could also at its election bring a tort action of conversion against the bank that had wrongfully honored a check with his forged signature.

4. Although the courts entertained defenses consisting of the payee's own negligence, acquiescence, or ratification, these apparently did not succeed very often....

ture, and further, that there is some historical extrinsic support evidencing an underlying intent on the part of the drafters that is consistent with this application of the provision....

We are in consequence not persuaded that the underlying policy served by the common law—the recognition of a single direct action by an owner-payee against the depositary or collecting bank and the avoidance of circuitous or chain litigation—overrides the plain terms of § 3–419(3). That policy was undoubtedly known to the drafters of the Code. It was presumably within their contemplation when § 3–419(3) was inserted granting immunity to these banks. We are constrained to adhere to the choice made by the Legislature in its enactment. It has not been shown that this choice leads to intolerable or absurd results, a factor that would have given us pause in applying § 3–419(3) in accordance with its terms.[5]

Accordingly, we conclude that N.J.S.A. 12A:3–419(3) recognizes that a depositary or collecting bank handling a forged check in the routine process of check collection acts in a representative capacity on behalf of its customer, who may be one other than the check's true owner or payee. Consequently, such a bank will not be disqualified from claiming, as a "representative," immunity against the owner-payee under N.J.S.A. 12A:3–419(3).

III

A further argument against granting immunity is drawn from the provision of § 3–419(3) that a depositary bank dealing with a check bearing a forged endorsement cannot be liable to the true owner "beyond the amount of any proceeds remaining in [its] hands." It can be contended that the proceeds of the checks should be considered as still in the control of Central Jersey, thus rendering the bank liable.
. . .

In Cooper v. Union Bank, supra, 9 Cal.3d 371, 507 P.2d at 613, 107 Cal.Rptr. 1, the court noted that the trial court had held the defendant depositary banks immune under § 3–419(3). It reversed, although offsetting the aggregate recovery to reflect the plaintiff's own contributory negligence. Id., 9 Cal.3d 371, at 620, 107 Cal.Rptr. 1. As partial support for this result, the court, relying on pre-UCC theory, observed that the bank still held the entire "proceeds" of the forged instruments, notwithstanding the fact that the forger's personal account with the bank in which the forged checks had been deposited was depleted. The

5. It is possible that the burdensome circuitous litigation deplored by many commentators may be mitigated today. The "circuity argument" has been criticized as being exaggerated and inconsequential in the modern era of long-arm jurisdiction, negotiated settlements, and liberal rules of impleader. See J. White and R. Summers, Handbook of the Law Under the Uniform Commercial Code, § 15–4 at 590–91 (1980). In addition, foreclosing a direct suit against a depositary bank and, instead, forcing the payee to sue his drawer or the drawee bank preserves in some instances the timely presentation of appropriate defenses that would have been unavailable to a depositary bank, such as that of the drawer's negligence in causing or detecting the forgery....

court reasoned that the bank perpetually retains the proceeds of the forged instrument in trust for the true owner, unless the bank's own assets dwindle below the amount of the check. Id., 9 Cal.3d 371, at 615, 107 Cal.Rptr. 1.

The "retained proceeds" position of ... *Cooper* has generated considerable academic debate.... Courts have resorted to the theory sparingly.... We concur.

"Proceeds" is that amount received from the drawee-payor bank in return for the check of its drawer.[6] See Comment, 5 Rut.–Cam.L.J., 319, 323 (1974); Comment, 45 U.Colo.L.Rev., supra, at 293. Remaining proceeds as used in § 3–419(3), we believe, connotes the amount, if any, the bank actually has left in its control as a consequence of dealing with the forged check. Thus, a bank could give the customer a provisional credit, which prevents the customer from withdrawing or obtaining actual credit for the instrument until the bank has effected collection. In that case, the bank would be liable under § 3–419(3) to the owner of the check for the amount, whether full or partial, of the check that remains on deposit in the account of the forger or his transferee....

In this case, plaintiff has not shown that any funds attributable to the forged instruments are still available in the customer's account. The checks were deposited in the account of the Cerrato law firm, the bank's customer and the transferee of the forger. In due course, the forged checks were transmitted for collection and the proceeds remitted. The funds or proceeds referable to these checks reflected in the customer's account were eventually withdrawn and the account ultimately depleted accordingly. Consequently, no proceeds remain for which this bank can be liable under § 3–419(3).

IV

In conclusion, we are satisfied that the Court may not disregard the plain language of N.J.S.A. 12A:3–419(3). The terms of this provision clearly and unmistakably designate a depository or collecting bank as a representative in the collection of a forged check. We are mindful of the objections to that interpretation. Nevertheless, we must infer that these objections were not ultimately important or persuasive to the Legislature. We rule therefore that generally a depository or collecting bank handling a forged check in the routine collection process may claim immunity against the true owner or payee under N.J.S.A. 12A:3–419(3). That immunity may be lost, however, under certain circumstances. A depository or collecting bank may become directly liable to an owner-payee in conversion of a forged check where it (1) acted in bad

---

6. The only definition of the term "proceeds" in the UCC appears at § 9–306(1):

"Proceeds" includes whatever is received upon the sale, exchange, collection or other disposition of collateral or proceeds.... Money, checks, deposit accounts, and the like are "cash proceeds." All other proceeds are "non-cash proceeds." [N.J.S.A. 12A:9–306(1).]

This Article Nine definition, however, was not incorporated into Article Three of the Code. See N.J.S.A. 12A:3–102.

faith; (2) failed to adhere to reasonable commercial standards of the banking profession applicable to such transactions; or (3) had given a provisional credit to the forger or his transferee and had not yet disbursed the entire amount of the collected proceeds.

None of these enumerated circumstances is present in the instant case. Accordingly, the judgment of the Appellate Division is reversed and summary judgment for the defendant reinstated.

Notes

(1) **Revised Article 3.** UCC 3–420(c) rejects the result in *Knesz* by excepting depositary banks from the protection that it affords to representatives. Comment 3 explains: "Subsection (3) of former Section 3–419 drew criticism from the courts, that saw no reason why a depositary bank should have the defense stated in the subsection. See Knesz v. Central Jersey Bank & Trust Co.... The depositary bank is ultimately liable in the case of a forged indorsement check because of its warranty to the payor bank under Section 4–208(a)(1) and it is usually the most convenient defendant in cases involving multiple checks drawn on different banks. There is no basis for requiring the owner of the check to bring multiple actions against the various payor banks and to require those banks to assert warranty rights against the depositary bank. In revised Article 3, the defense provided by Section 3–420(c) is limited to collecting banks other than the depositary bank. If suit is brought against both the payor bank and the depositary bank, the owner, of course, is entitled to but one recovery."

(2) **Delivery to Payee.** Can the payee maintain an action for conversion of a check if the check has not been delivered to the payee? In a leading case under former Article 3, the New York Court of Appeals answered this question in the negative, explaining that "most courts and commentators have concluded that either actual or constructive delivery to the payee is a necessary perquisite to a conversion action." The court noted that the payee "is not left without a remedy, inasmuch as it can sue on the underlying obligation" and rejected the payee's argument that permitting a conversion action "by a payee not-in-possession would promote judicial economy and avoid circuity of action." The drawers' delivery of the checks to their own accountant did not amount to "constructive delivery" because "putting a check in the hands of the drawer's own agent for purpose of delivery to the payee does not constitute delivery to the payee." State v. Barclays Bank, 76 N.Y.2d 533, 561 N.Y.S.2d 697, 563 N.E.2d 11 (1990).

The last sentence of UCC 3–420(a) follows this reasoning. According to Comment 1: "Until delivery, the payee does not have any interest in the check.... Normally the drawer of a check intends to pay an obligation owed to the payee. But if the check is never delivered to the payee, the obligation owed to the payee is not affected.... Since the payee's right to enforce the underlying obligation is unaffected by the fraud of the thief, there is no reason to give any additional remedy to the payee."

SECTION 3. EFFECT OF DRAWER'S FAULT

Prefatory Note. Under the usual rules seen thus far the drawer is free from the risk of loss due to forged and altered checks and checks bearing forged indorsements. A purchaser cannot shift the loss to the drawer in the event that the check is dishonored, and the payor bank cannot shift the loss to the drawer in the event that the check is paid by mistake. The usual rules, however, are subject to exceptions, the most important of which are considered in this section. See Phillips, The Commercial Culpability Scale, 92 Yale L.J. 228, 236–43 (1982).

The seminal case is Young v. Grote, 4 Bing. 253, 130 Eng.Rep. 764 (1827). Young, a depositor, contested the right of Grote, his banker, to charge a check to his account in the amount of £350.2s. During his absence, Young left five signed blank checks with his wife, who was not conversant with business. She gave one to Worcester, Young's clerk, who filled it up for £50.2s. and showed it to her. The word "fifty", as written, began in the middle of the line, and Worcester later added before it the words "Three hundred and," inserted the digit 3, and obtained payment for £350.2s. from Grote. The court held that Young must bear the loss. Best, C.J., first stated the general rule that "a banker who pays a forged check, is in general bound to pay the amount again to his customer, because, in the first instance, he pays without authority." He went on to say that, "In the present case, was it not the fault of Young that Grote and Co. paid 350*l.* instead of 50*l.*? ... It is urged, indeed, that the business of merchants requires them to sign checks in blank, and leave them to be filled up by agents. If that be so, the person selected for the care of such a check ought at least to be a person conversant with business as well as trustworthy.... [Such a person] would have guarded against fraud in the mode of filling it up; he would have placed the word fifty at the beginning of the second line; and would have commenced it with a capital letter, so that it could not have had the appearance of following properly after a preceding word; he would also have placed the figure 5 so near to the printed £ as to prevent the possibility of interpolation. It was by the neglect of these ordinary precautions that Grote and Co. were induced to pay." The Code counterpart of the rule in *Young v. Grote* is contained in UCC 3–406.

Problem 7. Empire uses a check-signing machine to sign checks drawn on its account. The machine is kept in an unlocked desk drawer together with Empire's checkbook. Does this subject Empire to any risk if the machine and checkbook are stolen? See Comment 3 to UCC 3–406.

Problem 8. Empire uses a check embossing machine to print the amount of the checks that it draws in the center of each check. The rest of the check, including the amount on the upper right-hand side is typed and it is then signed by hand. The machine is kept in an unlocked desk drawer, together with Empire's checkbook. Does this subject Empire to any risk if the machine is stolen?

Problem 9. A drew a check for $29 on X Bank, payable to B, leaving blanks to make it easy to raise it to $29,000. A had it certified by X Bank, raised it to $29,000, and gave it to B, who delivered to A goods worth $29,000. Can B recover $29,000 from X Bank? Would it make a difference if X Bank had indicated "$29.00" in its certification? See UCC 3–413(b).

THOMPSON MAPLE PRODUCTS v. CITIZENS NATIONAL BANK OF CORRY

Pennsylvania Superior Court, 1967.
211 Pa.Super. 42, 234 A.2d 32.

HOFFMAN, J. In this assumpsit action, the plaintiff, Thompson Maple Products, Inc., seeks to recover more than $100,000 paid out on a series of its checks by defendant bank, as drawee. The payee's signature on each of the checks was forged by one Emery Albers, who then cashed the checks or deposited them to his account with the defendant.

The case was tried to the court below sitting without a jury. That court entered judgment in favor of the plaintiff in the amount of $1258.51, the face amount of three checks which the defendant had paid without any endorsement whatever. It dismissed the remainder of the claim, and this appeal followed.

The plaintiff is a small, closely-held corporation, principally engaged in the manufacture of bowling pin "blanks" from maple logs. Some knowledge of its operations from 1959 to 1962 is essential to an understanding of this litigation.

The plaintiff purchased logs from timber owners in the vicinity of its mill. Since these timber owners rarely had facilities for hauling logs, such transportation was furnished by a few local truckers, including Emery Albers.

At the mill site, newly delivered logs were "scaled" by mill personnel, to determine their quantity and grade. The employee on duty noted this information, together with the name of the owner of the logs, as furnished by the hauler, on duplicate "scaling slips."

In theory, the copy of the scaling slip was to be given to the hauler, and the original was to be retained by the mill employee until transmitted by him directly to the company's bookkeeper. This ideal procedure, however, was rarely followed. Instead, in a great many instances, the mill employee simply gave both slips to the hauler for delivery to the company office. Office personnel then prepared checks in payment for the logs, naming as payee the owner indicated on the scaling slips. Blank sets of slips were readily accessible on the company premises.

Sometime prior to February, 1959, Emery Albers conceived the scheme which led to the forgeries at issue here. Albers was an independent log hauler who for many years had transported logs to the company mill. For a brief period in 1952, he had been employed by the plaintiff, and he was a trusted friend of the Thompson family. After procuring blank sets of scaling slips, Albers filled them in to show substantial, wholly fictitious deliveries of logs, together with the names of local timber owners as suppliers. He then delivered the slips to the company bookkeeper, who prepared checks payable to the purported owners. Finally, he volunteered to deliver the checks to the owners. The bookkeeper customarily entrusted the checks to him for that purpose.

Albers then forged the payee's signature and either cashed the checks or deposited them to his account at the defendant bank, where he was well known. Although he pursued this scheme for an undetermined period of time, only checks paid out over a three-year period prior to this litigation are here in controversy. See Uniform Commercial Code, Act of April 6, 1953, PL 3, as amended, § 4–406, 12A PS § 4–406.

In 1963, when the forgeries were uncovered, Albers confessed and was imprisoned. The plaintiff then instituted this suit against the drawee bank, asserting that the bank had breached its contract of deposit by paying the checks over forged endorsements. See UCC § 3–404, 12A PS § 3–404.

The trial court determined that the plaintiff's own negligent activities had materially contributed to the unauthorized endorsements, and it therefore dismissed the substantial part of plaintiff's claim. We affirm the action of the trial court.

Both parties agree that, as between the payor bank and its customer, ordinarily the bank must bear the loss occasioned by the forgery of a payee's endorsement. Philadelphia Title Insurance Company v. Fidelity–Philadelphia Trust Company, 419 Pa. 78, 212 A.2d 222 [2 UCC Rep. 1011] (1965); UCC § 3–404, 12A PS § 3–404.[1]

The trial court concluded, however, that the plaintiff-drawer, by virtue of its conduct, could not avail itself of that rule, citing § 3–406 of the Code: "Any person who by his negligence substantially contributes to ... the making of an unauthorized signature is precluded from asserting the ... lack of authority against ... a drawee or other payor

---

1. Section 3–404 of the Code provides: "Any unauthorized signature is wholly inoperative as that of the person whose name is signed unless he ratifies it or is precluded from denying it * * *."

who pays the instrument in good faith and in accordance with the reasonable commercial standards of the drawee's or payor's business." 12A PS § 3–406.

Before this court, the plaintiff Company argues strenuously that this language is a mere restatement of pre-Code law in Pennsylvania. Under those earlier cases, it is argued, the term "precluded" is equivalent to "estopped," and negligence which will work an estoppel is only such as "directly and proximately affects the conduct of the bank in passing the forgery...." See, e.g., Coffin v. Fidelity–Philadelphia Trust Company, 374 Pa. 378, 393, 97 A.2d 857, 39 A.L.R.2d 625 (1953); Land Title Bank and Trust Company v. Cheltenham National Bank, 362 Pa. 30, 66 A.2d 768 (1949). The plaintiff further asserts that those decisions hold that "negligence in the conduct of the drawer's business," such as appears on this record, cannot serve to work an estoppel.

Even if that was the law in this Commonwealth prior to the passage of the Commercial Code, it is not the law today. The language of the new Act is determinative in all cases arising after its passage. This controversy must be decided, therefore, by construction of the statute and application of the negligence doctrine as it appears in § 3–406 of the Code. Philadelphia Title Insurance Company v. Fidelity–Philadelphia Trust Company, supra, 419 Pa. at 84, 212 A.2d 222.

Had the legislature intended simply to continue the strict estoppel doctrine of the pre-Code cases, it could have employed the term "precluded," without qualification, as in § 23 of the old Negotiable Instruments Law, 56 P.S. § 28 (repealed).[2] However, it chose to modify that doctrine in § 3–406, by specifying that negligence which "*substantially contributes to ... the making of an unauthorized signature....*" will preclude the drawer from asserting a forgery [emphasis supplied]. The Code has thus abandoned the language of the older cases (negligence which "directly and proximately affects the bank in passing the forgery") and shortened the chain of causation which the defendant bank must establish. "[N]o attempt is made," according to the Official Comment to § 3–406, "to specify what is negligence, and the question is one for the court or jury on the facts of the particular case."

In the instant case, the trial court could readily have concluded that plaintiff's business affairs were conducted in so negligent a fashion as to have "substantially contributed" to the Albers forgeries, within the meaning of § 3–406.

Thus, the record shows that pads of plaintiff's blank logging slips were left in areas near the mill which were readily accessible to any of the haulers. Moreover, on at least two occasions, Albers was given

---

2. Thus, the Pennsylvania Bar Association Note on § 3–404 observes: "The ... phrase 'or is otherwise precluded' [in this section] continues the prior law as to estoppel, laches, and other grounds which prevent a person whose signature is forged from recovering. This is so because the same word 'precluded' was used in NIL § 23, 56 PS § 28 (repealed)...."

whole pads of these blank logging slips to use as he chose. Mrs. Vinora Curtis, an employee of the plaintiff, testified:

"Q. Did you ever give any of these logging slips to Mr. Albers or any pads of these slips to Mr. Albers?

"A. Yes....

"Q. What was the reason for giving [a pad of the slips] to him, Mrs. Curtis?

"A. Well, he came up and said he needed it for [scaling] the logs, so I gave it to him."

Mrs. Amy Thompson, who also served as a bookkeeper for the plaintiff, testified:

"Q. As a matter of fact, you gave Mr. Albers the pack of your logging slips, did you not?

"A. Yes, I did once.

"Q. Do you remember what you gave them to him for?

"A. I don't right offhand, but it seems to me he said he was going out to look for some logs or timber or something and he needed them to mark some figures on....

"Q. Well, if he was going to use them for scratch pads, why didn't you give him a scratch pad that you had in the office?

"A. That's what I should have done."

In addition, the plaintiff's printed scaling slips were not consecutively numbered. Unauthorized use of the slips, therefore, could easily go undetected. Thus, Mr. Nelson Thompson testified:

"Q. Mr. Thompson, were your slips you gave these haulers numbered?

"A. No, they were not.

"Q. They are now, aren't they?

"A. Yes.

"Q. Had you used numbered logging slips, this would have prevented anybody getting logging slips out of the ordinary channel of business and using it to defraud you?

"A. Yes."

Moreover, in 1960, when the company became concerned about the possible unauthorized use of its scaling slips, it required its own personnel to initial the slips when a new shipment of logs was scaled. However, this protective measure was largely ignored in practice. Mrs. Amy Thompson testified:

"Q. And later on in the course of your business, if you remember Mr. Thompson said he wanted the logging slips initialed by one of the so-called authorized people?

"A. Yes.

"Q. [D]idn't you really not pay too much attention to them at all?

"A. Well, I know we didn't send them back to be sure they were initialed. We might have noticed it but we didn't send them back to the mill.

"Q. In other words, if they came to you uninitialed, you might have noticed it but didn't do anything about it.

"A. Didn't do anything about it."

The principal default of the plaintiff, however, was its failure to use reasonable diligence in insuring honesty from its log haulers, including Emery Albers. For many years, the haulers were permitted to deliver both the original and the duplicate of the scaling slip to the company office, and the company tolerated this practice. These slips supplied the bookkeeper with the payees' names for the checks she was to draw in payment for log deliveries. Only by having the company at all times retain possession of the original slip could the plaintiff have assured that no disbursements were made except for logs received, and that the proper amounts were paid to the proper persons. The practice tolerated by the plaintiff effectively removed the only immediate safeguard in the entire procedure against dishonesty on the part of the haulers.[3]

Finally, of course, the company regularly entrusted the completed checks to the haulers for delivery to the named payees, without any explicit authorization from the latter to do so.

While none of these practices, in isolation, might be sufficient to charge the plaintiff with negligence within the meaning of § 3–406, the company's course of conduct, viewed in its entirety, is surely sufficient to support the trial judge's determination that it substantially contributed to the making of the unauthorized signatures.[4] In his words, that conduct was "no different than had the plaintiff simply given Albers a series of checks signed in blank for his unlimited, unrestricted use." Cf. Gresham State Bank v. O & K Construction Company, 231 Ore. 106,

---

3. We note that this procedure placed Albers in a position comparable to that of a trusted agent or employee, whose similar activities would have precluded his principal from asserting the forgeries, under § 3–405(1)(c). That section provides: "(1) An endorsement by any person in the name of a named payee is effective if ... (c) an agent or employee of the drawer has supplied him with the name of the payee intending the latter to have no such interest." The trial court's opinion characterizes Albers as an "agent" of the plaintiff, but makes no findings with reference to this section. We decline the invitation to do so now, since the decision must be affirmed on other grounds.

4. In this connection, the trial court also noted that the plaintiff at all times prior to the commencement of this litigation failed to keep an accurate inventory account. It could not therefore verify, at any given point in time, that it actually possessed the logs which it had paid for.

370 P.2d 726, 372 P.2d 187, 100 A.L.R.2d 654 (1962); Park State Bank v. Arena Auto Auctions, Inc., 59 Ill.App.2d 235, 207 N.E.2d 158 (1965).

Finally, the plaintiff argues that the defendant bank cannot rely on § 3–406 because it did not pay the checks in accordance with "reasonable commercial standards" as required by that section. All the checks were regular on their face and bore the purported endorsement of the named payee. It is asserted, however, that the defendant bank was required, as a matter of law, to obtain the second endorsement of Albers before accepting the checks for deposit to his account.

The short answer to that contention is that the trial court did not find, nor does the record show, that obtaining such a second endorsement is a reasonable, or even a general, commercial practice, where the depositor is well-known to the bank and where his identity can later be ascertained from code markings on the check itself.

Furthermore, under the Code, the bank did not have an unqualified right to a second endorsement. A check endorsed in blank is bearer paper. It is negotiable by delivery alone, without further endorsement. See UCC § 3–201, 3–204, 12A PS §§ 3–201, 3–204.

To the extent that banks do obtain such endorsements, they apparently do so for their own protection, over and above that provided by the warranties arising on presentment and transfer. Cf. UCC § 3–414, 12A PS § 3–414 (Contract of Indorser), with UCC § 3–417, 12A PS § 3–417 (Warranties). In short, the practice is not designed for the protection of the drawer.[5] We are reluctant to hold that the plaintiff may shift the loss to the defendant bank, in this case, merely because the bank failed to exercise an excess of caution on its own behalf.

Judgment affirmed.

Note

Revised Article 3. Comment 1 to UCC 3–406 explains that subsection (a) "is based on former Section 3–406" and that it "adopts the doctrine of Young v. Grote.... By issuing the instrument and 'setting it afloat upon a sea of strangers' the maker or drawer voluntarily enters into a relation with later holders which justifies imposition of a duty of care."

Comment 2 notes that the less stringent " 'substantially contributes' test of former Section 4–406 is continued ... in preference to a 'direct and proximate cause' test.... Conduct 'substantially contributes' to a material alteration or a forged signature if it is a contributing cause of the alteration or signature and a substantial factor in bringing it about. The analyses of 'substantially contributes' in former Section 3–406 by the court in Thompson Maple Products v. Citizens National

---

5. In any event, a second endorsement could not have protected this drawer, since the record shows that it was not plaintiff's practice to examine the backs of its checks when they were returned by the bank.

Bank of Corry ... states what is intended by the use of the same words in revised Section 3–406(b)."

Note that UCC 3–103(a)(7) contains a new definition of "ordinary care." Note too that UCC 3–406(b) introduces a concept of comparative negligence.

———

Prefatory Note. Critten employed a clerk named Davis, whose duty it was to fill out checks for Critten's signature and give them, together with the relevant bills, to Critten, who signed them, put them in envelopes, and placed them in the mailing drawer. Over a two-year period, Davis took twenty-four checks from the drawer, obliterated with acid the names of the payee and the amount, and made them payable to cash in a raised amount. He paid the bills himself and kept the excess. Since Davis was also entrusted with the verification of the bank balance, his peculations went unnoticed, although he usually failed to alter the check stubs to conceal them, until another clerk verified the balance when Davis was absent from work. Critten then sued the drawee for the excess it had paid on the checks. The court concluded that

> the depositor owes his bank the duty of a reasonable verification of the returned checks.... The practice of taking checks from check books and entering on the stubs left in the book the date, amount and name of the payee of the check issued has become general, not only with large commercial houses but with almost all classes of depositors in banks. The skill of the criminal has kept pace with the advance in honest arts and a forgery may be made so skillfully as to deceive not only the bank, but the drawer of the check as to the genuineness of his own signature. But when a depositor has in his possession a record of the checks he has given, with dates, payees, and amounts, a comparison of the returned checks with that record will necessarily expose forgeries or alterations. It is true that it will give no information as to the genuine character of the indorsements, and because the depositor has no greater knowledge on that subject than the bank, it owes the bank no duty in regard thereto.... It is also true that verification of the returned checks would not prevent a loss by the bank in the case of the payment of a single forged check, and probably not in many cases enable the bank to obtain a restitution of its lost money. It would, however, prevent the successful commission of continuous frauds by exposing the first forgeries.... While we hold that this duty rests upon the depositor, we are not disposed to accept the doctrine asserted in some of the cases that by negligence in its discharge or by failure to discover and notify the bank, the depositor either adopts the checks as genuine and ratifies their payment or estops himself from

asserting that they are forgeries.... If the depositor has by his negligence in failing to detect forgeries in his checks and give notice thereof caused loss to his bank, either by enabling the forger to repeat his fraud or by depriving the bank of an opportunity to obtain restitution, he should be responsible for the damage caused by his default, but beyond this his liability should not extend.

Therefore, although a comparison of returned checks with unaltered stubs would have thwarted subsequent alterations, Critten was not precluded from recovering for the first and second checks, which were returned together; comparison would have come too late to have prevented their payment. But comparison of the first and second checks with the stubs would have prevented payment of the third, fourth and fifth checks, and Critten was accountable for these. The sixth check, however, had been so mutilated by Davis that the bank was itself negligent in paying it, and the bank was therefore liable for that and subsequent checks. Furthermore, Davis had presented one of the checks for which Critten would have been accountable through a collecting bank, rather than directly to the payor bank. As to that check, the payor bank had recourse against the collecting bank and could not hold Critten. *Critten v. Chemical National Bank,* 171 N.Y. 219, 63 N.E. 969 (1902). In 1904, shortly after this decision, New York enacted a statute precluding a drawer from contesting payment of a forged or altered check, regardless of the drawer's exercise of reasonable care, unless the drawer had notified the payor bank within one year after return of the cancelled check.

Observe how closely UCC 4–406 tracks the *Critten* case and subsequent legislation. Subsections (c) and (d) deal with the duty of the depositor "to examine the statement or the items." Subsection (e) deals with the effect of the bank's lack of care. Subsection (f) contains the counterpart of the statutory period. Resolution of the controversy between payor bank and collecting bank is found in UCC 3–417(c) and 4–208(c).

Problem 10. Empire asks whether there is a specific period of time within which it must examine the Bank of New York's statement and its returned checks. If there is, Empire would like to know the consequences of any delay. Empire would also like to know, since it is a small company, if it runs any risk by having the same employee prepare checks for signature, enter them in the checkbook, and reconcile the statements and returned checks with the checkbook. Advise Empire. See UCC 4–406; *K & K Manufacturing, Inc. v. Union Bank,* infra.

Problem 11. The Bank of New York asks whether it must return its customers' checks to them after they have been paid and, if not, whether it must retain them. It also asks what, if any, the adverse consequences will be if it pays all checks under $5,000 by automated equipment without verifying the drawers' signatures. Advise The

Bank of New York.　See UCC 4–406; *K & K Manufacturing, Inc. v. Union Bank,* infra.

K & K MANUFACTURING, INC. v. UNION BANK

Court of Appeals of Arizona, 1981.
129 Ariz. 7, 628 P.2d 44.

HATHAWAY, CHIEF JUDGE.　In this case we must apply articles three and four of the Uniform Commercial Code to determine who should bear the risk of loss when a dishonest employee forges her employer's name as drawer on a number of checks on his business and personal checking accounts, then appropriates the proceeds for her personal use.

Appellant Bill J. Knight is the president and majority stockholder of both K & K Manufacturing, Inc. and Knight Foundry & Manufacturing, Inc.　Knight Foundry employed about 80 people at the time of trial, while K & K Manufacturing, which was formed to accomplish the contracting, buying and selling for the foundry business, employed only two persons when the events which form the basis of this action occurred.　These two employees were Knight and a bookkeeper, Eleanor Garza.　The bookkeeper's duties at K & K Manufacturing were very broad, including picking up the company mail and Knight's personal mail from a common post office box, preparing checks for Knight's signature to pay both company and personal bills, and making entries in a cash disbursement journal reflecting the expenses for which the checks were written.　Most importantly, it was her responsibility to reconcile the monthly statements prepared and sent by appellee Union Bank, where Knight kept both his business and personal checking and savings accounts.　No one shared these duties with Miss Garza.

Between March 1977 and January 1978, Miss Garza forged Knight's signature on some 66 separate checks drawn on his personal or business accounts at Union Bank.　The majority of these checks were made payable to her.　The total amount of the forgeries on the K & K Manufacturing account was $49,859.31.　The total on Knight's personal account was $11,350.　The bank paid each such check and Miss Garza received or was credited with the proceeds.

We need not concentrate on the details of the fraud, except to comment that it proved to be effective for nearly one year.　Miss Garza assured that the disbursement journal balanced by overstating legitimate expenditures, forging checks to herself for the difference, and later showing the forged check as "void."　Upon receipt of appellee's monthly statement and cancelled checks, she removed and concealed the bad checks.　The proceeds from most of the forgeries were deposited directly into her personal account rather than taken in cash.　She usually presented the bad checks to the bank tellers with numerous authorized checks, and spread her banking transactions among several tellers so that no one teller knew the extent of her business.

Eventually, an in-house audit showed the discrepancies in the 1977 disbursements. Appellants brought this action against appellee for breach of contract, seeking repayment of the funds the bank paid out on checks with unauthorized signatures. After a court trial, judgment was entered in favor of appellant Knight for $5,500, representing the amount paid out of his personal account on forged checks from March 28 to May 20, 1977. This figure included eight forged checks paid by the bank prior to the mailing of its monthly statement containing a record of the payments and the checks themselves to Knight on May 6, plus a 14–day period. Since no forged checks on the K & K Manufacturing account were paid prior to May 20, judgment was entered for appellee against it. In addition, the trial court made findings of fact and conclusions of law. Both Knight and K & K Manufacturing have appealed.

Appellants contend that findings 13, 14 and 15 are not supported by the evidence. They argue the record shows their actions were not negligent and that the bank's practices and procedures were negligent as a matter of law. The disputed findings are as follows:

"13. Defendant bank [appellee] paid all the checks in good faith and in accordance with reasonable commercial standards.

14. Defendant bank did not fail to exercise ordinary care in paying the checks.

15. The plaintiffs [appellants] did not exercise reasonable care and promptness to examine the bank statements and cancelled checks in order to discover the forgeries."

Our duty begins and ends with the inquiry of whether the trial court had before it evidence which reasonably supports its actions, viewed in a light most favorable to sustaining its findings. United Bank v. Mesa N.O. Nelson Co., 121 Ariz. 438, 590 P.2d 1384 (1979). We will not weigh conflicting evidence or set aside the trial court's findings unless they are clearly erroneous. Id. The determination of which actions are commercially reasonable and what constitutes ordinary care on the part of the bank, as well as reasonable care and promptness on the part of the depositor, are questions of fact for the trier of fact. See West Penn Administration, Inc. v. Union National Bank, 233 Pa.Super. 311, 335 A.2d 725 (1975).

The concept of which party bears the loss in a forgery situation such as the one presented here is addressed in articles three and four of the Uniform Commercial Code, covering commercial paper and bank deposits and collections. A.R.S. Sec. 44–2543 [U.C.C. § 3–406] provides:

"Negligence contributing to alteration or unauthorized signature

Any person who by his negligence substantially contributes to a material alteration of the instrument or to the making of an unauthorized signature is precluded from asserting the alteration or lack of authority against a holder in due course or against a drawee or other payor who pays the instrument in good faith and in accordance with the reasonable commercial standards of the drawee's or payor's business."

A.R.S. Sec. 44–2632 [U.C.C. § 4–406] provides in part:

"Customer's duty to discover and report unauthorized signature or alteration

A. When a bank sends to its customer a statement of account accompanied by items paid in good faith in support of the debit entries or holds the statement and items pursuant to a request or instructions of its customer or otherwise in a reasonable manner makes the statement and items available to the customer, the customer must exercise reasonable care and promptness to examine the statement and items to discover his unauthorized signature or any alteration on an item and must notify the bank promptly after discovery thereof.

B. If the bank establishes that the customer failed with respect to an item to comply with the duties imposed on the customer by subsection A the customer is precluded from asserting against the bank:

    1. His unauthorized signature or any alteration on the item if the bank also establishes that it suffered a loss by reason of such failure; and

    2. An unauthorized signature or alteration by the same wrongdoer on any other item paid in good faith by the bank after the first item and statement was available to the customer for a reasonable period not exceeding fourteen calendar days and before the bank receives notification from the customer of any such unauthorized signature or alteration.

C. The preclusion under subsection B does not apply if the customer establishes lack of ordinary care on the part of the bank in paying the item(s)."

These provisions impose a duty on the depositor to check his monthly statement for unauthorized signatures or alterations on checks. If the depositor fails to do so, after the first forged check and statement relating thereto is sent to him, plus a reasonable period not exceeding 14 days, he is precluded from asserting the unauthorized signature or alteration against the bank. U.C.C. Sec. 4–406, comment 3. The burden of proof of depositor's negligence is on the bank. Even if the bank succeeds in establishing the depositor's negligence, if the customer establishes that the bank failed to exercise ordinary care in paying the bad checks, the preclusion rule of [UCC 4–406(2)] does not apply. U.C.C. Sec. 4–406, comment 4.

We first address the issue of whether appellee met its burden of proof of showing that appellants "substantially contributed" to the forgeries or failed to exercise "reasonable care and promptness" in examining the monthly statements. The record shows that appellants trusted Miss Garza completely with both writing checks and reconciling the monthly statements. No spot checks were made by Knight or the controller at Knight Foundry, both of whom had access to the banking records. Knight was informed by a bank officer that his personal account was overdrawn on 12 occasions in 1977, yet did nothing to discover the reasons therefor. Knight testified he was aware Miss Garza's work was often inaccurate as well as tardy in 1977 and 1978.

Appellants argue they were not negligent in relying on a previously honest employee, citing Jackson v. First National Bank, 55 Tenn. App. 545, 403 S.W.2d 109 (1966).[1] We decline to follow *Jackson*, which held, contrary to the bulk of authority, that since a defalcating financial secretary had been a longtime faithful and trusted member of the church he cheated, the church could not be found negligent. Misplaced confidence in an employee will not excuse a depositor from the duty of notifying the bank of alterations on items paid from the depositor's account.... We adopt the majority view that the depositor is chargeable with the knowledge of all facts a reasonable and prudent examination of his bank statement would have disclosed if made by an honest employee.... The trial court's finding number 15 is amply supported by the evidence.

Secondly, we turn to the question of whether appellants met their burden of proof of demonstrating appellee did not exercise ordinary care in paying the bad checks, and did not act in good faith and in accordance with reasonable commercial standards. There appears to be no dispute regarding the good faith of appellee in paying the forgeries. The issue is whether its method of ascertaining unauthorized signatures on its depositor's checks met the standard of care under the circumstances.

Implied in the debtor/creditor relationship between a bank and its checking account depositor is the contractual undertaking on the part of the bank that it will only discharge its obligations to the depositor upon his authorized signature.... The mere fact that the bank has paid a forged check does not mean the bank has breached its duty of ordinary care, however....

At trial, an operations officer for appellee testified as to the methods employed during the period the forgeries occurred to discover unauthorized signatures on depositor's checks. She testified that checks were organized so that a bundle from the same account could be compared with the authorized signature on the bank's signature card. A staff of five filing clerks handled an average of approximately 1,000 checks each per hour in this manner. She testified it was common for a file clerk to become familiar with the drawer's signature in large accounts such as appellants'. An official of a large Arizona bank

---

1. *Jackson* was overruled in Vending Chattanooga, Inc. v. American National Bank & Trust Co., 730 S.W.2d 624 (Tenn. 1987). [Eds.]

testified that tellers and file clerks are not trained to be handwriting experts. He testified that in his opinion, because most large banks have completely abandoned physical comparison of checks with the signature card, the system employed by appellee was better than the norm of the banking community in Southern Arizona.

In view of this and other evidence, we conclude that there was sufficient evidence to support findings 13 and 14 and the judgment entered below. Similar methods of comparing drawer's signatures have been upheld as constituting ordinary care and being within reasonable commercial standards across the country.... Appellant Knight and his controller admitted the forgeries were quite good. Appellants also argue that because the bank tellers recognized Miss Garza was cashing large checks made to herself and her boyfriend and that she was driving an expensive sports car, they had a further duty to check the validity of the drawer's signature. This evidence was balanced by testimony that Miss Garza thoroughly explained the reasons for the large checks as increased salary, bonuses, and payment of Knight's expenses while he was out of town. Knight and Miss Garza were in the bank together on a regular basis and the tellers knew Miss Garza was authorized to handle large amounts of Knight's money. See Cooper v. Union Bank, 9 Cal.3d 123, 371, 507 P.2d 609, 107 Cal.Rptr. 1 (1973).

Finally, there was evidence that some K & K Manufacturing checks were forged with a rubber stamp facsimile of Knight's signature, which was only authorized for use with the Knight foundry account. Appellants argue appellee fell below the standard of ordinary care in honoring these checks. The trial court personally examined appellee's expert witness on this subject. There was testimony that if facsimile signatures appear "all of a sudden" on the checks, the depositor may be contacted, but there was sufficient evidence that the piecemeal use of the stamp here, which was at times authorized by appellants, was not such that appellee should be held to bring it to their attention. The finding of fact that appellee's acts, including those regarding the facsimile signature, did not fall below ordinary care or reasonable commercial standards was not clearly erroneous.

Affirmed.

Notes

(1) **Information to Customer Under Truncation.** Banks have traditionally returned each customer's paid checks together with a statement at monthly intervals. Doing so triggers the customer's duty under UCC 4–406 to discover and report an unauthorized signature or alteration. But if the check collection process is truncated at the depositary bank, the payor bank will not be able to do this.

In order to facilitate truncation, the revision of UCC 4–406 provides that the payor bank need only provide information "sufficient to allow the customer reasonably to identify the items paid." Comment 1 explains that under "a safe harbor rule" it will suffice if the item is described by item number, amount, and date of payment. "This information was chosen because it can be obtained by the bank's computer from the check's MICR line without examination of the items involved."

Is this fair to consumers? What more might a customer want? Comment 1 goes on to explain that accommodating "customers who don't keep records ... is not as desirable as accommodating others who keep more careful records" at "less cost to the check collection system and thus to all customers of the system." If technological advances make it possible for banks to give customers more information "in a manner that is fully compatible with automation or truncation systems," an amendment of the safe harbor requirements may be desirable.

(2) **Paid Checks as Evidence.** In order to facilitate truncation, UCC 4–406(b) allows a bank to destroy paid checks at any time after payment, as long as it maintains "the capacity to furnish legible copies of the items until the expiration of seven years after receipt of the items." Will such a copy always suffice as evidence of payment? Will it be stamped "paid"? Comment 3 to UCC 4–101 explains that "under various truncation plans customers will no longer receive their cancelled checks and will no longer have the cancelled check to prove payment. Individual legislation might provide that a copy of a bank statement along with a copy of the check is prima facie evidence of payment."

(3) **Missing Signatures.** Is a signature of an organization "unauthorized" under UCC 4–406 if the signature of more than one person is required to constitute the organization's authorized signature and one of the required signatures is missing? Authority was split under former UCC 4–406. The split is resolved by UCC 3–403(b) and 4–104(c). See Comment 4 to UCC 3–403.

(4) **New Definition of "Ordinary Care."** Even though a payor bank generally bears the loss on forged checks that it pays, it may find it cheaper to use automated payment procedures and absorb that loss for relatively small checks than to verify the drawer's signature on every check. At least this would be so if the loss were confined to the amount of the individual check. But if such a practice amounts to a failure to exercise ordinary care, the bank takes the much greater risk of bearing the loss on a series of checks as to which the customer would otherwise have been precluded under UCC 4–406. How far can a payor bank go in declining to verify drawer's signatures before it runs afoul of the standard of ordinary care?

In Medford Irrigation District v. Western Bank, 66 Or.App. 589, 676 P.2d 329 (1984), the court held that Western Bank had gone too far. The bank had concluded that "a small number of forgeries was detected by individual review of checks, while the cost of that review was approximately $200,000 per year.... Western utilizes a computer check payment system. Checks for a face amount under $5,000 are paid without human intervention or 'sight review' of the signatures. Checks are received for payment at Western's data processing center in Portland, and unless there is a 'hold' or a 'stop payment' order for a check, it is paid automatically by computer.... The computer is programmed to 'kick out' checks with a face amount of $5,000 or more. Absent specific instructions from a customer, only checks of $5,000 or more are individually reviewed for authorized signatures or alterations." As a matter of law, this was held not to be "ordinary care" under former UCC 4–406. "Although a procedure may be common throughout the banking industry, it is not, by that fact alone, a reasonable procedure."

Subsequent decisions showed some tolerance of bankers' reliance on automation. For example, in Rhode Island Hospital Trust National Bank v. Zapata Corp., 848 F.2d 291 (1st Cir.1988), the payor bank examined signatures on all checks for more than $1,000, and on checks between $100 and $1,000 if they were in a randomly selected one per cent or if the bank had reason to suspect a problem. This practice saved the bank about $125,000 annually. The bank "established that most other banks in the nation follow this practice and that banking industry experts recommended it." Indeed, most banks used a limit of $2,000 rather than $1,000. The court held that the bank had "made out a *prima facie* case of 'ordinary care' " under former UCC 4–103(3), now UCC 4–103(c), and that while the customer "might still try to show that the entire industry's practice is unreasonable," it had not shown this. Such cases did not, however, entirely allay the banking industry's fears.

To allay these fears, a new provision was added to revised Article 3, under which ordinary care does not require a payor bank that uses "automated means ... to examine the instrument if the failure to examine does not violate the bank's prescribed procedures and the bank's procedures do not vary unreasonably from general banking usage" not disapproved by Articles 3 or 4. Because this provision applies to the payor bank's exercise of ordinary care under UCC 3–406 as well as under UCC 4–406, it is tucked away in a new definition of "ordinary care" in UCC 3–103(a)(7), though it applies primarily to UCC 4–406. See Comment 5 to UCC 3–103. Comment 4 to UCC 4–406 explains "that sight examination by a payor bank is not required if its procedure is reasonable and is commonly followed by other comparable banks in the area.... The definition of 'ordinary care' ... rejects those authorities that hold, in effect, that failure to use sight examination is negligence as a matter of law. The effect ... is only to provide that in the small percentage of cases in which a customer's failure to examine its statement or returned items has led to loss ... a bank should not have to share that loss solely because it has adopted an automated ... payment procedure in order to deal with the great volume of items at a lower cost to all customers." Might this provision affect the incentive of banks to develop automated means for verification of signatures?

(5) Burden of Proof. Under UCC 4–406(d), it is up to the bank to prove the customer's failure to comply with the duties imposed on the customer. Under UCC 4–406(e), it is then up to the customer to prove the bank's failure to exercise ordinary care. If a payor bank seeks the protection of the "safe harbor" provision of UCC 3–103(a)(7) or 4–103(c), who has the burden of proving consistency or inconsistency with general banking usage? See Putnam Rolling Ladder v. Manufacturers Hanover Trust Co., 74 N.Y.2d 340, 547 N.Y.S.2d 611, 546 N.E.2d 904 (1989) (burden of proving general banking usage under former UCC 4–103(3) "should rest on the bank—the party seeking the advantage offered by the provision").

(6) Comparative Negligence. Note that UCC 4–406(e) introduces a comparative negligence rule like that in UCC 3–406(b).

UNAUTHORIZED ORDERS AND AUTOMATION

The Problem. Automation of the check collection process has had a profound practical effect on the payor bank's policing of unauthorized orders. The payor bank's computer can easily determine, with the aid of the information encoded on the check, whether the check is drawn on sufficient funds and whether payment has been stopped. Verifying the drawer's signature, however, must be done manually. On many checks, as we have seen, banks no longer verify drawers' signatures, since the cost of verification exceeds its benefit to the bank in terms of avoidance of the loss resulting from forged checks. Furthermore, under a system of check truncation in which checks are retained at the depositary bank, verification of the drawer's signature is not feasible.

Because the payor bank is not entitled to charge its customer's account on a forged check, banks must offset their losses on forged checks against their savings from increased automation. Other kinds of payment systems, however, operate on a different assumption. In these systems the user generally has a device, commonly a plastic card, that gives the user access to the system, and the user assumes some responsibility for retaining control of that device in order to prevent other persons from making unauthorized transfers. If the customer's numbered and encoded blank checks were regarded as analogous to the plastic card, it might be concluded that the payor bank should be entitled to charge its customer's account on a forged check, in at least some circumstances, if the forgery was the result of the customer's failure to keep blank checks within the customer's control.[1] But this is not the law for checks.

---

1. French law reaches just this conclusion. "The drawer who by his own fault loses a check form is responsible if his signature is subsequently forged on it unless he has notified the bank in time to prevent payment. The drawer has been held where checks were stolen from a desk in his place of business, from an unlocked drawer in a workroom, and from his briefcase in his hotel room." Farnsworth, The Check in France and the United States, 36 Tul.L.Rev. 245, 264 (1962).

Credit Cards. The law of bank credit cards offers an obvious comparison. Much of the early credit card litigation concerned the responsibility for the unauthorized use of lost or stolen cards. In 1970, Congress pre-empted the field, by legislation now found in the Consumer Credit Protection Act, 15 U.S.C. § 1643, implemented by Federal Reserve Board Regulation Z, 12 C.F.R. § 226.12.

That legislation limits to $50 the cardholder's liability for use of a card by a person "who does not have actual, implied or apparent authority for such use and from which the cardholder receives no benefit." 15 U.S.C. § 1602(*o*). For the consumer to be liable for even the $50, a number of conditions have to be met. One of the most important of these is that the card must be an "accepted credit card," one "which the cardholder has requested and received or has signed or has used, or authorized another to use." 15 U.S.C. § 1602(*l*). Another important condition was that the unauthorized use must have occurred prior to notification to the issuer that the card has been lost or stolen. Lack of fault on the part of the cardholder is not a condition.

Does the federal credit card legislation strike a fair balance between issuers and cardholders? Should fault play a role in the allocation of loss?

Electronic Fund Transfer Act. "One of the most hotly debated topics during consideration of federal EFT legislation was the allocation of liability for unauthorized fraudulent transfers. Industry groups, believing that much of the fraudulent activity arose as a result of consumers writing their PIN numbers on or near their EFT cards, argued that a negligence standard should be adopted. Under such a standard, the consumer would bear none of the loss unless his negligence substantially contributed to the unauthorized use; if it did, he would bear the entire loss. While this arrangement would encourage care in the handling and storing of EFT cards and PINs, consumer groups argued that it was unduly harsh on consumers and would enable financial institutions possessing greater legal resources to shift more than a fair share of the liability burden to consumers. They advocated a flat $50 limitation on liability like that applicable to credit cards under the Truth in Lending Act. These concerns ultimately carried the day, and although a pure $50 limit was rejected in favor of a compromise rule, the liability-allocation rule that was finally adopted will place strict limits upon consumer liability regardless of the consumer's negligence in safeguarding the account access devices.

"Under the EFT Act, an unauthorized transfer is defined as a transfer initiated by someone other than the consumer or a person to whom the consumer has given actual authority to initiate the transfer, and from which the consumer receives no benefit. Any transfer initiated by someone to whom the consumer furnishes his EFT card and PIN, however, is not to be considered unauthorized unless the consumer has notified the institution that transfers by that person are no longer permitted.

"As an initial matter, the amount of a consumer's liability for an unauthorized electronic transfer or related series of transfers will not exceed $50 or the amount of unauthorized transfers that occur before notice is given to the financial institution, whichever is less. Thus, the basic limitation on consumer liability is similar to the flat dollar-amount limitation of the Truth in Lending Act. There are two significant exceptions, however, that may escalate the initial $50 limitation on consumer liability.

"First, if the consumer fails to notify the financial institution within two business days after he discovers the loss or theft of an EFT card or PIN, the consumer may be liable for up to $500 of unauthorized use. This second tier of liability is intended to encourage prompt reporting of lost and stolen cards once the consumer becomes aware of the loss or theft. This scheme is designed to hold total system losses to a reasonable minimum, while protecting consumers from unlimited liability for indiscretions in safeguarding their EFT cards and PINs, or for slight delays in reporting a loss or theft.

"Second, there is no ceiling on consumer liability for subsequent unauthorized transfers that occur because the consumer has failed to report within 60 days of the transmittal of a periodic statement any unauthorized transfer that appears on the statement. This is intended to provide an incentive for consumers to read and verify their periodic statements, and thus thwart fraudulent users who might otherwise drain the account over a lengthy period of time. It also provides necessary encouragement for consumers to report in a reasonably prompt fashion suspected unauthorized transfers which do not arise out of any loss or theft of the access devices." Brandel & Olliff, The Electronic Fund Transfer Act: A Primer, 40 Ohio St.L.J. 531, 555–57 (1979).

What is the role of fault—on the part of the consumer or the financial institution—under the scheme just described? The scheme, along with some further qualifications, can be seen from Regulation E § 205.6. Regulation E is discussed in Connors, The Implementation of the Electronic Fund Transfer Act: An Update on Regulation E, 17 Wake Forest L.Rev. 329 (1981).

Suppose that a customer contests the right of her bank to charge her account for $800 that the bank claims were withdrawn at an ATM at a precise time by either the customer or someone authorized by her. The customer produces evidence that she was at work at the time in question and testifies that her card was never out of her possession and that she never told anyone her PIN and never even wrote it down. The bank produces evidence that the withdrawal could only have been made by someone using the customer's card together with her PIN. What result under the EFT Act and Regulation E? See Judd v. Citibank, 107 Misc.2d 526, 435 N.Y.S.2d 210 (1980) (not citing either the EFT Act or Regulation E [2]).

2. Under § 1693g(b) of the Act: "In any action which involves a consumer's liability for an unauthorized electronic fund transfer, the burden of proof is upon the

Article 4A. "A wire transfer is a very efficient method of payment. Large amounts of money can be paid at low cost and in a short time. But there is also risk of loss if there is fraud in the transaction or there is error by either the sender of the payment order or by one or more of the receiving banks through which the payment is made. The fraud cases involve unauthorized payment orders. A payment order might be sent in the name of a person by somebody who has no authority to act for the purported sender. Or, an unauthorized person might alter or amend a payment order of a sender. This kind of fraud is most likely to occur with respect to electronically transmitted payment orders. The law of agency is not very useful in determining whether the risk of loss with respect to an unauthorized payment order transmitted electronically will fall upon the receiving bank's customer, the purported sender of the fraudulent payment order, or the receiving bank that accepted it. Typically, the receiving bank is acting on the basis of a message that appears on a computer screen. There is no way of determining the identity or authority of the person who caused the message to be sent. The receiving bank is not relying on the authority of any particular person to act for its customer. The case is not comparable to payment of a check by the drawee bank on the basis of a signature that is forged. Rather, the receiving bank relies on a security procedure pursuant to which the authenticity of the message can be 'tested' by various devices which are designed to provide certainty that the message is that of the sender identified in the payment order.

"In the wire transfer business, the concept of 'authorized' is different from that found in agency law. A payment order is treated as the order of the person in whose name it is issued if it is properly tested pursuant to a security procedure [UCC 4A–201] and the order passes the test. Risk of loss rules regarding unauthorized payment orders with respect to which verification pursuant to a security procedure is in effect are stated in sections 4A–202 and 4A–203. The general rule is that a payment order is effective as the order of the customer, whether or not authorized, if the security procedure is commercially reasonable and the receiving bank proves that it accepted the order in good faith after verifying the order in compliance with the security procedure. There are certain exceptions and qualifications to this rule that are explained in the official comment following section 4A–203. The general rule is based on the assumption that losses due to fraudulent payment orders can best be avoided by the use of commercially reasonable security procedures, and that the use of such procedures should be encouraged. The most important element of this rule is the requirement that there be a commercially reasonable security procedure. If

financial institution to show that the electronic fund transfer was authorized or, if the electronic fund transfer was unauthorized, then the burden of proof is upon the financial institution to establish that the conditions of liability set forth in subsection (a) ... have been met, and ... that the disclosures required to be made to the consumer ... were in fact made...." (Regulation E does not contain a comparable provision.) Was this provision relevant to the *Judd* case? See Regulation E, § 205.2(a)(2)(i).

that requirement is not met, the rule does not apply and ordinary rules of agency apply. Thus, if the payment order was not authorized by the customer, the receiving bank acts at its peril in accepting the order.

"The rule is designed to protect both the customer and the receiving bank. A receiving bank needs to be able to rely on objective criteria to determine whether it can safely act on a payment order. Employees of that bank can be trained to 'test' a payment order according to the various steps specified in the security procedure. The bank is responsible for the acts of these employees. The rule assures that the interests of the customer will be protected by providing an incentive to a receiving bank to make available to the customer a security procedure that is commercially reasonable. Prudent banking practice may require that security procedures be utilized in virtually all cases, except for those in which personal contact between the customer and the bank eliminates the possibility of an unauthorized order. The burden of making available commercially reasonable security procedures is imposed on receiving banks because they generally determine what security procedures can be used and these banks are in the best position to evaluate the efficacy of procedures offered to customers to combat fraud. The burden on the customer is to supervise its employees to assure compliance with the security to restrict procedure, to safeguard confidential security information, and access to transmitting facilities so that the security procedure cannot be breached." Jordan & Warren, Introduction to Symposium: Revised Articles 3 & 4 and New Article 4A, 42 Ala.L.Rev. 373, 379–81 (1991).

SECTION 4. FICTITIOUS PAYEES AND EMPLOYER RESPONSIBILITY

Prefatory Note. This section is concerned with exceptions that have been developed primarily to place on employers the risk of check fraud by their employees.

We begin with the fictitious payee rule, which originated in the failure of several English commercial houses in the late eighteenth century. Lenders of credit had drawn or accepted bills of exchange payable to the order of imaginary firms, and given them to the houses which had indorsed them in the names of the imaginary firms and sold them to purchasers. The houses failed, and the lenders of credit, when sued by the purchasers of the drafts, claimed that the indorsements were forged. They lost in a number of suits and on a variety of theories. See Tatlock v. Harris, 3 T.R. 174, 100 Eng.Rep. 517 (1789); Minet v. Gibson, 3 T.R. 481, 100 Eng.Rep. 689 (1789), affirmed, 1 H.Bl. 569, 126 Eng.Rep. 326 (H.L.1791). During the next century the rule grew up that a bill payable to a fictitious person is payable to bearer as against all parties who knew that the payee was a fictitious person. When the Bills of Exchange Act was enacted in 1882, it provided, in Section 7(3), "Where the payee is a fictitious or nonexisting person the bill may be treated as payable to bearer." In Bank of England v. Vagliano Brothers, [1891] A.C. 107, reversing 23 Q.B.D. 243 (1889), the House of Lords decided that this changed prior law and lack of knowledge of the fictitious character of the payee was immaterial.

In 1896 the Commissioners on Uniform State Laws approved Section 9(3) of the Negotiable Instruments Law which rejected the rule in Vagliano's case: "The instrument is payable to bearer.... When it is payable to the order of a fictitious or nonexisting person, and such fact was known to the person making it so payable." Courts read "fictitious" to include a living person not intended by the maker or drawer to take any interest in the instrument. The prototype situation to which the rule applied was one of employee fraud, where the treasurer of a corporation, authorized to sign its checks, drew its check payable to a payee who was a living person but one whom the treasurer had fraudulently added to the payroll with no intention that that person receive the check. The treasurer then forged the payee's indorsement. The fictitious payee rule protected anyone who cashed the check as well as the payor bank that paid it, for, since the check was payable to bearer, no indorsement was necessary and the forgery was for these purposes, immaterial.

This situation was covered by former UCC 3–405(1)(b), which provided that if "a person signing as or on behalf of the maker or drawer intends the payee to have no interest in the instrument," an indorsement by any person in the payee's name is effective. That provision has now been replaced by UCC 3–404(b).

It was held that NIL 9(3) did not apply to the situation where an employee of the corporation, not authorized to sign its checks, fraudulently prepared the padded payroll containing the name of the payee, and the check was then signed by the innocent treasurer, and the indorsement of the payee forged by the employee. Since the fictitious character of the payee was not known to the treasurer, "the person making it so payable," the check was not payable to bearer, no person who cashed it took as a holder, and the payor bank that paid it could not charge the drawer's account. Banks objected to the injustice of this result, which placed on the payor bank a risk of employee fraud that they felt should properly be borne by the employer. The American Bankers Association recommended a Fictitious Payee Act, which amended NIL 9(3) to cover situations in which "such fact was known to the person making it so payable, or known to his employee or other agent who supplies the name of such payee." About half of the states adopted this amendment.

This situation was covered by former UCC 3–405(1)(c), which provided that if "an agent or employee of the maker or drawer has supplied him with the name of the payee intending the latter to have no such interest," an indorsement by any person in the payee's name was effective. Although former UCC 3–405 avoided the use of the term "fictitious payee," this descendant of the fictitious payee rule had been expanded to include the padded payroll case, just as the Fictitious Payee Act had done.

Revised Article 3 follows a very different course, UCC 3–404(b), now appearing under the traditional label "Fictitious Payees," is confined to the type of situation contemplated by the original NIL 9(3). The padded payroll situation, has now been moved to a separate section, UCC 3–405, which deals more generally with employer responsibility for employee fraud involving forged indorsements and shifts more loss to the employer. The impact of this change is suggested by the two problems and the case that follows.

Problem 12. Kim Kaller, Empire's treasurer drew a $25,000 check to the order of Quaker for a nonexistent delivery of goods. Kaller indorsed it in Quaker's name, deposited it in an account Kaller had opened in Quaker's name in Metro Bank, and The Bank of New York or Metro Bank paid it and charged it to Empire's account. Kaller has absconded with the proceeds. Does Empire have a claim against The Bank of New York or Metro Bank? See UCC 3–404(b) and Case # 2 in Comment 2.

Problem 13. Merideth Hussler, one of Empire's clerks, furnished Kim Kaller, Empire's treasurer, with a forged invoice from Quaker for a non-existent delivery of goods. Kaller drew a $25,000 check to the order of Quaker in payment of the invoice. Hussler stole the check before it was mailed to Quaker, indorsed it in Quaker's name, deposited it in an account Hussler had opened in Quaker's name in Metro Bank, and The Bank of New York or Metro Bank paid it and charged it to Empire's account. Hussler has absconded with the proceeds. Does Empire have a claim against The Bank of New York or Metro Bank? Would it make a difference if the invoice was a genuine one? Would it make a difference if Hussler, after indorsing the check in Quaker's name, had deposited it in his own account in Metro Bank? What if Hussler's indorsement in Quaker's name included "for deposit"? See UCC 3–405; *Danje Fabrics Division v. Morgan Guaranty Trust Co.,* infra.

Problem 14. Perini Corporation used a facsimile signature machine for writing checks. It authorized the banks in which it had accounts

> to honor and charge Perini Corporation for all such checks ... regardless of by whom or by what means the actual or purported facsimile signature thereon may have been affixed thereto, if such facsimile signature resembles the facsimile specimen from time to time filed with said banks.

Someone either gained access to the machine or developed a perfect copy of the facsimile and drew over a million dollars worth of checks payable either to "Quisenberry Contracting Co." or "Southern Contracting Co." These checks were deposited in the Habersham bank by a man calling himself "Jesse D. Quisenberry," who had already opened accounts in that bank in the names of the payees. The man did not, however, put indorsements of the payees on the checks that he deposited, indorsing them simply "Jesse D. Quisenberry" with no indication that he was acting for the payee. The checks were paid by the payor banks and the proceeds credited to the accounts in the Habersham bank, from which the man withdrew them. Has Perini any claim against the Habersham bank or the payor banks? See Case # 4 in Comment 2 to UCC 3–404; Perini Corp. v. First National Bank of Habersham County, 553 F.2d 398 (5th Cir.1977).

DANJE FABRICS DIVISION v. MORGAN GUARANTY TRUST CO.

Supreme Court of New York, New York County, 1978.
96 Misc.2d 746, 409 N.Y.S.2d 565.

LOUIS GROSSMAN, JUSTICE. This is a motion by defendant Citibank, N.A., sued herein as "First National City Bank" ("Citibank") for summary judgment under CPLR 3212 dismissing this action as against defendant Morgan Guaranty Trust Company ("Morgan"), and a cross-motion by plaintiff Danje Fabrics Division of Kingspoint International Corp. ("Danje") for summary judgment against defendant Morgan.

The facts in this case are essentially undisputed by the parties. In November 1974, plaintiff Danje, a family owned company that converted yarn into fabric, hired one Raymond Caulder ("Caulder") as its Accounts Payable Bookkeeper. Specialty Dyers ("Dyers") located in North Carolina, is in the business of dying fabrics, a service which Dyers has performed for Danje for several years and for which Danje has paid Dyers regularly, amounting to millions of dollars.

Dyers would submit invoices to Danje to secure payment for the services it had performed. These invoices were first reviewed in Danje's production department. The invoices would then be sent to Caulder who would record them in the accounts payable ledger and file the invoices by due date. When the due date came, Caulder, at times with the help of another employee, would manually prepare the necessary checks and write in the name of the payee. The checks were then submitted by Caulder to Ernest J. Michel ("Michel"), president of Danje, or to his son Stanley, for signature. Along with the checks given to Ernest or Stanley Michel for signature, the original invoices supporting each check and adding machine tapes of the invoices, if more than one, were submitted to the signatory.

On May 28, 1975, Caulder's employment was terminated by Danje for appearing for work drunk, unshaven and unruly. Shortly thereafter, it was discovered that between April 23, 1975 and May 21, 1975,

Caulder had taken twenty-seven checks totalling $49,645.82, made out to Dyers in payment of bona fide invoices for services actually performed and for which payments were actually due, after they had been signed, and diverted them into an account he or he and an accomplice had opened at Citibank in the name of Specialty Dyers. A private investigator hired by Danje to locate Caulder and obtain the return of the proceeds of the diverted checks reported to Danje that Caulder's true name was Raymond Flate. Caulder has not been found, nor has the money been retrieved. There is presently a balance of $6,435.29 in the Specialty Dyers account opened by Caulder at Citibank.

Thereafter, Danje commenced this action against Morgan as the payor or drawee bank and against Citibank as the collecting bank. Danje's complaint set forth three causes of action. The first was against defendant Morgan only for wrongfully debiting plaintiff's account for the twenty-seven checks which plaintiff alleged contained forged payee's endorsements. The second and third causes of action were against defendant Citibank only and alleged negligence on its part in permitting a fraudulent account to be opened by the forger. Citibank moved to dismiss the complaint as to itself for failure to state a cause of action, which was granted. The order dismissing the complaint as to Citibank was served with notice of entry. No appeal was ever taken from the said order and the time for plaintiff to appeal has expired. Thus, the only cause of action remaining is the one against Morgan as drawee bank. However, Citibank is still in the action since Morgan has cross-claimed against Citibank on its prior endorsements as the collecting bank. Citibank recognizes and concedes that if plaintiff has judgment against Morgan, then Morgan is entitled to judgment over against Citibank in like amount and has therefore brought this motion in which Morgan has joined.

Citibank contends that Morgan has a complete defense to the claim set forth by Danje in its complaint by reason of the provisions of § 3–405 of the Uniform Commercial Code.

This section provides in pertinent part:

"§ 3–405. *Imposters; Signature in Name of Payee*

(1) An endorsement by any person in the name of a named payee is effective if ... (c) an agent or employee of the maker or drawer has supplied him with the name of the payee intending the latter to have no such interest."

Since it was Caulder who was responsible for the preparation of checks based upon invoices given to him by plaintiff Danje's production department and who presented such checks to the individual who was authorized to sign them, Citibank argues, and Morgan agrees, that, based upon the facts as herein set forth, Caulder "supplied" the plaintiff with the name of the payee intending the latter to have no such interest and therefore the endorsements in question are effective. Danje's position is that, since the twenty-seven checks in question were prepared as a result of bona fide business transactions between Dyers, the named payee, and Danje, Caulder did not "supply" plaintiff with the name of the payee but simply converted the checks to his own use, and that therefore § 3–405(1)(c) of the Uniform Commercial Code has no application to the instant case.

Therefore, the issue to be decided in this case is what scope the word "supplied", as used in § 3–405(1)(c) of the Uniform Commercial Code was intended to have. Was it the legislature's intent for it to cover all instances where an employee presents an instrument to the maker for signature or must a line be drawn to distinguish between those instances where the instrument is based upon a fraudulent transaction and those where the instrument is based upon a bona fide transaction occurring in the regular course of business.

There are extremely few cases in any jurisdiction dealing with § 3–405(1)(c) of the Uniform Commercial Code and the court has found only three cases which bear any relation to the specific question raised herein. One is a New York case, Board of Higher Education v. Banker's Trust Co., 86 Misc.2d 560, 383 N.Y.S.2d 508, factually similar to the present case, which discusses the point in question but does not go into it in detail since the defendant did not seriously contest the applicability of the overall section. Another is a New Jersey case, Snug Harbor Realty Co. v. First National Bank of Toms River, N.J., 105 Super. 572, 253 A.2d 581, aff'd 54 N.J. 95, 253 A.2d 545, which presents a very similar fact pattern to the instant case and deals directly with the point in question. The third is a Federal Court of Appeals case in the Third Circuit applying Pennsylvania law, New Amsterdam Casualty Co. v. First Pennsylvania Banking & Trust Co. (3rd Cir.) 451 F.2d 892, which also presents similar facts with one distinction upon which the court rests its decision, and which sets forth a definition of the word "supplied" as used in § 3–405(1)(c) of the Uniform Commercial Code.

The law as set forth in § 3–405(1)(c) of the Uniform Commercial Code reads exactly the same in all of the three states in which the above-mentioned cases were decided. According to the official comment accompanying § 3–405(1)(c) of the Uniform Commercial Code as set forth in the official statutes of all three states:

> "Paragraph (c) is new. It extends the rule of the original subsection 9(3) to include the padded payroll cases, where the drawer's agent or employee prepares the check for signature or otherwise furnishes the signing officer with the name of the payee. The principle followed is that the loss should fall upon the employer as a risk of his business enterprise rather than upon the subsequent holder or drawee. The reasons are that the employer is normally in a better position to prevent such forgeries by reasonable care in the selection or supervision of his employees, or, if he is not, is at least in a better position to cover the loss by fidelity insurance; and that the cost of such insurance is properly an expense of his business rather than of the business of the holder or drawee."

Although the Official Comment quoted above, makes mention only of "padded payroll" cases, it is clear that the provisions of the Code extend beyond these to other "padded" cases where the operative facts are present, i.e., where the drawer's agent or employee prepares the checks, presumably drawn for payroll or other valid purposes, for signature or otherwise furnishes the signing officer with the name of the payee.

The Official Comment also provides two examples which illustrate situations in which § 3–405(1)(c) of the Uniform Commercial Code is applicable. Both examples use a fact pattern where an employee of a corporation prepares a padded payroll for the treasurer. In one instance, the employee adds a fictitious payee to the payroll without the knowledge of the treasurer, while in the other, the payee exists and the employee knows it but adds a check to the payroll intending the payee to have no interest in it. In both instances, any person could effectively endorse the payee's name and the loss would fall on the corporation rather than a subsequent holder or the drawee. The above illustrative situations are straightforward and clear. The problem with applying said illustrative situations to the instant case results from the fact that both of said situations are based on a payroll where an unauthorized check in each case has been added to it rather than a totally legitimate check. While it is clear that § 3–405(1)(c) of the Uniform Commercial Code applies to fraudulent checks, its application to a situation involving bona fide checks is not discussed in those examples.

In our present case, the checks stolen by Caulder were legitimate and bona fide payments due and owing to Dyers. The checks themselves involved in our case were not fraudulent in any respect and the facts herein indicate that proper and careful business procedures were followed in the drawing and making of said checks. The undisputed facts herein further show that it was only the criminal conduct of Caulder in appropriating, stealing and falsely endorsing said checks, which constituted legitimate payments to the named payee, that resulted in the loss herein incurred by Danje.

In Board of Higher Education v. Banker's Trust Co., supra, an employee of the plaintiff had as her duty the responsibility of preparing requisitions for checks to be issued by plaintiff for scholarships and other payments to students, to prepare the checks, to have them signed by the authorized personnel, and to send the checks to their recipients. On a number of occasions, the employee prepared duplicate requisitions and checks, which she retained after they had been signed. Also, in some instances, she retained checks which had been properly requisitioned instead of sending them. She then forged the endorsements of the named payees on these checks and cashed them. In arguing that these checks should not be debited against its accounts, plaintiff did not seriously contest the applicability of § 3–405(1)(c) of the Uniform Commercial Code to the facts of the case, but argued that the banks were estopped from relying on its provisions because of their gross negligence in allowing the forger to cash the checks. As a result, the court simply stated its conclusion that the forged endorsements were effective, lumping all of the checks together without distinguishing between the duplicate and the genuine checks, and proceeded to discuss the merits of the other arguments which were the main thrust of plaintiff's case.

In Snug Harbor Realty Co. v. First National Bank of Toms River, N.J., supra, plaintiff maintained a system under which parties asserting claims against it would submit invoices which were then given to its superintendent for verification. Upon verifying that the claims were valid, he would initial the invoices and forward them to the bookkeeper who would verify the contractual obligation and prepare the necessary checks. After the checks were signed by the company's authorized official, the superintendent would pick them up for delivery to the respective payees. Instead of delivering the checks, he proceeded to forge the endorsements of the named payees and cash the checks for his own personal use. The trial court found that the provisions of Section 3-405(1)(c) of the Uniform Commercial Code were "dispositive" and therefore the endorsements were effective and the bank not liable to the plaintiff. The appellate court reversed, stating:

> ". . . [the] unfaithful employee of the construction company did not supply to his employer 'the name of the payee intending the latter to have no such interest.' To the contrary, the payees were bona fide creditors of the company who had respectively submitted their invoices for work performed or materials furnished." (*Snug Harbor Realty Co.*, supra, 105 N.J.Super. at 574, 253 A.2d at 582).

Therefore, the creditors themselves "supplied" the plaintiff with the names of the payees, and the employee, in essence, stole the checks, thereby making his forged endorsements ineffective.

This Appellate Court decision in the *Snug Harbor* case, supra, appears to be on all fours with our instant case. In both situations, we are dealing with legitimate payments which were misappropriated and stolen by an employee instead of having them delivered or sent to the intended payee.

In New Amsterdam Casualty Co. v. First Pennsylvania Banking & Trust Co., supra, plaintiff was a stockbroker's insurer who had paid losses sustained by the stockbroker whose employee had forged endorsements on its checks and whose account had been debited by the drawee bank. The employee had submitted fraudulent sell orders to the trading room of the broker, thereby initiating the normal business procedure involved in the sale of items from various client's portfolios. The employee would then obtain the necessary confirmation slips, normally sent to the customer, by saying that he would deliver them personally. When the employee knew that the checks pursuant to the sale were ready, he would obtain them from the broker's cashier, stating that the customer had authorized his receipt of the checks. Instead of delivering the checks to the customer, he would then forge the endorsements of the named payees and cash the checks. The court decided that the endorsements were effective, relieving the drawee bank of liability. However, in explaining its decision, the court stated:

> "In the interest of business and bank stability, it is important that a reasonably clear line be drawn. Our decision places the burden on the drawer who, in the words of the official comment, is 'in a better position to cover the loss by fidelity insurance ...,' U.C.C. Section 3–405, comment 4.

> "For the purpose of giving meaning to the word 'supplied' in section 3–405(1)(c), we can find no viable place to draw the line within the business enterprise of the drawer. Accordingly, in the context of the facts here, the only rational distinction lies between bona fide and fraudulent transactions because it is only in the case of a bona fide transaction that anyone other than the faithless employee may be said to have supplied the name of the payee to the company." (*New Amsterdam Cas. Co.*, supra, at 897, 898)

Thus, although the court decided that Section 3–405(1)(c) of the Uniform Commercial Code was applicable to the facts of that case as presented to it, the court clearly stated that this was only because a fraudulent transaction had been involved. If a bona fide business transaction had been the basis for the issuance of the checks in question, the court indicated that it would have found differently.

This court believes that if the plaintiff in Board of Higher Education v. Banker's Trust Co., supra, had seriously contested the applicability of Section 3–405(1)(c) of the Uniform Commercial Code to the facts of that case, the New York Court would have been forced to distinguish between the genuine checks retained by the employee and the duplicate checks which she caused to be issued.

In our instant case, the checks involved were based upon bona fide transactions and obligations of the plaintiff which arose out of the normal business relationship with the payee named on said checks. In such instance, it cannot be claimed that the employee, Caulder, supplied his employer, Danje, with the name of the payee, Dyers, as said checks were legitimately based upon open invoices due and owing to the payee, Dyers.

Accordingly, on the basis of the fact pattern existing in our instant case considered along with the cases herein discussed and the manner in which those respective courts arrived at their conclusions, defendant's motion for summary judgment is denied and plaintiff's cross-motion for summary judgment against defendant, Morgan, is granted.

Morgan's cross claim against Citibank based upon Citibank's prior endorsements, as the collecting bank, of the checks in question and Citibank's admitted liability under its warranties as set forth in Section 4–207 of the Uniform Commercial Code is also granted.

Notes

(1) **Rationale of UCC 3–405.** Comment 1 to UCC 3–405 explains that the section "adopts the principle that the risk of loss for fraudulent indorsements by employees who are entrusted with responsibility with respect to checks should fall on the employer rather than the bank that takes the check or pays it, if the bank was not negligent in the transaction. Section 3–405 is based on the belief that the employer is in a far better position to avoid the loss by care in choosing employees, in supervising them, and in adopting other measures to prevent forged indorsements on instruments payable to the employer or fraud in the issuance of instruments in the name of the employer."

How would *Danje Fabrics* have been decided under UCC 3–405? Would UCC 3–405 apply to *Thompson Maple Products,* supra? (Was Albers an "employee" of Thompson? Did he have the requisite "responsibility"?)

(2) **Comparative Negligence.** Note that for the case in which the payor bank fails to exercise ordinary care, UCC 3–405(b) introduces a comparative negligence rule like that in UCC 3–404(d), 3–406(b), and 4–406(e).

(3) **Suit by Drawer Against Depositary Bank (Reprise).** We saw earlier (see Note 2, p. 314 supra) that under UCC 3–420 the drawer of a check paid over a forged indorsement has no action against the depositary bank for conversion. The drawer's recourse is against the payor bank. But what if the indorsement, though forged, is effective under UCC 3–404(b) or 3–405, so that the drawer has no recourse against the payor bank?

UCC 3–404(d) and 3–405(b) both provide that if the depositary bank has failed to exercise ordinary care and if that failure has substantially contributed to the loss, the drawer may recover from the depositary bank "to the extent the failure to exercise ordinary care contributed to the loss." For an illustration of the application of these rules, see Comment 4 to UCC 3–405; see also Comment 3 to UCC 3–404.

(4) **Subrogation of Insurer.** "It would be natural to assume upon a determination first of the allocation of loss among the parties in the absence of insurance, and then of the coverage of that loss by forgery or fidelity insurance, that the problem of the ultimate allocation of the loss among all the parties including insurers would be finally resolved. But this is not so because of the further question of subrogation of the insurer to the insured's rights against innocent third parties. Clearly both forgery and fidelity bonds, as forms of indemnity insurance, insure against the original loss, regardless of whether the insured may have the right to recover from the wrongdoer or from an innocent third party. Thus, for example, an insured drawer may recover from his insurer under a depositor's forgery or a fidelity bond on forged checks

written by an employee, even though he could have recovered from either the employee or the drawee bank. To be sure, as soon as the loss occurs, the insurer stands in the position of a surety with the wrongdoer as principal, and upon payment of that loss the insurer is subrogated to the insured's rights against the wrongdoer. Since this is usually a remedy of no great promise, the insurer will turn to the insured's claim against the drawee bank. The right of the insurer to enforce this claim has most frequently been viewed as that of a surety to be subrogated to the creditor's (the drawer's) rights against an innocent third party (the bank)." Farnsworth, Insurance Against Check Forgery, 60 Colum.L.Rev. 284, 316 (1960). Some cases have denied subrogation on the ground that the surety, having been paid by the drawer, is a "compensated surety." They are discussed and criticized in the cited article.

IMPOSTORS

Since the inception of the Code, the impostor rule has appeared in form as a Siamese twin of the fictitious payee rule, the two rules inseparably connected in the same section, initially in former UCC 3–405 and now in UCC 3–404. Yet in function the two rules have little in common, except to put the risk of a forged indorsement on the drawer.

As we have just seen, the primary function of the fictitious payee rule today is to shift the risk of employee dishonesty from the payor bank to the employer, which can guard against that risk by obtaining a fidelity bond. The primary function of the impostor rule is to shift the risk of confidence games practiced on the drawer from the payor bank to the gullible drawer, who has no available means of insuring against this risk.

We saw earlier that, under a similar impostor rule in UCC 2–403(1)(a), an owner of goods who was "conned" out of them by an impostor bore the loss as against a good faith purchaser who took them from the impostor. Is the impostor rule of UCC 3–404(a) as well founded? Is it significant that even a gullible drawer of a check expects to have the genuine indorsement of the payee, an expectation that has no counterpart in the sale of goods?

Problem 15. Cecil Conn approached Kim Kaller, Empire's treasurer, impersonating J.J. Sterling, a reputable merchant. Kaller drew a $5,000 check payable to Sterling as an advance payment for goods that Conn, as Sterling, promised to furnish to Empire. Conn indorsed it in Sterling's name, and The Bank of New York paid it and charged it to Empire's account. Conn absconded with the proceeds. Does Empire have a claim against The Bank of New York? See UCC 3–404(a). Would it make a difference if Kaller had drawn the check payable to "Sterling Industries, Inc." rather than to Sterling? What if Conn had not impersonated Sterling but had claimed to be the new president of

"Sterling Industries, Inc.," to which Kaller had made the check payable?

Note

Impersonation and Agency. UCC 3–404(a) covers impersonation not only of the payee but also of "a person authorized to act for the payee." The impostor rule of former UCC 3–405 did not go so far, as Comment 2 to that section made clear. " 'Impostor' refers to impersonation, and does not extend to a false representation that the party is the authorized agent of the payee. The maker or drawer who takes the precaution of making the instrument payable to the principal is entitled to have his indorsement."

Comment 1 to UCC 3–404 explains that subsection (a) "changes the former law in a case in which the impostor is impersonating an agent. Under former Section 3–305(1)(a), if ... Impostor impersonated Smith, the president of Smith Corporation, and the check was payable to the order of Smith Corporation, the section did not apply.... In revised Article 3, Section 3–404(a) gives Impostor the power to negotiate the check...." Was it wise to extend a rule of questionable justification to marginal cases? Does the extension cover the case, referred to in the former comment, of "a false representation that the party is the authorized agent of the payee"? Does such a false representation necessarily involve impersonation?

*

Part III

SALES TRANSACTIONS: DOMESTIC AND INTERNATIONAL LAW

INTRODUCTION

Our concern now shifts from payment by buyers to the distribution of goods by sellers. The fascination of the subject results in part from its astonishing variety: complex contracts negotiated between economic giants and clauses signed by unsuspecting consumers; face-to-face deals and cabled arrangements for imports and exports; sales "cash on the barrelhead" (facilitated by sophisticated banking devices) and sales on long-term credit. Such wild variations place heavy strain on the rules of law and on the ingenuity of counsellors.

This part centers on the performance of sales contracts. What quality of goods must the seller supply? How must shipment and delivery be handled? At what point must buyer pay for the goods? If the goods are destroyed, can the seller recover the price from the buyer or must the seller take the loss? If there is insurance, who gets the proceeds of the policy? One party becomes insolvent: can the other party get the goods? Goods obtained by fraud or theft are resold: who bears the loss? In dealing with hazards such as these, we need to take into account not only legal rules but also relevant commercial practices. Throughout, we must consider ways in which counselling may avoid some of these difficulties.

Scope of Article 2. Before looking at specific topics under Article 2, it is prudent to ask: What is the scope of Article 2? To what transactions does it apply? Article 2 itself declares that it "applies to transactions in goods." UCC 2–102. The principal transaction, reflected in the title of Article 2, is "sales." [1] The principal actors are "buyers," defined somewhat tautologically in UCC 2–103(1)(a), and "sellers," similarly defined in (1)(d). A "sale" is "the passing of title [to goods] from the seller to the buyer for a price." UCC 2–106(1). "Sales" result from "contracts for sale," defined in the same section and divided into "present sales" and "future sales." For the most part, these

---

1. Language purists might wonder why the simplified nomenclature is a noun derived from the sellers' side of transactions that are necessarily two-sided. The trans-actions could have been denominated "purchases" or, evenhandedly, "purchases and sales." Under much weight of history, the short form title, however, is simply "sales."

elementary concepts have clear meanings that do not often blur at the edges.

That cannot be said of "goods," the object of "sales," which has a clear core of meaning but bristles with difficulties in many settings. The Code defines "goods" as "all things (including specially manufactured goods) which are movable at the time of identification to the contract for sale other than the money in which the price is to be paid, investment securities (Article 8) and things in action." UCC 2–105(1).[2]

(*Query*: Are contracts between a utility and its customers for supply of electric power contracts for the sale of goods? See Singer Co. v. Baltimore Gas and Electric Co., 79 Md.App. 461, 558 A.2d 419 (1989).)

Goods and Services. Article 2 does not govern transactions in services, which remain essentially common-law contracts. Obviously, many familiar transactions require one party to deliver goods and render services for a single price. Would Article 2 or common law govern? Should the contracts be divided, with different law governing its parts, or should transactions treated by the parties as indivisible be placed entirely under or outside Article 2? The Code gives no guidance to the parties or the courts.[3] Not surprisingly, the result has been much unsatisfactory litigation.

Consider, for example, a contract to supply and install the structural steel necessary for a bridge. In one such case, three levels of the New York courts struggled inconclusively with the question of characterization; in the end, the Court of Appeals bypassed the issue on the view that the questions presented in that case would be decided the same way whether or not Article 2 applied. Schenectady Steel Co. v. Bruno Trimpoli General Construction Co., 34 N.Y.2d 939, 359 N.Y.S.2d 560, 316 N.E.2d 875 (1974).

Not all difficult cases can be so finessed. Driven to solve the problem, courts may treat contracts as divisible if that is feasible and, if not, tend to choose the governing law by measuring whether the goods or the services component is economically more dominant.[4] Compare

---

2. See Annot., What constitutes "goods" within the scope of UCC Article 2, 4 ALR 4th 912.

3. The Code does address transactions in which sellers perform services in contracts to manufacture goods to buyers' specifications. The definition of "goods" in UCC 2–105(1) expressly includes specially manufactured goods. In special-order contracts, typically the services would be performed at seller's place of business before the goods were tendered to buyer. See, e.g., California and Hawaiian Sugar Co. v. Sun Ship, Inc., 794 F.2d 1433 (9th Cir.1986) (construction of ocean-going barge).

4. Determining the relative value of the elements of sales/service transactions is more difficult than might first appear. In-

creasingly, the value of the physical elements of goods has diminished relative to the value of the technology or information needed to manufacture or process them. Consider the ubiquitous semi-conductor chip, essential for so many high-tech products. The raw materials in these chips have almost no economic value; value comes from the intelligence embedded in the chips. The value of the raw materials in a modern automobile, sold for many thousands of dollars, is a few hundred dollars. For many goods, it is not a mistake to say that their value represents "congealed services." Would it be feasible or desirable to make the applicability of Article 2 depend upon weighing manufacturers' costs of materials and labor?

Long Island Lighting Co. v. Transamerica Delaval, Inc., 646 F.Supp. 1442 (S.D.N.Y.1986), with Lucien Bourque, Inc. v. Cronkite, 557 A.2d 193 (Me.1989); see also Annot., Applicability of UCC Article 2 to mixed contracts for sale of goods and services, 5 ALR 4th 501.

(*Query:* Is a contract for sale of a "turn-key" computer system that includes hardware, software, installation and post-installation service governed by Article 2? See Neilson Business Equipment Center, Inc. v. Italo V. Monteleone, M.D., P.A., 524 A.2d 1172 (Del.1987). Is a contract to design and install a computer program in the buyer's existing hardware governed by Article 2?)

If these matters were to be resolved by statute, what would be a good Code solution?

Goods and Real Property. The line between real property and goods is necessarily somewhat artificial. Movability, the essential characteristic of things defined to be goods, is not uncharacteristic of land. Rocks and soil can be moved; top soil, gravel and "fill" are regularly bought and sold. The Code brings into Article 2 some things that are, by the terms of a contract, to be severed by the seller, including specifically minerals, growing crops, and timber. UCC 2–107(1). See, e.g., Manchester Pipeline Corp. v. Peoples Natural Gas Co., 862 F.2d 1439 (10th Cir.1988).

The Code is also helpful in characterizing transactions that go the other way, goods that are, by terms of a contract, to be affixed to realty. So long as the things are movable at the time of identification to a contract for sale, they are "goods" under UCC 2–105(1). The time of "identification" is set forth in UCC 2–501(1). Under this provision, a thing to be affixed to real estate is almost certain to be identified to the goods contract while still movable.

Contracts may involve transfer of both real estate and goods for a single price, the analogue of transactions in goods and services. Consider, for example, the sale of a new house in which the builder-developer has installed a stove, a refrigerator, other appliances and fixtures. Real estate sales are governed by common law.[5] Should Article 2 apply to any part of the contract?

(*Query:* Suppose the owner of a business, such as a jewelry store, contracts to sell all of the assets of the business, including the inventory, the display cases, the accounts receivable, the trade name under which the store has operated and other "goodwill," and the balance of a lease on the building. Is the contract governed by Article 2?)

Scope of CISG. In Part III we will be concerned not only with domestic sales under Article 2 but with international sales under the

---

One macroeconomic effect of the diminishing value of materials used to make goods has been a long term decline in the market value of primary commodities like copper, tin, iron, aluminum, rubber, etc. Economies of nations that depend upon extractive industries have suffered significantly.

5. The Commissioners on Uniform State Laws promulgated a Uniform Land Transactions Act in 1977. No state has adopted this act.

Convention on Contracts for the International Sale of Goods (CISG). What is the scope of CISG? The Convention provides that it "applies to contracts of sale of goods between parties whose places of business are in different States ... when the States are Contracting States," but does not apply to sales of goods "bought for personal, family or household use." CISG 1(a)[6] and 2(a).[7]

A nation becomes a Contracting State by ratification, acceptance, approval or accession. (We must adapt to the international usage of "state" to mean nation.) The nuances of these terms are not important for our purposes. The United States became a Contracting State when the Senate gave its advice and consent to the President's signing of the Convention.

Place of Business. Some parties to international sales contracts may have only one place of business, but many have more than one. When a party to a contract has more than one place of business, CISG refers to the place "which has the closest relationship to the contract and its performance." CISG 10(a).[8]

Goods, Seller and Buyer. CISG offers no definition of "goods." Indeed, the Convention defines none of the terms used in it. Although ships, vessels, hovercraft or aircraft are probably "goods," the Convention excludes sales of them from its scope. CISG 2(e). While investment securities, negotiable instruments and money are unlikely to be deemed "goods," sales of these are also expressly excluded by CISG 2(d).

The Convention defines neither "seller" nor "buyer," but sales by auction, on execution or otherwise by authority of law are expressly excluded from its scope. CISG 2(b) and (c).

Goods and Services. Unlike the Commercial Code, the Convention expressly recognizes contracts for mixed goods and services. CISG provides that it does not apply if "the preponderant part of the obligations of the party who furnishes the goods consists in the supply of labour and other services." CISG 3(2). Like the Commercial Code, CISG includes within its scope contracts for the supply of goods to be manufactured or produced, with a proviso that excludes any contract in which the buyer supplies a substantial part of the materials necessary for such manufacture or production. CISG 3(1).

Goods and Real Property. The Convention is silent on contracts for extraction or severance of property from real estate or for affixing property to real estate.

6. The Convention may apply to contracts when only one party's place of business is in a Contracting State if the choice of law rules of private international law lead to the application of the law of a Contracting State. CISG 1(b). Nations are permitted to ratify the Convention without agreeing to be bound by Article 1(b), and the United States has done so.

7. Contracts for consumer goods may be governed by the Convention if the seller neither knew nor ought to have known that they were bought for that purpose.

8. If a party has no place of business, applicability is determined by the party's "habitual residence." CISG 10(b).

Chapter 6

QUALITY AND TITLE: SELLERS' RESPONSIBILITY AND BUYERS' RIGHTS

SECTION 1. INTRODUCTION

Historical Background. The scope of sellers' responsibility to buyers has passed through a remarkable evolution of a curiously cyclical character. In the Middle Ages the authority of the Church and of guilds combined to impose heavy standards of quality upon sellers.[1] Thereafter, as we shall see, English law came to afford but little protection to buyers: *caveat emptor!* This outlook, in turn, has been reversed in modern law, but quaint language in current statutes cannot be understood without some appreciation of this development.

The law of sales is here, as at so many points, enmeshed with the larger body of contract law. Students of the development of contracts will recall the reluctance of early courts to enforce simple promises; in a static land economy, legal obligations were not to be assumed lightly. Although the specific undertakings in a document bearing the maker's seal received early legal protection, less formal undertakings had to wait for the ancient action "on the case" to develop beyond its tort ancestry into its contractual descendant, the action of special assumpsit.

The reluctance to give legal effect to simple informal statements is illustrated by the famous 1625 decision of Chandelor v. Lopus [2] in which a buyer brought an action on the case against a goldsmith for affirming that a stone he sold the buyer was a "bezoar" (or "bezar"), a stone found in the alimentary organs of goats and supposed to have remarkable medicinal qualities. (How the plaintiff proved that this was not a "true" bezoar does not appear.) The Exchequer Chamber ruled, after verdict for the plaintiff, that the declaration based on this affirmation was insufficient: " ... the bare affirmation that it was a bezar stone, without warranting it to be so is no cause of action." [3] Just how far the seller had to go to "warrant" was not stated; apparently he had to

---

1. Hamilton, The Ancient Maxim Caveat Emptor, 40 Yale L.J. 1133 (1931).

2. Cro. Jac. 4, 79 Eng. Rep. 3 (1625).

3. In view of the peculiar nature of the commodity, it may be worthwhile to record the further statement of the judges that, " ... every one in selling wares will affirm that his wares are good, or the horse which he sells is sound."

make an explicit statement like "I warrant that ..." or "I agree to be bound that...."

It is striking to find this curious decision dominating the New York court's thinking in the 1804 commercial case of Seixas v. Woods.[4] A dealer advertised and sold wood as "brazilletto," a wood valuable for manufacturing a chemical used in making dye; in fact the wood was worthless "peachum." A judgment for the buyer was reversed. Chancellor Kent's concurring opinion stated: "The mentioning the word, as Brazilletto wood, in the bill of parcels, and in the advertisement some days previous to the sale, did not amount to a warranty to the plaintiffs. To make an affirmation at the time of the sale, a warranty, it must appear by evidence to be so *intended,* and not to have been a mere matter of judgment and opinion, and of which the defendant had no particular knowledge. Here it is admitted, the defendant was equally ignorant with the plaintiffs, and could have had no such intention." [5]

Before many decades passed, cases like these were overturned. The *Seixas* ("brazilletto") case was rejected in New York in a 1872 case involving a dealer who bought barrels of "blue vitriol" and innocently resold them as such: when the material proved to be "salzburger vitriol" (a less valuable commodity) the dealer was held liable to the purchaser.[6] The opinions in such cases usually did not discuss the reasons of policy that produced the change in approach, but one may surmise that a greater volume and speed of trade called for firmer protection for contractual expectations. True, the dealer who resold may have been misled by its supplier; but the rule of law that made the dealer liable for its representations would normally give the dealer recourse against the supplier; certainly it would be difficult for the ultimate purchaser to recover from the dealer's supplier.[7]

When Professor Williston came to draft the Uniform Sales Act, one of his principal targets was the emphasis which some cases placed on the seller's "intent"—an offensive manifestation of a "subjective" view of contracts.[8] To obliterate this approach, Section 12 of the Uniform Sales Act provided: "Any affirmation of fact or any promise by the seller relating to the goods is an express warranty if the *natural*

---

4. 2 Caines 48 (1804).

5. Chief Justice Gibson, of Pennsylvania, used characteristically salty (and extreme) language to similar effect in McFarland v. Newman, 9 Watts 55 (Pa.1839). Gibson also drew a questionable analogy between a sale of goods and the deed for real estate. "A sale is a contract executed, on which, of course, no action can be directly founded." [Why not?] He added that warranty is "no more a part of the sale than the covenant of warranty in a deed is part of the conveyance." [Is it possible at the same time to convey property and undertake contractual obligations?]

6. Hawkins v. Pemberton, 51 N.Y. 198 (1872).

7. This practical point was emphasized in Jones v. Just, L.R. 3 Q.B. 197 (1868). Defendant sellers argued that they had relied on the selection of the goods by a supplier in Singapore; Mellor, J., replied that defendant sellers "had recourse against [the supplier] for not supplying an article reasonably merchantable."

8. The Commissioners' Note to USA 12 referred to the "intent" concept and stated that " ... the fundamental basis for liability on warranty is the justifiable reliance on the seller's assertions."

tendency of such affirmation or promise is to induce the buyer to purchase the goods, and if the buyer purchases the goods *relying thereon.*"[9] This language was well chosen to focus attention on the crucial question of reasonable reliance by the buyer on the seller's statements. This formulation also foreclosed difficult (and unprofitable) litigation over whether the seller's statement was a "promise" or an "affirmation of fact."

The Code in Section 2–313(1)(a) closely follows the above provision of the Uniform Sales Act. However, there is one puzzling change: There is no reference to reliance by the buyer; instead, an affirmation or a promise is an express warranty if it "becomes part of the basis of the bargain." The meaning of this phrase will be explored later.

Types of Warranties. It is orthodox learning, carried forward by the Uniform Sales Act and the Uniform Commercial Code, that warranties come in various "types." "Express" warranties (UCC 2–313) are to be distinguished from warranties that are "implied." Implied warranties of quality fall in two statutory categories: "merchantable quality" (UCC 2–314), and "fitness for particular purpose" (UCC 2–315).

Consider a simple example of each of the three types of warranties. *Case 1:* B and S, a Chevrolet dealer, sign an agreement of sale for a "new Corvair." After delivery, B discovers that the car had been used as a demonstrator with the odometer disconnected. *Case 2:* A car purchased by B has a defective crankshaft that promptly breaks. *Case 3:* B tells S, a paint dealer, that he wants paint for the outside of his house. S puts on the counter a can of "Lustro" which B buys. This paint is good for interior walls but is washed from exterior walls by the first rain. *Case 1* involves an express warranty (UCC 2–313), *Case 2* the warranty of merchantable quality (UCC 2–314), and *Case 3* the warranty of fitness for particular purpose (UCC 2–315).

In spite of the complexity and diversity of these statutory provisions it may help to consider whether they may be related—and possibly inspired by a common principle. For example, suppose that, just before the purchase, the seller had been asked these questions: In *Case 1*, "Has anyone been driving this car before?" In *Case 2*, "Is the crankshaft sound?" In *Case 3*, "Will the paint stand up under a rain?" Would the seller normally have given the undertakings requested by the buyer? If the seller had refused, would the buyer have purchased the goods?

Do buyers normally articulate such questions? If not, why not? Because they are unimportant? Or because the answers "go without saying"?[10] As we watch the *results* (as contrasted with the language) of the cases it will be useful to analyze the degree of kinship between the

---

9. USA 12 also included a sentence dealing with statements as to "value" or "opinion." This troublesome provision, and its overgrown offspring in UCC 2–313(2) will be considered later.

10. Are there analogous situations, outside the law of sale, where legal effect is given to understandings and expectations that are real, but normally are not fully expressed?

terms of the contract (including "express" warranties) and the various "types" of "implied" warranties.[11]

These seemingly simple-minded questions have larger impact than might be evident at first glance, for the answers may be relevant not only in defining the scope of a seller's undertaking but also in determining the effectiveness of contract terms purporting to disclaim and limit "warranties." These questions may even be relevant to the border warfare between the "fields" of sales (contract) and tort.

Commercial and Consumer Parties. With few exceptions, warranty law emerged historically in transactions between merchant buyers and merchant sellers, such as the "brazilletto" wood and the "blue vitriol" cases. (The most notable exception was horse trading, perhaps one of the earliest consumer goods transactions.) The commercial aspect of the cases explains the use of "merchantable" in the basic implied warranty of quality. Transactions between business sellers and business buyers, usually corporations, continue to be important in warranty law. Also important are warranties in sales of consumer products sold by retail dealers and bought by individuals for personal, family or household use. Consumer product warranties emerged initially on the same legal principles fashioned for commercial goods, but, increasingly, laws protective of ordinary consumers have become a special subpart of warranty law. The most litigated consumer product transactions involve retail sales of new cars, the modern counterpart of horse trading.[12]

Buyers' Monetary Remedies. The basic remedial principle of contract law applies in warranty cases. Aggrieved buyers are entitled to the benefit of their bargains. In simplest terms, this means that buyers' monetary recovery for breach of warranty is measured by the value of goods that would have met sellers' obligation. Since buyers commonly have received goods of *some* value and keep those goods, their value must be subtracted from the value of goods as warranted. One finds this formula in UCC 2–714(2).[13]

---

11. Randall v. Newson, 2 Q.B. 102 (Court of Appeal, 1877) held a seller liable on the sale of a defective carriage pole. Lord Justice Brett, after referring to various types of warranties that had been mentioned in earlier opinions, stated: "The governing principle ... is that the thing offered and delivered under a contract of purchase and sale must answer the description of it which is contained in words in the contract, or which would be so contained if the contract were accurately drawn out." This unified approach, however, was not sufficiently dominant in the English cases to be reflected in the drafting of the Sale of Goods Act. As a result, the different "types" of warranties, developed in the typical case-law process of distinguishing unwanted precedents, were cast into statutory form, and were carried into

the Uniform Sales Act and on into the Sales article of the Code. The Code does provide, however, that "warranties whether express or implied shall be construed as consistent with each other and as cumulative...." UCC 2–317.

12. Consumers are also frequent sellers, as occurs when a consumer "trades in" an existing car (or other "durable" good) on purchase of a new car (or good).

13. "Value" in this formulation means "market value" or "market price," the amounts that informed sellers and buyers have set or would have set for goods of the different levels of quality. In active markets for goods of the kind, "market price" is a statistical compilation of many actual contract prices. Where no active market of the precise goods exists, "value" must be

The market-oriented formula of UCC 2–714(2) is not an exclusive measure of buyers' damages. Buyers may seek recovery measured "in any manner which is reasonable." UCC 2–714(1). If the quality non-conformity is correctable, a buyer may seek to recover the cost of repairing the defect.[14]

Buyers who accepted goods with non-conformities may not be "made whole" by monetary recovery measured only by the value of goods as warranted or by the cost of repair. The Code authorizes buyers, "in a proper case," to recover "incidental damages" (UCC 2–715(1)) and "consequential damages." UCC 2–715(2). Potential liability for consequential damages is a major risk that faces buyers and sellers in some sales transactions. Sellers frequently seek to "contract out" of this potential liability. We will return to that subject later in this chapter.[15]

SECTION 2. WARRANTIES OF QUALITY: EXPRESS AND IMPLIED

(A) DOMESTIC SALES LAW

T.J. STEVENSON & CO. v. 81,193 BAGS OF FLOUR
United States Court of Appeals, Fifth Circuit, 1980.
629 F.2d 338, rehearing denied, 651 F.2d 77 (5th Cir.1981).

BROWN, C.J. With this decision we hopefully end, in all but a minor respect, an amphibious imbroglio and commercial law practitioner's nightmare involving three shiploads of enriched wheat flour. By a coincidence in this confusing case, each shipload of flour became infested, to varying degrees, with confused (*triboleum confusam*) and red rust (*triboleum casteneum*) flour beetles (sometimes called weevils). None of the parties involved—seller, buyer, and carrier—acted faultlessly over the course of the transaction. All brought their differences to the able District Judge for resolution. The District Judge carefully consid-

determined by extrapolation from other transactions. Sometimes this is done by expert appraisers.

14. See, e.g., Wat Henry Pontiac Co. v. Bradley, 202 Okl. 82, 210 P.2d 348 (1949) (pre-Code case). The reasonableness limitation no doubt precludes recovery of repair costs that greatly exceed the value added to a non-conforming product. Students may recall studying this as a common-law principle of damages in cases like Peevyhouse v. Garland Coal & Mining Co.,

382 P.2d 109 (Okl. 1962); Plante v. Jacobs, 10 Wis.2d 567, 103 N.W.2d 296 (1960).

15. Section 2–714 provides measures of recovery for buyers in regard to accepted goods, goods that belong to the buyers. A quite different measure of recovery is needed when goods have not been accepted by a buyer or, if accepted, are returned to the seller. Warranty law is deeply involved in such transactions, but we shall defer consideration of them until later when we deal with remedies under sales contracts.

ered five weeks of testimony presented by the parties, their numerous pleadings, motions, briefs and arguments, scores of interlocking mixed law-fact issues, and difficult questions of federal civil procedure, state commercial, and admiralty law. The Judge's careful and lengthy opinion, 449 F.Supp. 84 (S.D.Ala.1976), resolved the imbroglio but failed to fully convince the parties. The District Judge convinced us, however, and we affirm in almost all respects. Without pause to reflect on the complications that simple insects—confused flour beetles or otherwise—can create in the lives of men and Courts, we proceed to explain our decision.

I. The Life–Cycle of This Appeal: Inception,
Growth, and Development

A. The Documents

In April 1974 the Republic of Bolivia entered into two contracts for the purchase of 28,618 metric tons of American enriched wheat flour from ADM Milling Co. ADM owns a number of mills throughout the Midwest. Bolivia sought the flour for distribution to her citizens. The contracts were prepared on ADM's standard form, with quantity, chemical specifications, price, mode of shipment, payment terms, and delivery details filled in. The contracts required packing the flour in 100 pound capacity cotton bags and delivering it to Mobile, Alabama. Railcar shipment was contemplated to Mobile, followed by ocean carriage to South America. This was to take place from May to September 1974. The contracts contained the following delivery terms: "F.A.S. MOBILE, ALABAMA, for export;" and "Delivery of goods by SELLER to the carrier at point of shipment shall constitute delivery to BUYER. ..." Upon satisfactory delivery, the price was payable by irrevocable letter of credit.

Each contract contained an express warranty of merchantability:

Except as provided on the reverse side, SELLER MAKES NO WARRANTY, EXPRESS OR IMPLIED, THAT EXTENDS BEYOND THE DESCRIPTION ON THE FACE HEREOF, except that the product sold hereunder shall be of merchantable quality. ...

[The contracts of sale contained explicit specifications as to protein, ash and moisture content of the flour. There were no specifications as to insect infestation. The buyer agreed to pay the $6.6 million purchase price by a letter of credit, which was payable upon seller's presentation of documents, including an independent firm's certificate of quality concerning the protein, ash and moisture content of the flour immediately prior to loading on ships in Mobile. Seller engaged the services of an inspection firm to sample and evaluate the flour and to prepare certificates of quality.

[Full performance of the contract required eight shiploads of flour to be transported from Mobile to South America. No major problems arose with the first five shipments, which were shipped and paid for.

[As the sixth and seventh shipments were being loaded, the inspection firm noticed signs of infestation. The flour loaded on these vessels was fumigated to kill live insects and both ships sailed to South America. The inspection firm issued certificates stating that the flour complied with the contractual requirements and seller obtained payment under the letter of credit (approximately $1.7 million) for these two shiploads. As the flour was being unloaded at the port in Chile, buyer discovered live and dead weevils. Buyer refused to take possession of the flour. Buyer and seller subsequently agreed that buyer would take possession and sell the infested flour through a salvage broker in Bolivia. The net proceeds of this resale were $326,000 less than the contract price.

[Meanwhile, the eighth shipment was being loaded in Mobile. The inspection firm noticed that some of this flour was infested and these lots were fumigated before loading. After loading, the shipping company, on its own initiative, engaged an inspector to determine whether the cargo was infested. The buyer learned the results of that inspection report and declared it would not accept the shipment; the buyer also blocked the seller from obtaining payment under the letter of credit of the contract price ($850,000) for this final shipment. The shipment never went to South America. Seller eventually took it off the ship and sold it for $454,000 to a United States manufacturer of ceiling tiles.

[The District Court, sitting without a jury, found that the sixth, seventh and eighth shipments of flour had become infested either at the plants where it had been milled or on the rail cars used to transport the flour to Mobile. The court concluded that the flour in these shipments was unmerchantable and that buyer, therefore, had rightfully rejected them. On buyer's claim for damages for the sixth and seventh shipments, judgment was entered for buyer in the amount of $325,960.51. On seller's claim for the price of the eighth shipment, judgment was for the buyer.]

B. The Warranty

The District Judge held that the flour in each of the three shipments failed to meet the express warranty provisions of the contracts. ADM expressly warranted that the bagged flour would be "of merchantable quality" and that it would "comply with all of the applicable provisions of the Federal Food, Drug and Cosmetic Act ['FDA']." The District Judge decided that the infested flour breached both warranties. We, however, pretermit analysis of the FDA warranty since it is difficult to interpret and unnecessary to our resolution of this case. Instead we examine only ADM's warranty of merchantability.

The Code defines the minimum standards required of "merchantable" goods:

> Goods to be merchantable must be at least such as ...

(c) are fit for the ordinary purposes for which such goods are used....

UCC § 2–314(2) (emphasis supplied). Like the District Judge we consider only the subsection (c) portion of that definition, and do not reach the arguably applicable standards of subsections (a) and (b). The question is therefore whether the flour at various critical points in time was "fit for the ordinary purposes for which such goods are used."

Official Comments 2 and 8 provide helpful clues to divining the parties' intent (emphasis supplied):

> 2. The question when the warranty is imposed turns basically on the meaning of the terms of the agreement as recognized in the trade. Goods delivered under an agreement made by a merchant in a given line of trade *must be of a quality comparable to that generally acceptable in that line of trade under the description or other designation of the goods used in the agreement.*

. . .

> 8. Fitness for the ordinary purposes for which goods of the type are used is a fundamental concept of the present section and is covered in paragraph (c). As stated above, merchantability is also a part of the obligation owing to the purchaser for use. Correspondingly, protection, under this aspect of the warranty, of the person buying for resale to the ultimate consumer is equally necessary, and *merchantable goods must therefore be "honestly" resalable in the normal course of business because they are what they purport to be.*

These comments amplify what is implicit in the statute: "fit for ordinary purposes" merchantability is an ambiguous phrase which has little meaning unless trade usage and other extrinsic evidence is considered. A substantial amount of extrinsic evidence was accordingly admitted and considered by the District Judge in evaluating ADM's warranty of merchantability.

Before reviewing the facts, we observe that finding what the parties meant by "merchantability" requires some evaluation of standards in the commercial market and the state of the art in flour manufacturing. The merchantability of infested flour to be sold to consumers is a question of degree and kind. We have often recognized that no food is completely pure.[23] The FDA has long permitted very small amounts of insect fragments and other *dead* infestation in food products. To declare that any contamination of flour—even by small amounts of insect fragments, renders the flour unmerchantable would no doubt be out of step with commercial reality and would wreak havoc on food manufacturers and distributors while affording little or no additional protection to the consumer. What this case involves, however, is significant amounts of *live* infestation, by flour beetle eggs, larvae, pupae, and adults. Here the question is: How much live infestation

---

23. "A scientist with a microscope could find its filthy, putrid, and decomposed substances in almost any canned food we eat." United States v. 484 Bags, More or Less, supra, 423 F.2d at 841 (quoting United States v. 1,500 Cases, More or Less, 236 F.2d 208, 211 (7th Cir.1956)).

renders consumer-destined flour unfit for the ordinary purposes for which it is used?

The record in this case contains a number of relatively undisputed facts that shed light on the meaning of "merchantable" flour. First, flour beetle infestation in flour mills is an ever present and difficult to eliminate problem. Some flour buyers, such as the United States Government, have however been able to keep infestation problems in their flour to a bare minimum by using their own inspectors to test the flour during its manufacture and at various points thereafter. Also, the relatively stringent precautions taken in ADM-operated mills have reduced infestation problems in their flour to a very great degree. The record further shows that flour containing live infestation, though possibly not dead remains, must be completely fumigated before it can be sold to consumers. Such fumigation is, however, not a normal preparation undertaken by flour buyers. In this context, the fact that the flour involved in the instant case had to be fumigated takes on great significance. Cf. UCC § 1–205(1). As the District Judge stated, "Clearly, if wheat flour found to be infested with beetles would have passed the above [merchantable quality] test . . ., there would have been no need for the flour to have been fumigated. . . ." 449 F.Supp. at 126. We believe that the District Judge's observation closely tracks the Official Comments' statement that goods intended for resale to consumers, as here, are not merchantable unless " 'honestly' resalable in the normal course of business." The evidence in sum indicates that consumer-intended flour containing substantial amounts of live infestation is not merchantable under prevailing standards.

We are not aware of any precedent, in Illinois or elsewhere, which considers the issue of merchantability under circumstances similar to the instant case. . . .

Judicial interpretation, trade usage, and course of dealing point to but one conclusion as to flour infested with significant amounts of live flour beetles: although the flour may be "fit for human consumption" in the sense that it can be eaten without causing sickness, it is nonetheless not of merchantable quality. Such flour is not what is normally expected in the trade. It is not what ADM agreed to supply to Bolivia. Our holding is a narrow one. We do not say, for example, that one live beetle egg in a batch of 10,000 bags of flour renders that flour unmerchantable. Nor do we decide the merchantability of flour containing dead infestation in large or small amounts. Furthermore, we construe only the merchantability standard for flour which will be resold to consumers, not for flour sold directly to consumers. Finally, we emphasize that merchantability is an evolving standard, so that what is unmerchantable at one time and on one record may not be so in another case. In sum, we conclude that the District Judge was not erroneous in finding that the infested flour was not in conformity with ADM's warranty of merchantability. . . .

[Judgment affirmed.]

Notes

(1) Contract Interpretation. (a) The court's legal task was to interpret the express undertaking that the wheat flour would be "merchantable." The court turns to the Commercial Code, UCC 2–314, to search for the meaning of the contract term. Was this justifiable? The court relies particularly on Comments to 2–314. Is it likely that the representatives of the Bolivian government or of ADM Milling Co. were familiar with the Code or the Comments when the contract was drawn?

(b) The court also adverted to "standards in the commercial market" and "the state of the art in flour manufacturing." Did the court see these as significant to the meaning of UCC 2–314? The court noted that some buyers send their own inspectors to their sellers' plants to test flour being processed. Is this indicative of the quality standards in the marketplace?

(c) The court found that seller used relatively stringent precautions in its own mills and that this reduced infestation problems to a very great degree. The trial court opinion revealed that this was the flour in the first five shipments. ADM Milling Co. lacked capacity to mill the entire amount of the contract and contracted to buy the remainder from other milling companies. Is this relevant to determination of the seller's responsibility?

(d) Within the United States, the required degree of purity of flour sold is often the subject of trade association standards. For an interesting contract dispute that involved the differing standards of both the Millers' National Federation and the American Bakers' Association, see International Milling Co. v. Hachmeister, Inc., 380 Pa. 407, 110 A.2d 186 (1955).

(2) Inspection, Shipment and Payment. The *T.J. Stevenson* case reveals common commercial practices regarding performance of sales contracts when parties are at a distance from each other. Performance problems are taken up in Chapter 7.

———

SIDCO PRODUCTS MARKETING, INC. v. GULF OIL CORP.

United States Court of Appeals, Fifth Circuit, 1988.
858 F.2d 1095.

EDITH H. JONES, CIRCUIT JUDGE. At issue here is the grant of summary judgment for the defendant [Gulf] concerning claims for breach of express and implied warranties ... in the sale [by Gulf to Sidco] of a material called "middle layer emulsion" (MLE). Texas law applies in this diversity case. Concluding essentially that Gulf did not misrepresent the nature or qualities of MLE to the ultimate purchaser Sidco, we affirm.

I. BACKGROUND

According to Sidco, this is the story of a pig in a poke. On December 15, 1983, Gulf published a Bid Inquiry in which it invited bids from a selected group of purchasers for a product called "middle layer emulsion." One company on the bid list was Chemwaste, Inc. Several portions of the Bid Inquiry are relevant to our discussion. First, the product was defined as Middle Layer Emulsion [MLE], "a mixture of oil, water and particulate matter." Second, paragraph 10 of the Bid Inquiry afforded any prospective purchaser the opportunity to "inspect the tanks containing MLE and ... obtain a reasonable sample therefrom for testing." The bid price was to be gauged by the value of recoverable hydrocarbons estimated to be contained in the MLE. Third, a cautionary environmental note appeared as paragraph 14 of the Bid Inquiry:

> The solids in the middle layer emulsion are listed by the United States Environmental Protection Agency in 40 CFR Part 261 as a "Hazardous Waste from Specific Sources, Slop Oil emulsion solids from the petroleum refining industry" with an EPA hazardous waste number of K049. If the solids are removed from the middle layer emulsion, then the disposal of these solids are regulated by the Federal Government as well as many state and local governments. It will be the responsibility of the successful bidder to dispose of these solids and any waste water generated in accordance with all applicable Federal, State and local rules and regulations.

Sidco became interested in purchasing MLE for processing and resale of the oil in it when its president, Dirk Stronck, obtained and read a copy of the Bid Inquiry, including paragraph 14. Because Gulf was selling the product only to authorized bidders, Stronck contacted Romero Brothers Oil Exchange, Inc., which acquired from Chemwaste the right to sell MLE. Sidco availed itself of the opportunity to examine MLE chemically and engaged E.W. Saybolt & Company, Inc. for this purpose. Upon receipt of what it believed were satisfactory test results from Saybolt, Sidco signed a contract to purchase the MLE from Romero. The Romero contract was executed for Sidco by Ron Bougere, its then vice-president.

The sale from Gulf to Chemwaste, thence to Romero and Sidco, occurred January 24, 1984. Sidco paid $394,482 for MLE estimated to yield 28,077 barrels of recoverable hydrocarbons. Sidco then entered into a processing agreement with Texas Oil and Chemical Terminal, Inc. [TOCT] for "slop oil" without showing TOCT the Bid Inquiry or advising it that the product was MLE. TOCT's attempts to process MLE encountered serious difficulty—the product first plugged a pump screen and damaged TOCT's heater and later clogged a processing tower.

After further testing, Sidco was led to inquire of the Texas Department of Water Resources whether MLE might be a "hazardous waste" regulated by federal environmental law. The department answered affirmatively. [Sidco] protested this decision, but was ordered to and did remove the MLE from the TOCT refinery, which was not licensed to process hazardous waste, and paid for repairs to TOCT's heater. Nevertheless, hydrocarbon products were eventually extracted and sold by Sidco for gross revenue exceeding $400,000.

Sidco claims to have sustained over $13 million in damages, including $60,000 out-of-pocket costs, over $360,000 in lost revenues, the loss of $5 million in financial backing for proposed slop oil activities, and foregone business opportunities exceeding $8.6 million.

Sidco's lawsuit against Gulf alleged the following causes of action:

    1. Gulf breached an express warranty regarding the nature and quality of MLE, in violation of Tex. Bus. & Com. Code Ann. § 2.313;

    2. Gulf breached the implied warranty of merchantability in that MLE was not fit for the purpose for which slop oil is ordinarily sold, violating Tex. Bus. & Com. Code Ann. § 2.314 ....

II. DISCUSSION

The determination most critical to the success of Sidco's position is the nature of the misrepresentations or omissions by Gulf in its Bid Inquiry. Sidco concedes that the Bid Inquiry constitutes the only relevant communication between Gulf and Sidco's representatives prior to Sidco's purchase of MLE. Sidco charges that Gulf misrepresented three characteristics of the MLE: that it formed an unusually tight emulsion which was not susceptible to ordinary processing methods; that the product was not "ordinary slop oil," and that the product in its totality was a hazardous waste under applicable environmental regulations. Sidco alleges that all of its damages flowed from these misrepresentations. Sidco's breach of warranty claims ... depend upon the existence of these pleaded and vigorously argued misrepresentations of MLE's qualities.

Try as we may, we are unable to discern in the bare simplicity of Gulf's Bid Inquiry the false representations that Sidco asserts. The pertinent portions of the Bid Inquiry were quoted above. MLE is there described as an emulsion, which the dictionary alerts us is an "intimate mixture" of two incompletely miscible liquids, such as water and oil, or of a semisolid or solid dispersed in a liquid. Webster's Third New Int'l Dictionary. The MLE is defined to contain water, hydrocarbons and particulate matter. Prospective purchasers are offered the opportunity to sample a sufficient quantity of the MLE to determine its qualities. Finally, there is a cautionary note about the hazardous waste nature of solids contained in the MLE. There is, however, no affirmation of fact concerning the susceptibility of MLE to any particular hydrocarbon processing or refining technique. There is no representation that MLE is "ordinary slop oil." The term slop oil appears only once in the Bid Inquiry, as a descriptive term (in paragraph 14) in the title of the EPA regulation governing the nature of the solids. MLE itself is not represented in the Bid Inquiry as either environmentally hazardous or non-hazardous. The Bid Inquiry did, however, put the would-be purchaser on notice that he should sample and test the MLE in order to determine the nature and quantity of its hydrocarbon content and to calculate his bid price. To put the matter briefly, the Bid Inquiry described MLE much as would a want-ad for a "truck," in that it described the product generically and left the rest of the characteristics to be discerned by the purchaser in his test-drive or at his mechanic's shop.

A warranty is a promise or affirmation of fact concerning a product or a description of the product to which the product is represented to conform. Tex. Bus. & Com. Code Ann. §§ 2.313(a)(1) and (2). Gulf's Bid Inquiry made no promise or description of MLE with regard to its processability or its status as either "ordinary slop oil" or an EPA-regulated hazardous waste. Where there is no such representation, promise, or affirmation that becomes part of the basis of the parties' bargain, there is no express warranty to be breached. La Sara Grain Co. v. First National Bank, 673 S.W.2d 558, 565 (Tex.1984).

Sidco responds to this conclusion in two ways, which we believe are but versions of the same argument. Gulf, it says, "by its conduct" as well as by the Bid Inquiry, "acted as if" MLE was ordinary slop oil. Alternatively, the essence of Gulf's duplicitous conduct, Sidco contends, is that Gulf *omitted* to disclose that MLE could not be processed by ordinary refinery means, that it was not ordinary slop oil and that it was, irrespective of the solids it contained, a hazardous waste. Omissions, however, are not affirmative representations of any sort and thus cannot support a warranty claim, because express warranties must be explicit. ... On the record before us, it appears that Gulf's Bid Inquiry embodied no express warranty concerning the processability of MLE or its status as "ordinary slop oil" or a non-hazardous material.

Sidco also contends that MLE was sold under an implied warranty of merchantability or fitness for the purposes for which "ordinary slop oil" is used. Gulf moved for summary judgment on this issue, asserting that slop oil is bought and sold so that it can be processed to yield valuable petroleum products. Since the MLE did eventually produce $400,000 of such products for Sidco, the implied warranty of merchantability was fulfilled. This argument suffers from the lack of record evidence demonstrating that, if MLE were to be equated to "ordinary slop oil" for implied warranty purposes, the revenue earned for its petroleum contents represented a "quality comparable to that generally acceptable in that line of trade ..." Official Comment 2 to Tex. Bus. & Com. Code Ann. § 2.314. Alternatively, however, Gulf asserts that there can be no implied warranty of merchantability as requested by

Sidco, because Gulf nowhere expressly represented MLE as "ordinary slopoil." We find this latter rationale convincing and consistent with our previous discussion. . . .

For these reasons, the summary judgment granted by the district court is affirmed.

Notes

(1) **Merchantable Quality: Ordinary Purposes.** Goods may be useful for more than one purpose. Flour may be useful for human consumption, but can also be used in the manufacture of ceiling tiles. Sidco believed erroneously that the middle layer emulsion could be used as "slop oil," but the goods could be used as a source of hydrocarbons. Cows may be used as dairy animals, for breeding purposes, or for slaughter. What should determine the "ordinary purposes" of goods that have multiple uses? Can the answer be found in the words of the contract of the parties? Are there other sources?

(2) **Merchantable Quality: Fitness for Purpose.** Once purposes are identified, how good must goods be to be deemed "fit"? The Fifth Circuit said in *T.J. Stevenson* that it would not decide generally how much infestation could exist in flour that was still fit for human consumption. It declared that merchantability is an "evolving standard." What should determine the minimum standard of "fitness" of goods?

Problem 1. Buyer purchased a new Mustang automobile from a Ford dealer. After 30 months, during which Buyer had driven the car 75,000 miles, Buyer discovered that the way the taillight assembly gaskets had been installed permitted water to enter and cause severe rust damage. Did Seller breach the warranty of merchantability? On these facts, the Wisconsin Supreme Court held that the rust problem did not render the car unfit for the purpose of driving. "When a car can provide safe, reliable transportation it is generally considered merchantable." Taterka v. Ford Motor Co., 86 Wis.2d 140, 271 N.W.2d 653 (1978). If the car had been a Mercedes, would the same ruling be appropriate?

(3) **Merchantable Quality: Pass Without Objection in the Trade.** Section 2–314(2)(a) defines merchantability by reference to trade standards. The Code provides that trade usage (UCC 1–205(2)) becomes, by implication, part of the parties' bargain in fact (UCC 1–201(3) ("agreement")) which results in defining their legal obligations (UCC 1–201(11) ("contract")). If goods of a certain quality are regularly accepted without objection by buyers in the trade, this provides a contractual standard against which to measure the objection of a particular buyer in the same trade. See Comment 7 to UCC 2–314.

Does this suggest that the issue of sellers' responsibility should be decided as a matter of contract interpretation?

(4) Merchantable Quality: Fair Average Quality. UCC 2–314(2)(b) specifies that goods must be such as "in the case of fungible goods, are of fair average quality within the description." Comment 7 implies a limited scope for this provision: " 'Fair average' is a term directly appropriate to *agricultural* bulk products ..." (emphasis added). The statute, of course, extends to non-agricultural fungible goods; "fungible" goods, as defined in UCC 1–201(17), comprise not only various bulk products (like ores) but also most manufactured goods where "any unit is, by nature or usage of trade, the equivalent of any other like unit."

Comment 7 to UCC 2–314 seeks to shed light on the standard by stating that "fair average" means "goods centering around the middle belt of quality, not the least or the worst that can be understood in the particular trade by the designation, but such as can pass 'without objection.' Of course a fair percentage of the least is permissible but the goods are not 'fair average' if they are all of the least or worst quality possible under the description."

Does the text of the statute support the implication that goods fail to be of "merchantable quality" if they are below average quality but are "within the description"? Suppose that buyers had been accepting shipments of sugar which ranged in polarization between 75 and 80, with the various shipments averaging out at 77 ½. Would the shipment in that case which polarized at 75 ⅜ fail to meet the statutory standard? If buyers started rejecting shipments below 77 ½, so that the average quality of acceptable sugar rose to 79, would this in turn justify rejection of sugar below a polarization of 79? Can independent meaning be given to paragraph (b)? See 1 N.Y.L.R.C., Study of the Uniform Commercial Code 400–01 (1955). Are similar problems latent in paragraph (d)?

INTEGRATED CIRCUITS UNLIMITED, INC. v. E.F. JOHNSON Co., 691 F.Supp. 630 (E.D.N.Y.1988), affirmed, 875 F.2d 1040 (2d Cir.1989). Manufacturer of two-way taxi radios contracted to buy 2500 microprocessors to be used as components in the radios to be delivered in installments. After 1900 had been delivered, buyer notified seller that these items were unsatisfactory. Buyer asserted that it had had 130 (some 8%) of the microprocessors tested by an independent laboratory which reported that 2.6% of those tested had failed to perform. Buyer asserted that its acceptable quality level—the number of devices which can be defective without rendering the entire shipment unacceptable—was 1%.

Seller sued buyer for the unpaid price; buyer sought refund of the price paid.[1] After a bench trial, the court preliminarily accepted

---

1. Buyer contended it had not accepted the goods in question. Much of the legal analysis of the courts addressed the question whether buyer's rejection was rightful.

seller's expert witness' testimony that a defect rate of less than 5% was sufficient to make the goods conforming and rejected testimony of buyer's technicians who lacked industry-wide experience. On further reflection, the trial court observed that, in products containing only five components, a 5% failure rate for each part would result in a probability that one in four of the products had an inadequate component. The court held that credible evidence had shown an industry standard requiring a failure rate much lower than 1%. The court found for the buyer.

The trial court also addressed the adequacy of action based upon sampling of only 8% of the microprocessors. The court noted that the tests were expensive. While the sample had not been selected randomly, the court found that selection for sampling sufficed because it had been made without bias. The court concluded that the statistical probabilities were high enough and sufficiently reliable to warrant the buyer's action.

Notes

(1) **Merchantable Quality: Contract Description.** In *Sidco*, the advocate for the MLE buyer described the contract as a purchase of "a pig in a poke." Sales in which the parties use no description of the goods are not likely to occur. Normally, the goods would be described verbally.[2] "Any description of the goods which is made part of the basis of the bargain creates an express warranty that the goods shall conform to the description." UCC 2–313(1)(b). What is added to the idea of *express* warranty by the provisions in UCC 2–314(2) that define an *implied* warranty on the basis of the "contract description" (UCC 2–314(2)(a) and (b)) or "the agreement" (UCC 2–314(2)(d) and (e)? A satisfactory answer is not easy to find.

Section 2–314(2)(c) does not refer on its face to "contract description" or "agreement," but it declares sellers responsible for the ordinary utility of "such goods." To what antecedent could "such" goods refer? The goods described in the agreement or contract? The goods delivered?

(2) **Merchantable Quality of Manufactured Goods: Design Standards.** Manufacturers determine their own quality-control standards. Such standards, which may be high or low, are used to decide whether the manufacturer will sell a finished product in the marketplace. (Manufacturers of some goods, e.g., glass crystal or clothing, market some products that do not meet the firms' standards as "seconds.") If a manufacturer fails to detect that a product does not

---

On some microprocessors, the court found for the seller. As to materials rightly rejected, the buyer did not seek damages for seller's breach.

2. In a "present sale" (UCC 2–106(1)) words may be considerably less important than the parties' focus on the thing itself. So, too, in a sale by sample or model.

conform to its quality-control standards and, without notice of that fact, sells the product to a buyer, is the product, for that reason, unmerchantable?

Problem 2. A restaurant patron ordered and was served a platter that includes a portion of fish almondine. While eating, the patron choked on a fishbone, which lodged in his esophagus. The patron was rushed to a hospital where a bone, one centimeter long, was removed. Patron sued Restaurant for breach of the implied warranty of merchantability. (Note that serving food in a restaurant is a sale under UCC 2–314(1).) What result? See Morrison's Cafeteria v. Haddox, 431 So.2d 975 (Ala.1983) (jury verdict for patron reversed; as a matter of law, a one-centimeter bone in a fish fillet does not make the food unmerchantable). We consider sellers' liability for buyers' personal injuries further in Section 5 infra.

ROYAL BUSINESS MACHINES, INC. v. LORRAINE CORP.

United States Court of Appeals, Seventh Circuit, 1980.
633 F.2d 34.

BAKER, D.J. This is an appeal from a judgment of the district court entered after a bench trial awarding ... [Booher] $1,171,216.16 in compensatory and punitive damages against ... [Royal]. The judgment further awarded Booher attorneys' fees of $156,800.00. ... The judgment also granted Royal a set-off of $12,020.00 for an unpaid balance due on computer typewriters.

The case arose from commercial transactions extending over a period of 18 months between Royal and Booher in which Royal sold and Booher purchased 114 RBC I and 14 RBC II plain paper copying machines. [Booher bought the machines for the purpose of leasing them to its customers.] In mid-August 1976, Booher filed suit against Royal in the Indiana courts claiming breach of warranties and fraud. . . .

The issues in the cases arise under Indiana common law and under the U.C.C. as adopted in Indiana, Ind.Code § 26–1–102 et seq. (1976). . . .

EXPRESS WARRANTIES

We first address the question whether substantial evidence on the record supports the district court's findings that Royal made and breached express warranties to Booher. The trial judge found that Royal Business Machines made and breached the following express warranties:

(1) that the RBC Model I and II machines and their component parts were of high quality;

(2) that experience and testing had shown that frequency of repairs was very low on such machines and would remain so;

(3) that replacement parts were readily available;

(4) that the cost of maintenance for each RBC machine and cost of supplies was and would remain low, no more than 1/2 cent per copy;

(5) that the RBC machines had been extensively tested and were ready to be marketed;

(6) that experience and reasonable projections had shown that the purchase of the RBC machines by Mr. Booher and Lorraine Corporation and the leasing of the same to customers would return substantial profits to Booher and Lorraine;

(7) that the machines were safe and could not cause fires; and

(8) that service calls were and would be required for the RBC Model II machine on the average of every 7,000 to 9,000 copies, including preventive maintenance calls.

Substantial evidence supports the court's findings as to Numbers 5, 7, 8, and the maintenance aspect of Number 4, but, as a matter of law, Numbers 1, 2, 3, 6, and the cost of supplies portion of Number 4 cannot be considered express warranties.

Paraphrasing U.C.C. § 2–313 as adopted in Indiana, an express warranty is made up of the following elements: (a) an affirmation of fact or promise, (b) that relates to the goods, and (c) becomes a part of the basis of the bargain between the parties. When each of these three elements is present, a warranty is created that the goods shall conform to the affirmation of fact or to the promise.

The decisive test for whether a given representation is a warranty or merely an expression of the seller's opinion is whether the seller asserts a fact of which the buyer is ignorant or merely states an opinion or judgment on a matter of which the seller has no special knowledge and on which the buyer may be expected also to have an opinion and to exercise his judgment. ... General statements to the effect that goods are "the best," ..., or are "of good quality," ... or will "last a lifetime" and be "in perfect condition," ... are generally regarded as expressions of the seller's opinion or "the puffing of his wares" and do not create an express warranty.

No express warranty was created by Royal's affirmation that both RBC machine models and their component parts were of high quality. This was a statement of the seller's opinion, the kind of "puffing" to be expected in any sales transaction, rather than a positive averment of fact describing a product's capabilities to which an express warranty could attach. ...

Similarly, the representations by Royal that experience and testing had shown that the frequency of repair was "very low" and would remain so lack the specificity of an affirmation of fact upon which a warranty could be predicated. These representations were statements of the seller's opinion.

The statement that replacement parts were readily available is an assertion of fact, but it is not a fact that relates to the goods sold as required by Ind.Code § 26–1–2–313(1)(a) and is not an express warranty to which the goods were to conform. Neither is the statement about the future costs of supplies being 1/2 cent per copy an assertion of fact that relates to the goods sold, so the statement cannot constitute the basis of an express warranty.

It was also erroneous to find that an express warranty was created by Royal's assurances to Booher that purchase of the RBC machines would bring him substantial profits. Such a representation does not describe the goods within the meaning of U.C.C. § 2–313(1)(b), nor is the representation an affirmation of fact relating to the goods under U.C.C. § 2–313(1)(a). It is merely sales talk and the expression of the seller's opinion. See Regal Motor Products v. Bender, 102 Ohio App. 447, 139 N.E.2d 463, 465 (1956) (representation that goods were "readily saleable" and that the demand for them would create a market was not a warranty). ...

On the other hand, the assertion that the machines could not cause fires is an assertion of fact relating to the goods, and substantial evidence in the record supports the trial judge's findings that the assertion was made by Royal to Booher. The same may be said for the assertion that the machines were tested and ready to be marketed. ...

As for findings 8 and the maintenance portion of Number 4, Royal's argument that those statements relate to predictions for the future and cannot qualify as warranties is unpersuasive. An expression of future capacity or performance can constitute an express warranty. In Teter v. Shultz, 110 Ind.App. 541, 39 N.E.2d 802, 804 (1942), the Indiana courts held that a seller's statement that dairy cows would give six gallons of milk per day was an affirmation of fact by the seller relating to the goods. It was not a statement of value nor was it merely a statement of the seller's opinion. The Indiana courts have also found that an express warranty was created by a seller's representation that a windmill was capable of furnishing power to grind 20 to 30 bushels of grain per hour in a moderate wind and with a very light wind would pump an abundance of water. Smith v. Borden, 160 Ind. 223, 66 N.E. 681 (1903). Further, in General Supply and Equipment Co. v. Phillips, [490 S.W.2d 913 (Tex.App.1972)], the Texas courts upheld the following express warranties made by a seller of roof panels: (1) that tests show no deterioration in 5 years of normal use; (2) that the roofing panels won't turn black or discolor ... even after years of exposure; and (3) that the panels will not burn, rot, rust, or mildew. ...

Whether a seller affirmed a fact or made a promise amounting to a warranty is a question of fact reserved for the trier of fact. General Supply and Equip. Co. v. Phillips, supra. Substantial evidence in the record supports the finding that Royal made the assertion to Booher that maintenance cost for the machine would run 1/2 cent per copy and that this assertion was not an estimate but an assertion of a fact of performance capability.

Finding Number 8, that service calls on the RBC II would be required every 7,000 to 9,000 copies, relates to performance capability and could constitute the basis of an express warranty. There is substantial evidence in the record to support the finding that this assertion was also made.

While substantial evidence supports the trial court's findings as to the making of those four affirmations of fact or promises, the district court failed to make the further finding that they became part of the basis of the bargain. Ind.Code § 26–1–2–313(1) (1976). While Royal may have made such affirmations to Booher, the question of his knowledge or reliance is another matter.[7]

This case is complicated by the fact that it involved a series of sales transactions between the same parties over approximately an 18–month period and concerned two different machines. The situations of the parties, their knowledge and reliance, may be expected to change in light of their experience during that time. An affirmation of fact which the buyer from his experience knows to be untrue cannot form a part of the basis of the bargain. ... Therefore, as to each purchase, Booher's expanding knowledge of the capacities of the copying machines would have to be considered in deciding whether Royal's representations were part of the basis of the bargain. The same representations that could have constituted an express warranty early in the series of transactions might not have qualified as an express warranty in a later transaction if the buyer had acquired independent knowledge as to the fact asserted.

The trial court did not indicate that it considered whether the warranties could exist and apply to each transaction in the series. Such an analysis is crucial to a just determination. Its absence renders the district court's findings insufficient on the issue of the breach of express warranties.

Since a retrial on the questions of the breach of express warranties and the extent of damages is necessary, we offer the following observations. The court must consider whether the machines were defective upon delivery. Breach occurs only if the goods are defective upon delivery and not if the goods later become defective through abuse or neglect. ...

---

7. The requirement that a statement be part of the basis of the bargain in order to constitute an express warranty "is essentially a reliance requirement and is inextricably intertwined with the initial determination as to whether given language may constitute an express warranty since affirmations, promises and descriptions tend to become a part of the basis of the bargain. It was the intention of the drafters of the U.C.C. not to require a strong showing of reliance. In fact, they envisioned that all statements of the seller become part of the basis of the bargain unless clear affirmative proof is shown to the contrary. See Official Comments 3 and 8 to U.C.C. § 2–313." Sessa v. Riegle, 427 F.Supp. 760, 766 (E.D.Pa.1977), aff'd without op. 568 F.2d 770 (3d Cir.1978). ...

In considering the promise relating to the cost of maintenance, the district court should determine at what stage Booher's own knowledge and experience prevented him from blindly relying on the representations of Royal. A similar analysis is needed in examining the representation concerning fire hazard in the RBC I machines. The court also should determine when that representation was made. If not made until February 1975, the representation could not have been the basis for sales made prior to that date.

FRAUD AND MISREPRESENTATION

The district court found that beginning in April or May of 1974 and continuing throughout most of 1975, Royal, by and through its agents and employees acting in the course and scope of their employment, persuaded Booher to buy RBC I and RBC II copiers by knowingly making material oral misrepresentations which were relied upon by Booher to his injury.

Under Indiana law, the essential elements of actionable fraud are representations, falsity, scienter, deception, and injury.... A fraud action must be predicated upon statements of existing facts, not promises to perform in the future. ... Nor do expressions of opinion qualify as fraudulent misrepresentations. The district court made no specific findings as to which of the alleged representations it relied upon in finding fraud. If the court held all eight to be fraudulent misrepresentations, the court erred as to Numbers 1, 2, and 6 because, as discussed above, these were merely expressions of the seller's opinion rather than statements of material fact upon which a fraud action could be based. Numbers 3, 4, 5, 7, and 8, on the other hand, readily qualify as material factual representations. ...

The trial court, however, is silent on the remaining question, that of deception or reasonable reliance by Booher on the representations in the various transactions. ... This issue is virtually identical to the basis of the bargain question remanded under the express warranty theory.

The district court's finding of fraud, therefore, must be set aside, and the cause remanded for retrial on the questions of the specific misrepresentations relied upon by Booher in each transaction and the reasonableness of that reliance.

With regard to rescission as a remedy for fraud, rescission would be available only for those specific sales to which fraud attached. ...

IMPLIED WARRANTIES

The district court found that Royal breached the implied warranties of merchantability and of fitness for a particular purpose. We cannot agree that the record supports the court's findings.

A warranty of merchantability is implied by law in any sale where the seller is a merchant of the goods. To be merchantable, goods must, *inter alia,* pass without objection in the trade under the contract description, be of fair average quality, and be fit for the ordinary purposes for which such goods are used. Ind.Code § 26–1–2–314 (1976). They must "conform to ordinary standards, and ... be of the same average grade, quality and value as similar goods sold under similar circumstances." ... It was Booher's burden to prove that the copying machines were not merchantable. ... Booher failed to satisfy his burden of proof as to standards in the trade for either the RBC I or RBC II machine. No evidence supports the trial court's findings of a breach of the implied warranty of merchantability.

An implied warranty of fitness for a particular purpose arises where a seller has reason to know a particular purpose for which the goods are required and the buyer relies on the seller's skill or judgment to select or furnish suitable goods. Ind.Code § 26–1–2–315 (1976). The court found that Royal knew the particular purpose for which all the RBC machines were to be used and, in fact, that Royal had taken affirmative steps to persuade Booher to become its dealer and that occasionally its employees even accompanied Booher on calls to customers. ...

The district court, however, failed to distinguish between implied warranties on the RBC I and on the RBC II machines. Nor did the court differentiate among the different transactions involving the two machines. On remand the district court should make further findings on Booher's actual reliance on Royal's skill or judgment in each purchase of the RBC I and RBC II machines. We view it as most unlikely that a dealer who now concedes himself to be an expert in the field of plain paper copiers did not at some point, as his experience with the machines increased, rely on his own judgment in making purchases.

. . .

[Judgment reversed. Cause remanded for a new trial.]

Notes

(1) **Sellers' Talk; Affirmations of Fact.** The court considers six statements which were the basis of buyer's claim for breach of express warranty. Were any of the six statements "promises" of the seller? If a person makes a promise, which is supported by consideration, and does not perform the promise, is the person liable for breach of contract? Is there a difference between breach of contract and breach of warranty? Note that the Code defines an express warranty as either promises or affirmations of fact. In general contract law, does an affirmation of fact serve as the basis of liability for breach of contract?

(2) **"Opinion," "Value," "Commendation," and Express Warranties.** Professor Page Keeton outlined the wide variations in the impact of statements which might fall under the heading of "opinion." Quoting words of Learned Hand, Keeton observed that some statements are like the claims of campaign managers before election: "rather

designed to allay the suspicion that would attend their absence than to be understood as having any relation to objective truth." Keeton, The Rights of Disappointed Purchasers, 32 Tex.L.Rev. 1, 8 (1953). On the other hand, some statements of opinion may be expected to produce reliance.

In a slightly different connection, Keeton illustrated the effect of the nature of the recovery on the framing of the legal rule. A misrepresentation which is innocent ordinarily will not support an action for damages for deceit. But such a misrepresentation may more readily provide a defense to an action to enforce the agreement which it induced and even, in some cases, a basis for rescission of a completed transaction. Id. at 10. Is such shaping of the rule to the remedy feasible under current statutory structures?

The Code provides that "an affirmation" that is "merely of the value of the goods" or "a statement purporting to be merely the seller's opinion or commendation of the goods" does not create a warranty. UCC 2–313(2). Sales pitches of this genre are very common; would sellers continue this practice if it did not influence buyers? Are there reasons of public policy for negating buyers' protection if sellers' affirmations or statements are not true?

Does the exception in 2–313(2) apply to sellers' promises as to future value of goods?

(3) **Relationship to the Goods.** Under UCC 2–313(1)(a), an affirmation of fact or promise is not an express warranty unless it "relates to the goods." The court in *Royal Business Machines* found that three of seller's statements lacked this characteristic. Were any of these statements promises? Did the Code drafters mislead by including "or promise" in UCC 2–313(1)(a) without cross-reference to UCC 1–103?

(4) **Part of the Basis of the Bargain.** Under UCC 2–313(1)(a), an affirmation of fact or promise is not an express warranty unless it "becomes part of the basis of the bargain." Insofar as this applies to promises, is it consistent with general contract law? The Official Comment addressed to this phrase, Comment 3, does not refer to sellers' promises, but only to affirmations of fact. Is that indicative of the scope of the limiting concept of "part of the basis of the bargain"? Is there more justification for applying that limiting concept to affirmations of fact?

(5) **Reliance and Basis of the Bargain.** The Uniform Sales Act provision limited express warranty to an affirmation (or promise) that had "the natural tendency ... to induce the buyer to purchase the goods, and the buyer purchases the goods relying thereon." USA 12. The Code drafters deliberately dropped these elements and substituted the term, "part of the basis of the bargain." Comment 3 declares: no particular reliance need be shown. Nonetheless, courts like *Royal Business Machines* seek the meaning of "part of the basis of the bargain" in the idea of buyer reliance. See the court's footnote 7. In light of the deliberate legislative choice to drop a reliance requirement

from the text of the law, can the reasoning of the courts in reliance terms be explained? What is the meaning of the penultimate sentence in Comment 3?

Is the underlying problem different from any general contract inquiry seeking to find the nature of the parties' reasonable expectations? See Murray, Basis of the Bargain, Transcending Classical Concepts, 66 Minn.L.Rev. 283 (1982).

CIPOLLONE v. LIGGETT GROUP, INC., 893 F.2d 541 (3d Cir.1990).
[In a case brought on behalf of a woman whose illness and death allegedly had resulted from years of smoking cigarettes manufactured by the Liggett Group, Inc., plaintiff contended that the manufacturer had made certain express warranties in its advertisements and that those warranties had been breached.]

We turn now to another major area of dispute between the parties, one that implicates the conceptual basis of express warranty law. ... With respect to this issue, the district court gave the following instructions to the jury:

> [Plaintiff] must prove ... that Liggett, prior to 1966, made one or more of the statements claimed by the plaintiff and that such statements were affirmations of fact or promises by Liggett ... [and] that such statements were part of the basis of the bargain between Liggett and consumers like Rose Cipollone....
>
> The law does not require plaintiff to show that Rose Cipollone specifically relied on Liggett's warranties.
>
> Ordinarily a guarantee or promise in an advertisement or other description of the goods becomes part of the basis of the bargain if it would naturally induce the purchase of the product and no particular reliance by the buyer on such statement needs to be shown. However, if the evidence establishes that the claimed statement cannot fairly be viewed as entering into the bargain, that is, that the statement would not naturally induce the purchase of a product, then no express warranty has been created ....

The history of section 2–313(1)(a), although informative, fails to give a clear answer as to whether reliance is required. Section 2–313(1)(a) is an adaptation of section 12 of the Uniform Sales Act. A comparison of the two sections reveals that they are substantially the same except for the replacement of section 12's express reliance requirement with section 2–313(1)(a)'s basis of the bargain requirement.

... Comment 4 states that "the whole purpose of the law of warranty is to determine what it is that the seller has in essence agreed to sell." ... Reliance is irrelevant to what a seller agrees to sell.[28]

---

28. For example, imagine a tire merchant describing a tire to three different prospective purchasers, each listening to his sales talk at the same time. The seller

... We hold that once the buyer has become aware of the affirmation of fact or promise, the statements are presumed to be part of the "basis of the bargain" unless the defendant, by "clear affirmative proof," shows that the buyer knew that the affirmation of fact or promise was untrue. ...

Applying our interpretation of section 2–313 to the case at bar, we conclude that the district court's jury instructions were erroneous for two reasons. First, they did not require the plaintiff to prove that Mrs. Cipollone had read, seen, or heard the advertisements at issue. Second, they did not permit the defendant to prove that although Mrs. Cipollone had read, seen, or heard the advertisements, she did not believe the safety assurances contained therein. We must therefore reverse and remand for a new trial on this issue.*

Note

Other "Fields" of Law. UCC 1–103 provides that the principles of law and equity, including the law relative to "fraud, misrepresentation ... [and] mistake" supplement the Code unless displaced by particular provisions of it.

guarantees that the tire will (1) be safe for use even in heavily loaded vehicles; (2) last at least 20,000 miles; and (3) be the same style tire sold with a Rolls Royce. The first purchaser buys the tire relying on the seller's safety warranty. The second buys the tire relying on the seller's durability warranty. The third buys the tire relying on the seller's style warranty. None of the purchasers communicates to the seller the reason why he or she is purchasing one of the tires, although the reason for the purchase is communicated to the buyer's spouse, who will later come forward to testify truthfully regarding what the buyer relied on when making the purchase. It is implausible that each buyer has a different warranty, and that the second buyer, but not the first or third buyers, can sue if the tire wears out before 20,000 miles. [Footnote by court]

* The Supreme Court reviewed and reversed other aspects of the Third Circuit's decision. The only issue considered by the Supreme Court was the extent to which the Federal Cigarette Labeling and Advertising Act of 1965 and the Public Health Cigarette Smoking Act of 1969 superseded common-law damages claims under various warranty and tort theories. The Court held that these Acts did not supersede the plaintiff's express warranty claim and most of plaintiff's claims based on tort theories. Cipollone v. Liggett Group, Inc., 112 S.Ct. 2608 (1992).

The Court's analysis of the pre-emption issue under the 1969 Act regarding plaintiff's express warranty claims led to disagreement among the Justices regarding the nature of such warranties. That Act barred enforcement of requirements or prohibitions "imposed under State law." Construing that phrase, a plurality opinion by Stevens, J. (for four Justices) stated that liability under an express warranty is not imposed by law. A dissent by Scalia, J. (two Justices) declared that the background law, not the act of the warrantor, supplies the element of legal obligation and, therefore, liability under an express warranty is "imposed by State law" under the Act. Stevens, J. replied: "... [C]ommon understanding dictates that a contractual requirement, although only enforceable under state law, is not "imposed" by the state, but rather is "imposed" by the contracting party upon itself. A concurring opinion by Blackmun, J. (three Justices) supported the result of the non-supersession conclusions of the plurality opinion without stating a view on whether liability for breach of express warranty is self-imposed or imposed by law.

As *Royal Business Machines* demonstrates, factual situations giving rise to express warranty claims are likely to give rise as well to claims of fraud or misrepresentation. The Restatement (Second) of Torts (1977) provides:

§ 525. Liability for Fraudulent Misrepresentation

One who fraudulently makes a misrepresentation of fact, opinion, intention or law for the purpose of inducing another to act or to refrain from action in reliance on it, is subject to liability to the other in deceit for pecuniary loss caused to him by his justifiable reliance upon the misrepresentation.

An illustration to § 525 reveals the close relationship between the tort and the law of express warranty:

A, in order to induce B to buy a heating device, states that it will give a stated amount of heat while consuming only a stated amount of fuel. B is justified in accepting A's statement as an assurance that the heating device is capable of giving the services that A promises.

The Restatement, § 526, defines "fraudulently" in broad terms. The Restatement adds a provision for "negligent misrepresentation," § 552, and a special provision for "innocent misrepresentation" in certain transactions, including sales or rental of goods:

§ 552C. Misrepresentation in Sale, Rental or Exchange Transaction

(1) One who, in a sale, rental or exchange transaction with another, makes a misrepresentation of a material fact for the purpose of inducing the other to act or to refrain from acting in reliance upon it, is subject to liability to the other for pecuniary loss caused to him by his justifiable reliance upon the misrepresentation, even though it is not made fraudulently or negligently.

"Misrepresentation," as a part of general contract law, permits a party who has been misled by a fraudulent *or* material misrepresentation in the negotiation of a contract to avoid it. Restatement (Second) of Contracts § 164 (1981). See also E. Farnsworth, Contracts §§ 4.10—4.15 (2d ed. 1990).

Another "field" mentioned in UCC 1–103 is the law of mistake. The Restatement (Second) of Contracts provides:

§ 152. When Mistake of Both Parties Makes a Contract Voidable

(1) Where a mistake of both parties at the time a contract was made as to a basic assumption on which the contract was made has a material effect on the agreed exchange of performances, the contract is voidable by the adversely affected party unless he bears the risk of the mistake under the rule stated in § 154.

Comment *g* describes the "close relationship" between this principle and the law governing warranties.[3] See also E. Farnsworth, Contracts §§ 9.2, 9.3 (2d ed.1990).

———

Problem 3. Seller, a dealer in chemicals, told Buyer, "I've just received a shipment from Ace Chemical Co. in response to my order for Blue Vitriol. I can sell it to you at $60 per barrel." Buyer purchased 100 barrels. The barrels were sealed and it was not feasible or customary for Seller or Buyer to open the barrels before delivery. Seller had no reason to believe that the shipment from Ace did not conform with his order. When Buyer opened the barrels and tested the material it proved to be "Salzburger Vitriol," an inferior product.

Has Buyer a claim against Seller under UCC 2–313? (See Hawkins v. Pemberton, the 1872 Blue Vitriol decision discussed in Section 1, supra.) Has Buyer any alternative ground for recovery? See UCC 2–314(2)(a).

Problem 4. Seller, a car dealer, showed Buyer a car on display in the showroom. While Buyer was examining the car, Seller described the car as a "Model 57–V." Buyer agreed to buy the car for $3,000. The contract of sale described the car as a "Model 57–V." After the purchase, Buyer found that the car was a "Model 57–J." The two models were the same except that Model 57–V had four doors, chrome trim and a rug on the floor, while Model 57–J had two doors, no chrome trim and a rubber mat in place of a rug.

Has Buyer a claim under UCC 2–313? Under UCC 2–314(2)(a)? See UCC 2–316(3)(b). Cf. Best Buick v. Welcome, 18 UCC Rep. 75 (Mass.App.Div.1975) (1968 Mercedes, traded in on new car, described as "1970" model).

———

CHATLOS SYSTEMS, INC. v. NATIONAL CASH REGISTER CORP.

United States Court of Appeals, Third Circuit, 1982.
670 F.2d 1304.

[Chatlos Systems, Inc. (Chatlos) designed and manufactured cable pressurization equipment for the telecommunications industry. In the spring of 1974, Chatlos decided to buy a computer system and contacted several manufacturers, including National Cash Register Corp. (NCR). NCR recommended its 399/656 disc system. NCR's representative said

---

3. General contract law further provides relief, in limited circumstances, for unilateral mistake if the other party had reason to know of the mistake. See Restatement (Second) of Contracts § 153(b). In recent years, some courts have granted contract relief in limited circumstances even though one party's mistake was not palpable to the other. See also E. Farnsworth, Contracts § 9.4 (2d ed. 1990).

that the equipment would provide Chatlos with six accounting functions: accounts receivable, payroll, order entry, inventory deletion, state income tax, and cash receipts. The representative also told Chatlos that the system would solve inventory problems, result in direct savings of labor costs, and be programmed to be in full operation in six months. On July 24, 1974, Chatlos signed a written agreement in which NCR warranted the equipment "for 12 months after delivery against defects in material, workmanship and operational failure from ordinary use."

[NCR installed the equipment, but never succeeded in making it fully operational. In November 1976, Chatlos instructed NCR to remove the equipment. NCR refused.]

PER CURIAM. This appeal from a district court's award of damages for breach of warranty in a diversity case tried under New Jersey law presents two questions: whether the district court's computation of damages under N.J.Stat.Ann. § 12A:2–714(2) was clearly erroneous, and whether the district court abused its discretion in supplementing the damage award with pre-judgment interest. We answer both questions in the negative and, therefore, we will affirm.

Plaintiff-appellee Chatlos Systems, Inc., initiated this action in the Superior Court of New Jersey, alleging, *inter alia,* breach of warranty regarding an NCR 399/656 computer system it had acquired from defendant National Cash Register Corp. The case was removed under 28 U.S.C. § 1441(a) to the United States District Court for the District of New Jersey. Following a nonjury trial, the district court determined that defendant was liable for breach of warranty and awarded $57,-152.76 damages for breach of warranty and consequential damages in the amount of $63,558.16. Chatlos Systems, Inc. v. National Cash Register Corp., 479 F.Supp. 738 (D.N.J.1979), aff'd in part, remanded in part, 635 F.2d 1081 (3d Cir.1980). Defendant appealed and this court affirmed the district court's findings of liability, set aside the award of consequential damages, and remanded for a recalculation of damages for breach of warranty. Chatlos Systems, Inc. v. National Cash Register Corp., 635 F.2d 1081 (3d Cir.1980). On remand, applying the "benefit of the bargain" formula of N.J.Stat.Ann. § 12A:2–714(2) (Uniform Commercial Code § 2–714(2)), the district court determined the damages to be $201,826.50, to which it added an award of pre-judgment interest. Defendant now appeals from these damage determinations, contending that the district court erred in failing to recognize the $46,020 contract price of the delivered NCR computer system as the fair market value of the goods as warranted, and that the award of damages is without support in the evidence presented. Appellant also contests the award of pre-judgment interest.

... The district court relied ... on the testimony of plaintiff-appellee's expert, Dick Brandon, who, without estimating the value of an NCR model 399/656, presented his estimate of the value of a computer system that would perform all of the functions that the NCR

399/656 had been warranted to perform. Brandon did not limit his estimate to equipment of any one manufacturer; he testified regarding manufacturers who could have made systems that would perform the functions that appellant had warranted the NCR 399/656 could perform. He acknowledged that the systems about which he testified were not in the same price range as the NCR 399/656. Appellant likens this testimony to substituting a Rolls Royce for a Ford, and concludes that the district court's recomputed damage award was therefore clearly contrary to the evidence of fair market value—which in NCR's view is the contract price itself.

Appellee did not order, nor was it promised, merely a specific NCR computer model, but an NCR computer system with specified capabilities. The correct measure of damages, under N.J.Stat.Ann. § 12A:2–714(2), is the difference between the fair market value of the goods accepted and the value they would have had if they had been as warranted. Award of that sum is not confined to instances where there has been an increase in value between date of ordering and date of delivery. It may also include the benefit of a contract price which, for whatever reason quoted, was particularly favorable for the customer. Evidence of the contract price may be relevant to the issue of fair market value, but it is not controlling. ... Appellant limited its fair market value analysis to the contract price of the computer model it actually delivered.[3] Appellee developed evidence of the worth of a computer with the capabilities promised by NCR, and the trial court properly credited the evidence.[4]

Appellee was aided, moreover, by the testimony of Frank Hicks, NCR's programmer, who said that he told his company's officials that the "current software was not sufficient in order to deliver the program that the customer [Chatlos] required. They would have to be rewritten

---

3. At oral argument, counsel for appellant responded to questions from the bench, as follows:

Judge Rosenn: Your position also is that you agree, number one, that the fair market value is the measure of damages here.

Counsel for Appellant: Yes, sir.

Judge Rosenn: The fair market value you say, in the absence of other evidence to the contrary that is relevant, is the contract price. That is the evidence of fair market value.

Counsel: That's right.

Judge Rosenn: Now seeing that had the expert or had the plaintiff been able to establish testimony that there were other machines on the market that were similar to your machine—

Counsel: Yes.

Judge Rosenn: That the fair market value of those was $50,000, that would

have been relevant evidence but it had to be the same machine—same type machine.

Counsel: Well, I would say that the measure of damages as indicated by the statute requires the same machine—"the goods"—in an operable position.

4. We find the following analogy, rather than the Rolls Royce–Ford analogy submitted by appellant, to be on point:

Judge Weis: If you start thinking about a piece of equipment that is warranted to lift a thousand pounds and it will only lift 500 pounds, then the cost of something that will lift a thousand pounds gives you more of an idea and that may be—

Counsel for Appellee: That may be a better analogy, yes.

Judge Weis: Yes.

or a different system would have to be given to the customer." Appendix to Brief for Appellee at 2.68. Hicks recommended that Chatlos be given an NCR 8200 but was told, "that will not be done." Id. at 2.69. Gerald Greenstein, another NCR witness, admitted that the 8200 series was two levels above the 399 in sophistication and price. Id. at 14.30. This testimony supported Brandon's statement that the price of the hardware needed to perform Chatlos' requirements would be in the $100,000 to $150,000 range.

Essentially, then, the trial judge was confronted with the conflicting value estimates submitted by the parties. Chatlos' expert's estimates were corroborated to some extent by NCR's supporters. NCR, on the other hand, chose to rely on contract price. Credibility determinations had to be made by the district judge. Although we might have come to a different conclusion on the value of the equipment as warranted had we been sitting as trial judges, we are not free to make our own credibility and factual findings. We may reverse the district court only if its factual determinations were clearly erroneous. Krasnov v. Dinan, 465 F.2d 1298 (3d Cir.1972).[5]

Upon reviewing the evidence of record, therefore, we conclude that the computation of damages for breach of warranty was not clearly erroneous. We hold also that the district court acted within its discretion in awarding pre-judgment interest, Chatlos Systems, Inc. v. National Cash Register Corp., 635 F.2d at 1088.

The judgment of the district court will be affirmed.

ROSENN, CIRCUIT JUDGE, dissenting. The primary question in this appeal involves the application of Article 2 of the Uniform Commercial Code as adopted by New Jersey in N.J.S.A. 12A:2–101 et seq. (1962) to the measure of damages for breach of warranty in the sale of a computer system. I respectfully dissent because I believe there is no probative evidence to support the district court's award of damages for the breach of warranty in a sum amounting to almost five times the purchase price of the goods. The measure of damages also has been misapplied and this could have a significant effect in the marketplace, especially for the unique and burgeoning computer industry.[1]

In July 1974, National Cash Register Corporation (NCR) sold Chatlos Systems, Inc. (Chatlos), a NCR 399/656 disc computer system (NCR 399) for $46,020 (exclusive of 5 percent sales tax of $1,987.50). The price and system included:

---

5. The dissent essentially is based on disagreement with the estimates provided by Chatlos' expert, Brandon. The record reveals that he was well qualified; the weight to be given his testimony is the responsibility of the factfinder, not an appellate court.

1. Plaintiff's expert, Brandon, testified that generally 40 percent of all computer installations result in failures. He further testified that successful installations of computer systems require not only the computer companies' attention but also the attention of the customers' top management.

The computer (hardware)	$40,165.00
Software (consisting of 6 computer programs)[2]	5,855.00
	$46,020.00

NCR delivered the disc computer to Chatlos in December 1974 and in March 1975 the payroll program became operational. By March of the following year, however, NCR was still unsuccessful in installing an operational order entry program and inventory deletion program. Moreover, on August 31, 1976, Chatlos experienced problems with the payroll program. On that same day and the day following NCR installed an operational state income tax program, but on September 1, 1976, Chatlos demanded termination of the lease[3] and removal of the computer.

When this case was previously before us, we upheld the district court's liability decision but remanded for a reassessment of damages, instructing the court that under the purchase contract and the law consequential damages could not be awarded. Consequential damages, therefore, are no longer an issue here.

On remand, the district court, on the basis of the previous record made in the case, fixed the fair market value of the NCR 399 as warranted at the time of its acceptance in August 1975 at $207,826.50. It reached that figure by valuing the hardware at $131,250.00 and the software at $76,575.50, for a total of $207,826.50. The court then determined that the present value of the computer hardware, which Chatlos retained, was $6,000. Putting no value on the accepted payroll program, the court deducted the $6,000 and arrived at an award of $201,826.50 plus pre-judgment interest at the rate of 8 percent per annum from August 1975.

Chatlos contends before this court, as it had before the district court on remand, that under its benefit of the bargain theory the fair market value of the goods as warranted was several times the purchase price of $46,020. ...

[T]he sole issue before us now is whether the district court erred in fixing the fair market value of the computer system as warranted at the time of the acceptance in August 1975 at $207,826.50.

---

2. The six basic computer programs were: (1) accounts receivable, (2) payroll, (3) order entry, (4) inventory deletion, (5) state income tax, and (6) cash receipts. The contract price also included installation.

3. Chatlos decided to lease the system rather than purchase it outright. To per- mit this arrangement, NCR sold the system to Mid Atlantic National Bank in July 1975 for $46,020, which leased the system to Chatlos. Chatlos made monthly payments to Mid Atlantic in amounts which would have totaled $70,162.09 over the period of the lease.

II.

A.

I believe that the district court committed legal error. ...

There are a number of major flaws in the plaintiff's attempt to prove damages in excess of the contract price. I commence with an analysis of plaintiff's basic theory. Chatlos presented its case under a theory that although, as a sophisticated purchaser, it bargained for several months before arriving at a decision on the computer system it required and the price of $46,020, it is entitled, because of the breach of warranty, to damages predicated on a considerably more expensive system. Stated another way, even if it bargained for a cheap system, i.e., one whose low cost reflects its inferior quality, because that system did not perform as bargained for, it is now entitled to damages measured by the value of a system which, although capable of performing the identical functions as the NCR 399, is of far superior quality and accordingly more expensive.

The statutory measure of damages for breach of warranty specifically provides that the measure is the difference at the time and place of acceptance between the value "of the goods accepted" and the "value they would have had if they had been as warranted." The focus of the statute is upon "the goods accepted"—not other hypothetical goods which may perform equivalent functions. "Moreover, the value to be considered is the reasonable market value of the *goods delivered,* not the value of the goods to a particular purchaser or for a particular purpose." KLPR–TV, Inc. v. Visual Electronics Corp., 465 F.2d 1382, 1387 (8th Cir.1972) (emphasis added). The court, however, arrived at value on the basis of a hypothetical construction of a system as of December 1978 by the plaintiff's expert, Brandon. The court reached its value by working backward from Brandon's figures, adjusting for inflation ....

Although NCR warranted performance, the failure of its equipment to perform, absent any evidence of the value of any NCR 399 system on which to base fair market value, does not permit a market value based on systems wholly unrelated to the goods sold. Yet, instead of addressing the fair market value of the NCR 399 had it been as warranted, Brandon addressed the fair market value of another system that he concocted by drawing on elements from other major computer systems manufactured by companies such as IBM, Burroughs, and Honeywell, which he considered would perform "functions identical to those contracted for" by Chatlos. He conceded that the systems were "[p]erhaps not within the same range of dollars that the bargain was involved with" and he did not identify specific packages of software. Brandon had no difficulty in arriving at the fair market value of the inoperable NCR equipment but instead of fixing a value on the system had it been operable attempted to fashion a hypothetical system on which he placed a value. The district court, in turn, erroneously adopted that value as the fair market value for an operable NCR 399 system. NCR rightly contends that the "comparable" systems on which Brandon drew were substitute goods of greater technological power and capability and not acceptable in determining damages for breach of warranty under section 2–714. Furthermore, Brandon's hypothetical system did not exist and its valuation was largely speculation.

B.

A review of Brandon's testimony reveals its legal inadequacy for establishing the market value of the system Chatlos purchased from NCR. Brandon never testified to the fair market value which the NCR 399 system would have had had it met the warranty at the time of acceptance. . . .

Thus, the shortcomings in Brandon's testimony defy common sense and the realities of the marketplace. First, ordinarily, the best evidence of fair market value is what a willing purchaser would pay in cash to a willing seller. . . . In the instant case we have clearly "not . . . an unsophisticated consumer," . . . who for a considerable period of time negotiated and bargained with an experienced designer and vendor of computer systems. The price they agreed upon for an operable system would ordinarily be the best evidence of its value. The testimony does not present us with the situation referred to in our previous decision, where "the value of the goods rises between the time that the contract is executed and the time of acceptance," in which event the buyer is entitled to the benefit of his bargain. . . . On the contrary, Chatlos here relies on an expert who has indulged in the widest kind of speculation. Based on this testimony, Chatlos asserts in effect that a multi-national sophisticated vendor of computer equipment, despite months of negotiation, incredibly agreed to sell an operable computer system for $46,020 when, in fact, it had a fair market value of $207,000. . . .

Fourth, the record contains testimony which appears undisputed that computer equipment falls into one of several tiers, depending upon the degree of sophistication. The more sophisticated equipment has the capability of performing the functions of the least sophisticated equipment, but the less sophisticated equipment cannot perform all of the functions of those in higher levels. The price of the more technologically advanced equipment is obviously greater.

It is undisputed that in September 1976 there were vendors of computer equipment of the same general size as the NCR 399/656 with disc in the price range of $35,000 to $40,000 capable of providing the same programs as those required by Chatlos, including IBM, Phillips, and Burroughs. They were the very companies who competed for the sale of the computer in 1974 in the same price range. On the other hand, Chatlos' requirements could also be satisfied by computers available at "three levels higher in price and sophistication than the 399 disc." Each level higher would mean more sophistication, greater capabilities, and more memory. Greenstein, NCR's expert, testified without contradiction that equipment of Burroughs, IBM, and other vendors in the price range of $100,000 to $150,000, capable of performing Chatlos' requirements, was not comparable to the 399 because it was three levels higher. Such equipment was more comparable to the NCR 8400 series ....

III.

The purpose of the N.J.S.A. 12A:2–714 is to put the buyer in the same position he would have been in if there had been no breach. See Uniform Commercial Code 1–106(1). The remedies for a breach of warranty were intended to compensate the buyer for his loss; they were not intended to give the purchaser a windfall or treasure trove. The buyer may not receive more than it bargained for; it may not obtain the value of a superior computer system which it did not purchase even though such a system can perform all of the functions the inferior system was designed to serve. ...

VI.

On this record, therefore, the damages to which plaintiff is entitled are $46,020 less $6,000, the fair market value at time of trial of the retained hardware, and less $1,000, the fair market value of the payroll program, or the net sum of $39,020.

Accordingly, I would reverse the judgment of the district court and direct it to enter judgment for the plaintiff in the sum of $39,020 with interest from the date of entry of the initial judgment at the rate allowed by state law.

SUR PETITION FOR REHEARING

The petition for rehearing filed by appellant in the above entitled case having been submitted to the judges who participated in the decision of this court and to all the other available circuit judges of the circuit in regular active service, and no judge who concurred in the decision having asked for rehearing, and a majority of the circuit judges of the circuit in regular active service not having voted for rehearing by the court in banc, the petition for rehearing is denied. Judges Adams, Hunter and Garth would grant the petition for rehearing.

ADAMS, CIRCUIT JUDGE, dissents from the denial of rehearing, and makes the following statement:

Ordinarily, an interpretation of state law by this Court, sitting in diversity, is not of sufficient consequence to warrant reconsideration by the Court sitting in banc. One reason is that if a federal court misconstrues the law of a state, the courts of that state have an opportunity, at some point, to reject the federal court's interpretation. See Chuy v. Philadelphia Eagles Football Club, 595 F.2d 1265, 1286–87 (3d Cir.1979) (in banc) (Aldisert, J., dissenting). In this case, however, the majority's holding, which endorses a measure of damages that is based on what appears to be a new interpretation of New Jersey's commercial law, involves a construction of the Uniform Commercial Code as well. Rectification of any error in our interpretation is, because of the national application of the Uniform Commercial Code, significantly more difficult than it would be if New Jersey law alone were implicated. Moreover, the provision of the Uniform Commercial Code involved here is of unusual importance: the measure of damages approved by this Court may create large monetary risks and obligations in a wide range of commercial transactions, including specifically the present burgeoning computer industry. Because there would appear to be considerable force to the dissenting opinion of Judge Rosenn and because I believe that the principle articulated by the majority should be reviewed by the entire Court before it is finally adopted, I would grant the petition for rehearing in banc.

JAMES HUNTER, III and GARTH, CIRCUIT JUDGES, join in this statement.

Notes

(1) **Benefit of the Bargain: What Was the Bargain?** Was it reasonable for Chatlos to expect to receive goods worth five times the contract price? Should the price term be part of the "contract description" of goods sold? Consider Comment 7 to UCC 2–314: "In cases of doubt as to what quality is intended, the price at which a merchant closes a contract is an excellent index of the nature and scope of his obligation under the present section." Would it have been appropriate to probe more deeply into the probable expectations of the parties as to seller's obligation and buyer's remedy in the event that the computer system failed to perform? Should expectations as to (A) performance and (B) redress be considered in relation to each other? Are implied expectations as to redress less permissible that implied expectations as to performance, such as implied warranties of quality? Note that the court, in its earlier decision, gave full effect to the contract provision denying recovery for consequential damages. Does this shed light on the parties' allocation of the risks and benefits of the agreement?

(2) **Parol Evidence Rule.** In *Chatlos* and, apparently, in *Royal Business Machines,* sellers were charged with liability for breach of oral statements made by their representatives. When contracts of sale are reduced to writing, frequently sellers include in the document a declaration that the document contains the complete agreement of the parties and that there are no promises or representations not contained therein. These "integration" clauses are meant to invoke the parol evidence rule, which for sales contracts is codified in UCC 2–202. In addition to barring evidence that would *contradict* a writing intended as a final expression of a sales agreement, paragraph (b) bars "consistent additional terms" if the court finds "the writing to have been intended also as a complete and exclusive statement of the terms of an agreement." The parol evidence rule, and its codified sales version, are complex legal issues normally studied in the course on Contracts.

What might explain the absence of final written expressions with integration clauses in *Royal Business Machines* and *Chatlos?*

Problem 5. An agreement was signed for the sale of air conditioning equipment to Buyer. The written contract contained detailed specifications concerning the type of equipment, the horsepower of the motors and the tons of refrigeration to be produced. The machinery met the contract specifications, but it was not sufficiently large or powerful to cool Buyer's building. Seller refused to take back the equipment, and pointed out that Buyer received an efficiently operating unit of precisely the size called for in the contract.

Buyer tells his attorney that Seller had recommended the model and size, and had assured Buyer that it would cool Buyer's building. In preparing for trial, Buyer's attorney is concerned that Buyer's testimony with respect to the foregoing statements by Seller would be excluded under the parol evidence rule. The attorney asks you to develop a line of questions that would minimize this danger.

Examine carefully the language of UCC 2–202. Note that "Term" is defined (UCC 1–201(42)) as "that portion of an agreement which relates to a particular matter." Compare UCC 1–201(3) ("agreement" is defined as "the bargain of the parties in fact as found in their language or *by implication from other circumstances* ...") with UCC 1–201(11) ("contract" means "the total legal obligation which results from the parties' agreement as affected by this Act and any other applicable rules of law"). Does UCC 2–202 exclude the above evidence if offered to establish an *implied* warranty?

(3) Lease Transactions. The "buyer" in *Chatlos* was actually a lessee. Because Chatlos lacked sufficient credit to purchase the computer system on an installment basis, an intermediary company bought the system from NCR and leased it to Chatlos. The courts treated Chatlos as a buyer for purposes of the litigation. In 1987, Article 2A on Leases was added to the Code. Under UCC 2A–209(1), seller's warranties to a lessor extend to the lessee if the lease is a "finance lease" (UCC 2A–103(1)(g). This provision codifies the result in *Chatlos*.

The buyer of the copying machines in *Royal Business Machines* was an ordinary equipment lessor, not a financing lessor. As to its lessees, such a lessor's warranties of quality are provided in UCC 2A–210, –212, and –213. These sections parallel the warranty provisions in Article 2.

(4) Consequential Damages. A problem of large importance in sales transactions is the scope of sellers' liability for buyers' consequential damages. The legal issue is related to general contract law growing out of *Hadley v. Baxendale.*[3] The common-law principle is codified in the Code at UCC 2–715(2).

Within the context of sales transactions, buyers may suffer many types of consequential damages resulting from non-conformity of goods purchased. However, certain categories of damages tend to arise regularly. Merchants buying inventory may suffer consequential damages

---

3. A remarkable study of *Hadley v. Baxendale* discloses that the case, as decided, was not a contract case. See Danzig, *Hadley v. Baxendale:* A Study in the Industrialization of the Law, 4 J. Legal Studies 249 (1975).

in the form of lost revenues. Such a claim was advanced in *Sidco* and may explain the large amount of the compensatory damages awarded by the trial court in *Royal Business Machines*. Persons buying business equipment may incur expenses coping with the fall-out of the equipment's failure. Such a claim was advanced in *Chatlos*. Farmers buying seeds or herbicides may suffer damages in crop failures. We will see such cases later in this chapter.

A quite different set of consequential losses arises when buyers suffer personal injuries as a result of defects in the goods. This branch of warranty law has become integrally related to the law of strict tort liability and other facets of product liability law. We will consider this issue, along with others, in the later part of this chapter devoted to special laws of consumer protection.

CARNATION COMPANY v. OLIVET EGG RANCH

California Court of Appeal, First District, 1986.
189 Cal.App.3d 809, 229 Cal.Rptr. 261.

KLINE, J. Olivet Egg Ranch [Olivet] ... appeal[s] following jury trial on [its] claims of fraud and breach of various warranties arising out of [its] purchase and use of chicken feed produced by the Albers Milling Division of the Carnation Company [Albers] ....

[Olivet] ... controlled and managed an egg producing operation in Northern California.

For approximately five years, Olivet or its predecessors in interest purchased chickenfeed from Albers, which operated a mill in Santa Rosa. After unsuccessfully seeking payment of its bills, Carnation advised appellants they would no longer be allowed to purchase on credit. Appellants executed a note for the $606,382 balance owed to Carnation. When appellants defaulted on the note Carnation commenced this litigation. Appellants cross-complained on various theories, all premised on their assertion that the feed sold them was 'misformulated, mis-produced and nutritionally substandard' and, therefore, breached a variety of express and implied warranties made to appellants by Carnation and its employees. Appellants alleged that the feed's nutritional deficiencies had caused a decrease in Olivet's egg production revenues and sought to offset such losses against the amount due Carnation on the note.

After lengthy pretrial discovery, jury trial commenced in October 1979. Because the execution and terms of the note were uncontested, appellants proceeded as if plaintiffs and presented their case first. At the conclusion of Olivet's case Carnation successfully moved for nonsuit as to the loss of goodwill portion of Olivet's damage claim. The court granted a nonsuit on goodwill damages as to the breach of warranty causes of action only on the theory appellants had not met their burden of proving, under California Uniform Commercial Code section 2715, that they had made reasonable efforts to mitigate the damages flowing from the loss of their retail egg marketing accounts.

At the close of evidence Carnation was granted a directed verdict as to a portion of the damages suffered by Olivet's predecessor in interest in 1970.

The jury found that Carnation had breached its warranties and damaged Olivet in the amount of $225,000, but that the claim of fraudulent misrepresentation had not been established.

Separate judgments for both parties were entered and Olivet moved for a new trial on various grounds. ... The court denied the motion for new trial, granted a motion to vacate the two previously entered judgments and ordered nunc pro tunc entry of the net judgment after verdict. This appeal followed.

I.

Burden of Proof Under California Uniform Commercial Code Section 2715, subdivision (2)(a)

The nonsuit as to the $309,000 loss in goodwill appellants claimed due to their inability to service their egg marketing accounts[3] was granted upon the theory that California Uniform Commercial Code section 2715, subdivision (2)(a) places on the aggrieved party the burden of showing it took reasonable steps to mitigate its consequential damages. In granting nonsuit the court necessarily determined that, as a matter of law, Olivet failed to present evidence sufficient to meet its burden. It will be necessary to consider whether Olivet presented evidence sufficient to withstand nonsuit on this issue only if we first determine that the court's imposition of the burden on Olivet was legally correct. Olivet could not be penalized for failing to meet a burden which actually rested with Carnation. Thus, we are squarely faced with a question of first impression in California: which party bears the burden of proving the adequacy or inadequacy of efforts to mitigate consequential damages under California Uniform Commercial Code section 2715, subdivision (2)(a)?

Section 2715, subdivision (2)(a), which was adopted without change from the Uniform Commercial Code (UCC), simply declares that "[c]onsequential damages resulting from the seller's breach include ... [a]ny

---

3. Olivet had an arrangement with several large supermarket chains pursuant to which the markets invested in the ranch partnership and purchased all of their requirements directly from the ranch at a retail price. Olivet was thereby provided with an assured outlet for its eggs and was to derive a profit for the processing and marketing, as well as the egg sale. Due to Olivet's shortfall in egg production, it ultimately was unable to keep up with the requirements of its market accounts and Olivet transferred the accounts to Olson Egg Farms. Appellants claimed the loss of the goodwill value of the retail marketing arm of its operation as an additional element of damages.

The nonsuit was granted only as to the loss of goodwill attributable to the claimed breach of warranty. Because the burden of proof on mitigation as to the fraud cause of action is on the party asserting the defense, the court ruled that the issue remained in the case as to that claim.

loss resulting from general or particular requirements and needs of which the seller at the time of contracting had reason to know and which could not reasonably be prevented by cover or otherwise."

The official comment to the parallel provision of the UCC does not shed much light on allocation of the burden of proof. Paragraph 2 of the pertinent UCC comment provides in material part that: "The 'tacit agreement' test for the recovery of consequential damages is rejected. Although the older rule at common law which made the seller liable for all consequential damages of which he had 'reason to know' in advance is followed, the liberality of that rule is modified by refusing to permit recovery unless the buyer could not reasonably have prevented the loss by cover or otherwise. Subparagraph (2) [of the statute] carries forward the provision of the prior uniform statutory provision as to consequential damages resulting from breach of warranty, but modifies the rule by requiring first that the buyer attempt to minimize his damages in good faith, either by cover or otherwise." This comment does not demonstrate, as respondent asserts, that section 2715, subdivision (2)(a) was intended to act as "a restraint on the liberality of the common law."

Paragraph 4 of the UCC comment makes specific reference to the UCC's section on the liberal administration of remedies, indicating that the right to consequential damages should be broadly, not narrowly, construed. Furthermore, while paragraph 4 states that "[t]he burden of proving the extent of loss incurred by way of consequential damage is on the buyer ..." this statement does not determine the allocation of the burden of proof on the mitigation issue. It is entirely possible for the injured party to bear the burden of proving the extent of consequential damages while the breaching party has the duty of proving those items which limit the award of consequential damages.

The UCC's failure to allocate unambiguously the burden of proving mitigation has resulted in conflicting interpretations among those jurisdictions that have considered the question. Unfortunately, these cases are of little value to us since they do not analyze the problem nor explain why the burden should rest with one party or the other. By and large the cases merely state the unembellished conclusion that one or the other party has the burden of proof on this issue....

While the commentators do not unanimously support allocating the burden to the breaching party, there is substantial support among them for this position. Corbin, for example, declares that "[t]he burden of proving that losses could have been avoided by reasonable effort and expense must always be borne by the party who has broken the contract." (5 Corbin on Contracts (1964) § 1039 ...) White and Summers state that "consequential damages that the *defendant* proves the buyer could have avoided will not be allowed ..." (J. White and R. Summers, Uniform Commercial Code (2d ed. 1980) §§ 6–7, p. 250, italics added.) ...

Placing on the party who breaches the burden of showing that consequential losses could have been avoided is intuitively attractive, since proof that there has been a failure to mitigate adequately will reduce the damages awarded and, therefore, seems more in the nature of a defense than an element of the plaintiff's affirmative case. In this sense, proof of failure to mitigate is analogous to evidence showing comparative negligence in tort law, which must be alleged and proved by the defendant.... Moreover, it is sensible to require the defendant to prove those items which go to reduce the plaintiff's recovery, as plaintiffs would have little incentive to do so.

Respondent maintains that "[i]t makes more sense to place the burden of proving efforts to mitigate on the party best able to adduce evidence of such efforts." While this argument is on its surface appealing it does not stand up to closer scrutiny. As has been noted "[v]ery often one must plead and prove matters as to which his adversary has superior access to the proof. Nearly all required allegations of the plaintiff in actions for tort or breach of contract relating to the defendant's acts or omissions describe matters peculiarly in the defendant's knowledge. Correspondingly, when the defendant is required to plead contributory negligence, he pleads facts specially known to the plaintiff." (McCormick on Evidence (3d ed. 1984) ch. 36, § 337 at p. 950.)

Moreover, in cases such as this defendants do not genuinely lack the ability to ascertain the pertinent facts. A carefully drafted set of interrogatories could have provided Carnation with all the information it required about Olivet's efforts to mitigate its consequential damages. Since it therefore had access to the relevant evidence we see no reason why this consideration should prevent allocation to Carnation of the burden of showing that appellants failed to adequately mitigate their consequential damages.

For the foregoing reasons, we hold that while the burden of proving the extent of loss incurred by way of consequential damages rests with the injured party, section 2715, subdivision (2)(a) imposes upon the allegedly breaching party the burden of proving the inadequacy of efforts to mitigate consequential damages. Thus, Carnation, not Olivet, properly had the burden of proof on the issue of Olivet's mitigation of the consequential damages arising from Carnation's breach. Olivet therefore had no duty to present evidence of mitigation and the granting of the nonsuit on the basis of Olivet's asserted failure to produce such evidence was error. The nonsuit removed from the jury's consideration a $309,000 damage claim. Since Carnation never presented evidence on this issue there is no way of knowing whether appellants likely would have prevailed if the court had placed the burden of proof on Carnation. Accordingly, the judgment must be reversed.

(B) INTERNATIONAL SALES LAW

Having considered sellers' obligations for the quality of their goods under domestic United States law, we turn briefly to consider the analogous provisions of the Convention on International Sales. The first case studied in this chapter, an international sale of flour from a United States milling company to the Bolivian government, arose before the Convention existed and was decided under the Code. Would this case, and other cases and problems, be analyzed or decided differently if the law governing the matter is the CISG?

(1) Sellers' Obligations. The Convention sets forth sellers' quality obligations in Section II of Chapter II. The primary standards, in Article 35, resemble the warranty provisions of the Code, but there are substantial differences. The CISG does not use the term "warranty." Compare carefully the provisions in Article 35 with their counterparts in the Code and consider the Code provisions for which no counterparts exist in the CISG. What conclusions can be drawn from these comparisons? Are the quality obligations of sellers under CISG greater or less than their obligations under the Code?

The CISG does not contain a parol evidence provision comparable to UCC 2–202. Article 11 provides that a contract "need not be ... evidenced by writing" and "may be proved by any means, including witnesses." See also CISG 8(3). However, the parties by agreement may derogate from CISG 11 by an "integration clause" (CISG 6) or may agree that modification of a written agreement must be in writing (CISG 29(2)).

(2) Buyers' Remedies. Buyers' remedies under CISG are stated broadly in Article 45, which cross refers to Articles 74 to 77. How does the basic formula in the first sentence of Article 74 compare with UCC 2–714? What is the meaning of "loss ... suffered"? Does this permit a buyer to recover damages determined by the value the goods would have had if they had been conforming, the so-called "benefit of the bargain"? How does the formula in the second sentence of Article 74 compare with UCC 2–715(2)?

AWARD IN CASE NO. 3779 OF 1981
Collection of ICC Arbitral Awards 1974–85, p. 138

Arbitrator: Prof. Jacques H. Herbots (Belgium)

Parties: Claimant: Swiss seller
               Respondent: Dutch buyer

Published: Not (yet) published ....

[FACTS]

Three contracts were concluded in 1979 between the parties, all three concerning the same type of merchandise [whey powder] of which the quality was described in detail.

The merchandise, coming from a Canadian factory was to be delivered C.I.F. Rotterdam. The contracts were made in French and all contained—except for quantities—the same conditions, including an arbitral clause referring disputes to arbitration under the Arbitration Rules of the ICC. However, only the first two contracts were signed by the parties and executed. The third contract was not signed and before shipment from Canada took place, it was cancelled by the Respondent who complained that the merchandise delivered under the first two contracts was not in accordance with the quality prescribed in the contract.

The Canadian Factory sent one of its technicians, Dr. E., to the Netherlands and samples were taken and examined in an independent laboratory. It appeared that they were in accordance with the contractual requirements when analyzed under the North American method, but not when the European analytic method was used.

Arbitration followed in which the Swiss seller claimed US $55,000 (including *inter alia* $37,500 paid to the Canadian factory) in respect of the cancellation of the third contract. The Dutch buyer introduced a counterclaim of Hfl. 181,645.—covering losses in respect of the first two contracts.

[EXTRACT]

I. *Competence of Arbitrator*

The clause attributing jurisdiction to the ICC occurs in two preceding and similar contracts that were signed by both parties, as well as in the third contract, that, although it was not signed, was not protested against within a reasonable delay either.

Although the contracts are independent from one another from a juridical point of view, the three contracts form a group from an economic point of view.

If, in principle, silence does not mean acceptance, this meaning is, however, attributed to it in view of the circumstances, in particular, the previous business relations of the parties.

Consequently, within the context of their juridical relation and according to their obligations of good faith, the exception of incompetence does not apply.

II. *Law Applicable to the Contract*

... In an international sale of goods, when the parties remain silent, the domestic law of the country in which the seller has his place of residence is to be applied (see the Hague Convention on the International Sale of Goods of June 15, 1955); Kahn, J., Rep.Dall., Dr. internat., V° Vente commerciale; Lunz, Cours Acad. Dr. Internat. 1965, I, 1; Federal Court of Switzerland, 12th February 1952, R 1953, 390, note Flattet).

The chosen language, the place where the contract was entered into by correspondence together with applying the theory of reception, and the way of payment, all point in the same direction.

Consequently, Swiss law is applicable to the contract in dispute ....

IV. *With Respect to the Merits of the Dispute*

* * *

3. *The misunderstanding*

Both parties seem to have acted in good faith.

Actually, the Claimant had immediately declared his willingness to submit samples drawn by both parties to a test by a competent laboratory to be chosen by both parties, and to accept cancellation of the remaining contracts if this analysis proved that the Respondent's allegations had been well-founded.

The Respondent, on his part, also immediately reported the quality problems encountered, asked for an expert and sent samples to the Canadian factory. He agreed to pay for the goods that had already arrived in Rotterdam and he restricted himself to refusing to give any forwarding-instructions or to receive the goods ordered, but not yet loaded on board.

The dispute essentially arises from a misunderstanding.

The following conclusion is essential for understanding the matter: "The main conclusion of Dr. E. during his visit to the Dutch buyer was that the goods sent were not the product the Dutch buyer believed to have bought; the Dutch buyer maintains that, when the Swiss seller initially gave a description of the goods, no mention was made of a method of analysis. The Dutch buyer supposed that, since the description was given by a European firm, the European methods were to be applied ..." (quotation from document 24). To this the Claimant replies: "It goes without saying that the methods to be used should be those of the country of origin or those that are universally accepted, such as the (North American) method" (document 3).

It was only when the quality problems emerged that the Claimant announced the method of analyzing, *inter alia*, the solubility index, viz. the (North American) method that, according to him, is intentionally accepted (document 6 bis).

The Canadian factory was willing to send a technician but made the condition that first agreement should be reached on the method of analysis (document 7).

It is certain that the goods are in accordance with the contractual description, provided that the samples are analyzed according to the (North American) method.

It appears from the proceedings that, although it is not a sale on sample, a sample had been sent to the Respondent prior to the conclusion of the contracts.

The first deliveries were in accordance with this quality, the latter not, although they remained in accordance with the contractual description of the goods, which explains why it was only at a late stage that the misunderstanding came to light.

The misunderstanding is essentially about the solubility degree of the powder delivered.

The method of analysis must be carefully specified in order to be able to determine the solubility degree of the powder.

In Switzerland, methods of analysis are used that are incorporated in the Swiss Manual on Foods, of which Manual the chapter on goods like this particular powder has, unfortunately, not been published yet.

Although the North American method (actually designed for a different type of powder) is better known in the international powder industry involved than a French method, it cannot be considered, however, to be implicitly understood, at least, not on the European market.

The French method differs from the (North American) method with respect to the temperature during the dissolution and the technique of dissolution. The two methods are particularly different with respect to the method of expressing the result in a figure (the solubility index). The Canadian factory took this into account when it was too late, notably, when the Respondent complained about the quality of the goods and the question of analyzing the samples was raised.

4. Shared responsibilities with respect to the origin of the misunderstanding

From a telex from the Canadian factory to the Claimant ... it appears that the factory claims to have been clear as to the description of the goods and the methodology, and that the contractual (possibly insufficient) description of the goods, given by the Claimant to his own clients, does not concern him at all, from which it can be deduced that the factory leaves the total contractual responsibility to the Claimant in the case he had not done likewise with his own principal, that is to say, the Respondent.

The Claimant should have known that there was a possibility of error on the European market with respect to the appreciation of the description of the powder.

One cannot presume that there is agreement on the (North American) method between a Swiss seller and a Dutch buyer.

The Claimant should have mentioned that the contractual description was to be interpreted according to the (North American) method, as the Canadian supplier had done in his contract with the Claimant.

The Claimant should have informed the buyer of the conditions on which he contracted (see T.G.I., Argentan, 15th October 1970, D.S., 1971, p. 718, note of M. Ghestin, quoted by Lucas de Leyssac, *L'obligation de renseignements dans les contrats*, in: *L'information en droit privé*, L.G.D., J., 1978, p. 316).

With respect to the interpretation of the contract, the (also in Swiss law) traditional rule can be applied as well: "*in dubio, contra proferentem* ".

As Loysel wrote: "qui vend le pot, dit le mot".

The seller is obliged to state clearly what obligations he is undertaking.

The Respondent, on the other hand, knew very well that the goods were of Canadian origin, because he had had contact with the supplier.

Consequently, the error is equally due to his negligence, for he should have asked about the meaning of the symbols used in the contractual description of the powder of North American origin.

The dialectics between the right of being informed, and the obligation of informing oneself is thus at the heart of the problem in the present dispute.

The error of the Respondent is due to a negligence shared with the Claimant (in Swiss law one can find the following instances of shared negligence: A and B have concluded a sale, for which the price has been fixed on the basis of a tariff, the rectification of which has been published many times. A and B conclude a contract without informing themselves about the provisions of clearing that are applicable to their deal—see ENGEL, Pierre, *Traité des obligations en droit Suisse*, Neuchatel, 1973, p. 257).

The (North American) method being more frequently used than the other methods, the negligence of the Claimant as to the information seems less than that of the Respondent ....

THEREFORE:

We, Arbitrator, deciding in accordance with the provisions of the ICC Rules of Conciliation and Arbitration, within the limits of our mission, that was extended by decision of the Court of Arbitration;

> observe in the commercial relations of the parties the existence of an arbitration clause to settle the present dispute and consequently declare ourselves competent to decide and award with respect to the claim and the counterclaim;

With respect to the claim

> condemn the Respondent to pay to the Claimant the amount of $27,000 as indemnification for the invalidation (that is to say cancellation) of the third contract.

With respect to the counterclaim

reject the claim of the Respondent for indemnification because of the non-conformity of the goods delivered under the two preceding contracts.

Order that the costs of the arbitration, including costs and fee of the arbitrator, being $8,300, will be borne by the Claimant for 2/5 and by the Respondent for 3/5.

Notes

(1) **International Commercial Arbitration.** Many parties to international sales contracts elect by a clause in those contracts to have disputes resolved by arbitration. (The same is true for other kinds of international contracts.) One type of arbitration that may be chosen is arbitration pursuant to rules and procedures of the International Chamber of Commerce, which established in 1923 what is now called the International Court of Arbitration. Since its founding, the ICC Court has handled more than 6,700 cases. Most of those are unreported. However, since 1974, selected arbitral awards have been published. The initial collection, spanning eleven years, contained the whey powder determination. Since 1976, the International Council for Commercial Arbitration has been publishing Yearbooks of Commercial Arbitration which contain a selection of arbitral awards and other materials. These sources make it possible to compare commercial arbitration, its results and its method of dispute resolution, with the more familiar results and methods of adjudication.

Commercial arbitration is also widely used in the United States and elsewhere for the resolution of commercial disputes not involving international transactions. Domestic commercial arbitration tends to be done with high concern for privacy of the parties and the arbitrators in the United States are not expected to write reasoned awards. We lack even selected reports of arbitration awards of this kind.

(2) **Comparing Arbitration and Adjudication.** What aspects of the arbitrator's reasoning and award in the whey powder case are peculiar to the arbitration mode of dispute resolution? If this controversy had been submitted to a United States or other national court for disposition, would the court's reasoning have been the same? Would the outcome probably be the same?

AWARD MADE IN CASE NO. 2129 IN 1972, Collection of ICC Arbitral Awards 1974–1985, p. 23. A German seller contracted to deliver motor car accessories to a United States buyer. Buyer claimed relief for expenses incurred in altering the goods to make them usable on United States automobiles, which were larger than German automobiles. The arbitrator, applying the Ohio Commercial Code, found for the United States buyer:

The defendant's equipment had to be fit for the ordinary purposes for which it was to be used. Thus, the equipment manufactured for the German market had to be modified to service the U.S. market. At the time of contracting the defendant knew the purpose for which the equipment was required and the buyer relied upon him to furnish suitable machines.... This warranty of merchantability and fitness applies to sales for use as well as to sales for resale and can be invoked by the plaintiff as well as by his customers. The plaintiff is therefore entitled to be reimbursed for the money he spent repairing or altering the defendant's equipment pursuant to an implied warranty of merchantability and fitness.

AWARD OF SEPTEMBER 27, 1983, CASE NO. 3880
(Original in French)

Arbitrators:	Dr. Werner Wenger; Prof. Lucien Simont; Prof. Marcel Storme
Parties:	Claimant: Belgian buyer A Defendant: Belgian seller B
Published in:	110 *Journal du droit international (Clunet)* 1983, p. 897, with note Y. Derains and S. Jarvin, pp. 897–899.

[FACTS]

On January 26, 1979, claimant A and defendant B entered into a contract whereby B undertook to supply A with 150,000 pairs of ladies' boots between April and August 1979. On the same date, B entered into an identical contract (differing only in relation to the price) with a Romanian State trading enterprise C, who was to supply the same quantity of boots to B. When the Romanian enterprise C defaulted, arbitration proceedings were commenced by A who sought damages for late delivery and defective goods. The arbitrators rejected a request by defendant B to join the claim with an arbitration it had commenced separately against its supplier, the Romanian enterprise C, based on that company's default in delivery. Claimant A was successful as to 75% of its claim.

[EXTRACT]

[On *force majeure:*]

... [D]efendant B contends ... that to the extent that the contract obliged it to supply boots made at the factory D in Romania, the source proposed by its supplier, the Romanian enterprise C, the default of the latter constituted an insurmountable obstacle and an extraneous cause relieving it of any liability towards Claimant A ....

It follows that, B's obligations being in the nature of obligations of result, their non-fulfilment places B in default and involves it in liability vis-à-vis A, except for those cases where the latter company cancelled orders without justification....

[On the mitigation of damages:]

B argues, however, that A could have offered its clients in sufficient time merchandise equivalent to the subject-matter of the contract between the parties, in conformity with its obligation to take all appropriate steps to limit its damage and reduce its losses.

The boots which were the subject-matter of the contract have a seasonal character and could not be sold and delivered to A's client except at the beginning of the winter season at the latest. B, on the basis of promises made by its own supplier, had led A to believe, up to August 1979 and, at least for the major part of the order, even up to the first half of September 1979, that it would be in a position to deliver the goods, admittedly late, but before the last moment. Its failure to fulfil these promises only became apparent after it was too late to obtain the merchandise elsewhere. In effect, having regard to the changing fashions to which this type of product is subject, suppliers keep very little in stock. B omits to identify the sources to which A could have turned at the end of September 1979, to obtain merchandise equivalent to that described in the Contract.

In these circumstances it is not appropriate to reduce the compensation for damages suffered by reason of a violation of the creditor to observe its obligation to mitigate its damages.

[On loss of goodwill:]

Having regard to the fact that, out of a total of about 127,000 pairs of boots ordered by A from B, a significant number, 45,509 pairs, or about 35%, were the subject of justifiable complaints about failure to meet delivery dates and defects in quality. This percentage considerably exceeds what would normally be expected to be tolerated. Having regard to the seasonal character of the merchandise, A was only able to satisfy its clients from other sources to a limited extent. One's commercial reputation would seem to be affected when a business finds itself in the position of not being able to fulfil a significant proportion of its orders.

The nature of the effect on its reputation is such as to make it impossible, in the absence of precise criteria, to determine the exact extent of the damage caused by it; that such damage cannot be evaluated. In these circumstances, it appears that for the reasons stated above, and taking all aspects of the case into consideration, particularly the net margin of A and the trading figures with the clients mentioned above from 1980–1982 in comparison with previous years, A's claim can only be deemed to be partly founded, and the sum of Bfrs. 200,000 must be allowed to it as damages for any prejudice to its commercial reputation.

Note

Other "Fields" of Law (Reprise). The Convention (CISG 4) "governs only" the "obligations of the seller and the buyer arising from [the international sales] contract." Does the CISG displace rules of law that deal with defective goods under rubrics other than "contract"? To what extent is an international sales contract subject to law of fraud, misrepresentation or mistake, like those referred to earlier in United States law? Consider CISG 4(a). What issues are excluded from the CISG as going to the "validity of the contract"? The problems regarding the relationship between the Convention and domestic law are important and difficult. See J. Honnold, Uniform Law for International Sales §§ 64–67, 232–237 (2d ed. 1991).

SECTION 3. WARRANTIES OF TITLE

(A) DOMESTIC LAW

Introduction. Buyers of goods ordinarily expect to obtain "good" or "clean" title to the goods they have purchased.[1] Two types of cases may defeat that expectation: sales of stolen goods and sales of encumbered goods.[2] We have already dealt with stolen goods in Chapter 1.

Encumbrances on the title to goods (often called "liens") arise sometimes through the voluntary action of an owner, who creates or consents to the creation of an interest in the property. The principal example of this form of encumbrance is a "security interest" under Article 9 of the Code. Other times, an encumbrance arises by action of a third party, usually against the will of the owner. Thus, a judgment creditor may obtain a lien on property of the judgment debtor by the process of attachment or judgment execution. Alternatively, liens may arise by operation of law without a judgment. Examples are the liens that may be obtained by the Internal Revenue Service for unpaid federal taxes ("tax liens") or by repairers of goods for their services ("mechanics' liens").

A seller's responsibility to the buyer who is compelled to surrender goods to the rightful owner is stated in UCC 2–312(1)(a). A seller warrants that "the title conveyed shall be good, and its transfer rightful." The warranty against encumbrances is set forth in UCC 2–312(1)(b): "the goods shall be delivered free from any security interest or other lien or encumbrance of which the buyer at the time of contracting has no knowledge." Sellers' warranty can be excluded or

---

1. The Uniform Sales Act used the passing of title ("property") as the fulcrum for resolving a number of legal issues that may arise during the performance of sales contracts. The Commercial Code's rules on performance and remedies are not based on title passing. However, passing of title continues to be of primary importance to the parties to sales contracts because legal rights and duties not governed by the Code may turn upon the question of ownership. For example, tax obligations may fall upon the owner of property.

2. For property subject to a patent or trademark or other form of intellectual property, a seller may sell the goods without conveying the right to use them without infringement of the rights of the owner of the intellectual property. Intellectual property law often separates the physical thing from the right to use it. Rights to use are commonly conveyed by license by the patent holder or owner of the intellectual property right. Sellers' warranty with respect to infringement of intellectual property rights is found in UCC 2–312(3). See also UCC 2–607(5)(b).

modified "by specific language" in the agreement of sale or by certain "circumstances." UCC 2–312(2).

WRIGHT v. VICKARYOUS

Supreme Court of Alaska, 1980.
611 P.2d 20.

MATTHEWS, JUSTICE. On January 8, 1977, Vickaryous bought forty-five head of cattle from Wright at an auction sale. His bid was $13,032.50. Unknown to Vickaryous at the time, the Farmer's Home Administration, the Northwest Livestock Production Credit Association, and the State of Alaska Revolving Loan Fund each held perfected and filed security interests on the cattle. However, they had consented to the auction sale of the cattle in conversations with Wright. Thus, under the terms of section 9–306(2) of the Uniform Commercial Code as enacted in Alaska, their security interests were released by the sale.

Shortly after the auction, and on the same day that it was held, Wright and Vickaryous modified the sale contract to provide that Vickaryous would pay $1,000.00 down with the balance of the purchase price to be paid on or before delivery, no later than January 14th. Vickaryous then was told by a third party that there were liens on the cattle. The next day, an employee of Wright tendered delivery of the cattle to Vickaryous. He told the employee that he would not accept them because of the liens. On Monday, January 10th, Vickaryous contacted an attorney and asked him to determine whether the cattle were encumbered; the attorney discovered the filed security interests and advised Vickaryous of their existence. Vickaryous then stopped payment on the $1,000.00 check he had given as a down payment.

On Tuesday, January 11th, Wright served Vickaryous with a notice of intent to resell the cows and hold Vickaryous responsible for any deficiency. An auction resale was conducted on January 15th at which $3,166.00 was received. The expenses of resale were $1,025.00.

Wright brought this action to recover the difference between the contract price with Vickaryous and the resale price plus costs.

Trial was to the court. The court determined that although the security interests were released as a matter of law against Vickaryous, they remained of record and constituted "a substantial shadow" over the title to the cattle, sufficient to breach the warranty of freedom from encumbrances provided by section 2–312 of the U.C.C. The court found that since Wright made no effort to cure the uncertainty which constituted the breach of warranty he was not entitled to hold Vickaryous liable for breach of the sale contract.

Wright's main point on appeal is that there was no breach of the warranty of freedom from encumbrances since he had obtained the consent to sale of the secured parties and, therefore, their security interests were discharged as a matter of law. Vickaryous counters, and the court held, that the existence of apparently valid security interests on file constituted a cloud on the title and therefore a breach of warranty in the absence of an explanation by Wright that the security interests had been discharged.

Unless explicitly excluded, or the circumstances are such as to indicate otherwise, there is in every contract for the sale of goods a warranty that the title is good, and that the goods will be delivered free from encumbrances. This warranty is expressed in U.C.C. § 2–312(1) (AS 45.05.092(a)) which provides:

> Subject to (b) of this section there is in a contract for sale a warranty by the seller that
>
> (1) the title conveyed shall be good, and its transfer rightful; and
>
> (2) the goods shall be delivered free from a security interest or other lien or encumbrance of which the buyer at the time of contracting has no knowledge.

The official commentary to section 2–312 states:

> Subsection (1) makes provision for a buyer's basic needs in respect to a title which he in good faith expects to acquire by his purchase, namely, that he receive a good, clean title transferred to him also in a rightful manner *so that he will not be exposed to a lawsuit in order to protect it.* [emphasis added]

Uniform Commercial Code § 2–312, Comment 1. The emphasized language makes it clear that a marketable title concept is intended, for otherwise it would not be important whether a buyer was merely exposed to a lawsuit, but rather whether he could win it.

Cases decided in other jurisdictions confirm our view that section 2–312 expresses a concept of marketable title. In American Container Corp. v. Hanley Trucking Corp., 111 N.J.Super. 322, 268 A.2d 313, 318 (1970) the court stated the following with respect to the section 2–312 warranty:

> The purchaser of goods warranted as to title has a right to rely on the fact that he will not be required, at some later time, to enter into a contest over the validity of his ownership. The mere casting of a substantial shadow over his title, regardless of the ultimate outcome, is sufficient to violate a warranty of good title.

Accord, Ricklefs v. Clemens, 216 Kan. 128, 531 P.2d 94, 100 (1975). Other authorities involving the sale of personal property, not decided under the Uniform Commercial Code, likewise have concluded that a buyer need not complete a purchase which apparently will require a lawsuit to protect that which is acquired....

Under the facts of this case Wright could easily have saved the transaction by explaining that the sale was made with the consent of the secured parties and that their liens were discharged. Remarkably, he chose not to do so, and thus his breach stands....

Affirmed.

Notes

(1) **Inventory Finance.** Merchants and farmers commonly borrow money to finance their activities. Lenders often secure their loans with security interests in the goods to be sold. Seldom will any buyer knowingly take goods subject to a pre-sale encumbrance. Lenders' release of encumbrances on merchants' and farmers' inventory at the time of retail sale is routine commercial practice. Financers want the inventory sold (they get repaid from the proceeds of the sales) and therefore authorize the merchants or farmers to sell the goods to buyers free of security interests. This commercial practice is reflected in UCC 9–306(2), which provides that a security interest does not "continue" upon authorized sale of the goods.[3] In *Wright,* the court found that the secured parties had consented to the sale free of the encumbrances, but found further that the buyer was unaware of the release of security interests. The court treats the buyer as a surprised recipient of an intermeddler's report that encumbrances existed. How likely is it that an auction buyer of 45 head of cattle would be so unsophisticated in that marketplace as to be surprised by the information? How likely is it that such a buyer would not expect that encumbrances created by the seller would be released?

After buyer refused to accept them, the cattle were resold, in an apparently similar auction, one week after the first auction, but the price obtained in the second auction was sharply lower. Does this suggest that the buyer may have overbid in the first auction and, having realized this, wanted a way to escape the obligation to pay the contract price? If this were buyer's motive, would buyer's action be consistent with the obligation to act in good faith in the performance of the contract?

(2) **Clouds on Title.** The *Wright* court held that seller was in breach of the obligation under UCC 2–312 even though no third party ever pressed a claim against the buyer's title. Is this conclusion supported by the *text* of the section? Is it supported by the Comment? Is the Comment authorized to go beyond the text?

Third party claims of title to goods or claims of encumbrances on goods can range from being clearly plausible to quite fanciful. Where on this spectrum does sellers' responsibility end?

Should it matter whether the issue is raised before, or after, the buyer has accepted the goods and paid the price? After payment and acceptance, would a buyer have a right to damages under UCC 2–312

---

3. This matter is considered more fully in Part IV infra.

on the basis of an unsubstantiated concern that there was an encumbrance on the goods?

(3) Monetary Remedy for Breach. The Uniform Commercial Code does not provide clearly the measure of damages appropriate when a seller has breached the warranty of title. If a seller had no title to the goods and the rightful owner reclaimed the goods from the buyer, or if the goods were subject to a security interest and the secured party repossessed the goods, the buyer has suffered injury, but the correct statutory measure of damages is disputed. Buyers should be allowed to recover the value of the goods of which they have been deprived, but a question that often arises is on what date is value to be measured. A defect in title may be unknown to a buyer for a substantial period of time after goods have been purchased. Between the date of delivery and the date buyer loses possession, the value of the goods may have changed substantially. The direction of change could be up or down, and the rate of change can be slow or fast. For example, equipment generally depreciates steadily over time, whereas some works of art appreciate, occasionally precipitously, if the reputation of the artist is growing. The Code contains several provisions that might be invoked. One possible measure is that provided in UCC 2–714(2), which determines the value of the goods as warranted "at the time ... of acceptance." Another possible measure is that provided by UCC 2–711(1) in conjunction with UCC 2–713(1), which in effect determines the value of the goods "at the time when the buyer learned of the breach." [4]

A Maryland court faced the problem in a case arising from sale of certain patterns used to produce hardware. The patterns had depreciated in value while in buyer's possession. Buyer contended that UCC 2–714(2) should govern and that the value of the patterns on the date of acceptance should be used to fix the amount of damages. The court wrote:

> Scholars contend that § 2–714(2) does not regulate damages for breach of warranty of title, but that it in fact relates only to breach of warranty of quality.... This is said to be so because § 2–714(2) is based on § 69(6) and (7) of the Uniform Sales Act; those provisions pertained to breaches of warranty of quality, not title....
>
> It is suggested that because § 2–714(2) does not expressly apply to a breach of warranty of title, a court should look to pre-U.C.C. law in that situation by virtue of the "special circumstances" provision of § 2–714(2) and because the U.C.C. comment to that

---

4. To be entitled to a remedy measured by UCC 2–711 and 2–713, a buyer deprived of the goods by a rightful owner would have to revoke acceptance of the goods. Buyers are entitled to revoke their acceptances if the nonconformity in the goods substantially impairs their value, a standard easily met if buyers had to surrender the goods to a rightful owner or to a secured party. See Sumner v. Fel–Air, Inc., 680 P.2d 1109 (Alaska 1984). Once having rightfully revoked acceptance, a buyer may recover the price paid under UCC 2–711 plus the difference between the contract price and the value of the goods under UCC 2–711(1)(b) and 2–713(1). Revocation of acceptance is considered later.

section indicates it is not intended to provide for the exclusive measure of damages.... Pre-U.C.C. law is not too helpful, however. Under it decisions relating to the measure of damages for breach of warranty of title range from purchase price plus interest to value of the goods at time of dispossession, to value without specifying any time of determination, to value at time of sale (which may or may not be the same as the purchase price)....

Other jurisdictions have faced this problem. They have applied § 2–714(2) to breaches of warranty of title.... We shall do likewise. The statute is plain and unambiguous on its face and should be read according to its clear meaning....

The next question is whether to apply § 2–714(2)'s "difference at the time and place of acceptance between the value of the goods accepted and the value they would have had as warranted" or whether there are "special circumstances [that] show proximate damages of a different amount." We hold that there are special circumstances here.... [Buyer] had use and possession of the patterns for varying periods of time before it had knowledge of any title defects. And the patterns were unique; they were specially designed to produce castings to particular specifications.

Since we conclude that this case falls within the "special circumstances" clause of § 2–714(2), we must now decide what measure of damages to apply under it. Courts that have considered the question under the U.C.C. have almost uniformly rejected the view that the purchase price of the goods is the proper measure.... The value of the goods at the approximate date of dispossession, or something akin to that, is the measure of damages generally selected.

Metalcraft, Inc. v. Pratt, 65 Md.App. 281, 292–294, 500 A.2d 329, 335–336 (1985).

Suppose a different case in which the goods had appreciated significantly in value. Seller contends that UCC 2–714(2) limits damages to the value of the goods at the time of delivery and acceptance. Should a court permit the larger recovery that takes the appreciation into account? See Jeanneret v. Vichey, 693 F.2d 259 (2d Cir.1982); Menzel v. List, 24 N.Y.2d 91, 298 N.Y.S.2d 979, 246 N.E.2d 742 (1969).

Article 2 of the Uniform Commercial Code is under revision. Should the revisers develop a measure of damages for breach of UCC 2–312? What should that measure be?

Problem 1. After a sale of goods, a third party (X) contends that it holds a security interest that survived the sale from S to B; S contends that the security interest was invalid. If X brings an action against B, may B transfer some of the costs and risks of litigation to S by a third-party action (impleader) against S? See Rule 14, Federal Rules of Civil Procedure. If S is not subject to the jurisdiction of the court where B is sued, a "vouching" letter under UCC 2–607(5) may induce S to take over the defense—or at least provide B with a claim against S that could be vindicated without retrial of issues raised in the action by X v. B. But this is far from "quiet possession." Should B be subjected to the uncertainties and costs of even a disputed claim of title? How should the problem be solved?

Problem 2. The Hammer Auction Company operates a sales barn at which livestock are sold regularly at auction. Hammer sells the livestock on commission for many cattlemen. Buyers are aware that Hammer is not the owner and acts as the agent of some unnamed principal. William Buyer made the high bid on three heifers which had been left with Hammer by Sam Theft. After the purchase, Buyer learned that the heifers were stolen and had to return them to the true owner. Buyer sues Hammer to recover the amount of his bid.

What argument may be made for the defendant, Hammer, based on UCC 2–312(1)? Was Hammer "the seller" of the livestock? See UCC 2–103. Under common-law agency doctrine, one who contracts as agent for another without disclosing the identity of the principal is not merely an agent, but is deemed a "party to the contract." Restatement (Second) of Agency §§ 321–322. See Jones v. Ballard, 573 So.2d 783 (Miss.1990) (warranty of title); cf. Powers v. Coffeyville Livestock Sales Co., 665 F.2d 311 (10th Cir.1981) (warranty of quality). Does this doctrine from common law apply to transactions under UCC Article 2. Recall UCC 1–103.

What argument may be made for the defendant, Hammer, under UCC 2–312(2)? Does the statute displace the common-law of agency? Is "the seller" in 2–312(1) the same as "the person selling" in 2–312(2)? Should 2–312(2) be read to create an immunity for auctioneers and other agents of partially disclosed or undisclosed principals? See Comment 5.

Problem 3. Charles Creditor held a judgment against Daniel Debtor, and sued out a writ of attachment to levy on Debtor's property. Pursuant to the writ of attachment, Samuel Sheriff seized a tractor in Debtor's possession and sold it at an execution sale; Buyer bought the tractor for $500. Unknown to all parties, the tractor was subject to a perfected security interest held by Leo Lean to secure a $300 debt which Debtor owed Lean. Lean's security interest was binding after the sale, and Lean threatens to seize the tractor from Buyer unless Debtor's debt is satisfied. Has Buyer any recourse against Sheriff or Creditor? See UCC 2–312(2); Bogestad v. Anderson, 143 Minn. 336, 173 N.W. 674 (1919). Has Buyer any recourse against Debtor?

Problem 4. Marie Louise Jeanneret, a citizen of Switzerland, is a well-known art dealer in Geneva. Defendants Anna and Luben Vichey, wife and husband, are citizens of the United States. Anna's father, Carlo Frua DeAngeli, had an extensive and internationally recognized private collection of paintings in Milan, Italy. One of these was a painting, Portrait sur Fond Jaune, by the renowned French post-impressionist, Henri Matisse, who was born in 1869 and died in 1954.

Title to the Matisse painting ultimately vested in Anna Vichey. In 1970 the Matisse painting was brought to the Vicheys' apartment in New York City. In January 1973 Mme. Jeanneret began negotiations for the purchase of the painting, and an agreement was reached for its sale for 700,000 Swiss francs, then equivalent to approximately $230,-000. Luben Vichey delivered the painting to plaintiff in Geneva in March 1973.

Mme. Jeanneret included the Matisse painting in a large exhibit of 20th century masters at her gallery in Geneva. In November 1974, Mme. Jeanneret encountered Signora Bucarelli, superintendent in charge of the export of paintings from Italy, who declared she had been looking for the Matisse painting because she suspected its illegal exportation from Italy under laws designed to protect that nation's cultural heritage. Subsequently, the Assistant Minister of Culture issued a notification declaring the painting "an important work" of "particular artistic and historical interest" within the meaning of Italian law.

Mme. Jeanneret brought suit against the Vicheys for breach of warranty of title. At trial, John Tancock, a vice-president of Sotheby Parke Bernet auction house and head of its Department of Impressionist and Modern Painting and Sculpture, testified that, but for the question of illegal exportation, he would appraise the painting at $750,000. On the other hand, if the painting lacked "the necessary export documents from any country where it had been located," his opinion was that it would be impossible to sell the painting since "[n]o reputable auction house or dealer would be prepared to handle it." Hence "on the legitimate market its value is zero."

What should be the result of this action under UCC 2–312? Does Italy's cultural heritage law affect the owners' title to objects possessed in Italy that are restricted as to export? Would the 2–312 provision on infringement be invoked by an export restriction? Were sellers "merchants"? See UCC 2–104(1). If the trade usage of the reputable art dealers is self-imposed, in that they would incur no liability to the Italian government if they did handle such works, should that affect determination of Mme. Jeanneret's claim under 2–312? See Jeanneret v. Vichey, 693 F.2d 259 (2d Cir.1982).

Lease Transactions: Lessor's Warranty. The supplier of goods in a lease transaction does not contract to pass title to the goods. Under the Commercial Code, " 'lease' means a transfer of the right to possession and use of the goods for a term in return for consideration...." UCC 2A–103(1)(j). The related warranty of a lessor is found in UCC 2A–211:

(1) There is in a lease contract a warranty that for the lease term no person holds a claim or interest in the goods that arose

from an act or omission of the lessor ... which will interfere with the lessee's enjoyment of its leasehold interest.

(B) INTERNATIONAL SALES LAW

Sellers' Responsibility. The Convention on Contracts for the International Sale of Goods provides that, absent agreement otherwise, a seller must deliver goods that are "free from any right or claim of a third party." CISG 41. The Convention does not use the word "title." Does the Convention's formulation of the sellers' obligation differ from UCC 2–312 in any substantial way? [5]

The parties in *Jeanneret* were from different nations: United States sellers and a Swiss buyer. The buyer was a dealer who purchased the Matisse painting for resale. Would this transaction be within the scope of CISG? See CISG 2(a). Assuming that the Convention were applied in a case like *Jeanneret*, what would be the outcome?

SECTION 4. WARRANTY DISCLAIMERS AND LIMITATION OF DAMAGES CLAUSES

(A) DOMESTIC SALES LAW

Introduction. Neither the warranty provisions nor the provisions defining buyers' remedies, as set forth in the Code, preclude the parties from entering into contracts that provide otherwise.[1] Since the law of the United States and the United Kingdom took shape in the 19th century, sellers and buyers have regularly included contract terms on the extent of warranty obligation or damages recovery. In many kinds of sales transactions, patterns of warranty disclaimers or limitation of damages clauses have become so common that their absence in a given transaction would be remarkable.

Under the Code, express warranties arise only if sellers' words or conduct become "part of the basis of the bargain." UCC 2–313(1). When words or conduct tending to create an express warranty are found in the parties' agreements, but other words or conduct tend to negate such a warranty, the Code provides a standard for contract construction. UCC 2–316(1).

Both implied warranty provisions in the Code contain the conditioning language: "unless excluded or modified," which expressly permits the parties to agree that these warranties have been negated. As we will see, the Code further imposes certain *formal* requirements on

---

5. The Convention's provision on sellers' obligation with respect to intellectual property is found in Article 42.

1. UCC 1–102(3) provides the basic principle of contract autonomy. Only a few legal standards may not be varied by agreement.

sellers who seek to do so. UCC 2–316(2). An *implied disclaimer* of implied warranties is provided in the circumstances of a present sale. UCC 2–316(3)(b). Implied warranties can also be excluded or modified by course of dealing, course of performance, or usage of trade. UCC 2–316(3)(c).

The Code's treatment of clauses limiting sellers' liability for damages is found in UCC 2–718 and 2–719. The latter provides that the parties may agree to "limit or alter the measure of damages recoverable under this Article, as by limiting the buyer's remedies to return of the goods and repayment of the price or to repair and replacement of non-conforming goods or parts." UCC 2–719(1)(a). Consequential damages may be limited or excluded unless the limitation or exclusion is unconscionable. UCC 2–719(3).

In the marketplace for goods, would you expect that clauses limiting the damages that aggrieved buyers may recover and clauses disclaiming warranties are equally important? Do these clauses deal with the same or different economic risks? Which clause is more likely to cause a potential buyer to forego a purchase?

INSURANCE CO. OF NORTH AMERICA
v. AUTOMATIC SPRINKLER CORP.

Supreme Court of Ohio, 1981.
67 Ohio St.2d 91, 423 N.E.2d 151.

Appellee, Automatic Sprinkler Corporation of America ("Automatic Sprinkler"), purchased the components of a dry chemical fire protection system from appellant, The Ansul Company ("Ansul"). Both parties understood that Automatic Sprinkler would install this system in a building occupied by Youngstown Steel and Alloy Corporation ("Youngstown Steel").

A representative of Ansul signed a "Proposal," dated February 13, 1970. No one signed the proposal on behalf of Automatic Sprinkler. This document is five pages long. The front of each page includes typewritten or printed information which either describes the goods or states the price. Only the fifth and last page has printing on the back including:

"This sale is subject to the following terms and conditions:

" . . .

"9. The Ansul extinguisher is warranted to the original purchaser for five years from date of delivery against defects in workmanship and material. The Ansul Company will replace or repair any metal parts which in its opinion are defective and have not been tampered with or subjected to misuse, abuse or exposed to highly corrosive conditions. This warranty is *in lieu of* all other warranties express or implied. The Ansul Company assumes no liability for *consequential* or other loss or *damage* whatsoever arising out of injuries to or death of persons and damages to or destruction of property in any manner caused by, incident to, or connected with the use of the equipment, and the Buyer shall *indemnify* and save harmless the Seller from and against all such claims, loss, cost or damage. In addition, unless the Ansul equipment is maintained per Ansul's recommendations, Ansul hereby disclaims all liability whatsoever, including, but not limited to, any liability otherwise attaching under the warranty provisions of this paragraph." (Emphasis added.)

There are 15 paragraphs in all—each without a heading, each without extraordinary capitalization.

Ansul delivered the goods under a "Purchase Order," dated April 14, 1970, "per Ansul Quotation 8674 signed 2–13–70."

A fire occurred on September 9, 1974, at the building occupied by Youngstown Steel. The Ansul fire extinguisher system did not discharge.

None of the aforementioned facts is disputed. Two lawsuits did result, however.

Insurance Company of North America ("INA"), subrogee to the building owner, complained against Automatic Sprinkler and Ansul (case No. 80–619). Automatic Sprinkler ultimately cross-claimed against Ansul. Youngstown Steel and its insurer sued Automatic Sprinkler (case No. 80–620) Automatic Sprinkler then filed a third-party complaint against Ansul. In both cases, the claims alleged breach of warranty and negligence.

Later, the Court of Common Pleas consolidated these cases. The trial judge granted Ansul's motion for summary judgment and dismissed Automatic Sprinkler's claims against Ansul in both cases because (1) Ansul had disclaimed all warranties on sale and limited Automatic Sprinkler's remedies to repair and replacement of defective parts and (2) Automatic Sprinkler agreed to indemnify Ansul and hold it harmless from all claims. The Court of Appeals reversed the trial court, holding that the disclaimer and exclusion of consequential damages fail because they are not conspicuous.

The Court of Appeals also held that "there is no basis for summary judgment in favor of the Ansul Company on the indemnity provision question at this stage of the case," because paragraph 9 is not conspicuous. The court reversed and remanded the cause to the trial court for further proceedings on this issue.

The cause is now before this court pursuant to the allowance of motions to certify the record ....

LOCHER, JUSTICE. This case presents three issues: (1) whether Ansul has effectively disclaimed all implied warranties with Automatic Sprinkler; (2) whether Ansul has effectively excluded all liability for consequential damages; and (3) whether Automatic Sprinkler must indemnify Ansul against all claims arising in this litigation. Resolving each of these issues requires an interpretation of paragraph 9.

We hold that Ansul has neither disclaimed its liability for implied warranties nor excluded its liability for consequential damages.

I.

Ansul attempted to disclaim all liability to Automatic Sprinkler for breach of implied warranties by including the following language in paragraph 9: "This warranty is in lieu of all other warranties express or implied." Automatic Sprinkler argues that this language fails as a disclaimer because it does not mention merchantability and is not conspicuous as required by [UCC 2–316(2)]. Ansul, on the other hand, suggests that the "in lieu of" language is similar to "as is" under [UCC 2–316(3)(a)]. Under Ansul's view, the disclaimer is effective regardless of whether it is conspicuous or whether it mentions merchantability.

We hold that the "in lieu of" language is not similar to "as is"..... The effort to disclaim liability for all implied warranties fails because paragraph 9 is not conspicuous and because the disclaimer does not mention merchantability.

"As is" language describes the *quality of the goods* sold. As an example of "as is" language, [UCC 2–316(3)(a)] expressly includes "with all faults." ... Official Comment 7 ... further explains the intent of the drafters:

> "Paragraph [(a)] deals with general items such as 'as is,' 'as they stand,' 'with all faults,' and the like. Such terms in ordinary commercial usage are understood to mean that the buyer takes the entire risk as to the *quality of the goods* involved. ...." (Emphasis added.) . . .

We recognize that the courts have held that "in lieu of" language eliminates implied warranties. ... We reject this conclusion.

Under [2–316(3)(a)] "other language which, in common understanding, calls the buyer's attention to the exclusion of warranties and makes plain that there is no implied warranty" must be language which is consistent with the intention of the drafters and the General Assembly. This language must describe the *quality of the goods*.

Accordingly, the "in lieu of" language in paragraph 9 falls outside [2–316(3)(a)].

This "in lieu of" provision does not qualify, therefore, as a disclaimer of implied warranties under [2–316(2)]. There is no mention of merchantability. In addition, we have held that paragraph 9 is inconspicuous.

[UCC 1–201(10)] defines "conspicuousness" as follows:

" 'Conspicuous': A term or clause is conspicuous when it is so written that a reasonable person against whom it is to operate ought to have noticed it. A printed heading in capitals (as: NON-NEGOTIABLE BILL OF LADING) is conspicuous. Language in the body of a form is 'conspicuous' if it is in larger or other contrasting type or color. But in a telegram any stated term is 'conspicuous.' Whether a term or clause is 'conspicuous' or not is for decision by the court."

Paragraph 9 appears among 15 other paragraphs on the back of the last page of the Proposal. This is the only page with writing on the back and is unnumbered. None of these paragraphs has a heading, extraordinary capitalization or contrasting type. Furthermore, Ansul alone executed the Proposal which contained paragraph 9 approximately two months before Automatic Sprinkler submitted its purchase order. In light of all these circumstances, therefore, it is clear that paragraph 9 is inconspicuous.

Accordingly, we hold that the "in lieu of" provision in paragraph 9 does not disclaim all implied warranties.

II.

Ansul argues that, even if the purported disclaimer fails, paragraph 9 excludes "liability for consequential or other loss or damage...." We disagree.

[UCC 2–719(3) and 2–316(4)] permit parties to exclude consequential damages without expressly requiring that the exclusion be conspicuous. Nevertheless, courts and commentators have read U.C.C. 2–719[3] and U.C.C. 2–316[4] *in pari materia*. See e.g., Avenell v. Westinghouse Electric Corp. (Cuyahoga Cty., 1974), 41 Ohio App.2d 150, 324 N.E.2d 583; Zicari v. Joseph Harris Co., Inc. (1969), 33 App.Div.2d 17, 304 N.Y.S.2d 918; Nordstrom, Law of Sales, at 276; Special Project—Article Two Warranties in Commercial Transactions, 64 Cornell L.Rev. 30, 224. Nordstrom, supra, explains why these two statutes should be read together, as follows:

"The requirement that the agreement contain the alteration of basic Code remedies brings into play those ideas discussed in the prior section of this text [dealing with disclaimers of implied warranties]. The limitation [or exclusion of remedies] must be a part of the parties' bargain in fact. If it is contained in a printed clause which was not conspicuous or brought to the buyer's attention, the seller had no reasonable expectation that the buyer understood that his remedies were being restricted to repair and replacement. As such, the clause cannot be said to be a part of the bargain (or agreement) of the parties." (Citation omitted.)

Any other reading of these provisions would permit inconspicuous provisions excluding or limiting damage recovery to circumvent the protection for buyers in [2–316(2)]. ...

Paragraph 9 is inconspicuous in its entirety. The attempt to exclude liability for consequential damages, therefore, is also inconspicuous. Accordingly, Automatic Sprinkler may recover consequential damages from Ansul. . . .

Notes

(1) **Bargain in Fact.** Could Automatic Sprinkler Corporation of America contend persuasively that the language in the "Proposal" that disclaimed "all other warranties" was unclear to the buyer as a disclaimer of the warranty of merchantability? Could Automatic Sprinkler contend persuasively that it was reasonably unaware of the clause on Ansul's liability for consequential damages? Do you think it likely or unlikely that corporations like Automatic Sprinkler use such contractual clauses in transactions in which they are sellers?

(2) **Construction of UCC 2–316(2).** Why did the drafters of the Code include 2–316(2)? What did they intend by the requirement that a seller must "mention merchantability" to disclaim the 2–314 warranty?

The Ohio Supreme Court made no effort to resolve the controversy on the bargain in fact, but rather decided the case on the basis of Ansul's compliance with the "mention" clause in UCC 2–316(2) and with the court's implication of a statutory "conspicuousness" requirement in UCC 2–719. What is the public policy rationale of those *formal* requirements? Is it arguable that the legislation was designed to protect consumer buyers and not buyers like Automatic Sprinkler? Could a court properly exclude buyers who are large corporations?

(3) **Legislative History.** Consider the history of UCC 2–316. In the initial drafts of the Code, from 1940 to 1952, subsection (2) provided:

> (2) Exclusion or modification of the implied warranty of merchantability or of fitness for a particular purpose must be in specific language and if the inclusion of such language creates an ambiguity in the contract as a whole it shall be resolved against the seller; except that [the three subparagraphs now in (3) followed as exceptions].

Comments to the 1952 draft provided:

> 3. Disclaimer of the implied warranties of merchantability and of fitness for particular purpose is permitted under subsection (2), but with the safeguard that such disclaimers must be in specific terms and that any ambiguity must be resolved against the seller.

> 4. Implied warranties may not be excluded merely by the use of a clause disclaiming "all warranties express or implied." On the other hand, a clause such as "We assume no responsibility that the goods concerned in this contract are fit for any particular purpose

for which they are being bought outside of the general purposes of goods of the description," would normally be sufficient to satisfy the requirement that the disclaimer be in "specific terms."

5. The provision of subsection (2) that an ambiguity arising from the co-existence of words of disclaimer and evidence showing the creation of the implied warranties of merchantability or fitness for a particular purpose must be resolved against the seller is intended to pose the true issue in such cases. This section rejects that line of approach which presupposes the original existence of warranty and then attempts to deal with the question of whether it has been disclaimed by language in the agreement. ...

In 1955, after the Code had been adopted in Pennsylvania and was under consideration in a number of states, the Code was revised. The language above was deleted and the current provision substituted, with the exceptions set off in a new paragraph (3). The Editorial Board, which proposed the revision, gave this brief explanation:

Reason. The purpose of this change is to relieve the seller from the requirement of disclaiming a warranty of fitness in specific language and yet afford the buyer an adequate warning of such disclaimer.

No explanation was given for adding the requirements (i) that a valid disclaimer must "mention merchantability," (ii) that a disclaimer of the warranty of fitness for a particular purpose must be in writing and conspicuous, or (iii) that a disclaimer of warranty of merchantability, if in a writing, must be conspicuous. Comments to take account of the 1955 (and 1956) text changes were published in 1957. Comments 3, 4 and 5, in their present form, replaced the earlier comments.

Does the history shed light on the drafters' intention with regard to the necessary form of a disclaimer of the implied warranty of merchantability? What weight should a court place on such history in construing the Code as adopted by a particular legislature, such as the construction of the Ohio version of the Code in the *Insurance Company* case?

(4) Construction of UCC 2–719. In what sense is the *Insurance Company* decision a construction of 2–719? Is it conceivable that the drafters of the Code were unaware of the differences in the formulations of 2–316 and 2–719? Does the court's approach trespass on the legislature's prerogative?

UNIVERSAL DRILLING CO. v. CAMAY DRILLING CO.

United States Court of Appeals, Tenth Circuit, 1984.
737 F.2d 869.

McKAY, CIRCUIT JUDGE. The parties to this lawsuit are "experienced, sophisticated, intelligent business[men] with vast education and experience in petroleum engineering, ... oil and gas exploration, and ... [the] makeup and operation of oil drilling rigs and equipment." ... In June 1977 they entered into negotiations for the purchase and sale of two drilling rigs referred to by the parties as the Marthens Rig and Rig 10.

The negotiations resulted in a contract dated July 1, 1977, [which contained the following clauses:

18.01 The assets being purchased and sold hereunder are being sold by [defendant] in an "as-is" condition and without any warranty of operability or fitness ....

26.01 This Agreement and the exhibits hereto and the agreements referred to herein set forth the entire agreement and understanding of the parties in respect of the transactions contemplated hereby and supersede all prior agreements, arrangements and understanding relating to the subject matter hereof. No representation, promise inducement or statement of intention has been made by [defendant] or [plaintiffs] which is not embodied in this Agreement or in the documents referred to herein, and neither [defendant] nor [plaintiffs] shall be bound by or liable for any alleged representation, promise, inducement or statements of intention not so set forth.] *

... The contract defines the property to be sold as the personal property listed in Exhibits A, B and C to the contract. Rig 10 is defined as the property in Exhibit A and the Marthens Rig is defined as the property in Exhibits B and C. [The purchase price was $2,925,000.]

Subsequent to the delivery of the property, plaintiffs complained that the property they received did not conform to the contract alleging that they were to receive two used but nevertheless operable drilling rigs. Defendant, however, relying on the contract, argued that it delivered all of the property listed in the specific exhibits. This diversity lawsuit resulted.

At trial, [t]he trial court ... rejected plaintiffs' theory that there were breaches of express warranties based on the description of the goods contained in the contract. Plaintiffs appeal....

Breach of Express Warranties by Description

Approaching this issue it must again be remembered that the parties to this suit are experienced in the field of oil and gas explora-

---

* [The court reproduced the contract in a footnote. Eds.]

tion and drilling. Furthermore, none of the parties allege that they were in an inferior bargaining position.

Plaintiffs do not dispute the trial court's finding that the contract, specifically paragraph 18.01, effectively disclaimed all implied warranties. Plaintiffs do allege, however, that the description of the assets contained in the contract created an express warranty that the assets would conform to that description. In addition, plaintiffs argue that such an express warranty of description cannot be disclaimed, ... or at least was not effectively disclaimed.

Section 2–316 of the Uniform Commercial Code as adopted in Colorado provides for the modification and exclusion of warranties. Colo. Rev. Stat. § 4–2–315 (1973). In particular it provides that

> [w]ords or conduct relevant to the creation of an express warranty and words or conduct tending to negate or limit warranty shall be construed wherever reasonable as consistent with each other; but subject to the provisions of this article on parol or extrinsic evidence (section 4–2–202), negation or limitation is inoperative to the extent such construction is unreasonable.

Id. § 4–2–316(1). Accordingly, the initial inquiry must be whether express warranties were created under section 4–2–313 and if so how they are affected by section 18.01 of the contract.

Plaintiff argues that this case is controlled by Section 4–2–313(b) which provides that "[a]ny description of the goods which is made part of the basis of the bargain creates an express warranty that the goods shall conform to the description." Colo. Rev. Stat. § 4–2–313(b). The principles underlying section 4–2–313 are set out in comment four to that section:

> 4. In view of the principle that the whole purpose of the law of warranty is to determine what it is that the seller has in essence agreed to sell, the policy is adopted of those cases which refuse except in unusual circumstances to recognize a material deletion of the seller's obligation. Thus, a contract is normally a contract for a sale of something describable and described. A clause generally disclaiming "all warranties, express or implied" cannot reduce the seller's obligation with respect to such description and therefore cannot be given literal effect under Section 2–316.
>
> This is not intended to mean that the parties, if they consciously desire, cannot make their own bargain as they wish. But in determining what they have agreed upon in good faith is a factor and consideration should be given to the fact that the probability is small that a real price is intended to be exchanged for a pseudo-obligation.

Id. § 4–2–313 comment 4.

Similarly, Professors White and Summers argue that a seller should not be able to disclaim a warranty created by description.

We hope courts will reach similar conclusions and strike down attempted disclaimers in cases in which the seller includes a description of the article which amounts to a warranty and then attempts to disclaim all express warranties. To illustrate further: assume that the sales contract describes machinery to be sold as a "haybaler" and then attempts to disclaim all express warranties. If the machine failed to bale hay and the buyer sued, we would argue that the disclaimer is ineffective. In our judgment, the description of the machine as a "haybaler" is a warranty that the machine will bale hay and, in the words of 2–316, a negation or limitation ought to be "inoperative" since it is inconsistent with the warranty.

J. White & R. Summers, Handbook of the Law Under the Uniform Commercial Code § 12–3 at 433 (2d ed. 1980).

Plaintiff relies principally on two cases that follow this rationale. Century Dodge Inc. v. Mobley, 155 Ga.App. 712, 272 S.E.2d 502, 504 (1980) (cert. denied); Blankenship v. Northtown Ford, Inc., 95 Ill.App. 3d 303, 420 N.E.2d 167, 170–71 (1981). In both cases automobile dealers had sold "new" cars which for various reasons did not meet the description of a "new" car. Consequently the courts held that the boilerplate disclaimer provisions of the consumer sales contracts did not relieve the dealers of their responsibility to deliver a "new" car.

We do not question the rationale of the above authorities. Nonetheless, we find them not controlling the instant case. If in this case we were dealing with a consumer transaction, as in the cases just cited, we would be more inclined to follow those authorities. However, as noted in subsequent cases, "the courts are less reluctant to hold educated businessmen to the terms of contracts to which they have entered than consumers dealing with skilled corporate sellers." ...

Furthermore, both sections 4–2–313 and 4–2–316 express the policy of the statutory scheme to allow parties to make any bargain they wish. Comment four to section 4–2–313 states that if parties consciously desire they can disclaim whatever warranties they wish. Colo. Rev. Stat. § 4–2–313 comment 4 (1973). In addition, comment one to section 4–2–316 explains that its purpose is to "protect a buyer from unexpected and unbargained language of disclaimer." Id. § 4–2–316, comment 1. Consequently, we will not rewrite the contract in this case. The exhibits to the contract which described the goods must be read in conjunction with the contract itself. The contract states that the goods are used and there is no guarantee that they are fit or even *operable*.

If we were to hold the contract in the instant case created undisclaimable express warranties by description, we cannot think of alternative language that would memorialize the intent of the parties—to purchase and sell used "as is" equipment which has value but which may need repairs or additional parts to be fit and operable.

Our holding on this issue does not leave plaintiffs in general without remedy in similar contexts or the plaintiffs in this case with an "empty bargain." If the goods delivered do not meet the description in the contract there is a breach of the contract. In short, if no mast were delivered or if what was delivered was junk metal which in no way resembled a mast, plaintiffs would have a cause of action for breach of the contract.

Finally, plaintiffs did not receive an empty bargain. An appraisal which plaintiffs commissioned valued the goods received at an amount in excess of $3,000,000. .... The purchase price for the assets was $2,925,000.

The trial court did not err in excluding plaintiffs' evidence regarding breach of warranty....

Affirmed.

Notes

(1) **Contract Interpretation: UCC 2–316(1).** Buyer apparently argued, under UCC 2–316(1), that the words of negation of warranty in ¶ 18.01 were "inoperative" in light of the words of description. Could buyer have made its essential point differently? Could buyer have argued that the "operability" language in ¶ 18.01 referred to future performance of the rigs, but was not intended to declare that the rigs were presently not in operating condition?

Problem 1. In negotiations that led to the purchase of a mobile home, the seller showed a model mobile home to the buyer. The contract stated in capital letters that the sale was "AS IS." The buyer asserts that the mobile home delivered to him was not like the model. What result? See UCC 2–313(1)(c), 2–316(1); Consolidated Data Terminals v. Applied Digital Data Systems, Inc., 708 F.2d 385 (9th Cir.1983).

(2) **Commercial Sophistication of Buyers.** On the surface of the Uniform Commercial Code provisions defining sellers' responsibility for quality, the Code does not differentiate among buyers who are seasoned veterans in buying goods of the kind, buyers who are commercially naive, and buyers in between.[2] Nor does the Code's provision on exclusion or modification of warranties. What, then, explains the emphasis that the *Universal Drilling* court put on the experience and sophistication of the parties? The buyer relied principally on two decisions involving consumer retail sales of new automobiles. The Tenth Circuit expressed no question about the rationale of those decisions, but found them not controlling. Does the Code permit such different treatment for consumer retail sales and sales of business equipment?

---

2. The Code does differentiate among sellers on the basis of commercial experience in UCC 2–314. Only a seller who is "a merchant with respect to [the] goods" sold makes an implied warranty of merchantability. "Merchant" is defined in UCC 2–104(1).

The Code provision on contractual limitation or exclusion of consequential damages sets forth two standards, one for "injury to the person in the case of consumer goods" and another for "loss [that] is commercial." UCC 2–719(3). Is this provision sensitive to market levels of sales transactions?

(3) Oral Warranties and Written Negations: Parol Evidence and UCC 2–202. Cases frequently arise in which buyers and sellers executed contract documents containing clauses negating the existence of any warranties, particularly express warranties not contained in the documents, but buyers later contend that the sellers (or their sales personnel) had made oral affirmations or promises that would constitute warranties under UCC 2–313. A clause commonly inserted in writings of this kind, sometimes in the boilerplate of a printed form, asserts that the writing is a complete and exclusive statement.

Words in such documents cannot be construed as reasonably consistent with the words allegedly spoken. In providing a rule of contract construction for this type of case, UCC 2–316(1) cites the Code's parol evidence provision, UCC 2–202. Under the latter provision, if the words of negation of warranty are in a writing that a court finds to have been intended as the final expression of their agreement, those terms of negation may not be "contradicted by evidence of any prior agreement or of a contemporaneous oral agreement." This may exclude evidence of words or conduct relevant to the creation of an express warranty. Even if a buyer's evidence does not "contradict" a term in the written final expression, that evidence may be excluded if a court finds that the writing was intended by the parties to have been a complete and exclusive statement of the terms of the agreement.

Consider the following concern expressed about UCC 2–202: "To what extent should a 'merger' clause in a standard form contract be permitted to accomplish indirectly what cannot be done directly, e.g., the disclaimer of an express warranty. See 2–316(1). Other than § 2–302, there is no explicit control over the risk of unfair surprise [in the Commercial Code]. A possible solution is to require that a 'merger' clause in a standard form contract be 'separately signed' by the party against whom the clause operates. See § 2–205." Permanent Editorial Board Study Group on UCC Article 2 p. 60 (1990). Would you support the proposed solution?

For further reading, see E. Farnsworth, Contracts § 7.3 (2d ed. 1990); J. White & R. Summers, Uniform Commercial Code §§ 2–9 to 2–12 (3d ed. 1988).

WESTERN INDUSTRIES, INC. v. NEWCOR CANADA LIMITED

United States Court of Appeals, Seventh Circuit, 1984.
739 F.2d 1198.

POSNER, CIRCUIT JUDGE. Western Industries purchased several custom-built welding machines from Newcor Canada for use in manufacturing microwave oven cavities. The machines did not work right and Western brought this breach of contract action against Newcor, basing federal jurisdiction on diversity of citizenship. Newcor counterclaimed for the unpaid portion of the purchase price of the machines. The jury awarded Western damages of $1.3 million dollars and Newcor about half that (the full unpaid balance of the purchase price of the machines) on its counterclaim. Separate judgments were entered on the two claims and both parties have appealed. The appeals raise a variety of interesting substantive and procedural issues, the former being controlled (the parties agree) by the law of Wisconsin, including the Uniform Commercial Code, which Wisconsin has adopted.

The contract between Western and Newcor grew out of Western's contract with a Japanese manufacturer of microwave ovens, Sharp, to supply Sharp with cavities for microwave ovens. Sharp wanted Western to weld the cavities by a process known as projection welding, because that is how microwave oven cavities are made in Japan; and Western agreed. The projection method is not used in the United States to weld thin metal, such as the cavities of microwave ovens are made of; spot welding is the method used here. So when Western went to Newcor, a leading manufacturer of specialty welding machines, to explore the possibility of buying machines for use in fulfilling its contract with Sharp, it had to ask Newcor to design and build a type of welding machine that Newcor was unfamiliar with. Newcor agreed to do this, however, and after further discussions Western's director of engineering placed a purchase order by phone for eight machines with Newcor's sales engineer on May 17, 1979. According to the memoranda that both men made of the conversation, no specific terms other than the date of delivery were discussed; price was not discussed, for example. On May 23 Newcor delivered to Western a formal written quotation of terms for the sale. On the back of one page a number of standard contract terms were printed, including one disclaiming all liability for consequential damages. Western did not reply immediately, but in mid July it sent Newcor a formal purchase order, mysteriously pre-dated to May 15, that included on the back a set of printed terms one of which stated that the buyer (Western) was entitled to general as well as special damages in the event of a breach of the seller's warranties. On July 20 Newcor sent Western an acknowledgement form stating, "In conformity with our conditions of sale appearing in [the written quotation ...] furnished to you by us, this approves and accepts your order." Western did not respond. The parties never discussed any of the printed terms contained in the contract forms that they had exchanged. Three machines were bought later through a similar exchange of forms. The parties treat the sale of all 11 machines as one contract, as shall we.

The machines were built and delivered but turned out to be unusable for making microwave oven cavities. Newcor took the machines back and rebuilt them as spot welding machines, redelivering them to Western a year after the delivery date called for in the contract. As a result of the delay in getting machines that it could use, Western incurred unforeseen expenses in fulfilling its commitment to Sharp; for example, it had to manufacture cavities manually at much higher cost than it would have incurred if it has had proper machines. These expenses are the basis of its damage claim against Newcor.

Newcor's first ground of appeal is that the district judge improperly excluded evidence that the custom of the specialty welding machine trade is not to give a disappointed buyer his consequential damages but just to allow him either to return the machines and get his money back or (for example if the breach consists in delivering them late) keep the machines and get the purchase price reduced to compensate for the costs of delay. ... Newcor contends that it is not liable for any damages above the purchase price, however those damages are described; and if this is right, then even if Newcor had a contract with Western that it broke it is not liable for any of the damages that Western was awarded.

Although trade custom or usage is a question of fact, see UCC 1–205(2) and Official Comments 4 and 9; ... the district judge refused to allow Newcor's three principal witnesses on the existence of the alleged trade custom to testify, on the ground that they were incompetent to give such testimony; and having done this the judge later instructed the jury that there was no issue of trade custom in the case. Two of the three witnesses whom Newcor wanted to call were experienced executives of companies that manufacture specialty welding machines (one of them was also the president of those manufacturers' trade association), and between them the two had almost 75 years of experience in selling such machines. The third witness was a former executive of Western and had long experience in buying such machines. These witnesses were prepared to testify that consequential damages were unheard of in their trade. When a machine did not work the manufacturer would spend his own money to fix it or would take it back and refund the purchase price to the buyer, but he would not compensate the buyer for the disruption to the buyer's business caused by the defect....

Although we are in no position to determine whether the custom alleged by Newcor actually exists, we think it relevant to note that the hypothesis that it exists is certainly not so incredible that testimony on the subject could be excluded by analogy to the principle that excludes testimony in contradiction of the laws of nature. The relevant trade is the manufacture of a particular kind of custom-built machinery. A custom-built machine is quite likely either not to be delivered on time or not to work (not at first, anyway) when it is delivered; anyone who has ever had a house built for him knows the perils of custom design. If a custom-built machine is delivered late, or does not work as the buyer had hoped and expected it would, the buyer's business is quite likely to suffer, and may even be ruined; and as the buyers of these welding machines are substantial manufacturers to whose businesses the machines are essential, the potential costs of defective design or late delivery are astronomical.

... [A]ll we need find in order to conclude that Newcor's evidence of trade custom was admissible is that a rational jury could have concluded that, yes, it was the custom for manufacturers of specialty welding machines not to be liable for consequential damages. That contractual liability for such damages (in the absence of special notice) is of relatively recent vintage, that many breaches of contract are (as here) involuntary, that only the sky would be the limit to the amount of consequential damages that manufacturers of machinery indispensable to their customers' businesses might run up, that those manufacturers not only have a better idea of what the potential injury to them might be but also might be able to avert it more easily than their supplier— all these things make it not at all incredible that a custom might have evolved in this industry against a buyer's getting consequential damages in the event of a breach.

If there was such a custom, it would not take the manufacturers of specialty welding machines off the financial hook completely. When they have to take back and resell custom-built machines they face the prospect of a heavy loss. A machine custom-designed to one manufacturer's specifications may not fit any other's. That is no doubt why Newcor spent hundreds of thousands of dollars to rebuild these machines as spot-welding machines that Western could use. That is also why we reject Newcor's argument that Western should be estopped to claim damages because it induced Newcor to rebuild the machines. Newcor rebuilt them in its own interest, to mitigate the loss it would have incurred if it had had to take back the machines and refund the purchase price; if it had taken back the machines it would have had to rebuild them in order to be able to resell them.

But a disclaimer of liability for consequential damages would place some limit on the exposure of the manufacturers of specialty welding machines. It would also give buyers incentives to take their own precautions, which might be efficacious, against the disasters that might befall them if the machines did not work. ... There was much evidence that Western made a serious mistake in agreeing with Sharp (rather casually as it appears) to build microwave oven cavities by projection welding, a process which, it turned out, American safety standards made infeasible. Western would have been less likely to make such mistakes if it had known with certainty that it would not be able to get consequential damages if the machines didn't work....

Newcor has a second ground of appeal. It wanted to put before the jury not only the theory that trade custom had supplied a silent contractual term excluding liability for consequential damages, but also the theory that the explicit terms of the contract excluded such liability.... .

As a practical matter, however, Newcor's alternative theory is not very different from its main theory—that the custom of the trade excluded liability for consequential damages. Given an exchange of inconsistent forms, Newcor would have to present a reason why its form disclaiming liability for consequential damages should be accepted over Western's form asserting such liability; and the reason would have to be the custom of the trade, as that is the only substantial ground that Newcor has for claiming precedence for its disclaimer. ...

The parties raise some other issues, which we have considered but find to have no merit. The judgment in favor of Western on its claim and the judgment in favor of Newcor on its counterclaim are reversed and the case is remanded for a new trial on both claims, with no costs in this court.

Reversed and remanded.

Note

Implied Warranty Disclaimers or Limitation of Damages. The Code expressly declares that implied warranties can be excluded or modified by course of dealing, course of performance, or usage of trade. UCC 2–316(3)(c). Recall the decision in *Royal Business Machines*, Section 2, supra. No similar provision is found in 2–719. Is the omission significant?

KUNSTSTOFFWERK ALFRED HUBER v. R. J. DICK, INC.

United States Court of Appeals, Third Circuit, 1980.
621 F.2d 560.

WEIS, CIRCUIT JUDGE. In this diversity case, the district court concluded that under the Uniform Commercial Code the buyer has the burden of establishing that the seller agreed to pay consequential damages when goods proved defective. We hold that to avoid such liability the seller must prove an agreement that limits damages, and, in this instance, the course of dealing between the parties was not adequate to demonstrate such an understanding. Accordingly, we modify a judgment in favor of the plaintiff-seller for goods sold to allow credits for losses on resale incurred by the defendant-buyer.

The plaintiff brought suit in the United States District Court for the Eastern District of Pennsylvania to recover the cost of nylon industrial belting it sold to the defendant. Counterclaims asserted that some of the belting had been defective. After a bench trial, the district court entered judgment for the plaintiff, deducting from the requested damages portions of the amounts sought by two of the defendant's counterclaims.

The defendant, R.J. Dick, Inc., distributes nylon cord belting throughout the United States. Its principal place of business is in Iowa, and it maintains a warehouse in King of Prussia, Pennsylvania. The plaintiff is a sole proprietorship that manufactures nylon cord belting in Offenburg, West Germany under the trade name "Vis."

In September 1967 plaintiff's export manager, Alfred Ziegler, sent a letter to the defendant's president, quoting prices on belting and enclosing terms for delivery and payment. Included in the correspondence was a form entitled "General Terms of Sales II." One paragraph in the form limited the plaintiff's liability for defective merchandise to replacement or price reduction and excluded damages of any kind:

> [Reclamations must be made within 10 days after receipt of merchandise and prior to processing or use. Our guaranty is limited to replacement or price reduction and excludes damages of any kind. Also, we do not give a guaranty for specific utilization. Minor deviations do not provide grounds for reclamations.] *

In the following month, Ziegler and Vis's owner, Alfred Huber, visited King of Prussia and arranged for sale of their product to the Dick Company. At no time were the Vis general terms of sale discussed, and, consequently, Dick did not agree to be bound by the provisions of the form, including the limitation on damages recoverable for defective merchandise.

During the period from 1967 to 1974 there were occasions when the plaintiff's product did not meet the defendant's standards, either on initial inspection or after a period of use by defendant's customers. When the defendant issued a credit to a customer for belting that had manufacturing defects, a claim was made to the plaintiff for replacement or credit. If a difference arose between the parties over whether the defect was attributable to the manufacturer, the claim would be compromised.

In late 1973, Dick's problems with the belting increased, the most frequent being delamination, which made the product unusable. Beginning at that time and continuing through 1974, Ziegler complained about Dick's delay in payments. This suit followed the parties' inability to resolve these difficulties.

At trial, the plaintiff asserted that after making allowances for various credits to which it was agreeable, the defendant owed $30,-

* [The court reproduced the proposed contract clause in a footnote. Eds.]

910.29. Against this figure, however, the defendant asserted four counterclaims....

The court did allow partial recovery on the third and fourth counterclaims. The defendant contended in the third claim that it was entitled to $7,300.69, the amount it had credited its customers for defective material supplied by the plaintiff in 1974. The Court, however, awarded $3,398.25, a sum representing the price the defendant paid plaintiff. ... The fourth claim was for defective belting that one of Dick's distributors sold to a company called Wesco. Dick issued a credit of $7,092.80 on that transaction, but again the court allowed only the amount the defendant had paid plaintiff for the goods, $3,301.95. ... The defendant appeals....

The issue underlying the remaining two claims is straightforward: Was the defendant entitled to recover the credits granted customers when the product proved defective? In other words, was the defendant entitled to the profits it would have made on those sales? The parties agree that Pennsylvania law applies, particularly Article 2 of the Uniform Commercial Code....

There is no dispute that plaintiff was aware of the nature of defendant's business, i.e., that the goods were to be resold. In these circumstances, we conclude that under § 715(2)(a) the credits that defendant was obliged to extend to customers are proper consequential damages. ...

The plaintiff does not dispute this proposition but argues that the parties agreed to exclude recovery of such damages under U.C.C. § 2–719(1)(a). That section provides that the agreement between the parties may provide for limiting the measure of damages, as by restricting the buyer's remedy to return of the goods and repayment of the price or to repair and replacement nonconforming goods. Pa. Stat. Ann. tit. 12A, § 2–719(1)(a) (Purdon 1970).

There is insufficient evidence in the record to establish an express agreement to limit damages. The trial judge found that the only communication between the parties bearing on the subject was the form sent by plaintiff to defendant in September 1967. He stated that "Dick never expressly consented to the Huber contract" and therefore could not be held subject to it. Nevertheless, the trial judge reasoned that the form had put the defendant on notice that Huber did not intend to assume liability for consequential damages and that Dick therefore had the burden, which it failed to carry, of informing plaintiff that such damages might be demanded....

The plaintiff argues ... that there was a "course of performance" under U.C.C. § 2–208(1) which established an agreement to forgo consequential damages. Since there was no single contract between the parties, but rather a series of separate sales, we believe it more accurate to characterize the conduct as a "course of dealing," defined in U.C.C. § 1–205(1). The plaintiff's argument is not weakened by adopting the course of dealing route because the Code specifically permits a course of dealing or a usage of trade, unlike a course of performance, to "give particular meaning to and supplement or qualify terms of an agreement." U.C.C. § 1–205(3), Pa. Stat. Ann. tit. 12A, § 1–205(3) (Purdon 1970) (emphasis added).[6] In Posttape Associates v. Eastman Kodak Co., 537 F.2d 751 (3d Cir.1976), we concluded that a limitation of damages could be imposed by a trade usage; it follows that a course of dealing is a circumstance that may establish this term as part of the bargain of the parties in fact. U.C.C. § 1–201(3), Pa. Stat. Ann. tit. 12A, § 1–201(3) (Purdon 1970).

The inquiry then is whether the record establishes the course of dealing the plaintiff suggests. Initially we observe that the burden is on the plaintiff to prove the limitation agreement, ... especially where it is to be found in a course of dealing.[7]

In its findings the district court did not set out facts that would constitute a course of dealing establishing defendant's agreement to forgo consequential damages. On appeal, the plaintiff does not point to specific parts of the record where such facts may be found, nor has our independent review disclosed such evidence. It is not enough that the defendant accepted replacement or credits for the purchase price in many instances. Obviously, if the defects were detected before resale and supplies of belting were available to fill outstanding orders, the defendant might not have had a claim for lost profits. In other instances it may well be that even after resale, the defendant's customers were content to accept replacement rather than demand a refund. Moreover, the record does show that the parties compromised many of the claims for defects in workmanship.

We find no instances in which the defendant had made a claim for loss of profits on resale transactions other than those underlying the counterclaims. If such claims had been made and then been denied by the plaintiff without protest from the defendant, the argument that a course of dealing established such a limitation might have some force. Cf. U.C.C. § 2–208(1), Pa. Stat. Ann. tit. 12A, § 2–208(1) (Purdon 1970) ("any course of performance accepted or acquiesced in without objection shall be relevant to determine the meaning of the agreement").... . Absent such circumstances, however, we cannot say that the plaintiff has met the burden of proving a limitation agreement. Accordingly, the defendant is entitled to recover on the two counterclaims for loss of profits on actual sales.

6. By its own terms, a course of performance goes no further than being "relevant to determine the meaning of the agreement." U.C.C. § 2–208(1), Pa. Stat. Ann. tit. 12A, § 2–208(1) (Purdon 1970). Nevertheless, courts have generally allowed a course of performance to supplement and qualify the terms of an agreement as well. J. White & R. Summers, Uniform Commercial Code § 3–3 (1972).

7. In discussing terms supplied by a course of dealing, a usage of trade, and a course of performance, Professors White and Summers observed:

"Who has the burden of proof? The Code does not say. Yet courts are likely to impose the burden of proof on the party who seeks to benefit from evidence of course of dealing, trade usage, or course of performance."

J. White & R. Summers, Uniform Commercial Code § 3–3, at 88 (1972) (footnote omitted).

The total of the two counterclaims is $14,393.49. The parties agree that the increases sought by the defendant and contained in this figure accurately reflect the loss on sales. That total will therefore be deducted from the amount which plaintiff claimed to be due—$30,-910.29—thus resulting in an award to the plaintiff of $16,516.80. The case will be remanded to the district court so that it may modify its judgment accordingly.

Note

Choice of Forum. The German seller in *Kunststoffwerk* was litigating in a foreign court, the "home" court of the U.S. buyer. What led to this choice of forum? In counselling German or other non-U.S. sellers or buyers dealing with U.S. firms, would you recommend structuring transactions to obtain a more familiar or at least a neutral forum? How could this be done?

MILGARD TEMPERING, INC. v. SELAS CORP.

United States Court of Appeals, Ninth Circuit, 1990.
902 F.2d 703.

HALL, CIRCUIT JUDGE: This appeal marks the end of nearly seven years of litigation over a "sure fire" glass tempering furnace purchased over ten years ago. The seller, Selas Corporation of America ("Selas") appeals the judgment of the district court awarding the buyer, Milgard Tempering, Inc. ("Milgard"), damages resulting from its failure to repair serious defects in the furnace.... We have jurisdiction under 28 U.S.C. § 1291 (1988) and affirm.

I

... On June 11, 1979, [Milgard] entered into a carefully-negotiated contract with appellant/cross-appellee Selas to purchase a horizontal batch tempering furnace. ... Under the contract, Selas agreed to design and manufacture the furnace for $1.45 million. Its design was complex, and in Selas' eyes, experimental. However, Selas marketed it as a working piece of equipment. The contract provided a $50,000 bonus if Selas delivered all the major components before January 31, 1980. It also provided a penalty of $5,000 per week (not to exceed a total of $25,000) for every week of late delivery after March 31, 1980. Selas failed to meet either deadline, having completed delivery of major components in November, 1982.

Selas agreed to assemble the furnace at Milgard's plant and to assist in a "debugging period" that both parties expected would end June or July 1980. The contract also required Selas, in a series of preacceptance tests, to demonstrate that the furnace was capable of achieving designated yield and cycle rates. Section 28.5 of the contract limited Selas' liability for breach of warranty to repair or replacement of the furnace and barred liability for consequential damages. The parties modified the contract and agreed to forego the preacceptance tests and instead place the furnace in commercial production in July, 1980, thus making glass available for the "debugging" process.

By January 1982, Selas continued work on the furnace, but failed to achieve yield and cycle rates that substantially conformed with the contract specifications. Milgard then filed suit against Selas for breach of contract. In March 1982, the parties, without counsel, attempted to enter into a contractual agreement to settle the dispute. Under the proposed agreement, Selas would take over the tempering operation for 60 days to demonstrate the furnace's ability to achieve a 90 yield rate. It would also pay any operating losses Milgard incurred during that period. Then, if Milgard operated the furnace for six months without incident, Selas would "finetune" the furnace to achieve a 95 rate. Selas did the work and paid Milgard's operating losses. Milgard dismissed the suit without prejudice. However, during the six-month period, the furnace failed to perform to the specifications of either the contract or the attempted settlement agreement.

Milgard initiated a second lawsuit on March 4, 1983, alleging breach of contract and breach of warranty. On June 29, 1984, Judge Tanner in the district court granted summary judgment in favor of Selas. ... This court, in Milgard Tempering, Inc. v. Selas Corp. of America, 761 F.2d 553 (9th Cir.1985)[hereinafter Milgard I], reversed and remanded for trial. ...

On remand, after a five-week bench trial, Judge Bryan in the district court found that the furnace had never lived up to the specifications in the contract. He held that the limited repair remedy failed of its essential purpose and that Selas' default was sufficiently severe to expunge the cap on consequential damages. He awarded Milgard $1,076,268 in net damages. ...

Selas appeals the judgment and denial of its motion for new trial.... We affirm.

II

Selas ... argues that the district court erred in ruling that the limited repair remedy failed of its "essential purpose" and that such failure lifted the contractual cap on consequential damages.

A

Section 28.5 of the contract limited Milgard's remedies in the event of breach of warranty to repair or replacement of the defective equipment.

> [In the event of a breach of any warranty, express, implied or statutory, or in the event the equipment is found to be defective in workmanship or material or fails to conform to the specifications

thereof, [Selas'] liability shall be limited to the repair or replacement of such equipment as is found to be defective or non-conforming, provided that written notice of any such defect or non-conformity must be given to Selas within 1 year from the date of acceptance, or 15 months from completion of shipment, whichever first occurs. In the event that acceptance is delayed through the fault of Selas, then the Selas 1 year warranty shall be applicable and not begin until the date of acceptance. Selas assumes no liability for no [sic] consequential or incidental damages of any kind (including fire or explosion in the starting, testing, or subsequent operation of the equipment), and the Purchaser assumes all liability for the consequences of its use or misuse by the Purchaser or his employees. In no event will Selas be liable for damages resulting from the non-operation of Purchaser's plant, loss of product, raw materials or production as a result of the use, misuse or inability to use the equipment covered by this proposal or from injury to any person or property alleged to be caused by or resulting from the use of the product produced with the equipment to be supplied to Purchaser by Selas pursuant to this proposal whether the customer or Purchaser is mediate or immediate. Purchaser hereby releases [Selas] of and from and indemnifies [it] against, all liability not specifically assumed by [it] hereunder. (Emphasis added).] *

Such limitations on a party's remedies are permitted by Washington's version of the U.C.C., Wash.Rev.Code § 62A.2–719(1)(a) (West Supp. 1989).

An exclusive or limited remedy ... must be viewed against the background of § 62A.2–719(2).... . This section requires a court to examine the contract in general and the remedy provision in particular to determine what the remedy's essential purpose is and whether it has failed.

A limited repair remedy serves two main purposes. First, it serves to shield the seller from liability during her attempt to make the goods conform. Second, it ensures that the buyer will receive goods conforming to the contract specifications within a reasonable period of time. ...

A contractual provision limiting the remedy to repair or replacement of defective parts fails of its essential purpose within the meaning of § 62A.2–719(2) if the breaching manufacturer or seller is unable to make the repairs within a reasonable time period.... It is not necessary to show negligence or bad faith on the part of the seller, for the detriment to the buyer is the same whether the seller's unsuccessful efforts were diligent, dilatory, or negligent. ...

The district court in this case found that the furnace had never lived up to the specifications of the contract. ... Moreover, the court found that the few successful improvements were not made within a reasonable period of time, taking over two and one-half years. We

* [The court reproduced the contract in a footnote. Eds.]

agree that under these circumstances, the unreasonable delay and ultimate failure in repair made the repair remedy ineffective; thus, the remedy failed of its essential purpose.

Although the contract did not guarantee a specific time for completion of debugging, the court found that the writing was not completely integrated. ... Looking at the commercial context, the court found that both parties implicitly agreed that the complete period for start up and "debugging" would take about eight weeks. ...

B

Washington courts have not addressed the issue of whether failure of a limited repair remedy may serve to invalidate a consequential damages exclusion. Therefore, it is our responsibility to determine how the state's supreme court would resolve it. In undertaking this task, we may draw upon recognized legal sources including statutes, treatises, restatements, and published opinions. ... We may also look to "well-reasoned decisions from other jurisdictions." ...

1

We begin our analysis with Fiorito Bros., Inc. v. Fruehauf Corp., 747 F.2d 1309, 1314–15 (9th Cir.1984). In that case, we held that under Washington law, the failure of a repair remedy does not automatically remove a cap on consequential damages. We predicted that Washington courts would take a case-by-case approach and examine the contract provisions to determine whether the exclusive remedy and damage exclusions are either "separable elements of risk allocation" or "inseparable parts of a unitary package of risk-allocation." Id. at 1315 (quoting district court).

If the exclusions are inseparable, we reasoned, a court's analysis should track the Official Washington Comments to § 62A.2–719(2) [hereinafter Washington Comments], which explain that the subsection "relates to contractual arrangements which become oppressive by change of circumstances...." 747 F.2d at 1315. We then affirmed the district court's ruling that the seller's arbitrary and unreasonable refusal to live up to the limited repair clause "rendered the damages limitation clause oppressive and invalid." Id.

Fiorito relied heavily on this circuit's analysis ... in [S.M. Wilson & Co. v. Smith Int'l. Inc.,] 587 F.2d 1363. Wilson involved a contract between commercially sophisticated parties for a tunnel boring machine. The contract contained both a limited repair clause and a cap on consequential damages. After concluding that the repair remedy failed of its essential purpose within § 2719(2), this court held that the bar to consequential damages remained enforceable. We explained:

> Parties of relatively equal bargaining power negotiated an allocation of their risks of loss. Consequential damages were assigned to the buyer, Wilson. The machine was a complex piece of equipment designed for the buyer's purposes. The seller Smith did not ignore

his obligation to repair; he simply was unable to perform it. This is not enough to require that the seller absorb losses the buyer plainly agreed to bear. Risk shifting is socially expensive and should not be undertaken in the absence of a good reason. An even better reason is required when to so shift is contrary to a contract freely negotiated. The default of the seller is not so total and fundamental as to require that its consequential damage limitation be expunged from the contract.

Id. at 1375 (emphasis added). However this court in Wilson quickly pointed out that its holding was limited to the facts and was in no way intended to state that consequential damages caps always survive failure of limited repair remedies. Id. at 1375–76.

2

The district court in the instant case found Selas' default "fundamental, but not total." Nonetheless, it found the breach sufficiently fundamental to remove the cap on consequential damages. Selas claims that the court misunderstood the legal standard and that consequential damages may be allowed only when the seller's breach is both total and fundamental.

We agree that the district court's characterization of the case law was flawed. However, the analysis it employed was not. This court has found nothing magical about the phrase "total and fundamental" default in relation to U.C.C. 2–719(2). In Fiorito we eschewed such wooden analysis, leaving "[e]ach case [to] stand on its own facts." Id., 747 F.2d at 1314 (quoting Wilson, 587 F.2d at 1376). We further expressed our distaste for talismanic analysis in Milgard I, finding the "oppressive circumstances" analysis utilized by Fiorito and the Washington Comments and the "total and fundamental" default analysis in Wilson in accord with each other. 761 F.2d at 556.

The task before the district court was to examine the remedy provisions and determine whether Selas' default caused a loss which was not part of the bargained-for allocation of risk. ... This was the analysis that the district court actually employed.

We agree with the district court's decision to lift the cap on consequential damages. Milgard did not agree to pay $1.45 million in order to participate in a science experiment. It agreed to purchase what Selas represented as a cutting-edge glass furnace that would accommodate its needs after two months of debugging. Selas' inability to effect repair despite 2.5 years of intense, albeit injudicious,[9] effort

---

9. Selas exacerbated the repair problem by not providing a qualified process engineer during the initial debugging period and stubbornly refusing to replace the unproven ircon transfer system with more reliable methods that were available. We therefore agree with the district court's conclusion that "Selas did not make a completely open and honest effort to bring the furnace into compliance with the contract requirements." ... However, as noted earlier, the question of Selas' good faith is not dispositive of this appeal.

caused Milgard losses not part of the bargained-for allocation of risk. Therefore, the cap on consequential damages is unenforceable.

III

Next, Selas challenges the district court's determination of damages. The court had found that for 21 months (April 1, 1980 to December 31, 1982), the furnace was incapable of reaching any of the yield rates outlined in the contract. Thereafter, the furnace could reach a few with some regularity. Accordingly, the district court calculated damages for two time periods. First, it calculated Milgard's lost profits during the 21–month "damage" period. Second, it calculated losses Milgard did and would incur after December 31, 1982....

All three tests for loss of profits have been met in this case. First, the district judge made the factual finding that the parties contemplated the possibility of lost profits. Because § 28.5 of the contract refers to such profits, this finding is not clearly erroneous.

Second, the district court found that the failure of the machine to conform to the contract specifications proximately caused Milgard to lose profits. Selas does not challenge this finding and we do not disturb it.

Third, the district court had a sufficient factual basis upon which to make its computation of lost profits. ... Milgard's sole source of evidence in this area was its expert witness, Dr. Finch. Although the district judge found some of Dr. Finch's figures difficult to swallow, he pointed out that that did not negate them. ... [T]he court discounted the damage award in accordance with the weight of Finch's testimony. Therefore, we find no error....

VIII

For these reasons, the judgment of the district court is affirmed.

Notes

(1) **Repair or Replace Clauses.** Agreements in which sellers undertake to repair or replace the goods sold are very common in sales of business equipment and consumer goods. What do sellers seek to gain by use of such clauses? Are such clauses advantageous or disadvantageous to buyers?

How do repair or replace clauses relate to quality warranties? Did Selas purport to disclaim any warranties in the contract of sale? Why not? Even if a seller purports to disclaim all warranties, a repair or replace clause must contain some quality standard; typically that is found in the terms of the condition that activates seller's duty to repair or replace.[3] A condition frequently used in such clauses activates

---

3. In sales of consumer goods, some sellers undertake to replace some products if the customer requests. Customer satisfaction is the quality criterion. Similarly,

seller's duty "if the goods suffer defect in materials or workmanship." How does this standard compare with the criteria of merchantability? Does "defect" mean something different than "non-conformity"?

How do repair or replace clauses relate to contractual limitations of damages? Recall UCC 2–719(1)(a). In what sense is a seller's undertaking to repair or replace a "remedy" for the buyer?

(2) Failure of Essential Purpose. While a seller's repair or replace undertaking may be additive to buyer's other remedies, ordinarily agreements provide that the undertaking is in substitution for those remedies. What language in the furnace sale contract had that effect? The Code provides that statutory remedies become available to a buyer if an exclusive or limited remedy fails of its essential purpose. UCC 2–719(2).[4] What economic value is protected by repair or replacement? What statutory remedy is most analogous to the remedy of repair or replacement?

(3) Failure of Purpose and Consequential Damages. The terse language of UCC 2–719(2) gives little guidance on the issue decided in *Milgard.* "Remedy ... as provided in this Act" does not necessarily mean consequential damages. Comment 1 refers to occurrence of circumstances that "deprive either party of the substantial value of the bargain." Is the Ninth Circuit's approach consistent with seeking to protect the value of the bargain struck between seller and buyer?

S. M. WILSON & CO. v. SMITH INTERNATIONAL, INC., 587 F.2d 1363 (9th Cir.1978). Buyer purchased a tunnel boring machine which the buyer needed to construct mine shafts. Seller agreed to design, build and deliver the machine for a price of $550,000. Seller warranted that the machine was free from defects in materials and workmanship, but that is obligation under the warranty was limited to repair or replacement of defective parts returned to seller not later than 90–days after commencement of drilling operations using the machine. The sales document provided further that seller "shall not be liable for any loss or damage resulting, directly or indirectly, from the use or loss of use of the machine. Without limiting the generality of the foregoing this exclusion from liability embraces the purchaser's expenses for downtime or for making up downtime... ."

As delivered, the machine performed at a rate much slower than seller had promised. Apparently ignoring the 90–day clause in its warranty, seller tried but failed, for a substantial time after delivery, to repair the machine. Eventually, the defect was found and corrected.

some merchants sell consumer goods on "unconditional" money-back terms, the only condition being the buyer's return of the goods and request for the price paid. Merchants sometimes buy inventory from suppliers on terms that permit return of unsold goods. See UCC 2–326(1), 2–327.

4. Readers of UCC 2–719(2) may be puzzled by the notion that a "remedy" might have a "purpose." Human beings have objectives, abstractions do not. If the Code is referring to someone's purpose in an agreement for an exclusive or limited remedy, is it the buyer's purpose, or the seller's, or both parties'?

Because of problems with the machine, a drilling project expected by buyer to be completed in 80 days took 210 days to complete. Substantial consequential losses, alleged by buyer to have been $1.8 million, were sought by buyer. The trial court, making no finding of the amount of buyer's damages, held that such damages were precluded by the no-consequential damages clause in the contract of sale. The Court of Appeals, affirming, held that even though the replace/repair remedy had failed of its essential purpose, the contract provision barring recovery of consequential damages was enforceable. 587 F.2d 1363 (9th Cir.1978).

The Court of Appeals said:

The issue remains whether the failure of the limited repair remedy to serve its purpose requires permitting the recovery of consequential damages as sections 2714(3) and 2715 permit. We hold it does not. In reaching this conclusion we are influenced heavily by the characteristics of the contract.... . Parties of relatively equal bargaining power negotiated an allocation of their risks of loss. ... The seller ... did not ignore his obligation to repair; he simply was unable to perform it. This is not enough to require that the seller absorb losses the buyer plainly agreed to bear. ... The default of the seller was not so total and fundamental as to require that its consequential damage limitation be expunged from the contract.

CHATLOS SYSTEMS, INC. v. NATIONAL CASH REGISTER CORP., 635 F.2d 1081 (3d Cir.1980). Buyer, manufacturer of telecommunications equipment, purchased a computer system for its accounting needs. The contract price for the entire system was $46,000. The contract contained the following clause: "In no event shall NCR [the seller] be liable for special or consequential damages from any cause whatsoever." Eighteen months after the system was supposed to be operational, seller had been unable to make the system work properly and buyer asked seller to remove the computer. We previously considered this case in connection with the measure of the buyer's damages under 2–714(2). Another issue in that case was the enforceability of the clause excluding consequential damages.

At a bench trial, the court awarded buyer consequential damages in the amount of $63,500. The Court of Appeals for the Third Circuit reversed. The court said:

Whether the preclusion of consequential damages should be effective in this case depends upon the circumstances involved. The repair remedy's failure of essential purpose, while a discrete question, is not completely irrelevant to the issue of the conscionability of enforcing the consequential damages exclusion. ... Recognizing this, the question here narrows to the unconscionability of the buyer retaining the risk of consequential damages upon the failure of the essential purpose of the exclusive repair remedy.

... It is ... important that the claim is for commercial loss and the adversaries are substantial business concerns. We find no great disparity in the parties' bargaining power or sophistication. Apparently, Chatlos [the buyer], a manufacturer of complex electronic equipment, had some appreciation of the problems that might be encountered with a computer system. Nor is there a "surprise" element present here. The limitation was clearly expressed in a short, easily understandable sales contract. ...

... Some disruption of normal business routines, expenditure of employee time, and impairment of efficiency cannot be considered highly unusual or unforeseeable in a faulty computer installation. Moreover, although not determinative, it is worth mentioning that even though unsuccessful in correcting the problems within an appropriate time, NCR continued its efforts. Indeed, on the date of termination NCR was still actively working on the system at the Chatlos plant.

... We conclude, therefore, that the provision of the agreement excluding consequential damages should be enforced.... .

FIORITO BROS., INC. v. FRUEHAUF CORP., 747 F.2d 1309 (9th Cir.1984). Buyer, a heavy construction company, purchased thirteen dump truck bodies for use in carrying wet concrete to highway construction sites for the price of $66,600. Before the purchase agreement, seller's representative had assured buyer that the bodies were suitable for this purpose. The agreement was documented on seller's standard-form sales order, in which seller warranted that the goods were free from defects in materials and workmanship with the "sole remedy" of buyer being seller's five-year repair/replace promise. The form further provided that: "Seller and Customer agree that Seller shall have no liability for any cargo loss, loss of use or other incidental or consequential damages arising out of this order or which are alleged to have been caused by any of the goods delivered hereunder." None of the truck bodies was able to handle wet concrete. On buyer's complaint, seller's representative declared that the problems were not covered by the warranty. Later, seller wrote to buyer that its investigation had revealed that the product had been misused. Seller never acted to repair or replace the truck bodies. At trial, seller admitted that it had not conducted any investigation of buyer's use of the product. The jury awarded buyer $130,000 in damage. How much of this was for consequential damages does not appear in the opinion.

Affirming the judgment of the trial court, the Court of Appeals for the Ninth Circuit held that seller's repair/replace remedy had failed of its essential purpose. The court held further that the no-consequential-damages clause was unenforceable. 747 F.2d 1309 (9th Cir.1984).

The appellate court quoted with approval the trial court's opinion:

In the current case, it does not make sense to view the exclusive-remedy and consequential-damage provisions independently. The purpose of the parties in agreeing to this exclusive-remedy provision was to [i]nsure that the Plaintiff would not suffer from down time and other such consequential harms that follow from defective conditions in the trucks.... *It cannot be maintained that it was the parties' intention that Defendant be enabled to avoid all consequential liability for breach by first agreeing to an alternative remedy provision designed to avoid consequential harms, and then scuttling that alternative remedy through its recalcitrance in honoring the agreement.* (Emphasis added by Court of Appeals).

The Court of Appeals further upheld the trial judge's findings that the consequential-damages clause was not oppressive when the agreement was made, that the parties had relatively equal bargaining positions and sophistication, but that circumstances during performance rendered the damages limitation clause oppressive and invalid.

Note

Unconscionability and Consequential Damages. Would it be preferable to address the question of consequential damages limitation clauses in terms of unconscionability rather than failure of essential purpose? Does UCC 2–719(3) invite analysis of such clauses under the rubric of unconscionability? Which standard is more comprehensible to the parties and the courts? Consider the following case:

A & M PRODUCE CO. v. FMC CORP., 135 Cal.App.3d 473, 186 Cal.Rptr. 114 (1982). An experienced farmer, who operated as a corporation, decided to grow tomatoes for the first time and shopped for a weight-sizing machine to process his crop. After discussions with representatives of FMC, farmer ordered two machines for $32,000.00. The parties executed a contract document on a printed one-page FMC form, which provided on the back that seller warranted the machines to be free from defects in materials and workmanship under normal use and service for 12 months and, further, disclaimed all other express or implied warranties. The terms on the back of the document continued:

[Seller's] obligation under this warranty is limited to repairing or replacing any part of the equipment which is found to be defective.... .

SELLER IN NO EVENT SHALL BE LIABLE FOR CONSEQUENTIAL DAMAGES ARISING OUT OF OR IN CONNECTION WITH THIS AGREEMENT.... . CONSEQUENTIAL DAMAGES FOR PURPOSES HEREOF SHALL INCLUDE, WITHOUT LIMITATION, LOSS OF USE, INCOME OR PROFIT.... .

FMC delivered and installed the equipment. When the tomato crop ripened, the machines failed to work properly. Tomatoes piled up in front of the singulator belt and overflow tomatoes had to be sent through the machines again, causing damage to the crop. An FMC representative managed to control the overflow problem by stopping and starting the machine, but this significantly reduced the processing speed. After several weeks, the farmer ceased processing because the income from the tomatoes—some of which had been damaged—was inadequate to cover his costs.

The farmer offered to return the machines upon refund of his $5,000.00 down payment. FMC rejected this proposal and sued for the balance of the purchase price. The trial court held that it would be unconscionable to enforce the warranty disclaimer and limitation of consequential damages clauses and entered judgment upon a verdict for the farmer in excess of $260,000.00. The Court of Appeal affirmed.

> As to the exclusion of consequential damages, several factor combine to suggest that the exclusion was unreasonable on the facts of this case. Consequential damages are a commercially recognized type of damage actually suffered by A & M due to FMC's breach. ... If the seller's warranty was breached, consequential damages were not merely "reasonably foreseeable": they were explicitly obvious. All parties were aware that once the tomatoes began to ripen, they all had to be harvested and packed within a relatively short period of time. ...

> Another factor supporting the trial court's determination involves the avoidability of the damages and relates directly to the allocation of risks which lies at the foundation of the contractual bargain. It has been suggested that "[r]isk shifting is socially expensive and should not be undertaken in the absence of a good reason. An even better reason is required when to so shift is contrary to a contract freely negotiated." (S.M. Wilson & Co. v. Smith Intern., Inc. (9th Cir.1978) 587 F.2d 1363, 1375.) But ... FMC was the only party reasonably able to prevent this loss by not selling A & M a machine inadequate to meet its expressed needs.
> ...

> In summary, our review of the totality of circumstances in this case, including the business environment within which the contract was executed, supports the trial court's determination that the disclaimer of warranties and the exclusion of consequential damages in FMC's form contract were unconscionable and therefore unenforceable. When non-negotiable terms on preprinted form agreements combine with disparate bargaining power, resulting in the allocation of commercial risks in a socially or economically unreasonable manner, the concept of unconscionability as codified in Uniform Commercial Code sections 2–302 and 2–719, subdivision (3), furnishes legal justification for refusing enforcement of the offensive result.

A concurring opinion contained this:

Facts fly as "thick as autumnal leaves that strow the brooks of Vallombrose," in support of the trial court's conclusion that these contract clauses were oppressive, contrary to oral representations made to induce the purchase, and unreasonably favorable to the party with a superior bargaining position. No experienced farmer would spend $32,000 for equipment which could not process his tomatoes before they rot and no fair and honest merchant would sell such equipment with representations negated in its own sales contract.

HILL v. BASF WYANDOTTE CORP.

United States Court of Appeals, Fourth Circuit, 1982.
696 F.2d 287.

PHILLIPS, CIRCUIT JUDGE. In this diversity case controlled by South Carolina law BASF Wyandotte Corp. (BWC), manufacturer of Basalin, an agricultural herbicide, appeals from a judgment in favor of Hill, a farmer who bought Basalin from a retailer and used it with allegedly injurious consequences to his soybean crop. A jury, finding breach of warranty running from BWC as manufacturer to Hill as ultimate purchaser under relevant provisions of the state's version of the Uniform Commercial Code (U.C.C.), awarded Hill substantial direct and consequential damages.

Concluding that BWC was bound by no warranty save that expressed in writing on the cans of herbicide purchased by Hill and that under its terms Hill's remedy for breach was limited to direct damages, we vacate the judgment and remand for a new trial limited to the issues of liability and damages for breach of the express warranty on the herbicide cans.

I

In 1977, Hill was an experienced farmer with extensive farming operations in Richland County, South Carolina. Along with other crops he grew a substantial amount of soybeans. In recent years he had used a herbicide called Treflan, produced by a manufacturing rival of BWC's, to control weeds in producing this crop. In late January or early February of 1977 he met with a man named Pennington, who was a sales agent for BWC. They discussed the properties of BWC's herbicide, Basalin, which was then selling at a lower price than Treflan's. In the course of their discussions, in response to questioning by Hill, Pennington told Hill that "if you used Treflan, you [use Basalin] the same way ... the entire same way"; that "it would control the same weeds that Treflan will"; that "it would do the same way as Treflan, but it is cheaper"; "to put it down the same way, you don't have to change a thing, do it the same way."

Relying, according to his later testimony, upon these statements by Pennington, Hill decided to buy and use considerable quantities of Basalin in growing his 1977 soybean crop. BWC did not have a direct retail outlet in the area, and Hill made his purchases of Basalin from Kerr–McGee Chemical Corporation, a local agricultural chemical retailer. He made four separate purchases, the first on February 14, and the other three during April. In all he bought 365 gallons, all in 5–gallon cans, for a total purchase price of $8,382.35 which he paid in two separate installments.

On each of the cans of Basalin purchased there appeared a label containing a warranty and certain conditions of sale that included an allocation of risk, a disclaimer of any warranties other than the one expressly stated, and a limitation of remedies for breach of that warranty.

CONDITIONS OF SALE AND WARRANTY *

The Directions for Use of this product reflect the opinion of experts based on field use and tests. The directions are believed to be reliable and should be followed carefully. However, it is impossible to eliminate all risks inherently associated with use of this product. Crop injury, ineffectiveness or other unintended consequences may result because of such factors as weather conditions, presence of other materials, or the manner of use or application all of which are beyond the control of BASF WYANDOTTE CORPORATION ("BWC") or the seller. All such risks shall be assumed by the Buyer.

"BWC" warrants that this product conforms to the chemical description on the label and is reasonably fit for the purpose referred to in the Directions for Use subject to the inherent risks referred to above. "BWC" MAKES NO OTHER EXPRESS OR IMPLIED WARRANTY OF FITNESS OF MERCHANTABILITY OR ANY OTHER EXPRESS OR IMPLIED WARRANTY. In no case shall "BWC" or the Seller be liable for consequential, special or indirect damages resulting from the use or handling of this product. "BWC" and the Seller offer this product and the Buyer and user accept it, subject to the foregoing Conditions of Sale and Warranty which may be varied by agreement in writing signed by a duly authorized representative of "BWC." The purchase price of Basalin includes a royalty for a non-transferable license to practice the method of U.S. 3,854,927.

Read the entire label. Use only according to label instructions. Read "CONDITIONS OF SALE AND WARRANTY" before buying or using. If terms are not acceptable, return product at once, unopened.

After reading the label, Hill applied the herbicide to 1,450 acres of soybeans. He applied Treflan to approximately another 200 acres of

* [The court reproduced the text of the label in a footnote. Eds.]

soybeans. Following planting of this crop in May and June, Hill began in July to notice weed problems—particularly pig weed—in the Basalin fields. No corresponding problem was noted then or later in the Treflan fields. Efforts of various kinds were made to control the weed problem, but none were successful.

In the Basalin-treated fields, Hill had a bad crop, with lower yield than he had had in other years and a poorer quality that required greater-than-ordinary expense in harvesting. Ascribing this result to Basalin's failure to control weeds as warranted, Hill brought this action against BWC alleging breach of warranty and misrepresentation, and seeking $48,257.35 in direct and consequential damages.

BWC defended on several grounds: *inter alia,* that Hill's use of Basalin was not the proximate cause of any crop loss sustained; that BWC's sole warranty was that expressed on the label and that it was not breached; and that, in any event, under terms of the warranty, Hill's remedy was limited to recovery of the purchase price.

The case was first tried to Judge Chapman and a jury. On trial the evidence of causation was substantially conflicting. Hill's evidence indicated a significant difference in the yields on the Basalin-treated and Treflan-treated crops, and included testimony suggesting that Treflan in general was rated by experts as a better product and that other farmers in the area had had similar problems with Basalin during the same crop year. On the other hand, BWC's evidence included, *inter alia,* testimony that the two products were essentially identical in chemical composition and were rated of equal quality by experts; that the 1977 crop year had been a bad one generally in the area, with a drought at the critical time that might well have caused any diminished yield experienced; and that a significant portion of the Basalin-treated crop involved a seed variety more vulnerable to the drought conditions than was the variety used in Hill's smaller Trefland-treated crop.

Judge Chapman ruled as a matter of law that the only warranties in issue were the express warranties on the Basalin can which, by virtue of the applicable state U.C.C. provision ... 2–318 extended BWC's warranty beyond the retailer to Hill as a consumer; and that if breach of that warranty was proven, Hill's remedy was limited by its terms to direct damages as measured by the purchase price. On that basis the case was submitted to the jury which was then unable to reach a verdict, resulting in the declaration of a mistrial.

The case was then retried to Judge Anderson and a jury on substantially the same evidence. At the conclusion of the retrial, Judge Anderson, in direct disagreement with Judge Chapman's earlier critical rulings, instructed the jury that it might find BWC liable on the oral warranty of Pennington as well as any express warranty on the cans of Basalin, and that it might award consequential as well as direct damages if it found breach of warranty and damages proximately caused by the breach. This jury returned a general verdict for Hill of $209,725.

Following the denial of various post-trial motions by BWC, this appeal was taken.

II

BWC's contentions on appeal are essentially that Judge Anderson erred in his two rulings by which, in specific disagreement with those earlier made by Judge Chapman, he allowed the jury to treat Pennington's oral representations as an oral express warranty binding on BWC and to award consequential as well as direct damages for any breach found. We agree that there was error of law in both respects.

A

BWC contends that Pennington's oral representation did not amount to a warranty binding upon BWC for two reasons. First, as a matter of law, that the representation amounted to no more than sales puffing, as Judge Chapman had ruled on the first trial. Second, that in any event, BWC's express disclaimer of any express or implied warranties other than those expressed on the label was binding as a matter of law upon Hill as purchaser.

While we would be disposed to agree that under [UCC 2–313(2)] ... Pennington's representation was simply a "statement purporting to be merely the seller's opinion or commendation of the goods [that did] not create a warranty," we rest decision primarily on the conclusion that, in any event, Hill was bound by the disclaimer on the label of any warranties but those expressly stated there. Though on trial Hill attempted to discount the subjective effect of the label's contents upon him as he read them, he conceded that he did read the label before using any of the Basalin. There is, therefore, no question of either his actual notice of the disclaimer's existence as an express condition of the sale or that he was invited by another provision of the label to repudiate by return of the product if unwilling to accept the sale conditions.

Under controlling provisions of the U.C.C. as enacted in South Carolina, S.C.Ann.Code § 36–2–202 (Law.Co-op.1976) (parol or extrinsic evidence), and of the express conditions of the particular sale, the Pennington oral statements could not, as a matter of law, be allowed to vary the terms of the conditions of sale and warranty on the product label ... which alone controlled the legal relations of the parties to the executed sale.

Hill seeks to avoid the controlling effect of these statutory provisions by characterizing the disclaimer on the product label as a unilateral attempt by a seller following execution of a contract of sale or a consummated sale to disclaim express warranties made in conjunction with the sale or contract. The cases he cites in support of this proposition, e.g., Klein v. Asgrow Seed Co., 246 Cal.App.2d 87, 54

Cal.Rptr. 609 (Cal.Ct.App.1966), do support it, but they and that proposition are simply inapposite to the facts of this case. They deal with the effect of a post-contract or post-sale attempt unilaterally to avoid, by a later disclaimer, warranties embodied in or arising from an executory contract of sale or a completed sale. That is simply not the situation here in issue.

B

The district court also erred in allowing the jury to award consequential damages in the face of the express limitation of remedies on the label.

[UCC 2–719] ... authorizes remedy limitations such as that expressed here on the Basalin label unless those limitations are determined to be unconscionable, or not intended to be exclusive, or to have failed of their essential purpose. Id. Judge Anderson, as had Judge Chapman in the original trial, held the limitation in issue not to be unconscionable. Hill does not challenge that ruling on appeal. This leaves only the possibilities that the limitation expressed was not intended to be exclusive, or that the exclusive remedy as limited failed of its essential purpose within the meaning of the statute.

Hill urges that he never agreed that the limitation expressed should make the remedy as limited an exclusive one. He accepted, however, a product with a label proclaiming that damages in no case would exceed those contemplated on the label. The label extends to purchaser-users the privilege of returning Basalin cans unopened if the purchaser does not agree to the terms and conditions on the label. Hill read the label and chose not to return the product but to use it. He cannot defeat the warrantor's expressed intention to limit remedy by a privately held intention not to accept the limitation while accepting and using the product.

Hill's argument that such a limited remedy necessarily "fails of its essential purpose" [UCC 2–719(2)] is equally unavailing. The argument seems to be that because Hill *claims* damages in the amount by which his crop yield was allegedly reduced and cannot *obtain* such damages if the limitation on remedy is enforced, then the remedy "fails of its essential purpose." This would of course turn the provision on its head since it would always prevent imposition of any limitation that might prevent recovery of particular relief sought. The "fail of essential purpose" exception to the general right of sellers to limit liability under the U.C.C. applies most obviously to those situations where the limitation of remedy involves repair or replacement that cannot return the goods to their warranted condition. ... This exception does not apply here.

III

It is not possible to determine from the general verdict whether the jury found liability based solely upon breach of the Pennington oral "warranty" or of both that "warranty" and the express warranty on the label. It is therefore necessary to vacate the judgment in its entirety and remand for a new trial limited to the issues of whether BWC is liable for breach of the express warranty on the label and, if so, the amount of damages to which Hill is entitled for the breach under the limitation of remedies that we have held was validly imposed in the conditions of sale on the label.

It is so ordered.

Notes

(1) **Sales to Farmers.** The Code does not have special provision for sales of goods to farmers. Farmers who grow crops commonly purchase seed, fertilizer, and herbicides. Non-conformity of any of these supplies can result in substantial loss of the expected crops. The market value of each of these supplies tends to be a very small fraction of the value of the expected crops. In this setting, not surprisingly, suppliers try to avoid potential liability for the consequential damages of crop failure. Should the law provide specially for allocation of this risk between farmers and their suppliers? What would be the optimal legal standard? How significant is the fact that Hill was "an experienced farmer with extensive farming operations"?

(2) **Warranties by Manufacturers' Representatives.** Hill purchased the herbicide from a retailer, who is not a party to the litigation. Hill sued the manufacturer, BWC, and based his case in part on statements made by Pennington, a representative of the manufacturer. Putting aside for the moment the parol evidence exclusion, would a statement about the goods by someone who is not "the seller" be an express warranty under UCC 2–313? Could the statement become "part of the basis of the bargain"? If 2–313 does not apply, is there any other basis on which to find a warranty obligation?[5] Consider UCC 1–103.

The Fourth Circuit denied recovery on the claim based on Pennington's statements under UCC 2–202. If, as appears, Hill and BWC had no agreement between themselves, and certainly never adopted a writing as the final expression of an agreement, was the court correct in applying 2–202 to exclude Hill's claims based on Pennington's statements?

(3) **Manufacturers' Warranties on Labels.** BWC placed what purported to be a warranty on the labels of each can of Basalin. Conceivably Hill first saw and read the label after he had bought the goods from the retailer. Was the manufacturer's statement on the

5. In the marketing of consumer goods, a familiar transaction is the endorsement of goods given the Good Housekeeping Seal of Approval. The publisher of the magazine promises a remedy to consumers who buy endorsed products that turn out to be defective. Some credit card issuers, similarly, promise a remedy to consumers who, by use their credit cards, purchase products that turn out to be defective. Would such endorsements be enforceable under the Code?

label a warranty by BWC under UCC 2–313? See Massey–Ferguson, Inc. v. Laird, 432 So.2d 1259 (Ala.1983)(buyer of combine knew that manufacturer made a standard warranty, but did not examine the specific terms before contracting to purchase).

Note that a manufacturer's statement on the label would be a warranty by a retailer under UCC 2–314(f). As to retailers and their customers, the Code characterizes such statements as *implied* warranties.

(4) **Post-Purchase Disclaimers.** If a seller makes an express or implied warranty before or at the time of a contract of sale, does the seller have the power thereafter to limit or exclude the warranty? The parties have the power, by agreement, to modify a contract, UCC 2–209, but neither party has the unilateral power to decrease its contractual obligations to the other.

Was the purported disclaimer in the label in *Hill* a unilateral post-contract disclaimer? Could Hill seek to recover on basis of the express warranty in the label and not be bound by the disclaimer in the label?

The Basalin labels purport to disclaim implied warranties of merchantability and fitness for particular purpose. Hill apparently made no claim that either implied warranty existed or had been breached? What might explain that omission in plaintiff's case? What might explain the inclusion of disclaimers of these warranties in the labels?

Problem 2. Supreme Paint Company is a manufacturer of paint products. In response to an inquiry from Boyer Construction Co. about the price for a quantity purchase of ZX paint, Supreme wrote to Boyer:

> "Can quote you attractive price of $14 per gallon, freight prepaid to construction site, for immediate order for shipments of 100 gallons or more."

On September 10, Boyer replied:

> "Please ship 100 gallons of your ZX Paint for delivery at the construction site by November 1; unless we advise you to the contrary, make similar shipments to arrive December 1 and January 1."

The first shipment arrived on October 20. The invoice, which was received on the same day at Boyer's headquarters, noted the delivery of 100 gallons of ZX paint at a total price of $1400. The invoice bore at the bottom the following clearly printed statement:

> "Our paint products are prepared under carefully controlled manufacturing conditions, but if any of our products should be defective, we will gladly replace the product or refund the purchase price. We shall not be responsible for any other warranties, express or implied, including the warranty of merchantable quantity which extend beyond the description on the face hereof, and in no event shall be responsible for any special or consequential damages."

Boyer promptly paid for this shipment and for the two subsequent shipments that were made pursuant to the original schedule, and Boyer applied the paint to his construction job. The paint proved to be defective and peeled off. Early in January the November application began to peel, and the same developed for the later applications. Consequently Owner rejected Boyer's construction work, with the result that Boyer had to remove some of the siding for the building, clean off the original coat of paint by sand blasting and apply new paint. This extra work cost Boyer $150,000.

Did the disclaimer on the invoice become part of the contract with respect to some, or all, of the shipments? Is the disclaimer of consequential damages effective? See Geo. C. Christopher & Sons v. Kansas Paint & Color Co., 215 Kan. 185, 523 P.2d 709 (1974), modified on other grounds, 215 Kan. 510, 525 P.2d 626 (1974).

(5) Consequential Damages Clauses in Farm Supply Sales; Unconscionability. In the trial court, Hill contended that the limited remedy provided by BWC, pursuant to the terms of the Basalin labels, was unconscionable, but the contention was abandoned on appeal. How would you support an argument on this point for the farmer-buyer? See UCC 2–302, 2–719(3).

DURHAM v. CIBA-GEIGY CORP., 315 N.W.2d 696 (S.D.1982). Farmer purchased a herbicide, "Milogard," to control the growth of weeds in his milo crop. Due to a foxtail weed problem, the crop yield was low. An action was brought against the Milogard manufacturer on the basis of the labels on the cans, which stated: "Milogard 4L controls annual morningglory, carpetweed, lambsquarter, pigweed, ragweed, foxtail, smartweed, and velvetleaf." The labels also contained a warranty, disclaimer, and limitation of damages clause substantially identical to the label on the Basalin cans. The trial court held the limitation of damages clause unconscionable and the supreme court affirmed:

[T]he label represents that foxtail will be controlled by the pesticide but the user subsequently discovers that the pesticide is ineffective to control foxtail. To permit the manufacturer of the pesticide to escape all consequential responsibility for the breach of contract by inserting a disclaimer of warranty and limitation of consequential damage clause, such as was used herein, would leave the pesticide user without any substantial recourse for his loss. One-sided agreements whereby one party is left without a remedy for another party's breach are oppressive and should be declared unconscionable. ...

In this case, loss of the intended crop due to the ineffectiveness of the herbicide is inevitable and potential plaintiffs should not be left without a remedy. Furthermore, the purchasers of pesticides are not in a position to bargain with chemical manufacturers for contract terms more favorable than those listed on the pre-printed label, nor are they in a position to test the effectiveness of the pesticide prior to purchase. ...

The legislature of this state has spent considerable time and effort in establishing the law of warranty in South Dakota, and the damages that are recoverable for a breach of that warranty. Appellant seeks to restrict and abolish this established law on the label of the product to the point where there is no actionable warranty for the consumer. This is not acceptable.

We agree with the trial court's determination that appellant's disclaimer of warranty and limitation of consequential damages clause is invalid as unconscionable and contrary to the public policy of this state.

(B) INTERNATIONAL SALES LAW

The Convention on Contracts for the International Sale of Goods does not contain regulatory provisions comparable to UCC 2–316 and 2–719. Under CISG 6, the parties may "derogate from or vary the effect of" any of the Convention's provisions. Article 6 permits parties to agree to disclaimers of a quality warranty under CISG 35(2) [6] or to clauses limiting damages otherwise provided by the Convention, particularly by CISG 74. On the surface, therefore, it appears that the regulatory provisions of domestic law, like those of the Commercial Code, would not apply to international sales contracts.

However, the Convention does not purport to exclude application of all domestic laws to international sales contracts. Thus, Article 4(a) declares that the Convention is not concerned with "the validity of the contract or any of its provisions." Should CISG 4 be construed to permit challenge of warranty disclaimers or clauses limiting damages in international sales contracts as "invalid" under United States domestic law? [7]

"The answer should be No. ... It would be awkward to require [an international sales] contract to 'mention merchantability' in order to disclaim an implied obligation under [CISG] 35(2) that ... does not itself refer to 'merchantability.' ...

"The argument [that CISG 4(a) incorporates UCC 2–316(2) and (3)] proves too much for it leads to the conclusion that any domestic rule that denied full literal effect to a contract provision on the ground that it does not accurately represent the parties' understanding would constitute a rule of 'validity.' The reference to domestic rules of 'validity' in Article 4(a) cannot be carried this far without intruding on the

---

6. CISG 35(2) also contains a provision that the parties may agree otherwise.

7. CISG 7(2) refers to the rules of private international law for choice of law on questions not settled by the Convention. Since questions of "validity" are expressly not governed by the Convention, the law governing such questions would be found by application of the choice of law rules under private international law. In an appropriate case, United States domestic law might be chosen as the governing law.

Convention's rules for interpreting international sales contracts. More specifically, Article 8 addresses a basic question of interpretation in a manner somewhat similar to the rules of domestic law in UCC 2–316. ... The point is not, of course, that Article 8 of the Convention and UCC 2–316 are identical but rather that both address the same issue. It follows that the reference to 'validity' in Article 4(a) of the Convention may not be read so broadly as to import domestic rules that would supplant articles of the Convention such as Article 8." J. Honnold, Uniform Law for International Sales §§ 233–234 (2d ed. 1991). *Contra:* Note, 53 Fordham L. Rev. 863 (1985).

Whether or not CISG 4(a) incorporates regulatory provisions of the Uniform Commercial Code, counsel for sellers engaged in international sales transactions to which United States law may apply would be prudent to advise their clients to contract in accordance with the disclosure requirements of the Code. However, an international sales contract drafter should not rely on the Code rules that a disclaimer clause is sufficient if it mentions "merchantability" or uses the phrase "as is." A non-U.S. buyer, relying on CISG 8, could reasonably argue that the full import of these provisions had not been made clear to it.

———

Problem 3. The parties in *Western Industries* were a United States buyer and a Canadian seller. The transaction occurred prior to the CISG taking effect. If the case had been governed by the CISG, how would the battle of the forms be treated? See Art. 19. Is the CISG provision an improvement on the UCC 2–207? If the CISG had applied, would the outcome have changed?

Problem 4. The parties in *Kunststoffwerk* were a United States buyer and a German seller. The transaction occurred before the CISG took effect. If the CISG had applied, would the outcome have changed?

SECTION 5. LEGAL BARS TO ACTIONS FOR BREACH OF WARRANTY

———

(A) DOMESTIC SALES LAW

Introduction. A buyer may be barred from litigation of the merits of a warranty claim if the buyer fails to give the seller timely notice of the seller's breach. Even if a buyer's notice is timely, the buyer may be barred from relief if the buyer has not commenced a law suit within the statutory period of limitations. The notice-to-seller requirement is found in UCC 2–607(3)(a). The statute of limitations for transactions in goods is UCC 2–725.

(1) Notice of breach. Lawyers representing sellers in warranty litigation must be drawn to the "slam dunk" provision that results in buyers' being "barred from any remedy." UCC 2–607(3)(a). A buyer is subject to this result if, after acceptance of goods,[1] the buyer fails to notify seller of breach within a reasonable time after the buyer discovered or should have discovered the breach.

M.K. ASSOCIATES v. STOWELL PRODUCTS, INC.

United States District Court, for the District of Maine, 1988.
697 F. Supp. 20.

CARTER, DISTRICT JUDGE:

I. Introduction

M.K. Associates, a seller of wood products, has brought an action to recover the remainder of the purchase price due from a sale of ash dowels to the defendant Stowell Products, Inc. The defendant claims that the plaintiff breached the contract because the dowels were defective. The defendant argues that it is entitled to set off the remaining amount due as damages caused by the defective goods.

The case was tried before the court on September 19, 1988. For the reasons set forth below, the court finds for the plaintiff. The findings of fact and conclusions of law follow.

II. Findings of Fact

From December, 1986 through February, 1987, Stowell Products, through its purchasing manager, Wayne Curley, made a series of offers for ash dowels from M.K. Associates. The dowels were delivered during the period from December, 1986 to March, 1987. Stowell Products intended to use the dowels to manufacture products to fill a contract with another company, Mirro/Foley Corp., due in late August, 1987. Although Stowell Products made periodic payments to M.K. Associates on these orders up through the fall of 1987, it was substantially in arrears as early as March, 1987. The parties have stipulated that the amount still due for the purchase and delivery of the ash dowels is $10,518.40.

The employee who received the orders from M.K. Associates noticed that some of the dowels were defective because they were "out of round," and he reported this defect to Wayne Curley, the purchasing manager. The factory foreperson, Virginia Johnson, found she was

---

1. "Acceptance" of goods is defined in UCC 2–606. What conduct constitutes "acceptance" can be a difficult question. We will consider that subject later. Cases in which buyers claim sellers' breach of warranty typically involve problems not detected by buyers for some time after delivery of the goods, by which time "accep-

tance" will have occurred under 2–606. Sometimes, however, warranty problems surface before "acceptance." Of the cases studied, the *T.J. Stevenson* case (sale of flour to Bolivia), Section 2, supra, is a notable example of pre-acceptance warranty litigation.

unable to use the dowels because of the defects. From June to September, 1987, Johnson ran the dowels through a "seavey" machine in order to correct the defects. This corrective process enabled Stowell Products to use the dowels for the Mirro/Foley order, although the order was not shipped until September 25, 1987, about a month late.

In the spring of 1987, Wayne Curley, purchasing manager of Stowell Products, and Doug Bucy, general manager, had a series of conversations with M.K. Associates. These conversations discussed the fact that Stowell Products was behind on its payments for the order. Only one conversation, however, made any mention of problems with the dowels. This conversation occurred between Curley and Marshall Kates, owner of M.K. Associates, in March, 1987. At this time, Curley asked Kates if one of the orders could be cancelled because of problems in running the dowels through the production process. Kates answered that he couldn't cancel. They did not discuss the issue further.

Stowell Products made no other attempts to raise the issue of defects in the dowels to M.K. Associates. On September 2, 1987, M.K. Associates filed a complaint in this court for the remainder due from Stowell Products on the dowel order.

III. Conclusions of Law

The issue in this case is whether Stowell Products is entitled to deduct damages for defects in the dowels purchased from M.K. Associates against the amount owed for the orders. The defendant does not dispute that Stowell Products accepted the dowels from M.K. Associates, and that it did not revoke this acceptance. Instead, the defendant decided to keep the dowels and use them in its business. ...

Nonetheless, accepting defective goods does not preclude a buyer from pursuing remedies for breach of contract due to defects in goods. 11 M.R.S.A. § 2–607(2). "The buyer on notifying the seller of his intention so to do may deduct all or any part of the damages resulting from any breach of the contract from any part of the price still due under the same contract." 11 M.R.S.A. § 2–717. A buyer claiming a breach of contract after accepting goods must, however, notify the seller of the breach within a reasonable time after discovery of the breach, or the buyer will be barred from any breach of contract remedy. 11 M.R.S.A. § 2–607(3)(a).

The critical question in this case, therefore, is whether the defendant gave timely notice of the breach of contract claim. What constitutes reasonable time depends on the particular circumstances of a case. 11 M.R.S.A. § 1–204. The policies underlying the requirement of timely notice are first, to enable the seller to cure or replace, second, to give the seller an opportunity to prepare for negotiation and litigation, and third, to ensure finality. J. White & R. Summers, Uniform Commercial Code 421–22 (2d ed. 1980). See also In Re Morweld Steel Products Corp., 8 Bankr. 946, 951 (W.D.Mich.1981) (quoting Steel & Wire Corp. v. Thyssen Inc., 20 U.C.C. Rep. 892 (E.D.Mich.1976)). To further these purposes, "reasonable time" for notice is interpreted strictly for commercial buyers. See 11 M.R.S.A. § 2–607, Uniform Commercial Code (U.C.C.) Comment 4.

The defendant argues that notice of the breach was given by Wayne Curley, purchasing manager for Stowell Products, to Marshall Kates, owner of M.K. Associates, in their conversation in March, 1987. In this conversation, Curley told Kates that defects in some dowels were causing production problems, and Kates said he could not cancel the order. The defendant argues that Curley's conversation with Kates was sufficient notice. It is true that "no formality of notice is required." 11 M.R.S.A. § 2–717, U.C.C. Comment 2. "The content of the notification need merely be sufficient to let the seller know that the transaction is still troublesome and must be watched." 11 M.R.S.A. § 2–607, U.C.C. Comment 4. Nevertheless, after Kates responded that he would not be able to cancel the order, Curley let the matter rest and gave Kates no indication that Stowell Products pursued it further. Therefore, the defendant did not give adequate notice that the transaction was still troublesome.

Moreover, the U.C.C. Comments emphasize that notice of a claim of breach is crucial. "The notification which saves the buyer's rights under this Article need only be such as informs the seller that the transaction is claimed to involve a breach, and thus opens the way for normal settlement through negotiation." 11 M.R.S.A. § 2–607, U.C.C. Comment 4. Even if the seller knows of defects in the goods, the buyer must notify the seller of the buyer's claim that the defects constitute a breach. In Re Morweld Steel Products Corp., supra at 952 (quoting Standard Alliance Industries Inc. v. The Black Clawson Co., 587 F.2d 813 (6th Cir.1978), cert. denied, 441 U.S. 923 (1979)). The requirement that a commercial buyer's notice must include an indication that the buyer considers the contract breached is consistent with the policies behind the notice requirement, which include ensuring finality for transactions and allowing the seller to prepare for negotiation and settlement. In the conversation with Kates, however, Curley did not clearly let Kates know that Stowell Products considered the contract breached.

Finally, U.C.C. Comment 2 to 11 M.R.S.A. § 2–717 states that "any language which reasonably indicates the buyer's reason for holding up his payment is sufficient." Despite repeated conversations concerning late payments, no one from Stowell Products suggested to M.K. Associates that payments were being withheld to cover the costs of defects in the dowels.

Therefore, Stowell Products' only notice of the breach was in its answer to the plaintiff's complaint, filed on October 13, 1987, more than five months after the dowels were received and more than three months after the defendant began processing the dowels. The defendant argues that it was reasonable to wait until the Mirro/Foley order was completed in order to determine the total amount of damages.

The U.C.C. does not require, however, that the buyer give notice of the exact amount of damages that will be incurred. See Custom Automated Machinery v. Penda Corp., 537 F.Supp. 77, 86 (N.D.Ill.1982) (buyer not required to tell seller amount of damages as long as seller on notice of reason for withholding payment). At least by June, 1987, the defendant knew of significant costs that would be incurred by correcting the defective dowels. The defendant has given no reason to justify letting several months go by while it used the defective goods for its own business purposes before warning M.K. Associates that it considered the contract breached.

The defendant also claims that the delay was reasonable in light of the purposes of the notice requirement, since ample time for settlement remained after the plaintiff began this litigation. Courts have held, however, that waiting until the seller sues for the purchase price to claim a breach of contract fails to satisfy the requirement of timely notice. In Re Morweld Steel Products Corp., supra at 951–53; Pace v. Sagebrush Sales Co., 114 Ariz. 271, 560 P.2d 789 (1977).

IV. Conclusion

The defendant accepted and used the dowels from M.K. Associates despite any defects it found. The defendant failed to notify the plaintiff of any claim of a breach of contract until the plaintiff began this litigation. This delay was unreasonable, and therefore the defendant is barred from deducting damages for breach of contract.

Accordingly, the Court hereby ORDERS that judgment in this action be entered for the plaintiff in the amount of Ten Thousand Five Hundred Eighteen Dollars and Forty Cents ($10,518.40), plus interest and costs as provided by law.

Notes

(1) **UCC 2–607(3): Rationale and History.** Comment 4 states that "the rule of requiring notification is designed to defeat commercial bad faith... ." The court in *M.K. Associates* gives three quite different policies said to underlie the requirement. Does the *text* of 2–607(3)(a) support the positions in the comment or the opinion? What purpose could be important enough to justify totally barring a buyer's claim without regard to the degree of injury, if any, to the interest of the seller? Comment 4 declares that the necessary content of a buyer's notice is minimal: "merely sufficient to let the seller know that the transaction is still troublesome and must be watched ..., [not] a clear statement of all the objections that will be relied upon by the buyer ..., and [not] a claim for damages or of any threatened litigation or other resort to a remedy." [2] Can the extreme consequence be reconciled with that minimal information requirement?

2. Would a notice be sufficient if it stated in entirety: "Your delivery was non-conforming"?

As indicated in the comment (Prior Uniform Statutory Provision), 2–607(3) has an antecedent in USA 49, which also barred buyers who failed to give sellers timely notice of breach. But USA 49 had no counterpart in the Sale of Goods Act. Why did the drafters of the United States statute add this element? See S. Williston, The Law Governing Sales of Goods at Common Law and Under the Uniform Sales Act § 488 (1909). See also John C. Reitz, Against Notice: A Proposal to Restrict the Notice of Claims Rule in UCC § 2–607(3)(a), 73 Cornell L. Rev. 534, 540–541 (1988).

Some civil law jurisdictions impose a requirement of buyers' prompt notice of default. Some nations provide very short periods within which actions must be brought (statutes of limitation or "prescription") or notices given to sellers. G. Treitel, Remedies for Breach of Contract: A Comparative Account 141 (1988). Another technique is used in the German Commercial Code, §§ 377–378. In the case of commercial sales, buyers are required to examine goods promptly after delivery and to give notice of any discernible lack of conformity discovered; if a buyer fails to give such notice, goods are deemed to be in conformity with the contract. Id.

Could UCC 2–607(3)(a), in its present form, be construed to provide relief only if a seller can show that buyer's delay has prejudiced the seller and limiting the bar to recovery to the extent necessary to overcome the prejudice shown? One commentator argues for an affirmative answer:

> Many courts have in effect interpreted the "reasonable time" standard of the rule to reflect a rough balance of the interests of the buyer in obtaining a remedy against the interests [of the seller] served by the notice rule. Because the legislatures have not provided any guidance on the policy goals underlying the notice rule, the courts are free to construe them as broadly or narrowly as they think proper. ...

> The prejudice least likely to justify barring all of the buyer's claim is loss of opportunity to cure [the nonconformity]. When the seller demonstrates such a loss, the court might use the mitigation principle to justify barring only the costs that the seller could have avoided.

> [For the prejudice resulting from seller's loss of the opportunity to gather evidence of the goods conformity, courts should employ an evidentiary presumption in seller's favor.] Traditionally, courts place the burden of production of evidence on the party with the best access to the relevant evidence. Courts should also be free to employ presumptions to prevent the careless or deliberate behavior of one litigant from prejudicing the opposing litigant's defense or prosecution.

John C. Reitz, supra, 588–589. Do you agree with this analysis?

The Permanent Editorial Board UCC Article 2 Study Group stated in its Preliminary Report (pp. 168–169):

> Literal interpretation of the notice requirement should be rejected. Either the text of § 2–607(3)(a) or the comments should be revised to require only that the notice inform the seller that problems have arisen or continue to exist with regard to the accepted goods. Also, the comments should clarify that the buyer has no obligation to notify for breaches of which it has no knowledge.

Do you agree?

(2) **Statute of Limitations.** The Code generally shortened the period of limitations for warranty actions. The usual contract period is about six years. Section 2–725(1) provides a four-year period.[3] The period begins to run when a buyer's cause of action accrues, defined for most transactions as the date of tender of delivery. UCC 2–725(2). Buyer's knowledge or lack of knowledge of the breach is not material.

When does the period of limitations begin to run on seller's breach of implied warranty of merchantability? Of fitness for particular purpose? Could the period expire before a buyer has learned of the breach?

Determining when the period of limitations begin to run on seller's breach of an express warranty is more difficult. If a seller has provided a repair/replace type of express warranty, when does a buyer's cause of action accrue? Among other issues to be considered is the meaning of the exception clause in the second sentence of 2–725(2). That issue is presented in the case that follows.

———

TITTLE v. STEEL CITY OLDSMOBILE GMC TRUCK, INC.

Supreme Court of Alabama, 1989.
544 So.2d 883.

SHORES, JUSTICE. The plaintiff, Rodney K. Tittle, appeals a summary judgment entered in favor of defendants, Steel City Oldsmobile GMC Truck, Inc. (hereinafter "Steel City"), and General Motors Corporation (hereinafter "General Motors").

Tittle purchased a 1981 Oldsmobile automobile from Steel City on October 9, 1981, and accepted delivery of it the same day. With the purchase of his automobile, General Motors provided Tittle with a document entitled "1981 Oldsmobile New Car Warranty." This writing provided that Steel City, as Tittle's Oldsmobile dealer, would repair and adjust defects in material or workmanship that occurred during the

_____

3. The section also permits parties to a contract of sale to reduce the period (with   a one-year minimum) but not to extend it.

first 12 months or first 12,000 miles in which the car was in use. The document provided, further, that the warranty period would begin on the date the car was first delivered or placed in service. In addition to this warranty, Tittle purchased from General Motors Acceptance Corporation (hereinafter "GMAC"), the company with whom he financed the purchase of the car, a supplemental warranty that extended coverage of the original warranty to 36 months or 36,000 miles.

After Tittle accepted the automobile, he discovered numerous defects in it and repeatedly asked Steel City and GMAC to cure the problems. When Steel City proved unable, after a number of attempts, to repair the vehicle, Tittle met with the zone representative for GMAC, Don Ackerman. Tittle alleges that Mr. Ackerman, as agent for GMAC, offered to extend the existing warranty on the vehicle for an additional 12 months or 12,000 miles if Tittle would allow Steel City another opportunity to repair the defects in the vehicle. Tittle agreed, but following several unsuccessful attempts to repair the vehicle, Tittle returned the car to Steel City.

Tittle sued on January 29, 1986, in Jefferson County Circuit Court, alleging that Steel City, GMAC, and General Motors had breached their respective express warranties as well as implied warranties of merchantability and fitness. Tittle founded his claims upon the federal Consumer Product Warranty Act, known commonly as the Magnuson–Moss Act, 15 U.S.C. § 2301 et seq., and upon Alabama's version of the Uniform Commercial Code (hereinafter "U.C.C."), § 7-1-101 et seq., Ala. Code (1975). In their answers to the plaintiff's complaint, both Steel City and General Motors specifically pleaded the statute of limitations as an affirmative defense.

Steel City and General Motors filed motions for summary judgment based upon the statute of limitations defense. During the hearing on the motions, the trial judge asked the parties to present the court with additional authorities supporting their respective positions. The court requested that the parties submit these authorities on or before April 1, 1988. General Motors responded to the trial court's request by providing it with four cases. Tittle, however, filed both a supplemental brief opposing the defendants' motion for summary judgment and an affidavit containing facts not alleged at the time the court heard the summary judgment motions.

On April 4, 1988, the trial court entered summary judgment in favor of Steel City and General Motors. The court found that Tittle's claims were barred by the statute of limitations at the time his complaint was filed. The trial court specifically noted that the plaintiff's case remained pending as to defendant GMAC, but made its order final with respect to Steel City and General Motors. See, Ala. R. Civ. P. 54(b). It is from this summary judgment that the plaintiff appeals. Apparently anticipating Tittle's argument on appeal, General Motors filed a motion to strike the plaintiff's affidavit from the record, on June 20, 1988.

The issue presented this Court for review is whether the trial court erred in entering summary judgment for these two defendants on the ground that Tittle's claim for breach of an express warranty was barred by the statute of limitations. In arguing this issue, the parties raise five questions this Court must address: first, what statute of limitations applies in cases brought under the Magnuson–Moss Act or the breach of warranty claims brought under Alabama's version of the U.C.C.?; second, does Ala. Code (1975), § 8–20–12, toll the statute of limitations for breach of warranty in consumer cases until the breach is discovered?; third, does the warranty issued by General Motors explicitly extend to the future performance of the vehicle?; fourth, is a repair and replacement warranty breached upon tender of the car or upon refusal or failure to repair an alleged defect?; and fifth, was Mr. Tittle's affidavit properly submitted to the trial court and included in the record on appeal, and, if so, did the affidavit present a genuine issue of material fact precluding the trial court's summary judgment?

I.

The Magnuson–Moss Act authorizes civil actions by consumers in state or federal court when suppliers, warrantors, or service contractors violate its provisions. 15 U.S.C. § 2310(d)(1). The Act, however, does not provide a statute of limitations for claims that arise under this legislation. Where a federal statute grants a cause of action, but does not include a statute of limitations governing the scope of that statute's application, federal common law requires that the court apply the state statute of limitations governing the state action most closely analogous to the federal claim. DelCostello v. International Brotherhood of Teamsters, 462 U.S. 151 (1983). The state law action most analogous to Tittle's Magnuson–Moss warranty claim is an action for breach of warranty in a contract for sale. Thus, the statute of limitations that appropriately applies to Tittle's state breach of warranty action is the same statute of limitations that appropriately applies to his federal Magnuson–Moss claim. Under Alabama's version of the U.C.C., the statute of limitations that applies to an action for breach of any contract for sale is found in § 7–2–725, Ala. Code (1975)....

III.

Under § 7–2–725(2), a cause of action for breach of warranty accrues when the seller tenders to the buyer the goods made the basis of the warranty. Once the cause of action accrues, the statute provides a four-year limitations period in which the buyer may file suit, subject to two exceptions. First, a cause of action will not accrue, in the case of consumer goods, on a claim for damages for injury to the person until the injury occurs.* And, second, where the seller of consumer goods gives the buyer an express warranty that extends to the future perfor-

---

* [The Alabama version of UCC 2–725 contains a non-uniform amendment that establishes the date of a personal injury as the date on which the period of limitations begins to run with respect to such claims. Eds.]

mance of the goods, a cause of action will not accrue until the buyer discovers or should have discovered the defect in the goods.

Tittle argues that the trial court erred in entering summary judgment in this case even if the limitations period contained in § 7–2–725 is the one that appropriately applies to his cause of action, because, he says, the warranties given him by Steel City and General Motors explicitly extended to the future performance of his automobile. Consequently, Tittle claims that his cause of action did not accrue until he discovered or should have discovered the breach of the Steel City and General Motors warranties.

While Tittle's argument has been addressed in other jurisdictions, the question of whether a so-called "repair and replacement" warranty extends to the future performance of goods, so as to fall within the limited exception set out in § 7–2–725(2), is a case of first impression for this Court. Therefore, a brief analysis of the case law interpreting this section is appropriate. Before we analyze case law, however, it is critical that we consider exactly what the warranties given Tittle purport to guarantee.

Page 2 of Tittle's warranty is entitled, "1981 Oldsmobile New Car Limited Warranty." This document provides that "Oldsmobile Division, General Motors Corporation, warrants each new 1981 car," that "this warranty covers any repairs and needed adjustments to correct defects in material or workmanship," and that "the warranty period begins on the date the car is first delivered or put in use." The warranty further provides, "your Oldsmobile dealer will make the repairs or adjustments, using new or remanufactured parts." The warranty stipulates on page 3 that "it is our intent to repair under the warranty, without charge, anything that goes wrong during the warranty period that is our fault." The warranty then distinguishes the term "defects," which "are covered [under the warranty] because we, the manufacturer, are responsible," from the term "damages," which are not covered by the warranty because the manufacturer has "no control over damage caused by such things as collision, misuse and lack of maintenance which occurs after the car is delivered." Page 4 of the warranty, under the separate heading "Emission Components Defect Warranty, further provides:

> Oldsmobile ... warrants to owners of 1981 Oldsmobile passenger cars that the car (1) was designed, built, and equipped so as to conform at the time of sale with applicable regulations of the Environmental Protection Agency, and (2) is free from defects in materials and workmanship which cause the car to fail to conform with applicable Federal Environmental Protection Agency regulations for a period of use of 50,000 miles or 5 years, whichever occurs first.

In 1976, in the leading case of Voth v. Chrysler Motor Corp., 218 Kan. 644, 545 P.2d 371 (1976), the Supreme Court of Kansas spoke to Tittle's argument. The warranty in Voth read in pertinent part:

> Chrysler Corporation warrants this vehicle to the first registered owner only against defects in material and workmanship in normal use as follows: (1) the entire vehicle (except tires) for 12 months or 12,000 miles of operation after the vehicle is first placed in service, whichever occurs first, from the date of sale or delivery thereto; and (2) the engine block, head and all internal engine parts, water pump, intake manifold, transmission case and all internal transmission parts, torque converter (if so equipped), drive shaft universal joints, rear axle and differential, and rear wheel bearings for 5 years or 50,000 miles of operation after the vehicle is first placed in service, whichever occurs first, from the date of such sale or delivery. Any part of this vehicle found defective under the conditions of this warranty will be repaired or replaced, at Chrysler's option, without charge at an authorized Imperial, Chrysler, Plymouth, or Dodge dealership.

Voth, 218 Kan. at 647, 545 P.2d at 374–75 (quoting Chrysler's warranty from the record).

This warranty is similar to the warranty issued by General Motors in this case. The Kansas Supreme Court held that the Chrysler warranty did not explicitly extend to the future performance of the vehicle. Moreover, the court found that the warranty did not guarantee performance without malfunction during the term of the warranty, but warranted only that the manufacturer would repair or replace defective parts in the event the car malfunctioned. Voth, 218 Kan. at 648, 545 P.2d at 375. The Kansas court explains its rationale through a quotation from Owens v. Patent Scaffolding Co., 77 Misc.2d 992, 354 N.Y.S.2d 778 (Sup.Ct.1974), rev'd on other grounds, 50 A.D.2d 866, 376 N.Y.S.2d 948 (1975), in which an argument similar to Tittle's was rejected:

> In this case the warranty does not go to performance of the equipment. To warrant to make needed repairs to leased equipment is not a warranty extending to its future performance. All that the supplier promises is that if the equipment needs repairs he will make them. It does not promise that in the future the goods will not fall into disrepair or malfunction, but only that if it does, the supplier will repair it. [Underlying] the warranty to make needed repairs is the assumption that the goods may fall into disrepair or otherwise malfunction. No warranty that the goods will not is to be inferred from the warranty to make needed repairs.

Voth, 218 Kan. at 651, 545 P.2d at 378 (quoting Owens, supra, 77 Misc.2d at 999, 354 N.Y.S.2d at 785).

In articulating the distinction between a warranty to repair and a warranty extending to future performance, the court in Owens said:

> A promise to repair is an express warranty that the promise to repair will be honored [citations omitted]. The seller's warranty ... that ... [goods] "will give satisfactory service at all times" is

distinguishable from the supplier's warranty to "make modifications, alterations or repairs to the component parts of the equipment" when necessary. [The words in the former warranty] go to the performance of the goods; that it "will give satisfactory service at all times." When the time came that the [goods] did not give satisfactory service, the warranty was breached. [The former warranty] explicitly extended to future performance of the goods, and its breach could only be discovered at the time of such performance.

77 Misc.2d at 998, 354 N.Y.S.2d at 784.

In Ontario Hydro v. Zallea Systems, Inc. 569 F.Supp. 1261 (D.Del. 1983), Chief Judge Latchum expressed the distinction between these two types of warranties in this manner:

[T]he key distinction between these two kinds of warranties is that a repair or replacement warranty merely provides a *remedy* if the product becomes defective, while a warranty for future performance *guarantees the performance* of the product itself for a stated period of time. In the former case, the buyer is relying upon the warranty merely as a method by which a defective product can be remedied which has no effect upon his ability to discover his breach. In the latter instance, the buyer is relying upon the warranty as a guarantee of future performance and therefore has no opportunity to discover the breach until the future performance has been tested. (Emphasis in original.)

Ontario Hydro, at 1266.

Other courts and authorities support the same conclusion: a promise to repair is not necessarily a promise of future performance.... See also, W. D. Hawkland, Uniform Commercial Code Service, § 2–725:02 at 480 (the hardship to the buyer that may sometimes be created by the four-year limitations period as measured from tender of delivery is thought to be outweighed by the commercial benefit derived from an established limitations period).

Tittle, in response to the foregoing cases, proffers two cases that he suggests represent substantial authority from other jurisdictions directly contrary to Voth and similar cases. In the first case, Standard Alliance Industries, Inc. v. Black Clawsen Co., 587 F.2d 813 (6th Cir.1978), cert. denied, 441 U.S. 923 (1979) the seller of a forging machine, in addition to warranting specific performance levels for the operation of the machine, warranted that "the equipment manufactured by it would be free from defects in workmanship and material" for a period of one year. 587 F.2d at 816–17 (emphasis added). When the manufacturer failed, after numerous attempts, to repair the defective machinery, the buyer brought an action against the seller alleging breach of his express warranty. The Standard Alliance court held that the warranty at issue in the case extended to the future performance of the machine for a period of one year and that the buyer's cause of action accrued when the purchaser discovered or should have discovered that the machine was defective. Id., at 817.

In the second case, R. W. Murray Co. v. Shatterproof Glass Corp., 697 F.2d 818 (8th Cir.1983), the manufacturer's warranty provided:

Vision and spandrel glass shall be guaranteed by the glass manufacturer for a period of ten (10) years from the date of acceptance of the project to furnish and replace any unit which develops material destruction of vision between the interglass surfaces. This guarantee is for material and labor costs for replacing.

697 F.2d at 821–22 n. 2.

Shatterproof Glass Corporation warrants its insulating glass units for a period of twenty (20) years from the date of manufacture against defects in material or workmanship that result in moisture accumulation, film formation or dust collection between the interior surfaces, resulting from failure of the hermetic seal. Purchaser's exclusive remedy and Shatterproof's 'total' liability under this warranty shall be limited to the replacement of any lite failing to meet the terms of this warranty. Such replacement will be made F.O.B. Detroit to the shipping point nearest the installation.

697 F.2d 822 n. 3. The court construed these warranties as extending to the future performance of the goods for periods of 10 years and 20 years, respectively, and held that the purchaser's cause of action for breach of warranty accrued when the breach was, or should have been, discovered.

Despite the language used in the Shatterproof Glass warranties, guaranteeing for a specified period of time that a product is "free" from defects, as in Standard Alliance, seems to us altogether different from guaranteeing that product "against" defects, as in Voth. In the first instance, the manufacturer guarantees that the product possesses no defect whatsoever, while in the second instance the manufacturer guarantees that where defects emerge, he will remedy them, generally by repairing or replacing the defective part. While Shatterproof Glass used the term "against" in its warranty, we reconcile the holding in that case with Voth and Standard Alliance by noting the explicit nature of the remaining language in the warranty. Had the Shatterproof Glass court held that the warranties fell outside the U.C.C. § 2–725(2) "extends to future performance" exception, then despite the 10– and 20–year periods set out in the warranties, § 2–725(1) would have terminated the plaintiff's right of action four years after tender of the goods. (Section 2–725(1) provides in pertinent part, "By the original agreement the parties may reduce the period of limitation to not less than one year but may not extend it [beyond four years from the date of tender].")

In the present case, the warranty under which Tittle pursued his claim is even more free of ambiguity than that found in Voth and the other cases. The activating language of that warranty provides: "This warranty covers any repairs and needed adjustments to correct defects in material or workmanship." This language clearly does not guarantee that the car will perform free of defects for the term of the agreement. In fact, as the court in Voth recognized, the language of the guarantee anticipates that defects will occur. We, therefore, hold that the warranty provided Tittle upon the purchase of his car did not extend to the car's future performance.

We recognize that, under the analysis adopted by this Court, one might reasonably suggest that the language of the "Emission Components Defect Warranty" places it within our definition of a warranty that extends to future performance, at least within the limited scope of that separate provision. The emissions warranty provides: "Oldsmobile ... warrants ... that the car ... is free from defects in material and workmanship which cause the car to fail to conform with applicable Federal Environmental Protection Agency regulations for a period of use of 50,000 miles or 5 years, whichever comes first." We note, however, that although he enumerates an exhaustive list of defects, Tittle never alleged in his complaint or elsewhere that his vehicle failed to conform to EPA emissions standards. Hence, this provision is not applicable to the case before us.

IV.

Tittle next contends that even if the General Motors and Steel City warranties do not extend to the future performance of the vehicle, the cause of action does not accrue until there is a refusal or failure to repair. This contention, however, directly contradicts the plain meaning of the language in § 7-2-725, which states that a cause of action for breach of any contract for sale accrues when the breach occurs and that the breach occurs upon tender of delivery, regardless of the buyer's knowledge of the breach, unless the warranty explicitly extends to future performance. We have earlier determined that Tittle's warranty does not extend to the future performance of his car. The trial court, therefore, correctly determined that Tittle's cause of action, by statute and by the express terms of his warranty, accrued at the time Steel City delivered the vehicle to him.

V.

Finally, Tittle argues that even if we affirm the lower court's rulings regarding interpretation of § 7-2-725, the trial court still erred in granting summary judgment because, he says, a material issue of fact exists as to whether the defendants are estopped to assert the statute of limitations based upon their agent's representations....

... General Motors and Steel City argue that they should not be estopped from raising the statute of limitations defense because, they say, no evidence exists that the misrepresentations made by Mr. Ackerman were intentional or fraudulent, or that Tittle, relying on these representations, was induced not to file a lawsuit. ...

Tittle states in his affidavit that in 1984 a General Motors representative, Mr. Don Ackerman, represented that Steel City would repair the defects in his vehicle; that Mr. Ackerman indicated that if Tittle would allow Steel City another opportunity to repair the car, then Ackerman would extend the warranty 12 months or 12,000 miles; and that based on Mr. Ackerman's representations, he continued to attempt to have the car repaired rather than returning the car to the appellees. We find that a jury might conceivably construe Mr. Ackerman's statements as a promise to make repairs in return for a promise not to sue.

In reviewing a disposition of a motion for summary judgment, we use the same standard as that of the trial court in determining whether the evidence before the court made out a genuine issue of material fact. ... We do not here decide whether these defendants are estopped as a matter of law from asserting the statute of limitations as a defense; rather, we hold that a fact issue exists as to whether Ackerman acted as an agent for General Motors and Steel City and made a statement that Tittle reasonably relied on in delaying the filing of this lawsuit.

We, therefore, reverse the summary judgment in favor of General Motors and Steel City.

Reversed and remanded.

Notes

(1) **Magnuson–Moss Warranty Act.** The buyer in *Tittle* based his claim in part on the Magnuson–Moss Warranty Act. The court found nothing in that act that affected the statute of limitations issue. We will take up the Magnuson–Moss Act in the next section.

(2) **Construction of UCC 2–725(2).** The second sentence of UCC 2–725(2) poses obvious difficulties for interpretation. In a sense, all warranties of quality extend to performance of goods after tender of delivery, but the second sentence cannot be read properly as an exception that swallows the rule that the period of limitations ordinarily runs from the date of tender of delivery.

Consider the case in which the manufacturer promises to repair any defect in a car's drivetrain that occurs within two years or 24,000 miles, whichever occurs first. ... [M]any courts would interpret this as a warranty that extends to future performance and would therefore grant four years from the time of the occurrence of the defect. On the other hand, one might read the agreement to mean simply that the seller will repair any defect that comes to light within that period irrespective of its cause, but that the seller's liability ends at the earlier [of two years or] 24,000 miles and does not extend for four years beyond that time. The seller (and buyer if the truth be known) may construe such agreement not as a warranty at all but as an agreement to repair unrelated to any defect in the goods (as, for example, a wheel that breaks when it hits a pothole).

J. White & R. Summers, Uniform Commercial Code 479 (3d ed. 1988). Do you agree with the authors' analysis?

MOORMAN MANUFACTURING CO. v. NATIONAL TANK CO., 91 Ill.2d 69, 61 Ill.Dec. 746, 435 N.E.2d 443 (1982). In 1966 Moorman purchased a large grain-storage tank from National. The contract of sale contained the following:

Tank designed to withstand 60 lbs. per bushel grain and 100 m.p.h. winds.

In 1976 a crack developed in the tank; Moorman brought suit against National in 1977. One count of the complaint, based on the quoted language, alleged breach of express warranty. National contended that the claim was barred by the statute of limitations. The trial court, relying on the exception in 2–725(2), held that Moorman's claim was not time-barred. The Illinois Supreme Court reversed.

> The final issue is whether count IV, based upon breach of express warranty, was barred by the statute of limitations. ...

> Several appellate court decisions in this State have held that merely because it is reasonable to expect that a warranty of merchantability extends for the life of a product does not mean that such a warranty "explicitly extends to future performance." ...

> In Binkley Co. v. Teledyne Mid–America Corp. (E.D.Mo.1971), 333 F.Supp. 1183, aff'd (8th Cir. 1972), 460 F.2d 276, the seller of a welding machine expressly warranted that a welder would weld at a rate of 1,000 feet per 50–minute hour, which it never did. The court defined "explicit" under 2–725(2) as " ' "[n]ot implied merely, or conveyed by implication; distinctly stated; plain in language; clear; not ambiguous; express; unequivocal." ' " (333 F.Supp. 1183, 1186.) Although the warranty expressly stated that the welder would weld at 1,000 feet per hour, the court found that the statute had lapsed because there was no reference to future time in the warranty and, thus, no explicit warranty of future performance. In response to the buyer's argument that he was unable to test the product until after delivery the court pointed to the clear language of section 2–725(2) which provides that the breach occurs at the time of delivery "regardless of the aggrieved party's lack of knowledge."

> We agree with the decision in that case as well as the appellate decisions in this State adhering to the clear language of the statute.

> [Justice Simon concurred specially.]

MOORE v. PUGET SOUND PLYWOOD, INC., 214 Neb. 14, 332 N.W.2d 212 (1983). In 1970 the Moores purchased plywood for siding on their house. Problems in the siding developed in 1977; the Moores sued Plywood in 1981. The Nebraska Supreme Court held that the claim was not time-barred.

... England v. Leithoff, 212 Neb. 462, 323 N.W.2d 98 (1982), ... foreshadows the outcome of this case. We held therein that an oral representation concerning the origin of goods, made in the course of a sale, constitutes an express warranty under § 2–313(1)(b), which provides, among other things, that any description of goods which becomes a part of the basis of the bargain creates an express warranty that the goods shall conform to the description. According to the parties the description of the goods as "siding" carried with it the representation that it would last the lifetime of the house. Therefore, the requisite elements of § 2–313(1)(b) are present; that is, the description of the goods became a part of the bargain and created in the minds of the parties the expectation that the siding would last the lifetime of the house. Section 2–725(2) provides in part: ... The instant breach did not occur upon tender of delivery since, in light of the expectations of the parties, the warranty herein necessarily extended explicitly to future performance.

Note

Limitation Period for Implied Warranties. On what date does the period of limitations begin to run on a buyer's potential claim that the goods are unmerchantable? On a potential claim that the goods are not fit for the buyer's particular purpose? Could the second sentence UCC 2–725(2) be construed to apply to any implied warranty claims?

(B) INTERNATIONAL SALES LAW

(1) **Notice of Breach.** Assume that *M.K. Associates* had been an international sales transaction governed by CISG. Would the result have been the same or different? See CISG 39(1). The answer seems reasonably clear. Like the Code, CISG imposes a notice requirement with comparable elements of "reasonable time" and buyer's discovery. Instead of "barred from any remedy" CISG uses "loses the right to rely on a lack of conformity." Is there a different meaning?

A perceptive reader of CISG 39(1), familiar with the Code, would observe that the CISG demands more in the content of a buyer's notice than "of breach." How much factual detail must buyers include to "specify ... the nature of the lack of conformity"? If multiple non-conformities are discovered, must each be detailed? When a second non-conformity surfaces after a notice has been given, must another notice be sent?

Having worked through the CISG provision and made comparison to the Code, one might stop the legal analysis. To do so would be to commit a grave error. See CISG 44. What could explain drafting in this style? [4]

The danger continues beyond noticing that CISG 44 modifies CISG 39(1). On the face of CISG 44, a reader might conclude that relief from loss of the right to rely on a lack of conformity is available only if a buyer has not yet paid the full price. "[T]he buyer may reduce the price in accordance with article 50...." When one turns to CISG 50, however, one learns that a buyer can "reduce" a price "whether or not the price has already been paid." In short, a buyer who is excused under CISG 44 has not only the right to set off damages against the unpaid price, but also has an affirmative right to recover some or all of the price paid.

Fortunately these "traps" are not typical of the drafting of the CISG. However, they should alert those who use the Convention to the need for great care in its application.

The CISG imposes an outside limit on the time for a buyer's notice to the seller specifying the nature of the lack of non-conformity. Buyers must give notice within two years from the date the goods were "actually handed over" to them, whether or not the buyers discovered or ought to have discovered the non-conformities ("in any event"). CISG 39(2). An exception exists if this time limit is "inconsistent with a contractual period of guarantee." Note that the CISG 44 excuse provision is not available against the CISG 39(2) time bar.

The Code has no provision comparable to CISG 39(2).

FINAL AWARD IN CASE NO. 5713 of 1989

International Chamber of Commerce
15 Y.B. Comm. Arb. 70 (1990)

Parties: Claimant/counterdefendant: Seller
                     Defendant/counterclaimant: Buyer

Place of
   arbitration: Paris, France
Published in: Unpublished
Subject matters: — applicable law
                   — Art. 13(3) and (5) ICC Rules

---

4. In the last days of the diplomatic conference that produced the Convention, there was a major inter-regional disagreement regarding the notice requirement in CISG 39. Proposals by developing countries to relax the requirement had not been adopted. The proponents of modifying CISG 39 were sufficiently dissatisfied that the necessary two-thirds vote in favor of the Convention was in jeopardy. A compromise solution was proposed and became CISG 44. It was made a separate article so that the added provision would apply also to the notice requirements of CISG 43(1). J. Honnold, Uniform Law for International Sales § 261 (2d ed. 1991).

— Hague Convention of 1955 on the Law
  Applicable to the International Sales
  of Goods
— Vienna Sales Convention of 1980
— International trade usages
— set-off
— Art. 70 French New Code of Civil Proce-
  dure

Facts

In 1979, the parties concluded three contracts for the sale of a
product according to certain contract specifications. The buyer paid
90% of the price payable under each of the contracts upon presentation
of the shipping documents, as contractually agreed.

The product delivered pursuant to the first and third contracts met
the contract specifications. The conformity of the second consignment
was disputed prior to its shipment. When the product was again
inspected upon arrival, it was found that it did not meet the contract
specifications. The product was eventually sold by the buyer to third
parties at considerable loss, after having undergone a certain treatment
to make it more saleable.

The seller initiated arbitration proceedings to recover the 10%
balance remaining due under the contracts. The buyer filed a counterclaim alleging that the seller's claim should be set off against the
amounts which the buyer estimates to be payable to the buyer by the
seller, i.e., the direct losses, financing costs, lost profits and interest.

Excerpt

I. Applicable Law

The contract contains no provisions regarding the substantive law.
Accordingly that law has to be determined by the Arbitrators in
accordance with Art. 13(3) of the ICC rules.[1] Under that article, the
Arbitrators will "apply the law designated as the proper law by the rule
of conflicts which they deem appropriate".

The contract is between a Seller and a Buyer [of different nationali-
ties] for delivery [in a third country]. The sale was f.o.b. so that the
transfer of risks to the Buyer took place in [the country of the Seller].
[The country of the Seller] accordingly appears as being the jurisdiction
to which the sale is most closely related.

---

1. Art. 13 of the ICC Rules of 1975 (Not
amended by the 1988 amendments) reads
in relevant part:

"3. The parties shall be free to determine the law to be applied by the arbitrator to the merits of the dispute. In
the absence of any indication by the parties as to the applicable law, the arbitrator shall apply the law designated as the
proper law by the rule of conflict which
he deems appropriate....

5. In all cases the arbitrator shall take
account of the provisions of the contract
and the relevant trade usages."

The Hague Convention on the law applicable to international sales of goods dated 15 June 1955 (Art. 3) regarding sales contracts, refers as governing law to the law of the Seller's current residence.... [2] [The country of the Buyer] has adhered to the Hague Convention, not [the country of the Seller]. However, the general trend in conflicts of law is to apply the domestic law of the current residence of the debtor of the essential undertaking arising under the contract. That debtor in a sales contract is the Seller. Based on those combined findings, [the law of the country of the Seller] appears to be the proper law governing the Contract between the Seller and the Buyer.

As regards the applicable rules of [the law of the country of the Seller], the Arbitrators have relied on the Parties' respective statements on the subject and on the information obtained by the Arbitrators from an independent consultant.... The Arbitrators, in accordance with the last paragraph of Art. 13 of the ICC rules, will also take into account the "relevant trade usages".

II. Admissibility of the Counterclaim

  (a) Under [the law of the country of the Seller]...

  (b) Under the international trade usages prevailing in the international sale of goods

The Tribunal finds that there is no better source to determine the prevailing trade usages than the terms of the United Nations Convention on the International Sale of Goods of 11 April 1980, usually called "the Vienna Convention". This is so even though neither [the country of the Buyer] nor [the country of the Seller] are parties to that Convention. If they were, the Convention might be applicable to this case as a matter of law and not only as reflecting the trade usage.

The Vienna Convention, which has been given effect to in 17 countries, may be fairly taken to reflect the generally recognized usages regarding the matter of the non-conformity of goods in international sales. Art. 38(1) of the Convention puts the onus on the Buyer to "examine the goods or cause them to be examined promptly". The Buyer should then notify the Seller of the non-conformity of the goods within a reasonable period as of the moment he noticed or should have noticed the defect; otherwise he forfeits his right to raise a claim based on the said non-conformity. Art. 39(1) specifies in this respect that:

> In any event the buyer shall lose the right to rely on a lack of conformity of the goods if he has not given notice thereof to the seller within a period of two years from the date on which the goods were handed over, unless the lack of conformity constituted a breach of a guarantee covering a longer period.

---

2. Art. 3 of the Hague Convention on the Law Applicable to the International Sales of Goods reads in pertinent part: "In default of a law declared applicable by the parties under the conditions provided in the preceding article, a sale shall be governed by the domestic law of the country in which the vendor has his habitual residence at the time when he received the order...."

In the circumstances, the Buyer had the shipment examined within a reasonable time-span since [an expert] was requested to inspect the shipment even before the goods had arrived. The Buyer should also be deemed to have given notice of the defects within a reasonable period, that is eight days after the expert's report had been published.

Tribunal finds that, in the circumstances of the case, the Buyer has complied with the above-mentioned requirements of the Vienna Convention. These requirements are considerably more flexible than those provided under [the law of the country of the Seller]. This law, by imposing extremely short and specific time requirements in respect of the giving of the notices of defects by the Buyer to the Seller appears to be an exception on this point to the generally accepted trade usages.

In any case, the Seller should be regarded as having forfeited its right to invoke any non-compliance with the requirements of Arts. 38 and 39 of the Vienna Convention since Art. 40 states that the Seller cannot rely on Arts. 38 and 39, "if the lack of conformity relates to facts of which he knew, or of which he could not have been unaware, and which he did not disclose". Indeed, this appears to be the case, since it clearly transpires from the file and the evidence that the Seller knew and could not be unaware [of the non-conformity of the consignment to] contract specifications. . . .

Note

Period of Limitations. CISG contains no period of limitations. That is found in an entirely separate convention, the United Nations Convention on the Limitation Period of the International Sale of Goods. A sufficient number of nations had ratified this Convention for it to take effect in 1988. As of January 1992, the Convention was pending ratification by the Senate of the United States. Like UCC 2–725, the Convention sets a four-year limitation period. A convention is required to replace the greatly diverse limitation ("prescription") periods and subordinate rules, such as rules on "tolling," among various nations' domestic laws.

Article 11 of the Convention provides:

If the seller has given an express undertaking relating to the goods which is stated to have effect for a certain period of time, whether expressed in terms of a specific period of time or otherwise, the limitation period in respect of any claim arising from the undertaking shall commence on the date on which the buyer notifies the seller of the fact on which the claim is based, but not later than on the date of the expiration of the period of the undertaking.

SECTION 6. CONSUMER PROTECTION LAWS

Introduction. The Sales Article of the Uniform Commercial Code and its predecessor, the Uniform Sales Act, provided little, if any, special protection for consumers buying goods for ordinary personal, family or household purposes.[1] Consumer protection law has developed nonetheless, and the sales statutes have been substantially involved in those developments. One concern has been for the health of consumers. A second concern has focused on consumers' economic interest, particularly the concern that the value of goods purchased be commensurate with the price paid.

International Sales Law. The Convention on International Sales of Goods is explicitly not concerned with sales of ordinary consumer goods. CISG 2(a). Further, the Convention does not apply to a seller's liability for death or personal injury caused by the goods to any person. CISG 5.

(A) CONSUMER HEALTH: PRODUCT LIABILITY

Owners of products sometimes suffer traumatic injuries when they use or consume the goods they have bought. If a product poses a higher than expected risk of injuring someone, we are likely to say that that product has a "defect." For some time, injured persons have had a possible cause of action in negligence, but to prevail in such an action a plaintiff must prove, inter alia, that the defendant (or someone for whom the defendant is vicariously responsible) acted with a lack of due care.

Advocates of consumer protection, seeking a legal theory that did not require proof of defendants' fault, turned to warranty law. The prototypical injured plaintiff was a buyer who had consumed spoiled or adulterated food. In cases decided in the late 19th century and early 20th century, courts implied warranties in ordinary retail sales,[2] even

---

1. By contrast, the Code article on secured transactions provides particularly for credit transactions in consumer goods. See, e.g., 9–302(1)(d); 9–505; 9–507(1).

2. The British Sale of Goods Act and its United States counterpart, the Uniform Sales Act, posed a problem for buyers: the basic warranty of quality, merchantability, was not "implied" in ordinary retail sales of food or other goods. Caselaw codified by these statutes had found the warranty of merchantability arising in situations where sellers had contracted to supply goods that would fit contract descriptions; Mackensie Chalmers "restated" the cases by limiting merchantability to sales "by description." Protection had to be found under the rubric of fitness for particular purpose.

The change is well illustrated by developments in Massachusetts. Farrell v. Manhattan Market Co, 198 Mass. 271, 84 N.E. 481 (1908) (buyer suffered ptomaine poisoning from a fowl: buyer denied relief); Ward v. Great Atlantic & Pacific Tea Co., 231 Mass. 90, 120 N.E. 225 (1918) (buyer broke a tooth on a stone in a can of baked beans: buyer recovered); Flynn v. Bedell Co., 242 Mass. 450, 136 N.E. 252 (1922) (buyer contracted skin disease from dyed fur collar of coat: verdict for buyer upheld).

Consumers injured by unwholesome food or beverages served by a restaurant or hotel faced an additional legal hazard. At common law, some courts considered such transactions a service ("uttering") rather

in transactional settings where sellers of canned or packaged goods did not know, and had no practical way of finding out the true quality of the goods.[3] Once a warranty was breached, courts had no difficulty in broadening the classes of injury compensable as consequential damages from commercial losses, as in *Hadley v. Baxendale,* to personal injuries and property damage.

The move toward greater consumer protection did not end with establishment of retailers' warranty liability. Injured consumers needed, and eventually were allowed to obtain warranty relief directly from remote manufacturers of certain defective consumer goods that caused personal injuries. The list of such goods was confined to food, beverages, and other items of "intimate bodily use." In 1960, the New Jersey Supreme Court held that the owner of an automobile, injured when the steering failed, should have a warranty claim against the manufacturer. Henningsen v. Bloomfield Motors, Inc., 32 N.J. 358, 161 A.2d 69 (1960).

Two years later, the California Supreme Court created a new tort to protect the consumer-owner of a lathe injured by a piece of wood ejected from the equipment. Greenman v. Yuba Power Products, Inc. 59 Cal.2d 57, 27 Cal.Rptr. 697, 377 P.2d 897 (1963).[4] During this period, the American Law Institute was preparing a second edition of the Restatement of Torts. The new tort was inserted into the revision as § 402A, Special Liability of Seller of Product for Physical Harm to User or Consumer. More commonly, the tort is known as strict tort liability. As "restated," it is formulated as follows:

> (1) One who sells any product in a defective condition unreasonably dangerous to the user or consumer or to his property is subject to liability for physical harm thereby caused to the ultimate user or consumer, or to his property, if
>
> > (a) the seller is engaged in the business of selling such a product, and

than a sale and, therefore, not transactions in which a warranty of quality applied. Compare Friend v. Childs Dining Hall Co., 231 Mass. 65, 120 N.E. 407 (1918), with Nisky v. Childs Co., 103 N.J.L. 464, 135 A. 805 (1927). The Code declares that such transactions are sales under Article 2. UCC 2–314(1).

3. Compare Julian v. Laubenberger, 16 Misc. 646, 38 N.Y.S. 1052 (1896) (sale of can of salmon: since both parties knew that seller had not prepared the food, had not inspected it, and was entirely ignorant of the contents of the can, it would be unreasonable to say that the buyer had relied upon the superior knowledge of the seller), with Ward v. Great Atlantic & Pacific Tea Co., 231 Mass. 90, 120 N.E. 225

(1918) (sale of can of baked beans and pork: even though seller is not the manufacturer, seller is in a better position to ascertain the reliability of the manufacturer; the principle of retailers' liability may work apparent hardship in some instances, but that is no reason to change it).

4. *Greenman* had been tried on a warranty theory. The California Supreme Court found that it could not sustain the trial court judgment because the plaintiff had not given seller timely notice of the breach of warranty. See UCC 2–607(3)(a) similar provision existed in the Sales Act. Rather than reverse on this "intricacy" of sales law, the California court held that the judgment could be affirmed on the new tort theory.

(b) it is expected to and does reach the user or consumer without substantial change in the condition in which it is sold.

(2) The rule stated in Subsection (1) applies although

(a) the seller has exercised all possible care in the preparation and sale of his product, and

(b) the user or consumer has not bought the product from or entered into any contractual relation with the seller.

Reception of § 402A as new common law was rapid and widespread. Only a small number of state supreme courts have rejected strict tort liability.[5]

Judicial acknowledgment of the new tort did not displace consumers' warranty claims arising out of the same facts. What has emerged, therefore, is that consumer buyers in most states have substantially overlapping theories of possible recovery for personal injuries.[6]

For a number of reasons, consumers and their lawyers prefer to rely primarily upon strict tort liability. Suits can be brought directly against the manufacturers of the goods. The essential elements of the tort were derived entirely from earlier warranty cases, with the omission, of course, of the notice requirement of warranty law.[7] Proof of a defendant's liability on a strict tort theory is therefore less difficult than the proof under a warranty theory. The strict tort theory is also more protective of consumers with regard to contractual disclaimers or clauses limiting damages. Comment *m* to § 402A states that the "consumer's" cause of action "is not affected by any disclaimer or other agreement." [8]   A major difference in the two theories lies in the

---

5. E.g., Cline v. Prowler Industries of Md., Inc., 418 A.2d 968 (Del.1980); Swartz v. General Motors Corp., 375 Mass. 628, 378 N.E.2d 61 (1978); Prentis v. Yale Manufacturing Co., 421 Mich. 670, 365 N.W.2d 176 (1984). In New York, the Court of Appeals initially rejected the new tort. Mendel v. Pittsburgh Plate Glass Co., 25 N.Y.2d 888, 304 N.Y.S.2d 4, 251 N.E.2d 143 (1969). However, the New York court quickly joined the majority of states. Codling v. Paglia, 32 N.Y.2d 330, 345 N.Y.S.2d 461, 298 N.E.2d 622 (1973).

6. Section 402A is not limited to consumer-buyer plaintiffs, but rather extends to the "ultimate user or consumer" whether or not one who bought the product. A caveat attached to § 402A notes that the Institute expresses no opinion on whether the section should apply to persons other than users or consumers, typically casual bystanders. Contrast the Restatement's scope of protected persons with the scope of such persons under a warranty theory. The Code originally limited recovery for personal injuries to members of the family or household or house guests of the buyer.

UCC 2–318 (now Alternative A). In 1966, drafters of the Code offered state legislatures two broader alternatives. We will consider § 2–318 more fully later in this chapter, in the section on privity, infra.

7. Some states relax the notice requirement in cases of buyers claiming damages for personal injuries under a breach of warranty theory. In Illinois, for example, the notice requirement can be satisfied in some cases by pleadings in the litigation with sellers. E.g., Goldstein v. G.D. Searle & Co., 62 Ill.App.3d 344, 19 Ill.Dec. 208, 378 N.E.2d 1083 (1978); but see Wagmeister v. A.H. Robins Co., 64 Ill.App.3d 964, 24 Ill.Dec. 729, 382 N.E.2d 23 (1978); Allen v. G.D. Searle & Co., 708 F.Supp. 1142 (D.Or. 1989). Retail buyers are aided if dispute over the notice requirement is treated as an issue of fact to be decided by juries. E.g., Mullan v. Quickie Aircraft Corp., 797 F.2d 845 (10th Cir. 1986).

8. The Code permits use of warranty disclaimers (UCC 2–316) and of damage limitation clauses (UCC 2–719), with the exception that clauses limiting or exclud-

measure of recovery: plaintiffs proceeding in a tort theory ordinarily are permitted to recover damages for pain and suffering and, in extraordinary cases, may be permitted to recover punitive damages.

Moreover, a consumer who suffers an injury some considerable time after the good was sold may be unable to proceed successfully on a warranty theory while the strict tort theory is still available. The period of the tort statute of limitations does not commence until the injury, while the warranty statute of limitations begins to run at the time of delivery of the goods. UCC 2–725(1). If an injury occurs some years after delivery, the tort statute may be more favorable to plaintiffs.[9]

Personal injury claims, whether based on strict tort or warranty theory, give rise to an array of complex and difficult legal questions that we cannot explore in these materials. Private litigation of this type has become interrelated with federal and state regulatory laws on consumer product safety. In the remainder of this section, we will focus on issues of economic loss rather than personal injuries.

(B) MAGNUSON–MOSS WARRANTY ACT

The law of strict tort liability, together with warranty law, provided considerable relief for consumers who suffer personal injuries or property damage, but did little or nothing for consumers who bought and paid for goods that turned out to be disappointing in economic value. Many consumer goods were marketed under contracts that gave little or no effective relief to consumer buyers. This led to the 1975 enactment of a federal statute, the Magnuson–Moss Warranty Act (MMWA). The federal statute does not displace state warranty law. The federal act is a partial overlay on state law. Whenever the MMWA applies to a transaction, determination of a seller's responsibility will be governed basically by the Code warranty provisions, with which we are now familiar, but modified by the provisions of the federal statute. Both the Code and the MMWA must be considered in every transaction to which the MMWA applies.

The MMWA appears in Title 15, Chapter 50 of the U.S. Code, §§ 2301–2312. For purposes of this course, however, we will use the Act's section numbers, MMWA 101–112. The MMWA is interpreted and supplemented by Federal Trade Commission Regulations. For an

ing recovery for personal injuries are prima facie unconscionable (UCC 2–719(3)).

9. The claim of the plaintiff in *Mendel,* the early New York case that declined to recognize strict tort liability (note 5 *supra*), was held to be time barred under the four-year statute of limitations applicable to sales of goods. See UCC 2–725. New York's tort statute of limitations, however, would not have barred the claim.

The warranty statute of limitations may be more favorable to a plaintiff who suffers injury shortly after goods have been delivered but fails to institute legal proceedings within the one- or two-year limitation period generally provided for tort claims. Even though the tort claim is time-barred, the warranty period may not have elapsed as of the filing of suit.

overall review of MMWA, see C. Reitz, Consumer Product Warranties Under Federal and State Laws (2d ed. 1987).[10]

(1) Scope. The MMWA does *not* apply to all consumer purchases of consumer goods. While the Act has broad definitions of "consumer" (MMWA 101(3)) and "consumer product" (MMWA 101(1)), the federal statute applies only to transactions in which the seller has made a "written warranty" (MMWA 101(6) and FTC Reg. § 700.3) or "service contract" (MMWA 101(8)). These terms, particularly "written warranty," are of the utmost importance to understanding the effective scope of the MMWA.

Even without a close reading of the statute and regulations, note that the MMWA does not apply if the *only* warranty obligation of a seller is an implied warranty. Implied warranties cannot be a "written warranty" or "service contract." To bring a transaction within the Act, a seller must make an express warranty or undertake an express obligation with respect to the goods. However, again it is quite evident that not all express warranties would meet the definition of "written warranty." Express *oral* warranties are excluded regardless of the content of the seller's undertaking. The threshold question in all MMWA cases is whether an express warranty, in writing, meets the *content* elements of the Act's definitions.[11]

Problem 1. Eckstein purchased a new car from Maumee Valley Autos, Inc. The purchase order form, signed by the dealer and the buyer, declared that the dealer, at its option, would repair or replace any part that proved defective in materials or workmanship within twelve months from the date of purchase or 12,000 miles of use, whichever occurred first.

(a) If Eckstein's car were to prove defective, would he have the benefit of protection under the MMWA? See MMWA 101(6). The UCC?

(b) If Eckstein seeks only to enforce the dealer's repair/replace undertaking, does the MMWA provide him with more warranty protection than would be available under the Code?

Problem 2. Seller sold a used car to Buyer. Seller's salesman told Buyer that the car had gone only 60,000 miles, that the motor had been carefully checked out, and that the piston rings and brake linings had just been replaced. The only writing was a bill of sale transferring title to Buyer. The car proved to be in very bad shape, and the brakes failed, causing serious injury to Buyer and to the car.

---

10. Some parts of the MMWA have no counterparts in the Commercial Code. Federal law requires sellers to make warranty information available to potential buyers in advance of sale and in a way prescribed by law. (MMWA 102 and FTC Regs. 701 and 702). See C. Reitz, chapters 3 and 4.

11. "Certain representations, such as energy efficiency ratings for electrical appliances, care labeling of wearing apparel, and other product information disclosures may be express warranties under the Uniform Commercial Code. However, these disclosures alone are not written warranties under this Act." FTC Reg. § 700.3.

(a) Has Buyer any rights under the MMWA? See MMWA 101(6), 102(b)(2).

(b) Has the Buyer any rights? See MMWA 111(b)(1).

Problem 3. Seller sold and installed a furnace in Buyer's home. The only writing was an agreement of sale, signed by Seller and Buyer, which read:

> Seller agrees to deliver to Buyer and install one Cozy Furnace, for a total of $2,500. It is agreed that the Seller shall not be responsible to Buyer for any special or consequential damages resulting from the operation or malfunction of the furnace.

Three months after installation, the furnace exploded and soot was blown throughout the house, with the result that the house had to be redecorated at a cost of $3,000.

Has Buyer any rights under the MMWA or under the Code?

(2) "Truth in Warranting." The perceptive reader may now be asking: why did Congress pass the MMWA? Many (if not most) express warranties are excluded from the Act's coverage, seller's are permitted under the Act to sell without any warranty at all, and the Act adds nothing to the substance of seller's voluntary undertakings in a "written warranty" or "service contract." What consumer benefits *are* provided by this Act?

A partial answer is that Congress focused on certain transaction types in which it found need for reform. These were transactions in consumer durable goods, notably new automobiles, in which consumers received less warranty protection than they had been led to expect.

The MMWA objective was to create a marketplace in which there was "truth in warranting." In part, this explains the Act's requirement that every "written warranty" must be designated "clearly and conspicuously" as either a "limited" warranty or a "full" warranty (MMWA 103(a)). Moreover, if a warranty is designated as "full," the designation must also contain a "statement of duration" (MMWA 103(a)(1)). The FTC, by regulation, requires that the designations appear as a caption or prominent title, clearly separated from the text of the warranty. FTC Reg. § 700.6.[12]

The MMWA further provided that, for a "written warranty" to qualify as "full," it must meet "Federal minimum standards" provided in MMWA 104 (MMWA 103(a)(1)). Any "written warranty" that fails to meet all of these minimum standards must be designated as a

---

12. Pursuant to MMWA 102(a), the FTC regulation adds that the body of a "written warranty" must contain nine categories of specified information, must be in a "single document," and the language used must be "simple and readily understood." FTC Reg. § 701.3(a).

Neither the MMWA nor the FTC regulations have comparable provisions on the "limited warranty" (MMWA 103(a)(2)).[13]

Congress no doubt expected that "written warranties" would continue to be made on consumer durables. The definitions of the MMWA covered the printed warranties, often bordered in handsome filigree, that manufacturers of consumer durable goods tended to provide. In this expectation, Congress was correct. Congress may also have expected that consumers would come to understand the difference between "full" and "limited" warranties and, by exercise of market power, would induce sellers to avoid the pejoratively titled "limited warranty." In this expectation, Congress was incorrect. Only a few sellers ever offered "full" warranties on high-priced goods.[14]

(3) Implied Warranty Disclaimers. "The most dramatic provisions of the Magnuson–Moss Warranty Act may be those that unveil the implied warranties of quality, particularly the implied warranty of merchantability, with respect to consumer [durable] goods. For decades prior to the Act, manufacturers and dealers routinely marketed goods with contract language disclaiming all implied warranties of quality. [The MMWA] bars those disclaimers by any supplier who makes a *written warranty* or who, contemporaneously with sale, enters into a *service contract*." C. Reitz, supra, at 73–74. See MMWA 108(a).

If a disclaimer is improperly included in a contract of sale, notwithstanding MMWA 108(a), the Act declares it ineffective. MMWA 108(c).

The disclaimer preclusion provision in MMWA 108(a) applies to all "written warranties." The same rule applies, whether the warranty is "full" or "limited."

The MMWA does not speak to the content of the implied warranties of quality. The Act incorporates whatever meaning those warranties have under state law. MMWA 101(7).

Problem 4. Seller manufactures and installs central air conditioning systems. Buyer came into Seller's shop and described the size of his home to the salesman. The salesman drew Buyer's attention in Seller's catalog to the "HOMAIR," a unit that delivered 35,000 BTU of refrigeration. Buyer agreed to purchase the HOMAIR. The one-page sales contract stated at the bottom:

LIMITED WARRANTY

Seller expressly warrants against defects in materials, workmanship and installation if, and only if, such defects are brought to Seller's attention within one year of installation, whereupon Seller, at Seller's option, will repair or replace the defective part or parts.

---

designation or content of "service contracts." But see MMWA 106(a).

13. If a warrantor designates a warranty as "full," the MMWA declares that this designation incorporates the "Federal minimum standards" (MMWA 104(e)), whether or not those standards are explicitly contained in the warranty document.

14. A notable exception was American Motors Co., which offered "full" warranties on its new cars. The manufacturer did not survive. "Full" warranties are more prevalent in sales of relatively low-priced consumer goods if sellers are willing to undertake to replace a defective product or refund the price.

THERE ARE NO WARRANTIES, EITHER EXPRESS OR IM-
PLIED, INCLUDING THE WARRANTY OF MERCHANTABILI-
TY, WHICH EXTEND BEYOND THE DESCRIPTION ON THE
FACE HEREOF. IN NO EVENT SHALL SELLER BE LIABLE
FOR SPECIAL OR CONSEQUENTIAL DAMAGES.

(a) The air conditioning unit broke down eighteen months after the
date of installation. Seller informed Buyer that a new motor was
required, and that the cost to Buyer for the motor and installation
would be $350. What are Buyer's rights? See MMWA 108(a).

(b) After the system was installed and began to function, Buyer
discovered that the system did not generate enough cold air to cool his
house. He also learned that the problem was not due to any defect in
parts or operation, but was because the system was inadequate for the
size of his house. What rights does Buyer have against Seller for
breach of implied warranty of fitness for purpose? See MMWA 108(a).

(4) Clauses Limiting Damages. The position of the MMWA on
clauses limiting damages is explicit only in the Act's treatment of "full"
warranties. Section 104(a)(3) permits a "full" warrantor to exclude or
limit consequential damages if the clause appears conspicuously on the
face of the warranty.[15] The position with respect to "limited" warranties must be inferred.

Problem 5. Consider again the transaction in Problem 4. Suppose that a system of adequate size had been installed. A defect in the
tubing caused a leak of condensed moisture which damaged a wall of
the house; the repairs cost $1500. May Buyer recover from Seller for
this cost? See MMWA 108(a).

Is it reasonable to infer that Congress would require more consumer protection under a "limited" warranty than is required under a
"full" warranty? Must the formalities of conspicuousness and on-the-
face placement be met in a "limited" warranty?

Problem 6. Seller sold a new car to Buyer under a FULL (ONE
YEAR) WARRANTY which included on the face of the warranty a
conspicuous provision disclaiming responsibility for consequential damages. See MMWA 104(a)(3). Six months after the purchase the brakes
failed. The car was demolished and Buyer was seriously injured. May
Buyer recover (a) for the damage to the car and (b) for his personal
injuries? See MMWA 111(b) and UCC 2–719(3).

(5) Limited Duration of Implied Warranties. "In a most perplexing provision, the [MMWA] permits "limited" warrantors to limit
the duration of implied warranties of quality [MMWA 108(b)] ... The
notion of limiting duration connotes the shortening of a period of time.
Implied warranties of quality do not have any period of existence. An
implied warranty is breached or is not breached in the scintilla of time

---

15. Even for "full" warranties, this conclusion is a matter of inference. The Act's
formulation, "may not ... unless," must be
read to mean "may ... if". Is this is a
plausible interpretation of the statute?

that marks tender of delivery of the goods. A time period begins to run from that moment, the period of the statute of limitations. But plainly an implied warranty is not some kind of continuing promise ...

"At least five possible meanings might be ascribed to terms limiting the duration of implied warranties.

1. [S]hortening of the statute of limitations period.

2. [L]engthening the statute of limitations period.

3. [Defining] the time within which a buyer must give notice of breach or be barred from any remedy under [UCC 2–607(3)].

4. [Defining] a period of time after which a buyer cannot complain of non-conformities that later come to light even though they could not reasonably have been discovered earlier.

5. [Defining] a time during which buyer's remedy is to seek seller's repair or other promised post-delivery relief. ...

"None of the suggested meanings ... is entirely satisfactory as a matter of statutory construction. ... In my view, the fifth meaning comes closest to the spirit of the ... Act. It also makes sense in the marketplace." C. Reitz, supra, pp. 82, 86, 95.

(6) Recovery of Attorneys' Fees and Costs. The MMWA authorizes prevailing plaintiffs to recover, over and above other monetary remedies, an additional amount for attorneys' fees and costs. MMWA 110(d)(2). Allowance of fees and costs is not a matter of right; recovery lies in the discretion of the trial court. Courts may allow fees and costs only if actions are "brought" under MMWA 110(d)(1). Whether that condition has been met can be a difficult question. See C. Reitz, supra, pp. 134–143. In an ordinary breach of warranty case, the answer appears to turn on when and how plaintiff first mentions the MMWA.

A New Jersey case, which resulted in the consumer recovering damages in the amount of $6,745.59, concluded with an award of attorneys' fees of $5,165.00. Ventura v. Ford Motor Corp., 180 N.J. Super. 45, 433 A.2d 801 (1981). Similar awards have been made in other cases. See C. Reitz, supra, pp. 141–143. The largest recovery of fees and costs to date, nearly $2.5 million, occurred in the engine interchange class action against General Motors Corp. Id. at 140–141.

(7) Federal Forum for Warranty Litigation. The MMWA permits certain plaintiffs to bring warranty actions in federal courts. MMWA 110(d)(1)(B). This provision has limited usefulness to a single-plaintiff case because the amount in controversy must be at least $50,000.00 (MMWA 110(d)(3)(B)), and courts have held that amounts claimed for personal injuries are not counted for this purpose for this purpose. See Boelens v. Redman Homes, Inc., 748 F.2d 1058 (5th Cir.1984), rehearing denied, 759 F.2d 504 (1985); but see C. Reitz, supra, pp. 144–146.[16]

---

16. One district court allowed a claim for punitive damages to be counted toward the $50,000.00 threshold. Schafer v.

The amount in controversy in a class action may easily exceed the statutory threshold, but an odd formulation of MMWA 110(d)(1) may still foreclose jurisdiction in federal court. The following case illustrates.

SKELTON v. GENERAL MOTORS CORP.

United States Court of Appeals, Seventh Circuit, 1981.
660 F.2d 311.

CUDAHY, CIRCUIT JUDGE. Section 110(d) of Title I of the Magnuson–Moss Warranty–Federal Trade Commission Improvements Act ("Magnuson–Moss" or the "Act") creates a federal private cause of action for consumers damaged by the failure of a warrantor "to comply with any obligation under ... a written warranty." 15 U.S.C. § 2310(d)(1) (1976). The issue on this interlocutory appeal is whether a "written warranty" actionable under § 110(d) is limited to the particular promises, undertakings or affirmations of fact expressly defined as "written warranties" by Congress in the Act. The district court held that § 110(d) provides a federal cause of action not merely for breach of a "written warranty" as defined in the Act but also for breach of "all written promises presented in connection with the sale of a formally warranted product." 500 F.Supp. 1181, 1190 (N.D.Ill.1980). We reverse.

I.

Plaintiffs, purchasers of automobiles manufactured by defendant General Motors Corporation ("GM"), brought this action as a nationwide class action on behalf of all purchasers of GM automobiles manufactured from 1976 through 1979. In Count I of their amended complaint, plaintiffs allege that GM, through its "brochures, manuals, consumer advertising and other forms of communications to the public generally and to members of plaintiffs' class specifically," warranted and represented that 1976 through 1979 GM automobiles contained THM 350(M38) transmissions, or "transmissions of similar quality and performance. ... and that [such transmissions] would meet a specified level of performance." Plaintiffs charge in Count I that, contrary to these warranties and representations, GM substituted inferior THM 200(M29) transmissions for THM 350(M38) transmissions in GM automobiles manufactured from 1976 through 1979. This undisclosed substitution is alleged to constitute a violation of written ... warranties under § 110(d) of Magnuson–Moss. ...

General Motors moved to dismiss ... plaintiffs' complaint for failure to state a claim upon which relief could be granted. On October 1, 1980, the district court ... denied GM's motion to dismiss the

Chrysler Corp., 544 F.Supp. 182 (N.D.Ind.
1982); C. Reitz, supra, pp. 147–148.

"written warranty" claim in Count I.   500 F.Supp. 1181 (N.D.Ill.1980).
. . .

II.

[The plaintiffs did not deny that GM had given the buyer a formal warranty that was a "written warranty" as defined in § 101(6) of the Act. This written warranty did not refer to the type of transmission used in the automobile. The District Court concluded that the brochures and manuals that stated that the automobiles had THM 350(M38) transmissions were not "written warranties" under § 101(6)(A) since this written material did not relate "to the material or workmanship *and* [affirm] ... that such material or workmanship is *defect free* or will meet a specified level of performance *over a specified period of time*."

[The District Court, however, concluded that since GM had made a formal "express warranty" with the statements specified in § 101(6)(A), the Act should be construed to allow a federal remedy under the Act for misstatements made in written material other than "the paper with the filigree border." The substantial matters at stake included the Act's provisions in § 110(d), providing for private actions, class actions in the federal courts and the recovery of attorney's fees.]

Section 110(d) creates a private cause of action for breach of "written warranty," subject to the requirements that: (1) the consumer must have an individual claim of at least $25; (2) the total amount in controversy must equal or exceed $50,000; and (3) if brought as a class action, the complaint must name at least one hundred plaintiffs. 15 U.S.C. § 2310(d)(3) (1976). Section 110 also makes any failure to comply with the requirements of the Act a violation of § 5(a)(1) of the Federal Trade Commission Act (15 U.S.C. § 45(a)(1) (1976)), and empowers the FTC and the Attorney General to seek injunctive relief against (1) failure to comply with any obligation under the Act, and (2) written warranties which may be "deceptive" to a reasonable individual. 15 U.S.C. § 2310(c) (1976).

III.

The scope of the private action for breach of "written warranty" created by § 110(d) is the issue presented to us for resolution. Section 110(d) provides in part that:

> [A] consumer who is damaged by the failure of a supplier, warrantor, or service contractor to comply with any obligation under this title, or a written warranty, implied warranty, or service contract. may bring suit for damages and other legal and equitable relief [in any state court of competent jurisdiction or in an appropriate federal district court].

15 U.S.C. § 2310(d)(1) (1976).

The district court properly rejected plaintiffs' argument that the Act's draftsmen intended in § 110(d) to create a federal private cause of action for breach of all written express warranties. None of the legislative history offered by plaintiffs in this record provides the clear evidence of Congressional intent necessary to overcome the "familiar principle governing the interpretation of statutes ... that if a statutory definition of a word is given, that definition must prevail, regardless of what other meaning may be attributable to the word." ... Indeed, we are less than confident that it is possible to distill any unambiguous Congressional intent from the Act's legislative history. As the district court noted:

> [A review of the Act's legislative history] is the legal equivalent of an archaeological dig. Various consumer warranty bills were pending before the House and Senate for four years, during which each body defined, discarded, reintroduced and redefined concepts which in some fashion or another are related to the enacted legislation. Some provisions of the Act are vestigial reminders of concepts buried but not totally forgotten during the on-going legislative process. Both proponents and opponents of an expansive interpretation have cited compelling, to them, legislative history only dimly related to the language which finally emerged as law....

[The opinion included an extended discussion of the Act's legislative history, and concluded that this material did not support departure from a strictly literal construction of the provisions defining the scope of private actions under § 110(d).]

IV.

Although the district court properly declined to adopt plaintiffs' interpretation of § 110(d), it also rejected GM's argument that the only written warranties actionable under § 110(d) are those promises, representations or undertakings defined as "written warranties" in § 101(6). In its view:

> Congress ... indicated that although the Magnuson–Moss Act only regulates transactions involving written warranties as the term is narrowly defined in § 101(6), once a consumer is involved in such a transaction there is a policy of providing federal remedies beyond the four corners of the formal warranty.

500 F.Supp. at 1191. Thus, the district court concluded that, whenever a manufacturer elects to extend a "written warranty" to a consumer, "[o]ther written promises presented in connection with the same transaction should also be enforceable as part of the 'written warranty.'" 500 F.Supp. at 1190.

The district court's determination that "written warranty" in § 110(d) means something more than it was defined to mean in § 101(6) has two aspects. First, the court found that the "Act itself suggests several different possible meanings of the phrase 'written warranty'" and is therefore ambiguous. 500 F.Supp. at 1187. Second, because of this ambiguity, the district court looked to the purposes of the Act, as derived from its legislative history, and concluded that § 110(d) should be construed to provide "a remedy for all written promises presented in connection with the sale of a formally warranted product." 500 F.Supp. at 1190.

We believe that the three ambiguities identified by the district court, which we shall consider individually, are not sufficiently real or substantial to warrant rejection of the definition of "written warranty" provided by Congress in the Act. Moreover, as already discussed, we do not find in the Act's legislative history a clear Congressional intention that the term "written warranty" was meant to have different meanings in different sections of the Act. *See* Part III, supra. And, if anything is apparent from the statutory scheme, it is the importance of providing a clear, carefully circumscribed meaning to the term "written warranty." ...

There is no clear evidence that Congress intended for written warranty in § 102 to mean something different than the definition it ascribed to the term in § 101(6), and we consequently presume that Congress intended for "written warranty" to have the same meaning in both sections. We therefore decline to accept the position that "written warranty" means both a particular class of representations and some undefined "document" containing those representations. It is more appropriate to read the inconsistent phrase "inclusion in the written warranty" [emphasis supplied] to mean "inclusion *with* the written warranty" or "inclusion in *the document containing* the written warranty."

The term "written warranty" serves a central function in the Act of identifying the particular representations that are subject to the Act's disclosure and content requirements. Because of the function it serves, it is important that the term have a single, precise meaning. The § 101(6) definition provides that unambiguous meaning, and that definition is used (all things considered) with commendable aptness by the draftsmen in the forty-odd appearances of the term "written warranty" in every section of the Act. We cannot agree that syntactical slips such as the use of the preposition "in" in § 102, create ambiguities in the statutory scheme of sufficient weight to justify discarding the meticulously worded definition of "written warranty" in § 101(6) in favor of an undefined "document," or "pile of written documents," as urged by the district court. See 500 F.Supp. at 1190.

V.

In sum, we are constrained to interpret "written warranty" in § 110(d) in accordance with the definition of "written warranty" provided by Congress in § 101(6).

Reversed.

HARLINGTON WOOD, JR., CIRCUIT JUDGE, dissenting. This is a close case of statutory interpretation, but I respectfully dissent from the majority's conclusion that the Act must be so strictly and rigidly read as to exclude coverage of the alleged transmission substitution by General Motors.

Judge Moran, in the trial court, carefully pondered the arguments and concluded that the act was broader than General Motors argued, but not so broad as plaintiffs' urged. I generally agree with his interpretation.

As Judge Moran noted, 500 F.Supp. at 1184, he was not the first one to have some difficulty interpreting the Act. Others before him have characterized it as serving as no exemplar of legislative clarity. I would, therefore, not begin and end by viewing the Act's definition provisions in such isolation as to conclude that the beneficial consumer protection purposes of the Act are thereby completely limited. Were this a criminal statute, I might be bound to resolve the question in favor of General Motors, but it is not.

This Act needs some limited judicial first aid in order to be able to accomplish its remedial purposes. Therefore, I would interpret the Act to mean that those written documents of General Motors which made specific representations of substance about the product, not just advertising ballyhoo, and which were introduced by General Motors into the transaction became, as a practical matter, inferentially incorporated into the written warranty. The written warranty would then more fully deserve its gold filigree frame.

Notes

(1) **Federal Court Diversity Jurisdiction.** The Magnuson–Moss Warranty Act creates a new head of federal jurisdiction, which plaintiffs in *Skelton* sought to use. Without regard to that act, however, warranty litigation is often litigated in federal courts under diversity-of-citizenship jurisdiction, 28 U.S.C. § 1332. Diversity jurisdiction, however, is generally not available in warranty litigation arising out of retail sales because of the high level of the required amount in controversy, raised in 1988 to $50,000. (The federal courts' opinions we read before *Skelton* involved controversies over business goods of considerable value.)

(2) **Construction of MMWA 110(d)(1)(B).** The Court of Appeals concluded that the statute's omission of claims based on express warranties other than "written warranties" reflected a deliberate Congressional choice. Do you see any other explanation for the structure of MMWA 110(d)(1)(B)?

If a seller provided a "written warranty" to a buyer, may the buyer bring an action in federal court under MMWA 110(d)(1)(B) solely for breach of an implied warranty?

If a seller provided a "written warranty" and that document included warranty provisions in addition to those necessary to meet the definition of "written warranty," may the buyer sue for breach of the "definitional" terms and the additional terms in federal court under MMWA 110(d)(1)(B)?

(C) STRICT TORT LIABILITY FOR ECONOMIC LOSS

(1) Ordinary Consumer Buyers. We noted earlier that strict tort liability emerged principally to protect individuals who had suffered personal injuries caused by defective and unsafe products, but the drafters of Restatement (Second) of Torts § 402A added the possibility of recovery for "physical harm ... to ... property." As state courts fashioned their versions of this new tort, the scope of liability for economic losses became a matter of controversy. Most state courts have held that strict tort liability does not extend to claims for the economic value of the product itself. In Restatement terminology, the "property" for which recovery may be had is property other than the allegedly defective product. Some courts disagree.

Genesis of the disagreement is a 1965 New Jersey decision, based on breach of warranty, in which the buyer of carpet was permitted to recover damages when a buyer discovered a latent flaw in the carpet after its installation. Affirming judgment for the buyer, the New Jersey Supreme Court added, in dictum, that buyer could have cast the seller's liability "in simpler form," namely strict tort liability. Santor v. A & M Karagheusian, Inc., 44 N.J. 52, 207 A.2d 305 (1965).

Immediately thereafter, the California Supreme Court, the court which created strict tort liability, declared the New Jersey position to be an improper extension of the new tort. Seely v. White Motor Co., 63 Cal.2d 9, 45 Cal.Rptr. 17, 403 P.2d 145 (1965).

The ensuing controversy echoes down the years as state after state chooses sides and academics and others comment.

(2) Commercial Buyers. While strict tort liability arose in the cases about products purchased by individuals for personal, family or household use, the doctrinal formulation of the new tort did not restrict it to ordinary retail transactions. Products purchased for commercial purposes are also consumed or used. If the buyer is a corporation, that "person" [17] cannot suffer personal injuries. But an organization can suffer property damage. Moreover, if property damage compensable in tort includes loss of value of the product purchased, an organization would be a likely plaintiff in a strict tort liability suit. Even buyers of $125 million supertankers might try to recover on a strict tort liability theory.

---

17. "Person" is commonly defined to mean an individual or an organization.   See UCC 1–201(30).

EAST RIVER S.S. CORP. v. TRANSAMERICA DELAVAL, INC.

Supreme Court of the United States, 1986.
476 U.S. 858, 106 S.Ct. 2295, 90 L.Ed.2d 865.

BLACKMUN, J., delivered the opinion for a unanimous Court. In this admiralty case, we must decide whether a cause of action in tort is stated when a defective product purchased in a commercial transaction malfunctions, injuring only the product itself and causing purely economic loss. The case requires us to consider preliminarily whether admiralty law, which already recognizes a general theory of liability for negligence, also incorporates principles of products liability, including strict liability. Then, charting a course between products liability and contract law, we must determine whether injury to a product itself is the kind of harm that should be protected by products liability or left entirely to the law of contracts.

I

In 1969, Seatrain Shipbuilding Corp. (Shipbuilding), a wholly owned subsidiary of Seatrain Lines, Inc. (Seatrain), announced it would build the four oil-transporting supertankers in issue.... Each tanker was constructed pursuant to a contract in which a separate wholly owned subsidiary of Seatrain engaged Shipbuilding. Shipbuilding in turn contracted with respondent, now known as Transamerica Delaval Inc. (Delaval), to design, manufacture, and supervise the installation of turbines (costing $1.4 million each ...) that would be the main propulsion units for the 225,000–ton, $125 million ... supertankers. When each ship was completed, its title was transferred from the contracting subsidiary to a trust company (as trustee for an owner), which in turn chartered the ship to one of the petitioners, also subsidiaries of Seatrain. ... Each petitioner operated under a bareboat charter, by which it took full control of the ship for 20 or 22 years as though it owned it, with the obligation afterwards to return the ship to the real owner. See G. Gilmore & C. Black, Admiralty §§ 4–1, 4–22 (2d ed. 1975). Each charterer assumed responsibility for the cost of any repairs to the ships. ...

The Stuyvesant sailed on its maiden voyage in late July 1977. On December 11 of that year, as the ship was about to enter the Port of Valdez, Alaska, steam began to escape from the casing of the high-pressure turbine. That problem was temporarily resolved by repairs, but before long, while the ship was encountering a severe storm in the Gulf of Alaska, the high-pressure turbine malfunctioned. The ship, though lacking its normal power, was able to continue on its journey to Panama and then San Francisco. In January 1978, an examination of the high-pressure turbine revealed that the first-stage steam reversing ring virtually had disintegrated and had caused additional damage to other parts of the turbine. The damaged part was replaced with a part from the Bay Ridge, which was then under construction. In April 1978, the ship again was repaired, this time with a part from the Brooklyn. Finally, in August, the ship was permanently and satisfactorily repaired with a ring newly designed and manufactured by Delaval.

The Brooklyn and the Williamsburgh were put into service in late 1973 and late 1974, respectively. In 1978, as a result of the Stuyvesant's problems, they were inspected while in port. Those inspections revealed similar turbine damage. Temporary repairs were made, and newly designed parts were installed as permanent repairs that summer.

When the Bay Ridge was completed in early 1979, it contained the newly designed parts and thus never experienced the high-pressure turbine problems that plagued the other three ships. Nonetheless, the complaint appears to claim damages as a result of deterioration of the Bay Ridge's ring that was installed in the Stuyvesant while the Bay Ridge was under construction. In addition, the Bay Ridge experienced a unique problem. In 1980, when the ship was on its maiden voyage, the engine began to vibrate with a frequency that increased even after speed was reduced. It turned out that the astern guardian valve, located between the high-pressure and low-pressure turbines, had been installed backwards. Because of that error, steam entered the low-pressure turbine and damaged it. After repairs, the Bay Ridge resumed its travels.

II

The charterers' second amended complaint, filed in the United States District Court for the District of New Jersey, invokes admiralty jurisdiction. It contains five counts alleging tortious conduct on the part of respondent Delaval and seeks an aggregate of more than $8 million in damages for the cost of repairing the ships and for income lost while the ships were out of service. The first four counts, read liberally, allege that Delaval is strictly liable for the design defects in the high-pressure turbines of the Stuyvesant, the Williamsburgh, the Brooklyn, and the Bay Ridge, respectively. The fifth count alleges that Delaval, as part of the manufacturing process, negligently supervised the installation of the astern guardian valve on the Bay Ridge. ...

The District Court granted summary judgment for Delaval, and the Court of Appeals for the Third Circuit, sitting en banc, affirmed. East River S.S. Corp. v. Delaval Turbine, Inc., 752 F.2d 903 (1985). ...

III

... We join the Courts of Appeals in recognizing products liability, including strict liability, as part of the general maritime law. ...

IV

Products liability grew out of a public policy judgment that people need more protection from dangerous products than is afforded by the law of warranty. See Seely v. White Motor Co., 63 Cal.2d 9, 15, 403 P.2d 145, 149 (1965). It is clear, however, that if this development were allowed to progress too far, contract law would drown in a sea of tort. See G. Gilmore, The Death of Contract 87–94 (1974). We must determine whether a commercial product injuring itself is the kind of harm against which public policy requires manufacturers to protect, independent of any contractual obligation.

A

The paradigmatic products-liability action is one where a product "reasonably certain to place life and limb in peril," distributed without reinspection, causes bodily injury. See, e.g., MacPherson v. Buick Motor Co., 217 N.Y. 382, 389, 111 N.E. 1051, 1053 (1916). The manufacturer is liable whether or not it is negligent because "public policy demands that responsibility be fixed wherever it will most effectively reduce the hazards to life and health inherent in defective products that reach the market." Escola v. Coca Cola Bottling Co. of Fresno, 24 Cal., at 462, 150 P.2d, at 441 (opinion concurring in judgment).

For similar reasons of safety, the manufacturer's duty of care was broadened to include protection against property damage. ... Such damage is considered so akin to personal injury that the two are treated alike. ...

In the traditional "property damage" cases, the defective product damages other property. In this case, there was no damage to "other" property. Rather, the first, second, and third counts allege that each supertanker's defectively designed turbine components damaged only the turbine itself. Since each turbine was supplied by Delaval as an integrated package, ... each is properly regarded as a single unit. "Since all but the very simplest of machines have component parts, [a contrary] holding would require a finding of 'property damage' in virtually every case where a product damages itself. Such a holding would eliminate the distinction between warranty and strict products liability." Northern Power & Engineering Corp. v. Caterpillar Tractor Co., 623 P.2d 324, 330 (Alaska 1981). The fifth count also alleges injury to the product itself. ... The fifth count thus can best be read to allege that Delaval's negligent manufacture of the propulsion system— by allowing the installation in reverse of the astern guardian valve— damaged the propulsion system. ... Obviously, damage to a product itself has certain attributes of a products-liability claim. But the injury suffered—the failure of the product to function properly—is the essence of a warranty action, through which a contracting party can seek to recoup the benefit of its bargain.

B

The intriguing question whether injury to a product itself may be brought in tort has spawned a variety of answers. At one end of the spectrum, the case that created the majority land-based approach, Seely v. White Motor Co., 63 Cal.2d 9, 403 P.2d 145 (1965) (defective truck), held that preserving a proper role for the law of warranty precludes imposing tort liability if a defective product causes purely monetary harm. ...

At the other end of the spectrum is the minority land-based approach, whose progenitor, Santor v. A & M Karagheusian, Inc., 44 N.J. 52, 66–67, 207 A.2d 305, 312–313 (1965) (marred carpeting), held that a manufacturer's duty to make nondefective products encompassed injury to the product itself, whether or not the defect created an unreasonable risk of harm. ... The courts adopting this approach ... find that the safety and insurance rationales behind strict liability apply equally where the losses are purely economic. These courts reject the Seely approach because they find it arbitrary that economic losses are recoverable if a plaintiff suffers bodily injury or property damage, but not if a product injures itself. They also find no inherent difference between economic loss and personal injury or property damage, because all are proximately caused by the defendant's conduct. Further, they believe recovery for economic loss would not lead to unlimited liability because they think a manufacturer can predict and insure against product failure. ...

Between the two poles fall a number of cases that would permit a products-liability action under certain circumstances when a product injures only itself. These cases attempt to differentiate between "the disappointed users ... and the endangered ones," Russell v. Ford Motor Co., 281 Or. 587, 595, 575 P.2d 1383, 1387 (1978), and permit only the latter to sue in tort. The determination has been said to turn on the nature of the defect, the type of risk, and the manner in which the injury arose. See Pennsylvania Glass Sand Corp. v. Caterpillar Tractor Co., 652 F.2d, at 1173 (relied on by the Court of Appeals in this case). The Alaska Supreme Court allows a tort action if the defective product creates a situation potentially dangerous to persons or other property, and loss occurs as a proximate result of that danger and under dangerous circumstances. Northern Power & Engineering Corp. v. Caterpillar Tractor Co., 623 P.2d 324, 329 (1981).

We find the intermediate and minority land-based positions unsatisfactory. The intermediate positions, which essentially turn on the degree of risk, are too indeterminate to enable manufacturers easily to structure their business behavior. Nor do we find persuasive a distinction that rests on the manner in which the product is injured. We realize that the damage may be qualitative, occurring through gradual deterioration or internal breakage. Or it may be calamitous. Compare Morrow v. New Moon Homes, Inc., 548 P.2d 279 (Alaska 1976), with Cloud v. Kit Mfg. Co., 563 P.2d 248, 251 (Alaska 1977). But either way, since by definition no person or other property is damaged, the resulting loss is purely economic. Even when the harm to the product itself occurs through an abrupt, accident-like event, the resulting loss due to repair costs, decreased value, and lost profits is essentially the failure of the purchaser to receive the benefit of its bargain—traditionally the core concern of contract law. See E. Farnsworth, Contracts § 12.8, pp. 839–840 (1982).

We also decline to adopt the minority land-based view espoused by Santor .... Such cases raise legitimate questions about the theories behind restricting products liability, but we believe that the countervailing arguments are more powerful. The minority view fails to account for the need to keep products liability and contract law in separate spheres and to maintain a realistic limitation on damages.

C

Exercising traditional discretion in admiralty, ... we adopt an approach similar to Seely and hold that a manufacturer in a commercial relationship has no duty under either a negligence or strict products-liability theory to prevent a product from injuring itself.

"The distinction that the law has drawn between tort recovery for physical injuries and warranty recovery for economic loss is not arbitrary and does not rest on the 'luck' of one plaintiff in having an accident causing physical injury. The distinction rests, rather, on an understanding of the nature of the responsibility a manufacturer must undertake in distributing his products." Seely v. White Motor Co., 63 Cal.2d, at 18, 403 P.2d, at 151. When a product injures only itself the reasons for imposing a tort duty are weak and those for leaving the party to its contractual remedies are strong.

The tort concern with safety is reduced when an injury is only to the product itself. When a person is injured, the "cost of an injury and the loss of time or health may be an overwhelming misfortune," and one the person is not prepared to meet. Escola v. Coca Cola Bottling Co., 24 Cal.2d, at 462, 150 P.2d, at 441 (opinion concurring in judgment). In contrast, when a product injures itself, the commercial user stands to lose the value of the product, risks the displeasure of its customers who find that the product does not meet their needs, or, as in this case, experiences increased costs in performing a service. Losses like these can be insured. ... Society need not presume that a customer needs special protection. The increased cost to the public that would result from holding a manufacturer liable in tort for injury to the product itself is not justified. ...

Damage to a product itself is most naturally understood as a warranty claim. Such damage means simply that the product has not met the customer's expectations, or, in other words, that the customer has received "insufficient product value." See J. White & R. Summers, Uniform Commercial Code 406 (2d ed. 1980). The maintenance of product value and quality is precisely the purpose of express and implied warranties.[7] See UCC § 2–313 (express warranty), § 2–314 (implied warranty of merchantability), and § 2–315 (warranty of fitness for a particular purpose). Therefore, a claim of a nonworking product can be brought as a breach-of-warranty action. Or, if the customer

---

7. If the charterers' claims were brought as breach-of-warranty actions, they would not be within the admiralty jurisdiction. ...

prefers, it can reject the product or revoke its acceptance and sue for breach of contract. See UCC §§ 2–601, 2–608, 2–612.

Contract law, and the law of warranty in particular, is well suited to commercial controversies of the sort involved in this case because the parties may set the terms of their own agreements.[8] The manufacturer can restrict its liability, within limits, by disclaiming warranties or limiting remedies. See UCC §§ 2–316, 2–719. In exchange, the purchaser pays less for the product. Since a commercial situation generally does not involve large disparities in bargaining power, ... we see no reason to intrude into the parties' allocation of the risk.

While giving recognition to the manufacturer's bargain, warranty law sufficiently protects the purchaser by allowing it to obtain the benefit of its bargain. See White & Summers, supra, ch. 10. The expectation damages available in warranty for purely economic loss give a plaintiff the full benefit of its bargain by compensating for forgone business opportunities. ... Recovery on a warranty theory would give the charterers their repair costs and lost profits, and would place them in the position they would have been in had the turbines functioned properly. ... Thus, both the nature of the injury and the resulting damages indicate it is more natural to think of injury to a product itself in terms of warranty.

A warranty action also has a built-in limitation on liability, whereas a tort action could subject the manufacturer to damages of an indefinite amount. The limitation in a contract action comes from the agreement of the parties and the requirement that consequential damages, such as lost profits, be a foreseeable result of the breach. See Hadley v. Baxendale, 9 Ex. 341, 156 Eng. Rep. 145 (1854). In a warranty action where the loss is purely economic, the limitation derives from the requirements of foreseeability and of privity, which is still generally enforced for such claims in a commercial setting. See UCC § 2–715.... .

In products-liability law, where there is a duty to the public generally, foreseeability is an inadequate brake. ... Permitting recovery for all foreseeable claims for purely economic loss could make a manufacturer liable for vast sums. It would be difficult for a manufacturer to take into account the expectations of persons downstream who may encounter its product. In this case, for example, if the charterers—already one step removed from the transaction—were permitted to recover their economic losses, then the companies that subchartered the ships might claim their economic losses from the delays, and the charterers' customers also might claim their economic losses, and so on.

---

8. We recognize, of course, that warranty and products liability are not static bodies of law and may overlap. In certain situations, for example, the privity requirement of warranty has been discarded. ... In other circumstances, a manufacturer may be able to disclaim strict tort liability. See, e.g., Keystone Aeronautics Corp. v. R.J. Enstrom Corp., 499 F.2d 146, 149 (CA3 1974). Nonetheless, the main currents of tort law run in different directions from those of contract and warranty, and the latter seem to us far more appropriate for commercial disputes of the kind involved here.

"The law does not spread its protection so far." Robins Dry Dock & Repair Co. v. Flint, 275 U.S. 303, 309 (1927).

And to the extent that courts try to limit purely economic damages in tort, they do so by relying on a far murkier line, one that negates the charterers' contention that permitting such recovery under a products-liability theory enables admiralty courts to avoid difficult line drawing. . . .

D

For the first three counts, the defective turbine components allegedly injured only the turbines themselves. Therefore, a strict products-liability theory of recovery is unavailable to the charterers. Any warranty claims would be subject to Delaval's limitation, both in time and scope, of its warranty liability. . . . The record indicates that Seatrain and Delaval reached a settlement agreement. . . . We were informed that these charterers could not have asserted the warranty claims. . . . Even so, the charterers should be left to the terms of their bargains, which explicitly allocated the cost of repairs. . . .

Similarly, in the fifth count, alleging the reverse installation of the astern guardian valve, the only harm was to the propulsion system itself rather than to persons or other property. Even assuming that Delaval's supervision was negligent, as we must on this summary judgment motion, Delaval owed no duty under a products-liability theory based on negligence to avoid causing purely economic loss. . . . Thus, whether stated in negligence or strict liability, no products-liability claim lies in admiralty when the only injury claimed is economic loss. . . .

It is so ordered.

Notes

(1) **Hazardous Risks and Strict Tort Liability.** One court held that the line between tort and warranty liability should not be drawn in terms of the type of the loss, but should be determined rather by the nature of the defect and the type of risk it poses; thus, if a manufacturer so designs a product that a sudden, unexplained small fire spreads and destroys an expensive piece of equipment, a claim falls within the policy of tort law that manufacturers should not create safety hazards that pose a serious risk of harm to people and property. Pennsylvania Glass Sand Corp. v. Caterpillar Tractor Co., 652 F.2d 1165 (3d Cir.1981)

(2) **Disclaimers of Strict Tort Liability.** Courts in jurisdictions that permit buyers to recover for economic loss under the doctrine of strict tort liability have faced the further question of the effect of contract clauses purporting to modify or limit sellers' liability. One court held that it was permissible for sellers to contract out of strict tort liability, but a contract clause that disclaimed warranty liability

would not be effective as a disclaimer of tort liability. Keystone Aeronautics Corp. v. R.J. Enstrom Corp., 499 F.2d 146 (3d Cir.1974).

SECTION 7. PRIVITY BETWEEN OWNER
OR USER AND WARRANTOR
(A) DOMESTIC SALES LAW

Introduction. Until now, we have considered the issue of sellers' responsibility for the quality of their goods in situations where complaining buyers had bought the goods from sellers from whom they sought relief. (One significant exception: in *Hill v. BASF Wyandotte Corp.*, Section 3, supra, a farmer sought recovery not from his seller, but rather from the manufacturer of a herbicide.) In this section, we turn to the difficult legal issues that arise when owners of goods sue remote suppliers. The primary legal issue is whether such suits are possible even though there is no privity of contract between the parties.

Goods may be sold a number of times before reaching the ultimate owner or user. Chains of distribution link the sources of goods (e.g., manufacturers, growers, miners) and the eventual final users of those goods. Thus, a manufactured item may be sold by the manufacturer to a wholesaler, who in turn sells the item to a retailer, who then sells it to a customer.

One privity question arises when a buyer at the end of a chain of distribution sues a seller at or near the beginning of the chain. These problems are commonly characterized as issues of "vertical" privity.

A different set of problems, characterized as involving "horizontal" privity, arise when the last buyer in the chain of distribution of a product may not use the goods or may not fully consume them. The product may have been purchased as a gift; the owner-user would not be a buyer at all. A product bought by one family member may be used by other family members and guests. Partially used goods may re-enter the market as "trade-ins." Similar events occur regularly at the commercial level. (Recall the sale of the oil drilling rigs in *Universal Drilling Co.*, Section 3, supra.)

Notes

(1) Manufacturers' Advertisements as Express Warranties. One vertical privity issue, now quite well settled, permits retail buyers to enforce warranties made by manufacturers in advertising their products to the general public. A 19th century common-law contract principle established contractual relationships by treating some advertisements as "offers" that can be "accepted" by readers. The classic British case permitted recovery of a "reward" offered by the Carbolic Smoke Ball Company to any of their product's users who came down with one of the diseases supposedly prevented by the smoke. Carlill v.

Carbolic Smoke Ball Co., [1893] 1 Q.B. 256 (C.A.1892). In 1932, this took on modern warranty form in Baxter v. Ford Motor Co., 168 Wash. 456, 12 P.2d 409 (1932) (statement in manufacturer's promotional literature that windshields were "shatterproof" held to create an express warranty to retail buyer). Consider again the decision in cases like *Hill* that the terms of the labeling on the package became a manufacturer's express warranty.

Problem 1. M, a manufacturer of building materials, markets its products through independent distributors. However, M sends sales engineers to construction companies to explain the uses of M's products and promote their purchase. Following such a visit by one of M's sales engineers, the B construction company buys M's roofing material from distributor, D. B claims that the roofing material does not have the qualities described by M's sales engineer, and sues M for breach of express warranty. What result in a state which adheres to traditional rules of privity? See Ruud, Manufacturers' Liability for Representations made by their Sales Engineers to Subpurchasers, 8 U.C.L.A.L.Rev. 251 (1961). For numerous ways of finding privity, see Gillam, Products Liability in a Nutshell, 37 Ore. L. Rev. 119, 153 (1958).

(2) **Assignment and Third Party Beneficiary Law.** The general rules on assignment and of third party beneficiaries, which permit contract litigation to proceed between persons who did not contract with each other, applies to transactions in goods. Article 2 of the Commercial Code codifies to some extent both assignment and third party beneficiary law. UCC 2–210, 2–318. Sharp conflicts of policy are reflected in the latter which offers states three choices.[1] Are these principles more likely relevant to horizontal or vertical privity issues?

Problem 2. M, a manufacturer of industrial machinery, sold a power lathe to B Manufacturing Company. E, an employee of B, suffered physical injuries as a result of a defect in the lathe. Under which, if any, version of UCC 2–318 would E be assured a direct cause of action against M?

Problem 3. M sold a machine to D, a distributor; D resold the machine to B Manufacturing Company. The machine exploded and caused a fire which damaged B's property and led to an expensive shutdown. Which, if any, version of UCC 2–318 would assure B a direct cause of action against M?

(3) **Manufacturer's Implied Warranties.** The most difficult vertical privity problem arises when retail buyers or other persons seek recovery from remote suppliers on a warranty theory other than breach of express warranty.

This issue was central to many of the cases in which consumers were injured by unwholesome foods or beverages. In permitting recovery, courts declared that vertical privity was not necessary in that

---

1. UCC 2–318 as originally promulgated did not contain Alternatives B and C. What is now "Alternative A" was the only provision. In 1966, the Permanent Editorial Board added B and C.

limited category of cases. By 1960, William Prosser was able to write an extraordinarily influential article about the fall of the citadel of privity that had once shielded manufacturers from consumer suits. Prosser, The Assault Upon the Citadel (Strict Liability to the Consumer), 69 Yale L.J. 1099 (1960). In the same year, the New Jersey Supreme Court expanded the category of consumer products in which privity would not be required to include automobiles. Henningsen v. Bloomfield Motors, Inc., 32 N.J. 358, 161 A.2d 69 (1960). Two years later, the California Supreme Court announced strict tort liability. Greenman v. Yuba Power Products, Inc., 59 Cal.2d 57, 27 Cal.Rptr. 697, 377 P.2d 897 (1963). Fundamental to the new tort was the explicit omission of any requirement that the consumer or user have had a contract with the seller or manufacturer.[2] See Restatement (Second) of Torts § 402A(2)(b).[3]

While the privity issue in personal injury cases is largely removed by the advent of strict tort liability, the issue remains a matter of considerable uncertainty and disagreement in warranty cases involving claims of economic loss.

MORROW v. NEW MOON HOMES, INC.

Supreme Court of Alaska, 1976.
548 P.2d 279.

RABINOWITZ, CHIEF JUSTICE. This appeal raises questions concerning personal jurisdiction over, and the liability of, a nonresident manufacturer of a defective mobile home that was purchased in Alaska from a resident seller.

In October of 1969, Joseph R. and Nikki Morrow bought a mobile home from Golden Heart Mobile Homes, a Fairbanks retailer of mobile homes. A plaque on the side of the mobile home disclosed that the home had been manufactured in Oregon by New Moon Homes, Inc. The Morrows made a down payment of $1,800, taking out a loan for the balance of the purchase price from the First National Bank of Fairbanks. The loan amount of $10,546.49, plus interest of 9 percent per year, was to be repaid by the Morrows in 72 monthly installments of $190.13 each.

At the time of the purchase, the Morrows inspected the mobile home and noticed that the carpeting had not been laid and that several windows were broken. Roy Miller, Golden Heart's salesman, assured

2. A curious factual coincidence links the New Jersey decision in *Henningsen* and the California decision in *Greenman*. In both cases, the product that caused injury was purchased as a gift and the person injured was the donee.

3. The drafters of § 402A issued a caveat on the horizontal privity question whether bystanders or others who were neither users nor consumers should be permitted to recover.

them that these problems would be corrected and later made good his assurances. Miller also told the Morrows that the mobile home was a "good trailer," " . . . as warm as . . . any other trailer." After the sale, Miller moved the Morrows' mobile home to Lakeview Terrace, set it up on the space the Morrows had rented, and made sure that the utilities were connected. Then the troubles started.

On the first night that the mobile home's furnace was in use, the motor went out and had to be replaced. The electric furnace installed by the manufacturer had been removed by someone who had replaced the original with an oil furnace. The furnace vent did not fit, and consequently the "stove pipe" vibrated when the furnace was running. Subsequent events showed the furnace malfunction was not the primary problem with the mobile home.

About four days after the mobile home had been set up, the Morrows noticed that the doors did not close all the way and that the windows were cracked. The bathtub leaked water into the middle bedroom. In March of 1970 when the snow on the roof began to melt, the roof leaked. Water came in through gaps between the ceiling and the wall panels, as well as along the bottom of the wallboard. A short circuit developed in the electrical system; the lights flickered at various times. When it rained, water came out of the light fixture in the hallway. Other problems with the mobile home included the following: the interior walls did not fit together at the corners; the paneling came off the walls; the windows and doors were out of square; the door frames on the bedroom doors fell off and the closet doors would not slide properly; the curtains had glue on them; and the finish came off the kitchen cabinet doors.

Despite all these problems, the Morrows continued to live in the mobile home and make the loan payments. Golden Heart Mobile Homes was notified many times of the difficulties the Morrows were having with their mobile home. Roy Miller, the Golden Heart salesman with whom the Morrows had dealt, did put some caulking around the bathtub, but otherwise he was of little assistance. Finally, sometime before April 1, 1970, Nikki Morrow informed Miller that if Golden Heart did not fix the mobile home the Morrows wanted to return it. Miller said the Morrows would "[h]ave to take it up with the bank." Subsequently, Golden Heart went out of business.

The First National Bank of Fairbanks was more sensitive to the Morrows' plight. Upon being informed by the Morrows that they intended to make no further payments on the mobile home, bank personnel went out and inspected the home several times. In addition, on May 27, 1970, the bank wrote to New Moon Homes, Inc. in Silverton, Oregon. Its letter informed New Moon of the problems the Morrows were having with their New Moon mobile home and asked whether New Moon expected to send a representative to Fairbanks since Golden Heart, the dealer, was no longer in business. Apparently, New Moon did not respond to the bank's letter.

A short time later the Morrows' counsel wrote a letter to New Moon Homes notifying New Moon that the Morrows intended to hold the company liable for damages for breach of implied warranties. About a month later the Morrows separated, with Nikki Morrow continuing to live in the mobile home. She continued to make payments to First National because she "couldn't afford Alaskan rents." Nikki Morrow eventually moved out of the mobile home but made no effort to sell or rent it because she considered it "not fit to live in." In October of 1971 the Morrows filed this action against both New Moon Homes and Golden Heart Mobile Homes, alleging that defendants had breached implied warranties of merchantability and fitness for particular purpose in manufacturing and selling an improperly constructed mobile home. The complaint further alleged that New Moon "is a foreign corporation doing business in the State of Alaska." Although the record does not disclose the method by which New Moon was informed of the pending action, apparently the Morrows served a copy of the summons and complaint upon the Commissioner of Commerce, who forwarded the papers to New Moon in Oregon. In its answer New Moon *inter alia* raised the "affirmative defenses" of lack of personal jurisdiction and improper service of process.

The case was tried in July of 1973. No attorney appeared on behalf of Golden Heart Mobile Homes, but the Morrows proceeded to present their evidence against New Moon because they were looking primarily to the manufacturer for recovery. The Morrows offered the testimony of four witnesses which tended to identify the mobile home in question as a New Moon home. Neither side presented any evidence concerning New Moon's business connections with Alaska or the circumstances under which the New Moon mobile home came into Golden Heart's possession. The superior court granted the Morrows a default judgment against Golden Heart, but dismissed their claim against New Moon "for both failure of jurisdiction and failure of privity of contract." The Morrows then appealed from that portion of the superior court's judgment which dismissed their claim against New Moon.

The heart of this appeal concerns the remedies which are available to a remote purchaser against the manufacturer of defective goods for direct economic loss. The superior court held that the Morrows had no legal claim against New Moon because they were not in privity of contract with New Moon. The first argument advanced here by the Morrows amounts to an end run around the requirement of privity. The Morrows contend that their complaint asserted a theory of strict liability in tort. They further argue that they should have prevailed irrespective of any lack of privity of contract between New Moon and themselves, because lack of privity of contract is not a defense to a strict tort liability claim....

Under the Uniform Commercial Code the manufacturer is given the right to avail himself of certain affirmative defenses which can minimize his liability for a purely economic loss. Specifically, the manufacturer has the opportunity, pursuant to [UCC 2–316], to disclaim liability and under [UCC 2–719] to limit the consumer's remedies, although the Code further provides that such disclaimers and limitations cannot be so oppressive as to be unconscionable and thus violate [UCC 2–302]. In addition, the manufacturer is entitled to reasonably prompt notice from the consumer of the claimed breach of warranties, pursuant to [UCC 2–607(3)(a).]

In our view, recognition of a doctrine of strict liability in tort for economic loss would seriously jeopardize the continued viability of these rights. The economically injured consumer would have a theory of redress not envisioned by our legislature when it enacted the U.C.C., since this strict liability remedy would be completely unrestrained by disclaimer, liability limitation and notice provisions. Further, manufacturers could no longer look to the Uniform Commercial Code provisions to provide a predictable definition of potential liability for direct economic loss. In short, adoption of the doctrine of strict liability for economic loss would be contrary to the legislature's intent when it authorized the aforementioned remedy limitations and risk allocation provisions of Article II of the Code. To extend strict tort liability to reach the Morrows' case would in effect be an assumption of legislative prerogative on our part and would vitiate clearly articulated statutory rights. This we decline to do. Thus, we hold that the theory of strict liability in tort ... does not extend to the consumer who suffers only economic loss because of defective goods.

The principal theory of liability advocated by the Morrows at trial was that New Moon had breached statutory warranties which arose by operation of law with the manufacture and distribution of this mobile home. Specifically, the Morrows rely upon [UCC 2–314] and [UCC 2–315] of the Uniform Commercial Code as enacted in Alaska. The former section provides for an implied warranty of "merchantability" in the sale of goods governed by the Code; the latter establishes an implied warranty that the goods are fit for the particular purpose for which they were purchased. The superior court was of the view that these Code warranties operated only for the benefit of those purchasing directly from a manufacturer or seller. Since the Morrows were not in privity of contract with New Moon, the superior court concluded that a warranty theory based on [UCC 2–314] and [UCC 2–315] could not serve as a basis for liability. ...

It is equally clear that in this jurisdiction the Morrows, as immediate purchasers, can recover against their seller for breach of the Code's implied warranties. Indeed, this was the theory upon which the default judgment against Golden Heart Mobile Homes was predicated. The critical question in this case is whether the Morrows, as remote purchasers, can invoke the warranties attributable to the manufacturer which arose when New Moon passed title of the mobile home to the next party in the chain of distribution. In other words, do the implied warranties of merchantability and fitness run from a manufacturer only to those with whom the manufacturer is in privity of contract?

Although sometimes criticized, the distinction between horizontal and vertical privity is significant in this case. The issue of horizontal privity raises the question whether persons other than the buyer of defective goods can recover from the buyer's immediate seller on a warranty theory. The question of vertical privity is whether parties in the distributive chain prior to the immediate seller can be held liable to the ultimate purchaser for loss caused by the defective product. The Code addresses the matter of horizontal privity in [UCC 2–318], extending the claim for relief in warranty to any " ... person who is in the family or household of his buyer or who is a guest in his home if it is reasonable to expect that the person may use, consume, or be affected by the goods...." With regard to vertical privity, the Code is totally silent and strictly neutral, as Official Comment 3 to [UCC 2–318] makes eminently clear. The Code leaves to the courts the question of the extent to which vertical privity of contract will or will not be required.

This court has never previously confronted the question whether a requirement of privity of contract will preclude a purchaser from recovering against the original manufacturer on a theory of implied warranties. ... [W]e expressly held in Clary v. Fifth Avenue Chrysler Center, Inc., 454 P.2d 244 (Alaska 1969), that a manufacturer is strictly liable in tort for personal injuries attributable to his defective goods. In approving a theory based on strict liability in tort, we stressed the efficacy, simplicity, and comprehensiveness of that theory. Appellees in *Clary* had urged this court to limit the consumer's source of redress to possible application of the statutory provisions governing sales warranties, particularly [UCC 2–313: Express Warranties]. This we declined to do. As we have noted, under the statutory scheme an injured consumer is required to give notice of the defect to the warrantor within a relatively short period of time, and potential liability may be circumscribed by express disclaimers from the manufacturer. The *Clary* court was concerned that such provisions might operate as a trap for the unwary, and it expressed a preference for a tort theory more solicitous of the needs of the consumer in the modern, prepackaged, mass merchandised market place. However, this preference was never intended to imply that reliance on the statutory warranty provisions was not available as an alternative vehicle for relief. There is nothing incompatible in affording parallel consumer remedies sounding in tort and in contract, and several jurisdictions which have adopted strict liability in tort also make available an implied warranty theory without regard to privity of contract.

The dispute here is whether the requirement of vertical privity of contract should be abolished in Alaska. This battle has already been waged in many jurisdictions, and the results are well known: the citadel of privity has largely toppled. The course of this modern development is familiar history and we need not recount it at length here. Contrived "exceptions" which paid deference to the hoary doctrine of privity while obviating its unjust results have given way in more recent years to an open frontal assault. The initial attack came in Spence v. Three Rivers Builders & Masonry Supply, Inc., 353 Mich. 120, 90 N.W.2d 873 (1958), but the leading case probably remains Henningsen v. Bloomfield Motors, Inc., 32 N.J. 358, 161 A.2d 69 (1960), in which the New Jersey Supreme Court held liable for personal injuries and property damages both the manufacturer of an automobile and the dealer who sold the vehicle. The rationale for the widespread abolition of the requirement of privity stems from the structure and operation of the free market economy in contemporary society; it was succinctly summed up not long ago by the Supreme Court of Pennsylvania [in Kassab v. Central Soya, 432 Pa. 217, 246 A.2d 848, 853 (1968)]:

> Courts and scholars alike have recognized that the typical consumer does not deal at arms length with the party whose product he buys. Rather, he buys from a retail merchant who is usually little more than an economic conduit. It is not the merchant who has defectively manufactured the product. Nor is it usually the merchant who advertises the product on such a large scale as to attract consumers. We have in our society literally scores of large, financially responsible manufacturers who place their wares in the stream of commerce not only with the realization, but with the avowed purpose, that these goods will find their way into the hands of the consumer. Only the consumer will use these products; and only the consumer will be injured by them should they prove defective.

The policy considerations which dictate the abolition of privity are largely those which also warranted imposing strict tort liability on the manufacturer: the consumer's inability to protect himself adequately from defectively manufactured goods, the implied assurance of the maker when he puts his goods on the market that they are safe, and the superior risk bearing ability of the manufacturer. In addition, limiting a consumer under the Code to an implied warranty action against his immediate seller in those instances when the product defect is attributable to the manufacturer would effectively promote circularity of litigation and waste of judicial resources. Therefore, we decide that a manufacturer may be held liable for a breach of the implied warranties of [UCC 2–314] and [UCC 2–315] without regard to privity of contract between the manufacturer and the consumer.

The more difficult question before this court is whether we should extend this abolition of privity to embrace not only warranty actions for personal injuries and property damage but also those for economic loss. Contemporary courts have been more reticent to discard the privity requirement and to permit recovery in warranty by a remote consumer for purely economic losses. In considering this issue we note that economic loss may be categorized into direct economic loss and consequential economic loss, a distinction maintained in the Code's structure of damage remedies. One commentator has summarized the distinction:

Direct economic loss may be said to encompass damage based on insufficient product value; thus, direct economic loss may be "out of pocket"—the difference in value between what is given and received—or "loss of bargain"—the difference between the value of what is received and its value as represented. Direct economic loss also may be measured by costs of replacement and repair. Consequential economic loss includes all indirect loss, such as loss of profits resulting from inability to make use of the defective product.

The claim of the Morrows in this case is one for direct economic loss.

A number of courts recently confronting this issue have declined to overturn the privity requirement in warranty actions for economic loss. One principal factor seems to be that these courts simply do not find the social and economic reasons which justify extending enterprise liability to the victims of personal injury or property damage equally compelling in the case of a disappointed buyer suffering "only" economic loss. There is an apparent fear that economic losses may be of a far greater magnitude in value than personal injuries, and being somehow less foreseeable these losses would be less insurable, undermining the risk spreading theory of enterprise liability.

Several of the courts which have recently considered this aspect of the privity issue have found those arguments unpersuasive. We are in agreement and hold that there is no satisfactory justification for a remedial scheme which extends the warranty action to a consumer suffering personal injury or property damage but denies similar relief to the consumer "fortunate" enough to suffer only direct economic loss. . . .

The fear that if the implied warranty action is extended to direct economic loss, manufacturers will be subjected to liability for damages of unknown and unlimited scope would seem unfounded. The manufacturer may possibly delimit the scope of his potential liability by use of a disclaimer in compliance with [UCC 2–316] or by resort to the limitations authorized in [UCC 2–719]. These statutory rights not only preclude extending the theory of strict liability in tort, supra, but also make highly appropriate this extension of the theory of implied warranties. Further, by expanding warranty rights to redress this form of harm, we preserve " . . . the well developed notion that the law of contract should control actions for purely economic losses and that the law of tort should control actions for personal injuries." We therefore hold that a manufacturer can be held liable for direct economic loss attributable to a breach of his implied warranties, without regard to privity of contract between the manufacturer and the ultimate purchaser.[42] It was therefore error for the trial court to dismiss the Morrows' action against New Moon for want of privity.

---

42. We recognize that the arguments against the abolition of privity are more compelling when the injury alleged is damages of a consequential nature many times the value of the manufacturer's product. See, e.g., Note, Economic Loss in Products

Our decision today preserves the statutory rights of the manufacturer to define his potential liability to the ultimate consumer, by means of express disclaimers and limitations, while protecting the legitimate expectation of the consumer that goods distributed on a wide scale by the use of conduit retailers are fit for their intended use. The manufacturer's rights are not, of course, unfettered. Disclaimers and limitations must comport with the relevant statutory prerequisites and cannot be so oppressive as to be unconscionable within the meaning of [UCC 2–302]. On the other hand, under the Code the consumer has a number of responsibilities if he is to enjoy the right of action we recognize today, not the least of which is that he must give notice of the breach of warranty to the manufacturer pursuant to [UCC 2–607]. The warranty action brought under the Code must be brought within the statute of limitations period prescribed in [UCC 2–725]. If the action is for breach of the implied warranty of fitness for particular purpose, created by [UCC 2–315], the consumer must establish that the warrantor had reason to know the particular purpose for which the goods were required and that the consumer relied on the seller's skill or judgment to select or furnish suitable goods. In the case of litigation against a remote manufacturer, it would appear that often it will be quite difficult to establish this element of actual or constructive knowledge essential to this particular warranty.

In the case at bar the trial judge failed to enter written findings of fact.... We cannot determine from the record whether the Morrows would have prevailed on a theory of breach of implied warranties had the trial court not erred in raising the barrier of privity. Trial was had over two years ago. We are therefore of the opinion that, if the dismissal for want of jurisdiction was also erroneous, a new trial is warranted at which the Morrows will have the opportunity to assert their warranty theories free from the confines of privity. It is to the jurisdictional ruling that we now turn....

... Consequently, we order that this cause be remanded for a new trial in which Morrows will have the opportunity to establish every element of their case, including personal jurisdiction over New Moon.

Reversed and remanded for a new trial in accordance with this opinion.

ERWIN, JUSTICE (concurring). While I concur with the opinion, I would extend the concept of strict liability to cover "economic loss" rather than use the warranty theory advanced by the majority.

The history of products liability law does not justify a distinction between personal injury and property damage. The primary purpose of

Liability Jurisprudence, 66 Colum.L.Rev. 917, 965–66 (1965). We do not speak today to the issue of consequential economic loss, other than to note that [UCC 2–715] governs the recovery of such damages and requires, among other things, that said damages must have been foreseeable by the manufacturer. Adams v. J.I. Case Co., 125 Ill.App.2d 388, 261 N.E.2d 1 (1970).

the strict liability rule is to insure that the costs of injuries resulting from defective products are borne by the manufacturers that put such products on the market rather than by the consumers who are powerless to protect themselves.

Those in favor of the dichotomy between "economic loss" and other types of damage argue that an abolition of the distinction would result in manufacturers being liable for damages of unknown and unlimited scope. This concept is embraced by the majority, which notes that the manufacturer who may now minimize liability by relying on certain provisions in the Uniform Commercial Code, would be unable to do so if the doctrine of strict liability were applied. In essence, this position intimates that manufacturers' rights under the Uniform Commercial Code should be maintained in order to assure the predictability of their potential liability.

... [T]he concerns expressed by the majority in this case would for all intents and purposes be eliminated if the notion of "defective" in the strict liability doctrine is viewed as co-extensive with the concept of "unmerchantability" in the implied warranty field. The term has been well defined by case law and has a fixed meaning so far as the Uniform Commercial Code is concerned.

If the doctrine of strict liability were adopted for cases such as the present one, the ordinary consumer, whose bargaining power is seldom equal to the manufacturers', would have the opportunity to bring an action against the original wrongdoer, instead of the local retailer who served as little more than a conduit for the defective product. ...

Notes

(1) **Sequential Actions or Direct Action.** No vertical privity problems arise if a retail buyer of a manufactured product brings suit against the dealer from whom the product was purchased. If the buyer's complaint is based upon the condition of the product as it left the plant of the manufacturer, the retailer will have a cause of action against its supplier, and so in sequence up the chain of distribution to the manufacturer, who will bear ultimate liability.

Two procedural devices facilitate such back-to-back law suits. Modern procedures permit impleader. See, e.g., Fed.R.Civ.P. 14. Less well known is the Code's statutory version of the device of vouching-in, provided by UCC 2–607(5).

In light of this, what justifies permitting implied warranty actions by consumer buyers against remote manufacturers for the buyers' disappointment in the quality of their goods? Is the court's rationale in *Morrow* persuasive?

(2) **Contract Description and Merchantability.** When consumer buyers sue remote manufacturers for economic loss, the buyers are likely to rely principally on the warranty of merchantability as defined

in UCC 2–314(2)(c) (not fit for the ordinary purposes for which such goods are used). What determines "such goods"? Suppose a manufacturer sold certain goods as "seconds." Thereafter some of the goods came into the possession of a consumer buyer who was not told that they were not regular merchandise. Is the manufacturer liable to the consumer buyer for the difference between the value of regular merchandise and the value of the goods that are "seconds"?

(3) Change in Condition of the Goods After Manufacture. For many reasons, goods can deteriorate during the time they are in the chain of distribution. In warranty of merchantability actions for economic loss by consumer buyers against remote manufacturers, who has the burden of proving the quality of the goods as they left the manufacturers' plants?

Recall in *Morrow* that the mobile home had been modified at some time after the sale by the manufacturer to change the heating system. Is a manufacturer liable for modifications made by others? Suppose, for example, that a new car dealer agrees to sell a car from the dealer's inventory to a consumer buyer; the buyer, however, wants a car with a sun roof, which the seller agrees to install. Is the manufacturer of the car liable if the sun roof leaks?

Manufactured goods are commonly sold by manufacturers with the expectation that retail dealers or others will perform certain functions to make the goods ready for delivery to consumers. New car dealers undertake a large number of such tasks (the "dealer-prep" functions). Is a manufacturer liable for inadequate performance of these tasks by a retailer?

(4) Measure of Ordinary Damages for Economic Loss. Market value of a product at the retail level is normally considerably higher than the market value as the products first enter the chain of distribution. In a warranty action, a buyer's damages are measured by the value the goods would have had if they had been as warranted. UCC 2–714(2). If a remote manufacturer is held liable to a consumer buyer, which market level establishes the value of the goods as warranted?

(5) Consequential Economic Losses. In warranty actions by consumers buyers against remote manufacturers, can damages be recovered for buyers' consequential economic losses? Note the way the *Morrow* court dealt with this question. In what circumstances could a manufacturer, at the time of its sale of a product, have reason to know of the general or particular needs of an unknown consumer?

(6) Warranty Disclaimers and Clauses Limiting Damages. The *Morrow* court stated that its decision preserved manufacturers' statutory rights to define contractually their potential implied warranty liability to ultimate consumers. How would a manufacturer, who is making no express warranty to ultimate consumers, contract effectively with them? Must a disclaimer or damage limitation clause, to be binding on a consumer, be part of the retail contract with the consumer? Is a post-sale disclaimer or damage limitation clause binding? Recall UCC 2–316, 2–719; cf. *Hill v. BASF Wyandotte Corp.*

(7) Notice of Breach to Remote Manufacturers. The *Morrow* court stated that consumer buyers have responsibilities, not the least of which is the responsibility to give notice of breach to the manufacturer. Recall that the birth of strict tort liability for personal injury resulted from the failure of the Greenmans to give timely notice of breach to the manufacturer. Suppose a dissatisfied consumer gave timely notice to the retailer, but not to the remote manufacturer. Would the consumer be barred from any remedy against the manufacturer?

(8) Statute of Limitations on Manufacturers' Liability. The *Morrow* court stated that a consumer must bring action against a manufacturer within the time permitted by UCC 2–725. Under that provision, the period of limitations begins when tender of delivery is made. Does the statute run from the date of manufacturer's tender of delivery or from the date of the retailer's tender? See Heller v. U.S. Suzuki Motor Corp., 64 N.Y.2d 407, 488 N.Y.S.2d 132, 477 N.E.2d 434 (1985) (statute runs from date of manufacturer's tender).

(9) Fitness for Particular Purpose. The *Morrow* court "decided" that a manufacturer may be held liable for breach of either the implied warranty of merchantability or the implied warranty of fitness for particular purpose. How would a consumer buyer communicate to the remote manufacturer the buyer's particular purpose for which the goods are required and be in a position to rely reasonably on the manufacturer's skill and judgment in selecting or furnishing suitable goods? If the consumer buyer communicated to the retailer, would a manufacturer be liable for the retailer's lack of skill or judgment in selecting the wrong goods?

Problem 4. A home owner, needing paint for a masonry wall, went to a local paint store and described the project to the salesperson. The salesperson recommended Pierce's shingle-and-shake paint. Following the recommendation, home owner bought and applied that paint to the masonry wall. The results were totally unsatisfactory. Is Pierce Co., the paint manufacturer, liable to the home owner? Cf. Catania v. Brown, 4 Conn.Cir. 344, 231 A.2d 668 (1967).

(10) Components Suppliers. The image of vertical privity has products moving down a chain of distribution from manufacturers to consumers. In many instances, however, the final product contains many components made by others and sold to the manufacturer. May consumer buyers recover from the even more remote suppliers of components to the remote manufacturers?

(11) Remote Sellers of Primary Goods. If the goods in question are primary goods, such as crude oil or tomatoes, should remote sellers or farmers be liable to ultimate buyers?

SZAJNA v. GENERAL MOTORS CORP.

Supreme Court of Illinois, 1986.
115 Ill.2d 294, 104 Ill.Dec. 898, 503 N.E.2d 760.

JUSTICE RYAN delivered the opinion of the court. The plaintiff, John L. Szajna (Szajna), filed a suit in the circuit court of Cook County against the defendant, General Motors Corporation (GM), on his own behalf and on behalf of all others who bought 1976 Pontiac Venturas which were equipped with Chevette transmissions....

The following allegations were common to all three counts of Szajna's second amended complaint. In August 1976, he bought a 1976 Pontiac Ventura from Seltzer Pontiac, Inc. (Seltzer), in Chicago. Seltzer, as agent for GM, gave Szajna a folder which contained two warranties: one entitled a "Limited Warranty On 1976 Pontiac Car" and another entitled "1976 Pontiac Passenger Car Emission Control System." It was alleged that both warranties were made by GM to Szajna. It was also alleged that thousands of the cars sold as 1976 Pontiac Venturas, including Szajna's, were equipped with Chevette transmissions; that the use of Chevette transmissions in Pontiac Venturas necessitates higher amounts of repairs and that they have shorter service lives than do transmissions ordinarily used in Pontiac Venturas because the Chevette transmission was designed for use in a lighter weight car; that use of the Chevette transmission in Pontiac Venturas lessens the value of the cars; and that Szajna paid $375 to have the transmission in his car replaced.

The following allegations were also common to all three counts. GM manufactured, labeled and made available through its Pontiac Division the 1976 Pontiac Ventura. GM designed and engineered a transmission specifically for the 1976 Pontiac Ventura. "Through its brochures, parts catalogues and repair manuals, as well as through the release of automobile news and information from its public relations department," GM "advised the expert observers, testers and reporters of the nature of the '1976 Pontiac Ventura' model as including the transmission designed for that size of car." The public and Szajna, in buying the cars, relied on the experts and on GM for any noteworthy information on GM cars not readily observable. No information was given to the public or the experts that some of the 1976 Pontiac Venturas were equipped with Chevette transmissions.

Count I of Szajna's second amended complaint alleges breach of implied warranty under section 2–314 of the UCC. It alleges that 1976 Pontiac Venturas equipped with Chevette transmissions were not merchantable because they "would not pass without objection in the trade" under the contract description; "were not of fair average quality within the description, did not run within the variations permitted by the agreement of even kind and quality and did not conform to their labels" as Pontiac Venturas. (See Ill. Rev. Stat. 1975, ch. 26, pars. 2–314(2)(a), (b), (d), (f).) (The "description" referred to above was the name 1976 Pontiac Ventura.) Count I also alleges that the failure by GM to deliver 1976 Pontiac Venturas as warranted rendered them nonconforming goods for which Szajna and other purchasers could ... receive damages (Ill. Rev. Stat. 1975, ch. 26, par. 2–714).

Szajna also alleges in count I breach of implied warranty pursuant to section 110(d) of Magnuson–Moss, which provides that a consumer who is damaged by the failure of a supplier or warrantor to comply with any obligation under an implied warranty may bring suit for damages and other legal and equitable relief in any court of competent jurisdiction in any State. 15 U.S.C. sec. 2310(d)(1) (1976).

In dismissing count I of Szajna's second amended complaint, the trial court entered the following conclusions of law. First, privity of contract is a prerequisite in Illinois to a suit for breach of implied warranty alleging economic loss. Second, Magnuson–Moss, in permitting recovery for breach of implied warranty, incorporates State-law privity requirements. (15 U.S.C. sec. 2301(7) (1976).) Third, no privity of contract existed between Szajna and GM. Fourth, the limited written warranty extended by GM, although running to the ultimate purchaser, did not give rise to the implied warranty of merchantability. The appellate court, in essence, adopted the trial court's conclusions of law. It was of the opinion, however, that while Szajna and GM "were in privity for purposes of the provisions in the express limited warranty, they were not in privity for purposes of implied warranties, which were specifically disclaimed by the express warranty." Szajna v. General Motors Corp. (1985), 130 Ill.App.3d 173, 177....

Magnuson–Moss, enacted by Congress in 1975, ... does not require that warranty be given, but if there is a *written* warranty, Magnuson–Moss imposes certain requirements as to its contents, disclosures, and the effect of extending a written warranty. ... No supplier may disclaim or modify an implied warranty, except a supplier giving a limited written warranty may limit the duration of an implied warranty to the duration of the written warranty if such limitation is conscionable and is clearly set forth (15 U.S.C. sec. 2308 (1976).) ... In this case we are concerned only with the question of whether, under Magnuson–Moss, Szajna can maintain an action based on an implied warranty against the manufacturer of the automobile. ... Section 2301(7) defines implied warranty as follows:

> The term "implied warranty" means an implied warranty arising under State law (as modified by sections 2308 and 2304(a) of this title) in connection with the sale by a supplier of a consumer product. (15 U.S.C. sec. 2301(7) (1976).)

Focusing on that part of the definition stating the term means "an implied warranty arising under State law," some authors maintain that if the law of the State holds that privity is essential to implied warranty, then an action such as is involved in our case cannot be maintained. (Miller & Kanter, *Litigation Under Magnuson–Moss: New Opportunities in Private Actions,* 13 U.C.C. L.J. 10, 22 (1980).) However, the definition also states that the term means an implied warranty arising under State law "(*as modified by sections 2308 and 2304(a) of this title*)." (Emphasis added.) (15 U.S.C. sec. 2301(7) (1976).) Section 2308 provides:

> "No supplier may disclaim or modify (except as provided in subsection (b) of this section [limiting the duration of an implied warranty to the duration of a 'limited' written warranty]) any implied warranty to a consumer * * * if (1) such supplier makes any written warranty to the consumer * * * or (2) at the time of sale, or within 90 days thereafter, such supplier enters into a service contract with the consumer which applies to such consumer product." (15 U.S.C. sec. 2308(a) (1976).)

This section raises the question as to whether it modifies implied-warranty State-law provisions to the extent that any written warranty given by a manufacturer to a remote purchaser creates an implied warranty by virtue of Magnuson–Moss. At the very least we must acknowledge that the provisions of section 2308 clearly demonstrate the policy of Magnuson–Moss to sustain the protection afforded to consumers by implied warranties.

The Act broadly defines "consumer" in section 2301(3) as "a buyer (other than for purposes of resale) of any consumer product, any person to whom such product is transferred during the duration of an implied or written warranty * * * and any other person who is entitled by the terms of such warranty * * * or under applicable State law to enforce against the warrantor * * * the obligations of the warranty." (15 U.S.C. sec. 2301(3) (1976).) It has been suggested that this broad definition of "consumer" and the provisions of section 2310(d)(1) (15 U.S.C. sec. 2310(d)(1) (1976)), which section authorizes a "consumer" to maintain a civil action for damages for failure of a "supplier" or "warrantor" to comply with any obligation of a written or implied warranty, effectively abolish vertical privity. (See Comment, *Consumer Product Warranties Under the Magnuson–Moss Warranty Act and the Uniform Commercial Code,* 62 Cornell L. Rev. 738, 755–59 (1977).) We do not think we can focus on any one section of Magnuson–Moss but should read the sections referred to together to accomplish the purpose of Magnuson–Moss of furnishing broad protection to the consumer.

In resolving this murky situation we find helpful, and accept, Professor Schroeder's analysis and suggestion as a reasonable solution. In cases where no Magnuson–Moss written warranty has been given, Magnuson–Moss has no effect upon State-law privity requirements because, by virtue of section 2301(7), which defines implied warranty, implied warranty arises only if it does so under State law. However, if a Magnuson–Moss written warranty (either "full" or "limited") is given by reason of the policy against disclaimers of implied warranty expressed in Magnuson–Moss and the provisions authorizing a consumer to sue a warrantor, the nonprivity "consumer" should be permitted to maintain an action on an implied warranty against the "warrantor." (Schroeder, *Privity Actions Under the Magnuson–Moss Warranty Act*, 66 Calif.L.Rev. 1, 16 (1978).) The rationale of this conclusion, though not specifically articulated by Professor Schroeder in the article, would hold that under Magnuson–Moss a warrantor, by extending a written warranty to the consumer, establishes privity between the warrantor and the consumer which, though limited in nature, is sufficient to support an implied warranty under sections 2–314 and 2–315 of the UCC. The implied warranty thus recognized, by virtue of the definition in section 2301(7) of Magnuson–Moss, must be one arising under the law of this State. .... .

The appellate court in this case held that while the parties were in privity for purposes of the provisions of the express written limited warranty which General Motors had extended, they were not in privity for the purposes of implied warranty. (130 Ill.App.3d 173, 177.) This holding is in conflict with our holding herein and will therefore be reversed....

Notes

(1) **Rationale.** The Illinois Supreme Court based its holding in *Szajna,* regarding privity in implied warranty claims, on a policy perceived to underlie the Magnuson–Moss Warranty Act. Is the court's reading of the federal statute persuasive? Should the court have based its holding on state law? Suppose a manufacturer of a consumer good makes an express warranty to retail consumers, but the express warranty is not a "written warranty" under the Magnuson–Moss Act. Would the Illinois court conclude that privity exists for purpose of enforcing the express warranty, but would not exist for purpose of enforcing the implied warranty of merchantability?

(2) **UCC 2–318; Non–uniform Variations.** In an omitted portion of *Szajna,* the Illinois court agreed with the *Morrow* court that the Code does not address the privity problems presented in those cases. Both states had adopted the version of that section now referred to as Alternative A. Do Alternatives B or C address the privity problems in *Morrow* or *Szajna?*

Several legislatures have found all of the Editorial Board's proposals unsatisfactory. Some have deleted Section 2–318 entirely; others have revised 2–318, usually to lower the privity barrier. In this area there is little uniformity of even the statutory text, and case-law development has been even more individualistic. Local variations can be found in Uniform Laws Annotated.

———

COLLINS COMPANY, LTD. v. CARBOLINE COMPANY

Supreme Court of Illinois, 1988.
125 Ill.2d 498, 127 Ill.Dec. 5, 532 N.E.2d 834.

Justice Stamos delivered the opinion of the court. This cause is before us on a question of Illinois law certified by the United States Court of Appeals for the Seventh Circuit. The certified question is:

In the absence of original contractual privity, does an express warranty extend to an assignee's right to sue for purely economic loss and consequential damages?

For the reasons that follow and with the qualifications noted, we answer the question in the affirmative.

FACTS ...

In March 1981, Chicago Title and Trust Company, as trustee (Chicago Title), and Wachovia Bank and Trust Company, N.A. (Wachovia), owned a warehouse in Elk Grove Village, Illinois. The owners contracted with Flexible Roof Contractors, a wholly owned division of Pureco Systems, Inc. (Pureco), to replace the roofing system at the warehouse. The roofing system was to be replaced with one manufactured by Carboline Company (Carboline).

In manufacturing and supplying the system, Carboline issued an express written warranty, warranting the installed system against leakage for 10 years from the date of completing the installation, which was stated in the warranty as March 17, 1981. The warranty also stated that final inspection of the installation by Carboline occurred on March 19, 1981, and that the warranty would be effective only upon Carboline's inspection and acceptance of the installation. The warranty copy attached to the complaint does not appear to bear a signature in behalf of Carboline, but in its answer Carboline admitted that it issued "to Wachovia Bank & Trust Co., N.A." a warranty as exemplified by the copy and that the warranty "speaks for itself."

The warranty contained numerous terms, limitations, and conditions and disclaimed any warranty of merchantability or of fitness for a particular purpose. It provided that Carboline's sole warranty obligation should be to repair roofing leaks caused by defects in the roofing material or by the roofing applicator's workmanship and that Carboline's financial liability for the repairs should not exceed "the owner's original cost" of the installed system....

The warranty did not specifically identify the warrantee. In a blank labeled "Project Name and Location," the following legend was inserted: "Jarvis Ave. Job—1441 Jarvis Ave. Elk Grove Village, IL." On a second, unlabeled blank line immediately below was inserted "Chicago Title & Trust Co., Ancillary Trustee/Trust Agreement # 09–

64234." On a third blank line labeled "Owner" and appearing immediately below the second line, the name "Wachovia Bank & Trust Co., N.A." was inserted. As completed, the warranty form did not make clear whether the Chicago Title designation was meant to denote an additional "owner" or simply to further identify the "project name and location"; however, at the end of the form, in a blank labeled "OWNER ACCEPTANCE," the words "CT & T CO., as Trustee aforesaid" were inserted, followed by a signature and the designation "Vice President" under date of June 1, 1981. A warranty term provided that Carboline would not be liable under the warranty until "the owner" had accepted the roofing contractor's installation by signing the warranty form. Nowhere did the warranty state that it extended or was limited to the "owner," whoever or of whatever that might be. In fact, one term provided merely that the warranty should be void if reasonable care were not used "by the party occupying the building" in maintaining the roof.

It is also noteworthy that, despite the large number of terms and conditions expressed by the warranty form, no term forbade assignment of rights or obligations by any party.

In June 1984, Collins Company, Ltd. (Collins), acquired the warehouse building from Chicago Title and Wachovia. Beginning in or about May 1985, leaks developed in the roofing system, which have caused Collins to incur expense for temporary repairs, will require a complete replacement of the roofing system in the near future, and have interfered with the conduct of Collins' business. In 1986, Chicago Title and Wachovia assigned to Collins their rights under the warranty and any claims or rights they had against Pureco. The assignment was given in exchange for a covenant not to sue.

On March 6, 1986, Collins filed its three-count diversity complaint in the United States District Court for the Northern District of Illinois. . . .

In count I, Collins claimed $500,000 in damages from Carboline for breach of warranty. In that count, Collins asserted that the roofing system was defectively manufactured and installed and that Carboline was obliged under the warranty to replace the system and pay for any damages caused by leakage. Collins also asserted that it had relied on the warranty in deciding to purchase the building and that it had exercised due care in maintaining the roof. . . .

As affirmative defenses, Carboline asserted that the warranty was not assignable and therefore denied that Chicago Title and Wachovia had made an assignment to Collins. Carboline also asserted that the warranty was not issued to Collins. In addition, Carboline asserted that Collins' damages against it, if any, were limited by the warranty terms and that the latter barred Collins' claim. Finally, Carboline asserted that the roof leaks and other damage claimed were caused not by a roofing system defect but by sources beyond Carboline's control for which Carboline has no liability....

[B]ecause it found that Collins was not in privity with Carboline, the district court granted Carboline's motion for judgment. ...

On appeal, the Seventh Circuit court requested that we consider the certified question as one that may be determinative of the cause. ... We accepted the certification, pursuant to our Rule 20.... .

OPINION...

We ... hold that the assignee of a warrantee's rights under an express warranty, if the assignment is otherwise valid, succeeds to all those rights and thus stands in privity with the warrantor. ... Such an assignee's privity would generally enable it to sue for economic loss and consequential damages, just as an original contracting party might do....

We have previously stated that an express warranty is imposed by the parties to a contract and is part of the sale contract and that an action for breach of express warranty is an action ex contractu. ... It is clear that in its contractual nature an express warranty differs materially from an implied warranty. ...

An implied warranty is derived from the interplay of a transaction's factual circumstances with the foreseeable expectations of a buyer or other person who is protected by law in those expectations. ... This is a concept that the common law recognized long before promulgation of the UCC, albeit a concept that was originally rather limited in application. ... The implied warranty arises regardless of an affected seller's actual wishes.

By contrast, the warrantor is the master of the express warranty. ... The warranty arises only because the warrantor has willed it into being by making the requisite affirmation as part of a contract to which it is an adjunct. ...

In this difference between express and implied warranty can arguably be found justification for a differing treatment of the lack of privity when express-warranty claims are made by remote buyers or other persons. ...

While "[p]rivity requires that the party suing has some contractual relationship with the one sued" (Crest Container Corp. v. R.H. Bishop Co. (1982), 111 Ill.App.3d 1068, 1076), privity accompanies a valid assignment of the contract. ...

Once made, an assignment puts the assignee into the shoes of the assignor. ... Because the assignor was in privity with the opposite contracting party, so is the assignee. ...

Despite Carboline's and the district court's reliance for a contrary conclusion on our decision in Szajna v. General Motors Corp. (1986), 115

Ill.2d 294, the holding of that case is in harmony with our decision today.

In Szajna, we were asked to abolish the privity requirement in suits to recover for economic loss when breach of an implied warranty is alleged. ... This we chose not to do, noting our previously expressed preference that recovery for economic loss be had within the framework of contract law. ...

In Szajna we thus declined to extend to subsequent nonprivity buyers the UCC's implied warranties in sales of new automobiles. ... In so declining, we referred to the General Assembly's failure to adopt more expansive versions of the UCC's section 2–318 that would expressly attenuate privity requirements, and we observed that the UCC's overall contractual orientation would accommodate only with some difficulty the further extension of implied warranties to nonprivity parties. ...

Neither do we decide today whether an express warranty such as the one here ... can actually be interpreted to run beyond its original holder even in the absence of formal assignment....

Our decision also potentially gives effect to the ostensible promise of performance made by Carboline in its warranty, instead of rendering the promise illusory on the happenstance basis of a transfer of the warranted goods before the end of the stated warranty period. After all, Carboline could have included a limitation on assignment in its express 10–year warranty if it had so desired. ...

In addition, though the vouching-in procedure established by section 2–607(5) of the UCC ... remains available in proper cases ..., our decision potentially avoids the need for any such circuitous litigation in this case....

In answer to the question certified by the United States Court of Appeals for the Seventh Circuit, we conclude that, because the assignee of an express warranty acquires privity with the warrantor by virtue of a valid assignment, the express warranty does therefore "extend to an assignee's right to sue for purely economic loss and consequential damages."

Notes

(1) **Horizontal or Vertical Privity; UCC 2–318.** Would the privity problem presented in this case be more properly characterized as vertical or horizontal privity? If the issue is one of horizontal privity, could the current owner of the warehouse recover under any version of UCC 2–318? (Recall that Illinois has enacted Alternative A.) If 2–318 does not permit recovery, does that indicate a legislative judgment that recovery should be denied?

(2) **Express and Implied Assignments.** The Illinois court reserved decision on the importance of the former owner's formal assign-

ment of the roofer's repair warranty to the current owner of the warehouse. Should not transfer of a long-term roof warranty be implied in the sale of the building? Would the remaining years of that warranty be of value to the former owner?

(3) Warranty to Original Owner Only. Some sellers and manufacturers, who make repair or replace warranties, provide that the warranties extend to the first consumer purchaser only and do not extend to subsequent owners. Why would warrantors include such a limitation in their warranties? Are such provisions permitted under the Code? See UCC 2–318. Are such provisions permitted under the Magnuson–Moss Act? See 16 C.F.R. §§ 700.6(b), 701.3(a)(1).

If buyers of used goods could enforce express warranties, would they also be entitled to enforce implied warranties. See Bagel v. American Honda Motor Co., 132 Ill.App.3d 82, 87 Ill.Dec. 453, 477 N.E.2d 54 (1985) (second owner had no right to enforce implied warranty of merchantability); Johnson v. General Motors Corp., 349 Pa.Super. 147, 502 A.2d 1317 (1986) (widow of first consumer had no right to enforce implied warranty of merchantability).

(B) INTERNATIONAL SALES LAW

The Convention on International Sales of Goods has no specific provisions regarding privity of contract.

With regard to vertical privity, CISG provisions on the responsibilities of sellers and rights of buyers are drafted in terms of "the seller" and "the buyer" and "the contract," language which strongly implies a requirement of contractual privity. Suppose, however, that a manufacturer participates actively in marketing its products by providing dealers with the manufacturer's written "warranty" for delivery to buyers from those dealers. Even if it were held that the "warranty" created a contractual obligation to the ultimate buyers, should the rules of the Convention apply to that contractual relationship? See J. Honnold, Uniform Law for International Sales § 63 (2d ed. 1991).[4]

CISG lacks any provision relaxing privity requirements on the horizontal axis. Nothing comparable to UCC 2–318 exists in the Convention. Nor does CISG speak to assignments of unexecuted con-

---

4. In the first edition of this commentary on the Convention, the author concluded that the language of CISG did not reach remote sellers. The point was reconsidered in the second edition in light of the possibility that manufacturers may not only participate in, but may in fact dominate the way in which its products are ultimately sold.

While flexible interpretation of CISG may be urged as a general matter, the Convention's provisions on scope of application should be construed to achieve maximum predictability. J. Honnold, Uniform Law for International Sales § 60.5. Would predictability of CISG's application be endangered by flexible reading of "the seller" to include a remote seller in appropriate cases?

tracts. This may constitute a gap in the Convention for which no general principle is available under CISG 7(2). In that event, issues of assignability and recognition of third party beneficiaries would be governed by that domestic law "applicable by virtue of the rules of private international law."

Problem 5. A United States company enters into a contract to sell and deliver a quantity of crude oil to a French buyer in three months at a port to be specified by the buyer. Both France and the United States have ratified CISG. Before the date for delivery, the French buyer notifies the U.S. seller that it has assigned its rights to the crude oil to a British firm. The United Kingdom has not ratified CISG. Assuming that the assignment is valid, is the contract between the U.S. seller and British assignee governed by the Convention?

Chapter 7

EXECUTION OF SALES CONTRACTS: MANNER, TIME AND PLACE

SECTION 1. INTRODUCTION

Previous chapters were concerned with the "what" (title and quality and price) and the "who" (privity) of sales transactions. In this chapter we consider "when," "where," and "how" the parties execute the promises made in contracts of sale. Most sales involve physical handing over and receiving of goods. Title, a legal abstraction, cannot be delivered physically. However, sometimes title can be reified in a "document of title," a tangible thing that can be handed over to a buyer. Payment of the price may involve physical handing over of money, but payment commonly occurs with delivery of instruments that effect transfer to sellers of bank credits. How, where and when these steps take place can be as important to the parties as are issues of title, quality and price.

Agreed Terms and Default Rules. Buyers and sellers may fix the terms of manner, time and place of performance by agreement. Terms may be set by express agreement or by implication from trade usage, course of dealing, or course of performance. Agreed terms regarding execution may state specifically how, where and when each party is to perform, but it is not uncommon for agreements to confer on one party discretion to determine these matters unilaterally, perhaps within stated limits. Thus, the agreement may require seller to ship goods in March or April, with the exact date determined by the seller. Under domestic United States law, when an agreement "leaves particulars of performance to be specified by one of the parties, . . . specification must be made in good faith and within limits set by commercial reasonableness." UCC 2–311(1).

Buyers and sellers sometimes fail to agree, even by implication, on manner, time and place of each party's performance. To fill those gaps, domestic United States law and the Convention on International Sale of Goods set forth a number of default rules. In this sense, the law reduces the costs of transacting by providing standardized performance terms that become part of the sales contract.[1]

---

1. Recall the definition of "contract" in UCC 1–201(11): "the total legal obligation which results from the parties' agreement as affected by this Act and any other applicable rules of law."

Amount of the Price; "Open" Price Terms. Karl Llewellyn wrote that "Price is the heart of the sales contract." K. Llewellyn, Law of Sales 1 (1930). "Price" is a necessary element for a "sale" under the Commercial Code. UCC 2–106. Nevertheless, parties to sales contracts often agree to the transaction without establishing the price to be paid. The Code declares that the price in such transactions is a "reasonable price at the time for delivery." UCC 2–305(1). What is the relationship between "reasonable price" and market value? To what extent does 2–305 state rules that mirror the probable actual intention of the parties? Most students have explored the meaning of this provision in the course on Contracts.

Price Terms in Long–Term Supply Contracts. In contracting for supply of goods over an extended period of time, parties may fix prices that turn out, later, to be greatly different from the market value of the goods at the time of expected performance. The party disadvantaged by the unexpected rise or fall in market values may seek to be relieved from its obligation to deliver the goods or to pay the contract price.

Quality of the Money; "Legal Tender." Under general federal law, buyers meet their payment obligations if they deliver "legal tender," defined in 31 U.S.C.A. § 5103. For many reasons, buyers and sellers do not use, and do not expect to use "legal tender" in performance of the payment obligation of sales contracts.

Two–Party Execution. Execution of sales contracts often is accomplished by buyers and sellers without the intervention of third parties. Sellers and buyers may meet for handing over of the goods and the money. In retail sales customers commonly go to stores to pick up and pay for goods. Sometimes, sellers, using their own employees or agents, take goods to buyers; dealers' delivery of home heating oil is an example.

Execution Through Third Parties: Carriers and Banks. In other commercial settings, particularly when the parties are at a distance from each other, they will authorize or require use of carriers to transport goods from sellers to buyers. In some settings, the parties will authorize or require that payment of the sales price be made by banks.

Remedies for Non–execution or Improper Execution. Contractual terms on how, when and where sales contracts are to be executed are enforceable obligations. A party who fails, without excuse, to meet an obligation when due is in breach of contract; the aggrieved party will have one or more legal remedies. The terms of parties' agreements or the law's default rules provide the normative standards against which to measure whether sellers' or buyers' acts or omissions were in breach of their obligation to execute sales contracts.

(A) DOMESTIC SALES LAW

Basic performance obligations and related default rules are stated by the Code. The Code provisions are found largely in Parts 3 and 5 of Article 2.

Section 2–301 of the Code states the general obligation of both parties:

> The obligation of the seller is to transfer and deliver and that of the buyer is to accept and pay in accordance with the contract.

Presumably "transfer" refers to title and "deliver" refers to goods. On the buyers' side, the general obligation to "pay" is coupled with the obligation to "accept" the goods. This purport of the obligation to "accept" is, on the surface, strange;[2] if sellers are paid, would they care whether buyers "accept" the goods? We defer further consideration of that matter until the next section.

The parties' UCC 2–301 obligation is elaborated in the operational standards of *tender of delivery* and *tender of payment*. Tender connotes performance by the tendering party that satisfies its obligation and puts the other party in default if it fails to execute its obligation. See UCC 2–507(1) and 2–511(1). The Code's default rules on manner, time and place of the parties' obligations to execute sales contracts are based on the concept of tender.

(1) TWO–PARTY TRANSACTIONS

Manner of Sellers' Tender of Delivery of Goods. "Tender of delivery requires that the seller put and hold conforming goods at the buyer's disposition and give the buyer any notification reasonably necessary to enable him to take delivery." UCC 2–503(1). The "put and hold" formulation, which by implication excludes "let go," is the essence of the concept of tender of goods. Tender must be at a "reasonable hour" and tendered goods must be kept available for "the period reasonably necessary to enable the buyer to take possession." UCC 2–503(1)(a). "Tender" begins delivery, but effecting completed delivery usually requires buyers' response.

Place of Sellers' Tender. If the agreement is silent, the default rule establishes the place of delivery at a merchant seller's place of business. UCC 2–308(a). In this circumstance, a seller tenders by holding the goods at the place of business and notifying buyer that the

---

2. Students should be cautious to avoid confusing "acceptance of goods" with the concepts of offer and acceptance familiar from general contract law and found in the Code in UCC 2–206 and 2–207. "Acceptance of an offer" is a way of describing formation of contracts. "Acceptance of goods" is a concept used in connection with buyers' performance of sales contracts. Referring to "acceptance" without indicating whether one is referring to acceptance of an offer or of goods can be confusing, but context usually indicates which type of acceptance is meant. See, e.g., UCC 2–310.

goods are available.[3] Sellers may agree to take the goods to their buyers; in such transactions, the Code provides that buyers must furnish facilities reasonably suited to receipt of the goods.[4] UCC 2–503(1)(b).

Time of Sellers' Tender. Section 2–503(1)(a) provides that sellers' tender must be made at a reasonable hour and for a reasonable duration, but does not have a default rule for the date on which a seller is required to have the goods ready. The Code's answer is a "reasonable time" standard. UCC 2–309(1). Under this provision, a seller has some leeway before failure to tender delivery becomes a breach of contract. The outside limits of that period of time will be difficult to fix as an exact date.

Manner of Buyers' Tender of Payment. The Code refers to "tender of payment" in UCC 2–511, but does not define what constitutes such a tender. By analogy to tender of delivery, tender of payment occurs when a buyer "puts and holds" money or other instrument or payment device at the disposition of a seller. If a buyer tenders a personal check,[5] seller may insist on legal tender but must give buyer any additional time needed to procure it. UCC 2–511(2).

Time and Place of Tender of Payment. Sales contracts are more likely to have express or implied terms regarding buyers' tender of payment than sellers' tender of delivery. Commonly, parties agree to a time of payment that involves sellers' extending credit to buyers or buyers' making "down payments." Other reasons also explain the greater prevalence of agreed payment terms. Nonetheless, many sales contracts are silent on the manner, time and place of buyers' performance. The Code provides the default rules that fill those gaps in agreements.

Several Code provisions indicate the default rule regarding time and place for buyers' performance of their payment obligation. A buyer's payment is due "at the time and place at which the buyer is to receive the goods.... ." UCC 2–310(a). Before paying, a buyer has the right to inspect the goods. UCC 2–513(1).

Tender of Delivery in "Lots." Ordinarily, sellers must tender all goods at once, but the Code provides for exceptions of partial deliveries.[6]

---

3. The Code has no provision declaring that buyers are contractually obligated to take possession of tendered goods. When sellers put and hold goods at buyers' disposition, in the overwhelming majority of transactions the buyers will dispose of them. They want to have possession of the goods they agreed to buy. That may explain why the Code is silent on the matter.

4. This provision on buyers' obligation is oddly located in a section defining the manner of sellers' tender of delivery. Comment 4 to 2–503 states that this obligation of the buyer is no part of the seller's tender.

5. Personal checks would likely be considered a means of payment "current in the ordinary course of business." UCC 2–511(2). A buyer's personal check is an order by the buyer to a designated bank to pay money to a designated payee on demand. See UCC 3–104.

6. When a single article has been sold, delivery or tender of that article is the only performance possible. However, sometimes the goods sold are physically divisible into "lots." UCC 2–105(5). Under

If a seller properly delivers goods in installments, in the absence of agreement otherwise, a buyer must pay for each delivery if the contract price can be apportioned; otherwise the buyer can withhold payment until all the goods have been tendered. UCC 2–307.

To test your understanding of the performance rules, consider the following problems:

Problem 1. Wire Manufacturer ordered a quantity of certain copper from Copper Trading Co., which agreed to supply it. The sales agreement specified no delivery date. Manufacturer knew that Trading Co. would have to find a source of copper that met Manufacturer's needs, but assumed that no shortage of such copper existed. Trading Co. also assumed that it would have little difficulty locating the needed copper at a favorable price. Trading Co. discovers that the copper market is "tight" and spot prices are high. Trading Co. extends its search for copper to look for a relatively low price in the current market or, if necessary, to wait out what it hopes is a temporary peak in market prices.

(a) Manufacturer, whose inventory of copper is running low, demands that Trading Co. make immediate delivery. Trading Co. responds that it will deliver soon but gives no specific date.

(i) As counsel for Manufacturer, advise it on when Trading Co. was or will be in default.

(ii) As counsel for Trading Co., advise it as to the outside limit of its time for performance without breach.

(b) Manufacturer declares Trading Co. in default and institutes legal action. Which party has the burden of proving that a reasonable time had elapsed before Manufacturer's decision?

Problem 2. Plastics agreed to manufacture and deliver 40,000 pounds of special high-impact polystyrene pellets at 19 cents a pound for Industries. Industries agreed to accept delivery at the rate of 1000 pounds per day as the pellets were produced. Two weeks after the June 30 agreement, Plastics notified Industries that it was ready to deliver. Industries telephoned to say that labor difficulties and vacation schedules made it impossible to receive any pellets immediately; in that conversation Plastics replied that it would complete production and that it hoped that Industries would start taking delivery soon.

(a) On August 18, Plastics wrote to Industries: "We produced 40,000 pounds of high-impact pellets to your special order. You indicated that you would be using 1,000 lbs. per day. We have warehoused

what circumstances may a seller make a proper delivery or tender of less than all of the goods? The agreement may provide for multiple deliveries. In the absence of express agreement, the circumstances may indicate that this is not only proper but necessary. For example, the buyer of a large quantity of bricks needed to construct a large building may lack space at the site to store all the bricks if delivered at one time; when both seller and buyer are aware of this, multiple deliveries are proper. The default rule, however, is that all the goods must be delivered or tendered in a single lot. UCC 2–307.

these products for more than forty days. However, we cannot keep these products indefinitely and request that you begin taking delivery. We have done everything that we agreed to do." After another month, Industries has not taken any pellets. Plastics consults you for legal assistance. What advice would you give? Is UCC 2–610 applicable? Compare Multiplastics, Inc. v. Arch Industries, Inc., 166 Conn. 280, 348 A.2d 618 (1974).

(b) Suppose Plastics had consulted you before sending its August 18 letter. Would you have advised changes in the letter? Would you have set a specific date as a deadline for Industries to take delivery? Is UCC 2–311 helpful? Would you advise sending a written demand pursuant to UCC 2–609(1)?

Problem 3. Consumer and Car Dealer entered into a sales agreement for a new automobile. Three weeks after the agreement, Car Dealer notified Consumer that the specified car had arrived. Consumer went to Car Dealer's place of business, looked at and sat in the car, kicked the tires, lifted the hood and peered at the engine. Consumer asked for the keys in order to "take it for a trial" to see if the car performed satisfactorily. Car Dealer responded that Consumer could have the keys only after he had paid the price. Has Consumer had a reasonable opportunity to inspect? The Code declares that "tender of payment is a condition of the seller's duty to ... complete any delivery." UCC 2–507(1). Does this support Car Dealer's contention that Consumer's right to inspect includes only what Consumer can learn from examination of the goods while still in the Car Dealer's possession?

Problem 4. Recall the inspection arrangements in the flour sale transaction in *T.J. Stevenson & Son,* Chapter 6, Section 2, supra. What determined this method of inspection? Which party must pay the expenses of such inspections? See UCC 2–513(2).

Problem 5. Builder, constructing a new house, ordered appliances from Dealer. The sales contract required Dealer to deliver the appliances to the construction site on February 1. Builder agreed to pay 30 days after delivery. When Dealer's truck arrived, after 5 p.m., all Builder's employees had gone for the night. Dealer's truck driver put the appliances into the garage and locked it. Were Dealer's actions in conformity with the requirements of UCC 2–503? See Ron Mead T.V. & Appliance v. Legendary Homes, Inc., 746 P.2d 1163 (Okl.App.1987).

(2) TRANSACTIONS USING CARRIERS TO DELIVER GOODS

We turn now to transactions in which sellers perform through an intermediary, a carrier, and the necessary adaptation of the law governing performance of sales contracts.[7] Sellers surrender physical

---

7. Goods move to their markets on trucks, railroads, airplanes, and ships whose owners sell this transportation service. Some carriers hold themselves out as

possession of the goods to carriers who in turn surrender possession to buyers. The parties may include in their agreement terms regarding the manner, time and place of execution of contracts in which carriers provide transportation services. However, the Code provides default rules defining tender of delivery and payment in such transactions to fill gaps when agreements are silent.

When sellers are required or authorized by sales contracts to send goods by carrier, the Code recognizes two types of such contracts. Different tender rules apply to these types. If a seller is required to deliver the goods *at a particular destination,* the tender rules applicable to two-party transactions apply. UCC 2–503(3). If a seller is not required to deliver the goods at such destination another set of tender rules applies.[8] UCC 2–503(2) and 2–504.[9]

The Code's meaning of a sales contract requirement to deliver goods via carrier at a particular destination is found by considering other sections. Comment 1 to 2–504 declares that the general principles of the section cover the special cases of "F.O.B. point of shipment contracts." The Comment refers here to certain trade terms that parties to sales contracts commonly use in their agreements. The Code defines the meaning of these contract terms in UCC 2–319 and 2–320. Within those definitions, we find the manner, time and place of sellers' tender of delivery in transactions involving carriers' transport of the goods.

F.O.B. or Free on Board. Parties to sales contracts often use the F.O.B. term, or other similar terms, as convenient shorthand expressions. It is common in sales contracts contemplating land transport by rail or truck. To make sense an F.O.B. term must refer to a designated place where the goods are to be free on board. Choice of the place allocates between buyer and seller the carrier's charges to transport the freight; seller pays for the freight to the specified place.[10] More important for our present purposes, choice of place in an F.O.B. contract also defines sellers' tender obligations.[11]

available to the public; they are deemed "common carriers" and are regulated by federal and state laws. Others, "contract carriers," do not offer their services to the general public.

8. In the parlance of commercial law, the former are often called *destination contracts* and the latter *shipment contracts.* See Comment 1 to UCC 2–504.

9. On quick and careless reading, the phrase makes little sense. Would not every sales contract that requires a seller to ship via carrier be a destination contract? How can a seller send goods to the buyer via carrier without sending them to a named destination? If a seller is required to send the goods to a buyer at buyer's place of business or residence, would that not be sending them to a particular desti-

nation? Such questions misread the key language of the Code, which speaks of delivery at, not delivery to a particular designation.

10. Costs of transportation will probably be borne ultimately by buyers. When, by contract, a seller bears the cost of freight, as in an F.O.B. Buyersville contract, its cost of performance is raised by that amount. In a rational business, costs will be reflected in the price of the goods. Thus, freight costs initially allocated to sellers are likely to be passed through to their buyers.

11. This explains why the Code describes an F.O.B. term as a "delivery term," UCC 2–319(1), and not "merely a price term." Comment 1.

F.O.B. terms are one of several common contract terms defining sellers' tender obligations. A wide variety of terms are used in contracts that contemplate deep water transportation, including F.A.S., F.O.B. vessel, C.I.F., C. & F., Ex Ship. Each of these is defined by the Commercial Code. UCC 2–319(1)(c) and (2), 2–320, 2–321, 2–322.

"At a Particular Destination" Contracts. If the parties use an F.O.B. term and designate "the place of destination," the Code characterizes this as a contract in which seller is required to deliver at a particular destination. A seller must, at its own expense, transport the goods to "*the* place of destination" and "*there*" tender delivery of the goods to the buyer. UCC 2–319(1)(b). The tender rules are otherwise comparable to rules for sellers' tender in simple, two-party transactions, UCC 2–503(3), except the place of tender is at the destination of the transportation. In all likelihood, the seller will not be "there" in person to put and hold the goods at buyer's disposition. This is effected by the carrier acting pursuant to seller's instructions.

"The Place of Shipment" Contracts. If the parties use an F.O.B. term and designate "the place of shipment," the Code characterizes this as a contract in which seller is *not* required to deliver at a particular destination. A seller "must at that place ship the goods in the manner provided in this Article (Section 2–504)." [12] Similar provisions are found in the Code definitions of most deep water shipment terms.

Section 2–504(a) and (c) state two basic requirements. A seller must:

(1) put the goods in the possession of the carrier and make a contract for their transportation as may be reasonable having regard to the nature of the goods and other circumstances,[13] and

(2) promptly notify the buyer of the shipment.

If contracts with the carriers require them simply to deliver the goods to buyers, sellers complete their tender of delivery substantially before buyers receive the goods. For example, if the carrier is the U.S. Postal Service or Federal Express, a seller has made tender of delivery when the goods are mailed or handed over to the carrier. A similar result follows if the goods are shipped via a railroad or trucking line.

For a number of commercial reasons, sellers may hand over goods to carriers but not authorize the carriers simply to deliver the goods to buyers. Sellers may keep control of the carriers' duty to deliver after the goods have been shipped. This is feasible by use of the device of carriers' negotiable or "order" bills of lading. A bill of lading (originally a bill of "loading") is a document that a carrier (e.g., railroad, trucking company, ship owner, air freight carrier) issues when goods

---

12. The seller bears the expense of putting the goods into the possession of the carrier at the place of shipment; freight costs are added to the price of the goods as part of the buyer's obligation.

13. Specifications and arrangements relating to shipment are at the seller's option unless otherwise agreed. UCC 2–311(2).

are delivered to it for shipment.[14] An "order" bill of lading typically provides:

> The surrender of this Original Bill of Lading properly indorsed shall be required before the delivery of the property.

This states a carrier's contractual duty to the shipper, but it also restates the carrier's legal duty, once it has issued an "order" bill, under federal or state law.[15]

When a seller ships goods under an "order" bill of lading, UCC 2–504(b) adds a third requirement to seller's manner of execution of sales contracts. Seller must tender to buyer the bill of lading in a form that permits the buyer to obtain possession of the goods from the carrier. The Code provides that "tender [of such documents] through customary banking channels is sufficient." UCC 2–503(5). Through "banking channels" or otherwise, a seller can transmit documents to a buyer.

Time of Sellers' Tender. When sellers are authorized or required to ship goods to buyers via carriers, the matter of time of performance has multiple phases: when must seller deliver to carrier, when must seller give notice of shipment to buyer, and when must carrier deliver to buyer? If seller ships under an "order" bill of lading, when must seller tender that document?

If the sales contract is a "place of shipment" contract, it may provide that seller must ship within a stated time, but in the absence of agreement the reasonable-time standard would apply. UCC 2–309(1). Once a shipment is begun, notification to buyer must be made "prompt-

---

14. A bill of lading, in part, embodies the contract between the carrier and the shipper (often termed the *consignor*). A number of terms are printed on the front of printed bills of lading where terms describing specific shipments are filled in; the back contains more standard contract terms densely packed in small print. The bill of lading identifies the carrier receiving the goods, the shipper, the goods, the intended destination, the consignee, and possibly other terms. In this course, we are concerned with only those aspects of carriage contracts that are significant to the performance of sales transactions.

Carriers issue two kinds of bills of lading, the "order bill of lading" and the "straight bill of lading." Under the "straight" bill, the carrier undertakes to deliver the goods at the destination to a stated person, e.g., "to Buyer & Co." Under the "order" bill of lading, the carrier agrees to deliver *to the order of* a stated person, e.g., to "the order of Seller & Co."

When sales contracts use the trade terms, C.I.F. or C. & F., sellers are required to obtain negotiable bills of lading. UCC 2–320(2)(a); see also UCC 2–323(1).

15. The law governing interstate and export shipments is federal law, the 1916 Federal Bills of Lading (or Pomerene) Act, 49 U.S.C. App. §§ 81 to 124. Excerpts of the Pomerene Act are reprinted in footnotes 2, p. 603 infra, and 8, p. 605 infra. The most pertinent provisions are § 88(b)(carrier is bound to deliver goods under an order bill to one who surrenders the bill, properly indorsed, to the carrier), and § 90 (carrier is liable for delivery of the goods to a person not entitled thereto). See also §§ 89, 91.

The law governing intrastate carriage is state law, found in Article 7 of the Code. The relevant sections of Article 7 cover both bills of lading and their cousins, warehouse receipts. The legal responsibility of carriers (or warehousemen) to deliver is found in UCC 7–403 and 7–404. A key concept under the Code is "person entitled under the document," defined in 7–403(4), to whom the carrier must deliver under 7–403(1). Liability for failure to cancel an "order" bill of lading is stated in 7–403(3).

ly." UCC 2–504(c). Tender of any documents needed to obtain possession of goods must also be made "promptly" under UCC 2–504(b).

If the sales contract requires delivery at a particular destination, it may provide that seller must deliver there within a stated time, but again, in the absence of agreement, the reasonable-time standard would apply.

Manner, Time and Place of Buyers' Tender. The Code contains default rules for the manner, time and place of tender of payment when goods are delivered by carrier. Unless otherwise agreed, payment is due at the time and place at which the buyer is to receive the goods. UCC 2–310(a). This rule applies even though the place of shipment is the place of delivery, e.g., as in F.O.B. "the place of shipment" contracts.[16] Buyers ordinarily receive shipped goods at the termination of the carriage. Sellers may designate an agent to receive payment at that time and place, but in the absence of someone authorized to receive payment, buyers may send it to sellers. This is easily and commonly done by mailing checks.

The Code provisions create several difficult problems of construction. The Code gives some meaning to the distinction between "at a particular destination" contracts and other shipment contracts through the Code's definitions of certain common trade terms. If parties enter into contracts that authorize sellers to ship goods via carriers, but do not use the Code-defined trade terms, characterization of the contracts under UCC 2–503 and 2–504 poses difficulties.

Comment 5 to 2–503 declares that the drafters of the Code intentionally omitted the rule under prior uniform legislation that a contract term requiring a seller to pay the freight or costs of transportation was equivalent to an agreement to deliver to the buyer or at an agreed destination and regard the-place-of-shipment contract as "the normal one." The Comment continues:

> The seller is not obligated to deliver at a named destination ... unless he has specifically agreed so to deliver or the commercial understanding of the terms used by the parties contemplates such delivery.

Does the Comment go beyond the text of the Code? Does it provide a reasonable interpretation of the text?[17]

---

16. This rule applies whether or not sellers ship goods under negotiable or "order" bills of lading. If seller tenders a document of title, "the buyer may inspect the goods after their arrival before payment is due unless such inspection is inconsistent with the terms of the contract (Section 2–513)." UCC 2–310(b). Some buyers agree to pay against tender of documents. We will consider those agreements in a later section.

17. The Permanent Editorial Board Study Group on UCC Article 2 stated:

Without FOB terms in the agreement, § 2–319(1), it is not clear when a seller who is authorized to ship goods is "required to deliver at a particular destination." § 2–503(3). Comment 5 to § 2–503 provides a rule for construction. [We recommend] that this rule of construction be placed in the text of either § 2–319(1) or § 2–503.

Preliminary Report 134 (1990). See also id. at 115.

Problem 6. Buyer telephoned Catalogue Seller and ordered a compact disc player. In the conversation, Buyer said: "Please send the CD player by parcel post." Seller accepted the order without more being said about the price or delivery. Is the contract a place-of-shipment or at-a-particular-destination contract? Which party must pay the parcel post charges? See Pestana v. Karinol Corp., 367 So.2d 1096 (Fla.App. 1979).

Problem 7. National Heater Co., located in St. Paul, Minnesota, offered to sell heating units to Corrigan Co. to be used by the buyer in construction of an automobile plant in Fenton, Missouri. National Heater's written proposal of the terms of sale stated the price as $275,640, "F.O.B. St. Paul, Minn. with freight allowed." Corrigan then submitted a purchase order with the following: "Price $275,640—Delivered." National Heater sent an acknowledgment which included: "$275,640 Total Delivered to Rail Siding." Is the contract a place-of-shipment or at-a-particular-destination contract? See National Heater Co. v. Corrigan Co., 482 F.2d 87 (8th Cir.1973).

(3) TRANSACTIONS IN GOODS NOT TO BE MOVED

For many reasons, owners of goods, having put them into storage, may decide to sell them to buyers who want to keep the goods where they are. The person with custody of the goods, perhaps a warehouse operator, is characterized legally as a bailee. Performance rules for sales contracts in which goods are not to be moved require, in substance, that seller transfer to buyer the bailee's obligation to surrender the goods on demand. Such rules are provided in UCC 2–503(4) for transactions in which the parties have not specifically described the manner of sellers' performance.

An example of a market situation in which goods may be sold without intent to move them at the time of sale occurs in sales of propane and natural gas, which are held in huge underground storage facilities. Sellers and buyers perform contracts for sale of the goods by transfer to buyers of commitments to deliver by operators of the storage facilities. See., e.g., Commonwealth Petroleum Co. v. Petrosol International, Inc., 901 F.2d 1314 (6th Cir.1990).

An analogous transaction situation occurs when owners of goods, having put them into the possession of a carrier for transportation, decides to sell them to buyers. The carrier with custody of the goods is not generally characterized as a bailee and the goods are being moved as they are sold. While 2–503(4) is not literally applicable to transactions of goods sold in transit, seller's performance obligation must be to transfer to buyer the carrier's obligation to transport and deliver the goods.

In the oil business, crude oil in holds of supertankers moving across oceans is often bought and sold many times while the ships are en route.

Manner, Time, and Place of Sellers' Tender. Some bailees in possession of goods issue negotiable documents of title, similar to negotiable bills of lading issued by carriers, that control the right to obtain possession of the goods.[18] If goods are covered by such a document, seller performs its obligation under the sales contract by tendering the document. UCC 2–503(4)(a). The Code contains no provisions on the time or place for such tenders.

When goods are stored with a bailee who has not issued a negotiable document of title, tender occurs when seller's procure the bailee's acknowledgment of buyer's right to the goods. UCC 2–504(a). Sellers may tender by procuring that acknowledgment and notifying buyer or by giving buyer a document or written direction to the bailee to deliver goods to the buyer. The bailee's refusal to honor the document or direction "defeats" the tender. UCC 2–503(4)(b).

(B) INTERNATIONAL SALES LAW

The Convention on International Sale of Goods states the general obligation of buyers and sellers. Article 30 provides:

> The seller must deliver the goods, hand over any documents relating to them and transfer the property in the goods, as required by the contract and this Convention.

Article 53 is the reciprocal provision for buyers:

> The buyer must pay the price for the goods and take delivery of them as required by the contract and this Convention.

The Convention does not use the concept of *tender* for either party's performance.

Manner and Place of Delivery. Sales contracts between parties from different nations are highly likely to require use of carriers. Absent agreement on the nature of sellers' performance, sellers' obligation has the following three or four steps: Seller "must make such contracts as are necessary for carriage to the place fixed [by agreement] by means of transportation appropriate in the circumstances and according to the usual terms for such transportation." CISG 32(2). Seller must "hand ... the goods over to the first carrier for transmission to the buyer." CISG 31(a). If the goods are not clearly identified to the sales contract, by markings on the goods or by documents or otherwise, when handed over to the carrier, seller must give buyer notice of the consignment, CISG 32(1); the Convention does not require sellers to give notice of shipment in all transactions. Finally, seller "must ... hand over [to the buyer] any documents relating to [the goods]." CISG 30.[19]

---

18. The governing law is Article 7 of the Code. The prototypical document of title issued by a bailee is a warehouse receipt. UCC 1–201(45), 7–202.

19. Sellers are bound to hand over documents relating to the goods "at the time and place and in the form required by the contract." CISG 34. The Convention has

Unlike the Code the Convention does not distinguish between place-of-shipment and at-a-particular-destination contracts. The latter are not contemplated, no doubt in light of prevailing mercantile practice.

> [E]ven when the seller undertakes to pay freight costs to destination under "C.I.F." and "C. & F." ... quotations, it has long been settled that the seller ... completes his delivery duties ... when the goods are (at the latest) loaded on the carrier.

J. Honnold, Uniform Law for International Sales § 209 (2d ed. 1991). Moreover, the Convention, unlike the Code, contains no provisions regarding the meaning of shipment terms.[20]

The Convention provides default rules for performance of contracts that do not involve carriage of goods. Seller's obligation to deliver consists of "placing the goods at the buyer's disposal at the place where the seller had his place of business at the time of the conclusion of the contract," CISG 31(c), unless the parties knew from the circumstances of the contract that the goods would be placed at buyer's disposal at another location. CISG 31(b).

The CISG has no provision regarding the manner of delivery of goods held in storage or in transit.[21]

Time of Delivery. The Convention looks to the parties' contract as the primary source of the time term. CISG 33(a). Often, international sales contracts specify a period of time within which delivery is to occur. The agreement may provide further how an exact date will be set by one or both of the parties. If a period of time is stated without more, CISG 33(b) states a default rule that permits the seller to choose to perform "at any time within that period unless circumstances indicate that the buyer is to choose a date." When the contract is silent on time, CISG 33(c) requires a seller to perform "within a reasonable time after the conclusion of the contract."

---

no default rule for when and where this is to occur.

20. By contract, parties to international sales contracts may refer to a set of trade terms promulgated by the International Chamber of Commerce (ICC), which are known as *Incoterms*. The ICC is a nongovernmental organization with members from 110 countries.

Incoterms, last revised in 1990, categorize shipping or delivery terms into four principal categories: main carriage paid by seller (e.g., Cost and Freight, CFR, or CIF), main carriage paid by buyer (e.g., FOB, FAS), departure terms (Ex Works), and arrival terms (e.g., Delivered Ex Ship or DES). *Incoterms 1990* do not use FOB other than at port of shipment. Departure terms do not oblige sellers to contract for carriage. The arrival term, DES, requires a seller to place the goods at the disposal of

the buyer on board the vessel at the usual unloading point in the named port of destination.

During the drafting of the Convention, consideration was given to inclusion of a term that would have had the effect of incorporating trade terms in common usage, like *Incoterms*, into all international sales contracts. This proposal was opposed, in part because it would impose trade terms on a party, perhaps one from a developing country, whether or not it knew or ought to have known of them. The Convention's general provision on trade usage would direct tribunals to consider *Incoterms* if both parties knew or ought to have known of them. CISG 9(2). See J. Honnold, Uniform Law for International Sales § 118 and n. 5 (2d ed. 1991).

21. But see CISG 68 (risk of loss provision regarding goods sold while in transit).

Problem 8. Seller and Buyer contracted for sale of 12,000 tons of sugar to be delivered at the port of Dunkirk in May or June 1986 on board one or more ships provided by Buyer. The contract required Buyer to give Seller not less than 14 days' notice of the vessels' readiness to load. The contract also incorporated by reference the Rules of the London Refined Sugar Association. One Rule stated: "the seller shall have the sugar ready to be delivered at any time within the contract period." Another Rule provided: "the buyer, having given reasonable notice, shall be entitled to call for delivery of the sugar between the first and the last working days inclusive of the contract period." A third Rule stated that the buyer was responsible for costs incurred by the seller if the nominated vessel did not present herself within five days of the date specified in the buyer's notice. On May 15, Buyer gave notice calling on Seller to load the sugar on board the *Naxos,* estimated to arrive in Dunkirk between May 29 and 31. The *Naxos* was at the dock in Dunkirk and ready to load on May 29. Seller informed Buyer that the sugar would be available on June 3. Under the CISG, was Seller then in breach of contract? See Compagnie Commerciale Sucres et Denrees v. C. Czarnikow Ltd. (*The Naxos*), [1990] 1 W.L.R. 1337 (H.L.), reversing [1989] 2 Lloyd's Rep. 462 (C.A.).[22]

***Nachfrist* Provisions.** The Convention permits either party to a sales contract to extend the time for sellers' performance beyond that required in sales contracts. The provisions derive from German law, where the word, "*Nachfrist,*" is used. The dynamics of these provisions when exercised by buyers differ from the dynamics when exercised by sellers.

A seller may, even after the date for delivery, notify the buyer of intent to remedy a failure in performance and request additional time to do so.[23] The buyer may acquiesce or refuse seller's request, but if buyer does not respond within a reasonable time, seller may perform within the time indicated in its request. CISG 48(2).

The Convention provides that the buyer, too, "may fix an additional period of time of reasonable length for performance by the seller of his obligations." CISG 47(1). A commercial rationale for this provision is not quickly apparent; one can comprehend sellers needing and seeking additional time to remedy performance failures, but why would buyers thrust more time on sellers? As we will see in the next section, a *Nachfrist* notice "fixing" an additional but final period for performance plays an important role in the Convention's remedial system.

---

22. Applying British domestic sales law, the House of Lords held that seller was bound to have the sugar ready for loading immediately upon the ship's arrival. Seller contended that the contract permitted commencement of loading within a reasonable time after the ship had arrived. The House of Lords construed the notice provision of the agreement and the Rules to require the seller to have the sugar at the dock, ready to be loaded, when the ship arrived.

23. Seller's notice alone that it will perform within a specified period of time is assumed to include a request. CISG 48(3).

"Open" Price Terms. In a contract governed by CISG, is an agreement with an "open" price term enforceable? Article 55 declares that "in the absence of any indication to the contrary, [the parties are considered] to have impliedly made reference to the price generally charged at the time of the conclusion of the contract for such goods sold under comparable circumstances in the trade concerned."

Note that the time chosen for price determination under CISG is different from that under UCC 2–305. In what setting would this departure be important? Which approach is more likely to reflect the parties' probable intentions?

Buyers' Tender of Payment. The Convention does not have any provisions on the manner of buyers' payment beyond the requirement in CISG 54 that a buyer's obligation includes "taking such steps and complying with such formalities as may be required under the contract or any laws and regulations to enable payment to be made." To what kind of law or regulation does this provision refer?

Time and Place of Buyers' Tender. Unless otherwise agreed, a buyer must pay when the seller places either the goods or documents controlling their disposition at the buyer's disposal in accordance with the contract and this Convention." CISG 58(1). If payment is to be made against the handing over of goods or of documents, a buyer must pay "at the place where the handing over takes place." CISG 57(1)(b). Otherwise, payment must be made "at the seller's place of business." CISG 57(1)(a).

Choice of Currency. In sales contracts between sellers and buyers from different nations, what determines the currency of payment? The agreement may provide expressly or by implication that the price is to be paid in U.S. dollars, Canadian dollars, Deutsche marks, Japanese yen, British pounds, or Soviet rubles, etc. If, however, the agreement lacks an express or implied term of this kind, what legal rule fills the gap? Statutes like the Legal Tender Act of the United States govern domestic transactions, but what rule of law applies in an international transaction?

One aspect of the real value of a payment is bound up in the issue of choice of currency.[24] All nations' currencies commonly fluctuate in value as against each other. Among the most important commercial markets are the markets for exchange of currencies. The value of one currency in terms of another changes with great rapidity. A currency is said to be "strong" or "weak" depending upon the amount of other

---

24. A payee who wants to spend the payment in a particular place, where one currency is the common medium of payment, will be less concerned with fluctuations in currency exchange rates if payment is made in the currency that the payee plans to spend. Thus, to the extent that a French seller spends the price received for goods sold to pay its employees and its domestic French suppliers in French francs, the value of the franc against other currencies is not important if the price is paid in francs. If, however, the price is paid in another currency, the French seller will suffer any loss or gain that occurs when the currency of payment is converted into French francs.

currencies that can be bought with it. Recreational and business travellers are familiar with the daily variations at currency exchanges in airports and hotels. These reflect the movements of currency exchange rates in the major markets of the world.

If the date of payment under a sales contract is other than the date of the contract, the parties cannot know what the relative value of different currencies may be when the time for payment arrives. The longer the period of time before a payment is due, the greater becomes the uncertainty. Given a choice, buyers (or any debtors) would prefer to pay in a cheaper currency.[25] Sellers would prefer the opposite.

Restricted Convertibility; "Hard" and "Soft" Currencies. The major industrial nations of the world permit their currencies to "float" without significant legal restrictions. These currencies are the so-called "hard" currencies. Nations with weaker economies, however, tend not to permit free exchange of currencies because the international currency markets has limited demand for their domestic currencies. Such nations, which can acquire only limited amounts of the "hard" currencies through international sales of their domestic goods and services, often restrict the expenditure of the acquired "hard" currencies in order to meet the nation's priorities. Potential buyers in those countries, negotiating with foreign sellers, must obtain governmental permission to pay in "hard" currencies unless the sellers agree to accept a "soft" currency more easily available to the buyers.

National laws with respect to free convertibility of currency change over time.[26] A transactional risk for a seller is possible change in law by the government of the buyer's country, restricting the buyer's ability to pay the price, when due, in the contractually required currency.

Inspection of Goods Before Payment. Absent agreement to the contrary, buyers are not bound to pay the price until they have had opportunity to examine the goods. CISG 58(3).

---

25. Vastly simplified, this difference underlay the great 19th century controversy over "free silver" in the United States. The bimetallism movement championed by William Jennings Bryan, who rode to prominence on the famous "cross of gold" speech, would have made payment of long term debt less onerous by deflating the value of the U.S. dollar.

26. The former nations of the Communist bloc, and particularly the Soviet Union, have faced or are facing the need to change their laws on convertibility in order to enter the free world market. Making this change is difficult because of the resulting upheavals in the domestic economies of those nations.

SECTION 2.   ACCEPTANCE, REJECTION, AND CURE; AVOIDANCE

(A) DOMESTIC SALES LAW

---

(1) ACCEPTANCE AND REJECTION

Buyers' Duty to Accept Goods. UCC 2–301 declares that buyers are obligated to "accept" goods delivered by sellers, and UCC 2–507(1) states that: "tender entitles the seller to [buyer's] acceptance of the goods...." In this section, we consider the nature and significance of the obligation to accept goods.

Although not clearly stated, the Code's provisions cannot be read reasonably to impose on buyers the obligation to accept non-conforming goods or goods tendered in a manner, time or place that does not conform to sellers' obligation. Implicit in buyers' obligation is the condition that the tender and the tendered goods conform to the contract.

Buyers' Right to Reject Goods. The opposite of acceptance is rejection. Buyers may reject non-conforming goods or goods tendered other than in conformity with the contract. The provisions on rejection are found in UCC 2–601 and 2–612(2).

Significance of Acceptance or Rejection. Acceptance of goods is a significant legal watershed: at that moment the legal positions of a buyer and a seller change substantially. Acceptance precludes rejection. UCC 2–607(2). The buyer must pay at the contract rate for any goods accepted. UCC 2–607(3). If the buyer does not pay for accepted goods, seller has an action for the price. UCC 2–709(1)(a). In any subsequent litigation, such as an action for breach of warranty, the burden is on the buyer to establish any breach with respect to accepted goods. UCC 2–607(4). Acceptance of goods does not deprive buyers of monetary remedies if the goods do not conform to the requirements of the contract.[1] Unless time-barred under UCC 2–725 or barred for lack of notice under UCC 2–607(3)(a), aggrieved buyers may recover damages under UCC 2–714 and 2–715.[2]

---

1. Nearly all the breach of warranty of quality cases and problems in Chapter 3 and breach of the warranty of title cases and problems in Chapter 2 involved buyers who had accepted goods. Significant exceptions were the sale of cattle in Wright v. Vickaryous, Chapter 6, Section 3, supra and the Bolivian flour sale in T.J. Steven-son & Son v. 81,193 Bags of Flour, Chapter 6, Section 2, supra.

2. Monetary relief under UCC 2–714 and 2–715 is not the sole remedy for aggrieved buyers. Some are empowered to revoke their acceptances. UCC 2–608. We consider revocation of acceptance in a subsequent section.

Rejection of goods, if rightful, means that seller has failed to meet its obligation to make due tender of conforming goods. If seller does not make a conforming tender to "cure" whatever was amiss, UCC 2–508, buyer is released from obligation to pay the contract price, UCC 2–507(1), and is entitled to monetary remedies, which are catalogued in UCC 2–711. In addition to recovering any part of the contract price paid, UCC 2–711(1), buyer is entitled to damages measured by the cost of purchasing substitute goods ("cover") from another source, UCC 2–712, or by the differential between market price and contract price, UCC 2–713, together with incidental or consequential damages under UCC 2–715. Responsibility for disposition of rejected goods is on seller, although some buyers have the right or duty to act on seller's behalf in disposing of them.[3]

Manner of Buyers' Acceptance of Goods. The Code has a three-pronged definition of how buyers' accept goods: (1) overt statements to sellers, (2) estoppel resulting from buyers' handling of the goods, and (3) lapse of time after delivery or tender of delivery. UCC 2–606(1).

In most ordinary commercial and consumer transactions, acceptance is the result of mere lapse of time. Sometimes a buyer may "signif[y] to the seller that the goods are conforming or that he will take them or retain them in spite of their non-conformity," UCC 2–606(1)(a), but, more likely, buyers' receive goods and simply say nothing to the seller about conformity or non-conformity.[4] Continued silence becomes "failure to make an effective rejection," UCC 2–606(1)(b), because "rejection of goods must be within a reasonable time after their delivery or tender." UCC 2–602(1).[5]

Time of Acceptance: Inspection of Goods Before Acceptance. Acceptance by signification or by lapse of time cannot occur until buyers have had "a reasonable opportunity to inspect" the goods. UCC 2–606(1)(a) and (b), 2–513(1). We considered, in Section 1, buyers' right to inspect before the obligation to pay matured. The same provisions of

3. If a non-merchant buyer has taken possession of goods before rejecting them, buyer must hold the goods with reasonable care for a time sufficient to permit seller to remove them, UCC 2–602(2)(b), but has no further obligations with regard to the goods. UCC 2–602(2)(c). A merchant buyer in possession of rejected goods must follow seller's reasonable instructions. UCC 2–603(1). A merchant buyer in possession of perishable goods or goods whose market value may decline speedily, in the absence of seller's instructions, must make reasonable efforts to sell the goods for the seller's account. Id. If sellers give no instructions within a reasonable time after notification of rejection, buyers may store the goods, ship them back to sellers, or sell them for the sellers' accounts. UCC 2–604.

Resales of goods before rejection would normally constitute acceptances of the goods under the provision that an act inconsistent with sellers' ownership constitutes acceptance. UCC 2–606(1)(c). However, resale of rightfully rejected goods in conformity with the Code is neither acceptance nor conversion of them. UCC 2–603(3), 2–604.

4. Businesses courting good will sometimes inquire about customer satisfaction with the goods received. This may produce express responses, but thank-you notes or equivalent are not commonplace occurrences in marketplace transactions.

5. The third prong, "does any act inconsistent with the seller's ownership," UCC 2–606(1)(c), is based on buyers' conduct. Common acts that may fit this prong are buyers' consumption of the goods or transfer of them to a sub-purchaser.

the Code condition both the obligation to accept and the obligation to pay with buyers' right to inspect. The Code declares that buyers may inspect goods "in any reasonable manner," UCC 2–513(1), but offers no criteria for determining what inspection methods are reasonable.

ZABRISKIE CHEVROLET, INC. v. SMITH, 99 N.J. Super. 441, 240 A.2d 195 (1968). Buyer, who had paid by personal check, discovered a nonconformity after driving 7/10 of a mile from dealer's showroom. Buyer stopped payment on the check. Seller contended that buyer had accepted the car and sued for the purchase price. In deciding the buyer had not accepted the car, the court concluded that buyer had not completed his inspection of it when he paid and drove it away: "To the layman, the complicated mechanisms of today's automobiles are a complete mystery. To have the automobile inspected [in the showroom] by someone with sufficient expertise to disassemble the vehicle in order to discover latent defects ... is assuredly impossible and highly impractical. ... Consequently, the first few miles of driving become even more significant to the excited new car buyer. This is the buyer's first reasonable opportunity ... to see if it conforms to what it was represented to be.... . How long the buyer may drive the new car under the guise of inspection is not an issue in the present case."

PLATEQ CORP. v. MACHLETT LABORATORIES

Supreme Court of Connecticut, 1983.
189 Conn. 433, 456 A.2d 786.

PETERS, JUDGE. In this action by a seller of specially manufactured goods to recover their purchase price from a commercial buyer, the principal issue is whether the buyer accepted the goods before it attempted to cancel the contract of sale. The plaintiff, Plateq Corporation of North Haven, sued the defendant, The Machlett Laboratories, Inc., to recover damages, measured by the contract price and incidental damages, arising out of the defendant's allegedly wrongful cancellation of a written contract for the manufacture and sale of two leadcovered steel tanks and appurtenant stands. The defendant denied liability and counterclaimed for damages. After a full hearing, the trial court found for the plaintiff both on its complaint and on the defendant's counterclaim. The defendant has appealed.

The trial court, in its memorandum of decision, found the following facts. On July 9, 1976, the defendant ordered from the plaintiff two leadcovered steel tanks to be constructed by the plaintiff according to specifications supplied by the defendant. The parties understood that the tanks were designed for the special purpose of testing x-ray tubes and were required to be radiation-proof within certain federal standards. Accordingly, the contract provided that the tanks would be tested for radiation leaks after their installation on the defendant's premises. The plaintiff undertook to correct, at its own cost, any deficiencies that this post-installation test might uncover. The plaintiff had not previously constructed such tanks, nor had the defendant previously designed tanks for this purpose. The contract was amended on August 9, 1976, to add construction of two metal stands to hold the tanks. All the goods were to be delivered to the defendant at the plaintiff's place of business.

Although the plaintiff encountered difficulties both in performing according to the contract specifications and in completing performance within the time required, the defendant did no more than call these deficiencies to the plaintiff's attention during various inspections in September and early October, 1976. By October 11, 1976, performance was belatedly but substantially completed. On that date, Albert Yannello, the defendant's engineer, noted some remaining deficiencies which the plaintiff promised to remedy by the next day, so that the goods would then be ready for delivery. Yannello gave no indication to the plaintiff that this arrangement was in any way unsatisfactory to the defendant. Not only did Yannello communicate general acquiescence in the plaintiff's proposed tender but he specifically led the plaintiff to believe that the defendant's truck would pick up the tanks and the stands within a day or two. Instead of sending its truck, the defendant sent a notice of total cancellation which the plaintiff received on October 14, 1976. That notice failed to particularize the grounds upon which cancellation was based.[3]

On this factual basis, the trial court, having concluded that the transaction was a contract for the sale of goods falling within the Uniform Commercial Code, General Statutes §§ 42a–2–101 et seq., considered whether the defendant had accepted the goods. The court determined that the defendant had accepted the tanks, primarily by signifying its willingness to take them despite their nonconformities, in accordance with General Statutes § 42a–2–606(1)(a), and secondarily by failing to make an effective rejection, in accordance with General Statutes § 42a–2–606(1)(b). Once the tanks had been accepted, the defendant could rightfully revoke its acceptance under General Statutes § 42a–2–608 only by showing substantial impairment of their value to the defendant. In part because the defendant's conduct had foreclosed any post-installation inspection, the court concluded that such impairment had not been proved. Since the tanks were not readily resalable on the open market, the plaintiff was entitled, upon the defendant's wrongful revocation of acceptance, to recover their contract price, minus salvage value, plus interest. General Statutes

---

3. The defendant sent the plaintiff a telegram stating: "This order is hereby terminated for your breach, in that you have continuously failed to perform according to your commitment in spite of additional time given you to cure your delinquency. We will hold you liable for all damages incurred [sic] by Machlett including excess cost of reprocurement."

§§ 42a–2–703; 42a–2–709(1)(b). Accordingly, the trial court awarded the plaintiff damages in the amount of $14,837.92. . . .

Upon analysis, all of the defendant's claims of error are variations upon one central theme. The defendant claims that on October 11, when its engineer Yannello conducted the last examination on the plaintiff's premises, the tanks were so incomplete and unsatisfactory that the defendant was rightfully entitled to conclude that the plaintiff would never make a conforming tender. From this scenario, the defendant argues that it was justified in cancelling the contract of sale. It denies that the seller's conduct was sufficient to warrant a finding of tender, or its own conduct sufficient to warrant a finding of acceptance. The difficulty with this argument is that it is inconsistent with the underlying facts found by the trial court. Although the testimony was in dispute, there was evidence of record to support the trial court's findings to the contrary. . . . There is simply no fit between the defendant's claims and the trial court's finding that, by October 11, 1976, performance was in substantial compliance with the terms of the contract. The trial court further found that on that day the defendant was notified that the goods would be ready for tender the following day and that the defendant responded to this notification by promising to send its truck to pick up the tanks in accordance with the contract.

On the trial court's finding of facts, it was warranted in concluding, on two independent grounds, that the defendant had accepted the goods it had ordered from the plaintiff. Under the provisions of the Uniform Commercial Code, General Statutes § 42a–2–606(1), "[a]cceptance of goods occurs when the buyer (a) after a reasonable opportunity to inspect the goods signifies to the seller . . . that he will take . . . them in spite of their nonconformity; or (b) fails to make an effective rejection."

In concluding that the defendant had "signified" to the plaintiff its willingness to "take" the tanks despite possible remaining minor defects, the trial court necessarily found that the defendant had had a reasonable opportunity to inspect the goods. The defendant does not maintain that its engineer, or the other inspectors on previous visits, had inadequate access to the tanks, or inadequate experience to conduct a reasonable examination. It recognizes that inspection of goods when the buyer undertakes to pick up the goods is ordinarily at the seller's place of tender. See General Statutes §§ 42a–2–503, 42a–2–507, 42a–2–513; see also White & Summers, Uniform Commercial Code § 3–5 (2d Ed.1980). The defendant argues, however, that its contract, in providing for inspection for radiation leaks after installation of the tanks at its premises, necessarily postponed its inspection rights to that time. The trial court considered this argument and rejected it, and so do we. It was reasonable, in the context of this contract for the special manufacture of goods with which neither party had had prior experience, to limit this clause to adjustments to take place after tender and acceptance. After acceptance, a buyer may still, in appropriate cases, revoke its acceptance, General Statutes § 42a–2–608, or recover damages for breach of warranty, General Statutes § 42a–2–714. The trial court reasonably concluded that a post-installation test was intended to safeguard these rights of the defendant as well as to afford the plaintiff a final opportunity to make needed adjustments. The court was therefore justified in concluding that there had been an acceptance within § 42a–2–606(1)(a). A buyer may be found to have accepted goods despite their known nonconformity . . . and despite the absence of actual delivery to the buyer. . . .

Once the conclusion is reached that the defendant accepted the tanks, its further rights of cancellation under the contract are limited by the governing provisions of the Uniform Commercial Code. "The buyer's acceptance of goods, despite their alleged nonconformity, is a watershed. After acceptance, the buyer must pay for the goods at the contract rate; General Statutes § 42a–2–607(1); and bears the burden of establishing their nonconformity. General Statutes § 42a–2–607(4)."
. . . . After acceptance, the buyer may only avoid liability for the contract price by invoking the provision which permits revocation of acceptance. That provision, General Statutes § 42a–2–608(1), requires proof that the "nonconformity [of the goods] substantially impairs [their] value to him." . . . On this question, . . . the trial court again found against the defendant. Since the defendant has provided no basis for any argument that the trial court was clearly erroneous in finding that the defendant had not met its burden of proof to show that the goods were substantially nonconforming, we can find no error in the conclusion that the defendant's cancellation constituted an unauthorized and hence wrongful revocation of acceptance.

Finally, the defendant in its brief, although not in its statement of the issues presented, challenges the trial court's conclusion about the remedial consequences of its earlier determinations. Although the trial court might have found the plaintiff entitled to recover the contract price because of the defendant's acceptance of the goods; General Statutes §§ 42a–2–703(e) and 42a–2–709(1)(a); the court chose instead to rely on General Statutes § 42a–2–709(1)(b), which permits a price action for contract goods that cannot, after reasonable effort, be resold at a reasonable price.[19] Since the contract goods in this case were concededly specially manufactured for the defendant, the defendant cannot and does not contest the trial court's finding that any effort to resell them on the open market would have been unavailing. In the light of this finding, the defendant can only reiterate its argument, which we have already rejected, that the primary default was that of

---

19. . . . It should be noted that § 42a–2–709(1)(b) is not premised on a buyer's acceptance. Instead, it requires a showing that the goods were, before the buyer's cancellation, "identified to the contract." In the circumstances of this case, that precondition was presumably met by their special manufacture and by the defendant's acquiescence in their imminent tender. See White & Summers, Uniform Commercial Code, § 7–5 (2d Ed.1980). The defendant has not, on this appeal, argued the absence of identification.

It should further be noted that § 42a–2 709(1)(b), because it is not premised on acceptance, would have afforded the seller the right to recover the contract price even if the trial court had found the conduct of the buyer to be a wrongful rejection (because of the failure to give the seller an opportunity to cure) rather than a wrongful revocation of acceptance.

the plaintiff rather than that of the defendant. The trial court's conclusion to the contrary supports both its award to the plaintiff and its denial of the defendant's counterclaim.

There is no error.

Notes

(1) **Acceptance or Rejection of Goods Delivered by Carrier.** In "at a particular destination" contracts, when sellers tender goods through carriers at the stated place, buyers accept or reject in response to such tenders in the same way as they perform the acceptance obligation in transactions performed without carriers. Within a reasonable time after tender, they must elect to accept or reject the goods. UCC 2–606(1)(b).

In "the place of shipment" contracts, tender may be completed before arrival of the goods, but the time period for a buyer to accept or reject does not begin to run until buyer has had an opportunity to inspect the goods. UCC 2–606(1)(b). Unless the agreement designates a different time and place, the inspection opportunity begins when the goods have arrived. UCC 2–513(1). Thus, within a reasonable time after arrival of the goods, buyers must elect to accept or reject the goods. UCC 2–606(1)(b).

In "the place of shipment" contracts, sellers must do more than deliver conforming goods; sellers are also required to make proper contracts for transportation and to give buyers prompt notice of shipment. Sellers' failure on either score is a ground for rejection "only if material delay or loss ensues." UCC 2–504.

(2) **Manner and Time of Buyers' Rejection of Goods.** Rejection of goods is the antithesis of acceptance. It must be made before lapse of a reasonable time after tender or delivery. UCC 2–602(1). The only way for a buyer to reject effectively is to notify the seller seasonably. UCC 2–602(1). The Code does not prescribe the minimum content of an effective rejection notice, but does provide that certain buyers' failure to describe particular defects will preclude them from later relying on unstated defects to justify their rejection or to establish sellers' breach. UCC 2–605.[6]

(3) **Effective Rejection and Transfer of Possession.** Rejection decisions may be, and frequently are, made at the time of sellers' tender of goods, with the result that buyers refuse to take possession of the tendered goods. However, buyers who take possession of goods, without signifying that they accept them, may thereafter elect to reject them. Refusals to take possession of tendered goods usually occurs in

---

6. Compare the necessary content of buyers' notices to sellers with regard to non-conformity of accepted goods. UCC 2–607(3)(a) and Comment 4.

contexts that notify sellers of buyers' choice to reject. However, when change of possession occurs without buyers' choosing whether to accept or reject, what must buyers do to make an effective rejection? What must they do with the rejected goods in their possession? Consider the following problems.

Problem 1. Grain Supply and Miller made a contract for the sale to Miller of 1,000 bushels of wheat at $5.00 per bushel. The contract specified that the wheat would be delivered on June 1, and would be of No. 1 milling quality, free of weevil; Miller was to pay the price of $5,000 within 60 days after delivery. On delivery of the wheat, Miller inspected the wheat and found that it was "crawling" with weevils and was totally unfit for milling; Miller instructed a manager to sell the wheat for chicken feed. The manager suggested that they get in touch with Supply and work out some adjustment. Miller, thoroughly disgusted with Supply's performance, said: "I'm not having anything more to do with that outfit. Just let them try to collect for this rotten stuff." The wheat, sold for chicken feed, brought only $2,000—a fair price under the circumstances. Three months later, Supply called Miller and reminded him that the bill was overdue. Miller said "You should know that I won't pay for such a rotten shipment," and hung up.

Supply brought an action to recover the contract price for the wheat. Miller counterclaimed on grounds of breach of express and implied warranty and demanded damages resulting from the necessity of purchasing the No. 1 wheat elsewhere at $6.00 per bushel.

(a) What result in Supply's action to recover the contract price? UCC 2–709, 2–606.

(b) What result in Miller's counterclaim for damages? UCC 2–607(3)(a); Economy Forms Corp. v. Kandy, 391 F.Supp. 944 (N.D.Ga. 1974). For criticism see 15 UCC L.Rev. 105 (1982); 61 N.Car.L.Rev. 177 (1982).

Problem 2. Assume that in Problem 1, when the wheat arrived on June 1, Miller wired Grain Supply, "Wheat defective. Holding you responsible." Supply did not respond. Miller stored the wheat in a warehouse, and two months later (on August 1) Miller wired Supply, "What do you want done with your weevily wheat?" Supply wired back, "You bought the wheat, and I expect you to pay your bill," and brought suit. Miller interposed all available defenses and counterclaims.

By the time of trial, the wheat, which at delivery had been worth $2,000 for chicken feed, had been further damaged by the weevils; and in the meantime the price level for feed grains had dropped so that the shipment was worth only $300.

(a) May Miller defeat the claim for payment of the price on the ground that he has made an effective rejection of the goods? See UCC 2–607(1), 2–606(1)(b), 2–602(1); Boysen v. Antioch Sheet Metal, 16 Ill. App.3d 331, 306 N.E.2d 69 (1974); Louis Sherry Ice Cream Co. v.

Harlem River Consumers' Cooperative, 18 UCC Rep.Serv. 97 (City Civ.Ct.1975) (purchase of perishable commodity).

(b) Assume that the court finds that Miller's rejection was not effective. What judgment should be entered? Was Miller's brief wire of June 1 adequate to meet the requirements of UCC 2–607(3)(a)? (See Comment 4.) Who bears the loss from deterioration and price decline that occurred after delivery? See UCC 2–510(1), 2–606(1)(b), 2–714.

(2) RIGHTFUL REJECTION

One of most controverted issues in sales law is the standard for determining when buyers are entitled to reject goods that have been tendered or delivered. Sellers sometimes fail to carry out contract commitments, but margins of failure can be large or small. Do insignificant or minor failures justify rejections? Buyers dissatisfied with their bargains may be tempted to reject goods or tenders that are conforming, or almost so. A not surprising example occurs when the contract price for the goods is higher than the market price prevailing at the time of tender; a narrowly self-interested buyer will prefer to buy on the market and be relieved of the obligation to pay the higher contract price. These matters underlie the normative standards for rightful rejection.

The "Perfect Tender Rule." The basic standard that differentiates rightful from wrongful rejection is UCC 2–601.[7] In ordinary cases, a buyer is permitted to reject "if the goods or the tender of delivery fail in any respect to conform to the contract." Common legal usage refers to this standard as the "perfect tender rule."[8] Goods or the tender of delivery may fail to conform to the contract in many respects, but four tend to predominate: clouds on title, defects in quality, deficiencies or excesses in quantity, and late deliveries.

MOULTON CAVITY & MOLD, INC. v. LYN–FLEX INDUSTRIES, INC.

Supreme Judicial Court of Maine, 1979.
396 A.2d 1024.

DELAHANTY, JUSTICE. Defendant, Lyn–Flex Industries, Inc., appeals from a judgment entered after a jury trial by the Superior Court, York County, in favor of plaintiff, Moulton Cavity & Mold, Inc. The case

---

7. Buyers are permitted, of course, to accept goods known to be non-conforming. See UCC 2–607(2). There is no concept of wrongful acceptance.

8. Comment 2 to UCC 2–106(2)(definition of "conforming") states: "It is in general intended to continue the policy of exact performance by the seller of his obligations as a condition to his right to require acceptance."

concerns itself with an oral contract for the sale of goods which, as both parties agree, is governed by Article 2 of the Uniform Commercial Code, 11 M.R.S.A. §§ 2–101 et seq. For the reasons set forth below, we agree with defendant that the presiding Justice committed reversible error by instructing the jury that the doctrine of substantial performance applied to a contract for the sale of goods. We do not agree, however, that based on the evidence introduced at trial defendant is entitled to judgment in its favor as a matter of law. The appeal is therefore sustained and the case remanded for a new trial.

An examination of the record discloses the following sequence of events: On March 19, 1975, Lynwood Moulton, president of plaintiff, and Ernest Sturman, president of defendant, orally agreed that plaintiff would produce, and defendant purchase, twenty-six innersole molds capable of producing saleable innersoles. The price was fixed at $600.00 per mold. Whether or not a time for delivery had been established was open to question. In his testimony at trial, Mr. Moulton admitted that he was fully aware that defendant was in immediate need of the molds, and he stated that he had estimated that he could provide suitable molds in about five weeks' time. Mr. Sturman testified that "I conveyed the urgency to [Mr. Moulton] and he said 'within three weeks I will begin showing you molds and by the end of five weeks you will have [the entire order].' "

In apparent conformity with standard practice in the industry, plaintiff set about constructing a sample mold and began a lengthy series of tests. These tests consisted of bringing the sample mold to defendant's plant, fitting the mold to one of defendant's plastic-injecting machines, and checking the innersole thus derived from the plaintiff's mold to determine if it met the specifications imposed by defendant. After about thirty such tests over a ten-week period, several problems remained unsolved, the most significant of which was "flashing," that is, a seepage of plastic along the seam where the two halves of the mold meet. Although characterized by plaintiff as a minor defect, Mr. Moulton admitted that a flashing mold could not produce a saleable innersole.

It was plaintiff's contention at trial, supported by credible evidence, that at one point during the testing period officials of defendant signified that in their judgment plaintiff's sample mold was turning out innersoles correctly configured so as to fit the model last supplied by defendant's customer. Allegedly relying on this approval, plaintiff went ahead and constructed the full run of twenty-six molds.

For its part, defendant introduced credible evidence to rebut the assertion that it had approved the fit of the molds. It also noted that Moulton's allegation of approval extended only to the fit of the mold; as Moulton conceded, defendant had never given full approval since it considered the flashing problem, among others, unacceptable.

On May 29, some ten weeks after the date of the oral agreement and five weeks after the estimated completion date, Mr. Sturman met with plaintiff's foreman at the Moulton plant. A dispute exists regarding the substance of the ensuing conversation. Plaintiff introduced evidence tending to show that at that time, Mr. Sturman revoked defendant's prior approval of the fit of the sample mold and demanded that plaintiff redesign the molds to fit the last. Testimony introduced by defendant tended to show that it had never approved the fit of the molds to begin with and that on the date in question, May 29, plaintiff's foreman indicated that plaintiff simply would not invest any more time in conforming the molds to the contract. Mr. Sturman met the next day with Mr. Moulton, and Moulton ratified the position taken by his foreman. Thereupon, Mr. Sturman immediately departed for Italy and arranged to have the molds produced by the Plastak Corporation, an Italian mold-making concern, at a cost of $650.00 per mold. Plaintiff later billed defendant for the contract price of the molds, deducting an allowance for "flashing and shut-off adjustments." Upon defendant's refusal to pay, plaintiff brought this action for the price less adjustments. Defendant counterclaimed for its costs in obtaining conforming goods to the extent that they exceeded the contract price.

At trial, plaintiff's basic theory of recovery was that it had received approval with regard to the fit of the sample mold, that in reliance on that approval it had constructed a full run of twenty-six molds, and that defendant had, in effect, committed an anticipatory breach of contract within the meaning of Section 2–610 by demanding that the fit of the molds be completely redesigned. On its counterclaim, and in response to plaintiff's position, defendant advanced the theory that plaintiff had breached the contract by failing to tender conforming goods within the five-week period mentioned by both parties.

After the presiding Justice had charged the jury, counsel for plaintiff requested at side bar that the jury be instructed on the doctrine of substantial performance. Counsel for defendant entered a timely objection to the proposed charge which objection was overruled. The court then supplemented its charge as follows:

> The only point of clarification that I'll make, ladies and gentlemen, is that I've referred a couple of times to performance of a contract and you, obviously, have to determine no matter which way you view the contract to be, and there might even be a possible third way that I haven't even considered, whether the contract whatever it is has been performed and there is a doctrine that you should be aware of in considering that. That is the doctrine of substantial performance.
>
> It is not required that performance be in any case one hundred percent complete in order to entitle a party to enforcement of their contractual rights. That is not to say within the confines of this case that the existence of flashing would be excused or not be excused. It is just a recognition on the part of the law when we talk about performance, probably if we took any contract you could always find something of no substance that was not completed one

hundred percent. It is for you to determine that whether it has been substantially performed or not and what in fact constitutes substantial performance.

In your consideration, and as I say in this case, that's not to intimate that something like flashing is to be disregarded or to be considered. It's up to you based upon facts.

The jury returned a verdict in favor of plaintiff in the amount of $14,480.82.

I

In Smith, Fitzmaurice Co. v. Harris, 126 Me. 308, 138 A. 389 (1927), a case decided under the common law, we recognized the then-settled rule that with respect to contracts for the sale of goods the buyer has the right to reject the seller's tender if in any way it fails to conform to the specifications of the contract. We held that "[t]he vendor has the duty to comply with his order in kind, quality and amount." Id. at 312, 138 A. at 391. Thus, in *Smith,* we ruled that a buyer who had contracted to purchase twelve dozen union suits could lawfully refuse a tender of sixteen dozen union suits. Various provisions of the Uniform Sales Act, enacted in Maine in 1923, codified the common-law approach. R.S. (1954) ch. 185, §§ 11, 44. The so-called "perfect tender" rule came under considerable fire around the time the Uniform Commercial Code was drafted. No less an authority than Karl Llewellyn, recognized as the primum mobile of the Code's tender provisions (see, e.g., W. Twining, Karl Llewellyn and the Realist Movement 270–301 (1973); Carroll, Harpooning Whales, of Which Karl N. Llewellyn is the Hero of the Piece; or Searching for More Expansion Joints in Karl's Crumbling Cathedral, 12 B.C.Indus. & Comm.L.Rev. 139, 142 (1970)), attacked the rule principally on the ground that it allowed a dishonest buyer to avoid an unfavorable contract on the basis of an insubstantial defect in the seller's tender. Llewellyn, On Warranty of Quality and Society, 37 Colum.L.Rev. 341, 389 (1937). Although Llewellyn's views are represented in many Code sections governing tender,[6] the basic tender provision, Section 2–601, represents a rejection of Llewellyn's approach and a continuation of the perfect tender policy developed by the common law and carried forward by the draftsmen of the Uniform Sales Act. See Official Comment, § 2–106; Priest, Breach and Remedy for the Tender of Nonconforming Goods Under the Uniform Commercial Code: An Economic Approach, 91 Harv.L.Rev. 960, 971 (1978). Thus, Section 2–601 states that, with certain exceptions not here applicable, the buyer has the right to reject "if the goods or the tender of delivery fail *in any respect* to conform to the contract.... ." (emphasis supplied). Those few courts that have considered the question agree that the perfect tender rule has survived the enactment of the Code. Ingle v. Marked Tree Equipment Co., 244 Ark.1166, 428 S.W.2d 286

---

6. See, e.g., §§ 2–508 (seller's limited right to cure defects in tender), 2–608 (buyer's limited right to revoke acceptance), and 2–612 (buyer's limited right to reject nonconforming tender under installment contract).

(1968); Maas v. Scoboda, 188 Neb. 189, 195 N.W.2d 491 (1972); Bowen v. Young, 507 S.W.2d 600 (Tex.Civ.App.1974). We, too, are convinced of the soundness of this position.

In light of the foregoing discussion, it is clear that the presiding Justice's charge was erroneous and, under the circumstances, reversibly so. The jury was informed that "[i]t is not required that performance be in any case one hundred percent complete in order to entitle a party to enforcement of their contractual rights." Under this instruction, the jury was free to find that although plaintiff had not tendered perfectly conforming molds within the agreed period (assuming the jury found that the parties had in fact agreed on a specific time period for completion) it had nevertheless substantially performed the contract within the agreed time frame and was merely making minor adjustments when defendant backed out of the deal. Had the jury been instructed that plaintiff was required to tender perfectly conforming goods—not just substantially conforming goods—within the period allegedly agreed to and had they been instructed that, under Section 2–711, the buyer has the absolute right to cancel the contract if the seller "fails to make delivery," a different verdict might have resulted. Indeed, the supplemental instruction tended to encourage the jury to resolve the question by deciding whether "flashing" was or was not a substantial defect:

> It is not required that performance be in any case one hundred percent complete in order to entitle a party to enforcement of their contractual rights. That is not to say within the confines of this case that the existence of flashing would be excused or not be excused. ... It is for you to determine ... whether [the contract] has been substantially performed or not and what in fact constitutes substantial performance.

We find unpersuasive plaintiff's argument that the presiding Justice's instruction merely informed the jury that if it found that defendant had committed an anticipatory breach of the contract then plaintiff was not thereafter required to complete its performance as a condition precedent to recovery under the contract. Such an instruction might well have been appropriate and would certainly have been supportable under the applicable law. Dehahn v. Innes, Me., 356 A.2d 711, 719 (1976) ("When the other party has already repudiated the agreement, a tender would be a futile act and is not required by law."); §§ 2–610, 2–704. However, an examination of the passage of the charge in question leads us to reject plaintiff's interpretation. Without informing the jury that it must first find that defendant had committed an anticipatory repudiation, the presiding Justice, without qualification, stated that "performance [need not] be ... one hundred percent complete in order to entitle a party to enforcement of their contractual rights." Furthermore, the court drew a distinction between substantial and insubstantial defects, a distinction which, on these facts and under plaintiff's interpretation of the charge, would have been completely irrelevant. Finally, both the presiding Justice and counsel for plaintiff referred to the instruction at side bar as an explanation of the "substantial performance" doctrine. In legal parlance, that doctrine requires a buyer, under certain circumstances, to accept something less than a perfectly conforming tender. See, e.g., Rockland Poultry Co. v. Anderson, 148 Me. 211, 216, 91 A.2d 478, 480 (1952) (construction contract); Jacob & Youngs, Inc. v. Kent, 230 N.Y. 239, 129 N.E. 889 (1921) (Cardozo, J.) (construction contract). As such, it has no application to a contract for the sale of goods, and the jury should not have been permitted to consider it.

II

In his testimony at trial, Mr. Moulton indicated that he was aware that to defendant time was a critical factor. He also stated that he had given defendant an estimated delivery date of five weeks from the date the contract was formed. On appeal, defendant takes the position that the parties agreed on a five-week time period for delivery and that plaintiff's failure to tender conforming goods after ten weeks constitutes a breach as a matter of law and precludes plaintiff from recovering under the contract.

We disagree. While on the one hand Mr. Sturman testified that Mr. Moulton had told him that the goods would be delivered in five weeks, on the other hand Mr. Moulton testified that it was clear that he was merely making an estimate. The testimony thus left the jury at liberty to decide the factual question of whether the five-week time period was an agreed delivery date and thus a term of the contract or merely an estimate. While the interpretation of unambiguous language in a written contract falls within the province of the court, Blue Rock Industries v. Raymond International, Inc., Me., 325 A.2d 66 (1974), questions of fact concerning the terms of an oral agreement are left to the trier of fact, Carter v. Beck, Me., 366 A.2d 520 (1976).

The entry is: Appeal sustained. New trial ordered.

Notes

(1) Substantial Performance. Most students will recall from general contract law that a party is entitled to the full contract price if it has substantially performed its contractual obligations. To the extent that less than exact performance has been rendered, the other party is entitled to recoupment in the amount of any damages. A leading contracts case is Judge Cardozo's opinion in Jacob & Youngs, Inc. v. Kent, 230 N.Y. 239, 129 N.E. 889 (1921)(the Reading pipe case), cited by the Maine court. See also Restatement (Second) of Contracts §§ 237, 241, which puts the same performance standard in terms of material failure. On request of seller's counsel, the trial court in *Moulton Cavity & Mold* framed the jury charge on the substantial performance standard. What argument could be made in support of the trial court's decision?

(2) History of the Perfect Tender Rule. Historians identify a mid–19th century British decision as the origin of the perfect tender rule. Bowes v. Shand, [1876] 1 Q.B.D. 470, [1877] 2 Q.B.D. 112, [1877] 2 App. Cas. 455. Professor Grant Gilmore said that the perfect tender rule in the United States dates from October 26, 1885, when the Supreme Court decided Norrington v. Wright, 115 U.S. 188, 6 S.Ct. 12, 29 L.Ed. 366 (1885), and Filley v. Pope, 115 U.S. 213, 6 S.Ct. 19, 29 L.Ed. 372 (1885). See E. Peters, Commercial Transactions 33 (1971). A high (or low) water mark cited by Professor (now Connecticut Supreme Court Chief Justice) Peters was Frankel v. Foreman & Clark, 33 F.2d 83 (2d Cir.1929) (permitting rejection of a shipment of coats for trivial and inconsequential nonconformities in less than 2% of the coats). Id. at 34. For a comprehensive review of the perfect tender rule prior to the Commercial Code, see Honnold, Buyer's Right of Rejection, 97 U.Pa. L.Rev. 457 (1949).

(3) Retention of the Perfect Tender Rule in the Code. As the Code evolved, a major study was conducted under the aegis of the Law Revision Commission of the State of New York. The Commission recommended that "the right of rejection as stated in Section 2–601 be limited to material breach." The Editorial Board responsible for revising the Code following the New York study did not accept this recommendation. That Board relied on two grounds: "first, ... the buyer should not be required to guess at his peril whether a breach is material; second, ... proof of materiality would sometimes require disclosure of the buyer's private affairs such as secret formulas or processes." R. Braucher & E. Sutherland, Commercial Transactions (41 3d ed.) (1964). Are these reasons persuasive? In the pending revision of Article 2, would you recommend retention of UCC 2–601 in its present form? See Sebert, Rejection, Revocation, and Cure Under Article 2 of the Uniform Commercial Code: Some Modest Proposals, 84 Nw.L.Rev. 375 (1990); Lawrence, The Prematurely Reported Demise of the Perfect Tender Rule, 35 Kan.L.Rev. 557 (1987).

What arguments support favoring a liberal remedy of rejection rather than compelling aggrieved buyers to use price adjustments? Some of the considerations are canvassed in Honnold, Buyer's Right of Rejection, 97 U.Pa.L.Rev. 457, 466–72 (1949): e.g., (1) the hazard of securing redress when full cash payment is demanded on tender; (2) the difficulty in many cases of measuring, without controversy, the value of the deficiency in seller's performance. Do the rules of the Code fit these underlying interests as well as is feasible? See Peters, Remedies for Breach of Contracts Relating to the Sale of Goods Under the UCC, 73 Yale L.J. 199, 206–27 (1963); Miniter, Rejection, 13 Ga.L.Rev. 805 (1979); Priest, Breach and Remedy for the Tender of Nonconforming Goods; An Economic Approach, 91 Harv.L.Rev. 960 (1978); Schmitt & Frisch, 13 Toledo L.Rev. 1375 (1982).

(4) Installment Sales: A Different Set of Standards. The standards governing buyers' power to reject tendered goods change dramatically if the sales contract "requires or authorizes the delivery of goods in separate lots to be separately accepted," UCC 2–612(1), language which the drafters of the Code intended to have considerable breadth.[9] Such sales, termed "installment contracts," are not governed by the perfect tender rule in UCC 2–601. As each lot is tendered in a simple, two-party sale, a buyer may reject only if "the non-conformity substantially impairs the value of that installment and cannot be cured." UCC 2–612(2).[10]

Problem 3. Sellers can escape from the rigors of the perfect tender rule by eliciting from buyers express or tacit consent to divide full performance into more than one "lot." In making such arrangements, buyers may or may not be aware that they are surrendering a significant amount of leverage over the sellers when the time comes for performance. If you were counsel to a firm regularly engaged in selling or buying goods, what advice would you give on standard contracting terms?

Problem 4. Seller and Buyer have a long-term trading pattern whereby Buyer submits orders frequently for goods to be delivered some time later. Within the delivery time necessary for an order, Buyer usually makes one or more additional orders. Each purchase order results in a single delivery by Seller. Is Buyer's right to reject tendered goods governed by UCC 2–601 or 2–612(2)?

T.W. OIL, INC. v. CONSOLIDATED EDISON CO.
Court of Appeals of New York, 1982.
57 N.Y.2d 574, 457 N.Y.S.2d 458, 443 N.E.2d 932.

FUCHSBERG, JUDGE. In the first case to wend its way through our appellate courts on this question, we are asked, in the main, to decide whether a seller who, acting in good faith and without knowledge of any defect, tenders nonconforming goods to a buyer who properly rejects them, may avail itself of the cure provision of subdivision (2) of section 2–508 of the Uniform Commercial Code. We hold that, if seasonable notice be given, such a seller may offer to cure the defect within a reasonable period beyond the time when the contract was to be

9. Section 2–307 permits delivery in several lots "where the circumstances give either party the right to make or demand delivery in lots." The issue in 2–307, whether a seller may demand payment for partial deliveries, is not the same as the issue in 2–612(1), whether a seller may demand acceptance of partial deliveries. Comment 1 to 2–612 states that drafters of the Code intended to define installment contracts more broadly than did pre-Code law, and Comment 2 adds that provision for separate payment for each lot is not essential to an installment contract.

10. In an unusual "belt and suspenders" style of drafting, 2–612(2) continues to define circumstances in which a buyer "must accept an installment." Conceptually under the Code, buyers must accept goods that they may not reject. Therefore, the criteria for "may reject" should be the same as the criteria for "must accept." However, as stated the drafters failed to make the two clauses complementary. Consider a tender of non-conforming goods by a seller who has the ability to cure the non-conformity but who fails to give adequate assurance of doing so.

performed so long as it has acted in good faith and with a reasonable expectation that the original goods would be acceptable to the buyer.

The factual background against which we decide this appeal is based on either undisputed proof or express findings at Trial Term. In January, 1974, midst the fuel shortage produced by the oil embargo, the plaintiff (then known as Joc Oil USA, Inc.) purchased a cargo of fuel oil whose sulfur content was represented to it as no greater than 1%. While the oil was still at sea en route to the United States in the tanker *M T Khamsin*, plaintiff received a certificate from the foreign refinery at which it had been processed informing it that the sulfur content in fact was .52%. Thereafter, on January 24, the plaintiff entered into a written contract with the defendant (Con Ed) for the sale of this oil. The agreement was for delivery to take place between January 24 and January 30, payment being subject to a named independent testing agency's confirmation of quality and quantity. The contract, following a trade custom to round off specifications of sulfur content at, for instance, 1%, .5% or .3%, described that of the *Khamsin* oil as .5%. In the course of the negotiations, the plaintiff learned that Con Ed was then authorized to buy and burn oil with a sulfur content of up to 1% and would even mix oils containing more and less to maintain that figure.

When the vessel arrived, on January 25, its cargo was discharged into Con Ed storage tanks in Bayonne, New Jersey. In due course, the independent testing people reported a sulfur content of .92%. On this basis, acting within a time frame whose reasonableness is not in question, on February 14 Con Ed rejected the shipment. Prompt negotiations to adjust the price failed; by February 20, plaintiff had offered a price reduction roughly responsive to the difference in sulfur reading, but Con Ed, though it could use the oil, rejected this proposition out of hand. It was insistent on paying no more than the latest prevailing price, which, in the volatile market that then existed, was some 25% below the level which prevailed when it agreed to buy the oil.

The very next day, February 21, plaintiff offered to cure the defect with a substitute shipment of conforming oil scheduled to arrive on the *S.S. Appollonian Victory* on February 28. Nevertheless, on February 22, the very day after the cure was proffered, Con Ed, adamant in its intention to avail itself of the intervening drop in prices, summarily rejected this proposal too. The two cargos were subsequently sold to third parties at the best price obtainable, first that of the *Appollonian* and, sometime later, after extraction from the tanks had been accomplished, that of the *Khamsin*.

There ensued this action for breach of contract, which, after a somewhat unconventional trial course, resulted in a nonjury decision for the plaintiff in the sum of $1,385,512.83.... To arrive at this result, the Trial Judge, while ruling against other liability theories advanced by the plaintiff, which, in particular, included one charging the defendant with having failed to act in good faith in the negotiations for a price adjustment on the *Khamsin* oil (Uniform Commercial Code, § 1–203), decided as a matter of law that subdivision (2) of section 2–508 of the Uniform Commercial Code was available to the plaintiff even if it had no prior knowledge of the nonconformity. Finding that in fact plaintiff had no such belief at the time of the delivery, that what turned out to be a .92% sulfur content was "within the range of contemplation of reasonable acceptability" to Con Ed, and that seasonable notice of an intention to cure was given, the court went on to hold that plaintiff's "reasonable and timely offer to cure" was improperly rejected (sub nom. Joc Oil USA v. Consolidated Edison Co. of N.Y., 107 Misc.2d 376, 390, 434 N.Y.S.2d 623 [Shanley N. Egeth, J.]). The Appellate Division, 84 A.D.2d 970, 447 N.Y.S.2d 572, having unanimously affirmed the judgment entered on this decision, the case is now here by our leave. . . .

In support of its quest for reversal, the defendant now asserts that the trial court erred (a) in ruling that the verdict on a special question submitted for determination by a jury was irrelevant to the decision of this case, (b) in failing to interpret subdivision (2) of section 2–508 of the Uniform Commercial Code to limit the availability of the right to cure after date of performance to cases in which the seller knowingly made a nonconforming tender and (c) in calculating damages on the basis of the resale of the nonconforming cargo rather than of the substitute offered to replace it. For the reasons which follow, we find all three unacceptable.

I

[The court rejected objection (a).]

II

We turn then to the central issue on this appeal: Fairly interpreted, did subdivision (2) of section 2–508 of the Uniform Commercial Code require Con Ed to accept the substitute shipment plaintiff tendered? In approaching this question, we, of course, must remember that a seller's right to cure a defective tender, as allowed by both subdivisions of section 2–508, was intended to act as a meaningful limitation on the absolutism of the old perfect tender rule, under which, no leeway being allowed for any imperfections, there was, as one court put it, just "no room . . . for the doctrine of substantial performance" of commercial obligations (Mitsubishi Goshi Kaisha v. Aron & Co., 16 F.2d 185, 186 [Learned Hand, J.]; see Note, Uniform Commercial Code, § 2–508; Seller's Right to Cure Non–Conforming Goods, 6 Rutgers–Camden L.J 387–388).

In contrast, to meet the realities of the more impersonal business world of our day, the code, to avoid sharp dealing, expressly provides for the liberal construction of its remedial provisions (§ 1–102) so that "good faith" and the "observance of reasonable commercial standards of fair dealing" be the rule rather than the exception in trade (see § 2–

103, subd. [1], par. [b]), "good faith" being defined as "honesty in fact in the conduct or transaction concerned" (Uniform Commercial Code, § 1–201, subd. [19]). As to section 2–508 in particular, the code's Official Comment advises that its mission is to safeguard the seller "against surprise as a result of sudden technicality on the buyer's part" (Uniform Commercial Code, § 2–106, Comment 2; see, also, Peters, Remedies for Breach of Contracts Relating to the Sale of Goods under the Uniform Commercial Code: A Roadmap for Article Two, 73 Yale L.J. 199, 210; 51 N.Y.Jur., Sales, § 101, p. 41).

Section 2–508 may be conveniently divided between provisions for cure offered when "the time for performance has not yet expired" (subd. [1]), a precode concept in this State (Lowinson v. Newman, 201 App.Div. 266, 194 N.Y.S. 253), and ones which, by newly introducing the possibility of a seller obtaining "a further reasonable time to substitute a conforming tender" (subd. [2]), also permit cure beyond the date set for performance. ...

Since we here confront circumstances in which the conforming tender came after the time of performance, we focus on subdivision (2). On its face, taking its conditions in the order in which they appear, for the statute to apply (1) a buyer must have rejected a nonconforming tender, (2) the seller must have had reasonable grounds to believe this tender would be acceptable (with or without money allowance), and (3) the seller must have "seasonably" notified the buyer of the intention to substitute a conforming tender within a reasonable time.

In the present case, none of these presented a problem. The first one was easily met for it is unquestioned that, at .92%, the sulfur content of the *Khamsin* oil did not conform to the .5% specified in the contract and that it was rejected by Con Ed. The second, the reasonableness of the seller's belief that the original tender would be acceptable, was supported not only by unimpeached proof that the contract's .5% and the refinery certificate's .52% were trade equivalents, but by testimony that, by the time the contract was made, the plaintiff knew Con Ed burned fuel with a content of up to 1%, so that, with appropriate price adjustment, the *Khamsin* oil would have suited its needs even if, at delivery, it was, to the plaintiff's surprise, to test out at .92%. Further, the matter seems to have been put beyond dispute by the defendant's readiness to take the oil at the reduced market price on February 20. Surely, on such a record, the trial court cannot be faulted for having found as a fact that the second condition too had been established.

As to the third, the conforming state of the *Appollonian* oil is undisputed, the offer to tender it took place on February 21, only a day after Con Ed finally had rejected the *Khamsin* delivery and the *Appollonian* substitute then already was en route to the United States, where it was expected in a week and did arrive on March 4, only four days later than expected. Especially since Con Ed pleaded no prejudice (unless the drop in prices could be so regarded), it is almost impossible, given the flexibility of the Uniform Commercial Code definitions of "seasonable" and "reasonable" ..., to quarrel with the finding that the remaining requirements of the statute also had been met.

Thus lacking the support of the statute's literal language, the defendant nonetheless would have us limit its application to cases in which a seller *knowingly* makes a nonconforming tender which it has reason to believe the buyer will accept. For this proposition, it relies almost entirely on a critique in Nordstrom, Law of Sales (§ 105), which rationalizes that, since a seller who believes its tender is conforming would have no reason to think in terms of a reduction in the price of the goods, to allow such a seller to cure after the time for performance had passed would make the statutory reference to a money allowance redundant.[8] Nordstrom, interestingly enough, finds it useful to buttress this position by the somewhat dire prediction, though backed by no empirical or other confirmation, that, unless the right to cure is confined to those whose nonconforming tenders are knowing ones, the incentive of sellers to timely deliver will be undermined. To this it also adds the somewhat moralistic note that a seller who is mistaken as to the quality of its goods does not merit additional time (Nordstrom, loc. cit.). Curiously, recognizing that the few decisions extant on this subject have adopted a position opposed to the one for which it contends, Con Ed seeks to treat these as exceptions rather than exemplars of the rule (e.g., Wilson v. Scampoli, 228 A.2d 848 (D.C.App.) [goods obtained by seller from their manufacturer in original carton resold unopened to purchaser; seller held within statute though it had no reason to believe the goods defective]; Appleton State Bank v. Lee, 33 Wis.2d 690, 148 N.W.2d 1 [seller mistakenly delivered sewing machine of wrong brand but otherwise identical to one sold; held that seller, though it did not know of its mistake, had a right to cure by substitution]).

That the principle for which these cases stand goes far beyond their particular facts cannot be gainsaid. These holdings demonstrate that, in dealing with the application of subdivision (2) of section 2–508, courts have been concerned with the reasonableness of the seller's belief that the goods would be acceptable rather than with the seller's pretended knowledge or lack of knowledge of the defect (Wilson v. Scampoli, supra; compare Zabriskie Chevrolet v. Smith, 99 N.J.Super. 441, 240 A.2d 195).

---

8. The premise for such an argument, which ignores the policy of the code to prevent buyers from using insubstantial remedial or price adjustable defects to free themselves from unprofitable bargains (Hawkland, Sales and Bulk Sales Under the Uniform Commercial Code, pp. 120–122), is that the words "with or without money allowance" apply only to sellers who believe their goods will be acceptable with such an allowance and not to sellers who believe their goods will be acceptable without such an allowance. But, since the words are part of a phrase which speaks of an otherwise unqualified belief that the goods will be acceptable, unless one strains for an opposite interpretation, we find insufficient reason to doubt that it intends to include both those who find a need to offer an allowance and those who do not.

It also is no surprise then that the aforementioned decisional history is a reflection of the mainstream of scholarly commentary on the subject (e.g., 1955 Report of N.Y.Law Rev.Comm., p. 484; White & Summers, Uniform Commercial Code [2d ed.], § 8–4, p. 322; 2 Anderson, Uniform Commercial Code [2d ed.], § 2–508:7; Hogan, The Highways and Some of the Byways in the Sales and Bulk Sales Articles of the Uniform Commercial Code, 48 Cornell L.Q. 1, 12–13; Note, Uniform Commercial Code, § 2–508: Seller's Right to Cure Non–Conforming Goods, 6 Rutgers–Camden L.J. 387, 399; Note, Commercial Law—The Effect of the Seller's Right to Cure on the Buyer's Remedy of Rescission, 28 Ark.L.Rev. 297, 302–303).

White and Summers, for instance, put it well, and bluntly. Stressing that the code intended cure to be "a remedy which should be carefully cultivated and developed by the courts" because it "offers the possibility of conforming the law to reasonable expectations and of thwarting the chiseler who seeks to escape from a bad bargain" (op. cit., at pp. 322–324), the authors conclude, as do we, that a seller should have recourse to the relief afforded by subdivision (2) of section 2–508 of the Uniform Commercial Code as long as it can establish that it had reasonable grounds, tested objectively, for its belief that the goods would be accepted (ibid., at p. 321). It goes without saying that the test of reasonableness, in this context, must encompass the concepts of "good faith" and "commercial standards of fair dealing" which permeate the code (Uniform Commercial Code, § 1–201, subd. [19]; §§ 1–203, 2–103, subd. [1], par. [b]).[10] ....

Judgment affirmed.

Notes

(1) **Sellers' Right to Cure Non–conforming Tenders.** In a substantial departure from prior law, the Code authorizes sellers to make a second tender or delivery if the first is rightfully rejected. UCC 2–508(1).[11] To what extent does this power overcome the vices perceived by critics of the perfect tender rule?

Buyer was found to have reject the *Khamsin* oil rightfully, but its subsequent rejection of the *Appollonian* oil was wrongful. Thus buyer was in breach. We consider sellers' remedies for wrongful rejection later in this section.

10. Except indirectly, on this appeal we do not deal with the equally important protections the code affords buyers. It is as to buyers as well as sellers that the code, to the extent that it displaces traditional principles of law and equity (§ 1–103), seeks to discourage unfair or hypertechnical business conduct bespeaking a dog-eat-dog rather than a live-and-let-live approach to the marketplace (e.g., §§ 2–314, 2–315, 2–513, 2–601, 2–608). Overall, the aim is to encourage parties to amicably resolve their own problems (Ramirez v. Autosport, 88 N.J. 277, 285, 440 A.2d 1345; compare Restatement, Contracts 2d, Introductory Note to chapter 10, p. 194 ["the wisest course is ordinarily for the parties to attempt to resolve their differences by negotiations, including clarification of expectations [and] cure of past defaults"]).

11. Are sellers authorized to make a third tender if the first two are rightfully rejected? A fourth?

(2) Repair as Cure. Quality defects can be cured by tender of substitute goods, as in *T.W. Oil,* and quantity shortfalls by tender of additional goods. In a sale of a manufactured product, is seller's undertaking to replace a defective component a cure under UCC 2–508(1)? Does it matter whether the seller is the manufacturer or only a dealer? Suppose that a new automobile is rejected for transmission failures and car dealer replaces the transmission in its own service department? See Zabriskie Chevrolet, Inc. v. Smith, 99 N.J.Super. 441, 240 A.2d 195 (1968) (dealer's replacement did not effect cure). Should the possibility of cure by repair in sales of capital equipment be more liberal than in sales of consumer goods?

(3) Cure and Warranty Service. How does sellers' repair or replacement of rightfully rejected goods relate to sales contracts under which sellers undertake to repair or replace goods during a specified warranty period?

(4) Price Adjustment as Cure. In some trade settings, particularly sales of fungible goods, sellers offer take a lower price when goods may be rightfully rejected and buyers agree. Could a practice of this kind be the basis for concluding that trade usage permits sellers to cure defective tenders by price adjustment? Counsel for seller in *T.W. Oil* argued, in the trial court, that buyer should be held liable for breach of a duty to bargain in good faith for a price adjustment on the *Khamsin* oil. This argument was rejected by the trial court and is mentioned only in passing by the court of appeals. Does this argument have force under the present Code? Should the Code be amended to provide generally that sellers may cure by price adjustment?

MENDELSON–ZELLER CO. v. JOSEPH WEDNER & SON CO.

U.S. Department of Agriculture, 1970.
29 Agriculture Decisions 47, 7 UCC Rep.Serv. 1045.

FLAVIN, JUDICIAL OFFICER.

PRELIMINARY STATEMENT

This is a reparation proceeding under the Perishable Agricultural Commodities Act, 1930, as amended (7 U.S.C. 499a et seq.) A timely complaint was filed in which complainant seeks reparation against respondent in the amount of $2,480.73 in connection with a shipment of cantaloupes and lettuce in interstate commerce.

A copy of the formal complaint and of the Department's report of investigation were served upon the respondent, and respondent filed an answer denying liability. The answer included a counterclaim for $2,892.73. Complainant did not file a reply to the counterclaim and therefore it is deemed to be denied pursuant to section 47.9(a) of the rules of practice (7 CFR 47.9(a)).

An oral hearing at the request of respondent was held at Pittsburgh, Pennsylvania, on July 30, 1969. Respondent was represented by counsel at the hearing. One witness appeared for respondent. Complainant filed a brief.

FINDINGS OF FACT

1. Complainant, Mendelson–Zeller Co., Inc., is a corporation whose address is 450 Sansome Street, San Francisco, California. At the time of the transaction involved herein, complainant was licensed under the act.

2. Respondent, Joseph Wedner & Son Co., is a corporation whose address is 2018 Smallman Street, Pittsburgh, Pennsylvania. At the time of the transaction involved herein, respondent was licensed under the act.

3. On or about March 7, 1968, in the course of interstate commerce, complainant contracted orally to sell to respondent, a mixed truckload of produce consisting of 25 cartons of cantaloupes Jumbo size 45 at $17.75 per carton, 85 cartons of cantaloupes Jumbo size 56 at $15.25 per carton, and 574 cartons of lettuce size 24 at $3.45 per carton, delivered Pittsburgh, Pennsylvania. The total delivered price for the truckload, including $15.00 for top ice, was $4,116.55. It was agreed that shipment would begin on March 8. The parties estimated that delivery would be in time for the market of Tuesday morning, March 12, 1968.

4. Complainant shipped the lettuce at 9:40 a.m. March 8, 1968, from El Centro, California, and the cantaloupes were shipped at 10:00 p.m. the same day from Nogales, Arizona, in a truck operated by Arkansas Traffic Service, Inc., of Redfield, Arkansas. At 12:00 a.m. March 12, the truck driver called respondent stating that the truck would arrive about 3:00 or 3:30 p.m. and requesting that respondent's men wait to unload the truck. Respondent checked with its men, who said they would not wait, and then told the truck driver to arrive at 3:00 a.m. the morning of March 13th.

5. The truckload of produce arrived at respondent's place of business at 5:00 a.m., March 13, 1968, approximately 103 hours after leaving Nogales, Arizona.

6. Respondent unloaded and sold the commodities and remitted the net proceeds in the amount of $1,635.82 to complainant.

7. The formal complaint was filed on August 1, 1968, which was within 9 months after accrual of the cause of action.

CONCLUSIONS

Complainant seeks to recover the full delivered price for the truckload of produce sold to respondent and respondent contends that it was justified in remitting only the net proceeds resulting from its resale of the produce. The only material factual dispute relates to whether a delivery time of 3:00 a.m. March 12, 1968, was specified as a condition of the delivered sale contract. Complainant contends that such time was not specified as a contract condition but was merely the estimated time of arrival assuming normal condition, and that a 48 hour leeway is allowable by custom in such cases.

On March 13, 1968, the day the truck actually arrived, respondent's Manager, Norman Wedner, wrote to complainant's Sales Manager, Mr. E. A. Melia, Jr., in part as follows:

> The truck of mixed lettuce and cantaloupes was due for the market of Tuesday morning at 3:00 AM March 12, 1968.

> The truck driver called us at noon Tuesday and said he would be in at 3:00 or 3:30 PM Tuesday afternoon, and asked us to have the men wait to unload him. We held him on the phone and our warehouse men said they could not wait for him. We then told him to be at the warehouse at 3:00 AM Wednesday morning. He said fine, he would be there.

> He didn't arrive until 5:00 AM Wednesday Mar. 13, 1968. The lettuce wasn't available for delivery until 6:30 AM, causing us to miss a large chain store order.

Complainant's Traffic Manager, John Monk testified by deposition and referred to an exhibit which he said was a correct copy of his notes concerning instructions for the shipment of the produce. The exhibit is entitled "Loading and Delivery instructions," and in part gives the following information: "Delivery Date *Tues* Time *3:30 AM*." Mr. Monk stated that this exhibit reflected the estimated time of arrival and that he "was given no specific instructions as to actual time of delivery other than the delivery was to be planned so that if at all possible it would arrive in Pittsburgh on Tuesday morning." Complainant's Salesman, Irving Raznikov, stated that he was the actual recipient of the telephone order from Mr. Wedner. Although he stated that "Wedner requested a Tuesday a.m. arrival and I indicated to him that under normal circumstances there would be no problem with said delivery schedule," he also stated that he "stressed with Mr. Wedner that we could not and would not guarantee any specific arrival."

Respondent as the party alleging that a specified arrival time was a part of the contract of sale had the burden of proving by a preponderance of the evidence that its allegation was true. In view of the foregoing discussion we conclude that respondent has not met its burden of proof.

Section 2–309(1) of the Uniform Commercial Code provides that the time for delivery in the absence of an agreed time shall be a reasonable time. The load was tendered and accepted at 5:00 a.m. March 13, about 103 hours after the truck left Nogales, Arizona. Under the circumstances, we are unable to say the delivery was not within a reasonable time.

The failure of respondent to pay to complainant the full purchase price of $4,116.55 for the lettuce was in violation of section 2 of the act.

Respondent has already paid net proceeds of $1,635.82 to complainant. Reparation should therefore be awarded to complainant for the balance of the purchase price of $2,480.73, with interest. In the absence of any breach of contract on the part of complainant, respondent's counterclaim should be dismissed.

ORDER

Within 30 days from the date of this order, respondent shall pay to complainant, as reparation, $2,480.73, with interest thereon at the rate of 6 percent per annum from April 1, 1968, until paid.

The counterclaim should be dismissed.

Notes

(1) **Delay in Sellers' Tender of Delivery.** This case illustrates how much economic significance can attach to time of performance. Buyer resold lettuce and cantaloupes after 5:00 a.m. for $1,635.82, less than half of the original contract price. Moreover, buyer claimed damages of nearly $2,900.00, presumably profit that buyer allegedly would have made on resale to the large chain store. Assuming that the resale was reasonable [12] and the amount of the alleged damages is not exaggerated, goods delivered at 3:00 a.m. were worth $5,000 more than goods delivered at 5:00 a.m.

Buyer took the position that it was relieved of obligation to pay the contract price to seller because of the produce was received after the time permitted under the contract of sale. Did buyer contend that seller was late in handing over the produce to the carrier? Could seller be responsible for the carrier's delay in delivering the produce to buyer? See UCC 2–503(3).

(2) **Contract Interpretation.** Buyer apparently contended that the delivery term in the "Loading and Delivery instructions" was binding upon the seller. Was this document part of the contract of sale? On what theory might it reflect on the sales contract? [13]

(3) **Construction of UCC 2–309.** When buyer's principal contract argument failed, the seller's performance obligation was found in the default rule of UCC 2–309. Do you agree with the judicial officer's application of that provision to the facts of this case? If the truck driver could have delivered on the afternoon of March 12, was it not reasonable to require the goods to be delivered at 3:00 a.m. the next morning, in time to make the prime market for that day?

---

12. The opinion does not suggest that the buyer "dumped" the goods at less than their market value at the time of resale.

13. A different legal question is whether the terms of the document were part of the contract of carriage and binding on the carrier. Although the buyer was not a named party to the contract of carriage, the buyer might be able to seek a remedy from the carrier for its breach of that contract. Cf. UCC 2–722. In the principal case, of course, the carrier was not a party to the litigation.

(4) Buyer's Rejection and Resale. The Commercial Code imposes a duty on a merchant buyer, after rejection of perishable goods, to make reasonable efforts to sell them for the seller's account. UCC 2–603(1). If buyer in this case had rejected the produce, its actions would have been consistent with that duty. In interpreting the contract, the judicial officer concludes, in effect, that buyer lacked the right to reject the goods for late delivery.[14]

Problem 5. S, a fruit dealer with a place of business in Georgia, and B, of Providence, R.I., made a contract for the sale and shipment to B of a carload of peaches, known as "fancy Belles and Thurbers" at $2.25 per basket; at the contract price a carload cost $986.75. On arrival of the car, B paid the freight and examined the car, and found the peaches were not the varieties ordered. The varieties shipped would sell for $50 less than those specified. B wired S rejecting the car and advising S to ship to Boston, since Providence could not use peaches of that quality. S answered: "Car yours. Care not what you do with it. Gave you best colored stock possible as ordered and hold you responsible for amount of draft." B reshipped to Boston and ordered a Boston commission merchant to dispose of the car. B tendered S the proceeds, $638.13, less expenses (freight to Boston $362.63, expense of unloading $13.44 and commission of Boston agent $44.67) a balance of $217.39. The market price had dropped before arrival.

S sued B for the contract price of $986.75. If there had been no market decline, should it make any substantial difference whether B is held to have "accepted"? Does the decline in the peach market make the question of "acceptance" important? See UCC 2–607; Descalzi Fruit Co. v. William S. Sweet & Son, 30 R.I. 320, 75 A. 308 (1910); Askco Engineering Corp. v. Mobil Chemical Corp., 535 S.W.2d 893 (Tex.Civ.App.1976). Might B have been required to resell? See UCC 2–603.

FERTICO BELGIUM S.A. v. PHOSPHATE CHEMICALS EXPORT ASSOCIATION, INC.

Court of Appeals of New York, 1987.
70 N.Y.2d 76, 517 N.Y.S.2d 465, 510 N.E.2d 334.

BELLACOSA, J. A seller (Phoschem) breached its contract to timely deliver goods to a buyer-trader (Fertico) who properly sought cover

------

14. The law governing the *Mendelson–Zeller* case is the Commercial Code supplemented by a federal statute, the Perishable Agricultural Commodities Act. 7 U.S.C. §§ 499a–499s. The act and regulations issued under it determine the obligations of parties to sales contracts. Many trade terms used in sales agreements for perishable agricultural commodities are specially defined in 7 C.F.R. § 46.43. Some trade terms preclude buyers from rejecting goods on arrival. Among them are "f.o.b. acceptance final," "rolling acceptance," and "purchase after inspection." See, e.g., L. Gillarde Co. v. Joseph Martinelli & Co., 169 F.2d 60 (1st Cir.1948), cert. denied, 335 U.S. 885 (1948).

(under the Uniform Commercial Code that means acquiring substitute goods) from another source (Unifert) in order to avoid breaching that buyer-trader's obligation to a third-party buyer (Altawreed). The sole issue involves the applicable principles and computation of damages for breach of the Phoschem–to–Fertico contract.

We hold that under the exceptional circumstances of this case plaintiff Fertico, as a buyer-trader, is entitled to damages from seller Phoschem equal to the increased cost of cover plus consequential and incidental damages minus expenses saved (UCC § 2–712[2]). In this case, expenses saved as a result of the breach are limited to costs or expenditures which would have arisen had there been no breach. Thus, the seller Phoschem is not entitled to a credit from the profits of a subsequent sale by the first buyer-trader Fertico to a fourth party (Janssens) of nonconforming goods from Phoschem. Fertico's letter of credit had been presented by Phoschem and honored so, under the specific facts of this case, Fertico had no commercially reasonable alternative but to retain and resell the fertilizer. This is so despite Fertico's exercise of cover in connection with the first set of transactions, i.e., Phoschem to Fertico to Altawreed. The covering buyer-trader may not, however, as in this case, recover other consequential damages when the third party to which it made its sale provides increased compensation to offset additional costs arising as a consequence of the breach.

In October 1978 appellant Fertico Belgium S.A. (Fertico), an international trader of fertilizer, contracted with Phosphate Chemicals Export Association, Inc. (Phoschem), a corporation engaged in exporting phosphate fertilizer, to purchase two separate shipments of fertilizer for delivery to Antwerp, Belgium. The first shipment was to be 15,000 tons delivered no later than November 20, 1978 and the second was to be 20,000 tons delivered by November 30, 1978. Phoschem knew that Fertico required delivery on the specified dates so that the fertilizer could be bagged and shipped in satisfaction of a secondary contract Fertico had with Altawreed, Iraq's agricultural ministry. Fertico secured a letter of credit in a timely manner with respect to the first shipment.* After Phoschem projected a first shipment delivery date of December 4, 1978, Fertico advised Phoschem, on November 13, 1978, that the breach as to the first shipment presented "huge problems" and canceled the second shipment which had not as of that date been loaded, thus ensuring its late delivery. The first shipment did not actually arrive in Antwerp until December 17 and was not off-loaded until December 21, 1978. Despite the breach as to the first shipment, Fertico retained custody and indeed acquired title over that first shipment because, as its president testified "[w]e had no other choice"

* [A letter of credit is a commitment by a bank to pay a designated amount of money to a beneficiary of the letter of credit; the bank's obligation to pay is usually conditional upon the beneficiary's presentment of described documents. This device is commonly used in international sales as the means by which buyers pay the contract price for goods when sellers present to the banks documents indicating that the goods have been shipped. We consider this payment device further in Section 4. Eds.]

... as defendant seller Phoschem had presented Fertico's $1.7 million letter of credit as of November 17, 1978, and the same had been honored by the issuer... .

Fertico's predicament from the breach by delay of even the first shipment, a breach which Phoschem does not deny, was that it, in turn, would breach its contract to sell to Altawreed unless it acquired substitute goods. In an effort to avoid that secondary breach, Fertico took steps in mid-November to cover (UCC § 2–712) the goods by purchasing 35,000 tons of the same type fertilizer from Unifert, a Lebanese concern. The cost of the fertilizer itself under the Phoschem-to–Fertico contract was $4,025,000, and under the Unifert–to–Fertico contract $4,725,000, a differential of $700,000. On the same day Fertico acquired cover, November 15, 1978, Fertico's president traveled to Baghdad, Iraq, to renegotiate its contract with Altawreed. In return for a postponed delivery date and an additional payment of $20.50 per ton, Fertico agreed to make direct inland delivery rather than delivery to the seaport of Basra. Fertico fulfilled its renegotiated Altawreed contract with the substitute fertilizer purchased as cover from Unifert.

In addition to the problems related to its Altawreed contract, Fertico was left with 15,000 tons of late-delivered fertilizer which it did not require but which it had been compelled to take because Phoschem had received payment on Fertico's letter of credit. This aggrieved international buyer-seller was required to store the product and seek out a new purchaser. Fertico sold the 15,000 tons of the belatedly delivered Phoschem fertilizer to another buyer, Janssens, on March 19, 1979, some three months after the nonconforming delivery, and earned a profit of $454,000 based on the cost to it from Phoschem and its sale price to Janssens.

In 1981 Fertico commenced this action against Phoschem seeking $1.25 million in damages for Phoschem's breach of the October 1978 agreement. A jury returned a verdict of $1.07 million which the trial court refused to overturn on a motion for judgment notwithstanding the verdict. The Appellate Division vacated the damage award, ordered a new trial on the damages issue only and ruled, as a matter of law, (1) that the increased transportation costs on the Altawreed contract were not consequential damages; (2) that the higher purchase price paid by Altawreed to Fertico was an expense saved as a consequence of the Phoschem breach; and (3) that the Fertico damages had to be reduced by the profits from the Janssens' sale... . Fertico appealed to this court on a stipulation for judgment absolute. We disagree with propositions (2) and (3) in the Appellate Division ruling and conclude that the Uniform Commercial Code and our analysis support a modification and reinstatement of $700,000 of the damage award in a final judgment resolving this litigation between the parties.

Failure by Phoschem to make delivery on the contract dates concededly constituted a breach of the contract... . The Uniform Commercial Code § 2–711 gives the nonbreaching party the alternative of either seeking the partial self-help of cover along with recovery of damages (UCC § 2–712), or of recovering damages only for the differential between the market price and the contract price, together with incidental and consequential damages less expenses saved (UCC § 2–713...). Fertico exercised its right as the wronged buyer-trader to cover in order to obtain the substitute fertilizer it required to meet its obligation under its Altawreed contract (see, UCC § 2–712, comment 1).

A covering buyer's damages are equal to the difference between the presumably higher cost of cover and the contract price, plus incidental or consequential damages suffered on account of the breach, less expenses saved (UCC § 2–712[2]). Fertico is thus entitled to a damage remedy under this section because its cover purchase was made in good faith, without unreasonable delay, and the Unifert fertilizer was a reasonable substitute for the Phoschem fertilizer... .

Fertico's additional costs for delivering the fertilizer inland rather than at a seaport would usually constitute consequential damages because they resulted from Phoschem's breach, because Phoschem knew that Fertico would incur damages under its separate contract obligation and because the damages were not prevented by the cover (UCC § 2–715[2]). The increased costs attendant to the Altawreed contract are consequential damages because they did not "arise within the scope of the immediate [Phoschem–Fertico] transaction, but rather stem from losses incurred by [Fertico] in its dealings [with Altawreed] which were a proximate result of the breach, and which were reasonably foreseeable by the breaching party at the time of contracting".... . Inasmuch as Altawreed compensated Fertico for the additional delivery costs, Fertico was insulated from any loss in that respect as a result of Phoschem's breach, thereby eliminating this category of potential damages. On this question of consequential damages, the Appellate Division was correct.

The additional compensation to Fertico, an international trader, from Altawreed is not, however, an expense saved as a consequence of the seller Phoschem's breach for which Phoschem is entitled to any credit (UCC § 2–712[2]). In most instances, and particularly in this case, saved expenses must be costs or expenditures which would be anticipated had there been no breach.... . For example, if a seller were to breach a contract to deliver an unpackaged product to the buyer and the buyer were to cover with the same product prepackaged, the cost of packaging which the buyer would have had to perform is an expense saved as a consequence of the breach.... . The increased remuneration from Altawreed was compensation for the additiona¹ shipment responsibilities incurred by Fertico, not a cost or expenditure anticipated in the absence of a breach, and therefore was erroneously analyzed and credited in Phoschem's favor by the Appellate Division.

The third prong of the damages analysis relates to the profit made from the independent sale of the Phoschem fertilizer to Janssens. The Appellate Division erred in offsetting this profit against the damages otherwise suffered since that court mistakenly concluded that the sale stemmed from and was dependent upon Phoschem's breach. This offset, on these peculiar facts, would severely disadvantage Fertico, a trader in fertilizer who both buys and sells, and who would have pursued such commercial transactions had there been no breach by Phoschem. It would be anomalous to conclude that had it not been for Phoschem's breach Fertico would not have continued its trade and upon such reasoning to counterpoise the profits from the Janssens' sale against the damages arising from Phoschem's breach. Inasmuch as the facts here are exceptional because Fertico met its subsale obligations with the cover fertilizer and yet acquired title and control over the late-delivered fertilizer from Phoschem, our decision does not fit squarely within the available Uniform Commercial Code remedies urged by the dissent. . . .

Fertico learned of Phoschem's breach after Phoschem had negotiated Fertico's $1.7 million letter of credit, which constituted complete payment for the first shipment. With no commercially reasonable alternative, Fertico took custody of the first shipment but canceled the second (UCC § 2–601[c]), having previously notified Phoschem of its breach (UCC § 2–607). The loss resulting to Fertico by having to acquire cover, even in the face of its acceptance of a late-delivered portion of the fertilizer, is properly recoverable under section 2–714[1]. . . . At the same time, Uniform Commercial Code § 1–106 directs that the remedies provided by the Uniform Commercial Code should be liberally administered so as to put the aggrieved party in as good a position as if the other party had fully performed. Had Phoschem fully performed, Fertico would have had the benefit of the Altawreed transaction and, as a trader of fertilizer, the profits from the Janssens' sale as well. "Gains made by the injured party on other transactions after the breach are never to be deducted from the damages that are otherwise recoverable, unless such gains could not have been made, had there been no breach" (5 Corbin, Contracts § 1041, at 256 . . .). Fertico's profit made on the sale of a nonspecific article such as fertilizer, of which the supply in the market is not limited, should not therefore be deducted from the damages recoverable from Phoschem. . . .

Fertico was concededly wronged by Phoschem's breach and Fertico resorted to Uniform Commercial Code remedies which are rooted in what we perceive to be the realities of the marketplace. Fertico did what reasonable traders would do and would like to do in mitigating risks inflicted in this case by Phoschem and in exerting its commercial resourcefulness. That is, it took steps to save its business, its customers, its good will and its deals and ultimately to also recover appropriate damages from a wrongdoer. That did not produce a "windfall" or a "double benefit" to the aggrieved party as the dissenting opinion asserts. The result we reach today countenances no such thing. On the contrary, to deprive the buyer-trader Fertico of its rightful differential damages of $700,000 and to credit this transactionally independent profit to Phoschem would perversely enrich the wrongdoer at the expense of the wronged party, a result those in the marketplace would find perplexing and a result which the generous remedial purpose of the Uniform Commercial Code does not compel or authorize. The dissent's characterization of the recovery by an injured party of damages for a breach of contract as a "benefit" is wrong, since that functionally attributes a kind of lien against the independently pursued benefit derived out of that separate transaction.

Accordingly, the order of the Appellate Division affirming liability but vacating, on the law, the damage award and remanding the matter for a new trial on the issue of damages, as appealed to this court on a stipulation for judgment absolute, should be modified and damages awarded to Fertico in the amount of $700,000 in accordance with this opinion.

TITONE, J. (dissenting). At issue in this appeal is the relationship among the various remedies that article 2 of the Uniform Commercial Code provides for buyers aggrieved by sellers' defaults. Central to the analysis is the principle that the Code's remedies "shall be liberally administered to the end that the aggrieved party may be put in *as good a position* as if the other party had fully performed" (UCC § 1–106[1] [emphasis supplied]). Here, the majority has concluded that the aggrieved buyer may retain both cover damages and the profit from the resale of the late-delivered goods, in effect, securing the benefit of its bargain twice. Since that result is not required by, and indeed is not even consistent with, the purpose of Code's generous remedial provisions, I must respectfully dissent.[1]

I begin with the premise that an aggrieved buyer who has purchased substitute goods and sued for "cover" damages under UCC § 2–712 has impliedly rejected the seller's nonconforming performance and, consequently, holds the seller's goods only as security for any prepayments made to the seller (see, UCC § 2–706[6]; § 2–711[3]). I find the contrary position—that an aggrieved buyer may compatibly resort to cover and also retain and resell the nonconforming goods for its own account—to be legally insupportable and economically unsound. ... [F]rom an economic standpoint, the buyer receives the full benefit of his bargain when he obtains cover damages under UCC § 2–712. Allowing the buyer to retain and resell the goods in addition obviously leads to a windfall, since the buyer is receiving more than the benefit of the transaction it bargained for....

The majority has attempted to rationalize that result here by relying on a damages rule that has previously been applied only to aggrieved sellers. The rule permits a seller who regularly deals in goods of a particular type to sue the breaching buyer for lost profit even

---

1. My disagreement with the majority lies only in its conclusion that the Appellate Division erred by offsetting Fertico's damage award against the profit Fertico obtained on the resale of Phoschem's goods. I agree completely with the majority's conclusion concerning the proper application of the $20.50 per ton additional reimbursement that Fertico obtained from Altawreed.

though the wrongfully rejected goods have been sold to another buyer without loss. The rule applies only where the seller has an unlimited supply of standard-price goods.... In those situations, "it may safely be assumed that" the seller would have made two sales instead of one if the buyer had not breached, and, consequently, it can fairly be said that the buyer's breach deprived the seller of an opportunity for additional profit.... Thus, traditional remedies such as resale or market price differential are "inadequate to put the seller in as good a position as performance would have done," and the seller may sue for the lost profit (UCC § 2–708[2]).

The Code, however, does not contain an analogous provision allowing aggrieved buyers to recover profits from lost sales, and there is good reason for that omission, since neither of the conditions necessary for application of the sellers' lost-profit remedy may be satisfied in the case of an aggrieved buyer. ...

Indeed, this case illustrates the difficulty of applying the seller's lost-profit remedy to aggrieved buyers. Were it not for Phoschem's breach, Fertico would have delivered the 15,000 tons of fertilizer it had purchased from Phoschem to Altawreed and would have had to go into the marketplace again to acquire an additional 15,000 tons if it wished to make a second sale to Janssens. In this respect, Fertico's position here is really no different in principle from that of an aggrieved seller which had only one set of goods at its immediate disposal. In both instances, the breach of a prior agreement is what has made the goods available for a second sale.... And, while a second sale may have been theoretically possible even without the breach, the uncertainties occasioned by the buyer/seller's need to return to the marketplace for more goods of the same kind preclude the assumption, implicit in the majority's holding ... that the second sale and its accompanying profit would have been made on the same terms even if no breach had occurred.

Finally, I cannot agree with the majority's reliance on the supposedly "exceptional" circumstance that Fertico both "met its subsale obligations with the cover fertilizer and * * * acquired title and control over the late-delivered fertilizer".... First, the basis for and significance of the majority's conclusion that Fertico acquired title to the goods is left unclear. Certainly, the fact that Fertico had already paid for the goods cannot be controlling, since the Code clearly does not equate payment and receipt of the goods with passage of title. To the contrary, the Code expressly contemplates and accounts for these situations by permitting a wronged buyer who has rejected to retain and resell the goods in its possession to recover any down payment (UCC § 2–706[6]; § 2–711[3]). The Code also requires in these situations, however, that the buyer account to the breaching seller for any additional profit it has made on the resale (UCC § 2–706[6]). Nothing in the majority opinion satisfactorily explains why this remedy is insufficient.

Furthermore, the majority's emphasis on the asserted "exceptional facts" is unpersuasive because under the terms of the majority's holding the outcome in a given case would turn, in large measure, on the fortuity of which party had possession of the goods after the breach. In the case of a simple late delivery the buyer will ordinarily have possession after the breach. Under the majority's holding, that buyer may both obtain cover damages and resell the seller's goods, retaining any profit for itself. In the case of a complete failure to deliver, however, the seller will ordinarily have possession of the goods after the breach.... . [T]he repudiating seller may resell the undelivered goods in its possession for its own account.... . Since I cannot agree with a rule of law that ultimately imposes a greater penalty on the less serious of two similar breaches, I dissent and vote to affirm.

CHIEF JUDGE WACHTLER and JUDGES SIMONS, KAYE and HANCOCK, JR., concur with JUDGE BELLACOSA; JUDGE TITONE dissents and votes to affirm in a separate opinion in which JUDGE ALEXANDER concurs.

Notes

(1) **Anticipating Breach.** The opinion states that seller bound itself contractually that fertilizer to be shipped by ocean carriers would arrive in Antwerp on or before November 20 (15,000 tons) and November 30 (20,000 tons). Before November 20, buyer cancelled the second shipment and purchased "cover" goods for both (35,000 tons). What justified buyer's actions? Was seller in breach on November 13? Had seller repudiated the contract with respect to a performance not yet due? See UCC 2–610. Were buyer's expectations of receiving due performance impaired such that buyer had the right to invoke UCC 2–609?

Could buyer have rightfully rejected the shipment that arrived on December 17? Would UCC 2–601 or 2–612(2) apply? What Code provisions might justify buyer's cancellation of the second shipment? See UCC 2–610, 2–612(3).

(2) **Rejection of Goods Already Paid For; Buyers' "Security Interest."** Why did the majority conclude that buyer's right to reject was not a commercially reasonable solution? As the dissent notes, the Commercial Code provides that a buyer who has paid some or all of the price has a security interest in rejected goods in its possession, UCC 2–711(3). A buyer may enforce its security interest by selling the goods. Why would this not be a practical alternative for buyers who rightfully reject goods already paid for?

(3) **Construction of UCC 2–711(3).** The majority and dissent disagree about the proper disposition of the profit made on a resale. If an aggrieved *seller* resells under UCC 2–706 for a higher price than the original contract price, it is entitled to keep any profit made. UCC 2–706(6). The dissent erroneously asserts otherwise, but may have had in mind that a secured creditor who forecloses on a security interest under

Article 9 must turn over to the debtor proceeds obtained in liquidating the collateral in excess of the amount due to the creditor. UCC 9–504(2). Section 2–711(3) authorizes a buyer to resell "in the manner of an aggrieved seller (Section 2–706)." Should this be construed to authorize buyers generally to retain proceeds of resale in excess of the amounts of claims against sellers? Should a different result follow if the buyer, as in this case, is a trader, who regularly buys and sells fertilizer?

(3) WRONGFUL REJECTION

Sellers' Remedies. If buyers reject wrongfully and have not paid the full contract price, sellers are entitled to remedies, catalogued in UCC 2–703.

The Code provides for two remedies based upon sellers' actual or possible substitute transactions. A seller may resell the goods and recover monetary damages measured by the differential between the contract price and the net proceeds of the resale, UCC 2–706, or measured by the difference between the contract price and the market price of the goods, UCC 2–708(1).

The Code permits sellers the equivalent of specific enforcement in only limited circumstances. If, after reasonable effort, a seller is unable to resell wrongfully rejected goods or the circumstances reasonably indicate that such effort would be unavailing, the seller may be entitled to recover the contract price. UCC 2–709(1)(b). If buyers are compelled to pay the price, they are entitled to receive the goods. UCC 2–709(2).

The "wild card" remedy available under the Code to aggrieved sellers is recovery of damages measured by the "profit" the seller would have made if buyer had fully performed. UCC 2–708(2). "Profit" under this section is akin to the accounting formula of contract price less variable costs-of-goods-sold; "overhead" or so-called fixed costs are not included as an expense in calculations of "profit."

APEX OIL CO. v. THE BELCHER CO. OF NEW YORK, INC.

United States Court of Appeals, Second Circuit, 1988.
855 F.2d 997.

WINTER, CIRCUIT JUDGE. This diversity case, arising out of an acrimonious commercial dispute, presents the question whether a sale of goods six weeks after a breach of contract may properly be used to calculate resale damages under Section 2–706 of the Uniform Commercial Code, where goods originally identified to the broken contract were sold on the day following the breach. Defendants The Belcher Company of New York, Inc. and Belcher New Jersey, Inc. (together "Belcher") appeal from a judgment, entered after a jury trial before Judge McLaughlin, awarding plaintiff Apex Oil Company ("Apex") $432,-365.04 in damages for breach of contract and fraud in connection with an uncompleted transaction for heating oil. Belcher claims that the district court improperly allowed Apex to recover resale damages and that Apex failed to prove its fraud claim by clear and convincing evidence. We agree and reverse.

BACKGROUND

Apex buys, sells, refines and transports petroleum products of various sorts, including No. 2 heating oil, commonly known as home heating oil. Belcher also buys and sells petroleum products, including No. 2 heating oil. In February 1982, both firms were trading futures contracts for No. 2 heating oil on the New York Mercantile Exchange ("Merc"). In particular, both were trading Merc contracts for February 1982 No. 2 heating oil—i.e., contracts for the delivery of that commodity in New York Harbor during that delivery month in accordance with the Merc's rules. As a result of that trading, Apex was short 315 contracts, and Belcher was long by the same amount. Being "short" one contract for oil means that the trader has contracted to deliver one thousand barrels at some point in the future, and being "long" means just the opposite—that the trader has contracted to purchase that amount of oil. If a contract is not liquidated before the close of trading, the short trader must deliver the oil to a long trader (the exchange matches shorts with longs) in strict compliance with Merc rules or suffer stiff penalties, including disciplinary proceedings and fines. A short trader may, however, meet its obligations by entering into an "exchange for physicals" ("EFP") transaction with a long trader. An EFP allows a short trader to substitute for the delivery of oil under the terms of a futures contract the delivery of oil at a different place and time.

Apex was matched with Belcher by the Merc, and thus became bound to produce 315,000 barrels of No. 2 heating oil meeting Merc specifications in New York Harbor. Those specifications required that oil delivered in New York Harbor have a sulfur content no higher than 0.20%. Apex asked Belcher whether Belcher would take delivery of 190,000 barrels of oil in Boston Harbor in satisfaction of 190 contracts, and Belcher agreed. At trial, the parties did not dispute that, under this EFP, Apex promised it would deliver the No. 2 heating oil for the same price as that in the original contract—89.70 cents per gallon—and that the oil would be lifted from the vessel Bordeaux. The parties did dispute, and vigorously so, the requisite maximum sulfur content. At trial, Belcher sought to prove that the oil had to meet the New York standard of 0.20%, while Apex asserted that the oil had to meet only the specifications for Boston Harbor of not more than 0.30% sulfur.

The Bordeaux arrived in Boston Harbor on February 9, 1982, and on the next day began discharging its cargo of No. 2 heating oil at Belcher New England, Inc.'s terminal in Revere, Massachusetts. Later in the evening of February 10, after fifty or sixty thousand barrels had been offloaded, an independent petroleum inspector told Belcher that tests showed the oil on board the Bordeaux contained 0.28% sulfur, in excess of the New York Harbor specification. Belcher, nevertheless continued to lift oil from the ship until eleven o'clock the next morning, February 11, when 141,535 barrels had been pumped into Belcher's terminal. After pumping had stopped, a second test indicated that the oil contained 0.22% sulfur—a figure within the accepted range of tolerance for oil containing 0.20% sulfur. (Apex did not learn of the second test until shortly before trial.) Nevertheless, Belcher refused to resume pumping, claiming that the oil did not conform to specifications.

After Belcher ordered the Bordeaux to leave its terminal, Apex immediately contacted Cities Service. Apex was scheduled to deliver heating oil to Cities Service later in the month and accordingly asked if it could satisfy that obligation by immediately delivering the oil on the Bordeaux. Cities Service agreed, and that oil was delivered to Cities Service in Boston Harbor on February 12, one day after the oil had been rejected by Belcher. Apex did not give notice to Belcher that the oil had been delivered to Cities Service.

Meanwhile, Belcher and Apex continued to quarrel over the portion of the oil delivered by the Bordeaux. Belcher repeatedly informed Apex, orally and by telex, that the oil was unsuitable and would have to be sold at a loss because of its high sulfur content. Belcher also claimed, falsely, that it was incurring various expenses because the oil was unusable. In fact, however, Belcher had already sold the oil in the ordinary course of business. Belcher nevertheless refused to pay Apex the contract price of $5,322,200.27 for the oil it had accepted, and it demanded that Apex produce the remaining 48,000 barrels of oil owing under the contract. On February 17, Apex agreed to tender the 48,000 barrels if Belcher would both make partial payment for the oil actually accepted and agree to negotiate as to the price ultimately to be paid for that oil. Belcher agreed and sent Apex a check for $5,034,997.12, a sum reflecting a discount of five cents per gallon from the contract price. However, the check contained an endorsement stating that "[t]he acceptance and negotiation of this check constitutes full payment and final settlement of all claims" against Belcher. Apex refused the check, and the parties returned to square one. Apex demanded full payment; Belcher demanded that Apex either negotiate the check or remove the discharged oil (which had actually been sold) and replace it with 190,000 barrels of conforming product. Apex chose to take the oil and replace it, and on February 23 told Belcher that the 142,000 barrels of discharged oil would be removed on board the Mersault on February 25.

By then, however, Belcher had sold the 142,000 barrels and did not have an equivalent amount of No. 2 oil in its entire Boston terminal.

Instead of admitting that it did not have the oil, Belcher told Apex that a dock for the Mersault was unavailable. Belcher also demanded that Apex either remove the oil *and* pay terminalling and storage fees, or accept payment for the oil at a discount of five cents per gallon. Apex refused to do either. On the next day, Belcher and Apex finally reached a settlement under which Belcher agreed to pay for the oil discharged from the Bordeaux at a discount of 2.5 cents per gallon. The settlement agreement also resolved an unrelated dispute between an Apex subsidiary and a subsidiary of Belcher's parent firm, The Coastal Corporation. It is this agreement that Apex now claims was procured by fraud.

After the settlement, Apex repeatedly contacted Belcher to ascertain when, where and how Belcher would accept delivery of the remaining 48,000 barrels. On March 5, Belcher informed Apex that it considered its obligations under the original contract to have been extinguished, and that it did not "desire to purchase such a volume [the 48,000 barrels] at the offered price." Apex responded by claiming that the settlement did not extinguish Belcher's obligation to accept the 48,000 barrels. In addition, Apex stated that unless Belcher accepted the oil by March 20, Apex would identify 48,000 barrels of No. 2 oil to the breached contract and sell the oil to a third party. When Belcher again refused to take the oil, Apex sold 48,000 barrels to Gill & Duffus Company. This oil was sold for delivery in April at a price of 76.25 cents per gallon, 13.45 cents per gallon below the Belcher contract price.

On October 7, 1982, Apex brought this suit in the Eastern District, asserting breach of contract and fraud. The breach-of-contract claim in Apex's amended complaint contended that Belcher had breached the EFP, not in February, but in March, when Belcher had refused to take delivery of the 48,000 barrels still owing under the contract. The amended complaint further alleged that "[a]t the time of the breach of the Contract by Belcher the market price of the product was $.7625 per gallon," the price brought by the resale to Gill & Duffus on March 23. ... In turn, the fraud claim asserted that Belcher had made various misrepresentations—that the Bordeaux oil was unfit, and unusable by Belcher; and that consequently Belcher was suffering extensive damages and wanted the oil removed—upon which Apex had relied when it had agreed to settle as to the 142,000 barrels lifted from the Bordeaux. Apex asserted that as a result of the alleged fraud it had suffered damages of 2.5 cents per gallon, the discount agreed upon in the settlement.

The case went to trial before Judge McLaughlin and a jury between February 3 and February 13, 1986. As it had alleged in its pleadings, Apex asserted that its breach-of-contract claim was based on an alleged breach occurring *after* February 11, 1982, the day Belcher rejected the oil on board the Bordeaux. Judge McLaughlin, however, rejected this theory as a matter of law. His view of the case was that Belcher's rejection of the Bordeaux oil occurred under one of two circumstances:

(i) either the oil conformed to the proper sulfur specification, in which case Belcher breached; or (ii) the oil did not conform, in which case Apex breached. Judge McLaughlin reasoned that, if Belcher breached on February 11, then it could not have breached thereafter. If on the other hand Apex breached, then, Judge McLaughlin reasoned, only under the doctrine of cure, see N.Y.U.C.C. § 2–508 (McKinney 1964), could Belcher be deemed to have breached. Apex, however, waived the cure theory by expressly disavowing it (perhaps because it presumes a breach by Apex). Instead, Apex argued that, regardless of whether the Bordeaux oil had conformed, Belcher's refusal throughout February and March 1982 to accept delivery of 48,000 barrels of conforming oil, which Belcher was then still demanding, had constituted a breach of contract. Judge McLaughlin rejected this argument, which he viewed as si.nply "an attempt to reintroduce the cure doctrine."

In a general verdict, the jury awarded Apex $283,752.94 on the breach-of-contract claim, and $148,612.10 on the fraud claim, for a total of $432,365.04. With the addition of prejudgment interest, the judgment came to $588,566.29.

Belcher appeals from this verdict. Apex has not taken a cross-appeal from Judge McLaughlin's dismissal of its post-February 11 breach theories, however. The parties agree, therefore, that as the case comes to us, the verdict concerning the breach can be upheld only on the theory that, if Belcher breached the contract, it did so only on February 11, 1982, and that the oil sold to Gill & Duffus on March 23 was identified to the broken contract.

DISCUSSION

... Belcher's principal argument on appeal is that the district court erred as a matter of law in allowing Apex to recover resale damages under Section 2–706. Specifically, Belcher contends that the heating oil Apex sold to Gill & Duffus in late March of 1982 was not identified to the broken contract. According to Belcher, the oil identified to the contract was the oil aboard the Bordeaux—oil which Apex had sold to Cities Service on the day after the breach. In response, Apex argues that, because heating oil is a fungible commodity, the oil sold to Gill & Duffus was "reasonably identified" to the contract even though it was not the same oil that had been on board the Bordeaux. We agree with Apex that, at least with respect to fungible goods, identification for the purposes of a resale transaction does not necessarily require that the resold goods be the exact goods that were rejected or repudiated. Nonetheless, we conclude that as a matter of law the oil sold to Gill & Duffus in March was not reasonably identified to th᛫ contract breached on February 11, and that the resale was not commercially reasonable.

Resolving the instant dispute requires us to survey various provisions of the Uniform Commercial Code. ... The Bordeaux oil was unquestionably identified to the contract under Section 2–501(b), and Apex does not assert otherwise. Nevertheless, Apex argues that Section 2–501 "has no application in the context of the Section 2–706 resale remedy," because Section 2–501 defines identification only for the purpose of establishing the point at which a buyer "obtains a special property and an insurable interest in goods." N.Y.U.C.C. § 2–501. This argument has a facial plausibility but ignores Section 2–103, which contains various definitions, and an index of other definitions, of terms used throughout Article 2 of the Code. With regard to "[i]dentification," Section 2–103(2) provides that the "definition[ ] applying to *this Article*" is set forth in Section 2–501. Id. § 2–103 (emphasis added).

Section 2–501 thus informs us that the Bordeaux oil was identified to the contract. It does not end our inquiry, however, because it does not exclude as a matter of law the possibility that a seller may identify goods to a contract, but then substitute, for the identified goods, *identical* goods that are then identified to the contract. ... Belcher relies upon Section 2–706's statement that "the seller may resell the *goods concerned,*" N.Y.U.C.C. § 2–706(1) (emphasis added), and upon Section 2–704, which states that "[a]n aggrieved seller ... may ... identify to the contract conforming goods *not already identified* if at the time he learned of the breach they are in his possession or control." Id. § 2–704(1) (emphasis added). According to Belcher, these statements absolutely foreclose the possibility of reidentification for the purpose of a resale. Apex, on the other hand, points to Section 2–706's statement that "it is not necessary that the goods be in existence or that any or all of them have been identified to the contract before the breach." Id. § 2–706(2). According to Apex, this language shows that "[t]he relevant inquiry to be made under Section 2–706 is whether the resale transaction is reasonably identified to the breached contract and not whether the goods resold were originally identified to that contract." Apex Br. at 25.

None of the cited provisions are dispositive. First, Section 2–706(1)'s reference to reselling "the goods concerned" is unhelpful because those goods are the goods identified to the contract, but which goods are so identified is the question to be answered in the instant case. Second, as to Section 2–704, the fact that an aggrieved seller may identify goods "not already identified" does not mean that the seller may not identify goods as substitutes for previously identified goods. Rather, Section 2–704 appears to deal simply with the situation described in Section 2–706(2) above, where the goods are not yet in existence or have not yet been identified to the contract. Belcher thus can draw no comfort from either Section 2–704 or Section 2–706(1). Third, at the same time, however, Section 2–706(2)'s reference to nonexistent and nonidentified goods does not mean, as Apex suggests, that the original (prebreach) identification of goods is wholly irrelevant. Rather, the provision regarding nonexistent and nonidentified goods deals with the special circumstances involving anticipatory repudiation by the buyer. See N.Y.U.C.C § 2–706 comment 7. Under such circumstances, there can of course be no resale remedy unless the seller is allowed to identify goods to the contract after the breach. That is obviously not the case here....

[F]ungible goods resold pursuant to § 2–706 must be goods identified to the contract, but need not always be those *originally* identified to the contract. In other words, at least where fungible goods are concerned, identification is not always an irrevocable act and does not foreclose the possibility of substitution. ... Nevertheless, as [§ 2–706] expressly states, "[t]he resale must be *reasonably* identified as referring to the broken contract," and "every aspect of the sale including the method, manner, time, place and terms must be commercially reasonable." Moreover, because the purpose of remedies under the Code is to put "the aggrieved party ... in as good a position as if the other party had performed," id. § 1–106(1), the reasonableness of the identification and of the resale must be determined by examining whether the market value of, and the price received for, the resold goods "accurately reflects the market value of the goods which are the subject of the contract." Servbest [Foods, Inc. v. Emssee Industries, Inc., 82 Ill.App. 3d 662,] 671, [403 N.E.2d 1], 8....

Apex's delay of nearly six weeks between the breach on February 11, 1982 and the purported resale on March 23 was clearly unreasonable, even if the transfer to Cities Service had not occurred. Steven Wirkus, of Apex, testified on cross-examination that the market price for No. 2 heating oil on February 12, when the Bordeaux oil was delivered to Cities Service, was "[p]robably somewhere around 88 cents a gallon or 87." (The EFP contract price, of course, was 89.70 cents per gallon.) Wirkus also testified on redirect examination that the market price fluctuated throughout the next several weeks:

Q. Sir, while you couldn't remember with particularity what the price of oil was on a given day four years ago, is it fair to say that prices went up and down?

A. Definitely that's fair to say.

Q. From day-to-day?

A. Yes.

Q. Towards the end of February prices went down?

A. That's correct.

Q. Then in early March it went back up?

A. In early March, yes.

Q. Then they went back down again towards the middle of March; isn't that correct?

MR. GILBERT: I object to the form of this, your Honor, on redirect.

THE COURT: Yes.

Q. Did they go back down in mid March, Mr. Wirkus?

A. My recollection, yes.

Q. In late March what happened to the price?

A. Market went back up.

Moreover, Wirkus testified that, on March 23, in a transaction unrelated to the resale, Apex purchased 25,000 barrels of No. 2 oil for March delivery at 80.50 cents per gallon, and sold an equivalent amount for April delivery at 77.25 cents per gallon. Other sales on March 22 and 23 for April delivery brought similar prices: 100,000 barrels were sold at 76.85 cents, and 25,000 barrels at 76.35 cents. The Gill & Duffus resale, which was also for April delivery, fetched a price of 76.25 cents per gallon—some eleven or twelve cents below the market price on the day of the breach.

In view of the long delay and the apparent volatility of the market for No. 2 oil, the purported resale failed to meet the requirements of Section 2–706 as a matter of law. ...

... Apex's only asserted justification, which the district court accepted in denying Belcher's motion for judgment notwithstanding the verdict, was that the delay was caused by continuing negotiations with Belcher. We find that ruling to be inconsistent with the district court's view that Belcher's breach, if any, occurred on February 11. The function of a resale was to put Apex in the position it would have been on that date by determining the value of the oil Belcher refused. The value of the oil at a later date is irrelevant because Apex was in no way obligated by the contract or by the Uniform Commercial Code to reserve 48,000 gallons for Belcher after the February 11 breach. Indeed, that is why Apex's original theory, rejected by the district court and not before us on this appeal, was that the breach occurred in March.

The rule that a "resale should be made as soon as practicable after ... breach," ... should be stringently applied where, as here, the resold goods are not those originally identified to the contract. In such circumstances, of course, there is a significant risk that the seller, who may perhaps have already disposed of the original goods without suffering any loss, has identified new goods for resale in order to minimize the resale price and thus to maximize damages. That was not the case in Servbest, for example, where the resale consisted of the first sales made after the breach. See 82 Ill.App.2d at 675, 403 N.E.2d at 11. Here, by contrast, the oil originally identified to the contract was sold the day after the February 11, 1982 breach, and no doubt Apex sold ample amounts thereafter in the six weeks before the purported resale. ... Because the sale of the oil identified to the contract to Cities Service on the next day fixed the value of the goods refused as a matter of law, the judgment on the breach-of-contract claim must be reversed.

We turn finally to Apex's fraud claim. ... Belcher claims that the evidence was insufficient to support the jury's finding that Apex, in agreeing to the settlement with Belcher, had relied upon Belcher's misrepresentations in ignorance of their falsity and had suffered injury accordingly.

In support of the finding of reliance, Apex relies primarily, if not exclusively, upon the testimony of its president, Anthony Novelly. Novelly testified that he had delegated the task of negotiation to in-house counsel, Harold Lessner. Lessner nevertheless kept Novelly abreast of Belcher's various demands and representations because it was Novelly, as president, "who had to approve the settlement ultimately." To this effect, Novelly testified as follows:

Q. During your discussion with Mr. Lesner [sic], did he say anything to you concerning whether Belcher had used the oil?

A. No, he said the oil was off spec and not useable.

Q. He said that is what Belcher had told him?

A. Correct.

Q. During your conversation with Mr. Lesner [sic], did he tell you anything about whether Belcher was claiming damages, as a result of the delivery?

A. Yes, they were.

Q. And did you rely on all the matters that were conveyed to you in approving the settlement?

A. Yes, I did.

According to Apex, this testimony regarding its alleged reliance is "unrebutted." That may be true so far as other witnesses are concerned, but Novelly candidly modified his testimony on cross-examination as follows:

Q. At the time you approved the settlement, one of the terms was that Belcher was going to get a discount off the agreed price for the BORDEAUX oil of two and a half cents per gallon, is that correct?

A. Yes.

Q. Did you believe they were intitled [sic] to a two and a half cent per gallon discount based on the facts you know?

MR. WEINER: Objection.

THE COURT: Overruled.

A. Not really.

Q. You did not believe that?

A. No.

Q. Did you believe they were intitled [sic] to any discount?

A. I wouldn't have thought so.

Q. You agreed to the settlement for other reasons, did you not?

A. I agreed to the settlement to get the thing settled.

Q. You wanted to get it behind you, is that correct?

A. Yes.

Q. You had a number of items—

A. Whole bunch of them.

Q. You didn't like to leave all these open items?

A. I didn't want a mess hanging around.

Q. You wanted to get everything cleaned up?

A. That's correct.

Q. You had another idea—withdrawn. You had another motivation, didn't you sir?

A. Coastal [Belcher's parent] was a big company, I don't like to have problems with big companies. I try to settle things and avoid litigation.

Q. You want to get all the open items closed, for you to do business with Coastal and its subsidiaries, is that correct?

A. That is a good statement, yes....

Q. At the time you were discussing the settlement with Mr. Lesner [sic] or anybody else you talked about it with, did you have the belief that the oil delivered to Belcher aboard the BORDEAUX was in fact not useable by Belcher?

A. I never had that belief, no.

However much this display of refreshing candor ought to be rewarded, we must conclude that, in light of the concessions that Novelly was seeking a compromise of all outstanding disputes and did not believe Belcher's misrepresentations as to the oil delivered on February 11, a reasonable jury could not find by clear and convincing evidence that Apex believed and relied upon Belcher's misrepresentations.

Reversed.

Notes

(1) **Commodities Futures.** This case illustrates how products may be traded through "exchanges" that permit buyers and sellers to anticipate future deliveries of certain standardized products. Many participants in these futures markets have no expectation of either delivering or receiving goods under their contracts; before the closing date, these traders take offsetting buy-sell positions so that no performance occurs. These participants may be investors seeking profits from changes in market prices of the commodities or merchants "hedging" planned transactions against shifts in market prices. The buyer and seller in *Apex Oil* did not close out their positions and were "matched" by the N.Y. Mercantile Exchange as seller and buyer. Once "matched" the parties became obligated as if they had chosen to contract with each other. Thereafter, they negotiated a modification of the place of performance for part of the oil.

(2) Construction of UCC 2–706 and 2–708. Seller's counsel sought unsuccessfully to fix damages under UCC 2–706 by the March 23 sale to Gill & Duffus. When a seller claims but fails to qualify for relief under 2–706, may recovery be had under UCC 2–708(1)? Under 2–708(2)? See Comment 2 to UCC 2–706. Should a seller-plaintiff plead and seek to prove damages under all possible statutory provisions in the alternative?

Problem 6. Suppose seller in *Apex* had sought damages measured by UCC 2–708(1). Buyer counters that seller's damages should be measured, under UCC 2–706, by the price of the resale to Cities Service. Is there any statutory basis for an argument that seller may not recover a larger amount under 2–708(1) than it would receive if damages were measured by 2–706? See Sebert, Remedies Under Article Two of the Uniform Commercial Code: An Agenda for Review, 130 U.Pa.L.Rev. 360, 380–383 (1981).

R.E. DAVIS CHEMICAL CORP. v. DIASONICS, INC.

United States Court of Appeals, Seventh Circuit, 1987.
826 F.2d 678.

CUDAHY, CIRCUIT JUDGE. Diasonics, Inc. appeals from the orders of the district court denying its motion for summary judgment and granting R.E. Davis Chemical Corp.'s summary judgment motion.... We ... reverse the grant of summary judgment in favor of Davis and remand for further proceedings.

I.

Diasonics is a California corporation engaged in the business of manufacturing and selling medical diagnostic equipment. Davis is an Illinois corporation that contracted to purchase a piece of medical diagnostic equipment from Diasonics. On or about February 23, 1984, Davis and Diasonics entered into a written contract under which Davis agreed to purchase the equipment. Pursuant to this agreement, Davis paid Diasonics a $300,000 deposit on February 29, 1984. ... Davis ... [subsequently] refused to take delivery of the equipment or to pay the balance due under the agreement. Diasonics later resold the equipment to a third party for the same price at which it was to be sold to Davis.

Davis sued Diasonics, asking for restitution of its $300,000 down payment under section 2–718(2) of the Uniform Commercial Code (the "UCC" or the "Code"). Ill. Rev. Stat. ch. 26, para. 2–718(2) (1985). Diasonics counterclaimed. Diasonics did not deny that Davis was entitled to recover its $300,000 deposit less $500 as provided in section 2–718(2)(b). However, Diasonics claimed that it was entitled to an offset under section 2–718(3). Diasonics alleged that it was a "lost volume seller," and, as such, it lost the profit from one sale when Davis breached its contract. Diasonics' position was that, in order to be put in as good a position as it would have been in had Davis performed, it was entitled to recover its lost profit on its contract with Davis under section 2–708(2) of the UCC. ...

The district court ... entered summary judgment for Davis. The court held that lost volume sellers were not entitled to recover damages under 2–708(2) but rather were limited to recovering the difference between the resale price and the contract price along with incidental damages under section 2–706(1). ... Davis was awarded $322,656, which represented Davis' down payment plus prejudgment interest less Diasonics' incidental damages. Diasonics appeals the district court's decision respecting its measure of damages as well as the dismissal of its third-party complaint.

II.

We consider first Diasonics' claim that the district court erred in holding that Diasonics was limited to the measure of damages provided in 2–706 and could not recover lost profits as a lost volume seller under 2–708(2). Surprisingly, given its importance, this issue has never been addressed by an Illinois court, nor, apparently, by any other court construing Illinois law. Thus we must attempt to predict how the Illinois Supreme Court would resolve this issue if it were presented to it. Courts applying the laws of other states have unanimously adopted the position that a lost volume seller can recover its lost profits under 2–708(2). Contrary to the result reached by the district court, we conclude that the Illinois Supreme Court would follow these other cases and would allow a lost volume seller to recover its lost profit under 2–708(2).

We begin our analysis with 2–718(2) and (3). Under 2–718(2)(b), Davis is entitled to the return of its down payment less $500. Davis' right to restitution, however, is qualified under 2–718(3)(a) to the extent that Diasonics can establish a right to recover damages under any other provision of Article 2 of the UCC. Article 2 contains four provisions that concern the recovery of a seller's general damages (as opposed to its incidental or consequential damages); 2–706 (contract price less resale price); 2–708(1) (contract price less market price); 2–708(2) (profit); and 2–709 (price). The problem we face here is determining whether Diasonics' damages should be measured under 2–706 or 2–708(2). To answer this question, we need to engage in a detailed look at the language and structure of these various damage provisions.

The Code does not provide a great deal of guidance as to when a particular damage remedy is appropriate. The damage remedies provided under the Code are catalogued in section 2–703, but this section does not indicate that there is any hierarchy among the remedies. One method of approaching the damage sections is to conclude that 2–708 is relegated to a role inferior to that of 2–706 and 2–709 and that one can turn to 2–708 only after one has concluded that neither 2–706 nor 2–

709 is applicable.[6] Under this interpretation of the relationship between 2–706 and 2–708, if the goods have been resold, the seller can sue to recover damages measured by the difference between the contract price and the resale price under 2–706. The seller can turn to 2–708 only if it resells in a commercially unreasonable manner or if it cannot resell but an action for the price is inappropriate under 2–709. The district court adopted this reading of the Code's damage remedies and, accordingly, limited Diasonics to the measure of damages provided in 2–706 because it resold the equipment in a commercially reasonable manner.

The district court's interpretation of 2–706 and 2–708, however, creates its own problems of statutory construction. There is some suggestion in the Code that the "fact that plaintiff resold the goods [in a commercially reasonable manner] does *not* compel him to use the resale remedy of § 2–706 rather than the damage remedy of § 2–708." Harris, A Radical Restatement of the Law of Seller's Damages: Sales Act and Commercial Code Results Compared, 18 Stan.L.Rev. 66, 101 n.174 (1965) (emphasis in original). Official comment 1 to 2–703, which catalogues the remedies available to a seller, states that these "remedies are essentially cumulative in nature" and that "whether the pursuit of one remedy bars another depends entirely on the facts of the individual case." See also State of New York Report of the Law Revision Comm'n for 1956, 396–97 (1956).[7]

---

6. Evidence to support this approach can be found in the language of the various damage sections and of the official comments to the UCC. See § 2–709(3) ("a seller who is held not entitled to the price under this Section shall nevertheless be awarded damages for non-acceptance under the preceding section [§ 2–708]"); UCC comment 7 to § 2–709 ("if the action for the price fails, the seller may nonetheless have proved a case entitling him to damages for non-acceptance [under § 2–708]"); UCC comment 2 to § 2–706 ("failure to act properly under this section deprives the seller of the measure of damages here provided and relegates him to that provided in Section 2–708"); UCC comment 1 to § 2–704 (describes § 2–706 as the "primary remedy" available to a seller upon breach by the buyer); see also Commonwealth Edison Co. v. Decker Coal Co., 653 F.Supp. 841, 844 (N.D.Ill. 1987) (statutory language and case law suggest that "§ 2–708 remedies are available only to a seller who is not entitled to the contract price" under § 2–709); Childres & Burgess, Seller's Remedies: The Primacy of UCC 2–708(2), 48 N.Y.U.L.Rev. 833, 863–64 (1973). As one commentator has noted, 2–706 "is the Code section drafted specifically to define the damage rights of aggrieved reselling sellers, and there is no suggestion within it

that the profit formula of section 2–708(2) is in any way intended to qualify or be superior to it." Shanker, The Case for a Literal Reading of UCC Section 2–708(2) (One Profit for the Reseller), 24 Case W. Res. 697, 699 (1973).

7. UCC comment 2 to 2–708(2) also suggests that 2–708 has broader applicability than suggested by the district court. UCC comment 2 provides: "This section permits the recovery of lost profits in all appropriate cases, which would include all standard priced goods. The normal measure there would be list price less cost to the dealer or list price less manufacturing cost to the manufacturer."

The district court's restrictive interpretation of 2–708(2) was based in part on UCC comment 1 to 2–704 which describes 2–706 as the aggrieved seller's primary remedy. The district court concluded that, if a lost volume seller could recover its lost profit under 2–708(2), every seller would attempt to recover damages under 2–708(2) and 2–706 would become the aggrieved seller's residuary remedy. This argument ignores the fact that to recover under 2–708(2), a seller must first establish its status as a lost volume seller. . . .

The district court also concluded that a lost volume seller cannot recover its lost

Those courts that found that a lost volume seller can recover its lost profits under 2–708(2) implicitly rejected the position adopted by the district court; those courts started with the assumption that 2–708 applied to a lost volume seller without considering whether the seller was limited to the remedy provided under 2–706. None of those courts even suggested that a seller who resold goods in a commercially reasonable manner was limited to the damage formula provided under 2–706. We conclude that the Illinois Supreme Court, if presented with this question, would adopt the position of these other jurisdictions and would conclude that a reselling seller, such as Diasonics, is free to reject the damage formula prescribed in 2–706 and choose to proceed under 2–708.

Concluding that Diasonics is entitled to seek damages under 2–708, however, does not automatically result in Diasonics being awarded its lost profit. Two different measures of damages are provided in 2–708. Subsection 2–708(1) provides for a measure of damages calculated by subtracting the market price at the time and place for tender from the contract price.[9] The profit measure of damages, for which Diasonics is asking, is contained in 2–708(2). However, one applies 2–708(2) only if "the measure of damages provided in subsection (1) is inadequate to put the seller in as good a position as performance would have done...." Ill. Rev. Stat. ch. 26, para. 2–708(2) (1985). Diasonics claims that 2–708(1) does not provide an adequate measure of damages when the seller is a lost volume seller. To understand Diasonics' argument, we need to define the concept of the lost volume seller. Those cases that have addressed this issue have defined a lost volume seller as one that has a predictable and finite number of customers and that has the capacity either to sell to all new buyers or to make the one additional sale represented by the resale after the breach. According to a number of courts and commentators, if the seller would have made the sale represented by the resale whether or not the breach occurred, damages measured by the difference between the contract price and market price cannot put the lost volume seller in as good a position as it would have been in had the buyer performed. The breach effectively cost the seller a "profit," and the seller can only be made whole by awarding it damages in the amount of its "lost profit" under 2–708(2).

profit under 2–708(2) because such a result would negate a seller's duty to mitigate damages. This position fails to recognize the fact that, by definition, a lost volume seller cannot mitigate damages through resale. Resale does not reduce a lost volume seller's damages because the breach has still resulted in its losing one sale and a corresponding profit. ...

9. There is some debate in the commentaries about whether a seller who has resold the goods may ignore the measure of damages provided in 2–706 and elect to proceed under 2–708(1). Under some circumstances the contract-market price differential will result in overcompensating such a seller. See J. White & R. Summers, Handbook of the Law under the Uniform Commercial Code § 7–7, at 271–73 (2d ed. 1980); Sebert, Remedies under Article Two of the Uniform Commercial Code: An Agenda for Review, 130 U.Pa.L.Rev. 360, 380–83 (1981). We need not struggle with this question here because Diasonics has not sought to recover damages under 2–708(1).

We agree with Diasonics' position that, under some circumstances, the measure of damages provided under 2–708(1) will not put a reselling seller in as good a position as it would have been in had the buyer performed because the breach resulted in the seller losing sales volume. However, we disagree with the definition of "lost volume seller" adopted by other courts. Courts awarding lost profits to a lost volume seller have focused on whether the seller had the capacity to supply the breached units in addition to what it actually sold. In reality, however, the relevant questions include, not only whether the seller could have produced the breached units in addition to its actual volume, but also whether it would have been profitable for the seller to produce both units. Goetz & Scott, Measuring Sellers' Damages: The Lost–Profits Puzzle, 31 Stan.L.Rev. 323, 332–33, 346–47 (1979). As one commentator has noted, under the economic law of diminishing returns or increasing marginal costs[,] ... as a seller's volume increases, then a point will inevitably be reached where the cost of selling each additional item diminishes the incremental return to the seller and eventually makes it entirely unprofitable to conclude the next sale. Shanker, supra, at 705. Thus, under some conditions, awarding a lost volume seller its presumed lost profit will result in overcompensating the seller, and 2–708(2) would not take effect because the damage formula provided in 2–708(1) does place the seller in as good a position as if the buyer had performed. Therefore, on remand, Diasonics must establish, not only that it had the capacity to produce the breached unit in addition to the unit resold, but also that it would have been profitable for it to have produced and sold both. ...

One final problem with awarding a lost volume seller its lost profits was raised by the district court. This problem stems from the formulation of the measure of damages provided under 2–708(2) which is "the profit (including reasonable overhead) which the seller would have made from full performance by the buyer, together with any incidental damages provided in this Article (Section 2–710), due allowance for costs reasonably incurred and due credit for payments or *proceeds of resale*" (emphasis added). The literal language of 2–708(2) requires that the proceeds from resale be credited against the amount of damages awarded which, in most cases, would result in the seller recovering nominal damages. In those cases in which the lost volume seller was awarded its lost profit as damages, the courts have circumvented this problem by concluding that this language only applies to proceeds realized from the resale of uncompleted goods for scrap. See, e.g., Neri [v. Retail Marine Corp.,] 30 N.Y.2d [393,] at 399 & n.2, 285 N.E.2d [311,] at 314 & n.2; see also J. White & R. Summers, Handbook of the Law under the Uniform Commercial Code § 7–13, at 285 ("courts should simply ignore the 'due credit' language in lost volume cases") (footnote omitted). Although neither the text of 2–708(2) nor the official comments limit its application to resale of goods for scrap, there is evidence that the drafters of 2–708 seemed to have had this more limited application in mind when they proposed amending 2–708 to include the phrase "due credit for payments or proceeds of resale." We conclude that the Illinois Supreme Court would adopt this more restrictive interpretation of this phrase rendering it inapplicable to this case.

We therefore reverse the grant of summary judgment in favor of Davis and remand with instructions that the district court calculate Diasonics' damages under 2–708(2) if Diasonics can establish, not only that it had the capacity to make the sale to Davis as well as the sale to the resale buyer, but also that it would have been profitable for it to make both sales. Of course, Diasonics, in addition, must show that it probably would have made the second sale absent the breach....

Notes

(1) **Subsequent Decision:** On remand, Diasonics proved its average costs of manufacturing through expert testimony by accountants. It introduced evidence that the contract price was $1,500,000 but offered no specific evidence of the cost of manufacturing the equipment intended for Davis and resold to the third party. Using average cost data, the district court found that Diasonics profit would have been $453,000. The court of appeals affirmed. 924 F.2d 709 (7th Cir.1991).[15]

(2) **Construction of UCC 2–708(2).** As indicated in the court's opinion, the academic debate about the proper reading of UCC 2–708(2) has been and continues to be vigorous. Some explanation must be found for the enormous difference in the amount of damages recoverable in a case like *Davis,* under UCC 2–708(2) ($453,000), under UCC 2–706 ($–0–), under UCC 2–708(1) (probably $–0–). The remarkably laconic Comment to UCC 2–708(2) gives no indication of appreciating the sheer force of this section. Much of the academic debate is in the mode of law-and-economics analysis, based upon models of "lost volume" sellers. Others argue that the basic remedial principle requires putting an aggrieved seller into as good a position as buyer's performance would have done, UCC 1–106, and that market-based damages under UCC 2–706 and 2–708(1) fail to mirror full performance. In addition to the materials referred to by the court, see Sebert, Remedies Under Article Two of the Uniform Commercial Code: An Agenda for Review, 130 U.Pa.L.Rev. 360 (1981); Goldberg, An Economic Analysis of the Lost–Volume Retail Seller, 57 S.Cal.L.Rev. 283 (1984); Cooter and Eisenberg, Damages for Breach of Contract, 73 Cal.L.Rev. 1434 (1985); J. White & R. Summers, Uniform Commercial Code §§ 7–8 to 7–14 (3d ed. 1988); Scott, The Case for Market Damages: Revisiting the Lost Profits Puzzle, 4 U.Chi.L.Rev. 1155 (1990).

Although the UCC 2–708 Comment states that the section is a rewriting of a provision in the Uniform Sales Act, that act had no provision comparable to UCC 2–708(2). The cited section, USA 64,

---

15. The court of appeals remanded for further consideration of a contract term that buyer contended would have lowered the purchase price by a post-payment rebate of $255,000.

provided generally for recovery of loss resulting in the ordinary course of events from buyer's breach (64(2)) and stated the specific formula of market-based damages in 64(3); it added in 64(4):

> (4) If, while labor or expense of material amount are necessary on the part of the seller to enable him to fulfill his obligations under the contract to sell or the sale, the buyer repudiates the contract or the sale, or notifies the seller to proceed no further therewith, the buyer shall be liable to the seller for no greater damages than the seller would have suffered if he did nothing towards carrying out the contract or the sale after receiving notice of the buyer's repudiation or countermand. The profit the seller would have made if the contract or the sale had been fully performed shall be considered in estimating such damages.

The Code revised the USA 64(4) allocation of risk if a manufacturing seller elects, upon repudiation, to complete the process. UCC 2–704(2). The manufacturer who exercises reasonable commercial judgment for the purposes of avoiding loss and "effective realization" is protected even if the value added thereby is less than the costs incurred.

Is it accurate to describe UCC 2–708 as a rewriting of USA 64?

(3) Revision of Article 2. The Permanent Editorial Board Study Group on Article 2 recommended revision of UCC 2–708(2) to state, explicitly, that a seller may invoke the profit-measure of damages (1) when seller can show "lost volume," i.e., that but for the breach seller would probably have made two sales, or (2) or when a "middleman" seller reasonably stopped performance before the goods were obtained or a manufacturing seller stopped performance before the goods were completed. Preliminary Report 214–216 (1990). The Study Group recommended, further, that different measures be used for these two categories: The "due allowance ... due credit ..." clause should apply only to "stopped performance" cases and not to "lost volume" cases, but consideration should be given to economic analyses of declining margins of profit in multiple transactions. Id. 217–218. Do you agree?

(B) INTERNATIONAL SALES LAW

---

(1) BUYERS' AVOIDANCE FOR SELLERS' BREACH

The Convention on International Sale of Goods does not use the concepts of buyers' acceptance and rejection of goods and for the most part eschews any performance standard like the perfect tender rule. The Convention permits buyers to throw goods back on sellers on two grounds: (1) if sellers' performances are so deficient as to constitute "fundamental breach" as defined in CISG 25, or (2) if seller does not deliver goods within an extended time fixed by buyers under the *Nachfrist* provision of CISG 47. If either ground exists, a buyer may declare the contract avoided. CISG 49. For deficiencies that do not amount to "fundamental breach" or delays that are not within the *Nachfrist* provisions, buyers must take and keep or dispose of the goods. Buyers may, of course, seek monetary relief through price reduction or damages.

Buyers' exercise of the power to avoid contracts for fundamental breach is analogous to buyers' power to revoke acceptance under domestic United States law. We defer discussion of the manner, time, and effect of avoidance until the next section. We consider here the power to avoid for delay in performance.

Avoidance for Sellers' Late Performance. Sellers who deliver goods substantially after the time required for performance under the contracts may thereby commit fundamental breach. Aggrieved buyers may declare contracts avoided for fundamental breach whether the result of sellers' delay or other non-conformity.

However, the Convention underscores buyers' right to timely performance by sellers with additional provisions that do not depend upon fundamental breach. These provisions permit strict enforcement, not with regard to the time terms of the sales contracts, but rather with regard to the extensions of time that buyers can set under the Convention's *Nachfrist* provisions. Article 49(1)(b) empowers a buyer to avoid a sales contract if the seller has not delivered the goods within the "additional time" fixed by the buyer under CISG 47(1). In this facet of sellers' performance, buyers can effectively demand something akin to the exact performance of the perfect tender rule. Under what circumstances would buyers be specially concerned about the time of sellers' performance? See J. Honnold, Uniform Law for International Sales §§ 288, 305 (2d ed. 1991).

Time of Avoidance. The avoiding power of CISG 49(1)(b) is explicitly limited to cases of non-delivery. Once a seller has delivered, a buyer's power to throw the goods back on seller turns upon the degree of injury; buyer can avoid only for fundamental breach. Thus, here as elsewhere, CISG tends to restrict remedies for breach to monetary damages rather than permitting destruction of the duty to perform—a policy choice that responds to the waste that may result from contract-avoidance after extended international transport.

Manner of Avoidance. To avoid a contract under CISG 49(1)(b), a buyer must declare the contract avoided and give notice to the seller. CISG 26.

Effect of Avoidance. In cases of non-delivery, a buyer who declares the contract avoided is released from its obligations under the contract. CISG 81. Particularly, a buyer is released from the CISG 53 obligations to take delivery of the goods and pay the price. If buyer has already paid the price, it is entitled to restitution. CISG 81(2). Whether or not the price has been paid, buyer is entitled to damages. CISG

81(1). If the goods have arrived at their destination and placed there at buyer's disposal, even though the buyer has exercised the right to avoid the contract, the buyer must take possession of the goods on behalf of the seller, provided that this can be done without payment of the price and without unreasonable inconvenience or expense. CISG 86(2). Buyer must take steps to preserve the goods, CISG 87, and, under circumstances defined by the Convention, may or must sell them. CISG 88.

Problem 7. Assume the international sales transaction in *Fertico Belgium* had been governed by CISG. Would the *Nachfrist* provisions affect the outcome? Does CISG permit a buyer, who does not avoid the contract, to "cover" for a late delivery and recover damages? In calculating buyer's damages under CISG, would seller be entitled to a reduction for the amount of buyer's profit on resale of the late arriving goods?

(2) SELLERS' AVOIDANCE FOR BUYERS' BREACH

The Convention contains provisions that permit sellers to declare contracts avoided on grounds analogous to those that permit buyers to do so. CISG 64. Sellers' primary concern is, of course, payment of the price. Commonly in international sales, agreements provide that buyer must open bank letters of credit, to assure sellers of payment, before sellers ship the goods. (We have seen such a term in the *Fertico Belgium* case.) Failure of a buyer to obtain a letter of credit pursuant to its contract may, in some circumstances, constitute fundamental breach. Sellers, like buyers, may exercise a *Nachfrist* provision that fixes an additional time for buyers to meet their obligations regarding payment. CISG 63(1). If a buyer fails to act properly within that time, the seller may avoid the contract whether or not the delay constitutes fundamental breach. CISG 64(1)(b).[16]

SECTION 3. REVOCATION OF ACCEPTANCE

(A) DOMESTIC SALES LAW

Buyers who accepted non-conforming goods may still throw the goods back at sellers under the conditions set forth in UCC 2–608. Revocation of acceptance is a powerful legal tool in the hands of buyers.

---

16. In dealing with buyers' obligation to pay, CISG 64(1)(b) is not limited to contracts that contemplate payment by bank letter of credit.

The *Nachfrist* provision of 64(1)(b) refers not only to buyers' obligation to pay the price, but alternatively refers to the obligation to take delivery of the goods. This is a somewhat anomalous provision; a seller who is paid is not likely to be much concerned with the timeliness of buyer's taking delivery. For discussion of this aspect of CISG 64(1)(b), see J. Honnold, Uniform Law for International Sales § 354 (2d ed. 1991).

If justified in revoking acceptance buyers are entitled to recover the contract price and damages, UCC 2–711(1), measured by a substitute purchase, UCC 2–712, or by market prices, UCC 2–713. Further disposition of the goods becomes sellers' problem; revocation of acceptance gives buyers the same rights and duties with regard to the goods as if they had rejected them. UCC 2–608(3).

McCULLOUGH v. BILL SWAD CHRYSLER–PLYMOUTH, INC.

Supreme Court of Ohio, 1983.
5 Ohio St.3d 181, 449 N.E.2d 1289.

On May 23, 1978, appellee, Deborah A. McCullough (then Deborah Miller), purchased a 1978 Chrysler LeBaron from appellant, Bill Swad Chrysler–Plymouth, Inc. (now Bill Swad Datsun, Inc.). The automobile was protected by both a limited warranty and a Vehicle Service Contract (extended warranty). Following delivery of the vehicle, appellee and her (then) fiance informed appellant's sales agent of problems they had noted with the car's brakes, lack of rustproofing, paint job and seat panels. Other problems were noted by appellee as to the car's transmission and air conditioning. The next day, the brakes failed, and appellee returned the car to appellant for the necessary repairs.

When again in possession of the car, appellee discovered that the brakes had not been fixed properly and that none of the cosmetic work was done. Problems were also noted with respect to the car's steering mechanism. Again, the car was returned for repair and again new problems appeared, this time as to the windshield post, the vinyl top and the paint job. Only two weeks later, appellant was unable to eliminate a noise appellee complained of that had developed in the car's rear end.

On June 26, 1978, appellee returned the car to appellant for correction both of the still unremedied defects and of other flaws that had surfaced since the last failed repair effort. Appellant retained possession of the vehicle for over three weeks in order to service it, but even then many of the former problems persisted. Moreover, appellant's workmanship had apparently caused new defects to arise affecting the car's stereo system, landau top and exterior. Appellee also experienced difficulties with vibrations, the horn, and the brakes.

The following month, while appellee was on a short trip away from her home, the automobile's engine abruptly shut off. The car eventually had to be towed to appellant's service shop for repair. A few days later, when appellee and her husband were embarked on an extensive honeymoon vacation, the brakes again failed. Upon returning from their excursion, the newlyweds, who had prepared a list of thirty-two of the automobile's defects, submitted the list to appellant and again requested their correction. By the end of October 1978, few of the enumerated problems had been remedied.

In early November 1978, appellee contacted appellant's successor, Chrysler–Plymouth East ("East"), regarding further servicing of the vehicle. East was not able to undertake the requested repairs until January 1979. Despite the additional work which East performed, the vehicle continued to malfunction. After May 1979, East refused to perform any additional work on the automobile, claiming that the vehicle was in satisfactory condition, appellee's assertions to the contrary notwithstanding.

On January 8, 1979, appellee, by letter addressed to appellant, called for the rescission of the purchase agreement, demanded a refund of the entire purchase price and expenses incurred, and offered to return the automobile to appellant upon receipt of shipping instructions. Appellant did not respond to appellee's letter, and appellee continued to operate the car.

On January 12, 1979, appellee filed suit against appellant, East, Chrysler Corporation, and City National Bank & Trust Co., seeking rescission of the sales agreement and incidental and consequential damages. By the time of trial, June 25, 1980, the subject vehicle had been driven nearly 35,000 miles, approximately 23,000 of which were logged after appellee mailed her notice of revocation. The trial court dismissed the action as to East, the bank and Chrysler Corporation, but entered judgment for appellee against appellant in the amount of $9,376.82, and ordered the return of the automobile to appellant. The court of appeals subsequently affirmed, determining that appellee had properly revoked her acceptance of the automobile despite her continued use of the vehicle, which use the appellate court found reasonable.

The cause is now before this court pursuant to the allowance of a motion to certify the record.

Locher, Justice. The case at bar essentially poses but a single question: Whether appellee, by continuing to operate the vehicle she had purchased from appellant after notifying the latter of her intent to rescind the purchase agreement, waived her right to revoke her initial acceptance. After having thoroughly reviewed both the relevant facts in the present cause and the applicable law, we find that appellee, despite her extensive use of the car following her revocation, in no way forfeited such right.

The ultimate disposition of the instant action is governed primarily by R.C. 1302.66[UCC 2–608]. . . .

Appellant essentially argues that appellee's revocation of her initial acceptance of the automobile was ineffective as it did not comply with the mode prescribed for revocation in [UCC 2–608]. Specifically, appellant asserts that appellee's continued operation of the vehicle after advising appellant of her revocation was inconsistent with her having relinquished ownership of the car,[2] that the value of the automobile to appellee was not substantially impaired by its alleged nonconformities, and that the warranties furnished by appellant provided the sole legal remedy for alleviating the automobile's defects. Each of appellant's contentions must be rejected.

Although the legal question presented in appellant's first objection is a novel one for this bench, other state courts which have addressed the issue have held that whether continued use of goods after notification of revocation of their acceptance vitiates such revocation is solely dependent upon whether such use was reasonable. ... Moreover, whether such use was reasonable is a question to be determined by the trier of fact. ...

The genesis of the "reasonable use" test lies in the recognition that frequently a buyer, after revoking his earlier acceptance of a good, is constrained by exogenous circumstances—many of which the seller controls—to continue using the good until a suitable replacement may realistically be secured. Clearly, to penalize the buyer for a predicament not of his own creation would be patently unjust. As the court stated in Richardson v. Messina (1960), 361 Mich. 364, 369, 105 N.W.2d 153, 156:

     ... It does not lie in the seller's mouth to demand the utmost in nicety between permissible and impermissible use, for the perilous situation in which the purchaser finds himself arises from the imperfections of that furnished, for a consideration, by the seller himself. ...

In ascertaining whether a buyer's continued use of an item after revocation of its acceptance was reasonable, the trier of fact should pose and divine the answers to the following queries: (1) Upon being apprised of the buyer's revocation of his acceptance, what instructions, if any, did the seller tender the buyer concerning return of the now rejected goods? (2) Did the buyer's business needs or personal circumstances compel the continued use? (3) During the period of such use, did the seller persist in assuring the buyer that all nonconformities would be cured or that provisions would otherwise be made to recompense the latter for the dissatisfaction and inconvenience which the defects caused him? (4) Did the seller act in good faith? (5) Was the seller unduly prejudiced by the buyer's continued use. ...

It is manifest that, upon consideration of the aforementioned criteria, appellee acted reasonably in continuing to operate her motor vehicle even after revocation of acceptance. First, the failure of the seller to advise the buyer, after the latter has revoked his acceptance of the goods, how the goods were to be returned entitles the buyer to retain possession of them. ... Appellant, in the case at bar, did not

---

2. [UCC 2–608(3)] requires that a buyer who revokes his acceptance must treat the subject goods as if he had rejected them pursuant to [UCC 2–602]. Under [2–602(2)(a)], a buyer's continued exercise of ownership rights *vis-a-vis* the rejected goods is a wrong against the seller.

respond to appellee's request for instructions regarding the disposition of the vehicle. Failing to have done so, appellant can hardly be heard now to complain of appellee's continued use of the automobile.

Secondly, appellee, a young clerical secretary of limited financial resources, was scarcely in position to return the defective automobile and obtain a second in order to meet her business and personal needs. A most unreasonable obligation would be imposed upon appellee were she to be required, in effect, to secure a loan to purchase a second car while remaining liable for repayment of the first car loan. ...

Additionally, appellant's successor (East), by attempting to repair the appellee's vehicle even after she tendered her notice of revocation, provided both express and tacit assurances that the automobile's defects were remediable, thereby, inducing her to retain possession. Moreover, whether appellant acted in good faith throughout this episode is highly problematic, especially given the fact that whenever repair of the car was undertaken, new defects often miraculously arose while previous ones frequently went uncorrected. Both appellant's and East's refusal to honor the warranties before their expiration also evidences less than fair dealing.

Finally, it is apparent that appellant was not prejudiced by appellee's continued operation of the automobile. Had appellant retaken possession of the vehicle pursuant to appellee's notice of revocation, the automobile, which at the time had been driven only 12,000 miles, could easily have been resold. Indeed, the car was still marketable at the time of trial, as even then the odometer registered less than 35,000 miles. In any event, having failed to reassume ownership of the automobile when requested to do so, appellant alone must bear the loss for any diminution of the vehicle's resale value occurring between the two dates.

[UCC 2–711(3)] provides an additional basis for appellee's retention after revocation of the automobile. A buyer who possesses, as appellee does in the instant action, a security interest in the rejected goods may continue to use them even after revoking his acceptance. .... . Consequently, appellee's continued use of the defective vehicle was a permissible means of protecting her security interest therein.

Appellant maintains, however, that even if appellee's continued operation of the automobile after revocation was reasonable, such use is "*prima facie* evidence" that the vehicle's nonconformities did not substantially impair its value to appellee, thus precluding availability of the remedy of revocation. Such an inference, though, may not be drawn. As stated earlier, external conditions beyond the buyer's immediate control often mandate continued use of an item even after revocation of its acceptance. Thus, it cannot seriously be contended that appellee, by continuing to operate the defective vehicle, intimated that its nonconformities did not substantially diminish its worth in her eyes.

We must similarly dismiss appellant's assertion that, as appellee's complaints primarily concerned cosmetic flaws, the defects were trivial. First, the chronic steering, transmission and brake problems which appellee experienced in operating the vehicle could hardly be deemed inconsequential. Moreover, even purely cosmetic defects, under the proper set of circumstances, can significantly affect the buyer's valuation of the good. ...

Whether a complained of nonconformity substantially impairs an item's worth to the buyer is a determination exclusively within the purview of the factfinder and must be based on objective evidence of the buyer's idiosyncratic tastes and needs. ... Any defect that shakes the buyer's faith or undermines his confidence in the reliability and integrity of the purchased item is deemed to work a substantial impairment of the item's value and to provide a basis for revocation of the underlying sales agreement. Durfee v. Rod Baxter Imports, Inc. (Minn.1977), 262 N.W.2d 349, at 354; Asciolla v. Manter Oldsmobile–Pontiac, Inc., supra, 370 A.2d at 274. Clearly, no error was committed in finding that the fears occasioned by the recurrent brake failings, steering malfunctions and other mechanical difficulties, as well as the utter frustration caused by the seemingly endless array of cosmetic flaws, constituted nonconformities giving rise to the remedy of revocation.

. . .

Judgment affirmed.

HOLMES, J., dissents in part and concurs in part. I concur in the syllabus law as set forth in this case, but would remand to the trial court for a determination of the amount due the dealer from the buyer as a setoff due to the buyer's use of the goods after revocation. Both the court of appeals and this court state that Swad should be entitled to such an offset against the judgment for the reasonable value of the use of the automobile after the revocation. However, both courts summarily dispense with such an offset by stating that Swad introduced no evidence to establish the reasonable value of the automobile's use.

The need for any such evidence when the appellant was asserting that the buyer had waived any right to revoke acceptance would, from the standpoint of trial procedure, have been highly questionable. The seller should be given an opportunity to present evidence of the reasonable value of such use, or the trial court should take judicial notice of the fair market value of the use of such an automobile.

Notes

(1) **Substantial Impairment; Measure of Conforming Goods and Identity of Warrantor.** Since the right to revoke acceptance is conditioned upon substantial non-conformity of the goods, it is necessary to begin with the measure of conforming goods. Revocations are

most likely to involve dissatisfaction with the quality of the goods. Thus, the measure of conformity is found in express or implied warranties of quality. Identifying the warranty that was breached in *McCullough,* and further identifying the warrantor of the breached warranty, is not a simple matter.

The opinion notes, at the outset, that "the automobile was protected by both a limited warranty and a Vehicle Service Contract (extended warranty)," but does not indicate that either was breached. Is it likely that the revocation occurred during the active coverage of the extended warranty? If not, consider the limited warranty. The manufacturer is almost certain to have made the limited warranty. Is Chrysler Corporation a party to the case in the Ohio Supreme Court?

Only Bill Swad Chrysler–Plymouth is a defendant on appeal. For what quality warranty is the dealer responsible? If a dealer is not a co-warrantor of a manufacturer's limited warranty, the Magnuson–Moss Warranty Act does not foreclose the dealer from selling cars with a disclaimer of all implied warranties, including the warranty of merchantability. Typically, car dealers include such disclaimers in sales agreements with their customers, who are informed that the only quality warranties are those of the manufacturer or, in some instances, components suppliers (e.g., tires). If Bill Swad's agreement with McCullough contained such a disclaimer, what would be the measure of conforming goods vis-a-vis Bill Swad?

(2) Manner and Time of Buyers' Revocation of Acceptance. Revocation of acceptance occurs when buyers give notice of it to the sellers.[1] UCC 2–608(2). Buyers are not required to offer to hand back the goods to effect a revocation; buyers who have paid part or all of the price have security interests in the goods that entitle them to keep the goods and, if necessary, to sell them to recover the price paid. UCC 2–711(3), 2–608(3). The Code provides that buyers must act "within a reasonable time" after they discover or should have discovered the ground; the time is defined in part by deterioration in the condition of the goods not caused by their defects.

(3) Cure After Revocation. After buyers give notice of revocation of acceptance, do sellers have the right to cure? No such right is mentioned in UCC 2–608 and UCC 2–508, literally construed, is limited to cure after buyers' rejections.

The issue is not novel. Numerous courts ... have confronted it and have generally agreed that in most circumstances the right to cure is lost once acceptance has occurred. The Mississippi [Supreme Court] decided otherwise in *Fitzner Pontiac–Buick–Cadillac Inc. v. Smith,* [523 So.2d 324 (1988)], holding that the buyer of an automobile that had been plagued with infirmities since its purchase could not revoke unless the seller was first afforded an opportunity to cure.

---

1. This is by inference from the actual language of the Code, which states that a revocation is "not effective until" a buyer gives notice. UCC 2–608(2).

Undaunted by the reality that neither the language of the Code nor the weight of authority sanction this extension of the right to cure, the court reasoned that its holding was justified by the general policy of the law favoring the prevention of economic waste.

Frisch & Wladis, General Provisions, Sales, Bulk Transfers, and Documents of Title, 44 The Business Lawyer 1445, 1464 (1989). See also U. S. Roofing, Inc. v. Credit Alliance Corp., 228 Cal.App.3d 1431, 279 Cal.Rptr. 533 (1991).

The Permanent Editorial Board Study Group on UCC Article 2 recommended that UCC 2–608 be amended to provide the seller with a right to cure only until the time for performance has expired. Preliminary Report 171 (1990).

(4) Buyers' Legal Actions Following Revocation. Buyers who revoke acceptance often find it necessary or desirable to bring law suits to obtain relief. Buyers who have paid all or part of the price may seek to recover those sums from the sellers. Even if, as in *McCullough*, buyer has a security interest in goods retained following revocation, buyer may elect not to resell the car and may choose instead to sue the seller (and others). What might induce buyers to seek recovery through litigation rather than by self-help relief through foreclosures of their security interests? See UCC 2–711(1).

(5) Actions Against Manufacturers. Buyers who revoke acceptance often elect to bring post-revocation legal actions against the manufacturers, in addition to or instead of suing the immediate sellers. McCullough did so; the trial court dismissed that part of buyer's case and apparently buyer did not appeal. Does UCC 2–608 contemplate or authorize revoking buyers to bring legal actions against manufacturers? Courts deciding the issue are sharply divided.[2] One set of commentators argues that revocation against remote sellers should be permitted:

> There is certainly nothing in Article 2 that would be inconsistent with such an approach. Moreover, the concept of "remote revocation" is gaining a foothold elsewhere. In the Magnuson–Moss Federal Warranty Act, a manufacturer who markets consumer products under a "full warranty" heading must permit the consumer/buyer to elect either a refund of the full purchase price or

---

2. *Compare* Andover Air Ltd. Partnership v. Piper Aircraft Corp., 7 UCC Rep. Serv. 2d 1494 (D.Mass.1989); Gasque v. Mooers Motor Car Co., 227 Va. 154, 313 S.E.2d 384 (1984); Seekings v. Jimmy GMC of Tucson, Inc., 130 Ariz. 596, 638 P.2d 210 (1981); Edelstein v. Toyota Motors Distributors, 176 N.J. Super. 57, 422 A.2d 101 (1980); Conte v. Dwan Lincoln–Mercury, Inc., 172 Conn. 112, 374 A.2d 144 (1976); Voytovich v. Bangor Punta Operations, Inc., 494 F.2d 1208 (6th Cir.1974), *with*

Gochey v. Bombardier, Inc., 153 Vt. 607, 572 A.2d 921 (1990); Ford Motor Credit Co. v. Harper, 671 F.2d 1117 (8th Cir.1982); Volkswagen of America, Inc. v. Novak, 418 So.2d 801 (Miss.1982); Murray v. Holiday Rambler, Inc., 83 Wis.2d 406, 265 N.W.2d 513 (1978); Volvo of America Corp. v. Wells, 551 S.W.2d 826 (Ky.App.1977); Durfee v. Rod Baxter Imports, Inc., 262 N.W.2d 349 (Minn.1977); Asciolla v. Manter Oldsmobile–Pontiac, Inc., 117 N.H. 85, 370 A.2d 270 (1977).

replacement goods if the product contains a "defect" or "malfunction" that cannot be cured after a "reasonable number of attempts" by the manufacturer. Thus, revocation against the remote manufacturer is a remedy under *federal* law in some situations. Similarly, a number of state legislatures are enacting "lemon" statutes that give revocation rights against the manufacturer of a defective motor vehicle without regard to limits in the written warranty accompanying the goods.

B. Clark & C. Smith, The Law of Product Warranties ¶ 7.03(3)(d) (1984). Cf. J. White & R. Summers, Uniform Commercial Code 376–77 (3d ed. 1988).

(6) **Actions Against Lenders.** Most retail car buyers pay part of the price at delivery (including, perhaps, the agreed value of a trade-in) but arrange to pay the balance of the price in installments over a period of years. Commonly, the loans that finance buyers' purchases are made by banks or finance agencies. We can infer that the buyer in *McCullough* entered into such an arrangement; one of the parties sued was a bank, presumably the bank to which buyer was obligated to make installment payments. What relief would buyers likely seek from lenders? Refund of previous payments? Release from obligation to pay future installments? Damages for breach of warranty?

The trial court dismissed the suit against the bank and apparently buyer did not appeal. Under what theory might a buyer's revocation of acceptance affect the buyer's rights against or obligations to a bank or finance company? See Smith v. Navistar International Transportation Corp., 714 F.Supp. 303 (N.D.Ill.1989) (manufacturer, financer, and dealer were part of one corporate family).

In retail installment-purchase transactions, typically the contract of sale provides for buyer's deferred payments; promptly after the sale, the retailer assigns the buyer's debt to a bank or finance company. Since 1975, a Federal Trade Commission rule requires sellers of consumer goods to insert into their contract documents a provision that makes lenders subject to all claims and defenses that buyers could assert against sellers. Preservation of Consumers' Claims and Defenses, 16 C.F.R. § 433. If buyers have claims or defenses against their immediate sellers, the lenders would be subject to them as well.[3] In such transactions, would lender be subject to buyers' claims or defenses against remote sellers?

(7) **Use After Revocation and the Code.** Did the *McCullough* court give adequate attention to the incorporation by 2–608(3) of the "rights and duties" applicable to rejection—particularly the prohibition by 2–602(2)(a) of "any exercise of ownership" and the duty under 2–602(2)(b) "to hold" the goods for the seller? See also 2–606(1)(c): "any act inconsistent with the seller's ownership."

3. The rule provides that buyer's recovery against a lender "shall not exceed amounts paid by the debtor hereunder."

Do these words indicate that the law-makers faced and decided the issues presented in the *McCullough* case? Do your answers lead to any conclusions concerning "literal reading" of Article 2? Have you encountered other statutes where a "literal" reading is more or less acceptable?

(8) Compensation for Use After Revocation. In Johnson v. G.M. Corp., 233 Kan. 1044, 668 P.2d 139 (1983), the buyers of a 1979 Chevrolet pick-up truck, after extended and unsuccessful attempts at repair, notified GM that they revoked acceptance and thereafter drove the truck an additional 14,619 miles. The court awarded the buyers a judgment for return of the price less an offset for the value of their use of the truck. In fixing the offset the court relied on a Federal Highway Administration Booklet, "Cost of Owning and Operating Automobiles and Vans 1982." How would the cost of operation compare with rental costs?

(9) Magnuson–Moss "Full" Warranties; "Lemon Laws." The Magnuson–Moss Warranty Act, in § 104(a)(4), permits consumers to elect a "refund" for a defective product if a "reasonable number of attempts" fail to remedy a defect or malfunction. However, this remedy depended on the granting of a "full" federal warranty. Most sellers of expensive goods that they do not want thrown back after acceptance have chosen to grant "limited" warranties.

A large number of states have enacted "lemon laws" that give special protection, including the right to revoke acceptance, when defects in motor vehicles are not corrected within a reasonable time. While non-uniform in their language, these statutes tend to allow consumers, for a limited period, to demand from manufacturers refund of the purchase price or a replacement car when the "same defect" continues to exist after four attempts to repair it or the car was out of service for 30 days during the year after it was sold. See C. Reitz, Consumer Product Warranties Under Federal and State Laws, ch. 14 (2d ed. 1987).

(B) INTERNATIONAL SALES LAW

The Convention on International Sale of Goods does not use the concept of buyers' acceptance and, therefore, has no provision for revocation of acceptance. The comparable CISG provisions are those permitting buyers to avoid contracts. As discussed in the previous section, CISG permits buyers to avoid contracts in two circumstances. We previously considered avoidance in connection with delays in performance in connection with CISG's *Nachfrist* provisions. In this section, we are concerned with buyers' right to avoid contracts, particularly contracts that have been executed, on the ground that the goods are non-conforming. The Convention relates this power to avoid to the concept of fundamental breach.

Avoidance for Fundamental Breach. The Convention's default performance rules contemplate that buyers must keep goods received unless sellers' performance failures constitute fundamental breach. A breach is "fundamental" if the detriment in performance substantially deprives the aggrieved party of what it was entitled to expect under the contract. CISG 25.

Manner of Avoiding. If goods received are so non-conforming that sellers' performance amounts to fundamental breach, buyers may declare contracts avoided. CISG 49(1). For a declaration of avoidance to be effective, it must be made by notice to the seller. CISG 26.[4]

Time of Avoidance. A buyer's time to decide whether to declare a contracted avoided for fundamental breach is determined by the time needed to discover the deficiency. Power to avoid for quality or quantity defects expires a reasonable time after buyer knew or ought to have known of the breach. CISG 49(2)(b)(i). Power to avoid for late delivery that constitutes fundamental breach expires a reasonable time after buyer has become aware that delivery has been made. CISG 49(2)(a).

Effect of Avoidance. Avoidance of a contract generally releases both parties from their obligations under it. CISG 81(1). The aggrieved buyer is entitled to damages that have accrued prior to avoidance, id., but must account to the seller for benefits derived from the goods. CISG 84. A party who has performed the contract in whole or in part may claim restitution. CISG 81(2). A buyer who elects to avoid must be able generally to return the goods delivered substantially in the condition in which it received them. CISG 82(1). Exceptions exist (1) if buyer is unable to return the goods and the impossibility is not due to its act or omission, or (2) if the goods were sold in the normal course of business or consumed or transformed by the buyer before it discovered or ought to have discovered the lack of conformity, or (3) if the goods deteriorated or perished as a result of buyer's examination of them. CISG 46(2). A buyer must act, on behalf of the seller, to preserve goods in the buyer's possession or placed at its disposal at their shipping destination. CISG 86.[5] The buyer may warehouse the goods. CISG 87. A buyer need not return goods if seller fails to repay the price or the cost of preservation of the goods. CISG 88(1). If seller delays unreasonably in taking the goods back, buyer may sell them by any appropriate means, CISG 88(1), and must do so if the goods are subject to rapid deterioration or their preservation would involve unreasonable expense. CISG 88(2).

Cure of Non–conforming Deliveries. Without power to reject goods and only limited power to avoid, buyers are not in a strong position to use self-help to compel sellers to cure non-conforming deliveries. However, the Convention permits buyers to seek court

---

4. Notices under the Convention are effective, whether or not received, if dispatched "by means appropriate in the circumstances." CISG 27.

5. Note that CISG 86 uses the word "reject" in connection with buyers' rights.

That word does not appear elsewhere in the Convention. It does not have the connotation of "rejection" under domestic United States law. See J. Honnold, Uniform Law for International Sales § 455 (2d ed. 1991).

orders compelling sellers to perform. CISG 46(1). Article 46 differentiates sharply between court orders to compel delivery of substitute goods and court orders to repair. Substitute goods may be ordered only if the deficiency in the original delivery was a fundamental breach. CISG 46(2). An order to repair is permitted unless repair is unreasonable in the circumstances. CISG 46(3).

The Convention's authorization of court-ordered relief may be of little value to buyers in the United States or other common-law nations where equitable relief, by injunction or specific performance, is denied if the aggrieved party has an adequate remedy at law, i.e. monetary damages. See, e.g., UCC 2–716. The Convention accepts that some nations' laws limit parties' access to specific relief. CISG 28.

Even if not faced with buyers' avoidance or not ordered to cure non-conforming deliveries, sellers may elect to try to remedy failures in their performances. Buyers must permit sellers to do so if the sellers act without unreasonable delay and without causing buyers unreasonable inconvenience. CISG 48(1). What might motivate sellers to act in this way?

Problem 1. Telecommunications Company (TCo) in an African country contracted to buy a high power microwave amplifier (HPA) from a United States supplier (SCo). The agreement contained extensive technical specifications for the HPA. The agreement provided, further, that SCo would install and test the HPA at the site in Africa within 15 months. When the HPA had been manufactured, TCo inspected it at the factory and found that it met the contract specifications. SCo installed the HPA in Africa. Before the HPA was operational, TCo again inspected the equipment and indicated that it was satisfactory. After six months of SCo's effort to get the HPA into service, SCo realized that it would not work because it had been designed for a grounded neutral power supply system, whereas the power supply at the site was an isolated neutral power system. The contract specifications were silent on the nature of the power supply. Rebuilding the HBA to operate with the available power supply would delay installation for more than a year. Assuming CISG is the governing law, may TCo declare the contract avoided for fundamental breach? See Awards of June 1984 and May 1985 in Case No. 4567, 11 Yearbook Commercial Arbitration 143 (1986).

Problem 2. Buyer and seller contracted for sale of a computer. Seller shipped the computer to buyer. On arrival, buyer discovered that three major components of the equipment were defective. Buyer immediately informed seller of the defects and of its election to avoid the contract. Seller wired back: "All defects can promptly and completely corrected. Will send top-level team next week." Assume that the deficiencies in the computer, as delivered, would constitute fundamental breach. If the seller has the ability to correct the problems without unreasonable delay and without causing buyer unreasonable convenience, may it do so despite buyer's declaration of avoidance?

What is the meaning of "subject to article 49" in CISG 48(1)? See J. Honnold, Uniform Law for International Sales § 296 (2d ed. 1991)("The seller's right to cure should also be protected if, ... where cure is feasible, the buyer hastily declares the contract avoided before the seller has an opportunity to cure the defect. ... [W]here cure is feasible and where an offer of cure can be expected, one cannot conclude that the breach is "fundamental" until one knows the answer to this question: Will the seller cure?")

Problem 3. In performance of a contract for the sale of sugar with an average polarization of 78, seller shipped sugar which buyer tested and determined to average 73. Buyer immediately wired seller a notice that the sugar received did not conform to contract specifications on polarization. What purpose would this notice serve? Recall CISG 39(1). Would this notice constitute a declaration of avoidance? May sellers combine, in one communication, notice of a lack of conformity and declaration of avoidance? What content would such a communication have? Must a buyer use the word "avoid"?

Problem 4. Buyer received goods that are sufficiently deficient in quality that seller has committed a fundamental breach. Buyer sent notice to the seller specifying the lack of conformity (CISG 39) and declaring the contract avoided (CISG 26). One week later, buyer sought a court order directing the seller to deliver substitute goods on the ground that seller had delivered goods whose lack of conformity constitutes a fundamental breach and that buyer was entitled to "require" seller to deliver substitute goods under CISG 46(2). Seller counters that its obligations under the contract were released when buyer declared the contract avoided. Is seller correct? See J. Honnold, Uniform Law for International Sales § 440.2 (2d ed. 1991).

SECTION 4.   PERFORMANCE AND THE CREDIT RISK

Introduction. Unless the parties to sales contracts tender and complete delivery and payment simultaneously, one incurs the credit risk inherent in having surrendered something of value without having received the expected thing of value. If a seller delivers goods without receiving the price, the seller has incurred a credit risk. Conversely, if a buyer pays the price without receiving goods, the buyer has incurred a credit risk.

In many commercial situations, one of the parties willingly and openly assumes the credit risk of performing first. Sales on short-term or long-term credit are common. The tremendous volume of domestic commercial credit is encouraged by highly organized channels for credit information and the transactional efficiency of delivery on open billing. An important asset of businesses who sell goods (or services) on credit is their accounts receivable, generated typically by delivering goods to buyers on terms that require payment at the end of the month, within 30 days of delivery, etc. Long-term credit sales tend to involve installment payment arrangements, familiar in consumer purchasing of automobiles and other relatively expensive durable goods.

Similarly, buyers' prepayments are commonly made in certain types of transactions. (In a service contract familiar to students, tuition is paid at the beginning of an academic term.) Sales contracts for goods to be manufactured by sellers are one of the most common settings in which buyers pay some of the price before delivery. "Down payments" are also found in other transaction situations.

The two principal topics for this section are: (1) How and to what extent do the default rules of performance supplied by law, i.e., gap-filling provisions that apply in the absence of agreement on the matter, impose credit risks on buyers or sellers who have not agreed to assume such risks? (2) What protections are available to parties exposed to loss from credit risk?

Credit risks generally fall into two categories: obligors who *cannot* or who *will not* perform. The former are sometimes thought of in terms of bankruptcy risk. The latter are a more commercial risk. Risk avoidance strategies do not distinguish between unable and unwilling promisors. However, the potential relief once a credit risk has materialized depends greatly on the distinction.

(A) DOMESTIC SALES LAW

(1) **Simultaneous Exchanges.** The Code's default rules on performance tend to avoid or minimize credit risk to either buyers or sellers through the complementary provisions of 2–507(1) and 2–511(1). Under the former, a buyer's duty to pay is conditional upon a seller's tendering delivery. Under the latter, a seller's duty to tender and complete delivery is conditional upon a buyer's tender of payment. These conditions can be satisfied if the parties tender their reciprocal performances simultaneously.

In face-to-face performances, the "put and hold" manner of tender of the goods and the price permits the parties to "let go" at the same time. Events at the check-out counter of a food store are an example of a relatively simple simultaneous exchange. In more complex transactions, simultaneous exchanges may occur at meetings scheduled for that purpose, sometimes called "closings." (This is a normal event in the performance of real estate sales contracts, contracts for the issuance of securities, and the like.)

(2) **Sequential Exchanges.** Simultaneous exchange is not feasible in some situations even though the parties may be in direct contact. Some sales contracts with a service component, such as contracts to sell and install goods, cannot be performed in the "put and hold" manner. The seller's performance necessarily occurs over a period of time. Simultaneous exchange of goods plus service for money is therefore impractical. The Code states no performance rule for this type of

transaction. Common-law contract principles presumably would apply (UCC 1–103).

(3) Documentary Transactions. Face-to-face performance is not feasible when the goods are to be sent via carriers to buyers. In this transactional setting, however, the marketplace developed and the law reinforces a performance scenario that comes remarkably close to eliminating credit risk for either party in non-simultaneous performances. The Code assists sellers and buyers to set up simultaneous performances in the form of "documentary transactions," but the parties must agree to do so. This mode of performance is not prescribed by the Code as a default rule.

The parties to sales contracts who elect to enter into "documentary transitions" enlist the aid of carriers and banks to accomplish the result. Underlying the services of carriers and banks is the law of negotiable instruments and negotiable documents of title. The document of title is typically a negotiable bill of lading. The negotiable instrument is typically a negotiable draft ordering the buyer to pay the purchase price. With this mix of services and documents, sellers and buyers are able to effect simultaneous transfer of documents of title in exchange for payment of the price.

Negotiable Bills of Lading. In section 1, we considered the Code's default rules on the manner of sellers' performance of contracts in which they are authorized or required to ship goods by use of carriers. Carriers issue bills of lading upon receipt of goods from sellers in either "straight bill" or "order bill" form.[1] If sellers choose to take "order bills," carriers incur the contract duty, undergirded by federal or state statutes, to deliver the goods only to persons who duly present the "order bills" and to cancel the bills on delivery of the goods. 49 U.S.C. App. 88–91[2], UCC 7–104(1)(a).

---

1. Trucking concerns have found it awkward to accept goods under order bills of lading because of lack of terminal facilities at the points of destination.

2.

§ 88. Duty to deliver goods on demand; refusal

A carrier, in the absence of some lawful excuse, is bound to deliver goods upon a demand made either by the consignee named in the bill for the goods or, if the bill is an order bill, by the holder thereof, if such a demand is accompanied by—

(a) An offer in good faith to satisfy the carrier's lawful lien upon the goods [for freight and other charges];

(b) Possession of the bill of lading and an offer in good faith to surrender, properly indorsed, the bill which was issued for the goods, if the bill is an order bill; and

(c) A readiness and willingness to sign, when the goods are delivered, an acknowledgment that they have been delivered, if such signature is requested by the carrier.

In case the carrier refuses or fails to deliver the goods, in compliance with a demand by the consignee or holder so accompanied, the burden shall be upon the carrier to establish the existence of a lawful excuse for such refusal or failure.

§ 89. Delivery; when justified

A carrier is justified, subject to the provisions of sections 90–92 of this title, in delivering goods to one who is—

(a) A person lawfully entitled to possession of the goods, or

(b) The consignee named in a straight bill of lading, or

(c) A person in possession of an order bill for the goods, by the terms of which

By keeping control of an "order bill" until buyer tenders payment of the price, a seller can avoid the credit risk of delivering without receiving payment. By keeping control of the money until seller tenders the "order bill," a buyer can avoid the credit risk of paying without receiving title to the goods and the power to get them from the carrier.

Negotiable Drafts. "Documentary transactions" commonly require a document, other than the negotiable bill of lading, to facilitate the transfer of the purchase price. For this purpose sellers and buyers use drafts. A draft is drawn by the seller on the buyer for the amount of money due to the seller in exchange for the goods. Typically, the seller's draft will order buyer to pay the price when the draft is presented to buyer ("at sight"); drafts payable on demand are called "sight drafts."

Banks' Services. Sellers and buyers typically employ the services of banks to effect simultaneous exchange of the negotiable bill of lading and the contract price. A seller first delivers the goods to a carrier and obtains an "order bill of lading." Seller then prepares a "sight draft" for the price of the goods, attaches to it the "order bill," and delivers both documents to its local bank for transmission to the buyer "through banking channels." [3] The receiving bank forwards the documents through the network of bank-to-bank relationships that exists for this, and many other purposes. [4] In due course, the draft and bill of lading arrive at a bank in buyer's city. [5] It is the function of that bank to effect the exchange of goods for money by turning over the bill of lading

the goods are deliverable to his order; or which has been indorsed to him, or in blank by the consignee, or by the mediate or immediate indorsee of the consignee.

§ 90. Liability for delivery to a person not entitled thereto

Where a carrier delivers goods to one who is not lawfully entitled to the possession of them, the carrier shall be liable to anyone having a right of property or possession in the goods if he delivered the goods otherwise than as authorized under subdivisions (b) and (c) of section 89....

§ 91. Liability for delivery without cancellation of bill

Except as provided in section 106 of this title [permitting carriers' to dispose of goods to collect the freight or other charges], and except where compelled by legal process, if a carrier delivers goods for which an order bill had been issued, the negotiation of which would transfer the right to the possession of the goods, and fails to take up and cancel the bill, such carrier shall be liable for failure to deliver the goods to anyone who for value and in

good faith purchases such bill, whether such purchaser acquired title to the bill before or after the delivery of the goods and notwithstanding delivery was made to the person entitled thereto.

3. Seller's actions comply with its performance obligations under UCC 2–308(c) and 2–503(5), which permit use of "customary banking channels," and with 2–504.

4. Article 4 of the Code, supplemented by Article 3, governs bank deposits and collections. The bank taking the paper from seller is authorized to present the draft to buyer or to send it via another bank or banks to buyer. UCC 4–202(a)(1). Banks who handle the paper are agents and subagents of sellers. See UCC 4–201. Each bank that handles a seller's draft becomes a "collecting bank" (UCC 4–105(5)), with the duties set out in UCC 4–202, 4–501, and 4–503. The last bank in the chain is the "presenting bank." UCC 4–105(6).

5. Often the bank selected to make presentment is the bank with which the buyer has an ongoing banking relationship and which the buyer had told seller would be the appropriate bank to which documents should be forwarded.

when buyer has paid the amount of the draft.[6]   After payment is made, it is transferred back to seller's bank and eventually to seller, again through normal banking channels.[7]

Negotiation; Rights of Holders. Both the "order bill" and the negotiable draft move through these steps by the process of negotiation, not by mere transfer. "Holders" of negotiable documents of title or of negotiable instruments may receive greater legal protection than mere transferees. In Chapter 1, we noted that the concept of good faith purchase has developed in a wider setting than purchase of goods. Commercial law offers very significant legal protection to holders in due course of negotiable instruments, UCC 3–305, and to holders of negotiable documents of title to whom the documents have been duly negotiated. 49 U.S.C. App. 108, 111(b)[8]; UCC 7–502. These protections are often significant to buyers and sellers as well as to the banks whose services they use in carrying out "documentary transactions."

6. Unless otherwise instructed, the bank presenting a "sight draft" is authorized to send buyer a written notice that it holds a draft for payment; buyer has three days to make payment. UCC 4–212. If, instead of sending notice, the bank presents the draft to buyer at its place of business or residence UCC 3–501(b)(1), 3–111). Payment is due no later than the third day following presentment. UCC 3–502(c). The bank may deliver the bill of lading accompanying the draft "only on payment." UCC 4–503(a).

An alternative transaction involves use of a "time draft," which orders a buyer to pay a specified time after presentment. A buyer's choices on presentment of a time draft are to accept or to dishonor the draft. See UCC 3–409, 3–413 (definition and operation of acceptance), 3–410 (acceptance varying draft), 3–502(c) (dishonor). Accepted "time drafts," known as "trade acceptances," tend to be marketable negotiable instruments. Sellers often sell accepted drafts before their due date, albeit for less than their face value; this process is often called "discounting" of drafts.

7. Air Freight. The speed of carriage of goods by air required adaptation of the method of issuing and transmitting bills of lading. Taking a bill of lading at the point of shipment and forwarding it through banking channels to the destination to be exchanged for the price would be too slow. A solution is found by using electronic communications. The Commercial Code permits a carrier, at the request of a consignor, to issue a bill of lading at the point of destination, UCC 7–305(1), and to deliver it to a local bank. Meanwhile, seller (or seller's bank) wires a draft on the buyer to the bank holding the bill. Within hours, the bank notifies buyer who pays the draft and obtains the bill.

8.

§ 108. Negotiation of order bill of lading by indorsement

An order bill may be negotiated by the indorsement of the person to whose order the goods are deliverable by the tenor of the bill. Such indorsement may be in blank or to a specified person. If indorsed to a specified person, it may be negotiated again by the indorsement of such person in blank or to another specified person. Subsequent negotiation may be made in like manner.

§ 111. Title and right acquired by transferee of ordinary bill

A person to whom an order bill has been duly negotiated acquires thereby—...

(b) The direct obligation of the carrier to hold possession of the goods for him according to the terms of the bill as fully as if the carrier had contracted directly with him.

DIAGRAM OF A DOCUMENTARY TRANSACTION

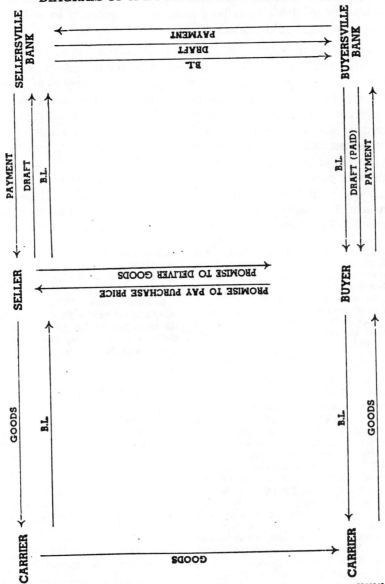

[B2934]

STEPS IN COLLECTION OF DOCUMENTARY DRAFT

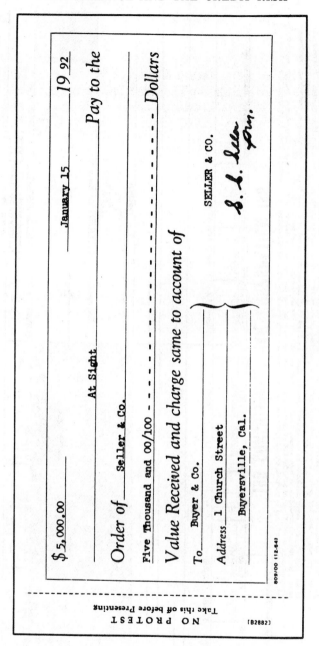

SIGHT DRAFT

FD 2534 R4 1-76
PRINTED IN USA

(Uniform Domestic Order Bill of Lading, adopted by Carriers in Official, Southern, Western and Illinois Classification territories, March 15, 1922, as amended August 1, 1930, June 15, 1941, September 21, 1944, January 9, 1946, and July 14, 1949.)

UNIFORM ORDER BILL OF LADING — ORIGINAL

RECEIVED, subject to the classifications and tariffs in effect on the date of the issue of this Bill of Lading, the property described below, in apparent good order, except as noted (contents and condition of contents of packages unknown), marked, consigned, and destined as indicated below, which said company (the word company being understood throughout this contract as meaning any person or corporation in possession of the property under the contract) agrees to carry to its usual place of delivery at said destination, if on its own road or its own water line, otherwise to deliver to another carrier on the route to said destination. It is mutually agreed as to each carrier of all or any of said property over all or any portion of said route to destination, and as to each party at any time interested in all or any of said property, that every service to be performed hereunder shall be subject to all the conditions not prohibited by law, whether printed or written, herein contained, including the conditions on back hereof, which are hereby agreed to by the shipper and accepted for himself and his assigns.

The surrender of this Original ORDER Bill of Lading properly indorsed shall be required before the delivery of the property. Inspection of property covered by this bill of lading will not be permitted unless provided by law or unless permission is indorsed on this original bill of lading or given in writing by the shipper.

190 CONSOLIDATED RAIL CORPORATION 190

1

| CAR INITIAL | CAR NUMBER | | | | | |

| TRAILER INITIALS | TRAILER NUMBER | TV | LGH | TV | | |

STOP THIS CAR

| TRAILER INITIALS | TRAILER NUMBER | TV | LGH | TV | | |

AT _____ FOR _____

AT _____ FOR _____

AT _____ FOR _____

ORDERED	FURNISHED		
LENGTH/CAPACITY OF CAR		WEIGHT IN TONS PROPERTY	WAYBILL DATE	WAYBILL NO.

CONSIGNEE AND ADDRESS AT STOP

SHIPPER	FULL NAME OF SHIPPER	ORIGIN	STATE
	Seller & Co.		

BILL OF LADING DATE	BILL OF LADING NO.	INVOICE NO.	CUSTOMER NO.
2/6/92	102	A – 21	32 – B

CONSIGNED TO Seller & Co.

ORDER OF

DESTINATION	STATE OF	COUNTY OF
Buyerville	Cal.	Sonora

NOTIFY Buyer & Co.
Buyerville, California

WHEN SHIPPER IN THE UNITED STATES EXECUTES NO-RECOURSE CLAUSE OF SECT. 7 OF BILL OF LADING CHECK (x) ⟶   YES ☐

RECEIVED $_____ TO APPLY AS PREPAYMENT OF CHARGES ON THE PROPERTY DESCRIBED HEREON

WEIGHED AT		
GROSS	TARE	ALLOWANCE

AT

STATE OF   COUNTY OF

1 Church St., Buyersville, California

ROUTE (FOR SHIPPER'S USE ONLY)   DELIVERY CARRIER
SP

PC – C&NW – UP – SP

Subject to Section 7 of Conditions, if this shipment is to be delivered to the consignee without recourse on the consignor, the consignor shall sign the following statement: The carrier shall not make delivery of this shipment without payment of freight and all other lawful charges.

Signature of Consignor

Note—Where the rate is dependent upon value, shippers are required to state specifically in writing the agreed or declared value of the property. The agreed or declared value of the property is hereby specifically stated by the shipper to be not exceeding PER

If the shipment moves between two ports by a carrier by water, the law require that the bill of lading shall state whether it is "carrier's or shipper's weight."

SHIPPERS SPECIAL INSTRUCTIONS (INCLUDE ICING, VENTILATION, HEATING, MILLING, WEIGHING, ETC.)

AGENT OR CASHIER

PER

(THE SIGNATURE HERE ACKNOWLEDGES ONLY THE AMOUNT PREPAID)

CHARGES ADVANCED

$

If CHARGED ARE TO BE PREPAID WRITE OR STAMP HERE

"TO BE PREPAID"

NO. PKGS.	DESCRIPTION OF ARTICLES, SPECIAL MARKS AND EXCEPTIONS	COMMODITY CODE NO.	* WEIGHT (SUBJECT TO COR.)	RATE	FREIGHT	ADVANCES	NET	PREPAID
50 ctns.	Bags, paper		1,000 lbs.	$4.60	$46.00			$46.00

SHIPPER   Seller & Co.   PER|AGENT

PERMANENT POST OFFICE ADDRESS OF SHIPPER   1 Main Street, Sellersville, N.Y.   PER

[D626]

NEGOTIABLE BILL OF LADING
[Printed on yellow paper; front]

ENDORSEMENTS

CONTRACT TERMS AND CONDITIONS

NEGOTIABLE BILL OF LADING
[*Reverse*]

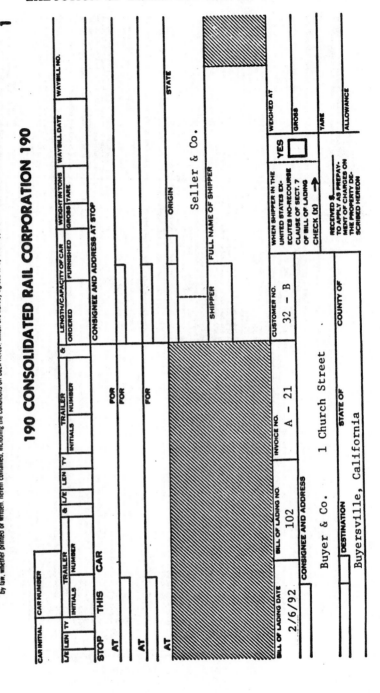

ROUTE (FOR SHIPPER'S USE ONLY)

PC – C&NW – UP – SP

DELIVERY CARRIER

SP

AGENT OR CASHIER

PER

(THE SIGNATURE HERE ACKNOWLEDGES ONLY THE AMOUNT PREPAID)

CHARGES ADVANCED

$

NET

IF CHARGES ARE TO BE PREPAID WRITE OR STAMP HERE:

'TO BE PREPAID'

Subject to Section 7 of Conditions, if this shipment is to be delivered to the consignee without recourse on the consignor, the consignor shall sign the following statement: The carrier shall not make delivery of this shipment without payment of freight and all other lawful charges.

_____
Signature of Consignor

Note—Where the rate is dependent upon value, shippers are required to state specifically in writing the agreed or declared value of the property. The agreed or declared value of the property is hereby specifically stated by the shipper to be not exceeding _____ PER _____

"If the shipment moves between two ports by a carrier by water, the law requires that the bill of lading shall state whether it is "carrier's or shipper's weight".

SHIPPERS SPECIAL INSTRUCTIONS (INCLUDE ICING, VENTILATION, HEATING, MILLING, WEIGHING, ETC.)

NO. PKGS.	DESCRIPTION OF ARTICLES, SPECIAL MARKS AND EXCEPTIONS	COMMODITY CODE NO	*	WEIGHT (SUBJECT TO COR.)	RATE	FREIGHT	ADVANCES	PREPAID
50 ctns.	Bags, paper			1,000 lbs.	$4.60	$46.00		$46.00

THIS IS TO CERTIFY THAT THE ABOVE NAMED MATERIALS ARE PROPERLY CLASSIFIED, DESCRIBED, PACKAGED, MARKED AND LABELED, AND ARE IN PROPER CONDITION FOR TRANSPORTATION, ACCORDING TO THE APPLICABLE REGULATIONS OF THE DEPARTMENT OF TRANSPORTATION.

_____ SIGNED

SHIPPER   Seller & Co.   PER **AGENT**

PERMANENT POST OFFICE ADDRESS OF SHIPPER   1 Main Street, Sellersville, N.Y.   PER _____

NON–NEGOTIABLE BILL OF LADING
[Printed on white paper; front]

CONTRACT TERMS AND CONDITIONS

Sec. 1. (a) The carrier or party in possession of any of the property herein described shall be liable as at common law for any loss thereof or damage thereto, except as hereinafter provided.

(b) No carrier or party in possession of all or any of the property herein described shall be liable for any loss thereof or damage thereto or delay caused by the act of God, the public enemy, the authority of law, or the act or default of the shipper or owner, or for natural shrinkage.

(c) In case of quarantine the property may be discharged at risk and expense of owners into quarantine station or place.

Sec. 2. (a) No carrier is bound to transport said property by any particular train or vessel, or in time for any particular market or otherwise.

(b) As a condition precedent to recovery, claims must be filed in writing with the receiving or delivering carrier.

(c) Any carrier or party liable on account of loss of or damage to any of said property shall be subject to the full benefit of any insurance that may have been effected upon or on account of said property.

Sec. 3. Except where such service is performed under arrangements made with the carrier.

Sec. 4. (a) Property not removed by the party entitled to receive it within the free time allowed by tariffs.

(b) Where a part of a shipment is perishable property.

(c) Where perishable property which has been transported to destination hereunder is refused by consignee.

(e) The provisions hereof respecting disposition of the property.

(f) Property destined to or taken from a station, wharf, or landing at which there is no regularly appointed freight agent.

Sec. 5. No carrier hereunder will carry or be liable in any way for any documents, specie, or for any articles of extraordinary value not specifically rated in the published classifications or tariffs unless a special agreement to do so and a stipulated value of the articles are indorsed hereon.

Sec. 6. Every party, whether principal or agent, shipping explosives or dangerous goods, without previous full written disclosure to the carrier of their nature, shall be liable for and indemnify the carrier against all loss or damage caused by such goods, and such goods may be warehoused at owner's risk and expense or destroyed without compensation.

Sec. 7. The owner or consignee shall pay the freight and average, if any, and all other lawful charges accruing on said property; but, except in those instances where it may lawfully be authorized to do so, no carrier by railroad shall deliver or relinquish possession at destination of the property covered by this bill of lading until all tariff rates and charges thereon have been paid. The consignor shall be liable for the freight and all other lawful charges, except that if the consignor stipulates, by signature, in the space provided for that purpose on the face of this bill of lading that the carrier shall not make delivery without requiring payment of such charges and the carrier, contrary to such stipulation, shall make delivery without requiring such payment, the consignor (except as hereinafter provided) shall not be liable for such charges. Provided, that, where the carrier has been instructed by the shipper or consignor to deliver said property to a consignee other than the shipper or consignor, such consignee shall not be legally liable for transportation charges in respect of the transportation of said property (beyond those billed against him at the time of delivery for which he is otherwise liable) which may be found to be due after the property has been delivered to him, if the consignee (a) is an agent only and has no beneficial title in said property, and (b) prior to delivery of said property has notified the delivering carrier in writing of the fact of such agency and absence of beneficial title, and, in the case of a shipment reconsigned or diverted to a point other than that specified in the original bill of lading, has also notified the delivering carrier in writing of the name and address of the beneficial owner of said property; and, in such cases the shipper or consignor, or, in the case of a shipment so reconsigned or diverted, the beneficial owner, shall be liable for such additional charges. If the consignee has given to the carrier erroneous information as to who the beneficial owner is, such consignee shall himself be liable for such additional charges. On shipments reconsigned or diverted by an agent who has furnished the carrier in the reconsignment or diversion order with a notice of agency and the proper name and address of the beneficial owner, and where such shipments are refused or abandoned at ultimate destination, the said beneficial owner shall be liable for all legally applicable charges in connection therewith. If the reconsignor or diverter has given to the carrier erroneous information as to who the beneficial owner is, such reconsignor or diverter shall himself be liable for all such charges.

If a shipper or consignor of a shipment of property (other than a prepaid shipment) is also the consignee named in the bill of lading and, prior to the time of delivery, notifies, in writing, a delivering carrier by railroad (a) to deliver such property to another party, (b) that such party is the beneficial owner of such property, and (c) that delivery is to be made to such party only upon payment of all transportation charges in respect of the transportation of such property, and delivery is made by the carrier to such party without such payment, such party shall, if the carrier shall be liable (as shipper, consignor, consignee, or otherwise) for such transportation charges but the party to whom delivery is so made shall in any event be liable for such transportation charges billed against the property at the time of such delivery, and also for any additional charges which may be found to be due after delivery of the property, except that if the arbitrary, prior to such delivery, has notified in writing the delivering carrier that he is not the beneficial owner of the property, and has given in writing to such delivering carrier the name of the party to whom delivery is made has given to the carrier erroneous information as to the beneficial owner, such party shall nevertheless be liable for such additional charges. If the shipper or consignor has given to the delivering carrier erroneous information as to who the beneficial owner is, such shipper or consignor shall himself be liable for such transportation charges, notwithstanding the provisions of this paragraph and irrespective of any provisions as to who the beneficial owner is in the contract of transportation under which the shipment was made.

The term "delivering carrier" means the line-haul carrier making ultimate delivery.

Nothing herein shall limit the right of the carrier to require at time of shipment the prepayment or guarantee of the charges. If upon inspection it is ascertained that the articles shipped are not those described in this bill of lading, the freight charges must be paid upon the articles actually shipped.

Where delivery is made by a common carrier by water the foregoing provisions of this section shall apply, except as may be inconsistent with Part III of the Interstate Commerce Act.

Sec. 8. If this bill of lading is issued on the order of the shipper, or his agent, in exchange or in substitution for another bill of lading, the shipper's signature to the prior bill of lading as to the statement of value or otherwise, or election of common law or bill of lading liability, in or in connection with such prior bill of lading, shall be considered a part of this bill of lading as fully as if the same were written or made in or over this bill of lading.

Sec. 9. (a) If all or any part of said property is carried by water over any part of said route, and loss, damage or injury to said property occurs while the same is in the custody of the carrier by water the liability of such carrier shall be determined by the bill of lading of the carrier by water (this bill of lading being such bill of lading if the property is transported by such water carrier thereunder) and by the laws and the regulations applicable to transportation by water. Such water carriage shall be performed subject to all the terms and provisions of, and all the exemptions from liability contained in, the Act of the Congress of the United States, approved on February 13, 1893, and entitled "An act relating to the navigation of vessels, etc.," and of other statutes of the United States according carriers by water the protection of limited liability, as well as to the following substitutions of this section: and to the conditions contained in this bill of lading not inconsistent with this section, when this bill of lading becomes the bill of lading of the carrier by water.

(b) No such carrier by water shall be liable for any loss or damage resulting from any fire happening to or on board the vessel, or from explosion, bursting of boilers or breakage of shafts, unless caused by the design or neglect of such carrier.

(c) If the owner shall have exercised due diligence in making the vessel in all respects seaworthy and properly manned, equipped, and supplied, no such carrier shall be liable for any loss or damage resulting from the perils of the lakes, seas, or other waters, or from latent defects in hull, machinery, or appurtenances whether existing prior to, at the time of, or after shipment, or from collision, stranding, or other accidents of navigation, or from prolongation of the voyage. And, when for any reason it is necessary, any vessel carrying any or all of the property herein described shall be liberty to call at any port or ports, in or out of the customary route, or to deviate for the purpose of saving life or property, and for docking and repairs. Except in case of negligence such carrier shall not be responsible for any loss or damage to property if it be necessary or is usual to carry the same upon deck.

(d) General Average shall be payable according to the York-Antwerp Rules of 1924, Sections 1 to 15, inclusive, and Sections 17 to 22, inclusive, and as to matters not covered thereby according to the laws and usages of the Port of New York. If the owners shall have exercised due diligence to make the vessel in all respects seaworthy and properly manned, equipped and supplied, it is hereby agreed that in case of danger, damage or disaster resulting from faults or errors in navigation, or in the management of the vessel, or from any latent or other defects in the vessel, her machinery or appurtenances, or from unseaworthiness, whether existing at the time of shipment or at the beginning of the voyage (provided the latent or other defects or the unseaworthiness was not due and discoverable by the exercise of due diligence), the shippers, consignees and/or owners of the cargo shall nevertheless pay salvage and any special charges incurred in respect of the cargo, and shall contribute with the shipowner in general average to the payment of any sacrifices, losses or expenses of a general average nature that may be made or incurred for the common benefit or to relieve the adventure from any common peril.

(e) If the property is being carried under a tariff which provides that any carrier or carriers party thereto shall be liable for loss from perils of the sea, then as to such carrier or carriers the provisions of this section shall be modified in accordance with the tariff provisions, which shall be regarded as incorporated into the conditions of this bill of lading.

(f) The term "water carriage" in this section shall not be construed as including lighterage in or across rivers, harbors, or lakes, when performed by or on behalf of rail carriers.

Sec. 10. Any alteration, addition, or erasure in this bill of lading which shall be made without the special notation hereon of the agent of the carrier issuing this bill of lading, shall be without effect, and this bill of lading shall be enforceable according to its original tenor.

EFFECTIVE JUNE 15, 1941

NON–NEGOTIABLE BILL OF LADING
[Reverse]

(1) THE SITUATION OF BUYERS

Documentary transactions in the form just described reduce the credit risk for buyer and sellers in many ways, but they leave buyers in a precarious position in a number of respects. The following problems are intended to examine the situation of buyers who are expected to pay the purchase price in exchange for a negotiable bill of lading.

Problem 1. Seller & Co. of Sellersville, N.Y., agreed to sell a large quantity of paper bags to Buyer & Co., of Buyersville, California, who agreed to pay $5,000.00, F.O.B. Buyersville. The parties agreed to a payment term: "sight draft against order bill of lading." Seller & Co. turned over the goods to Conrail and received a negotiable bill of lading made out to the order of Seller & Co. Seller & Co. prepared a draft for the purchase price, indorsed the bill of lading "in blank," [10] and forwarded the draft and bill through Sellersville Bank to Buyer & Co.

(a) Before the goods have arrived in Buyersville, Buyersville Bank received the draft and bill of lading. Buyersville Bank promptly notified Buyer & Co. that it had a draft and bill of lading. Buyer & Co. refused to pay the draft on the ground that it had not had an opportunity to inspect the goods. Is Buyer & Co. permitted to refuse to pay pending arrival of the goods and inspection of them? See UCC 2–513(3)(b); see also 2–310(b).

(b) Assume that Buyer & Co. paid when the sight draft was presented and obtained the bill of lading. Subsequently, the railroad car containing the 50 cartons of paper bags arrived in Buyersville and the railroad so notified Buyer & Co.[11] Buyer & Co. surrendered the bill of lading and took possession of the goods. Upon opening the boxes, Buyer & Co. discovered that a large percentage of the paper bags had been improperly glued. May Buyer & Co. reject the goods under UCC 2–601? See UCC 2–512(2). If Buyer & Co. has the power to reject the goods, to what extent are buyer's rights affected by the fact that it has already paid the price?

(c) Assume that Buyer & Co. paid when the sight draft was presented and obtained the bill of lading. The goods did not arrive within the expected time. When buyer asked the railroad for information, the railroad disclosed that the car containing the goods had been attached to the wrong train in St. Louis. The goods arrived in California three

---

10. A negotiable document of title running to the order of a named person can be negotiated by indorsement and delivery. An indorsement "in blank" permits further negotiation by delivery alone. 49 U.S. Code App. 89(c); UCC 7–501(1). Negotiation of documents of title within banking channels is facilitated by "in blank" indorsements. This permits a document to move forward without the necessity that each bank sign it and identify the next bank in the chain.

11. Order bills of lading usually indicate the person to be notified upon arrival of the goods at their destination. (See the face of order bill of lading form in the prototype transaction.) The "notify" provision does not authorize the carrier to deliver goods to the party listed without surrender of the bill of lading.

weeks later than anticipated. May Buyer & Co. reject the goods under UCC 2–601?

Rejection of Tender of Documents. In shipment contracts with negotiable bills of lading, buyers are first tendered documents that control the right to obtain possession of the goods from the carriers. Before seeing the goods, buyers accept or reject the tender of documents. Acceptance of a tender of the documents does not signify acceptance of the goods. Acceptance and rejection of goods by signification or lapse of time occurs only after buyers have had a reasonable opportunity to inspect them upon arrival. UCC 2–513(1).

Under UCC 2–601, a buyer may reject "the whole" if "the tender of delivery" fails in any respect to conform to the contract. Documents, like goods, may or may not conform to the contract; tendered documents must be in "correct" and "due" form. UCC 2–503(5), 2–504(b). The Code's most explicit reference to non-conformity of documents is found in the installment contract provision. UCC 2–612(2). The perfect tender rule is associated historically with cases in which buyers were tendered documents.

Contracting for Documentary Transactions. In the prototype transaction, buyer pays the price upon seller's tender of a negotiable bill of lading. Recall that this arrangement is not a default rule of performance; it result from the agreements of the parties. What terms in sales contracts are sufficient to commit buyers to pay at this stage in performance? See UCC 2–310, 2–513(3).

(a) A commonly used contract term is: "sight draft against order bill of lading." Does this satisfy the Code requirements?

(b) If a sales contract uses the term C.I.F. or C. & F., must the buyer pay the price upon tender of an order bill of lading? See UCC 2–320(4).

(c) If the sales contract uses the term F.O.B. Sellersville or F.O.B. Buyersville, must the buyer pay the price upon tender of an order bill of lading? What explains the difference between the F.O.B. term and C.I.F. or C. & F. terms? Is it significant that the latter are used most commonly in shipments by water? See Comment 4 to UCC 2–310. For other terms in contracts contemplating shipment by water, see UCC 2–319(4), 2–321, 2–322.

Inspection by Third Party. Parties to documentary transactions may agree that the goods will be inspected by a third party before shipment or at some point en route. The sales contract may specify that results of the inspection must be reflected in the inspector's certificate of quality which must be tendered to the buyer with the bill of lading. See UCC 2–513(4).

Inspection by Carrier. Carriers have some duties regarding the quality and quantity of goods not in packages or sealed containers. Thus a carrier must ascertain the kind and quantity of bulk freight, and may be liable for misdescription or nonreceipt of the goods. 49

U.S.C. App. 100, 102, UCC 7–301(2). To protect themselves against claims that goods were damaged en route, carriers may add notes on bills of lading about the condition of the goods or packages.

In the paper bags transaction, would Buyer & Co. have a cause of action against the railroad for delivering goods that do not conform to the sales contract? Does the description of the goods in the bill of lading, "Bags, paper," create a basis for carrier liability for the quality of the goods? See UCC 7–301(1). Read again the RECEIVED paragraph at the head of the order bill of lading.

(2) THE SITUATION OF SELLERS

Sellers who engage in documentary exchange transactions incur certain risks of transaction failure. Vis-a-vis buyers, risk exists that buyers will not make payment against tender of documents. Sellers may want to stop the goods, then en route to buyers' locations, and either get them back or divert them to other destinations. Carriers permit consignors to modify the routing of goods, but sellers lose time and incur expenses in making these changes.

Sellers are dependent upon banks and carriers to carry out their respective services. If they should fail to do so, sellers might be deprived of their goods without having received the promised payments.

Problem 2. Buyer and Seller agreed on sale of a lathe No. 3X from Seller's current catalogue with payment to be made against documents. The next day, Seller delivered a No. 3X lathe to the railroad, obtained a bill of lading that calls for delivery to "order of Seller," indorsed the bill in blank, and gave it along with a sight draft drawn on Buyer to its local bank for transmittal to Buyer. The documents were forwarded to a bank in Buyer's city, which sent a notice to Buyer that it held these documents for Buyer's payment. Buyer ignored the notice. What is the nature of the bank's obligation?

(a) Has Buyer dishonored the draft by not responding to the bank's notice? See UCC 3–502(c)?

(b) Is the bank obliged to do more than inform Seller of a Buyer's dishonor? See UCC 4–503(b). What might be the reason for this provision?

Problem 3. Assume the same facts as above, except that the presenting bank gave Buyer the bill of lading in exchange for the Buyer's uncertified check in the amount of the draft. Before the Buyer's check was paid, Buyer obtained the lathe from the railroad and stopped payment on its check. See UCC 4–403(a). What are Seller's rights?

(a) Does Seller have a claim against the railroad? See 49 U.S.C. App. 89(c), UCC 7–404.

(b) Does Seller have a claim against the presenting bank? See UCC 4–202(a), 4–213, 4–103(e). And see Bunge v. First National Bank of Mount Holly Springs, 118 F.2d 427 (3d Cir.1941).

(c) Does Seller have a claim against its local bank for the actions of the presenting bank? See UCC 4–202(c) and Comment 4.

(d) Does Seller have a claim against Buyer? See UCC 2–301, 2–507. Of what practical value to Seller is 2–507(2)?

Problem 4. Assume the same facts as in the original problem, except that Buyer, without paying the draft or obtaining the bill of lading from the presenting bank, gets possession of the lathe from railroad. What are Seller's rights?

(a) Does Seller have a claim against the railroad? See 49 U.S.C. App. 88(b), 90; UCC 7–403(1). What would be the proper measure of damages? See Alderman Bros. Co. v. New York, etc. R. Co., 102 Conn. 461, 129 A. 47 (1925).

(b) Does Seller have a claim against any Bank?

(c) Does Seller have a claim against Buyer?

Sellers' Use of Drafts to Obtain Credit. Sellers engaging in documentary transactions sometimes seek to speed up the inflow of cash by getting the amount of the drafts, less a discount, from the banks who take them for presentation and collection. The context of documentary transactions gives banks reasonable assurance that credit extended to sellers will be repaid promptly from proceeds of the drafts. Moreover, the drafts are negotiable instruments on which the sellers are liable as drawers. UCC 3–414(b). Not uncommonly, therefore, banks taking drafts for collection will "discount" them. At the same time they also receive the "order bills" indorsed in blank.

(a) If a carrier delivers the goods to the wrong person under an "order bill," is the discounting bank entitled to a remedy against the carrier? See 49 U.S.C. App. 90, 91; UCC 7–403.

(b) Is the discounting bank liable to the buyer if the goods do not conform to the seller's obligations under the sales contract? See UCC 7–507, 7–508; cf. UCC 2–210(4).

Sellers may also "discount" drafts to anticipate payment when underlying documentary transactions require buyers to accept "time drafts" upon presentment rather than make immediate payment. Accepted drafts establish liability on both the drawer and the drawee/acceptor. UCC 3–409, 3–413, 3–414.

(3) SELLERS' POWER TO RECLAIM GOODS

Introduction. Sellers who delivered goods without being paid may, in some limited circumstances, reclaim the goods from their buyers. The power to reclaim is essentially lost in credit sales, i.e., transactions in which sellers voluntarily agree to deliver before payment.

One exception, already explored, is sellers' power to avoid transactions induced by buyers' fraudulent misrepresentation. Avoidance and its accompanying *in rem* remedies are associated with the law of torts and restitution as much as with contract law. Article 2 of the Commercial Code, which assumes the common-law power to avoid for fraud, also creates for sellers statutory power to reclaim in some circumstances. Effective exercise of that power reduces sellers' credit risk.

Problem 5. Buyer induces Seller to deliver goods on credit by promising to pay for them in 30 days. Shortly after delivering the goods, Seller discovers that Buyer is insolvent. May Seller recover the goods? See UCC 2–702(2). What difference, if any, would it make if:

(a) Two months prior to delivery Seller had received from Buyer its financial statement showing Buyer to be solvent?

(b) Two months prior to delivery Seller had received a report from a credit reporting agency erroneously showing Buyer to be solvent?

Problem 6. Buyer and Seller contract for sale of an antique brass chandelier. Seller delivers the chandelier in exchange for Buyer's personal check for the price, $7,500.00. Seller deposits the check the next day. A week later, Seller's bank informs Seller that the deposited check had been dishonored by Buyer's bank, that the provisional credit to Seller's account has been reversed, and that Seller's account has been charged a fee for the transaction. May Seller recover the chandelier? See UCC 2–507(2).

Originally, Comment 3 to UCC 2–507 declared that the ten day time limit for sellers' reclamation in UCC 2–702(2) is also applicable in here. That Comment was withdrawn by the Permanent Editorial Board in 1990. See PEB Commentary No. 1, Section 2–507(2):

> There is no specific time limit for a cash seller to exercise the right of reclamation. The right may be exercised as long as there has not been excessive delay causing inequitable prejudice to the buyer.

Is the 1990 commentary persuasive? Is it any more or less binding on a court than the original Comment?

Problem 7. A contract for sale between Seller in San Francisco and Buyer in New York calls for shipment of a carload of Sunkist oranges at $3000, f.o.b. San Francisco. Payment terms are: Cash 30 days after delivery. Seller ships oranges in conformity with the contract on a "straight bill of lading" naming buyer as consignee. After the carload arrives in the New York freight yards but before the oranges are unloaded, Seller learns that Buyer's creditors have begun to obtain judgments against Buyer and judicial liens against Buyer's property.

(a) Has Seller a chance to keep the oranges for itself? See UCC 2–705. Note the Code's extension of the grounds for stoppage beyond insolvency, for carload and similarly large shipments.[12]

12. Would you advise a seller to ship on credit to a shaky buyer in reliance on the seller's stoppage rights? Would sellers likely hear of insolvency during the time

(b) Assume Seller instructs the railroad not to deliver the oranges to Buyer but rather to transport them to another consignee in Philadelphia.

(i) If the railroad refuses to release the oranges to Buyer, would it be liable to Buyer for failing to honor the terms of its bill of lading? See UCC 7–403; UCC 7–303.

(ii) Under what circumstances, if any, may the railroad ignore Seller's instructions without incurring liability to Seller? See UCC 2–705; UCC 7–303. See also Butts v. Glendale Plywood Co., 710 F.2d 504 (9th Cir.1983) (carrier's rerouting of shipment to buyer's buyer, made at buyer's direction while goods still in transit, held to be "reshipment" under UCC 2–705(2)(c)).

(B) INTERNATIONAL SALES LAW

Introduction. Grappling with international sales transactions runs some of the hazards of navigating among icebergs. The elements, while broadly standardized, have infinite variations in particular transactions. In reported decisions of courts and arbitrators, many critical facts may be invisible. Seldom do these tribunals give the complete setting from which the controversies arose. To provide a basis for understanding the fundamental mechanics of international sales transactions, this section opens with a prototype transaction that follows the sale, step by step, through its most important stages.

Management of credit risk is more important in international sales transactions than in domestic transactions, where both seller and buyer are in the same country and subject to the same domestic laws. The marketplace developed a payment device, the bank letter of credit, which serves well the parties' needs to control credit risks in the performance of export-import sales.

As noted in previous sections, the Convention on Contracts for the International Sale of Goods has few provisions on the manner, time, and place for performance of buyers' payment obligation that are not dependent upon the agreement of the parties. However, the Convention contains a default rule that, absent agreement otherwise, buyers need not pay until they have had an opportunity to examine the goods. CISG 58(3). Agreement to pay before inspection may be inferred from agreement on "the procedures for delivery or payment." Id. If the contract involves carriage of goods, sellers may dispatch the goods on terms whereby the goods, or documents controlling their disposition, will not be handed over to the buyer except against payment of the

required for shipment? On the other hand, a lawyer would probably be liable for malpractice if a client presented the facts in the preceding Problem and the lawyer could think of no course of action other than taking a day or so to research the point.

price. CISG 58(2). Since examination of goods can occur before they are "handed over" to buyers, Article 58(2) does not override 58(3).

The Convention makes no mention of payment by letter of credit. Parties who wish to use this payment device must do so by their agreement.

Agreements on payment terms, like other contract terms, may be express or implied. No implication arises from the parties' use of the ICC's *Incoterms,* which describe the buyer's payment obligation in documentary transactions to be: pay the price as provided in the contract of sale. However, common-law courts have long held that an obligation to pay against documents is implicit in international sales. The leading case is E. Clemens Horst Co. v. Biddle Bros., [1912] A.C. 18 (H.L.) (sale of hops shipped from San Francisco C.I.F to London, Liverpool, or Hull). Recall that this common-law rule was incorporated into the Code, which provides that contractual use of terms associated with water transport (C.I.F., C. & F., F.A.S., F.O.B. vessel) creates a duty on buyers to pay against documents. UCC 2–319(4), 2–320(4), 2–321(3).

(1) BALL BEARINGS FOR BRAZIL: A PROTOTYPE EXPORT TRANSACTION[13]

SKF Industries, Inc., is a Philadelphia manufacturer of ball and roller bearings. On December 4, 1992, SKF receives a letter from Companhia Importadora Brasileira, a distributor of bearings in Rio de Janeiro, Brazil (hereinafter called "Brasileira"), requesting a price quotation for 1200 ball bearings (catalogue number 187B) and 2400 roller bearings (catalogue number 839R). On December 15 SKF replies by letter (FORM 1) explaining the quotation as set forth in the enclosed proforma invoice (FORM 2).

---

13. Mr. B.A. Tassone, Director of International Marketing, and Mr. H.J. Gupfinger, Manager of Material Flow, SKF Industries, Inc., were exceedingly helpful in explaining their practices and in preparing the sample forms. Thanks are also owing to Mr. Robert S. Adamson, Assistant Vice President, Philadelphia National Bank, for preparing the letter of credit. Of course, any errors in presenting the transaction are our own responsibility.

SKF INDUSTRIES, INC.
INTERNATIONAL MARKETING/BEARINGS GROUP

December 15, 1992

Companhia Importadora Brasileira
Caixa Postal 10
Rio de Janeiro, Brazil

Re: <u>CIB - 43H2</u>

Gentlemen:

We are very pleased to acknowledge receipt of your above inquiry
dated December 4 requesting our quotation on a total quantity of
3,600 ball and roller bearings.

We are attaching hereto our proforma invoice in quadruplicate
showing the net price for each size, along with the total f.a.s.
Philadelphia or New York City value. For your convenience, we
have also estimated the insurance charges, ocean freight and
handling charges as well as the consular fees. We have, therefore, arrived at a total estimated c.i.f. Rio de Janeiro value.
We wish to call your attention specifically to the fact that our
quotation is an f.a.s. Philadelphia or New York City quotation
and the total c.i.f. value shown is simply as an estimated value
which we have included for your convenience in obtaining your
Import License and opening the Letter of Credit. The shipping
and handling charges will be for your account and we will invoice
the exact charges whether they are higher or lower than those
estimated.

We have been able to quote a January delivery for both sizes, but
have to point out that this promise is valid only if your firm
order will be received by return air mail. Even though the delivery
has been promised for January, we suggest that your Letter of Credit
be valid until February 28, 1993, so that there will be no necessity
to request an extension unless some unforeseen difficulties should
arise. Needless to say, the Letter of Credit should be for a minimum
of 10,950 United States dollars. As all of the bearings which you
require are available for shipment in January, we have estimated
shipping expenses for only one shipment. Therefore, it is not
necessary to allow for partial shipments in the Letter of Credit.

We appreciate very much this opportunity of quoting and will look
forward to the early receipt of your firm order.

Very truly yours,

E. L. Derry
E. L. Derry
General Supervisor

[D628]

FORM 1
LETTER TRANSMITTING QUOTATION

SKF INDUSTRIES, INC.
FRONT STREET AND ERIE AVENUE
PHILADELPHIA, PA. 19132

CABLE ADDRESS
"SKAYEF" – PHILADELPHIA

REFER CORRESPONDENCE TO
EXPORT SALES DEPT.
P.O. BOX NO. 6731
PHILADELPHIA, PENNA. 19132

TELEX 83-4539

OUR PROFORMA INVOICE
NUMBER: IA/100
DATE: 12/15/92

YOUR INQUIRY
NUMBER: CIB-43R2
DATE: 12/4/92

Companhia Importadora Brasileira

Caixa Postal 10

Rio de Janeiro, Brazil

ITEM NO.	MANUFACTURER'S PART NUMBER	MATERIAL SPECIFICATIONS SIZE DESCRIPTION	QUANTITY	PRICE UNIT	PRICE TOTAL	AVAILABILITY STOCK	AVAILABILITY	WEIGHT IN LBS.
1	187 B		1200	2.15	2,580.00		January	
2	839 R		2400	3.37	8,088.00		January	

Os precos acima indicados sao os correntes no mercado de exportacao para qualquer pais.

Nao ha comissao.

Nao sao publicados catalogos e/ou lista de preco para o material acima indicado.

Est. total net weight - 4520 lbs. - 2050 kilos
Est. total gross weight - 5010 lbs. - 2272 kilos

Schedule B Commodity Code - 7197010

TOTAL MAT'L. VALUE F.A.S. VESSEL PHILA. OR N.Y.C.	$10,668.00
ESTIMATED FREIGHT FORWARDER'S CHARGES	19.00
ESTIMATED CONSULAR CHARGES	58.00
ESTIMATED F.O.B. VESSEL	
ESTIMATED INSURANCE CHARGES	48.50
ESTIMATED TRANSPORTATION CHARGES	156.50
ESTIMATED C.I.F.	10,950.00

THIS OFFER SUBMITTED SUBJECT TO PRIOR SALE AND CONFIRMATION OF TERMS AND PRICES AT TIME OF RECEIPT OF ORDER.

BCSP INDUSTRIES, INC.

(82890)

TERMS:

DELIVERY - FAS VESSEL PHILADELPHIA/NEW YORK CITY

PAYMENT   LETTER OF CREDIT

CONDITIONS: Prices shown are those in effect at time of quotation. Prices in effect at time of shipment will prevail.

PH-3718-F

FORM 2
PROFORMA INVOICE

TERMS AND CONDITIONS

Any order resulting from this quotation will be subject to the following conditions:

1. Delivery dates are approximate. Seller shall not be liable for any delay in, or inability to complete delivery because of any of the following causes: Acts of God; suspension or requisition of any kind; strikes or other stoppages of labor or shortage in the supply thereof; inability to obtain fuel, material or parts; fire, casualties or accidents; failure of shipping facilities; riot; or any cause, whether the same or a different character, beyond Seller's control.

2. Prices indicated are based on the prices in effect as of the date hereof. They are subject to change in accordance with the prices in effect as of the date of shipment.

3. Products are not returnable for credit or replacement, unless authorized in writing by Seller.

4. If, for any reason whatsoever, this order or any part thereof, is terminated by the Buyer, such termination shall be effected with the understanding that termination charges may result therefrom.

5. Orders for special products are subject to shipment of any overrun or underrun not to exceed 10%. The Buyer will pay, in full, for such overshipment, and in the event of an undershipment the Buyer will consider the order completed with such undershipment.

(828911)

6. Goods manufactured by Seller shall conform to the description, shall be fit for the ordinary purposes for which such goods are used, and shall be free of defects in material and workmanship at time of shipment. THERE ARE NO WARRANTIES OF MERCHANTABILITY OR OTHERWISE, EXCEPT OF TITLE, WHICH EXTENDS BEYOND THAT STATED ABOVE.

7. Seller's liability and Buyer's remedy for breach of warranty or otherwise is expressly limited to the replacement of any products sold hereunder which Seller determines, by laboratory examination is non-conforming, provided said non-conforming products are returned F.O.B. Seller's warehouse within twelve (12) months of shipment hereunder. Seller retains the right to render credit for the purchase price in lieu of furnishing a replacement product.

8. IN NO EVENT SHALL SELLER BE LIABLE HEREUNDER OR OTHERWISE FOR LOSS OF PROFITS, SPECIAL, INCIDENTAL, OR CONSEQUENTIAL DAMAGES OF ANY KIND.

9. Shipments hereunder shall be at all times subject to the approval of Seller's Credit Department.

10. The terms and conditions on the face and reverse side hereof constitute the entire agreement between Buyer and Seller. No reference herein to Buyer's inquiry or order shall in any way incorporate different or additional terms or conditions which are hereby objected to. No modification hereto shall be binding upon Seller unless made in writing by Seller's authorized representative. Receipt of this acknowledgment by Buyer without prompt written objection thereto shall constitute an acceptance of these terms and conditions by Buyer.

[Reverse]

PROFORMA INVOICE

FORM 2

Examination of the proforma invoice will show that it contains all the particulars for the proposed shipment which are then known to SKF. (It will be useful to consider whether this communication constitutes an offer which, on acceptance, would create a binding contract. Compare the letter with the printed language in the bottom right-hand corner of the proforma invoice.)[14]

The Price Quotation: F.A.S. and C.I.F. One will note that the proforma invoice in the bottom left-hand corner has a blank after "TERMS: DELIVERY" and that SKF inserted the following: "F.A.S. PHILA/NEW YORK CITY". "F.A.S." stands for "Free Along Side"; this means that the seller will be responsible for the cost and risks of bringing the goods "Along Side" an overseas vessel at the stated location: the buyer bears the costs and risks from that point.[15] Therefore, under this quotation the Brazilian buyer will understand that its total costs will include not only the quoted F.A.S. price of $10,668, but also freight charges from Philadelphia to Brazil, the cost of insurance and any other expenses of bringing the goods into Brazil.

It is necessary to pause in the description of this transaction to note that instead of quoting a price "F.A.S. Philadelphia," the price might have been quoted "C.I.F. Rio de Janeiro." The initials "C.I.F." stand for "Cost, Insurance, and Freight" and mean, among other things, that in exchange for this stated price the seller undertakes not only to supply the goods ("cost") but also to obtain and pay for insurance and bear the freight charges to the stated point.[16] In spite of the widespread use of C.I.F. quotations in foreign trade, sellers in the position of SKF often prefer to quote on a F.A.S. basis since this relieves them of the burdens and hazards of variations and fluctuations in freight and insurance costs for shipments to widely scattered points. This preference is reflected in the "F.A.S." quotation in the transaction which we are following. (Note the explanation in the second paragraph of the letter in FORM 1.)

Buyer's Purchase Order. In response to SKF's letter of December 15, on January 5, Brasileira sent SKF the Buyer's Purchase Order that follows (FORM 3).

---

14. If the seller were a middleman purchasing goods for export could it safely leave the transaction open at this point?

15. See International Chamber of Commerce's INCOTERMS F.A.S.; UCC 2–319(2).

16. See International Chamber of Commerce's INCOTERMS C.I.F.; UCC 2–320. From the fact that the contract price includes the freight, do not leap to any conclusion about who has the risk of loss.

EXPORT SALES
DATE REC'D DIRETOS
JAN 10 1944 REGULAMENTOS

COMPANHIA IMPORTADORA BRASILEIRA

Caixa Postal, 10   Fone 2-1881   End. Teleg. ROLESFER

RIO DE JANEIRO, BRAZIL

Fornecedor: S K F Industries, Inc.
(Supplier)

Pedido No. 42
(Order)

Endereço: P.O.Box 6731 - Philadelphia 32, Pa. USA
(Address)

Data: 5/1/93
(Date)

Condições Pagamento: Irrevocable Letter of Credit
(Payment Terms)

Banco: Advise
(Bank) C.I.B.

Embarque: Ship to Rio de Janeiro
(Shipment)

Marca: Rio de Janeiro
(Shipping Mark)

Embarcador: Pierce-Byron, Inc., 325 Chestnut St., Phila., PA
(Forwarder)

Declaração Consular: Rolamento de esfera, rolete cone ou agulhas para mancal
(Consular Declaration)

Licença de Importação No. DG-59/10000   Valôr: $10,950.00
(Import License) (Value)

Validade: 2/28/93
(Validity)

Seguro: Against all usual risks including theft and
(Insurance) marine up to clients warehouse.

Embalagem: Packing export
(Packing) in wood cases

[B2913]

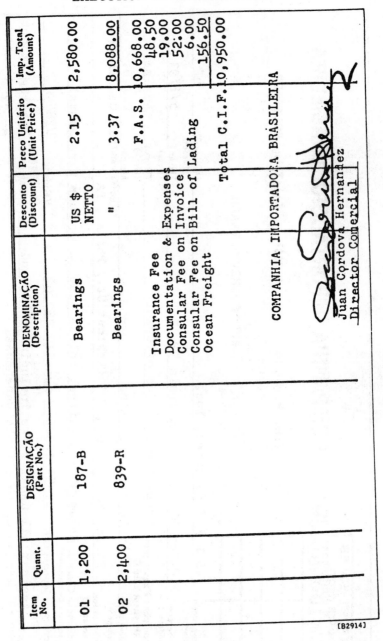

Item No.	Quant.	DESIGNAÇÃO (Part No.)	DENOMINAÇÃO (Description)	Desconto (Discount)	Preço Unitário (Unit Price)	Imp. Total (Amount)
01	1,200	187-B	Bearings	US $ NETTO	2.15	2,580.00
02	2,400	839-R	Bearings	"	3.37	8,088.00
					F.A.S.	10,668.00
			Insurance Fee			48.50
			Documentation & Expenses			19.00
			Consular Fee on Invoice			52.00
			Consular Fee on Bill of Lading			6.00
			Ocean Freight			156.50
					Total C.I.F.	10,950.00

COMPANHIA IMPORTADORA BRASILEIRA

Juan Córdova Hernández
Director Comercial

[B2914]

FORM 3
BUYER'S PURCHASE ORDER

The Letter of Credit. The proforma invoice (FORM 2), which SKF enclosed with its letter of December 15, under "TERMS ... PAYMENT" contained the notation "Letter of Credit". Letters of credit play a central role in most exporting transactions and deserve careful attention. In following the domestic documentary transaction between Sellersville, New York and Buyersville, California, Sec. A, supra, we saw that one way for a seller to be assured of payment is to ship goods under a negotiable bill of lading and arrange for a bank in buyer's city to hold the bill of lading until the buyer pays the draft. In the usual foreign sale (and in some domestic sales) this arrangement for securing payment of the price is not adequate. For example, in our current SKF export it probably will not be advisable for SKF to allow payment to be delayed until the bearings reach Brazil. Under such an arrangement Brasileira might reject the bearings in Rio de Janeiro; at this point substantial shipping costs would have been incurred and the bearings would be at a location where it might be awkward and expensive for the seller to arrange for redisposition. Of course, the seller would have a claim against the buyer for this loss, but litigation is always hazardous and in a foreign country the hazards multiply. Moreover, in dealing with the many countries which control foreign exchange, it may be difficult to get the local money converted into usable dollars.

In some situations, sellers may need assurance of payment even before the time for shipment. This problem arises in contracts (either foreign or domestic) which call for the manufacture of goods to the buyer's specifications (electric generators; locomotives; steel girders to be cut in non-standard lengths). In these contracts the seller will need firm assurance of payment before it starts to manufacture.

Strong protection against these hazards can be created if the contract provides that, at a specified point in the transaction before the seller incurs costs it cannot readily recoup, the buyer must establish an irrevocable letter of credit. By such a letter of credit, a bank promises to honor the seller's draft for the price; in our export transaction the bank's promise will be conditioned upon seller's presenting specified documents, one of which will be a negotiable bill of lading evidencing shipment of the goods.

Although the proforma invoice did not so specify, SKF will expect the letter of credit to be "confirmed" by a local bank in the United States. (Cf. UCC 2–325.) It is easy to see why SKF wants the undertaking by a bank of known solvency and responsibility. But why does the local bank only "confirm," rather than "issue," the letter of credit? The answer arises from this practical consideration: the bank that issues a letter of credit needs assurance that it will be reimbursed by the buyer, on whose behalf it pays the seller. The Philadelphia bank will probably not know the Brazilian buyer, and cannot be sure of reimbursement. But the buyer's own bank (Banco do Brasil) can take steps to minimize or remove these hazards. As we shall see, it will receive the negotiable bill of lading controlling the goods which will provide security for the customer's obligation to reimburse the bank; in addition, the buyer's own bank can judge whether security is needed before it issues the letter of credit.

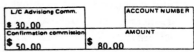

L/C Advising Comm.		ACCOUNT NUMBER
$ 30.00		
Confirmation commission		AMOUNT
$ 50.00	$ 80.00	

CABLE ADDRESS: PHILABANK TELEX: 845-355

IRREVOCABLE DOCUMENTARY CREDIT

OUR CREDIT NO.	CR NO—CORRESPONDENT	DATE	EXPIRY DATE	LETTER OF CREDIT AMOUNT
E 4450	164	JAN.11,1993	FEB.28,1993	US$10,950.00

BENEFICIARY	CORRESPONDENT
SKF INDUSTRIES, INC.	BANCO do BRAZIL S.A.
PHILADELPHIA, PA.	RIO de JANEIRO, BRAZIL

MAIL TO

Gentlemen:

We are instructed by the above correspondent to advise you that they have opened their irrevocable credit in your favor for account of COMPANHIA IMPORTADORA BRASILEIRA, CAIXA POSTAL 10, RIO de JANEIRO, BRAZIL available by your drafts on THE PHILADELPHIA NATIONAL BANK AT SIGHT accompanied by the following documents:

1. FULL SET OF CLEAN ON BOARD OCEAN BILLS OF LADING STATING "FREIGHT PREPAID" MADE OUT TO ORDER OF BANCO do BRAZIL S.A.
2. INSURANCE POLICY OR CERTIFICATE COVERING MARINE AND WAR RISK.
3. PACKING LIST.
4. COMMERCIAL INVOICE IN SEXTUPLICATE OF WHICH THREE COPIES MUST BE LEGALIZED BY THE BRAZILIAN CONSUL AND VISAED BY THE LOCAL CHAMBER OF COMMERCE.

COVERING: 1200 BALL BEARING NO. 187-B AND 2400 ROLLER BEARINGS NO. 839-R.
          TOTAL VALUE $10,950.00 CIF RIO de JANEIRO
          IMPORT LICENSE DC-59/10000 EXPIRES 2/28/93

SPECIAL INSTRUCTIONS:

A. ALL DRAFTS SO DRAWN MUST BE MARKED "DRAWN UNDER ADVICE NO. E 4450/164".

SHIPMENT FROM: PHILADELPHIA   TO: RIO de JANEIRO

PARTIAL SHIPMENTS: ARE NOT PERMITTED   TRANSHIPMENTS: ARE NOT PERMITTED

THE ABOVE CORRESPONDENT ENGAGES WITH YOU THAT ALL DRAFTS DRAWN UNDER AND IN COMPLIANCE WITH THE TERMS OF THIS CREDIT WILL BE HONORED ON DELIVERY OF DOCUMENTS AS SPECIFIED IF PRESENTED AT THIS OFFICE ON OR BEFORE THE EXPIRATION DATE SHOWN ABOVE.

IF DESIRED, DRAFTS AND DOCUMENTS MAY BE PRESENTED AT PHILADELPHIA INTERNATIONAL BANK, 55 BROAD STREET, NEW YORK, N.Y. 10004.   (D629)

[Letter of Credit continued on next page]

PNB Philadelphia National Bank INTERNATIONAL DIVISION P O Box 13866 Phila PA 19101	☐ To be collected at negotiation. ☐ We have debited your Account/ H. O. Account	L/C Advising Comm. $ Confirmation commission $	ACCOUNT NUMBER AMOUNT

CABLE ADDRESS: PHILABANK TELEX: 845-355

IRREVOCABLE DOCUMENTARY CREDIT

ATTACHED TO AND FORMING PART OF DOCUMENTARY CREDIT NO. E4450 DATE: JANUARY 11, 1993
CR. NO. CORRESPONDENT 164

MAIL TO ▶

DOCUMENTS MUST CONFORM STRICTLY WITH THE TERMS OF THIS CREDIT, IF YOU ARE UNABLE TO COMPl
WITH ITS TERMS, PLEASE COMMUNICATE WITH YOUR CUSTOMER PROMPTLY WITH A VIEW TO HAVING THE
CONDITIONS CHANGED. THIS WILL ELIMINATE DIFFICULTIES AND DELAY WHEN YOUR DOCUMENTS ARE
PRESENTED FOR NEGOTIATION.

X WE CONFIRM THIS CREDIT AND THEREBY UNDERTAKE THAT ALL DRAFTS DRAWN IN ACCORDANCE
   WITH TERMS THEREOF WILL BE DULY HONORED ON PRESENTATION.

ALL DRAFTS AND DOCUMENTS MUST INDICATE THE REFERENCE NUMBER OF THE CORRESPONDENT BANK
AND THE REFERENCE NUMBER OF THE PHILADELPHIA NATIONAL BANK.

Carrie Cash
AUTHORIZED SIGNATURE

EXCEPT SO FAR AS OTHERWISE EXPRESSLY STATED, THIS DOCUMENTARY CREDIT IS SUBJECT TO THE
"UNIFORM CUSTOMS AND PRACTICE FOR DOCUMENTARY CREDITS: (1983 REVISION), INTERNATIONAL
CHAMBER OF COMMERCE, PUBLICATION NO. 400.

(D630)

FORM 4
LETTER OF CREDIT

By this process, something remarkable happens: large hazards inherent in a transaction between a seller and a remote buyer can be reduced almost to the vanishing point by breaking the transaction into steps, and by assigning each step to a party who is in a position to avoid mishap. Thus, the seller is assured of payment by the engagement of the confirming Philadelphia bank; the Philadelphia bank is assured of reimbursement by the undertaking of the issuing Brazilian bank; this Brazilian bank can take steps to assure reimbursement by its local customer. Unhappily, as will soon be seen, not every risk can be removed. But the success of these arrangements is shown by their widespread use by sellers and by the minimal rates charged by banks for the risks which remain.[17]

To meet SKF's letter of credit requirements, Brasileira requests its local bank, Banco do Brasil, to arrange for the issuance of a letter of credit which will comply with the terms of the proforma invoice. Brasileira will sign a detailed Application and Agreement for Commercial Credit prepared by the bank.[18] Banco do Brasil, after approving Brasileira's credit standing, transmits a letter of credit by cable to the Philadelphia confirming bank. The Philadelphia bank then delivers to SKF a document (FORM 4) advising SKF that Banco do Brasil has opened a described letter of credit in favor of SKF and adding the Philadelphia bank's confirmation. (See the end of FORM 4.)

By this arrangement, SKF, the beneficiary of the credit, is assured of payment of its sight drafts drawn on the local Philadelphia bank in the amount of the total cost of the sale, provided it presents the documents called for in the letter of credit. An examination of this letter of credit also reveals that the bill of lading is to be consigned to the "order of Banco do Brasil," thereby giving this bank control over the goods, with the consequent security for its claim against the buyer which has already been discussed.

---

17. In domestic or import letters of credit, an American bank might typically charge an opening commission of $20 and, for negotiations, 1/4% (minimum of $10 for clean drafts and $30 for documentary drafts). A typical commission for accepting an export letter of credit would be 1½% (rate varying with risk; minimum $50), and for confirming a foreign letter of credit 1/10% (minimum $50). For paying under an export letter of credit, the charge might be 1/10% ($35 minimum).

18. A typical American bank's Application and Agreement for Commercial Letter of Credit calls for the buyer to specify which documents should be required by the Letter of Credit, and other essential information such as the amount and expiration date of the credit. The form of agreement then contains two or more closely-printed pages of provisions most of which are designed to assure the bank of reimbursement from its customer for the bank's outlays under the credit in spite of various mishaps. The form also may provide that, except for points covered by the agreement, the operation of the credit will be governed by the Uniform Customs and Practice for Commercial Documentary Credits (1983 Revision in force from 1 October 1984).

This Application, of course, governs only the relationship between the bank and its customer requesting the credit (Brasileira). The obligation of the bank to the beneficiary (SKF) will be governed by the terms of the Letter of Credit which the bank thereafter issues.

CUSTOMER	CUSTOMER ORDER NO.		SKF ORDER NO.	SHPT. NO.
Companhia Importadora Brasileira	CIB-43H2	•	W-77	1

ADDRESS	CUSTOMER ORDER DATE	CUSTOMER NO.	DATE
Caixa Postal 10 Rio de Janeiro, Brazil	1/5/93	88831	1/12/93

	TERRITORY NO.		IND. NO.
	824	X4	100

SOLD TO • Companhia Importadora Brasileira
of Caixa Postal 10
Rio de Janeiro, Brazil

TERMS • Letter of Credit   EXPORT LICENSE G-DEST

IMPORT LICENSE • DG-59/10000 expires 2/28/93   LETTER OF CREDIT • No. E 4450/164 expires 2/28/93

MARKS AND CASE NUMBERS	QUANTITIES		DESCRIPTION OF GOODS	SELLING PRICE	
	ORDERED	SHIPPED		UNIT	TOTAL
	1,200	1,200	187-B Bearings	2.15	2,580.00
	2,400	2,400	839-R Bearings	3.37	8,088.00
					10,668.00

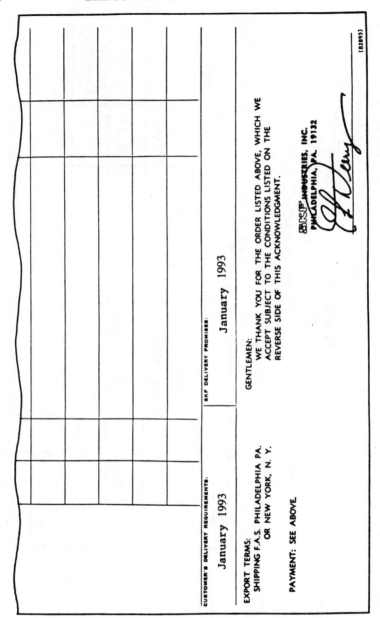

FORM 5
ORDER ACKNOWLEDGEMENT
*[The reverse side of this form is the same as the reverse side
of Form 2]*

SKF INDUSTRIES, INC.
FRONT STREET AND ERIE AVE.
PHILADELPHIA, PA. 19132
P. O. BOX 6731

CUSTOMER ORDER NO NUMERO DE PEDIDO DEL CLIENTE	SKF ORDER NO NUMERO DE PEDIDO DE SKF	SHPT. NO. DESPACHO
CIB-43H2	W-77	1

EXPORT SALES DEPT.
CABLE ADDRESS   **"SKAYEF"**

SKF INVOICE DATE
FECHA DE LA FACTURA   1/12/93

SOLD TO
VENDIDO A   Companhia Importadora Brasileira

OF   Caixa Postal 10
DE   Rio de Janeiro, Brazil

TERMS
PLAZOS   Letter of Credit

FAS/   Philadelphia

IMPORT LICENSE
LICENCIA DE
IMPORTACION   DG-59/10000   expires   2/28/93

LETTER OF CREDIT
CARTA DE CREDITO   No. E 4450/164   expires   2/28/93

MARKS AND CASE NUMBERS MARCAS Y NUMEROS DE CAJA	QUANTITY SHIPPED CANTIDAD EMBARCADA	DESCRIPTION OF GOODS "ROLAMENTOS COMPLETOS DE ESFERAS" DESCRIPCION DEL MATERIAL		SELLING PRICE PRECIO DE VENTA	
				UNIT UNIDADES	TOTAL TOTAL
				US$	US$
C.I.B. RIO DE JANEIRO #1/25	1,200	187-B	Bearings	2.15	2,580.00
	2,400	839-R	Bearings	3.37	8,088.00
					10,688.00
		Consular Fees			58.00
		Freight Forwarders Chrgs.			19.00
		Insurance Charge			48.50
		Transportation Charge			156.50
				TOTAL C.I.F.	10,950.00

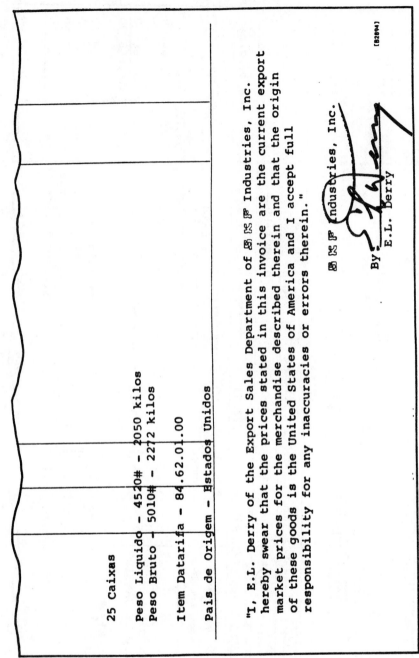

25 Caixas

Peso Liquido - 4520# - 2050 kilos
Peso Bruto - 5010# - 2272 kilos

Item Datarifa - 84.62.01.00

Pais de Origem - Estados Unidos

"I, E.L. Derry of the Export Sales Department of B K F Industries, Inc. hereby swear that the prices stated in this invoice are the current export market prices for the merchandise described therein and that the origin of these goods is the United States of America and I accept full responsibility for any inaccuracies or errors therein."

B K F Industries, Inc.

By: E.L. Derry

[B2894]

FORM 6
COMMERCIAL INVOICE

Acceptance; Shipment. On receipt of the confirmed letter of credit, SKF sends Brasileira its Order Acknowledgment (FORM 5). This document repeats the description and price of the goods which had also appeared on the proforma invoice and states the number and expiration date of the letter of credit. Note the provision in the lower right hand corner that the buyer's order is accepted, "Subject To The Conditions Listed On The Reverse Side Of This Acknowledgment." (Note especially the conditions dealing with the effect of contingencies beyond the seller's control, fluctuations in the price of the goods, and liability for defective merchandise.)

The arrival of the letter of credit is the "go ahead" signal for SKF to make the shipment. SKF then prepares the Commercial Invoice (FOP.M 6) which provides a complete record of the transaction and is an important source of information to such interested parties as a bank discounting a draft or an underwriter extending insurance. Note that all data on the commercial invoice conforms to that found in the other shipping documents. By scanning it, one should be able to form a complete picture of the nature of the packing (number of packages, weights, etc.), the commodities being shipped, and the value of the shipment.

As the time for actual shipment of the bearings approaches, SKF contacts Pierce–Byron Inc., the forwarder who will act as the agent of the shipper in attending to the details of shipment and further documentation. Since SKF is located in a port city there are no problems regarding inland transportation to the port of export. SKF sends shipping instructions to Pierce–Byron that inform the forwarder that to comply with the requirements of the letter of credit, the bill of lading must be drawn to the "order of Banco do Brasil." In addition to these shipping instructions, SKF also sends its forwarder copies of the commercial invoice, a packing list and a Shipper's Export Declaration (a Department of Commerce form designed to give the government data from which foreign trade statistics can be compiled). When the forwarder receives these documents, it takes over all further documentation as the agent of the shipper; the latter merely has to dispatch the goods from the factory in accordance with the forwarder's instructions.

In shipments to many countries one of the documents specified in the letter of credit will be a "Consular Invoice," which is required by the buyer's government for foreign customs and statistical purposes. In the case of Brazil, such a separate invoice is not necessary. Instead, a notarized statement is set forth at the end of the Commercial Invoice (FORM 6, supra) and this document is visaed by the Brazilian consul in Philadelphia.

MOORE McCORMACK LINES, Incorporated

COMBINED TRANSPORT
PORT TO PORT
BILL OF LADING

NOT NEGOTIABLE UNLESS
CONSIGNED "TO ORDER"

SHIPPER/EXPORTER

SKF INDUSTRIES, INC
1100 FIRST AVENUE
KING OF PRUSSIA, PA 19406

DOCUMENT NO.

EXPORT REFERENCES

EXPORT DEC. NO.

CONSIGNEE
ORDER OF

BANCO DO BRAZIL, S.A.
RIO DE JANEIRO, BRAZIL

FORWARDING AGENT · REFERENCES

PIERCE BYRON, INC.
325 CHESTNUT ST. PHILA., PA

MMC NO.

POINT AND COUNTRY OF ORIGIN

NOTIFY PARTY

COMPANHIA IMPORTADORA BRASILEIRA
CAIXA POSTAL 10
RIO DE JANEIRO, BRAZIL

DOMESTIC ROUTING/EXPORT INSTRUCTIONS

DELIVERY TO STEAMER
BY DELAIR TRUCKING CO.

PRECARRIAGE BY

PACKER AVENUE

PLACE OF RECEIPT

EXPORTING CARRIER (SHIP)

S/S MORMACOAK

USA FLAG

AM

PORT OF LOADING

PHILA., PA

ONWARD INLAND ROUTING

PORT OF DISCHARGE

RIO DE JANEIRO

PLACE OF DELIVERY

RIO DE JANEIRO

[*Ocean Bill of Lading continued on following pages.*]

PARTICULARS FURNISHED BY SHIPPER OF GOODS

MARKS AND NUMBERS	NO. OF PKGS.	SHIPPERS DESCRIPTION OF PACKAGES AND GOODS	GROSS WEIGHT		MEASUREMENT
			KILOS	POUNDS	
C.I.B. RIO DE JANEIRO #1/25	25	(TWENTY-FIVE) CASES OF: STEEL AND ROLLER BEARINGS "IMPORT LICENSE DG-59/10000 EXPIRES FEBRUARY 28, 1993" LETTER OF CREDIT NO E4450/164 "EVIDENCING SHIPMENT OF 1200 BALL BEARINGS NO 187-B AND 2400 ROLLER BEARINGS NO 839-R" FREIGHT PREPAID "ON BOARD" JANUARY 12, 1993 "O R I G I N A L"	2272 KGS	5010 LBS	

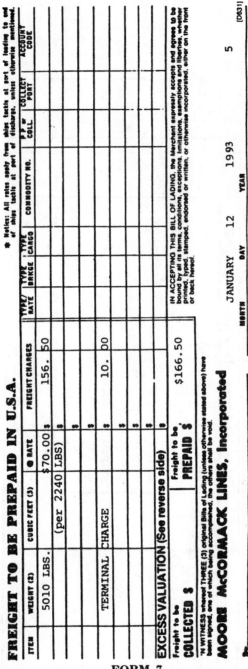

FREIGHT TO BE PREPAID IN U.S.A.

* Notice: All rates apply from ships tackle at port of loading to end of ships tackle at port of discharge, unless otherwise mentioned.

ITEM	WEIGHT (2)	CUBIC FEET (3)	@ RATE	FREIGHT CHARGES	TYPE/ RATE	TYPE BRKGE	TYPE CARGO	COMMODITY NO.	PP or COLL	COLLECT PORT	ACCOUNT CODE
	5010 LBS.		$70.00	$ 156. 50							
		(per 2240 LBS)		$							
				$							
	TERMINAL CHARGE			$ 10. 00							
				$							
				$							
				$							

EXCESS VALUATION (See reverse side)

Freight to be COLLECTED $	Freight to be PREPAID $	$166.50

"IN WITNESS whereof THREE (3) original Bills of Lading (unless otherwise stated above) have been signed, one of which being accomplished, the others shall be void.

IN ACCEPTING THIS BILL OF LADING, the Merchant expressly accepts and agrees to be bound by all its terms, conditions, exceptions, limitations, exemptions and liberties, whether printed, typed, stamped, endorsed or written, or otherwise incorporated, either on the front or back hereof.

MOORE McCORMACK LINES, Incorporated

JANUARY	12	1993
MONTH	DAY	YEAR

By..................

[D631]

FORM 7
OCEAN BILL OF LADING
[*Front; reverse on following pages*]

SHORT FORM BILL OF LADING

Received the Goods, or containers, vans, trailers, vehicles, transportable tanks, flats, palletized units, skids, platforms, frames, cradles, sling-loads or other packages said to contain the Goods herein mentioned in apparent external good order and condition, except as otherwise indicated herein, to be transported to the port of discharge named herein and/or such port or place as authorized or permitted hereby or so near thereunto as the vessel can get, lie and leave, always in safety and afloat under all conditions of tide, water and weather and there to be delivered to the Merchant or on-Carrier on payment of all charges due thereon.

This short form Bill of Lading issued for the Merchant's convenience and at its request instead of the Carrier's regular long form Bill of Lading, shall have effect subject to the provisions of the United States Carriage of Goods by Sea Act approved April 16, 1936 or, if this Bill of Lading is issued in any other locality where there is in force a compulsorily applicable Carriage of Goods by Sea Act, Ordinance or Statute of a nature similar to the International Convention for the Unification of Certain Rules Relating to Bills of Lading, dated at Brussels, August 25, 1924, it shall be subject to the provisions of said Act, Ordinance or Statute and rules thereto annexed.

All the terms and conditions of the Carrier's regular long form Bill of Lading, including any clauses presently being printed, typed, stamped, endorsed or written thereon, are incorporated herein by reference with the same force and effect as if they were written at length herein, and all such terms and conditions so incorporated by reference are agreed by Merchant to be binding and to govern the relations, whatever they may be, between all who are or may become parties or holders of this Bill of Lading or owners of the Goods, or containers or other packages covered thereby, as fully as if this Bill of Lading had been prepared on the Carrier's regular long form Bill of Lading.

At all times when the Goods, or containers or other packages are in the care, custody or control of a participating Carrier, such Carrier shall be entitled to all the rights, privileges, liens, limitations and exonerations from liability, granted or permitted to such participating Carrier under its Bill(s) of Lading, tariff(s) and law compulsorily applicable, and nothing contained in this Bill of Lading shall be deemed a surrender thereof by such participating Carrier.

Each Carrier shall, subject to the terms and conditions of this Bill of Lading and the applicable tariff, laws, rules and regulations, be responsible for any loss or damage to the Goods, or containers or other packages only during the time the Goods, or containers or other packages are in its actual care, custody and control, except as otherwise expressly provided herein.

In making any arrangements for transportation by participating Carriers of the Goods, or containers or other packages carried hereunder, either before or after ocean carriage, it is understood and agreed that the ocean Carrier acts solely as agent of the Merchant, without any other responsibility whatsoever as Carrier for such transportation.

The Merchant's attention is directed to the fact that the Carrier's regular long form Bill of Lading contains a number of provisions giving the Carrier and participating Carriers certain rights and privileges and certain exemptions and immunities from and limitations of liability additional to those provided by the said United States Carriage of Goods by Sea Act, 1936 and/or Convention and/or such other Act, Ordinance or Statute as may be applicable and, in addition, extends the benefit of its provisions to-stevedores and other independent contractors. The Carrier's regular long form Bill of Lading is on file with the Federal Maritime Commission and Interstate Commerce Commission in Washington, D.C. and copies can be obtained from the Carrier or from the Federal Maritime Commission or, if covering Intermodal Transporation, from the Interstate Commerce Commission if applicable.

In case of any loss or damage to or in connection with Goods exceeding in actual value the equivalent of $500 lawful money of the United States, per package, or in case of Goods not shipped in packages, per shipping unit, the value of the Goods shall be deemed to be $500 per package or per shipping unit. The Carrier's liability, if any, shall be determined on the basis of a value of $500 per package or per shipping unit or pro rata in case of partial loss or damage, unless the nature of the Goods and a valuation higher than $500 per package or per shipping unit shall have been declared in writing by the shipper before shipment and inserted in this Bill of Lading, and extra freight or charge paid. In such case, if the actual value of the Goods per package or per shipping unit shall exceed such declared value, the value shall nevertheless be deemed to be declared value and the Carrier's liability, if any, shall not exceed the declared value and any partial loss or damage shall be adjusted pro rata on the basis of such declared value.

The words "shipping unit" shall mean and include physical unit or piece of cargo not shipped in a package, including articles or things of any description whatsoever, except Goods shipped in bulk, and irrespective of weight or measurement unit employed in calculating freight charges.

Where containers, vans, trailers, vehicles, transportable tanks, flats, palletized units, skids, platforms, frames, cradles, sling-loads and other such packages are not packed by the Carrier, each individual such container, van, trailer, vehicle, transportable tank, palletized unit, skid, platform, frame, cradle, sling-load and other such package, including in each instance its contents, shall be deemed a single package and Carrier's liability limited to $500 with respect to each such package.

A signed original Bill of Lading, duly endorsed, must be surrendered to the Carrier on delivery of the Goods, or container or other packages.

All agreements with respect to the Goods, or containers or other packages carried hereunder are superseded hereby and none of the terms hereof shall be deemed waived or surrendered unless in writing and signed by a duly authorized agent of the Carrier.   [D632]

FORM 7
OCEAN BILL OF LADING
[*Reverse*]

SKF then sends the cases of bearings by truck to the pier where they are delivered to the ocean carrier's receiving clerk who signs a dock receipt. The dock receipt is a form, supplied by the ocean carrier, which contains information relevant to the shipping of the bearings, such as the number of the pier and (if known) the name of the ship. The dock receipt is non-negotiable; as its name suggests, when signed by the receiving clerk, the dock receipt serves as a temporary receipt for the goods until they are loaded on board.

The S.S. Mormacoak is soon ready to receive cargo. When the bearings are loaded on board, the steamship line issues a Bill of Lading (FORM 7, supra) which, to comply with the letter of credit, is "CONSIGNED TO ORDER OF *Banco do Brasil*." The bill of lading is initially prepared by the forwarder on a form supplied by the ocean carrier; it sets forth the markings and numbers of the packages, a description of the goods, and the number and weight of the packages. The reverse side of the bill of lading states that the goods are "Received for Shipment," but a statement "FREIGHT PREPAID *ON BOARD*" is initialed by a representative of the steamship line after loading. (Note carefully this indorsement; the distinction between a "Received for Shipment" and an "on board" bill of lading may be important. See infra.) The forwarder delivers the bill of lading and the commercial invoice to SKF.

Insurance. It was noted above that in this transaction the price was quoted "F.A.S. Philadelphia," whereas in many overseas transactions the price is quoted as "C.I.F". One of the important differences between these two forms of quotation relates to the handling of insurance. Under the C.I.F. quotation the seller is obliged to obtain and pay for insurance on the shipment. Receiving this insurance coverage is, of course, important to the buyer; to assure this the letter of credit under C.I.F. transaction would require the seller to present an appropriate insurance policy covering the shipment, along with the shipping and other documents, when seller presents its draft to the bank for payment.

The present F.A.S. transaction of itself imposes no such obligation. However, one will note that the letter of credit (FORM 4) requires SKF to present "Insurance Policy or Certificate covering marine and war risk." If there were no letter of credit, the buyer might arrange independently for insurance. But a bank issuing a letter of credit needs insurance to protect its interest in the goods as security for the buyer's obligation to reimburse the bank for its payments under the credit. As the first step towards complying with this requirement, you may have noted that on the proforma invoice SKF computed an "estimated value—C.I.F. which included an item for "estimated insurance charges" of $48.50.

A STOCK COMPANY

MARINE INDEMNITY INSURANCE COMPANY OF AMERICA
Wm. H. McGEE & CO., Inc., Managers, 4 World Trade Center, New York, N. Y. 10048

SPECIAL CARGO POLICY
R-32251   OC   970788

In correspondence refer to these letters and numbers

SUM INSURED	ASSURED'S REFERENCE	PLACE AND DATE
$ 10,950.00	CIB-43H2	KING OF PRUSSIA, PA 19406 JANUARY 12, 1993

This Company, in consideration of an agreed premium and subject to the terms and conditions below and on the reverse hereof or stamped or endorsed hereon, does insure

SKF INDUSTRIES, INC.

in the sum of TEN THOUSAND NINE HUNDRED FIFTY AND ——————————00/100 US Dollars

on TWENTY-FIVE (25) CASES CONTAINING: STEEL BALL AND ROLLER

BEARINGS GROSS WT: 5010 LBS

MARKS AND NUMBERS

valued at sum insured, to be shipped subject to an "Under Deck" Bill of Lading unless otherwise specified hereon,

by S.S MORMACOAK   or other vessel, and successive conveyances   B/L date JANUARY 12, 1993

at and from PHILADELPHIA, PA USA   via

to RIO DE JANEIRO, BRAZIL

Loss, if any, payable to the order of the Assured.

C.I.B.
RIO DE JANEIRO #1/25
IMPORT LICENSE DG-59/10000
EXPIRES FEBRUARY 28, 1993
L/C NO E 4450/164

—————— SPECIAL TERMS AND CONDITIONS ——————

SHIPMENTS ON DECK, AIR CARGO and MAIL or PARCEL POST SHIPMENTS, when insured under this Policy are subject to average terms and conditions specified in clauses 18, 19 and 20 hereof. SHIPMENTS SUBJECT TO AN "UNDER DECK" BILL OF LADING AND SHIPMENTS IN CONTAINERS SUBJECT TO AN "UNDER DECK" BILL OF LADING OR A BILL OF LADING WHICH DOES NOT DISCLOSE THE NATURE OF STOWAGE ARE INSURED:—

Machinery, Tools, Ball Bearing Parts, Factory Instruments, Steel and Raw Materials incidental to the business of the Assured are Insured:—

To cover against all risks of physical loss or damage from any external cause or spontaneous combustion (excepting such risks as are excluded by the F. C. & S. Warranty and S. R. & C. C. Warranty in this policy) irrespective of percentage.

This insurance is also subject to the following American Institute Clauses current on the date of issuance of this policy:—			When goods are so destined this insurance is subject to:—
MARINE EXTENSION CLAUSES	S. R. & C. C. ENDORSEMENT	WAR RISK INSURANCE	SOUTH AMERICAN 60 DAY CLAUSE

ORIGINAL — DUPLICATE UNPAID

This Policy not transferable unless countersigned by an authorized representative of this Company or the Assured

Countersigned SKF Industries, Inc.

IN WITNESS WHEREOF, this Company has executed and attested the presents.

Secretary   _Presid_

IDS

FORM 8

MARINE INSURANCE POLICY
[Continued on following pages]

TERMS AND CONDITIONS REFERRED TO ON THE FACE OF THIS POLICY

This insurance is against the perils of the seas, fire, assailing thieves, jettisons, barratry of the master and mariners, and all other like perils, losses or misfortunes that have or shall come to the hurt, detriment or damage of the property insured except as otherwise provided for herein.

AMERICAN INSTITUTE CARGO CLAUSES (February, 1949)

(F. C. & S. Warranty Clause, 1946)

[B3311J]

FORM 8

MARINE INSURANCE POLICY

[*Reverse*]

SKF, like most sellers who ship goods abroad, has an "open" policy of insurance which covers all goods in transit from warehouse to warehouse plus 30 days; the premiums depend on the volume of shipments reported to the insurer and covered by the policy. SKF fills out a Marine Insurance Policy (FORM 8) stating the necessary details of the specific shipment. Since the insurance policy will pass through various hands which may need its protection, the policy provides that it "does insure SKF Industries, Inc., For account of whom it may concern ... Loss, if any, payable to assured *or order*." The policy will be countersigned by the insurance company to provide evidence to third persons of its obligation under the policy.

Payment; the Draft. The Philadelphia bank stated in its letter that the estimated C.I.F. price of $10,950 would be "available by your drafts on us at sight" when accompanied by the listed documents. SKF accordingly draws a sight draft for $10,950 on the Philadelphia bank (FORM 9, infra). The draft together with the commercial invoice (in sextuplicate), insurance certificate (original and duplicate), full set of ocean bills of lading (three originals) and the packing list (original and duplicate) are presented to the Philadelphia bank. When the bank receives these documents it issues its bank draft to SKF's order for $10,950 and transmits the documents by air mail to Banco do Brasil, which will reimburse the Philadelphia bank.

The documents, sent by air mail, will reach the Brazilian bank well ahead of the ocean shipment. The time for the release of the documents to buyer and its reimbursement to the bank will depend upon the arrangement which was made between the bank and buyer when the letter of credit was initially established. If the buyer plans to resell the bearings, it may not be able to reimburse the bank until the goods arrive and it resells the goods. In this event, the Brazilian bank may need to take further steps to secure its claim against the buyer. Happily, such added complications need not concern us now.

$ 10,950.00

PHILADELPHIA, JANUARY 12 1993

At Sight

PAY TO THE ORDER OF

SKF INDUSTRIES, INC.

TEN THOUSAND NINE HUNDRED FIFTY--------------------00/100 DOLLARS

THE PHILADELPHIA NATIONAL BANK
DRAWN UNDER ADVICE NO. E 4450/164

To FOR THE ACCOUNT OF: COMPANHIA
IMPORTADORA BRASILEIRA, CAIXA
POSTAL 10, RIO DE JANEIRO
BRAZIL

SKF INDUSTRIES, INC.

[signature]

FORM 86 1/70

[D634]

FORM 9
DRAFT

(2) RESPONSIBILITY OF BUYERS AND SELLERS WHO AGREE TO DOCUMENTARY SALES USING LETTERS OF CREDIT

Sales Contracts' Provisions for Letters of Credit. The Convention on Contracts for International Sales of Goods is silent on payment devices; it does not set a default rule that buyers must open letters of credit nor the terms of satisfactory letters of credit.

Sellers who wish to be paid by letter of credit must obtain not only their buyers' contract commitment to do so, but must also establish in the sales contract what will be the nature and terms of those letters of credit. Buyers who agree to pay by letter of credit are also concerned about the letter of credit terms because buyers want to assure, insofar as feasible, that they will receive the contracted for goods after the letters of credit have been paid. To do this, buyers need to establish the conditions on the banks' duty to pay that tend to show sellers have performed before banks are permitted and required to pay under their letters of credit; a prime condition usually is a bill of lading or comparable shipping document that shows that seller has delivered the goods to a carrier. The conditions, initially agreed upon in the sales contracts, later become the conditions in the banks' commitment letters.

Sellers typically require buyers to open letters of credit for an amount in excess of the contract price so that sellers can recover incidental expenses incurred on buyers' behalf. Sellers typically require that letters of credit be issued or confirmed before shipping the goods; if a seller must specially manufacture or procure the goods to be delivered, the seller may negotiate to require the buyer to open a letter of credit well before the estimated date for shipment of the goods to buyer. If the date of shipment is uncertain at the time of the sales contract, the parties may negotiate for the length of time during which a letter must remain open. Sellers typically do not identify banks that must be the issuing bank or the confirming bank, but they may specify that buyers use banks of recognized standing in the banking community. If sellers do not negotiate for the commitment of local banks as confirming banks, enforcement of the issuing banks' obligation may require litigation in foreign countries.[19] Sellers who want a local bank's commitment must negotiate buyers' obligation to obtain a letter of credit from an issuing bank that will, in turn, secure a confirming bank.[20] Finally, the sales contract determines whether a letter of

---

19. See Pacific Reliant Industries, Inc. v. Amerika Samoa Bank, 901 F.2d 735 (9th Cir.1990)(Oregon seller of building materials to Samoa buyer agreed to letter of credit issued by Samoan bank; seller's suit to enforce the credit in Oregon federal district court dismissed for lack of personal jurisdiction over the bank).

20. In making its commitment to the beneficiary of a confirmed credit, the con-

firming bank is relying entirely on the credit of the issuing bank. This work. better when the banks have a continuing relationship. "It is customary that the issuing bank requests a bank of its choice to advise and, as the case may be, to confirm its credit to the beneficiary." ICC, Case Studies on Documentary Credits, Case 26, p. 39 (J. Dekker 1989).

credit is required under the Uniform Customs and Practices for Documentary Credits (UCP).[21]

Problem 8. Why was not SKF content to deliver under a documentary transaction like that between Buyersville and Sellersville described in Subsection (A), supra? What risk does SKF avoid by requiring a letter of credit? How do the parties expect that claims for defects in the goods will be handled?

Problem 9. In the letter of credit (FORM 4), what is the scope of the Philadelphia Bank's commitment in the first paragraph? Where is its liability stated? If the Brazilian Bank failed, who would bear the loss? Are there other risks that SKF avoids by having an American bank confirm the letter of credit?

Problem 10. Is SKF expressly entitled under the contract to have the letter of credit confirmed by a local bank? Can the obligation be implied? See UCC 2–325. What change in the forms would avoid any question?

Problem 11. After establishment of the letter of credit but before shipment by SKF, suppose that ocean freight rates rise. Who bears the added expense? How should the payment be handled?

Problem 12. Under an F.A.S. quotation, is the seller obliged to take out an insurance policy covering the shipment? Compare UCC 2–319 with 2–320. Was such an obligation imposed in this case?

Problem 13. Could SKF effectively tender a "Received for Shipment" bill of lading? See UCC 5–114. Which provision of the bill of lading (FORM 7) shows its conformity to the letter of credit in this regard? What is the importance of such a requirement in a letter of credit?

Problem 14. A contract for the sale of 3000 tons of Brazilian groundnuts called for shipment from Brazil for Genoa between February 1 and April 30, at the option of the sellers. The contract further provided: "Payment: By opening of a confirmed, irrevocable, divisible, transmissible and transferable credit opened in favour of the sellers and utilisable by them against delivery of the following documents." The buyer established a letter of credit on April 22. The seller had already resold the goods on the ground that the credit was established too late in the light of the seller's privilege to ship in February or March. Seller sued the buyer for damages. What evidence of custom and what arguments concerning seller's need for the letter of credit would be relevant? See Pavia & Co. v. Thurmann–Nielsen, [1952] 1 All Eng.L.R. 492 (C.A.).

If the buyer has the obligation to arrange for shipping and has the privilege of selecting the date for shipment within a designated period, may the buyer delay establishing the letter of credit until the end of

---

21. The Uniform Customs and Practices for Documentary Credits, promulgated by the International Chamber of Commerce, are discussed below in the materials dealing with the responsibility of banks under their letters of credit.

the period? What would be the effect of a showing by seller that it was customary in this trade to use the letter of credit in order to raise funds to pay the seller's supplier? See Ian Stach, Ltd. v. Baker Bosly, Ltd., [1958] 1 All E.R. 542 (interesting and instructive opinion by Diplock, J., on the practical problems presented by using the ultimate buyer's letter of credit to finance "a string of merchants' contracts between the manufacturer or stockist and the ultimate user"); 108 L.J. 388 (1958).

Once sales contracts have set the nature and terms of letters of credit that buyers must obtain and that sellers must accept in the performance of their contracts, those undertakings can and do give rise to disputes between sellers and buyers over the sufficiency and timeliness of buyers' performance. If buyer fails seasonably to furnish an agreed letter of credit, what are the consequences on seller's obligations to perform and on seller's right to remedy? Domestic United States law, the Code, declares that the buyer is in breach. UCC 2–325(1). Would the same result follow under CISG?

Revocable Letters of Credit. Banking practice developed two types of letters of credit, revocable and irrevocable. Issuing banks and their customers choose whether the customers have power to revoke without the consent of the beneficiaries of the credits. As between sellers and buyers, revocable letters of credit are akin to buyers' personal checks; payment can be stopped by instructions to the bank. Thus, revocable letters of credit are not satisfactory to sellers who want to be free of credit risk. If a sales contract requires only that buyer furnish a letter of credit, does buyer meet that obligation by obtaining a revocable letter of credit? Domestic United States law, the Code, declares that buyer must provide an irrevocable letter of credit. UCC 2–325(3). Would the same result follow under CISG? [22]

Bankers' Acceptances and Letters of Credit. If the buyer in the letter of credit transaction does not wish to pay upon presentment, a slightly different transaction may be arranged. The seller will draw a time draft rather than a sight draft on the issuing bank, which will accept it, return it to the seller, and release the documents to the buyer on open credit or perhaps against trust receipts. The buyer has its goods; the seller has a "banker's acceptance" which can easily be discounted; the issuer has lent its credit but has paid no money. Before the maturity date of the draft, the buyer will place the necessary funds in the hands of the issuing bank. See also: P. Oppenheim, International Banking 195–96 (4th ed. 1983).

Among the cases that follow, many are transactions in which sellers agreed to bankers' acceptances rather than insisting upon immediate payment under sight drafts. As a result, buyers learned about

---

22. A similar, but quite different question arises of interpreting a letter of credit that does not declare whether or not it is revocable.

the nature of sellers' performances before the credits had been paid and took action to prevent payment altogether or to prevent the proceeds of payment from reaching sellers.

"Back–to–Back" Credits. Assume that Buyer agrees to buy a large shipment of goods from Seller, and establishes a letter of credit covering the purchase with Seller as beneficiary. Seller will buy goods to fill this contract from Distributor. Distributor requires cash for the goods and Seller lacks sufficient cash until it delivers to Buyer. Can the assurance of payment under the letter of credit give Seller the credit it needs to make the purchase? (Distributor may face the same credit problem in arranging a purchase from Manufacturer. Indeed, in some cases a long string of transactions needs to be financed on the strength of the letter of credit established by the ultimate buyer.)

A dilemma appears. The initial letter of credit from Buyer to Seller needs to be utilized as a source of credit before Seller gets the goods; on the other hand, tender of these goods is a condition of the bank's obligation to pay. Ingenious attempts to answer this problem have produced the so-called "back-to-back" credits. The bank which has issued the initial credit to Seller issues a second letter of credit to Distributor, contingent on Distributor's presenting documents which either satisfy the initial letter of credit or which can readily be made to satisfy the letter of credit, as by getting a new bill of lading evidencing shipment from Seller to Buyer. Distributor is thus assured of payment; and credit strain on Seller and the bank are avoided since Distributor will not be paid until (a) Seller's right to obtain funds under the credit, and (b) the bank's right to reimbursement from Buyer have both been established.

Added flexibility may be achieved if the rights under a letter of credit may be assigned. In this area, as in others, there is possible conflict between the Code and the ICC Uniform Customs if the latter's language is given its full, literal sweep. Article 54 of the Uniform Customs provides: "A credit can be transferred only if it is expressly designated as 'transferable' by the issuing bank." UCC 5–116(1) establishes a similar rule as to "the right *to draw* under a credit." But subsection (2) states: "Even though the credit specifically states that it is nontransferable or nonassignable the beneficiary may before performance of the conditions of the credit assign his *right to proceeds*." The balance of the subsection contains interesting rules regulating such assignments. Compare UCC 2–210(2) and 9–318(4) which similarly invalidate "restraints on alienation" of the right to receive cash proceeds.

(3) RESPONSIBILITY OF BANKS UNDER
THEIR LETTERS OF CREDIT

The commercial linchpin in setting up sales transactions using letters of credit is the degree of certainty with which parties can expect that the banks, particularly confirming banks, will pay when drafts are presented to them. From sellers' perspective, that translates into the question of ease of enforcement of the banks' commitments. Sellers' aim is to divorce the banks' duty to pay from any question of sellers' performance on the underlying sales contracts beyond presentation of documents. From buyers' perspective, the question is whether they can effectively "stop payment" by the banks. Buyers' aim is to retain some control over the banks' paying in the event that sellers are seen to be defaulting on their obligations to deliver the goods. The clash between these two objectives is addressed in the law and practice governing banks' obligations under their letters of credit.

The ICC Uniform Customs and Practice for Documentary Credits (UCP). About 1930, the international banking community began to promulgate rules to harmonize the issuance and performance of letters of credit. Published by the International Chamber of Commerce, the Uniform Customs and Practice or UCP have been revised a number of times, and most recently in 1992.[23] The UCP, adhered to by banks in over 145 nations, are practically universal in application. Bankers from throughout the world have been organized by the ICC into a Commission on Banking Technique and Practice which issues opinions on interpretation of the UCP and, through a group of experts, responds to queries about the UCP.[24]

A common practice emerged whereby banks issuing or confirming letters of credit referred explicitly to the UCP. See, e.g., Form 4 in the Prototype transaction.

The UCP do not deal with the rights or obligations of parties to the contracts underlying letters of credit. "Credits, by their nature, are separate transactions from the sales or other contract(s) on which they may be based and banks are in no way concerned with or bound by such contract(s), even if any reference whatsoever to such contract(s) is included in the credit." UCP 1983, Article 3.

UCP provisions are not laws. They are standard contractual terms adopted by the international banking community and enforceable only as terms of contracts. In common-law courts, banks that issue or confirm letters of credit might argue that their promises to the beneficiaries of the credits are unenforceable for want of consideration. Domestic United States law, the Code, responded that no consideration is necessary. UCC 5–105.

Article 5; New York Exclusion. Drafters of the Code elected to attempt to codify the law on letters of credit by including in the Code Article 5 on that subject. Prior to that time, letters of credit had not

23. The 1983 version of the UCP are found in ICC Brochure No. 400. See also M. Davis, The Documentary Credits Handbook (1988).

24. Opinions of the Banking Commission are published regularly by the ICC.

See ICC Publications 371, 399, 434 and 469. For a set of responses to recent queries, see Case Studies on Documentary Credits: Problems, Queries, Answers (J. Dekker, 1989).

been subject to statutory enactment in the United States or elsewhere. Article 5 differs from the UCP in a number of respects. When the Commercial Code was presented to the states for enactment, in New York there was concern about displacement of the UCP. Much letter of credit practice, particularly in international sales, was centered in that state. New York eventually adopted the Code, but added a non-uniform provision, 5–102(4), rendering the entire article inapplicable to a letter of credit if by its terms or by agreement, course of dealing or usage of trade the letter of credit is subject in whole or in part to the UCP. The Permanent Editorial Board for the Code reacted vigorously (Report No. 2 (1964)):

PERMANENT EDITORIAL BOARD COMMENT

Reasons for Rejection. The New York Clearing House Association (NYCHA) in its report of December 1, 1961 recommended the entire elimination of Article 5 on letters of credit. The above variation in Section 5–102(1), as the Code was enacted in New York, represents a continuation of the views of the NYCHA. Article 5 is still printed as a part of the Code but the variation as enacted provides that "Article 5 does not apply to a letter of credit or a credit if by its terms or by agreement, course of dealing or usage of trade such letter of credit or credit is subject in whole or in part to the Uniform Customs and Practice for Commercial Documentary Credits fixed by the Thirteenth or by any subsequent Congress of the International Chamber of Commerce" (Uniform Customs). This point of view and the action in New York constitutes a sufficiently fundamental departure from the Code that it needs to be dealt with on fundamental lines.

1. The underlying and basic concept behind the NYCHA position is that there should be no legislation in the letter of credit field. The reasoning is that it is better for banks, if not for all interested parties, to have the determination of rights and duties of parties under letters of credit left to the present combination of case law, Uniform Customs, agreements, practices and customs in the field.

This underlying point of view is contrary to the fixed policy of the sponsoring organizations of the Uniform Commercial Code, long considered and carefully determined. The Editorial Board sees no good reason to reverse this policy. ...

2. A second basic position taken by the NYCHA is that most letters of credit finance international shipments of merchandise and are, therefore, international in character, with the result that there should be no unilateral legislation on the subject in the United States. Conversely, the NYCHA appears to contend that the only controlling rules governing letters of credit should be international rules. The NYCHA further contends that if one or more American states sees fit to enact statutory legislation in this field, other countries may do likewise to the detriment of the United States.

The Editorial Board considers this view to be totally unrealistic. Carried to its logical conclusion, under this view no court in the United States should render a decision in a letter of credit case because such a decision, which clearly creates law in the United States, is unilateral. An equally logical extension of the same argument is that there should be neither statutory law nor case law in the United States in any international field because such law is necessarily unilateral.

Assuming that letters of credit are used preponderantly to finance international shipments of goods, in the absence of a world order and world courts, the problems of society and commerce can only be solved by the various instrumentalities of law available in the several sovereign nations. The great preponderance of what law there is today controlling international transactions is exactly "unilateral" law, established either by courts or legislatures, in independent, sovereign nations. Recognizing the imperfections in this process, the conflict of laws questions arising from it, and the uncertainties and confusion involved in it, this process has done fairly well to establish rules of law and, in any event, absent a world order and world courts, it is all that society has except for a very limited number of treaties. ...

3. The third basic position taken by the NYCHA is that, recognizing the need of some rules as to "international" letters of credit, the Uniform Customs which are now in existence, and have been for twenty or more years, fill all needs and work well.

The Editorial Board approves of the effort to provide rules governing letters of credit by way of the drafting and promulgation of the Uniform Customs. The Editorial Board considers that the Uniform Customs contribute materially to the aggregate body of rules making more definite and certain letter of credit operations. However, the Board does not agree that the Uniform Customs constitute the only set of rules and guide lines that are available and needed.

Of paramount importance is that the Uniform Customs do not have the status of "law." Not being law they are subject to all of the weaknesses and vicissitudes of what they purport to be, namely, "customs." Have they been accepted by, are they binding upon, all interested parties? ...

4. A fourth basic position advanced by the NYCHA is that the Uniform Customs have preempted the field of rules dealing with letters of credit and, consequently, no state legislation can or should be enacted in this field. The argument is that New York and the other several states must have either the Uniform Customs or Article 5; they cannot have both.

The Editorial Board cannot agree with this reasoning. A fundamental concept of the Code as a whole is that there can be a set of statutory rules (with varying degrees of completeness of coverage) in the fields of the different articles but there is also room and need for customs, course of dealing, usages of trade, agreement of parties and business practices. See Sections 1–102(2)(b), 1–205, 4–103 and 5–102(3).

The Code also recognizes the need of supplementary principles of law other than the specific terms of the Code itself. See Sections 1–103, 9–104 and 9–203(2). ...

5. The Editorial Board considers that the attempt, through the New York variation in Section 5–102(4), to find a compromise between the Code position on Article 5 and that of the NYCHA, is highly confusing, unwise and potentially productive of substantial litigation. Of first importance, the New York variation adopts the mutually exclusive concept that if the Uniform Customs in any way apply, then Article 5 is totally inapplicable. Aside from the general wisdom of any state legislature's enacting comprehensive and serious legislation, all of which can be rendered completely nugatory by the election of individual persons, the Board considers that the determination of when a credit is "by agreement, course of dealing or usage of trade ... subject in whole or in part to the Uniform Customs ..." will be a matter of great difficulty. The added New York language is almost a direct invitation to litigation. If Article 5 and the Uniform Customs overlap only to the extent of, let us say, 25% of their respective provisions and, of such overlapping, the rules of Article 5 and the Uniform Customs are, in substance, the same, with inconsistency occurring in only two instances, the Board entirely fails to see why, whether there is a large or trifling application of the Uniform Customs, Article 5 should be rendered totally inapplicable. The Board considers the New York variation both unacceptable and unsound.

PETRA INTERN. BANKING CORP. v. FIRST AMER. BANK OF VA.

United States District Court, Eastern District of Virginia, 1991.
758 F. Supp. 1120.

Ellis, United States District Judge. This dispute grows out of the use of two documentary letters of credit to finance the purchase of T-shirts by a Virginia corporation from the manufacturer in Amman, Jordan. In essence, following the delivery of poor quality T-shirts, the purchaser refused to pay the issuing bank and the issuing bank then refused to pay the confirming bank, which had honored drafts drawn under the letters of credit. The purchaser and the issuing bank rely on their receipt of technically nonconforming documents under the letters as grounds for nonpayment. The purchaser and the manufacture. settled their dispute over the poor quality T-shirts, but the remaining parties were not able to resolve their differences. Thus, here the confirming bank seeks recovery against the issuing bank and the purchaser for payments it made under the letters of credit, and the issuing bank seeks recovery against the purchaser for any sums it must pay to the confirming bank.

Before the Court are cross-motions for summary judgment. The motions raise, inter alia, the seldom litigated issue of what remedy an account customer has when an issuing bank inadvertently accepts nonconforming documents under a letter of credit. All material facts are undisputed. These facts, the terms of the letters of credit, other relevant contractual agreements, and existing law require that defendant First American Bank, the issuer of the letters, reimburse the confirming bank for payments made under the letters, and that First American Bank's account customer, the purchaser of the T-shirts, reimburse First American. Both First American and the purchaser, by failing to object to documentary inconsistencies in timely fashion, have waived their right to do so. All other issues raised in this case with the exception of costs and attorney's fees are also disposed of on summary judgment.

Facts

In 1987 Dameron International, Inc., a Virginia corporation ("Dameron"), purchased T-shirts from National Marketing–Export Co. ("National Marketing") of Amman, Jordan. To facilitate the transaction, Dameron sought issuance of two letters of credit by First American Bank of Virginia ("First American"). To this end, Dameron executed two documents, each entitled Application and Agreement for International Commercial Letter of Credit ("the Agreements"), and signed two commercial notes, each in the amount of $135,000.00, to secure the letters of credit. Richard Pitts, the president of Dameron, and his wife, son, and daughter-in-law, executed continuing guaranties to further secure any debts of Dameron owed to First American. First American issued its Irrevocable Letters of Credit Nos. 1–629 and 1–630 ("the Letters"), each for $135,000, on December 17, 1987. The Letters stated that they were issued "in favor of National Marketing–Export Co.," of Amman, Jordan and "for the account of Dameron Intl., Inc." of McLean, Virginia. The Letters authorized drafts to be drawn on First American within thirty days of submission to First American of specific, listed documents. At the request of National Marketing and National's bank in Jordan, Petra Bank, the Letters were amended on December 22, 1987, to provide that drafts under the Letters could be drawn directly on Petra International Banking Corporation of Washington, D.C. ("PIBC"), Petra's American affiliate. In the vernacular of letters of credit transactions, PIBC became a "confirming bank," First American an "issuing bank," Dameron the "account customer," and National Marketing the "beneficiary" of the Letters.

When initially issued, the Letters required that an "inspection certificate from [an] independent inspector certifying number and quality of pieces per sample" of the T-shirts be among the documents presented for payment. This provision subsequently was amended to require both a certificate from a specific independent inspection company and a "statement by the beneficiary," National Marketing, attesting to the quality of the T-shirts.

Dameron received several T-shirt shipments from National Marketing in 1988. Several corresponding payments were made under the Letters by PIBC to National Marketing. In late September 1988, another shipment was begun and National Marketing made a demand for payment under the Letters. This demand was relayed from Petra Bank in Amman to PIBC as two documentary time drafts drawn against the Letters in the aggregate amount of $95,904. PIBC sent a telex to First American on October 7, 1988, noting certain discrepancies between the documents submitted and those required by the Letters, including the fact that the certificate from the independent inspection company was missing. First American forwarded PIBC's telex to Dameron, which waived the discrepancies listed by PIBC on condition that the drafts were drawn 150 days from the date of the bill of lading, i.e., from the date of shipment. First American sent a telex message to PIBC on October 19, 1988, stating "ACCOUNT PARTY HAS WAIVED ALL DISCREPANCIES PROVIDED DRAFTS ARE DRAWN AT 150 DAYS BILL OF LADING." First American sent a second telex message on October 24, 1988, stating in relevant part: "DISCREPANCIES HAVE BEEN WAIVED BY A/P [i.e., Dameron]. PLEASE ACCEPT DRAFT AND FORWARD DOCS TO US." Between receipt of the first and second telexes, on October 21, 1988, PIBC discounted and accepted the documentary time drafts. On October 25, 1988, PIBC sent a telex to First American that confirmed receipt of First American's telex of October 24th, informed First American that the drafts had been accepted with the proviso that they be drawn 150 days from the date of the bill of lading, i.e., on February 21, 1989, and transmitted the documents to First American. First American forwarded the documents to Dameron shortly after receiving them. Dameron kept the documents and took possession of the T-shirts. On November 16, 1988, First American sent an acknowledgement letter to PIBC stating that the documentary drafts for $95,904 were "accepted and, at maturity, we will remit proceeds according to your cover letter."

Dameron was dissatisfied with the quality of the T-shirts received from National Marketing. It undertook negotiations with National concerning the $95,904 payment. As the February 21, 1989 deadline for drawing on the time drafts approached, Dameron requested that First American obtain an extension of payment. First American then sent a telex to PIBC requesting an extension to May 21, 1989. The telex stated that National Marketing had agreed to this delay in receiving payment. PIBC informed First American that it would delay and refinance the payment provided that First American pay interest during the delay at the prime rate plus two percent. Dameron and First American agreed. As the new May 21, 1989 deadline drew near, Dameron requested that First American seek an additional extension of thirty days. First American requested the extension, explaining that "SPECIAL ARRANGEMENTS REGARDING THESE PAYMENTS WERE MADE BY BUYERS AND SELLERS ALLOWING THE 30 DAY EXTENSION." PIBC agreed to this second extension on the condition that it continue to receive interest at prime plus two percent, and First American and Dameron accepted this requirement.

In June or July, 1989, Richard Pitts informed First American that Dameron did not want to pay National Marketing because of the poor quality of the T-shirts. William von Berg of First American informed Pitts that First American would be obligated to pay under the Letters unless the bank were sued by Dameron and enjoined from doing so. While the parties are uncertain as to when this conversation occurred, it is clear that in late June, when Dameron requested a third extension, Dameron and National Marketing continued to be hopeful that they would settle their differences concerning the $95,904. Dameron planned to obtain additional T-shirts of suitable quality from National at a reduced price, and it so informed First American. On June 20, 1989, Richard Pitts requested that First American seek a third extension. On the same day, Bassem Farouki, the principal of National Marketing, informed PIBC that Dameron would be requesting an additional thirty-day extension. Although PIBC initially took the position that First American should finance Dameron, it eventually agreed to an extension to July 21, 1989, under the same interest payment conditions as were attached to the previous two extensions.

Dameron's negotiations with National Marketing did not bear fruit. On July 20, 1989, Dameron obtained an Order of Attachment from the Fairfax County Circuit Court, directing First American not to pay PIBC under the Letters. First American claims that it did not immediately learn of the existence of the writ. Nevertheless, First American did not pay PIBC on July 21, 1989. Rather, on that day, at Dameron's request, First American requested an extension of payment to the following week. PIBC responded by demanding payment. Payment was not made. Instead, on July 28th, First American informed PIBC that it had been enjoined by the Fairfax County Circuit Court from making payments under the Letters until further notice.

From July 20, 1989 until April 13, 1990, Dameron pursued a law suit against National Marketing in the Fairfax County Circuit Court. In the course of this litigation, and more than one year after its receipt of the documents, Dameron noticed and then informed First American that the "Statement of the Beneficiary" was not among the documents that First American forwarded pertaining to the $95,904 shipment. First American informed Dameron that it had forwarded all documents it had received. The absence of the Statement of the Beneficiary from the documents was not noted as a discrepancy by PIBC or First American when each had examined the documents. Both Dameron and First American agree that the Statement of the Beneficiary was never among the documents presented by National Marketing to PIBC, and that PIBC, First American, and Dameron each inadvertently failed to notice the missing Statement of the Beneficiary when each received the documents.

Dameron and National Marketing eventually settled their suit. Dameron kept the T-shirts, but received an undisclosed amount of cash from National Marketing related, it appears, to the shipment here at issue and to other shipments and disputes between the parties. The precise terms of the settlement remain confidential and have not been disclosed to the Court. On April 13, 1990, the Fairfax County Circuit Court vacated the Order of Attachment. On the same day, PIBC requested payment from First American of $95,904 of principal and $14,079.24 of interest. First American has refused to make the payment, relying primarily on PIBC's alleged failure to note the missing Statement of the Beneficiary. Dameron, in turn, has refused to reimburse First American if payment is made under the Letters, despite having signed the Agreements and commercial notes, kept the documents accompanying the relevant drafts, taken possession of the T-shirts, and recovered settlement compensation from National Marketing. The Pitts, in turn, have refused First American's demands for reimbursement under the Continuing Guarantees....

I. First American's Obligation to Pay PIBC

PIBC requests summary judgment on Count I of its Complaint, which alleges that First American wrongfully refused to honor the Letters and pay the $95,904 plus interest to PIBC. First American contends that PIBC's failure to note the missing Statement of the Beneficiary relieves it of any obligation to honor the drafts drawn under the Letters. The threshold issue is the choice of governing law. The Letters state on their face that they are to be governed by the Uniform Customs and Practices for Documentary Credits (1983 Revision), International Chamber of Commerce Publication No. 400 ("the UCP"). Given this, the Court finds that the UCP should be applied in this case. Neither PIBC nor First American objects to application of the UCP, though they differ in interpreting its provisions.

The pertinent UCP provision is Article 16, which states that if an issuing bank desires to "refuse documents," it must do so "without delay" by stating the discrepancies it has found and "holding the documents at the disposal of, or ... returning them to, the presentor (remitting bank or the beneficiary, as the case may be)." If the issuing bank fails to perform these requirements, it "shall be precluded from claiming that the documents are not in accordance with the terms and conditions of the credit."[26] Numerous courts have held that Article 16

---

26. The full text of Article 16 of the UCP is as follows:

(a) If a bank so authorized effects payment, or *incurs a deferred payment undertaking,* or accepts or negotiates *against documents which appear on their face to be in accordance with the terms and conditions of a credit,* the party giving such authority *shall be bound* to reimburse the bank which has effected payment, or incurred a deferred payment undertaking, or has accepted or negotiated, and *to take up the documents.*

(b) If, upon receipt of the documents, the issuing bank considers that they appear on their face not to be in accordance with the terms and conditions of

and its predecessor, Article 8 of the 1974 UCP, preclude an issuing bank from asserting the noncompliance of documents presented by a beneficiary where the bank delays in raising this claim. Bank of Cochin v. Manufacturers Hanover Trust Co., 808 F.2d 209 (2d Cir.1986), a case precisely on point, presents a striking example of this principle in operation between an issuing and a confirming bank. There, the issuing bank, on the very day of its receipt of a documentary draft from the confirming bank, telexed its intention to dishonor the draft. But the issuing bank did not supply the confirming bank with a reason for the dishonor until twelve-to-thirteen-days later. This delay, the Court found, violated Article 8(d)'s command that an issuing bank intending to dishonor a documentary draft "notify [the confirming bank] 'expeditiously' and 'without delay' of specific defects and of the disposition of the documents, and ... precluded [the issuing bank] from asserting noncompliance...." Id. at 213. The same result should obtain here because the issuing bank's notice was delayed even longer than in Bank of Cochin. In the instant case, First American received the documents on or about October 25, 1988. Not only did it fail to note any discrepancies or to hold the documents at PIBC's disposal, it transferred the documents to its account customer and formally notified PIBC on November 16, 1988 that "the transaction was accepted and, at maturity, we will remit proceeds...." First American did not mention any discrepancies to PIBC until more than one year after receipt of the documents. In the interim, it made several promises to pay in exchange for extensions of time. First American is therefore precluded by Article 16 from asserting noncompliance.

First American seeks to avoid application of Article 16 by arguing that Article 16 applies to drafts passing from beneficiaries or advising banks to issuing banks, but not to drafts passing from confirming banks to issuing banks. In support, First American points to Virginia Code § 8.5–107(2), which states that a confirming bank "becomes directly obligated on the credit to the extent of its confirmation, *as though it*

the credit, *it must determine, on the basis of the documents alone, whether to take up such documents, or to refuse them* and claim that they appear on their face not to be in accordance with the terms and conditions of the credit.

(c) The issuing bank shall have *a reasonable time* in which to examine the documents and to determine as above whether to take up the documents or to refuse the documents.

(d) *If the issuing bank decides to refuse the documents it must give notice to that effect without delay* by telecommunication or, if that is not possible, by other expeditious means, to the bank from which it received the documents (the remitting bank), or to the beneficiary, if it received the documents directly from him. *Such notice must state the discrep-*

ancies in respect of which the issuing bank refuses the documents *and must also state whether it is holding the documents at the disposal of, or is returning them to, the presenter* (remitting bank or the beneficiary, as the case may be). The issuing bank shall then be entitled to claim from the remitting bank any refund of any reimbursement which may have been made to that bank.

(e) *If the issuing bank fails* to act in accordance with the provisions of paragraphs (c) and (d) of this article and/or fails *to hold the documents at the disposal of,* or to return them to, *the presenter, the issuing bank shall be precluded from claiming that the documents are not in accordance with the terms and conditions of the credit.*

(Emphasis added.)

were its issuer and acquires the rights of an issuer." (Emphasis added.) From this, First American argues that it should be viewed as PIBC's account customer in the transaction at issue, while PIBC should be deemed to be the issuing bank subject to Article 16. It is true that PIBC, upon becoming a confirming bank, has the rights and duties of an issuing bank and is therefore subject to Article 16. It is also true that First American may be viewed as PIBC's customer. Even so, neither of these points changes First American's status as an issuing bank nor relieves it from its Article 16 duties. In short, as one or more confirming banks are inserted in the chain between the original issuing bank and the beneficiary, each bank, including the original issuer, is an issuing bank subject to Article 16. This conclusion finds support in the language of Article 16 and makes good commercial sense. On its face, Article 16 uses broad language, the plain meaning of which covers documentary draft transfers between confirming and issuing banks. Sensible policy considerations support this construction. To hold otherwise and accept First American's reading of Article 16 would render the UCP devoid of standards governing transactions between confirming and issuing banks. This would make no business sense. For similar reasons, the Court rejects First American's odd claim that PIBC's acceptance of the documentary drafts before First American had received and reviewed the documents should absolve First American of its obligation to honor the draft.[32] Finally, even if the Court were to find that First American should be treated as a "customer" of PIBC, First American would still be liable for the reasons given below in Part III for holding Dameron liable to reimburse First American....

III.　Dameron's Obligation to Reimburse First American

Having found that PIBC has a legal right to payment from First American, ... the Court turns next to First American's claim that Dameron must reimburse it for any amount it must pay PIBC under the Letters. First American relies on the Agreements executed by Dameron to obtain the Letters. In the Agreements, Dameron pledged to indemnify First American for the latter's acts with respect to the Letters as long as such acts were taken in good faith. And, First American correctly notes that Dameron has not shown any bad faith on

---

32. Under the scheme of Article 16, it appears that a confirming bank becomes obligated to pay a documentary credit when it transfers documents on to the issuing bank. The confirming bank may, if it finds discrepancies, dishonor a documentary draft and return the documents to the beneficiary or to a prior confirming or advising bank in the chain of transfer. The confirming bank, like the issuing bank, appears to be required to accept or reject the documents "on the basis of the documents alone." Article 16(b). It is not permitted to pass them on perfunctorily to the issuing bank to obtain that bank's opinion on the documents' compliance with the letter of credit. If it could so operate, it would be no more than an advising bank. Furthermore, First American can claim no harm from PIBC's acceptance of the draft before First American received the documents. Under Article 16, First American was still entitled to review the documents upon receipt and to reject and return them as nonconforming to PIBC. ...

the part of First American with respect to accepting the documents. Dameron argues, however, that the good faith standard in the Agreements violates Virginia law and hence is void. Therefore, Dameron continues, First American's failure to note the missing Statement of the Beneficiary, though not a breach of good faith, nevertheless relieves Dameron of any obligation to reimburse First American.

It is not necessary to reach the unsettled, thorny question whether the Agreements, which appear to be standard form contracts employed by First American, violate Virginia law. Even assuming first that the Agreements run afoul of Virginia law, next that First American is obligated, as Dameron contends, by Virginia Code § 8.5–109(2) to "examine documents with care so as to ascertain that on their face they appear to comply with the terms" of the Letters, and finally that First American breached this duty by failing to note the absence of the Statement of the Beneficiary, the Virginia UCC and the common law of letters of credit still bar Dameron's claim because Dameron accepted the documents and used them to gain control of the T-shirts. Under these circumstances, Dameron cannot rely on documentary discrepancies to avoid honoring its Agreements with First American.

The Agreements between First American and Dameron state that they shall be governed by Virginia law. Title 8.5 of Virginia's UCC, which pertains to Letters of Credit, contains no provision governing an account customer's remedies for wrongful honor by an issuing bank. Section 8.5–102(3), however, frankly admits that Title 8.5 "deals with some but not all of the rules and concepts of letters of credit...." The section invites the application of "rules or concepts ... developed prior to this act or ... hereafter" to "a situation not provided for ... by this title." Id. ... Thus, in ascertaining Dameron's remedies as an account customer for First American's wrongful honor, this Court is directed by Virginia law to apply the "fundamental theory" of letters of credit and the "canon of liberal interpretation" in Virginia Code § 8.1–102. ...

A review of the few existing, apposite cases indicates that under the common law of letters of credit an account customer, by accepting documents from the issuing bank and subsequently "surrendering the documents [to shippers or customs officials] and accepting a substantial portion of the goods ... waives its right to seek strict enforcement of the letter of credit." *Dorf Overseas Inc. v. Chemical Bank*, 91 A.D.2d 895, 457 N.Y.S.2d 513, 514 (1983). This result "is the only one consistent with principle and common sense." H. Harfield, Bank Credits and Acceptances 107 (5th ed. 1974). Fundamental to letter of credit transactions is the principle that both the letter of credit and also the separate agreement between account customer and issuing bank are transactions in documents entirely independent from the underlying sale of goods. ... An account customer, if it desires to claim discrepancies, has a duty to return documents to the issuing bank rather than use them to obtain control over the goods. The documents provide some compensation to a bank which has inadvertently honored nonconforming documents. "The bank's loss will be the amount of the payment which it has made under the credit less any amount which it may realize from disposition of the documents which it has purchased." Id. at 105. The result is equitable. The beneficiary/seller is paid by the bank for the goods; the bank owns the documents and title to the goods; and the account customer has avoided paying for goods that, because of discrepancies in the documents, it feared accepting. This rule also avoids the inequitable result of a windfall for the account customer in the form of obtaining goods never paid for. While some commentators have favored less stringent rules with respect to an account customer's acceptance of documents,[42] the rule just stated has gained the widest acceptance in American case law and best reflects the fundamental theory underlying letters of credit.

The undisputed facts of this case are that shortly after October 25, 1988, First American transferred the documents at issue to Dameron. Dameron did not note any discrepancies; rather, it used the documents to take possession of the T-shirts. Until July 1989, when it brought suit against National Marketing, Dameron attempted to sell the T-shirts, apparently with disappointing results, and to work out a deal

---

42. Harfield, quoted in the text, presents the most in-depth analysis found of an account customer's remedies for an issuing bank's inadvertent acceptance of nonconforming documents. Harfield's conclusion, discussed supra, is that an account party must reject and return nonconforming documents within a reasonable period or be deemed to have waived its right to object to documentary inconsistencies. ... Some commentators have favored other rules.

In an early treatise, Finkelstein contended that an account customer should be able to accept nonconforming documents, reimburse the issuing bank, but deduct any direct or consequential damages flowing from the bank's acceptance of nonconforming documents. Finkelstein likened this to a buyer's ability to keep nonconforming goods, retain its right of action against the seller for breach of contract, and recover consequential damages. Finkelstein, Legal Aspects of Commercial Letters of Credit 195–97 (1930). ...

More recently, Kozolchyk took a middle ground between Finkelstein and Harfield. Kozolchyk, Commercial Letters of Credit in the Americas 322–26 (1966). Kozolchyk ... believed ... that an account customer might be permitted to receive "direct and foreseeable" damages, and urged American courts to adopt the practice found in some other countries of permitting an account customer to accept documents while expressly reserving a right of action against the bank for document inconsistencies. Id. at 316, 324. See also J. White and R. Summers, Handbook of the Law Under the Uniform Commercial Code § 19–8 at 864–65 (3d ed. 1988) (suggesting that an account customer might recover damages pertaining to defective goods from an issuing bank that wrongfully honors a draft, but providing no case law or reasons for this conclusion and observing that "because customers are so infrequently successful in suing issuing banks for wrongful honor, the law here is quite undeveloped"); Dolan, The Law of Letters of Credit para. 9.03 at 9–35, 9–36 (1984) (observing merely that disputes between issuing banks and account parties should be governed by "contract remedy rules" unless such rules are inadequate). ...

[E]ven if the Court were to accept the notion that an account customer should be able to accept documents and goods and then sue for direct damages resulting from a bank's acceptance of nonconforming documents, it would not permit Dameron to reduce the payment owed to First American by any damages stemming from National Marketing's delivery of faulty goods. Such damages stem from the seller's breach, not First American's. Moreover, even if the court were to hold that an account customer could receive damages from the issuing bank stemming from the receipt of faulty goods, Dameron has already been compensated for such receipt through its settlement with National Marketing. There is no reason in this case for Dameron not to reimburse First American for the full amount First American paid for the goods.

with National to compensate Dameron for the nonconforming goods. On three occasions during this period, Dameron pledged to reimburse First American for honoring the drafts related to the T-shirts in exchange for extensions of time for payment. Furthermore, Dameron obtained a court order attaching payment of the drafts, which order was not lifted until Dameron had settled its law suit with National Marketing. The terms of this settlement have been kept confidential by Dameron, although it stated that it received some monetary compensation under the settlement. It is reasonable to assume that a portion of the settlement was intended to compensate Dameron for the substandard quality of the T-shirts. Not until approximately a year or more after receipt of the documents and goods, did Dameron raise the issue of the missing Statement of the Beneficiary. The undisputed facts therefore show that Dameron delayed informing First American of any discrepancies for more than a reasonable period of time. It failed to return the documents to First American and instead took control of the goods. By these acts, Dameron waived its right to reject nonconforming documents and bound itself to reimburse First American for the amount of the drafts. ... First American's cross-claim against Dameron should be granted, and Dameron will be ordered to reimburse First American for the amount of the drafts plus interest. ...

Notes

(1) **Nature of Terms Conditioning Banks' Obligations.** In theory, the parties to letter of credit transactions could make any fact or event the condition that unlocks a bank's duty to pay or accept a demand for payment. Banking practice, however, strongly favors limiting the fact or event to the presentation of described documents. UCP Article 4 declares: "In credit operations all parties deal in documents, and not in goods, services and/or other performances to which the documents may relate." For example, parties to a sales contract may agree that goods must be shipped by conference line vessels but should not expect a bank to verify that this has occurred. The ICC experts advise: "It should be remembered that banks are to check documents, not facts. Therefore the condition ... should be expressed as a requirement for a certificate of the carrier that the vessel is a conference line one." ICC Case Studies on Documentary Credits 20 (J. Dekker 1989).

The parties in *Petra* established a documentary requirement that seller provide its statement that the goods shipped were of the quality of the samples on which buyer had relied. This statement, which the court refers to as the Statement of the Beneficiary, was not presented to the banks. Of what value to buyer would such statement be?

(2) **Bills of Lading: "Clean" and "Foul."** Bills of lading are obviously important to buyers concerned that payments may be made for goods not shipped. Letters of credit usually call for "clean" bills of

lading; in any event, such a requirement may be implied. British Imex Industries Limited v. Midland Bank Limited, [1958] 1 Q.B. 542. If a carrier receives a shipment in torn or leaky cartons, it will note that fact on the bill of lading to protect itself from the claim that it damaged the goods. A bill of lading with such a notation is not "clean," and a bank need not pay under a letter of credit when such bills of lading are tendered.

Article 34 of the 1983 ICC Uniform Customs deals with this question as follows:

> a. A clean transport document is one which bears no super-imposed clause or notation which expressly declares a defective condition of the goods and/or the packaging.

> b. Banks will refuse transport documents bearing such clauses or notations unless the credit expressly states the clauses or notations which may be accepted.

Suppose that a bill of lading covering a shipment of oil well casing and tubing is tendered under a letter of credit. In the bill of lading the phrase "in apparent good order and condition" has been deleted and the following inserted: "Ship not responsible for kind and condition of merchandise." The bill also bears the stamped notation, "Ship not responsible for rust." If the ICC Uniform Customs are applicable, may the bank decline to pay under the letter of credit? See Liberty National Bank & Trust Co. v. Bank of America National Trust & Savings Association, 218 F.2d 831 (10th Cir.1955), affirming 116 F.Supp. 233 (W.D.Okl.1953).

Problem 15. Seller, in London, agreed to sell "Coromandel groundnuts" to a Danish buyer. Pursuant to the contract Bank opened a letter of credit in Seller's favor. Seller tendered documents to Bank which conformed to the letter of credit except that the bill of lading described the goods as "machine shelled groundnut kernels" instead of "Coromandel groundnuts." The invoice described the goods in the manner called for in the letter of credit. The war intervened, and Bank refused to honor Seller's draft because of the discrepancy between the bill of lading and the letter of credit. In action by Seller against the Bank, Seller proved that in the London produce market the two terms referred interchangeably to the same commodity. What result? See Rayner & Co. v. Hambros Bank, [1942] 2 All E.R. 694 (C.A.). Compare UCC 5–109(1) (preamble) with paragraph (1)(c) of that section. But cf. Temple–Eastex Inc. v. Addison Bank, 672 S.W.2d 793, 38 UCC Rep.Serv. 971 (Tex.1984) (letter of credit called for presentation of "draft" but plaintiff presented demand letter; presentation was consistent with banking practice).

The 1983 UCP provide in Article 41(c):

The description of the goods in the commercial invoice must correspond with the description in the credit. In all other documents the goods may be described in general terms not inconsistent with the description of the goods in the credit.

In the above problem, were the goods described in "general terms" in the bill of lading? Will the distinction drawn by the Uniform Customs, Art. 41 be binding under the Code? See UCC 5–109.

(3) Bills in a Set. A practice of carriers' issuing bills of lading in a set of parts grew up in overseas transportation in an era when the transmission of any document across the ocean was more hazardous than it is today. To cope with the risk of non-arrival of the documents, each part of the set could be sent separately. If only one part arrived, the carrier would honor it. Bills of lading in a set are now governed by UCC 7–304, which limits their issuance to overseas transportation. Once bills of lading are issued in more than one copy, the separate parts can be negotiated to different persons. Some of the problems associated with this possibility are addressed in 7–304(3) and (5).

When sellers and buyers have agreed to payment by letter of credit, the question arises of the banks' treatment of bills in a set when only one part of the set is presented for payment. Commercial banking practice developed whereby issuing or confirming banks would pay against presentation of part of the set, even though the letter of credit presentation of the "full set," provided the presenting bank agreed to indemnify the paying banks against loss. In a World War II era case, an issuing bank in New York refused to pay against part of the set. The Court of Appeals held that the bank's refusal was wrongful:

> It is absolutely essential to the expeditious doing of business in overseas transactions in these days when one part of the bill of lading goes by air and another by water. Unless an indemnity can be substituted for the delayed part, not only does quick clearance of such transactions become impossible but also the universal practice of issuing bills of lading in sets loses much of its purpose.

Dixon, Irmaos & Cia v. Chase National Bank, 144 F.2d 759 (2d Cir. 1944), cert. denied, 324 U.S. 850 (1945). The *Dixon* case was sharply criticized and defended. Backus & Harfield, Custom and Letters of Credit: The Dixon, Irmaos Case, 52 Colum.L.Rev. 589 (1952); Honnold, Letters of Credit, Custom, Missing Documents and the Dixon Case: A Reply to Backus and Harfield, 53 Colum.L.Rev. 504 (1953).

The 1983 Uniform Customs and Practices provide, in Article 26(iii), that banks will accept a transport document which "consists of the full set of originals issued to the consignor if issued in more than one original." The ICC group of exports, responding to an inquiry about how to determine the number of parts to a set, replied that the number of originals must be ascertainable from each copy of the bill of lading itself. ICC Case Studies on Documentary Credits 82 (J. Dekker 1989).

The Code took account of bills in a set only in Article 2. Tender rules, as between seller and buyer, are set forth in UCC 2–323(2). The

Code takes no position as to whether banks are subject to a similar rule under letters of credit. Cf. UCC 5–113.

UNION EXPORT CO. v. N.I.B. INTERMARKET, A.B.

Supreme Court of Tennessee, 1990.
786 S.W.2d 628.

DROWOTA, C.J. This case involves an international letter of credit. Union Export Company (Union) had First American National Bank (First American) issue an irrevocable letter of credit in the amount of $345,000 to N.I.B. Intermarket, A.B. (N.I.B.), a Swedish exporter, to insure payment for calcium chloride that Union had purchased from N.I.B. In this appeal, First American argues that the Court of Appeals erred in affirming the Chancellor's issuance of a permanent injunction enjoining First American from paying a draft drawn pursuant to the letter of credit. Union also appeals, arguing that the injunction was proper but that it was error for the Court of Appeals to remand the case to the trial court for a determination of whether a Swedish bank, to whom the draft had been negotiated before it was presented to First American, was a holder in due course. For the reasons that follow, we reverse the decision of the Chancellor and the Court of Appeals.

I.

Union commenced this action against N.I.B. and First American, seeking, as to N.I.B., damages for breach of contract, and, as to First American, a temporary restraining order and a permanent injunction barring First American from honoring a $345,000 letter of credit issued on Union's account in favor of N.I.B., as well as attachment of any proceeds of the letter of credit owing to N.I.B. The trial court granted Union a temporary restraining order on April 29, 1987, and a preliminary injunction on June 17, 1987.

Thereafter, First American filed its answer and a counterclaim in which it sought to have the preliminary injunction vacated. First American also sought a judgment against Union for Union's reimbursement obligation once First American paid the draft it had accepted under the letter of credit.

Union then moved for a partial summary judgment against First American, requesting that the injunction in its favor be made permanent. First American also filed a motion for summary judgment, in which it alleged that Union owed it reimbursement for Union's liability under the letter of credit.

The Chancellor held a hearing on both motions for summary judgment, after which he granted Union's motion, permanently enjoining First American from making any payment under the letter of credit. In so doing, the trial court found that there was fraud in the underlying transaction, that fraudulent documents had been presented to First American, and that the fraud perpetrated by N.I.B. entitled Union to have payment of the draft drawn under the letter of credit permanently enjoined under Tenn. Code Ann. § 47–5–114(2).

First American subsequently moved to alter or amend the judgment and also sought an indemnity bond from Union in the amount of $345,000 plus ten percent (10) interest from June 18, 1987, payable in the event that Union succeeded in its appeal. The Chancellor denied this motion.

First American then appealed to the Court of Appeals. The Court of Appeals sustained the Chancellor's provision of injunctive relief but ordered that the case be remanded to the trial court and that an attempt be made to join Skanska Banken, a Swedish bank, a claimant to First American's enjoined acceptance, as a party. The Court of Appeals held that if Skanska could prove it were a holder in due course, then, under § 47–5–114(2)(a) the injunction must be vacated.

II.

The facts in this case are undisputed. Sometime prior to August 26, 1986, Union, a Nashville based company, agreed to purchase 1500 metric tons of calcium chloride, a chemical used in snow removal, from N.I.B., a Swedish exporter. In order to guarantee payment, Union had First American issue N.I.B. an irrevocable letter of credit in the amount of $345,000. The letter of credit required the presentment of a draft payable 150 days after sight along with certain other documents.

On December 1, 1986, First American received from Skanska Banken (Skanska) a $345,000 time draft, drawn and endorsed in blank by N.I.B., together with other documents, all of which complied with the letter of credit. First American accepted the draft on December 1, 1986 by affixing its signature thereto, and on the next day, December 2, sent notice of its acceptance by Telex to Skanska. The acceptance had a maturity date of April 30, 1987.

Upon receiving notice of the acceptance, Skanska made two loans to N.I.B. totaling $345,000, taking as security N.I.B.'s claim under the letter of credit.

In February, 1987, Union notified First American that the shipment of chemicals it purchased from N.I.B. was defective. Because First American indicated it would pay its acceptance when it matured, Union commenced this action.

III.

A commercial letter of credit transaction involves three separate contractual relationships: (1) the underlying contract between the buyer (in this case, Union) and the seller (N.I.B.); (2) the agreement between the issuer (First American) and its customer (Union) in which the issuer agrees to issue the letter of credit in return for the customer's promise to reimburse it and pay a commission; and (3) the letter of credit itself which is an engagement by the issuer that it will honor drafts presented by the beneficiary or a transferee beneficiary upon compliance with the terms and conditions specified in the letter of credit. ...

The fundamental principle governing these transactions is the doctrine of independent contracts, which provides that the issuing bank's obligation to honor drafts drawn on a letter of credit by the beneficiary is separate and independent from any obligation of its customer to the beneficiary under the sale of goods contract and separate as well from any obligation of the issuer to its customer under their agreement. ...

In the case at bar, both the trial court and the Court of Appeals found that the injunction against payment under the letter of credit was proper under the limited exception to the doctrine of independence found at Tenn. Code Ann. § 47–5–114(2) ... .

Under the general rule the issuer must honor the draft when the documents presented comply with the terms of the letter of credit. Tenn. Code Ann. § 47–5–114(1). Under this limited exception of § 5–114(2), however, when a required document does not conform to the necessary warranties, is forged, is fraudulent, or there is fraud in the transaction, an issuer acting in good faith is not required to, but may honor a draft drawn under a letter of credit if the documents presented appear on their face to comply with the terms of the letter of credit. In addition, a court may enjoin an issuer from honoring such a draft if the issuer fails to do so on its own. Tenn. Code Ann. § 47–5–112(2)(b). ... Notwithstanding this exception, if the person presenting a draft drawn on a letter of credit is a holder in due course (Tenn. Code Ann. § 47–3–302), the issuer must pay the draft, whether or not it has notice of forgery or fraud. Tenn. Code Ann. § 47–5–114(2)(a) ... .

In this case, the element of fraud is undisputed. For this reason, the Chancellor enjoined payment under Tenn. Code Ann § 5–114(2)(b). The Court of Appeals remanded for a determination of whether Skanska, to whom the draft had been negotiated, is a holder in due course, and thus entitled to the proceeds under Tenn. Code Ann. § 5–114(2)(a) despite the element of fraud.

First American appeals this decision, arguing that the injunction is inappropriate regardless of whether or not Skanska is a holder in due course because the injunction was issued after First American accepted the time draft, and thus was untimely under Tenn. Code Ann. § 47–4–303.

Tenn. Code Ann. § 47–4–303(1) provides in relevant part:

(1) Any ... legal process served upon ... a payor bank, *whether or not effective under other rules of law* to terminate, suspend, or modify the bank's right or duty to pay an item or to charge the customer's account for the item, comes too late to so terminate,

suspend or modify such right or duty if the ... legal process is received or served and a reasonable time for the bank to act thereon expires or the setoff is exercised after the bank has done any of the following: (a) accepted or certified the item. [Emphasis added.]

Acceptance is defined in § 47–3–410(1) as:

(1) Acceptance is the drawee's signed engagement to honor the draft as presented. It must be written on the draft, and may consist of his signature alone. It becomes operative when completed by delivery or notification.

In the case at bar, it is undisputed that First American is the payor bank, and that it accepted the draft within the meaning of Tenn. Code Ann. § 47–3–410(1) prior to the issuance of legal process. Union argues that the injunction was timely, because Tenn. Code Ann. § 47–5–114(2)(b) provides that "a court ... may enjoin such honor," and "honor" is defined in the general definitional section of the U.C.C. as "to pay or to accept and pay." Tenn. Code Ann. § 47–1–201(21). Thus, there is an apparent conflict between Tenn. Code Ann. § 47–5–114(2)(b) and Tenn. Code Ann. § 47–4–303 under the facts of this case.

Article 4 of the U.C.C. governs bank deposits and collections. U.C.C. § 47–4–101. Section 102 of article 4 specifically provides that if provisions in article 4 conflict with those in article 3 then article 4 governs, but in the event article 4 provisions conflict with article 8, then article 8 governs. There is no provision in the Code providing which article would apply in the event of a conflict between articles 4 and 5.

In First Commercial Bank v. Gotham Originals, Inc., 475 N.E.2d at 1260, the New York Court of Appeals held that § 4–303 governed. It relied on the express language of § 4–303(1), which states "whether or not effective under other rules of law" legal process is not effective under the specified circumstances. The Court found further support from the language of § 5–102(3) and comment (2) thereto, on the limited controlling authority of article 5.

The facts in Gotham Originals are similar to the facts in the present case. The issuing bank accepted two drafts drawn under a letter of credit. The drafts were payable after sight in 60 days. After acceptance, but before payment, the customer discovered fraud in the transaction, and the trial court enjoined the issuer from payment. The intermediate appellate court reversed and vacated the injunction, and the Court of Appeals affirmed, both acting under § 4–303.

In addition to holding that § 4–303 prevailed by its own terms, the Court noted the following policy reason supporting the result:

Important policy considerations suggest the result also. Letters of credit provide a quick, economic and predictable means of financing transactions for parties not willing to deal on open accounts by permitting the seller to rely not only on the credit of the buyer but also on that of the issuing bank. By its terms, the credit often reflects a conscious negotiation of risk allocation between customer and beneficiary and its utility rests heavily on strict adherence to the agreed terms and the doctrine of independent contract (see, J. White & R. Summers, Handbook on Uniform Commercial Code § 18–1, at 704–08[2d ed.]). It is this predictability of credit arrangements which permits not only the financing of sale of goods transactions between widely separated parties in different jurisdictions but also has permitted the development of a market in trade or bankers' acceptances of time drafts. Once a draft payable in the future is accepted by a bank, it becomes known as a bankers' acceptance, and such acceptances can be, and regularly are, sold in conjunction with letter of credit transactions to obtain financing prior to the date of maturity in a market sanctioned by the Federal Reserve Board (see, 12 U.S.C. § 372; PLI, Letters of Credit and Bankers' Acceptances 231–34, 236). If the courts intervene to enjoin issuing banks from paying drafts they have previously accepted they seriously undermine this market and limit the use of acceptances as a financing tool.

Id. at 1261.

The same policy considerations apply in Tennessee. We therefore hold that, under Tenn. Code Ann. § 47–4–303(1), Union's injunction against payment of the time draft drawn pursuant to the letter of credit was untimely because it was issued after First American had already accepted the draft. We therefore reverse the decision of the Court of Appeals, and we order the injunction vacated.

IV.

Union next argues that, should the injunction be vacated, the proceeds owing to N.I.B. under the letter of credit are subject to attachment since they represent personal property of either legal or equitable nature. Tenn. Code Ann. § 29–6–132. Attachment of the proceeds would also enable Union to obtain Tennessee jurisdiction over N.I.B. as an out-of-state defendant pursuant to Tenn. Code Ann. § 29–6–101(1).

For the same reasons we above vacated the injunction against payment of the draft drawn under the letter of credit, we now hold that Union is not entitled to an attachment of the letter of credit's proceeds. The attachment issued after First American accepted the draft, and thus is invalid under Tenn. Code Ann. § 47–4–303.

Accordingly, the judgment of the Court of Appeals is reversed, and the trial court's injunction against the payment of the accepted time draft drawn pursuant to Union's letter of credit is hereby vacated. Costs will be taxed to Union Export Company.

Notes

(1) "Holder in Due Course" Protection for Collecting Banks. In the *Union Export* case the bank collecting the seller's draft argued that UCC 5–114(2)(a) barred injunctive relief on the ground that the collecting bank "had taken the draft under conditions that would make it a holder in due course."

UCC 5–114(2)(a) carries "holder in due course" protection beyond that conferred by Article 3. Under UCC 3–305 and 3–306 a holder in due course of an instrument (e.g., a draft) is protected against claims to that instrument and defenses of the obligor. In other words, a bank collecting a draft would be protected against ownership claims to *the draft* and defenses of the obligor. UCC 5–114(2)(a) goes further since the bank that issues a letter may not be a party to the draft drawn by the seller. In *Union Export,* the bank which had issued the letter of credit accepted the draft when it was presented. By that acceptance, the bank became a party to the draft, indeed became the primary party obligated *on the draft.* UCC 3–413. The provision in 5–114 applies to an issuing bank's liability on its *letter of credit* undertaking even though the bank is not a party to the draft.

This extension of the concept of holder in due course accounts for the fact that UCC 5–114(2)(a) does not state that the negotiating bank has the rights of a holder in due course; instead, UCC 5–114(2)(a) protects a bank which has taken the draft under circumstances that "*would* make it a holder in due course," and extends that type of protection to cut off defenses under a different instrument—the letter of credit.

This extension might be justified on the ground that the issuing bank has promised, under specified circumstances, to honor a draft drawn by the seller; thus the issuing bank might be analogized to a bank that "certifies" a check by putting its signed "acceptance" on the check; the certifying bank then becomes a party to the check and is subject to the rights of a holder in due course.

There remain questions of policy as to whether a collecting bank should be given the immunity from injunctive relief granted by UCC 5–114(2)(a). To qualify for this immunity the collecting bank must have given value (UCC 3–303)—either by "discounting" the draft or by taking the draft as security for an antecedent debt the seller owed to the bank. And the collecting bank must have taken the draft in "good faith" (UCC 3–302(a)(2)(ii), 1–201(19)).

(2) Attachment of Proceeds of Letters of Credit. The buyer in *Union Export* proceeded on two remedial paths: injunction against the bank to stop payment or seizure of the proceeds of the bank's payment before transmission to the seller. The Tennessee court held that the injunction remedy was untimely because Skanska was a holder in due course of the draft accepted by First American. The court then summarily rejected buyer's alternative remedy of attachment of the proceeds *after* First America had paid; the court explains that "the same reasons" apply. Given the seller's fraud, why are the funds that represent the purchase price not subject to attachment? See also the decision of the French Cour de Cassation in SA Discount Bank v. Teboul, Recueil, 1982, 382 (attachment of funds at intermediary bank was violation of French Civil Code Article 1134 and of Article 3 of the UCC); see Goldman, The Applicable Law: General Principles of Law— the *Lex Mercatoria,* in Contemporary Problems in International Arbitration 119 (J. Lew ed. 1987).

ANDINA COFFEE, INC. v. NATIONAL WESTMINSTER BANK, USA

Supreme Court of New York, Appellate Division, First Department, 1990.
160 A.D.2d 104, 560 N.Y.S.2d 1.

MILONAS, J. Plaintiff Andina Coffee, Inc., a New York corporation, was engaged in the importation of coffee from defendant Gonchecol, Ltda., at one time a major Colombian exporter of coffee. To pay for its purchases, Andina delivered to Gonchecol letters of credit which it obtained from a number of commercial banks in New York, including defendants National Westminster Bank USA (NatWest) and Coopera- tieve Centrale Raiffeisenboerenleenbank B.A. (Rabobank). As the ben- eficiary of the letters of credit, Gonchecol apparently used all or some of the funds to borrow money from defendant Banco Credito y Commer- cio de Colombia (BCCC) and other Colombian banks in order to finance its business operations. In June 1986, BCCC advanced $2,100,000 to Gonchecol in exchange for which it was to be reimbursed through a $2,100,000 check drawn on a Panamanian bank. However, Gonchecol's check bounced, and BCCC was left with an unpaid $2,100,000 loan. According to NatWest and Rabobank, this event could only have served to confirm what BCCC had already learned from its own sources; that is, that Gonchecol had already lost millions of dollars and was experi- encing severe financial difficulties. As was the situation with most of the moneys made available by BCCC to Gonchecol, the source of repayment would have to be proceeds from the letters of credit provided to Gonchecol from the issuing banks.

Beginning in May of 1986, coffee financed under the various letters of credit, which were to be paid on the presentation of interior truck bills of lading, failed to materialize. Consequently, representatives of the New York banks were dispatched to Colombia in August of 1986 when it was discovered that Gonchecol had caused fraudulent truck bills of lading to be furnished for large quantities of coffee which were, in fact, never shipped, thereby resulting in substantial financial losses to New York banks. The four letters of credit involved here are the last outstanding instruments which were not drawn against prior to the disclosure of the exporter's dishonest practices. In that regard, NatWest and Rabobank had each supplied two of the letters of credit, one for $2,104,000 and the other three in the amount of $1,000,000, pursuant to which they agreed to make payment upon the presentation within a specified period of time of drafts and certain documents, among which were to be the "original railroad and/or truck bill of lading." The bill of lading was supposed to show that the coffee was actually in existence, that it had left the control of the growers and that it was in the hands of the shipper and en route from the interior of Colombia to a seaport.

On July 9, 1986, 15 days after BCCC had already advanced $2,100,-000 to Gonchecol against the latter's bad check, it received from NatWest a letter of credit in the amount of $2,104,000. The following day, almost six weeks before the earliest possible date for presentment under that instrument, BCCC accepted from Gonchecol its draft and accompanying documents. These documents included truck bills of lading which were dated August 22, 1986, almost six weeks after the date submitted to BCCC, and purported to show that 8,000 bags of coffee had been delivered to a trucking company for transport to a Colombian port. BCCC sent the draft and documents to NatWest with a cover letter dated July 15, 1986. By telex dated July 22, 1986, NatWest advised BCCC that it would not pay under the letter of credit because of four enumerated discrepancies in the documents, including the fact that the draft and documents were presented prior to the earliest date mentioned in the letter of credit and that the truck bills of lading were postdated.

BCCC thereupon requested that the bills of lading and other documents be returned to it by mail. It then reviewed the documents received under the other three letters of credit and perceived that the bills of lading in those instances were similarly postdated. Consequently, it sent all of the bills of lading back to Gonchecol so that the exporter could revise the dates to comply with the letters of credit. Indeed, some of the changes were made twice in an attempt to bring the documents into conformity with both the form and date mandates of the letters of credit. Thus, it appears that the documents were designed more to effect payment under the letters of credit than to reflect accurately the business transactions that they were intended to evince. In any event, by the time that the documents had been altered and realtered, the full extent of Gonchecol's fraud had been detected, and payment was rejected by NatWest and Rabobank on the ground that, in part, the bills of lading were postdated and fraudulent.

The instant appeal concerns respective motions and cross motions for summary judgment with respect to the letters of credit. The Supreme Court, in granting BCCC's cross motion for summary judgment and denying the motions of NatWest and Rabobank for the same relief, was persuaded that BCCC took the drafts for value, in good faith and without any knowledge of any fraud defenses and was, therefore, a holder in due course entitled to payment under the letters of credit. In the view of the court, there is no evidence to support the assertions by NatWest and Rabobank that BCCC possessed actual knowledge of Gonchecol's fraud and that it did not accept the drafts in good faith. Finally, the court concluded that the "transactions involved in this case must be considered against a background of haphazard permissive and careless negotiations and payment of prior letters of credit by the issuing banks over a year and a half period. First of all, it is not denied that the same discrepancies alleged in the documents submitted by BCCC were the same one [sic] which the banks had accepted for the aforementioned period ... . Secondly, it cannot be denied that the letters of credit involved are not based upon underlying arms-length transactions." The court proceeded to criticize the issuing banks for assuming a high risk by merely demanding trucking bills of lading rather than on-board bills of lading, since it "appears that the port forwarder and the trucking company were all part of Gonchecol's enterprises and that the importer, Andina Coffee, Inc., although a separate corporate entity, belonged to the same overall organization as the exporter."

Yet, notwithstanding the questionable nature of the financing arrangement undertaken by NatWest and Rabobank, and, certainly, the record is replete with indications of dubious business judgment by the various issuing banks, the soundness of the lenders' financial practices is not at issue here. What is crucial is whether BCCC accepted drafts drawn upon letters of credit "under circumstances which would make it a holder in due course" (Uniform Commercial Code 5–114[2][a]). ...

The mere fact that the documents presented in connection with the letters of credit may have been complete forgeries and that no coffee was delivered to the trucker for export is insufficient to avoid payment under the letter of credit ... . What is critical is whether the bills of lading complied with the requirements of the letters of credit or whether BCCC possessed actual knowledge of the fraud ... or otherwise acted in bad faith. ... Thus according to the Court of Appeals in First Commercial Bank v. Gotham Originals, Inc., 64 N.Y.2d [287], at 295:

> But when a required document does not conform to the necessary warranties or is forged or fraudulent or there is fraud in the transaction, an issuer acting in good faith may, but is not required to, refuse to honor a draft under a letter of credit when the documents presented appear on their face to comply with the terms of the letter of credit. .... Notwithstanding this exception, if the person presenting a draft drawn on a letter of credit is a holder in due course ..., the issuer *must* pay the draft, whether it has notice of forgery or fraud or not.

It is settled that New York law mandates strict compliance with the terms of a letter of credit ... . The postdating of bills of lading is not only a departure from the requirements of the letters of credit but also constitutes a form of fraudulent practice. Contrary to the Supreme Court's characterization that the objections to the accompanying documents raised by NatWest and Rabobank were frivolous and highly technical, the discrepancies were, in reality, material. At the very least, they would have had the effect of concealing the actual shipment dates (even assuming that they had represented genuine, and not fictitious, transactions) and, in fact, did not, as required by the letters of credit, "evidence shipment" of the coffee. Further, while there is authority that by its previous acceptance of nonconforming documents, as admittedly occurred herein, the issuing bank does not waive the right to reject future defects ... and the preclusion rule contained in the UCP (Uniform Customs and Practice for Documentary Credits) is by no means absolute, at most the failure to assert an objection on a previous occasion presents a question of fact as to whether there was a waiver ... .

Unless the postdating was expressly allowed under the letters of credit, and there is no indication that this is the situation, or the parties' prior course of conduct conclusively demonstrates otherwise, the documents provided under the letters of credit did not comply with the terms thereof, and BCCC may not compel payment. Equally significant is the BCCC's apparently active role in obtaining the revisions of the documents, particularly after it was confirmed with definite proof of Gonchecol's financial instability in the form of a bad check, raises questions of fact as to whether it was acting in good faith and without actual knowledge of the exporter's fraud. The record of the present matter clearly presents sufficient unresolved matters precluding summary judgment as to whether BCCC participated in a scheme whereby the bills of lading were altered simply to render them in conformity with the letters of credit. Once it has been "shown that a defense exists a person claiming the rights of a holder in due course has the burden of establishing that he or some person under whom he claims is in all respects a holder in due course" (Uniform Commercial Code 3–307[3]). Since NatWest and Rabobank have demonstrated a viable defense with respect to the letters of credit, BCCC must now prove that it is a holder in due course, and, consequently, summary judgment in its favor is not warranted.

(4) "STANDBY" (OR "GUARANTY") LETTERS OF CREDIT

New Wine in Old Bottles. The classical letter of credit is a device for routine, safe exchange; something of value, usually a negotiable bill of lading controlling the delivery of goods, is exchanged for cash. In recent years, banks have been issuing "Letters of Credit" that promise to pay large sums on the presentation of pieces of paper that are scarcely marketable—statements of non-performance or default. Even when the "Letter of Credit" does not mention default but instead promises payment on presentation of a certificate of *performance* (e.g., the completion of a building project), in actual operation the bank is asked to pay only when a party who was expected to pay (e.g., the one for whom a building was constructed) fails to do so. The fact that the bank's obligation is normally used only when something goes wrong has led these devices to be called "standby" or "guaranty" letters of credit.

Standby letters of credit are used in sales transactions. But whereas it is the seller who is the beneficiary of the ordinary documentary letter of credit, it is the buyer who is the beneficiary of the standby letter of credit. The standby letter may be given to secure performance by the seller and, if the buyer has paid something in advance, to secure the buyer's advance.

The label "Letter of Credit" and statements in the instrument that payment is to be made in presentation of a draft accompanied by a "certificate" or other "document" (no matter how worthless) respond to the fact that many state laws prohibit banks from guaranteeing debts. However, there seems to be need for such undertakings, and the volume and form of these instruments have multiplied. See Baird, Standby Letters of Credit in Bankruptcy, 49 U.Chi.L.Rev. 130 (1982); Verkuil, Bank Solvency and Guaranty Letters of Credit, 25 Stan.L.Rev. 716 (1973); Symposium: Letters of Credit and Standbys, 24 Ariz.L.Rev. 235–369 (1982).

GROUND AIR TRANSFER, INC. v. WESTATES AIRLINES, INC.

United States Court of Appeals, First Circuit, 1990.
899 F.2d 1269.

BREYER, CIRCUIT JUDGE. The two parties before us—Westates and Charter One—signed a "charter air service" contract. As the contract required, Charter One arranged for a bank to issue a $50,000 "standby" letter of credit in Westates' favor, a letter designed, in part, to make certain Westates would not suffer harm should Charter One fail to carry out its contractual obligations. ... Subsequently, a dispute arose; each party claimed the other broke the contract.

Westates, the beneficiary of the letter of credit, would now like to "call" the letter, thereby obtaining the $50,000, which it hopes to keep, at least while the courts litigate the parties' various "breach of contract" claims. The federal district court, however, has issued an injunction, forbidding Westates to call the letter of credit.

Westates appeals from the issuance of the injunction. It says that the law prohibits a court from enjoining a call on a standby letter of credit, at least in a typical case, where the beneficiary's position in the underlying contract dispute is colorable and where the beneficiary can satisfy the terms that the letter of credit itself sets forth as conditions for its call. ... We agree with Westates that the record before us indicates that this case presents the typical commercial circumstances (in respect to the underlying contract, the dispute, and the letter of credit), in which commercial law, as embodied in the Uniform Commercial Code, prohibits an injunction. ... Consequently, we reverse the district court.

I.

Background

We set forth several background circumstances so that the reader can see that this case (as far as the record here reveals) is one in which commercial law normally would prohibit an injunction. That is to say, the underlying contract is a simple, typical commercial contract; Westates' claim that Charter One broke the contract is at least "colorable"; and Westates seems able to satisfy the terms that the letter of credit itself sets forth as conditions for its call.

1. *The contract.* Westates provides airplanes and related services for charter flights. Charter One sells charter flights to travelers. In mid–1989 Westates and Charter One signed a contract under which Westates promised to provide planes and crews for Charter One's new service between Providence, Rhode Island, and Atlantic City, New Jersey, and also (by later amendment to the contract) for its new service between Worcester, Massachusetts, and Atlantic City. The contract required Charter One to pay Westates each month a fee calculated on the basis of the number of hours flown, with a minimum fee of about $105,000 (based on 70 hours flown), which was increased to about $209,000 (150 hours flown) when the Worcester service was added. The contract contained a special "default" clause, which says,

> upon any default by Charter One as defined in this agreement, Westates may immediately terminate all service. ... Westates shall immediately notify Charter One of the default. ... If the default is not cured by Charter One within ten (10) days from the date of mailing the *notice of default,* Westates shall have the right to immediately declare Charter One's default to be a material breach of this agreement and declare this agreement to be terminated without further notice to Charter One.

(Emphasis added.) The contract also required speedy transmission of each monthly payment. It said that late payment was "considered a default."

2. *The contract dispute.* Each party now says that the other party broke this contract. The record reveals a dispute that began in August 1989, when the contract was less than one month old. Charter One's president says that Westates' owner called him and threatened to cancel the contract unless Charter One would pay a higher minimum fee. Charter One refused. Westates then sent Charter One a "ten day default" notice, under the contract's special "default" provision. The "ten day notice" said that Westates would not provide planes for Charter One's Worcester/Atlantic City service after September 4. Wes-

tates, even before September 4, provided only one plane, rather than two planes (as the contract required), but Westates says that maintenance problems, not contract-cancellation efforts, were responsible.

Subsequently, Westates, apparently under pressure from Charter One, changed its mind about cancelling the contract. Charter One's attorney wrote to Westates suggesting that "Westates reconsider its decision to cancel the contract and instead perform its obligations as required." The letter adds:

> Please advise the undersigned by close of business on Wednesday, August 30, 1989, whether Westates intends ... cancellation of the Worcester program. If we do not hear from [you] ... by that time, we will assume that Westates does not intend to abide by its contract, and Charter One will take such measures as are necessary to protect its rights.

On August 30 a Westates attorney, in California, called Charter One's attorney, in Washington, D.C. She says that she told Charter One that Westates indeed intended to abide by the contract and that it rescinded its cancellation. She did not call, however, until 3 p.m. California time, which was 6 p.m. Washington, D.C., time. Charter One then decided that it would not go through with the contract; and it wrote back to Westates that Westates' call had come "too late" (apparently meaning that the call had arrived after "close of business"). The letter added that Charter One would therefore "reject your verbal offer to rescind cancellation of the Worcester program...."

Westates then stopped providing Worcester/Atlantic City service. It continued, however, to provide Providence/Atlantic City service. In mid-September Charter One withheld about $32,000 from the monthly fees due Westates for that Providence service. Westates said that the contract did not permit Charter One to withhold this money. On September 22 it sent Charter One another "ten day default" notice. After ten days it cancelled the contract.

The parties have not yet litigated the merits of their contract disputes. We therefore need not decide whether Westates did, or did not, break the contract in mid-August, or whether it successfully reinstated the contract on August 30, or whether, irrespective of the status of the Worcester/Atlantic City portion of the contact, the Providence/Atlantic City portion remained in effect, or whether Charter One did, or did not, have the right to withhold $32,000 in mid-September. We need only decide that the record, so far, indicates that Westates' position, in respect to the contract dispute, is not obviously without merit, that its position is "colorable," and that, in arguing that it was entitled to receive the $32,000 and (not having received the money) to send a "ten day default" letter, Westates is not acting "fraudulently."

3. *The letter of credit.* The letter of credit here at issue is a typical, commercial letter designed to guarantee a beneficiary against harm caused by a contractual "default." The air service contract described above requires Charter One to arrange for a "letter of credit"

as a "default guarantee." It says specifically in the section dealing with "default" that

> Charter One must provide Westates with a Irrevocable Letter of Credit acceptable to Westates in the amount of $50,000.   ...

It adds that:

> Upon termination of the agreement by Westates ... it is agreed that Westates may take the irrevocable Letter of Credit as liquidated damages for the breach of this agreement by Charter One.

Charter One arranged for a Michigan bank to issue the letter. The letter itself says that Westates may "call" the letter and obtain the money by asking the bank for the money and providing the bank with a copy of the ten day default notice. It reads:

> the credit amount is available to you [Westates] by your drafts on us at sight accompanied by: Dated notarized copy of the ten (10) day notice described in [the Westates/Charter One contract].

The record indicates that Westates can easily meet the terms in this letter of credit. It can provide the bank with a draft and with the "dated notarized copy of the ten ... day notice" that it sent to Charter One on September 22.

II.

Ordinary Principles of Commercial Law

As we have previously explained, parties to commercial contracts often arrange for "standby" or "guarantee" letters of credit. The beneficiary of such a letter typically wants to make certain that, if the other party to the contract defaults, the beneficiary can gain access to a secure fund of money which he can use, say, to satisfy the other party's debt to him (if he is a "seller"), or to purchase a substitute performance (if he is a "buyer"). He may also wish to make certain that, should any contractual dispute arise, it will "wend [its] way towards resolution with the money in [his] pocket, rather than in the pocket" of his adversary. Itek [Corp. v. First National Bank of Boston], 730 F.2d [19], at 24. In order to permit the parties to agree to achieve these objectives, courts have typically considered the letter of credit as "independent" of the contract. That is to say, they have considered it a separate agreement with, say, the issuing bank, that permits the beneficiary to present the documents that satisfy the "call" conditions, and that requires the bank to honor the letter when the beneficiary does so. ... Whether in satisfying those conditions—say, as here, by presenting a draft and a copy of a ten day notice—the beneficiary is, or is not, violating the terms of some other document, such as an underlying contract, is normally beside the point, for to prevent the beneficiary from obtaining the money while the court decides the "underlying contract" question may deprive the beneficiary of the very benefit for which he bargained, namely that any such underlying contract dispute will be "resolved while he is in possession of the money." Itek, 730

F.2d at 24 ... . That is why the Uniform Commercial Code explicitly states that an "issuer must honor a ... demand for payment which complies with the terms of the relevant contract regardless of whether the ... documents conform to the underlying contract ... between the customer and the beneficiary." U.C.C. § 5–114(1), Cal.Com. Code § 5114(1) (West 1989). And, that is why the U.C.C. narrowly circumscribes the circumstances under which a court can enjoin the issuer from making such a payment. See U.C.C. § 5–114(2). Courts have also proved about as reluctant to issue injunctions against beneficiaries calling, as against issuers paying, letters of credit. ... Given the policy reasons against enjoining payment, the random happenstance as to whether beneficiary or issuer is within the court's jurisdiction, and the practical fact that, in any such case, the real parties in interest are likely the contracting parties (with issuing bank as neutral observer), the roughly parallel reluctance to enjoin both issuer and beneficiary is understandable. ...

We have said throughout that courts may not "normally" issue an injunction because of an important exception to the general "no injunction" rule. The exception, as we also explained in Itek, 730 F.2d at 24–25, concerns "fraud" so serious as to make it obviously pointless and unjust to permit the beneficiary to obtain the money. Where the circumstances "plainly" show that the underlying contract forbids the beneficiary to call a letter of credit, Itek, 730 F.2d at 24; where they show that the contract deprives the beneficiary of even a "colorable" right to do so, id. at 25; where the contract and circumstances reveal that the beneficiary's demand for payment has "absolutely no basis in fact," id.; ... where the beneficiary's conduct has " ' "so vitiated the entire transaction that the legitimate purposes of the independence of the issuer's obligation would no longer be served," ' " Itek, 730 F.2d at 25 ...; then a court may enjoin payment. The Uniform Commercial Code, as adopted in most states, says:

> Unless otherwise agreed when documents appear on their face to comply with the terms of a credit but a required document ... is forged or fraudulent or there is fraud in the transaction: ...
>
> (b) [except in certain circumstances listed in subsection (a) not here applicable] an issuer acting in good faith may honor the draft or demand for payment despite notification from the customer of fraud, forgery or other defect not apparent on the face of the documents *but a court of appropriate jurisdiction may enjoin such honor.*

U.C.C. 5–114(2) (emphasis added).

The "fraud" exception does not apply in this case, however, for the record shows nothing "fraudulent" about Westates' demand for payment, nor did the district court find to the contrary. As our earlier discussion of the contract dispute makes clear, ... the record reveals that Westates' claims and defenses are, at the least, "colorable." ...

III.

California Law

California letter of credit law quite obviously differs from the norm in one important respect, but in a respect that must make a court more reluctant, not less reluctant, to issue an injunction. When California adopted the Uniform Commercial Code, it consciously refused to adopt the language permitting an injunction that we underlined when we quoted U.C.C. 5–114(2) .... By omitting this language, California underscored the principle of the "independence" of the letter of credit. The California Code's drafters explicitly stated that the U.C.C.'s "provision for a protective injunction was omitted because: 'By giving the courts power to enjoin the honor of drafts drawn upon documents which appear to be regular on their face, the Commissioners on Uniform State Laws do violence to one of the basic concepts of the letter of credit, to wit, that the letter of credit agreement is independent of the underlying commercial transaction.'" Cal.Com. Code § 5114, comment 6 (West 1989) .... Thus California would seem even more hostile than the typical state to an injunction in the circumstances before us....

[W]e do not believe the California Supreme Court would permit an injunction where other states (applying the traditional "fraud" exception) would not do so. After all, California's state legislature has altered the U.C.C. to make it more difficult in California than elsewhere to enjoin an issuer's payment of a letter of credit; to make it significantly easier than elsewhere to enjoin a call by a beneficiary would undercut that underlying legislative policy.

For these reasons the judgment of the district court is

Reversed.

Notes

(1) Independence From Underlying Transactions. The "standby" credit, which in fact (though not in form) is used when there is default in the underlying transaction, places heavy strain on the classic doctrine that the letter of credit is "independent" from the contractual obligations of the parties. See, for example, Roman Ceramics Corp. v. Peoples National Bank, 714 F.2d 1207 (3d Cir.1983). A letter of credit called for the bank to pay S on S's certification that invoices for S's sales to B had not been paid. The bank refused to pay on the basis of evidence from B that the invoices covered by the bank had been paid. A majority of the court, per Garth, J., ruled that the demand for payment was "fraud in the transaction" under UCC 5–114(2)(b); a dissent, by Adams, J., argued that there was no fraud, and that sustaining the bank's refusal (in contrast to an injunction against payment) further impaired the certainty of payment needed in commercial transactions. See Bank of Newport v. First National Bank & Trust Co., 687 F.2d 1257 (8th Cir.1982) (refusal by issuing bank); Becker, Standby Letters of Credit, Will the Independence of the Credit Survive? 13 U.C.C.L.J. 335 (1981).

(2) General References. See J. Dolan, The Law of Letters of Credit: Commercial and Standby Credits (1984); H. Harfield, Bank Credits and Acceptances (5th ed.1974). For a shorter treatment, see H. Harfield, Letters of Credit (1979). For a comparative work, see B. Kozolchyk, Commercial Letters of Credit in the Americas (1966).

Chapter 8

RISK OF LOSS

SECTION 1. INTRODUCTION

The Problem. Casualty to goods—as by fire, theft, or flood—may occur at any one of several stages in the performance of the sales contract. The casualty may occur on the seller's premises, either after the making of a contract for the sale of specific (identified) goods or after the seller has identified goods as those intended for performance of the contract. More frequently, the loss occurs while the goods are in transit or after their arrival but before the buyer takes possession. Problems can arise even after the buyer receives the goods if casualty occurs during a period of testing or inspection, or following the buyer's rejection (or revocation of acceptance) of the goods on the ground that they were not in conformity with the contract.

Dispute between the seller and buyer is often avoided by the availability of insurance coverage, and sometimes by the legal responsibility of the carrier for damage occurring during transit. Even in these situations, problems may arise as to whether the seller or the buyer has the responsibility to take over and salvage damaged goods, press a claim against the insurer or carrier, and bear any loss from inadequacy in insurance coverage or from limitations on the liability of the carrier. The point at which the risk of loss passes is thus of greater practical significance than would be indicated by the volume of litigation.

In addition, rules on risk of loss may determine whether the seller has performed its warranty and other contractual obligations. Suppose, for instance, that a contract calls for No. 1 wheat and that water damage during the rail shipment makes the wheat grade only No. 4; in such a case the rules on risk of loss in transit will determine whether the buyer has a claim against the seller for breach of contract. Anglo–American statutory formulations do not bother to express this obvious relationship between rules on risk and warranty; the Convention on International Sale of Goods is more articulate: "The seller is liable ... for any lack of conformity which exists at the time when the risk passes to the buyer, even though the lack of conformity becomes apparent only after that time." [1]

Historical Background; Early Common Law. English law, at an early stage, seemed to conclude that risk of loss did not pass to the

---

1. CISG 36(1); see also CISG 36(2), 66.

buyer until the goods were delivered to it. Such was the view expressed in the thirteenth century by Bracton in De Legibus, " ...
because in truth, he who has not delivered a thing to the purchaser, is
still himself the lord of it;" Bracton illustrated the point with the death
of an ox and the burning of a house prior to delivery to the purchaser.[2]

Long before the first codification of English sales law, a different
approach had developed. This change probably was not designed to
accelerate the transfer to the buyer of risk of loss, but rather to
strengthen the buyer's remedies against the seller and against third
persons who may attempt to take the goods. The difficulty stemmed
from the fact that the buyer had no common law remedy to take the
goods from a recalcitrant seller, or from third persons (such as the
seller's creditors), unless the buyer could be said to have "property" or
"title." A claim for damages against a seller who is plagued by
creditors is, of course, of little value; what is needed is a remedy to
seize the goods, or a legal claim (e.g., for conversion) against a third
person who is not judgment-proof. There is evidence that, to mitigate
this deficiency in the common law remedial system, courts at an early
date developed the view that when a contract is made for the sale of
specific (identified) goods, the buyer thereupon has the "property."[3]

Once it was concluded that the buyer had "property" in the goods,
it seemed to follow that it bore the risk if "its" goods were destroyed.
The famous 1827 King's Bench decision in *Tarling v. Baxter* involved
the sale of a stack of hay which burned prior to the time for delivery
and payment.[4] The opinion by Bayley, J., opened with the basic
premise: "It is quite clear that the loss must fall upon him in whom the
property was vested at the time when it was destroyed by fire." All
that remained was to find where "the property" was located. The
answer was that "the property" vested in the buyer when the contract
was made, even though the buyer did not have possession and would
not have even the right to possession until it paid (or tendered) the
price. The opinion recognized that more was at stake than risk of loss:
"*All* the consequences resulting from the vesting, of the property
follow, *one* of which is, that if it be destroyed, the loss falls upon the
vendee." (Emphasis added.) As we have seen, the other consequences
included the strong proprietary remedies given to the buyer.[5]

---

2. Bracton, De Legibus, Twiss Ed.1878,
Ch. XXVII, p. 493. Compare Glanville,
Laws and Customs (Cir.1187–89) Book X,
Ch. XIV, 216 (Beames ed. 1900). The joint
treatment of goods and realty did not survive later developments in the common
law, but to some extent has persisted in
civil law formulations.

3. Holdsworth, History of English Law
355–56 (3d ed. 1923). Holdsworth suggests
that such remedies led to "the doctrine
that a contract of sale of specific goods
passes the property in the goods." See
also: Blackburn, The Contract of Sale 188–

189 (1845); 2 Pollock & Maitland, History
of English Law 210 (2d ed. 1898); P. Ati-
yah, The Rise and Fall of Freedom of Contract 103, 106 (1979) (present ownership,
with possession postponed, used as tool for
effective future planning).

4. 6 B & C 360, 108 Eng.Rep. 484 (K.B.
1827).

5. Another remedial consequence was
that the seller could recover the full price
from the buyer in an action of debt, as
contrasted with a damage claim in assumpsit. The action of debt was reserved for
executed transactions in which the defen-

"Property" and Risk in the Sale of Goods Act and the Uniform Sales Act. The use of the "property" concept was brought to the New World as part of the common-law heritage, and dominated the handling of sales problems in both England and the United States long before the onset of codification. Chalmers conscientiously transcribed the case-law rules in preparing the (British) Sale of Goods Act (1893)—a set of rules which is on the statute-books in substantial parts of the world.[6] Under Section 20, unless the parties have agreed otherwise, when "the property" in goods "is transferred to the buyer, the goods are at the buyer's risk whether delivery has been made or not." Under Section 17, where there is a contract for the sale of "specific or ascertained" goods, the property is transferred when the parties so intend. Section 18 lays down five rules (when no different intention appears) "for ascertaining the intention of the parties as to the time at which the property in the goods is to pass to the buyer." Rule 1 codifies the approach of *Tarling v. Baxter*:

> Where there is an unconditional contract for the sale of specific goods, in a deliverable state, the property in the goods passes to the buyer when the contract is made, and it is immaterial whether the time of payment or the time of delivery, or both, be postponed.

In preparing the Uniform Sales Act, Professor Williston closely followed the British model. The general rule that risk of loss passes when "the property" is transferred was placed in Section 22; the rules for ascertaining the parties' intent appear in Article 19—with the rule of the *Tarling* Case reproduced as Rule 1.[7] The Uniform Sales Act retained the crucial role of "property" in other settings. For example, under Section 66, where the property has passed, the buyer may "maintain any action allowed by law to the owner of goods of similar kind when wrongfully converted or withheld;" under Section 63(1) the seller may bring an action to recover the price (as contrasted with damages for breach of contract) where "the property has passed to the buyer." Thus, the solution of a variety of sales problems under the Uniform Sales Act was entangled with the question whether "the property" in the goods remained with the seller or whether "it" had passed to the buyer.

Difficulty With the "Property" Concept; The Code. "Property" in goods is, of course, a legal conclusion and can serve as a tool for decision only when it is implemented by rules referring to events, such as the making of a contract, completion of an agreed performance,

---

dant had received a quid pro quo. But this requirement was met by the conclusion that the buyer had the "property" even though it did not have the goods.

6. E.g., the provinces of Canada other than Quebec, Australia, New Zealand, India, Pakistan, Singapore, Nigeria, Ghana, Kenya, and various other jurisdictions where the common law tradition was established.

7. The Uniform Sales Act made a significant (and unfortunate) deviation from the British Act by adding as Rule 5 a provision holding risk in transit on the seller where the contract "requires the seller to deliver the goods to the buyer ... or to pay the freight or cost of transportation to the buyer. ..."

delivery to a carrier, or receipt by a buyer. The "property" concept thus was highly malleable, and probably would have served as well as any other label for the development of rules addressed to a single problem such as risk of loss. Difficulty, however, developed because this one concept was employed to solve different problems which sometimes called for different solutions. For instance, as we have noted, there was reason to speed the passage of "property" to the buyer to provide him with effective remedies against a recalcitrant seller. Very different practical considerations bear on the question as to who should bear casualty loss while the goods are still held by the seller. The use of "property" in sales law thus suffered from a difficulty that has arisen in various parts of the legal structure when a single concept is pressed into service to solve disparate problems.

The most radical departure of the Sales Article of the Code from the approach of the Uniform Sales Act is the Code's virtual abandonment of "property" (or "title") as a vehicle for deciding sales controversies. Instead, the Code provides separate rules to govern risk, replevin rights, recovery of the full price, and other problems which the Uniform Sales Act referred to the "property" concept. Professor Williston characterized this step as "the most objectionable and irreparable feature" of the Sales Article; even apart from other objections, this was sufficient reason for rejecting Article 2.[8] Most students have come to a different conclusion.[9] The crucial test, of course, is the appropriateness of the Code's rules for concrete situations.[10]

1980 Convention on International Sales of Goods. The Convention provisions on risk of loss are found in Chapter IV. The most important articles are 67 and 69. Article 67 applies when the sales contract involves carriage of goods; the special situation of goods sold while in transit is covered in Article 68. Article 69 applies when the sales contract requires the buyer to come for the goods. For a useful account of the Convention's rules, see Roth, The Passing of Risk, 27 Am.J.Comp.L. 291 (1979).

SECTION 2. CASUALTY IN TWO-PARTY TRANSACTIONS

(A) DOMESTIC SALES LAW

Introduction. We begin with the structure of the Code's provisions allocating risk of loss in two-party transactions, sales in which

---

8. See Williston, The Law of Sales in the Proposed Uniform Commercial Code, 63 Harv.L.Rev. 561, 569–71 (1950).

9. Corbin, The Uniform Commercial Code—Sales; Should it be Enacted? 59 Yale L.J. 821, 824–27 (1950); Latty, Sales and Title and the Proposed Code, 16 Law & Contemp.Prob. 3 (1951). Some interesting

comparisons are provided by Tanikawa, Risk of Loss in Japanese Sales Transactions, 42 Wash.L.Rev. 463 (1967).

10. See White, Evaluating Article 2 of the UCC: A Preliminary Empirical Expedition, 75 Mich.L.Rev. 1262 (1977).

delivery of the goods occurs without the use of third-party carriers. The nature of the problem and the basic rules can be seen in the following problem, which is suggested by the facts of the famous English case of *Tarling v. Baxter*, discussed in Section 1, supra.

Problem 1. John Smith, a dairy farmer, usually grows a small amount of alfalfa hay to feed to his dairy cows. This summer his alfalfa field did unusually well and he found he had a stack of hay he did not need. On June 1, a neighbor, Brown, came and looked at the stack of hay in Smith's field, and a contract was made for the sale of the stack to Brown for $400; Brown was to pay for the hay and remove it during the first week in July. On June 15, the stack burned.

(a) Smith sues Brown to recover the agreed price of $400. What result? See UCC 2–509; 2–104(1) and the *Martin* case, infra. Would the result be different if the seller was the Smith Alfalfa Company?

(b) At the trial, Smith's lawyer calls Smith to the stand and asks questions that would elicit testimony that Brown specifically requested and received assurances that Smith "would hold the hay in the pasture for Brown and would not sell it to anyone else." Brown's lawyer objects to the evidence as irrelevant. Smith's lawyer answered that the evidence was relevant to show that Brown had received the goods under UCC 2–509(3). What ruling? See UCC 2–103(1)(c).

(c) Suppose the fire had occurred on July 10? See UCC 2–503, 2–510.

MARTIN v. MELLAND'S INC.

Supreme Court of North Dakota, 1979.
283 N.W.2d 76.

ERICKSTAD, CHIEF JUSTICE. The narrow issue on this appeal is who should bear the loss of a truck and an attached haystack mover that was destroyed by fire while in the possession of the plaintiff, Israel Martin (Martin), but after certificate of title had been delivered to the defendant, Melland's Inc. (Melland's). The destroyed haymoving unit was to be used as a trade-in for a new haymoving unit that Martin ultimately purchased from Melland's. Martin appeals from a district court judgment dated September 28, 1978, that dismissed his action on the merits after it found that at the time of its destruction Martin was the owner of the unit pursuant to Section 41–02–46(2), N.D.C.C. (Section 2–401 U.C.C.). We hold that Section 41–02–46(2), N.D.C.C., is inapplicable to this case, but we affirm the district court judgment on the grounds that risk of loss had not passed to Melland's pursuant to Section 41–02–57, N.D.C.C. (Section 2–509 U.C.C.).

On June 11, 1974, Martin entered into a written agreement with Melland's, a farm implement dealer, to purchase a truck and attached haystack mover for the total purchase price of $35,389. Martin was given a trade-in allowance of $17,389 on his old unit, leaving a balance owing of $18,000 plus sales tax of $720 or a total balance of $18,720. The agreement provided that Martin "mail or bring title" to the old unit to Melland's "this week." Martin mailed the certificate of title to Melland's pursuant to the agreement, but he was allowed to retain the use and possession of the old unit "until they had the new one ready." The new unit was not expected to be ready for two to three months because it required certain modifications. During this interim period, Melland's performed minor repairs to the trade-in unit on two occasions without charging Martin for the repairs.

Fire destroyed the truck and the haymoving unit in early August, 1974, while Martin was moving hay. The parties did not have any agreement regarding insurance or risk of loss on the unit and Martin's insurance on the trade-in unit had lapsed. Melland's refused Martin's demand for his new unit and Martin brought this suit. The parties subsequently entered into an agreement by which Martin purchased the new unit, but they reserved their rights in any lawsuit arising out of the prior incident.

The district court found "that although the Plaintiff [Martin] executed the title to the ... [haymoving unit], he did not relinquish possession of the same and therefore the Plaintiff was the owner of said truck at the time the fire occurred pursuant to [UCC 2–401]."

Martin argues that the district court erroneously applied ... [UCC 2–401], regarding passage of title, to this case and that ... [UCC 2–509], which deals with risk of loss in the absence of breach, should have been applied instead. Martin argues further that title (apparently pursuant to [UCC 2–401(1)]) and risk of loss passed to Melland's and the property was then merely bailed back to Martin who held it as a bailee. Martin submits that this is supported by the fact that Melland's performed minor repairs on the old unit following the passage of title without charging Martin for the repairs. Melland's responds that [UCC 2–401(2)], governs this case and that the district court's determination of the issue should be affirmed.

One of the hallmarks of the pre-Code law of sales was its emphasis on the concept of title. The location of title was used to determine, among other things, risk of loss, insurable interest, place and time for measuring damages, and the applicable law in an interstate transaction. This single title or "lump" title concept proved unsatisfactory because of the different policy considerations involved in each of the situations that title was made to govern. Furthermore, the concept of single title did not reflect modern commercial practices, i.e. although the single title concept worked well for "cash-on-the-barrelhead sales," the introduction of deferred payments, security agreements, financing from third parties, or delivery by carrier required a fluid concept of title with bits and pieces held by all parties to the transaction.

Thus the concept of title under the U.C.C. is of decreased importance. The official comment to Section 2–101 U.C.C. [§ 41–02–01, N.D.C.C.] provides in part:

> The arrangement of the present Article is in terms of contract for sale and the various steps of its performance. The legal consequences are stated as following directly from the contract and action taken under it without resorting to the idea of when property or title passed or was to pass as being the determining factor. The purpose is to avoid making practical issues between practical men turn upon the location of an intangible something, the passing of which no man can prove by evidence and to substitute for such abstractions proof of words and actions of a tangible character. Uniform Commercial Code (U.L.A.) § 2–101.

Section 41–02–46, N.D.C.C. (§ 2–401 U.C.C.), which the district court applied in this case, provides in relevant part:

> Each provision of this chapter with regard to the rights, obligations and remedies of the seller, the buyer, purchasers or other third parties applies irrespective of title to the goods except where the provision refers to such title. Insofar as situations are not covered by the other provisions of this chapter and matters concerning title become material the following rules apply ...

[UCC 2–509] is an "other provision of this chapter" and is applicable to this case without regard to the location of title. Comment one to Section 2–509 U.C.C. provides that "the underlying theory of these sections on risk of loss is the adoption of the contractual approach rather than an arbitrary shifting of the risk with the 'property' in the goods."...

Before addressing the risk of loss question in conjunction with [UCC 2–509], it is necessary to determine the posture of the parties with regard to the trade-in unit, i.e. who is the buyer and the seller and how are the responsibilities allocated. It is clear that a barter or trade-in is considered a sale and is therefore subject to the Uniform Commercial Code. ... It is also clear that the party who owns the trade-in is considered the seller. [UCC 2–304] provides that the "price can be made payable in money or otherwise. If it is payable in whole or in part in goods each party is a seller of the goods which he is to transfer."
...

Martin argues that he had already sold the trade-in unit to Melland's and, although he retained possession, he did so in the capacity of a bailee (apparently pursuant to [UCC 2–509(2)]). White and Summers in their hornbook on the Uniform Commercial Code argue that the seller who retains possession should not be considered bailee within Section 2–509:

> "The most common circumstance under which subsection (2) will be applied is that in which the goods are in the hands of a

professional bailee (for instance, a warehouseman) and the seller passes a negotiable or a non-negotiable document of title covering the goods to the buyer. That case is simple enough. One question remains, however. Can the seller ever be a 'bailee' as the word is used in subsection (2)? The facts in a pre-Code case ... well illustrate the problem. There seller had reached an agreement with buyer for the sale of a colt. The parties had agreed that the seller would hold the colt for the buyer and, depending upon the terms of the payment of the price, would or would not charge him a fee for stabling the colt. The colt was killed without any fault on the part of the seller, and the seller sued the buyer for the purchase price. In such a case the seller could certainly argue that he was a bailee and that risk had passed since he had acknowledged the buyer's 'right' to possession of goods under (2)(b). The case would be a particularly appealing one for that argument if the seller were receiving payment from the buyer for the boarding of the horse.

We believe that such an interpretation of the word bailee should be rejected by the courts, and except in circumstances which we cannot now conceive, a seller should not ever be regarded as a bailee. To allow sellers in possession of goods already sold to argue that they are bailees and that the risk of loss in such cases is governed by subsection (2) would undermine one of the basic policies of the Code's risk of loss scheme. As we have pointed out, the draftsmen intended to leave the risk on the seller in many circumstances in which the risk would have jumped to the buyer under prior law. The theory was that a seller with possession should have the burden of taking care of the goods and is more likely to insure them against loss.

If we accept such sellers' arguments, that is, that they are bailees under subsection (2) because of their possession of the goods sold or because of a clause in the sale's agreement, we will be back where we started from, for in bailee cases the risk jumps under (2)(b) on his 'acknowledgment' of the buyer's right to possession. By hypothesis our seller has acknowledged the buyer's right and is simply holding the goods at buyer's disposal. Thus, to accomplish the draftsmen's purpose and leave risk on the seller in possession, we believe that one should find only non-sellers to be 'bailees' as that term is used in 2–509(2). Notwithstanding the fact that a seller retains possession of goods already sold and that he has a term in his sale's contract which characterizes him as a "bailee" we would argue that he is not a bailee for the purposes of subsection (2) of 2–509 and would analyze his situation under subsection (1) or subsection (3) of 2–509." J. White & R. Summers, Handbook of the Law Under the Uniform Commercial Code, 144–45 (1972) ...

It is undisputed that the contract did not require or authorize shipment by carrier pursuant to [UCC 2–509(1)]; therefore, the residue section, subsection 3, is applicable:

In any case not within subsection 1 or 2, the risk of loss passes to the buyer on his receipt of the goods if the seller is a merchant; otherwise the risk passes to the buyer on tender of delivery.

Martin admits that he is not a merchant; therefore, it is necessary to determine if Martin tendered delivery of the trade-in unit to Melland's. Tender is defined in [UCC 2–503(1)] . . . .

It is clear that the trade-in unit was not tendered to Melland's in this case. The parties agreed that Martin would keep the old unit "until they had the new one ready." . . .

We hold that Martin did not tender delivery of the trade-in truck and haystack mover to Melland's pursuant to (§ 2–509 U.C.C.); consequently, Martin must bear the loss.

We affirm the district court judgment.

Notes

(1) **Insurance Coverage.** Comment 3 declares that the underlying theory of UCC 2–509(3) is based on expectations as to casualty insurance coverage on the goods. Merchants, it is said, can be expected to have effective coverage on merchandise in their possession, while buyers cannot be expected to have insurance on property purchased but not yet delivered. This follows from standard fire and casualty insurance policies, sold to business concerns, that provide coverage for specified buildings including, generally, all contents. Policies typically include expressly "property sold but not removed."[1] Does either the text of UCC 2–509(3) or the Comment's theoretical explanation state or imply the further rule that merchant-sellers may obtain relief for the loss from their insurance carriers primarily or exclusively?

(2) **Effect of Casualty on Parties' Contract Obligations: UCC 2–613.** The Code does not declare, in UCC 2–509, that sellers are discharged of obligation to deliver because certain goods have been lost or damaged while the risk of loss was on sellers. Under contracts of sale, there are a number of possibilities that bear on the question of discharge. (a) The goods lost or damaged were the only goods that the seller might have tendered properly under the contract. (b) The goods lost or damaged were part of a supply of substitutable goods, any of which the seller might have tendered properly under the contract, but the seller had identified the specific goods lost or damaged as those it planned to deliver. (c) The goods lost or damaged were among a supply of substitutable goods, but the seller had not yet identified any specific goods lost or damaged as those it planned to deliver. Should seller be discharged from its contractual obligation in any or all of these circumstances?

---

1. In recent years, business concerns have had access to even broader insurance coverage through "multiple line" or "package" policies.

The Code provides a partial answer in UCC 2–613, which provides that contracts may be totally or partially "avoided" depending upon the degree of the physical loss. When contracts are avoided, according to Comment 1, the parties are relieved from obligation. Section 2–613 fits, to large extent, the first of the three circumstances we hyothesized. Would UCC 2–613 apply on the facts of *Martin?*[2] If so, did Melland's have a claim against Martin for breach of his promise to deliver the haystack mover? What line of reasoning leads to the conclusion that Melland's should be excused from performing its promise to deliver the new haystack mover? If Martin had not allowed the insurance coverage to lapse and tendered the insurance proceeds plus $18,720 (the agreed cash balance owed) to Melland's, could Melland's refuse to deliver the new haystack mover without being in breach of contract?

What happens to the contract obligations of sellers who have incurred risk of loss but whose contracts are not avoided under UCC 2–613? See UCC 2–615.

(3) **Insurance Carrier Subrogation.** A seller who suffers loss or casualty to goods on which it has effective insurance coverage is likely to submit a claim under the insurance policy even if the risk of loss has passed to the buyer. If an insurance company pays a claim, may it seek to be subrogated to seller's claim for the price under UCC 2–709(1)? Would seller be entitled to the proceeds of the policy from the insurance company and recovery of the price from the buyer? Should it matter whether the buyer has caused the loss or casualty? These interrelated questions have been answered most clearly in the context of real property transactions. In an executory contract, if only the vendor has effective insurance on property that suffers loss or casualty after risk of loss has passed to the vendee, the vendor's insurance should ultimately benefit the vendee. See R. Keeton & A. Widiss, Insurance Law 324 (1988).

(4) **Insurance at Less Than Market Value.** Typically, insurance companies do not insure goods for the full market value. When insureds do not retain significant risk, the insurers face what is commonly called moral hazard. Thus sellers who recover on their insurance policies are likely to receive less compensation than they would have received from their buyers under the sales contracts. On what theory is the difference between insured coverage and contract price (or market value) allocated between sellers and buyers? See UCC 2–510(1) and (3)?

(5) **Risk of Loss in Non–merchant Seller Transactions.** The most natural transactional description of the parties in the *Martin* case would characterize the farmer, Martin, as the buyer, and the dealer, Melland's Inc., as the seller. In trade-in transactions, however, each party is both a seller and buyer of the separate goods involved. See

---

2. Query: Could Melland's Inc. argue persuasively that Martin's allowing the insurance coverage to lapse was a "fault" that should deprive him of the protection of 2–613?

UCC 2–304(1). For purposes of risk of loss analysis under UCC 2–509(3), would the owner of a good being traded in be a merchant? UCC 2–104(1). If not, is the contention plausible that he had made a tender of delivery to the dealer who was not yet prepared to tender the reciprocal performance? UCC 2–503(1), 2–511(1).

How should UCC 2–509(3) be applied when trade-in equipment is lost or damaged after contract but before completed performance? Is the underlying theory that allocates risk on expectation of insurance coverage appropriate in this context? Would it be reasonable to fashion a risk of loss rule on the expectation that non-merchant sellers of trade-in goods will have fire and casualty insurance coverage on things of sufficient value to be worth trading in? Does UCC 2–509(3) permit such a rule to be fashioned?

In *Martin*, the farmer had effective insurance at the time of contract, but allowed that insurance to lapse. Whatever the general rule on risk of loss for trade-ins, should a decision to drop coverage, without notifying the dealer, affect the allocation of risk of loss in this particular situation?

Problem 2. S Company made a contract for the sale to B of a specified machine tool which S had been using in its manufacturing operations; prior to this transaction S had never sold a machine tool. The contract permitted B to remove the tool within a month. One week after the contract was made, the tool was destroyed by a fire in S's plant. Both S and B are insured under the standard fire policy. How should the interests of the parties be adjusted?

The Permanent Editorial Board Study Group on Article 2 recommended that the Code be revised to eliminate the distinction between merchant and non-merchant sellers. "We assume that the non-merchant seller in possession will be in a much better position than the buyer to obtain insurance." Preliminary Report 148 (1990).

UNITED AIR LINES, INC. v. CONDUCTRON CORP.

Appellate Court of Illinois, First District, 1979.
69 Ill.App.3d 847, 26 Ill.Dec. 344, 387 N.E.2d 1272.

GOLDBERG, PRESIDING JUSTICE: United Air Lines, Inc. (plaintiff), brought an action for breach of contract against Conductron Corporation, McDonnell Douglas Electronics Company, a subsidiary of McDonnell Douglas Corporation, and McDonnell Douglas Corporation (defendants). ... The case involves sale by defendants to plaintiff of an aircraft flight simulator. This machine was destroyed by fire while on plaintiff's property. [At the time of the fire, plaintiff had paid $1,043,-434.33 as partial payment of the purchase price. Plaintiff sought recovery of its payments, liquidated damages for defendants' breach of contract, and interest.] The trial court entered summary judgment in favor of plaintiff for $1,326,573.20. Defendants appeal.

Defendants contend that the trial court erred in entering summary judgment for plaintiff because the risk of loss of the simulator was upon plaintiff at the time of its destruction. ...

Plaintiff contends that at the time the simulator was destroyed the risk of loss was upon defendants. In this regard, plaintiff urges that defendants defaulted under the terms of the contract by failing to deliver a conforming aircraft flight simulator; this default was never cured; the simulator was never accepted by plaintiff because of its deficiencies and plaintiff at all times retained the right of rejection.

...

Many of the facts which appear from the pleadings, interrogatories, depositions, and affidavits are undisputed. The purchase agreement between plaintiff and defendants, some 65 pages in length, was executed on December 30, 1966. The agreement contains 19 articles and was supplemented by a number of change orders. It required defendants to deliver a Boeing 727 digital flight simulator to plaintiff on January 13, 1968. A flight simulator is a highly sophisticated electro-mechanical device operated by computers. It is designed to simulate the experiences of a pilot in the cockpit of a jet airplane during flight. As flight simulators are used for training pilots, they must meet the requirements necessary for approval by the Federal Aviation Administration (FAA). The contract so provided. In addition the contract provided that the simulator would conform to plaintiff's specifications.

The original contract provided for inspection and testing of the simulator by plaintiff at defendants' plant prior to its shipment to plaintiff's Flight Training Center in Denver, Colorado. The defendants agreed to correct any deficiency or discrepancy appearing from such inspection. The agreement further provided that when delivery of the simulator was made title would pass to plaintiff but that such delivery would not constitute acceptance of the simulator by plaintiff. Final acceptance by plaintiff was subject to satisfactory completion and also to certification by the FAA.

Defendants failed to complete fabrication of the simulator by the agreed upon date. This resulted in a request by plaintiff that the simulator be delivered to the plaintiff's training center in Colorado for the testing process which, under the original agreement, could have been completed at defendants' plant. On February 20, 1969, the parties entered into a modification of the contract referred to as Change Order Number 3. This order provided for disassembly of the machine, its delivery to plaintiff by common carrier not later than February 28, 1969, and reassembly by defendants on plaintiff's premises not later than March 15, 1969. From July 1, 1969 to August 1, 1969, the simulator was to be available to plaintiff for demonstration purposes and for correction by defendants of deviations noted by plaintiff in the above mentioned testing. The documents stated that in the event the defendants were unable satisfactorily to correct all deviations prior to November 1, 1969, the plaintiff would have the right to cancel the agreement and receive a refund of all payments made to the defendants as buyer plus liquidated damages. The Change Order also gave plaintiff the right to use the simulator for personnel training purposes.

While the simulator was still in possession of defendants upon their facilities, plaintiff's personnel noted some 647 deficiencies in its operation. These difficulties were recorded and reported to defendants by means of written reports referred to as "squak sheets." The simulator was delivered to plaintiff's facility and was reassembled by defendants on March 14, 1969, in accordance with Change Order Number 3. Since the machine had not received FAA approval, it could not be used as an aircraft flight simulator. It was used for training purposes to acquaint and familiarize pilots with instrument location in the cabin of a Boeing 727 aircraft.

On April 18, 1969, the simulator was tested for 10 hours by two of plaintiff's test pilots. About 10 p.m. a fire was discovered in the machine. The simulator was substantially damaged. The origin of the fire is unknown. After the fire, plaintiff requested that defendants dismantle and ship the simulator back to their plant for repairs at plaintiff's expense. On May 16, 1969, plaintiff notified defendants that they considered there was a breach by defendants of the warranties contained in the purchase agreement. On June 4, 1969, the parties amended the agreement by Change Order Number 4. This document provided that the plaintiff would receive $60,000 as liquidated damages for the late delivery of the simulator to be deducted from the remaining payments due defendants. Plaintiff commenced this action on May 11, 1973, seeking rescission of the contract and damages. On January 28, 1977, plaintiff filed Count VII as an amendment to the complaint. This amendment alleged that the risk of loss of the simulator was upon defendants at the time it was destroyed.

. . . Summary judgment in favor of plaintiff was entered by the trial court based on the theory that the simulator had never been accepted by plaintiff and, therefore, the risk of loss remained upon defendants. The order allowed plaintiff $1,043,434.33 as a refund of partial payments made, $60,000 as liquidated damages for delay and prejudgment interest of $223,138.78; a total of $1,326,573.20. No issue is raised on computation of these damages. . . .

III.

We turn next to the merits of summary judgment in favor of plaintiff based on the theory that defendants should bear the risk of loss for the destruction of the simulator. . . .

To evaluate the risk of loss issue, attention must be given to the impact of both the Uniform Commercial Code and the contract terms.

Section 2–510 of the Code (Ill.Rev.Stat.1977, ch. 26, par. 2–510(1)), provides:

> (1) Where a tender or delivery of goods so fails to conform to the contract as to give a right of rejection the risk of their loss remains on the seller until cure or acceptance.

Few cases involve this section of the Code and those that do merely cite the Code with little explanation. ... The official Uniform Commercial Code Comment provides some guidance by stating that the purpose of this section is to make clear that "the seller by his individual action cannot shift the risk of loss to the buyer unless his action conforms with all the conditions resting on him under the contract." (S.H.A. ch. 26, par. 2–510(1) at page 398.) Of primary importance, then, is the determination of whether or not the simulator so failed to conform to the contract provisions as to vest the right of rejection in plaintiff and whether or not there was acceptance of the simulator by plaintiff.

The purchase agreement provided in part that the simulator would "accurately and faithfully simulate the configuration and performance of ..." a certain specified Boeing aircraft and that final acceptance of the simulator would be "subject to satisfactory completion of the reliability demonstration requirements ..." and to Federal Aviation Administration certification. The affidavit of John Darley, an employee of plaintiff who tests and evaluates flight simulators to determine whether they meet plaintiff's and the FAA specifications, states that the simulator at no time met those requirements and that plaintiff was never able to begin acceptance testing. His affidavit states clearly that the machine was destroyed by fire "before that time when United [plaintiff] was to begin acceptance testing ... ." The affidavit of Phil C. Christy, employed by plaintiff as a technical assistant regarding simulators, reaffirms that as late as February 1969 there were "numerous discrepancies" in the operation of the simulator. These affidavits stand uncontradicted by counteraffidavit. Therefore they "are admitted and must be taken as true." ... On February 23, 1977, J.M. Gardner, Director of Contracts & Pricing for defendant McDonnell Douglas Electronics Company wrote a letter to plaintiff's attorney in which he stated that the simulator was "destroyed prior to final acceptance."

Defendants contend that Change Order Number 3, which provided for delivery of the simulator at plaintiff's training center in Denver, resulted in waiver of plaintiff's right to object to predelivery nonconformities. We reject this contention. The Change Order simply provides that the testing and inspection, which under the original agreement would have occurred at defendants' plant, would take place in Denver. Sections of the original agreement which provide that delivery does not constitute acceptance remain unchanged by this Change Order Number 3. Also, the language of the Change Order that testing and inspection would be completed in Denver and that the seller would have access to the simulator to demonstrate compliance are inconsistent with the idea that plaintiff had waived the right to object to nonconformity of the simulator.

Defendants do not contest the fact that there were technical difficulties with the simulator, as evidenced by the hundreds of discrepancy reports, actually 645, prepared by plaintiff's employees during the testing period. Instead, defendants stress the complex nature of the device and urge that plaintiff accepted the simulator despite its manifest deficiencies. In support of this contention defendants look to the six week period of inspection of the simulator in Denver and cite Uniform Commercial Code section 2–606 (Ill.Rev.Stat.1977, ch. 26, par. 2–606), which provides:

Acceptance of goods occurs when the buyer

(a) after a reasonable opportunity to inspect the goods signifies to the seller that the goods are conforming or that he will take or retain them in spite of their non-conformity; or

(b) fails to make an effective rejection (subsection (1) of Section 2–602), but such acceptance does not occur until the buyer has had a reasonable opportunity to inspect them; or

(c) does any act inconsistent with the seller's ownership; but if such act is wrongful as against the seller it is an acceptance only if ratified by him.

Defendants thus wish this court to hold that plaintiff had a reasonable opportunity to inspect the simulator and to reject it prior to its destruction. This approach completely ignores the terms of the contract. The purpose of the Uniform Commercial Code is set forth in section 1–102 (Ill.Rev.Stat.1977, ch. 26, par. 1–102), which states that the provisions of the act may be varied by agreement. This court expressed the same principle in First Bank & Trust Co., Palatine v. Post (1973), 10 Ill.App.3d 127, 131, 293 N.E.2d 907, 910, where we stated:

[t]he Uniform Commercial Code was enacted to provide a general uniformity in commercial transactions conducted in this state and was never intended to be used by courts to create a result that is contrary to the clearly understood intentions of the original parties.

The clear intent of the parties before this court, as stated in the purchase agreement, was that physical delivery of the simulator and payments received by the defendants were not to constitute acceptance of the simulator. Acceptance was to be predicated on successful completion of acceptance testing and also upon receipt of FAA certification. The contract terms definitely anticipated and sanctioned use of the simulator by plaintiff to enable it to determine whether this complex and expensive device met the contract specifications. If use of goods is necessary to allow proper evaluation of them, such use does not constitute acceptance. ...

This record shows that the simulator at no time conformed to the specifications agreed to in the purchase agreement and it remained nonconforming until its destruction. Although plaintiff had use and possession of the simulator for six weeks that arrangement was expressly sanctioned by the contract to allow testing. Retention of the simulator for testing purposes did not constitute acceptance so as to shift the risk of loss to the plaintiff. The simulator was destroyed before completion of acceptance testing and before receipt of FAA certification. Both were conditions precedent to acceptance of the simulator. In this situation the risk of loss remained on the defendants as seller. On the issue of risk of loss, there is no genuine issue regarding any material fact. On the contrary, in our opinion, plaintiff's right to summary judgment in this regard is clear beyond question. We conclude that the plaintiff is entitled to summary judgment as a matter of law....

Judgment affirmed.

Notes

(1) **Risk of Loss After Buyers Have Received Goods.** Assuming that UCC 2–509(3) governs passage of the risk of loss on the facts of *United Air Lines*, the merchant-seller provision provides that risk passes to the buyer on "receipt of the goods." "Receipt" means "taking physical possession" of goods. UCC 2–103. Without referring to UCC 2–509, the court analyzed the case not in terms of buyer's receipt of the simulator, but in terms of buyer's acceptance of it. On what basis could the court determine that risk of loss remained upon sellers until buyer accepted the simulator? Should UCC 2–509(3) be read to mean that risk of loss passes to a buyer only upon receipt of *conforming* goods? See the caption to UCC 2–509 and UCC 1–109.

The court in *United Air Lines* based its opinion on UCC 2–510(1). Does this section apply to the facts of that case? When Conductron delivered the simulator to United Air Lines pursuant to Change Order Number 3, did the parties expect that it would conform to the contract requirements? Was Conductron then in breach? Was Conductron in breach when the fire occurred on April 18? If Conductron was not in breach, is UCC 2–510 pertinent? (We consider UCC 2–510 further after the following case.)

If neither UCC 2–509(3) nor UCC 2–510(1) is applicable, what risk of loss rule does apply?

(2) **Alternative Analysis Under UCC 2–711(1).** Why should risk-of-loss analysis be used at all in a case like *United Air Lines*? Buyer seeks to recover so much of the price as has been paid plus damages, remedies available under UCC 2–711(1) "where the seller fails to make delivery ... or the buyer rightfully rejects [the goods]." United Air Lines would not accept the fire-damaged simulator; if Conductron tendered the simulator in that condition, United Air Lines would

certainly reject it. If Conductron fails to tender a conforming simulator within the time permitted under the contract, it will have failed to make delivery. Is application of UCC 2–711(1) affected by risk-of-loss rules?

Problem 3. B agreed to buy a mobile home of S. In accordance with the agreement, S put the mobile home in place on B's lot and made the sewer and gas connections. B moved into the home. S had not yet made the furnace and electrical hook-ups when a gas explosion and an ensuing fire destroyed the mobile home. Who bears the loss? See Southland Mobile Home Corp. v. Chyrchel, 255 Ark. 366, 500 S.W.2d 778 (1973); William F. Wilke, Inc. v. Cummins Diesel Engines, Inc., 252 Md. 611, 250 A.2d 886 (1969).

Problem 4. The S Chevrolet Company delivered a car to B under a "Conditional Sales Contract." B paid S $700 in cash and in the contract agreed to pay the balance of $1500 in 15 monthly installments. The contract provided that S held a security interest in the car which S could exercise to enforce its right to receive payment. In addition, the contract provided:

> It is expressly understood and agreed that the title to the above-described automobile shall remain in the seller until the aforesaid sums of money shall be paid as herein provided, and that the seller may at any time, either personally or by agent, using so much force as is necessary, enter in or upon the premises where said automobile may be, with or without the issuance of any writ of replevin, and take possession of said automobile on default in any of the payments herein provided or on failure to comply with one or all of the conditions of this contract.

A month after delivery, the car is wrecked beyond repair without any fault by B. Must he continue to make the payments to S? Does the language of the Conditional Sales Contract evidence an intent by the parties to exercise their power, under UCC 1–102(3), to vary by agreement the Code's rules on risk of loss? Can the policy of the Code be drawn, by analogy, from UCC 2–505, 2–509(1)(a), 1–201(37) (second sentence)? What, apart from constructional aids in the statute, is the most sensible reading of this language? (In actual practice, unless there has been some mishap in the drafting, printing or assembling of the form, the contract will say in so many words that the buyer bears all casualty risks.)

––––––

RON MEAD T.V. & APPLIANCE v. LEGENDARY HOMES, INC.

Oklahoma Court of Appeals, Division Three, 1987.
746 P.2d 1163.

HANSEN, PRESIDING JUDGE. Plaintiff, Ron Mead, is a retail merchant selling household appliances. Defendant, Legendary Homes, is a home builder. Defendant purchased appliances from Plaintiff for installation in one of its homes. The appliances were to be delivered on February 1, 1984. At five o'clock on that day the appliances had not been delivered. Defendant closed the home and left. Sometime between five and six-thirty Plaintiff delivered the appliances. No one was at the home so the deliveryman put the appliances in the garage. During the night someone stole the appliances.

Defendant denied it was responsible for the loss and refused to pay Plaintiff for the appliances. This suit resulted.

After a non-jury trial the court issued a "Memorandum Opinion" finding § 2–509 of the Uniform Commercial Code, 12A O.S. 1981 controlled. This section provides: "The risk of loss passes to the Buyer on his receipt of the goods." The trial court found Defendant had not received the goods, thus the risk of loss remained with Plaintiff. Plaintiff appeals the judgment rendered in favor of Defendant....

Plaintiff ... submits the trial court erred in concluding Plaintiff did not establish usage of trade in leaving appliances unattended at a building site. The trial court found the record was void of any evidence which would show the method of delivery used by Plaintiff was pursuant to a "course of dealing" between the parties which would waive or excuse the requirements of 12A O.S. 1981 § 2–503.

Section 1–205(2) defines "usage of trade" as any "practice or method of dealing having such regularity of observance in a place, vocation or trade as to justify an expectation that it will be observed with respect to the transaction in question." Although there was testimony some builders allow deliveries to be made to unattended job sites, nothing indicated such practice was uniformly observed after working hours unless specifically agreed to by the parties.

Although there was conflicting testimony between witnesses whether Defendant advised Plaintiff to deliver the appliances before noon, nothing appears in the record to indicate there was any agreement the appliances would be accepted after hours.

Section 2–103 defines "receipt" of goods as taking physical possession of them. We agree with the trial court "(t)he act by the deliveryman of placing the goods in an unlocked garage, in a house under construction, and then locking the door did not give the Buyer the opportunity to take physical possession (of them)."

Credibility of witnesses and weight and value to be given to their testimony is for the trial court on waiver of a jury, and conclusions there reached will not be disturbed on appeal, unless appearing clearly to be based upon caprice or to be without any reasonable foundation. Accordingly, the trial court is affirmed.

Notes

(1) Basis of the Decision: Analytical Confusion. The problem presented in this case can be analyzed in three ways: under the Code's rules for tender of delivery or under the Code's two rules allocating risk of loss. The Oklahoma courts, and presumably the lawyers arguing the case, did not resolve which of these standards they were applying.

If seller had not made a tender of delivery, buyer had no duty to pay the price. UCC 2–507(1). Seller tried and failed to establish a course of dealing or trade usage that permitted tender of delivery by the method it employed. Thus, buyer's duty to pay the price never matured.

Alternatively, the case can be analyzed under the risk of loss rules in UCC 2–509(3). Since seller unquestionably was a merchant, risk of loss would pass only on receipt of the goods. The appellate court, citing UCC 2–103, concludes that "receipt" had not occurred. Seller's action for the price depends on risk of loss passing. ⁊CC 2–709(1)(a). Absent receipt, risk of loss did not pass, and the price action must fail.

A third line of analysis has been offered:

> Although the court manages to properly conclude that the risk of loss had not passed to the buyer, it does so despite misapplication of the Code's risk of loss provisions. Both the trial court and the court of appeals incorrectly cited section 2–509 as the controlling section. Because of the improper tender by the seller, the risk of loss issue in this case should have been resolved by application of section 2–510(1). Regardless of whether the goods have been received, under section 2–510(1) the buyer does not bear risk of loss where the tender is so nonconforming as to give a right of rejection. . . . One must wonder how this case would have ended if, all other things being the same, the court had decided that the buyer had received the goods. In view of the court's apparent ignorance of both section 2–510 and the immateriality of the possession issue, it would seem that, notwithstanding the defective tender, the seller would have wrongfully prevailed.

Frisch & Wladis, Uniform Commercial Code Annual Survey: General Provisions, Sales, Bulk Transfers, and Documents of Title, 44 Bus. Law. 1445, 1467 (1989).

(*Query*: Which, if any, of these lines of analysis is correct?)

(2) Proposed Repeal of UCC 2–510. The Permanent Editorial Board Study Group on Article 2 found numerous flaws in UCC 2–51ʋ and recommended that it be repealed. Preliminary Report 149 (1990). The Study Group noted that the section requires no showing of any causal connection between the breach and the loss and may allocate risk from the party in the best position to insure the goods to the party who is not. Moreover, the Study Group declared, the section is "complex, incomplete and difficult to apply." Id. See also Howard, Allocation of Risk of Loss Under the UCC: A Transactional Evaluation of §§ 2–509 and 2–510, 15 U.C.C.L.J. 334 (1983).

(3) Sellers' Price Action. The remedy sought in *Ron Mead* was the contract price for the appliances. On what basis could seller seek to recover the price of the stolen appliances? See UCC 2–709(1)(a). Could seller argue successfully that it was entitled to the price on the ground that the appliances were "conforming goods" even though the manner of their tender did not conform to the contract?

MULTIPLASTICS, INC. v. ARCH INDUSTRIES, INC.

Supreme Court of Connecticut, 1974.
166 Conn. 280, 348 A.2d 618.

BOGDANSKI, J. The plaintiff, Multiplastics, Inc., brought this action to recover damages from the defendant, Arch Industries, Inc., for the breach of a contract to purchase 40,000 pounds of plastic pellets. From a judgment rendered for the plaintiff, the defendant has appealed to this court.

The facts may be summarized as follows: The plaintiff, a manufacturer of plastic resin pellets, agreed with the defendant on June 30, 1971, to manufacture and deliver 40,000 pounds of brown polystyrene plastic pellets for nineteen cents a pound. The pellets were specially made for the defendant, who agreed to accept delivery at the rate of 1000 pounds per day after completion of production. The defendant's confirming order contained the notation "make and hold for release. Confirmation." The plaintiff produced the order of pellets within two weeks and requested release orders from the defendant. The defendant refused to issue the release orders, citing labor difficulties and its vacation schedule. On August 18, 1971, the plaintiff sent the defendant the following letter: "Against P.O. 0946, we produced 40,000 lbs. of brown high impact styrene, and you have issued no releases. You indicated to us that you would be using 1,000 lbs. of each per day. We have warehoused these products for more than forty days, as we agreed to do. However, we cannot warehouse these products indefinitely, and request that you send us shipping instructions. We have done everything we agreed to do." After August 18, 1971, the plaintiff made numerous telephone calls to the defendant to seek payment and delivery instructions. In response, beginning August 20, 1971, the defendant agreed to issue release orders but in fact never did.

On September 22, 1971, the plaintiff's plant, containing the pellets manufactured for the defendant, was destroyed by fire. The plaintiff's fire insurance did not cover the loss of the pellets. The plaintiff brought this action against the defendant to recover the contract price.

The trial court concluded that the plaintiff made a valid tender of delivery by its letter of August 18, 1971, and by its subsequent requests for delivery instructions; that the defendant repudiated and breached the contract by refusing to accept delivery on August 20, 1971; that the period from August 20, 1971, to September 22, 1971, was not a commercially unreasonable time for the plaintiff to treat the risk of loss as resting on the defendant under General Statutes § 42a–2–510(3), and that the plaintiff was entitled to recover the contract price plus interest.

General Statutes § 42a–2–510, entitled "Effect of breach on risk of loss," reads, in pertinent part, as follows: "(3) Where the buyer as to conforming goods already identified to the contract for sale repudiates or is otherwise in breach before risk of their loss has passed to him, the seller may to the extent of any deficiency in his effective insurance coverage treat the risk of loss as resting on the buyer for a commercially reasonable time." The defendant contends that § 42a–2–510 is not applicable because its failure to issue delivery instructions did not constitute either a repudiation or a breach of the agreement. The defendant also argues that even if § 42a–2–510 were applicable, the period from August 20, 1971, to September 22, 1971, was not a commercially reasonable period of time within which to treat the risk of loss as resting on the buyer. The defendant does not claim that the destroyed pellets were not "conforming goods already identified to the contract for sale," as required by General Statutes § 42a–2–510(3), nor does it protest the computation of damages. With regard to recovery of the price of goods and incidental damages, see General Statutes § 42a–2–709(1)(a).

The trial court's conclusion that the defendant was in breach is supported by its finding that the defendant agreed to accept delivery of the pellets at the rate of 1000 pounds per day after completion of production. The defendant argues that since the confirming order instructed the defendant to "make and hold for release," the contract did not specify an exact delivery date. This argument fails, however, because nothing in the finding suggests that the notation in the confirming order was part of the agreement between the parties. Since, as the trial court found, the plaintiff made a proper tender of delivery, beginning with its letter of August 18, 1971, the plaintiff was entitled to acceptance of the goods and to payment according to the contract. General Statutes §§ 42a–2–507(1), 42a–2–307.

The defendant argues that its failure to issue delivery instructions did not suffice to repudiate the contract because repudiation of an executory promise requires, first, an absolute and unequivocal renunciation by the promisor, and, second, an unambiguous acceptance of the repudiation by the promisee. ... Anticipatory repudiation is now governed by General Statutes §§ 42a–2–609 to 42a–2–611, which in some respects alter the prior law on the subject. The present case does not involve repudiation of an executory promise, however, since the defendant breached the contract by failing to accept the goods when acceptance became due.

The defendant next claims that the plaintiff acquiesced in the defendant's refusal to accept delivery by continuing to urge compliance with the contract and by failing to pursue any of the remedies provided aggrieved sellers by General Statutes § 42a–2–703. In essence, the defendant's argument rests on the doctrines of waiver and estoppel, which are available defenses under the Uniform Commercial Code. General Statutes §§ 42a–1–103, 42a–1–107, 42a–2–209; Mercanti v. Persson, 160 Conn. 468, 477–79, 280 A.2d 137 . . . . The defendant has not, however, shown those defenses to apply. Waiver is the intentional relinquishment of a known right. . . . Its existence is a question of fact for the trier. . . . The trial court did not find that the plaintiff intentionally acquiesced in the defendant's breach of their agreement, thereby waiving its right to take advantage of that breach. Indeed, the plaintiff's repeated attempts to secure compliance seem inconsistent with the possibility of waiver. . . .

Nor has the defendant made out a case of estoppel. "The two essential elements of estoppel are that 'one party must do or say something which is intended or calculated to induce another to believe in the existence of certain facts and to act on that belief; and the other party, influenced thereby, must change his position or do some act to his injury which he otherwise would not have done.' Dickau v. Glastonbury, 156 Conn. 437, 441, 242 A.2d 777; Pet Car Products, Inc. v. Barnett, 150 Conn. 42, 53, 184 A.2d 797." Mercanti v. Persson, supra, 477. Neither element of estoppel is present in the record of this case. The plaintiff's requests for delivery instructions cannot be said to have misled the defendant into thinking that the plaintiff did not consider their contract breached. In fact, General Statutes § 42a–2–610, entitled "Anticipatory repudiation," specifically provides that the aggrieved seller may "resort to any remedy for breach as provided by section 42a–2–703 . . ., even though he has notified the repudiating party that he would await the latter's performance and has urged retraction." Although the present case is not governed by General Statutes § 42a–2–610, that section does demonstrate that the plaintiff's conduct after the defendant refused to accept delivery was not inconsistent with his claim that the contract was breached.

The remaining question is whether, under General Statutes § 42a–2–510(3), the period of time from August 20, 1971, the date of the breach, to September 22, 1971, the date of the fire, was a "commercially reasonable" period within which to treat the risk of loss as resting on the buyer. The trial court concluded that it was "not, on the facts in this case, a commercially unreasonable time," which we take to mean that it was a commercially reasonable period. The time limitation in § 42a–2–510(3) is designed to enable the seller to obtain the additional requisite insurance coverage. . . . The trial court's conclusion is tested by the finding. . . . Although the finding is not detailed, it supports the conclusion that August 20 to September 22 was a commercially reasonable period within which to place the risk of loss on the defendant. As already stated, the trial court found that the defendant repeatedly agreed to transmit delivery instructions and that the pellets were specially made to fill the defendant's order. Under those circumstances, it was reasonable for the plaintiff to believe that the goods would soon be taken off its hands and so to forego procuring the needed insurance.

We consider it advisable to discuss one additional matter. The trial court concluded that "title" passed to the defendant, and the defendant attacks the conclusion on this appeal. The issue is immaterial to this case. General Statutes § 42a–2–401 states: "Each provision of this article with regard to the rights, obligations and remedies of the seller, the buyer, purchasers or other third parties applies irrespective of title to the goods except where the provision refers to such title." As one student of the Uniform Commercial Code has written: "The single most important innovation of Article 2[of the Uniform Commercial Code] is its restatement of ... [the parties'] responsibilities in terms of operative facts rather than legal conclusions; where pre-Code law looked to 'title' for the definition of rights and remedies, the Code looks to demonstrable realities such as custody, control and professional expertise. This shift in approach is central to the whole philosophy of Article 2. It means that disputes, as they arise, can focus, as does all of the modern law of contracts, upon actual provable circumstances, rather than upon a metaphysical concept of elastic and endlessly fluid dimensions." Peters, "Remedies for Breach of Contracts Relating to the Sale of Goods Under the Uniform Commercial Code: A Roadmap for Article Two," 73 Yale L.J. 199, 201.

There is no error.

In this opinion the other judges concurred.

(B) INTERNATIONAL SALES LAW

Two-party transactions may occur in international sales. The Convention on International Sale of Goods establishes risk of loss rules for this type transaction in Article 69. The general principle is that risk passes when a buyer "takes over the goods." CISG 69(1). This phrase is more clear in its connotation of positive buyer action than is the Code's "receipt." Recall, for example, the conceptual difficulty posed in the *United Air Lines* case. Moreover the Convention standard applies to all sellers. The Convention does not contemplate non-merchant sellers.

The Convention also addresses the possibility that buyers, having opportunity to do so, will fail to "take over" goods. Although the Convention does not generally use the concepts of tender of delivery, it incorporates a similar idea here only for the purpose of allocating risk of loss to such buyers. Risk of loss thus remains on sellers until buyers' failure to take over goods placed at their disposal is breach of contract.

The Convention explicitly relates buyers' duty to pay to the risk of loss rules. Buyers' duty to pay is not discharged if casualty or loss occurs after risk of loss has passed. CISG 66. An inference can be drawn that payment obligations are discharged if risk of loss had not passed.[3] The Convention has no counterpart provision that relates sellers' duty to deliver to the rules of risk of loss. However, the Convention provides broadly that sellers (and buyers) may not be liable for failures to perform if the failures were due to impediments beyond their control. CISG 79.[4]

Problem 5. On June 1, Seller handed over goods to Buyer. Buyer's inspection on June 2 disclosed that the goods were not in conformity with the contract. On June 3 a fire in Buyer's warehouse injured the goods.

(a) Buyer claims damages from Seller for the non-conformity of the goods and for the injury to the goods. What result under CISG? See CISG 36(1), 69(1), 74.

(b) Buyer contends that the non-conformity was so substantial as to constitute a fundamental breach and, on June 4, declares the contract avoided. Assuming that Buyer is correct in characterizing the non-conformity as a fundamental breach, to what remedies is Buyer entitled under CISG? See CISG 70, 81, 84. See also J. Honnold, Uniform Law for International Sales § 383 (2d ed. 1991).

SECTION 3. CASUALTY DURING SHIPMENT

(A) DOMESTIC SALES LAW

Introduction. In many sales transactions, sellers are authorized or required to ship goods to buyers via carriers. While en route, goods may of course suffer loss or damage. The principal subject in this Section is the allocation of risk of such losses between sellers and buyers. A subordinate question is the extent of the carriers' liability for goods that suffer casualty while in their possession.

Shipment and Destination Contracts. Sales contracts that contemplate delivery of goods by carrier are generally characterized as place-of-shipment or at-a-particular-destination contracts. In the former, the cost of transportation is borne by the buyer; in the latter, freight charges are paid by seller. Risk of loss is allocated in the same characterization. UCC 2–509(1).

Under UCC 2–319, sales contracts that use the F.O.B. term are shipment contracts if the term is F.O.B. the place of shipment; seller bears the risk of putting the goods into the carrier's possession. UCC 2–319(1)(a). Risk passes when the goods are duly delivered to the

---

3. Under CISG 66, a buyer is discharged from the obligation to pay the price if the loss or damage is due to an act or omission of the seller.

4. CISG 79 adds other conditions that sellers must meet to be protected from liability.

carrier. UCC 2–509(1)(a). Conversely, if the contract term is F.O.B. the place of destination, seller must at its own risk transport the goods to that place. UCC 2–319(1)(b). Risk passes when the goods are there duly tendered. UCC 2–509(1)(b).

Shipping terms commonly associated with water transport pose difficult problems for risk of loss. Even though the price includes the cost of transportation, sellers expressly bear the risk of putting the goods into the carriers' possession, loading the goods on board, or delivering them alongside a vessel, as the terms require. UCC 2–319(1)(b) and (2), 2–320(2) and (3). Contracts that use the terms F.O.B. vessel or F.A.S. can be recognized as shipment contracts; thus the risk passing provision of UCC 2–509(1)(a) applies. However contracts that use the terms C.I.F. and C. & F. cannot easily be characterized as shipment contracts. Nor is it plausible to construe them as destination contracts with risk passing at the place of destination.[1] A different result follows if the term used is "delivery ex-ship." UCC 2–322.

Risk of loss and contract performance problems tend to arise when sales contracts are ambiguous as to whether they are shipment or destination contracts.

Problem 1. Seller Manufacturing Company, in Sellersville, Pennsylvania, has distributed a catalogue giving descriptions and prices for a line of garden tractors which Seller makes and sells. Buyer Garden Supply Company, in Birmingham, Alabama, an enterprise with stores in various cities in Alabama, wired Seller, "Please ship to us in Birmingham, 10 Garden Tractors, Catalogue No. 103X, priced at $1,430 each." Seller replied: "Order accepted. Tractors being shipped this week." Neither the catalogue nor the correspondence dealt with methods or costs of delivery.

Seller promptly hauled the 10 garden tractors in his truck to the freight station of the Conrail Railroad in Sellersville and delivered them to the freight agent in the freight yards. Seller received a "straight" (non-negotiable) bill of lading providing that the goods were "Consigned to Buyer Garden Supply Co., Birmingham, Ala." Freight costs of $310 were noted on the bill of lading as "C.O.D." (Collect on Delivery).

One of the tractors was stolen from the Conrail freight yard in Sellersville. Another was damaged in a freight car en route to Birmingham.

(a) Buyer paid for eight tractors, but refused to pay for the tractor that was stolen or for the damaged tractor. Seller sues for the price of the two tractors. Buyer interposes all available defenses to the price action and, in addition, counterclaims for the freight costs of $610 which he had to pay the railroad in order to receive delivery of the

---

1. The Code provision on the C.I.F. term imposes a duty on sellers to contract for casualty insurance for the benefit of the buyers. UCC 2–320(2)(c).

tractors. What result? See UCC 2–509, 2–504, 2–709(1)(a); *Pestana v. Karinol Corporation*, infra.

(b) Suppose Seller's truck had overturned and burned while the tractors were being taken from Seller's factory to the freight yards. May Seller recover the price for the tractors destroyed by fire?

PESTANA v. KARINOL CORP.

District Court of Appeal of Florida, Third District, 1979.
367 So.2d 1096.

HUBBART, JUDGE. This is an action for damages based on a contract for the sale of goods. The defendant seller and others prevailed in this action after a non-jury trial in the Circuit Court for the Eleventh Judicial Circuit of Florida. The plaintiff buyer appeals.

The central issue presented for review is whether a contract for the sale of goods, which stipulates the place where the goods sold are to be sent by carrier but contains (a) no explicit provisions allocating the risk of loss while the goods are in the possession of the carrier and (b) no delivery terms such as F.O.B. place of destination, is a shipment contract or a destination contract under the Uniform Commercial Code. We hold that such a contract, without more, constitutes a shipment contract wherein the risk of loss passes to the buyer when the seller duly delivers the goods to the carrier under a reasonable contract of carriage for shipment to the buyer. Accordingly, we affirm.

A

The critical facts of this case are substantially undisputed. On March 4, 1975, Nahim Amar B. [the plaintiff Pedro P. Pestana's decedent herein] who was a resident of Mexico entered into a contract through his authorized representative with the Karinol Corporation [the defendant herein] which is an exporting company licensed to do business in Florida and operating out of Miami. The terms of this contract were embodied in a one page invoice written in Spanish and prepared by the defendant Karinol. By the terms of this contract, the plaintiff's Amar agreed to purchase 64 electronic watches from the defendant Karinol for $6,006. A notation was printed at the bottom of the contract which, translated into English, reads as follows: "Please send the merchandise in cardboard boxes duly strapped with metal bands via air parcel post to Chetumal. Documents to Banco de Commercio De Quintano Roo S.A." There were no provisions in the contract which specifically allocated the risk of loss on the goods sold while in the possession of the carrier; there were also no F.O.B., F.A.S., C.I.F. or C & F terms contained in the contract. See §§ 672.319, 672.320, Fla.Stat. (1977). A 25% downpayment on the purchase price of the goods sold was made prior to shipment.

On April 11, 1975, there is sufficient evidence, although disputed, that the defendant Karinol delivered the watches in two cartons to its agent American International Freight Forwarders, Inc. [the second defendant herein] for forwarding to the plaintiff's decedent Amar. The defendant American insured the two cartons with Fidelity & Casualty Company of New York [the third defendant herein] naming the defendant Karinol as the insured. The defendant American as freight forwarder strapped the cartons in question with metal bands and delivered them to TACA International Airlines consigned to one Bernard Smith, a representative of the plaintiff's decedent, in Belize City, Belize, Central America. The shipment was arranged by Karinol in this manner in accord with a prior understanding between the parties as there were no direct flights from Miami, Florida to Chetumal, Mexico. Mr. Smith was to take custody of the goods on behalf of the plaintiff's decedent in Belize and arrange for their transport by truck to the plaintiff's decedent Amar in Chetumal, Mexico.

On April 15, 1975, the cartons arrived by air in Belize City and were stored by the airline in the customs and air freight cargo room. Mr. Smith was duly notified and thereupon the plaintiff's decedent made payment on the balance due under the contract to the defendant Karinol. On May 2, 1975, Mr. Smith took custody of the cartons after a certain delay was experienced in transferring the cartons to a customs warehouse. Either on that day or shortly thereafter, the cartons were opened by Mr. Smith and customs officials as was required for clearance prior to the truck shipment to Chetumal, Mexico. There were no watches contained in the cartons. The defendant Karinol and its insurance carrier the defendant Fidelity were duly notified, but both eventually refused to make good on the loss.

The plaintiff Pedro P. Pestana, as representative of the Estate of Nahim Amar B., deceased, filed suit against the defendant Karinol as the seller, the defendant American as Karinol's agent freight forwarder, and the defendant Fidelity as the defendant Karinol's insurer. The complaint alleged that the defendant Karinol entered into a contract to ship merchandise from Miami, Florida to Chetumal, Mexico with the plaintiff's decedent, that the defendant American as freight forwarder and agent of the defendant Karinol accepted shipment of such merchandise, that the merchandise was lost, stolen or misplaced while in the care and custody of the defendant Karinol and the defendant American, that the defendants Karinol and American failed to make delivery to the plaintiff's decedent at Chetumal, Mexico, and that there existed a liability policy with the defendant Fidelity for the benefit of the plaintiff's decedent. The complaint sought damages together with court costs and reasonable attorneys fees. All the defendants duly filed answers to the complaint wherein liability was denied. The defendant Karinol filed a cross-complaint against the defendant American. The trial court after a non-jury trial found for all of the defendants in this cause. This appeal follows.

B

There are two types of sales contracts under Florida's Uniform Commercial Code wherein a carrier is used to transport the goods sold: a shipment contract and a destination contract. A shipment contract is considered the normal contract in which the seller is required to send the subject goods by carrier to the buyer but is not required to guarantee delivery thereof at a particular destination. Under a shipment contract, the seller, unless otherwise agreed, must: (1) put the goods sold in the possession of a carrier and make a contract for their transportation as may be reasonable having regard for the nature of the goods and other attendant circumstances, (2) obtain and promptly deliver or tender in due form any document necessary to enable the buyer to obtain possession of the goods or otherwise required by the agreement or by usage of the trade, and (3) promptly notify the buyer of the shipment. On a shipment contract, the risk of loss passes to the buyer when the goods sold are duly delivered to the carrier for shipment to the buyer. §§ 672.503 (Official U.C.C. comment 5), 672.504, 672.509(1), Fla.Stat. (1977). ...

A destination contract, on the other hand, is considered the variant contract in which the seller specifically agrees to deliver the goods sold to the buyer at a particular destination and to bear the risk of loss of the goods until tender of delivery. This can be accomplished by express provision in the sales contract to that effect or by the use of delivery terms such as F.O.B. (place of destination). Under a destination contract, the seller is required to tender delivery of the goods sold to the buyer at the place of destination. The risk of loss under such a contract passes to the buyer when the goods sold are duly tendered to the buyer at the place of destination while in the possession of the carrier so as to enable the buyer to take delivery. The parties must explicitly agree to a destination contract; otherwise the contract will be considered a shipment contract. §§ 672.319(1)(b), 672.503 (Official U.C.C. comment 5), 672.509(1), Fla.Stat. (1977) ... .

Where the risk of loss falls on the seller at the time the goods sold are lost or destroyed, the seller is liable in damages to the buyer for non-delivery unless the seller tenders a performance in replacement for the lost or destroyed goods. On the other hand, where the risk of loss falls on the buyer at the time the goods sold are lost or destroyed, the buyer is liable to the seller for the purchase price of the goods sold. White and Summers, Uniform Commercial Code 134 (1972).

C

In the instant case, we deal with the normal shipment contract involving the sale of goods. The defendant Karinol pursuant to this contract agreed to send the goods sold, a shipment of watches, to the plaintiff's decedent in Chetumal, Mexico. There was no specific provision in the contract between the parties which allocated the risk of loss on the goods sold while in transit. In addition, there were no delivery terms such as F.O.B. Chetumal contained in the contract.

All agree that there is sufficient evidence that the defendant Karinol performed its obligations as a seller under the Uniform Commercial Code if this contract is considered a shipment contract. Karinol put the goods sold in the possession of a carrier and made a contract for the goods safe transportation to the plaintiff's decedent; Karinol also promptly notified the plaintiff's decedent of the shipment and tendered to said party the necessary documents to obtain possession of the goods sold.

The plaintiff Pestana contends, however, that the contract herein is a destination contract in which the risk of loss on the goods sold did not pass until delivery on such goods had been tendered to him at Chetumal, Mexico—an event which never occurred. He relies for this position on the notation at the bottom of the contract between the parties which provides that the goods were to be sent to Chetumal, Mexico. We cannot agree. A "send to" or "ship to" term is a part of every contract involving the sale of goods where carriage is contemplated and has no significance in determining whether the contract is a shipment or destination contract for risk of loss purposes. ... As such, the "send to" term contained in this contract cannot, without more, convert this into a destination contract.

It therefore follows that the risk of loss in this case shifted to the plaintiff's decedent as buyer when the defendant Karinol as seller duly delivered the goods to the defendant freight forwarder American under a reasonable contract of carriage for shipment to the plaintiff's decedent in Chetumal, Mexico. The defendant Karinol, its agent the defendant American, and its insurer the defendant Fidelity could not be held liable to the plaintiff in this action. The trial court properly entered judgment in favor of all the defendants herein.

Affirmed.

Notes

(1) **Allocation of Freight Costs as Allocation of Risk of Loss.** If freight from Sellersville to Buyersville is $12 per ton, quotations of "$100 F.O.B. Sellersville," "$112 F.O.B. Buyersville," and "$112 F.O.B. Sellersville, freight allowed" all have the same effect with respect to the buyer's costs. However, the first and third allocate transit risk to the buyer, while the second allocates transit risk to the seller. It seems likely that the parties, in negotiating the contract, are more likely to concentrate on immediate cost and return factors rather than on the relatively unusual feature of risk of loss. Hence, there is ground for skepticism that choice among the above forms of quotation reflects an express agreement as to risk.

Price quotations that include freight may, on occasion, be employed to meet competition from a seller that is close to the buyer. If a seller wishes to be in a position to quote prices that include freight, but with transit risk allocated to the buyer, how could the order forms be structured? Would it be adequate to include a form clause dealing with risk of loss? Since negotiating agents cannot be expected to remember technical instructions, should the form include a special notation at the point where the price is to be inserted? What would you recommend?

(2) Policy Considerations Relevant to Risk Allocation Rules. Comment 5 to UCC 2–503 regards the "shipment" contract as normal and the "destination" contract as a variant. Under UCC 2–509(1) the "normal" shipment contract places transit risks on the buyer. Are there considerations of policy that bear on this result?

In considering risk allocation while the seller remains in possession, we asked whether the seller or the buyer has the better opportunity to guard against casualty and to insure against loss. Are these considerations significant in transportation cases? It has been suggested that the seller should bear transit loss since he is in a better position to select and bargain with the carrier. In evaluating this argument would it be relevant to inquire into the amenability of railways, truckers and ocean carriers to negotiate concerning the terms and conditions for transport?

Would it be relevant to consider which party can more readily cope with the consequences of transit damage? At which point in the transaction will transit damage be discovered? Is the seller or the buyer in a better position to salvage the goods, assess the damage, and press a claim against the carrier or insurer? Would the answer be the same for (a) raw materials, such as cotton shipped to a textile manufacturer and (b) a complex machine manufactured by the seller?

Note that considerations of policy as to who can most efficiently handle transit losses is relevant not only in the construction of ambiguous contracts but also in the process of negotiating and drafting contract provisions.

Problem 2. Seller agreed to sell Buyer an accumulation of brass scrap, with terms "f.o.b. Seller's city, payable by sight draft on arrival." Seller shipped and took a bill of lading running to "Seller or order." The brass was stolen during transit. Must Buyer pay the price? Does the fact that the bill of lading is a "document of *title*" and ran in Seller's name affect the risk of loss? See UCC 2–509(1)(a) ("even though the shipment is under reservation").

What considerations of policy underlie this result? (Suppose that the bill of lading is to be transferred to the buyer in exchange for payment while the goods are in transit.)

Problem 3. Seller in Seattle and Buyer in Boise made a contract calling for Seller to ship Buyer one hundred bags of "No. 1 Cane Sugar," F.O.B. Seattle. When the shipment was unloaded at Buyer's place of business Buyer inspected the sugar and immediately wired Seller "Sugar grades No. 2, will hold you responsible for reduced value of shipment." The next day the sugar was destroyed by a fire in the buyer's warehouse.

(a) On the above facts, who has risk of loss? See UCC 2–510(1), 2–606(1)(a).

(b) Suppose the buyer had wired: "Sugar grades No. 2. Will reject sugar unless you allow price reduction of 50 cents per hundredweight." If the casualty occurred before Seller replied, who would bear the risk?

Problem 4. Seller is a sugar refiner located in San Francisco; Buyer is a Boston candy manufacturer. Seller and Buyer made a contract for the sale to Buyer of 1000 tons of No. 1 beet sugar at $160 per ton. The contract terms were "C.I.F. Boston, ocean carriage via the Panama Canal. Shipment during June; payment 60 days after arrival of ship in Boston."

During the ocean voyage, water leaked into the hold and seriously damaged half of the sugar. On arrival Buyer noticed not only the water damage, but also concluded that the sugar had been poorly refined and that it contained excessive impurities, so that the sugar graded No. 2 and was unsuitable for use in making candy. The sugar undamaged by water would bring $110 per ton; the water-soaked sugar was worthless. Buyer rejected the entire shipment and refused to pay the price.

(a) Seller sues for the price, and claims that the sugar conformed to the contract when it was loaded on board in San Francisco. Seller also contends that, in any event, the loss from the water damage fell on the Buyer, and that the Buyer may not reject since he cannot return the goods to the Seller in the same condition as when risk of loss passed to the Buyer. What result? See UCC 2–320, 2–509, 2–510, 2–601, 2–709(1)(a).

(b) Assume that Seller delivered No. 1 sugar to the ocean carrier, but had completed delivery to the ship on July 3. As in the above problem, the sugar is seriously damaged in transit by ocean water. Seller sues Buyer for the price. What result?

Notes: Liability of Domestic U.S. Carriers

(1) **Rail and Truck.** Uniform bills of lading used by rail carriers in this country contain the following provision:

Sec. 1(a) The carrier or party in possession of any of property herein described shall be liable as at common law for any loss thereof or damage thereto, except as hereinafter provided.

(b) No carrier or party in possession of all or any part of the property herein described shall be liable for any loss thereof or damage thereto or delay caused by the Act of God, the public enemy, the authority of law, or the act or default of the shipper or owner, or for natural shrinkage. The carrier's liability shall be that of warehouseman, only, for loss, damage, or delay caused by fire occurring after the expiration of the free time allowed by tariffs lawfully on file (such free time to be computed as therein

provided) after notice of the arrival of the property at destination
or at the port of export (if intended for export) has been duly sent
or given, and after placement of the property for delivery at
destination, or tender of delivery of property to the party entitled
to receive it, has been made. Except in case of negligence of the
carrier or party in possession (and the burden to prove freedom
from such negligence shall be on the carrier or party in possession),
the carrier or party in possession shall not be liable for loss,
damage, or delay occurring while the property is stopped and held
in transit upon the request of the shipper, owner, or party entitled
to make such request, or resulting from a defect or vice in the
property, or for country damage to cotton, or from riots or strikes.

The liability "as at common law" to which the bill of lading refers
is one of absolute responsibility for the safety of the freight.[2]

The bills of lading issued by truck carriers employ the same
language as that quoted above, but add at the end exculpation from
liability for delay resulting from highway obstruction or impassability,
etc., unless the carrier is negligent.

A general *caveat* is necessary with respect to the dollar amount of
recovery. Examination of the bills of lading discloses the provision that
goods are

RECEIVED, subject to the classification and tariffs in effect on the
date of issue of this Bill of Lading.

The "classifications" are set forth in a thick book which lists the
myriads of things which may be hauled by a railroad, and classifies
them for rate purposes. These classifications are filed with the Interstate Commerce Commission and are part of the rate structure; the
carrier may not deviate from them, under penalty of the stern rules
against discrimination. Some of the items are classified under rates
with sharply limited liability. Owners of valuable goods have to their
dismay learned of these limitations buried in the book on freight
classification.

(2) **Air Carriers.** The liability of carriers of air freight for shipments within the United States has not been fully developed. The
problem is, however, minimized since the tariffs filed by domestic air
carriers with the Civil Aeronautics Board, which the airbills incorporate, assume virtually absolute liability, subject to a monetary limit
based on weight; responsibility for value exceeding the limit calls for
added charges.

Note: Insurers v. Carriers

As we have seen, the seller or the buyer may have insurance that
covers damage to the goods that occurs during transit. In cases where

---

2. See Guandolo, Transportation Law
934 (2d ed. 1973); Miller, Law of Freight
Loss and Damage Claims § 101 (2d ed.
1961). Carrier liability for human cargo is
lighter, and is limited to negligence. What
might explain the difference?

rules of law provide that the carrier is also responsible for the damage, interesting jockeying for position has occurred to determine whether the loss should fall ultimately on the insurer or on the carrier. The situation has been summarized by Professors Robert E. Keeton and Alan I. Widiss as follows:

Claims Against Common Carriers

For many years insurers and common carriers (such as truckers and railroads) engaged in an extended struggle with regard to the insurers' assertion of claims against carriers for damage to goods covered by insurance obtained by shippers. The following description of some main events in this struggle indicates the nature of the controversy and its relation to subrogation.

One of the early events in the conflict was the adoption by carriers of a bill-of-lading clause giving a carrier the benefit of insurance effected by a shipper. Insurers responded to this clause in the bill-of-lading with a policy clause providing for nonliability of an insurer upon shipment under a bill of lading that gave a carrier the benefit of a shipper's insurance. Since carriers then had nothing to gain and shippers had much to lose by retention of the clause previously used in bills of lading, the carriers modified the bill-of-lading clause to give a carrier the benefit of any insurance effected on the goods so far as this did not defeat the insurer's liability. This strategic retreat by the carriers still left the insurers with a problem. If an insurer paid a shipper, would it be a "volunteer" and therefore not entitled to subrogation to the shipper's claim against the carrier? If it did not pay the shipper, how could it maintain good business relations with an insured who wanted prompt payment from somebody and did not like waiting for the carrier and insurer to resolve a dispute as to ultimate responsibility for the loss? To avoid this problem, insurers resorted to loan receipts: an insurer paid a shipper an amount equal to the promised insurance benefits, but the transaction was cast as a loan repayable out of the prospective recovery from the carrier. The effectiveness of a loan receipt in preserving rights against a common carrier has been recognized in a number of judicial decisions. Thus, at least as reflected in such precedents, the insurers prevailed in the struggle with carriers over form provisions concerning responsibility for losses of insured property during shipment. And this result is also fortified by decisions that a "benefit of insurance" clause in a bill of lading is invalid under statutory prohibitions against rate discrimination, since a carrier would be receiving greater compensation from a shipper who had insurance than from one who did not.

R. Keeton & A. Widiss, Insurance Law 250–251 (1988).

(B) INTERNATIONAL SALES LAW

Introduction. Risk of loss rules for international sales are provided in Articles 67 and 68. Compare these articles with the provisions in UCC 2–509(1) and 2–510. See Berman & Ladd, Risk of Loss or Damage in Documentary Transactions Under the Convention on the International Sale of Goods, 21 Cornell Int'l L.J. 423 (1988).

Problem 5. In April, Continental entered into a contract with the Commodity Credit Corporation (C.C.C.), to sell cement to C.C.C. for delivery to Vietnam. The prices were quoted "CFR" Vietnam. Simultaneously with the signing of the contract, Continental entered into a contract with a company in Taiwan to supply the concrete; the Taiwanese supplier shipped the goods with States Marine Lines, Inc. On May 28, the shipping line announced that war risk surcharges would be added to freight costs; for this contract the surcharges amounted to $371,000. Who bears the burden of the surcharges?

Does CISG allocate the responsibility to purchase casualty insurance on goods in transit? If the sales contract incorporates *ICC Incoterms* (1990), use of the term, CFR,[3] (cost and freight to a named port of destination), means (p. 44):

> The seller must ... contract on usual terms at his own expense for the carriage of the goods to the named port of destination by the usual route in a seagoing vessel (or inland waterway vessel as appropriate) of the type normally used in the transport of goods of the contract description, [but seller has] no obligation [as to purchase of insurance]

If the parties use the term, CIF, *Incoterms* 1990 has a different set of sellers' obligations (pp. 50, 52):

> The seller must ... obtain at his own expense cargo insurance as agreed in the contract, that the buyer, or any other person having an insurable interest in the goods, shall be entitled to claim directly from the insurer and provide the buyer with the insurance policy or other evidence of insurance cover.
>
> The insurance shall be contracted with underwriters or an insurance company of good repute and, failing agreement to the contrary, be in accordance with the minimum cover of the Institute Cargo Clauses (Institute of London Underwriters) or any similar set of clauses. ... When required by the buyer, the seller shall provide at buyer's expense war, strikes, riots and civil commotion risk insurances if procurable. The minimum insurance shall cover the price provided in the contract plus ten per cent (i.e. 110%) and shall be provided in the currency of the contract.

3. *Incoterms* (1990) does not use the term, C. & F., found in UCC 2–320, 2–321. The ampersand, which could be replaced by an "A", would be confusing in international usage. In French, the English "insurance" translates to "assurance." Without knowing which language is implied, use of CAF creates unnecessary ambiguity. Thus the ICC uses CFR in lieu of C. & F.

Problem 6. Seller in San Francisco made a contract with Buyer in Bombay for the sale of a machine to Buyer. The contract included the provision: "Price $10,000. CIF Bombay." The machine was damaged during the ocean voyage. Who bears the risk of loss?

For purposes of applying CISG 67(1), is Seller "bound to hand [the goods] over at a particular place," i.e., Bombay? Compare CISG 31.

The matter is dealt with more clearly if the parties have incorporated the *ICC Incoterms* into their sales contracts. *Incoterms* (1990) specify when risk of loss passes in three categories of common shipping terms, which the ICC categorizes as "F" terms, "C" terms, and "D" terms. The "F" category are the terms in which the contract price does not include cost of carriage (e.g., FOB or FAS). In the "C" category are terms under which sellers must paid the costs of carriage (e.g., CFR and CIF). Under any of the "F" or the "C" terms of CFR and CIF, risk of loss passes at the time of shipment. A different result follows if the parties use other "C" terms, such as CPT (carriage paid to place of destination) or CIP (carriage and insurance paid to place of destination) or "D" terms, such as DES (delivered ex ship), DEQ (delivered ex quay), and DDP (delivered duty paid). Sellers bear risk of loss until the goods are delivered at the specified place.

Precision in Defining the Moment of Risk Passing. Loading and offloading goods pose special risks of damage to the goods in that process. Allocation of this risk of loss between buyer and seller requires precision in knowing exactly when risk passes.

In an FOB vessel contract, for example, risk passes when the goods pass the ship's rail. This traditional usage is retained in *ICC Incoterms* (1990) at 38. The same point is designated in CFR and CIF contracts. Id. at 46, 52. In an FAS contract, risk passes when the goods have been placed alongside the vessel on the quay or in lighters. Id. at 32.

Use of other terms puts the moment of risk passing when goods are delivered into the possession of carriers, including delivery to a terminal facility, e.g., FCA (free carrier). Id. at 26–28. In the "D" terms, sellers bear the risks of offloading under the term, DEQ (delivered ex quay), but not under DES (delivered ex ship). Id. at 74, 82.

RHEINBERG–KELLEREI GMBH v. VINEYARD WINE Co., 53 N.C.App. 560, 281 S.E.2d 425 (1981). Rheinberg, a West German wine importer, and Vineyard, a North Carolina wine distributor, made a contract for Rheinberg to sell 620 cases of wine to Vineyard. The contract called for Rheinberg to ship the wine to Vineyard, and on 29 November 1978 Rheinberg delivered a container containing the wine to a shipping company for shipment to Wilmington, Delaware, freight payable by Vineyard at destination. Early in December the shipment left Germany via the M.S. Munchen, which in mid-December was lost in the North Atlantic with all hands and cargo. The sales contract provided: "Insurance to be covered by purchaser." Rheinberg notified Sutton, its agent, of the shipment, and forwarded shipping documents to a correspondent bank in Charlotte, North Carolina. Vineyard received no notice of the shipment until after the ship and cargo had been lost.

Vineyard refused to pay for the wine, and Rheinberg sued for the price in a North Carolina court. The case was litigated under domestic United States law.

Judgment for the defendant was affirmed by the Court of Appeals. The transfer of risk of loss to buyer was negated by UCC 2–504(c) since the seller did not "promptly notify the buyer of the shipment." It would not be practical "to attempt to engraft into [2–504] a rigid definition of prompt notice ... which must be determined on a case-by-case basis, under all the circumstances." However, in this case Vineyard was not notified "within the time in which its interest could have been protected by insurance or otherwise"; the notice had not been "prompt."

Queries: The opinion did not discuss the ambiguities latent in the last phrase of UCC 2–504(c): "if material loss or delay *ensues*." On these facts, would loss have "ensued" from the failure to notify if the buyer was covered by insurance under a blanket policy? Or did loss "ensue" from the loss at sea of the ship and cargo? Who should have the burden to show that loss had "ensued"?

How would the case be decided if CISG were the applicable law?

Notes: Liability of Carriers in International Transport

(1) **Ocean Carriers.** The development of liability of ocean carriers is a story of sharp international bargaining; an early phase involved the conflict between British case-law enforcing standard bill of lading clauses that disclaimed carrier liability, and American case-law that invalidated clauses that exempted the carrier from responsibility for negligent loss or damage to cargo.

Attempts to solve the problem by international agreements at Liverpool in 1882 and at Hamburg in 1885 failed to satisfy American shipper interests. There ensued the so-called Harter Act, which was enacted by Congress in 1893, 46 U.S.C. §§ 190–195. This Act drew a distinction between the obligation of the carrier to "exercise due diligence to make the ... vessel in all respects seaworthy and properly manned, equipped and supplied" and the freedom from liability for "damage or loss resulting from faults or errors in navigation or in the management of said vessel. ..." Sections 1 and 2 limited the power to contract out of the responsibility which the Act imposed. Australia, Canada and New Zealand copied this legislation, but England kept its rules permitting further limitation of liability, even as applied to American bills of lading.

The Hague Rules. Further attempts for agreement finally culminated, at the Fifth International Conference on Maritime Law held in Brussels in 1924, in an international convention usually called the

"Hague Rules." The United States Government and many other countries signed this Convention. However, ratification by the United States Senate was delayed until 1936, and was then given in connection with the enactment by Congress of the Carriage of Goods by Sea Act, 1936, 46 U.S.C. §§ 1300–1315. This Act followed the language of the 1924 Brussels Convention, with a few minor modifications. The Brussels Convention has now been ratified by most of the important commercial countries. United States coastwise shipping (e.g., Seattle to San Diego) and some aspects of international shipping are subject to the Harter Act which, at significant points provides stronger legal protection for cargo. See Gilmore and Black, Admiralty 145 (2d ed. 1975).

One accustomed to the heavy responsibility of domestic rail carriers will be surprised at the rules which govern ocean carriers. For example, Article 4 the Brussels Convention (as embodied in Section 4(2) of the Carriage of Goods by Sea Act) sets forth a "catalogue" of seventeen grounds for exempting the carrier from liability. This article provides in part:

> Neither the carrier nor the ship shall be responsible for loss or damage arising or resulting from—
>
> (a) Act, neglect, or default of the master, mariner, pilot or the servants of the carrier in the navigation or in the management of the ship;
>
> (b) Fire, unless caused by the actual fault or privity of the carrier;
>
> (c) Perils, dangers, and accidents of the sea or other navigable waters; ..."

The Hamburg Rules. The special exemptions for the carrier in The Hague Rules of 1924 were virtually eliminated from the United Nations Convention on the Carriage of Goods by Sea, finalized in 1978 at Hamburg ("The Hamburg Rules"). For discussion and text of the Convention see Symposium, UNCITRAL's First Decade, 27 Am. J.Comp.L. 353–419 (discussion), 421–440 (text). The United States was one of the twenty-seven States that signed the Convention, but ratification by the United States and several other signatories has been delayed by opposition from ocean carriers.

The twentieth ratification needed to bring the Hamburg Convention into force occurred on October 7, 1991; the Convention will enter into force for these twenty States on 1 November 1992. With few exceptions, the initial parties to the Convention are small, developing countries. However, the Convention's impending entry into force has stimulated consideration in additional States. Thus, a British solicitor wrote in 1991:

> The claim that the Hamburg Rules overly favour cargo owners is predictable, ... but so far as the effect of the Rules is concerned it does not bear close scrutiny. This is no system of strict carrier liability, it has, at its core, the principle of liability based on carrier

fault. It is true that in general carrier fault is presumed but this is subject to important exceptions. The imposition of the burden of proof upon carriers (except in the case of fire, an important exception) is hardly an unbearable burden as they will be in a position to control the carriage and ascertain the cause of any loss. They need only show that they were not negligent. ... Despite its weaknesses, an international momentum now seems to be developing which will lead to the Convention's operation in the near future and it is quite possible that its acceptance by a major trading nation would give it the critical mass it needs to overthrow the ancient regime based on the Hague Rules.

Waldron, The Hamburg Rules—A Boondoggle for Lawyers?, [1991] J. Bus. Law 305, 318–319.

Marine Insurance. Problems resulting from the restricted responsibility of the ocean carrier may be solved but are not necessarily simplified by a marine insurance policy. For instance, one of the common and important clauses in marine policies is "free of particular average" (F.P.A.): hardly a word in this phrase means what a layman would suppose. "Free of" means without insurance coverage; "average" is a corruption of a French term (derived from the Arabic) which means loss or damage; "particular average" refers to partial losses which are not "general." (But a "general average" or loss does not mean total loss, but rather (roughly speaking) those losses incurred when some part of a marine venture is sacrificed to save the rest, as when part of a cargo is jettisoned to lighten a ship in peril.) The point of this illuminating explanation is to suggest that even in dealing with marine policies a specialist is needed. See Gilmore & Black, Admiralty 76–79 (2d ed., 1975); MacDonald, Practical Exporting and Importing 318–31 (1959).

(2) Air Carriers. Rules for liability for international air shipments were prescribed by the Warsaw Convention of 1929. The Convention has now been accepted by the United States and over 90 other countries. Article 20 of this Convention in part provides (in translation):

> (1) The carrier shall not be liable if he proves that he and his agents have taken all necessary measures to avoid the damage or that it was impossible for him or them to take such measures.

> (2) In the transportation of goods and baggage the carrier shall not be liable if he proves that the damage was occasioned by an error in piloting, in the handling of the aircraft, or in navigation and that, in all other respects, he and his agents have taken all necessary measures to avoid the damage.

Article 22 sets forth monetary limits on damage awards. The most controversial limits apply to recovery for personal injury and death—issues that are not relevant here. Unless damage to cargo is caused by wilful misconduct, recovery was initially limited to approximately $16 per kilogram—a figure that was augmented by devaluation of the dollar.

Continuing dissatisfaction with the Convention brought about its revision by the Guatemala City Protocol of 1971. Should this agreement go into effect, air carriers would no longer have the benefit of the exceptions for errors in piloting, and the like, set forth in Article 20(2), above. Under this revision, Article 20 would provide:

> In the carriage of cargo the carrier shall not be liable for damage resulting from destruction, loss, damage or delay if he proves that he and his servants and agents have taken all necessary measures to avoid the damage or that it was impossible for them to take such measures.

The Guatemala City Protocol would raise the maximum liability for personal injury and wrongful death but the limits on liability for cargo would be preserved, subject to unlimited liability for losses resulting from certain intentional or reckless conduct of the carrier. See S. Sorkin, How to Recover for Loss or Damage to Goods in Transit §§ 9.15–9.21, 13.08 (1978, with supplements). The Protocol has not been acted upon by the U.S. Senate.

*

Part IV

SECURED TRANSACTIONS

The dominant theme of this part is the extension of credit. The transactions are greatly varied in context and size: complex financings in corporate merger and acquisition settings, involving millions (even billions) of dollars; short-term credit extended in business settings by sellers of goods and providers of services; credit given to consumers who wish to buy automobiles, furniture, and many other kinds of goods.

Chapter 9 covers the fundamentals of the legal rights of creditors. It also addresses the resolution of a variety of conflicting claims to personal property—tangible and intangible—among owners, buyers, sellers, and creditors. For example, goods are delivered to the buyer on credit. To protect against the risk that the buyer may fail to pay, can the seller who is financing the sale obtain a claim to the goods that will permit the seller to recapture them from the buyer or from the buyer's other creditors?

With the fundamentals in tow, the remainder of this part centers on legal arrangements that give a creditor powers over personal property of the debtor. It embraces an enormous variety of financing transactions, some of which have little or nothing to do with the distribution of goods. For example, a business needs more cash in order to operate profitably. Can a loan at an acceptable interest rate be arranged if the borrower agrees that the lender will have a claim on the borrower's equipment, inventory of goods held for sale, accounts receivable, and other personal property that will survive attack by other creditors? What is the impact of this arrangement on the borrower's suppliers and other creditors? Will courts permit the lender to enforce against the borrower the full range of rights that lenders write into credit agreements? If the debtor defaults, may the creditor seize and resell the borrower's personal property and, if the loan is not satisfied, recover any shortfall?

Chapter 9

RIGHTS OF CREDITORS, OWNERS,
AND PURCHASERS

SECTION 1. THE RIGHTS OF UNSECURED CREDITORS

Much of law school is devoted to determining whether one person is legally obligated to another and, if so, the amount of damages recoverable or other appropriate remedy. The subject of secured transactions is one of the few that generally assumes the defendant's liability and explores how the aggrieved party can turn its claim into cash.

Consider a simple case: Bank lends Dana $1,000, which Dana agrees to repay, together with stated interest, in one year. At the end of the year, Dana fails to pay. What can Bank do to recover its claim?

Above all, and particularly when the claim is very small, Bank wishes to avoid incurring the expense and delay inherent in legal proceedings. Accordingly, it strongly prefers to encourage Dana to pay voluntarily. Bank's first approach is likely to be informal. It may write one or more **dunning letters** to Dana, in which it demands payment and threatens suit if payment is not forthcoming immediately. The letter may suggest that failure to pay will adversely affect Dana's ability to obtain credit in the future. It may suggest also that, if Dana cannot make full payment, Bank would be willing to enter into an arrangement for Dana to pay in installments. Rather than attempt to collect the claim itself, Bank may refer the claim to a **collection agency**, which, for a fee, will attempt collection. The collection agency's first approach also is likely to be informal.

Employees of Bank or its collection agency may be tempted to induce Dana to pay by "making an offer you can't refuse." The criminal law, the common law of tort, and federal and state statutes regulating debt collection provide some check against the overexuberance of those who wish to collect what is due and owing, particularly when the debtor is a consumer. For example, the Fair Debt Collection Practices Act, 15 U.S.C. §§ 1692–1692o (1988 & Supp. I 1989), affords remedies to persons who are subjected to harassment, misrepresentations, and certain other unfair practices by collection agencies. Some states have extended similar protection against abuses by creditors themselves, as well as by collection agencies. See, e.g., Wis. Stat. Ann. §§ 427.104, 427.105 (West 1988).

728

It is worth noting what may be obvious to some: Bank has a right to be paid; however, it has no interest whatsoever in any particular property that Dana may own. Bank may not simply send its agents to Dana's house to take whatever they can find. To collect a claim in this way would be to engage in both tortious and criminal conduct. If Dana does not pay voluntarily, Bank is relegated to the judicial process. Its lawyers will prepare a complaint and summons, which they will file with the clerk of the court and cause to be served upon Dana. Dana will have a period of time in which to respond. In many cases of this kind, where the facts are simple and the defenses are likely to be few, the debtor may fail to respond at all. If so, the creditor will be able to obtain the entry of a **default judgment** upon an ex parte showing that the debt is owed. If the debtor does respond, then the case will proceed through the motion and discovery stages and, if settlement is not forthcoming, to trial and the entry of judgment.

Assume that, whether by default or after trial, Bank obtains judgment in the amount of $1,000 plus interest and costs. Dana, the **judgment debtor**, ignores the entry of the judgment and continues to fail to pay. What can Bank do? Is Dana in contempt of court for failing to pay?

A judgment is an adjudication that the judgment debtor owes a particular amount to the **judgment creditor**. It is not an order requiring the judgment debtor actually to pay. Even so, a judgment is not without value. Without a judgment, a creditor must rely on persuasion and other informal techniques to induce a debtor to pay. A judgment entitles the judgment creditor in addition to invoke the "long arm of the law" to dispossess the debtor from property (other than property that is exempt from the reach of creditors [1]) and cause the property to be applied toward the satisfaction of the claim. [2]

We leave to courses in creditors' rights a detailed examination of the collection of judgments. For our purposes, the following, highly simplified overview should suffice. Collecting a judgment through the judicial process typically involves two steps. The first is to obtain a **judicial lien** on particular property of the judgment debtor. The second is to turn the lien into cash. [3]

---

1. All states have laws providing that certain property of individuals (as opposed to partnerships or corporations) is **exempt** from the reach of creditors. These laws vary widely: some award liberal **exemptions** and other afford only meager protection. Exempt property typically includes the home, household and personal effects, and tools of the trade. Often, the extent to which property is exempt is limited to a specified dollar amount (e.g., up to $750 in jewelry; up to $10,000 of the value of one's home).

2. The focus of this part of the book is on credit transactions. We refer, there-

fore, to the process by which an unsecured creditor becomes a judgment creditor. Note, however, that any claimant who obtains a judgment for money is a judgment creditor. For example, a successful plaintiff in a tort action for damages becomes a judgment creditor.

3. Although the following discussion focuses on postjudgment liens, most states make some provision for prejudgment liens under limited circumstances, e.g., upon a showing that the defendant is about to abscond from the jurisdiction or hide property otherwise available to creditors. Many of the restrictions on the availability

A lien is a property interest of a particular kind. The holder of the lien (the **lienor**) may use the property subject to the lien for only one purpose, to apply toward satisfaction of the debt it secures. Although state laws and procedures governing postjudgment liens vary, generally speaking a judgment creditor acquires a lien in one of two ways. The creditor may obtain from the clerk of the court a **writ of execution**, instructing the sheriff to **levy** upon (seize) assets of the judgment debtor located within the sheriff's bailiwick (usually a county). In the majority of states, the creditor acquires an **execution lien** on whatever property the sheriff levies upon before the writ expires. In a minority of states, an **inchoate** execution lien arises on all property of the judgment debtor within the bailiwick when the writ is delivered to the sheriff; however, the inchoate lien cannot be enforced against specific property until the sheriff levies upon the property and the lien becomes **consummate**. If the sheriff fails to levy before the writ expires, the inchoate lien is discharged.[4]

In most states, a judgment creditor may obtain a **judgment lien** simply by recording a memorandum or abstract of the judgment in the real estate records or (depending on local law) having the court clerk enter the judgment in the docket book. Upon the recordation or docketing, a judgment lien arises on all of the debtor's interests in real property in the county. In only a few states does the judgment lien extend to personal property. See, e.g., Cal. Code Civ. Proc. § 697.530 (West 1987) (judgment lien arises on most nonexempt personal property upon filing a notice with the Secretary of State). Because this book is concerned almost exclusively with personal property, we shall have no more to say about judgment liens.

An execution lien affords two important advantages to the judgment creditor. First, it provides a means for applying the judgment debtor's property to satisfaction of the judgment. To turn the lien into cash, the judgment creditor usually looks to the sheriff, who will sell

---

of prejudgment remedies, including those affording the debtor notice of the exercise of the remedy and an opportunity to be heard, reflect cases decided under the due process clause of the fourteenth amendment. See, e.g., North Georgia Finishing, Inc. v. Di–Chem, Inc., 419 U.S. 601 (1975) (discussing constitutional requirements surrounding prejudgment garnishment of corporate debtor's bank account). See also Note on Replevin, Due Process, and State Action, Chapter 15, Section 1, infra. Prejudgment liens are similar in many ways to the postjudgment liens discussed below. The principal difference is that the creditor ordinarily cannot cause the former to be turned into cash until judgment is entered against the defendant-debtor.

4. While levy may be a suitable means for acquiring a lien upon **tangible** personal property, a different method is necessary when the creditor seeks to acquire a lien on a debtor's **intangible** personal property, which, by its very nature, cannot be seized. A common example of intangible property is a claim against a third party. Suppose, for example, that Bank has reason to know that Kerry owes Dana $100. Bank could cause the clerk of the court to issue a **writ of garnishment** directed to Kerry, instructing Kerry to inform the court whether Kerry is indebted to Dana and, if so, for how much. In most jurisdictions, a **garnishment lien** on Kerry's debt to Dana arises when the writ is served upon Kerry.

the property at a **sheriff's sale**.[5] Because the sale usually is poorly advertized (often in a legal newspaper), because the sheriff makes no warranty of title, and because the judgment debtor is an unwilling seller, the price paid at a sheriff's sale rarely, if ever, approaches the price that the property would command in the marketplace. The first two reasons also explain why few, if any, buyers appear at the sale other than the judgment creditor. Inasmuch as the judgment creditor is entitled to the proceeds of the sale (less the costs of sale), the judgment creditor need not pay cash. Rather, the creditor may **bid in the judgment**, i.e., simply reduce the amount of the judgment debt by the amount it wishes to pay for the property. If the judgment creditor is the successful bidder, it becomes the owner of the property and must thereafter resell the property to obtain cash.

An execution lien enables the judgment creditor not only to apply particular property toward the satisfaction of its claim against the debtor but also to reach the property to the exclusion of other, competing creditors who have not obtained liens. Although more than one execution lien may attach to particular property, liens generally rank in temporal order; that is, the holder of the debt secured by the earliest lien is entitled to be paid first from the proceeds of the sale of the property. Thus, by winning the "race of diligence" and obtaining a lien on specific assets, Bank generally acquires not only a property interest in those assets but also **priority** over other, subsequently arising liens.

Any consideration of the judicial collection system should take into account its costs. These include Bank's out-of-pocket expenses as well as the cost of delay. How much would it cost to obtain and collect a judgment against Dana? How long would it take? What risks attend the delay?

All things being equal, Bank would be in a better position if it could acquire a lien without first having to obtain a judgment and invoke the power of the sheriff. At the time Bank extended credit, or at any time thereafter, Bank and Dana could have *agreed* that Bank would have a limited interest in particular property. The nature of this interest could be such that if Dana failed to pay, Bank could cause the property to be sold and apply the proceeds to the satisfaction of its claim without the need to incur the costs and delay attendant to obtaining a judgment and collecting it through the judicial process. When the property concerned is personal property, this kind of **consensual lien**, which arises by the agreement of the parties, is called a **security interest**. (A consensual security interest must be distinguished from a **judicial lien**, which arises through the exercise of judicial process, and a **statutory lien**, which arises by operation of law in favor of certain suppliers of goods and services.) A security interest affords yet another benefit to the holder that a judicial lien does not. Whereas the law governing judicial liens differs from state to state, the

---

5. To turn a garnishment lien into cash, the court will order the **garnishee** (Kerry, in the example in footnote 4) to pay the debt to Bank, either directly or through a judicial officer.

law governing security interests, including the rights and duties of the immediate parties (debtor and creditor) and the rights of third parties, is found largely in Article 9. Security interests under Article 9 are the principal focus of this part of the book.

SECTION 2. SELLER'S POWER OVER THE GOODS AS AGAINST BUYER

As Section 1 suggests, unless the borrower agrees to grant the lender a security interest, the lender must resort to the judicial process if the borrower does not repay the debt voluntarily. Is a seller of goods in any better position with respect to a buyer?

Generally, the answer is "no." If the seller delivers goods on credit to the buyer and the buyer, having received a conforming tender, fails to pay, the law affords the seller exactly what the seller bargained for: the right to recover the price from the buyer. See UCC 2–709. The seller ordinarily has no right to recover the goods themselves (except, of course, if it can do so through **execution** or other judicial remedy). See generally UCC 2–703.

Suppose that the seller advances the following argument: Buyer promised to pay for the goods and broke that promise. For such a serious (indeed, fundamental) breach I should have a right to rescind the transaction and recover the goods by a possessory remedy, such as **replevin.**[1]

This argument is consistent with a common misunderstanding. Many people believe that if they don't pay for a purchase, the seller can "take it back." This argument may be sound in some civil-law legal systems, but it is not supported by common law. Any attempt by a seller to replevy goods sold on credit would have failed under the English common law, which was codified in the (British) Sale of Goods Act, which in turn was followed in the Uniform Sales Act. The drafters of the UCC did not dream of overturning the basic common-law approach. The catalogue of the seller's remedies in UCC 2–703 does not mention recovery of the goods.

Although a credit seller ordinarily may not recover goods delivered to the buyer and must instead enforce the buyer's promise to pay, the law does afford to some sellers certain power over delivered goods that a simple creditor does not enjoy. The discussion that follows builds on materials previously addressed.

---

1. Replevin, like sequestration and claim and delivery, is a judicial remedy to recover possession of personal property. Replevin statutes are procedural: They do not create the right to possession but rather aid those who are entitled to possession under other law.

(A) The Right to Withhold Delivery

Problem 1. On January 3, Seller and Buyer entered into a contract for the sale of a garden tractor, which Buyer agreed to pay for and take away by January 30. The agreement specified that "title" passed to Buyer on January 3. On January 30, Buyer demands the tractor but declines to pay. Is Seller justified in denying Buyer possession of "Buyer's" goods? May Seller close out the transaction by reselling "Buyer's" tractor to another customer? See UCC 2–401; UCC 2–511(1); UCC 2–703; UCC 2–706.

Problem 2. On January 3, Seller and Buyer entered into a contract for the sale of a power lathe. Seller agreed to deliver the lathe on January 30, and Buyer agreed to pay for the lathe within 30 days thereafter. On January 15, Seller received an updated credit report, showing that Buyer recently had become extremely slow in paying its debts. Seller is concerned that Buyer will take delivery and will not pay. What can Seller do? See UCC 2–609; UCC 2–702(1); UCC 1–201(23).

(B) The Right to Stop Delivery

Problem 3. A contract for sale between Seller in San Francisco and Buyer in New York called for shipment of a carload of oranges at $12,000, f.o.b. San Francisco. (See UCC 2–319(1)(a).) Terms: Cash 30 days after delivery. Seller shipped oranges in conformity with the contract on a **straight (non-negotiable) bill of lading** (see UCC 1–201(6)) naming Buyer as **consignee** (i.e., as the person to whom delivery is to be made, see UCC 7–403(1), (4)).

After the carload arrives in the New York freight yards but before the oranges are unloaded, Seller learns that Buyer's creditors have begun to obtain judgments against Buyer and judicial liens against Buyer's property.

(a) Has Seller a chance to keep the oranges for itself? See UCC 2–705; UCC 1–201(23); UCC 2–609. (Note the Code's extension of the grounds for stoppage beyond insolvency, for carload and similarly large shipments.) See also In re National Sugar Refining Co., 27 B.R. 565 (S.D.N.Y.1983) (rejecting, in buyer's bankruptcy, several challenges to seller's rights of stoppage under UCC 2–702(1) and UCC 2–705(1), but not discussing the significance of the fact that seller held the negotiable bill of lading).

(b) Assume Seller instructs the railroad not to deliver the oranges to Buyer but rather to transport them to Philadelphia.

(i) If the railroad refuses to release the oranges to Buyer, would it be liable for failing to honor the terms of its bill of lading? See UCC 7–403; UCC 7–303.

(ii) Under what circumstances, if any, may the railroad ignore Seller's instructions with impunity? See UCC 2–705; UCC 7–403(1);

UCC 7–303. See also Butts v. Glendale Plywood Co., 710 F.2d 504 (9th Cir.1983) (carrier's rerouting of shipment to buyer's buyer, made at buyer's direction while goods still in transit, held to be "reshipment" under UCC 2–705(2)(c)).

Would you advise a seller to ship on credit to a shaky buyer in view of the seller's stoppage rights? Would sellers often hear of insolvency during the time required for shipment? On the other hand, an attorney would probably be liable for malpractice if a client presented the facts in the preceding Problem, and the attorney could think of no course of action other than taking a day or so to research the point.

(C) The Right to Recover Delivered Goods

Prior to the Code, the sharpest controversy over reclamation of goods by the seller grew out of attempts to base reclamation not on overt fraud by the buyer but on an implied false representation of an intent to pay. See Keeton, Fraud—Statements of Intention, 15 Tex. L.Rev. 185 (1937) (decisions in Illinois, Missouri, Indiana, Pennsylvania and Vermont refused to base fraud remedies on such an "implied" misrepresentation). As the following Problem suggests, the drafters of the Code addressed this controversy directly. (One wonders whether the drafters were so bemused by this vexing question that they failed to set their solution to this narrow question in a wider context. Perhaps that approach to drafting statutes is in the "common-law tradition.")

Problem 4. Buyer induced Seller to deliver goods on credit and promised to pay for them in 30 days.

(a) Shortly after delivering the goods, Seller discovered that Buyer was insolvent at the time of delivery. Seller seeks to recover the goods. May Seller do so? See UCC 2–702(2); UCC 1–201(23).

(b) Two months prior to delivery Buyer gave to Seller a **financial statement** showing Buyer to be solvent. May Seller recover the goods?[2]

(c) Two months prior to delivery Seller sought and received a report from a credit reporting agency erroneously showing Buyer to be solvent. May Seller recover the goods?

Problem 5. Seller and Buyer made a contract for the sale of a quantity of mink pelts. The contract required Seller to send the pelts to Buyer immediately by air freight and required Buyer to transfer the agreed price of $250,000 to Seller's account in Firstbank before obtaining the pelts from the air carrier. Relying on Buyer's honesty, Seller consigned the goods to Buyer by a straight (non-negotiable) bill of lading, which permitted the air carrier to deliver the goods to Buyer. The shipment arrived in Buyer's city on June 1; on the same day, without paying the price, Buyer took the pelts from the air carrier and

---

2. Would your answer depend upon when the sales contract was formed?

placed them in its warehouse. May Seller recover the pelts? See UCC 2–507(2); UCC 2–702(2). Are both provisions applicable to this case?

Problem 6. Angie and Mark Rook, on their tenth wedding anniversary, decided impulsively to buy from Sorbet Jewelers, Inc. a diamond "anniversary ring" that Sorbet had on display for the price of $2,500.00. Over a number of years, the Rooks had bought and paid for a number of items from Sorbet Jewelers. The ring from the display case fit Angie and the Rooks told the sales clerk that they would take it immediately to cap their celebration. Mark Rook gave his check for the price to the clerk. Mr. Sorbet, owner of Sorbet Jewelers, who had recognized the Rooks from prior transactions, congratulated them on their choice of a fine ring and authorized the clerk to accept the check. A few days later, Sorbet Jewelers received notice from its bank that Mark Rook's check had been returned unpaid by their bank for "insufficient funds" and that, accordingly, the $2,500.00 credit previously entered into the Sorbet Jewelers account had been reversed. May Sorbet Jewelers, Inc. recover the anniversary ring? See UCC 2–507(2); UCC 2–511(3) cf. UCC 2–403(1) (third sentence).

Note on the "Cash Seller's" Right to Reclaim

UCC 2–507(2) deals with transactions in which sellers have not agreed to extend credit. In such transactions, "tender of payment is a condition to the seller's duty to tender and complete any delivery." UCC 2–511(1). As we have seen, such transactions are called "cash sales" and the sellers are called "cash sellers." We consider here the relief available to cash sellers who have delivered the goods but have not received the price. UCC 2–702(2) expressly grants a credit seller the right to reclaim goods under certain circumstances. UCC 2–507(2), in contrast, refers cryptically to the buyer's "right as against the [cash] seller to retain or dispose of" the goods as being "conditional upon his making the payment due." Courts routinely have concluded that the unpaid cash seller enjoys a right to reclaim goods from the buyer. One court has referred to the cash seller's reclamation right as "judicially-confected." In re Samuels & Co., 526 F.2d 1238 (5th Cir.1976) (en banc), cert. denied, 429 U.S. 834 (1976). Is this a fair characterization? Can you articulate a statutory basis for the cash seller's reclamation right? Does it help to characterize reclamation as a remedy for enforcing a statutory right to possession of the goods? Is the fact that the seller enjoyed such a right under pre-Code law relevant?

Assuming that the Code affords a reclamation right to cash sellers, does it also impose a time limit on the exercise of that right? From the 1951 Official Text of the Code until 1990, Comment 3 to UCC 2–507 provided that "[t]he provision of this Article for a ten-day limit within which the seller may reclaim goods delivered on credit to an insolvent buyer is also applicable here." The Code itself, however, imposed no such limitation.

The time limit, if any, for reclamation under UCC 2–507 has been litigated most often under facts like the following: Buyer and Seller agree for payment on delivery. Buyer tenders its check (see UCC 2–511(2)), which Seller deposits and Buyer's bank dishonors ("bounces"). Having not received payment (see UCC 2–511(3)), Seller seeks to reclaim the goods. Seller fails to demand their return within ten days after their delivery to Buyer, perhaps because Seller did not learn of the dishonor within that time.

Some courts followed Comment 3 and permitted a seller to reclaim only when demand was made within the ten-day period. See, e.g., Szabo v. Vinton Motors, 630 F.2d 1 (1st Cir.1980) ("Comment 3 does not contradict, but merely complements and explains the Code."). Others, observing that the text of the Code itself contains no time limit, refused to apply the limit contained in the Comment. See, e.g., Burk v. Emmick, 637 F.2d 1172 (8th Cir.1980) ("the only limitation imposed upon the seller's [reclamation] right is a reasonableness requirement").

All probably would agree that even a seller who exchanges goods for a check (drawn on insufficient funds) or who is the victim of active fraud should not have an unlimited time for reclamation. One way to fill gaps in the Code is to extend other Code provisions by analogy. If rules of limited scope (e.g., the time limits in UCC 2–702(2)) are to be extended by analogy, surely one should use the provision that is most analogous to the problem posed by the gap in the Code. Dealing with the gap in UCC 2–507 by analogical extension of the time limits in UCC 2–702 leads to these questions: (a) Under UCC 2–702(2) is the ten-day rule applicable to all reclamations? (Suppose the buyer gave the seller a written misrepresentation of solvency.) (b) Is a seller who agrees to deliver only for cash and exchanges the goods for a worthless check more comparable to (i) a seller who delivers to a buyer who proves to be insolvent or (ii) a seller who delivers to a buyer who has made a written misrepresentation of solvency?

Another approach to gap-filling, suggested by UCC 1–103, is to turn to the common-law rule. At common law an attempt to reclaim after excessive delay would be defeated by doctrines such as waiver, estoppel, or ratification of the buyer's property interest. See, e.g., Frech v. Lewis, 218 Pa. 141, 67 A. 45 (1907). The Permanent Editorial Board adopted this approach in PEB Commentary No. 1. Please read the Commentary. Is it persuasive? If not, is it any more or less binding on a court than the original Comment?

Problem 7. Buyer acquired goods under circumstances giving Seller a right to reclaim. Before Seller could exercise its rights, Buyer resold the goods to Purchaser, who took delivery in good faith and without notice of Seller's rights. Buyer extended credit to Purchaser, who has not yet paid Buyer. As we saw in Chapter 1, this cuts off Seller's property right in the goods. Does Seller's property (reclamation) right against the goods shift to the property received by Buyer upon resale of the goods—Buyer's claim against Purchaser for the price? (Although it is intangible, a right to payment is property and can be transferred.)

Neither UCC 2–507 nor UCC 2–702 refers to a seller's claim against what the buyer receives upon disposition of the goods (the **proceeds** of the goods). Does the absence of a statutory reference to proceeds necessarily mean that Seller has no claim to them? Or, should a court validate such a claim by reference to the common law or by analogy? The cases are divided, but the majority permit sellers with reclamation rights to reach proceeds. Compare, e.g., United States v. Westside Bank, 732 F.2d 1258 (5th Cir.1984) (credit seller who complies with all the requirements of UCC 2–702 retains claim against traceable proceeds from the sale of the goods) with, e.g., In re Coast Trading Co., Inc., 744 F.2d 686 (9th Cir.1984) (UCC 2–702 does not in and of itself create a right to reclaim proceeds). The Article 2 Study Group's "tentative conclusion is that a reclaiming seller should not have a right to proceeds." PEB Article 2 Report 200. Do you agree?

SECTION 3. SELLER'S POWER OVER THE GOODS AS AGAINST THIRD PARTIES

The Problems in Section 2, supra, deal with the seller's power over goods when only two parties (Seller and Buyer) are involved. Often, however, a third party claims an interest in the goods. This third party may claim an interest through Seller (e.g., one of Seller's creditors may levy upon the goods while they are in transit) or through Buyer (e.g., Buyer may contract to resell the goods. The rights of secured creditors of Seller are discussed below in Chapter 13, Section 2. You should review the materials on good faith purchase in Chapter 1. This section builds on that foundation.

(A) RIGHTS OF RECLAIMING SELLERS AS AGAINST THIRD PARTIES

Problem 1. Recall Problem 3, Section 2, supra, concerning the sale of a carload of oranges between Seller in San Francisco and Buyer in New York on terms of: Cash 30 days after delivery. Assume now that the carload arrived in the New York freight yards on January 15. The next day Buyer obtained the oranges from the railroad. On January 18, Buyer sold and delivered the oranges to Great Dane Supermarkets. On January 22, having learned that Buyer's creditors have begun to obtain judgments against Buyer and judicial liens against Buyer's property, Seller demanded that Great Dane Supermarkets surrender the oranges to Seller. Great Dane refused. In Seller's action against Great Dane for conversion, what result? See UCC 2–705(2)(a).

Problem 2. Recall Problem 4 in Section 2, supra. Assume a sale and delivery of goods on credit extended in reliance upon a misleading financial statement given to Seller by Buyer. Upon Seller's learning that Buyer has misled Seller and was hopelessly insolvent, Seller sought to reclaim the goods. Seller found the goods in the possession of a Third Party who had bought them from Buyer. In Seller's action to replevy the goods from Third Party, what result? See UCC 2–702(3); UCC 2–403.

Problem 3. Recall Problem 5 in Section 2, supra. Assume that Seller learned from Firstbank that no funds had been transferred by Buyer on June 1 and that Buyer had sold and delivered the mink pelts to Coat Manufacturer. In Seller's action to replevy the pelts from Coat Manufacturer, what result? See UCC 2–403.

Problem 4. Recall Problem 6 in Section 2, supra. Sorbet Jewelers instituted an action in replevin to recover the diamond ring from Angie Rook. What result? See UCC 2–403. Was Angie Rook a "purchaser"? See UCC 1–201(32) and (33)? Did she give "value"? See UCC 1–201(44).

Problem 5. Buyer, who had only recently entered business as a cotton broker and had no established credit rating, went to Seller's place of business with a forged reference and financial statement ostensibly from Firstbank. Relying on these documents, Seller delivered cotton to Buyer who promised to pay $100,000 for the cotton within two weeks. Even before approaching Seller, Buyer had contracted to sell the cotton to Textile Co. for $105,000. Buyer promptly delivered the cotton to Textile Co. Three weeks later, still unpaid, Seller learned that the cotton it had delivered to Buyer was in the possession of Textile Co., which has paid only $10,000 to Buyer. Seller brought an action against Textile Co. to replevy the cotton. What result?

(a) Would Textile Co. be protected as a buyer in the ordinary course of business under UCC 2–403(2)? Did Seller entrust the goods to Buyer? See UCC 2–403(3). Did Textile Co. buy from "a person in the business of selling goods of that kind"? See UCC 1–201(9). Must a buyer have paid the price for goods in order to qualify as a buyer in the ordinary course of business? Is it significant that Buyer delivered the cotton to Textile Co. pursuant to their pre-existing sales contract? Is it significant that Textile Co. is a corporation buying for a business purpose, rather than a consumer buying for a personal, family or household purpose? Is it significant that Textile Co. had never dealt with Buyer before and took no measures to check on Buyer's background?

(b) Would Textile Co. be protected as a good faith purchaser for value under UCC 2–403(1)? Are any of the factors mentioned in (a) significant?

(c) Why should the law give security of property to a buyer who has not yet paid for goods? If a buyer is not protected, does the buyer have an adequate defense to enforcement of its promise to pay?

(d) Could Seller obtain relief comparable to replevying the cotton by "seizing" the $95,000 debt owed by Textile Co. to Buyer? If Seller were already a **judgment creditor** of Buyer, Seller could **garnish** any of Buyer's assets, one of which is the debt owed to Buyer by Textile Co. On the facts assumed, however, Seller is merely a creditor; by the time Seller obtains a judgment against Buyer, the particular asset (Textile Co.'s debt) and, indeed, all Buyer's assets may have become unavailable or may have been subject to earlier liens by other creditors of Buyer. Could Seller proceed *in rem* to seize Textile Co.'s debt as *proceeds* of goods that cannot be replevied? Recall Problem 7, Section 2, supra.

(B) Scope of "Purchase" in Good Faith Purchase

Introductory Note. For the most part, we have been considering the paradigmatic sequence of events involving transfers of goods from *A* to *B* to *C* and the relative positions of *A* and *C* on the premise that *C* was a buyer who bought the goods under a contract of sale. The definitions of "purchase" and "purchaser" in UCC 1–201(32) and (33) are much broader than the definitions of "sale" and "buyer" in UCC 2–103(1)(a) and UCC 2–106(1). In this subsection, we consider what classes of persons might be "purchasers" and therefore potentially entitled to the protection afforded to good faith purchasers.

Problem 6. Recall Problem 5 above. Suppose that, instead of Textile Co. buying the cotton, it had obtained a judgment against Buyer and had caused the sheriff to levy on the cotton pursuant to a writ of execution. Before the sheriff has sold the goods, Seller discovered the fraud and demanded that the sheriff surrender the cotton. Who has the better claim to the cotton? Is Textile Co., for whom the sheriff is acting, a good faith purchaser for value under UCC 2–403(1)? See Oswego Starch Factory v. Lendrum, infra.

Problem 7. Suppose that Textile Co. had extended a loan to Buyer six months earlier. Instead of buying the cotton or having the sheriff levy on it, assume that Buyer granted Textile Co. a security interest in the cotton. Would Textile Co. be a purchaser of the cotton by virtue of acquiring the security interest in it?

OSWEGO STARCH FACTORY v. LENDRUM
57 Iowa 573, 10 N.W. 900 (1881).

Action of replevin by Oswego Starch against sheriff Lendrum. Plaintiff's petition alleged that plaintiff had sold and shipped goods to Thompson & Reeves, and that this firm prior to the purchase was knowingly insolvent and intended to defraud plaintiff of the purchase price. Defendant Lendrum levied on the goods for creditors of Thompson & Reeves and thereafter plaintiff elected to rescind the sale because of fraud.

Lendrum demurred on the ground, inter alia, that he and the attaching creditors had no knowledge of the alleged fraud and that therefore the contract could not be rescinded after the levy. From a decision for Lendrum, plaintiff appealed.

BECK, J. ... [T]he point of contest involves the rights of an attaching creditor without notice.

The title of the property was not divested by the attachment, but remained in the vendees. The seizure conferred upon the creditors no right to the property as against plaintiff other or different from those held by the vendee. The sole effect of the seizure was to place the property in the custody of the law, to be held until the creditors' execution. They parted with no consideration in making the attachment, and their condition as to their claims were in no respect changed. Their acts were induced by no representation or procurement originating with plaintiff which would in law or equity give them rights to the property as against plaintiff. Plaintiff's right to rescind the sale inhered in the contract and attached to the property. It could not be defeated except by a purchaser for value without notice of the fraud....

Our position is simply this, that as an attaching creditor parts with no consideration, and does not change his position as to his claim, to his prejudice, he stands in the shoes of the vendee. ... The innocent purchaser for value occupies a different position, and his rights are, therefore, different. [Reversed.]

Notes on Reliance and Nonreliance Parties

(1) **The Position of a Creditor Who Levies.** The *Oswego Starch* decision represents the preponderant view of the pre-Code case law. See 3 Williston, Sales § 620 (1948). Is it persuasive? What is the basis of the distinction the court draws between a judicial lien creditor, against whom the right to rescind may be exercised, and a "purchaser for value," who would defeat this right? Is the court correct that "an attaching creditor parts with no consideration"? If so, then how can the creditors in *Oswego Starch* obtain judgment against Thompson & Reeves, the debtor?

Does UCC 2–403(1) change the pre-Code result? *B*'s rights to the goods are subject to *A*'s right to rescind the transaction and recover the goods. But does *B* have *power* to convey greater rights? Even if *B* has "voidable title," the answer is "no," unless the lien creditor is a "good faith purchaser for value."

A lien creditor is likely to meet the good faith and value requirements. See UCC 1–201(19); UCC 1–201(44). Is the lien creditor a "purchaser"? The Code defines "purchase" (UCC 1–201(32)) to include "taking by sale, discount, negotiation, mortgage, pledge, lien, issue or re-issue, gift or any other voluntary transaction creating an interest in property." One will note that the list of transactions includes "taking by ... *lien*," and a judgment creditor who levies execution on property often is called a "*lien* creditor." See UCC 9–301(3). But the word "lien" is a chameleon; prior to the Code voluntary transactions creating mortgages and similar security interests were often said to create a "lien." In the setting of the types of transactions listed in the definition of "purchase" and the concluding characterization that the list applies to "any other *voluntary* transaction," it seems fairly clear that the drafters did not mean to say that the seizure of a debtor's property by a sheriff acting for a creditor makes the creditor a "purchaser." This conclusion becomes inescapable in the light of Code sections that distinguish between, on the one hand, lien creditors and, on the other, transferees or purchasers. See UCC 9–301(1) and (2).

Does any policy justify distinguishing between a judicial lien creditor and a buyer? Consider some of the ways in which the two are different. Unlike a buyer, who contracts to purchase all of the rights to the goods, a lien creditor acquires only a limited interest in (i.e., a **lien** on) the goods. And unlike a buyer, whose rights arise by virtue of its contract, a judicial lien creditor acquires its rights through the judicial process (a overview of which appears in Section 1). Finally, whereas a buyer typically acquires its rights in exchange for new consideration (current payment or a promise to pay), a lien creditor's extension of credit is divorced from the property on which it subsequently obtains a lien. Is any of these distinctions relevant?

(2) The Position of an Article 9 Secured Party. Like the lien creditor, the Article 9 secured party can be expected ordinarily to meet the good faith and value requirements.[4] Is the secured party a "purchaser"? Interestingly, the definition of purchase does not specifically include "taking by security interest." One might argue that the drafters' exclusion of this form of transfer, which is the subject of one of the Code's major articles, evidences a decision to exclude Article 9 secured parties from the class of "purchasers." On the other hand, one might conclude that the creation of an Article 9 security interest is an "other voluntary transaction creating an interest in property," if not a "lien."

If, as it appears, the Code provides that a judicial lien creditor is not a "purchaser," and thus takes subject to *A*'s right to rescind the transaction and recover the goods, whereas an Article 9 secured party (like a buyer) is a "purchaser," and thus may cut off *A*'s rights, can one justify this distinction?

Although most of the remainder of this book is devoted to the rights of a secured party, for present purposes one can draw several comparisons with buyers and judicial lien creditors. An Article 9

---

4. The most serious challenge to a secured party's good faith is likely to arise from its knowledge or notice of competing claims.

secured party is like a buyer, in that its rights in the goods (a security interest, defined in UCC 1–201(37)) arise by contract. See UCC 9–102(2). It is like a judicial lien creditor in that it acquires only a limited interest in the goods. This limited interest entitles the secured party, upon its debtor's (*B*'s) default, to repossess the goods, sell them, and apply the proceeds to its claim against the debtor.

Sometimes, an Article 9 secured party takes a security interest in specific goods owned by the debtor at the time the loan is made.[5] In this respect a secured party is like a buyer, exchanging new consideration for an interest in goods. Other times, as in Problem 4, an Article 9 secured party takes a security interest to secure an antecedent debt, i.e., a debt owed before the security interest is taken. This secured party seems to be analogous to a judicial lien creditor—it has extended credit on an unsecured basis, and its acquisition of rights in particular property is not a *quid pro quo* for the loan (although it may have taken the security interest in exchange for its forbearance in exercising its remedies).

Sometimes a secured party takes a security interest in both property existing at the time credit is extended as well as **after-acquired property**, i.e., property the debtor may acquire after the loan is made. See UCC 9–204. A security interest covering both existing and after-acquired property (often referred to as a **"floating lien"**) is particularly common when the collateral is inventory (goods held for sale) or accounts receivable (rights to payment for goods sold or services rendered). The rights of a reclaiming seller as against a buyer's secured creditor who claims a "floating lien" are considered in Chapter 14, Section 5, infra.

(3) The Role of Reliance in Resolving Competing Claims. Personal property law often distinguishes among third-party claimants on the basis of whether they gave value in reliance upon the transferor's (in our case, *B*'s) apparent ownership of particular property. This distinction is reflected in *Oswego Starch*, supra, as well as in *Mowrey v. Walsh*, which you read in Chapter 1 supra ("The judgment creditor had not advanced money upon these goods, and his loss placed him in no worse situation than he was in before the fraud.") It also underlies the delivery requirement in the third sentence of UCC 2–403(1).

Should the strength of a person's claim to goods turn on whether the person actually relied, or should it turn on (i) whether the person belongs to a class that generally relies and on (ii) whether, had the

---

5. Two variations of this paradigm are common. In one, the seller of goods retains a security interest to secure the purchase price. In the other, a lender takes a security interest in goods acquired with the borrowed funds. A security interest arising under either of these circumstances is called a "purchase money security interest" ("PMSI") and receives special treatment under both the UCC and the Bankruptcy Code. See, e.g., UCC 9–107 (definition of "purchase money security interest"); UCC 9–312(3), (4) (priority rules for PMSI's); BC 547(c)(3) (protecting certain PMSI's that otherwise would be avoidable as preferences). PMSI's are discussed in Chapter 13, Section 1(A), infra.

person investigated, it would have uncovered facts that would have formed the basis for reasonable reliance upon the transferor's ownership (e.g., the goods in question were located in the transferor's warehouse in boxes addressed to the transferor)? Do buyers generally give value in reliance upon their seller's ownership of particular property? Do judicial lien creditors? Do Article 9 secured parties?

Chapter 10

INTRODUCTION TO SECURED FINANCING

The remainder of this book deals primarily with consumers and businesses that need credit and the lenders and credit sellers who extend credit to them. In particular, the focus is on transactions in which creditors obtain consensual liens—"security interests"—on personal property (both goods and intangibles). Section 1 describes the contexts in which extensions of credit take place and the patterns and participants involved. Section 2 provides an overview of the principal statute that regulates security interests, Article 9 of the Uniform Commercial Code. Finally, Section 3 considers the variety of roles lawyers play in secured transactions.

SECTION 1. SECURED FINANCING IN CONTEXT

(A) Unsecured and Secured Credit

Although the following materials focus primarily on the legal regulation of secured credit, the legal regime can be understood only by approaching secured credit as a subset of credit extensions generally. Why is credit sought and given? The likely intuitive answer of most North American consumers would be essentially correct: Both consumers and businesses need funds, goods, or services *now*, not later, and often they choose to enjoy the fruits of credit while paying over time. Creditors extend credit not only to increase profit directly, by earning interest, but also indirectly, by increasing the sale of their goods and services.

Many of the problems in this book focus on the Prototype transaction described in Chapter 11, Section 1, infra. As you will see, the Prototype includes detailed examples of both consumer and business credit transactions. In the Prototype, Lee Abel purchased a new car from Main Motors under an **installment purchase** arrangement. After making a down payment (consisting of a trade-in), Abel signed an agreement containing a promise to pay the balance of the purchase price, plus **carrying charges** (comparable to interest charges on a loan) and insurance charges. Main Motors, on the other hand, itself required financing in order to buy the car that it sold to Abel as well as the other cars in its inventory. On average, Main Motors maintains an inventory of cars that cost (wholesale) about $2,400,000; it does not have capital sufficient to enable it to invest that much money for extended periods. Consequently, Main buys automobiles with funds that it borrows from Firstbank.

In the Prototype, Lee Abel granted a security interest in the new car to Main Motors in order to secure the obligations under the installment purchase contract. Similarly, Main Motors granted a security interest in its automobile inventory to Firstbank in order to secure its obligation to repay the loan. Although it is clear enough why Abel and Main Motors needed credit, why was the credit given to Abel and Main *secured*, as opposed to *unsecured*, credit? Before venturing an answer to that question, one must consider three aspects of secured and unsecured credit: (i) enforcement against the borrower or buyer (the "debtor"), (ii) priorities among creditors and buyers competing to satisfy their claims from the same property of the debtor, and (iii) enforcement of the security interest in a bankruptcy proceeding of the debtor.

A secured creditor with an Article 9 security interest has the right to satisfy its claim against the debtor from the collateral (the property subject to the security interest). The Article 9 secured party's rights include the right to take possession of the collateral upon the debtor's default in payment or performance of the obligation secured. See UCC 9–503. Unsecured creditors, however, have *no* property rights in the debtor's property. Their remedies generally depend on first obtaining a judgment against the debtor and subsequently obtaining a lien through the judicial process. Only at that time would a formerly unsecured creditor become secured by the **judicial lien**.[1]

In general, an Article 9 secured party can acquire rights in the debtor's personal property that are senior to later-in-time secured creditors (including judicial lien creditors) and buyers. (Note, however, that much of Article 9—and consequently much of these materials—is concerned with conditions, qualifications, and exceptions to this generalization.) An unsecured creditor, on the other hand, is subject to the "race of diligence"—it generally is junior to earlier-in-time secured creditors and must obtain a judicial lien in order to take priority over later-in-time secured creditors.

How does a debtor's bankruptcy affect security interests and other liens? Bankruptcy law is complex and interesting enough to be the subject of a separate course. Although the following brief overview of bankruptcy is greatly simplified, it will suffice for our immediate purposes. Chapter 14 details many of the ways in which a debtor's bankruptcy affects Article 9 secured parties.

The substantive law of bankruptcy is contained in the federal Bankruptcy Code (title 11, U.S. Code). Enacted in 1978, the Bankruptcy Code superseded the Bankruptcy Act of 1898, which had been amended many times and substantially overhauled in 1938. The filing

---

1. The rights of other kinds of secured creditors, such as holders of **statutory liens** and mortgagees of real estate (land and buildings), vary enormously according to the law of each state. Those creditors may enforce some of their rights against the debtor's property only through judicial proceedings.

of a petition by or against a debtor commences a bankruptcy case (see BC 301; BC 302(a); BC 303(b)), and creates an "estate" comprised of all the legal and equitable interests of the debtor in property as of the commencement of the case. BC 541(a). When the petition is filed under Chapter 7 of the Bankruptcy Code, which contemplates liquidating the debtor's nonexempt assets and distributing the proceeds to creditors, the United States trustee [2] appoints an interim trustee, who will continue to serve as *the* trustee in bankruptcy unless the creditors elect another person to the position. See BC 701; BC 702.

The bankruptcy trustee is a representative of creditors, primarily unsecured creditors. The trustee is charged with the duty, inter alia, of collecting and reducing to money the property of the estate and distributing the money to creditors. See BC 704. The Bankruptcy Code affords to the trustee the power to avoid (i.e., undo) certain valid prebankruptcy transactions, including those that have the effect of improperly preferring one creditor to another and those that are fraudulent. See generally BC 544–548; Chapter 14, infra.

Chapter 11 cases contemplate that the debtor's enterprise will be reorganized; that is, the enterprise will continue and the claims against the debtor will be scaled down or extended or both. In Chapter 11, the debtor's management ordinarily remains in control of the enterprise as the "debtor in possession." A trustee normally is appointed only when management has been guilty of fraud, dishonesty, incompetence, or gross mismanagement. See BC 1104(a). The debtor in possession enjoys the avoiding powers of a trustee. See BC 1107(a).

One important, and immediate, effect of a bankruptcy filing is the automatic stay of virtually all activities of creditors directed toward collection of their debts. See BC 362(a). This means that the state law "race of diligence" for unsecured creditors ends when the debtor enters bankruptcy.

Except for some special priority rules for certain types of claims, unsecured creditors share pro rata in their common debtor's bankruptcy. In contrast, federal bankruptcy law generally respects a secured creditor's claim to the value of its collateral. The following example may assist in comparing the treatment of secured and unsecured claims in bankruptcy: [3]

> A debtor in a bankruptcy case has three creditors, each owed $100, for a total of $300 of debt. One creditor is secured by $100 of assets (i.e., fully secured), and the other two creditors are unsecured. The debtor's trustee in bankruptcy sells all the assets for cash and, after payment of all fees and expenses, $150 in cash (of which $100 is attributable to the property that

---

2. The Attorney General appoints one United States trustee and one or more assistant United States trustees for each of 21 regions. See 28 U.S.C. § 581 (1988). The United States trustee serves for a term of five years and, like the assistants, is subject to removal by the Attorney General.

3. The treatment of secured claims in bankruptcy is dealt with in detail in Chapter 14, infra.

was subject to the security interest) remains. What result? The fully secured creditor would have its claim satisfied in full, leaving $50 to be distributed between the two remaining creditors, each of which claims $100. Each unsecured creditor, then, would receive a distribution of $25 or "25 cents on the dollar."

Given these obvious advantages of secured credit for creditors, it is easy to see why in the Prototype Main Motors and Firstbank preferred to have a security interest in collateral. Because Abel's purchase of a new automobile and Main Motors' automobile inventory purchases represent very large dollar amounts when compared with their respective net worths and incomes, they had little choice but to agree to give collateral as a condition to obtaining the credit. Virtually all consumer automobile installment financing and automobile dealer inventory financing is done on a secured basis. Even if unsecured credit had been available, the absence of collateral could have resulted in a much higher interest rate to compensate the financers for the additional risk.

These observations lead to yet other questions: Why do some creditors extend unsecured credit? By conferring senior status (in and out of bankruptcy) on Firstbank, would Main Motors' unsecured creditors charge higher interest rates that would offset any reductions in interest rates paid by Main Motors to Firstbank as a result of providing collateral? Suffice it to observe, for now, that factors such as disparities in bargaining power and information, the relative size and duration of credit extensions, the costs of creating secured financings, disparities among creditors in their ability to monitor the debtor's financial activities and use of collateral, and market competition all serve to explain current financing patterns, to be addressed shortly, which involve a mix of secured and unsecured credit.

A related question should be raised here, although its answer must be deferred. A positive explanation of why debtors sometimes give and creditors sometimes take secured credit under current law does not provide a normative justification for the advantages the current legal regime affords to secured claims. Secured credit imposes costs, particularly on the hapless unsecured creditors of a financially distressed debtor. As we shall see, whether and how the social benefits conferred by secured credit can justify those costs has inspired a lively scholarly debate. See Chapter 14, Section 6, infra.

Although collateral provides important advantages for a creditor, its significance in the extension of credit should not be overemphasized. For example, a lawyer who thinks that the security interest is the most important part of a credit transaction will be corrected quickly by a banker or merchant. From the point of view of a lender or seller, the most important safeguard for the credit is the likelihood that the debtor will pay voluntarily. Evaluation of this likelihood requires mature judgment of the debtor's character, ability, and financial status, and sometimes of the business outlook generally. Recourse to the most ironclad security interest is sure to be costly. Executives and lawyers must spend valuable time to enforce the security interest (perhaps fighting off claims of other creditors in the process) and dispose of such diverse collateral as steel, oil, cattle, and blouses—unwieldy merchandise for a banker, whose stock in trade is money. Indeed, enforcement of a security interest in collateral represents a serious breakdown of the financing operation, whose profit depends on a rapid and routine flow of money. Creditors regard the opportunity to enforce a security interest with something of the zest with which a merchant regards the opportunity to file a claim under an insurance policy.

This does not suggest that security arrangements are without value or that bankers and merchants so regard them. The most canny banker or credit manager makes errors in judgment; business conditions shift. While recourse to security ranks far below voluntary payment, it stands well above loss of the entire claim or receipt of a small dividend at the conclusion of extended bankruptcy proceedings. In addition, in consumer transactions the security device often is used as leverage against the debtor. The threat of depriving the debtor of goods that he or she needs or prizes (such as a refrigerator or fur) often encourages "voluntary" payment, even though the used goods would realize little for the creditor upon sale. In 1985 the Federal Trade Commission sought to limit the "hostage value" of certain consumer collateral by prohibiting as an unfair trade practice the taking of security interests in household goods unless the secured party maintains possession of the collateral or has extended the credit that enabled the debtor to acquire it. See FTC Rule on Credit Practices, 16 C.F.R. § 444.2(a)(4) (1991).

(B) Patterns of Financing

The 1980's witnessed profound changes in the patterns of consumer and business financing and in the financial services industry generally. Nonetheless, some useful generalizations about financing patterns remain possible.

Unsecured Consumer Credit. "Consumer credit" generally refers to credit extended to natural persons for personal, family, or household purposes. Much consumer credit is unsecured. Examples are credit extended pursuant to bank and other **lender credit card** arrangements,[4] credit extended by department stores and gasoline companies under **seller credit cards** or charge accounts,[5] and personal

---

4. Charges made pursuant to lender credit cards constitute loans by the card issuer to the cardholder. The loans are advanced when the card issuer pays the merchant who accepts the credit card in connection with the sale of goods or services.

5. Some "private label" credit cards nominally issued by sellers of goods actually are issued by third-party lenders who may or may not be affiliated with the seller. Also, some credit cards and charge account arrangements provide that the seller receives a security interest in goods sold to secure the price.

or **signature loans** extended by finance companies, banks, thrift institutions, and credit unions. Consumer credit usually is extended with the expectation that it will be repaid from the consumer's future earnings, an expectation often based on satisfactory credit reports obtained from private credit reporting services.

Unsecured Business Credit; Trade Credit. Many business borrowers also obtain unsecured credit. The most creditworthy corporations issue short-term (i.e., 30– to 90–day) debt instruments known as **commercial paper.** Holders of these instruments who wish to dispose of them before they become due can trade (sell) them in a secondary market. As long as the issuer's credit remains satisfactory (according to **rating agencies** such as Moody's and Standard & Poor's), the debt typically is repaid by issuing and selling new commercial paper as the old paper matures. Corporations also issue longer-term debt securities (**bonds** or **debentures**), many of which are publicly traded.

Creditworthy business borrowers obtain both medium- and long-term financing from commercial banks, as well. Bank credit is extended in a variety of forms. Arrangements known as **revolving credits** ("revolvers") allow a borrower to borrow, repay, and reborrow amounts as needed during an agreed time period, provided that the aggregate unpaid amount of loans does not at any time exceed the agreed cap. Some revolvers obligate the bank to extend loans (a **committed credit facility**), subject to certain conditions precedent (such as the absence of any default by the borrower). Others create a **line of credit**, pursuant to which the lending bank is not obligated to lend. The line of credit agreement ("line letter") governs the terms and conditions of the loans that the borrower requests and the lender, in its discretion, elects to make from time to time. Loans outstanding under lines of credit often are to be repaid on the lender's demand or within a relatively short time following demand. Under other credit arrangements, known as **term loans**, the loan advances are to be paid back in installments over a period of time.[6] Some revolvers automatically convert into term loans after a specified period of time, such as two or three years.

Bank credit agreements typically contain provisions dealing with (i) the amount of credit, interest rate, commitment fee, repayment terms, and the like; (ii) conditions precedent (in committed facilities); (iii) affirmative covenants (e.g., the borrower will comply with the law, pay all taxes, give financial statements to the lender periodically); (iv) negative covenants (e.g., the borrower will not incur debt or create security interests except within agreed limits, will not merge with another entity, will not sell substantially all of its assets); (v) events of default (e.g., bankruptcy, nonpayment of the loan when due, default on debt owed to another lender); and (vi) remedies (e.g., acceleration of entire amount of loan).

---

6. Many term loans also are made by insurance companies, although the transactions usually are structured as a purchase of a note by the insurance company—a "private placement."

For most businesses, the banks, finance companies, and other professional lenders are not the most significant source of short-term credit. Instead, the most important providers of short-term credit are other businesses that typically give extended terms (usually 30 to 90 days) for payment for goods and services—**trade credit**.[7] Most businesses not only receive trade credit in their purchases of goods and services but also grant trade credit in connection with sales of their own goods and services. Principal advantages of trade credit are its general availability and the absence of costly negotiations or formalities associated with longer-term arrangements such as bank credits. From the standpoint of the trade creditor, the credit extensions facilitate the sales of goods and services to those who are not in a position to pay cash or who otherwise would patronize a competitor.

Secured Financing of Sales of Goods. As we have seen, unsecured credit is common and important in both the consumer and the business environments. We shall see, next, that the same can be said of secured credit. We turn first to secured financing in its most familiar (at least to consumers) and historically significant role— secured credit extended to buyers of goods (including consumer goods, equipment used in business, and inventory held for sale or lease).

Consumer Goods. Lee Abel was not unique in entering into a secured installment purchase of a car; most automobiles are sold on a secured, installment basis. Consider the volume of consumer credit extended in the United States. By the end of 1990, outstanding consumer installment credit obligations stood at over $750 billion, with more than one third of that amount being automobile installment credit.[8] This staggering figure is even more startling when compared with $4.5 billion in 1939 and $15 billion in 1951. Increases in these figures reflect both inflation and the expansion of the economy. For example, annual disposable income rose from $226.1 billion in 1951 to $3,945.6 billion in 1990, an increase of 1,645%. But in 1951 installment credit was equal to approximately 6.6% of disposable income; in 1990 the percentage was 19%. United States consumers obviously have been increasingly willing to encumber their future earnings.[9]

In the case of consumer goods, secured credit commonly is extended by the seller (dealer), who retains a security interest in the goods to secure payment of the purchase price (or the balance of the price remaining after a down payment). Because dealers usually prefer to obtain the sale price immediately after the sale, rather than in installments over time, dealers commonly enter into an arrangement with a secured financer, such as a bank or finance company, whereby the

---

7. Of course, many consumers also receive short-term, unsecured credit from businesses such as the electric company, lawn care service, plumber, cable TV company, and newspaper delivery service.

8. The figure includes both secured and unsecured credit; however, consumer automobile financing typically involves secured

credit. Also, the figure includes installment credit extended in connection with services; it is not limited to goods-related credit.

9. 77 Fed. Res. Bull., May, 1991, at A38, A53; 42 Fed. Res. Bull., Dec., 1956, at 1352, 1370.

dealer assigns to the financer the buyer's payment obligation and the security interest and the financer pays the dealer the unpaid portion of the purchase price for the goods. To facilitate this arrangement, which is similar to the accounts receivable financing discussed in Chapter 12, Section 2, infra, the financer usually supplies the dealer with the form of credit application and retail installment sale/security agreement and often approves the consumer's credit before the dealer makes the sale. The Prototype transaction presents the entire operation (secured sale by the dealer and assignment to the financer) in greater detail in the concrete setting of automobile financing. When expensive consumer goods, such as motor vehicles and boats, are involved, it is not unusual for a third-party lender to make a secured loan directly to the buyer to cover a substantial portion of the purchase price. For example, instead of obtaining credit from Main Motors, Abel might have obtained a secured purchase-money loan from Abel's regular bank: the bank would have provided funds for the specific purpose of enabling Abel to pay for the new car, and Abel would have secured the repayment obligation by giving the bank a security interest in the new car.

An increasingly varied group of creditors holds consumer installment credit obligations. Probably the most significant trend during the last several decades has been the growing dominance of commercial banks in the installment credit market. More recently, deregulation has permitted savings institutions to enter the consumer installment credit market, and by the end of 1990 almost 10% of the installment credit obligations were held in "pools of securitized assets." [10] The following table reflects the shifting market shares in the consumer installment credit market.[11]

Table 1

Type of Institution	Credits Outstanding (In Millions)					
	1940	1950	1960	1970	1982	1990
Commercial Banks	1,452	5,798	16,672	45,398	152,069	351,695
Finance Companies	2,278	5,315	15,435	27,678	94,322	136,154
Credit Unions	171	590	3,923	12,986	47,253	91,203
Retail Outlets	1,596	2,898	6,295	13,900	51,154	46,858
Savings Institutions						49,594
Pools of Securitized Assets						75,437

The legal regulation of consumer credit is extensive and complex enough to warrant a separate course at many law schools. Special consumer protection rules are discussed at several places in this book.

Business Equipment. When consumer goods are bought on credit the financing necessarily anticipates that the debtor will earn income from other sources, usually wages or salary. Business equipment (taxicabs, trucks, computers, commercial refrigerators), however, is intended to assist in generating income that will help repay the credit and even leave a profit for the user. The installment financing of sales

10. Securitization is discussed below in this Section.

11. 77 Fed. Res. Bull., May, 1991, at A38; 69 Fed. Res. Bull., Nov., 1983, at A40; 60 Fed. Res. Bull., May, 1974, at A50.

of business equipment does not match the mammoth scope of consumer financing, but it has played an important role in aiding productive activity—particularly by small businesses.[12] The financing patterns for buyers of business equipment are similar in many respects to those for consumer buyers. Both dealer-arranged financing, in which the dealer takes the security interest and assigns it to a secured financer, and third-party direct secured lending to buyers are common.

Inventory. Sellers of goods extend secured credit routinely to wholesalers and dealers who hold the goods for sale as their inventory; however, seller-financed sales of inventory are much less common than seller-financed sales of consumer goods and business equipment. Sellers of expensive items that will become the buyer's inventory (e.g., the manufacturers of construction equipment and automobiles) normally insist on cash payment of the purchase price upon delivery. Other sellers, as we have seen, typically extend unsecured, short-term trade credit to buyers of inventory. Dealers and wholesalers who need longer-term inventory financing typically look to third-party secured financers, much as Main Motors looks to Firstbank for inventory financing in the Prototype.

Other Secured Financing. Much secured credit is extended for purposes other than to finance buyers' purchases of consumer goods, business equipment, and inventory. Many business, large and small, must supplement their capital by borrowing, in order to obtain adequate funds to remain in operation. Funds borrowed under **working capital** or **operating capital** lending arrangements may be used for payment of salaries, rent, utilities, and other expenses of operation as well as for the purchase of equipment, supplies, and inventory. Many of these financings are secured, especially in cases of small- to medium-sized borrowers. These loans frequently are structured as uncommitted lines of credit or as revolving credit arrangements that, at some point, convert into term loans, not unlike the unsecured credit arrangements discussed above. Other secured financings are highly specialized and bear little resemblance to traditional unsecured lending arrangements.

Following are descriptions of some typical financing patterns that, although common, are particularly complex. They are included here with a view toward giving you a "taste" for the diverse contexts in which secured financing plays a central role and introducing you to some transactions about which you may have heard or read and in which you someday may play a role. We do not expect you to memorize these materials, or even to understand them fully at first reading. As will become apparent, the descriptions present only the basics; important details and qualifications have been omitted in the

---

12. Secured financing has been significant in aiding smaller business enterprises to buy a wide range of equipment, such as printing presses, laundry equipment, mining and oil field equipment, drink dispensing and bar equipment, commercial refrigerators, machine tools, power shovels, cranes, road-building equipment of all types, agricultural equipment, bottling machines, electronic data processing equipment, dental and medical equipment, hairstyling equipment, trucks, diesel engines, and generators. This list can only suggest the wide variety of equipment involved.

interest of brevity and comprehensibility. Please remember that while the essential elements of many transactions conform to these descriptions, the variations in terms, structure, collateral, and purposes of these secured financings are infinite.

Inventory and Receivables Financings. Consumer goods and business equipment, both of which are purchased for use, must be contrasted with goods held for sale. Goods held for sale include not only inventory, such as cars, trucks, and refrigerators in a dealer's showroom or warehouse, but also raw materials and components awaiting or in the course of manufacture: nuts and bolts to be used for assembly and bales of cotton held by a spinner or going through the spindles. The distinctive fact about inventory, and one that creates complex and fascinating legal problems, is that all parties hope for rapid turnover and liquidation of the goods into cash. The goods often will be (re)sold on credit, thereby creating an account receivable to which the secured creditor's security interest may be transferred.

In many cases creditors who make loans secured by inventory and receivables rely heavily on the collateral as their "way out"—their source of repayment. The current jargon used to refer to transactions in which the lender relies heavily on the value of its collateral is **asset-based financing**. In a typical arrangement a borrower would be required to maintain at all times a **borrowing base** value of inventory and qualifying (not in default) receivables that is at least equal to the outstanding loan balance. Normally the borrowing base would be a percentage (say, 60%) of the book value of inventory plus a percentage (say, 75%) of the face amount of receivables. The excess of collateral value over the outstanding loan balance provides the lender with a "cushion" that offers protection if the borrower defaults. Reporting requirements and, in some cases, inspections of inventory put the lender in a position to monitor the collateral and act to protect its interests if the borrower experiences a financial downslide. In many instances a borrower's receivables, which usually represent its most liquid assets (other than cash), are the principal collateral on which secured lenders rely.[13] For a useful treatment of the manifold aspects of asset-based financings, see H. Ruda, Asset Based Financing: A Transactional Guide (1991).

"All Assets" Secured Financing. A pattern has emerged in certain credit markets whereby lenders routinely take a security interest in all of a borrowers assets.[14] A typical example is a commercial bank loan to a small business. The individual controlling shareholders of a closely-held corporate borrower generally are required to give a guaranty of payment as additional security. Compared to asset-based lenders, these "all assets" lenders may place relatively slight reliance on the collateral's value and the individuals' guaranties as a source of repayment.

---

13. The general setting for accounts receivable financing is developed in detail in Chapter 12, Section 2, infra.

14. The borrower's real property may or may not be taken as collateral, depending on its value and the attendant costs.

Instead, they tend to rely heavily on the borrower's predicted cash flow and overall ability to pay. Like those financers who take consumer goods collateral for its hostage value instead of its market value, the "all asset" lenders probably look to the collateral and guaranties primarily as a tool for obtaining power over the borrower so as to inhibit business decisions and investments that could undermine their position.[15]

Acquisition Financing: Leveraged Buyouts. Another financing pattern involves obtaining a security interest in virtually all of a debtor's assets, but that is its only similarity to the "all assets" financings just mentioned. The "takeover" phenomenon of the 1980's fueled demand for secured credit to finance acquisitions of controlling interests in publicly held corporations. Although the transaction structures are quite varied, these **leveraged buyouts** ("LBO's") exhibit certain common patterns. Usually a substantial percentage of the purchase price of the corporate stock of the entity to be acquired (the "target") is borrowed (hence, the **leverage**); those borrowings typically are secured by substantially all of the assets of the *target*, once it is acquired.[16] Many of these secured loans, usually made by **syndicates** of commercial banks, have involved hundreds of millions of dollars and, in some cases, billions. The LBO secured lenders typically rely heavily on collateral value. In many cases unsecured debt also is incurred in order to fund a portion of the purchase price. Because of the high leverage and the dominant position of the secured lender, this unsecured debt became known as **junk bonds** (or, even more bluntly, "junk").[17]

"Special Purpose Vehicle" Financing: Leveraged Leasing. Some very innovative forms of receivables financings involve the use of a type of borrower called a **special purpose vehicle** ("SPV"). In these financings the SPV, which may be a corporation, partnership, or trust, is organized for the specific purpose of participating in the financing.[18] **Leveraged leasing** is one such form of financing.

A business entity may choose to lease equipment instead of buying it for a variety of reasons (often including its inability to use the tax benefits of ownership, such as accelerated depreciation, because it lacks sufficient taxable income). For example, long-term leasing is a typical means by which airlines obtain the use of commercial aircraft. The lessor often will be an SPV (typically a trust) formed by "equity"

---

15. Professor Robert Scott has dubbed these lenders "relational" creditors because the value of the collateral seems to be primarily in its impact on the relationship between the borrower and the lender. See Scott, A Relational Theory of Secured Financing, 86 Colum.L.Rev. 901 (1986).

16. Because the assets of the target are used as collateral, these transactions have long been known as "bootstrap" transactions, reflecting the notion that the target seems to be "buying itself." The vanities

of the 1980's investment bankers being what they were, the "bootstrap" label was replaced by the "LBO" nomenclature.

17. The investment bankers, of course, prefer another term: "high-yield securities."

18. Hence the "vehicle" denomination, reflecting the SPV's role as an tool or implement necessary for the financing structure.

investors who (through the SPV) invest in the equipment and lease it to the lessee. These investors often wish to obtain, through the SPV, the tax benefits of ownership that the lessee cannot use. The investors capitalize the SPV with only a portion (say, 20%) of the funds necessary to purchase the equipment. The SPV then borrows the additional necessary funds, pays for the equipment, and enters into a lease with the lessee. By causing the SPV to borrow a substantial portion of the purchase price (i.e., "leveraging" the investment), the investors achieve 100% of the tax benefits of ownership by putting up only a fraction of the cash necessary to buy the equipment. As collateral for its borrowing, the SPV grants to the lender a security interest in the equipment (subject to the lessee's rights under the lease, of course) and in the lease itself (including the rental stream, payable over time by the lessee).

Because the equipment and the lease are the SPV's only assets, the lender must be satisfied with the value of the equipment and the creditworthiness of the lessee.[19] The lessee is instructed to make the lease payments directly to the lender, as assignee of the lease, and those payments are applied by the lender against the SPV's secured debt. If for any reason (such as the lessee's default combined with unanticipated obsolescence of the equipment) the equipment and the lease are not adequate to satisfy the SPV's debt, then the lender will suffer a loss. It will have no recourse against any of the investors. If the lessee does not default and the secured debt is satisfied, then the SPV (and, indirectly, the investors) will be entitled to the **residual value** of the equipment at the end of the lease. The investors expect that value (combined with any tax savings arising out of the SPV's ownership of the equipment, which are passed on to the investors) to be sufficient for them to recover their investments and enjoy a return thereon. Depending on the value of the equipment at the end of the lease term, however, that expectation may or may not be realized. Because the lender's repayment turns on its ability to collect the rental stream from the lessee and on the value of the equipment, the lender must be assured that its security interest will withstand attack by any creditor of, or trustee in bankruptcy for, the SPV, any investor, or the lessee.

"Special Purpose Vehicle" Financing: Securitization. **Securitization** transactions (sometimes called "structured finance") are similar in some respects to leveraged leasing transactions, but there are some important distinctions. First, securitization involves the creation of debt securities that are backed by "pools" of receivables (rights to payment); traditional leveraged leasing transactions involve one or more equipment leases to the same lessee. Almost any kind of receivable can support securitization financings. Second, whereas professional

---

19. In some transactions the lessor is not an SPV but is an operating company that has other assets and other liabilities. In those transactions the debt of the lessor to the lender normally is **limited recourse** debt. That is, the lending agreement provides that the lender is entitled to look only to the collateral—the equipment and the lease—for satisfaction of the debt. The lender is not entitled to satisfy the debt out of other assets of the lessor.

lenders (usually banks and finance companies) typically engage in leveraged leasing transactions, securitization involves the issuance of debt securities that can be sold to other kinds of investors. Third, the receivables involved in a securitization transaction initially are owned by a non-SPV operating company, whereas in a leveraged lease the SPV-lessor normally is the original lessor.

A typical securitization transaction begins with a business entity that originates receivables. For example, the originator could be a bank that holds consumer installment sale contracts (as Firstbank holds Lee Abel's contract in the Prototype) or it could be a financial institution that generates credit card receivables (rights to payment from holders of credit cards issued by the institution). The first receivables used in securitization transactions were home mortgage loans secured by residential real estate. These transactions probably remain the most commercially significant securitizations.

> The first structured financing came in 1970 when the newly created Government National Mortgage Association began publicly trading "pass-through" securities. In a mortgage pass-through security, the investor purchases a fractional undivided interest in a pool of mortgage loans, and is entitled to share in the interest income and principal payments generated by the underlying mortgages. Mortgage lenders originate pools of mortgages with similar characteristics as to quality, term, and interest rate. The pool is placed in a trust. Then, through either a government agency, a private conduit, or direct placement, certificates of ownership are sold to investors. Income from the mortgage pool passes through to the investors.[20]

A similar pattern is followed in most other securitizations: The originator transfers a large number of receivables (usually referred to as a "pool") to an SPV, and the SPV issues debt securities. As in the leveraged leasing transaction, because the SPV's only assets are the receivables, collections of the receivables are the only source of payment of interest on, and repayment of principal of, the securities. The funds generated by the sale of the securities are used to pay the originator for the receivables it sells to the SPV. (The financial intermediaries that arrange the transaction take their shares of the funds as well.) Although the investors are not necessarily knowledgeable enough to evaluate, on their own, the quality of the receivables, disclosure documents provide information concerning the quality of the receivables (e.g., past history of collections of similar receivables) and the risks that the investors are undertaking. Investors in publicly traded securities also may be guided by a rating agency's ratings of the securities.

As in leveraged leasing transactions, the investors must be assured that neither the SPV's nor the originator's insolvency will interfere

---

20. S. Schwarcz, Structured Finance 3–4 (1990).

with the collection of the receivables and the application of those collections to payments to the investors. But, the fact that the receivables originally were owned by the originator, an operating company with liabilities, creates a problem that the lender in a typical leveraged lease transaction does not encounter: making sure that the SPV and the operating company are not linked and that the transfer of the receivables to the SPV will be effective against creditors of the operating company (i.e., making sure that the SPV is **bankruptcy remote** from the originator). Indeed, in securitization transactions it is not unusual for the SPV's obligations to the investors, on the securities, to be *unsecured*. It is the transfer of the receivables from the originator to the SPV that is of particular concern.[21]

Securitization can provide an originator with a lower cost of borrowing than a conventional loan secured by the receivables. Even the fully secured, conventional secured lender faces a variety of risks in the event of a borrower's bankruptcy or other financial distress. By removing the receivables entirely from the asset base of the originator, however, securitization of the receivables may produce less risk and, consequently, a lower interest rate for the originator.

Agricultural Financing. The agricultural industry, including the proverbial "family farmers," the large, corporate "agri-business" concerns, and the myriad other businesses in the chain of production, processing, and distribution, depends heavily on secured credit. Farms, like many other businesses, need expensive equipment; what has been observed above about financing sales of business equipment applies as well to farm equipment. Agricultural financing also presents some unique characteristics:

> Like Caesar's Gaul, agricultural lending is divided into three parts: (1) long-term credit to finance the purchase or improvement of real estate by a farmer or rancher; (2) intermediate production credit to finance the purchase of equipment and livestock; and (3) short-term loans to cover current operating expenses, including annual crop production....
>
> The variety of collateral put up by farmers and ranchers as security for loans is very broad; it includes the farmland itself, fixtures, growing and future crops (including those pledged to landowner-lessors), products of crops, such as harvested grain, livestock, equipment, and a wide assortment of intangibles, including accounts receivable and U.S. Department of Agriculture "entitlements."[22]

Article 9 and a wide variety of other statutes, both state and federal, contain rules specifically addressing some perceived special problems of agricultural financing.

---

21. As we shall see in Chapter 12, Section 2, infra, applicable law may characterize the transfer as a sale or a security interest, depending on the purpose.

22. B. Clark, The Law of Secured Transactions Under the Uniform Commercial Code ¶ 8.01, at 8–2 to 8–3 (2d ed. 1988).

Secured Financing in the Securities Markets. Secured financing plays an indispensable role in modern securities markets. The transactional patterns vary widely, and most cannot be explained and understood in the absence of a broad and deep treatment of the operations of securities markets. However, some very general examples follow:

(i)   An individual investor who has physical possession of a stock certificate registered in the investor's own name with the issuing corporation wishes to borrow from a local bank and **pledge** (i.e., grant a security interest in) the stock certificate to the bank.

(ii) An individual investor who has a securities account with a stockbroker wishes to borrow from a local bank and pledge to the bank stocks and bonds "in" the investor's account.

(iii) In order to buy securities on **margin**, an individual investor who has a securities account with a stockbroker wishes to obtain credit from the stockbroker and pledge to the stockbroker the securities to be purchased.

(iv) A stockbroker wishes to obtain an "overnight" secured loan from a bank in order to obtain funds needed to settle (pay) its end-of-day payment obligations to other professional securities industry participants.

In the securities markets, secured financing, including **repo** financing,[23] involves truly staggering amounts each day, especially in the United States government securities markets. One expert "guestimate[d]" that in 1987 the average *daily* volume of repo transactions was at least $560 billion. M. Stigum, The Repo and Reverse Markets 7–8 (1989). The legal and operational aspects of taking collateral in the third and fourth examples mentioned above are likely to be encountered only by securities market professionals and their specialized counsel; however, lenders and their lawyers confront the first two examples with great frequency. As we shall see in Chapter 11, Section 2(B), infra, the applicable law (Articles 8 and 9) is problematic.

---

23. "Repurchase agreements," or "repos," are an important means of financing, especially for government securities dealers.

In a repo, a seller of a security (a funds borrower) transfers the security to a buyer (a funds lender) under an arrangement whereby the securities seller agrees to repurchase the security on a specified date (often the next day) at a specified price, and the securities buyer agrees to resell the security back to the seller. From the perspective of the buyer, the transaction is a reverse repurchase agreement (reverse repo). Repos serve the function of secured borrowings and loans, although they are denominated as sales and resales. The economics of the transaction are such that when the seller (funds borrower) pays the repurchase price (i.e. repays the loan), the buyer (funds lender) receives a profit (a return on the money loaned). The legal characterization of repos ... is not clear.

Mooney, Beyond Negotiability: A New Model for Transfer and Pledge of Interests in Securities Controlled by Intermediaries, 12 Cardozo L. Rev. 305, 324 n. 51 (1990).

(C) Real Property Collateral, Guaranties of Payment, and Other Credit Enhancements

Although the focus here is on personal property collateral, one must keep in mind that both consumers and businesses also obtain credit on the strength of real estate collateral, e.g., through home mortgage loans, second mortgage "home equity" loans, construction loans, long-term "permanent" mortgage loans, etc. Moreover, there are other means of supporting an extension of credit, such as a third-party's guaranty of payment or a bank's letter of credit. In many cases personal property collateral is taken in a transaction that also involves real property collateral, guaranties of payment, or other credit enhancements. The interplay between the law governing security interests in personal property (Article 9) and that governing the other aspects of the transaction can give rise to some interesting problems to be explored later.

SECTION 2. A ROADMAP TO SECURED TRANSACTIONS UNDER UNIFORM COMMERCIAL CODE ARTICLE 9

(A) Background; Ongoing Code Revision

Article 9 of the Uniform Commercial Code substantially rewrote the law of secured transactions; it was the most revolutionary of the Articles of the Code. By virtually abandoning the concept of "title," Article 2 required a drastic change in the focus of legal thinking about sales. But Article 9 even more sharply changed the focus of legal thought about secured transactions.

Prior to the Code, a creditor seeking security had to choose among a bewildering variety of legal "devices"—pledge, chattel mortgage, conditional sale, trust receipt, assignment of accounts receivable, factor's lien. Each "device" operated within complex (and often unclear) rules governing its scope and the procedures for its validation and enforcement; the choice of the wrong "device" was subject to perils reminiscent of common-law pleading.

The Code swept away the separate security "devices." The old names (pledge, conditional sale) may still be used, but the label does not control the result. Instead, Article 9 prescribes general rules for all secured transactions, with some variations depending on the type of transaction. The decision to establish a unitary approach to secured transactions was one of the Code's most important contributions to the legal system. The important questions that remain relate, for the most part, to whether the maximum possible benefit has been gained from what most agree was a brilliant idea.

Article 9 was the first part of the Code to undergo significant revision by the Code's sponsors. Although for a time the Code's sponsors held the line against most proposed improvements in the Code, by 1966 the pressure to modify Article 9 became irresistible. The work of the Article 9 Review Committee began in 1967; its efforts culminated in the 1972 Official Text. Without affecting the basic structure of Article 9, the 1972 revisions effected numerous changes (some of them very important) to the Article. As of the writing of this book, the 1972 revisions had become law in every state except Vermont. The 1978 Official Text made additional material changes to Article 9 as it dealt with investment securities. Forty-seven states have adopted these changes.

Revision of Article 9 now appears imminent once more. Drafting committees working on the revision of Article 5 (Letters of Credit) and Article 8 (Investment Securities) are almost certain to propose some conforming amendments to Article 9. Moreover, it appears likely that the Permanent Editorial Board's Article 9 Study Committee, whose report is due in mid–1992, will recommend further revisions to Article 9; if so, a drafting committee probably will be working on those revisions by early 1993.[1]

We turn now to an overview of the substance of Article 9. You should read through it several times, to glean a general understanding of the principal terms and concepts. As the course progresses and the details mount up, reference to the overview may restore a needed perspective.

(B) Scope of Article 9; Security Interests in Collateral

Article 9 "applies ... to any transaction (regardless of its form) which is intended to create a security interest in personal property or fixtures." UCC 9–102(1). This provision makes sense only if we consult UCC 1–201(37), which defines the term "security interest," in pertinent part, as "an interest in personal property or fixtures which secures payment or performance of an obligation."[2] The broad reach of Article 9 is limited by various exclusions set forth in UCC 9–104. The scope of Article 9 is discussed in Chapter 12, infra.

Article 9 tells us nothing about the obligation that is secured, leaving that to other law. Although we usually think of the obligation

----

1. Any revisions of Article 9 that may be forthcoming are unlikely to render nugatory your efforts in this course. A revised Article 9 will derive from the current version; by understanding the shortcomings and gray areas of the latter, you will gain a deeper comprehension of the former. In any event, the revisions will take at least two years to write and probably a few more to gain widespread adoption.

2. Certain other transactions—sales of accounts and chattel paper—also are embraced by the definition of "security interest" and by Article 9's basic scope provision, UCC 9–102. We shall defer consideration of those transactions for now and focus on interests that secure obligations.

as being a contractual promise to repay a loan or to pay the price of goods bought, in theory a security interest could secure virtually any obligation—liquidated or unliquidated, contingent or noncontingent.

"[T]he property subject to a security interest" is the "collateral." UCC 9–105(1)(c). Property can be "carved up" in many ways. Two or more persons might own property "in common," as owners of undivided fractional interests. Or, property can be divided temporally, as in a lease, where the lessee owns the right to use and possession during the lease term and the lessor owns the residual interest that remains at the end or the term. See UCC 2A–103(1)(m), (1)(q) (defining "leasehold interest" and "lessor's residual interest"). A security interest that secures an obligation, however, can be measured in two dimensions at any given point in time: the *value of the collateral* and the *amount of the obligation secured*. The following figure illustrates these two dimensions:

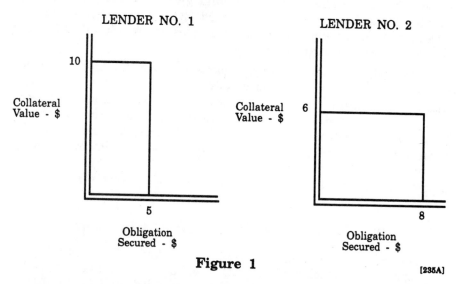

Figure 1

[235A]

As you can see, Lender # 1 has a security interest in collateral valued at $10 and is owed $5; at this point in time Lender # 1 is **oversecured**. Lender # 2, on the other hand, is owed $8 but its security interest extends only to collateral with a value of $6; Lender # 2 is **undersecured**. Keep in mind that the value of collateral securing an obligation can change (e.g., by appreciation, depreciation, or the acquisition of additional collateral), as can the amount of the obligation secured (e.g., by additional borrowings, the accrual of interest, and repayments).

(C) THE CAST OF CHARACTERS

The chief protagonists in a secured transaction are the "debtor" and the "secured party." The secured party is "a lender, seller or other person in whose favor there is a security interest." UCC 9–105(1)(m).

The debtor is "the person who owes payment or other performance of the obligation secured, whether or not he owns or has rights in the collateral." UCC 9–105(1)(d). The definition goes on to provide that

> [w]here the debtor and the owner of the collateral are not the same person, the term "debtor" means the owner of the collateral in any provision ... dealing with the collateral, the obligor in any provision dealing with the obligation, and may include both where the context so requires[.]

There are many possible variations from the straightforward scenario in which a debtor is the sole obligor on secured debt and also is the sole owner of the only collateral securing the debt. For example, a corporation might grant a security interest in collateral it owns to secure the indebtedness of its subsidiary. Or, parents might cosign a promissory note with their child, thereby becoming obligated for the same debt as the child, while the child gives a security interest in collateral that he or she owns. In each of these examples it will be necessary to determine which party or parties are the "debtor" for purposes of various Article 9 provisions.

The Code also deals with the rights of some, but not all, third parties who may claim an interest in collateral covered by a security interest. Consider a priority contest between a secured party, as a good faith purchaser, and a seller seeking to reclaim goods from a debtor-buyer who has voidable title. And think of the trustee in bankruptcy—often a significant player in secured credit when the debtor becomes financially distressed. Other third parties whose rights Article 9 addresses will be mentioned shortly in the discussion of priorities.

(D) Creation of a Security Interest: Attachment

The creation of a security interest under Article 9 is embodied in the concept of "attachment." UCC 9–203(2) provides that "[a]ttachment occurs as soon as all of the events specified in [UCC 9–203(1)] have taken place." UCC 9–203(1) sets forth three conditions to attachment, which may be met in any order. First, the debtor must agree that a security interest will attach *and* either the collateral must be in the secured party's possession or the debtor must have signed a security agreement (UCC 9–105(1)(*l*)) containing a description of the collateral (UCC 9–110). Second, "value" (UCC 1–201(44)) must have been given, and third, the debtor must have "rights in the collateral." Until all these elements have been satisfied, a security interest does not attach and "is not enforceable against the debtor or third parties with respect to the collateral." UCC 9–203(1). See generally Chapter 11, Section 2, infra.

Although not mentioned as a condition to attachment, the debtor's agreement must address the obligation that is secured by collateral— otherwise one of the two dimensions that mark the borders of a security interest would be missing. Article 9 affords the parties considerable freedom to determine which obligations are secured: "Obligations covered by a security agreement may include future advances or other value." UCC 9–204(3). In addition, "a security agreement may provide that any or all obligations covered by the security agreement are to be secured by after-acquired collateral." UCC 9–204(1).[3] But recall that no security interest can attach to the collateral under UCC 9–203(1) until the debtor has "rights" in it.

(E) Types of Collateral

Although Article 9's "unitary" approach to security interests generally treats all security interests the same, different types of collateral receive different treatment in several respects. Before mentioning some of those differences, which derive primarily from differences in the nature of the collateral and in the financing patterns that prevailed when Article 9 was first written, it will be useful to identify the various "types" of Article 9 collateral.[4] "Goods" (UCC 9–105(1)(h)) are subdivided into "consumer goods," "equipment," "farm products," and "inventory." UCC 9–109. Intangible collateral includes "accounts" and "general intangibles." UCC 9–106. Types of paper representing or embodying intangible rights include "chattel paper," "documents," and "instruments." UCC 9–105(1)(b), (f), & (i). Goods affixed to real estate can become "fixtures," although Article 9 leaves to real estate law the determination of what constitutes fixtures. UCC 9–313(1). Property acquired by a debtor upon the exchange or disposition of collateral, such as the account (right to payment) that arises when inventory is sold on unsecured credit, constitutes "proceeds." UCC 9–306(1). See generally Chapter 11, Section 4, infra.

Although we shall revisit the various types of collateral later in these materials (most of them on several occasions), it would be useful for you to review the statutory definitions at this point in your reading.

(F) Perfection and Priority

A secured party who wishes to rely on the benefits of a security interest in collateral will be concerned about whether conflicting claims to the collateral could come ahead of its security interest. A baseline rule of Article 9 can be found in UCC 9–201: "Except as otherwise provided by this Act a security agreement is effective according to its terms between the parties, against purchasers of the collateral, and against creditors." That (somewhat awkward) statement generally is understood to mean that an attached security interest in collateral will be senior to conflicting claims unless a provision in the Code provides otherwise. Much of the remainder of this book is devoted to an examination of the substantial number of provisions otherwise.

---

3. UCC 9–204(2) limits security interests in after-acquired consumer goods.

4. Comment 5 to UCC 9–102 contains a useful index of Article 9 sections containing special rules for each type of collateral.

In many cases a security interest's priority over other conflicting claims to collateral will depend on whether the security interest is "perfected." Perfection occurs when a security interest has attached and when the applicable steps specified in Article 9, Part 3 (specifically, UCC 9–302, UCC 9–304, UCC 9–305, and UCC 9–306) have been taken. UCC 9–303(1). If those steps are taken before attachment, perfection occurs upon attachment. Id. Although there are some specialized means of perfection, the two principal means are (i) the filing of a "financing statement" and (ii) the secured party's taking possession of the collateral. A security interest in some types of collateral can be perfected by either filing or possession (e.g., goods); other types can be perfected only by possession (e.g., instruments) or only by filing (e.g., accounts). See generally Chapter 11, Section 2, infra.

Part 4 of Article 9 deals with filing. Of particular importance are UCC 9–402 (dealing with what to file—the "formal requisites of a financing statement") and UCC 9–401 (dealing with where to file). See also UCC 9–103 (dealing with what state's law governs perfection and the effect of perfection or non-perfection). See generally Chapter 11, Sections 2 and 3, infra.

Article 9 includes several important priority rules. For example, under UCC 9–301(1) an attached but unperfected security interest is subordinate to the rights of certain non-ordinary course, good-faith buyers of collateral and, significantly, to the rights of a "lien creditor." (A "lien creditor" is a creditor with a judicial lien. UCC 9–301(3). We shall see in Chapter 14 that a debtor's trustee in bankruptcy can assume the seniority of a judicial lien creditor and set aside security interests that are unperfected when the debtor enters bankruptcy.) Under Article 9's priority rules, even perfected security interests are not perfect. For example, they usually are subordinate to competing Article 9 security interests under the first-in-time rule of UCC 9–312(5), which, however, is subject to long list of exceptions. See generally Chapter 13, Section 1, infra. Also, perfected security interests can be cut off by a "buyer in ordinary course of business." UCC 1–201(9); UCC 9–307(1). See generally Chapter 13, Section 2, infra.

Notwithstanding the apparent breadth of the baseline priority rule in UCC 9–201 and the large number of priority rules found elsewhere in the Article, many priority contests between Article 9 security interests and competing claimants to collateral are not addressed in Article 9 (or elsewhere in the Code). Examples are priority contests with federal tax liens and a growing variety of other statutory liens.

(G) ENFORCEMENT

The right and ability of a secured party to satisfy its claim out of the collateral already has been mentioned in general terms. Part 5 of Article 9 regulates in detail a secured party's enforcement rights. See generally Chapter 15, infra. These rights arise upon a debtor's "default." Just as Article 9 is silent concerning the nature and scope of the obligation secured by a security interest, so Article 9 does not define what constitutes a default in that obligation. Defining default is left primarily to the agreement of the debtor and secured party. In addition to failure to make a payment when due, sometimes with a grace period, typical defaults include the debtor's insolvency, bankruptcy, and breach of a loan covenant, and the existence of a conflicting lien on the collateral.

A menu of the rights and remedies of secured parties and debtors after default appears in UCC 9–501. Notwithstanding the Code's general deference to freedom of contract, see UCC 1–102, Article 9 prohibits debtors from waiving certain of their rights before default. UCC 9–501(3). As an empirical matter, the secured party's most important enforcement tools are its rights (i) to collect on intangible collateral, such as accounts, from the obligors (called "account debtors"), (ii) to take possession of collateral on default, and (iii) to dispose of collateral (typically, by sale or lease). UCC 9–105(1)(a) (defining "account debtor"); UCC 9–502 (secured party's collection rights); UCC 9–503 (secured party's right to take possession); UCC 9–504 (disposition of collateral). In the case of collections and dispositions, the secured party is entitled to apply funds received to the obligation secured, leaving the debtor obligated for a "deficiency" should the funds be insufficient. UCC 9–502(2); UCC 9–504(2). The debtor is entitled to any "surplus" that remains after satisfaction of the secured obligation and certain junior security interests. Id. In addition, a secured party may propose to retain collateral in satisfaction of the secured debt, but the debtor and certain junior secured parties are entitled to object to that proposal, thereby forcing the secured creditor to turn to another remedy, such as disposition. UCC 9–505.

To increase the likelihood that a fair price will be obtained upon the disposition of collateral, the secured party must give advance notice of the disposition to the debtor and certain junior secured parties, and every aspect of the disposition must be "commercially reasonable." UCC 9–504(3). Similarly, collections on intangible collateral must be undertaken in a commercially reasonable manner. UCC 9–502(2).

A debtor is entitled to "redeem" collateral at any time before the secured party disposes (or contracts to dispose) of the collateral or collects upon the collateral. UCC 9–506. This redemption right derives from the "equity of redemption" developed by the English courts of equity with respect to real estate. It recognizes that at some point the debtor's equitable right must be "foreclosed." Even today, people commonly use the term "debtor's equity" to refer to the positive remainder obtained when the amount of the secured obligation is subtracted from the value of the collateral and usually speak of "foreclosure" as the means of enforcing a lien. These terms can be traced historically to the foreclosure of a debtor's equity of redemption.

A secured party who fails to comply with Part 5 can be held liable to a debtor in damages and subjected to judicial restraint. UCC 9–507. Courts in some jurisdictions have held that a secured party who fails to comply with Part 5 loses its right to claim a deficiency, regardless of the amount of actual harm or damage (if any) caused by the noncompliance.

(H) REFERENCE MATERIALS

This field has been blessed by a book destined to join the short list of classics in legal literature: G. Gilmore, Security Interests in Personal Property (1965) (cited herein as Gilmore, Security). Those of you who wish to probe deeply should consult this work for perspective and for intensive examination of the history of personal property security law as well as the policies and provisions of the Code (and when you are in the mood for the refreshment offered by writing that combines charm with insight). Although dated (it deals with the 1962 Official Text of the Code), Professor Gilmore's treatise remains an important resource. Chapters 21–25 of J. White & R. Summers, Uniform Commercial Code (3d ed. 1988) deal incisively with the essential issues raised by Article 9. D. Baird & T. Jackson, Security Interests in Personal Property (2d ed. 1987), although nominally a casebook, includes extensive and valuable analyses of basic policy issues. Perhaps the most comprehensive narrative treatment of the law of secured financing, and one that frequently is updated with supplements, is B. Clark, The Law of Secured Transactions under the Uniform Commercial Code (2d ed. 1988 & Supp.) (cited herein as Clark, Secured Transactions). A clear and thorough explanation of many of the transactional patterns in secured financing, with numerous examples of documentation, is found in J. Dolan, Uniform Commercial Code: Terms and Transactions in Commercial Law 179–337 (1991).

Counsel for banks and finance companies that operate on a multistate basis need current and readily accessible material on developments in each state. This need has given rise to loose-leaf services not unlike those dealing with developments in taxation law. See, e.g., Commerce Clearing House (CCH), Secured Transactions Guide and Consumer Credit Guide. The General Introduction, supra, mentioned the valuable service that the Uniform Commercial Code Reporting Service (U.C.C. Rep. Serv.) provides in gathering cases decided under all Articles of the Code. That service also tracks adoptions of both official and nonuniform amendments to the Code on a state-by-state basis. (The other reference materials cited in the General Introduction also are valuable resources for study and research concerning secured transactions.) For many of the difficult issues posed by secured financing under Article 9, the most thorough treatment will be found in legal periodicals; many of these are cited in the Notes that follow the cases and Problems.

SECTION 3. THE ROLES OF LAWYERS IN SECURED TRANSACTIONS

We have met tax lawyers, litigators, securities lawyers, and patent lawyers, but we have never met a self-styled "secured transactions" lawyer. To be sure, we have met many who held themselves out as experts on secured transactions (and most of them really were). But the law governing secured transactions never represents more than one slice of any pie, significant and complex as that slice may be.

Consider, for example, a large, syndicated bank financing, in which several banks in a "syndicate" are extending credit to a corporation under the same credit agreement. The lawyers who represent each of the parties in such a large, sophisticated transaction well might refer to themselves as "financing lawyers" or "commercial lawyers," but would be just as likely, perhaps, to observe that they are "corporate lawyers" who "do deals." As counsel for the lenders and the borrower, they would be expected to prepare and negotiate the wording of the documentation and render formal, written legal opinions on the enforceability of the documentation and on various other aspects of the transaction. Counsel would consult frequently with their clients and advise them concerning legal risks. Counsel almost certainly would need not only a sound understanding of business matters, such as how the banks obtain funds to make their loans and the accounting principles featured in various covenants, but also expertise in diverse areas of the law: regulations affecting the bank lenders, restrictions on interest rates that can be charged, rights of setoff against bank accounts, liens arising out of the Employee Retirement Income Security Act ("ERISA"), federal and state tax liens and a variety of other federal and state lien statutes, securities regulation laws affecting the borrower, conflict of laws, equitable principles that limit the enforceability of agreements, tort law relating to the behavior of lenders, the effects of the borrower's or lender's insolvency, etc. (the list could go on and on). The collateral may be an indispensable part of the transaction and may occupy much of the time of the lawyers involved, but it is only one part of the deal.

Assume now that the borrower in our syndicated bank financing becomes financially distressed; it is in default under that financing, as well as under various other financings, and is behind in paying its trade debt. If the borrower is not in bankruptcy, counsel for many of the creditors and counsel for the debtor might undertake negotiations (usually called a **workout**) leading to a restructuring of credit extensions. Much of the same expertise and many of the same lawyering skills brought to bear in the original financings will be called upon in the workout context. If the borrower becomes a debtor under the Bankruptcy Code, the nature of the work of many of the lawyers will be essentially the same as in the out-of-court workout. However, some disputes or claims may require litigation, in which case lawyers skilled in trial practice will be utilized.

Now consider an individual consumer's purchase of an automobile financed by a commercial bank. The bank will present several "forms" to the individual borrower for signature (e.g., credit application, promissory note, security agreement). It would be quite rare for the bank's loan officer or the borrower to retain and consult counsel to assist in this financing. Indeed, it is unlikely that the bank would agree to one-time changes to its forms under any circumstances. Although the parties need not worry about securities laws that apply to the borrower or about complicated financial covenants, it would be a serious mistake to think that lawyers had not played an essential role in this consumer transaction. Federal and state regulation of consumer credit (including disclosure requirements and mandatory and prohibited practices and terms) is so complex and pervasive that only highly specialized and knowledgeable counsel are equipped to prepare and approve consumer credit forms.[1]

If the consumer buyer defaults in the monthly payments or files for bankruptcy, the bank may retain a "collection" lawyer who specializes in collections of consumer debts. The lawyer might resort to legal proceedings or, if the debtor is in bankruptcy, might assist the bank in obtaining possession of the collateral or in working out a mutually acceptable resolution between the borrower and the bank. At that stage, the borrower also might have retained a lawyer (if the borrower could afford the cost); the borrower's lawyer would be sure to examine closely the transaction with the bank to uncover potential attacks on the validity of the bank's claim and security interest and any possible counterclaim against the bank arising out of regulatory noncompliance or otherwise.

In sum, the roles of legal counsel in financings, including secured financings, involve much more than the ex post analysis of facts for the purpose of predicting (or advocating) an appropriate judicial resolution (i.e., *A* sues *B*; who wins?). As you work your way through the following materials, from time to time you will be asked to identify problems and propose ex ante solutions. You will also have an opportunity to consider how you might counsel your client in a variety of circumstances.

---

1. We have seen the FTC's anti-holder in due course rule in Chapter 2, Section 1(B), and its rule prohibiting nonpossesso- ry, non-purchase money security interests in household goods in Section 1 of this Chapter.

Chapter 11

ESTABLISHMENT AND PERFECTION
OF SECURITY INTERESTS

SECTION 1. FINANCING AUTOMOBILES:
A PROTOTYPE

The preceding chapter briefly mentioned some aspects of the auto-mobile financing transactions illustrated in this Section. The following Prototype portrays in more detail the legal and related business practic-es employed in financing the marketing of automobiles.[1] This picture may suggest ways to avoid legal pitfalls through proper handling of business transactions generally; it also provides a good setting for dealing with the legal problems that arise in this and other important types of financing. You should read this Section quickly at this point to get an overview of the basic transactions. We shall return to this Prototype at various points later in these materials when dealing with specific problems.

The following pages present a typical example of automobile fi-nancing at two levels: (i) while the dealer holds the cars as inventory (financing the acquisition of a dealer's inventory of durable goods sometimes is called **floorplanning**) and (ii) upon the sale of one of the cars to an individual consumer who buys the car "on time." The dealer is Main Motors, Inc., a Pontiac dealer; credit for the dealer's inventory financing is supplied by a lending institution named Firstbank. The consumer buyer is Lee Abel; secured credit for Abel's purchase also is provided by Firstbank, but in a transaction that is separate and distinct from the inventory financing for Main Motors.

(A) Financing the Dealer's Inventory: The Setting

Main Motors sells about 700 new Pontiacs each year at a retail value of close to $10,500,000; Main's sales of used cars (most taken by Main as "trade-ins" on new cars) come to about one half of this amount. To meet varied tastes for model, color, and combinations of accessories, and to facilitate sales to eager buyers, Main carries an inventory averaging 175 new cars, with a wholesale cost to Main of about $2,400,000. Main has a physical plant (land and buildings, including

---

1. The Prototype does not necessarily describe the practices of any particular bank, automobile dealer, or automobile manufacturer.

showroom, service facility, and parking lots; tools and other equipment; etc.) valued at $2,100,000, and carries about $300,000 worth of parts and accessories required for its service department. More than one-half of Main's sales of new cars are installment credit sales; for used cars the proportion is greater. Most of the installment contracts for new cars run 48 months, and for used cars 30 months. Consequently, without financing assistance, Main's investment in new cars would be tied up for extended periods even after their sale. Like most car dealers, Main lacks capital to meet all of these needs and relies heavily on financing.

Firstbank has field representatives who solicit dealers to establish financing arrangements. One of them contacts Main Motors and proposes terms on which the bank will (i) finance (floorplan) Main's inventory of new cars, thereby enabling Main to acquire cars on credit, and (ii) purchase the consumer installment contracts generated by Main's installment sales, thereby eliminating Main's burden of waiting for payment until each installment comes due.

Finding the terms of Firstbank's proposal more attractive than Main's existing financing arrangements with another lender, Main's management indicates its willingness to accept Firstbank's terms.

(B) CREATING AND PERFECTING FIRSTBANK'S SECURITY INTEREST

At this point, Main signs several documents, including a *financing statement* and a *security agreement*.

The Financing Statement. Firstbank will file a financing statement (Form 1) in the appropriate filing office;[2] the completed form is designed to meet the requirements of UCC 9–402.

The Security Agreement. You will recall that perfection of a security interest requires, in addition to filing a financing statement, that the security interest attach. UCC 9–303(1). Recall as well that one element of attachment is that the debtor sign a security agreement describing the collateral. UCC 9–203(1)(a). The security agreement signed by Main Motors is a detailed, **blanket lien** (i.e., very broad coverage) agreement, the "Dealer Inventory Security Agreement" (Form 2). This comprehensive contract between the parties includes language not only evidencing the bank's continuing security interest in Main's inventory and related collateral (see ¶ 5), but also authorizing the bank to endorse notes and sign financing statements on behalf of Main (see ¶ 6). It also contains provisions relating to the terms of the lending arrangements (see ¶¶ 1, 2, and 8), defining the "Events of Default" (see ¶ 12), and setting forth Firstbank's remedies (see ¶ 13).

---

2. For the place of filing within a state, see UCC 9–401(1); as to the applicability, here, of Pennsylvania law, see UCC 9–103(1). Both sections are discussed in Section 3, infra. Firstbank will file both with the Secretary of the Commonwealth of Pennsylvania, in Harrisburg, and also (because Main Motors has only one place of business) with the Prothonotary of the County of Philadelphia pursuant to UCC 9–401(1)(c) (third alternative, as adopted by Pennsylvania).

FORM 1
FINANCING STATEMENT

PARTIES	FINANCING STATEMENT
	FINANCING STATEMENT Uniform Commercial Code Form UCC-1 **IMPORTANT — Please read instructions on** **reverse side of page 4 before completing**

PARTIES

Debtor name (last name first if individual) and mailing address:

MAIN MOTORS, INC.
237 North Seventh Street
Philadelphia, PA 19116

1

Debtor name (last name first if individual) and mailing address:

1a

Debtor name (last name first if individual) and mailing address:

1b

Secured Party(ies) name(s) (last name first if individual) and address for security interest information:

FIRSTBANK, N.A.
Broad and Spruce Streets
Philadelphia, PA 19110

2

Assignee(s) of Secured Party name(s) (last name first if individual) and address for security interest information:

2a

Special Types of Parties (check if applicable):

☐ The terms "Debtor" and "Secured Party" mean "Lessee" and "Lessor," respectively.

☐ The terms "Debtor" and "Secured Party" mean "Consignee" and "Consignor," respectively.

☐ Debtor is a Transmitting Utility

3

SECURED PARTY SIGNATURE(S)

This statement is filed with only the Secured Party's signature to perfect a security interest in collateral (check applicable box(es)) —

a ☐ acquired after a change of name, identity or corporate structure of the Debtor.

b ☐ as to which the filing has lapsed.

c already subject to a security interest in another county in Pennsylvania —
  ☐ when the collateral was moved to this county.
  ☐ when the Debtor's residence or place of business was moved to this county.

d already subject to a security interest in another jurisdiction —
  ☐ when the collateral was moved to Pennsylvania.
  ☐ when the Debtor's location was moved to Pennsylvania.

e ☐ which is proceeds of the collateral described in block 9, in which a security interest was previously perfected (also describe proceeds in block 9, if purchased with cash proceeds and not adequately described on the original financing statement)

Secured Party Signature(s)
(required only if box(es) is checked above):

_____

_____

_____

4

Filing No. (stamped by filing officer):   Date, Time, Filing Office (stamped by filing officer):

5

This Financing Statement is presented for filing pursuant to the Uniform Commercial Code, and is to be filed with the (check applicable box):

☒ Secretary of the Commonwealth.
☐ Prothonotary of _____ County.
☐ real estate records of _____ County.

6

Number of Additional Sheets (if any): 7

Optional Special Identification (Max. 10 characters): 8

COLLATERAL

Identify collateral by item and/or type:
  All of the following, whether now owned or hereafter acquired: Inventory; accounts, chattel paper, general intangibles, and all obligations of sureties and guarantors for the payment and satisfaction thereof; contracts of lease, sale, rental or other dispositions of inventory; books and records; rights in connection with the residual value of inventory leased, rented, sold or otherwise disposed of, including proceeds of any third party's exercise of an option to purchase; replacements or substitutions of any of the foregoing, including cash and non-cash proceeds thereof, proceeds of proceeds, all insurance thereon and proceeds of such insurance, trade-ins, returned goods, and repossessed goods.

☐ (check only if desired) Products of the collateral are also covered.

9

Identify related real estate, if applicable: The collateral is, or includes (check appropriate box(es)) —

a. ☐ crops growing or to be grown on —
b. ☐ goods which are or are to become fixtures on —
c. ☐ minerals or the like (including oil and gas) as extracted on —
d. ☐ accounts resulting from the sale of minerals or the like (including oil and gas) at the wellhead or minehead on —

the following real estate:
Street Address:

Described at: Book _____ of (check one) ☐ Deeds ☐ Mortgages , at Page(s) _____ .
for _____ County. Uniform Parcel Identifier _____
☐ Described on Additional Sheet.
Name of record owner (required only if no Debtor has an interest of record):

10

DEBTOR SIGNATURE(S)

Debtor Signature(s):

1   MAIN MOTORS, INC.

1a   *G. S. Gessell*

By: G. S. Gessell, President

1b

RETURN RECEIPT TO

FIRSTBANK, N.A.
Broad and Spruce Streets
Philadelphia, PA 19110

11

12

STANDARD FORM — FORM UCC 1
Approved by Secretary of Commonwealth of Pennsylvania
PRINTED FOR AND SOLD BY JOHN C. CLARK CO.

FILING OFFICE ORIGINAL   [G11025]

FORM 2
DEALER INVENTORY SECURITY AGREEMENT

FIRSTBANK, N.A., a national banking association with a place of business located at Broad & Spruce Streets, Philadelphia, Pennsylvania

("Bank"), and   Main Motors, Inc.   a   Delaware corporation

whose principal place of business is

   237 North Seventh Street, Philadelphia, PA   19116

("Dealer"), intending to be legally bound, hereby agree as follows:

1. BACKGROUND.

     Dealer hereby requests Bank from time to time to make loans and advances to Dealer ("Loan(s)") acceptable to Bank to finance the purchase of Inventory, as that term is defined herein, from suppliers thereof ("Suppliers") for sale or lease in the ordinary course of Dealer's business. Subject to the terms and conditions of this agreement ("Agreement"), Bank expects to finance Dealer's purchase of Inventory, but reserves in its sole discretion, the right to decline to make any Loan(s) requested by Dealer for any reason. Loan(s) may be disbursed either directly to Dealer, to Dealer's demand deposit account at Bank, or by Bank's paying, at Dealer's request and for Dealer's account, drafts of, or other demands for payment by, a Supplier properly presented to Bank when accompanied by the manufacturer's invoice or bill of sale and adequate documentation of proper ownership.

2. LOAN(S) AND NOTE.

     Subject to the terms and conditions hereof, and Bank's continuing satisfaction with the financial and other conditions of Dealer, Bank will from time to time during the continuance of the Agreement make Loan(s) to Dealer, as Dealer may from time to time request, on not less than five (5) days prior notice, by submitting to Bank a properly completed Loan Request Form in the form attached hereto ("Loan Request Form") (or by complying with any other means of requesting Loans as may be agreed upon by Bank and Dealer in writing), to finance Dealer's purchase of Inventory, provided, however, the aggregate principal amount outstanding of such Loan(s) shall not, at any one time, exceed the sum of $2,400,000.   ("Loan Limit"). Bank may, from time to time, raise or lower the Loan Limit upon five (5) days' written notice to Dealer. Bank expressly reserves, in its sole discretion, the right to decline to make any Loan(s) requested by Dealer for any reason. Dealer agrees to execute and deliver to Bank a demand note in an amount equal to the Loan Limit, in the form attached hereto ("Note(s)") and, at Bank's request, to execute from time to time such additional or substituted Note(s) as are necessary to evidence any change in the Loan Limit. The actual amount due under the Note(s) shall be that amount as shown on the Bank's books and records. Bank will from time to time render to Dealer statements of all amounts due Bank under the Note(s) which statements shall be deemed conclusive and irrefutable evidence of the actual amounts due Bank, unless Dealer notifies Bank in writing to the contrary within fifteen (15) days of Bank's sending such statements to Dealer.

3. INVENTORY.

     For purposes of this Agreement, "Inventory" means any new or used inventory (as that term is defined in the Pennsylvania Uniform Commercial Code (the "UCC"), Article 9) that is owned or possessed by Dealer and shall include all tangible personal property held by Dealer for sale or lease or to be furnished under contracts of service, tangible personal property that the Dealer has so leased or furnished, tangible personal property held by others for sale on consignment for the Dealer, tangible personal property sold by the Dealer on a sale or return or consignment basis, tangible personal property returned to the Dealer or repossessed by the Dealer following a sale thereof by Dealer, and tangible personal property represented by a document of title, including, but not limited to, automobiles, parts and accessories, together with all materials, additions, equipment, accessions, accessories and parts installed in, related, attached or added thereto or used in connection therewith and all substitutions and exchanges for and replacements thereof whether installed prior to receipt or after receipt by Dealer. An Item of Inventory financed hereunder is an "Item".

4. FINANCING TERMS.

     The percentage of the purchase price of any Item that Bank, in its discretion, elects to lend to Dealer to finance the purchase thereof pursuant to this Agreement will be established by Bank from time to time by prior written notice to Dealer ("Financing Terms").

5. GRANT OF SECURITY INTEREST.

     As security for the prompt and punctual payment and performance of all liabilities and obligations of Dealer to Bank, including, but not limited to, the Note(s), and the performance by Dealer of all of Dealer's obligations as set forth herein and/or in any and all documents and instruments executed or delivered in conjunction herewith, and the complete satisfaction of all existing and future liabilities and obligations of Dealer to Bank or of Dealer and others to Bank of any nature whatsoever, whether matured or unmatured, absolute or contingent, direct or indirect, sole, joint or several, and any extensions, modifications or renewals thereof, including, but not limited to, all of Bank's expenses incurred in connection with the collection and performance of Dealer's liabilities and obligations hereunder, Bank's reasonable attorney's fees and the costs of curing any Event of Default (as specified below in paragraph 12) that Bank elects to cure, all of which Dealer hereby agrees to pay (collectively, "Dealer's Liabilities to Bank"), Dealer hereby grants and conveys to Bank a continuing lien upon and security interest in all of Dealer's property described below now owned or hereafter acquired:

     (a) Inventory;
     (b) Accounts, chattel paper, and general intangibles (each as defined in the Pennsylvania UCC, Article 9) and all obligations of sureties and guarantors for the payment and satisfaction thereof;
     (c) Contracts of lease, sale, rental or other disposition of Inventory in which Dealer has an interest;
     (d) Books and Records (herein defined to mean all books and records of original or final entry, including, without limitation: invoices; receipts; instruments; documents; account ledgers and journals (both due and payable); minutes; resolutions; correspondence with regard to the Collateral; tax returns; bank checks, receipts and financing statements; contracts; agreements; and any other books and records maintained by Dealer in the normal course of Dealer's business, including all such books and records as have been photocopied, reduced to film images or otherwise, or encoded into electronic or mechanical impulses in or

[G11026]

upon computer tapes, programs, software, and data banks associated therewith, or accounting or recording machines or the like, and without regard to whether such books and records are maintained at Dealer's place of business or elsewhere);

(e) Rights in connection with the residual value of any of Dealer's Inventory leased, rented, sold or otherwise disposed of, including but not limited to the proceeds of any third party's option to purchase any portion of Dealer's Inventory;

(f) Balances on deposit with or held in any capacity by Bank at any time and any other property of any nature of Dealer that Bank may at any time have in its possession wherever located, now or hereafter acquired; and

(g) All replacements and substitutions of all or any of the foregoing, all cash and non-cash proceeds thereof, proceeds of proceeds thereof, all insurance thereon, and all proceeds of such insurance, including, but not limited to trade-ins, returned, and/or repossessed goods.

Bank's rights in all of the above property (collectively, "Collateral") shall be independent of any right of set-off or appropriation that Bank may have or acquire under paragraph 13 hereof or otherwise.

6. POWER OF ATTORNEY.

Dealer hereby appoints any employee, officer or agent of Bank as Dealer's true and lawful attorney-in-fact, with power:

(a)   To endorse the name of Dealer upon:

(i)   Any Note(s), security agreement, UCC financing statement and continuations thereof, certificates of origin and certificates of title to any motor vehicle or other property evidenced by such a certificate and any other instrument or document required by Bank to perfect and continue perfection of the liens and security interests granted to Bank hereunder or otherwise in connection with Loan(s);

(ii)   Any and all other notes, checks, drafts, money orders or other instruments of payment;

(iii) Instruments received by Dealer in connection with the sale or other disposition of any Collateral;

(iv)   Any check that may be payable to Dealer on account of returned or unearned premiums or the proceeds of insurance (and any amount so collected may be applied by Bank toward satisfaction of any of Dealer's Liabilities to Bank).

(b)   To sign and endorse the name of Dealer upon any: drafts against all persons obligated to pay, directly or indirectly any account, chattel paper, general intangible, or instrument ("Account Debtors"); assignments, verifications and notices in connection with any Collateral; and invoices, freight or express bills, bills of lading, and storage or warehouse receipts relating to any Collateral;

(c)   To give written notices in connection with accounts, chattel paper, general intangibles, or instruments;

(d)   To give written notices to officers and officials of the United States Postal Service to effect a change or changes of address so that all mail addressed to Dealer may be delivered directly to Bank (Bank will return all mail not related to the Dealer's Liabilities to Bank or the Collateral to Bank); and

(e)   To open all such mail.

Dealer hereby grants unto said attorney full power to do any and all things necessary to be done with respect to the above as fully and effectively as Dealer might or could do with full power of substitution and hereby ratifying and confirming all its said attorney or its substitute shall lawfully do or cause to be done by virtue hereof. This power of attorney shall be deemed to be coupled with an interest and irrevocable until all of Dealer's Liabilities to Bank are paid or performed in full, and shall survive any dissolution, termination or liquidation of Dealer.

7. DOWN PAYMENT; ASSIGNMENT OF TITLE.

Dealer agrees that on or before accepting delivery of any Item it will pay Supplier, in cash and not by credit whether extended by Supplier or any other person, the amount(s) required pursuant to the Financing Terms. Dealer hereby requests and authorizes Bank to pay the proceeds of the Loan(s) to Supplier. Dealer acknowledges that it acquires each Item subject to Bank's lien and security interest therein and Dealer hereby irrevocably authorizes Supplier to deliver to Bank, upon Bank's written request, a certificate of origin, certificate of title or other evidence of ownership evidencing a first perfected security interest in favor of Bank in or unencumbered title to each Item and all other documents and certificates necessary to evidence the same.

8. DEALER'S PAYMENTS TO BANK.

Without Bank's prior written consent, Dealer will not sell any Item for a price less than the then outstanding principal balance of the Loan(s) plus accrued and unpaid interest thereon made to enable Dealer to acquire that Item ("Release Price"). When Dealer sells an Item it will promptly pay to Bank the Release Price of such Item.

Dealer agrees to make such payments to Bank from time to time to reduce the principal balance of any Loan(s) made hereunder to enable Dealer to purchase an Item that Dealer has not sold as Bank and Dealer shall agree to, in writing, from time to time.

Provided, however, that nothing herein shall be construed to amend in any way the terms of the Note(s) which is, and is intended to remain, payable ON DEMAND, it being understood that Bank may demand payment at any time of the Note(s). Without first paying Bank in full the Release Price, Dealer will not return for credit, exchange or consign any Item.

9. INVENTORY RISKS.

Bank assumes no responsibility for the existence, character, quality, quantity, condition, value and/or delivery of any Item. Dealer shall not be relieved of any of Dealer's Liabilities to Bank because any Item fails to conform to the manufacturer's, Supplier's, or Dealer's warranties, or because any Item may be lost, stolen destroyed or damaged. Dealer will promptly notify Bank of the loss, theft or destruction of or damage to any Item and will forthwith pay to Bank the Release Price of such Item.

10. INDEMNIFICATION.

Dealer agrees to comply with all requirements of the federal Truth in Lending Act and the federal Equal Credit Opportunity Act, and Regulations Z and B of the Board of Governors of the Federal Reserve System, Trade Regulation Rules of the Federal Trade Commission, the federal Fair Debt Collection Practices Act and Fair Credit Reporting Act, the Pennsylvania Model Act for the Regulation of Credit Life Insurance and Credit Accident and Health Insurance, the Pennsylvania Unfair Trade Practices and Consumer Protection Law, the Motor Vehicle Sales Finance Act, the Goods and Services Installment Sales Act, and all regulations promulgated by all governmental units and agencies thereunder, and all other applicable state, federal and local laws, regulations and ordinances regulating the credit sale of goods and/or services by Dealer and at all times to carry on its business in a lawful manner. Dealer

[G11027]

hereby agrees to indemnify, defend and hold Bank harmless from and against all liability and claims asserted against Bank by any person in connection with:

    (a)   any sale, lease, enforcement or other disposition of any Collateral;

    (b)   any alleged violation of any law, regulation or ordinance by Dealer or Bank in connection with this Agreement or any other contract between Dealer and Bank;

    (c)   any personal injury alleged to have been suffered by any person in connection with any sale, lease, enforcement or other disposition of any Collateral;

    (d)   any claim by any person arising out of Dealer's breach of warranty or failure to perform any of Dealer's obligations under any contract regarding the sale, lease, enforcement or disposition of any Collateral; or

    (e)   any claim by any person arising from a claim made by a consumer under the Federal Trade Commission's Trade Regulation Rule to Preserve Consumer Defenses on any loan made by Bank to said consumer, whether referred to Bank by Dealer or not.

Dealer further agrees to reimburse Bank for all interest, counsel fees and costs expended by Bank in connection with the foregoing, including, but not limited to, those incurred in any bankruptcy or insolvency proceedings, and any subsequent proceedings or appeals from any order or judgment entered therein. This indemnification shall survive termination of this Agreement.

11. WARRANTIES, REPRESENTATIONS AND COVENANTS.

To induce Bank to enter into this Agreement and to extend credit, Dealer warrants, represents and covenants (which warranties, representations and covenants shall survive this Agreement) that:

    (a)   Dealer will keep complete and accurate Books and Records and make all necessary entries thereon to reflect all transactions respecting the Collateral. Dealer will keep Bank informed as to the location of all Books and Records and will permit Bank, its officers, employees and agents, to have access to all Books and Records and any other records pertaining to Dealer's business and financial condition that Bank may request and, if deemed necessary by Bank, permit Bank, its officers, employees and agents, to remove them from Dealer's places of business or any other places where the same may be found for the purposes of examining, auditing and copying same. Any Books and Records so removed by Bank will be returned to Dealer by Bank as soon as Bank shall have completed its inspection, audit or copying thereof.

    (b)   All of Dealer's offices where it keeps its Books and Records concerning the Collateral and all locations at which it keeps its Inventory, and all locations at which it maintains a place of business are listed in Schedule A attached hereto. Dealer will promptly notify Bank in writing of any change in the locations of its Books and Records, of the Collateral, of any place of business or of the closing or establishment of any new place of business. If any of the Collateral or any Books and Records are at any time to be located on premises leased by Dealer or on premises owned by Dealer subject to a mortgage or other lien, Dealer will obtain and deliver or cause to be delivered to Bank, prior to delivery of any Collateral or Books and Records to such premises, an agreement, in form and substance satisfactory to Bank, waiving the landlord's, mortgagee's or lienholder's rights to enforce any claim against Dealer for monies due under the landlord's lien, mortgagee's mortgage, or other lien by levy or distraint, or other similar proceedings against the Collateral or Books and Records and assuring Bank's ability to have access to the Collateral and Books and Records in order to exercise Bank's rights to take possession thereof and to remove them from such premises.

    (c)   Dealer has, and at all times will have, good, marketable and indefeasible title to the Collateral, free and clear of all liens or encumbrances (except for taxes not in default or contested in good faith, for which adequate reserves have been set aside, and Bank's liens and security interests). All accounts, chattel paper, general intangibles, and instruments included in the Collateral arose in the ordinary course of Dealer's business and are not subject to any defense, set-off or counterclaim.

    (d)   Dealer will, at its sole cost and expense, preserve the Collateral and Dealer's rights against Account Debtors free and clear of all liens and encumbrances except those created pursuant hereto. Dealer will not grant to anyone other than Bank any lien upon or security interest in the Collateral nor allow any person other than Bank to obtain a lien upon the Collateral. At Dealer's sole expense, Dealer will keep the Collateral in good condition and repair at all times.

    (e)   Dealer will at all times keep itself and the Collateral insured against all hazards in such amounts and by such insurers as are satisfactory to Bank together with full casualty and extended coverage in amount not less than one hundred ten percent (110%) of the Loan Limit. Dealer will cause Bank's security interests in the Collateral to be endorsed on all policies of insurance thereon in such manner that all payments for losses will be paid to Bank as loss payee and Dealer will furnish Bank with evidence of such insurance and endorsements. Such policies shall be payable to Dealer and Bank as their respective interests appear and shall contain a provision whereby they cannot be cancelled except after ten (10) days' written notice to the Bank. In the event that Dealer fails to pay any such insurance premiums when due, Bank may, but is not required to, pay such premiums and add the costs thereof to the amounts due Bank by Dealer under the Note(s), which costs Dealer hereby agrees to pay to Bank with interest at the rate specified in the Note(s). Dealer hereby assigns to Bank any returned or unearned premiums that may be due Dealer upon cancellation of any such policies for any reason whatsoever and directs the insurers to pay Bank any amounts so due.

    (f)   Dealer will promptly notify Bank if there is any change in the status or physical condition of any Collateral or the ability of any Account Debtor to pay or preserve the Collateral, or of any defense, set-off or counterclaim asserted by any person. If any Collateral is sold, leased, rented, released for demonstration, transferred or otherwise moved from the place where such Collateral is normally kept by Dealer, Dealer will notify Bank forthwith.

    (g)   Dealer will permit Bank to inspect and audit the Collateral at all reasonable times. In the event that Bank and Dealer cannot agree within seventy-two (72) hours as to what shall be a reasonable time to inspect and audit Collateral, Bank's decision shall be controlling, and upon oral notice, Dealer will permit such inspection and audit.

    (h)   Dealer hereby irrevocably assigns to Bank all of its rights of stoppage in transit with respect to any item sold on credit to any Account Debtor, which rights shall be paramount to Dealer's.

    (i)   Dealer will, at such intervals as Bank may require, submit to Bank:

        (i)   a schedule reflecting, in form and detail satisfactory to Bank, the names and addresses of all Account Debtors together with the amounts due for all of Dealer's outstanding accounts; and

[G11026]

(ii)   copies of all invoices evidencing the sale or lease of any Item or Items to Account Debtors pertaining to any or all of its accounts, with evidence of shipment of the Item or Items, the sale or the leasing of which have given rise to such accounts.

(j)   Dealer will file all tax returns that Dealer is required to file and pay when due all taxes and license and other fees with respect to the Collateral and Dealer's business, except taxes contested in good faith and for which adequate reserves have been established by Dealer.

(k)   If a certificate of title is required to be issued for any Item, Dealer will file all documents necessary to obtain such a certificate from the appropriate governmental authority within three (3) days after the date of the Loan made to enable the Dealer to purchase that item. Dealer will cause a notation of the Bank's lien and security interest to be made and noted on such certificate at Dealer's sole expense. If Dealer fails or refuses to so file such document or note Bank's liens and security interests thereon, Bank may, at Dealer's expense, file such documents as Bank, in its sole discretion, deems appropriate to perfect its lien and security interest.

(l)   The proceeds of each Loan will be used solely to finance the purchase price of Inventory in accordance with the Financing Terms.

(m)   Dealer, if a corporation, is duly organized, validly existing and in good standing under the laws of the state of its incorporation, has the power and authority to make and perform this Agreement, and is duly qualified in all jurisdictions in which it conducts its business or where such qualification is required. The execution, delivery and performance of this Agreement, and the execution and delivery of the Note(s) and all other documents required hereunder have been duly authorized and will not violate any provision of law or regulation or of the articles of incorporation, by-laws or partnership agreement of Dealer or of any agreement, indenture or instrument to which Dealer is a party, or result in the creation or imposition of any security interest, lien or encumbrance in any of the Collateral. This Agreement, the Note(s) and all other documents related hereto, when executed and delivered by Dealer, will be valid and binding obligations of Dealer, enforceable against Dealer in accordance with their terms.

(n)   Within ninety (90) days after the end of each fiscal year of Dealer, Dealer will furnish Bank with annual financial reports relating to the financial condition of Dealer and its affiliates (including but not limited to consolidated and consolidating balance sheets, earnings or profit or loss statements and surplus statements), each in reasonable detail and prepared by an independent certified public accountant ("CPA") in accordance with generally accepted accounting principles consistently applied. In addition, Dealer will obtain from such independent CPA and deliver to Bank, within ninety (90) days after the close of each fiscal year, such CPA's written statement that in making the examination necessary to the certification, the CPA has obtained no knowledge of the occurrence or imminent occurrence of any Event of Default (as specified in paragraph 12 below) by Dealer hereunder, or disclosing all Events of Default of which such CPA has obtained knowledge; provided, however, that in making the examination such CPA shall not be required to go beyond the bounds of generally accepted auditing procedures for the purposes of certifying financial statements. Bank shall have the right, from time to time, to discuss Dealer's affairs directly with Dealer's independent CPA after notice to Dealer and opportunity for Dealer to be present at any such discussions. Dealer agrees that the CPA selected by Dealer shall be acceptable to Bank, it being agreed that Bank will not unreasonably withhold its consent of the accountants selected by Dealer.

(o)   On or before the fifteenth (15th) day of each month Dealer will furnish to Bank (in form satisfactory to Bank) unaudited statements of the financial condition and operations of Dealer and its affiliates for the preceding calendar month.

(p)   Dealer will furnish Bank promptly with such information in addition to that specified in subparagraphs (n) and (o) above respecting the financial condition and affairs of Dealer and its affiliates as Bank may, from time to time, reasonably require.

(q)   No Event of Default, as specified in paragraph 12 below, has occurred or is about to occur and no event has occurred or is about to occur that, with the passage of time or giving of notice or both, could be an Event of Default.

(r)   There are no suits in law or equity or proceedings before any tribunal or governmental instrumentality now pending or, to the knowledge of Dealer, threatened against Dealer or any guarantor or surety for Dealer's Liabilities to Bank, the adverse result of which would in any material respect affect the property, finances or operations of Dealer or of any surety or guarantor for Dealer, or their ability to satisfy Dealer's Liabilities to Bank.

(s)   No statement, warranty, representation, covenant, information, document or financial statement made, presented or asserted by Dealer to Bank in connection with this Agreement or as an inducement to Bank to make Loan(s) hereunder was or is incorrect, incomplete, false or misleading in any material respect nor has Dealer failed to advise Bank of any information affecting materially Dealer's business, operations or financial condition.

(t)   In the event that Bank, for any reason, determines that the value of the Collateral is insufficient to secure adequately the actual amount due Bank under the Note(s), Dealer will, upon ten (10) days' written notice:

    (i)   deliver or cause to be delivered to Bank additional Collateral in an amount sufficient, in Bank's sole discretion, to secure adequately such amounts due Bank; or

    (ii)   reduce the outstanding aggregate balance of Loan(s) by an amount satisfactory to Bank.

(u)   Dealer will not permit:

    (i)   any of the Collateral to be levied or distrained upon under any legal process;

    (ii)   any of the Collateral to become a fixture unless that fact has been disclosed to Bank in advance in writing; or

    (iii)   any Item to be subject to any lease or rental agreement if the Account Debtor's obligations thereon have not been assigned to Bank pursuant to the provisions hereof, unless Dealer has paid Bank in full the Loan made to enable Dealer to purchase that Item.

12. EVENTS OF DEFAULT.

Dealer shall be in default hereunder upon the occurrence of any one or more of the following ("Events of Default"):

(a)   The failure of Dealer at any time to observe or perform any of its agreements, warranties, representations, covenants or obligations contained in this Agreement, the Note(s) or any other document related hereto, or if any statement, warranty, representation, covenant, signature or information made herein or contained in any

[G11029]

application, exhibit, schedule, statement, certificate, financial statement or other document executed or delivered pursuant to or in connection with this Agreement or the Note(s), was or is incorrect, incomplete, false or misleading;

(b) The failure of Dealer to furnish promptly to Bank such financial or other information as Bank may reasonably request;

(c) The failure to pay the outstanding balance of Loan(s) and all accrued interest thereon to Bank UPON DEMAND by Bank or the nonpayment when due of any amount payable on any of Dealer's Liabilities to Bank of whatsoever nature;

(d) The failure of Dealer to observe or perform any agreement of any nature whatsoever with Bank or any other party; or the occurrence of any event of default, or any event that, with the passage of time or giving of notice or both, would be an event of default by Dealer under any other agreement;

(e) Dealer, or any surety or guarantor for Dealer's Liabilities to Bank, becomes insolvent, or makes any assignment for the benefit of creditors, or any petition is filed by or against Dealer, or any surety or guarantor for Dealer's Liabilities to Bank, under the federal Bankruptcy Code or under any provision of any other law or statute alleging that Dealer, or any surety or guarantor for Dealer's Liabilities to Bank, is insolvent or unable to pay debts as they mature;

(f) The entry of any judicial or tax lien against Dealer, or any surety or guarantor for Dealer's Liabilities to Bank, or against any of their respective properties, whether such lien is junior or senior to Bank's security interest, or the appointment of any receiver, trustee, conservator or other court officer over the Dealer, or any surety or guarantor for Dealer's Liabilities to Bank, or against any of their respective properties, for any purpose, or the occurrence of any change in the financial condition of Dealer or any surety or guarantor for Dealer's Liabilities to Bank, which, in the sole judgment of Bank, is materially adverse;

(g) The Collateral or any rights therein shall be subject to or threatened with any judicial process, condemnation or forfeiture proceedings;

(h) The dissolution, merger, consolidation or reorganization of Dealer;

(i) A substantial change, as determined by Bank in its sole judgment, in the identity, ownership, control or management of Dealer;

(j) The cancellation, termination or other loss of any franchise held by Dealer, or any restriction on such franchise that affects adversely, as determined by Bank in its sole judgment, Dealer's continued existence, operations or financial condition;

(k) The borrowing of any money by Dealer from any source other than Bank, whether or not subordinate to this Agreement or the Note(s) executed in conjunction herewith, without Bank's prior written consent;

(l) Bank believes, in good faith, subject only to its own business judgment, that the prospect of any payment or performance of any obligation hereunder is or may become impaired.

13. BANK'S RIGHTS UPON DEFAULT.

Upon the occurrence of any Event of Default, Bank may, without notice and at its option, do any or all of the following:

(a) Exercise from time to time any and all rights and remedies available to Bank under the UCC or otherwise available to Bank, including the right to collect, settle, compromise, adjust, sue for, foreclose or otherwise realize upon any of the Collateral and to dispose of any of the Collateral at public or private sale(s) or other proceedings, and Dealer agrees that Bank or its nominee may become the purchaser at any such public sale(s) and that ten (10) days' prior notice of any such disposition constitutes reasonable notification. The proceeds of any Collateral shall be applied to the payment of Dealer's Liabilities to Bank, in such order as Bank may, in its sole discretion, elect. Dealer waives and releases any right to require Bank to collect any of Dealer's Liabilities to Bank from any other Collateral under any theory of marshaling of assets or otherwise, and specifically authorizes Bank to apply any Collateral in which Dealer has any right, title or interest against any of Dealer's Liabilities to Bank in any manner that Bank may determine.

(b) Declare all of Dealer's Liabilities to Bank to be immediately due and payable.

(c) Reduce Dealer's Liabilities to Bank to judgment.

(d) Appropriate, set-off and apply, on account of any of Dealer's Liabilities to Bank, all balances of Dealer on deposit with, or held in any capacity by Bank at any time, and any other property of any nature of Dealer that Bank may at any time have in its possession, including but not limited to, certificates of deposit and savings, demand and other deposit accounts, securities and personal property.

(e) Take possession of all or any Collateral with or without legal process, for the purpose of which Bank through its representatives may enter any premises wherein the Collateral may be found and Dealer, on Bank's request, will assemble the Collateral and make it available to Bank at a place designated by Bank that is reasonably convenient to both Dealer and Bank.

(f) Bank may send notices in Dealer's name or instruct Dealer to send notices and Dealer agrees to send such, advising any and all Account Debtors that the accounts have been assigned to Bank and that all payments thereon are to be made directly to Bank.

14. MISCELLANEOUS.

(a) This Agreement shall inure to the benefit of and is and shall continue to be binding upon the parties, their successors, representatives, receivers, trustees, heirs and assigns, but nothing contained herein shall be construed to permit Dealer to assign this Agreement or any of Dealer's rights or obligations hereunder without first obtaining Bank's express written approval.

(b) Until all of Dealer's Liabilities to Bank are paid in full and all of Dealer's obligations hereunder are satisfactorily performed in full, all obligations, representations, warranties, covenants, undertakings and agreements of Dealer hereunder and under the Note(s) and all other documents executed in connection herewith or related hereto shall remain in full force and effect.

(c) This Agreement and the Note(s) have been executed pursuant to, delivered in and shall be governed by and construed under the laws of the Commonwealth of Pennsylvania. The parties acknowledge the jurisdiction of

[G11030]

the state, federal and local courts located within the Commonwealth of Pennsylvania over controversies arising from or relating to this Agreement.

(d) If any provision of this Agreement shall for any reason be held to be invalid or unenforceable, such invalidity or unenforceability shall not affect any other provision hereof.

(e) All rights, powers and remedies of Bank hereunder or under any other obligation are cumulative and not alternative and shall not be exhausted by any single assertion thereof. The failure of Bank to exercise any such right, power or remedy will not be deemed a waiver thereof nor preclude any further or additional exercise of such right, power or remedy, now or in the future, upon any obligation of Dealer. The waiver of any default hereunder shall not be a waiver of any subsequent default. This paragraph shall be applicable to Dealer and any person liable with respect to any of Dealer's obligations.

(f) All notices provided for herein shall be deemed to have been given:

(i)   If by Bank to Dealer, when deposited in the mail or delivered to the telegraph company addressed to:

MAIN MOTORS, INC.
237 NORTH SEVENTH STREET
PHILADELPHIA, PA 19116

; and

(ii)   If by Dealer to Bank upon receipt by Bank at:

FIRSTBANK, N.A.
DEALER FINANCE DEPARTMENT
BROAD AND SPRUCE STREETS
PHILADELPHIA, PA 19110

(g) This Agreement:

(i)   is the complete written Agreement of the parties hereto, supersedes any prior understandings or written agreement; and

(ii)   cannot be varied, changed or otherwise modified except by written permission of Bank; and no oral promises, conditions or representations made by either party shall vary the terms and conditions herein.

(h) This Agreement:

(i)   may be executed in any number of counterparts and all of such counterparts taken together shall be deemed to constitute one and the same document; and

(ii)   shall become effective when each of the parties hereto shall have signed a copy hereof (whether the same or different copies) and shall have delivered the same to Bank or shall have sent to Bank a facsimile, telex or telegraph stating that the same has been signed and mailed to it. Complete sets of counterparts shall be lodged with Dealer and with Bank.

IN WITNESS WHEREOF, the parties have hereunto caused this Agreement to be executed and sealed by their proper and duly authorized representatives as of this _____19th_____ day of _____March_____ 19 _91__ .

FIRSTBANK, N.A.   NAME OF DEALER_____MAIN MOTORS, INC._____

By: _*Sandy Stern*_____   By: _*G. S. Gessel*_____
    Vice President   G. S. Gessel, President

                              (Name and Title)

                           Attest: _*Stacey Scribe*_____
                               Stacey Scribe, Secretary

                               (Name and Title)

(If a corporation, Dealer's corporate seal must be affixed and its Secretary, Assistant Secretary, Treasurer or Assistant Treasurer must sign on the line marked "Attest".)

[G11031]

The Dealer's Line of Credit; The Demand Note. A "Demand Note" (Form 3) is issued in conjunction with the Dealer Inventory Security Agreement (see ¶ 2). This note evidences the obligation of Main Motors to repay loans made to it under the **line of credit** arrangement (Firstbank makes each advance in its discretion, not pursuant to a commitment). The maximum amount of the line of credit set by the bank and reflected in the Dealer Inventory Security Agreement and the Demand Note is $2,400,000. Main executes only one note throughout the course of this business relationship with Firstbank. However, should the principal amount of Firstbank's loans to Main Motors rise above the stipulated principal amount, the Demand Note (second paragraph) and the Dealer Inventory Security Agreement (¶ 2) protect Firstbank by virtue of Main's promise therein to repay the actual amount of the loans "as shown on the bank's books and records."[3]

"Picking Up" a Floor Plan. Main Motors decided to change its financing relationship from its current lender (Old Bank) to Firstbank. When this happens, Firstbank is said to "pick up a floor plan."

Before picking up the floor plan Firstbank performs a physical inspection of Main Motors' premises. The bank's representative checks all units in stock by listing the serial number of each unit and taking possession of all invoices held by the dealer. These invoices reflect the wholesale price that has been paid for each unit. Old Bank will send Firstbank a list of all units upon which Main has an outstanding indebtedness, and Firstbank will compare this list with the list compiled by its own representative. When the two lists match dollar for dollar and cent for cent, Main completes a "Loan Request Form" (Form 4). Firstbank requires this document only when it refinances an outstanding indebtedness of a dealer; the form functions as a record of those units in which Firstbank initially takes a security interest.

3. Firstbank and other lenders require borrowers to execute and deliver promissory notes largely by custom. For most purposes Firstbank's position would be identical if it were to rely only on a borrower's agreement to repay contained in a Dealer Inventory Security Agreement.

FORM 3
DEMAND NOTE

<u>March 19, 1991</u>
Philadelphia, Pennsylvania

$ * * * 2,400,000.00 * * *

FOR VALUE RECEIVED AND INTENDING TO BE LEGALLY BOUND HEREBY, the undersigned (each jointly and severally if more than one and jointly and severally referred to as "Dealer") promises to pay to the order of FIRSTBANK, N.A., Philadelphia, Pennsylvania ("Bank") in lawful money of the United States of America, at any of its banking offices, the principal sum of

TWO MILLION FOUR HUNDRED THOUSAND

Dollars ("Loan Limit") to be repaid ON DEMAND, but until such time as demand is made by Bank, to be repaid in accordance with the terms and conditions of a certain Dealer Inventory Security Agreement between Dealer and Bank dated   March 19, 1991   ("Agreement") together with interest on the outstanding principal balance hereof payable monthly, as billed, at a fluctuating rate per annum equal at all times to   one percent (1)   % per annum over the rate of interest announced by the Bank publicly, from time to time, in Philadelphia, Pennsylvania, as the Bank's base rate, but in no event in excess of the maximum rate permitted by applicable law. Each change in the fluctuating rate shall take effect simultaneously with such change in the Bank's base rate. Interest shall be calculated hereunder for the actual number of days that the principal balance is outstanding, based on a year of three hundred sixty (360) days, unless otherwise specified in writing.

The principal balance due hereunder plus all accrued interest due thereon at any time and from time to time shall be that amount as shown on the Bank's books and records and the statements submitted to Dealer by Bank in accordance with paragraph 2 of the Agreement, which shall, if no timely objection is made, be conclusive and irrefutable evidence of the amount of principal and interest due Bank.

THE AGREEMENT. This Note is the Note(s) referred to in and is issued in conjunction with and under and subject to, the terms and conditions of the Agreement, and is secured by, among other things, the Collateral, as that term is defined in the Agreement and a mortgage on all the real property of   N/A   . Upon the happening of an Event of Default, as specified in the Agreement, Bank will be entitled to all of Bank's Rights Upon Default as specified in the Agreement.

PREPAYMENT. The principal sum due under this Note may be repaid by Dealer in whole or in part without penalty at any time.

MISCELLANEOUS. Dealer hereby waives protest, notice of protest, presentment, dishonor and notice of dishonor. In addition to all other amounts due hereunder, Dealer agrees to pay to Bank all costs (including reasonable attorney's fees) incurred by Bank in connection with the enforcement hereof. The rights and privileges of Bank under this note shall inure to the benefit of Bank's successors and assigns

[G11032]

forever. All obligations shall bind Dealer's heirs, successors and assigns forever. If any provision of this Note shall be held to be invalid or unenforceable, such invalidity or unenforceability shall not affect any other provision hereof, but this Note shall be construed as if such invalid or unenforceable provision had never been contained herein. This Note has been delivered in, shall be construed in accordance with, and shall be governed by the laws of the Commonwealth of Pennsylvania. The waiver of any default hereunder shall not be a waiver of any other or subsequent default.

      Dealer has duly executed this Note the day and year first above written and has hereunto set hand and seal.

IF INDIVIDUAL(S), SIGN BELOW

_____

_____

_____

IF GENERAL OR LIMITED PARTNERSHIP,
SIGN BELOW

_____(SEAL)

_____(SEAL)

_____(SEAL)

IF A CORPORATION, SIGN BELOW

NAME OF CORPORATION: __MAIN MOTORS, INC.__

BY: _G.S. Gessel_____(SEAL)   (AFFIX CORPORATE SEAL HERE)
     G. S. Gessel, President

     (NAME AND TITLE)

ATTESTED:_____Stacey Scribe_____
     Stacey Scribe, Secretary

     (SIGNATURE AND TITLE)   [G11033]

     Upon completion of the Loan Request Form, Firstbank will send Old Bank a check for the total debt on all listed units. In return, Old Bank will sign a release, by which it releases all interest in the units listed, and will provide for filing a *termination statement* (see UCC 9–404) to the effect that it no longer claims a security interest in connection with its financing statement.

FORM 4
LOAN REQUEST FORM

This Loan Request Form is the Loan Request Form referred to in Paragraph 2 of the Agreement and is issued in conjunction with and under and subject to the terms and conditions of the Agreement. All terms used herein shall be defined as such terms are defined in the Agreement. The Loan(s) requested hereunder are the Loan(s) referred to in Paragraph 2 of the Agreement and the Items of Inventory described herein are the Items of Inventory referred to in the Agreement, which is part of the Collateral as that term is defined in the Agreement.

As an inducement to Bank to make the Loan(s) requested hereby, Dealer hereby reaffirms and restates all of Dealer's agreements, liabilities, representations, warranties, covenants and obligations under the Agreement and further covenants that if the Loan(s) requested hereunder are made by Bank they are and will be received by Dealer under and subject to all the terms and conditions of the Agreement.

IF INDIVIDUAL(S), SIGN BELOW

_____

_____

_____

IF GENERAL OR LIMITED PARTNERSHIP,
SIGN BELOW

_____(SEAL)

_____(SEAL)

_____(SEAL)

IF A CORPORATION, SIGN BELOW

NAME OF CORPORATION: __MAIN MOTORS, INC.__

BY:___*G. S. Gessel*_____(SEAL)   (AFFIX CORPORATE SEAL HERE)
    G. S. Gessel, President

(NAME AND TITLE)

ATTESTED:___*Stacey Scribe*_____
    Stacey Scribe, Secretary

(SIGNATURE AND TITLE)   [G11034]

March 19_____, 19_91_
(Date)

MAIN MOTORS, INC._____
(Dealer Name)

237 North Seventh Street_____
(Street Address)

Philadelphia_____   PA   19116_____
(City or Town)   (State)

Dealer hereby requests FIRSTBANK, N.A., Philadelphia, Pennsylvania ("Bank") to make the following Loan(s), as the term Loan(s) is defined in a certain Dealer Inventory Security Agreement and Power of Attorney between Dealer and Bank dated   March 19, 1991 ("Agreement"), in accordance with and under and subject to the terms and conditions of the Agreement. Pursuant to the Agreement, Dealer confirms that it has granted to Bank and hereby affirms and grants to Bank a lien and security interest in the Items of Inventory described below together with all materials, additions, equipment, accessions, accessories and parts installed in, related, attached or added thereto or used in connection therewith and all substitutions and exchanges for and replacements thereof as security for all of "Dealer's Liabilities to Bank".

Loan No.	Description of Item	Serial No.	New or Used	Dealer Cost	Less Down Payment	Loan Amount
871	Pontiac	103399	New	13,123.22	None	13,123.22
871	Pontiac	103821	New	9,839.44	None	9,839.44
871	Pontiac	104745	New	13,123.22	None	13,123.22
871	Pontiac	104838	New	12,740.20	None	12,740.20
871	Pontiac	200215	New	9,839.44	None	9,839.44
871	Pontiac	507704	New	13,252.50	None	13,252.50

                                    TOTALS   71,918.02
                                                                        [G11035]

Figure 1 diagrams the documentation and payment involved when Firstbank picks up Main Motors' floor plan from Old Bank.

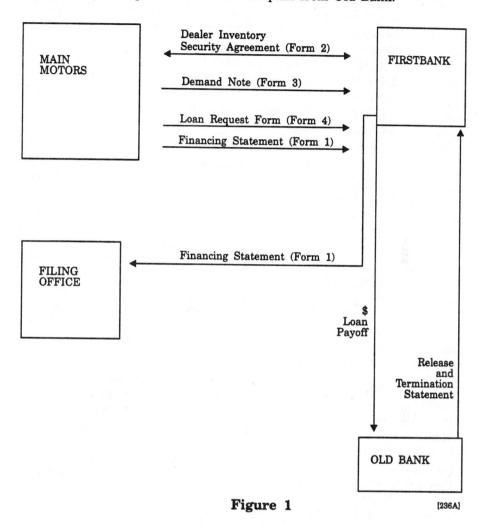

Figure 1   [236A]

Financing of New Deliveries. Firstbank will make loans to finance new deliveries of automobiles from the Pontiac Division of General Motors Corporation by advancing the wholesale price of each automobile directly to General Motors. The details of that procedure are addressed below.

(C) DELIVERY OF AUTOMOBILES: ASSURING THE MANUFACTURER OF PAYMENT

General Motors, like other automobile manufacturers, does not extend credit to automobile dealers. Consequently, General Motors must either be paid or be assured of payment before delivery.

At one time it was customary to ship new cars by rail, and to send a **sight draft** (instruction to pay upon presentment), accompanied by a negotiable bill of lading, to a local bank that would release the bill of lading to the dealer upon the dealer's payment of the draft. Today, new cars usually are delivered by highway trailer. These highway carriers, unlike the railroads, do not have facilities to store cars during periods of delay that may occur when negotiable bills of lading, with sight drafts attached, pass through banking channels into the hands of the dealer. This relatively cumbersome method of controlling delivery until payment is unnecessary because of the assurance of payment that Firstbank's letter of credit (described next) affords General Motors.

Bank Letter of Credit; Addendum to Dealer Inventory Security Agreement. In order to provide assurance of payment, Firstbank issues a **letter of credit** in favor of General Motors. The letter of credit provides that from time to time, subject to a stated limitation on amount, upon receipt of General Motors' draft drawn on Firstbank accompanied by an automobile invoice for the cars being shipped, Firstbank will pay to General Motors the amount of the invoice. In addition, Firstbank and Main Motors enter into an Addendum pursuant to which Main Motors agrees to reimburse Firstbank for all amounts advanced to General Motors under the letter of credit and further agrees that all such amounts constitute loans made under the line of credit established under the Dealer Inventory Security Agreement (Form 2) and the Demand Note (Form 3).

On receipt of an order for new cars from Main Motors, General Motors sends the cars and the related certificates of origin [4] directly to Main Motors and, through the bank collection system, sends to Firstbank an invoice describing the shipment (giving models, serial numbers, and prices of cars) and its draft calling on Firstbank to pay under the letter of credit. Upon receipt of these documents, Firstbank pays General Motors by sending funds to General Motors' bank, for credit to General Motors' account. Under an alternative arrangement, General Motors would maintain a bank account with Firstbank and, upon receipt of the documents, Firstbank would credit that account.

Figure 2 diagrams the documentation and payment involved each time Firstbank makes an advance for a new delivery of cars by General Motors to Main Motors.

4. The function of the certificates of origin is explained below in connection with financing sales to consumers.

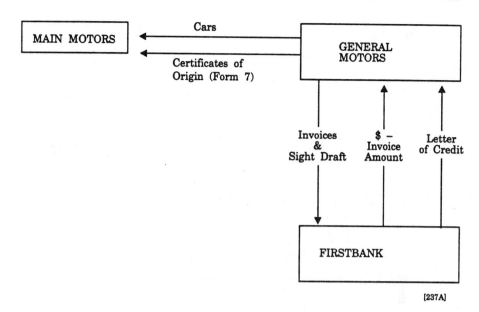

Figure 2

Option to Repurchase. Although the letter of credit arrangement just described provides General Motors with assurance of payment, General Motors also has an interest in protecting its reputation. Specifically, General Motors wishes to ensure that new General Motors automobiles are sold only by authorized dealers who maintain certain standards. Consequently, General Motors requires its dealers to obtain secured financing from lenders who enter into an agreement affording General Motors a repurchase option. Under that agreement (which is not to be confused with securities "repos," discussed in Chapter 10, Section 1(B), supra), if Main Motors defaults and Firstbank takes possession of its inventory of automobiles, then General Motors will have an option to repurchase the automobiles for the original wholesale price. Firstbank is not averse to that arrangement; General Motors' exercise of its option to repurchase would provide a convenient means for Firstbank to recover the principal amount of its outstanding loans on new automobiles.

(D) DIAGRAM OF AUTOMOBILE DEALER INVENTORY FINANCING

Figure 3 diagrams all of the transactions and documentation involved in the Prototype automobile dealer inventory financing.

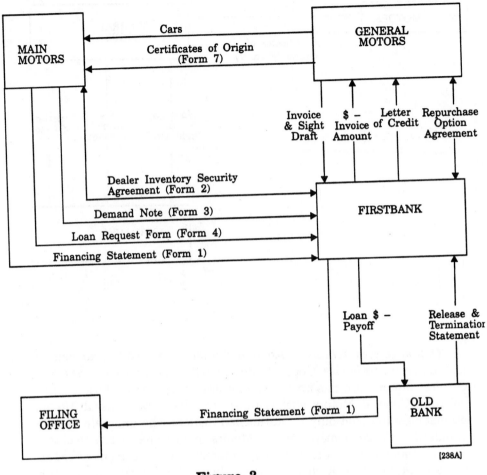

Figure 3

(E) SALES TO CONSUMERS

Lee Abel drives a 1987 Buick LeSabre to Main's showroom and, after negotiating a $5,100 trade-in allowance for the used car, reaches an agreement with one of Main's salespersons for the purchase of a 1991 Pontiac Firebird for a cash price of $14,250. Like most car buyers, Abel will buy on credit.

The Credit Decision. The relationship between Firstbank and Main Motors concerning consumer installment sales agreements is developed in detail below. For the moment, recall that Main Motors is not in a position to wait for Abel to pay for the new car over 48 months. It follows that Main's decision to sell to Abel on credit depends on whether a third-party financer (here, Firstbank) is willing to purchase Abel's installment obligation from Main, thereby putting Main in funds at the inception of the transaction.

Main Motors asks Abel to fill out an "Installment Credit Application" supplied by Firstbank. That form calls for information concerning Abel's place and length of employment, salary, number of dependents, banking relationships, and other credit outstanding, as well as other information relevant to Firstbank's credit decision. Main Motors then faxes the application to Firstbank's consumer credit department. Firstbank's staff reviews the application, obtains information about Abel's credit history and creditworthiness from a centralized **credit reporting agency,** and (within a matter of hours) reaches a decision about whether to extend credit to Abel.

Typically Firstbank's credit investigation shows that the prospective buyer is a satisfactory risk for the amount of credit requested. If so, Firstbank agrees to purchase the installment contract, provided that the amount of the down payment and other terms meet its standard requirements. One typical requirement is that the down payment reduce the amount owing for the car to not more than the dealer's cost. In this case, the trade-in allowance of $5,100 for Abel's used car reduces the unpaid balance to $9,150—comfortably less than the $13,252.50 wholesale cost of the new Pontiac. Nevertheless, the present case does deviate from the customary pattern in that the credit investigation shows that Abel, although honest and reliable, occasionally has been slow in meeting installment obligations.

Alternative Assignment Plans. The method for dealing with this problem depends in part upon the underlying arrangement between a dealer and a purchaser of installment paper for the allocation of the risk of default by buyers. There are five common forms of agreements between a dealer and an assignee of installment credit contracts: (1) without recourse, (2) repurchase, (3) partial guaranty, (4) limited repurchase, and (5) full guaranty. The details of each of these alternatives are found in an "Assignment and Repurchase Agreement" (Form 5).

Note that Form 5 refers to an arrangement called the "Firstbank Retail Plan." That arrangement consists of a set of standard provisions that Firstbank and Main Motors (and Firstbank's other dealer customers) have agreed will apply to all purchases of consumer installment contracts. It contemplates that in the normal case Firstbank would purchase contracts of buyers on a **non-recourse** basis (i.e., Firstbank will not look to the dealer-assignor in the event of a buyer's nonpayment), thereby relieving Main Motors of liability or risk by reason of a buyer's failure to pay. In this case, however, because of the "slow pay" reports on Abel, Firstbank and Main Motors agree to allocate the risk of default differently. Firstbank requests Main to execute the "repurchase" portion of the Assignment and Repurchase Agreement.

FORM 5
ASSIGNMENT AND REPURCHASE AGREEMENT

A. For value received, the undersigned does hereby sell, assign and transfer to Firstbank, N.A. his, its or their entire right, title and interest in and to the attached contract, herewith submitted to Firstbank, N.A. for acceptance, and the property covered thereby, described as follows:

DESCRIPTION OF CONTRACT

Type of Contract	Date of Contract	Customer's Name
Motor Vehicle Installment Sales Contract	5/15/91	Lee Abel

Covering the following property

Year	Make	New or Used	Model	Serial No.
1991	Pontiac	New	Firebird	1G2AS87160N507704

and authorizes Firstbank, N.A. to do every act and thing necessary to collect and discharge obligations arising out of or incident to said contract and assignment. In order to induce Firstbank, N.A. to accept assignment of the contract, the undersigned warrants that: the contract arose from the sale of the within described property; the contract was complete in all respects and the undersigned made all disclosures required by law, including all disclosures required by Title 1 of the Consumer Credit Protection Act of 1968, as amended, and by local law, prior to execution thereof by the Customer; the Customer is not a minor and has capacity to contract; the contract and personal guaranty by third party, if any, are genuine, legally valid and enforceable and comply with all applicable requirements of state and federal law; title to the contract is vested in the undersigned free of all liens and encumbrances and the undersigned has the right to assign such title; the property is as represented to the Customer by the undersigned; statements made by the Customer in the contract are true to the best of the undersigned's knowledge and belief, and the undersigned has no knowledge of any fact that would impair the validity or value of the contract; the down payment paid by the Customer and received by the undersigned was as stated in the contract; a certificate of title to the property showing the lien or encumbrance for the benefit of Firstbank, N.A. or the undersigned has been or will be applied for forthwith, if permitted by law. If there is a breach of any such warranty, without regard to the undersigned's knowledge or lack of knowledge with respect thereto or Firstbank, N.A.'s reliance thereon, the undersigned hereby agrees unconditionally, notwithstanding the numbered paragraph below executed by the undersigned, to purchase said contract from Firstbank, N.A., upon demand, for the full amount then unpaid whether said contract shall then be, or not be, in default. The undersigned further agrees that in the event the Customer or any other person or governmental agency makes a claim against Firstbank, N.A. alleging facts which, if true, would constitute a breach of any of the foregoing warranties or representations, the undersigned shall assume the defense of such claim and shall indemnify and save Firstbank, N.A. harmless from all loss, cost and expenses arising therefrom, and, at Firstbank, N.A.'s option, the undersigned will repurchase the contract for the full amount then unpaid. Liability of the undersigned arising out of or incident to this assignment shall not be affected by any indulgence, compromise, settlement, extensions, or variations of terms of said contract effected with, or by, the discharge or release of the obligation of the Customer or any other person interested, by operation of law or otherwise. The undersigned waives notice of acceptance of this assignment and notices of non-payment and non-performance of the contract. The acceptance or approval of the contract by Firstbank, N.A. shall not constitute an agreement, representation or warranty by Firstbank, N.A. as to the legal sufficiency thereof or of the disclosures therein contained or a waiver of Firstbank, N.A.'s right to rely on the foregoing warranties or representations with respect thereto.

B. As part of the foregoing assignment, the undersigned's obligations are further defined in the particular numbered paragraph below executed by the undersigned, and signature of any such numbered paragraph shall constitute signature of the entire assignment.

---

1. "Without Recourse" (See paragraphs A and B above)

The assignment of said contract is and shall be without recourse against the undersigned, except as otherwise provided above and by the terms of the Firstbank, N.A. Retail Plan in effect at the time this assignment is accepted.

Seller Signs _____ By _____
(If corporation or partnership) (Title)

---

2. "Repurchase" (See paragraphs A and B above)

The undersigned guarantees payment of the full amount remaining unpaid under said contract, and covenants if default be made in payment of any installment thereunder to pay the full amount then unpaid to Firstbank, N.A., upon demand, except as otherwise provided by the terms of the Firstbank, N.A. Retail Plan in effect at the time this assignment is accepted.

Main Motors, Inc.

Seller Signs _G. S. Gessell_____ By _G. S. Gessell, President_____
(If corporation or partnership) (Title)

---

3. "Partial Guaranty" (See paragraphs A and B above)

Notwithstanding the terms of the Firstbank, N.A. Retail Plan, the undersigned unconditionally guaranties payment of the full amount remaining unpaid under said contract, and agrees to purchase said contract from Firstbank, N.A. for the full amount then unpaid whether said contract shall then be, or not be, in default, provided, however, at the time of any such demand by Firstbank, N.A. the undersigned may, at his election, pay to Firstbank, N.A. the sum of $_____ in consideration of being released from such guaranty obligation, and in such event, the assignment of said contract is without recourse against the undersigned, except as otherwise provided above and by the terms of the Firstbank, N.A. Retail Plan in effect at the time this assignment is accepted.

Seller Signs _____ By _____
(If corporation or partnership) (Title)

---

4. "Limited Repurchases" (See paragraphs A and B above)

The undersigned guaranties payment of the full amount remaining unpaid under said contract, and covenants if default be made in payment of any installment thereunder to pay the full amount then unpaid to Firstbank, N.A. upon demand, except as otherwise provided by the terms of the Firstbank, N.A. Retail Plan in effect at the time this assignment is accepted provided, that if the Customer satisfactorily pays each of the first _____ installments coming due under the within contract, this assignment shall thereafter be without recourse against the undersigned, except as otherwise provided above and by the terms of the Firstbank, N.A. Retail Plan in effect at the time this assignment is accepted.

Seller Signs _____ By _____
(If corporation or partnership) (Title)

---

5. "Full Guaranty" (See paragraphs A and B above)

Notwithstanding the terms of the Firstbank, N.A. Retail Plan, the undersigned unconditionally guaranties payment of the full amount remaining unpaid under said contract, and agrees to purchase said contract from Firstbank, N.A., upon demand, for the full amount then unpaid, whether said contract shall then be, or not be, in default.

Seller Signs _____ By _____
(If corporation or partnership) (Title)

NOTE: If a corporation, assignment must be executed in the name of the corporation by an officer having proper authority from the Board of Directors. If a partnership, assignment must be executed by a partner.

[0311096]

Under the "repurchase" terms, if a default occurs under Abel's contract, Main Motors agrees to repurchase the contract from First-bank by paying the entire unpaid amount thereunder. Although not reflected in the Assignment and Repurchase Agreement, the terms of the Firstbank Retail Plan provide that Main would not be required to repurchase the contract until after Firstbank takes possession of the car from Abel. Thus this arrangement divides the burdens and risks of default between Firstbank and Main Motors: Firstbank assumes the burden of repossession and also the risk of loss in the event the car cannot be located for repossession; Main Motors assumes the burdens and losses involved in any foreclosure proceedings and in collecting any deficiency from Abel.

The Dealer's Contract With the Consumer. With financing arrangements completed, Main Motors is in a position to make delivery to Abel. As we have seen, Main Motors and Abel have agreed on a cash price of $14,250 for the Pontiac. Main has agreed to take Abel's 1987 Buick for a trade-in credit of $5,100, leaving a balance of $9,150. In addition, Abel has elected to assume the cost of credit life and accident and health insurance ($799.79) and must pay state taxes ($855.00) and fees ($60.00); these costs bring Abel's unpaid obligation for the car to $10,864.79.

Abel also must pay a finance charge. In this instance, Abel agrees to pay an Annual Percentage Rate of 12.5% on the amount financed, which amounts to $2,996.94 for the four years the contract is to run. This finance charge brings the total of payments to $13,861.73, payable in 48 installments of $288.79. Main Motors and Abel sign an "Installment Sale Contract" (Form 6) that evidences this obligation. Form 6 would be used in Pennsylvania; certain of its provisions, such as the Notice to Buyer, are included in order to comply with the Motor Vehicle Sales Finance Act (Pa. Stat. Ann., tit. 69 §§ 601–637 (1991)). Other provisions, such as disclosure of the Total Sale Price and the Annual Percentage Rate, are included in order to comply with the Truth In Lending Act (Title I of the United States Consumer Credit Protection Act of 1968, 15 U.S.C. §§ 1601–1667e (1988 & Supp. I 1989)).

In addition to providing for Abel's payment obligations, the Installment Sale Contract also contains a security agreement in which Abel grants a security interest in the new car to Main Motors to secure those payment obligations. When the assignment by Main to Firstbank is effected, Firstbank becomes Abel's creditor and is the new secured party in the transaction.[5]

---

5. You may note that at the end of the Installment Sale Contract there is an assignment form that contains terms and provisions substantially the same as the general terms in the Assignment and Repurchase Agreement (Form 5). When there is no need for special recourse provisions between Main and Firstbank, the assignment contained in the Installment Sale Contract will suffice. Note, as well, the notice of assignment to Firstbank near the top of the face of the Installment Sale Contract (Form 6).

FORM 6
INSTALLMENT SALE CONTRACT

| IMPORTANT: YOU MUST circle date you wish payment to fall due each month.   5   10 (15) 20   25   30 | FIRSTBANK, N.A.
MOTOR VEHICLE INSTALLMENT SALE CONTRACT
SECURITY AGREEMENT AND DISCLOSURE STATEMENT | Date of Contract __5-15__ , 18__91__ |

Buyer(s) (hereinafter whether one or more, jointly and severally liable and called "Buyer", "I", "me", "my", or "mine"):

Lee Abel	123 E. 10th Street	Phila.		PA.
(Name)	(No. and Street)	(City)	(County)	(State and Zip Code)
(Name)	(No. and Street)	(City)	(County)	(State and Zip Code)

Seller (hereinafter called "Seller", "you", or "your"):

Main Motors, Inc.	237 North Seventh Street, Phila., PA 19116		
(Name)	(No. and Street)	(City)	(County) (State and Zip Code)

ASSESSMENT: You have advised me that you, the Seller, intend assigning this Motor Vehicle Installment Sale Contract (hereinafter called the "Contract") and all your rights under the Contract to Firstbank, N.A. Philadelphia, Pennsylvania (hereinafter called "Bank"). In the event that the Contract is assigned to Bank, I agree to render performance of all my obligations under the Contract to Bank.

I hereby agree to purchase from you, and you hereby agree to sell to me, on the following terms and conditions, the following described motor vehicle and equipment (hereinafter called the "Vehicle"):

New or Used	Year and Make	Series	Body Style	No. Cyl.	If Truck, Ton Capacity	Manufacturer's Serial No.	Key No.
New	91 Pontiac	Firebird	CP	6		1G2AS87160N507704	7650, 1821

Including the following equipment (check box(es) if applicable): ☒ AM   ☒ FM Stereo   ☒ Air Conditioning   ☒ Automatic Transmission   ☒ Power Steering   ☐ Power Brakes   ☐ Power Windows   ☐ Power Seats   ☐ Vinyl Top   ☐ Other (describe) _____ which I represent is purchased primarily for (check one): ☒ Personal, family or household use; ☐ Business Use; ☐ Agricultural use; ☐ Other (specify) _____ for the Deferred Payment Price computed below.

[This portion of the form is omitted. It contains disclosures of the terms of the transaction in the manner required by the Truth In Lending Act (Title I of the United States Consumer Credit Protection Act of 1968, 15 U.S.C. 1601–1667e (1988 & Supp. I 1989)) and Regulation Z issued thereunder. See 12 C.F.R. § 2266.18 (1990) (content of disclosures for closed-end credit transactions). The terms that must be disclosed in this transaction include the annual percentage rate (12.5%), the total amount of finance charge ($2,996.94), the amount financed ($10,864.79), the total of payments ($13,861.73), the total sale price ($18,961.73), the total number of payments (48 monthly payments), and the amount of each payment ($288.79).]

DEFAULT CHARGES AND COLLECTION COSTS: I agree to pay you a default charge at the rate of **2%** per month of the amount of any installment payment or payments in arrears for each month or fractional part thereof exceeding **10** days. Upon the occurrence of any event of default as set forth in paragraph 5 of the ADDITIONAL PROVISIONS on the reverse side of this Contract, you may declare immediately due and payable all sums lawfully due under the Contract (that is you may "accelerate the maturity of the Contract") and you will be entitled to reimbursement for actual costs incurred for proceedings to collect on the Contract including, but not limited to, court costs and reasonable attorney's fees of **20%** of the amount due if the Contract is referred to an attorney not a salaried employee of yours for collection. Even if you have accelerated the maturity of the Contract, I shall receive a refund of unearned **FINANCE CHARGE** computed in accordance with Sum of Digits Method, commonly called the Rule of **78's**, whenever the unpaid balance is liquidated in full prior to the originally scheduled maturity date as if I had prepaid the Contract on that date, whether such payment is made voluntarily or involuntarily, or by termination, cash payment, or surrender or repossession and resale of the Vehicle, unless the refund is less than **$1.00** or would result in a net minimum earned **FINANCE CHARGE** of less than **$10.00.**

REFUND FOR PREPAYMENT: I may prepay the Contract in full or in part at any time without penalty or premium and if I prepay in full, I shall receive a refund of the unearned portion of the **FINANCE CHARGE** determined as of the next succeeding installment due date in accordance with the Sum of the Digits Method, commonly called the Rule of **78's**, but not refund will be made if it amounts to less then **$1.00** or would result in a net minimum earned **FINANCE CHARGE** of less than **$10.00.**

SECURITY AGREEMENT: In order to secure payment of the Total of Payments and all other amounts lawfully due or to become due under the Contract, I hereby grant to you a security interest under the Pennsylvania Uniform Commercial Code in the Vehicle, including all accessories, attachments and parts used in the Vehicle now or hereafter installed in or affixed to the Vehicle (which, if installed hereafter, will constitute after-acquired property), and in the proceeds of the Vehicle, including an assignment of insurance proceeds and returned unearned insurance premiums. Upon the occurrence of any event of default as set forth in paragraph 5 of the ADDITIONAL PROVISIONS on the reverse side hereof, I hereby affirm that you have the right to set off against the balance owed under the Contract any property of mine which is now or later in your possession, which means that you can apply my deposits or sell and apply the proceeds of any other of my property in the your possession to pay the balance due on this Contract. The right of set off will cover after-acquired property and secure other and future indebtedness to the you. Intending to be legally bound and notwithstanding any language to the contrary in any other agreement or obligation between us and existing on the date of this Contract, except for its right of set off you hereby waive the right to treat as security for the Contract any other collateral which, by the terms of such other agreement or obligation, would otherwise be the security for the Contract.

REDEMPTION RIGHT AFTER REPOSSESSION: I may redeem the Vehicle following repossession for default at any time for a period of **15** days after you mail lawful notice to me of repossession of the Vehicle, and at any time thereafter before you have disposed of, or contracted to dispose of, the Vehicle. The redemption price shall be the then unpaid balance of the Contract plus any accrued default charges and other amounts lawfully due under the Contract, and if default at the time of repossession exceeded **15** days, I shall also pay your expenses of retaking, transporting, repairing and storing authorized by law.

This Contract is subject to the **ADDITIONAL PROVISIONS** set forth on the reverse side which are a part of this Contract. **NOTICE:** See other side for important information.

NOTICE: ANY HOLDER OF THIS CONSUMER CREDIT CONTRACT IS SUBJECT TO ALL CLAIMS AND DEFENSES WHICH THE DEBTOR COULD ASSERT AGAINST THE SELLER OF GOODS OR SERVICES OBTAINED PURSUANT HERETO OR WITH THE PROCEEDS HEREOF. RECOVERY HEREUNDER BY THE DEBTOR SHALL NOT EXCEED AMOUNTS PAID BY THE DEBTOR HEREUNDER.

NOTICE TO BUYER: DO NOT SIGN THIS CONTRACT IN BLANK.
YOU ARE ENTITLED TO AN EXACT COPY OF THE CONTRACT YOU SIGN.
KEEP IT TO PROTECT YOUR LEGAL RIGHTS.

Executed the day and year first above written by the below named Seller and Buyer and assigned by Seller to Firstbank, N.A. pursuant to the terms of the Seller's Assignment on the reverse side.

MAIN MOTORS, INC.
Seller

Lee Abel
Buyer

A. Flour ____(SEAL)
By A. Flour, Mgr.

_____(SEAL)
Buyer

RECEIPT IS ACKNOWLEDGED OF A TRUE AND CORRECT COPY OF THIS CONTRACT.

Buyer _Lee Abel_ _____   Buyer_____

ORIGINAL TO BANK   [G11036]

[Face of Form 6 concluded]

[Reverse of Form 6 on following pages]

ADDITIONAL PROVISIONS

1.   You may assign the Contract and, upon assignment, your assignee shall acquire all of your interest in the Contract and the Vehicle and shall be entitled to all of your rights and privileges under the Contract. After I receive written notice of any such assignment, I shall make all payments under the Contract directly to the assignee of the Contract and you shall not be the agent of the assignee for transmission of payments or otherwise.

2.   I agree: to keep the Vehicle free from all encumbrances, including but not limited to liens for storage, services or materials; to pay you forthwith upon demand, with interest at the highest lawful contract rate, any amount you actually pay in order to release or discharge the Vehicle from any encumbrance; not to sell, assign or encumber, without your prior written consent, any of my rights under the Contract or in the Vehicle, nor to grant any further security interest in the Vehicle, nor permit my rights in the Contract or in the Vehicle to be reached by judicial process; to notify you promptly of all changes in the place where the Vehicle is permanently kept (and I represent that until further notice, the Vehicle will be kept at the address I have given you on the face of the Contract); not to use or permit the Vehicle to be used illegally or for hire (unless specifically provided for in the Contract); and that no injury to or loss, destruction or damage of or to the Vehicle shall release me from any of my obligations under the Contract.

3.   ALL OF YOUR REPRESENTATIONS AND WARRANTIES, EXPRESS OR IMPLIED, REGARDING THE VEHICLE AND THIS TRANSACTION ARE SET FORTH IN THE CONTRACT. Manufacturer's warranties, if any, will be available at your place of business prior to purchase and copies will be supplied to me at the time of delivery of the Vehicle.

4.   The Vehicle shall be at my risk. Until all monies payable under the Contract are paid in full, I shall keep the Vehicle insured against fire, theft and collision, in an amount at least sufficient to cover your interest in the Vehicle, with a carrier acceptable to you, and with a loss payable clause in favor of you and me as our interests appear. If I have not authorized you to purchase such insurance, I shall, upon request, promptly furnish you with satisfactory evidence of such insurance. If I have authorized you to purchase such insurance, I understand that such authorization does not relieve me of my obligation to obtain and maintain such insurance but only authorizes you to attempt to obtain the requested coverages on my behalf through an authorized agent, and that if you are unable to obtain the requested coverages for the terms and amounts included in the Contract, you may, at your option (i) obtain such coverages for such term, if any, as the insurance carrier to whom you shall apply therefore will provide for such amount, or (ii) credit such amount to the final maturing installments under the Contract in inverse order of maturity or as otherwise required by law.

    If I fail to obtain or maintain such insurance, or fail to furnish satisfactory evidence of such insurance upon request, you may, at your option and without prejudice to your rights under the Contract if you do not, obtain such insurance protecting either our interests or your interests only. In either event, I agree to reimburse you for the cost of such insurance upon demand together with interest thereon at the highest lawful contract rate.

    I hereby assign to you any monies payable under such insurance, by whomever obtained, including returned and unearned insurance premiums, and you are hereby authorized on my behalf to receive or collect the same, to endorse checks or drafts in my name in payment thereof, to cancel such insurance or to release or settle any claim with respect thereto. The proceeds of such insurance, by whomever obtained, not in excess of the then unpaid balance of the Contract, whether paid by reason of loss, injury, return premium or otherwise, shall be applied towards the replacement of the Vehicle or payment of the indebtedness under the Contract, at your option; provided that unexpired premiums received by you as a result of cancellation of insurance originally placed at my expense shall be credited to any matured unpaid installments.

5.   The occurrence of any of the following shall, at your option, constitute an event of default under the Contract: my death, my failure to make any payment under the Contract in full punctually on or before its due date, my failure to comply with any other provision of the Contract, institution of a proceeding in bankruptcy, receivership or insolvency by or against me or my property, or you deem the Vehicle in danger of confiscation. Upon the occurrence of any event of default, you shall have the following rights: to declare all amounts due or to become due under the Contract to be immediately due and payable, with reasonable attorney's fees (20% if permitted by law) if the Contract is referred to an attorney for collection; to require me, upon demand, to deliver the Vehicle to you at a place reasonably convenient to both of us; to take immediate possession of the Vehicle wherever found; with or without recondition, to sell the Vehicle at public or private sale; and in taking possession you may peaceably enter any premises where the Vehicle may be found and take possession of the Vehicle and anything found in it. I shall give you notice by registered mail within 24 hours after repossession if I claim that any articles were contained in the Vehicle at the time of repossession which are not covered by the Contract, and failure to do so shall be a bar to any subsequent claim therefor.

6.   If the Vehicle is repossessed other than by legal process, I shall be liable for your costs incurred in retaking, transporting, storing and repairing the Vehicle only if the default exceeded 15 days at the time of repossession, if such costs are actual, necessary and reasonable (excluding charges for services of your full time employees), and if such costs are supported by satisfactory evidence of payment. Upon repossession of the Vehicle by legal process, I shall be liable for costs of suit and reasonable attorney's fees as are provided by the laws governing such proceedings.

7.   If the Vehicle is consumer goods as defined in the Pennsylvania Uniform Commercial Code, and if I have prior to repossession for default paid 60% of the Cash Price of the Vehicle, you shall sell the Vehicle at public or private sale after the expiration of the aforesaid 15 day redemption period and not later than 90 days from the date of repossession. If the Vehicle is not consumer goods as so defined, or if it is but I have not paid 60% of the Cash Price of the Vehicle, you may, at your option, following repossession: (a) sell or otherwise dispose of the Vehicle at public or private sale; or (b) retain the Vehicle in satisfaction of my obligation under the Contract by sending me a written notice of your proposal to so retain the Vehicle but, if I object in writing to such proposal within 21 days of receipt of notice thereof, you shall sell or otherwise dispose of the Vehicle at public or private sale. In the event of any public sale of the Vehicle, you shall send me reasonable notice of the time and place of such sale; in the event of any private sale of the Vehicle, you shall send me reasonable notice of the time after which any such sale is to be made. You shall apply the proceeds of any such sale or other disposition first to defray the reasonable expenses of selling, transporting, retaking and storing the Vehicle, and then to the unpaid balance of the Contract plus any then lawfully accrued default charges. After any lawful application of the proceeds, I shall be entitled to any surplus, but I shall also be liable for any deficiency.

8.   The Contract constitutes the entire agreement between the parties and no modification of the Contract shall be valid in any event, and I expressly waive the right to rely on any such modification unless made in a writing signed by you. The Contract shall bind the heirs, personal representatives, successors and assigns of the parties hereto. Waiver of any default shall not constitute waiver of any subsequent default. Your rights and remedies are cumulative and not alternative. Any provision of the Contract prohibited by applicable law shall be ineffective to the extent of such prohibition without invalidating any other provision of the Contract. All words used in the Contract shall be of such gender or number as the circumstances require. The Contract shall be governed by the laws of Pennsylvania.

NOTICE OF PROPOSED CREDIT INSURANCE: The Signer(s) of the Contract hereby take(s) notice that group credit life insurance coverage and/or group credit accident and health insurance coverage will be applicable to the Contract if so marked on the face of the Contract and each type of coverage will be written by the insurance company named on the face of the Contract. The insurance, subject to acceptance by the insurer, covers only the person signing the request for such insurance. The amount of charge is indicated for each type of credit insurance to be purchased. The term of insurance will commence as of the date the FINANCE CHARGE begins to accrue and will expire on the originally scheduled maturity date of the indebtedness. Within 30 days, subject to acceptance by the insurer, there will be delivered to the insured debtor a certificate of insurance more fully describing the insurance. In the event of the indebtedness, a refund of insurance charges will be made where due.   [G11039]

SELLER'S ASSIGNMENT

For value received, and intending to be legally bound, Seller (meaning the Seller whose signature to the foregoing Contract and this Assignment appears on the face of said Contract) hereby sells, assigns and transfers to Firstbank, N.A. its successors or assigns (herein called "Assignee"), the foregoing Contract, and all monies due or to become due thereunder, and all right, title and interest in the Vehicle therein described, with full power in Assignee in its or Seller's name to take all such legal or other action as Seller might take, save for this Assignment. Seller warrants that: (1) Seller's title to the Contract and the Vehicle covered thereby is absolute, free of all liens, encumbrances and security interests, subject only to the rights of the Buyer as set forth therein; (2) the Contract is genuine, arising from the sale of the Vehicle therein described, and all parties to the Contract are of full age and had capacity to contract; (3) a Certificate of Title showing a first lien or encumbrance in favor of Assignee has been or will be forthwith applied for as required by law; (4) the Vehicle and all extra equipment described in the Contract was delivered to and accepted by Buyer; (5) the cash down payment and/or trade-in were actually received by Seller and no part thereof consisted of notes, post-dated checks or other credit advanced by Seller to Buyer; (6) all warranties and statements in the Contract and Disclosure Statement are true and correct; (7) there is owing on the Contract the Total of Payments set forth therein; (8) Seller is duly licensed under the Pennsylvania Motor Vehicle Sales Finance Act and Seller has complied in every respect with said Act; (9) the form and content of the Contract, the Disclosure Statement provided Buyer in connection with the Contract and the transaction from which they arose comply in every particular with all applicable statutes, regulations, rulings and proclamations, Federal or State, controlling the sale of motor vehicles and the extension of credit in connection therewith, including, without limitation, the Pennsylvania Motor Vehicle Sales Finance Act, the Federal, Truth-in-Lending Act and Regulation Z of the Board of Governors of the Federal Reserve System, as amended by the Truth-in-Lending Simplification and Reform Act and Revised Regulation Z, the Federal Equal Credit Opportunity Act and Regulation B of the Board of Governors of the Federal Reserve System, as amended, Trade Regulation Rules and Cease and Desist Orders of the Federal Trade Commission, and the Federal Magnuson-Moss Warranty Act; (10) an executed copy of the Contract and Federal Disclosure Statement containing the disclosures conforming to and complete in accordance with the above-mentioned laws and regulations has been received by Buyer; and (11) Seller has no knowledge of any facts impairing the validity or value of the Contract. If any of the foregoing warranties at any time appear, in the opinion of Firstbank, N.A., to be breached, the Seller shall repurchase the Contract from Assignee upon demand, and shall pay therefor the amount owing thereon plus any and all costs and expenses paid or incurred by Assignee in respect thereof. Should Buyer establish a bona fide claim or defense to payment against Assignee which would be valid against Seller, subject to any other agreement between Assignee and Seller, Seller shall indemnify, defend, save and hold Assignee harmless of and from all loss, cost and expense (including court costs and attorney's fees) and, at the option of Assignee, Seller shall repurchase the Contract upon demand, whether or not the Buyer is then in default, and shall pay therefor the amount owing thereon.

(SELLER'S SIGNATURE ON FACE OF CONTRACT IS AN EXECUTION OF THIS ASSIGNMENT)

NOTICE TO BUYER: SEE OTHER SIDE FOR IMPORTANT INFORMATION   [G11040]

[Reverse of Form 6 concluded]

Figure 4 diagrams the documentation and deliveries involved when Main Motors sells the new car to Lee Abel and assigns Abel's Installment Sale Contract to Firstbank.

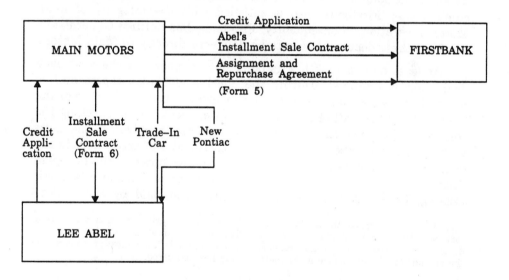

Figure 4

[239A]

(F) Perfecting the Security Interest in the New Car; The Certificate of Title

One of the terms of Firstbank's purchase of Abel's Installment Sale Contract is that the security interest in Abel's Pontiac is to be perfected. All states now have "certificate of title" laws; although these laws vary materially, in general they provide that the normal method of perfecting a security interest in an automobile (or other vehicle required to be titled) is by causing the security interest to be reflected on the certificate of title issued by a central state office (e.g., in Pennsylvania, the Bureau of Motor Vehicles). An exception is made for vehicles held by a dealer in inventory, as to which the usual financing statement filing rules apply. See UCC 9–302(3)(b).

Certificates of Origin and Control Over Dealer Operations. A "Certificate of Origin" (Form 7) is a document that is issued by the manufacturer of a new vehicle.

Because a certificate of title for a new vehicle cannot be issued without presenting a certificate of origin, the latter document is a useful device to ensure that a dealer is operating in conformity with its financing agreement. For this reason, some lenders hold certificates of origin in their own files until they receive word from a dealer that a particular car has been sold. Firstbank, like many other lenders, has decided that holding each certificate of origin for each car would be too cumbersome; Firstbank also is satisfied with the integrity of Main Motors' operation. Consequently, Firstbank has notified General Motors that these documents are to be delivered directly to Main Motors.

At least once a month Firstbank does a floorplan check at each dealership it finances. During the check the bank's representative looks at every new car listed on the invoices it has received from the manufacturer (i.e., all of the cars it has financed). After checking the collateral, the representative matches the serial numbers of the units with the serial numbers printed on the certificates of origin kept in the dealer's files. This is done to make sure that each car on the floorplan financing remains untitled. If either a certificate of origin or a car is missing, Firstbank probably should have been paid by the dealer.[6]

---

6. Under the terms of the Dealer Inventory Security Agreement (Form 2, ¶ 8), a dealer is required to repay immediately the amount loaned to finance a car (here, the wholesale price) when a car is sold. The absence of a car or a certificate of origin would be an indication that a sale may have occurred.

FORM 7
CERTICATE OF ORIGIN

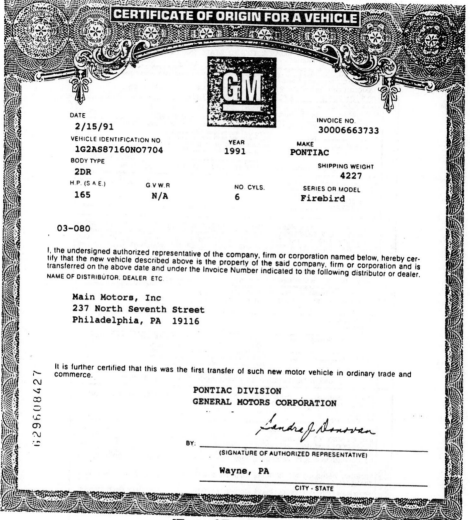

CERTIFICATE OF ORIGIN FOR A VEHICLE

GM

DATE
2/15/91

INVOICE NO.
30006663733

VEHICLE IDENTIFICATION NO.
1G2AS87160NO7704

YEAR
1991

MAKE
PONTIAC

BODY TYPE
2DR

SHIPPING WEIGHT
4227

H.P. (S A E.)
165

G.V.W.R
N/A

NO. CYLS.
6

SERIES OR MODEL
Firebird

03-080

I, the undersigned authorized representative of the company, firm or corporation named below, hereby certify that the new vehicle described above is the property of the said company, firm or corporation and is transferred on the above date and under the Invoice Number indicated to the following distributor or dealer.

NAME OF DISTRIBUTOR. DEALER. ETC.

Main Motors, Inc
237 North Seventh Street
Philadelphia, PA   19116

It is further certified that this was the first transfer of such new motor vehicle in ordinary trade and commerce.

PONTIAC DIVISION
GENERAL MOTORS CORPORATION

BY: _____
(SIGNATURE OF AUTHORIZED REPRESENTATIVE)

Wayne, PA
_____
CITY - STATE

G296 08427

[Face of Form 7]

[Reverse of Form 7 on following page]

DISTRIBUTOR-DEALER ASSIGNMENT NUMBER 1

FOR VALUE RECEIVED, I THE UNDERSIGNED, TRANSFER THE VEHICLE DESCRIBED ON THE FACE OF THIS CERTIFICATE TO

NAME OF PURCHASER(S)   Lee Abel

ADDRESS   123 E. 10th Street, Philadelphia, PA

AND CERTIFY TO THE BEST OF MY KNOWLEDGE INFORMATION AND BELIEF UNDER PENALTY OF LAW THAT THE VEHICLE IS NEW AND HAS NOT BEEN REGISTERED IN THIS OR ANY STATE AND AT THE TIME OF DELIVERY THE VEHICLE WAS SUBJECT TO THE FOLLOWING SECURITY INTERESTS AND NONE OTHER AND WARRANT TITLE TO THE VEHICLE.

FEDERAL REGULATIONS REQUIRE YOU TO STATE THE ODOMETER MILEAGE UPON TRANSFER OF OWNERSHIP

I certify to the best of my knowledge that the odometer reading is ___002___ and reflects the actual mileage of the vehicle unless one of the following statements is checked ☐ 1 the amount of mileage stated is in excess of 99,999 or ☐ 2 The odometer reading is not the actual mileage

AMOUNT OF LIEN	DATE OF LIEN	KIND OF LIEN	IN FAVOR OF
$13,861.73	5/15/91	Inst. Sale	Firstbank, N.A.

LIENHOLDER'S ADDRESS   Broad & Spruce, Philadelphia, PA

DEALER   Main Motors, Inc.   BY *C. G.*   Pres.

Name of Dealership   Dealer's License No.   Authorized Signature of Dealer   Title or Position

State of _____

County of _____

Being duly sworn upon oath says that the statements set forth are true and correct. Subscribed and sworn to me before me this ____ day of ____ 19__

_____ Notary Public   Notary Seal

USE NOTARIZATION ONLY IF REQUIRED IN TITLING JURISDICTION

DISTRIBUTOR-DEALER ASSIGNMENT NUMBER 2

FOR VALUE RECEIVED, I THE UNDERSIGNED, TRANSFER THE VEHICLE DESCRIBED ON THE FACE OF THIS CERTIFICATE TO

NAME OF PURCHASER(S) _____

ADDRESS _____

AND CERTIFY TO THE BEST OF MY KNOWLEDGE INFORMATION AND BELIEF UNDER PENALTY OF LAW THAT THE VEHICLE IS NEW AND HAS NOT BEEN REGISTERED IN THIS OR ANY STATE AND AT THE TIME OF DELIVERY THE VEHICLE WAS SUBJECT TO THE FOLLOWING SECURITY INTERESTS AND NONE OTHER AND WARRANT TITLE TO THE VEHICLE.

FEDERAL REGULATIONS REQUIRE YOU TO STATE THE ODOMETER MILEAGE UPON TRANSFER OF OWNERSHIP

I certify to the best of my knowledge that the odometer reading is _____ and reflects the actual mileage of the vehicle unless one of the following statements is checked ☐ 1 the amount of mileage stated is in excess of 99,999 or ☐ 2 The odometer reading is not the actual mileage

AMOUNT OF LIEN	DATE OF LIEN	KIND OF LIEN	IN FAVOR OF

LIENHOLDER'S ADDRESS _____

DEALER _____   BY _____

Name of Dealership   Dealer's License No.   Authorized Signature of Dealer   Title or Position

State of _____

County of _____

Being duly sworn upon oath says that the statements set forth are true and correct. Subscribed and sworn to me before me this ____ day of ____ 19__

_____ Notary Public   Notary Seal

USE NOTARIZATION ONLY IF REQUIRED IN TITLING JURISDICTION

DISTRIBUTOR-DEALER ASSIGNMENT NUMBER 3

FOR VALUE RECEIVED, I THE UNDERSIGNED, TRANSFER THE VEHICLE DESCRIBED ON THE FACE OF THIS CERTIFICATE TO

NAME OF PURCHASER(S) _____

ADDRESS _____

AND CERTIFY TO THE BEST OF MY KNOWLEDGE INFORMATION AND BELIEF UNDER PENALTY OF LAW THAT THE VEHICLE IS NEW AND HAS NOT BEEN REGISTERED IN THIS OR ANY STATE AND AT THE TIME OF DELIVERY THE VEHICLE WAS SUBJECT TO THE FOLLOWING SECURITY INTERESTS AND NONE OTHER AND WARRANT TITLE TO THE VEHICLE.

FEDERAL REGULATIONS REQUIRE YOU TO STATE THE ODOMETER MILEAGE UPON TRANSFER OF OWNERSHIP

I certify to the best of my knowledge that the odometer reading is _____ and reflects the actual mileage of the vehicle unless one of the following statements is checked ☐ 1 the amount of mileage stated is in excess of 99,999 or ☐ 2 The odometer reading is not the actual mileage

AMOUNT OF LIEN	DATE OF LIEN	KIND OF LIEN	IN FAVOR OF

LIENHOLDER'S ADDRESS _____

DEALER _____   BY _____

Name of Dealership   Dealer's License No.   Authorized Signature of Dealer   Title or Position

State of _____

County of _____

Being duly sworn upon oath says that the statements set forth are true and correct. Subscribed and sworn to me before me this ____ day of ____ 19__

_____ Notary Public   Notary Seal

USE NOTARIZATION ONLY IF REQUIRED IN TITLING JURISDICTION

[D1344]

[Reverse of Form 7]

In the event that Firstbank finances a dealer with serious financial problems, Firstbank will be particularly careful to see that it gets paid for each car sold. Firstbank's physical inventory checks will be more frequent—perhaps even daily. In protecting its interests, one of the first things that Firstbank will do is take possession of all certificates of origin. Because a dealer cannot title cars it sells without such certificates, Firstbank thereby achieves some comfort that it will be paid upon a dealer's sale of each vehicle.

Issuance of the Certificate of Title. Main Motors, as seller, executes an assignment of the Certificate of Origin to Abel, indicating that Firstbank is to have a lien (security interest) in the new car (see the reverse side of Form 7). (If Main were going to retain the contract it would list itself as lienholder.) Main Motors then sends the Certificate of Origin to the Bureau of Motor Vehicles, which, in turn, issues a Certificate of Title (Form 8). Here, the Certificate of Title is issued in the name of Lee Abel, and it states that the vehicle is subject to an encumbrance in favor of Firstbank. The Certificate of Title is then forwarded to Firstbank.[7]

---

7. In some states the certificate of title is forwarded to the owner, not the lienholder, and in others a duplicate is forwarded to the owner.

FORM 8
CERTIFICATE OF TITLE

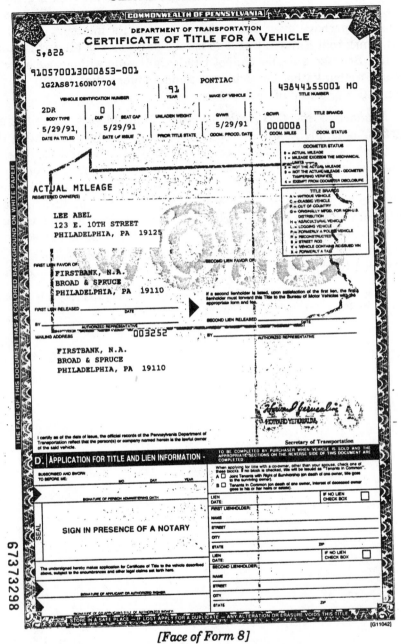

[Face of Form 8]

[Reverse of Form 8 on following page]

(TYPE OR PRINT) Certificate of Title must be submitted within 20 days, unless the purchaser is a registered dealer holding the vehicle for resale.

WARNING — FEDERAL AND STATE LAWS REQUIRE THAT YOU STATE THE MILEAGE IN CONNECTION WITH THE TRANSFER OF OWNERSHIP. FAILURE TO COMPLETE OR PROVIDING A FALSE STATEMENT MAY RESULT IN FINES AND/OR IMPRISONMENT.

A. ASSIGNMENT OF TITLE — Registered dealers must complete forms MV27A or MV27B as required by law. If purchaser is NOT a registered dealer, Section D on the front of this form must be completed.

I / We certify to the best of my / our knowledge that the odometer reading is _____ , _____ ✕ miles and reflects the actual mileage of the vehicle, unless one of the following boxes is checked.

☐ Reflects the amount of mileage in excess of its mechanical limits   ☐ Is NOT the actual mileage WARNING Odometer discrepancy

I / We further certify that the vehicle is free of any encumbrance and that ownership is hereby transferred to the person(s) or the dealer listed

SUBSCRIBED AND SWORN TO BEFORE ME: MO   DAY   YEAR

SIGNATURE OF PERSON ADMINISTERING OATH

	LAST FIRST M.I.
PURCHASER OR FULL BUSINESS NAME	
CO-PURCHASER	
STREET ADDRESS	
CITY	
STATE ZIP PURCHASE PRICE OR DIN	

PURCHASER SIGNATURE

CO-PURCHASER SIGNATURE

PURCHASER AND / OR CO-PURCHASER MUST HANDPRINT NAME HERE

SIGNATURE OF SELLER

SIGNATURE OF CO-SELLER

SELLER AND / OR CO-SELLER MUST HANDPRINT NAME HERE

SEAL — DO NOT NOTARIZE UNLESS SIGNED IN PRESENCE OF A NOTARY AND PURCHASER'S NAME IS LISTED

B. RE-ASSIGNMENT OF TITLE BY REGISTERED DEALER — If purchaser listed in Block A is NOT a registered dealer Section D on the front of this form must be completed.

I / We certify to the best of my / our knowledge that the odometer reading is _____ , _____ ✕ miles and reflects the actual mileage of the vehicle, unless one of the following boxes is checked.

☐ Reflects the amount of mileage in excess of its mechanical limits   ☐ Is NOT the actual mileage WARNING Odometer discrepancy

I / We further certify that the vehicle is free of any encumbrance and that ownership is hereby transferred to the person(s) or the dealer listed

SUBSCRIBED AND SWORN TO BEFORE ME: MO   DAY   YEAR

SIGNATURE OF PERSON ADMINISTERING OATH

SEAL — DO NOT NOTARIZE UNLESS SIGNED IN PRESENCE OF A NOTARY AND PURCHASER'S NAME IS LISTED AND SELLER IS A DEALER

RE-ASSIGNMENT OF TITLE BY REGISTERED DEALER — If purchaser is NOT a registered dealer Section D on the front of this form must be completed.

I / We certify to the best of my / our knowledge that the odometer reading is _____ , _____ ✕ miles and reflects the actual mileage of the vehicle, unless one of the following boxes is checked.

☐ Reflects the amount of mileage in excess of its mechanical limits   ☐ Is NOT the actual mileage WARNING Odometer discrepancy

I / We further certify that the vehicle is free of any encumbrance and that ownership is hereby transferred to the person(s) or the dealer listed

SUBSCRIBED AND SWORN TO BEFORE ME: MO   DAY   YEAR

SIGNATURE OF PERSON ADMINISTERING OATH

SEAL — DO NOT NOTARIZE UNLESS SIGNED IN PRESENCE OF A NOTARY AND PURCHASER'S NAME IS LISTED AND SELLER IS A DEALER

RE-ASSIGNMENT OF TITLE BY REGISTERED DEALER — If purchaser is NOT a registered dealer Section D on the front of this form must be completed.

I / We certify to the best of my / our knowledge that the odometer reading is _____ , _____ ✕ miles and reflects the actual mileage of the vehicle, unless one of the following boxes is checked.

☐ Reflects the amount of mileage in excess of its mechanical limits   ☐ Is NOT the actual mileage WARNING Odometer discrepancy

I / We further certify that the vehicle is free of any encumbrance and that ownership is hereby transferred to the person(s) or the dealer listed

SUBSCRIBED AND SWORN TO BEFORE ME: MO   DAY   YEAR

SIGNATURE OF PERSON ADMINISTERING OATH

SEAL — DO NOT NOTARIZE UNLESS SIGNED IN PRESENCE OF A NOTARY AND PURCHASER'S NAME IS LISTED AND SELLER IS A DEALER

C. ☐ CHECK HERE IF APPLICATION FOR DEALER TITLE AND COMPLETE SECTION D. TITLING FEES $ _____

ALL SELLERS SIGNATURES ON THIS SIDE MUST BE NOTARIZED. SIGN ONLY IN THE PRESENCE OF AN OFFICER EMPOWERED TO ADMINISTER OATHS.

[Reverse of Form 8]

Figure 5 diagrams the assignment of the certificate of origin and the issuance of the certificate of title.

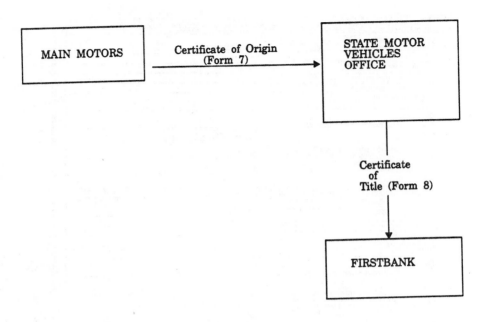

Figure 5

[240A]

(G) Repayment of Inventory Loan and Assignment of Consumer Paper; Notification of Assignment and Payment Instructions

In the Dealer Inventory Security Agreement (Form 2, ¶ 8) Main Motors agreed that when it sells one of the cars in which Firstbank holds a security interest, it will pay the amount advanced by Firstbank for that car. Main's cost for Abel's Pontiac, advanced by Firstbank, was $13,252.50. Had Abel paid cash for the car, Main Motors would send its check for $13,252.50 to Firstbank. In the more typical situation, as in this sale to Abel, Main Motors has sold the car under an Installment Sale Contract.

In order to obtain funds to pay Firstbank, Main has assigned the contract to a purchaser. Main well might have obtained funds by assigning Abel's contract to a purchaser *other* than Firstbank (e.g., a finance company or another bank). However, Main "just happens" to have assigned the contract to Firstbank and Firstbank "just happens" to be the inventory financer that is owed payment upon the sale of the car. For this reason, Firstbank can make entries in Main's bank account with Firstbank to effectuate both Firstbank's payment of the purchase price of Abel's contract and Main's repayment to Firstbank of the inventory loan. Main sends Abel's contract to Firstbank, and Firstbank credits Main's account with the price it is to pay for the contract. The $5,100 allowance given for Abel's trade-in reduced the

Unpaid Balance of Cash Price for the car to $9,150. That amount, plus the amount of the insurance charges and state taxes and fees, approximates the amount that Firstbank will pay to Main as the purchase price for Abel's contract, since Firstbank expects to earn the finance charges that Abel is to pay. After crediting Main's account in that amount, the Bank then debits the account for the amount due on the inventory loan. Note that the amount of the debit ($13,252.50, which Firstbank advanced to Main against the car) exceeds the amount Firstbank pays for an assignment of the contract. Under these circumstances Main will be expected to enclose its check, or authorize Firstbank to debit its account, for the difference.

Main has not yet received as much cash for the Pontiac sold to Abel as it has paid for that car. It is evident that Main's profit on this transaction will depend in part on the price it gets from the sale of Abel's 1987 Buick, which Main took in trade. Not so obvious is the opportunity for further profit that Main Motors enjoys. Competition among banks and finance companies to purchase installment sale contracts leads to arrangements with a dealer that enhance the dealer's return. The reasons for this competition become evident when one considers the relatively high finance charges that can be charged on consumer automobile installment paper.

Firstbank may make an informal arrangement for sharing this return with Main Motors. The portion of the finance charges returned to Main (**dealer participation**) will depend on factors such as the level of interest rates generally, the bank's cost of money, and the degree of competition to obtain financing arrangements with Main. Now we can see that it was not a pure coincidence that Firstbank purchased Abel's contract and also provided Main Motors with inventory financing. Many banks and finance companies provide inventory financing, sometimes even as a "loss leader," in order to get the first crack at the lucrative retail installment contract financing.

On receipt of Abel's contract, Firstbank writes to Abel and directs that payments are to be made to Firstbank; along with the letter is a coupon book containing coupons to be enclosed with each of the 48 installment payments. When (and if) Abel completes the payments, Firstbank will return the Certificate of Title, marked "encumbrance satisfied."

Figure 6 diagrams (i) Firstbank's payment to Main Motors for Abel's installment sale contract; (ii) Main's payment to Firstbank of the amount of the inventory loan made against the Pontiac;[8] (iii) Firstbank's communication to Abel, notifying Abel that the contract has been assigned to Firstbank, instructing Abel to make all payments to Firstbank, and enclosing payment coupons; and (iv) Abel's monthly payments.

---

8. As the text observes, Firstbank and Main Motors effect payments to one another by debits and credits to the bank account Main Motors maintains with Firstbank.

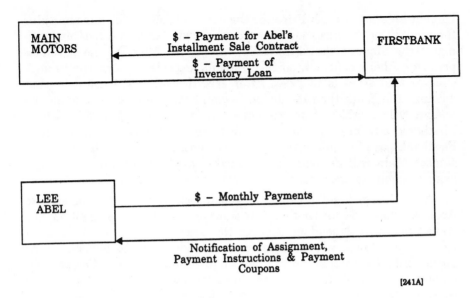

[241A]

Figure 6

(H) DIAGRAM OF AUTOMOBILE INSTALLMENT SALE CONTRACT FINANCING

Figure 7 diagrams all of the transactions and documentation featured in the Prototype installment sale contract financing.

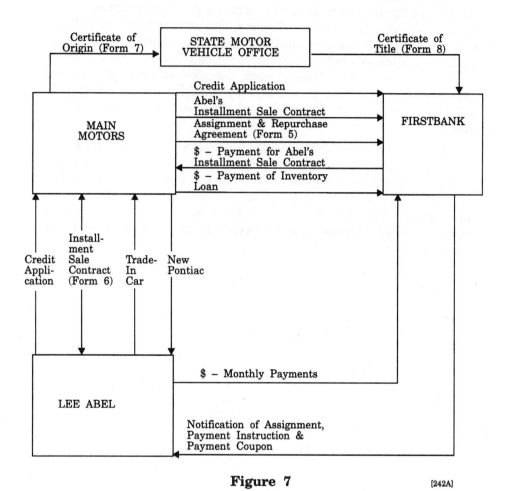

Figure 7   [242A]

(I) THE CONSUMER FAILS TO PAY

At this point the transaction with Lee Abel departs from the typical pattern, in which the buyer makes the payments when due. We now shall assume that after 12 months Abel is unable to keep up the monthly payments.

Collection Efforts. If Abel does not respond to one or two dunning letters from Firstbank, a collector calls Abel on the telephone to encourage prompt payment; if letters and telephone calls fail, the collector may demonstrate Firstbank's seriousness of purpose by making a house call. (In special circumstances, the creditor and debtor may execute a new contract (a **refinancing agreement**) that reduces the amount of each monthly payment by extending the payments over a longer period.)

Repossession. In this case we shall assume that there is no hope for prompt improvement in Abel's financial position; Firstbank takes steps to repossess the Pontiac. Two methods are available: (i) self help and (ii) judicial proceedings such as a replevin action. In most cases creditors employ self help as the less expensive method. Often debtors voluntarily surrender collateral upon the secured creditor's request. Otherwise, an employee of the secured creditor or of a third-party collection service normally will be able to locate the car and take it away.

After Abel's car is repossessed, Firstbank sends Abel a registered letter to the effect that Firstbank has taken the car. The letter also notifies Abel of the right to redeem the car upon payment of a specified amount and of a proposed resale of the car if that amount is not forthcoming. This letter follows as Form 9. (Several items in this letter are required under the Pennsylvania Motor Vehicle Sales Finance Act, supra.)

FORM 9
NOTICE OF REPOSSESSION

Date of Repossession: 8/28/92

TO: Lee Abel
      123 E 10th Street
      Phila., PA 19125

FROM: FIRSTBANK, N.A.
      Broad and Spruce Streets
      Phila., PA 19110

Re: Account No. 253-876543

Make of Vehicle: 1991 Pontiac Firebird
(Mfg.) Serial No: 1G2AS87160N50774

Date of Installment Contract: 5-15-91
Vehicle is now stored at: Storage Garage
                            1112 E. Susquehanna
                            Phila., PA 19125

CHARGES

Unpaid Time Balance	$ 10,396.25
Default Charges	Included
Repair Costs	00.00
Repossession Costs	250.00
Storage Costs	150.00
(Less rebate)	(1,345.50)
TOTAL DUE	$ 9,450.75

We have lawfully repossessed the above vehicle. If you do not pay the total due set forth above within 15 days of the postmark of the envelope in which this notice was sent (i.e., on or before __9/12/92__), we intend to: (1) sell the vehicle at a private sale on or after __9/13/92__ , (2) credit your account with the net proceeds of sale; and (3) take action against you for any deficiency balance remaining.

At any time before we have sold the vehicle or entered into a contract for its disposition, you may redeem the vehicle by payment in full of the charges set forth above, subject to adjustments in the applicable rebate on account of payments received after __9/15/92__ . Payment must be made at the above address (9 a.m. to 5 p.m., Monday through Friday, except legal holidays).

If you believe you were not in default under your contract or if you are have temporary problems meeting this obligation and need help, you may discuss the matter with ____L. Null____ by calling (215) 585- __5035__ and perhaps we can arrange a different payment schedule.

FIRSTBANK, N.A.

L. Null

REGISTERED MAIL -
RETURN RECEIPT REQUESTED

L. Null
Consumer Lending Department   [G11044]

At this point Firstbank calls upon Main Motors to repurchase the contract as Main agreed to do under the terms of the assignment. Main then assumes the rights and duties of a secured party. After the specified notice period expires, Main will sell the car. The rights of parties in these situations are developed more fully in Chapter 15, infra.

SECTION 2. ATTACHMENT AND PERFECTION: IN GENERAL

(A) PROBLEMS UNDER THE PROTOTYPE; ADEQUACY OF THE FINANCING STATEMENT AND SECURITY AGREEMENT

Introduction. The Prototype, Financing Automobiles, may have given the impression that financing transactions proceed with little concern for rules of law—as a ship may seem (from the shore) to proceed without regard for charts or buoys. The following Problems are designed to expose some of the legal planning that underlies the Prototype; the Problems also consider variations on the Prototype that reveal hazards arising from the failure to take account of the underlying rules of law. In particular, the Problems focus on the purposes and adequacy of financing statements and security agreements.

Problem 1. The transaction followed precisely the steps described in the Prototype. Lean, the holder of a judgment against Main Motors, subsequently caused the sheriff to levy on the cars in Main's inventory. Is Lean's execution lien senior or junior to Firstbank's security interest in the cars? See UCC 9–201; UCC 9–301(1)(b); UCC 9–303; UCC 9–203(1); UCC 9–302(1)—(4); UCC 9–402(1); UCC 9–109(4); UCC 9–401(1); Note (1) on Attachment and Perfection by Filing, infra.

Problem 2. One of Firstbank's clerks neglected to file the Financing Statement (Form 1, Section 1, supra) in the public offices specified in UCC 9–401. Lean, the judgment creditor, caused the sheriff to levy on Main's inventory of cars.

(a) Is Lean's execution lien senior or junior to Firstbank's security interest? See UCC 9–301(1)(b); UCC 9–302(1); UCC 9–401. (The proper place of filing—i.e., the appropriate state and the proper office(s) within that state—is considered in more detail in Section 3, infra.)

(b) Now assume that on March 19 Main executed and delivered the documents described in the Prototype and Firstbank advanced funds to General Motors for a trailer-load of new cars. The new cars were delivered to Main on March 23; that same day Lean levied on the newly-delivered cars. On March 26 Firstbank filed the Financing Statement in the proper offices. Is Lean's execution lien senior or junior to Firstbank's security interest? See UCC 9–301(1)(b); UCC 9–301(2); UCC 9–107; Note (1) on Attachment and Perfection by Filing, infra.

Problem 3. Firstbank established the financing arrangement with Main Motors as described in the Prototype. Subsequently, Main Motors was approached by Secondbank, which was interested in providing floorplan financing to Main Motors. Secondbank asks you, its counsel, to check the public record to discover whether, and to what extent, Main's assets may be subject to security interests.

(a) What does the public record reveal? Does it show whether any motor vehicles are subject to Firstbank's security interest and, if so, which ones? Does it show whether Main is obligated to Firstbank and, if so, the amount of that obligation?

(b) Does the Financing Statement (Form 1, Section 1, supra) provide more information than UCC 9–402(1) requires? Would the Financing Statement be adequate to perfect a security interest in Main's inventory of automobiles if the only reference to collateral were "inventory"? What answer if the only reference were to "motor vehicles"? See UCC 9–402(1) ("indicating the types, or describing the items"). Is "motor vehicles" a "type" of collateral? See UCC 9–109 (classifying "goods" as "consumer goods," "equipment," "farm products," and "inventory"). See Note 3 on Attachment and Perfection by Filing, infra.

(c) When a Financing Statement merely "indicates the types" of collateral, how can an interested party such as Secondbank discover the relevant facts? See UCC 9–208. (Do not overlook the obvious while pondering this question!)

(d) Should the Code require more complete information to appear in the public record? Should the answer turn on the purpose(s) of Article 9 filing? See Note 2 on Attachment and Perfection by Filing, infra. Should the answer turn on the type of collateral involved? Would it be feasible to require more detailed filing in the setting of inventory financing like that involved in the Prototype? See UCC 9–402, Comment 2. On the other hand, insofar as filing is intended to alert interested parties to the possibility that the secured party may claim a security interest, how could anyone be misled by a filing covering "all personal property"? Would such a description be sufficient?

(e) If Secondbank were to extend financing to Main Motors secured by Main's existing inventory, and if Secondbank failed to "pick up" Firstbank's floor plan by satisfying Main's indebtedness to Firstbank, would Secondbank's security interest in the cars be senior or junior to Firstbank's security interest? See UCC 9–312(5)(a); [1] Note 1 on Attachment and Perfection by Filing, infra.

---

1. Chapter 13, Section 1, infra, focuses in detail on priorities among conflicting Article 9 security interests, including the baseline, first-to-file-or-perfect rule of UCC 9–312(5)(a). In that connection, we shall see that a secured party who acquires a purchase money security interest (as defined in UCC 9–107) may qualify for priority over earlier-filed secured parties. See UCC 9–312(3), (4); Chapter 13, Section 2(B), infra.

Problem 4. Firstbank obtained the documentation and followed the procedures in the Prototype, except that Main Motors' president, G.S. Gessell, failed to sign the Financing Statement. Gessell, Firstbank's loan officer, and the clerks in the filing offices (who accepted and duly indexed the Financing Statement) all failed to notice this oversight. Lean, the holder of a judgment against Main Motors, subsequently caused the sheriff to levy on the cars in Main's inventory.

(a) Is Lean's execution lien senior or junior to Firstbank's security interest in the cars? See UCC 9–402(1); UCC 1–201(39); Note (3) on Attachment and Perfection by Filing, infra.

(b) Suppose that Firstbank required Gessell (the sole shareholder of Main Motors, Inc.) to provide additional collateral for the loan to Main Motors—Gessell's yacht. Who should sign the financing statement covering the yacht? Who is the "debtor"? Whose creditors may have an interest in discovering claims against the yacht? See UCC 9–105(1)(d).

(c) Would your answers to the questions in part (b) change if you discover that the yacht is jointly owned by Gessell and Gessell's spouse, Teryl Gessell?

Problem 5. Firstbank obtained the documentation and followed the procedures in the Prototype. However, after Firstbank delivered the Financing Statement to the proper public filing offices, an error in the process of inputing data into a computer resulted in the Financing Statement being erroneously indexed, in one of the offices, so as to reflect Firstbank as *debtor* and Main Motors as *secured party*. This error was reflected in a receipt mailed to Firstbank by the filing officer, but none of Firstbank's staff noticed the error.

(a) Was the filing effective? See UCC 9–403(1); In re Flagstaff Foodservice Corp., 16 B.R. 132 (Bkrtcy.S.D.N.Y.1981) (filing officer's complete failure to index financing statement did not impair effectiveness of filing, notwithstanding that three years after the filing the secured party had not yet received a copy of the filed financing statement and its check for the filing fee had not cleared). What result better promotes the purposes of the filing system?

(b) Do other creditors or lienholders who may be damaged by the erroneous indexing have any recourse other than to attack the effectiveness of the security interest? See UCC 9–403(4); UCC 9–407(2); Mobile Enterprises, Inc. v. Conrad, 177 Ind.App. 475, 380 N.E.2d 100 (1978) (complaint against Indiana's Secretary of State and Director of the Uniform Commercial Code Division for negligent failure to disclose to plaintiff the existence of a filed financing statement was sufficient to withstand a motion to dismiss); Note (3) on Attachment and Perfection by Filing, infra.

Problem 6. The documentation and procedures in the Prototype were followed, except that the Financing Statement filed by Firstbank set forth the name of the debtor as "Main Motors"; Main's exact corporate name is "Main Motors, Inc." Lean, Main's judgment creditor, caused the sheriff to levy on all the cars. Is Lean's execution lien senior or junior to Firstbank's security interest? See UCC 9–301(1)(b); UCC 9–402(1); UCC 9–402(7) (1st sentence). Was the error in the name a "minor error" that is "not seriously misleading"? See UCC 9–402(8). Does application of the "seriously misleading" standard depend on the characteristics of a particular search system? What if a search for "Main Motors, Inc." *invariably* would turn up all filings against "Main Motors"? What if such a search *never* would reveal those filings? See Note (3) on Attachment and Perfection by Filing, infra.

Problem 7. (a) Assume that Main's business is operated (i.e., signs, letterhead, business forms, telephone listing, advertising) under the name (a "trade name") "Center City Pontiac Sales and Service." Would the filing against "Main Motors, Inc." be sufficient to perfect Firstbank's security interest? Would a filing against "Center City Pontiac Sales and Service" be sufficient? See UCC 9–402(1); UCC 9–402(7) (1st sentence) & Comment 7 (first paragraph); Note (3) on Attachment and Perfection by Filing, infra.

(b) Assume that Firstbank's operations are carried out under the trade name "Phirst of Philly" and that the Financing Statement set out that trade name in the box for the secured party's name. Is the Financing Statement sufficient? See UCC 9–105(1)(m); UCC 9–402(1); UCC 9–402(8); In re Cushman Bakery, 526 F.2d 23 (1st Cir.1975), cert. denied, 425 U.S. 937, 96 S.Ct. 1670, 48 L.Ed.2d 178 (1976) (holding that a financing statement setting forth the name of the secured party's nominee, selected to avoid concern by the debtor's other creditors, satisfied the requirement that the financing statement state the name of the secured party and that the "good faith" requirement of UCC 1–203 did not impair perfection of the security interest); cf. UCC 9–302(2). Consider the fact that Article 9 filing systems normally provide no system for searching against a *secured party's* name.

Notes on Attachment and Perfection by Filing

(1) The Elements of Attachment and Perfection; Article 9's Basic Conveyancing Principles.

Attachment. "Attachment" is one of the fundamental concepts in Article 9. When the conditions giving rise to attachment are satisfied, then a security interest is created. See UCC 9–203(1). A security interest is a property interest. See UCC 1–201(37). Unless and until a security interest attaches to particular property, the putative secured party has no enforceable security interest—and thus no property right—in the collateral. That is, until the security interest attaches, the putative secured party is, in fact, unsecured.

UCC 9–203(1) provides that "a security interest is not enforceable against the debtor or third parties with respect to the collateral and does not attach" unless the three conditions specified in therein occur.

The first condition is the debtor's agreement that a security interest attach. Inasmuch as Article 9 is devoted to security interests that arise from the consent of the debtor, see UCC 9–102(2), this condition should come as no surprise. UCC 9–203(1)(a) requires that the requisite agreement either be embodied in a signed "security agreement" (defined in UCC 9–105(1)(*l*)) or be accompanied by the secured party's possession of the collateral. When, as is typical, a debtor signs a written security agreement (see, e.g., the Dealer Inventory Security Agreement, Form 2, Section 1, supra), this condition is satisfied easily. However, as Problems 9 to 12 below illustrate, things sometimes go awry in the real world.

The second condition for attachment is that "value has been given." UCC 9–203(1)(b). By definition, a security interest "secures payment or performance of an obligation." UCC 1–201(37). Before a security interest can attach, there must be an obligation (usually a money debt) to secure. Like the first condition, the "value" condition normally is satisfied easily; that the secured party extended credit usually is clear. See UCC 1–201(44) (defining "value" to include present consideration as well as antecedent debt). Any issue that arises with respect to the "value" condition is likely to concern *which* debt is secured rather than whether *any* debt is outstanding.

The third condition for attachment is that "the debtor has rights in the collateral." UCC 9–203(1)(c). This condition is best conceptualized and understood as a specialized aspect of the familiar principle of *nemo dat quod non habet* (one cannot give what one does not have): A debtor can give a security interest in collateral only if it has rights in that collateral. Straightforward as this may seem, more than a few courts and commentators have confounded the application of the "rights in the collateral" condition in the context of Article 9's basic conveyancing principles.

One source of the confusion has been the first sentence of UCC 9–201: "Except as otherwise provided by this Act a security agreement is effective according to its terms between the parties, against purchasers of the collateral and against creditors." This principle often is paraphrased to the effect that a security interest in collateral is "good as against the world" except as the UCC provides otherwise. Broad as this statement may be, it is important to mind its limitations. We discuss below, particularly in Chapter 13, many of the specific instances where the Code expressly limits the operation of UCC 9–201. For present purposes you should realize that *UCC 9–201 generally operates only with respect to the debtor's rights in collateral—however limited or expansive they might be.* For example, assume that Debtor is the owner of a 25% undivided interest in an item of equipment. Having "rights in the collateral," Debtor can cause a security interest to attach to that item of equipment. Assume further that Debtor signs a security agreement purporting to grant a security interest in the equipment to Bank to secure a loan. Does UCC 9–201 afford Bank a security interest "good against the world" in the 75% interest that Debtor does not own as well as the 25% interest owned by Debtor? Of course not. The "collateral" addressed by UCC 9–201 consists only of the debtor's rights in the equipment. Again, the *nemo dat* principle applies; Debtor cannot give more than it has.

Perfection. The concept of "perfection" gives rise to perhaps the broadest exception to the rule of UCC 9–201. Once attached, a security interest is enforceable against the debtor; however, a security interest is unlikely to be effective against third parties claiming an interest in the collateral unless it is "perfected."

A security interest is "perfected" when the security interest has attached *and* "the applicable steps required for perfection have been taken" as "specified in Sections 9–302, 9–304, 9–305 and 9–306." UCC 9–303(1). For the most part, these "applicable steps" consist of methods by which a secured party gives notice of its security interest to the public. The filing of a financing statement is the most common method—so common, in fact, that UCC 9–302(1) provides that "[a] financing statement must be filed to perfect all security interests," with certain specified exceptions. Section 2(B) of this Chapter deals with the most important exceptions, including perfection by possession under UCC 9–305.

The various elements of perfection and attachment can occur in any order. For example, a secured party first might comply with UCC 9–302 by filing a financing statement. (Firstbank did so in the Prototype.) Next, the debtor might sign a security agreement covering collateral (say, inventory) in which the debtor has rights. Finally, the secured party might give value (e.g., by making a loan) to the debtor. In this example, upon the occurrence of the last step, the giving of value, the security interest simultaneously would attach and become perfected. Now assume that, subsequent to the initial attachment and perfection as to the debtor's existing inventory, the debtor acquires a new item of inventory. If the security agreement covers "after-acquired" as well as existing collateral, e.g., "all inventory now owned or hereafter acquired," then immediately upon the debtor's acquisition of rights in the new inventory, the security interest would attach and become perfected in the new inventory. The last step would be the debtor's acquisition of "rights in the collateral."

Priority Rules and Conveyancing Principles. For practical purposes, a secured party who fails to take the "applicable steps" for perfection is likely to be no better off than one whose security interest did not attach. An unperfected security interest is vulnerable, in particular, to the rights of a "lien creditor," such as a creditor who obtains an execution or other judicial lien. See UCC 9–301(1)(b) (unperfected security interest is subordinate to lien creditor); UCC 9–301(3) (defining "lien creditor").[2] Even worse, from the secured party's per-

---

2. An unperfected security interest also is subordinate to the rights of certain good-faith buyers and transferees. UCC 9–301(1)(c); UCC 9–301(1)(d); see Chapter 13, Section 2(B), infra.

spective, is that an unperfected security interest will not be effective when it is needed most—in the debtor's bankruptcy. See BC 544(a)(1); UCC 9–301(1)(b); UCC 9–301(3); Chapter 14, Section 2(A), infra.

The priority rule of UCC 9–301(1)(b) constitutes an important exception to the general rule of UCC 9–201. It also represents an exception to the *nemo dat* principle. Although the debtor already has conveyed an attached and enforceable security interest to an unperfected secured party, the lien creditor can achieve rights that are senior to those of the secured party, thereby receiving greater rights than those of the debtor!

UCC 9–301(2) creates an exception to UCC 9–301(1)(b). It creates a grace period for purchase money security interests, whereby a security interest perfected by filing "before or within ten days after the debtor receives possession of the collateral" is senior to the interest of one who becomes a lien creditor (or transferee in bulk) "between the time the security interest attaches and the time of filing." UCC 9–301(2); see also UCC 9–301, Comment 5. UCC 9–107 defines "purchase money security interest" to include a security interest retained by a seller to secure the price of collateral sold, such as Main's security interest (which subsequently was assigned to Firstbank) in the car sold to Lee Abel in the Prototype. That term also embraces a security interest taken by a third-party lender who advances funds to enable a debtor to acquire collateral, such as Firstbank's advances to General Motors for cars bought by Main in the Prototype. The priority rule in UCC 9–301(2) balances the interests of purchase money financers, who may find it inconvenient or impossible to file before the debtor receives possession of collateral, against those of (presumably) nonreliance lien creditors. Is the balance struck an appropriate one? (The rights of a purchase money secured party when the debtor's bankruptcy intervenes before the secured party has filed a financing statement are considered in Chapter 14, Section 2, infra.)

Consideration of another priority rule rounds out this overview of Article 9's basic conveyancing principles. Assume that *SP*–1 extends credit to Debtor and receives a security interest in Debtor's equipment pursuant to a written security agreement, and further assume that *SP*–1 fails to perfect its security interest by filing or otherwise. Next, assume that, for whatever reason, Debtor grants an enforceable security interest in its equipment to another secured party (*SP*–2); *SP*–2 perfects its security interest by a proper filing (see Note (3) on Attachment and Perfection by Filing, infra). Under the "first-to-file-or-perfect" rule that generally applies among conflicting Article 9 security interests, *SP*–2's security interest is senior to that of *SP*–1, even though *SP*–1's security interest was created (i.e., attached) first and even if *SP*–1 eventually files a financing statement. UCC 9–312(5)(a). Once again, the subordination of *SP*–1's security interest reflects an exception to the general rule of UCC 9–201 as well as to the *nemo dat* principle. Although Debtor's rights in its equipment were subject to

SP–1's (unperfected) security interest, Debtor conveyed greater rights to SP–2.

(2) Fraud, Ostensible Ownership, and Filing. Why does the filing of a proper (UCC 9–402) financing statement play such an important role in the Article 9 priority scheme? What purpose or purposes motivated the Code drafters to impose a filing system? Do the actual benefits of that system outweigh the costs? The answers to these and related questions are complex and uncertain, as the following brief exploration of the historical background of the filing system suggests.

Retention of Possession and the "Fraud in Law" Doctrine. Consider the following facts:

> P was indebted both to C and T. C brought an action on the debt against P. In the meantime, P transferred all of P's personal property to T in full satisfaction of P's debt to T. However, P retained possession of the personal property and continued to use it and treat it as P's own, with T's acquiescence. Subsequently, C obtained a judgment against P and the sheriff attempted to levy on P's property. P's friends resisted the levy, claiming that the property had been transferred to T for good consideration.

These are the facts of Twyne's Case, 76 Eng. Rep. 809 (Star Ch. 1601), in which T (Twyne) was held convicted of a violation of the Statute of 13 Elizabeth, ch. 5. That statute provided that transfers made with the "intent[ ] to delay, hinder or defraud creditors and others" were void, provided for the recovery from the transferee of the "whole value of ... goods and chattels" transferred, and provided criminal sanctions against the parties to the transfer. *Twyne's Case* is best known for setting forth what have become known as "badges of fraud"—in particular, a seller's retention of possession of personal property after its sale. The court in *Twyne's Case* simply could not believe that P (Pierce) and Twyne really contemplated the general transfer of all of Pierce's personal property ("without exception of his apparel"—underwear, toothbrush, and all) to Twyne; in short, the transaction was a sham.

The Statute of 13 Elizabeth was either received into the common law or expressly adopted by statute in most jurisdictions in the United States. See, e.g., Sturtevant v. Ballard, 9 Johns. 337 (N.Y.Sup.Ct.1811) ("[A] voluntary sale of chattels, with an agreement ... that the vendor may keep possession, is, except in special cases, and for special reasons, to be shown to and approved of by the court, fraudulent and void, as against creditors."). Subsequent to the *Sturtevant* case, New York law (after various vicissitudes) became more favorable to buyers who could establish their good faith. See 2 Williston, Sales § 385 (rev. ed. 1948). Several other states, however, continued to articulate the view that a seller's retention of tangible personal property constituted "fraud *per se*." Other jurisdictions rejected this "fraud in law" approach in favor of a more lenient, "fraud in fact" version of the vendor-in-possession doctrine. Modern "fraudulent conveyance" or "fraudulent transfer" law, epitomized by the Uniform Fraudulent Transfer Act (UFTA), adopts the "fraud in fact" approach. Under this approach, the seventeenth-century "badges of fraud" retain their vitality. UFTA 4(b)(2) provides that, in determining whether a transfer is made "with actual intent to hinder, delay, or defraud any creditor of the debtor" and, thus, whether an aggrieved creditor may be able to set the transfer aside, the court may consider various factors, including "whether ... the debtor retained possession or control of the property transferred after the transfer."

Common-law courts typically viewed a transfer for security purposes, such as a mortgage, as a species of sale, which was to be scrutinized for fraud and possibly avoided (set aside) based upon the debtor-transferor's continued possession. Clow v. Woods, 5 Serg. & Rawle 275 (Pa.1819), is an early example. Relying on the rule of the Statute of 13 Elizabeth, the court held a mortgage of all of a tanner's equipment and inventory to be "fraudulent and void" where the debtor was to remain in possession, in the absence of default, under the terms of the mortgage. The court was concerned primarily with the potential for such a transaction to be used for dishonest purposes: "I do not suppose the parties had in fact a fraudulent view, but as such a transaction might be turned to a dishonest use, it was their duty, as far as in their power, to secure the public against it."

Cases like *Clow* proved to be most inconvenient for debtors and secured parties. To be absolutely sure that a creditor could not obtain a judicial lien senior to its interest in the collateral, the creditor could have taken the collateral into its possession; however, for many kinds of collateral (e.g., the bark, tools, skins, and unfinished leather in *Clow*) a possessory security interest (**pledge**) would have been most impractical. Do you see why?

The Problem of "Ostensible Ownership." The potential for a sham transaction—perhaps a conveyance by the debtor that the transferee (a friendly relative or creditor) would assert only if creditors attempted to levy on the debtor's assets—is but one aspect of the fraud that concerned judges from *Twyne's Case* through the early twentieth century. During the same period, reported decisions and commentary dealing with a seller's or debtor's retention of possession typically intermixed expressions of concern about bogus transactions with apprehension about another perceived problem—"ostensible ownership." The ostensible ownership problem involves the risk that a debtor's retention of possession will deceive its creditors into believing that the debtor owns the property free of conflicting claims.

A sham transaction presents a problem distinct from that engendered by ostensible ownership. In the former, the debtor "really" owns the goods free and clear but attempts to deceive creditors into believing that the goods have been conveyed to a third party; in the latter, a third party really has an interest in the goods, but the debtor's continued possession deceives creditors into believing that the debtor owns the goods free and clear.[3] Notwithstanding this distinction, the courts and commentators frequently failed to draw a clear line between the two aspects of fraud, often referring to them interchangeably when determining that a secured transaction constituted a fraudulent conveyance.

Consider, on the one hand, the points made by two judges in *Clow v. Woods*: "In every case where possession is not given, the parties must leave *nothing* unperformed, within the compass of their power, to secure third persons from the consequences of the apparent ownership of the vendor." (Gibson, J.) "There is no way of coming at the knowledge of who is the owner of goods, but by seeing in whose possession they are." (Duncan, J.). On the other hand, the court indicated that it would have approved an arrangement whereby the mortgagee would have bought the goods and leased them to the mortgagor:

> The object of the parties might have been attained without any (at least with less) risk to the public, by the landlord [mortgagee] himself becoming the purchaser in the first instance, and permitting the tenant [mortgagor] to have the use of the property: in which case, the transaction would have been a safe and fair one; and that course should have been pursued.

5 Serg. & Rawle at 280 (Gibson, J.). Thus, Justice Gibson would have been content with the **sale-leaseback** arrangement, even though it would have created the same problem of ostensible ownership as the "secret" mortgage created.[4] Perhaps leases and other bailments, which

---

3. The distinction can be seen particularly clearly when intangibles, rather than chattels, are the subject of the challenged transfer. For example, in Benedict v. Ratner, 268 U.S. 353, 45 S.Ct. 566, 69 L.Ed. 991 (1925), the Court struck down as fraudulent a financing arrangement involving the assignment of accounts receivable, pursuant to which the debtor-assignor was permitted to collect the receivables and use the proceeds in the usual course of its business without accounting to the lender-assignee. The Court held that the fraud consisted of "the reservation [by the debtor] of dominion inconsistent with the effective disposition of title and the creation of a lien." In other words, as in *Twyne's Case*, the perceived inconsistency between what the debtor *did* and what the debtor *said* it was doing, led the Court to conclude that the purported financing arrangement was a sham. Much to the chagrin of the District Court (L. Hand, J.), whose decision was reversed, the Court specifically denied that the fraud rested "upon seeming ownership because of possession retained." Indeed, any fraud concerning assignments of intangibles, which by their nature cannot be possessed or observed, could not derive from misleading appearances. An analogous genre of deception could result, however, when a debtor's books are not marked to reflect an earlier assignment.

4. Commentary likewise failed to come to grips fully with the sham-ostensible ownership dichotomy. For example, Garrard Glenn argued that the relationship between the English reputed ownership doctrine—never widely adopted by statute in the United States—and the avoidance of fraudulent conveyances based on the vendor-in-possession doctrine, was grounded in estoppel. See 1 G. Glenn, Fraudulent Conveyances and Preferences §§ 346–48, at 606–07 (rev. ed. 1940). But Glenn was forced to concede that the courts, in their application of the vendor-in-possession doctrine, were less than faithful to the ostensible ownership rationale. For a brief account of the development of filing statutes and their relationship to fraud and ostensible ownership concerns, see Mooney, The Mystery and Myth of "Ostensible Owner-

already had become established commercial devices, seemed a less hospitable environment for sham transactions.

The judiciary's concern for unsecured creditors and hostility toward nonpossessory security devices (i.e., devices in which the debtor remains in possession of the collateral) extended beyond ostensible ownership and fraud (more generally). At least some courts feared that, rather than facilitate commerce, the widespread use of these devices would wreak economic havoc, depriving debtors of their ability to pay unsecured claims and, perhaps, of their ability to obtain credit in the first instance.[5]

We will never know the extent to which nonpossessory security devices actually posed serious risks to creditors. We do know that, nearly a century and a half ago, one court expressed skepticism about the empirical basis for the doctrine of ostensible ownership and concern over the impediments to commerce that the doctrine itself might impose:

> The truth is, there is something rather loose and indefinite in the idea of a delusive credit gained by the possession of personal property. Such inconvenience may spring from this source, to be guarded against by prudent enquiries on the part of those concerned, and to some extent by legislative enactments, tending to a degree of notoriety in regard to the title. More than this seems to me a remedy worse than the disease; and it is obvious that to prohibit altogether the separation of the title from the possession of personal property, would be incompatible with an advanced state of society and commerce, and productive of much inconvenience and injustice in the pursuits and business of life.

Davis v. Turner, 45 Va. (4 Gratt.) 422, 441 (1848).

Dispelling Fraud Through "Public Notice." Although the judiciary's approach to nonpossessory security interests was somewhat muddled, the legislative responses have been abundantly clear. Beginning with the chattel mortgage statutes in the early nineteenth century and culminating with Article 9, state legislatures enacted statutes that legitimized a wide variety of personal property security devices, including chattel mortgages, conditional sales, accounts receivable financings, and trust receipt financings.[6] These statutes generally imposed (under penalty of avoidance or subordination) an obligation of what came to be

---

ship" and Article 9 Filing: A Critique of Proposals to Extend Filing Requirements to Leases, 39 Ala. L. Rev. 683, 725–38 (1988).

5. See, e.g., Zartman v. First Nat'l Bank of Waterloo, 189 N.Y. 267, 82 N.E. 127 (1907) (refusing to give effect to chattel mortgage on after-acquired inventory "if the result would deprive the general creditors ... of their only chance to collect debts"; observing that "[i]f it is understood that a corporate mortgage given by a manufacturing corporation may take everything except accounts and debts, such corporations, with a mortgage outstanding, will have to do business on a cash basis or cease to do business altogether.").

6. For a survey of the development of pre-Code security devices, see 1 Gilmore, Security chs. 1–8.

known as "public notice," requiring the secured creditor to make a filing or recording in a public office as a substitute, or proxy, for taking possession of the collateral. Article 9's provision for perfection by filing (UCC 9–302(1)) is a direct descendant of these earlier statutes.

The Role of Public Notice in the 1990's. Perhaps it is of no great moment (but surely it is of historical interest) whether the judicial hostility toward nonpossessory security interests and the demonstrated legislative bias toward "public notice" were motivated primarily by general fraud concerns or by more narrowly focused concerns about ostensible ownership (even if such motivations actually could be identified). However, for those who would evaluate and propose changes to the Article 9 scheme and for those who must interpret and live with that scheme, it is important to obtain the broadest possible understanding of what Article 9's "public notice" requirements actually achieve and fail to achieve. Professors Baird and Jackson see the Article 9 filing system as little more than a solution to the problem of "ostensible ownership." Their somewhat narrow view leads them to argue for an expanded reach of the Article 9 filing regime:

> [O]nce one realizes that these [ostensible ownership] problems have a common source, simple solutions to them become apparent. In proposing these simple solutions to problems that have consumed hundreds of pages of law review commentary, we are not advocating a radical departure from established wisdom. Rather, we are urging only that rulemakers apply more generally the principle that has shaped the law of security interests in personal property for four hundred years: A party who wishes to acquire or retain a nonpossessory interest in property that is effective against others must, as a general matter, make it possible for others to discover that interest.

> ... An ostensible ownership problem ... exists whenever there is a separation of ownership and possession. Article 9's treatment of the ostensible ownership problem created by secured credit naturally leads one to ask whether the ostensible ownership problem created by leases or other bailments is different. We believe the answer is simple: The two ostensible ownership problems are not different in any relevant respect. They impose the same costs on third parties, and if a filing system is an appropriate response to the first problem, it is an equally appropriate response to the second.

Baird & Jackson, Possession and Ownership: An Examination of the Scope of Article 9, 35 Stan.L.Rev. 175, 178, 186 (1983). As you ponder the attributes of the Article 9 filing system, addressed next, consider whether this "simple" analysis is a useful, or sufficient, normative baseline. Does it expose all of the costs and benefits? On what empirical assumptions does it depend?

The Attributes of Article 9 Filing. A brief consideration of the operation of the Article 9 filing regime may provide useful insight into the "theory" and "purpose" of that system. Benefits that tend to justify or explain the filing system derive from the following attributes:

(i) The system *provides useful information to prospective purchasers* of personal property—both buyers and secured parties. For example, a prospective non-ordinary course buyer of an item of equipment [7] or a prospective secured lender can, by searching the proper files, determine whether a security interest in the equipment may have been perfected by filing. The absence of a filing thereby allows the prospective transferor to offer some evidence tending to establish a negative—that no (perfected) security interest has been given to another party. Even if no filing is found, however, the prospective purchaser also must ascertain that the equipment is not in the possession of a secured party. See UCC 9–305. Moreover, even a "clean" search does not provide comfort that the prospective transferor owns the equipment or that it acquired its title free of claims that would be senior to those of the prospective purchaser. Finally, the Code filing records generally cover only security interests; they do not reveal many other claims to the property, including tax and other statutory liens that may be senior to the rights of the prospective purchaser.

(ii) The filing system also *provides information to existing and prospective creditors generally.* This attribute is related to the preceding one; the filing system reduces the costs of obtaining information. (And, if one believes that prospective creditors and purchasers are misled by a debtor's possession of personal property, the information provided by filing can be viewed as reducing the "problem of ostensible ownership.") That unsecured creditors somehow are "entitled" to accessible information concerning claims of secured creditors may explain, in part, the priority rule that subordinates unperfected security interests to judicial liens. See UCC 9–301(1)(b). Yet no one really knows the extent to which unsecured creditors use or rely upon the filing system. The position of unsecured creditors is unlike that of purchasers, who normally take steps to ensure their seniority to later-arising claims to the purchased property. Ascertaining that there is no filing against a debtor would not provide an existing or prospective unsecured creditor with any protection against the debtor subsequently encumbering some or all of its assets.[8] Unsecured creditors sometimes may be interested in whether there are filings against a debtor for other reasons, however. For debtors in some lines of business, a filing against receivables or inventory may be seen by trade creditors as a

---

7. See UCC 9–306(2) (security interest normally continues notwithstanding sale); UCC 9–301(1)(c) (buyer not in ordinary course of business sometimes takes free of unperfected security interest); UCC 1–201(9) (defining "buyer in ordinary course of business").

8. An unsecured creditor might bargain for the debtor's agreement not to create security interests in its property; however, any security interest created in violation of this agreement ordinarily will be valid. See Note (4) on the Role of Knowledge in Priority Contests, Chapter 13, Section 1(A), infra.

signal of financial distress, while a filing against equipment would be viewed differently.   On the other hand, debtors in other lines of business may be expected to give a security interest in "all assets" as a routine matter.   Interestingly, reports issued by business credit reporting agencies such as Dun & Bradstreet frequently include information concerning Article 9 filings.

(iii) Article 9's filing system can *provide some protection against fraudulent assertions that a debtor gave a security interest when no security interest was given (or that a security interest was given later than asserted).*   A filed financing statement constitutes irrefutable evidence that a debtor took steps relating to a security interest on or prior to the date of filing.   Consequently, the filing rules make it less likely that a debtor and creditor would collude to claim that a security interest was created earlier than it was.   A financing statement can be filed even though no security interest has attached.   But the fact that important priority rules are based on the time of filing, rather than the time of creation (attachment), reduces the risk of collusion as to the time of creation.   In part, the reduction of fraud and collusion through filing, as a substitute of sorts for a change of possession, derives from *Twyne's Case.*   Publicity overcomes secrecy—one of the "badges" of fraud.

(iv) Article 9's priority rules based on the time of filing also *reduce evidentiary costs and disputes in connection with determination of security interest priorities.*   The public office filing system memorializes the time of filing and constitutes a visible and (generally) reliable "scoreboard."

(v) Article 9's filing rules *create a hurdle that a secured party must clear in order to justify its entitlement to collateral at the expense of a debtor's unsecured creditors.*   It is arguable that, as a normative matter, the benefits of security should not be easily obtained.   However, this "hurdle" argument is a poor justification for a filing requirement; most would support efforts to make compliance with filing requirements even less difficult and costly.

(vi) No matter how simple Article 9's requirements may be or become, secured parties from time to time will fail to comply with the filing rules—either by failing to file in the proper locations or by filing defective financing statements.   In many cases this noncompliance results in the subordination of security interests to lien creditors or, more often, to trustees in bankruptcy.   Consequently, the Article 9 filing rules *enable unsecured creditors to capture assets that otherwise would be allocated to secured parties.*   This distributional attribute of the filing regime is related to the "hurdle" rationale just mentioned; seniority to unsecured creditors requires that a secured party "play the game according to the rules."   Although those who benefit from the inevitable instances of noncompliance undoubtedly would oppose the abolition of filing requirements, it seems wrong to characterize the inevitability of noncompliance and resulting subordination as a "benefit" of filing. Similar results could be obtained more directly, e.g., by requiring that each debtor maintain a pool of unencumbered assets.[9]

(3) What to File: The Adequacy of Financing Statements; Filing Systems. The formal requisites for a financing statement are found in UCC 9–402(1):

> A financing statement is sufficient if it gives the names of the debtor and the secured party, is signed by the debtor, gives an address of the secured party from which information concerning the security interest may be obtained, gives a mailing address of the debtor and contains a statement indicating the types, or describing the items, of collateral.

UCC 9–402(8) provides additional guidance: "A financing statement substantially complying with the requirements of this section is effective even though it contains minor errors which are not seriously misleading." This seemingly straightforward system of "notice filing" was borrowed in large part from the Uniform Trust Receipts Act, promulgated in 1933. It is surprising, perhaps, that determining the adequacy of financing statements under UCC 9–402 has proven perplexing to courts, commentators, and practitioners alike.

The preceding Note summarizes several plausible positive explanations for what the filing system actually does and does not do. The courts, however, generally have measured the adequacy of financing statements against a narrow paradigm consisting of an interested person who wishes to discover whether there are filings against a debtor and, if there are filings, the collateral that they cover. Can an interested person find the financing statement in question? Is the information contained in the financing statement sufficiently complete and meaningful?

Debtor's Name. Filing officers index financing statements "according to the name of the debtor." UCC 9–403(4). Consequently, whether an interested person can find a financing statement is a function of (i) the debtor's name as it appears on the financing statement, (ii) the name against which the interested person requests a search of the filing officer's records, and (iii) the financing statements disclosed by the filing officer as a result of that search request. Individual names are particularly problematic: Consider an individual whose birth certificate refers to Kelly Livingston Jones, who normally goes by "K. Livingston Jones" for personal affairs and "K. L. Jones" for professional and business purposes, and who is called "Kelly Jones" by friends. What is this individual's "real name"? Can a single debtor have more than one name for purposes of UCC 9–402(1)? Is a filing that names "Kelly Jones" adequate? Would it be "seriously misleading" under the UCC 9–402(8) test?

---

9. Exemption laws are intended to preserve a pool of assets for individual (i.e., human) debtors; however, otherwise exempt property ordinarily may be encumbered by a purchase money security interest.

In some filing offices, search requests are processed by individuals who search the files for filings against the name(s) submitted by a party requesting a search. In such a system, whether a search request for filings against "Kelly Jones" would result in identification of filings against any or all of the other variations just mentioned will depend on the formal or informal procedures adopted by that office and, perhaps, the judgment of the particular employee conducting the search. When you consider that many filing systems now are "computerized" to some extent, determining whether a financing statement sufficiently shows the name of the debtor can become even more difficult. For example, will a search against K. L. Jones uncover a filing against K L Jones? KL Jones? Kelly L. Jones? Kelly Jones? The answers depend on the search logic employed by a given system. This means that a lawyer or banker can know whether searching against a particular name will uncover filings against different, but similar, names only if that lawyer or banker understands the manner in which the particular search system has been programmed to respond. In most states, however, the search logic is not a matter of public record. Nevertheless, the courts generally test the adequacy of the name used in a financing statement by considering whether a search made in a reasonable manner would, in the applicable system, uncover the financing statement in question.

Apart from inaccuracies in the debtor's name, there is the problem of "trade names," under which individuals, partnerships, and corporations may choose to conduct business. (For example, the Chicago National League Ball Club, Inc., has adopted the trade name "Chicago Cubs.") The first sentence of UCC 9–402(7) seems to make it clear enough that use of a "real" name is adequate and that use of a trade name is not necessary. Comment 7 goes further; it indicates that use of a trade name instead of a "real" name is insufficient (although the statute does not so provide explicitly).

Should the risks and burdens of investigating and listing the exact name of a debtor be placed on the secured party who files? Or, should the risks of investigating and searching against trade names and names similar to a debtor's "real" name lie with those who search? Is it possible to generalize about which class of parties—secured parties who file or searchers—can protect themselves better against these risks and burdens? For which class of parties is such protection less costly?

References to Collateral. A secured party must do more than ensure that a financing statement correctly states the debtor's name. A financing statement must "contain[ ] a statement indicating the types, or describing the items, of collateral." UCC 9–402(1). As Comment 2 explains,

> [UCC 9–402] adopts the system of "notice filing" which proved successful under the Uniform Trust Receipts Act. What is required to be filed is not, as under chattel mortgage and conditional sales acts, the security agreement itself, but only a simple notice which may be filed before the security interest

attaches or thereafter. The notice itself indicates merely that the secured party who has filed may have a security interest in the collateral described. Further inquiry from the parties concerned will be necessary to disclose the complete state of affairs.

Case law generally upholds financing statements that refer to collateral by a defined Code category, such as "equipment" or "inventory". The cases also generally support the sufficiency of financing statements that refer to generic categories of collateral other than the Code "types," such as "grain" or "new boats".

Some courts have taken a narrower view, however. For example, a financing statement that referred to "Honda parts" was held insufficient to perfect a security interest in—of all things—Honda parts! In re Cilek, 115 B.R. 974 (Bkrtcy.W.D.Wis.1990). Relying on the definition of "type" found in the Random House College Dictionary (1982) (the term is not defined in the Code), the court concluded that "type," as used in UCC 9–402(1) includes only the Code-defined types of collateral—e.g., "account," UCC 9–106, or "inventory," UCC 9–109(4). Relying on the same dictionary's definition of "item," the court determined that the financing statement was defective because it failed to describe each particular item of collateral.

Liberal standards of "notice filing" notwithstanding, a financing statement's complete omission of a description of collateral will be fatal. And the overwhelming majority of cases refuse to uphold financing statements containing only "super-generic" descriptions, such as "all personal property," "all assets," and the like.

Addresses. The courts generally have imposed a less exacting standard for the addresses of debtors and secured parties than they have with respect to debtors' names and identifications of collateral. Although contrary authority exists, there is support for upholding the sufficiency of financing statements even when addresses are missing entirely. The significance of an address may depend on the circumstances. For example, an address may be of great assistance to one who is searching against the name "John Smith," and less so to one searching against, say, Phineas T. Bluster or a well-known corporate debtor.

Debtor's Signature. A financing statement must be "signed by the debtor." UCC 9–402(1). It is not difficult to satisfy this requirement in the usual case; nonetheless, slip-ups do occur. One purpose of requiring a debtor's signature is obvious: a debtor has a strong interest in the content of the public records that disclose possible claims against the debtor's property. The courts generally have applied the (relatively forgiving and broad) definition of "signed" in UCC 1–201(39) in cases where the debtor's signature on a financing statement has been called into question. As to how an inanimate business entity may sign a financing statement, one must resort to non-UCC law of partnerships, corporations, or agency. See UCC 1–103.

Filing Systems. Personal property filing systems based upon an index of debtor names have been utilized at least since the time of the chattel mortgage laws of the nineteenth century. The "modern" system of "notice filing" embraced by Article 9 dates back to the promulgation of the Uniform Trust Receipts Act in 1933—almost sixty years ago. Although "computerized" systems now are common, there seems to be a consensus that the existing filing systems generally do not work well and fail to take full advantage of the benefits of existing technology. In particular, the speed and accuracy of the existing systems leave something to be desired. See generally Report of the Uniform Commercial Code Article 9 Filing System Task Force to the Permanent Editorial Board's Article 9 Study Committee 6–10 (1991).

Problem 8. Assume that Firstbank "picked up" the floorplan financing for Main Motors, on September 3, 1991, as described in the Prototype, and that, effective October 1, 1991, Main changed its corporate name from "Main Motors, Inc." to "Center City Pontiac Sales and Service, Inc." Main received new shipments of cars on November 15 and December 20, 1991, and on February 14, 1992. Firstbank took no action to perfect its security interest subsequent to filing the original Financing Statement (Form 1, Section 1, supra). Lean, Main's judgment creditor, caused the sheriff to levy on all the remaining cars in Main's inventory on February 20, 1992. Is Lean's execution lien senior or junior to Firstbank's security interest? See UCC 9–402(7) (2d sentence). Does the answer depend on whether Firstbank knew that Main had changed its name? Should it?

Professor Jay Westbrook has observed that the operation of the second sentence (to the extent a secured party is absolved indefinitely from refiling against a new name) and the third sentence would constitute a classic "glitch"—were it not for the fact that the Comments make clear that the sentences mean what they say. He sees them as creating a "loophole" that is "inconsistent with the entire statutory scheme." See Westbrook, Glitch: Section 9–402(7) and the U.C.C. Revision Process, 52 Geo. Wash. L. Rev. 408, 411, 416–17 (1984). Professor Stephen Knippenberg, on the other hand, has argued that the drafters' assumptions and perceptions must be evaluated before deciding whether UCC 9–402(7) should be changed; he suggests that the provision may be grounded on the assumption that there are very few second-in-time searchers who would be misled by "old name" financing statements and many first-in-time secured parties whose perfection would be jeopardized by a system that requires them to monitor name changes. See Knippenberg, Debtor Name Changes and Collateral Transfers Under 9–402(7): Drafting From the Outside–In, 52 Mo.L.Rev. 57, 113–115 (1987). What reasons can you think of for imposing more diligence on a secured party at the time a filing is made (i.e., get the debtor's name *right*) than is imposed on a secured party subsequently?

Problem 9. Assume that the only documents signed by Main Motors were the Financing Statement (Form 1, Section 1, supra) and a simple promissory note. Firstbank paid General Motors for a trailerload of new cars delivered to Main; Main orally agreed that Firstbank had a security interest in these cars.

(a) Is the Financing Statement an adequate basis for enforcement of the security interest? Compare UCC 9–203(1)(a) with UCC 9–402(1); see UCC 1–201(3), UCC 9–105(1)(*l*); Note 1 on Adequacy of Security Agreements, infra. Why would anyone sign a financing statement, as debtor, without intending to create a security interest in the property described therein? See UCC 9–312(5)(a).

(b) Would Firstbank have an enforceable security interest if the promissory note signed by Main contained the notation: "Collateral: Motor Vehicles"?

Problem 10. Assume that by error a new Pontiac Firebird was omitted from the Loan Request Form (Form 4, Section 1, supra), and that this form, the Financing Statement, and a simple promissory note were the only documents executed by Main.

(a) Does Firstbank have an enforceable security interest in the omitted Firebird, for which it has paid General Motors? See UCC 9–203(1)(a).

(b) Would the Dealer Inventory Security Agreement cover the slip-up? See Dealer Inventory Security Agreement (Form 2, Section 1, supra) ¶ 5.

(c) Would your answer to part (b) be the same if the Dealer Inventory Security Agreement covered only "motor vehicle inventory located at Dealer's address set forth above" and, in fact, the omitted Firebird was stored at another location? Should the reference to location be construed as a limitation on the collateral covered or merely a reference to the location where the parties expected the collateral to be kept? Compare In re Little Puffer Billy, Inc., 16 B.R. 174 (Bkrtcy. D.Or.1981) (collateral described as "[a]ll inventory of [debtor], Valley River Center, Eugene, Oregon" included inventory at other locations; location intended merely as place of inquiry) with In re California Pump & Manufacturing Co., 588 F.2d 717 (9th Cir.1978) (collateral described as "[a]ll furniture . . . located at" a specified address did not include collateral never located at that address).

Problem 11. Assume that Firstbank "picked up" the floorplan financing for Main Motors as described in the Prototype. Subsequently, Firstbank paid General Motors for a new shipment of cars to Main Motors. Does Firstbank have an enforceable security interest in the newly arrived cars? See UCC 9–203(1); UCC 9–204(1). Is the security interest perfected? See UCC 9–302(1); UCC 9–402(1). Would it make any difference if the only references to collateral in the Dealer Inventory Security Agreement and the Financing Statement were to "all inventory"? See Note 2 on Adequacy of Security Agreements, infra. As to the adequacy of general descriptions, see UCC 9–110.

Notes on Adequacy of Security Agreements

(1) Signed Security Agreement or Secured Party's Possession: Article 9's "Statute of Frauds." A security interest cannot attach unless "the collateral is in the possession of the secured party pursuant to agreement, or the debtor has signed a security agreement." UCC 9–203(1)(a); see UCC 9–105(1)(*l*) (defining "security agreement" as "an agreement which creates or provides for a security interest"); UCC 1–201(39) (defining "signed" to include "any symbol executed or adopted by a party with present intention to authenticate a writing"). Because the attachment of a security interest is a transfer—a conveyance—of a property interest from the debtor to the secured party, the necessity for the debtor's agreement is apparent. The Comments indicate that the requirement of a writing (implicit in the "signature" requirement) "is in the nature of a Statute of Frauds"—i.e., a formal requisite that both enhances the veracity of claims to secured party status and serves to caution a debtor. UCC 9–203, Comment 5; see E.A. Farnsworth, Contracts § 6.1, at 394 (2d ed. 1990) (discussing functions of Statute of Frauds). Professors White and Summers explain that the written security agreement requirement also serves another protective function—providing additional information to those who examine a security agreement. See J. White & R. Summers, Uniform Commercial Code (3d ed. 1988) § 22–3, at 966. But any comfort drawn from that information could be illusory and any protection might be fleeting. Other security agreements covering additional collateral or securing other indebtedness might then exist or thereafter be entered into, and it is the date of *filing* that generally determines priorities.

A secured creditor who fails to obtain a written, signed security agreement, but is in possession of the collateral, nonetheless must provide evidence that its possession is "pursuant to agreement" (read: security agreement). See, e.g., Reinhardt v. Nikolaisen, 775 S.W.2d 284 (Mo.App.1989) (oral security agreement is enforceable when secured party is in possession of collateral). According to the Comments, "[w]here the collateral is in the possession of the secured party, the evidentiary need for a written record is much less than where the collateral is in the debtor's possession...." UCC 9–203, Comment 3. Do you agree?

Printed forms of security agreements are readily available; when properly completed and signed they easily satisfy the minimal requirements of UCC 9–203(1)(a). Moreover, a security agreement need not contain any "magic words" to create a security interest. The courts generally have been generous to secured parties who have used inartful language. Nevertheless, the debtor's failure to sign an "agreement which creates or provides for a security interest" will be fatal to the assertion of an attached (nonpossessory) security interest. For example, many cases have held that a debtor's signature on a financing statement alone does not satisfy UCC 9–203(1)(a) when the financing statement meets only the minimum requirements of UCC 9–402 and does not contain additional language constituting an appropriate "agreement." See UCC 1–201(3) (defining "agreement" as "the bargain of the parties in fact as found in their language or by implication from other circumstances").

Does a debtor's signing of a financing statement create an "implication" that the debtor has agreed to create a security interest? A "technical" answer is found in UCC 9–402(1): "A financing statement may be filed before a security agreement is made or a security interest otherwise attaches." Why else would a debtor sign a financing statement if not to create a security interest? As a practical matter, prospective secured parties frequently file before a secured loan or sale is consummated (i.e., they "pre-file") so that a filing office search report reflecting the financing statement can be obtained before value is given. That a financing statement is filed does not necessarily mean that any security interest has been or will be created. See UCC 9–402, Comment 2 (quoted in part in Note 3 on Attachment and Perfection by Filing, supra).

Why do putative secured parties sometimes fail to take the relatively simple step of requiring a debtor to sign a security agreement? The reported decisions, at least, indicate that inadvertence and clerical or administrative errors are most often to blame (although examples of mistakes by truly "amateur" creditors also can be found). In the slightly altered words of a famous bumper sticker: "It happens."

As to what constitutes a signature on a security agreement, the approach taken by the courts generally has been forgiving—not unlike that taken in connection with financing statements. See Note 3 on Attachment and Perfection by Filing, supra.

(2) **Description of the Collateral; After–Acquired Property.** A security agreement signed by the debtor must "contain[ ] a description of the collateral" in order to satisfy UCC 9–203(1)(a). Cases dealing with what constitutes an adequate description are, in many respects, of the same genre as those dealing with the sufficiency of references to collateral in financing statements. See Note 3 on Attachment and Perfection by Filing, supra. But keep in mind the different functions performed by financing statements and security agreements. A financing statement is supposed to put a searcher on notice that a security interest *may* be claimed so that the interested person can make further inquiry. A security agreement, on the other hand, provides evidence that a security interest *in fact* has been created in certain collateral. (The identification function also is served by the alternative of possession by the secured party, which serves as an evidentiary proxy for a security agreement that describes the collateral.)

The requirement that a security agreement contain a description of the collateral reflects the functional differences between a financing statement and a security agreement. Although a financing statement need only indicate the "types" of collateral covered (UCC 9–402(1)), the description of collateral in a security agreement must meet a stricter standard, specified in UCC 9–110: "[A]ny description of personal property ... is sufficient whether or not it is specific if it reasonably identifies what is described." The Comments indicate that a description in a security agreement must "do the job assigned to it—... *make possible* the identification of the thing described," while rejecting the notion that a description must be "of the most exact and detailed nature, the so-called 'serial number' test," as applied in earlier chattel mortgage cases. UCC 9–110, Comment (emphasis added).

Is it necessary for a description to identify the collateral itself? Or, is a description sufficient if it provides enough information so that someone, by *additional* investigation, *could* identify it? How does the latter test differ from the test for an adequate notice filing under UCC 9–402? Some courts seem to make little or no distinction. See, e.g., In re Amex–Protein Development Corp., 504 F.2d 1056 (9th Cir.1974) (under UCC 9–110 a collateral description in security agreement is adequate "if it provides such information as would lead a reasonable inquirer to the identity of the collateral"). Other courts have rejected the notion that a security agreement serves a notice function. See, e.g., First State Bank v. Shirley Ag Service, Inc., 417 N.W.2d 448 (Iowa 1987) (security agreement provides evidence of agreement and addresses Statute of Frauds problems, but does not serve any notice function).

As they have with respect to financing statements (see Note 3 on Attachment and Perfection by Filing, supra), some courts have held that "super-generic" collateral descriptions (such as "all property of every description") used in security agreements are inadequate. However, these descriptions generally have fared better in the security agreement context than when used in financing statements. See FDIC v. Hill, 13 Mass.App. 514, 434 N.E.2d 1029 (1982), appeal denied, 386 Mass. 1104, 440 N.E.2d 1177 (1982) (description of collateral as "all personal property" in security agreement was sufficient to cover equipment). When it is determined that the bargain-in-fact of the parties is that the security agreement covers all personal property of the debtor, why should it be necessary to resort to more detail? In *every* case where attachment is in dispute it will be necessary to determine that a debtor has "rights in the collateral." UCC 9–203(1)(c). If all personal property is to be covered, then, the distinguishing factor between collateral and non-collateral is the existence of those rights.

Generic descriptions, both by Article 9 "type" and otherwise, usually have been considered sufficient when used in a security agreement. One recurring issue is whether a description such as "all of debtor's equipment" covers not only equipment of the debtor at the time the security agreement is executed but also equipment subsequently acquired by the debtor. Pursuant to UCC 9–204(1) "a security agreement may provide that ... obligations ... are to be secured by after-acquired collateral." Whether conceptualizing the issue as one concerning the adequacy of the collateral description or as one concerning whether the parties agreed to cover after-acquired collateral, some courts have refused to uphold claims to after-acquired property in the absence of an explicit reference in the security agreement. Others have been more generous, especially when the collateral concerned has been accounts or inventory, which turn over continually and for which it would make little commercial sense for the parties to limit the collateral to that on hand at the inception of the transaction.

Problem 12. Several months after Firstbank and Main Motors established the inventory financing arrangements as described in the Prototype, Main fell behind in payments to its unsecured trade creditors. Main requested a short-term (60–day) loan from Firstbank in the amount of $100,000. Firstbank agreed and advanced that sum to Main; the only documentation was a promissory note signed by Main that contained no reference to any of the inventory financing documentation. Main failed to pay the note when due and also defaulted under the inventory financing arrangement. Subsequently, Lean, a judgment creditor of Main, caused the sheriff to levy on Main's automobile inventory.

As counsel for Lean, you conclude that Lean's execution lien is junior to Firstbank's security interest. However, you learn that the value of the automobile inventory probably is sufficient to satisfy all amounts outstanding on Main's inventory loans from Firstbank, with surplus value available for Lean. On the other hand, if the automobile inventory secures not only the inventory loans but also the $100,000 term loan, there would be little, if anything, left for Lean.

(a) What are the best arguments that the automobile inventory does not secure the $100,000 loan? See UCC 9–204(3) & Comment 5; Dealer Inventory Security Agreement (Form 2, Section 1, supra) ¶ 5; Note on Obligations (Including Future Advances) Covered by Security Agreements, infra.

(b) Assuming that the $100,000 loan would be secured, what result if Main's $100,000 obligation to Firstbank arose not out of a loan but out of an accident in which one of Main's tow-trucks ran through Firstbank's plate glass window, into its lobby, and over its president?

(c) As Firstbank's counsel, how could you draft the Dealer Inventory Security Agreement so as to ensure that the collateral would secure Main's obligations to Firstbank in both of these circumstances?

Note on Obligations (Including Future Advances) Covered by Security Agreements

The term "security interest" is defined in UCC 1–201(37) to include "an interest in personal property or fixtures which secures payment or performance of an obligation." The Code leaves it to the parties to agree as to what obligations are secured by a security interest. Although the Code does not define or regulate generally the obligations that are secured, UCC 9–204(3) does address one aspect of the obligations that may be secured by a security interest: "Obligations covered by a security agreement may include future advances or other value whether or not the advances or value are given pursuant to commitment (subsection (1) of Section 9–105)." This provision might seem superfluous, were it not for the pre-UCC treatment of future advance provisions in the courts. Comment 5 to UCC 9–204 notes that "[a]t common law and under chattel mortgage statutes there seems to have been a vaguely articulated prejudice against future advance agreements comparable to the prejudice against after-acquired property interests." The following passage reveals the source and flavor of at least some of that prejudice:

> **Validity of future advance arrangements under pre-Code law: The "dragnet" cases.** A convenient starting point will be the type of situation which regularly calls down the thunderings of judicial wrath: the lender's claim that obligations of the mortgagor [debtor] which are in no sense related to the financing transaction which the mortgage [security interest] was given to secure are, nevertheless, covered by the mortgage. Cases of this type, which often are indistinguishable from cases of outright fraud, keep coming along in numbers just sufficient to keep fresh in the judicial mind the ease with which the future advance device can be exploited by the overreaching mortgagee [secured party] to crush the impoverished but no doubt honest debtor.

> A standard boiler-plate clause provides in substance: the mortgaged property [collateral] shall stand as security for any indebtedness of any sort which may now or hereafter be owing by mortgagor to mortgagee. In polite society this is sometimes referred to as a "cross-security" clause; it can serve many useful and legitimate purposes. A court which proposes to invalidate a claim asserted under such a clause will refer to it less politely as a "dragnet" clause, with the remark that such clauses "are not highly regarded in equity. They should be 'carefully scrutinized and strictly construed.'" Or as the Arkansas court [Berger v. Fuller, 180 Ark. 372, 21 S.W.2d 419, 421 (1929)] put it in a colorful passage:

>> Mortgages of this character have been denominated "Anaconda mortgages" and are well named thus, as by their broad and general terms they enwrap the unsuspecting debtor in the folds of indebtedness embraced and secured in the mortgage which he did not contemplate ...

> What often happens in dragnet cases is that a mortgagee who holds a mortgage given to secure a small claim on an otherwise impoverished debtor's one valuable piece of property—which may be his homestead—buys up, no doubt at a large discount, other claims against the mortgagor and adds these to the mortgage debt. A variant is that the mortgagee, after his

debt has been largely paid, will assign the mortgage to another creditor, who asserts that his previously unsecured claim is now, by virtue of the dragnet clause, the debt secured.

2 Gilmore, Security § 35.2, at 917–18.

It is clear enough that the Code itself legitimizes future advance provisions and puts no restrictions on what obligations can be secured. Yet Professor Gilmore argued that the pre-Code law has survived, at least to the extent that only future advances that are similar and related to an initial, principal obligation should be given the benefit of broad future advance and "all obligations" provisions. Id. § 35.5, at 932. Numerous cases have taken the approach urged by Professor Gilmore. See, e.g., Community Bank v. Jones, 278 Or. 647, 566 P.2d 470 (1977) (citing, inter alia, Gilmore, Security; applying "general test" of whether indebtedness was of same class as primary obligation).

As may be the case when determining what collateral is covered by a security agreement, a better approach might be to apply conventional rules of contract interpretation to the task at hand. See, e.g., In re Public Leasing Corp., 488 F.2d 1369 (10th Cir.1973) (parol evidence should not have been admitted to construe a "cross-collateralization clause" that was "clear and unambiguous"). If the bargain-in-fact of the parties is that a security agreement is to secure all of a debtor's obligations, should that bargain be disregarded merely because a putative secured obligation is somehow dissimilar or unrelated to earlier obligations? If so, the result would offend the freedom-of-contract principle that the Code appears to respect in the context of what obligations are to be secured. Cf. UCC 1–102(3) (affording parties substantial freedom to vary Code provisions and to agree on standards of performance). Nevertheless, it seems likely that in many cases the same results would obtain regardless of the approach taken.

On the subject of broad "all obligations" clauses, see generally Campbell, Contracts Jurisprudence and Article Nine of the Uniform Commercial Code: The Allowable Scope of Future Advance and All Obligations Clauses in Commercial Security Agreements, 37 Hastings L.J. 1007 (1986) (arguing that the courts should reject the "same class" or "relatedness" test advocated by Professor Gilmore).

(B) PERFECTION BY MEANS OTHER THAN FILING

Problem 13. Lee Abel purchased a Pontiac from Main Motors and executed a Motor Vehicle Installment Sale Contract (Form 6, Section 1, supra). Main assigned to Firstbank its rights under this contract and the parties followed the other procedures described in the Prototype. Note that no financing statement naming Abel as debtor was filed with respect to Abel's new Pontiac.

(a) Friendly Finance, a judgment creditor of Abel, caused the sheriff to levy on the car. Is Friendly's execution lien senior or junior to Firstbank's security interest? See UCC 9–301(1)(b); UCC 9–302(1)(d); UCC 9–109(1); UCC 9–302(3)(b), (4); Uniform Motor Vehicle Certificate of Title and Anti–Theft Act §§ 20, 3. Is the result consistent with the policy of requiring public notice as a condition to prevailing over judicial liens and the claims of many other third parties?

(b) The facts are the same, except that Abel purchased a tractor for use on a farm that Abel operates. Under the applicable Motor Vehicle Code, the tractor is not a motor vehicle that must be licensed, registered, or covered by a certificate of title. Again, no financing statement was filed and Friendly caused the sheriff to levy on the tractor. Is Friendly's execution lien senior or junior to Firstbank's security interest in the tractor? See UCC 9–301(1)(b); UCC 9–302(1)(d); UCC 9–302(?)(b), (4); UCC 9–107; UCC 9–109.

(c) The facts are the same as in part (b), except that Abel, who lives in a house surrounded by several acres of rolling lawn, bought the tractor to pull a lawn mower. Is Friendly's execution lien senior or junior to Firstbank's security interest? See UCC 9–301(1)(b); UCC 9–302(1)(d); UCC 9–107; UCC 9–109. Can you reconcile the result with the result in part (b)? With Article 9's policy in favor of public notice? Are Abel's other creditors likely to assess the tractor differently under the facts of part (c) than under the facts of part (b)? Federal law views nonpossessory, non-purchase money security interests in consumer goods with disfavor. See FTC Rule on Credit Practices, 16 C.F.R. § 444.2(a)(4) (1991) (taking a nonpossessory, non-purchase money security interest in household goods constitutes an "unfair act or practice" under Federal Trade Commission Act § 5); BC 522(f) (nonpossessory, non-purchase money security interests in certain consumer goods can be avoided in bankruptcy).

(d) The facts are the same as in part (c), except that after Abel used the tractor around the house for a few months, Abel decided that it could be put to better use at the farm. Thereafter, Abel used the tractor exclusively for farming operations. As in part (b), the sheriff levied on the tractor at the farm. Is Friendly's execution lien senior or junior to Firstbank's security interest? See UCC 9–301(1)(b); UCC 9–302(1)(d); UCC 9–107; UCC 9–109. When is the use of collateral determined for purposes of classifying collateral "types"? What is the effect of a change in use? Cf. UCC 9–401(3). Compare UCC 9–401(3) (alternative).

Problem 14. Dooley, an amateur numismatist, applied to Castle Finance Company for a loan. In response to Castle's request for security, Dooley delivered to Castle a valuable coin collection and received a loan for $1,000. No financing statement was filed.

(a) Lean, a judgment creditor of Dooley, levies on the coin collection held by Castle. Who has priority? Does Castle even have an interest in the coins? See UCC 9–201; UCC 9–301(1)(b); UCC 9–303; UCC 9–203(1); UCC 9–302(1)(a); UCC 9–305; UCC 1–201(24).

(b) What result if Castle filed a financing statement conforming to UCC 9–402(1) but did not take delivery of the coins? See UCC 9–304(1).

(c) What result if Castle itself did not take delivery of the coin collection but instead appointed Dooley its agent for the purpose of holding the coins on its behalf? Dooley's lawyer? See UCC 9–305 & Comment 2; In re Copeland & Notes following, infra; Note on Possession by Agents and Bailees, infra.

(d) What result if Dooley's coin collection was on display at Museum, which received a letter from Dooley stating: "Castle Finance Company holds a security interest in my coin collection, which is now in your possession"? See UCC 9–305 & Comment 2; Note on Possession by Agents and Bailees, infra. Does it matter whether Museum responds?

(e) Assume the facts in part (d) and that Museum fails to respond. Upon the closing of the exhibit, Museum returns the coins to Dooley; shortly thereafter Lean levies. Is Lean's execution lien senior or junior to Castle's security interest? If Lean's lien takes priority, does Castle have a claim against Museum?

(f) Assume the facts in part (d) and that Museum fails to respond. Upon Dooley's default, Castle demands in writing that Museum turn over the coins for sale by Castle pursuant Article 9. See UCC 9–503; UCC 9–504. If Museum returns the coins to Dooley, would it become liable to Castle?

(g) Would the result in part (d) change if Castle, rather than Dooley, notified the museum of the security interest?

(h) What additional or different steps, if any, would you have advised Castle to take in this transaction?

IN RE COPELAND[*]

United States Court of Appeals, Third Circuit, 1976.
531 F.2d 1195.

SEITZ, CHIEF JUDGE. This is a consolidated appeal from two separate orders of the district court in a Chapter XI bankruptcy proceeding instituted by Lammot duPont Copeland, Jr. (hereinafter "Copeland" or "debtor"). The appeals are united by a common factual basis. In July of 1967, Copeland personally guaranteed payment on a $2,700,000 loan by Pension Benefit Fund, Inc. ("Pension Benefit") to two corporations and entered into an agreement which required him to pledge as collateral security 18,187 shares of Christiana Securities Co. stock. An "escrow agreement" was simultaneously executed between Copeland, Pension Benefit and Wilmington Trust Company ("Wilmington Trust")

[* The court's citations are to the applicable pre–1972 version of the Code.]

which designated Wilmington Trust as escrow holder of the pledged stock. [The stock was thereupon delivered to Wilmington Trust.]

Nearly three years later, in April, 1970, there was a default on the loan. Following written demand upon the principal corporations for payment, Pension Benefit notified Copeland and Wilmington Trust by letter of September 11, 1970 of the uncured default and of its intention to demand the surrender of the escrowed stock in accordance with the pledge agreement. Copeland did not respond to this letter, but on October 20, 1970, filed a petition for an arrangement under Chapter XI of the Bankruptcy Act, 11 U.S.C. §§ 701 et seq., and an application to stay enforcement of Pension Benefit's lien on the Christiana stock. Thereafter, Copeland withdrew his objection to the delivery of the stock to Pension Benefit, and the stock was turned over by Wilmington Trust on December 1, 1970. ...

[D]ebtor filed an independent application for an order requiring Pension Benefit to surrender the stock itself and dividends received with respect thereto. Debtor's application was denied by the district court, sitting as a bankruptcy court, by order dated February 3, 1975. Debtor and the Statutory Creditors' Committee appealed.

I. DEBTOR'S APPEAL

We shall consider first the issues raised in debtor's appeal since, if he is successful in recovering the stock, Pension Benefit's appeal will be rendered moot.

Copeland asserts a superior right to possession of the stock by virtue of his status as debtor-in-possession which enables him to exercise all the powers of a trustee in bankruptcy, Bankruptcy Act § 342 [the predecessor to Bankruptcy Code § 1107], and specifically, to avail himself of all rights and remedies of any creditor—real or hypothetical—who had or could have obtained a lien on the debtor's property on the date of bankruptcy. Bankruptcy Act § 70c [the predecessor to Bankruptcy Code § 544(a)]. The rights of a lien creditor must be determined by reference to state law. Pertinent here is § 9–301(1)(b) of the Uniform Commercial Code as enacted in Delaware, 6 Del. C. § 9–301(1)(b), which provides:

"(1) Except as otherwise provided in subsection (2), an unperfected security interest is subordinate to the rights of

. . .

"(b) a person who becomes a lien creditor without knowledge of the security interest and before it is perfected."

Since under § 70c of the Bankruptcy Act the trustee has all rights of an ideal lien creditor under § 9–301(1)(b) of the Code, his rights in the stock are superior to Article 9 claimants whose interests were unperfected as of the date of bankruptcy.

Copeland contends that Pension Benefit's security interest in the Christiana stock was unperfected on the date of bankrupcty. He asserts that the district court therefore erred in denying his application for an order requiring Pension Benefit to surrender the stock and dividends received with respect thereto.

A. Attachment

Copeland first argues that Pension Benefit's security interest was unperfected because it had not attached as of October 20, 1970, the date on which debtor filed his Chapter XI petition. The district court determined to the contrary.

Section 9–303 provides that a "security interest is perfected when it has attached and when all of the applicable steps required for perfection have been taken." Attachment occurs under § 9–204 [UCC 9–203(1)] when there is an agreement that the security interest attach, value is given, and the debtor has rights in the collateral. A security interest attaches immediately upon the happening of these events "unless explicit agreement postpones the time of attaching." § 9–204(1) [UCC 9–203(2)]. Although the aforementioned prerequisites to attachment had been fulfilled on the date the pledge agreement was executed in 1967,[3] Copeland contends that the parties explicitly agreed to postpone the time of attachment. In support of this contention, he relies upon paragraph 8 of the pledge agreement which states:

> "8. In the event there is a default by the Pledgor in the performance of any of the terms of this Agreement, or if there is a default in the payment of the loan as provided in the note and if such default continues for a period of fifteen (15) days, the Pledgee shall have the right, upon fifteen (15) days notice, sent by registered mail to the Pledgor, to call upon The Wilmington Trust Company to forthwith deliver all of the stock and stock powers which it is holding as security hereunder to Pledgee, or such other party as Pledgee may designate, and thereupon, without any liability for any diminution in price which may have occurred, and without further consent by the Pledgor, the said Pledgee may sell all or part of the said stock in such manner and for such price or prices as the said Pledgee may be able to obtain. At any bonafide public sale, the Pledgee shall be free to purchase all or any part of the pledged stock. Out of the proceeds of any sale, the Pledgee shall retain an amount equal to the entire unpaid principal and interest then due on the loan plus the amount of the actual expenses of the sale and shall pay the balance to the Pledgor. In the event that the proceeds of any sale are insufficient to cover the entire unpaid principal and interest of the loan plus the expenses of the sale, the Pledgor shall be liable for any deficiency."

---

3. The pledge and escrow agreements together constituted the requisite agreement. Value was given by Pension Benefit's binding commitment to extend credit. § 1–201(44). The debtor had rights in the collateral in that he remained owner of record and was empowered to vote the shares and receive the dividend income even after the stock was transferred to Wilmington Trust.

Copeland argues that by the terms of this paragraph, Pension Benefit's security interest did not attach until each of the following events had occurred: (1) the debtor had defaulted; (2) default had continued for fifteen days; (3) fifteen days written notice by registered mail had been sent to the debtor by Pension Benefit; (4) proper demand had been made upon Wilmington Trust to deliver the stock and stock powers; and (5) the stock and stock powers had been delivered to Pension Benefit. Since the stock was not turned over to Pension Benefit until December 1, 1970, he maintains that the security interest had not attached, and consequently was not perfected, on the pivotal date of bankruptcy, October 20, 1970.

We believe that the relevant language of paragraph 8 which debtor urges postpones the date of attachment merely establishes an orderly procedure for enforcement of the security interest upon default. It is understandable that debtor would seek to protect his stock to the fullest extent possible from hasty and premature foreclosure attempts by Pension Benefit. Indeed, § 9–501 of the Code, with exceptions not here relevant, specifically recognizes the right of parties to a security agreement to agree among themselves as to the duties and responsibilities of a secured party when default occurs. To read paragraph 8 as anything other than an attempt to safeguard debtor's interest in the valuable pledged stock against unwarranted claims of default and improper attempts to enforce the security interest would distort the nature of the transaction envisioned by the parties and would render Pension Benefit's security for repayment of the loan largely meaningless. We say this because Pension Benefit's interest in the stock would be subordinate to any intervening creditors who had obtained and perfected a security interest in the stock after Pension Benefit but before bankruptcy, a result clearly not intended by either party. We therefore conclude that the pledge agreement was not intended to delay the date of attachment of Pension Benefit's security interest, but rather was designed to protect debtor's interest in the stock from improper attempts by Pension Benefit to obtain its possession in the event there was a claim of default.

. . .

B. Perfection

Relying on § 9–304(1) and § 9–305, Copeland next argues that even assuming the security interest had attached, it was not properly perfected on the date of bankruptcy. Section 9–304 provides that a security interest in instruments, defined in § 9–105(g) and § 8–102 to include corporate securities such as the Christiana stock, can only be perfected by the secured party's taking possession. Section 9–305 modifies this rule by permitting a secured party to perfect his security interest through the possession of his bailee. Section 9–305 states in pertinent part:

"A security interest in letters of credit and advices of credit (subsection (2)(a) of Section 5–116), goods, instruments, negotiable documents or chattel paper may be perfected by the secured party's taking possession of the collateral. If such collateral other than goods covered by a negotiable document is held by a bailee, the secured party is deemed to have possession from the time the bailee receives notification of the secured party's interest...."

Debtor maintains that Pension Benefit's security interest was not perfected by Wilmington Trust's possession of the stock because Wilmington Trust was the agent of both parties. He asserts that this position is inconsistent with the degree of possession needed to perfect under the "bailee with notice" provision of § 9–305. To satisfy the requirement of this section, he urges, possession must be maintained by an agent under the sole control of the secured party.

In support of this contention, debtor places considerable emphasis upon what would have been the nature of the relationship between the parties at common law. Since the stock was held by Wilmington Trust as agent for both parties, he argues that the arrangement must be characterized as an escrow, rather than a perfected pledge which requires possession by the pledgee or an agent under his absolute dominion and control. Citing In re Dolly Madison Industries, Inc., [351 F.Supp. 1038 (E.D.Pa.1972) aff'd mem., 480 F.2d 917 (3d Cir.1973),] he further stresses that the simultaneous existence of an escrow and a pledge is a legal impossibility. Since the transaction fails as a common law pledge for lack of possession by the pledgee or his agent, and since the Code, he asserts, has incorporated the requirement of the common law pledge that the pledgee or an agent under his absolute control maintain possession of the collateral, Pension Benefit's security interest was unperfected under § 9–304 and § 9–305 on the date of bankruptcy.

Although concluding that Wilmington Trust was an escrow agent at common law and hence incapable of becoming Pension Benefit's agent for the purpose of perfecting the pledge, the district court held that the provision of § 9–305 permitting perfection by a "bailee with notice" had been satisfied, and that the security interest was consequently perfected under the Code. The court rejected debtor's argument that § 9–305 had incorporated the restrictive possession requirement of the common law pledge, finding that an acceptance of this proposition would frustrate the parties' intent to collateralize the loan as against third party creditors, would be in disregard of the policy considerations underlying both the law of pledge and the Code, and would unduly restrict the use of the escrow device.

We find it unnecessary to consider the parties' rights at common law because we believe that the language and policy underlying § 9–305 support the district court's conclusion that Pension Benefit's security interest was perfected upon delivery of the stock to Wilmington Trust in July, 1967. While it is true that the Code does not wholly displace the common law, § 1–103, nor abolish existing security devices,

Official Comment 2, § 9–102,[4] Article 9 simplifies pre-Code secured financing by providing for the unitary treatment of all security arrangements. It eliminates many of the antiquated distinctions between various security devices in favor of a single "security interest", §§ 9–102, 1–201(37), and a single set of rules regarding creation and perfection, designed to govern "any transaction (regardless of its form) which is intended to create a security interest in personal property or fixtures including goods, Documents, Instruments...." § 9–102. Since neither party denies that the pledge and escrow agreements were intended to create a security interest in the stock within the meaning of the Uniform Commercial Code, we attach no particular significance to the common law distinctions between the pledge and the escrow which debtor stresses, except insofar as they bear on the question of whether Pension Benefit's security interest was properly perfected under § 9–305 of the Code through Wilmington Trust's possession of the stock.

It is to that question which we now turn. Historically and prior to the Code, possession of collateral by a creditor or third party has served to impart notice to prospective creditors of the possessor's possible interest therein. The Code carries forward the notice function which the creditor's possession formerly provided. Notice to future lenders is furnished under the Code by a filed financing statement, § 9–302, or by the possession of the property subject to the security interest by a secured party or his agent, §§ 9–304, 9–305, depending upon the nature of the collateral.

Where the Code requires perfection by possession of the secured party or his bailee, it is clear that possession by the debtor or an individual closely associated with the debtor is not sufficient to alert prospective creditors of the possibility that the debtor's property is encumbered. See, In re Black Watch Farms, Inc., 9 UCC Rep.Serv. 151 (Ref. Dec. S.D.N.Y.1971). Thus, Official Comment 2 to § 9–305 states:

> "Possession may be by the secured party himself or by an agent on his behalf: it is of course clear, however, that the debtor or a person controlled by him cannot qualify as such an agent for the secured party. ...."

It does not follow from this statement or from the policy underlying § 9–305, however, that possession of the collateral must be by an individual under the sole dominion and control of the secured party, as debtor urges us to hold. Rather, we believe that possession by a third party bailee, who is not controlled by the debtor, which adequately informs potential lenders of the possible existence of a perfected security interest satisfies the notice function underlying the "bailee with notice" provision of § 9–305.

---

4. While Delaware has not adopted the Official Comments prepared by the drafters of the Uniform Commercial Code, these comments are nevertheless useful in interpreting the Code, as it is to be applied in Delaware, in view of the Code's expressed purpose of making uniform the law among the various jurisdictions. § 1–102(2)(c)....

In the case presently before us, the collateral was held by Wilmington Trust pursuant to the terms of both the pledge and escrow agreements. Regardless of whether Wilmington Trust retained the stock as an escrow agent or as a pledge holder, its possession and the debtor's lack of possession clearly signaled future creditors that debtor's ownership of and interest in the stock were not unrestricted. As an independent, institutional entity, Wilmington Trust could not be regarded automatically as an instrumentality or agent of the debtor alone. There was consequently no danger that creditors would be misled by its possession.

The fact that debtor remained owner of record and was empowered to vote the shares and receive current income does not compel a different finding. The location of title to collateral is immaterial with respect to the rights and obligations of the parties to a security transaction. § 9–202; Barney v. Rigby Loan & Investment Co., 344 F.Supp. 694 (D.Idaho 1972).

Nor do we believe our summary affirmance of the district court's decision in *In re Dolly Madison Industries, Inc.*, supra, dictates a contrary conclusion. In reversing a decision by the referee denying the trustee's application for a turnover order, the district court in *Dolly Madison* rested its decision on a finding that the security agreement ... postponed the attachment of the security interest asserted by a creditor of the bankrupt until after bankruptcy. In support of this decision, the court noted that the parties had evidenced their intent to delay attachment by placing the collateral in the neutral custody of an escrow agent pending payment or default. Statements by the court indicating that the simultaneous existence of an escrow and a pledge is a legal impossibility were merely intended to underscore the parties' deliberate choice of the escrow device rather than a pledge in order to assure that attachment would be postponed. Since the district court found that attachment had been delayed by specific agreement of the parties, it was not called upon to determine whether an attached security interest had been perfected. Hence, any statements suggesting that the placement of collateral in escrow precludes a creditor from perfecting his security interest for lack of sufficient possession under § 9–305 are mere uncontrolling dicta.

Having found that Wilmington Trust's possession of the stock afforded the requisite notice to prospective creditors, we conclude that it was a "bailee with notice" within the meaning of § 9–305 and that its possession therefore perfected Pension Benefit's security interest. Hence, perfection occurred in July, 1967, more than three years in advance of bankruptcy, on the date the stock was delivered to Wilmington Trust with notification of Pension Benefit's interest therein. For this reason, the district court correctly concluded that debtor's interest in the stock as debtor-in-possession was subordinate to that of Pension Benefit and properly denied debtor's application for a turnover order.

. . .

Notes on *In re Copeland*

(1) The Role of Pre–Code Law. Counsel for Copeland "placed considerable emphasis on what would have been the nature of the relationship between the parties at common law." They argued that the escrow would have failed as a common-law pledge "for lack of possession by the pledgee or his agent." Does the court disagree with this assessment? Assuming that counsel's assertions about the common-law rules were correct, what justifies the court's departure from the common law? See UCC 1–102; UCC 1–103; UCC 9–205.

(2) The Effect of Post–*Copeland* Amendments to the Code. The 1977 amendments to the Code removed the rules on attachment and perfection of security interests in investment securities (e.g., stocks and bonds) from Article 9 and placed them in Article 8. See UCC 8–321; UCC 8–313. The Notes on Perfection of Security Interests in Investment Securities, infra, discuss these rules in some detail. For present purposes, please observe that possession of a certificate by or on behalf of the secured party remains an effective method by which to perfect a security interest in securities under Article 8. See UCC 8–321(1); UCC 8–313(1)(a). The drafters of Article 8 did not intend that the relocation and rephrasing of the attachment and perfection provisions relating to investment securities would modify the law as it had developed under UCC 9–304(1) and UCC 9–305. See Aronstein, Haydock & Scott, Article 8 *Is* Ready, 93 Harv.L.Rev. 888, 893 (1980) (explaining that the drafters of the 1977 amendments attempted to preserve existing legal relationships except as necessary to accommodate securities not represented by instruments); id. at 905–07 (explaining that the drafters did not address persistent problems concerning perfection by notification that had arisen under UCC 9–305). Thus, *Copeland*'s discussion of perfection by possession remains "good law," even though UCC 8–321 and 8–313 have replaced UCC 9–304(1) and UCC 9–305 as the applicable Code sections.

Note on Possession by Agents and Bailees

The possessory security interest, or **pledge**, was the prototypical common-law security device. In contrast to nonpossessory arrangements, where Debtor remained in possession of the collateral, the pledge was thought not to give rise to significant ostensible ownership or other fraud problems. Possession by Secured Party put to rest any notion that Debtor owned the property free and clear; it also was consistent with Secured Party's assertion that it was relying on the collateral for repayment of its claim against Debtor. See generally Note (2) on Attachment and Perfection by Filing, supra.

It is not much of a stretch to conclude that if possession by Secured Party is sufficient for an effective pledge, then possession by its agent would suffice as well. Article 9 apparently adopts this common-law view. See UCC 9–305, Comment 2. Of course, possession by certain agents—most notably, Debtor itself—would not alleviate one's concerns that the purported secured transaction is a sham or that other creditors might mistakenly rely on Debtor's possession as an indication that Debtor's ownership rights were unencumbered. See UCC 9–305, Comment 2; Restatement of Security § 11 & Comment *b* (1941).

Consider what happens when the collateral consists of property that a third party (Bailee) holds for Debtor. UCC 9–305 states that "the secured party is deemed to have possession from the time the bailee receives notification of the secured party's interest." [11] In this regard, UCC 9–305 follows Restatement of Security § 8 (1941), which states: "Where the chattel is in the possession of a third person a pledge may be created by assent of the pledgor and notification by either pledgor or pledgee, to the third person, that the chattel has been pledged to the pledgee."

In what way is Bailee's receipt of notification akin to possession by Secured Party? Does notification adequately allay concerns that the purported security interest is merely a sham? The fact that a (presumably disinterested) third party has been informed of the transaction would seem to lend credence to Secured Party's assertion that the parties actually contemplated a secured transaction. The notification makes it less likely that the parties are engaging in after-the-fact fabrication.

Does notification to Bailee address the ostensible ownership problem? Does it make Debtor less of an ostensible owner than does the original bailment? Suppose Lender wishes to extend credit to Debtor and seeks to determine whether Debtor owns the bailed goods free and clear. Lender could ask Debtor, but the perfection rules of Article 9 are designed to afford creditors a means to obtain information without having to rely solely on the debtor's honesty. (In fact, the drafters rejected an early proposal to scrap public files and introduce appropriate safeguards to protect people misled by false or incomplete financial statements. See 1 Gilmore, Security § 15.1, at 464–65.) Lender could ask Bailee. Need Bailee pay any attention to a notice it has received from *Secured Party*, with which Bailee has not contracted? If not, does this argue against the rule of Restatement of Security § 8, under which the "notification" is effective even if it is given by Secured Party? (This rule may apply to Article 9 pledges by virtue of UCC 1–103.) Does receipt of notification from Debtor impose upon Bailee a legal duty to convey accurate information to third parties with whom it has not contracted? If not, then would it be a sufficient solution to the ostensible ownership problem that most bailees tell the truth most of the time?

---

11. By notifying a "bailee" (as defined by UCC 7–102(1)(a)) that a non-negotiable document of title issued by the bailee has been transferred, the transferee can prevent certain parties from defeating its rights. See UCC 7–504(2).

UCC 9–305 and the Comments thereto are silent concerning whether receipt of notification imposes upon Bailee any duty to Secured Party. Of particular concern in the context of perfection is whether, notwithstanding Bailee's receipt of notice, Debtor maintains control over the goods. For example, if Bailee has issued to Debtor an Article 7 document of title covering bailed goods, then Bailee "must deliver" them to Debtor or pursuant to Debtor's written instructions unless Bailee establishes an excuse. See UCC 7–403. Thus, there may be a major practical difference between actual possession by Secured Party (or its agent) and "deemed" possession by notification to Bailee: Unless Secured Party voluntarily relinquishes the collateral in its actual possession, Debtor cannot retake it without engaging in theft; however, notification to Bailee does not ipso facto deprive Debtor of its right to take possession of, and dispose of, the bailed property.

Just as UCC 9–305 apparently follows the Restatement of Security and makes Bailee's acknowledgement to Secured Party irrelevant to Secured Party's perfection by "deemed" possession (see Comment 2), the section *could* create a world in which the scope of Bailee's duties to Secured Party likewise is irrelevant. Does it do so? Clearly, once Debtor obtains possession of the collateral from Bailee, the security interest no longer is perfected by Secured Party's "deemed" possession. But is the fact that Debtor has the right *as against Bailee* to obtain possession sufficient to defeat Secured Party's "deemed" possession? Should the effectiveness of the notification to Bailee turn on whether Debtor has the right *as against Secured Party* to obtain possession, e.g., on whether the security agreement requires Debtor to keep the goods with Bailee? With the possible exception of UCC 9–205, Article 9 is silent.

One might argue that UCC 9–305 by its terms indicates that notification is sufficient to perfect, regardless of whether Debtor has the right or the power to obtain delivery from Bailee. Debtor's unexercised ability to recover the collateral from Bailee arguably should not defeat perfection by notification and "deemed" possession, any more than Secured Party's unexercised ability to return collateral to Debtor would defeat perfection by actual possession. Does UCC 9–205 support this argument? That section rejects the pre-Code view, whose most famous articulation appears in Benedict v. Ratner, 268 U.S. 353, 45 S.Ct. 566, 69 L.Ed. 991 (1925), that a debtor's unfettered dominion and control over collateral is inconsistent with the creation of a lien and thus fraudulent. Under this view, Debtor's retention of control over goods in the possession of Bailee cannot of itself be the reason why notification is insufficient to perfect.

Can this view be squared with UCC 9–305, Comment 2 ("it is of course clear … that the debtor or a person controlled by him cannot qualify as such an agent for the secured party")? Is it consistent with the second sentence of UCC 9–205, which provides that "[t]his section does not relax the requirements of possession where perfection of a security interest depends upon possession of the collateral by the secured party *or by a bailee* " (emphasis added)?

Assume that the Restatement of Security accurately articulates the common law (or, at least, the "better view") and consider the import of the following paragraph from § 8 Comment *a* :

> While ordinarily an agency cannot be created without consent of the agent (Restatement of Agency, § 15) it is not considered desirable to require the consent of the third person as a condition precedent to the creation of the pledge. *The third person's duties are not altered in any material respect by the pledge.* To make the third person's consent a test of the creation of the pledge would invest him with an arbitrary power of affecting the interests of the other parties. The third person of course may surrender the possession *if he does not wish to be under any duty to the pledgee.*

(Emphasis added.)

Observe that the Restatement speaks of "the creation of the pledge." Is it possible that notification of a third person in possession of collateral is sufficient to establish the secured party's possession for purposes of creation (i.e., to satisfy the first condition for attachment in UCC 9–203(1)(a)) but is insufficient for purposes of perfection? For an affirmative answer, see In re Kontaratos, 10 B.R. 956 (Bkrtcy.D.Me. 1981) (refusing to read UCC 9–305 in "such a 'loose and relaxed' way as to conscript [the senior secured party in possession] into involuntary service as the agent through whose possession a prohibited secondary security interest becomes perfected and interested third persons are to derive notice of the [junior] encumbrance").

Taken as a whole, the reported cases, one of which is reproduced above, afford neither clear nor consistent guidance on the foregoing issues. To what extent can they be solved by contract?

Problem 15. Dallar, a coin dealer, applies to Creative Finance Company for a loan. Creative is willing to make the loan, but insists on being secured by Dallar's inventory of coins. Assuming that Dallar and Creative can agree to the terms of the financing, how would you advise Creative to perfect its security interest? See UCC 9–109; UCC 9–105(1)(h); Note on the Rise and Decline of Field Warehousing, infra. Cf. UCC 2–105(1).

Note on the Rise and Decline of Field Warehousing

The difficulty for Creative Finance in Problem 15 arises because Dallar's need to retain the collateral for sale in its business conflicts with Article 9's requirement that a secured party must take possession of "money" in order to perfect a security interest in it. This problem arises under the Code only rarely. In the vast majority of cases, the debtor has no need to retain possession of collateral consisting of money or instruments, as to which possession by the secured party is the exclusive means of perfection. Conversely, filing is an alternative means of perfection for other types of tangible collateral; thus, the debtor's retention of possession of, say, a power lathe or auto parts does not preclude the secured party's becoming perfected.

Before the advent of "notice" filing (as distinguished from "transactional" filing) systems, however, the conflict between the debtor's need to retain possession of the collateral and the law's requirement that a secured party take possession of the collateral in order to enjoy a property right that was valid against other creditors arose with greater frequency. One solution was the complex and colorful "pledge" arrangement known as a "field warehouse."

The notion of a field warehouse derives from the creative application of the principle that a secured party may take possession of collateral through its agent, which might be a warehouse. Rather than suffer the adverse consequences of moving the debtor's inventory to a warehouse, inventory lenders moved the warehouse to the inventory. Typically, the debtor's inventory was placed in a fenced area (the "warehouse") within its premises. The "warehouse" usually was the debtor's stockroom, but might be a tank of oil or whiskey with a padlock on the outlet vale or a fenced-in pile of coal; there has been an astonishing variety of settings. See Van Vlissingen, A Better Look at Field Warehousing 14 (Burroughs Clearing House, July 1936). More recent uses have included "field warehouse feedlots," in which cattle are held, and leased rooms for warehousing a variety of "instruments," as to which possession is the exclusive means of perfection under Article 9. See McGuire, The Impact of the UCC on Field Warehousing, 6 UCC L.J. 267 (1974). Under the traditional arrangement, a specialized field warehouse company leased the premises from the debtor for a nominal amount, posted signs indicating that the goods in the fenced area were in the custody of the warehouse, and administered the flow of goods in and out of warehouse. Typically, the company issued non-negotiable warehouse receipts naming the secured party as the person entitled to delivery. As such, the secured party could cause the warehouse to release inventory by issuing written delivery orders (or a single, standing delivery order). See UCC 7–403.

The fencing and the administration of the "warehouse" added to the cost of the loan. But prior to Article 9, in many situations there was no reliable alternative for security in collateral that was subject to constant turnover. To minimize both the costs of the arrangement and the disruption to the debtor's business, the person in immediate charge of the "warehouse" usually was an employee of the debtor who was placed on the payroll of the field warehouse company (subject, of course, to reimbursement by the debtor).

In spite of grounds for questioning the substance of the "pledgee's" possession and control, attacks by other creditors on field warehousing usually failed—a tribute to the elaborate and impressive indicia of warehousing developed by its administrators, aided, perhaps, by judicial sensitivity for the need for a security arrangement where nothing else would work.

Early drafts of Article 9 included a frontal attack on the field warehouse: public filing was required for the perfection of security interests in goods "stored under a field warehousing or similar arrangement on premises which are part of the place of business of the debtor." See UCC 9–305(2) (1952) & Comment 4, 17 Kelly, Drafts 244, 246–47. In 1956, field warehouse interests succeeded in eliminating this provision; the Code's general rule protecting security interests in "collateral in the possession of the secured party under Section 9–305" seemed to provide a legal basis for the continuation of field warehousing. See UCC 9–302(1)(a).

Article 9 does not relax the common-law rules on the degree and extent of possession that are necessary to constitute a valid field warehouse. See UCC 9–205 (2d sentence) and Comment 6. Nevertheless, the Code has had an indirect, but basic, impact on field warehousing. By providing for the perfection of security interests in fluctuating assets by the filing of a simple financing statement, Article 9 undercut the principal reason for the establishment of the field warehouse. Thus, in 1963, Lawrence Systems, then the leading operator of field warehouses, in a dramatic reversal of policy, began to encourage lenders holding its receipts to file under Article 9. The basic reason was the danger that the holder of a competing security interest who filed would have a prior claim to new assets. See UCC 9–312(5)(a). (The rules governing priority of competing security interests will be examined more fully in Chapter 13, Section 1.)

Widespread adoption of Article 9 deprived the field warehouse of a significant "perfection" function; however, there still was a job for field warehousing organizations that had developed skills in watching over the ebb and flow of inventory: "certified (or 'verified') inventory control." Although filing can perfect a security interest in inventory, it does not prevent the debtor from selling the inventory and absconding with or dissipating the proceeds. The lender may not have the skills and resources needed to keep a close watch on the assets of a borrower of questionable financial standing or integrity. "Certified inventory control" eliminates the bailment trappings (such as the fence and signs). It replaces the warehouse receipt with a certificate or statement to the lender that certifies to the value of the inventory on the borrower's premises; the certifier by contract engages to comply with the lender's delivery instructions (administered, as in field warehousing, by "custodians" on the borrower's premises) and also accepts liability for any loss that may result from reliance on the certificates or from failure to observe the lender's delivery instructions. (A service similar in function to certified inventory control includes guaranteeing the validity of accounts receivable used for security, coupled with contractual protection to the lender against loss from the diversion of proceeds when the borrower's customers pay their bills. McGuire, supra, 6 UCC L.J. at 280–83.)

Problem 16. Diggins Construction Company entered into a contract to build a small office building for Realty for a total price of $1,000,000. The contract called for step-by-step progress payments to Diggins as the building reached specified stages of completion. Firstbank is willing to lend Diggins $900,000, to be secured by a security interest in the contract with Realty and the payments due and to become due under the contract.

Diggins prefers not to reveal this transaction to the public, and so it suggests to Firstbank that no financing statement be filed. It proposes instead that (i) the security agreement be entitled "Pledge of Contract," (ii) the original signed contract with Realty be delivered to Firstbank by way of pledge, and (iii) upon Diggins's default, Firstbank would have the right to notify Realty to make payments directly to Firstbank.

As counsel to Firstbank, how would you respond to this suggestion? See UCC 9–302(1)(a); UCC 9–305; UCC 9–105(1)(i); UCC 9–106; UCC 9–502.

Problem 17. Equipco is in the business of selling construction equipment. It sells to its very best customers on unsecured credit: the customer pays 20 percent down and gives a negotiable promissory note for the balance. To secure a line of credit, Firstbank took a security interest in "all Equipco's existing and after-acquired rights to payment in every form whatsoever, whether or not represented by a writing, and including, without limitation, accounts receivable, general intangibles, chattel paper, and instruments." The security agreement obligates Equipco to deliver to Firstbank all writings evidencing rights to payment within seven days after Equipco receives them. Firstbank filed a financing statement containing the same description of the collateral.

(a) Equipco received a promissory note from Buyer on June 15 and neglected to turn it over to Firstbank. Equipco filed a bankruptcy petition on July 1. Is Firstbank's security interest perfected? See UCC 9–302(1); UCC 9–304(1); 9–304(4); UCC 9–108. (Do not assume that, if the security interest is perfected, it necessarily will be valid in bankruptcy. The ability of the trustee in bankruptcy to avoid security interests, both perfected and unperfected, is discussed in Chapter 14, Sections 2 and 3, infra.)

(b) What answer if, on June 15, Equipco sold the equipment on secured credit: Buyer paid 10 percent down, signed a promissory note for the balance, and signed a security agreement covering the equipment? (Again, Equipco failed to deliver the note to Firstbank.) See UCC 9–105(1)(b).

(c) What answers in parts (a) and (b) if Equipco enters bankruptcy on July 15?

Problem 18. Delgado imports whiskey in large quantities, which Delgado stores in storage tanks at a warehouse bonded by the U.S. Customs Service. (Under applicable law, the whiskey may remain in a bonded warehouse for up to five years before Delgado is obligated to pay the import duty. See 19 U.S.C. § 1557(a) (1988).) Each time Delgado stores a quantity of whiskey, Delgado receives a warehouse receipt running "to the order of Delgado."

(a) Firstbank is willing to take the whiskey as collateral for a loan and asks you for advice on how to perfect its security interest. Among the possibilities are (i) filing a financing statement; (ii) taking delivery of the warehouse receipts; and (iii) notifying the warehouse of Firstbank's security interest. What do you recommend? See UCC 9–304(2); UCC 9–304(3); UCC 9–305; UCC 7–502(1); UCC 9–309; UCC 9–304(5).

One way to approach this question is to begin by determining which, if any, of the possibilities would satisfy the requirements of UCC 9–302(1). Next, consider the potential advantages and disadvantages of each course of action. For example, does one approach afford Firstbank the most protection against claims of third parties? Does one approach enhance Delgado's ability to obtain needed access to the whiskey, e.g., when Delgado wishes to bottle some of it?

(b) Assume that Firstbank decides to perfect its security interest by filing a financing statement. How should Firstbank describe the collateral?

(c) Assume that Firstbank decides to perfect its security interest by taking delivery of the warehouse receipt. Should Firstbank require Delgado to indorse the warehouse receipt before delivery? See UCC 7–502; UCC 7–501; UCC 7–504. If Delgado delivers the warehouse receipt to Firstbank but neglects to indorse it, is Firstbank perfected? See UCC 9–304(2). If Firstbank wishes to take possession of the whiskey upon Delgado's default, see UCC 9–503, will the warehouse permit Firstbank to remove the whiskey without Delgado's indorsement? See UCC 7–403. If Firstbank makes the loan and later wishes to obtain Delgado's indorsement, what can Firstbank do? See UCC 7–506.

Problem 19. Dalrymple borrowed $100,000 from Secondbank on an unsecured basis. After suffering financial reversals, Dalrymple defaulted on its obligation. As part of an effort to restructure its debts out of court, Dalrymple offers to bring interest current, make a $20,000 reduction in principal, and secure the $80,000 balance with one of its major assets, a $1,400,000 promissory note payable to Dalrymple's order. Firstbank holds a possessory security interest in the note to secure a claim of $750,000. Secondbank is content to take a junior security interest but wishes to insure that its security interest is perfected.

Advise Secondbank. See UCC 9–304(1); UCC 9–305; UCC 7–102(1)(a). Would it be necessary or helpful to obtain Firstbank's assistance in effectuating the transaction? Why might Firstbank be willing to cooperate? What concerns might it have? What might be done to alleviate those concerns? See Note on Possession by Agents and Bailees, supra.

Problem 20. Recall that in the Prototype, Firstbank filed a financing statement (Form 1, Section 1, supra) to perfect its security interest in Main's inventory of automobiles. Given that Firstbank took possession of the manufacturer's certificates of origin (Form 7, Section 1, supra), was the filing unnecessary? See In re Haugabook Auto Co., 9 U.C.C. Rep. Serv. 954 (Bkrtcy.M.D.Ga.1971) (possession of certificates of origin held not to constitute possession of motor vehicles); cf. Lee v. Cox, 18 U.C.C. Rep. Serv. 807 (M.D.Tenn.1976) (possession of registration papers for Arabian horses held not to constitute possession of horses). If the filing perfects Firstbank's security interest, then what purpose, if any, is served by Firstbank's taking possession of the certificates of origin? See Section 1(F), supra.

Problem 21. Drahman is the owner of 1,000 shares of General Motors common stock. The stock certificates, in registered form, are in Drahman's safe deposit box. On July 1, Drahman borrowed $10,000 from Lender and signed a security agreement granting Lender a security interest in "all my General Motors common stock." On July 15, Lean, one of Drahman's judgment creditors, acquired an execution lien on the stock (see UCC 8–317).

(a) Who has the superior claim to the stock? See UCC 9–301(1)(b); UCC 8–102(1); UCC 9–203; UCC 8–321; UCC 8–313(1)(i); UCC 9–108; Note 1 on Perfection of Security Interests in Investment Securities, infra.

(b) What result if the execution lien arose on August 1?

(c) What result if Lender had taken possession of the stock certificate? Does taking possession afford Lender any other advantages? Would you advise Lender to insist on obtaining Drahman's indorsement or executed **stock power** as well? See UCC 8–302; UCC 8–301; UCC 8–308(1); UCC 8–307; UCC 8–321(4); UCC 8–313(1)(a); UCC 9–503.

Problem 22. Drabek is the owner of 1,000 shares of General Motors common stock. A stock certificate covering 50,000 shares of General Motors stock was issued to Central Depositary Systems and is located in CDS's warehouse. CDS's books show that it is holding 7,000 of these shares for Broker, whose books show that it is "holding" 1,000 shares for Drabek and 6,000 for another customer.

To secure a loan from Lender, Drabek signed a written security agreement on May 1 describing the collateral as "1,000 shares of General Motors common stock in my account with Broker." At the time, Drabek's account contained only 1,000 shares. Lender sent a copy of the signed security agreement to Broker, who received it on May 2 but did not acknowledge receipt. On June 1, Lean acquired an execution lien on the stock.

(a) Who has the superior claim to the stock? See UCC 8–321; UCC 8–313(1)(h); Notes on Perfection of Security Interests in Investment Securities, infra.

(b) The facts are as in part (a) except that Drabek, in violation of the security agreement, instructed Broker to sell 600 shares. Broker dutifully followed Drabek's instructions and sold the shares to a bona fide purchaser (see UCC 8–302(1)). Is Broker liable to Lender for having sold Lender's collateral?

(c) The facts are as in part (a) except that the security agreement covered "all securities now or hereafter in my account with Broker" and Drabek's account contained 1,000 shares of General Motors and 500 shares of AT&T on June 1. What result? See UCC 8–321; UCC 8–313; UCC 9–110. Does the security agreement contain a "description of *the* security"? "At the time" the Broker received a copy of the security agreement, did Drabek have "rights in *the* security"?

Notes on Perfection of Security Interests In Investment Securities

(1) Certificated Securities. As the Note on *Copeland* and Problem 21 suggest, the rules on attachment and perfection of security interests in certificated securities are found in Article 8 rather than Article 9. Even attorneys conversant with Article 9 have difficulty applying the attachment and perfection rules of Article 8. The difficulty stems primarily from the condition to attachment that UCC 8–321(1) adds: a "transfer" under UCC 8–313(1) must occur before a security interest is enforceable.

In the simple case, where the debtor is in possession of a stock certificate or bond, the secured party (or its designee) may effect a transfer under UCC 8–313(1)(a) by taking possession of the security. Similarly, a transfer occurs when the secured party's "financial intermediary" (see UCC 8–313(4)) acquires possession of a certificated security specially indorsed to the secured party or issued in the secured party's name. UCC 8–313(1)(c). This is akin to possession by an agent.

UCC 8–313(1) becomes a trifle easier to understand when one realizes that many of the other transfers it describes are analogous to methods of perfection by possession described in UCC 9–305 and discussed in the Note on Possession by Agents and Bailees, supra, in connection with other Article 9 "instruments." Thus, the transfers in UCC 8–313(1)(d)(i) and (ii), (1)(e), and (1)(h)(ii) all are variations of the idea expressed in the second sentence of UCC 9–305: the secured party is deemed to have possession of collateral held by a bailee from the time the bailee receives notice of the secured party's interest. The same can be said for the transfers described in subsections (1)(d)(iii), (1)(g), and (1)(h)(i). To understand why this is so, one must have some familiarity with the manner in which securities are marketed.

By the late 1960's, the volume and speed of transactions in the securities markets reached proportions that posed a crisis for the customary processes of transfer, i.e., physical transfer of certificates. This "paperwork crunch" generated important proposals to provide a legal framework for transactions in "certificateless" shares. These proposals and a supporting study were embodied in a Report issued on September 15, 1975, by the Committee on Stock Certificates of the ABA Section on Corporation, Banking and Business Law. The Report proposed amendments to the Model Business Corporation Act and also set forth proposed revisions of portions of the UCC—principally in Article 8 and related sections of Article 9.

The Report identifies the central problem as follows:

> In the typical market transaction, the buyer and seller are unknown to each other and may be geographically separated by thousands of miles. On the other hand, the marvels of electronic communication make it possible to transmit instructions and acknowledge their receipt in a matter of minutes. The physical delivery of a piece of paper has become the time-consuming unsafe process, passing, as it must, through the hands of intermediaries and spanning, as it might, an entire continent. Thus, the negotiable stock certificate, an instrument almost indispensable in the environment in which it grew, has become a serious impediment to the very transaction it was designed to promote.

Report, ABA Stock Certificate Committee 2–3 (1975).

To address this situation, the scope of Article 8 was extended in 1977 to include "uncertificated" securities, as defined in UCC 8–102(1)(b). See Note (2), infra. The securities markets, however, could not wait for a legislative solution and developed a practical one. Stock certificates and bonds would be issued in the name of, and held in a warehouse by, a central depository. Each depository (which Article 8 calls a "clearing corporation," see UCC 8–102(3)), would maintain books showing the person on whose behalf it held each of the securities in its possession. In most cases, the depository holds for other institutional participants in the securities markets, such as stockbrokers and banks (which Article 8 calls "financial intermediaries," see UCC 8–313(4)). Each of these persons, in turn, would maintain books showing the person on whose behalf it "held" each of securities.

Consider the "simple" case in which Debtor maintains a securities account with Broker A (a "financial intermediary") and wishes to use the securities in the account as collateral for a loan from Bank. Bank will be unlikely to take possession of securities themselves, because they are not likely to be in Broker A's possession. Rather, the securities are likely to in the possession of Depository (a "clearing corporation"), whose books may show Broker B as the owner. Books maintained by Broker B (another "financial intermediary"), in turn, show Broker A as owner, and Broker A's books show Debtor as owner.

In other words, Depository is holding for Broker *B*, which is "holding" for Broker *A*, which is "holding" for Debtor. The situation becomes even more complex when one takes into account the fact that this chain is likely to be different for each type of security, or even for different quantities of the same issue of stock. Not only might different depositories and financial intermediaries be involved, but some of the financial intermediaries might be in possession of some of the securities. In the example, Bank will be able to receive a transfer through Broker *A* as if Broker *A* were a bailee (see UCC 8–313(1)(d)(iii) and UCC 8–313(1)(h)(i)) or, if Bank is a participant with Depository, on the books of Depository (see UCC 8–313(1)(g)).

UCC 8–313(1) contains two other noteworthy types of transfers. Subsection (1)(j) is designed to provide an easy method for a financial intermediary to take a security interest in securities "held" in an account with that financial intermediary. Under this subsection, the secured party itself is in the position of "bailee."

Under subsection (1)(i), a transfer occurs at the time "new value" is given (see UCC 9–108), if the debtor has signed a security interest describing the security. This provision is analogous to the temporary perfection provision applicable to instruments other than certificated securities (UCC 9–304(4)). As is the case under Article 9, the security interest becomes unperfected after 21 days unless it is perfected by another method. Compare UCC 9–304(4) & (6), with UCC 8–313(1)(i) & 8–321(2). Perfection under UCC 8–313(1)(i) is used primarily by those who lend to broker-dealers and other institutional participants.

(2) **Uncertificated Securities.** The principal reason for the 1977 amendments to Article 8 was to provide a means for transferring interests (including security interests) in "uncertificated securities," which are not represented by a certificate. See UCC 8–102(1)(b). Under the pre–1977 Code, this type of collateral would have been classified as a general intangible, as to which perfection could be accomplished by filing. The drafters of the amendments took pains to develop perfection provisions that were parallel to those applicable to certificated securities; the latter, as we have seen, derive from the concept of possession. For trenchant criticism of this basic approach, see Coogan, Security Interests in Investment Securities Under Revised Article 8 of the Uniform Commercial Code, 92 Harv.L.Rev. 1013 (1979). The drafters' more measured response appears in Aronstein, Haydock & Scott, Article 8 *Is* Ready, 93 Harv.L.Rev. 889 (1980).

(3) **Good Faith Purchase of Securities.** A secured party may not be indifferent to the manner in which the transfer of a security interest occurs. A secured party who qualifies as a "bona fide purchaser" of a security not only acquires the rights in the security that the debtor had or had actual authority to convey but also takes free of any adverse claim and enjoys priority over competing Article 9 security interests. See UCC 8–301(1); UCC 8–302(3); UCC 8–302(2) (explanation of "adverse claim"); UCC 9–309. The concept of "bona fide purchaser"

is quite similar to those of "holder in due course" in Article 3 and "holder to whom a negotiable document of title has been duly negotiated" in Article 7. See generally Chapter 1, supra. Observe, however, that a bona fide purchaser need not be a "holder." Indeed, one can be a bona fide purchaser of an uncertificated security. See UCC 8–302(1)(b), (1)(c). In this regard, too, the drafters of the 1977 amendments sought to afford transferees of interests in uncertificated securities rights comparable to those enjoyed with respect to certificated securities.

(4) Proposals for Change. Debtors who maintain securities accounts with brokers and other financial intermediaries may wish to use the securities as collateral. One legislative proposal currently under consideration is to revise the Code to add a "securities account" as a separate type of collateral. In 1991 the National Conference of Commissioners on Uniform State Laws appointed a drafting committee to revise Article 8. The law governing security interests in investment securities also may be influenced by developments at the federal level. The Market Reform Act of 1990, Pub. L. No. 101–432 (1990), amended the Securities and Exchange Act of 1934 so as to authorize the Securities and Exchange Commission, upon its making certain findings of fact, to issue preemptive federal regulations covering the transfer and pledge of securities. Pursuant to the Act, the SEC has formed a committee to advise it concerning the exercise of that rulemaking authority. In addition, there seems to be renewed interest in changes to federal regulations issued by the Treasury Department covering the transfer and pledge of United States Treasury securities. For the current regulations, see 31 C.F.R. §§ 306.115–306.122, 350.2–350.6 (1990). The Treasury Department issued two versions of proposed amended regulations in 1986 but has yet to issue final amendments.

Note on Rights and Duties of Secured
Party in Possession of Collateral

UCC 9–207 affords certain rights to, and imposes certain duties upon, a secured party who perfects a security interest by possession. The most significant of these duties is a requirement to "use reasonable care in the custody and preservation of collateral in his possession." UCC 9–207(1). As with all obligations of reasonableness in the Code, that duty "may not be disclaimed by agreement." UCC 1–102(3); see also UCC 9–501(2) (rights of debtor after default).

SECTION 3. WHERE TO FILE A
FINANCING STATEMENT

One generally acknowledged purpose of the Article 9 filing system is to provide information to third parties. See Note 2 on Attachment and Perfection by Filing, Section 2(A), supra. A well-fashioned system affords prospective purchasers of the collateral (including prospective secured parties) the opportunity to discover, with relative ease, whether the debtor may have encumbered particular property with a security interest. But a prospective purchaser or other searcher will be unable to commence a search of the public records to determine whether a financing statement has been filed against a debtor without first knowing which records to search.

The Code is state law; each state maintains its own filing offices. With a few exceptions each state maintains a single "central" (or "state-wide") filing office and dozens of "local" offices, one in each county. Thus, before it can begin to search, a searcher must determine not only the state in which a financing statement would have been filed but also the particular office within that state in which a financing statement would have been filed. And because a financing statement that is filed in the wrong place ordinarily is insufficient to perfect a security interest,[1] a secured party who attempts to perfect by filing likewise must make the same determinations. The following materials address Article 9's answers to the problems of where to file and search.

(A) MULTIPLE-STATE TRANSACTIONS: WHERE TO FILE

Notes on Choice-of-Law

(1) **The Need for Choice-of-Law Rules.** Owner sells or mortgages Blackacre to Purchaser. Owner lives in State X; Blackacre is in State Y; Purchaser lives in State Z. Where should the transaction be placed on the public record? What law governs perfection of Purchaser's interest against third persons? The answer is clear: the law of the place where Blackacre is (*lex rei sitae*). See Restatement (Second) of Conflict of Laws § 223 (1969). This rule is so firmly established that it may seem to be "in the nature of things," but its strength lies in its practicality. Even if Owner and Purchaser move, Blackacre stays. The rules and the records at the place where Blackacre is located provide a reliable point of reference.

For personal property the answer is not so easy. Debtor sells goods on credit to Buyer; to secure a loan, Debtor assigns the account (right to payment) to Secured Party. Debtor is in State X, Buyer is in State Y, and Secured Party is in State Z. Where should notice of the transaction be filed? Which law applies? Those used to thinking about transactions in land may say, "wherever the *res* is." But where is the debt that Buyer owes Debtor? In State X with Debtor, the obligee? In State Y with Buyer, the obligor? Or in State Z with Secured Party, the assignee? The questions multiply when each of the three parties is a corporation with offices in several states.

---

1. UCC 9–401(2), which validates certain misfiled financing statements against specified persons, is discussed in Chapter 13, Section 1(A), infra.

Even tangible goods—cotton, furniture, railroad cars—present vexing problems. The goods may be moving from state to state at the time of the transaction, or they may be moved after the transaction. They may be resold to buyers in another, possibly distant, state. And goods usually leave no trail, in the public records or elsewhere, that will disclose where they have been or what has happened.

These problems carry us into a large field (known as conflict of laws, choice of law, and private international law) where, for the most part, solutions must be sought in an amorphous and evolving body of case law. See R. Leflar, L. McDougal & R. Felix, American Conflicts Law ch. 18 (4th ed. 1986). However, statutes on substantive rules sometimes deal with "conflicts" problems by specifying when the statute's rules are applicable to transactions that have contacts with other states. Even after general adoption of "uniform" laws, these conflicts rules are useful because of the proclivity of both legislatures and courts to develop local variations in the "uniform" law.

UCC 1–105(1) contains two general choice-of-law rules: the parties enjoy the right to agree that the law of any state bearing a "reasonable relation" to the transaction shall govern their rights and duties; absent such agreement, the Code as enacted by the state in which the litigation is brought "applies to transactions bearing an appropriate relation to [such] state." These general rules may be suitable for controversies between the debtor and creditor, e.g., to determine which state's version of Article 9 applies to the exercise of the secured party's rights on default. They are wholly unsuitable for controversies concerning the effectiveness of a security interest against third parties, i.e., controversies whose outcome depends on whether a security interest is perfected. For the Article 9 filing system to work effectively, searchers must be able to determine where to search. Enabling the parties to the transaction to agree between themselves as to the applicable law would be foolhardy. How could a searcher discover whether any such agreement had been made? And even if a searcher could assure itself of the absence of such an agreement, how could the searcher predict which state's law a court would apply in the event of litigation?

Recognizing that the debtor and secured party should not be able to choose the applicable law so as to affect the rights of third parties, the Code's drafters created a special set of rules that determine the law applicable to perfection and the effect of perfection or non-perfection of security interests. These rules are in UCC 9–103, whose provisions govern notwithstanding an agreement of the parties to the contrary. See UCC 1–105(2).

(2) An Approach to Solving Choice–of–Law Problems. Thinking about choice-of-law problems under the Code is subject to a subtle trap. In the classroom we have in our hands only one statute book—the "uniform" Code. We can easily forget that the conflicts rules we see in our version of UCC 9–103 may invoke "perfection" rules that are quite different from those we see in our version of UCC 9–302 and UCC

9–401. State legislatures routinely have made the Code nonuniform. For example, several states have gagged at the rule of UCC 9–302(1)(d) that perfects purchase money security interests in consumer goods without filing. Moreover, we may not safely forget that all the world does not have Article 9: Goods may move into the Code domain from foreign countries that have a wide variety of rules governing what we (but not they) call the "perfection" of "security interests."

In short, having only one "uniform" code in our hands can seduce us into forgetting what we are doing in this area—working with *two* legal systems. In law practice we would not fall into this trap, for we would work with at least two different statute books on our desks: (1) one with the conflicts rules of UCC 9–103 and (2) a second with the "perfection" rules (e.g., UCC 9–302, UCC 9–401) of the jurisdiction whose law is made applicable by the conflicts rules of the first book. In the classroom it may help those of us who are visually-minded to imagine that (as in practice) we are working with these two statute books.

Applying the conflicts rules of UCC 9–103 is not easy, even when one has recourse to two statute books. Thinking about the relationship between two legal systems requires some intellectual strain, as we shall see again in Chapter 14, when we try to mesh state property law with the federal bankruptcy law. That the drafters completely rewrote UCC 9–103 in 1972, and that the principal drafter of the 1972 revision now wishes he could "do things over again," are ample testimony to the difficulty of the task. See Kripke, A Draftsman's Wishes That He Could Do Things Over Again—U.C.C. Article 9, 26 San Diego L.Rev. 1 (1989).

The wide range of assets—tangible and intangible—embraced by Article 9 and the extent to which financing transactions straddle many states generate problems of amazing subtlety and complexity. Most of the problems cannot be tackled here. The most that is feasible is to lay a foundation for thinking about multiple-state problems, to see the Code's approach to them in a few common situations, and to appreciate the crucial importance of UCC 9–103 both to planning a secured transaction and to litigating over priorities.

Problem 1. Party Press, Inc., is in the printing business. In need of additional funds, it borrowed $100,000 from Carlucci Credit Co. and secured the loan with one of its presses. The press is located in Illinois; Party is incorporated in Indiana, has plants in Indiana, Illinois, and Ohio, and has its corporate headquarters in Ohio; and Carlucci is incorporated in Delaware but has its corporate headquarters in New Jersey and has representatives in all 50 states. Carlucci filed a financing statement with the Illinois Secretary of State.

(a) After Carlucci filed, Lean acquired an execution lien on the press. Is the security interest perfected? Consider the following approach to the question: If the issue is litigated in Illinois, which state's version of UCC 9–103 will the court apply? To which state's version of

UCC 9–401(1) would that state's UCC 9–103(1) refer? (In working through these Problems, you may assume that each state has enacted the uniform version of UCC 9–103.)

(b) In an ideal world, the forum in which the litigation is brought would not affect the status of the security interest as perfected or unperfected. How does UCC 9–103(1) measure up in this regard? Suppose that, five months after Carlucci filed a financing statement, Party filed a bankruptcy petition in Ohio. Party's bankruptcy trustee argues that Carlucci's security interest is unperfected. If the bankruptcy court applies Ohio's version of UCC 9–103, which state's version of UCC 9–401(1) would the court consult to determine whether Carlucci is perfected?

Problem 2. The facts are the same as in Problem 1, except that after the loan closed (i.e., after the documentation was signed and the funds were advanced) but before the financing statement was filed, Party moved the press from Illinois to Indiana. Ignorant of this fact, Carlucci filed the financing statement in Illinois. Is the security interest perfected? Would the answer change if Carlucci had known that the press had been relocated before filing the financing statement?

Problem 3. The facts are the same as in Problem 1, except that before the loan closed Carlucci filed a financing statement in Illinois. Shortly thereafter, Party moved the press to Indiana; then the documents were signed and the loan was funded. Is the security interest perfected?

Problem 4. Under the facts of the Prototype (Section 1, supra) Firstbank filed its financing statement against Main Motors in Pennsylvania. General Motors periodically ships replacement parts to Main from its factory in Michigan. Inasmuch as value already has been given and Main has signed the Dealer Inventory Security Agreement (Form 2, Section 1, supra), Firstbank's security interest in each shipment of parts attaches when Main acquires "rights in the collateral." See UCC 9–203(1). Assume that Main acquires such rights when General Motors delivers the parts to a carrier. On May 15, General Motors delivered a shipment of replacement parts to the carrier.

(a) Is Firstbank's security interest in the shipped parts perfected while the shipment is still en route to Pennsylvania? See UCC 9–103(1)(b), (1)(c); UCC 9–107; cf. Joint Holdings & Trading Co. v. First Union National Bank, 50 Cal.App.3d 159, 123 Cal.Rptr. 519 (1975) (applying 1962 version of UCC 9–103).

(b) Is Firstbank's security interest in the shipped parts perfected once the shipment arrives in Pennsylvania? What is the "last event . . . on which is based the assertion that the security interest is perfected"? See UCC 9–303 (explaining when a security interest is perfected). The principal drafter of the "last event" test believes that the term includes "the arrival of the collateral in a jurisdiction where there is already an appropriate filing." Kripke, A Draftsman's Wishes That He Could Do Things Over Again—U.C.C. Article 9, 26 San Diego

L.Rev. 1, 7 (1989). See also Kripke, The "Last Event" Test for Perfection of Security Interests Under Article 9 of the Uniform Commercial Code, 50 N.Y.U.L.Rev. 47 (1975). Is that interpretation sensible? Does it comport with the statute?

Problem 5. The facts are the same as in Problem 4 except that the collateral consists of a shipment of automobiles rather than parts.

(a) Are the automobiles "ordinary goods" subject to UCC 9–103(1), goods "covered by a certificate of title" subject to UCC 9–103(2), or "mobile goods" subject to UCC 9–103(3)? Why doesn't UCC 9–103 follow the classification of goods in UCC 9–109?

(b) Is Firstbank's security interest in the shipped autos perfected while the shipment is still en route to Pennsylvania? Recall that General Motors would not ship the cars to Main Motors on credit, and that Firstbank was obligated to pay General Motors for each shipment of cars upon proper demand. See UCC 9–107; UCC 9–103(1)(c).

(c) Would it make any difference if the shipment is delayed for two months in Ohio?

(d) What result in parts (b) and (c) if Firstbank had filed in Michigan instead of Pennsylvania?

Problem 6. Dunston is a custom harvester. Unlike a farmer, Dunston owns no land. Rather, Dunston uses combines (specialized machinery) to harvest grain grown by others. Although Dunston's home in Nebraska also serves as the office, Dunston works in Iowa and Kansas as well.

(a) When Dunston entered the business, Seller sold Dunston two new combines and retained a security interest to secure their price. The combines are not covered by a certificate of title. Seller filed a financing statement in Nebraska. Is Seller perfected? See UCC 9–103(3).

(b) Seller sold Dunston an additional combine. The combine is not covered by a certificate of title. Seller and Dunston agreed that this combine is to be used only in Kansas. Seller filed a financing statement in Kansas. Is Seller perfected? Would the result change if Dunston were a farmer who used the combine to harvest Dunston's own grain?

Problem 7. Cellar Equipment, located in Chicago, retained a security interest in two presses it sold on credit to Party Press. The presses were delivered to Indianapolis, where Party agreed to keep them. Cellar filed a proper financing statement in Indiana. Without Cellar's knowledge or consent, Party removed one of the presses from Indianapolis to its plant in Cleveland on June 1. It is now December 1, and Cellar has yet to discover the removal.

(a) On August 30, Eck acquired an execution lien on the press. Is the execution lien senior or junior to Cellar's security interest? See UCC 9–103(1)(d) (containing not only a choice-of-law rule but also a rule of substantive law); UCC 9–301(1)(b); UCC 1–201(33), (32). Cf. Prairie State Bank v. Internal Revenue Service, 155 Ariz. 219, 745 P.2d 966 (App.1987) (holding, erroneously, that the holder of a federal tax lien is a "purchaser"). What could the loser have done to protect itself?

(b) What result if Eck acquired an execution lien on November 15? See UCC 9–103(1)(d).

(i) What could the loser have done to protect itself? Under most circumstances, the law of the state into which goods are brought and kept will require the secured party to take some "action . . . to perfect the security interest." Suppose Cellar had discovered the removal in August but Party refused to sign a new financing statement for filing in Ohio. What "action" could Cellar have taken? See UCC 9–302(1); UCC 9–305; UCC 9–402(2)(a); UCC 9–503.

(ii) Suppose the security agreement required Party to keep the press at a specified location in Indianapolis. (Provisions of this kind are common in security agreements.) Suppose further that Party removed the press to Cleveland for the purpose of rendering Cellar's security interest unperfected. Would the result change? See In re Howard's Appliance Corp., 874 F.2d 88 (2d Cir.1989) (imposing a constructive trust on collateral subject to an unperfected security interest where secured party failed to file in appropriate state as a consequence of debtor's misconduct, and holding that secured party's rights as beneficiary of constructive trust were superior to those of judicial lien creditor); UCC 1–103.

(c) What result if Bayer bought and took delivery of the press from Party on August 30? Note that UCC 9–103(1)(d) addresses only perfection; it does not address the priority of third-party claims to the collateral. The rights of buyers of collateral are discussed in Chapter 13, Section 2, infra. For present purposes you may assume that Bayer would take free of an unperfected security interest but subject to a perfected security interest. See UCC 9–306(2); UCC 9–301(1)(c). What could the loser have done to protect itself?

(d) What result if Bayer bought and took delivery of the press on November 15? What could the loser have done to protect itself?

(e) Would the result in part (d) change if Party had moved the press to Cleveland for storage while the Indianapolis plant was being renovated? Were the goods being "kept in" Cleveland? See UCC 9–103, Comment 3; In re Potomac School of Law, Inc., 16 B.R. 102 (Bkrtcy.D.D.C.1981) (UCC 9–103(1)(d) inapplicable to out-of-jurisdiction storage of library books intended to be transitory, notwithstanding that books remained in storage more than four months). Should Bayer's rights turn on Party's subjective intentions or on the objective fact that the goods had been in Cleveland for more than four months? Should they turn on whether the storage *appeared* to be transitory?

(f) Can you reconcile UCC 9–103's treatment of Eck with the treatment it affords to Bayer? Why does the retroactive unperfection rule of UCC 9–103(1)(d) run only in favor of "purchasers"? (The different treatment afforded to non-purchasers may give rise to an intractable problem of circular priorities. See Note (3) on the Role of Knowledge in Priority Contests, Chapter 13, Section 1(A), infra.)

(B) Where to File Within a State

Each state's version of UCC 9–401(1) dictates whether one must file a financing statement with the central office, with a local office, or with both.

Please turn to UCC 9–401(1). As you can see, the official text of the Code itself invites nonuniformity with regard to where to file within a state. Professor Gilmore explained:

> [T]here was an irreconcilable diversity of opinion on the place-of-filing provisions, particularly with respect to the merits of state-wide filing as opposed to the traditional system of filing by local units. Representatives of finance companies and large banks, who had become familiar with the advantages of state-wide filing under the Uniform Trust Receipts Act and some of the factor's lien and accounts receivable statutes, strongly urged the adoption of state-wide filing for security interests in all types of collateral except fixtures [which are real estate and covered by local real estate records] and possibly consumer goods and farm products.... But, with respect to business or commercial debtors (who were neither individual consumers nor farmers), except where fixtures were involved, the argument was strongly made that an exclusive state-wide filing system (with no requirement of additional local filings) should be adopted. This argument was strongly resisted by those who remained unconvinced that the asserted advantages of state-wide filing outweighed the need of local creditors for locally available credit information. The attempt at drafting a single set of place-of-filing provisions was ultimately abandoned....

1 Gilmore, Security § 18.1, at 517.

The three official versions of UCC 9–401(1) range from requiring very little in the way of local filing to requiring local filing in many cases, often in addition to central filing. The intermediate position, reflected in the second alternative, has proven to be the most popular, having been adopted by 25 states. (The other states that have enacted one of the "uniform" alternatives are about equally divided between the first alternative and the third.) As the Problems below suggest, the local filing requirements impose upon filers and searchers additional burdens.

Problem 8. Dale Drake buys a refrigerator from Seller on secured credit. Under each version of UCC 9–401(1), where should Seller file:

(a) if Drake is a dentist and uses the refrigerator to store chemicals?

(b) if Drake is a dairy and egg farmer and uses the refrigerator to store eggs that the hens lay? Cf. UCC 9–109(3).

(c) if Drake owns and operates an appliance store and has bought the refrigerator for resale?

(d) if Drake enjoys football and uses the refrigerator to store beer?

Problem 9. Main Motors acquires diagnostic equipment for its service department subject to a security interest in favor of Secondbank. At all relevant times, the equipment is in Philadelphia County, Pennsylvania. Pennsylvania has adopted the third alternative subsection (1) to UCC 9–401.

(a) In which office(s) should Secondbank file the financing statement?

(b) Main Motors moves its business to Montgomery County, Pennsylvania, and moves the diagnostic equipment to the new location. What must Secondbank do to continue the perfected status of its security interest? See UCC 9–401(3); cf. UCC 9–103(1)(d). Only five states have adopted the alternative subsection (3), and Pennsylvania is not among them. Which alternative do you prefer?

Problem 10. Consider the facts of Problem 6 above. Assume that the relevant state has adopted the second alternative UCC 9–401(1). In which office should Seller file the financing statement? Would the result change if Dunston were a farmer who used the combine to harvest Dunston's own grain? See UCC 9–401, Comment 3. Cf. UCC 9–109(3) (using the term "farming operations").

UCC 9–103(3) applies only to goods "of a type normally used in more than one jurisdiction." This suggests that the application of the subsection turns on the nature of the goods rather than on the use to which the particular debtor puts them. In contrast, the second and third alternative versions of UCC 9–401(1) refer to "equipment used in farming operations." Does this mean "equipment that the particular debtor actually uses in farming operations," or does it mean "equipment of a type normally used in farming operations"? Konkel v. Golden Plains Credit Union, 778 P.2d 660 (Colo.1989), ruled that the inherent quality of the goods determines whether UCC 9–103(3) applies, whereas the debtor's actual use of the goods is determinative for purposes of UCC 9–401(1). The first point is generally acknowledged; the second is a matter of some dispute. Compare, e.g., In re Tinker, [1973–1980 Transfer Binder] Secured Transactions Guide (CCH) ¶ 52,-400 (Bkrtcy.E.D.Tenn.1974) (creditor who made central filing against machinery used to feed livestock was unperfected, notwithstanding that machinery normally was used for nonagricultural purposes), with, e.g., Sequoia Machinery, Inc. v. Jarrett, 410 F.2d 1116 (9th Cir.1969) ("the drafters of the Code carefully avoided defining 'equipment used in farming operations' in terms of the occupational status or contractual arrangements of the debtor-use"). Which rule affords greater certainty?

Problem 11. Del and Dot Dascenzo purchased a mobile home from Syd Seller. On July 23, the Dascenzos signed a security agreement, under which Seller retained a security interest to secure the balance of the purchase price. The security agreement showed the Dascenzos' residence to be in Herkimer County, New York, although they actually were living in neighboring Fulton County at the time. The Dascenzos decided to refer to the Herkimer County address for two reasons: They were planning to move into the mobile home upon its delivery to the site in Herkimer County and had so informed Seller; and the tax rate in Herkimer County was substantially lower than that prevailing in Fulton County.

The mobile home was delivered as planned to its Herkimer County site on August 1. On August 3, the Dascenzos moved into it. On August 6, Seller filed a financing statement in the office of the County Clerk of Fulton County. Two years later, the Dascenzos entered bankruptcy.

Assume that under New York law, the mobile home is a motor vehicle required to be registered but is not subject to a certificate of title statute. New York has adopted the third alternative subsection (1) to UCC 9–401.

(a) Is the security interest perfected? See UCC 9–302(1)(d); UCC 9–401(1). Does UCC 9–401(1) contain a "timing" provision (i.e., a provision that explains the time at which one determines where to file)? If not, what considerations are relevant in fashioning a rule? Should the courts borrow the "last event" test from UCC 9–103(1)(b)? See UCC 9–401, Comment 4. The cases are in conflict. See In re Knapp, 575 F.2d 341 (2d Cir.1978) (place of residence at the time the security interest attached was controlling); In re Roy, 21 UCC Rep.Serv. 325 (N.D.Ala.1977) (place of residence at time of filing is controlling); In re Hammons, 614 F.2d 399 (5th Cir.1980) (adopting "last event" test).

(b) What result if Seller had filed in Herkimer County on July 28? See generally Frisch, U.C.C. Filings: Changing Circumstances Can Make a Right Filing Wrong. But Can They Make a Wrong Filing Right?, 56 S.Cal.L.Rev. 1247 (1983).

Note on Amending Article 9 to Solve Problems of Where to File

In the more than forty years since the early development of the Article 9 filing system, much has changed. The credit market has become more national (indeed, international) in scope. The practice of taking a security interest in "all assets" has developed and flourished.

Data can be transmitted and stored in electronic rather than tangible form. To what extent should the rules governing where to file, UCC 9–103 and UCC 9–401(1), reflect these changes?

The Future of Local Filing Offices. Thirty years' experience with local filing has convinced most users of the Article 9 filing system that requiring a local filing instead of or in addition to a central filing serves no commercial purpose. Local filings typically are more difficult to access than central filings. Moreover, as the Problems above suggest, determining which local office is the appropriate office has proven problematic.

The Future of the "Last Event" Test. One prime candidate for revision is the "last event" test of UCC 9–103(1)(b). Although the test's lack of clarity is manifest, it has posed more problems for the commentators than it has for the courts. Under the current rule, an inventory lender will need to file in a multiplicity of jurisdictions if the debtor's goods are located in many states; one whose collateral consists of inventory and accounts may need to make two filings even though all the inventory is located in a single state. Rather than rephrase the test to clarify its meaning, would the UCC's sponsors do better to eliminate the test altogether? Would a choice-of-law rule that looked to the debtor's location, as UCC 9–103(3)(b) now does, be appropriate for the collateral now covered by the "last event" test in UCC 9–103(1)?

The Prospects for a Nationwide Filing System. Many of the problems associated with determining where to file and whether and when to refile could be solved by scrapping state filing systems and adopting a single, nationwide system. One way to establish a nationwide system would be through preemptive federal legislation. A less intrusive (and probably more feasible) route would be through developments in the private sector: one or more corporations might provide search and filing systems and services to states pursuant to contract. Even if several such nongovernmental systems were to be developed, a de facto nationwide system might emerge if the systems were to share their information. Who might oppose a national filing system? On what basis?

(C) MOTOR VEHICLES AND CERTIFICATES OF TITLE: UCC 9–103(2)

Introduction. In the Prototype (Section 1, supra) when Main Motors sold the car to Lee Abel, an application was made to the Bureau of Motor Vehicles not only for a registration (or "owners") card and license plate (a device for tax collection and law enforcement) but also for a Certificate of Title (Form 8, Section 1, supra). Since the sale called for payment in installments secured by the Pontiac, Main made sure that the application for the Certificate of Title gave the name of the holder of the security interest (Firstbank, to whom the security interest had been assigned) and the amount of the debt. The Bureau recorded this information and printed it on the Certificate of Title. Normally, the certificate is sent to the secured creditor.

Under certificate of title systems, one who plans to buy or lend against a motor vehicle must first inspect the certificate to make sure it is "clean"—or run the risk of purchasing a car that was stolen or subject to a prior encumbrance. In legal terms, Article 9 makes this certificate system the exclusive means for public notification of security interests; UCC 9–302(3) states that, when the collateral is subject to a certificate of title statute, the filing of a financing statement "is not necessary or effective to perfect a security interest."

The certificate system was designed to make transactions in motor vehicles not only safe but also convenient. If the owner exhibits a "clean" certificate, a buyer or lender can close a transaction without the delay and cost of going to a public office (perhaps in another city) to check the records.

For decades the failure of many states to adopt the certificate system impaired the success of the system, as did deficiencies in the drafting and administration of those statutes that had been enacted. Now every state has a certificate system. The principal problem that remains is the skill of thieves or skip-state owners in obtaining clean certificates by the use of false affidavits—often to the effect that the certificate issued by another state has been lost.

Certificates issued by two different states—e.g., a "foul" certificate issued by State A and a "clean" certificate issued by State B—call for choice-of-law rules. These appear in subsection (2) of UCC 9–103. The Problems that follow examine these rules. They assume that both State A and State B provide for notation of security interests on the certificate of title. For an example of such a statutory provision, see Uniform Motor Vehicle Certificate of Title and Anti–Theft Act § 21.

Problem 12. On June 1, Bilk purchased a car in State A with money loaned by Firstbank. State A issued a certificate of title noting Firstbank's security interest and sent the certificate to Firstbank. On June 15 Bilk, by means of a fraudulent affidavit, obtained a clean State A certificate. With State A license plates still on the car, on June 16 Bilk drove the car to State B. Using the clean State A certificate, on that afternoon Bilk sold the car to Bushing, a used car dealer.

(a) Does Bushing take free of or subject to Firstbank's security interest? See UCC 9–103(2)(b). For purposes of this Problem and the following one, you may assume that buyers take free of unperfected security interests but subject to perfected security interests. See UCC 9–306(2); UCC 9–301(1)(c). What could the loser have done to protect itself?

(b) What result if Bilk moved to State B on June 15 but did not sell the car to Bushing until November? See UCC 9–103(2)(b) ("and thereafter until the goods are registered in another jurisdiction"). What could the loser have done to protect itself?

(c) Would it make any difference in part (b) if Bilk sold the car to Broom, a laborer, who bought the car for personal use? What could the loser have done to protect itself?

Problem 13. On June 1, Bilk purchased a car in State A with money loaned by Firstbank. State A issued a certificate of title noting Firstbank's security interest and sent the certificate to Firstbank. On July 1, Bilk registered the car in State B and obtained State B license plates for the car. By a false affidavit, Bilk also obtained from State B a clean certificate of title. On July 2 Bilk sold the car to Broucher, a used car dealer.

(a) Does Broucher take free of or subject to Firstbank's security interest? See UCC 9–103(2)(b), (d). Note that there are two certificates. Which is "the jurisdiction issuing *the* certificate"? Consider the context: continuing perfection "after the goods are removed from *that* jurisdiction." Under UCC 9–103(2)(b), does a new registration cut short the four-month period? What could the loser have done to protect itself?

(b) What result if the sale to Broucher occurred on November 1? What could the loser have done to protect itself? In this setting, is Broucher more or less deserving of protection than was Bushing in Problem 12(b)? Is Firstbank more or less deserving?

Some states permit the "registration" of a motor vehicle without the issuance of a certificate of title. This "registration" may include the issuance of license plates. Suppose that Bilk had registered the car in State B but had not obtained a State B certificate prior to selling the car to Broucher on November 1? Courts disagree as to whether or not a certificate of title must have been issued for a car to be "registered" as that term is used in UCC 9–103(2)(b). Which reading better allocates the risk between Firstbank and Broucher?

(c) Would it make any difference in part (a) or (b) if Bilk sold the car to Brice, a laborer, who bought the car for personal use? Assume that Brice and Firstbank litigate their rights in State B. What result? What could the loser have done to protect itself? Would the same result obtain if litigation proceeds in State A?

SECTION 4. PROCEEDS OF COLLATERAL

Introduction. Creditors who have ongoing relationships with business debtors often secure their loans with interests in the debtor's inventory. The Prototype automobile financing transaction that opened this Chapter is an example. When, as both parties hope and expect, the inventory is sold, the creditor's security interest rarely can be asserted against the buyer. See UCC 9–307(1); Chapter 13, Section 2, infra. Instead, the secured party must enforce its security interest against the "proceeds" of its collateral—whatever is received upon the sale. See UCC 9–306(1) & (2).

Financers of inventory and accounts expect that their collateral will be sold or collected. For them, the creation of proceeds is a normal—indeed, desirable—aspect of the financing; proceeds are the means by which the debtor will be able to repay the loan. In contrast, for those who finance the acquisition of equipment, the creation of proceeds may signal a breakdown in the financing relationship; it may mean that the debtor has disposed of the collateral in violation of the security agreement. Even though the security interest in the equipment may survive the sale, see UCC 9–306(2) (discussed in Chapter 13, Section 2, infra), the secured party may be unable to locate the collateral to enforce its security interest. Under those circumstances, the secured party's only remaining hope for protection may lie in the proceeds.

The problem of wrongful dispositions is not confined to security interests. In a wide variety of settings in which *B* wrongfully disposes of *A*'s property, basic remedial principles have accorded *A* a property interest in traceable proceeds—not only proceeds held by *B* but also those held by third persons who do not have a strong claim for protection, e.g., persons who lack the reliance interest of a good faith purchaser. For a discussion of the legal tools used to protect *A*'s interest, including the doctrines of "constructive trust" and "equitable lien," see Restatement of Restitution § 202 (1937); D. Dobbs, Remedies §§ 4.3, 5.16 (1973).

As you work through the following materials, it will be useful to consider the extent to which the detailed "proceeds" rules of Article 9 (UCC 9–306) constitute particularized responses to a basic and pervasive remedial problem and the extent to which the rules serve to fill gaps in the articulated bargain between the debtor and the secured party.[1]

Problem 1. In the setting of the Prototype transaction, a new Pontiac financed by Firstbank was traded by Main Motors for a Lincoln. Subsequently, Main traded the Lincoln for a Cadillac.

(a) Does Firstbank have a security interest in the Cadillac? If so, is it perfected? See UCC 9–204(1); Dealer Inventory Security Agreement (Form 2, Section 1, supra); Financing Statement (Form 1, Section 1, supra).

(b) Suppose that both the Security Agreement and the Financing Statement covered only the motor vehicles financed by Firstbank (here, the Pontiac). Does Firstbank have a security interest in the Cadillac? If so, is it perfected? See UCC 9–306(2) & (3); Notes on Security Interests in Proceeds, infra.

(c) Now suppose, additionally, that neither the Security Agreement nor the Financing Statement mentioned proceeds of the collateral. Is the claim to proceeds lost? See UCC 9–306(2) & (3); UCC 9–203(3).

Problem 2. Firstbank financed the purchase of new cars by Main Motors in the manner described in the Prototype transaction, except

---

1. Bankruptcy and other insolvency proceedings pose special risks and afford special protection for claims to proceeds. Those matters are addressed in Chapter 14, Section 3(B), infra. This section focuses on the treatment of proceeds claims outside of insolvency proceedings.

that the financing statement referred to the collateral as "Motor Vehicles." On June 1 Main sold to Computer Storehouse, Inc. (CSI), a computer dealer, a new Pontiac that had been financed by Firstbank. CSI paid for the Pontiac, in part, by delivering to Main certain computer equipment; CSI installed the equipment in Main's office. On June 15 one of Main's trade creditors, LC Co., had the sheriff levy on all of Main's office equipment, including the computer equipment.

(a) Does Firstbank's security interest extend to the computer equipment? See UCC 9–306(1) & (2). If so, is Firstbank's security interest senior to LC's execution lien? See UCC 9–306(3)(a); UCC 9–301(1)(b); Notes on Security Interests in Proceeds, infra.

(b) Now assume that instead of swapping the computer equipment for a portion of the price of the Pontiac, CSI paid cash for the Pontiac. The next day, June 2, Main Motors used a portion of the cash to purchase the computer equipment. Firstbank took no further action to perfect a security interest in the computer equipment. LC then had the sheriff levy on June 15. Does the result in part (a) change? See UCC 9–306(3)(a).

(c) Would the result in part (b) change if LC levied on June 5? Are the relative rights of LC and Firstbank fixed as of the date of levy, or can they change as time passes? Compare UCC 9–403(2) (security interest that becomes unperfected upon lapse is deemed to have been unperfected as against a person who became a *purchaser or lien creditor* before lapse) with UCC 9–103(1)(d)(i) (security interest that becomes unperfected after collateral is removed to another jurisdiction is deemed to have been unperfected as against a person who became a *purchaser* after removal).

Problem 3. Dealer sells auto parts to retailers on unsecured credit. The parts are located in Dealer's warehouses in Gary, Indiana; Memphis, Tennessee; and Compton, California. Finance Company perfected its security interest in the auto parts by filing financing statements covering "inventory of auto parts" in those three states. Does Finance Company have a perfected security interest in any or all of Dealer's rights to payment for auto parts sold to its customers? See UCC 9–306(2) & (3); Notes on Security Interests in Proceeds, infra. Do you need additional information to answer this question?

HOWARTH v. UNIVERSAL C.I.T. CREDIT CORP.[*]

United States District Court, Western District of Pennsylvania, 1962.
203 F.Supp. 279.

MARSH, DISTRICT JUDGE. The plaintiff, trustee in bankruptcy of Spohn Motor Company, Inc. (Spohn), brought this action, pursuant to

[* The court's citations are to the applicable pre–1972 version of the Code.]

§ 60 of the Bankruptcy Act, as amended March 18, 1950, 11 U.S.C.A. § 96 (1961 Supp.), to recover from the defendant, Universal C.I.T. Credit Corporation (UCIT) the value of property transferred to UCIT from Spohn within four months of filing the petition in bankruptcy.

The underlying facts stipulated by the parties are adopted by the court. From these facts it appears that an involuntary petition in bankruptcy was filed against Spohn on January 6, 1958, and it was adjudicated a bankrupt on February 13, 1958.

On February 5, 1957, pursuant to a Loan Agreement (Ex. H), UCIT advanced to Spohn the sum of $75,000. On the same day, Spohn executed a Chattel Mortgage (Ex. I) covering certain chattels. Shortly thereafter UCIT perfected a security interest therein by properly filing a Financing Statement (Ex. J) under the provisions of the Uniform Commercial Code—Secured Transactions, Act of April 6, 1953, P.L. 3, § 9–101 et seq. . . . (hereinafter referred to as U.C.C.).

Prior to September 28, 1957, Spohn also executed in favor of UCIT used car Trust Receipts (Ex. D) and assigned to UCIT certain Bailment Leases (Ex. E).

During August of 1957, and for some months prior thereto, UCIT had advanced to Spohn, or to Ford Motor Company for the benefit of Spohn pursuant to an Agreement for Wholesale Financing (Ex. A), dated December 13, 1954, the principal sum of $437,972.84 for 201 new motor vehicles, each secured under the terms of new car Trust Receipts (Ex. G). On March 3, 1955, UCIT perfected a security interest in, inter alia, new and used motor vehicles, equipment, accessories or replacement parts, and proceeds by properly filing a Financing Statement (Ex. B).

Prior to September 28, 1957, 110 of the new motor vehicles had been sold out of trust by Spohn, leaving 91 new vehicles which UCIT repossessed and sold for $188,268.32, leaving a remainder of $249,704.52 due by Spohn to UCIT for new vehicles sold out of trust.

Between September 28, 1957 and October 31, 1957, Spohn being thus indebted to UCIT, transferred to it the following items, to which the plaintiff-trustee concedes he has no claim: the proceeds of the sale of 15 vehicles subject to bailment leases; office furniture, fixtures and equipment; shop equipment; accounts receivable from UCIT; accounts receivable from Ford Motor Company for wholesale incentive; warranty and policy claims receivable from Ford Motor Company; and other receivables from Ford Motor Company. The facts show conclusively that UCIT had a perfected security interest in each of these items.

In addition to these items, during the same period, Spohn transferred to UCIT, either voluntarily or involuntarily the following: bank cash, shares of stock, customers receivables, 70 used vehicles, and motor parts and accessories. These transfers were made by Spohn for its antecedent debts, at a time when Spohn was insolvent and UCIT had reason to so believe. The plaintiff-trustee contends that these transfers constituted preferences within the meaning of § 60 of the Bankruptcy Act, since their effect was to enable UCIT to obtain a greater percentage of its debt that Spohn's unsecured creditors, except as to those items in which UCIT held a perfected security interest.

We take up the disputed items seriatim.

BANK CASH

Spohn's bank account in the Peoples First National Bank & Trust Company in the sum of $6,734.21 was garnisheed and transferred to UCIT pursuant to a writ of attachment execution issued on a judgment in favor of UCIT in the sum of $75,000. The lien against the bank cash obtained by the attachment within four months of bankruptcy and while Spohn was insolvent is null and void. Section 67 of the Bankruptcy Act, 11 U.S.C.A. § 107.

Spohn's bank account was not under the control of UCIT, and the source of this money has not been identified. Apparently UCIT has not been able to trace any of the money in the bank to proceeds from the sales of collateral on which it held a security interest. The defendant argues that the money must have come from the sale of property in which it had a security interest. This is an unwarranted assumption for all of it could have come from services rendered, sale of Spohn's common stock, or loans to Spohn.

The court may not assume the source of the money in the bank. The burden is upon UCIT to trace cash proceeds received by Spohn from the disposition of secured collateral into the bank deposits. This it has not done. This cash was received by Spohn, the debtor, and deposited more than 10 days prior to the bankruptcy proceeding (cf. U.C.C. § 9–306(2); it is not identifiable cash proceeds received from the sale or disposition of any collateral. Thus it is free from any security interest of UCIT and is subject to the claims of general creditors represented by the plaintiff-trustee.

We hold the bank cash garnisheed by UCIT is a voidable preference and the plaintiff-trustee is entitled to recover $6,734.21.

ACCOUNTS RECEIVABLE

Spohn collected customers receivables by cash and checks in the sum of $10,847.75 and transferred this amount to UCIT within four months of bankruptcy. Of this sum $1,100.00 was identified as cash proceeds from the sale of two new vehicles on which UCIT held a perfected security interest, leaving in dispute the sum of $9,747.75. This remainder comprises commingled cash proceeds arising from the sale of motor vehicles, parts and services.

From the Stipulated Facts and Exhibit L, it cannot be ascertained whether any of the articles sold were covered by a perfected security interest in favor of UCIT. Exhibit L gives only the name of the person owing the account, the amount paid, and the date the money was transferred to UCIT. Moreover, even if it were to be assumed that some of the accounts arose from the sale of parts and vehicles, it still could not be ascertained whether or not any portion of any account arose from services performed by Spohn. As UCIT did not hold a security interest in proceeds received from the sale of services, it is not entitled to retain proceeds which may have come from this source.

Furthermore, as we understand the Uniform Commercial Code, in insolvency proceedings the secured creditor is only entitled to commingled cash when it is received as proceeds of collateral within ten days of the filing of the petition.

For these reasons, we hold that the plaintiff-trustee is entitled to $9,747.75.

17 USED VEHICLES

These 17 used vehicles were taken in trade by Spohn toward the purchase price of 17 new vehicles. On each of the new vehicles sold, UCIT held a perfected security interest by virtue of the Agreement for Wholesale Financing (Ex. A), new car Trust Receipts (Ex. G), and Financing Statement (Ex. B). The 17 new vehicles were sold out of trust by Spohn.[**] ...

. . .

The plaintiff-trustee contends that according to the Motor Vehicle Code no lien can be obtained on a "trade-in" unless the lien is noted on the title certificate. It is the opinion of the court that a finance company such as UCIT engaging in wholesale financing of new and used vehicles held for resale by a dealer, and having obtained a security interest in new vehicles and the proceeds thereof, may perfect its security interest in the proceeds by filing in compliance with § 9–302(1) of the U.C.C., and, in view of § 207(c) of the Motor Vehicle Code, need not require the dealer to procure title certificates for each "trade-in" on which to show its lien....

. . .

The security interest of UCIT in these proceeds was created at the times the Agreement and the Trust Receipts were executed and perfected by the filing of the Financing Statement in March, 1955. Pursuant to § 9–306(1) of the U.C.C., this security interest continued up to the time UCIT took possession, within four months of bankruptcy, of the 17 "trade-ins", i.e., identifiable proceeds. In our opinion § 9–306(1) is not in conflict with § 60 of the Bankruptcy Act, and the perfected security interest of UCIT in these proceeds is enforceable.

[** Selling inventory "out of trust" is an expression frequently used in financing circles, perhaps because of appealing connotations that the sale was a breach of "trust" that should invoke the powerful remedies available against defalcating trustees. (The debtor actually was denominated a "trustee" under the Uniform Trust Receipts Act, which governed much pre-Code inventory financing. See generally 1 Gilmore, Security ch. 4.) However, as you probably surmised, there was nothing wrong with the *sale* of the cars; the only thing that went wrong was that the *dealer failed promptly to pay* the debt to UCIT attributable to the vehicles that it sold.]

We hold that UCIT is entitled to retain the money received from the sale of the 17 used vehicles.

42 USED VEHICLES

These 42 used vehicles were taken in trade for new vehicles, which had been financed by UCIT, under the terms of the Agreement for Wholesale Financing (Ex. A) and the Trust Receipts (Ex. G). These vehicles must also be regarded as identifiable proceeds in which, as previously shown, UCIT had perfected a security interest by filing the Financing Statement (Ex. B).

It was not stipulated that the new vehicles were sold out of trust by Spohn. However, as we interpret the pertinent security agreements, UCIT created a security interest in *all proceeds*, which would include these 42 "trade-ins", until *all the indebtedness* due by Spohn to UCIT was paid. As heretofore quoted, the Agreement for Wholesale Financing (Ex. A) provided that until payment in full, Spohn would hold all proceeds separately and in trust for UCIT. Likewise, the Trust Receipts (Ex. G), after providing that UCIT could accelerate all indebtedness then owing to it by Spohn in the event of insolvency, further provided that UCIT "may require the respective amount on any chattel to be paid to it in cash. Until such payment we [Spohn] will hold *all proceeds* of sale separately and in trust for * * * Universal C.I.T." (Emphasis supplied.) Since Spohn owed UCIT upwards of $400,000 on all the chattels which it had financed at the time of the transfers, we think these 42 used cars were proceeds to which UCIT is entitled.

The other arguments advanced by the plaintiff-trustee to recover the value of these used vehicles have been disposed of in the preceding section of this opinion.

We hold that UCIT is entitled to retain the money received from the sale of the 42 used vehicles....

Notes on Security Interests in Proceeds

(1) **"Automatic," Perfected Security Interests.** Prior to the 1972 amendments, UCC 9–203 provided that "[i]n describing collateral, the word 'proceeds' is sufficient without further description to cover proceeds of any character." This created an ambiguity when read with the (apparently) automatic continuation of a security interest in proceeds pursuant to UCC 9–306(2). See pre–1972 UCC 9–203(1)(b) & 9–306(2). That ambiguity was remedied in 1972 by the addition of UCC 9–203(3), which makes it clear that no mention of proceeds is necessary in a security agreement.

Under the pre–1972 UCC 9–306(3)(a), a right to proceeds became unperfected ten days after the debtor's receipt of the proceeds unless "a filed financing statement covering the original collateral also covers proceeds." For the same reason that motivated the changes to UCC 9–

203, the 1972 revision removed this requirement that the financing statement "cover" (i.e., claim) proceeds: A claim to proceeds of the collateral was considered so basic that (like implied warranties) this understanding "goes without saying." Moreover, the drafters thought the absence of a claim to proceeds in the financing statement would not mislead third persons. See UCC 9–306, Reasons for 1972 Change, Uniform Commercial Code, 1990 Official Text with Comments, App. II, at 1066 ("automatic right to proceeds" based on the "theory that this is the intent of the parties, unless otherwise agreed").

(2) **Security Interests in Proceeds and in After–Acquired Property: A Comparison.** In many cases a perfected security interest in proceeds could be achieved simply by covering after-acquired property of the appropriate type in the security agreement and financing statement. For example, the security agreement of an inventory financer might (and often does) cover after-acquired accounts. However, the "automatic right to proceeds" affords additional benefits to a secured party if after-acquired property qualifies as "proceeds." As explained in the preceding Note, a secured party has an automatic security interest in proceeds even if (through oversight or otherwise) the security agreement does not cover the proceeds as original collateral. Does this benefit represent more than statutory generosity? In addition to rescuing some secured parties from careless omissions, might the "automatic" approach save the costs of extended negotiations? Might it also inhibit abuse and overreaching by some secured parties who, if it were necessary to protect one's claim to proceeds in the security agreement, might use unnecessarily broad language?

As to perfection, UCC 9–306(3) provides that if property constitutes proceeds of collateral in which a security interest is perfected, the security interest in proceeds is "continuously perfected." [2] But the security interest in proceeds ceases to be so perfected "ten days after receipt ... by the debtor," subject to three exceptions.

The first exception, UCC 9–306(3)(a), generally makes it unnecessary for a financing statement to cover the type or items of collateral that proceeds represent (except when proceeds are acquired with cash proceeds). For example, a filing covering inventory is sufficient to ensure continued perfection in proceeds consisting of accounts, as long as filings against inventory and accounts are to be made in the same office. (To determine where to file, one must consult UCC 9–103 and UCC 9–401(1); see Section 3, supra.) Of course, when proceeds are of a type in which a security interest can be perfected by filing, a secured party could achieve the same result as that provided by UCC 9–306(3)—

---

2. Some of you may find it curious that UCC 9–306(2) and (3) provide that a security interest "*continues* in any identifiable proceeds" and "is *continuously* perfected." This suggests that the security interest in proceeds is (somehow) the *same* security interest as the security interest in the orig-

inal collateral. UCC 9–306, Comment 2(b) offers a glimpse of the perceived bankruptcy implications of this approach under the Bankruptcy Act of 1898. The treatment of security interests in proceeds under the current federal bankruptcy law is considered in Chapter 14, Section 3(B), infra.

continued perfection—merely by filing a financing statement covering that type of collateral, in advance.

Another exception to the ten-day limitation is made for "identifiable cash proceeds" when "a filed financing statement covers the original collateral." UCC 9–306(3)(b). A security interest in "cash proceeds" (UCC 9–306(1) (3d sentence)) as original collateral ordinarily cannot be perfected by filing: deposit accounts (as original collateral) are excluded from Article 9 and other cash proceeds are likely to be money or instruments. See UCC 9–104(*l*); UCC 9–304(1). It follows that the continued perfection conferred by UCC 9–306(3)(b) provides greater protection for proceeds, as such, than would be available under the after-acquired property approach. (If permissive perfection by filing were available for deposit accounts and other cash proceeds, however, this advantage would disappear.)

It is worth emphasizing that the important protection afforded by UCC 9–306(3)(b) does not apply when a security interest in the original collateral is perfected by a means other than filing. Consequently, cash proceeds of collateral in which a security interest cannot be perfected by filing, e.g., instruments and securities, are covered by subsection (c), discussed next. Why the less favorable treatment for cash proceeds of collateral subject to possessory security interests? Did the drafters consider possession by the secured party to be a "second class" form of public notice? Probably not; the drafting history of the 1972 revisions suggests that the drafters simply did not focus their attention on the treatment of cash proceeds of collateral in which a security interest had been perfected by possession. Instead, they worried that pre–1972 UCC 9–306(3)(a), which provided that a security interest in proceeds was "continuously perfected" if "a filed financing statement covering the original collateral also covers proceeds," could be read to confer a perfected security interest in proceeds consisting of instruments. They wished to preserve the status quo—possession, not filing, is the means of perfection for instruments—although they made an exception for instruments that are cash proceeds. See Uniform Commercial Code, 1990 Official Text with Comments, App. II, General Comment on the Approach of the Review Committee for Article 9, ¶¶ E.5. & E.22, at 1012–13, 1017.

The third exception, UCC 9–306(3)(c), permits continued perfection beyond the ten-day period if the security interest in proceeds is perfected before the period expires. A security interest in after-acquired property other than proceeds also can be perfected following the debtor's acquisition of the property; but the temporary perfection provided by UCC 9–306(3)(c) can be important for purposes of priority. See, e.g., UCC 9–301(1), UCC 9–312(6). If a secured party acts within the ten-day period, there will be no "gap" during which the security interest is unperfected. Again, to the extent proceeds consist of property not excluded from the scope of Article 9, and in which a security interest can be perfected by filing, the same advantage could be had by an initial filing covering the after-acquired property. Moreover, unless the debtor cooperates or the secured party monitors the debtor's activities closely, the secured party is not likely to discover the need to perfect in proceeds prior to the expiration of the ten-day period.

Problem 4. Continental Construction Co. bought a new backhoe; Palmetto Bank loaned Continental the purchase price, and perfected a security interest in the backhoe by filing.

(a) An employee of Iceberg Masonry, Inc., negligently dropped a load of bricks on the backhoe at a job site; the damaged backhoe was beyond repair. Continental's insurer, Everystate Insurance Co., sent its check covering the value of the backhoe ($100,000) to Continental. Does Palmetto's security interest extend to the check? See UCC 9–306(1) & (2). If so, is it perfected? See UCC 9–306(3).

(b) Would the result in part (a) be the same if the $100,000 check had been sent by *Iceberg's* liability insurance carrier? What result if the check had been sent by Iceberg itself?

(c) Suppose instead that the backhoe malfunctioned and that Continental pressed a claim against Manufacturer for damages resulting from negligent design and breach of implied warranty; the claim included evidence of damage resulting from the malfunctions and loss of profits resulting from loss of use of the backhoe. Manufacturer settled for $50,000 and sent a check to Continental for that sum. Palmetto Bank claims the check as proceeds of its collateral. What result? See In re Continental Trucking, Inc., 16 UCC Rep.Serv. 526 (M.D.Fla.1974) (check issued by truck manufacturer to satisfy judgment on claim for damages (including loss of profits) based on negligence and breach of warranty theories did not constitute proceeds of truck); Note (1) on What Constitutes Proceeds, infra.

(d) Now suppose that the backhoe was not damaged. Instead, a sluggish economy reduced Continental's business and its equipment needs. Continental leased the backhoe to Deep Dig Corp. for a one year term pursuant to a written lease. Does Palmetto's security interest extend to the lease? To checks sent to Continental by Deep Dig as lease payments? Would the answers be different if the lease had been an oral one, not reduced to writing? Would it matter if the lease were for a day or a month instead of a year?

Problem 5. Busy Bee Co. operates an interstate bus company. Firstbank has a security interest in Busy's existing and after-acquired equipment, inventory and accounts, perfected by filing. Every day, thousands of riders pay Busy and independent travel agents for tickets. Does Firstbank acquire a security interest in these payments? See Notes on What Constitutes Proceeds, infra. If so, is the security interest perfected?

Problem 6. United Entertainment Group, Inc. (UEG), operates coin-operated music and entertainment machine "routes." UEG supplies coin-operated jukeboxes, video games, pool tables, and the like to establishments (called "joints," in the trade) such as restaurants, taverns, and clubs. The operators of the joints receive no interest in the machines (other than the right to possession) and pay nothing for the machines. However, once or twice each week, an employee of UEG stops by each joint. The joint manager and the UEG employee "rob" the machine and, together, count the money. The joint keeps one half of the money and UEG takes the other half. Either party can terminate the arrangement for any reason upon five-days' notice.

Firstbank has a security interest in UEG's existing and after-acquired equipment, inventory, and accounts, perfected by filing. Does Firstbank acquire a security interest in the funds obtained from the machines? See Notes on What Constitutes Proceeds, infra. If so, is the security interest perfected?

Problem 7. On June 1 Dale Bookbinder obtained a short-term (six-month) loan from Firstbank in the amount of $25,000. Bookbinder delivered to Firstbank, as collateral, a certificate for 2,000 shares of General Motors Corporation (GMC) common stock. On June 3 GMC declared a stock dividend: each stockholder became entitled to receive one additional share of stock for each four shares owned. Because Bookbinder remained the registered owner of the shares, GMC mailed a new certificate for 500 shares directly to Bookbinder, who received it on July 15. Does Firstbank acquire a security interest in the new certificate? See Notes on What Constitutes Proceeds, infra. If so, is the security interest perfected? See UCC 9–306; UCC 8–321; UCC 8–313; FDIC v. W. Hugh Meyer & Associates, 864 F.2d 371 (5th Cir.1989) (UCC 8–321(1) requires transfer under UCC 8–313(1) for attachment; automatic creation and perfection provisions for proceeds do not apply to security interests in investment securities). For a discussion of the *W. Hugh Meyer* case, see Schroeder & Carlson, Security Interests Under Article 8 of the Uniform Commercial Code, 12 Cardozo L. Rev. 557, 618–25 (1990). What could Firstbank have done to improve its position? (Hint: Consider why GMC sent the new certificate to Bookbinder instead of Firstbank.)

Notes on What Constitutes Proceeds

(1) **Exchange and Replacement; Insurance Payments.** The definition of proceeds is transactional. Each of the triggering events— "sale, exchange, collection or other disposition of collateral or proceeds"—contemplates that proceeds are actually received in place of and in substitution for the original collateral, which has been disposed of or reduced in value (such as by collections).[3] Applying this "replacement" standard, a lease of goods would seem to be an "other disposition" giving rise to proceeds consisting of rentals; however, the authori-

---

3. A security interest also may continue in the original collateral under UCC 9–306(2). Unauthorized dispositions "subject to" security interests are considered in Chapter 13, Section 2, which also deals more generally with priorities as among secured parties and buyers of collateral.

ties are not uniform on this point. Compare Proposed Permanent Editorial Board Commentary on Section 9–306(1) (taking the position that lease rentals constitute proceeds) with In re Cleary Brothers Construction Co., 9 B.R. 40 (Bkrtcy.S.D.Fla.1980) (rents are not proceeds of equipment subject to preexisting security interest). Certainly a lessee receives a property interest in the leased goods and, to that extent, the lessor has "disposed of" an interest in the goods. See UCC 2A–103(1)(j) (defining "lease" to be "a transfer of the right to possession and use of goods for a term in return for consideration") & (1)(m) (defining "leasehold interest" as "the interest of the lessor or the lessee under a lease contract"); UCC 9–504(1) (after default, secured party may "sell, lease or otherwise *dispose*" of collateral). The same conclusion would seem to follow for royalties received in exchange for a debtor's licensing of intellectual property such as copyrights and trademarks.

How does the "replacement" standard apply to insurance payments? The *Continental Trucking* case, cited in Problem 4(c), was decided under the pre–1972 version of UCC 9–306(1). That version did not contain what is now the second sentence of that subsection, indicating that "[i]nsurance payable by reason of loss or damage to the collateral is proceeds ...." The Reasons for 1972 Change state that the new second sentence was "intended to overrule various cases to the effect that proceeds of insurance on collateral are not proceeds of the collateral." Is the policy of the second sentence sound? See Henson, Insurance Proceeds as "Proceeds" Under Article 9, 18 Cath. U.L.Rev. 453, 461 (1969) (arguing for judicial inclusion of insurance proceeds as Article 9 "proceeds," in part on the ground that "[t]here is no reason for general creditors to get a windfall in the form of insurance proceeds when they would have had no claim on the collateral had it not been destroyed."). Does the policy extend to insurance payments in compensation for loss of the use of the collateral (e.g., lost profits) as opposed to diminution in the collateral's value? Are these two losses the same?

The second sentence of UCC 9–306(1) is limited to insurance; it does not extend to payments received directly from those who damage collateral. Should a court read the sentence as limiting the scope of "proceeds" of damaged collateral to insurance payments, or should it conclude that a payment from a tortfeasor in compensation for damage to the collateral meets the "replacement" standard and thus constitutes "proceeds"? See In re Territo, 32 B.R. 377 (Bkrtcy.E.D.N.Y.1983) (the payment in settlement of claim for damage to collateral was proceeds within the 1972 definition, even though not paid under an insurance policy.).[4]

---

4. In the "proceeds" context, it is important to distinguish between the payment of a claim for damage to collateral and the claim itself. To the extent that a tort claim constitutes "proceeds" of, say, negligently damaged goods, no Article 9 security interest would seem to attach at all. The exclusion from Article 9 of tort claims is absolute; it contains no exception for proceeds. See UCC 9–104(k). The exclusion differs in this regard from the exclusion of interests in insurance policies, which does contain an exception for "proceeds." See UCC 9–104(g); UCC 9–306(1). Compare also UCC 9–104(h) (general exclusion of rights that are the subject of judg-

Other examples of property received by a debtor in replacement of collateral, on account of a diminution in value of collateral, or to supplement collateral, do not seem to fit the "other disposition" criterion of UCC 9–306(1). Consider, for example, a breach of warranty claim against a seller of goods. The debtor acquires a chose in action that replaces the value of collateral that would have (or should have) been available to the secured party. Is the similarity of this intangible to the insurance payments that UCC 9–306(1) explicitly includes in the definition of "proceeds" sufficient to justify including the intangible within the definition?

Do the disposition and collection standards unduly restrict what constitutes proceeds in this exchange and replacement paradigm? Assuming they do, can the acquisition of assets by a debtor, even if due in part to a diminution in value of collateral, be too attenuated from the diminution for those assets to be considered proceeds? For example, would anyone think that accounts generated by a construction contractor would (or should) be considered proceeds of the contractor's construction equipment, even though the equipment depreciates as a result of its use in earning the accounts? Similarly, would (or should) inventory fabricated by a debtor's factory equipment be considered proceeds of that equipment? What about cash earned from music or video machines? Has the equipment merely provided a service, or is the better analogy that of a short-term rental? Should the result turn on whether the equipment user has acquired a *property* interest in the machine under non-Code law?

(2) Property Closely Associated With Original Collateral. Another plausible way to conceptualize what are or should be proceeds does not depend on the exchange concept. Instead, one can view proceeds as property that is so necessarily and obviously associated with an interest in the original collateral that a security agreement and financing statement ought not to be required to mention them explicitly. After all, "automatic" attachment and perfection are the principal effects that flow from classifying property as proceeds. If the debtor, by virtue of its interest in the original collateral, is necessarily entitled to additional property, then a secured party likewise would be entitled to the additional property as proceeds.

Claims for damage or loss of collateral seem to fit this characterization. The same could be said for all forms of distributions on account of securities, partnership interests, and other intangibles (which may or may not already be covered as "collections" proceeds), government subsidies, and other payments that do not, technically, involve an "exchange" or disposition.

Whether various kinds of government farm subsidies qualify as proceeds has been one of the most litigated aspects of UCC 9–306

ments does not exclude "a judgment taken on a right to payment which was collateral").

during recent years. The "close association" conceptualization of proceeds might underlie some cases that hold government "payment in kind" (PIK) benefits are proceeds of crops. See, e.g., Production Credit Association of Fairmont v. Martin County National Bank, 384 N.W.2d 529 (Minn.App.1986). The PIK program involves a governmental "payment" of grain, in kind, in exchange for a farmer's agreement *not* to grow crops on part of its land. Other cases hold that PIK benefits are not proceeds of crops because the farmers never grew any crops that could have been disposed of in exchange for such benefits. See, e.g., In re Schmaling, 783 F.2d 680 (7th Cir.1986). In any event, most of the reported decisions concerning farm subsidies as proceeds involved security agreements and financing statements that never mentioned the subsidies as collateral. See generally Annotation, Secured Transactions: Government Agricultural Program Payments as "Proceeds" of Agricultural Products Under UCC § 9–306, 79 A.L.R.4th 903 (1990). In these cases, whether the subsidies were classified as proceeds determined whether the secured party had a security interest at all. In many of these cases a properly drawn security agreement and financing statement covering the rights to the subsidies would have saved the secured party's claim without implicating the proceeds issue (assuming that the subsidies were assignable under applicable federal laws and regulations).

Problem 8. Firstbank has a security interest, perfected by filing, in all of the restaurant equipment of The Bus Corp., the operator of a small restaurant. The Bus wrongfully sold a used oven to the operator of another restaurant, The Light Dog Co. (Because the sale by The Bus was not authorized, Firstbank's security interest in the oven continued and The Light Dog's interest remains subject to that security interest. See UCC 9–306(2); Chapter 13, Section 2(A), infra.) Light Dog then resold the stove to another restaurant operator, The New Neck, Inc. In payment, New Neck gave Light Dog its check for $1,500.

(a) Does Firstbank have a security interest in the $1,500 check? UCC 9–306(1) & (2); Note on Cash Proceeds and the Meaning of "Received by the Debtor" in UCC 9–306(2), infra.

(b) Assuming an affirmative answer in part (a), is Firstbank's security interest perfected? See UCC 9–306(3).

(c) Now assume that the collateral involved was not an oven but was a delivery van, in which Firstbank perfected its security interest by complying with the relevant motor vehicle certificate of title law. Does Firstbank have a perfected security interest in the $1,500 that New Neck paid for the van? See UCC 9–306(3)(b); UCC 9–302(1)(d), (3) & (4).

Problem 9. In the setting of the Prototype transaction, Main Motors sold one of the Firstbank-financed automobiles to Buyer for $12,000. Buyer took out a large roll of hundred dollar bills, peeled off one hundred twenty bills, and handed them to Main's cashier. Main immediately took this cash and paid $1,000 to Landlord for overdue rent, and $11,000 to Secondbank, which had been pressing Main to repay an unsecured loan.

(a) Did Firstbank's security interest extend to the cash that Main received from Buyer? If so was it perfected? See UCC 9–306(1)–(3); Note on Cash Proceeds and the Meaning of "Received by the Debtor" in UCC 9–306(2), infra.

(b) Assuming that Firstbank held a perfected security interest in the automobile and the cash proceeds, does it necessarily follow that Firstbank may reclaim the funds from Landlord or Secondbank or hold those parties liable for money had and received? [5]

Note on Cash Proceeds and the Meaning of "Received by the Debtor" in UCC 9–306(2)

The definition of "proceeds" in UCC 9–306(1) refers to "whatever is received." But the operative rule of UCC 9–306(2) provides that "a security interest . . . continues in any identifiable proceeds including collections *received by the debtor.*" Does "received by the debtor" modify "proceeds" or only "collections"? The phrase "including collections" was added to the 1957 official text of the Code only as a clarification, suggesting that "received by the debtor" modifies "proceeds" generally. See 1956 Recommendations of the Editorial Board for the Uniform Commercial Code, 18 Kelly, Drafts 280, 282; Uniform Commercial Code, 1957 Official Text with Comments, 9–306, 20 Kelly, Drafts 181. What constitutes the debtor's "receipt" of proceeds also must be determined for purposes of the ten-day temporary perfection provision in UCC 9–306(3)—a security interest "becomes unperfected ten days after *receipt of the proceeds by the debtor.*"

Some courts have held that only proceeds that are physically received by a debtor qualify for a continuing security interest under UCC 9–306(2). Consider In re Halmar Distributors, Inc., 116 B.R. 328 (Bkrtcy.D.Mass.1990). That case held (among other alternative holdings) that a secured party with a first priority security interest in accounts had no security interest in collections of those accounts made by a junior secured party because the proceeds were never "received by the debtor." However, the court did not explain the basis upon which the junior secured party acquired a security interest in the collections— if not as proceeds. It merely observed that the collections were undertaken by the junior secured party "in its own right and not by the Debtors." Why should a security interest in proceeds cease to continue merely because, for example, the collections on accounts collateral are received by a competing claimant or by an escrow agent, or are paid into court?

---

5. The gravamen of an action for "money had and received" is that the defendant received money that should have been paid to the plaintiff and under circumstances such that the defendant should pay it over to the plaintiff.

It is commonly recognized that intangibles, such as accounts arising from the sale of inventory, are subject to a continuing security
interest under UCC 9–306(2) even though they cannot be "received by
the debtor" in the sense of physical possession. Is it plausible that the
drafters used the word "received" to mean "acquired"? If so, UCC 9–
306(2) could be read, in pertinent part, as follows: A security interest
continues in any identifiable proceeds, including collections, *in which
the debtor acquires rights.* Would even that approach be too narrow?
Suppose, for example, that Buyer buys equipment subject to a security
interest granted by Seller to Bank. Would Bank's proceeds include
what *Buyer* receives when it resells the goods? Arguably Seller would
have no rights in what Buyer receives because Seller relinquished its
rights (but not Bank's rights) in the original collateral. Presumably
this approach also would capture what is received upon a transfer by a
thief who steals collateral from a debtor. On the other hand, some
might think that allowing a secured party to claim what a debtor's
transferee receives upon a retransfer gives a claim to proceeds too
broad a reach.

Be that as it may, several reported cases have concluded that,
under current law, a security interest continues in proceeds received by
the original debtor's transferee. The reason: having acquired the
collateral, the transferee *is a debtor.* See UCC 9–105(1)(d) (" 'debtor'
means the owner of the collateral in any provision ... dealing with the
collateral"). Among the cases adopting this reasoning are Centerre
Bank, N.A. v. New Holland Div. of Sperry Corp., 832 F.2d 1415 (7th
Cir.1987), and In re San Juan Packers, Inc., 696 F.2d 707 (9th Cir.1983).

The Permanent Editorial Board has implicitly taken the position
that collections made by one secured party (*SP*–2) are, nevertheless,
proceeds in which the security interest of a competing secured party
(*SP*–1) continues. See Permanent Editorial Board Commentary No. 7.
To say that *SP*–1's security interest continues in the proceeds is not to
say, however, that the priorities applicable to the underlying collateral
also will obtain as to the proceeds. As we shall see in more detail—
particularly in Chapter 13, Section 2—various purchasers of collateral
may be protected under rules analogous to and including those encountered in Chapter 1 concerning good faith purchasers. See UCC 9–307;
UCC 9–308; UCC 9–309.

Permanent Editorial Board Commentary No. 7 considers the situation in which *SP*–1 has a senior interest in accounts that are collected
in good faith by *SP*–2, which has a junior security interest. It explains
that *SP*–2 may achieve priority in the collected checks either as a
holder in due course (UCC 3–306 [UCC 3–305 in the pre–1990 version of
Article 3]) or as a qualifying purchaser under UCC 9–308. The Code
does not address comprehensively the rights of those who receive
money (as opposed to checks). Nevertheless, one ought not assume that
the law affords no protection to recipients of money constituting cash
proceeds claimed by another person's secured party. See UCC 1–103;
UCC 9–306, Comment 2(c). Would one expect the Code to subject those
who receive cash to constructive notice based on public filing? Cf. UCC

9–309 (filing does not constitute notice for purposes of determining whether purchaser of collateral is a protected purchaser of an instrument, document, or security). PEB Commentary No. 7 takes the position that *SP*–2's rights to cash that it collects can be senior to those of *SP*–1 under non-UCC principles of law and equity and by way of analogy to UCC 9–309.

––––––––

The *Howarth* case, supra, illustrates the consequence of a secured party's inability to demonstrate that the collateral it claims constitutes "identifiable proceeds": loss of a security interest. The problem of security interests in proceeds of collateral takes new twists when the proceeds are cash, or its equivalent, deposited in the debtor's bank accounts and commingled with other funds. The remaining portion of this Section explores these twists in the nonbankruptcy context. The debtor's entry into bankruptcy may affect the analysis and the results. See Chapter 14, Section 3(B), infra.

Problem 10. In the setting of the automobile financing Prototype, assume that Firstbank's security interest in Main's inventory was perfected by a filed financing statement that referred to the collateral only as "Motor Vehicles" (as in Problem 2, supra). Moreover, the security agreement covered only new motor vehicles financed by Firstbank, not used vehicles.

Main deposited cash received from the sale of new and used cars and from its repair department into a checking account maintained with Firstbank. As in the Prototype, when financed cars were sold, Main promptly sent Firstbank a check covering the amount Firstbank had advanced to the manufacturer for those cars. However, in June, when Main owed $1,500,000 to Firstbank, Main became short of cash and used proceeds from the sale of financed cars to meet payroll, rent, utilities, and other pressing obligations. On June 1 Main had a balance of $1000 in its checking account. The following table shows the deposits (+) and withdrawals (-) for the first few days of June; "PC" indicates proceeds of collateral subject to Firstbank's security interest.

June		Debit or Withdrawal		Balance E.O.D.
1				$ 1,000.
2	+	$15,000.	Sale of one new Pontiac (PC)	16,000.
3	+	9,000.	Sale of one new Pontiac (PC)	25,000.
4	−	4,000.	Rent on off-site storage lot	21,000.
5	−	12,000.	Payroll	9,000.
6	−	2,000.	Fuel oil	7,000.
7	−	1,000.	Telephone; electricity	6,000.
8	+	2,000.	Collections for body repairs	8,000.
9	+	6,000.	Sale of used cars (Not PC)	14,000.
10	+	12,000.	Loan from relative	26,000.

During this period Main made no payments to Firstbank.

On June 12 Caesar, a creditor of Main with a judgment for $50,000, garnished the checking account by serving a garnishment summons on

Firstbank. Is Caesar's garnishment lien senior to Firstbank's security interest in Main's checking account? If so, to what extent? See Universal C.I.T. Credit Corp. v. Farmers Bank of Portageville, infra; Note on Tracing and Commingled Cash Proceeds, infra. (Ignore any right of setoff that Firstbank may enjoy.)

UNIVERSAL C.I.T. CREDIT CORP. v. FARMERS BANK OF PORTAGEVILLE [*]

United States District Court, Eastern District of Missouri, 1973.
358 F.Supp. 317.

WEBSTER, DISTRICT JUDGE. Plaintiff, a Delaware corporation, brings this action against defendant Farmers Bank of Portageville, a Missouri banking corporation. Jurisdiction is founded upon diversity of citizenship under 28 U.S.C. § 1332. The amount in controversy exceeds $10,000.

Plaintiff's amended complaint is in three counts. In the first count, plaintiff seeks to recover $22,390.19 as the unpaid balance on checks drawn to plaintiff as payee and thereafter endorsed and presented to defendant, which refused payment. In count II plaintiff contends that it had a perfected security interest in the proceeds of sales of certain automobiles, which proceeds were deposited in the debtor's account in defendant bank and which plaintiff contends were thereafter permitted by defendant to be withdrawn with knowledge of plaintiff's claim. The third count, denominated "alternative for improper failure and refusal to honor drafts" was abandoned at the trial.

Facts

Gerald W. Ryan, doing business as Ryan–Chevrolet and Olds Co., a proprietorship, operated an automobile dealership in Portageville, Missouri. On or about June 18, 1968, Ryan entered into an agreement with plaintiff for wholesale financing, commonly known as floor plan financing. Under the terms of this agreement, plaintiff from time to time advanced funds to pay the manufacturer's invoice on new automobiles, acquiring a security in such automobiles. As each automobile was sold by Ryan, he was required to remit plaintiff's advance. These remittances were in the form of checks drawn on Ryan's checking account at defendant's bank. The financing statements filed in New Madrid County reflect the security interest in the proceeds of the sale of the automobiles. Proper filing is not disputed.

Toward the end of 1969, plaintiff decided for reasons of policy, but primarily because it had not been supplied with current financial

[* The court's citations are to the applicable pre–1972 version of the Code.]

statements, to terminate the floor plan arrangement. Ryan was notified that the floor plan would be terminated December 31, 1969.

Sometime after 3:00 p.m. on January 15, 1970, Ryan had a conversation with Richard L. Saalwaechter, President of defendant bank. Ryan told Saalwaechter that he was being put out of business by plaintiff since plaintiff had revoked the floor plan, and that he wanted to be sure that the bank got paid, He said "let C.I.T. be last—they put me out of business." Ryan discussed his debt to the bank on a demand promissory note. He told Saalwaechter that he wanted the bank to be safe on its loan. Ryan asked Saalwaechter to debit his account and credit the bank with $12,000 from his checking account. Saalwaechter then verified Ryan's checking account and determined that there was a balance of $16,340.00. When Saalwaechter suggested that Ryan write a check to the bank, Ryan told him that he preferred that the bank run a debit against the account because C.I.T. was after him and he didn't know what they could do to him. Ryan further told Saalwaechter that C.I.T. had checks out, and that he wanted to make a cash withdrawal to keep C.I.T. from getting its checks. Thereupon, although the bank's business day had closed at 3:00 p.m., Saalwaechter debited Ryan's account in the amount of $12,000.00. The next morning, January 16th, Ryan came to the bank and made a cash withdrawal of $3,100.00. Saalwaechter testified that he had no knowledge that any of Ryan's checks to C.I.T. were in the bank until after the debit and the withdrawal.

The funds in dispute derive from the sale by Ryan of six motor vehicles. In some cases, a trade-in was involved with which we are not concerned. In each case, Ryan received a check from the purchaser in payment of the cash portion of the deal. Each check was deposited in Ryan's account with defendant bank and he received full credit therefor. Each automobile sold and the proceeds thereof were subject to plaintiff's security interest. The checks representing the proceeds of the six automobiles sold by Ryan were all deposited on or prior to January 15, 1970 and aggregate $18,112.44....

Liability Under Count I

Plaintiff contends that defendant bank failed to give timely notice of dishonor or make timely settlement and is therefore liable for the full amount of the checks under the applicable provisions of the Uniform Commercial Code in force in Missouri.

[The court rejected the plaintiff's contentions based on Count I.]

Liability Under Count II

It is not disputed that plaintiff had a continuously perfected security interest in six automobiles and their proceeds. See § 400.9–306(3) V.A.M.S. Ryan sold separately each of these automobiles and deposited the amount received on each sale in his checking account at the defendant bank. Funds from other sources were deposited in the checking account prior to and contemporaneously with such deposits.

Numerous checks were issued on the account between the time of the first and last sale. Plaintiff contends that the defendant bank was not entitled to debit Ryan's checking account in the amount of $12,000 on January 15, 1970, relying upon Section 400.9–306(2), which provides:

"Except where this article otherwise provides, a security interest continues in collateral notwithstanding sale, exchange or other disposition thereof by the debtor unless his action was authorized by the secured party in the security agreement or otherwise, and also continues in any *identifiable* proceeds including collections received by the debtor." (Emphasis supplied.)

Defendant contends that the proceeds from the sales of the six automobiles were not "identifiable" within the meaning of § 400.9–306(2). Defendant argues that when the proceeds were deposited and thereby commingled with other funds in Ryan's account and thereafter substantial withdrawals were made exceeding the amount of the deposited proceeds, the proceeds completely lost their identity. No Missouri case defines the term "identifiable" as used in this section. It is provided in § 400.1–103 that all supplemental bodies of law continue to apply to commercial contracts except insofar as displaced by the particular provisions of the Uniform Commercial Code. Applying § 400.1–103, this court concludes that proceeds are "identifiable" if they can be traced in accordance with the state law governing the transaction. Missouri has recognized in an analogous situation—suits to impose a constructive trust—that special funds may be traced into commingled funds. Perry v. Perry, 484 S.W.2d 257 (Mo.1972). The mere fact that the proceeds from the sales of the six automobiles were commingled with other funds and subsequent withdrawals were made from the commingled account does not render the proceeds unidentifiable under Missouri law. As the court said in Perry v. Perry, supra at 259:

"... where a defaulting trustee has first commingled the trust funds with his own and then paid them out in satisfaction of his own debts, it will be presumed that the payment was made from his own contribution to the commingled fund, 'and not out of the trust money,' so that whatever is left is the money for which he is accountable in his fiduciary capacity. Lolordo v. Lacy, 337 Mo.1097, 88 S.W.2d 353, 358; Cross v. Cross, 362 Mo.1098, 246 S.W.2d 801, 803." Perry v. Perry, 484 S.W.2d 257, 259 (Mo.1972).

Before tracing the proceeds, it is necessary to decide whether under the circumstances in this case the defendant bank was entitled to debit Ryan's checking account if the account contained proceeds from the sales of the six automobiles. Comment 2(c) to § 400.9–306 provides:

"Where cash proceeds are covered into the debtor's checking account and paid out in the operation of the debtor's business, recipients of the funds of course take free of any claim which the secured party may have in them as proceeds. What has been said relates to payments and transfers in ordinary course. *The law of fraudulent conveyances would no doubt in appropriate cases support recovery of proceeds by a secured party from a transferee out of ordinary course or otherwise in collusion with the debtor to defraud the secured party.*" (Emphasis supplied)

There are no Missouri cases on point. However, Missouri has long recognized that one indicia of a fraudulent conveyance is a transaction outside the usual course of doing business. Bank of New Cambria v. Briggs, 236 S.W.2d 289, 291 (Mo.1951). In Missouri, "fraud, like any other fact, may be established by circumstantial evidence [and][t]here are circumstances which have come to be recognized as indicia or badges of fraud, one of which circumstances alone may not prove fraud, but may warrant an inference of fraud, especially where there is a concurrence of several indicia of fraud." Id. Ryan told Saalwaechter that plaintiff had revoked the floor plan and that he wanted the bank to be safe on its loan. Ryan asked Saalwaechter to debit his account. When Saalwaechter suggested that Ryan write a check to the bank, Ryan indicated that he preferred the bank run a debit against the account and further informed Saalwaechter that he had issued checks to plaintiff and wished to keep plaintiff from collecting on the checks. All of these events, including the debit to Ryan's account, transpired after the close of business on January 15, 1970. These facts clearly show that the debit of Ryan's account was not in the ordinary course of business. Although, as indicated above, there are no Missouri cases directly on point, this court concludes that the Missouri courts would not, under these circumstances, permit the defendant bank to retain the amount debited outside the usual course of business and thereby defeat the security interest of plaintiff in the identifiable proceeds of the sale of the six automobiles.

Support for this conclusion is also found in the law governing a bank's right of set-off. As a general rule an account constituting a general deposit is subject to the bank's right of set-off. First National Bank of Clinton v. Julian, 383 F.2d 329, 338 (8th Cir.1967), applying Missouri law and following Adelstein v. Jefferson Bank & Trust Company, 377 S.W.2d 247, 251 (Mo.1964). An exception to that general rule is that a bank is not entitled to a set-off where it has "sufficient knowledge of facts relating to the interests of others in the account as to put the bank on inquiry to ascertain the trust character of the account." Northern Ins. Co. v. Traders Gate City National Bank, 259 Mo.App. 132, 186 S.W.2d 491, 497 (1945) following Brown v. Maguire's Real Estate Agency, 343 Mo. 336, 121 S.W.2d 754 (1938). The *Northern Insurance Company* case indicates that the bank's knowledge of the "trust character" of a deposit can be shown by indirect evidence or by showing that the bank would have sufficient information to put it on inquiry as to the trust character of the deposit. 186 S.W.2d at 498. The bank's knowledge that Ryan had floor plan financing with plaintiff, that Ryan had issued checks to plaintiff which Ryan did not want collected by plaintiff, and Ryan's insistence that the bank run a debit against his account, coupled with the communication of such facts after banking hours, were sufficient to put the bank on inquiry as to the possible trust character of all or part of the funds deposited in Ryan's account....

This court's final task is to trace the proceeds of the sales of the six automobiles to determine if they were taken by the bank when it debited Ryan's account after the close of business on January 15, 1970. As indicated above, Perry v. Perry, supra, 484 S.W.2d at 259, stated the general rule that in tracing commingled funds it is presumed that any payments made were from other than the funds in which another had a legally recognized interest. This is commonly referred to as the "lowest intermediate balance" rule. Restatement of Trusts, Second, § 202, Comment *j* provides in pertinent part:

> "*j. Effect of withdrawals and subsequent additions.* Where the trustee deposits in a single account in a bank trust funds and his individual funds, and makes withdrawals from the deposit and dissipates the money so withdrawn, and subsequently makes additional deposits of his individual funds in the account, the beneficiary cannot ordinarily enforce an equitable lien upon the deposit for a sum greater than the lowest intermediate balance of the deposit...."

Illustration 20 to Comment *j* is as follows:

> "*A* is trustee for *B* of $1,000. He deposits this money together with $1000 of his own in a bank. He draws out $1500 and dissipates it. He later deposits $1000 of his own in the account. He is entitled to a lien on the account for $500, the lowest intermediate balance." Comment *j*, Illustration 20, Restatement of Trusts § 202 at 544 and Restatement of Trusts, Second, § 202 at 451.

The situation in the instant case differs from Comment *j* and the Illustration in one respect. We have not one, but six, separate deposits of funds of a "trust character" spanning a period of nearly a month, during which time a substantial number of withdrawals and deposits of other funds were made in the account. Comment *m* to the Restatement of Trusts, Second, § 202 at 453 provides:

> "*m. Subsequent additions by way of restitution.* Where the trustee deposits trust funds in his individual account in a bank, and makes withdrawals from the deposit and dissipates the money so withdrawn, and subsequently makes additional deposits of his individual funds in the account, *manifesting an intention to make restitution* of the trust funds withdrawn, the beneficiary's lien upon the deposit is not limited to the lowest intermediate balance.
>
> "Where the deposit of trust funds and of his individual funds was *in an account in the name of the trustee as such, and not in his individual account,* and he withdraws more than the

amount of his individual funds, and subsequently deposits his individual funds in the account, the beneficiary's lien upon the deposit is not limited to the lowest intermediate balance since the new deposit will be treated as *made by way of restitution of the trust funds previously withdrawn.*" (Emphasis supplied.)

Thus, individual funds subsequently deposited to a trust account by the trustee are presumed to be by way of restitution. Perry v. Perry, supra at 259. Subsequent deposits by the trustee to his own account, on the other hand, are not so treated unless the trustee "manifests an intention to make restitution." No such manifestation of intent was shown in this case. Therefore, subsequent deposits of funds not relating to the proceeds from the sales of the six automobiles in Ryan's individual d/b/a account will not be treated as made by way of restitution of trust funds previously withdrawn.

However, each deposit of the proceeds of the sales of the six automobiles will be treated as additions to the trust fund, and the lowest intermediate balance theory will be followed.

It was stipulated at trial that the following deposits were received by Ryan from the sale of the six automobiles and their proceeds in which plaintiff held a continuously perfected security interest:

	Vehicle	Serial No.	Purchaser	Date of Deposit	Amount
1.	1969 Chev.	866578	Campbell	12–19–69	$5,700.00
2.	1970 Olds.	217371	Faulkner	12–20–69	4,125.00
3.	1969 Chev.	890453	Hunter	1–09–70	1,599.94
4.	1970 Chev.	138013	Carlisle	1–12–70	2,237.50
5.	1970 Olds.	160314	Rone	1–15–70	2,700.00
6.	1970 Chev.	141638	Hendricks	1–15–70	1,750.00

The court has examined the banking records of the Ryan account and finds that the identifiable proceeds in which plaintiff held a continuously perfected security interest on January 15, 1970 prior to the bank's $12,000 debit entry was $11,429.11. This amount may be traced according to the following summarization:

Date		"Proceeds" Deposited	End Balance	"Proceeds" Remaining in Account
12–18–69			$ 710.74	
12–19–69	(1)	$5,700.00	9,100.58	$ 5,700.00
12–20–69	(2)	4,125.00	9,709.90	*9,709.90
12–24–69			6,201.41	*6,201.41
1–02–70			4,715.30	*4,715.30
1–09–70	(3)	1,599.94	11,987.65	6,315.24
1–12–70	(4)	2,237.50	15,426.72	8,552.74
1–14–70			6,979.11	*6,979.11
1–15–70	(5)	2,700.00		
	(6)	1,750.00	16,340.00	11,429.11

* Lowest Intermediate Balance

On January 15, 1970, the bank debited against the Ryan account checks aggregating $516.65 and in addition made the $12,000.00 debit entry in its favor. The $12,000.00 debit entry was made at 3:00 p.m.

after the close of business. It may, therefore, be inferred that the checks aggregating $516.65 were received prior thereto in the ordinary course on January 15, 1970 during banking hours. The pro forma balance prior to the $12,000.00 debit entry was, therefore, $15,823.35. Subtracting from this amount the "proceeds" remaining in the account ($11,429.11), the amount which the bank was entitled to debit was $4,394.24. Accordingly, plaintiff is entitled to recover from the bank he excess amount debited, or $7,605.76. That amount is identified as proceeds in which plaintiff had a perfected security interest, and plaintiff is entitled to recover this amount, together with interest at 6% from October 26, 1970, the filing date of the complaint. The Clerk will enter judgment in favor of plaintiff on Count II in accordance with this Memorandum.

This Memorandum constitutes the court's Findings of Fact and Conclusions of Law.

So ordered.

Note on Tracing and Commingled Cash Proceeds

We have seen that a security interest "continues in any *identifiable* proceeds" and "is continuously perfected" in "*identifiable* cash proceeds" when the original collateral is covered by a filed financing statement. UCC 9–306(2) & (3)(b). Problems 1 through 9 in this section involved proceeds (or putative proceeds)—goods, intangibles, and cash proceeds such as money or checks—that clearly were "identifiable." Problem 10 and the *Farmers Bank* case, however, considered bank accounts in which proceeds and non-proceeds had been commingled. As you know, a depositor has no property interest in specific coins or currency deposited in a bank. Clearly, then, once cash proceeds are deposited in a bank account containing non-proceeds, the cash proceeds are not "identifiable" in the same sense as the proceeds considered earlier in this section. They become even less "identifiable" as the debtor makes withdrawals from, and deposits into, the bank account.

The *Farmers Bank* court reached for a legal fiction—the "lowest intermediate balance rule" (LIBR)—in order to identify what otherwise would not have been identifiable. Courts have developed tracing rules, including LIBR, in an effort to afford an equitable, restitutionary remedy to victims of wrongdoing. Is the case for tracing as strong in the context of proceeds of a secured creditor's collateral as it is when, for example, a trustee has misappropriated trust funds? Might the courts easily have concluded that cash proceeds lose their identity upon commingling? In his treatise Professor Gilmore took the position that proceeds cease to be identifiable upon deposit in a commingled bank account, and there is some early authority supporting that result. 2 Gilmore, Security § 27.4, at 735–36; Morrison Steel Co. v. Gurtman, 113 N.J.Super. 474, 274 A.2d 306 (App.Div.1971) ("Generally, as is true here, proceeds will have been rendered unidentifiable by having been commingled with other funds in a single bank account.") (dictum). But since 1973 the reported cases uniformly have allowed a secured party to employ tracing principles in order to claim a continuing perfected security interest in a commingled deposit account. But cf. In re Littleton, 106 B.R. 632 (Bkrtcy.9th Cir.1989) (secured party who allowed debtor to commingle proceeds in a general account rather than segregate them in separate account as required by security agreement held to have waived security interest in proceeds and made identifiability impossible), affirmed on other grounds (per curiam) 942 F.2d 551 (9th Cir.1991). The case law all seems to be directly or indirectly traceable to the *Farmers Bank* case, and the cases generally invoke LIBR as the tracing principle.

Chapter 12

THE SCOPE OF ARTICLE 9

The discussion in Chapters 10 and 11 of the law governing attachment, perfection, and priorities was premised upon the assumption that Article 9 applies to the transactions. Article 9 does not, however, apply to *all* secured transactions. And some of its provisions apply to transactions that do not create security interests. This Chapter examines more closely the scope of Article 9.

Substance, rather than form, controls whether a transaction is within the scope of Article 9. Article 9 applies "to *any* transaction *(regardless of its form)* which is intended to create a security interest in personal property." UCC 9–102(1)(a). To make clear the applicability of Article 9 to the wide variety of pre-Code security devices, UCC 9–102(2) provides that the Article applies to "security interests created by contract" and sets forth a list of different forms that secured transactions took before the Code was enacted. We have encountered some of these transactions previously. See, e.g., Chapter 10, Section 1(A), supra; Chapter 11, Section 3(B), supra.

What exactly is the substance of a "security interest"? When does a transaction that the parties consider not to be for security nevertheless create a security interest? Whose intent is relevant in determining whether a transaction is "intended to create" a security interest?

UCC 1–201(37) defines the term "security interest." The length of the definition (it runs nearly two pages) suggests the difficulty of defining the term. The first sentence explains that a security interest is "an interest in personal property ... which secures payment or performance of an obligation." As Professor Gilmore pointed out, "[t]his, like most definitions of basic terms, is essentially a declaration of faith." 1 Gilmore, Security § 11.1, at 334.

Declarations of faith, however, are not meaningless. The materials in this Chapter explore how courts have attempted to discern the line between security interests, as to which Article 9 applies, and other, similar property interests that are not security interests and as to which Article 9 generally is inapplicable. (As we shall see, particular provisions of Article 9 may apply to certain transactions even though they do not create security interests.) Section 1 of this Chapter focuses on interests in goods. It not only attempts to refine the definition of "security interest" but also examines the legal treatment of nonpossessory interests in goods that are not "security interests." Section 2 addresses transactions in accounts and chattel paper. Certain transactions in those kinds of rights to payment create "security interests" under Article 9, even though they do not "secure[ ] payment or performance of an obligation." See UCC 1–201(37) (3d sentence); UCC 9–102(1)(b). Finally, Section 3 looks at transactions that Article 9 excludes, even though they do create security interests.

SECTION 1. BAILMENTS

Introductory Note

Much of Article 9 addresses problems that may arise when one person claims an interest in goods in the possession of another. Secured transactions are not the only occasion for nonpossessory interests in goods. These interests arise in a wide variety of settings. Individuals often leave goods with third parties: watches are repaired; clothing is cleaned; tools are loaned to neighbors; film is developed. Commercial transactions, too, often give rise to nonpossessory interests: grain is stored and milled; cattle are fattened in feed lots and sold; metals are refined; construction equipment is leased.

Many of these interests may pose problems similar to those posed by nonpossessory security interests: they may be sham transactions; they may create "ostensible ownership" problems. See generally Chapter 11, Section 2(A), supra. Part 3 of Article 9 contains the Article's "solution" to the problems of nonpossessory security interests. As you know, security interests as to which no public notice has been given generally are unperfected, see UCC 9–302(1), and unperfected security interests generally are subordinate to the rights of third parties who claim an interest in the collateral. See UCC 9–301(1); UCC 9–312. See also Chapter 13, infra. To what extent does the Code impose this solution on transactions that create nonpossessory interests in goods but are not for security? To what extent should it do so? These are two of the questions that are the focus of this Section.

The law applicable to most nonpossessory interests in goods contains no public notice requirement akin to the Article 9 perfection rules. Rather, third parties take subject to a nonpossessory interest even if the holder of that interest does not publicize it. But see, e.g., UCC 2–403(2) (buyer in ordinary course takes rights of entruster of goods) (discussed in Chapter 1, supra). Debtors and secured parties desirous of avoiding the application of Article 9's filing and priority rules may be tempted to document a secured transaction in another way (say, as a lease). Similarly, a secured party who has failed to perfect a security interest may argue in retrospect that the transaction does not create a security interest and so the failure to file was irrelevant.

The law distinguishes between security interests and most other nonpossessory interests in goods not only with respect to perfection and priority rules but also with regard to the enforcement rights of the person not in possession. Article 9 affords debtors certain rights and imposes upon secured parties certain duties that cannot be waived. See UCC 9–501(3); Chapter 15, infra. The law applicable to other, similar transactions may afford no such protection to the person in possession of the goods. This disparity, too, may prompt secured parties to assert that their interests are not security interests.

The scope provisions of Article 9 preclude debtors and secured parties from overriding the substantive provisions of the Article (whether relating to the secured party's remedies or the relative rights of competing claimants to the collateral) by characterizing what is in essence a security interest as something else. In order to determine whether to reject the parties' characterization of a particular transaction, however, one must have an idea of what a security interest is.

Many of the transactions that create nonpossessory interests in goods are bailments. This Section examines several common types of bailments with a view toward determining (i) whether the transaction creates a "security interest" and (ii) if not, what law regulates the nonpossessory interest.

(A) Leases

Introductory Notes

(1) **The Role of Personal Property Leasing.** A firm that wishes to acquire equipment may be reluctant (or unable) to pay with cash on hand. One option is to acquire the equipment on secured credit. Even a firm with strong credit may prefer, however, to acquire the use of the equipment by entering into a lease. The following are among the reasons that prompt firms to lease goods: the lessor may be able to purchase equipment in large quantity at advantageous rates and may have efficient outlets for disposing of used equipment; the lessor (Xerox and IBM are examples) may have special skill in servicing technical equipment; a leasing arrangement may give the lessee a higher tax deduction than the rate of depreciation on equipment that it purchases; the lessee may have promised other creditors (e.g., in a credit agreement or bond indenture) that it would not grant security interests in its property. In some situations leasing has tax advantages for the lessor, who is able to pass a portion of the tax savings along to the lessee. For example, a lessor who has substantial income from other sources may wish to take advantage of tax deductions for accelerated depreciation.

These various factors have produced in recent decades a tremendous growth in equipment leasing. To appreciate the significance of this growth, consider Professor Boss's observations:

> In the thirty-five years since the adoption of the Code, the leasing industry, which was in its infancy during the drafting

of the Code, has grown explosively and now represents a sizeable sector of our economy. Equipment leasing grew at an estimated rate of thirty percent a year during the 1950s and has exceeded the thirty percent per annum growth rate several times during the past two decades. In the five-year period from 1975 to 1980, the total original cost of industrial equipment on lease in the United States rose from 80 billion dollars to 150 billion dollars. The volume of new equipment leases in the United States rose steadily from 43.5 billion dollars in 1980 to an estimated 74.4 billion dollars in 1984. Today, approximately twenty percent of all capital investment in the United States is directly attributable to equipment leasing, with over 310 billion dollars in lease receivables currently outstanding. In 1986 alone over 90 billion dollars of equipment was financed through leasing in the United States. Indeed, of the new equipment currently accepted for delivery in the United States, approximately one-third is leased.

Boss, The History of Article 2A: A Lesson for Practitioner and Scholar Alike, 39 Ala. L.Rev. 575, 576–77 (1988).

Leasing also plays an important role in the acquisition of consumer goods. These transactions range from week-to-week "rent to own" leases of television sets to long-term leases of expensive automobiles.

(2) The Legal Consequences of Distinguishing Leases From Secured Transactions. One might argue that the lessor's interest under a lease "secures payment or performance of an obligation" and is therefore always a "security interest" within the meaning of UCC 1–201(37): If the lessee fails to comply with its obligations under the lease, e.g., fails to pay rent, then the lessor may retake the goods. Despite this potentially broad reading of "security interest," the second, third, and fourth paragraphs of the definition in UCC 1–201(37), which are devoted to distinguishing between leases and security interests, make clear that not every lease creates a security interest.[1]

How does one determine whether Article 9 applies to a particular transaction that has been documented as a lease? Before answering this important question, it is useful to have in mind some of the consequences of the distinction between putative leases that are within the scope of Article 9, and other ("true") leases.

A lease for security is nothing other than an Article 9 secured transaction dressed up in lease terminology. The "lessee," who is obligated to make periodic payments, is an Article 9 "debtor." The "lessor," who is entitled to payment and who enjoys the right to recove.

---

1. The recent amendment of UCC 1–201(37) (see the discussion of Article 2A, infra) deleted the reference to leases that are "intended as security." Although UCC 9–102(2), which addresses the scope of Article 9, continues to contain the phrase, one can be certain that the drafters intended to eliminate the parties' intentions as a factor in determining whether a putative lease creates a security interest. See UCC 1–201(37), Comment 37 (seventh paragraph); Note (2) on Distinguishing Leases from Secured Transactions, infra.

the leased goods upon the "lessee's" default, is an Article 9 secured party. The attachment, perfection, priority, and remedial rules of Article 9 apply to the transaction, just as if the parties had used the secured transaction form.

In contrast, a "true lease" is not an Article 9 transaction. Article 2A governs the rights of the lessor and lessee in a true lease transaction. To some extent, Article 2A also governs the rights of third parties. Article 2A was added to the UCC in 1987 and has yet to be as widely adopted as the preceding amendments. The Article derives in large part from Article 2. The 1987 version of Article 2A gave rise to substantial criticism, some of which was addressed in the nonuniform versions of Article 2A that were enacted in a few states, including California. See Flick, Article 2A—Leases, 44 Bus. Law. 1501 (1989). The dispute between critics and sponsors of Article 2A delayed its widespread enactment. In 1990 the UCC's sponsors amended the Official Text to the general satisfaction of the critics. California has since adopted the uniform version, and widespread enactment should be forthcoming in the near term. Until Article 2A is enacted in a particular jurisdiction, the rights of parties to a lease transaction will continue to be governed by the common law, which often borrows from Articles 2 and 9, and occasional nonuniform statutes. In fashioning the common law, a court may look to Article 2A for guidance even if the Article has not been enacted in that jurisdiction.

The need to distinguish between a lease for security and a true lease arises in a variety of contexts. Of primary importance is that the "lessor's" interest in goods under a lease for security is an Article 9 security interest. To protect its interest against the claims of third parties, the "lessor" must file a financing statement; otherwise, the "lessor's" security interest will be unperfected and the competing claimant probably will take priority over the "lessor." See UCC 9–301(1). (Perfecting by taking possession of the goods is an alternative to filing, but it is of virtually no practical use in a transaction, like a lease for security, which is characterized by the debtor ("lessee") using the goods.) In contrast, absent a statute to the contrary, filing is irrelevant as to true leases.

If the "lessee" under a lease for security enters bankruptcy, the "lessor's" failure to file a financing statement will result in the avoidance of the "lessor's" interest by the bankruptcy trustee. See BC 544(a)(1) (discussed in Chapter 14, Section 2, infra). The failure of a lessor under a true lease to file a financing statement will not affect the lessor's rights in bankruptcy.

Another consequence of the application of Article 9 to leases for security is that the "lessor" under such a lease must comply with Part 5 of Article 9 upon the "lessee's" default. (Part 5 is discussed in Chapter 15, infra.) In contrast, the rights and obligations of a lessor under a true lease upon the lessee's default are described in UCC 2A–523 to 2A–532. In those jurisdictions where Article 2A has not yet been enacted, the rights and obligations of a lessor under a true lease are uncertain; in particular, case law is confused and conflicting in its resolution of such basic issues as whether the lessor who repossesses upon the lessee's default must dispose of the goods and the measure of the lessor's damages.

UCC 1–201(37), which defines "security interest," affords some guidance on the question whether a particular lease is a security interest subject to Article 9 or is a lease (i.e., a "true lease") subject to Article 2A. Coincident with the promulgation of Article 2A in 1987, UCC 1–201(37) was amended to clarify the distinction between secured transactions and leases. Despite its apparent complexity, the revised definition has met with general approval.

The following Problems address the lease-security interest distinction.

Problem 1. Smith and Jones entered into a written agreement concerning a machine having a useful life of ten years. No financing statement was filed with respect to the machine. Six months after Jones took possession, Lean, one of Jones's creditors, acquired an execution lien on the machine. Under which of the following scenarios, if any, is Lean's lien senior to Smith's interest? In any case where Lean's lien is senior, what, if anything, could Smith have done to avoid the loss?

(a) Smith agreed to sell the machine to Jones for $120,000, payable $10,000 monthly. Smith retained title until Jones made all 12 payments. See UCC 1–201(37) (2d sentence); UCC 9–102(2); UCC 9–301(1)(b); UCC 9–302(1); UCC 2A–307(1).

(b) Smith agreed to lease the machine to Jones for one year at $10,000 per month. The lease gives Jones the option to buy the machine at the end of the year for $10.

(c) Smith agreed to lease the machine to Jones for one year at $1,200 per month. The lease gives Jones the option to buy the machine at the end of the year for $110,000.

(d) Smith agreed to lease the machine to Jones for ten years at $1,200 per month. At the end of the lease term, Jones must return the goods to Smith.

(e) Smith agreed to lease the machine to Jones for one year at $10,000 per month, with an option to renew the lease at $1 per month for each of the following nine years. At the end of the lease term, Jones must return the goods to Smith.

(f) Smith agreed to lease the machine to Jones for ten years at $10,000 per month for the first year and $1 per month thereafter. At the end of the lease term, Jones must return the goods to Smith.

Problem 2. Grace agreed to lease a bread wrapping machine to Royer's Bakery for one year at $10,000 per month. Royer's has the option to purchase the machine at the end of the lease term for $1.

Royer's also has the right to terminate the lease at any time without penalty, provided it gives thirty days' advance notice to Grace. No financing statement was filed with respect to the machine.

(a) At the end of the first month of the lease, Lean acquired an execution lien on Royer's interest in the machine. Is the execution lien senior or junior to Grace's interest?

(b) Assume that the transaction creates a security interest in favor of Grace and that Royer's defaults after making only one monthly payment. If the property is sold pursuant to UCC 9–504 for $110,000, how are the proceeds of the sale to be allocated? (Under UCC 9–504(2), the debtor is entitled to any surplus after satisfaction of the secured indebtedness and any related costs of sale. What is the size of the secured indebtedness?)

(c) Would your answer to part (a) change if Lean acquired the lien during the eleventh month?

(d) If you believe that Grace's interest is junior in part (a) or part (c), what could Grace have done to avoid the loss?

Problem 3. Manufacturer agreed to lease a $6 million aircraft to Airline for three years at $2.3 million a year. Airline has the option to purchase the aircraft at the end of the lease term for $500,000.

(a) Is Manufacturer an Article 9 secured party?

(b) Assume that the transaction creates a security interest in favor of Manufacturer and that Airline defaults after making the payment for year two.

(i) If the property is sold pursuant to UCC 9–504 for $4 million, how are the proceeds of the sale to be allocated? (Under UCC 9–504(2), the debtor is entitled to any surplus after satisfaction of the secured indebtedness and any related costs of sale. What is the size of the secured indebtedness?)

(ii) If the property is sold pursuant to UCC 9–504 for $2.2 million, what is the size of Manufacturer's deficiency claim? I.e., how much more, if anything, does Airline owe Manufacturer? See UCC 9–504(2) (debtor is liable for any deficiency).

Problem 4. Developer was constructing a new office building. A local ordinance required Developer to install sprinklers throughout the building. Developer agreed to lease a sprinkler system from Wetco for three years at $1,000 per month. No financing statement was filed with respect to the sprinkler system. Developer has the option to purchase the system at the end of the lease term for $10,000. If Developer does not exercise the purchase option, then it must return the system to Wetco. To remove the system from the building, Developer would incur costs (including the costs of repairing the damage to the building caused by the removal) totalling approximately $50,000.

Lean acquires an execution lien on Developer's interest in the sprinkler system.

(a) Is the execution lien senior or junior to Wetco's interest?

(b) If you believe that Lean's lien is senior in part (a), what, if anything, could Wetco have done to avoid the loss?

IN RE MARHOEFER PACKING CO.[*]

United States Court of Appeals, Seventh Circuit, 1982.
674 F.2d 1139.

PELL, CIRCUIT JUDGE. This appeal involves a dispute between the trustee of the bankrupt Marhoefer Packing Company, Inc., ("Marhoefer") and Robert Reiser & Company, Inc., ("Reiser") over certain equipment held by Marhoefer at the time of bankruptcy. The issue presented is whether the written agreement between Marhoefer and Reiser covering the equipment is a true lease under which Reiser is entitled to reclaim its property from the bankrupt estate, or whether it is actually a lease intended as security in which case Reiser's failure to file a financing statement to perfect its interest renders it subordinate to the trustee.

I

In December of 1976, Marhoefer Packing Co., Inc., of Muncie, Indiana, entered into negotiations with Reiser, a Massachusetts based corporation engaged in the business of selling and leasing food processing equipment, for the acquisition of one or possibly two Vemag Model 3007-1 Continuous Sausage Stuffers. Reiser informed Marhoefer that the units could be acquired by outright purchase, conditional sale contract or lease. Marhoefer ultimately acquired two sausage stuffers from Reiser. It purchased one under a conditional sale contract. Pursuant to the contract, Reiser retained a security interest in the machine, which it subsequently perfected by filing a financing statement with the Indiana Secretary of State. Title to that stuffer is not here in dispute. The other stuffer was delivered to Marhoefer under a written "Lease Agreement."

The Lease Agreement provided for monthly payments of $665.00 over a term of 48 months. The last nine months payments, totaling $5,985.00, were payable upon execution of the lease. If at the end of the lease term the machine was to be returned, it was to be shipped prepaid to Boston or similar destination "in the same condition as when received, reasonable wear and tear resulting from proper use alone excepted, and fully crated." The remaining terms and conditions of the agreement were as follows:

    1. Any State or local taxes and/or excises are for the account of the Buyer.

[* The court's citations are to the applicable pre–1972 version of the Code.]

2. The equipment shall at all times be located at

> Marhoefer Packing Co., Inc.
>
> 1500 North Elm & 13th Street
>
> Muncie, Indiana

and shall not be removed from said location without the written consent of Robert Reiser & Co. The equipment can only be used in conjunction with the manufacture of meat or similar products unless written consent is given by Robert Reiser & Co.

3. The equipment will carry a ninety-day guarantee for workmanship and materials and shall be maintained and operated safely and carefully in conformity with the instructions issued by our operators and the maintenance manual. Service and repairs of the equipment after the ninety-day period will be subject to a reasonable and fair charge.

4. If, after due warning, our maintenance instructions should be violated repeatedly, Robert Reiser & Co. will have the right to cancel the lease contract on seven days notice and remove the said equipment. In that case, lease fees would be refunded pro rata.

5. It is mutually agreed that in case of lessee, Marhoefer Packing Co., Inc., violating any of the above conditions, or shall default in the payment of any lease charge hereunder, or shall become bankrupt, make or execute any assignment or become party to any instrument or proceedings for the benefit of its creditors, Robert Reiser & Co. shall have the right at any time without trespass, to enter upon the premises and remove the aforesaid equipment, and if removed, lessee agrees to pay Robert Reiser & Co. the total lease fees, including all installments due or to become due for the full unexpired term of this lease agreement and including the cost for removal of the equipment and counsel fees incurred in collecting sums due hereunder.

6. It is agreed that the equipment shall remain personal property of Robert Reiser & Co. and retain its character as such no matter in what manner affixed or attached to the premises.

In a letter accompanying the lease, Reiser added two option provisions to the agreement. The first provided that at the end of the four-year term, Marhoefer could purchase the stuffer for $9,968.00. In the alternative, it could elect to renew the lease for an additional four years at an annual rate of $2,990.00, payable in advance. At the conclusion of the second four-year term, Marhoefer would be allowed to purchase the stuffer for one dollar.

Marhoefer never exercised either option. Approximately one year after the Vemag stuffer was delivered to its plant, it ceased all payments under the lease and shortly thereafter filed a voluntary petition in bankruptcy. On July 12, 1978, the trustee of the bankrupt corporation applied to the bankruptcy court for leave to sell the stuffer free and clear of all liens on the ground that the "Lease Agreement" was in fact a lease intended as security within the meaning of the Uniform Commercial Code ("Code") and that Reiser's failure to perfect its interest as required by Article 9 of the Code rendered it subordinate to that of the trustee. Reiser responded with an answer and counterclaim in which it alleged that the agreement was in fact a true lease, Marhoefer was in default under the lease, and its equipment should therefore be returned.

Following a trial on this issue, the bankruptcy court concluded that the agreement between Marhoefer and Reiser was in fact a true lease and ordered the trustee to return the Vemag stuffer to Reiser. The trustee appealed to the district court, which reversed on the ground that the bankruptcy court had erred as a matter of law in finding the agreement to be a true lease. We now reverse the judgment of the district court.

II

The dispute in this case centers on section 1–201(37) of the Uniform Commercial Code, I.C. 26–1–1–201.[1] In applying this section, the bankruptcy court concluded that "the presence of the option to renew the lease for an additional four years and to acquire the Vemag Stuffer at the conclusion of the second four-year term by the payment of One Dollar ($1.00) did not, in and of itself, make the lease one intended for security."

The district court disagreed. It held that the presence of an option to purchase the stuffer for one dollar gave rise to a conclusive presumption under clause (b) of section 1–201(37) that the lease was intended as security. Although it acknowledged that the option to purchase the stuffer for only one dollar would not have come into play unless Marhoefer chose to renew the lease for an additional four-year term, the district court concluded that this fact did not require a different result. "It would be anomalous," said the court, "to rule that the lease was a genuine lease for four years after its creation but was one intended for security eight years after its creation."

Reiser, relying on Peter F. Coogan's detailed analysis of section 1–201(37), Coogan, Hogan & Vagts, Secured Transactions Under the Uniform Commercial Code, ch. 4A, (1981) (hereinafter "Secured Transactions Under U.C.C."), argues that the district court erred in constru-

---

1. Section 1–201(37) of the Uniform Commercial Code states:

'Security interest' means an interest in personal property or fixtures which secures payment or performance of an obligation.... Unless a lease or consignment is intended as security, reservation of title thereunder is not a 'security interest' but a consignment is in any event subject to the provisions on consignment sales. Whether a lease is intended as security is to be determined by the facts of each case; however, (a) the inclusion of an option, to purchase does not of itself make the lease one intended for security, and (b) an agreement that upon compliance with the terms of the lease the lessee shall become or has the option to become the owner of the property for no additional consideration or for a nominal consideration does make the lease one intended for security.

ing clause (b) of that section as creating a conclusive presumption that a lease is intended as security where the lease contains an option for the lessee to become the owner of the leased property for no additional consideration or for only nominal consideration. It contends that by interpreting clause (b) in this way, the district court totally ignored the first part of that sentence which states that "[w]hether a lease is intended as security is to be determined by the facts of each case." Reiser claims that because the totality of facts surrounding the transaction indicate that the lease was not intended as security, notwithstanding the presence of the option to purchase the stuffer for one dollar, the district court erred in reversing the bankruptcy court's determination.

We agree that the district court erred in concluding that because the Lease Agreement contained an option for Marhoefer to purchase the Vemag stuffer at the end of a second four-year term, it was conclusively presumed to be a lease intended as security. However, in our view, the district court's error lies not in its reading of clause (b) of section 1–201(37) as giving rise to such a presumption,[2] but rather in its conclusion that clause (b) applies under the facts of this case.

The primary issue to be decided in determining whether a lease is "intended as security" is whether it is in effect a conditional sale in which the "lessor" retains an interest in the "leased" goods as security for the purchase price. 1C Secured Transactions Under U.C.C. § 29A.05[1][C], p. 2939. By defining the term "security interest" to include a lease intended as security, the drafters of the Code intended such disguised security interests to be governed by the same rules that apply to other security interests. *See* U.C.C., Art. 9. In this respect, section 1–201(37) represents the drafter's refusal to recognize form over substance.

Clearly, where a lease is structured so that the lessee is contractually bound to pay rent over a set period of time at the conclusion of which he automatically or for only nominal consideration becomes the owner of the leased goods, the transaction is in substance a conditional sale and should be treated as such. It is to this type of lease that clause (b) properly applies. Here, however, Marhoefer was under no contractual obligation to pay rent until such time as the option to purchase the Vemag stuffer for one dollar was to arise. In fact, in order to acquire that option. Marhoefer would have had to exercise its earlier option to renew the lease for a second four-year term and pay Reiser an addition-

---

2. This reading of section 1–201(37) is not without support in the reported cases. In Peco v. Hartbauer Tool & Die Co., 262 Or. 573, 500 P.2d 708 (1972), for example, the court noted that

[a]t first glance the provisions of . . . section [1–201(37)] may be somewhat confusing, probably because they are stated in the inverse order of importance. However, upon a careful reading of the entire section it is clear that the first question to be answered is that posed by

clause (b)—whether the lessee may obtain the property for no additional consideration or for a nominal consideration. If so, the lease is intended fo: security. If not, it is then necessary to determine "by the facts of each case" whether . . . the fact that the lease contains an option to purchase "does not (of itself) make the lease one intended for security." Id. at 575, 500 P.2d at 709–10, quoting Ore.Rev.Stat. § 71–2010(37) (1969).

al $11,960 in "rent." In effect, Marhoefer was given a right to terminate the agreement after the first four years and cease making payments without that option ever becoming operative.

Despite this fact, the district court concluded as a matter of law that the lease was intended as security. It held that, under clause (b) of section 1–201(37), a lease containing an option for the lessee to purchase the leased goods for nominal consideration is conclusively presumed to be one intended as security. This presumption applies, the court concluded, regardless of any other options the lease may contain.

We think the district court's reading of clause (b) is in error. In our view, the conclusive presumption provided under clause (b) applies only where the option to purchase for nominal consideration necessarily arises upon compliance with the lease. *See* 1C Secured Transactions Under U.C.C. § 29.05[2][b] pp. 2947–49. It does not apply where the lessee has the right to terminate the lease before that option arises with no further obligation to continue paying rent. But see In re Vaillancourt, supra, 7 U.C.C. Rep. 748; In re Royers Bakery, Inc., 1 U.C.C. Rep. 342 (Bankr.E.D.Pa.1963). For where the lessee has the right to terminate the transaction, it is not a conditional sale.

Moreover, to hold that a lease containing such an option is intended as security, even though the lessee has no contractual obligation to pay the full amount contemplated by the agreement, would lead to clearly erroneous results under other provisions of the Code. Under section 9–506 of the Code, for example, a debtor in default on his obligation to a secured party has a right to redeem the collateral by tendering full payment of that obligation. The same right is also enjoyed by a lessee under a lease intended as security. A lessee who defaults on a lease intended as security is entitled to purchase the leased goods by paying the full amount of his obligation under the lease. But if the lessee has the right to terminate the lease at any time during the lease term, his obligation under the lease may be only a small part of the total purchase price of the goods leased. To afford the lessee a right of redemption under such circumstances would clearly be wrong. There is no evidence that the drafters of the Code intended such a result.

We therefore hold that while section 1–201(37)(b) does provide a conclusive test of when a lease is intended as security, that test does not apply in every case in which the disputed lease contains an option to purchase for nominal or no consideration. An option of this type makes a lease on intended as security only when it necessarily arises upon compliance with the terms of the lease.

Applying section 1–201(37), so construed, to the facts of this case, it is clear that the district court erred in concluding that the possibility of Marhoefer's purchasing the stuffer for one dollar at the conclusion of a second four-year term was determinative. Because Marhoefer could have fully complied with the lease without that option ever arising, the district court was mistaken in thinking that the existence of that option alone made the lease a conditional sale. Certainly, if Marhoefer had elected to renew the lease for another term, in which case the nominal purchase option would necessarily have arisen, then the clause (b) test would apply.[6] But that is not the case we are faced with here. Marhoefer was not required to make any payments beyond the first four years. The fact that, at the conclusion of that term, it could have elected to renew the lease and obtain an option to purchase the stuffer for one dollar at the end of the second term does not transform the original transaction into a conditional sale.

This fact does not end our inquiry under clause (b), however, for the trustee also argues that, even if the district court erred in considering the one dollar purchase option as determinative, the lease should nevertheless be considered a conditional sale because the initial option price of $9,968 is also nominal when all of the operative facts are properly considered. We agree that if the clause (b) test is to apply at all in this case, this is the option that must be considered. For this is the option that was to arise automatically upon Marhoefer's compliance with the lease. We do not agree, however, that under the circumstances presented here the $9,968 option price can properly be considered nominal.

It is true that an option price may be more than a few dollars and still be considered nominal within the meaning of section 1–201(37). Because clause (b) speaks of nominal "consideration" and not a nominal "sum" or "amount," it has been held to apply not only where the option price is very small in absolute terms, but also where the price is insubstantial in relation to the fair market value of the leased goods at the time the option arises.[7]

Here, however, the evidence revealed that the initial option price of $9,968 was not nominal even under this standard. George Vetie, Reiser's treasurer and the person chiefly responsible for the terms of the lease, testified at trial that the purchase price for the Vemag stuffer at the time the parties entered into the transaction was $33,225. He testified that the initial option price of $9,968 was arrived at by taking thirty percent of the purchase price, which was what he felt a four-year-old Vemag stuffer would be worth based on Reiser's past experience.

The trustee, relying on the testimony of its expert appraiser, argues that in fact the stuffer would have been worth between eighteen

---

6. Reiser concedes that had Marhoefer elected to renew the lease after the first term, the transaction would have been transformed into a sale.

7. The trustee argues that the determination of whether the option price is nominal is to be made by comparing it to the fair market value of the equipment at the time the parties enter into the lease, instead of the date the option arises. Although some courts have applied such a test, In re Wheatland Electric Products Co., 237 F.Supp. 820 (W.D.Pa.1964); In re Oak Mfg., Inc., 6 U.C.C. Rep. 1273 (Bankr. S.D.N.Y.1969), the better approach is to compare the option price with the fair market value of the goods at the time the option was to be exercised. In re Universal Medical Services, Inc., 8 U.C.C. Rep. 614 (Bankr.E.D.Pa.1970). See 1C Secured Transactions Under U.C.C. § 29A.05[2][b].

and twenty thousand dollars at the end of the first four-year term. Because the initial option price is substantially less than this amount, he claims that it is nominal within the meaning of clause (b) and the lease is therefore one intended as security.

Even assuming this appraisal to be accurate, an issue on which the bankruptcy court made no finding, we would not find the initial option price of $9,968 so small by comparison that the clause (b) presumption would apply. While it is difficult to state any bright line percentage test for determining when an option price could properly be considered nominal as compared to the fair market value of the leased goods, an option price of almost ten thousand dollars, which amounts to fifty percent of the fair market value, is not nominal by any standard.

Furthermore, in determining whether an option price is nominal, the proper figure to compare it with is not the actual fair market value of the leased goods at the time the option arises, but their fair market value at that time as anticipated by the parties when the lease is signed. 1C Secured Transactions Under U.C.C. § 29A.05[2][b], p. 2953. Here, for example, Vetie testified that his estimate of the fair market value of a four-year-old Vemag stuffer was based on records from a period of time in which the economy was relatively stable. Since that time, a high rate of inflation has caused the machines to lose their value more slowly. As a result, the actual fair market value of a machine may turn out to be significantly more than the parties anticipated it would be several years earlier. When this occurs, the lessee's option to purchase the leased goods may be much more favorable than either party intended, but it does not change the true character of the transaction.

We conclude, therefore, that neither option to purchase contained in the lease between Marhoefer and Reiser gives rise to a conclusive presumption under section 1–201(37)(b) that the lease is one intended as security. This being so, we now turn to the other facts surrounding the transaction.

III

Although section 1–201(37) states that "[w]hether a lease is intended as security is to be determined by the facts of each case," it is completely silent as to what facts, other than the option to purchase, are to be considered in making that determination. Facts that the courts have found relevant include the total amount of rent the lessee is required to pay under the lease, Chandler Leasing Corp. v. Samoset Associates, supra, 24 U.C.C. Rep. at 516; whether the lessee acquires any equity in the leased property, Matter of Tillery, 571 F.2d 1361, 1365 (5th Cir.1978); the useful life of the leased goods, In re Lakeshore Transit–Kenosha, Inc., 7 U.C.C. Rep. 607 (Bankr.E.D.Wis.1969); the nature of the lessor's business, In re Industro Transistor Corp., 14 U.C.C. Rep. 522, 523 (Bankr.E.D.N.Y.1973); and the payment of taxes, insurance and other charges normally imposed on ownership, Rainier National Bank v. Inland Machinery Co., 29 Wash.App. 725, 631 P.2d

389 (1981). *See generally* 1C Secured Transactions Under U.C.C. § 29A.05[2][e]; and Annot., 76 ALR 3d 11 (1977). Consideration of the facts of this case in light of these factors leads us to conclude that the lease in question was not intended as security.

First, Marhoefer was under no obligation to pay the full purchase price for the stuffer. Over the first four-year term, its payments under the lease were to have amounted to $31,920. Although this amount may not be substantially less than the original purchase price of $33,225 in absolute terms, it becomes so when one factors in the interest rate over four years that would have been charged had Marhoefer elected to purchase the machine under a conditional sale contract.[8] The fact that the total amount of rent Marhoefer was to pay under the lease was substantially less than that amount shows that a sale was not intended. 1 Secured Transactions Under U.C.C. § 4A.01.

It is also significant that the useful life of the Vemag stuffer exceeded the term of the lease. An essential characteristic of a true lease is that there be something of value to return to the lessor after the term. 1C Secured Transactions Under U.C.C. § 29A.05[2][c], p. 2959. Where the term of the lease is substantially equal to the life of the leased property such that there will be nothing of value to return at the end of the lease, the transaction is in essence a sale. In re Lakeshore Transit–Kenosha, Inc., supra. Here, the evidence revealed that the useful life of a Vemag stuffer was eight to ten years.

Finally, the bankruptcy court specifically found that "there was no express or implied provision in the lease agreement dated February 28, 1977, which gave Marhoefer any equity interest in the leased Vemag stuffer." This fact clearly reveals the agreement between Marhoefer and Reiser to be a true lease. See Hawkland, The Impact of the Uniform Commercial Code on Equipment Leasing, 1972 Ill. L. Forum 446, 453 ("The difference between a true lease and a security transaction lies in whether the lessee acquires an equity of ownership through his rent payments."). Had Marhoefer remained solvent and elected not to exercise its option to renew its lease with Reiser, it would have received nothing for its previous lease payments. And in order to exercise that option, Marhoefer would have had to pay what Reiser anticipated would then be the machine's fair market value. An option of this kind is not the mark of a lease intended as security. See In re Alpha Creamery Company, 4 U.C.C. Rep. 794, 798 (Bankr.W.D.Mich. 1967).

Although Marhoefer was required to pay state and local taxes and the cost of repairs, this fact does not require a contrary result. Costs such as taxes, insurance and repairs are necessarily borne by one party

---

8. The bankruptcy court found that Reiser was originally willing to sell Marhoefer the stuffer under a conditional sale contract the terms of which would have been $7,225 down and monthly installments of $1,224 over a twenty-four month period. The total payments under such an agreement would have amounted to $36,-601, substantially more than the amount Marhoefer was required to pay over four years under the lease.

or the other. They reflect less the true character of the transaction than the strength of the parties' respective bargaining positions. See also Rainier National Bank, supra, 631 P.2d at 395 ("The lessor is either going to include those costs within the rental charge or agree to a lower rent if the lessee takes responsibility for them.").

IV

We conclude from the foregoing that the district court erred in its application of section 1–201(37) of the Uniform Commercial Code to the facts of this case. Neither the option to purchase the Vemag stuffer for one dollar at the conclusion of a second four-year term, nor the initial option to purchase it for $9,968 after the first four years, gives rise to a conclusive presumption under clause (b) of section 1–201(37) that the lease is intended as security. From all of the facts surrounding the transaction, we conclude that the agreement between Marhoefer and Reiser is a true lease. The judgment of the district court is therefore reversed.

Notes on Distinguishing Leases From Secured Transactions [2]

(1) The "Factors" Approach Under Revised UCC 1–201(37). Few commercial law issues have spawned as much litigation and provided as much uncertainty as the determination whether a purported lease of goods creates a security interest or a true lease. The pre–1987 version of UCC 1–201(37) stated that "[w]hether a lease is intended as security is to be determined by the facts of each case...." Although the courts usually take cognizance of the facts of the cases before them, they often exhibit great difficulty in determining which facts are relevant and which are not. The scores of reported cases on the subject identify no fewer than two dozen factors that courts have used in drawing the lease/security interest distinction, most of which are consistent with both a lease and a secured transaction.

Revised UCC 1–201(37) does not draw a precise line between true leases and security interests. Instead, it continues to state that whether a transaction creates a lease or security interest is determined by the facts of each case. Nevertheless, the revised section goes a long way toward clarifying the distinction between the two transactions. One of its major contributions is to state unequivocally that some of the factors upon which courts have relied in holding that a transaction creates a security interest do not, of themselves, create a security interest. These factors, which appear in UCC 1–201(37) (second a)-(e), are:

• the discounted present value of the rental stream equals or exceeds the fair market value of the goods at the time the lease is entered into (often known as a "full-payout" lease);

2. These Notes are drawn substantially from Harris, The Interface Between Articles 2A and 9 Under the Official Text and the California Amendments, 22 UCC L.J. 99, 104–10 (1989).

• provisions whereby the lessee assumes risk of loss of the goods, or agrees to pay taxes, insurance, filing, recording, or registration fees, or service or maintenance costs with respect to the goods (these provisions are commonly found in "net" leases);

• an option for the lessee to renew the lease, including an option for a fixed rent that equals or exceeds the reasonably predictable fair market rent at the time the option is to be performed; and

• an option for the lessee to become the owner of the goods, including an option for a fixed price that equals or exceeds the reasonably predictable fair market value of the goods at the time the option is to be performed.

(2) **Revised UCC 1–201(37) Eliminates Language of Intention.** A second major contribution of revised UCC 1–201(37) is the substitution of the term "security interest" for the phrase "intended as security." That phrase prompted some courts to distinguish between leases and security interests by reference to the subjective intentions of the parties rather than by analysis of the economics of the transaction. Because the characterization of the transaction may affect the rights of third parties, reliance upon the subjective intentions of the parties to the lease transaction is inappropriate. Rather, as *Marhoefer* recognizes, the economic substance of the transaction should determine its characterization.

(3) **The Importance of the Lessee's Contractual Obligation.** In explaining the difference between a lease and a security interest, revised UCC 1–201(37) focuses on economic realities. The revised section sets forth four specific cases in which a transaction creates a security interest. Each case is characterized by two elements, the first of which is the existence of a debt owed by the "lessee" to the "lessor." Without a debt to secure, there can be no security interest. Revised UCC 1–201(37) states this point as follows: "the consideration the lessee is to pay the lessor ... is an obligation for the term of the lease not subject to termination by the lessee."

(4) **The Importance of a Meaningful Residual Interest for the Lessor.** In addition to an unconditional obligation to pay, each secured transaction described in revised UCC 1–201(37) includes a second element—the absence of a meaningful residual interest for the lessor. In a true lease, the lessor is the owner of the goods. The lessee acquires the right to use the goods for a limited period of time. When the lease term ends, the lessor expects the property to be returned so that the lessor can use it, relet it, or otherwise dispose of it. The lessor's interest in the goods after expiration, cancellation, or termination of the lease is called the "lessor's residual interest." See UCC 2A–103(1)(q). In contrast, if the lease affords the lessee the right to use the goods for their entire economic life, then the lessee (and not the lessor)

is in effect the owner of the goods. The goods have been sold to the lessee, and the lessor does not expect to recover them unless the lessee fails to pay for them. In other words, the lessor has only a security interest.

Determining whether the lessor retains a meaningful residual interest in the goods can be difficult. Revised UCC 1–201(37) (first a)-(d) sets forth four specific cases in which the lessor lacks a meaningful residual interest and that, therefore, create security interests if the lessee has a noncancellable obligation to pay. These cases are:

• the original term of the lease equals or exceeds the remaining economic life of the goods;

• the lessee is bound to renew the lease for the remaining economic life of the goods or is bound to become the owner of the goods;

• the lessee has an option to renew the lease for the remaining economic life of the goods for no additional consideration or nominal additional consideration upon compliance with the lease agreement; and

• the lessee has an option to become the owner of the goods for no additional consideration or nominal additional consideration upon compliance with the lease agreement.

In the first two cases the lessee acquires the right to use the goods until the goods have no further economic life. At the end of the lease term or renewal term, the goods will have no value to the lessor, who therefore is a secured party.

The third and fourth cases address an issue with which the courts have grappled, with varying degrees of success, under pre–1987 UCC 1–201(37): the effect of renewal and purchase options. The fourth case follows pre–1987 UCC 1–201(37), and the third case is a variation on the same theme. But rather than refer to an option to become the owner, the third case refers to its equivalent—an option to renew the lease for the remaining economic life of the goods.

Although not specifically mentioned in revised UCC 1–201(37), the remedies that a "lease" affords to the "lessor" upon the "lessee's" default may deprive the "lessor" of its residual and thus be indicative of a secured transaction. Consider a lease that requires the lessor to sell the property upon the lessee's default and to apply the proceeds of sale to the lessee's obligation under the lease. The proceeds of the sale represent the value of the use of the goods for their entire useful life. The useful life consists of two portions—the portion covered by the lease term, for which the lessee bargained, and the portion commencing with the expiration of the lease, which the lessor retains as the lessor's residual interest. A lessor who credits to the lessee the entire amount of the proceeds received upon a sale following the lessee's default has, in effect, allocated none of the value of the property to its residual interest. This suggests that the lessor never enjoyed a residual interest (businesses rarely give away property for other than eleemosynary purposes), which, in turn, suggests that the transaction was not really a lease to begin with.

(5) The Meaning of "Nominal Consideration." Although pre–1987 UCC 1–201(37) spoke of "nominal consideration," it failed to define the term. When confronted with option prices that were not nominal in absolute terms, courts adopted a variety of tests, some of which overlapped.

Revised UCC 1–201(37) follows the better-reasoned case law in determining what consideration is nominal. UCC 1–201(37)(x) provides that "[a]dditional consideration is nominal if it is less than the lessee's reasonably predictable cost of performing under the lease agreement if the option is not exercised." "Reasonably predictable" costs "are to be determined with reference to the facts and circumstances at the time the transaction is entered into." UCC 1–201(37)(y). In other words, if it would appear to the parties at the outset of the lease that it would cost the lessee less to exercise the option than not to exercise it, one reasonably can assume that the lessee will exercise the option and become the owner of the goods, leaving no meaningful residual for the lessor.

Revised UCC 1–201(37)(x) also gives two examples of when additional consideration is not nominal:

• when the consideration for an option to renew is stated to be the fair market rent for the use of the goods for the term of the renewal, determined at the time the option is to be performed; and

• when the consideration for an option to become the owner of the goods is stated to be the fair market value of the goods determined at the time the option is to be performed.

A lessee faced with either of these "fair-market" options cannot necessarily be expected to exercise them and deprive the lessor of a residual interest.

(6) Dealing With Uncertainty. Although revised UCC 1–201(37) is likely to reduce the confusion and uncertainty that prevailed in the cases construing its predecessor, some uncertainty is likely to remain. This uncertainty is likely to derive not only from unavoidable infelicities of drafting but also from the decision of the drafters not to draw a precise line between security interests and leases or to create safe harbors for transactions that meet certain requirements. One can anticipate that close cases will arise in which, for example, reasonable people might differ over whether the lessee enjoys an option to become the owner of the goods for "nominal consideration." The extensive case law construing the pre–1987 version is likely to provide another source of uncertainty, as is the fact that many of the reported opinions emanate from bankruptcy courts, where the economics of litigating sometimes results in issues not being briefed as fully as they otherwise might be.

A cautious lessor may wish to plan in advance for the possibility that a court will recharacterize what the lessor believes to be a "lease" as a secured transaction. The lessor's principal concern in this regard is that, if its interest in the goods is held to be a security interest, then its failure to file a financing statement would render the security interest unperfected. The lessor might be reluctant to file a financing statement in the form approved by UCC 9–402(3); a court might consider the use of the terms "debtor" and "secured party" as evidence that the transaction creates a security interest. UCC 9–408, added to the UCC in 1972, suggests the solution: File a precautionary financing statement using the terms "lessee" and "lessor" instead of "debtor" and "secured party." The fact of filing "shall not of itself be a factor in determining whether or not the ... lease is intended as security.... However, if it is determined for other reasons that the ... lease is so intended, a security interest of the ... lessor which attaches to the ... leased goods is perfected by such filing." UCC 9–408.

Note on Leases and "Ostensible Ownership"

One way to eliminate much of the litigation over the lease-security interest distinction would have been to create a set of rules under which third parties take free of a lessor's interest as to which there had been no public notice (e.g., by filing a financing statement). Indeed, the imposition of a filing requirement for leases has been urged by prominent members of the current generation of Article 9 scholars as well as by some of those who were present at the creation of Article 9. These commentators generally have argued that a lessor's nonpossessory interest in leased goods gives rise to the same problems of "ostensible ownership" as does a nonpossessory security interest. From the perspective of third parties, goods held subject to lease appear identical to goods held subject to a security interest. Creditors of the lessee, like creditors of the Article 9 debtor, may be misled into thinking that the person in possession of the goods owns them free and clear. Why, then, should the rights of third parties differ, depending on whether the holder of the nonpossessory interest enjoys a meaningful residual interest and the unconditional right to receive payment for the goods?

The Article 2A drafting committee was not moved by this strong support for the imposition of a filing requirement for leases. Rather, Article 2A generally reflects the longstanding common-law rule that creditors of, and other transferees from, the lessee take subject to the lessor's interest in the goods, regardless of whether the lessor's interest has been publicized. See, e.g., UCC 2A–307(1) (creditors); UCC 2A–305 (buyers and sublessees).

Can one develop a principled justification of the drafting committee's decision? Is it simply a response to pressures brought by the leasing industry, or perhaps the reflection of unthinking conservatism? Consider the premise of those who would extend the filing system to leases: Do leases and secured transactions present equivalent problems of ostensible ownership? Were the Article 9 filing system to be abolished, would it be as difficult to determine whether a person in possession of goods in fact is the owner as it would be to determine whether the person owns them free of a security interest? The absence of an outcry from creditor groups suggests that the secret interests held by lessors of personal property have not resulted in losses to third parties claiming through lessees.

Imposing a filing requirement is easier than articulating the consequences that flow from a failure to file. For example, would the non-filing lessor lose its residual interest, which it may never have agreed to convey and which may be of substantial value relative to the lessee's rights under the lease? To the extent that the consequences of failing to file with respect to a true lease would differ from those with respect to a security interest, parties will retain the incentive to litigate over the characterization of the transaction and a major incentive for imposing a filing requirement would be lost.

(B) Consignments

Introductory Note. The preceding part of this Chapter explored leases—bailments in which the bailee was to *use* the goods. As we saw, these bailments bear a resemblance (sometimes a very close resemblance) to purchase money security interests in *equipment*. This part of the Chapter addresses consignments—bailments in which the bailee is to *sell* the goods. These bailments resemble purchase money security interests in *inventory*. As you work through the following materials, you will see that the Code's treatment of consignments differs considerably from its treatment of leases. Should the drafters have afforded the same treatment to both consignments and leases? If so, what should that treatment be?

Problem 5. The Corona Company has just developed what it believes to be its crowning achievement: Cal–Trak, a portable instrument that can measure and record calories as they are expended. Corona wishes to market this product to joggers and others concerned with fitness. It entered into the following agreement with Spartners: Corona will deliver a specified quantity of Cal–Traks to Spartners "on consignment." Title will remain in Corona. Spartners will use best efforts to sell the Cal–Traks to retail stores. Spartners has no obligation to pay for the Cal–Traks until they are sold, at which time Spartners will remit the sale price, less its commission. Spartners may return unsold Cal–Traks at any time without penalty and must return them upon Corona's demand.

Two months later, one of Spartners's judgment creditors caused the sheriff to levy upon all its inventory, including 10,000 Cal–Traks. Corona seeks to recover the Cal–Traks from the sheriff, arguing that they are not property of the judgment debtor, Spartners.

(a) What result? See UCC 1–201(37) (5th sentence); UCC 9–102(2); UCC 2–326(3), (2); In re Zwagerman, infra; Notes on Consignments, infra.

(b) What could the loser have done to avoid the loss?

(c) Suppose that, prior to taking delivery of the Cal–Traks, Spartners had granted a security interest in all its inventory, existing and after-acquired, to Bank. Would Bank's security interest attach to the Cal–Traks (which, recall, are still owned by Corona)? See UCC 9–203(1); UCC 2–326. (Do not assume that, if Bank's security interest attaches then Bank necessarily defeats Corona. See Chapter 11, Section 2(A), Note (1) on Attachment and Perfection by Filing (discussing "rights in the collateral"). As to the relative priority of Corona's ownership interest and Bank's security interest, see UCC 9–114, discussed in Chapter 13, Section 1(B), infra.)

(d) Would the result in part (a) change if Spartners were required to obtain Corona's approval of the terms of each sale?

(e) Would the result in part (a) change if Spartners were free to determine the price at which the Cal–Traks were sold?

Problem 6. Corona (of Problem 5) entered into the following agreement with Wholesaler: Wholesaler will take delivery of 10,000 Cal–Traks "on consignment" and will use best efforts to sell the Cal–Traks to retail stores. Wholesaler will pay the wholesale price 30 days after delivery; however, after three months Wholesaler may return to Corona any goods that Wholesaler is unable to sell. Wholesaler will receive a refund for these returned goods.

Two months later, one of Wholesaler's judgment creditors caused the sheriff to levy upon all its inventory, including 8,000 unsold Cal–Traks. Corona seeks to recover the Cal–Traks from the sheriff, arguing that they are not property of the judgment debtor, Wholesaler.

(a) What result? See UCC 2–326(1), (2).

(b) What could the loser have done to avoid the loss? The last sentence of UCC 2–326(3) makes the subsection inapplicable if one of the specified events occurs. If subsection (3) is inapplicable, what is the source of Corona's rights? Does Corona have a "security interest" in the Cal–Traks? If not, would a financing statement covering the transaction have any legal effect? The Article 2 Study Group recommended that UCC 2–326 be revised to provide that creditors of a buyer who holds goods delivered on "sale or return" are unable to reach the goods if the seller gives public notice by filing a financing statement. PEB Article 2 Report 122.

Problem 7. Corona entered into the following agreement with Distributor: Distributor will take delivery of 10,000 Cal–Traks "on consignment" and will use best efforts to sell the Cal–Traks to retail stores. Distributor will pay the wholesale price 30 days after delivery; if Distributor fails to pay, Corona may demand return of all unsold Cal–Traks.

Two months later, one of Distributor's judgment creditors caused the sheriff to levy upon all its inventory, including 8,000 unsold Cal–Traks. Corona seeks to recover the Cal–Traks from the sheriff, arguing that they are not property of the judgment debtor, Distributor.

(a) What result? See Note (2) on Consignments, infra.

(b) What could the loser have done to avoid the loss?

IN RE ZWAGERMAN

United States Bankruptcy Court, W.D. Michigan, 1990.
115 B.R. 540, affirmed, 125 B.R. 486 (W.D.Mich.1991).

OPINION

DAVID E. NIMS, JR., BANKRUPTCY JUDGE. This case comes before the court on the complaint filed by James D. Robbins, the Trustee in this estate, for a determination as to the respective interests in proceeds from the sale of cattle present on the farm of Gordon and Joan Zwagerman, doing business as Zwagerman Farms, the Debtors herein, at the time of the filing of the petition....

FACTS

Gordon and Joan Zwagerman filed their Chapter 7 bankruptcy petition on December 30, 1985. Other than at a 341 Meeting held on February 5, 1986, the Debtors have refused to testify, claiming their privilege against self-incrimination. David Bradley claims that all proceeds belong to him because he owned the cattle on the Debtors' farm. Comerica Bank–Detroit, the Bank herein, argues that based on their properly perfected security interest in the cattle, they are entitled to the proceeds.

Since approximately 1969, the Debtors operated a farm at which they fattened hogs and cattle and then sold them for slaughter. Originally, the Debtors fattened livestock which they personally owned. At some point in the early 1980's the Debtors apparently had a cash flow problem and started to bring some cattle into their feedlots[1] in which they did not have an ownership interest. Those cattle were furnished by David Bradley, a man the Debtor met while buying cattle out of the South. Bradley agreed to deliver cattle to the Zwagerman farm in order for the cattle to be fattened. The first delivery to the Debtors was on or about November 27, 1981. Both the number of head per shipment and the number of shipments per month were sporadic. Each shipment was accompanied by a contract, generally including the following pertinent provisions:

---

[1] A "feed lot" is an area where the operator keeps his cattle while fattening them. A "custom feed lot" physically appears the same, but the operator does not own the cattle.

1. That Red River will deliver a specified number of cattle on a specified date, with the expense of hauling to be paid by Red River.

2. Zwagerman agrees to feed such cattle and to be paid fifty-five (55) cents per pound for the poundage the cattle gain after being delivered.

3. Any loss of cattle by death shall be borne by Zwagerman.

4. Zwagerman agrees to feed the cattle until the weights reach approximately one thousand one hundred (1,100) pounds and when sold, the proceeds will be delivered to Red River. Red River will send to Zwagerman its check for the number of pounds gained by the cattle from time of delivery to Zwagerman to time of sale.

5. The parties agree that should any dispute arise in this agreement that the forum for settling such dispute will be Sumner County, Tennessee.

. . .

Bradley never visited the farm, but called the Debtor two to six times a week to discuss the best time to sell based on the market and cattle conditions. Although no amount of time was set for the fattening of the cattle, Bradley estimated that it took 90–140 days. The purchasers made checks out to the Debtor who then deposited the check into one of his personal checking accounts. Pursuant to the contract, the Debtor was supposed to send a check to Bradley for the full amount of the sale. Once Bradley received a check for the sale of cattle, he would send a weight gain check in return to the Debtor. ...

In the spring of 1983, the Debtor contacted Phillip Roberts, an agricultural loan officer at Comerica Bank, to pursue the refinancing of his debt to P.C.A. and F.M.B. The cattle on the farm were to be part of the security for the Comerica loan, just as they were for the existing P.C.A. loan. In deciding to recommend to the loan committee that a revolving credit loan for $1,300,000.00 and a term loan for $200,000.00 be given to the Debtor, Roberts testified that he took many things into consideration. He went out to the farm and saw cattle which the Debtor referred to as "my cattle." Parties mentioned on the various documents were contacted for verification, including Michigan Livestock Exchange which informed the Bank that Zwagerman bought cattle through them. Lien searches were done at the Register of Deeds. Various financial records, including bank statements and tax returns, were reviewed. A balance sheet paralleling statements dated 12/31/82 and 3/31/83, accompanied by an earnings work sheet, was submitted by the Debtor. Production of the Bills of Sale for the cattle was not required since Comerica was refinancing a debt owed to P.C.A.

The balance sheet bearing dates of 12/31/82 and 3/31/83 indicated in the assets section an increase of 715 cattle in three months and a decrease in liabilities. Roberts commented that it is typical for banks to have problems interpreting the figures submitted by farmers, particularly those who do a large amount of buying and selling, as farmers are usually poor bookkeepers. Therefore, it was left up to an analyst to reconcile the figures. The accompanying earnings work sheet showed "custom cattle" as an entry separate from "cattle" in the amount of $208,232.00 for the period ending 3/31/83. Roberts admitted that in 1983 he knew the term "custom cattle" meant that the farmer didn't own the cattle, but rather would be compensated for feed and care of the cattle pursuant to an agreement with the owner. Furthermore, he stated that he would have red flagged any documents with such an entry to require more information regarding ownership. The only explanation Roberts proffered to the Court was that when the loan application was being reviewed in 1983, no one from the Bank, including himself, caught the entry.

On November 10, 1983, a note and security agreement were signed. The security agreement purportedly gave the Bank a security interest in the livestock. The following paragraph was also contained within that document,

> 2.4 At the time any Collateral becomes subject to a security interest in favor of Bank, Debtor shall be deemed to have warranted that (i) Debtor is the lawful owner of such Collateral and has the right and authority to subject the same to a security interest in Bank ...

A financing statement was filed by the Bank on November 17, 1983....

On December 3, 1985, Bradley received a call from Gordon Zwagerman who disclosed that many Bradley cattle had been sold without accounting for them to Bradley. ... The 90–140 day turnaround period had become a 13–14 month turnaround period. No cattle were shipped and no checks were sent or received by Bradley after that December 3, 1985, telephone call. A few days later, the Zwagermans' attorney told Bradley that approximately 458 cattle were on the farm. In contrast, Bradley's records showed that 3,141 cattle should have been on the farm.

On December 11, 1985, Comerica was contacted by the Zwagermans' attorney who relayed that the Zwagermans had encountered financial difficulties due to losses in the commodity futures market, the number of cattle presently on the farm was much lower than the Bank records reflected, and a David Bradley owned at least some of the cattle. Two days later the Bank "took possession" of the cattle, but actually left them on the farm and paid Gordon Zwagerman $500.00 a week to take care of them....

DISCUSSION

Bradley contends that because he retained ownership in the cattle and the relationship between himself and the Debtor was only a bailment, the proceeds are held for his benefit by constructive trust. Comerica claims that the Bradley/Debtor relationship was not a bailment, but rather a consignment subject to [UCC 2–326], and therefore their properly perfected security interest gives them an interest in the proceeds which has priority over Bradley. The Trustee argues that the nature of Bradley's interest is either a consignment subject to [UCC 2–326] or a security interest, and not a bailment. Thus, the Trustee asserts that Comerica has a superior interest in the proceeds, or in the alternative, based on his status as hypothetical lien creditor under 11 U.S.C. § 544,[*] the proceeds are property of the estate; and all the payments the Debtors made to Bradley for cattle sales within ninety days of the bankruptcy are preferences.

Although Count I of the Complaint suggested that the contract between Zwagerman and Bradley created a security interest under Article 9 of the U.C.C., I assume that such a claim has been abandoned since there were no arguments at trial advancing that position. In addition, the evidence does not indicate that there was any intent between the contracting parties that Bradley would retain a security interest in the cattle.

Bailment

... A bailment is nothing more than a delivery of goods for some purpose, upon a contract, express or implied, to be redelivered to the bailor upon fulfillment of the purpose or to be dealt with according to the bailor's direction. Similarly, an agency is a relationship arising from a contract, express or implied, by which one of the parties confides to the other the transaction or management of some business or other activity in his name, or on his behalf, and whereby the other party assumes so to act and to render an account thereof. Thus in both situations, the title to the property remains in the bailor or principal, and the bailee or the agent holds the property under the bailment or agency for the owners' benefit. Consequently, it became well settled under the Bankruptcy Act that absent state statutory enactment to the contrary, if property was in a debtor's hands as bailee or agent, the trustee held it as such, and the bailor or principal could recover the property or its proceeds.

4 Collier on Bankruptcy § 541.08[2] (15th ed. 1990). Bradley has suggested in his briefs that Zwagerman was an agister and the contract was an agistment. The term agistment is an ancient one derived from the old Germanic word *giest* meaning guest. The Random House Dictionary of the English Language (1973) indicates agistment as being an obsolete word meaning the act of feeding or pasturing for a fee. Black's Law Dictionary 61 (5th ed. 1979) defines agistment as:

Agistment. A contract whereby a person, called an agister, has control of animals and retains possession of land. The taking in and feeding or pasturing of horses, cattle, or similar animals for a reward and is a species of bailment.

[* BC 544 is discussed in Chapter 14, Section 2(A), infra.]

Delivery of animals pursuant to a contract of agistment has been held to be a bailment of the animals.

"Bailment," in its ordinary legal signification, imports the delivery of personal property by one person to another in trust for a specific purpose, with a contract, express or implied, that the trust shall be faithfully executed and the property returned or duly accounted for when the special purpose is accomplished.

The contracts and the practice of the parties seem to clearly indicate their intent. Bradley had cattle to be fed. Zwagerman had good feed. Not only was Michigan grass superior to Tennessee grass but also Zwagerman had access to good silage and even discarded cookies. Bradley delivered the cattle to Zwagerman who fed them until they reached a certain weight. Then, by mutual agreement they were sold at an agreed price. Zwagerman, as a bailee or agister, never had title to the cattle.

Effect of U.C.C. § 2–326

The Bank and Trustee claim that because of Bradley's failure to give notice under Uniform Commercial Code (U.C.C.) § 2–326, his interest is subordinate to theirs. The written contracts seem to imply that Tennessee law will apply. However, both Tennessee and Michigan have adopted the U.C.C. and I find no material differences between Tenn. Code Ann. § 47–2–326 (1989) and Mich. Comp. Laws § 440.2326 (1989) . . . .

Section 2–326(1) is limited to transactions where delivered goods may be returned by the buyer even though they conform to the contract. There was never any intent that Zwagerman could return the cattle to Bradley. Costs, together with the shrinkage loss, would have made a return economically unfeasible.

In this case, delivery was never made to a buyer. U.C.C. § 2–103(1)(a) provides: "(1) In this article unless the context otherwise requires (a) 'Buyer' means a person who buys or contracts to buy goods." The U.C.C. does not seem to define "buy." Black's Law Dictionary 181 (5th ed. 1979) defines "buy" as "to acquire the ownership of property by giving an accepted price or consideration therefor; or by agreeing to do so; to acquire by the payment of a price or value; to purchase."

There was no agreement between Bradley and Zwagerman that Zwagerman would acquire ownership in the cattle. No price was agreed upon. Sale was not to take place until sometime in the future at which time Zwagerman would sell as agent for Bradley, at a price agreeable to Bradley, and the entire proceeds of the sale would be sent to Bradley less a shrinkage fee.

Section 2–326(1)(b) would restrict the operation of § 2–326 "Sale or return" transactions to those instances where the goods were delivered "primarily" for resale. The word "primarily" is not defined in the U.C.C. XII The Oxford English Dictionary 472 (2d ed. 1989) defines "primarily" as "[w]ith reference to other temporal order: In the first place, first of all, pre-eminently, chiefly, principally; essentially."

In this case I find that delivery was not primarily for resale. The cattle were shipped for feeding and fattening. If it were primarily for resale, it would have been much more reasonable to sell them in Tennessee and avoid the expense of transporting, shrinkage, and other loss unless an unusual market condition existed in the Southwestern Michigan area; and there were no proofs to that effect.

Thus, for all the reasons stated, the court finds that this case does not involve a "sale or return" under § 2–326(1).

This brings us to § 2–326(3). Undisputedly, the exclusions found in subsections 2–326(3)(a),(b), and (c) do not affect this case. No applicable sign law exists, the Debtors were not known by their creditors to be engaged in selling the goods of others, and Bradley stipulated that he did not file a financing statement. Therefore, a determination must be made as to whether or not the facts of this case fall within the parameters of U.C.C. § 2–326(3).

The court finds that the goods were not delivered to Zwagerman "for sale." It is not clear whether "for sale" refers to the sale to the buyer or resale by the buyer to third parties. But, delivery was not "for sale" in either event. As stated above, the delivery was for the care, feeding, and fattening the cattle. It would have been far more economical for Bradley to sell or to have someone in Tennessee sell the cattle and save shipping and shrinkage costs.

There is a closer question as to whether Zwagerman maintained a place of business at which he dealt in cattle. He was a farmer, who for many years raised his own cattle and custom fed the cattle of others. Eventually, he sold the cattle delivered to him by Bradley, as Bradley's agent, at a time, place, and price controlled by Bradley. There were no proofs that sales took place at the farm, even though this would have been possible.

I do not find a definition of consignment in the code. A "consignment contract" is defined in Black's Law Dictionary 278 (5th ed. 1979) as "[c]onsignment of goods to another (consignee) for sale under agreement that consignee will pay consignor for any sold goods and will return any unsold goods." A consignment contract, as defined above, is common. This type of consignment has not given courts a lot of trouble, and is the subject of many of the cases cited to by the Trustee and the Bank. I have read and agree with the conclusion of those cases.

BFC Chemicals, Inc., v. Smith–Douglas, Inc., 46 Bankr. 1009 (E.D.N.C.1985) is slightly different from the cases noted above. A certain chemical was placed by BFC, the creditor, in a large storage tank from which the debtor withdrew its needs from time to time to formulate agricultural chemicals for resale to its customers. The debtor then paid BFC for chemical taken. The debtor filed under

Chapter 11. BFC filed what was treated by the bankruptcy judge as a motion for relief from stay [in order to recover the chemicals]. This was denied. The district judge held that N.C.G.S. § 25–2–326 was applicable because the goods were delivered "for sale" and the matter was remanded for reconsideration and a determination whether BFC complied with N.C.G.S. 25–2–326(3)(a). While this is somewhat different than the above cited consignment cases, I believe I would be inclined to agree with the district judge.

In Simmons First National Bank v. Wells, 279 Ark. 204, 650 S.W.2d 236 (1983), the bank had a perfected security interest in inventory and after acquired property of Western Rice Mills. Western defaulted on its loan and a receiver was appointed. Wells intervened. Until about four months prior to the receivership, Wells sold his rice to Western which milled and resold it. But, because of Western's financial inability to buy the rice outright, Wells had orally agreed that Western would mill for a certain price, market at an agreed price, and turn over the proceeds less Western's charge for milling. The trial court held for Wells. The state supreme court held that here was a clear consignment but remanded to determine whether Wells was protected by the state statute pertaining to grain warehousemen. This case differs from our case in that Western marketed the rice at an agreed minimum price. It could be said that in the Wells case delivery was primarily for resale.

O'Brien v. Chandler, 765 P.2d 1165 (N.M.1988) involved an oral agreement between McCoy, a cattle dealer, and Chandler, a cattle broker, whereby McCoy agreed to ship cattle to a feedlot for delivery to Chandler. Delivery was made and McCoy furnished invoices to Chandler which set out the sales price. Without knowledge to McCoy, Chandler obtained a loan from a bank and pledged the cattle as security. This security interest was perfected. The bank claimed that it had no knowledge of any interest of McCoy. McCoy sued to recover the cattle. The trial court held that the bank had a perfected security interest superior to any rights of McCoy. The New Mexico Supreme Court affirmed, holding that the contract was a sale. This case differs from ours in two important facts. First, a price was set, and secondly, invoices were furnished. If the bank had requested proof of ownership, Chandler had the proof in the invoices. In our case, if any creditor had requested proof of ownership, all Zwagerman could have furnished would have been contracts that indicated that he had no interest in the cattle. . . .

In Eastman Kodak Co. v. Harrison (In re Sitkin Smelting & Refining, Inc., 639 F.2d 1213 (5th Cir.1981), reh'g en banc denied, 645 F.2d 72 (1981), Sitkin entered into an agreement with Eastman by which it would process film waste and purchase the silver content recovered. Sitkin filed under Chapter XI. Eastman filed an adversary proceeding against the trustee in bankruptcy and C.I.T. Corp., a secured creditor. The bankruptcy referee held that possession should be entrusted to the [sic] C.I.T. The court of appeals reversed, concluding that the agreement between Kodak and Sitkin provided for a bailment of the unprocessed waste, and therefore, Kodak was entitled to reclaim possession. The court stated:

> The transaction between Kodak and Sitkin is not a sale or return within the meaning of section 2–326, since the goods were not delivered for resale with an option to return. C.I.T., then, fails to overcome the presumption against the application of section 2–326.

Id. at 1218. I would agree with the result reached in Sitkin but not on the basis for the decision. Even if this was a "sale or return," the print waste was not "delivered primarily for resale."

In Union State Bank of Hazen v. Cook (In re Cook), 63 Bankr. 789 (Bankr.D.N.D.1986), parents, a son and his wife, and a partnership of which the father and son were partners filed petitions under Chapter 11. These debtors operated a family farm on which they raised Angus cattle and maintained a custom feed lot. Another son, Tom, did not stay on the farm but cattle he had raised as part of a 4–H project were left on the farm. He spent about one week each year on the farm. The court found that the business relationship between Tom and the debtors was quite loose. Tom's cattle were not separated from the debtors' cattle. The debtors were allowed to cull and market Tom's cattle, and even retain some of the proceeds of his cattle, but he never gave them authority to mortgage his cattle. The plaintiff bank was granted a security interest by the debtors in all livestock owned by them, including the increase thereof. The bank was not aware of Tom's interest until the bankruptcy was filed. Partnership schedules indicated 36 head were held for Tom, valued at approximately $22,000.00. While there were other issues before the court in determining ownership, the court noted that the cattle were all branded with the partnership brand. Although North Dakota has a branding statute, a brand is only prima facie evidence of ownership. N.D. Cent. Code § 36–09–19 (1980). The testimony of Tom and his brother was found to be convincing and supported by the fact that some of the cattle were registered by the American Angus Association in Tom's name. The court held that the parties' intent was crucial, and the intent was that Tom retain ownership. The burden was on the bank to demonstrate that the debtors possessed sufficient rights in Tom's cattle for the security interest to attach. The debtors' authority to sell Tom's cattle did not give them the authority to encumber the cattle.

In *Cook*, as in our case, the bank was casual about its loan. Although the bank representative made inspections of the operation, he never counted the cattle. The bank's officer admitted that other cattle besides debtors' could have been on the ranch and that he relied only on the financial statements submitted. The court held that Tom's cattle were not subject to the bank's lien.

In First National Bank of Blooming Prairie v. Olsen, 403 N.W.2d 661 (Minn.Ct.App.1987), Olsen owned and operated a feedlot for which the bank provided financing. The bank had a perfected security interest in Olsen's farm property including livestock. There were approximately 2,500 cattle on the farm, all of which were owned by third-party investors. The owner-investors did not perfect under § 2–326. The bank filed a replevin action and the trial court held that § 2–326 did not apply because the cattle were not delivered for sale. The court of appeals held that the § 2–326 did apply, relying on the official comment that "Subsection (3) resolves all reasonable doubts as to the nature of the transaction in favor of the general creditors of the buyer." However, the court found for the investors because the bank had actual knowledge that Olsen custom-fed a substantial number of cattle....

In Walter E. Heller & Co. S.E. v. Riviana Foods, Inc., 648 F.2d 1059 (5th Cir.1981) Riviana entered into a warehouse agreement with Amos Brokerage Company to store and eventually deliver the goods to Riviana's customers. Amos was not permitted to sell these goods but did maintain a place where it sold like goods under another name. Heller and Amos entered into an inventory security agreement and accounts financing security agreement. Subsequently, Amos filed bankruptcy. The court held that the goods were not delivered "for sale" as required by U.C.C. § 2–326 for a "sale and return." It drew a comparison to Allgeier v. Campisi, 117 Ga.App. 105, 159 S.E.2d 458 (1968), where the plaintiff entrusted her car to a dealer who was authorized to receive offers but lacked authority to sell without the approval of the plaintiff. The defendant, a security interest holder in the plaintiff dealer's inventory, sought possession of the car. The court held for the plaintiff since the car was not delivered "for sale" under U.C.C. § 2–326.

As can be noted from the cases mentioned above, there has been little uniformity in the court decisions on § 2–326. There is much to be said for extension of the section to situations that were not anticipated or intended by the drafters of the law. If I could interpret the law as I think it should be written, I would probably hold that 2–326 should be applied to every situation where there may be secret interests in property which would be harmful to those dealing with the person having possession. One of the purposes of Article 9 was to eliminate the secret lien, and an aim of 2–326 was to protect third parties in consignment cases. However, cattle cases are not as serious as some of the situations faced by courts in the cases above. Any prudent, prospective lender or purchaser is well aware that cattle may be custom fed or cows may be leased. More disturbing are the inventory cases in which it is not common practice to deliver goods while retaining title.

I am well aware of the provision in § 1–102 of the U.C.C. which provides that, "This Act shall be liberally construed and applied to promote its underlying purposes and policies." Nevertheless, radical changes in the unambiguous provisions of the law should not be made by judicial interpretation. The result would be to uproot the drafters' intent to promote uniformity and certainty. It is much better that such changes be brought about by legislation after much discussion both inside and outside the legislative bodies concerned. It was no accident that the Michigan U.C.C. Act of 1962, 1962 Mich. Pub. Acts 174, did not become effective until over a year later on January 1, 1964. Those of us who were around at that time can recall the many seminars which were held for lawyers, accountants, financial institutions, trade associations, and many others to prepare the commercial world for this new law. Because the U.C.C. was so superior to what it replaced it was not surprising that some lawyers and jurist expected a miraculously all-encompassing statute. However, the U.C.C. has been amended many times and I am sure it will be amended many more times in the future.

R. Anderson, Anderson on the Uniform Commercial Code § 1-102:20–21 (1981) states:

When a section of the code is clear and unambiguous there is "no occasion" to engage in statutory construction.

Contrary to the rule of liberal construction stated in the preceding sections, there is some authority that the Code is to be strictly construed where in derogation of the common law, and a statute should be construed in harmony with the common law unless there is a clear legislative intent to abrogate the common law. In many states there are special statutory construction acts that expressly repudiate this principle of statutory construction, so that it is extremely doubtful whether strict construction should be made solely because of conflict with the common law.

A better reason for strict construction is that if the court does not adhere to the letter of the Code, the objective of certainty will be defeated. Thus where the Code is unambiguous, it should be applied according to its letter, as to do otherwise would merely produce confusion in the business world.

When the provisions of the Code are unambiguous they are to be followed by the courts. . . .

A court should adhere strictly to the provisions of the Code in order to achieve stability, consistency, and predictability. And an "overly" liberal interpretation of the Code should be avoided as creating uncertainty among businessmen and their legal advisors who believe themselves to be entering into transactions on the basis that the Code means what it says.

Loose construction of the Code cannot be justified on the basis of the direction to construe the Code liberally as a mandate for liberal construction is not a "license to legislate."

Later Anderson continues:

The certainty of commercial practices and relations is essential to furthering trade. Consequently as a variant of the objective of furthering trade, a court should so interpret the Code as to further certainty in commercial dealings.

The dangers of expanding the boundaries of § 2–326 cannot be better illustrated than the case before us. Bradley, at the time of trial, was an 80 year old man who had been in the cattle business his entire life except for a few years in service during World War II. He had also served as a vice president of a local bank. While he was aware of the practice of custom feeding of cattle, he never actually engaged in it before his arrangement with the Debtors. He then did what any prudent businessman should do—he visited his lawyer who "was good," according to Bradley, because he subsequently became a judge. His lawyer set up a group of forms to be used and instructed Bradley as to the procedure to be followed, but he never instructed Bradley to perfect his transaction by filing with a register of deeds. Bradley had never heard of requiring the filing of a financing statement as to these transactions. Testimony during the trial indicated that there was little custom feeding going on in Michigan at the time Zwagerman and Bradley entered into their joint undertaking. In the fall of 1986, Michigan Livestock, a large cattle dealer, commenced delivering their cattle for feeding in an operation similar to that of Bradley and Zwagerman. It is possible they may have heard of Bradley's operation and problems by this time. Before that, most of the custom lots were carried out by the big lots out West. Michigan Livestock filed a sort of financing statement; the form used did not comply with the U.C.C. but did give notice. However, testimony indicated that most persons delivering cattle for custom feeding did not file financing statements.

Twenty states have branding laws and dispose of title matters as to cattle through these laws. Neither Michigan or Tennessee have adopted such a statute.

From the clear terms of § 2–326, related sections of the U.C.C., the general commercial practice, and the fact that a number of states have felt that control in this area should be by a separate branding statute outside of the U.C.C., I find that the transaction with which we are concerned is not a "sale or return" under the meaning of § 2–326 and that the title to the cattle delivered to the Zwagermans by Bradley remained in Bradley.

[In the remainder of the opinion, the court determined which cattle were Bradley's and whether certain pre-bankruptcy payments from Zwagerman to Bradley were recoverable as preferences under BC 547. Preferences are discussed in Chapter 14, Section 2(B), infra.

The District Court affirmed on both the consignment issue and the preference issue. Its conclusion as to the former was as follows: "While the question is a close one, the factual finding that the delivery was not 'for sale' is not clearly erroneous and will not be upset on appeal." Having determined that Zwagerman did not hold the cattle "for sale," the court did not address whether Zwagerman maintained a place of business at which he dealt in cattle.]

Notes on Consignments

(1) Consignments Under Pre–Code Law. The delivery of goods on "consignment" has an ancient and honorable history. The consignee (sometimes called a "factor") was a selling agent who did not undertake entrepreneurial risks. To the extent the consigned goods were sold, the consignee received a commission or a margin above a stated price; unsold goods could be returned to the owner.

The agreement between consignor and consignee clearly provided that the consignor remained the owner of the goods; when the consignee, as selling agent, effected a sale to a buyer, title passed from the consignor to the buyer. Under this arrangement, creditors of the *consignor* could, of course, levy on the goods while they were held by the consignee. By the same token, most courts held that creditors of the *consignee* had no right to levy on the consignor's goods. Possession often did not imply ownership. On the other hand, courts usually would rebel when the agreement made the "consignee" an entrepreneur rather than a selling agent, as when the agreement required the consignee to pay for the goods even though the consignee was unable to sell them. See 1 Gilmore, Security § 3.5.

The law of a few states reflected a wider concern for creditors of the consignee by enacting the "Trader's Acts." These Acts typically dealt with the situation where a person transacted business "as a trader" in its own name and without disclosing the name of its principal or partner by a conspicuous sign at the place of business. In these circumstances, all the property used in the business was made liable for the debts of the "trader." (The model for such legislation was a Virginia statute first enacted in 1839; this Virginia statute was repealed in 1973.) For some of the problems presented by statutes of this kind, see Note, The Mississippi Business Sign Statute—Necessity of Agency or Partnership Relations, 18 Miss.L.J. 417 (1947).

(2) Consignments Under the Code: "True" Consignments versus Consignments "Intended as Security." Does Article 9 govern an orthodox ("true") consignment, where the consignee has no obligation to pay for the goods? It is difficult to conclude that the consignor's ownership of the goods is a "security interest"—an "interest in personal property ... which secures payment or performance of an obligation." UCC 1–201(37). The duty of a bailee to return bailed goods is not the kind of obligation that supports a security interest. If it were, then *all* consignments, leases, and other bailments would create security interests; we know this is not the case.

The drafters of the Code recognized, however, that *some* "consignments" might create security interests, i.e., that the parties to inventory financing might describe the transaction in their documents as a "consignment." We have seen that the common law provided an incentive to do so: By retaining title, a consignor immunized the goods from the reach of the consignee's creditors.[3] The Code follows pre-Code law in treating as secured transactions those "consignments" that are "intended as security." See UCC 1–201(37) (5th sentence); UCC 9–102(2). For example, a "consignment" that requires the "agent-consignee" to pay for goods that the consignee is unable to sell is likely to be characterized as "intended as security"; if so, then the transaction creates an Article 9 security interest and is subject to Article 9 in its entirety: the rules concerning attachment, perfection, priority and remedies all apply. See, e.g., Clark Oil & Refining Co. v. Liddicoat, 65 Wis.2d 612, 223 N.W.2d 530 (1974) ("consignment" of petroleum products to service station operator was intended for security, thus making applicable Article 9's priority rules).

How does the Code affect true consignments (those not "intended as security"), in which the consignor's retention of title does not create a "security interest"? The fifth sentence of UCC 1–201(37) refers one to UCC 2–326. One might infer from the reference to "Consignment Sales" in the caption to UCC 2–326 that the section applies to sales dressed up as consignments (i.e., to consignments for security), and not to true consignments, which, as we have seen, are bailments. See UCC 1–109 (section captions are part of the UCC). That inference would be mistaken: Notwithstanding its caption, UCC 2–326 applies to true consignments; Article 9 applies to consignments for security.

The drafters of the Code concluded that, even in true consignments, the creditors of the consignee deserve protection from undisclosed interests in goods. UCC 2–326 affords that protection in a rather complicated way, by assimilating a consignment to a "sale or return."

(3) A Closer Look at UCC 2–326(3). *The Effect of UCC 2–326(3).* Suppose *A* delivers goods to *B* on "consignment" for sale, and *B* "maintains a place of business at which he deals in goods of the kind involved, under a name other than the name of the person making delivery" (here, a name other than "*A* "). UCC 2–326(3). Suppose further that the transaction between *A* and *B* is a "true consignment"—that it does not create a security interest. UCC 2–326(3) changes the common-law rule and provides that *A's* goods are subject to the claims of *B's* creditors. More specifically, UCC 2–326(3) *deems* consigned goods to be delivered on "sale or return" in the circumstances specified in that subsection. Goods *actually* sold on sale or return (i.e., goods that are delivered to a buyer who may return them if they cannot be resold) are subject to the claims of the buyer's creditors while in the buyer's possession. See UCC 2–326(1)(b), (2). Likewise, creditors of the consignee may levy upon consigned goods that UCC 2–

---

3. In addition, because the consignor remained the owner of consigned goods, the consignee was free to fix the price at which they were to be sold. However, a consignor fixing prices should be aware of the possible antitrust implications, as to which the law is not entirely clear. For a general discussion, see Harrington, The Law of Consignments: Antitrust and Commercial Pitfalls, 34 Bus. Law. 431, 445–53 (1979). See also Mesirow v. Pepperidge Farm, Inc., 703 F.2d 339 (9th Cir.1983), cert. denied, 464 U.S. 820, 104 S.Ct. 83, 78 L.Ed.2d 93 (1983) (concerning price fixing at the wholesale level).

326(3) *deems* to be on sale or return while they are in the consignee's possession.

Avoiding the Application of UCC 2–326(3). What can *A* do to avoid this result? UCC 2–326(3) affords the cautious consignor three methods of protection. Technically, a consignor who uses one of these three methods renders subsection (3) inapplicable. If subsection (3) is inapplicable, then the goods are not "deemed to be on sale or return" and are not subject to the claims of the consignee's creditors (assuming the applicable non-Code law is to that effect). See UCC 2–326, Comment 2.

One method is a litigator's nightmare: The consignor must "establish [cf. UCC 1–201(8) (definition of "burden of establishing")] that [the consignee] is *generally* known by his creditors to be *substantially* engaged in selling the goods of others." UCC 2–326(3)(b). Would you advise a client to rely on this subsection? According to Professors White and Summers, "[i]n only two cases has a consignor established general knowledge that the consignee sold the goods of others, and one of those cases was wrongly decided under present law." J. White & R. Summers, Uniform Commercial Code (3d ed. 1988) § 21–4, at 939. The Article 2 Study Group recommended that this provision be eliminated. PEB Article 2 Report 121.

A second method by which a consignor may protect its ownership interest against creditors of the consignee is to comply with "an applicable law providing for a consignor's interest or the like to be evidenced by a sign." UCC 2–326(3)(b). Resort to this method is likely to be futile: There is authority to the effect that the phrase "applicable law" refers only to a statute and not to a common-law rule, see, e.g., Vonins, Inc. v. Raff, 101 N.J.Super. 172, 243 A.2d 836 (App.Div.1968), and only two states (Mississippi and North Carolina) have enacted such statutes. J. White & R. Summers, Uniform Commercial Code (3d ed. 1988) § 21–4, at 939 n. 8. The Article 2 Study Group recommended that this provision be limited to cases where goods are delivered to an auctioneer for sale. PEB Article 2 Report 121.

The only realistic alternative for a consignor is to "compl[y] with the filing provisions of the Article on Secured Transactions (Article 9)." UCC 2–326(3)(c). Like a lessor (see Note 6 on Distinguishing Leases from Secured Transactions, Section (1)(A), supra), a consignor may file a financing statement showing itself as "consignor" and the party in possession as "consignee" without prejudicing the determination whether the transaction is a consignment or a security interest. See UCC 9–408.

Compliance With Article 9. By filing a financing statement, a consignor under a "true" consignment would seem to escape the effect of UCC 2–326(3) and insulate the consigned goods from the reach of the consignee's creditors. (The Code does not explicitly provide for this result.) While this is true as to creditors who subsequently obtain judicial liens on the goods, it is not completely true as to secured parties who take a security interest in the consignee's inventory (which would include the consigned goods). UCC 9–114, which was added in 1972, contains special rules determining the priority contest between the consignor and the consignee's inventory financer. These rules, which require that an existing inventory lender receive notice of the consignment, are modeled upon UCC 9–312(3), governing the priority of purchase money security interests in inventory. They are discussed in Chapter 13, Section 1(B), infra.

The Scope of UCC 2–326(3). The first sentence of UCC 2–326(3) describes those consignments that are deemed to be on "sale or return." As the *Zwagerman* case, supra, indicates, courts have had difficulty determining whether a particular transaction meets the description in UCC 2–326(3): Were the goods delivered "for sale"? Does the person in possession (the putative consignee) "maintain[ ] a place of business at which he deals in goods of the kind involved"? Does the putative consignee deal in goods "under a name other than the name of the person making delivery"?

What purpose do these phrases serve? Comment 2 to UCC 2–326(3) suggests that public notice is required for transactions where creditors of the consignee may reasonably be deemed to have been misled by the secret reservation of title in the consignor. Did the *Zwagerman* court, which professed to be sympathetic to "ostensible ownership" concerns, construe these requirements too narrowly?

The Article 2 Study Group's recommendations in this regard are as follows (PEB Article 2 Report 122):

> (2) The phrase "delivered to a person for sale" in § 2–326(3) should be expanded to include all deliveries of goods pursuant to which the parties expect the consignee ultimately to sell to others, even though further processing or prior consent to sale is required.

> (3) Clarification of whether the consignee must, as § 2–326(3) now provides, "maintain a place of business at which he deals in goods of the kind involved" should be made. As written, this restricts the scope of protection to third parties. Section 2–326(3) should also be broadened to include delivery to an possession by a "merchant who deals in goods of that kind." Compare § 2–403(2).

(4) "Sale or Return" Transactions. What is the effect of filing a financing statement against a buyer in a transaction that is a "sale or return," as defined in UCC 2–326(1)? UCC 2–326(3) provides that filing makes "this subsection . . . not applicable." When a transaction is a "sale or return" on its own terms, however, the filing seemingly would provide no protection to the seller from claims of the buyer's creditors. On the other hand, in a true consignment transaction (i.e., one in which the bailee is to attempt to sell the goods on the bailor's behalf, but the bailee never becomes a "buyer") that is not deemed to be a "sale or return" under UCC 2–326(3), the bailor seems to be protected against claims of the bailee's creditors even without filing. Is it likely that the drafters contemplated or intended these different results in transactions that, from the perspective of third parties, may be identical?

(5) Rethinking the Code's Treatment of Consignments. Most people would agree that "[t]he Uniform Commercial Code's provisions regarding consignments are not models of draftsmanship." In re State Street Auto Sales, Inc., 81 B.R. 215 (Bkrtcy.D.Mass.1988). Although the present text may create unnecessary difficulties, there appears to be no easy solution for the problems presented by transactions that do not meet the definition of "security interest" but are functionally similar.

The Code's sponsors have established a drafting committee to revise Article 2. What approach to consignments should that committee take? Should it clarify in the statute the distinction between true consignments and those intended as security, much as the 1987 amendments clarified the distinction between true leases and security interests? See Section 1(A), supra. Should the Code be revised to subject *all* consignments to Article 9's filing provisions? To Article 9 in its entirety, except, perhaps, for a few specific provisions? (As we shall see in Section 2, infra, the Code adopts a similar approach with respect to assignments of accounts and chattel paper.)

The Article 2 Study Group recommended that the scope of UCC 2–326(3) be clarified and broadened (see the above recommendations) and that the filing rules of Article 9 continue to apply to true consignments. In addition, "[a]n effort to distinguish a 'true' consignment from a consignment for security should be made in the comments." PEB Article 2 Report 121.

Problem 8. Crispin is a stereophile who acquires new speakers every six months or so. Crispin leaves the old speakers with Dealer, who agrees to try to sell them on commission. Acting pursuant to an execution writ issued at the request of one of Dealer's judgment creditors, the sheriff levies on the speakers. Is the levy effective against Crispin? If so, then the sheriff's sale would cut off Crispin's ownership interest. See UCC 2–326(3).

In Chapter 1, we saw that Factor's Acts and UCC 2–403(2) empower Dealer to make even an unauthorized sale of the speakers. Should Crispin's ownership interest also be subject to the claims of Dealer's creditors?

Although UCC 2–326, literally applied, subjects Crispin to this threat, Professor John Dolan has observed that the cases generally protect the consumer consignor. See Dolan, The UCC Consignment Rule Needs an Exception for Consumers, 44 Ohio St. L.J. 21 (1983). Professor Dolan approves of the results of those cases but not their reasoning, which does not depend on the fact that the consignor was a consumer. He argues that contemporary credit practices no longer justify rules based on ostensible ownership concerns. Whatever validity remains in requiring consignors to file financing statements derives from antifraud concerns not present when consumers are the consignors: There is little risk that a consumer is cloaking what is essentially inventory financing in the guise of a consignment.

The Article 2 Study Group was persuaded by Professor Dolan's argument. See Permanent Editorial Board Article 2 Report 122. What should judges do under current law? The Code arguably invites them to apply the principle of *cessante ratione legis, cessat ipsa lex* (the reason of the law ceasing, the law itself also ceases). See UCC 1–102(2). Do you agree with Professor Dolan that the reason for the rule of UCC 2–326(3) fails where consumer consignments are concerned? If so, is this an appropriate setting for judges to ignore the language of UCC 2–326(3)?

(C) BAILMENTS FOR PROCESSING

The Code directly addresses two prototypical types of bailments: leases and consignments. But many transactions in which one person is in possession of goods "owned" by another do not fit within these prototypes. Among these are arrangements whereby the person in possession is to return the goods (or something extracted from them) to the owner—or deliver them to a third party—only after the goods are repaired, processed, refined, fabricated, or similarly dealt with. Regardless of the form these arrangements take (and they may take an infinite variety of forms), if the "owner's" interest in the goods "secures payment or performance of an obligation" (UCC 1–201(37)), then the "owner" holds a security interest subject to Article 9. See UCC 9–102(1)(a). As observed above, if the *only* performance that the goods secure is the obligation to return them to the owner, then the transaction would not be a security interest; otherwise, all bailments would be Article 9 transactions.

As the following materials suggest, drawing the line among secured transactions, consignments, and other bailments is quite difficult.

Problem 9. Grower delivers rice to Miller. Miller agrees to pay for the rice in three installments. Concerned about Miller's ability to make the payments, Grower retains title to the rice.

(a) Is this transaction a security interest or a bailment?

(b) The sheriff levies on the rice pursuant to an execution writ procured by Elsie, a judgment creditor of Miller. Whose rights are senior, Grower's or Elsie's? Although a judicial lien creditor ordinarily acquires no better rights to the goods than its debtor enjoyed, however, an unperfected security interest is subordinate to the rights of a person who becomes a lien creditor before the security interest is perfected. See UCC 9–301(1)(b).

Problem 10. Grower delivers rice to Miller. Miller agrees to mill it for a fee and return it to Grower.

(a) Is this transaction a security interest or a bailment?

(b) While Miller is in possession of the rice, the sheriff levies on it pursuant to an execution writ procured by Elsie, a judgment creditor of Miller. Whose rights are senior, Grower's or Elsie's?

(c) Assume that Lender holds a security interest in all Miller's existing and after-acquired inventory and equipment. Will the security interest attach to the rice? See UCC 9–203(1); Note (1) on Attachment and Perfection by Filing, Chapter 11, Section 2(A). If so, will Lender be able to cut off Grower's interest in the rice? See UCC 2–403(1) (1st sentence); Note on Bailments for Processing, infra.

Problem 11. Grower delivers rice to Miller. Miller agrees to mill it for a fee and deliver it at Grower's direction to Grower's customers. The customers are to pay Miller, who will deduct the milling fee and remit the balance to Grower.

(a) Is this transaction a security interest or a bailment? If it is a bailment, is it a consignment subject to UCC 2–326?

(b) While Miller is in possession of the rice, the sheriff levies on it pursuant to an execution writ procured by Elsie, a judgment creditor of Miller. Whose rights are senior, Grower's or Elsie's?

Problem 12. What results in Problem 11 if Miller delivers the rice to its own customers, rather than Grower's? See Simmons First National Bank v. Wells, 279 Ark. 204, 650 S.W.2d 236 (1983) (holding arrangement whereby miller was obligated to sell at an agreed minimum price to be subject to UCC 2–326(3)).

Note on Bailments for Processing

Article 9 applies to secured transactions; it does not apply to bailments.[4] Two important consequences follow from this observation. First, if the person in possession of goods claimed by another is a bailee, then the bailor's ownership interest in the goods generally is enforceable against third parties even in absence of public notice. See UCC 2–403(1) (1st sentence) (*nemo dat* principle). But see UCC 2–403(2) (entrustment rule).[5] If, however, the person in possession is an Article 9 debtor, then the secured party must file a financing statement to protect its security interest against most third parties. See UCC 9–301(1)(b), (c) (lien creditors, certain buyers); UCC 9–312(5) (perfected secured parties).[6] Second, a bailor's remedies against the bailee and the bailed goods are determined by common law and scattered statutes,

---

4. The possessory security interest (**pledge**), whereby a debtor's property is delivered to a creditor to secure an obligation, is a bailment that is subject to Article 9; however, the pledge differs from the bailments under consideration in this Chapter. If any of the "bailments" discussed here create security interests, the person in possession of the goods would be the debtor, not the secured party.

UCC 9–114 applies to a particular type of bailment—a consignment of the type described in UCC 2–326(3). See Chapter 13, Section 1(B) (discussing UCC 9–114).

5. In some cases, the common law of accession and confusion may operate to subordinate the rights of the bailor to claims of creditors of, and purchasers from, the bailee. See R. Brown, The Law of Personal Property ch. VI (Raushenbush ed., 3d ed. 1976).

6. Of course, if a putative bailment is a secured transaction, the secured party will have no security interest at all unless the requirements for attachment are met. See UCC 9–203(1) (discussed in Chapter 11, Section 2(A)).

whereas Article 9 governs a secured party's remedies against the debtor and the collateral.

As we have seen, the Code expounds at length about the distinction between leases ("bailments for hire" at common law) and security interests, see UCC 1–201(37) (last three paragraphs), and it singles out certain types of consignments (bailments for sale) for special treatment. See UCC 2–326. The Code does not, however, give any other guidance for distinguishing between bailments and security interests. Some cases are easy to characterize: No one would seriously contend that a security interest is created when, for example, Lee Abel brings the Pontiac to Main Motors for an oil change or Benny Stolwitz brings Arnie Becker's suits to the cleaners. But as one moves away from the "pure" bailment, characterizing the transactions becomes more difficult and the results become harder to predict.

As with the lease/security interest distinction, courts have looked to a variety of factors when distinguishing between a bailment for processing and a secured transaction. Two of these factors seem particularly irrelevant. First, some courts appear to have been influenced by the perception that creditors of the bailee (including Article 9 secured parties) may rely to their detriment on the bailee's possession of bailed goods. Although one might argue, as some commentators have, that public notice of bailments *should* be required as a prerequisite for protection against creditors and purchasers, the law simply is not to that effect: Bailors generally are not required to cure any "ostensible ownership" problems by filing or otherwise.

Second, courts may become concerned with the subjective intentions, or purposes, of the parties. The learning in the context of leases is relevant here: Because the characterization of the transaction affects not only the rights of the parties but also the rights of third parties, subjective intentions should be irrelevant. See Note 2 on Distinguishing Leases from Secured Transactions, supra. Nevertheless, some reported decisions attempt to divine the "intention," "motivation," or "purpose" of the parties.

What can a putative bailor do to protect itself against the risk that a court will determine its interest in the goods to be a security interest? The easiest step is to file a financing statement; in the event the arrangement is held to be a secured transaction, the security interest will be perfected. (Under some loan agreements, the filing of a financing statement against the debtor is a default; if the bailee is a debtor under such an agreement, it may refuse to cooperate with the bailor in this regard.) Will the fact that a financing statement has been filed affect the court's characterization of the transaction? To reduce this risk, a bailor might be tempted to file a financing statement referring to itself as "bailor" and to the person in possession as "bailee." UCC 9–408, which permits precautionary financing statements of this kind to be filed for leases and consignments, does not cover other bailments.

Nevertheless, one hopes a court would extend the rule. See UCC 1–102(1), (2), & Comment 1.

A filed financing statement will protect the "bailor's" interest against lien creditors of the "bailee" and, as we shall see in Chapter 14, Section 2(A), infra, against the "strong arm" of the "bailee's" bankruptcy trustee. But, as Chapter 13 makes clear, perfection of a security interest does not guarantee priority over conflicting security interests. The bailment-security interest issue often is litigated between a putative bailor and the "bailee's" inventory financer. In that setting, if the arrangement is characterized as a secured transaction rather than a bailment, the "bailor's" security interest may be subordinate to that of the inventory financer. See UCC 9–312(3) (discussed in Chapter 13, Section (1)(B), infra).

SECTION 2. ACCOUNTS AND CHATTEL PAPER FINANCING

Introductory Note. Consider the following, common scenario: Dealer provides services on unsecured credit to a variety of customers. Dealer needs cash to continue to operate. Rather than wait for payment, Dealer approaches Financer, who agrees to buy dealer's rights under its contracts with its customers. Inasmuch as Financer has become the owner of the accounts (rights to payment), one might jump to the conclusion that Article 9 is irrelevant to the transaction. In doing so, one would be making a serious mistake.

As we have seen, most questions as to the applicability of Article 9 are dominated by the concept of "security interest." This unitary approach is expressed in the basic rule of UCC 9–102(1)(a): Article 9 applies "to any transaction (regardless of its form) which is intended to create a *security interest*." The approach to accounts (and chattel paper) is startlingly different: Immediately after the general provision, quoted above, UCC 9–102(1)(b) states that Article 9 also applies "to *any sale* of accounts or chattel paper." (The sharply different treatment of sales of other property is illustrated by the specific provision in UCC 1–201(37) (4th sentence) that the property interest of a buyer of *goods* "is not a 'security interest'.")

As we shall see, the sweep of the provision bringing "any sale" of accounts or chattel paper within Article 9 is slightly narrowed by a set of exclusions from Article 9, see UCC 9–104(f), as well as by a narrow exemption from the filing requirement in UCC 9–302(1)(e). But it is evident that the framers of the Code concluded that the selling of accounts and chattel paper had unique features that made it unwise, in this setting, for Article 9 to apply only to transfers of "an interest ... which secures payment or performance of an obligation." UCC 1–201(37).

What led the drafters to abandon, for most Article 9 purposes, the distinction between an assignment for collateral purposes and an outright sale?[1] According to Comment 2 to UCC 9–102, "[c]ommercial financing on the basis of accounts and chattel paper is often so conducted that the distinction between a security transfer and a sale is blurred, and a sale of such property is therefore covered by subsection (1)(b) whether intended for security or not[.]" To appreciate why this might be so, it will be useful to have a bird's-eye-view of accounts receivable financing. The following was written, on the basis of first-hand practical experience, shortly after the completion of the Code. Although some details have become dated and some new practices have developed, the discussion of the mechanics of accounts financing, including the allocation of risks between the assignor and assignee, retains its utility as an introduction to the field. Moreover, the discussion of pre-Code rules on the effectiveness of assignments and priority among assignees has not been wholly superseded by the Code. As we shall see, some assignments are left outside the scope of Article 9; for these cases it will be necessary to look to pre-Code law.

KUPFER, ACCOUNTS RECEIVABLE FINANCING: A LEGAL AND PRACTICAL LOOK–SEE

Prac. Law., Nov. 1956, at 50, 50–65.

Less than half a century ago, a mere moment of transit in our Anglo–Saxon legal and economic history, accounts receivable financing was virtually unknown. It now approximates an annual volume of ten billion dollars. The office of this paper will be to dissect the economic structure of the mechanism and to analyze the details of the legal blueprints that make it tick. . . .

Purposes of Accounts Receivable Financing. A borrower normally will first seek unsecured credit to the extent to which he can obtain it. But the overwhelming majority of our industrial and commercial units constitute "small business," and require accommodation for which unsecured credit is not readily available. They may require liquid funds for more working capital; or for expansion purposes; or to take discounts on merchandise purchased. For these needs, they will usually resort to their most liquid asset other than cash—their accounts receivable.

Generally speaking, because of its inherently self-liquidating and revolving nature, accounts receivable financing is not an apt permanent source of capital, although it is frequently so employed on a temporary basis. . . .

The greater part of accounts receivable financing covers sales of manufacturers and merchants, and, historically, it was confined, in its early development, to that area. In recent years, however, its opera-

------

    1. The distinction may affect the assignee's remedies against the assignor.   See UCC 9–502(2); Chapter 15, Section 5, infra.

tion has been expanded into much wider, and at times greener, fields. Illustrations are the financing of deferred-payment sales and the leasing plans of commercial and industrial equipment; the financing, for department stores, of retail budget-instalment and charge accounts; the rediscounting of the paper of small-loan companies and the smaller consumer-finance companies; and even the financing of mergers and acquisitions of businesses. Its operation in the purely service field is by no means unknown, although the author has yet to hear of lawyers' accounts receivable being accepted as collateral! It could, however, happen, and probably will before we know it.

The Different Types of Accounts Receivable Financing:

The Parties. To every accounts receivable operation there are necessarily three parties: (1) the lender upon, or purchaser of, the accounts; (2) the borrower upon, or seller of, them; and (3) the debtor upon the accounts assigned. For semantic uniformity and brevity, these three parties will be respectively called the "*assignee*," the "*assignor*," and the "*account-debtor*," unless the context otherwise indicates. (Occasionally, the words "*lender*" or "*secured creditor*" will connote the assignee, and the word "*borrower*," the assignor. Only exceptionally—and then obviously—will there be any departure from the use of "*account-debtor*.")

The Two Basic Forms. There are two essential requirements to the payment of any account receivable. First, the assignor must comply with the terms of his agreement with, or the order of, the account-debtor, and secondly, the latter must be financially able and willing to pay. The first requirement is called the "merchandise risk," and the second, the "credit risk." And out of this dichotomy arise the two basic forms of accounts receivable financing. These are respectively known as "*recourse*" and "*non-recourse*" financing, and the terminology in itself differentiates them.

In *both*, the assignor necessarily retains the *merchandise* risk, because the fabrication of the goods or the rendition of the service in accordance with his commitment to the account-debtor at all times rests solely within his control.

In *recourse* financing, the *assignor* also retains the *credit* risk; he guarantees to the assignee that the account will be paid at its maturity. Therefore, both in economics and in law, the financing transaction, however the contract may be set up, constitutes a loan upon the security of the assigned accounts.

In the *non-recourse* operation, the *assignee* assumes the *credit* risk, and, in legal consequence, the operation constitutes a purchase. (Non-recourse financing is sometimes called "*factoring*." Historically, factoring was first associated solely with inventory financing. When accounts receivable financing—usually on a non-recourse basis—developed as an adjunct to inventory financing, the term was originally applied to the combined operation. Latterly, it is occasionally used to cover both recourse and non-recourse accounts receivable financing, with or without a precedent inventory loan. Therefore, except to the highly initiated and in the context of a specific operation, the use of the term is only apt to confuse, and will be eschewed in this paper.)

The distinction between recourse and non-recourse financing is of great importance in the application of interest and usury laws.

Combining With Inventory Financing. Inventory financing can be combined with either the non-recourse or recourse financing of accounts; traditionally, it was more intimately associated with the former, although it may, but need not, be employed in connection with either type, as the economic "lead line" which ultimately becomes solely the accounts receivable operation. When inventory financing is absent, the operation is called "pure" accounts receivable financing, and this is the more usual form that it takes.   ...

Function of Banks. The function of banks in accounts receivable financing is also a matter of considerable interest. In the first place they constitute the wholesalers of credit to the account receivable companies. Secondly, a number of them are engaged directly in the accounts receivable field. The competition is not at all unwelcome to finance companies, although, from the standpoint of the banks, it presents both advantages and disadvantages which are beyond the ambit of this paper. And finally, the banks frequently participate with finance companies in specific operations because it minimizes the risk and puts at their disposal the specialized know-how of accounts receivable companies, thus reducing the overall cost of the lending operation. . . .

Implementation of the Operation:

The Underlying Contract and the Assignments. Every accounts receivable operation starts with the execution of an underlying contract between the assignor and the assignee. It spells out in detail the rights of the parties, and its contents have become more or less standard.

When the accounts to be assigned have been created by the assignor, they are listed on assignment forms or "schedules." Since the assigned accounts constitute the very lifeblood of the assignee's security, all the material documents pertaining to the assigned accounts must accompany the assignment schedule and be contemporaneously delivered to the assignee at the time when it makes its advance to the assignor upon them. These documents vary with the nature of the assigned accounts but must always include copies of the relevant invoices; the original bills of lading or express receipts evidencing the delivery of the merchandise or (where applicable) proof of the rendition of the service; and all other papers necessary to effect collection of the assigned accounts. It is vital that the assignee satisfy himself as to the authenticity and legal competence of these documents.

The assignment-schedules as a rule must cover specific accounts; in most jurisdictions [prior to the Code], blanket assignments [were] of little, if any, legal value. See, illustratively, State Factors Corp. v. Sales Factors Corp., 257 App.Div. 101, 12 N.Y.S.2d 12 (1st Dep't 1939). However, under the so-called "floating lien" provisions of the Uniform Commercial Code (§§ 9–108 and 9–204) ... general, or blanket, assignments are permitted and recognized. ...

Indirect and Direct Collections. There are two methods—indirect or direct, so-called, for the actual collection of the assigned accounts.

In the indirect collection program, the account-debtors are not notified of the assignments, and remittances are made to the assignor, who is obligated promptly to endorse and transmit them in specie to the assignee—customarily on the day of their receipt. If it has not already become apparent, we shall, a little later, appreciate the economic and legal necessity [prior to the Code] for the imposition of this requirement.

In the direct collection program, the account-debtors are forthwith notified of the assignments, and are instructed to make their remittances directly to the assignee.

Indirect collection is much more frequently found in recourse financing, and direct collection in non-recourse financing, but the association is by no means inevitable. Indeed, one of the larger and most respected financing agencies has recently instituted a non-notification, non-recourse program, for assignors whose operations and standing make it adaptable to their business.

In all accounts receivable programs, the assignee, at periodic intervals (usually monthly) makes an audit of the assignor's books and operations, through one of the members of its own staff. In addition, when the collection program is indirect, the assignee causes periodic spot verification to be made of the existence of the assigned accounts and the amounts due upon them. This is accomplished by direct correspondence between an auditing concern and a random selection of the account-debtors.

Causes of Loss. Experience has demonstrated that the incidence of loss in an accounts receivable operation is minimal, almost to the vanishing point, if: the adaptability of the assignor's business to accounts receivable financing has been soundly analyzed and conceived; the credit standing of the account-debtors has been sensibly evaluated at the time when the assignments are tendered for advances upon them; and the operation is properly conducted within the framework above outlined. Of course, losses do take place, but, when they do, they are attributable, largely, if not solely, to what, in air-travel, would be called "pilot failure" in one of three aspects:

(1) Over-concentration. The first such cause, over-concentration, is purely economic and is by no means indigenous to the accounts receivable field. It is basic (a) that the assignee should diversify, as among the types and selection of assignors whose business he finances, and (b) that the accounts receivable of any one assignor should be diversified as

much as the nature of its business permits. If the author were charged with operational responsibility (which none of his clients has ever "threatened" to entrust to him), he would view, with a highly piscatorial eye, financing a borrower who had only three large customers, however, financially "good" these customers might be. All of this is purely an economic matter, but a very important one.

(2) Fictitious Accounts. The second cause of loss—the assignment of fictitious accounts—brings us into the legal area. Obviously, if an assignor ships goods on consignment or, worse yet, purports to assign "accounts" against "account-debtors" to whom no merchandise has been shipped at all, the assignee has no security for his advances. Neither the nature of the operation nor the rates charged for it permit the assumption of any such hazard, and it is this signpost which points the path to the importance of checking the shipping and other documents adverted to above. ...

One final feature of this whole matter is so obvious as merely to require mention. If the account-debtor, without notice of either of the duplicate assignments, pays the assignor or either of the assignees, he is fully protected and naturally need not pay any of them, all over again.

(3) Conversions. The last cause of loss is the conversion by the assignor of the proceeds of assigned accounts. It can occur only when the collection method is indirect. ...

Although there is no substitute for watchfulness, relatively simple techniques exist to guard against and obviate the hazard of over-concentration, fictitious accounts and duplicate assignments, and conversions. Assuming the original soundness of the assignor's business operation, no financing assignee who makes a reasonable realistic check of the account-debtor's credit is apt to sustain any serious loss if he will just watch these three matters.

Compliance With Formal Requirements of the Assignment:

[Prior to the Code, the] requirements for the perfection of an assignment of an account, so as to vest title to it in the assignee as against all the world, [varied] from state to state.

This perfection matter is of no importance from the account-debtor's standpoint, because, as already observed, if in good faith and without notice of the assignment, he makes payment either to the assignor or to the assignee he is fully protected.

Neither is it of much, if any, consequence as between an assignee and a solvent assignor, because the assignment is good between the parties, whether or not it has been technically "perfected" as against others.

Therefore, the practical significance of the perfection concept arises principally in the event of the assignor's bankruptcy, because the date of such perfection is the cut-off date for the application of the four-months' period under section 60, the preference provision of the Bankruptcy Act.

Case Law. Until the comparatively recent past, the perfection of title was governed solely by case law. The states fell into two classes.

Following the English case of Dearle v. Hall, 3 Russ 1 [38 Eng. Rep. 475 (Ch. 1828)], the first group, constituting the minority, held that notification to the account-debtor was essential to the perfection of an assignment. The principle is known as the *"English"* or *"notification"* rule. In such states, unless the first assignee notified the account-debtor of the assignment, a second assignee of the account, who took his assignment for value and without notice of the prior assignment (and, of course, himself first gave notice) prevailed. ...

Legally, notification to the *account-debtor* would hardly seem to constitute any "overt" act of import because it furnishes no protection to the assignor's suppliers or other unsecured creditors. Therefore— still remembering that we are dealing with the situation before many legislatures recently moved in and took hold—the majority of the states embraced the so-called *"American"* or *"validation"* rule, obtaining in New York. It dispenses with notices as a necessary element to the perfection of title, and holds that the first assignment in point of time prevails, regardless of the order in which notice, if any, to the account-debtor is given.

A variant of this rule, as set forth in section 173 of the Restatement of the Law of Contracts, prevailed in Massachusetts and several other states. Although no longer obtaining in the state of its origin, it is known as the "Massachusetts" [or "Four Horsemen"] rule. It accords priority to the first assignee unless the second assignee, without notice of the prior assignment, obtains (1) payment or satisfaction of the account-debtor's obligation; or (2) judgment against the account-debtor; or (3) a new contract with the account-debtor, by means of a novation; or (4) delivery of a tangible token or writing (such as a promissory note), surrender of which would be required by the account-debtor's contract for its enforcement.

So far, so good.

The Klauder Case and the Resulting State Statutes. In 1938, the Chandler Act amended section 60a of the Bankruptcy Act [11 U.S.C. § 96(a) (1952)] so as to step up the position of a trustee in bankruptcy from that of a hypothetical judgment-creditor or execution-creditor to that of a hypothetical *bona fide* purchaser. And in 1943, a bombshell was thrown into the area of all secured lending (and particularly accounts receivable) by the United States Supreme Court's opinion in Corn Exchange Nat'l Bank & Trust Co. v. Klauder, 318 U.S. 434[, 63 S.Ct. 679, 87 L.Ed. 884] (1943), interpreting the Chandler Act amendment.

Without attempting to follow what many regard as the circuitous legal gyrations by which the *Klauder* result was arrived at, suffice it to say that it placed accounts receivable financing at great risk, by destroying the efficacy of the existing signposts of perfection and leaving the field without a landmark.

The matter was finally set aright generally by the 1950 amendment to section 60a, but, since the perfection of title rests upon state law it was necessary to resort to the legislatures to stake out anew workable signposts in the accounts receivable area. (So far as known, only Ohio regulated the matter by statute at the time of the *Klauder* decision.)

The majority of states, therefore, regulated the matter by statute, and the method of perfection to be required became a warmly debated policy question. It was generally agreed that, as an *indicium* of perfection, from a practical standpoint, neither notice to the account-debtor nor the marking of the assignor's books meant anything. The choice, therefore, narrowed down to the adoption of either (a) the validation rule, with or without its Massachusetts variant; or (b) notice-filing (also called "recording") of a general notice of intention to assign, along the lines prescribed by the Uniform Trust Receipts Act.

[In 1956, prior to the general adoption of the Code, statutes in] twenty-one states [required] notice-filing: Alabama; Arizona; California; Colorado; Florida; Georgia; Idaho; Iowa; Kansas; Louisiana; Missouri; Nebraska; North Carolina; Ohio; Oklahoma; Pennsylvania (under the Uniform Commercial Code); South Carolina; Texas; Utah; Vermont; and Washington.

The statutes in fifteen states [prior to the Code, prescribed] the validation rule: Arkansas; Connecticut; Illinois; Indiana; Maine; Maryland; Massachusetts; Michigan; Minnesota; New Hampshire; Oregon; Rhode Island; South Dakota; Virginia; and Wisconsin.

One (North Dakota) requir[ed] the marking of the account-debtor's books.

Case-law [governed] in the rest. It will be noted that neither New York nor New Jersey, the original "homes" of the validation rule, [had] any statute on the subject. This for the reason that the rule, as laid down in their cases, [was] so clear that no legislation on the subject seemed necessary. The Uniform Commercial Code embodies the notice-filing principle.

Notes on Sales of Accounts and Chattel Paper

(1) **Reasons for the Broad Scope of Article 9.** As Kupfer's description indicates, accounts are used as a source of current capital through two primary types of arrangements. (1) One arrangement is a loan, with repayment secured by the assignment of accounts. This transaction may be expressed as a sale of the account (at a discount), with recourse by the "buyer" against the "seller" to the extent that any obligor (account debtor) fails to pay. (2) A second arrangement pro-

vides for the sale of the accounts without a right of recourse; however, even in a "non-recourse" sale (sometimes called **factoring**), the assignor is responsible if an obligor (account debtor) has a claim for breach of warranty or for some other reason returns the goods for credit. Between these two prototypical arrangements lies a range of transactions, tailored to suit the appetite of the parties for accepting (or sharing) the credit risk—the risk that the account debtor will be financially unable to pay the entire amount of the account in a timely manner.

When goods are sold on *secured* credit and the resulting *chattel paper* is sold, as in the case of the automobile financing Prototype in Chapter 11, the parties must agree to allocate not only the credit risk but also the risks attendant to enforcing the security interest that the seller (assignor of the chattel paper) has retained in the goods and assigned to the financer. For an example of some of the ways in which this risk may be allocated, see Form 5, Chapter 11, Section 1, supra.

Suppose the drafters of Article 9 had divided the world of accounts and chattel paper financing in two: (1) "recourse" arrangements that would be treated like security interests and would be subject to Article 9 and (2) "non-recourse" arrangements that would be excluded from the Article. A sharp eye would be needed to distinguish between the two arrangements; a fair amount of time and money would be expended on classifying ambiguous arrangements after the fact. The number of ambiguous arrangements might increase, since parties planning these transactions would have incentives to camouflage the substance in order to pull themselves in or out of Article 9.

Indeed, non-Code law sometimes provides these incentives, adding to the confusion. Even where the transaction in substance clearly is a loan, the lender may wish to make the transaction look like a sale: The lender's return for the loan may exceed the statutory limit for "interest." Usury statutes do not, of course, regulate the *price* for *sales* of accounts. And such a "sale" at a discount coupled with a "warranty" by the "seller" that the account is "good" and will be paid at maturity might conceivably lead a sympathetic (or dull) judge to conclude that the transaction really was a sale and not a usurious loan.

Against this background, it is less surprising that even the pre-Code statutes on the assignment of accounts covered not only assignments for security but also outright sales. See 1 Gilmore, Security § 8.7. The Code uses a similarly broad brush: With respect to accounts and chattel paper, Article 9 applies not only to the transfer of a security interest (UCC 9–102(1)(a)) but also to "any sale" (UCC 9–102(1)(b)).

(2) Narrowing the Scope Through Exclusions. From the outset, the Code's drafters recognized that the inclusion of all sales of accounts and chattel paper would go too far. UCC 9–104(f) excludes a few specific types of transfers of accounts and chattel paper. Excluded transfers include the assignment of a right to payment together with a delegation of the duty of performance giving rise to the payment, and the transfer of a single account to an assignee in whole or partial satisfaction of a preexisting indebtedness. UCC 9–104, Comment 6 suggests that the excluded transfers, "by their nature, have nothing to do with commercial financing transactions."

Although UCC 9–104(f) reintroduces the problem of line-drawing that the inclusion of "any sale" eliminates, as a practical matter the problem has not proven to be particularly difficult one. The amount of litigation on this issue is trivial; it is dwarfed by that concerning the lease-sale distinction and the other ambiguous transactions in goods discussed in Section 1 above.

(3) Sales of Instruments and General Intangibles; Credit Card Receivables. Not all rights to payment are accounts or chattel paper; some are instruments, others are general intangibles. Like accounts and chattel paper, instruments and general intangibles are the subject of both secured financings and outright sales. For example, to increase its liquid assets, a bank may wish to utilize its portfolio of **credit card receivables**—unsecured obligations of its cardholders to pay for credit they received through the use of the card. If these receivables are "accounts," then Article 9 will apply regardless of whether the receivables are sold or are used to secure a loan. On the other hand, if the receivables are general intangibles, then Article 9 would apply to the financing only if it is a secured transaction.

With respect to general intangibles, Professor Kripke long ago observed that the exclusion of non-sale- and non-service-related rights to payment from the definition of "account" was an anomaly and did not reflect the intent of the drafters. Kripke, Suggestions for Clarifying Article 9: Intangibles, Proceeds, and Priorities, 41 N.Y.U.L.Rev. 687, 690–91 (1966). Notwithstanding Professor Kripke's major role in the Article 9 Review Committee (he was the Associate Reporter), the 1972 revisions did not correct the situation.

The exclusion of sales of general intangibles from Article 9 gives rise to several problems. The most obvious is that exclusion from Article 9 excuses assignees from compliance with the public notice (filing) provisions of the Article. See UCC 9–302; Note on Public Notice of Transfers of Accounts, infra.

The excluded transactions are governed by non-Code law, typically the common law dealing with the assignment of choses in action. This law may be both hard to find and unclear. (Some of these transactions would have been governed by pre-Code statutes dealing with assignments of accounts receivable; however, those statutes were repealed in the course of enacting the Code. See UCC 10–102.) This non-Code law may include the doctrine of Benedict v. Ratner, 268 U.S. 353, 45 S.Ct. 566, 69 L.Ed. 991 (1925), which held that the grant of a security interest in accounts receivable was fraudulent where the assignor retained unfettered dominion over the proceeds, and which UCC 9–205 repealed insofar as it might apply to Article 9 transactions (security interests in all kinds of collateral and sales of accounts and chattel paper). For discussions of *Benedict*, see Chapter 11, Sections 2(A) and (B), supra; and Chapter 14, Section 3(A), infra.

Moreover, as Note (1), supra, suggests, determining whether a transaction should be characterized as a true sale or as a secured transaction often is difficult. Courts have used a number of factors, including the existence and nature of recourse against the assignor. According to one writer, the cases addressing the dichotomy "are not easily harmonized, and different readers may argue as to which factors are relevant and which are entitled to greater weight." S. Schwarcz, Structured Finance 19 (1990). As a result of this uncertainty, parties must proceed on alternative assumptions, thereby further complicating transactions and increasing costs. In a similar vein, classifying certain types of property as accounts, chattel paper, general intangibles, or instruments, may be difficult.

The easy fix—adding sales of general intangibles (and, perhaps, instruments) to the scope of Article 9—would be disastrous. Many general intangibles do not consist of a right to the payment of money; sales of these types of property typically are not financing transactions. Moreover, even if Article 9 were expanded to cover the sale of only those general intangibles for money due or to become due, the drafters would need to exclude the vast range of transactions that do not constitute commercial financing.

Problem 1. The Pullit Co. is in the business of manufacturing conveyor belts that it sells on open credit to a variety of customers. Many of these belts are sold to manufacturers of drill presses and similar equipment; they are installed in these machines and used to carry out metal scraps. In need of immediate cash, Pullit entered into a written agreement with Financer, pursuant to which Financer agreed to purchase certain accounts meeting specified characteristics (e.g., not overdue) for an amount equal to 70% of the face amount of the account. Pullit sold these accounts on a non-recourse basis; however, it warranted that the accounts were genuine and that none of the account debtors had defenses to payment.

(a) Lean, a judgment creditor of Pullit, served a **garnishment** summons on three of Pullit's biggest customers. The summons instructs each **garnishee** to inform the court of the amount it owes to Pullit; service of the summons gives rise to a lien in favor of the judgment creditor (here, Lean) in that amount. If a garnishee answers that it is indebted to Pullit, the court will enter judgment in that amount in favor of Lean, and the customer will be obligated to pay Lean instead of Pullit. Prior to the entry of judgment, Financer intervenes, asserting that it is the owner of the accounts, that the customers owe Pullit nothing, and that Lean is not entitled to payment from the customers. What result? See UCC 9–102(1)(b); UCC 1–201(37) (3d sentence); UCC 9–301(1)(b); UCC 9–302(1).

(b) Would the result in part (a) change if, before service of the garnishment summons, Financer had notified Pullit's customers that it had purchased their accounts? If Financer had taken possession of the contracts for the sale of the conveyors?

(c) Would the result in part (a) change if Pullit had retained purchase money security interests in the conveyors and sold Financer the secured rights to payment? See UCC 9–105(1)(b); UCC 9–102(1)(b).

Problem 2. You are partner at a law firm (Firm). One of Firm's clients (Client) owes Firm several hundred thousand dollars, most of which is past due. Client has been manufacturing some custom equipment under one of its larger contracts; it expects to pay Firm once its buyer pays for the equipment. Firm is willing to wait (it has little choice), but it wants to be sure that when Client is paid, Firm will be paid. You prepare a security agreement and a financing statement for Client to sign.

(a) Client is reluctant to have a financing statement filed against it. How would you respond to each of the following alternative suggestions?

(i) Client could sell the account to Firm, instead of granting a security interest in it. See UCC 9–104(f) (last clause).

(ii) Firm does not need to file a financing statement to protect its security interest. See UCC 9–302(1)(e) & Comment 5; In re Tri–County Materials, Inc., infra; Note on Public Notice of Transfers of Accounts, infra.

(b) Other than taking the security agreement and filing the financing statement, are there any other steps you would advise Firm to take to bolster its position? See UCC 9–318(3); Note on Rights of Account Debtors, infra.

IN RE TRI–COUNTY MATERIALS, INC.

United States District Court, C.D.Illinois, 1990.
114 B.R. 160.

MIHM, DISTRICT JUDGE. . . .

FACTS

Tri-County Materials, the Debtor below, operated a sand and gravel pit. Ladd Construction Company was a general contractor which had a contract with the State of Illinois to construct a portion of Interstate 39. Ladd and Tri–County entered into a contract according to which Tri–County would supply Ladd with 100,000 tons of sand and gravel at $2.50 per ton. In order to complete its contractual obligations, Tri–County needed certain equipment to process the sand and gravel from the land it leased. As a result, KMB, Inc. leased equipment to Tri–County for that purpose. . . .

Although initially the agreement between Tri–County and KMB for the lease of the equipment was oral, that agreement was reduced to writing in June of 1988. In the agreement, Tri–County assigned part of its account with Ladd Construction Company to KMB for the purpose of securing the rental charges which Tri–County owed to KMB. Ladd was notified of the assignment and received bi-weekly notification of the amount due to KMB by Tri–County. KMB did not file a Uniform Commercial Code financing statement regarding the assignment.

Tri-County filed a voluntary petition for bankruptcy under Chapter 11 in October of 1988. At that time, Ladd owed Tri–County $43,413.71 for previously supplied material while Tri–County owed KMB $30,484.

The bankruptcy court found that KMB did not have a security interest in the funds due from Ladd because they had failed to perfect that interest as required under Article 9 of the Uniform Commercial Code. ...

PERFECTION OF SECURITY INTEREST

Tri-County owed KMB $30,484 at the time of filing bankruptcy. KMB claims that, because Tri–County assigned its right to receive payments from Ladd to the extent that it owed money to KMB, it had a security interest in the money owed to Tri–County.

Ill.Rev.Stat. ch. 26, § 9–302 provides as follows:

(1) a financing statement must be filed to perfect all security interests except the following: ... (e) an assignment of accounts which does not alone or in conjunction with other assignments to the same assignee transfer a significant part of the outstanding accounts of the assignor.

KMB takes the position that it is entitled to rely on § 9–302(1)(e) because it is not regularly engaged in accounts receivable financing, thus making this a casual and isolated transaction, and because the amount which Tri–County owed to KMB, when compared to the $250,-000 which Tri–County was entitled to receive from Ladd was a mere 12%, thus making it an insignificant transfer. Appellant argues that because KMB fails to meet either test it did not have a perfected security interest in the Ladd account.

The burden of proving the applicability of § 9–302(1)(e) rests on the party asserting the exception. See, Consolidated Film Industries v. United States, 547 F.2d 533 (10th Cir.1977). Although the Code does not define "significant part," case law has developed two tests.

The first test is referred to as the percentage test. This test focuses on the size of the assignment in relation to the size of outstanding accounts. In re B. Hollis Knight Co., 605 F.2d 397 (8th Cir.1979); Standard Lumber Company v. Chamber Frames, Inc., 317 F.Supp. 837 (E.D.Ark.1970).

The second test is the "casual or isolated" test. This test is suggested by the language of Comment 5 to UCC § 9–302 which states that:

> The purpose of the subsection (e)(1) exemptions is to save from ex post facto invalidation casual or isolated assignments: some accounts receivable statutes have been so broadly drafted that all assignments, whatever their character or purpose, fall within their filing provisions. Under such statute many assignments which no one would think of filing may be subject to invalidation. The subsection (1)(e) exemptions go to that type of assignment. Any person who regularly takes assignments of any debtor's accounts should file.

The totality of circumstances surrounding the transaction determines whether an assignment was casual or isolated. If the transaction was not part of a regular course of commercial financing then under this test filing is not required. The rationale appears to be the reasonableness of requiring a secured creditor to file if assignment of debtor's accounts is a regular part of business and the corresponding unreasonableness of a filing requirement for casual or isolated transactions.

There is no authoritative determination of whether both tests must be met in order to claim the exemption or whether either by itself is sufficient. The bankruptcy court agreed with the *Hollis Knight* court which held that both tests must be met. This Court agrees with that assessment. The statutory language specifically requires that the assignment be an insignificant part of the outstanding account. Thus, at the very least, this test must be met in every instance. A showing of a casual or isolated assignment of a significant part of outstanding accounts would not be entitled to the exemption given this clear statutory requirement. On the other hand, given the comments to the UCC regarding the purpose of this exemption, in a case involving the transfer of an insignificant part of outstanding accounts to a creditor whose regular business is financing, such accounts should not fall within this exemption. Thus it is a logical result of the language and purpose of this section to require that both tests be met.

Under the UCC, an account is "any right to payment for goods sold or leased or for services rendered which is not evidenced by an instrument or chattel paper, whether or not it has been earned by performance." Ill.Rev.Stat. ch. 26, § 9–106.

The Debtor's bankruptcy schedules indicate that Tri–County had ten accounts at the time of the Chapter 11 filing, of which the largest by far was the Ladd contract for $250,000. The assignment to KMB permitted KMB to:

> request that the Ladd Construction Company ... make any and all payments to [Tri–County] by including on said check payment the name of [KMB] who shall have said check negotiated and endorsed by [Tri–County] and said check shall be deposited in [KMB's]

account with [Tri–County's] endorsement, at which time [KMB] shall issue a check to [Tri–County] for the difference between the amount of the check issued and the rental payment owed to [KMB]."

Equipment Rental Agreement p. 5.

It is thus clear that the assignment was not of the entire Ladd account but only of that portion of the account necessary to cover the balance due to KMB. At the time the parties entered into the Agreement, the total rental amount was estimated at $30,000; the actual figure turned out to be $30,484. The ratio of the amount assigned to the total account, even assuming that the Ladd contract was the *only* account, is approximately 12%.

Although there is no bright line marking the division between significant and insignificant, the 12% figure is surely on the "insignificant" side. See, Standard Lumber Co. v. Chamber Frames, Inc., 317 F.Supp. 837 (D.C. Ark.1970) (16% insignificant). Thus, the first test, contrary to what the bankruptcy court found, has been satisfied. The bankruptcy court based its finding on the assumption that Tri–County had assigned the entire Ladd account to KMB, an assumption that is not supported by the record.

The record also shows without contradiction that KMB was not in the business of accepting contract assignments, nor had either party to the assignment engaged in such a transaction at other times. The bankruptcy court found that despite the "isolated" nature of this assignment, it was "a classic secured transaction," Op. p. 9, and thus failed to fall within the "casual and isolated" exception to the filing requirement.

This Court agrees with that assessment. This is not the type of "casual" transaction in which reasonable parties would fail to see the importance of filing. Rather, it was evidenced by a formal, written agreement between two corporations; notice of the agreement was sent to Ladd, and other conduct engaged in by KMB indicates the degree of formality attached to it. This is the type of transaction for which the UCC requires filing in order to perfect.

Because KMB failed to perfect its security interest, this Court affirms the bankruptcy court's ruling.

CONCLUSION

As stated above, this Court AFFIRMS the bankruptcy court in its finding that ... KMB did not have a perfected security interest in the Ladd account.

· · ·

Note on Public Notice of Transfers of Accounts

As the *Tri–County Materials* case indicates, courts have disagreed over the meaning of UCC 9–302(1)(e), which exempts certain transfers of accounts from the general rule that filing is necessary to perfect a security interest. The range of opinions is even broader than *Tri–County Materials* suggests. See, e.g., Park Avenue Bank v. Bassford, 232 Ga. 216, 205 S.E.2d 861 (1974) (dollar amount of assigned accounts "significant" without regard to percentage); Architectural Woods, Inc. v. Washington, 88 Wash.2d 406, 562 P.2d 248 (1977) (en banc) (applying only "casual and isolated" test). One way to evaluate the proper scope of the exemption is to determine which types of transfers do not implicate the need for public notice. This, in turn leads one to examine the reason or reasons underlying the general rule.

Note (2) on Attachment and Perfection by Filing, Chapter 11, Section 2(A), supra, explores a number of these reasons. Please review it now. Do the reasons justifying a filing requirement for security interests in tangible collateral apply equally to secured parties (including buyers, see UCC 9–105(1)(m)), whose collateral consists of intangible property, such as accounts? If so, does any of these reasons support an exemption for a transfer of accounts having insubstantial value? Insubstantial value relative to the assignor's total accounts? Does any of these reasons support an exemption for "casual or isolated assignments"? Assignments as to which "no one would think of filing"? UCC 9–302, Comment 5. Assignments as to which only professionals would think of filing?

Problem 3. Assume the facts in Problem 1, supra, in which Pullit sold its accounts to Financer. (Ignore the facts in paragraphs (a)-(c), dealing with Lean.) Assume also that the agreement between Financer and Pullit gives Financer the right to notify Pullit's customers to make payment directly to Financer.

(a) Two weeks after its account is sold to Financer, Customer # 1 pays Pullit in full. Is Financer out of luck? See UCC 9–318(3).

(b) Would the result in part (a) change if, prior to paying Pullit, Customer # 1 received a letter from Financer stating as follows: "You are hereby advised that all amounts owing from yourself to The Pullit Co. have been sold to the undersigned. Kindly remit all future payments to the undersigned at the address shown on the letterhead."?

(c) Would the result in part (a) change if the letter described in part (b) did not contain the second sentence? Compare Vacura v. Haar's Equipment, Inc., 364 N.W.2d 387 (Minn.1985) (notification of assignment will not cut off account debtor's right to pay assignor unless it contains explicit direction that payment is to be made to assignee) with First National Bank of Rio Arriba v. Mountain States Telephone & Telegraph Co., 91 N.M. 126, 571 P.2d 118 (1977) (unconditional language of assignment, which was accepted in writing by account debtor, was notice that payment was to be made to assignee). Courts often read UCC 9–318(3) strictly, to protect account debtors from having to pay twice.

(d) Customer # 2 received the letter described in part (b) but refuses to pay Financer, citing a provision of its contract with Pullit stating that "this contract is not assignable." Is Financer out of luck? See UCC 9–318(4).

(e) Would the result in part (d) change if Pullit had retained a purchase money security interest in the conveyors purchased by Customer # 2 and had sold Financer the secured rights to payment? See UCC 9–318(4); Note on Rights of Account Debtors, infra.

(f) Customer # 3 received the letter described in part (b) but refuses to pay Financer, claiming that it doesn't believe Pullit has stooped so low as to "hock its receivables." What, if anything, can Financer do? See UCC 9–318(3). What can Customer # 3 do if it remains dubious? See Note on Rights of Account Debtors, infra.

(g) Customer # 4 received the letter from Financer. In response it informed Financer that, two weeks before it received the letter, the conveyor it bought from Pullit malfunctioned. A manufacturing defect caused sparks to fly from the machine; these sparks set off a fire causing damage to Customer's plant, thereby cutting Customer's manufacturing capacity by 20% for three days. Accordingly, Customer # 4 not only refuses to pay for the conveyor (which does not operate) but also seeks compensation from Financer for property damage and loss of profits.

(i) Is Customer obligated to pay for the conveyor? See UCC 9–318(1).

(ii) Is Customer entitled to compensation from Financer for its loss? See UCC 9–318(1). Is Customer's demand a "defense or claim arising" from the contract between the account debtor and the assignor? See Note on Rights of Account Debtors, infra.

(h) Would the result in part (g) change if Customer # 4 had paid in full for the conveyor that malfunctioned and the account that Financer was assigned was for the sale of a different conveyor? See UCC 9–318(1).

(i) Would the result in part (g) change if the conveyor malfunctioned three days *after* Customer # 4 received the letter? See UCC 9–318(1). Would it make any difference if both conveyors were the subject of a single contract between Pullit and Customer? If there was a master agreement containing general terms, supplemented by separate agreements containing the specifications for each conveyor?

Note on Rights of Account Debtors

As the excerpt from Kupfer, supra, suggests, some accounts financing is done on a notification basis, i.e., the account debtors are notified to remit payment directly to the assignee (secured party). Not surprisingly, Article 9 provides that such an agreement is effective against both the debtor and the account debtor. See UCC 9–318(3); UCC 9–502(1). When accounts financing is done on a non-notification basis, upon the debtor's (assignor's) default, the secured party likewise is entitled to notify account debtors to make payment to the secured party. See UCC 9–502(1).

The Account Debtor's Problem: Whom to Pay? UCC 9–318 addresses a variety of issues that may arise in the collection of accounts. Subsections (3) and (4) set forth the circumstances under which the account debtor must pay the secured party, who may be a stranger to the transaction, rather than the assignor, with whom the account debtor has dealt. Knowing the proper party to pay is (or should be) a major concern for the account debtor. If the account debtor pays the wrong party, it does not discharge its obligation on the contract and will have to pay again—this time to the proper party. (Although the mistaken account debtor will be entitled to recover its payment from a party who is not entitled to it, see Restatement of Restitution § 17 (1937), the account debtor would prefer not to litigate the issue, particularly with a person who wrongfully kept funds to which it was not entitled.) Subsection (3) helps protect the account debtor from having to pay twice.

The account debtor on a contract may wish to avoid entirely the risk of paying the wrong party by simply making the contract non-assignable, or by conditioning assignment on its advance consent. However, UCC 9–318(4) makes provisions of this kind, which are not terribly common, "ineffective." UCC 9–318(4) is one of several Code rules promoting free alienability of property. See also UCC 9–311 (debtor's rights in collateral may be transferred notwithstanding a prohibition in the security agreement). An "ineffective" prohibition on assignment will not prevent the assignment from taking effect; that is, the prohibition will not prevent a security interest from attaching to the account. The fact that the prohibition is ineffective against the assignee does not necessarily mean that it is of no effect whatsoever. The contract between the account debtor and the assignor may provide that violation of the prohibition on assignments constitutes a default under the contract. Does UCC 9–318(4) render this default clause ineffective? If the prohibition is effective as between the account debtor and the assignor, is the value of the account as collateral substantially impaired? See the discussion of claims and defenses of the account debtor, infra.

Observe that UCC 9–318(4) refers only to accounts and certain general intangibles; it is silent as to chattel paper. The failure to include chattel paper may have been inadvertent; security agreements and personal property leases rarely prohibit the creditor from assigning its rights, and the drafters may have ignored or been oblivious to the potential problem. The effectiveness of prohibitions on the transfer of chattel paper eventually came to the fore under the 1987 version of

Article 2A. As originally promulgated, UCC 2A–303(1) provided that contractual prohibitions on the voluntary transfer of lessor's interest under a lease would be effective. Under this section, a secured party who purchased a debtor's portfolio of leases ran the risk (undoubtedly a very small one) that its security interest never attached to some of the leases. This section was one of several that gave rise to a protracted dispute over the desirability of amending Article 2A before attempting to secure its widespread enactment. In 1990, the Code's sponsors relented and amended UCC 2A–303 to reflect the policy of UCC 9–318(4). For a discussion of the pre–1987 version of UCC 2A–303 and the dispute it helped to engender, see Harris, The Interface Between Articles 2A and 9 Under the Official Text and the California Amendments, 22 UCC L.J. 99 (1989).

The Secured Party's Problem: Claims and Defenses of the Account Debtor. UCC 9–318(1) generally reflects the *nemo dat* principle. The assignee (secured party) generally takes its interest in the account subject to defenses of the account debtor. If, for example, the account debtor has a defense to payment, it may assert the defense against the assignee. By notifying the account debtor of the assignment, the assignee may deprive the account debtor of certain defenses that may arise in the future. See UCC 9–318(1)(b). And, as we saw in Chapter 2, an assignee may take free of nearly all defenses if the account debtor agrees. See UCC 9–206(1). (Of course, the account debtor retains its rights against the assignor.)

Suppose an account debtor makes payments to the assignee and then discovers that the goods are worth only half what the account debtor has paid for them. The account debtor seeks to recover the overpayment from the assignee. Had the account debtor known of the defense before payment, it could have asserted a defense to the assignee's demand for payment. Do the legal positions of the account debtor and assignee change simply because the account debtor discovers the goods are defective after it has paid for them?

Yes, according to the Restatement of Restitution (1937). Section 14(2) provides as follows:

> An assignee of a non-negotiable chose in action who, having paid value therefor, has received payment from the obligor is under no duty to make restitution although the obligor had a defense thereto, if the transferee made no misrepresentation and did not have notice of the defense.

Similarly, payment made by mistake that was induced by the fraud or material misrepresentation of a third person cannot be recovered unless "the payee has notice of the fraud or representation before he has given or promised something of value." Restatement of Restitution § 28(d). Are these rules premised on the negotiability of money? On need for finality in commercial transactions?

UCC 9–318 indicates that assignees take subject to "claims" as well as "defenses." Does the inclusion of "claims" change what appears to be the non-Code law? Does it mean that an assignee must disgorge payments it has received for defective goods? Payments induced by the assignor's fraud? Does the inclusion of "claims" mean that the assignee becomes accountable for damages caused by the goods whose sale gave rise to the assigned account?

The First Circuit had occasion to address some of these issues in Michelin Tires (Canada) Ltd. v. First National Bank of Boston, 666 F.2d 673 (1st Cir.1981). Michelin entered into a contract for the design and installation of a carbon black handling and storage system, which was to form part of a Michelin tire factory in Nova Scotia. Michelin agreed to pay the contractor, JCC, periodic progress payments. JCC granted a security interest in its rights under the contract to FNB. FNB notified Michelin of the assignment, and Michelin paid FNB a total of $724,-197.60. Thereafter, Michelin discovered that JCC had submitted fictitious invoices and fraudulent sworn statements showing that JCC had paid its subcontractors. JCC filed a bankruptcy petition, and Michelin sued to recover the payments from FNB.

The majority found that Michelin was not entitled to recover under principles of restitution and that UCC 9–318(1), despite its reference to "claims," did not create affirmative rights of recovery against assignees who did not actively participate in the fraudulent transactions. The court found this result to be consistent with sound policy:

> While it is our judgment that analysis of the statutory language, taken in context, indicates that no affirmative right was contemplated and further that those cases that have permitted such a right are factually inapposite, we also believe it would be unwise to permit such suits as a matter of policy. [A]llowing affirmative suits would "make every Banker, who has taken an assignment of accounts for security purposes, a deep pocket surety for every bankrupt contractor in the state to whom it had loaned money."
>
> We are unwilling to impose such an obligation on the banks of the Commonwealth without some indication that this represents a considered policy choice. By making the bank a surety, not only will accounts receivable financing be discouraged, but transaction costs will undoubtedly increase for everyone. The case at hand provides a good example. In order to protect themselves, FNB would essentially be forced to undertake the precautionary measures that Michelin attempted to use, independent observation by an intermediary and sworn certifications by the assignor. FNB would have to supervise every construction site where its funds were involved to ensure performance and payment. We simply do not believe that the banks are best suited to monitor contract compliance. The party most interested in adequate performance would be the other contracting party, not the financier. Given this natural interest, it seems likely to us that while the banks will be given

additional burdens of supervision, there would be no corresponding reduction in vigilance by the contracting parties, thus creating two inspections where there was formerly one. Costs for everyone thus increase, without any discernible benefit. It is also difficult to predict the full impact a contrary decision would have on the availability of accounts receivable financing in general.

Our holding, of course, is not that § 9–318 *prohibits* claims against the assignee. We hold merely that § 9–318 concerns only the preservation of defenses to the assignee's claims and, as such, is wholly inapposite in an affirmative suit against an assignee.

666 F.2d at 679–80.

In dissent, Judge Bownes concluded that under UCC 9–318(1)(a), "an assignee's rights to retain payments made to it under an assignment are subject to, or are exposed to, affirmative actions brought by the account debtor to recover payments mistakenly made."

This interpretation of section 9–318(1)(a), that the account debtor has rights of action against the assignee, is the fairest way to reconcile the rights of account debtors and secured creditors, particularly where, as here, credit is advanced through a line of credit. This case boils down to the question of whether the secured creditor or the account debtor should bear the cost of not finding out that JCC falsely claimed that it had paid its subcontractors. The secured creditor is in a better position than the account debtor to determine whether the assignor/borrower is complying with the terms of the contract in which the creditor has an interest. The reason is that the secured creditor can employ an effective sanction without having to initiate litigation and without risking any loss itself to ensure compliance; it can threaten to cut off credit unless it is satisfied with the borrower's performance. The other party, the account debtor, has no similar sanction. If he is not satisfied, he must litigate and bear the expense of litigation and the sure delay in completion of the contract. The creditor/assignee is not deterred from enforcing compliance by such costs. Obviously, either the secured creditor or the account debtor can make inquiries regarding compliance with the contract, but at some point both will have to rely on the representations of others, which creates opportunities for fraud, as occurred here. The secured creditor is accustomed to looking over the borrower's shoulder on an ongoing basis and can check compliance. By virtue of his control over credit, the creditor can ensure compliance with the contract. The account debtor can only investigate and if it holds up payments, it puts the contract in jeopardy.

666 F.2d at 684–85. Had JCC negligently constructed the facility, do you suppose Judge Bownes would have permitted Michelin to recover compensatory damages from FNB? See UCC 9–317 (mere existence of a security interest does not impose contract or tort liability upon the secured party for the debtor's acts or omissions).

Which view do you find more persuasive? More in keeping with the language of UCC 9–318(1)(a)? Under pre-Code law, account debtors generally were able to assert setoff rights against innocent assignees but were not entitled to recover payments made by mistake. Do you suppose the drafters intended to expand the rights of an account debtor to include the right to recover mistaken payments?

The same problem may arise with regard to negotiable promissory notes under Article 3. The 1990 revision yields a result consistent with *Michelin Tires:* "[T]he claim of the obligor may be asserted against a transferee of the instrument only to reduce the amount owing on the instrument at the time the action is brought." UCC 3–305(a)(3).

SECTION 3. EXCLUSIONS FROM ARTICLE 9 OR ITS FILING PROVISIONS

The provisions of Article 9 are not limited to interests that "secure[ ] payment or performance of an obligation." UCC 1–201(37). For example, as we saw in Section 2, supra, Article 9 applies in its entirety to many sales of accounts and chattel paper. We also saw, in Section 1(B), supra, that a consignor may use the Article 9 filing system to give effective public notice of its ownership interest in consigned goods.

This Section discusses two other aspects of the scope of Article 9: transactions that create security interests, but as to which Article 9 nevertheless is inapplicable; and transactions that create security interests covered by Article 9, but as to which public notice is given by filing or recording in a non-Article 9 system.

UCC 9–104 excludes certain types of transactions from Article 9. We had occasion to consider subsection (f), relating to certain transfers of accounts and chattel paper, in Section 2, supra.

Many of the other exclusions follow directly from the scope provisions, UCC 9–102(1) and (2). For example, Article 9 applies to "any transaction ... intended to create a security interest in personal property or fixtures." See UCC 9–313. UCC 9–104(j) reflects the converse: "Article [9] does not apply ... to the creation or transfer of an interest in or lien on real estate," except to the extent that provisior. is made for fixtures. Security interests in real estate (i.e., mortgages and trust deeds) are governed by real estate law.

In a similar fashion, UCC 9–102(2) provides that Article 9 applies to "security interests created by contract," and UCC 9–104 specifically excludes from the applicability of Article 9 two types of nonconsensual liens: landlord's liens, see UCC 9–104(b), and liens given by statute or other rule of law for services or materials. See UCC 9–104(c). The creation, priority, and enforcement of most nonconsensual liens is governed by the statutory and common law of each jurisdiction. However, Article 9 contains a provision governing priority contests between an Article 9 security interest and a lien for services or materials. See UCC 9–310. When UCC 9–310 does not apply, non-Code law governs priorities; that law often is not well developed.

Another exclusion that one might think to be self-evident is that of UCC 9–104(a): Article 9—state law—does not apply "to a security interest subject to any statute of the United States, to the extent that such statute governs the rights of parties to and third parties affected by transactions in particular types of property." The phrase "to the extent that" is a signal that the provision creates delicate problems of meshing state and federal law. The federal statutes that touch on security interests—e.g., those governing copyrights, patents, ships, and aircraft—do not contain a complete set of rules governing creation, perfection, priority, and enforcement. The courts must determine the extent to which any particular federal statute touching upon a secured transaction governs the specific issue in question.

Related, but not identical, to the exclusion from the *applicability* of Article 9 in UCC 9–104(a) is the exclusion from the Article 9 *filing system* in UCC 9–302(3)(a). If "a statute or treaty of the United States . . . provides for a national or international registration or a national or international certificate of title or . . . specifies a place of filing different from that specified in this Article [9] for filing of [a] security interest" in particular property, then the filing of an Article 9 financing statement is neither necessary nor effective to perfect a security interest in that property. UCC 9–302(3). Even so, Article 9 would continue to apply to questions other than perfection (unless, of course, UCC 9–104 excludes the entire transaction).

UCC 9–104, Comment 8, explains that Article 9 does not apply to security interests in certain "types of claims which do not customarily serve as commercial collateral: judgments under paragraph (h), set-offs under paragraph (i) and tort claims under paragraph (k)." Even if the Comment is accurate, does it justify relegating to the common law those secured parties who do take an interest in, say, a tort claim?

Professor Gilmore, the principal drafter of Article 9, had the following observations about the exclusion for setoffs:

> This exclusion is an apt example of the absurdities which result when draftsmen attempt to appease critics by putting into a statute something that is not in any sense wicked but is hopelessly irrelevant. Of course a right of set-off is not a security interest and has never been confused with one: the statute might as appropriately exclude fan dancing. A bank's right of set-off against a depositor's account is often loosely referred to as a "banker's lien," but the "lien" usage has never led anyone to think that the bank held a security interest in

the bank account. Banking groups were, however, concerned lest someone, someday, might think that a bank's right of set-off, because it was called a lien, was a security interest. Hence the exclusion, which does no harm except to the dignity and self-respect of the draftsmen.

1 Gilmore, Security § 10.7, at 315–16. Professor Gilmore may not have recognized all the costs of excluding "any right of set-off" from Article 9.

Chapter 13

CONFLICTING CLAIMS TO COLLATERAL: ARTICLE 9's BASIC PRIORITY RULES

Chapter 11 dealt primarily with whether a security interest is enforceable against the debtor and would withstand attack from judicial lien creditors. This chapter and the next deal with other conflicting claimants to the collateral. This chapter discusses claims by holders of conflicting security interests and by buyers of the collateral from the debtor. Chapter 14 focuses on the rights of the debtor's trustee in bankruptcy.

SECTION 1. COMPETING SECURITY INTERESTS

Introductory Note. Prior to enactment of the Code, conflicts between security interests had to be resolved under circumstances that approached anarchy. Only some of the security "devices" (chattel mortgage, conditional sale, trust receipt, assignment of accounts, factor's lien) had the benefit of statutory priority rules; even these rules almost invariably were rudimentary and were confined to conflicts between security interests created by the same "device." When separate security worlds would collide (e.g., conditional sale vs. trust receipt; assignment of accounts vs. factor's lien), the outcome was wildly unpredictable. The total effect was bearable only for one who had a taste for case-law improvisation or for chaos.

In bringing all personal property security under one roof, the Code exposed the wide variety of priority problems that had been lurking in the crannies among the various types of chattel security; the drafters met a scene that makes one think of Noah when he came to the room in the Ark reserved for snakes.

Even in the initial version of Article 9, by a happy marriage of theory and practical experience, the drafters developed a priority system that created a kind of order. Experience and further thought during the Code's first two decades produced significant refinements that are reflected in the 1972 revision of the great priority schema, UCC 9–312.

Most of the significant priority problems that experience and lively imaginations have exposed seem susceptible of solution under the 1972 version of Article 9. However, the current study of that Article has identified several examples of priority contests that warrant additional refinements. In this area, perhaps all that a student should try to carry into practice is a feel for Article 9's system of ordering priorities.

A lawyer who faces these problems in practice usually will have time to examine the Code and the case law to determine whether new problems have arisen in the cracks between the subsections.

Interestingly, Article 9 does not define or explain (at least not directly) the concept of "priority." What does it mean to say that one claim has "priority" over another or that one claim is "senior" or "junior" to another? One answer is that the claimant with priority, the senior claimant, is entitled to have its claim satisfied first from the value of the collateral involved. The junior claimant, then, could look to the remaining value, if any. However, as we shall consider in Chapter 15, Section 3(B), even in the absence of any action or participation by a senior claimant, a junior claimant sometimes can enforce its security interest by collecting or disposing of collateral after the debtor's default.

The following materials address the subject of conflicting security interests in several groups of Problems that are to be solved by a careful examination of the Code and the Notes and cases that follow the Problems. The statutory scheme is not limpid; the order of presentation in UCC 9–312 was not designed for comfort. The Problems are designed to lead you through the system step by step. The order in which the Problems appear is not accidental: you should solve the first Problem before taking on the second, and so on.

(A) THE FIRST-TO-FILE-OR-PERFECT RULE

Problem 1. On June 1 *D*, a dealer in mink pelts, obtained a $50,000 loan from *SP*–1 and as security delivered to *SP*–1 pelts of equivalent value. *SP*–1 did not file a financing statement.

On July 1 *D* obtained a $50,000 loan from *SP*–2 and executed a security agreement granting to *SP*–2 a security interest in all mink pelts owned by *D*. *SP*–2 immediately filed a financing statement covering "mink pelts."

(a) *D* defaults on the debts to *SP*–1 and *SP*–2. *D*'s principal assets are the pelts delivered to *SP*–1. Do both *SP*–1 and *SP*–2 have a security interest in the pelts? Is each security interest perfected? Whose security interest is senior? See UCC 9–312(5); UCC 9–302(1)(a); Notes (1) and (2) on the First–to–File–or–Perfect Rule, infra. What could the losing party have done to avoid the loss?

(b) Reverse the order of the transactions in part (a): The transaction with *SP*–2 (including filing) occurred on June 1, and the transaction with *SP*–1 occurred on July 1. In this setting whose security interest is senior? What could the losing party have done to avoid the loss?

(c) Now assume that *SP*–2 filed the financing statement on June 1 but did not make the loan or obtain a security agreement at that time. On July 1 the transaction with *SP*–1 occurred (including the loan and delivery of the pelts). On August 1 *SP*–2 made the loan to *D* and *D* signed the security agreement. Whose security interest is senior? What could the losing party have done to avoid the loss?

Problem 2. On June 1 *D*, a dealer in soybeans, borrowed $200,000 from *SP*–1. *D* granted to *SP*–1 a security interest in all soybeans that *D* then owned or might thereafter acquire, to secure the $200,000 loan and any other indebtedness of *D* to *SP*–1 that might arise in the future. *SP*–1 filed a financing statement covering "soybeans, now owned or hereafter acquired." On June 1 *D* owned and held in its granaries approximately 50,000 bushels of soybeans with a market price of $5.00 per bushel (i.e., with an aggregate value of $250,000). During the summer and fall *D* made many purchases and sales of soybeans, but the amount held in the granaries remained in the vicinity of 50,000 bushels; also, the price remained in the neighborhood of $5.00 per bushel.

By September 1 *D*'s payments to *SP*–1 had reduced the debt from $200,000 to $25,000. On that date *D* applied to *SP*–2 for a loan and showed *SP*–2 cancelled checks showing payments to *SP*–1 and current statements from *SP*–1 to *D* that accurately reported the current balance of $25,000 owing to *SP*–1. *SP*–2 thereupon loaned *D* $150,000, took a written security agreement covering *D*'s soybeans, and filed a financing statement.

On September 15 *SP*–1 made a further loan to *D* of $175,000; *SP*–1's financing statement of June 1 remained on file throughout.

(a) On October 1 *D* defaulted on the loans to both *SP*–1 and *SP*–2. Who has the senior security interest in the 50,000 bushels of soybeans in *D*'s granaries? See UCC 9–204(3); UCC 9–312(5), (7), & Comments 5–7; Note (3) on the First–to–File–or–Perfect Rule, infra. What should the losing party have done to protect itself? See UCC 9–316; UCC 9–404(1); UCC 9–405.

(b) Would the result in part (a) change if, on September 1, *SP*–2 gave written notice of its transaction to *SP*–1?

(c) Would the result in part (a) change if *SP*–1's security agreement secured payment of "all amounts due and to become due under D's promissory note in the amount of $200,000 of even date herewith" and *SP*–1's September 15 loan was evidenced by a new promissory note in the amount of $175,000? If so, what should the losing party have done to protect itself?

(d) In preparing to apply for a loan from *SP*–2, *D* presented to *SP*–1 on September 1 a signed statement under UCC 9–208 indicating "the aggregate amount of unpaid indebtedness" on September 1 of $25,000, with the "request that the statement be approved or corrected" by *SP*–1 and returned to *D*. *SP*–1 wrote "approved" on the statement, signed it, and returned it to *D*. *D* showed this statement to *SP*–2 in applying for the $175,000 loan that *SP*–2 thereupon extended to *D*. On September 15 *SP*–1 extended to *D* a further loan of $175,000, as described above. On D's default on October 1, who has the senior security interest in D's 50,000 bushels of soybeans? What should the losing party have done to protect itself?

(e) The facts are as in part (a), except that on September 1, when SP-2 made the loan of $150,000 to D, D's debt to SP-1 had been reduced to zero; the financing statement, however, remained on file and, as stated above, on September 15 SP-1 made a further loan of $175,000. Under these circumstances, who has priority? See UCC 9–312(7) (future advance while "a security interest is *perfected* "); UCC 9–303(1) ("security interest is *perfected* when it has *attached* "); UCC 9–203(1)(b) (a security interest "does not attach unless ... value has been given"). Under this chain of provisions, would large consequences turn on whether a $1.00 debt remained outstanding? Should one assume that such a result was intended? Can there be any period of time during which SP-1's September 15 advance is outstanding and during which SP-1's security interest is unattached and, consequently, not "perfected"? If there cannot be, can you fashion an argument that the advance was made "while" SP-1's security interest was perfected?

Notes on the First–to–File–or–Perfect Rule

(1) **Article 9's Basic Rule on Priority Among Competing Security Interests: A Complex Excursus to Explain a Basic Rule.** UCC 9–312(5)(a) gives legal priority to a security interest that is prior in time with respect to either "filing or perfection." It may seem odd, at first glance, that legal priority is given to the interest that is first in time with respect to *either* filing *or* perfection. Wouldn't the party who *files* first also be first as to *perfection* of a security interest? If so, why not omit the reference to perfection? To state the basic rule solely in terms of who files first would not be adequate, since in some situations security interests can be perfected without filing. See Chapter 11, Section 2(B), supra.

A more complex question is this: Why doesn't Article 9 simply say that legal priority is given to the security interest that is *perfected* first? Why is there also a reference to filing? For most ordinary security transactions, the simpler first-to-perfect rule would be adequate. But in many common commercial transactions, particularly those in which the collateral includes after-acquired property (see, e.g., Problem 2, supra), filing may precede "perfection."

This distinction between filing and perfection results from the interplay of UCC 9–303 and 9–203. UCC 9–303(1) provides that a security interest is not "perfected" until it has "attached." UCC 9–203(1) lays down a series of requirements for "attachment": (a) execution of a security agreement (or the secured party's possession of the collateral pursuant to agreement); (b) the giving of value by the secured party; and (c) the debtor's having rights in the collateral. Consider the following example: Bank files a financing statement on

June 1 and makes a loan (i.e., gives "value") to Debtor on July 1. UCC 9–203(1)(b) tells us that the security interest did not "attach" until July. And we have just learned from UCC 9–303(1) that a security interest must "attach" before it is "perfected." Thus, "perfection" did not occur until July 1, although filing took place a month earlier.

Why does Article 9 go to such lengths to provide that "perfection" of a security interest, in some circumstances, will not occur at filing? Was all this designed to lead to the result that a security interest that is filed before any other security interest will be subordinate to a security interest that is filed later but is the first to reach "perfection"? Quite the contrary. Let us return to the basic priority rule in UCC 9–312(5)(a): "Conflicting security interests rank according to priority in time of filing *or* perfection." Suppose that *A* files on June 1, that *B* files and lends on June 15, and that *A* lends on July 1. Under the basic rule of UCC 9–312(5)(a), the prevailing security interest is the one that is first *either* to file *or* to perfect. *A* filed before *B* either filed *or* perfected. Consequently, *A* 's security interest prevails over *B* 's. See UCC 9–312, Comment 5, Example 1.

The drafters thought these intricacies necessary in order to address the setting of continuing financing arrangements where credits and collateral ebb and flow—the "floating lien." (The financing of Main Motors' inventory in the Prototype is an example of the "floating lien." This type of financing is discussed in detail in Chapter 14, Section 3(A), infra.) In many ordinary financings the creditor extends "value" at a time when the other elements of "attachment" (UCC 9–203) and "perfection" (UCC 9–303) have been satisfied. When filing and perfection occur together, there is no occasion to distinguish between the separate elements in the basic rule of UCC 9–312(5)(a): filing *or* perfection. Perhaps it would have been better to state Article 9's basic rule on priority in a way so that it could be applied to simple financing transactions without worrying about the significance of language that was designed for more complex (albeit not uncommon) situations. Be that as it may, the current rule affords secured parties the opportunity to fix their place in line by filing a financing statement even before the details of a secured loan have been finalized.

(2) Guarding Against Prior Security Interests: The Two–Step Ideal. Assume that Bank is considering making a loan to Debtor, and that the loan will be extended only if secured by certain assets of Debtor. How can Bank be sure that there is no outstanding security interest that will take priority? As we have seen from Chapter 11, Section 2(B), supra, and from UCC 9–302(1)(a), checking the public records will not, alone, give Bank the assurance it desires. But let us suppose that the cautious Bank takes two steps: (1) It ascertains that Debtor is in possession of the collateral; and (2) it checks the public records and finds that no other creditor has filed a financing statement.[1] Under these circumstances is Bank safe from outstanding

1. Checking the public record may prove to be easier said than done. We have seen several Code provisions under which financing statements remain effec-

security interests? The answer is: Yes—in most situations, but not in all. For instance, a creditor who wants to be sure there is no outstanding security interest that will receive priority also will need to consider whether the collateral, or the situation, is of a type that might fall within one of the other exceptions from the filing requirement that are listed in UCC 9–302(1). Fortunately, these exceptions are limited either as to type of collateral or as to the period of temporary perfection.

(3) **Future Advances.** A strict application of the first-to-file-or-perfect rule of UCC 9–312(5) to Article 9 security interests would seem to leave no room for determining priority based on the time that value is given.[2] (Of course, if a first-filed secured party *never* gives value, it will not be entitled to any of the benefits of a security interest.) Nevertheless, the drafters of the 1972 amendments to Article 9 thought it necessary to drive home this point (as well as an exception to the rule) by adding UCC 9–312(7). The drafters explained as follows:

> While, under the existing [pre–1972] Code, the position of an intervening [possessory] pledge in reference to a subsequent advance by an earlier-filed secured party is debatable, the proposed unified priority rule of Section 9–312(5)(a) ... would indicate that the subsequent advances by the first-filed party have priority, and subsequent advances under a security interest perfected by possession likewise have priority over an intervening filed security interest. These priority rules are expressly stated in proposed Section 9–312(7). That proposal also deals with the rare case of the priority position of a subsequent advance made by a secured party whose security interest is temporarily perfected without either filing or possession, against an intervening secured party. Since there is no notice by the usual methods of filing or possession of the existence of the security interest, the subsequent advances rank only from the actual date of making unless made pursuant to commitment.

General Comment on the Approach of the Review Committee for Article 9, ¶ E–43, Uniform Commercial Code 999, 1022–23 (12th ed., West 1990). In adding UCC 9–312(7) the drafters were inspired, in part, by their desire to overturn certain reported decisions that reached results contrary to that provision.

tive even though the facts governing the location of the filing and the content of the statement have changed. See, e.g., UCC 9–103(1)(d) (financing statement remains effective after collateral is removed from the jurisdiction) (discussed in Chapter 11, Section 3, supra); UCC 9–306(2) (financing statement covering one type of collateral may be effective to perfect a security interest in another type of collateral constituting proceeds) (discussed in Chapter 11, Section 4, supra); UCC 9–402(7) (financing statement remains effective as to certain collateral even after debtor's name changes) (discussed in Chapter 11, Section 2(A), supra).

2. The timing of advances can be important in sorting out priority contests between secured parties and lien creditors (see UCC 9–301(4), in connection with federal tax liens) and certain buyers (see UCC 9–307(3), discussed in Section 2, infra).

The most famous of these decisions, and one that the Article 9 Review Committee specifically disapproved, is Coin–O–Matic Service Co. v. Rhode Island Hospital Trust Co., 3 UCC Rep.Serv. 1112 (R.I. Super.Ct.1966). In *Coin–O–Matic*, Trust Company held a perfected (by filing) security interest in Debtor's automobile. Coin–O–Matic then took a security interest in the same collateral and also perfected by filing. Thereafter, Trust Company made a new loan secured by a new security agreement and filed a new financing statement. Debtor used a portion of the proceeds of the new loan to pay off the original indebtedness to Trust Company, and Trust Company cancelled the original security agreement.

Trust Company argued that its original financing statement was sufficient to protect not only the original security agreement but also the subsequent agreement, despite the fact that Coin–O–Matic's security agreement and filed financing statement intervened. The court rejected Trust Company's argument, holding that "a single financing statement in connection with a security agreement when no provision is made for future advances is not an umbrella for future advances based upon new security agreements, notwithstanding the fact that involved is the same collateral."

The court seemed particularly concerned about the leverage that a contrary rule would create. The Trust Company's argument, the court wrote, "places a lender in an unusually strong position, vis-a-vis, the debtor and any subsequent lenders. In fact, it gives the lender a throttle hold on the debtor." Nevertheless, the court observed that "a lender can protect himself against the situation involved herein by providing in the original security agreement for future advances."

Does a future advance clause give the lender any less of a "throttle hold" on the debtor? How can one justify the distinction the court drew between a single security agreement with a future advance clause (as to which Trust Company would have enjoyed priority) and two separate security agreements (as to only the first of which Trust Company would have enjoyed priority)? Once both lenders know the applicable rules, won't they adjust their behavior?

The court observed that Debtor and Trust Company intended the second transaction to be "an entirely new transaction when the additional loan was made and they considered the original transaction as terminated. They did not intend to affect an intervening creditor." The court suggested further that Debtor "might well have not agreed to a new transaction if such new transaction was to have the effect of cutting out the intervening creditor." Should the intentions of Debtor and Trust Company affect Trust Company's priority against Coin–O–Matic? Note that upon Debtor's satisfaction of its secured obligations under the first transaction, Debtor was entitled to have Trust Company terminate its financing statement filing. UCC 9–404(1).

Problem 3. *SP*–1 perfected a security interest in certain collateral by filing a financing statement in May, 1987. *SP*–2 perfected a security interest in the same collateral by filing in April, 1992. *SP*–2 had actual knowledge of *SP*–1's security interest. In May, 1992, the effectiveness of *SP*–1's filing lapsed by expiration of the five-year period specified in UCC 9–403(2). The 1972 version of UCC 9–403(2) makes clear the consequence of lapse: the security interest becomes unperfected (unless it is perfected without filing) and "is deemed to have been unperfected as against a person who became a purchaser or lien creditor before lapse."

Should one inclined toward the "good faith" principle, discussed in the *Shallcross* and *Lowry* cases, infra, apply that principle to preserve *SP*–1's priority over *SP*–2 notwithstanding UCC 9–403(2)? Cf. Frank v. James Talcott, Inc., 692 F.2d 734 (11th Cir.1982) (under 1962 UCC 9–403, lapse of first-filed financing statement rendered secured party unperfected and subordinate to second-to-file secured party; the latter's knowledge of the earlier-in-time security interest was not relevant). Has *SP*–2 misbehaved in any way that would warrant continued subordination of *SP*–2's security interest notwithstanding the lapse of *SP*–1's financing statement?

Problem 4. In January *SP*–1 loaned $25,000 to *D*, a dentist. *D* executed to *SP*–1 a security agreement covering *D*'s dental equipment. *SP*–1 promptly filed a financing statement, in proper form, in the Clerk's Office of Rockland County, New York, but failed to file with the Department of State in addition, as required by New York's version of UCC 9–401(1)(c). See UCC 9–401(1) (third alternative).

Thereafter *D* applied to *SP*–2 for a loan. When *SP*–2 inquired about security, *D* said, "Everything I have is hocked—lock, stock and barrel" to *SP*–1. Nevertheless, *SP*–2 made a loan to *D* secured by *D*'s dental equipment and properly filed financing statements in the two locations required by New York's UCC 9–401.

Whose security interest in the equipment is senior? See UCC 9–312(5); UCC 9–401(2); UCC 1–201(25) (definition of "knowledge"). Did *SP*–2 have "knowledge of the contents of [*SP*–1's] financing statement"?

In re Davidoff, 351 F.Supp. 440 (S.D.N.Y.1972), on which this Problem is based, held that a financing statement filed in only one of two required filing offices was sufficient to confer priority over a subsequent secured party that made proper filings because the second-in-time secured party had knowledge of the earlier-in-time security interest. Other courts have held that knowledge of the *security interest* does not constitute "knowledge of the *contents of the financing statement.*" Reported decisions vary regarding how much more the second filer must know in order to lose priority. No court has gone so far as to limit the application of UCC 9–401(2) only to secured parties who actually have seen the competing secured party's financing statement.

One might construct a priority system in which knowledge is irrelevant. See Notes on the Role of Knowledge in Priority Contests, infra. Even if one finds a role for knowledge to play, the policy behind UCC 9–401(2) is opaque. Assume that UCC 9–401(2) has the effect, as *Davidoff* suggests, of denying priority to *SP*–2 because *SP*–2 knows of *SP*–1's competing security interest. What explains the fact that, if *SP*–1 failed to file *any* financing statement, then *SP*–2 would enjoy priority notwithstanding its knowledge? On the other hand, under a more narrow reading of UCC 9–401(2), *SP*–2 enjoys priority if it knows only that *D* previously has encumbered property in which *SP*–2 is about to take a security interest but loses priority if it knows in addition the identity of the secured party. What accounts for this distinction?

Problem 5. In January *SP*–1 loaned $25,000 to *D*. *D* executed to *SP*–1 a security agreement covering *D*'s equipment. *SP*–1 promptly filed a financing statement, in proper form, in the Clerk's Office of Rockland County, New York, but failed to file with the Department of State in addition, as required by New York's version of UCC 9–401(1)(c). See UCC 9–401(1) (third alternative). (These are essentially the facts of Problem 4.)

On June 1 *D* signed and delivered to *SP*–2 a security agreement under which the same equipment secured a previously unsecured loan made by *SP*–2. Shortly thereafter, *SP*–2 received a report of filings made against *D* in the Clerk's Office of Rockland County; the search report included a copy of *SP*–1's financing statement. *SP*–2 immediately made proper filings in accordance with UCC 9–401(1).

(a) Whose security interest in the equipment is senior? See UCC 9–312(5); UCC 9–401(2); Notes on the Role of Knowledge in Priority Contests, infra; First National Bank & Trust v. First National Bank of Greybull, 582 F.2d 524 (10th Cir.1978) (*SP*–1 had senior security interest as the first-to-file, where *SP*–1 learned of *SP*–2's improperly filed financing statements *after SP*–1 had made loan and taken security interest (which had become unperfected) and *before* re-filing; court refused to give UCC 9–401(2) "the literal interpretation urged" by *SP*–2).

(b) Suppose that a court has held that on the facts in part (a) *SP*–2's prior filing gave *SP*–2 priority over *SP*–1 pursuant to UCC 9–312(5)(a). Would the court be bound by that decision in a case where *SP*–2 made its loan *after SP*–2 had seen *SP*–1's financing statement? Does UCC 9–312(5)(a) offer any hope of different treatment for these two cases? See Notes on the Role of Knowledge in Priority Contests, infra.

SHALLCROSS v. COMMUNITY STATE BANK & TRUST CO.[*]

Superior Court of New Jersey, Law Division, 1981.
180 N.J.Super. 273, 434 A.2d 671.

LONG, J. S. C. This case involves a novel issue arising out of a priority dispute between two secured creditors. The facts are as follows:

Plaintiff is Lawrence Shallcross, the president of Shallcross and Pace Sheet Metal Works. In February 1977 Shallcross had a discussion with Raymond Dunphey, president of R. Dunphey Sheet Metal Works, Inc., concerning a Wysong shear owned by Shallcross and an RAS shear owned by Dunphey. According to Shallcross, Dunphey wanted to purchase plaintiff's shear but could not then afford it. It was agreed that Shallcross would deliver the Wysong shear to Dunphey, and if Dunphey paid the purchase price of $13,500 within six months, Shallcross would transfer title to him. It was also agreed that if Dunphey sold its RAS shear within the six-month period, Shallcross was to be paid at that time. Dunphey took possession of the Wysong shear on or about February 25, 1977 and the terms of the above oral agreement were set forth in a letter dated March 4, 1977.

In January 1978 Dunphey sold its RAS shear and Shallcross sought payment for the Wysong shear. In June, 1978, Shallcross and Dunphey renegotiated the price of the Wysong shear downward to $11,250 when Dunphey indicated that only $10,000 had been received for its RAS shear. Dunphey agreed to make monthly payments of $356.95. On June 29, 1978 a bill of sale, promissory note, financing statement and security agreement were signed by plaintiff and Dunphey, and on July 12, 1978 the financing statement was filed. Dunphey made three of the monthly payments and then defaulted.

In the interim, defendant Community State Bank and Trust Company (hereinafter, the bank) entered into a loan transaction and security agreement with Dunphey on June 19, 1978. The Wysong shear was listed as one of the items of collateral for the loan, and the security agreement contained an after-acquired property clause. Pursuant to this agreement the bank loaned Dunphey $50,000 on the date of the agreement and an additional $40,000 on December 15, 1978, in accordance with the provision for future advances. This security agreement was filed on June 23, 1978. Dunphey defaulted in the payment of the loan and the shear was sold by the bank to offset the debt under the terms of this security agreement. When Shallcross attempted to satisfy Dunphey's obligation to him by obtaining possession of the shear, he found that the collateral was no longer available. Shallcross has sued the bank for wrongful conversion of the shear. The bank now moves for summary judgment, claiming that there are no genuine issues of

[* The court's citations are to the applicable pre–1972 version of the Code.]

fact and that it clearly had priority in the collateral under the provisions of Article 9 of the Uniform Commercial Code, N.J.S.A. 12A:9–101 et seq.

Article 9 lays out the framework upon which competing security interests can be evaluated and priorities established. In this regard, N.J.S.A. 12A:9–312(5) provides in relevant part that

> In all cases not governed by other rules stated in this section (including cases of purchase money security interests which do not qualify for the special priorities set forth in subsections (3) and (4) of this section), priority between conflicting security interests in the same collateral shall be determined as follows: (a) in the order of filing if both are perfected by filing, regardless of which security interest attaches first under 12A:9–204(1) and whether it attaches before or after filing . . . .

Here, it is undisputed that the bank filed first in time and therefore perfected its security interest prior to Shallcross. Shallcross maintains that this provision does not establish the relative positions of the parties, for several reasons which will be discussed serially. . . .

Shallcross must . . . proceed under the general priority rules of N.J.S.A. 12A:9–312(5). As has previously been noted, that statute clearly provides that the priority is to be determined by the order of filing when both security interests are perfected by filing. In order to avoid the effect of the statute, Shallcross has suggested that the bank's knowledge of his prior interest in the collateral prevents the bank from obtaining a priority. Factually, Shallcross asserts that the bank knew of his interest in the shear before it loaned Dunphey the money and accordingly took the shear as collateral subject to his interest. In support of this position, Shallcross claims that he was present in Dunphey's shop when a representative of the bank came to inspect the shop and equipment, and that he personally heard Dunphey inform the representative that he still owed Shallcross money on the shear.

Although no New Jersey court has yet to pass on this issue, a review of the statute, decisions from other jurisdictions and the Official Code Comments adopted by the New Jersey Study Commission leads to the conclusion that knowledge of a prior interest does not affect the priority provisions of the act.

First, it should be noted that there is no suggestion in the language of N.J.S.A. 12A:9–312(5) that knowledge or notice of a prior interest is a bar to the invocation of the priorities established therein. The absence of a notice provision in this section of the act is particularly significant since the drafters of the act saw fit to specifically include knowledge or notice provisions in other sections of it. One such example is N.J.S.A. 12A:9–301(1)(b), dealing with the priority between an unperfected security interest and a lien creditor.

Except as otherwise provided in subsection (2), an unperfected security interest is subordinate to the rights of ... (b) a person who becomes a lien creditor without knowledge of the security interest and before it is perfected.

[Compare the current version of 9–301(1)(b).]

Obviously, the drafters contemplated that, in certain cases, knowledge of another interest would bar the subsequent interest from obtaining priority. Had they intended that this be an element of N.J.S.A. 12A:9–312(5), they would have specifically provided so. Even in N.J.S.A. 12:9–312(3), which governs a purchase money security interest in inventory collateral, there is a notice provision. There is, however, no such provision in clause (5). Hence, it seemed clear that the failure to set forth a "knowledge" or "notice" provision in 9–312(5) was intentional and that such a provision is not to be implied. This conclusion is consistent with the weight of decisional authority. First Nat'l Bank and Trust Co. v. Atlas Credit Corp., 417 F.2d 1081 (10 Cir.1969); In re Smith, 326 F.Supp. 1311 (D.Minn.1971); National Bank of Sarasota v. Dugger, 335 So.2d 859 (Fla.App.1976); Madison Nat'l Bank v. Newrath, 261 Md. 321, 275 A.2d 495 (Ct.App.1971); Bloom v. Hilty, 427 Pa. 463, 234 A.2d 860 (Sup.Ct.1967); Noble Co. v. Mack Financial Corp., 107 R.I. 12, 264 A.2d 325 (Sup.Ct.1970).

The leading out-of-state case on the subject is *In re Smith*, supra, where the court discussed these issues at length. There, Smith purchased an automobile, and a conditional sales contract was executed by the dealer and subsequently assigned to the First National Bank of Minneapolis. No financing statement was filed. A few months later Community Credit Co. lent Smith money and Smith executed a chattel mortgage on the automobile and a financing statement was filed. Community Credit Corp. had actual knowledge of the unperfected security interest held by First National in the automobile. Id. at 1312. The court concluded that prior knowledge was irrelevant for several reasons equally applicable here. First, the court discussed the integrity of the filing system, a point raised by Professor Gilmore in his treatise, Security Interests in Personal Property, § 34.2 (1965). The court commented:

> It is desirable that perfection of interests take place promptly. It is appropriate then to provide that a secured party who fails to file runs the risk of subordination to a later but more diligent party. In this regard it should be pointed out that filing is of particular importance with respect to notice to other parties. It is agreed that where the later party has actual notice there is no need to rely upon a filing to notify him of a prior interest. The problem, however, cannot be analyzed in this narrow context. Some parties may rely on the record in extending credit and obtaining a security agreement in collateral. Although they will prevail over the unperfected prior interest in time if a dispute arises, it is entirely possible that

they wanted to avoid the dispute altogether. In other words, they may not have relied in ultimately prevailing in the event of a dispute but they may have relied on the complete absence of a prior interest perfected or otherwise out of which a dispute could arise. The only way this kind of record expectation can be protected is by prompt perfection of all security interests. [326 F.Supp. at 1313–1314].

In conjunction with this, the *Smith* court also recognized the evidentiary problems created by a knowledge requirement, which is subjective and is much more difficult to establish than an objective criterion such as the date of filing. Id. at 1314. Finally, the court in *Smith* analyzed the Official Comments accompanying the Code and determined that they supported the view that knowledge is not an element for consideration in this connection.

The official comments to § 9–312 contain several examples which illustrate the resolution of priority disputes under clause (5). These examples, adopted by the New Jersey Study Commission in its comment to the section, comport with the conclusion in *Smith*. Example 2 is perhaps closest in point.

A & B [make] non-purchase money advances against the same collateral. The collateral is in the debtor's possession and neither interest is perfected when the second advance is made. Whichever secured party first perfects his interest (by taking possession of the collateral or by filing) takes priority and *it makes no difference whether he knows of the other interests at the time he perfects his own.* [Emphasis supplied]

The language of this example is clear—it makes no difference whether the secured party knows of the other's interest at the time he perfects his own. The point of the example and the statutory scheme itself is to encourage the prompt perfection of security interests as an unequivocal method of establishing priorities with certainty and without opening the flood gates of litigation, no more or no less.

Nothing in this interpretation can be considered to controvert the good faith requirement of N.J.S.A. 12A:1–203. For this record is devoid of any evidence to show a leading on, bad faith or inequitable conduct on the part of the bank which would justify what in essence is estoppel against the assertion of a priority. This is not to say that the priorities established under N.J.S.A. 12A:9–312(5) would never be affected by a showing of bad faith. That is simply not the question presented here.

For the foregoing reasons the motion for summary judgment is hereby granted.

GENERAL INSURANCE CO. v. LOWRY [*]

United States District Court, Southern District of Ohio, 1976.

412 F.Supp. 12, affirmed 570 F.2d 120 (6th Cir. 1978).

CARL B. RUBIN, DISTRICT JUDGE. This is an action to compel specific performance of an agreement. It was heard on June 20, 1975, for purposes of a preliminary injunction and on the merits on February 2, 1976. In accordance with Rule 65(a)(2), evidence presented at the hearing for preliminary injunction was deemed to be evidence on the merits as well and has been considered by the Court in reaching its determination. Pursuant to Rule 52 of the Federal Rules of Civil Procedure the Court does submit herewith its findings of fact and conclusions of law.

I

FINDINGS OF FACT

1. Prior to January 14, 1972, plaintiff General Insurance Company of America issued surety bonds on which George A. Hyland, Edward F. Lowry and C. M. Dingledine were indemnitors. Pursuant to obligations credited by such bonds the plaintiff paid out various sums of money for which it sought indemnity from the named indemnitors.

2. On January 14, 1972, a cognovit note in the sum of $564,566.79 was executed by the three named indemnitors. Twelve items of collateral security were given to secure such promissory note. For purposes of this litigation, only one such is of any significance. Item III in the list of collateral securities is stated to be "shares of common stock owned by Edward F. Lowry in Pico, Inc., an Ohio corporation." On the same date the above indemnitors executed a Memorandum Agreement (Plaintiff's Exhibit 1) which contained the following language:

> Hyland, Lowry and Dingledine each agree that he will do no act which will reduce or impair the security listed and that each will cooperate in the preparation and execution of the instruments necessary to perfect the security.

3. Subsequently on October 12, 1972, and on July 3, 1973, other notes were executed by the indemnitors and in each instance Item III of the collateral security was a pledge of shares of common stock owned by Edward F. Lowry in Pico, Inc. (Plaintiff's Exhibits 2 and 3). At no time were the shares of stock ever delivered to the plaintiff and no further written agreement regarding such shares was ever executed by the defendant.

4. Throughout these proceedings defendant was represented by attorney Jacob Myers, both as an individual practitioner and as President and sole shareholder in Kusworm & Myers Company, LPA. Mr. Myers attended the meeting of January 14, 1972, examined the documents signed by his client and actively represented defendant Lowry throughout the time involved in this litigation. Subsequent meetings of the

---

[* The court's citations are to the applicable pre–1972 version of the Code.]

parties were held in July, 1972, September, 1972, and May, 1973. Mr. Myers attended the meetings of September 27, 1972, and May 8, 1973, but did not attend the meeting in July of 1972. Other than a letter in January of 1972 from counsel for plaintiff to Mr. Myers requesting delivery of the shares of stock, no other written demand for such shares was ever made by plaintiff's counsel.

5. On January 8, 1974, Edward Lowry executed a promissory note to Kusworm & Myers Company, LPA, in the sum of $12,555.65 (Joint Exhibit I). To secure such note defendant Lowry likewise signed an agreement pledging 19 shares of stock in Pico Development Company, Inc. to Kusworm & Myers Company, LPA, (Joint Exhibit IV) and endorsed at the appropriate place Certificate No. 4 of Pico Development Company (Joint Exhibit II). The stock was subsequently transferred on the books of such company to the name of Kusworm & Myers Company, LPA, and Jacob Myers individually had knowledge of the agreements that had been signed, the reference to the stock in Pico Development Company and the fact that such shares had not been transmitted to plaintiff. The note signed by Edward Lowry to Kusworm & Myers Company, LPA, was given for valuable consideration, to-wit: attorney fees rendered and to be rendered by both Kusworm & Myers Company, LPA, and Jacob Myers.

6. Pursuant to preliminary injunction issued by this Court on June 26, 1975, physical possession of 19 shares of Pico Development Company still remain with Jacob A. Myers, conditioned upon an injunction against sale, assignment, transfer, hypothecation or other disposition without prior approval of this Court.

OPINION

Were it not for the unusual circumstances surrounding this case, its resolution would be a simple matter. The Memorandum of Agreement and the list of collateral which it incorporates by reference from the note fulfill the requirements of a binding security agreement .... General Insurance Company gave value for this security interest. Lowry had rights in the stock and accordingly the security interest did attach under [UCC 9–204]. But since this was a security interest in an instrument as defined in [UCC 9–105], and General Insurance never took possession of the Pico stock, the security interest was never perfected under [UCC 9–304].

By taking possession of Lowry's stock pursuant to its 1974 pledge agreement, Kusworm & Myers, LPA, did perfect their security interest. Under [UCC 9–312] defendants' rights in the stock prevail over the plaintiff's unperfected security interest, even though they had knowledge of the plaintiff's interest. In re Smith, 326 F.Supp. 1311 (D.Minn. 1971).

If the integrity of the concept of "good faith" is to be maintained, we do not believe that such a result can be tolerated. Defendant Myers is not merely a disinterested creditor who attempted to protect his commercial interests. He is the plaintiff's attorney and he and his client as witness and obligor respectively signed the memorandum of agreement. Under the circumstances herein, when the parties signed that agreement and executed the note, the plaintiff obtained an equitable lien against the 19 shares of Pico stock superior in priority to the later perfected security interest held by Kusworm & Myers, LPA.

Although courts should hesitate to invoke equity powers to disturb the operation of a statute, nothing in the Uniform Commercial Code precludes the imposition of an equitable lien in narrowly-circumscribed situations. Aetna Casualty & Surety Co. v. Brunken & Son, Inc., 357 F.Supp. 290 (D.S.D.1973); Warren Tool Company v. Stephenson, 11 Mich.App. 274, 161 N.W.2d 133 (1968); see [UCC 1–103].

All of the prerequisites to the establishment of an equitable lien by plaintiff are present here: all of the parties intended that the Pico stock then in Lowry's possession be given to the plaintiff as security for the debt; an instrument was signed by the parties memorializing this intent; and the present holder of the stock, Mr. Myers, had knowledge of the agreement. The defendants may not use their own dereliction in failing to turn over the stock to the plaintiffs as a defense of their actions.

Faced with facts similar to the instant case, the Supreme Court of Ohio imposed an equitable lien on stock which a defendant failed to deliver according to its agreement with the plaintiff stating that:

> *What good conscience requires, equity should require,* and while we are able to find no adjudicated case upon parallel facts, we are persuaded from the nature of the transaction, the relations and rights of the parties, good conscience and sound morals among men in every-day business, that Klaustermeyer should have his lien for his loan. (emphasis added)

Klaustermeyer v. Cleveland Trust Company, 89 Ohio St. 142, 105 N.E. 278 (1913).

The Court finds this reasoning sound and adopts it *in toto*.

CONCLUSIONS OF LAW

A. This Court has jurisdiction in accordance with 28 U.S.C. § 1332.

B. Where defendant Edward F. Lowry as first party for consideration agrees to secure a bond issued by plaintiff General Insurance Company of America as second party with collateral security and agrees further not to impair such security, he creates an equitable lien on such collateral in favor of such second party.

C. The Uniform Commercial Code does not preclude the imposition of an equitable lien under appropriate circumstances.

D. Defendants Jacob A. Myers and Kusworm & Myers, LPA, as third party with full knowledge of the agreements referred to in Conclusion of Law B and occupying an attorney-client relationship to first party may not under the circumstances of this case obtain by pledge under the U.C.C. a security interest superior to the equitable lien of second party General Insurance Company of America.

E. The prayer of the amended complaint should be and is hereby GRANTED. Defendant Edward F. Lowry is hereby ordered to pledge the shares of Pico, Inc., referred to herein to Plaintiff. Defendant Jacob A. Myers and Kusworm & Myers, LPA, are hereby directed to endorse, transfer and deliver to plaintiff the shares of Pico, Inc.

Costs to be assessed against defendants.

Let Judgment Issue in Accordance With the Foregoing.

[The opinion of the United States Court of Appeals, affirming the District Court, included the following]:

PHILLIPS, CHIEF JUDGE. The issue in this diversity suit is whether the priority provision of the Ohio Uniform Commercial Code, Ohio Rev. Code Ann. § 1309.31 (UCC 9–312), precludes the imposition of an equitable lien under the unusual facts of the present case. In comprehensive findings of fact and conclusions of law, District Judge Carl B. Rubin allowed an equitable lien under the "narrowly-circumscribed" situation here presented. General Insurance Company of America v. Lowry, 412 F.Supp. 12 (S.D.Ohio 1976). Reference is made to the reported decision of the district court for a detailed recitation of pertinent facts.

In diversity cases, federal courts must apply the law of the State as pronounced by its highest court. See Erie R. R. v. Tompkins, 304 U.S. 64, 58 S.Ct. 817, 82 L.Ed. 1188 (1938). We conclude that because of the peculiar circumstances involved in this case, the Supreme Court of Ohio would uphold the imposition of an equitable lien notwithstanding the priority provisions of [UCC 9–312]. We reach this conclusion based upon two considerations.

First, § 1301.09 (UCC 1–203) provides: "Every contract or duty within [Chapter 1309] of the Revised Code, imposes an obligation of good faith in its performance of enforcement." Section 1301.01(S) defines good faith as "honesty in fact in the conduct or transaction concerned." See In re Samuels & Co., 526 F.2d 1238, 1243–44 (5th Cir.1976) (en banc), cert. denied, Stowers v. Mahon, 429 U.S. 834, 97 S.Ct. 98, 50 L.Ed.2d 99 (1976). In Thompson v. United States, 408 F.2d 1075, 1084 (8th Cir.1969), the Eighth Circuit held that the good faith provision of the UCC "permits the consideration of the lack of good faith ... to alter priorities which otherwise would be determined under Article 9."

The district court emphasized that this case involves the attorney for one of the parties, not a disinterested creditor attempting to protect his commercial interests. We agree with the district court that the record discloses facts which do not meet the good faith standards of the Uniform Commercial Code.

Second, an equitable lien was created by appellants in favor of appellee. In 1913, the Supreme Court of Ohio dealt with facts strikingly similar to the present suit. In Klaustermeyer v. The Cleveland Trust Co., 89 Ohio St. 142, 105 N.E. 278 (1913), each member of the Board of Directors of Euclid Avenue Trust Company loaned $5,000 to the company when the trust company began having financial difficulties. Stock owned by the company was to be delivered to the directors as security for each member of the Board of Directors of Euclid Avenue Trust for the benefit of creditors to the Cleveland Trust Company before the stock was delivered to Klaustermeyer, one of the board members. The Supreme Court of Ohio held that Klaustermeyer had an "equitable lien on the securities in the possession of the Euclid Avenue Trust Company, which were assigned and transferred to The Cleveland Trust Company...." 89 Ohio St. at 144, 105 N.E. at 279. In holding that the trust company had a duty to deliver the securities to Klaustermeyer, the court said:

> In modern times the doctrine of equitable liens has been liberally extended for the purpose of facilitating mercantile transactions, and in order that the intention of the parties to create specific charges may be justly and effectually carried out. Bispham's Principles of Equity (8 ed.), Section 351.

> What good conscience requires, equity should require, and while we are able to find no adjudicated case upon parallel facts, we are persuaded from the nature of the transaction, the relations and the rights of the parties, good conscience and sound morals among men in everyday business, that Klaustermeyer should have his lien for his loan. 89 Ohio St. at 153, 105 N.E. at 282.

We disagree with appellants' argument that the enactment of the Uniform Commercial Code overruled *Klaustermeyer* and eliminated equitable liens in all situations. Section 1301.03 (UCC 1–103) states in pertinent part: "Unless displaced by the particular provisions of [Chapter 1309] of the Revised Code, the principles of law *and equity* ... shall supplement its provisions." (emphasis added).

Discussing the doctrine of equitable liens and citing *Klaustermeyer*, the Ohio Court of Appeals held in Syring v. Sartorius, 28 Ohio App.2d 308, 309–10, 277 N.E.2d 457, 458 (1971):

> The doctrine may be stated in its most general form that every express executory agreement in writing whereby a contracting party sufficiently indicates an intention to make some particular property, real *or personal*, or fund, therein described or identified, *a security for a debt* or other obligation, or whereby the party promises to convey, assign, or transfer the property as security, creates an equitable lien upon the property so indicated, which is enforceable against the property in the hands not only of the original contractor, but of his purchasers or encumbrancers with notice. Under like circum-

stances, a merely verbal agreement may create a similar lien upon personal property. The doctrine itself is clearly an application of the maxim "equity regards as done that which ought to be done." Cf. Klaustermeyer v. Cleveland Trust Co., 89 Ohio St. 142, 105 N.E. 278. (emphasis added).

This court has recognized the continuing validity of *Klaustermeyer*. See In re Easy Living, Inc., 407 F.2d 142, 145 (6th Cir.1969). See also In re Troy, 490 F.2d 1061, 1065 (6th Cir.1974).

Construing Texas law, the Fifth Circuit implicitly found that the existence of an equitable lien does not conflict with Article Nine of the UCC. See Citizens Co-Op Gin v. United States, 427 F.2d 692, 695–96 (5th Cir.1970). Other Circuits construing various state laws have recognized the doctrine of equitable liens. See Casper v. Neubert, 489 F.2d 543, 547 (10th Cir.1973); Awkwright Mutual Insurance Co. v. Bargain City, U. S. A., Inc., 373 F.2d 701 (3d Cir.1967); Cherno v. Dutch American Mercantile Corp., 353 F.2d 147, 151–53 (2d Cir.1965). But cf. Shelton v. Erwin, 472 F.2d 1118 (8th Cir.1973).

We, therefore, are convinced that the Ohio Supreme Court, if it were deciding this case, would follow its earlier opinion in *Klaustermeyer* holding that General Insurance Company is entitled to an equitable lien on the Pico stock in possession of appellant Myers.

Affirmed.

Notes on the Role of Knowledge in Priority Contests

(1) **The "Pure Race" Priority Rule of UCC 9–312(5)(a).** In holding that knowledge of an earlier, unperfected security interest is irrelevant to a priority contest governed by the first-to-file-or-perfect rule of UCC 9–312(5)(a), the *Shallcross* case is in accord with the majority of reported decisions that have considered the issue. The commentary also generally supports that reading of the statute. A recording system (such as UCC 9–312(5)(a)) that awards priority to the first party to file irrespective of that party's knowledge of an unfiled, earlier-in-time interest is called a "pure race" system. The priority rule of UCC 9–301(1)(b), which affords priority to a lien creditor who becomes such before a competing security interest is perfected, whether or not the lien creditor knows of the security interest, is another "pure race" rule.

(2) **"Race–Notice" and "Notice" Priority Systems.** Most of Article 9's priority rules are not "pure race" rules, but are more accurately described as "race-notice" or "notice" rules. In a "race-notice" system, a subsequent claimant becomes senior to an earlier, unperfected security interest only if the subsequent party takes its interest without notice of the earlier interest and *also* is the first to perfect its interest. For example, UCC 9–401(2) provides an exception to the otherwise applicable "pure race" rule. Under that provision, a secured

party who is the first to (properly) file is senior to an earlier-in-time secured party who has attempted to file (but did so improperly) only if the first-to-properly-file secured party did not have "knowledge of the contents of" the improperly filed financing statement.

In a "notice" system, a subsequent purchaser who takes with notice of an earlier-in-time claim is subordinated to that claim even if the earlier-in-time claimant has failed to give any public notice, such as by filing. For example, UCC 9–301(1)(c) and (1)(d) give certain non-secured party transferees priority over an unperfected security interest only if the transferees do not have "knowledge of the security interest" at the specified relevant time.[3]

(3) **Circular Priority.** Peculiar priority problems may arise when more than two creditors claim an interest in particular collateral. Assume, for example, that under the applicable priority rules, $C-1$ takes priority over $C-2$ and $C-2$ takes priority over $C-3$. One might be tempted to jump to the conclusion that $C-1$ takes priority over $C-3$. One ought not yield to this temptation. The transitive law of mathematics (i.e., if $A > B$ and $B > C$, then $A > C$) does not necessarily apply to priority rules. It is possible that $C-1$ prevails over $C-2$, $C-2$ prevails over $C-3$, and $C-3$ prevails over $C-1$! This unhappy state of affairs is called a "circular priority."

One problem with "race notice" and "notice" systems is that they can generate circular priorities. Consider, for example, the operation of UCC 9–401(2). Assume that (i) $SP-1$ files improperly; (ii) $SP-2$ subsequently files properly but is junior to $SP-1$ because $SP-2$ has "knowledge of the contents" of $SP-1$'s improperly filed financing statement; and (iii) lien creditor (LC) then obtains an execution lien on the collateral involved. In this situation, LC is senior to $SP-1$, whose security interest is unperfected. UCC 9–301(1)(b). $SP-1$ is senior to $SP-2$ by virtue of $SP-2$'s knowledge of the improperly filed financing statement. UCC 9–401(2). And $SP-2$ is senior to LC because $SP-2$'s security interest is perfected. UCC 9–301(1)(b). LC beats $SP-1$, $SP-1$ beats $SP-2$, and $SP-2$ beats LC.

Article 9 provides no solution for this, or any other, circular priority puzzle. In the absence of a controlling statutory rule, how should a court determine the priority? Possibilities might include allocating the value of the collateral pro rata and subordinating the party (or parties) that the court deems least deserving (because of carelessness or some other reason that the court finds compelling). See 2 Gilmore, Security ch. 39; Note, Circular Priority Systems Within the Uniform Commercial Code, 61 Tex.L.Rev. 517 (1982).

(4) **Certainty, Good Faith, and Extra–Code Principles.** A few commentators have called for tempering the "pure race" rule of UCC 9–312(5)(a) with some sort of knowledge qualification. See Felsenfeld,

---

3. If one conceptualizes the "delivery" requirement in UCC 9–301(1)(c) as a form of compliance with a "public notice" re- quirement, then UCC 9–301(1)(c) arguably is a "race-notice" rule.

Knowledge as a Factor in Determining Priorities Under the Uniform Commercial Code, 42 N.Y.U.L.Rev. 246 (1967); Nickles, Rethinking Some U.C.C. Article 9 Problems, 34 Ark. L. Rev. 1, 72–103 (1980). Professors Baird and Jackson, on the other hand, have defended the "pure race" rule. Baird & Jackson, Information, Uncertainty, and the Transfer of Property, 13 J. Legal Stud. 299 (1984).

Baird and Jackson argue that judicial inquiries into the question of knowledge would be costly and would cause delay. Among the costs of "notice" systems are the costs of determining whether and when a person acquired knowledge of a competing claim and the uncertainty costs arising from the possibility that a court would make an erroneous determination. Baird and Jackson also argue that knowledge of an earlier-in-time interest is not equivalent to bad faith. In their view, parties should not be penalized for obtaining knowledge; acquiring knowledge should be encouraged. They point out that "notice" systems do not provide any incentive for a knowledgeable second-in-time party to cause the public records to be corrected so as to reflect the earlier, unfiled security interest.

By way of contrast, Professor Carlson's study offers the harshest critique of the "pure race" rule. Carlson, Rationality, Accident, and Priority Under Article 9 of the Uniform Commercial Code, 71 Minn. L.Rev. 207 (1986). To Carlson, a knowledgeable second-in-time party who achieves seniority under UCC 9–312(5)(a)'s first-to-file-or-perfect rule is much like a thief. Carlson explains that cost-benefit analyses such as those of Baird and Jackson fail to consider all of the pertinent costs, including the costs to the parties who are subordinated and the social costs of a rule that is inconsistent with well-accepted morality. Moreover, his analysis of the drafting history suggests that the drafters of UCC 9–312(5) may not have intended to create a strict "pure race" rule!

Interestingly, Carlson stops short of proposing a modification of what generally has been construed to be a "pure race" statutory scheme. Instead, he seems satisfied that courts can import, through UCC 1–103, extra-Code doctrine that is sufficient to deprive the truly bad-faith actors of the fruits of their wrongful actions. The *Lowry* case is an example.

One hopes that the case-by-case application of extra-Code doctrines to a "pure race" reading of UCC 9–312(5) will result in a just, workable, and sufficiently predictable system of priorities. To a considerable extent, the success of the system depends on the ability of judges to override UCC 9–312(5) judiciously, i.e., only in appropriate cases and only with appropriate techniques. In the *Lowry* case, the court resorted to the doctrine of "equitable lien" in order to justify subordinating the perfected security interest of Kusworm & Myers. That doctrine carries with it a considerable amount of baggage, including a set of priority rules that may have been appropriate for the case at bar but inappropriate in another Article 9 case. (See the excerpt from Syring

v. Sartorius quoted in the opinion of the Sixth Circuit.) Rather than giving the unperfected secured party an additional property right (an "equitable lien") that took priority over Kusworm & Myers' perfected security interest, could the court have reached the same result by applying the good faith requirement of UCC 1–203 in order to subordinate Kusworm & Myers' perfected security interest? Would that approach have created fewer potential problems?

As Baird and Jackson point out, acting with knowledge that an earlier-in-time interest exists is not *necessarily* equivalent to bad faith. Indeed, what Carlson condemns is acting with the knowledge that achieving seniority over that interest is *wrongful* as to the earlier-in-time claimant. The knowledgeable second-in-time secured party may be exposed to liability for tortious interference with the contractual relations between the earlier-in-time secured party and the common debtor. See First Wyoming Bank v. Mudge, 748 P.2d 713 (Wyo.1988) (imposing liability for tortious interference on bank that took security interest with knowledge that transaction caused debtor to violate a covenant in agreement between debtor and another creditor). Well-drafted security agreements typically contain provisions requiring debtors to maintain the perfection and priority of security interests and prohibiting debtors from giving senior interests (and often *any* competing interests) to other parties. In most cases, then, one might argue that knowledge of the earlier, unperfected interest is essentially equivalent to knowledge that subordination of the earlier party's interest is wrongful. Does this argument give knowledge too great a role to play in rearranging the "pure race" priorities of UCC 9–312(5)?

(B) Purchase Money Security Interests

Problem 6. On June 1 *D*, a construction company, obtained a $100,000 loan from *SP*–1, and executed in favor of *SP*–1 a security agreement covering "all construction equipment now owned or hereafter acquired" by *D*. *D* owned construction equipment such as bulldozers, cranes and trucks. *SP*–1 immediately filed a financing statement covering "construction equipment."

(a) On July 1 *D* bought a new Cletrac bulldozer from the manufacturer, *M*, and paid *M* the price of $100,000. On July 2 *D* obtained a $90,000 loan from *SP*–2, and executed to *SP*–2 a security agreement covering the new bulldozer. *SP*–2 promptly filed a financing statement covering the Cletrac bulldozer (bulldozers are not subject to the relevant certificate of title act). *D* defaulted on the loans to *SP*–1 and *SP*–2. Who has priority as to the new bulldozer? See UCC 9–312(5); UCC 9–312(4); UCC 9–107.

(b) Suppose that *D* on July 1 had told *SP*–2 of the need for a loan to buy the new bulldozer from *M*. *SP*–2 then made a loan to *D* in the form of a $90,000 check payable jointly to *D* and *M*; *D* then endorsed the check to *M* and paid *M* the remaining $10,000 of the price. On July

2 *M* delivered the bulldozer to *D*. *SP*–2 filed on July 8. Who has priority as to the new bulldozer? What, if anything, could the losing party have done to avoid the result?

(c) What policy considerations underlie the legal rules that decide parts (a) and (b)? See UCC 9–312, Comment 3; Note (2) on Purchase Money Priority and the Definition of "Purchase Money Security Interest," infra.

(d) Would the results in parts (a) and (b) change if the security agreement in favor of *SP*–1 contained the following provision?

> Debtor shall not create or suffer to exist any security interest (including any purchase money security interest) in any collateral that is, at any time, covered by this agreement, and any such prohibited security interest that Debtor may attempt to create shall be null and void.

See UCC 9–311.

Problem 7. *D*, a wholesaler, sells textiles to retail stores from substantial stocks of textiles maintained in *D*'s warehouse.

On June 1 *D* obtained a $100,000 loan from *SP*–1 and executed a security agreement granting a security interest to *SP*–1 in all the textiles that *D* then owned or might thereafter acquire. *SP*–1 immediately filed a financing statement covering "textiles."

Late in June *D* needed to purchase $20,000 worth of additional textiles from the manufacturer, *M*. *M* would not sell to *D* on credit. *D* lacked the necessary cash and *SP*–1 refused to enlarge the existing $100,000 loan.

Because of these difficulties, on July 1 *D* applied to *SP*–2 for a loan to pay *M* for the textiles. *SP*–2 agreed and made out a check for $20,000 payable jointly to *D* and *M*; *D* endorsed the check to *M*. On July 2 *SP*–2 filed a financing statement. On July 5 *M* delivered the textiles to *D*, who placed them in the warehouse.

Shortly after the $20,000 shipment of textiles arrived, *D* defaulted on the loans to *SP*–1 and *SP*–2. Whose security interest is senior as to this shipment of textiles? See UCC 9–312(3), (4), and (5). What, if anything, could the losing party have done to improve its position?

For a discussion of Article 9's policies with respect to the situation posed by this Problem, see UCC 9–312, Comment 3; Note (2) on Purchase Money Priority and the Definition of "Purchase Money Security Interest," infra. For detailed guidance on operating procedures to ensure compliance with 9–312(3), see Baker, The Ambiguous Notification Requirement of Revised UCC Section 9–312(3): Inventory Financers Beware!, 98 Banking L.J. 4 (1981).

Problem 8. *D* is a wholesale distributor of toys. On June 1 *D* obtained a $100,000 loan from *SP*–1 and signed a security agreement covering "all inventory now owned or hereafter acquired." On June 2 *SP*–1 properly filed a financing statement.

On July 1 *D* signed a security agreement in favor of *SP*–2, a toy marble manufacturer, covering "all marbles that *SP*–2 sells to Customer from time to time" and securing "the purchase price of marbles sold from time to time by SP–2 to Customer." That same day *SP*–2 properly filed a financing statement and sent a notice to *SP*–1 in compliance with the requirements of UCC 9–312(3).

On July 15, at *D*'s request, *SP*–2 shipped 100,000 marbles to *D* in 1,000 bags containing 100 marbles each, and sent *D* an invoice for $1,000 (a unit price of 1 cent per marble). On July 30 *SP*–2 filled another order from *D* by shipping another 100,000 marbles, packaged in 100 boxes of 1,000 marbles each. *SP*–2 then sent to *D* an invoice for another $1,000.

After making three payments in the aggregate amount of $700, *D* failed to make further payments to *SP*–2. It is now September 1 and *D* is in possession of 350 bags of marbles from the first order and 25 boxes of marbles from the second order—the other marbles having been sold.

Is *SP*–2's perfected security interest in the marbles senior to the security interest of *SP*–1? If so, to what extent? Do you need additional facts in order to determine the priority issue? See Southtrust Bank of Alabama, National Association v. Borg–Warner Acceptance Corp., infra; Note (6) on Purchase Money Priority and the Definition of "Purchase Money Security Interest," infra.

SOUTHTRUST BANK v. BORG–WARNER ACCEPTANCE CORP.[*]

United States Court of Appeals, Eleventh Circuit, 1985.
760 F.2d 1240.

TUTTLE, SENIOR CIRCUIT JUDGE: Borg-Warner Acceptance Corporation ("BWAC") appeals from a decision of the district court denying its motion for summary judgment and granting summary judgment to Southtrust Bank ("the Bank") in a diversity suit. The Bank filed a declaratory judgment action to ascertain which of the parties has priority in the inventory of four debtors, Molay Brothers Supply Company, Inc., Gulf City Distributors, Inc., Standard Wholesale Supply Company and Crest Refrigeration, Inc.[1] These debtors, which are no longer in existence, defaulted on obligations they owed to one or the other party.

Both the Bank and BWAC have perfected security interests in the inventory of the debtors. In each case, the Bank filed its financing

----

[* The court's citations are to the pre–1972 version of Alabama's Code and to the 1972 version of Georgia's Code.]

1. The inventory of debtor Crest was in Georgia and all financing statements regarding Crest were filed there. Therefore, Georgia law applies as to Crest. The inventory of the other three debtors and all filings concerning them were in Alabama. Thus, Alabama law controls as to these debtors. Ala.Code § 7–9–103(1)(b) (1975).

statement first.   BWAC contends that as a purchase money lender it falls within the purchase money security interest exception to the first to file rule and therefore is entitled to possession of the inventory.[2] The Uniform Commercial Code (UCC) as adopted in both Alabama and Georgia, provides in pertinent part:

> A security interest is a "purchase money security interest" to the extent that it is:
>
> (a) Taken or retained by the seller of the collateral to secure all or part of its price; or
>
> (b) Taken by a person who by making advances or incurring an obligation gives value to enable the debtor to acquire rights in or the use of collateral if such value is in fact so used.

Ala.Code § 7–9–107 (1975); O.C.G.A. § 11–9–107 (1981).

BWAC engages in purchase money financing.   Here, BWAC purchased invoices from vendors who supplied inventory items to the debtors in question.   The security agreements between BWAC and each of the debtors contained the following provision:

> In order to secure repayment to Secured Party of all such extensions of credit made by Secured Party in accordance with this Agreement, and to secure payment of all other debts or liabilities and performance of all obligations of Debtor to Secured Party, whether now existing or hereafter arising, Debtor agrees that Secured Party shall have and hereby grants to Secured Party a security interest in all Inventory of Debtor, whether now owned or hereafter acquired, and all Proceeds and products thereof.

The term "Inventory" was defined as "all inventory, of whatever kind or nature, wherever located, now owned or hereafter acquired ... when such inventory has been financed by Borg–Warner Acceptance Corporation."

BWAC and the debtors employed a scheduled liquidation arrangement to reduce the debt owed BWAC.   Under this arrangement a debtor was permitted to pay a percentage of the invoice each month, without regard to whether the item was actually sold.   If an unpaid item was sold, then the remaining inventory served as collateral to secure the unpaid balance.

The key issue for decision by this Court is whether inclusion of an after-acquired property clause and a future advances clause in BWAC's security agreements converted its purchase money security interest (PMSI) into an ordinary security interest.

The district court held that inclusion of after-acquired property and future advances clauses ("the clauses") in the security agreement

---

2. A purchase money security interest in inventory has priority over a conflicting security interest in the same inventory.   Ala.Code § 7–9–312(3) (1975); O.C.G.A. § 11–9–312(3) (1981).

converted BWAC's PMSI into an ordinary security interest. The court relied on In re Manuel, 507 F.2d 990 (5th Cir.1975) (holding, in a consumer bankruptcy context, that PMSI must be limited to the item purchased at time of the agreement and cannot exceed the price of that item); In re Norrell, 426 F.Supp. 435 (M.D.Ga.1977) (same); and In re Simpson, 4 U.C.C.Rep.Serv. 243 (W.D.Mich.1966) (inclusion of future advances clause in security agreement for farm equipment destroys PMSI).

BWAC argues that the cases relied on by the court are distinguishable. First, BWAC notes that almost all the cases following the "transformation" rule (i.e., inclusion of the clauses transforms a PMSI into an ordinary security interest) are consumer bankruptcy cases. It argues that the rationale of those cases, which is to protect the consumer, does not apply in commercial cases such as the case at bar. See In re Mid–Atlantic Flange, 26 U.C.C.Rep.Serv. 203, 208 (E.D.Pa. 1979). BWAC argues that the policy considerations in a commercial setting, promoting commercial certainty and encouraging credit extension, do not support the application of the transformation rule. According to BWAC, applying the transformation rule to inventory financiers would require them to police inventory constantly and to see that inventory corresponds on an item-by-item basis with debt.

The Bank argues that the transformation rule is not a product of special bankruptcy considerations, and that if the drafters had intended to limit the rule to consumer transactions, they would have said so, as they did in other sections of the Code. The Bank contends that a holding that inclusion of the clauses destroys a PMSI would not have a serious negative effect on inventory financiers. It points out that such financiers could retain priority by obtaining a subordination agreement from the first-to-file creditor.

We see no reason to limit the holding of In re Manuel to consumer bankruptcy cases. In that case, the Fifth Circuit stated:

> A plain reading of the statutory requirements would indicate that they require the purchase money security interest to be in the item purchased, and that, as the judges below noted, the purchase money security interest cannot exceed the price of what is purchased in the transaction wherein the security interest is created. . . .

Id. at 993. Nothing in the language of U.C.C. § 9–312(3) or § 9–107 distinguishes between consumer and commercial transactions or between bankruptcy and nonbankruptcy contexts. We see no policy reasons for creating a distinction where the drafters have not done so.

Second, BWAC contends that the cases supporting the transformation rule involve situations in which the clauses were actually exercised, e.g., Manuel (agreement covered preexisting debt); Simpson (future advances actually made). BWAC argues that mere inclusion of the clauses does not void a PMSI. In re Griffin, 9 B.R. 880 (Bankr. N.D.Ga.1981) (when creditor is seller, mere existence of unexercised future advances clause does not destroy PMSI); Mid Atlantic Flange (same). We need not reach the issue of whether mere inclusion of unexercised future advances and after-acquired property clauses voids a PMSI because we find that BWAC exercised the clauses here. After entering the security agreements with the debtors, BWAC regularly purchased inventory for the debtors and now claims that the debtors' BWAC-financed inventory secures these purchases. This is an exercise of the future advances clause. Similarly, BWAC claims as collateral not only the inventory purchased at the time the security agreements were entered, but all BWAC-financed inventory. This is an exercise of the after-acquired property clause. We hold, therefore, that BWAC's exercise of the future advances and after-acquired property clauses in its security agreements with the debtors destroyed its PMSI.

We note, as did the district court, that BWAC retains a security interest in the goods. It merely loses its priority status as a purchase money secured lender. The concept of the floating lien under the U.C.C. remains intact. We hold, merely, that such a floating lien is inconsistent with a PMSI. A PMSI requires a one-to-one relationship between the debt and the collateral.

BWAC's final argument is that the court should adopt a "to the extent" rule, based on the literal language of UCC, § 9–107:

> A security interest is a "purchase money security interest" *to the extent* that it is ... (b) Taken by a person who by making advances or incurring an obligation gives value to enable the debtor to acquire rights in or the use of collateral if such value is in fact so used. (emphasis added.)

Some courts have held that the clauses, even if exercised, do not invalidate a PMSI if there is some method for determining the extent of the PMSI. For example, in re Staley, 426 F.Supp. 437 (M.D.Ga.1977), the court held that the PMSI was valid because the security agreement specified that payments be allocated first to items bought first. Thus, it was easy for the court to ascertain which items had been fully paid for and hence no longer served as collateral. Here, however, nothing in the contract or in state law allocates payments to particular items of inventory. BWAC, in fact, claims all BWAC- financed inventory as its collateral without regard to payments made by the debtors. We agree with the court in In re Coomer, 8 B.R. 351, 355 (Bankr.E.D.Tenn.1980), that

> Without some guidelines, legislative or contractual, the court should not be required to distill from a mass of transactions the extent to which a security interest is purchase money.

Unless a lender contractually provides some method for determining the extent to which each item of collateral secures its purchase money, it effectively gives up its purchase money status.

Because we hold that BWAC's exercise of the after-acquired property and future advances clauses in its security agreements voided its

PMSI, we need not reach the other issues raised by the Bank. We also do not reach the issue raised by BWAC concerning the district court's reference to proceeds from sales of the inventory being held "in trust." Whether the proceeds are held "in trust" is relevant only to the issue of damages. The district court entered final judgment only on the claim for declaratory relief and referred the damage claim to a magistrate. Because no final judgment has been entered as to damages, that issue is not properly before this Court.

AFFIRMED.

Notes on Purchase Money Priority and the Definition of "Purchase Money Security Interest"

(1) Contexts in Which the Distinction Between "Purchase Money Security Interests" and Non–purchase Money Security Interests Is Relevant. Whether a security interest meets the definition of "purchase money security interest" ("PMSI") in UCC 9–107 is important in several contexts. We saw above in Chapter 11, Section 2(A), that a PMSI perfected by filing "within ten days after the debtor receives possession of the collateral" receives priority over the interests of bulk transferees and lien creditors arising "between the time the security interest attaches and the time of filing." UCC 9–301(2). We also saw that PMSI's in most consumer goods are "automatically" perfected without filing or possession by the secured party. See UCC 9–302(1)(d).

This Section of the materials addresses the priority of PMSI's as against competing security interests. In particular, it looks at priority rules that provide exceptions to the first-to-file-or-perfect rule of UCC 9–312(5)(a), thereby allowing qualifying PMSI's to achieve seniority over security interests perfected by earlier-in-time filings. See Note (2), infra.

(2) Purchase Money Priority Under UCC 9–312(3) and (4). The PMSI priority rules—UCC 9–312(3) for inventory collateral and UCC 9–312(4) for other collateral—override the otherwise-applicable first-to-file-or-perfect rule of UCC 9–312(5). When the requirements for PMSI priority are not met, however, a PMSI will be subject to UCC 9–312(5).

Procedural Requirements. UCC 9–312(3) and (4) apply only to PMSI's that meet the definition in UCC 9–107. In addition, certain procedural requirements are necessary for purchase money priority.

Timing of Perfection. Each of the two PMSI priority rules establishes a temporal standard for perfection. For non-inventory collateral, the security interest must be "perfected at the time the debtor receives possession of the collateral or within ten days thereafter." UCC 9–312(4).[4] The standard for inventory collateral is less flexible. An

---

4. A substantial number of states have extended the ten-day period in UCC 9– 312(4) to twenty days. Many states also have extended the ten-day period in UCC

inventory PMSI must be "perfected at the time the debtor receives possession of the inventory"; there is no ten-day period of grace. UCC 9–312(3)(a).

Applicability to Collateral Other Than Goods. One may draw two inferences from the references in UCC 9–312(3) and (4) (and UCC 9–301(2)) to a debtor's receipt of "possession" of collateral. First, these priority rules apparently do not apply to collateral, such as accounts and general intangibles, that cannot physically be possessed. Second, these priority rules could be applied not only to goods but also to collateral such as documents, instruments, and chattel paper. The application of the PMSI rules to priorities in "paper collateral" is more theoretical than real, however. In most cases the appropriate priorities for those types of collateral can be established without resort to the PMSI priority rules. See, e.g., UCC 9–304(2); UCC 9–308; UCC 9–309. The drafters probably contemplated that PMSI priorities would be employed primarily (and, perhaps, exclusively) in the acquisition of goods.

Notification to Conflicting Secured Parties. For inventory collateral only, UCC 9–312(3)(b), (c), and (d) provide a detailed scheme that requires a PMSI financer to give a written notification to certain conflicting secured parties (see paragraph (b)). The notification must be received by those parties before (but not more than five years before) the debtor receives possession of the inventory (see paragraph (c)). Finally, the notification must state that the PMSI financer has or may obtain a PMSI in specified items or types of inventory (see paragraph (d)). (You should study these notification requirements with care.)

Comment 3 to UCC 9–312 explains the rationale for the notification requirement of subsection (3) as follows:

> The reason for the additional requirement of notification is that typically the arrangement between an inventory secured party and his debtor will require the secured party to make periodic advances against incoming inventory or periodic releases of old inventory as new inventory is received. A fraudulent debtor may apply to the secured party for advances even though he has already given a security interest in the inventory to another secured party. The notification requirement protects the inventory financer in such a situation: if he has received notification, he will presumably not make an advance; if he has not received notification (or if the other interest does not qualify as a purchase money interest), any advance he may make will have priority. Since an arrangement for periodic advances against incoming property is unusual outside the inventory field, no notification requirement is included in subsection (4).

9–301(2), which addresses purchase money priority over certain lien creditors and transferees in bulk.

Do you find this explanation of the notification requirement persuasive? Should that requirement be extended to other collateral, such as equipment? See Baird & Jackson, Possession and Ownership: An Examination of the Scope of Article 9, 35 Stan.L.Rev. 175, at 194–96 (1983), where the authors argue that a notification requirement should be added to UCC 9–312(4) for non-inventory PMSI's. Apparently they believe that the reliance of secured creditors on after-acquired equipment warrants a notification requirement. Although they base their argument on ostensible ownership grounds, they fail to address the empirical question of whether secured creditors typically are aware of debtors' possession of after-acquired equipment. For a different view of reliance on after-acquired equipment, see Harris, A Reply to Theodore Eisenberg's *Bankruptcy in Law Perspective*, 30 UCLA L. Rev. 327, at 338 n.66 (1982) (defending the application of the two-point test in BC 547(c)(5) only to accounts and inventory):

> [T]hose who take equipment as collateral typically expect the original collateral to remain in the debtor's possession so that he can use it to generate income that will enable him to repay the loan. Although they may easily take a security interest in after-acquired equipment, ordinarily these lenders do not expect to rely upon it and would be protected without it.

Why Purchase Money Priority? The most commonly advanced justification for PMSI priority is that it provides a means for a debtor to obtain additional secured financing when the first-to-file secured party is unwilling to provide it. In this sense, PMSI priority ameliorates the "situational monopoly" of a first-to-file secured creditor who has the benefit of an after-acquired property clause. See Jackson & Kronman, Secured Financing and Priorities Among Creditors, 88 Yale L.J. 1143, at 1167 (1979) ("Although the after-acquired property clause saves costs, it also creates what economists call a 'situational monopoly,' in that a creditor with a security interest in after-acquired property enjoys a special competitive advantage over other lenders in all his subsequent dealings with the debtor.").

It is understandable that a debtor might prefer the flexibility that purchase-money financing affords. What price does the first-to-file secured party (and, indirectly, the debtor) pay for this flexibility? Do the PMSI priority rules place a substantial risk on the first-to-file secured creditor? If so, does the first-to-file secured creditor react to the risk by charging higher rates (discounting, in effect, the value of collateral) to offset the risks? In fact, several safeguards are available to first-to-file lenders who might otherwise perceive that the PMSI priority rules present material risks to their positions. For example, we already have seen that inventory lenders are entitled to notification from later PMSI financers. That notification puts the inventory lender in a position to protect itself by not relying on the PMSI-financed collateral. Also, first-to-file financers can bargain for covenants and events of default that restrict or prohibit the debtor from obtaining PMSI financing. Although these contractual obligations and remedies do not entirely eliminate the risk (see UCC 9–311), they are considered important nonetheless in the credit markets.

There is a more fundamental reason why PMSI priority does not seriously impair the position of first-to-file secured creditors. The PMSI financer contributes new value that *in fact is used by the debtor to acquire a new asset.* The debtor's balance sheet reflects both a new debt and a new asset. Neither the first-to-file secured creditor's existing collateral nor its overall position are affected. (This rationale also assumes that non-notified first-to-file secured creditors do not rely materially to their detriment on after-acquired, non-inventory collateral.) This explanation highlights the importance of the tracing requirement in UCC 9–107's definition of PMSI, discussed below in Note (5). Consider the effect of a rule to the contrary, under which a debtor could borrow funds, fail to acquire a new asset, and confer on the lender a super-priority in a first-to-file secured creditor's existing collateral: it would undercut the core basis of secured credit. Would the result of that sort of "last-in-time" priority rule be that no one would go to the trouble of obtaining collateral? Would all credit be unsecured credit? An affirmative answer to each of these questions is developed in Jackson & Kronman, Secured Financing and Priorities Among Creditors, 88 Yale L.J. 1143, at 1162–64 (1979).

(3) Priorities in Consignment Transactions; UCC 9–114. In the discussion of consignments (Chapter 12, Section 1(B), supra) we observed that filing a financing statement generally protects the consignor's ownership interest from the reach of the consignee's creditors. See UCC 2–326(2) & (3). By implication, that interest should be senior to later-in-time judicial lien creditors of the consignee.

What priority rules apply as between the consignor and the consignee's secured parties? Article 9 did not address this question until the 1972 revisions added UCC 9–114. Under that section, the consignor can achieve priority over an earlier-filed inventory secured party by filing and giving the earlier-filed party notice before the consignee receives the consigned goods. UCC 9–114(1). As Comment 1 to UCC 9–114 indicates, this approach "conforms closely to the concepts and the language of Section 9–312(3)." Because consignments to merchants are functionally similar to purchase-money inventory financing, the similar treatment seems sound.

Unfortunately, UCC 9–114 leaves much to be desired. Not only is it incomplete in its treatment of priorities, but its language, if read literally, could produce bizarre results. Some of these defects are identified in recommendations made by the Article 2 Study Group:

> The Study Group recommends that the Article 9 Study Committee consider the following revisions to § 9–114 and, where appropriate, to other sections of Article 9.
>
> (1) If a consignor has filed a proper financing statement but has not met the additional conditions in § 9–114(1), the priority provisions of § 9–312(5) rather than § 9–114(2) should

control.   The consignor should not be automatically subordinated.

(2) It should be made clear that priority between a lien creditor and a consignor who files but does not meet the conditions in § 9–114(1) should track the priority rules in § 9–301(1)(b).

(3) It should be made clear that a consignor's interest in the goods attaches to their proceeds and what the priority of the consignor's interest should be.

Permanent Editorial Board Article 2 Report 122–23.

One court managed to overcome the infelicities of UCC 9–114 in one recent case. In re Mobile Traveler, Inc., 117 B.R. 651 (Bkrtcy. D.Kan.1990). In that case, the consignor failed to give notice to a bank that earlier had filed a financing statement covering inventory of the consignee. Because the earlier-filed bank had no claim against the consignee, it did not challenge the consignor's priority. However, a *later*-filed inventory secured party claimed priority. The later-filed party relied on the language of UCC 9–114(2), which provides that the interest of a consignor who fails to comply with subsection (1) is "subordinate to a person who would have a perfected security interest in the goods if they were the property of the debtor," and which makes no distinction based on when the conflicting claimant files or acquires its interest. Chalking up the dilemma to poor drafting, the court refused to reach the nonsensical result urged upon it and awarded priority to the consignor.

(4) **Competing PMSI's in the Same Collateral.** Consider the following scenario: Debtor wishes to acquire equipment. To do so, Debtor borrows a down payment from Lender and finances the balance of the purchase price with Seller. Lender and Seller each takes a security interest in the equipment and perfects by filing within ten days after Debtor takes possession. What is the relative priority of the two PMSI's in the same collateral, each of which qualifies for priority under UCC 9–312(4)? The Code provides no clear answer.

Is there any reason to favor one secured party over the other on the basis of status (seller or lender)? One might argue that the two PMSI's should enjoy equal priority, inasmuch as each secured party has some reason to believe that it enjoys first priority. Moreover, as a practical matter, in many cases it is likely that a PMSI financer will be unable to discover the filing (or, in the case of consumer goods, the automatically perfected security interest) of its competitor. On the other hand, there may be good reasons to award priority to the first secured party to file or perfect.[5] In particular, a rule of equal priority could create unneces-

---

5. In the case of PMSI's in consumer goods, attachment, and consequently perfection, of a seller's security interest and a lender's security interest may occur simul- taneously upon the debtor's acquisition of rights in the collateral.   See UCC 9–203(1)(c); UCC 9–302(1)(d).

sary complications when one secured party tries to enforce its security interest.[6]

(5) Definition of "Purchase Money Security Interest"; The Tracing Requirement. UCC 9–107 provides for two types of PMSI's: those "taken or retained by the seller of the collateral to secure all or part of its price," UCC 9–107(a), and those taken by a lender who "gives value to enable the debtor to acquire rights in or the use of collateral if such value is in fact so used." UCC 9–107(b).

For a security interest taken by a lender to qualify as a PMSI, the value (i.e., the loan—or **enabling loan** as it often is called) (i) must be given for the purpose of enabling the debtor to acquire the collateral and (ii) must actually be used for that purpose. It follows from the second component of this rule that, in order to achieve PMSI status, a secured lender must trace the loaned funds and establish that they actually were used to pay the purchase price for the collateral. The secured lender typically accomplishes this by advancing the loaned funds directly to the seller of the collateral or by issuing a check payable jointly to the seller and the buyer-debtor. Does the rationale of the purchase money priority rules, considered above in Note (2), explain this strict tracing requirement? Normally there is no tracing problem when a PMSI is created in favor of a seller.

Does PMSI status require a close temporal connection between the incurrence of purchase-money debt (the obligation to pay the price or to repay an enabling loan) and the attachment and perfection of the security interest? Suppose, for example, that a seller sells goods on unsecured credit (an **open account**) or a lender makes an unsecured enabling loan. Sometime (months, or even years) later, the buyer gives the seller (or the enabling lender) a security interest in the goods to secure the balance of the purchase price (or unpaid balance of the loan). Is the security interest a PMSI? A literal application of the definition in UCC 9–107 would seem to result in PMSI status. See In re Cerasoli, 27 B.R. 51 (Bkrtcy.M.D.Pa.1983) (security interest taken to secure enabling loan several months after enabling loan was made, held a PMSI). But see In re Brooks, 29 UCC Rep.Serv. 660 (Bkrtcy. D.Me. 1980) (security interest taken several months after the making of enabling loans, held not a PMSI). (Note that in most cases the delay would mean that the PMSI would not qualify for purchase money *priority* under UCC 9–312(3) or (4). See Note (2) supra; Note on Debtor's Receipt of Possession of Collateral, infra.)

(6) The "Transformation" and "Dual Status" Rules. UCC 9–107 provides that a security interest is a PMSI "to the extent" that it meets the criteria of paragraphs (a) or (b) of that section. The implication of the quoted phrase is that a security interest in the PMSI-financed collateral is *not* a PMSI "to the extent" that it also secures debt other than the price or an enabling loan. Likewise, that language

---

6. See Chapter 15, Section 3(B), infra, which considers the duties that secured parties who enforce their security interests owe to other secured parties.

suggests that a security interest in collateral other than the PMSI-financed collateral is not a PMSI even though it secures a purchase-money debt for other collateral.

Several cases support the retention of PMSI status for a security interest in PMSI-financed collateral when that collateral also secures obligations other than the purchase-money debt. Those cases recognize security interests having a "dual status": they are part PMSI (i.e., to the extent that they secure the price or an enabling loan) and part non-PMSI (i.e., to the extent that they secure other indebtedness). See, e.g., In re Gibson, 16 B.R. 257 (Bkrtcy.D.Kan.1981). However, there is a substantial body of case law holding that what otherwise would be a PMSI is transformed into a non-PMSI whenever the PMSI-financed collateral secures any obligations other than the price or an enabling loan or whenever other collateral, in addition to the PMSI-financed collateral, secures the purchase-money debt. See, e.g., In re Norrell, 426 F.Supp 435 (M.D.Ga.1977); In re Simpson, 4 UCC Rep.Serv. 243 (Bkrtcy.W.D.Mich.1966).

A number of cases also have applied this "transformation" rule to deny PMSI status when the price or an enabling loan has been **refinanced** (i.e., extended or combined with other indebtedness), even when the secured party could identify a portion of the collateral as PMSI-financed collateral and a portion of the secured indebtedness as the price or as an enabling loan for that collateral. In re Matthews, 724 F.2d 798 (9th Cir.1984), is typical of those cases. In *Matthews*, the debtors owed $3,902.64 to Transamerica. The debt was secured by a PMSI in a piano and a stereo. The parties agreed to refinance the loan: the term was extended and the monthly payment was reduced in amount. Transamerica's books showed a new secured loan to the debtors in the amount of $4,245.01, of which $3,902.64 was applied to pay off the old delinquent loan. The court observed that the debtors did not use the proceeds of the new loan to acquire rights in or the use of the piano or stereo; they already owned them. "The new security interest in the piano and stereo taken by Transamerica at the time of the refinancing was therefore not a 'purchase money security interest' as the [Code] has defined it."

Southtrust Bank v. Borg–Warner Acceptance Corp, supra, held that the inclusion of a future advance clause and an after-acquired property clause transformed the putative PMSI into an "ordinary" security interest. Does *Southtrust* support the transformation rule? The court seemed to leave the door open to PMSI status, even when future advances purport to be secured by PMSI collateral, when there is a contractual "method for determining the extent to which each item of collateral secures its purchase money." The most difficult aspect of this determination may be the allocation of payments made by the debtor to the various components of the secured obligations. For a case upholding the parties' agreement on a formula for allocating payments, see In re Breakiron, 32 B.R. 400 (Bkrtcy.W.D.Pa.1983). In some jurisdictions there is a statutory method of allocation. See, e.g., Pristas v.

Landaus of Plymouth, Inc., 742 F.2d 797 (3d Cir.1984) (applying formula provided by Pennsylvania's Goods and Services Installment Sales Act to a dual-status security interest). In the absence of explicit agreement or statutory guidance, some courts have devised a method of allocation. See, e.g., In re Conn, 16 B.R. 454 (Bkrtcy.W.D.Ky.1982) (allocation based on first-in, first-out method).

Southtrust is one of the relatively few cases holding that a PMSI was transformed into a non-PMSI in the commercial context. Most cases that have confronted the issue, including *Matthews*, supra, have arisen in the context of BC 522(f)(2), which permits the avoidance of certain non-PMSI security interests in certain types of collateral, primarily consumer goods.[7]

Which approach—transformation or dual-status—is more consistent with the policies that underlie Article 9? Consider two important principles of the Article 9 scheme that seem to be well-accepted. First, parties are given great flexibility to agree as to what collateral (any combination of now-owned and after-acquired property) will secure what obligations (any combination of now-existing or later-arising debt). See UCC 9–204. But see UCC 9–204(2) (limiting the effect of an after-acquired property clause with respect to consumer goods). Second, PMSI's are given favored treatment. See UCC 9–301(2); UCC 9–302(1)(d); UCC 9–312(3), (4). Should parties to a secured transaction be forced to sacrifice flexibility for PMSI treatment or PMSI treatment for flexibility? Should consensual refinancing and restructuring of debt, including secured debt, be discouraged by the threat of the loss of PMSI status? See In re Billings, 838 F.2d 405 (10th Cir.1988) (transformation rule discourages creditors holding PMSI's from helping their debtors work out of financial problems without the need to enter bankruptcy or surrender collateral).

On the other hand, a security interest is a PMSI only "to the extent" that it secures purchase-money obligations, the amount of which must be determined in each case. Should the secured party invoking PMSI status have the burden of proving that amount? Courts generally say "yes."

Problem 9. Lee is in the data processing business. *SP*–1 has a perfected security interest in "all equipment now owned or hereafter acquired" by Lee. On June 1, 1989, Lee and Lor entered into a "true lease" of a computer for a three-year term. The lease agreement provides that Lee, as lessee, has an option to purchase the computer at the end of the lease term for its "fair market value." In accordance with the lease, on May 1, 1992, Lee notified Lor of Lee's intention to

---

7. BC 522(f)(2) permits debtors to avoid "nonpossessory, nonpurchase-money security interest[s]" in certain types of exempt property. It is likely that fewer and fewer cases involving BC 522(f)(2) will be reported because the FTC's Rule on Credit Practices now restricts the taking of certain nonpossessory, non-PMSI's. See 16 C.F.R. § 444.2(a)(4) (1991) (making it an unfair practice for lenders or retail installment sellers to obtain from consumers nonpossessory security interests, other than PMSI's, in household goods).

exercise that option. Thereafter Lee and Lor reached agreement that the fair market value of the computer—and therefore the sale price—is $1,000.

Lee requests financing from your client, *SP*–2, for Lee's purchase of the leased computer. Your search of the records uncovers *SP*–1's financing statement covering "all equipment." Lee is reluctant to ask *SP*–1 to subordinate its security interest to that of *SP*–2 because Lee does not want to pay the fees that *SP*–1's lawyers will charge for drawing up the subordination agreement. However, Lee has assured your client that Lee's agreement with *SP*–1 permits Lee to give PMSI's in equipment to other financers.

How can you assure *SP*–2 that it will achieve purchase money priority? See UCC 9–105(1)(d), UCC 9–312(4); Note on Debtor's Receipt of Possession of Collateral, infra.

Note on Debtor's Receipt of Possession of Collateral

We have seen that a PMSI does not qualify for purchase money priority under UCC 9–312(3) unless it is perfected "at the time the debtor receives possession of the inventory." Likewise, purchase money priority in non-inventory collateral under UCC 9–312(4) depends on perfection of the PMSI "at the time the debtor receives possession of the collateral or within ten days thereafter." The Code does not contain a definition of "possession" for these purposes. The courts have struggled with various scenarios, such as the one presented by Problem 9, in which a prospective debtor in a PMSI transaction is *already* in possession of collateral in a capacity other than that of buyer-owner.

Relying on the references to possession by the "debtor" in UCC 9–312(3) and (4), several courts have concluded that the 10–day period does not begin to run until the party in possession becomes a "debtor," as defined in UCC 9–105(1)(d). See, e.g., Commerce Union Bank v. John Deere Industrial Equipment Co., 387 So.2d 787 (Ala.1980) (lessee under true lease, with option to purchase, did not become a "debtor," thereby starting UCC 9–312(4)'s 10–day period to run, until date that lessee exercised purchase option); Brodie Hotel Supply, Inc. v. United States, 431 F.2d 1316 (9th Cir.1970) (possession of equipment pending agreement to purchase did not trigger 10–day period under Alaska's UCC 9–312(4), because possessor did not become a "debtor" until he became obligated to pay for equipment); Petition of Board of Trustees, 49 Mich. App. 106, 211 N.W.2d 561 (1973) (10–day period under UCC 9–312(4) did not begin to run until party in possession of equipment became contractually bound to purchase it).

Do the cases that delay the commencement of the ten-day period undercut the policy of favoring public notice and the policy against "secret" liens? Or, are some of these cases better characterized as being consistent with current law that does *not* require public notice in the case of leases and various other bailments? We have seen in Chapter 12, Section 1, supra, that there is disagreement over whether some of those bailments should be subjected to Article 9's filing regime. But, inasmuch as filing is not required, isn't it appropriate to delay commencement of the ten-day period until the relationship of the parties falls within the scope of Article 9?

Note on "Cross–Collateral" Agreements, Payment Allocation Formulas, and Consumer Protection

Used home furnishings and other used consumer goods bring relatively little at liquidation sales when compared with their use value to the installment buyer. This "hostage value" aspect of collateral consisting of consumer goods provided much of the inspiration for the Federal Trade Commission's Rule on Credit Practices, which makes it an unfair practice for lenders or retail installment sellers to receive nonpossessory, non-PMSI's in household goods. See 16 C.F.R. § 444.-2(a)(4) (1991). The FTC regulations have the effect of prohibiting **cross-collateral** provisions—agreements whereby each item of collateral secures not only its own price (and, absent application of the transformation rule, would be subject to a PMSI to that extent) but also the price of other items of collateral sold by the financer (to that extent, a non-PMSI).

Secured parties may be able to preserve much of the leverage that comes from the threat of repossessing many of the debtor's most valued consumer goods without violating the FTC regulations, if the system of allocating installment payments among a series of purchases means that the debt for none of the goods is paid until all debts are paid. For example, a consumer buyer and a secured seller (or enabling lender) could agree that each payment made by the buyer would be allocated proportionately among the outstanding balances for all items purchased. In this way, any default in payment would constitute a default under each transaction, and the secured creditor would be entitled to take possession of all of the items of collateral. That type of arrangement with a consumer debtor was attacked as "unconscionable" in the famous case of Williams v. Walker–Thomas Furniture Co., 350 F.2d 445 (D.C.Cir.1965) (remanded to trial court for factual determinations on issue of unconscionability).

Uniform Consumer Credit Code (U3C) 3.303, which has not been widely enacted, deals with this problem by providing that payments shall be "applied first to the payment of the debts arising from the sales first made." Is this a reasonable and appropriate regulation of the parties' freedom to contract?

(C) Proceeds

Problem 10. The facts are as in Problem 6(b), supra: *SP*–1 holds a security interest in present and future construction equipment; *SP*–1 filed on June 1. *SP*–2 holds a security interest in the new Cletrac bulldozer purchased in July with the loan from *SP*–2. *SP*–2 filed on July 8.

Late in July *D* found that, to meet the special requirements of a new construction job, *D* needed a bulldozer with a power attachment that the Cletrac bulldozer lacked. On August 1, without consulting *SP*–1 or *SP*–2, *D* traded the Cletrac bulldozer for a used Caterpillar bulldozer that met *D*'s needs.

Shortly thereafter *D* ran out of cash and defaulted on the debts to *SP*–1 and *SP*–2. Who has priority as to the Caterpillar bulldozer? See UCC 9–312(4); UCC 9–306.

Problem 11. *D* is a wholesaler of textiles whose business is like that described in Problem 7. *D* makes many sales on credit to retail stores. The retail stores, in a period of recession, began to take more and more time to pay, with the result that *D* ran short of operating funds.

On June 1, when accounts receivable due *D* from retail stores amounted to $60,000, *D* applied to *SP*–1 for a loan. *SP*–1 extended *D* a loan of $50,000, and *D* executed a security agreement covering "all present and future accounts." *SP*–1 promptly filed a financing statement covering "accounts receivable currently existing or arising hereafter."

On July 1, finding itself in need of additional funds, *D* applied to *SP*–2 for a loan. *D* offered its inventory as collateral. *SP*–2 searched the files and found only *SP*–1's financing statement covering accounts, not inventory. *SP*–2 made a loan of $20,000 to *D*, and *D* executed a security agreement covering "all inventory now owned or hereafter acquired." *SP*–2 promptly filed a financing statement covering "inventory."

In September *D* defaulted on the loans to *SP*–1 and *SP*–2. At that time there were on hand (i) inventory valued at $5,000; (ii) accounts (that arose out of the sale of inventory) valued at $25,000; and (iii) a bank account containing $5,000 that came from the collection of accounts.

(a) Who has the senior security interest in each of these three groups of property? See UCC 9–312(5) & (6); UCC 9–306. See Note on Conflicting Security Interests of Accounts Financers and Inventory Financers, infra.

(b) Now assume that *SP*–2 was the first to file a financing statement. What result?

Note on Conflicting Security Interests of Accounts Financers and Inventory Financers

Before concluding that the answers to Problem 11 are the result of accident or whimsy, read the following excerpts from a 1973 panel discussion by some of the drafters of the 1972 revisions to UCC 9–312.[8]

PROFESSOR KRIPKE: ... A prospective debtor goes to the bank and asks, "Will you lend me $1,000,000 on my accounts receivable?" The bank asks its counsel to check the filings against the debtor. He finds no filings of any kind against this debtor, and the bank is prepared as a matter of credit to make the loan, but it says to its counsel, "Are you sure that we'll have a first security interest on these accounts?" and counsel says, "Yes, of course, there's nothing on file against this debtor. You will therefore be first." Then the counsel says, "On second thought I don't know, because even though you now file first on accounts, I don't know what the answer will be if someone else later files on inventory and claims the accounts as proceeds." That problem exists today under the Code and we think we have a very serious problem if counsel can't give that opinion. ... From my point of view, next to the fixture problem which was causing a great deal of public difficulty, the solution to this problem before it got into the cases was the principal reason for undertaking this amendment process. It was not a purely theoretical question. Sitting in New York as I do where a number of the commercial lenders are situated, every time they get a difficulty under the Code they call me up and bawl me out for it. This was one of the particular problems that they constantly came back to—this whole group of problems as to the relationship between inventory financing and accounts receivable financing.

The first step to solve it was to do something about the two different rules for priority problems which are contained in the existing [1962] Code in Section 9–312(5). One of those rules is the first to file rule and the other is the first to perfect rule. One can never see ahead to the answers to priority problems unless he can visualize what the rules of the game are going to be. Here are two different rules of the game and you don't know which game you're going to play. ...

We collapsed the effect of filing and the effect of perfection, and the basic principle is that the priority ranks from the time at which either of these events occurs.... Applying this to the simple fact situation that I have suggested, if the accounts receivable secured party lends on accounts and files before anything else happens, he will win even though someone else enters the chain of production earlier and files on inventory and its proceeds. Similarly, if someone files on inventory and has through it a claim to proceeds, he will have the first right to

---

8. A Second Look at the Amendments to Article 9 of the UCC, 29 Bus. Law. 973,   1001–03 (1974).

accounts even though someone else later comes along and claims accounts. In that latter case the inventory financer has it because he gets there first by perfecting a claim to inventory through possession or through filing. We rejected the notion that I think caused this difficulty and which is implied in certain writings under the Code that the person who handles inventory has a prior claim simply because inventory precedes accounts in the cycle of a business. We thought that if we recognized such a principle we could never give an accounts financer any certainty as to his position. It was important to give him certainty so we make the inventory right depend on his first filing or perfection and not on the fact that inventory comes ahead of accounts in the cycle of a business.

... It's more important to have a clear rule that everyone can accommodate to than it is to have a vague rule that no one is sure of even though you might argue that some different rule is theoretically correct.

MR. COOGAN: I would stress again that this is a purely empirical answer. I think everybody said that if one could practically protect the financer who furnishes new inventory, without cutting the heart out of accounts financing, we would have been willing to do it, but the difficulty is that if you protected the inventory financer you make the accounts financing so problematical that you cut off the most likely source of cash that is going to be used to pay the inventory financer.

MR. HAYDOCK: It does seem unfair to some people where an inventory financer comes in later with a purchase money security interest to have him defeated, when we have adopted a different rule with respect to other types of collateral.

SOMEONE IN AUDIENCE: In the case of an inventory financer would you ever go into inventory financing if you had checked the records and knew that there was an accounts receivable financing statement on file?

MR. HAYDOCK: No.

PROFESSOR KRIPKE: I think there are people who do that.

AUDIENCE: Is it normal business procedure? Would you ever advise your client to do inventory financing without getting a waiver on it? When they do it they take a credit risk.

PROFESSOR KRIPKE: They take a credit risk. That raises a point that I think is worth mentioning and which was the subject of a quite vehement attack on our drafting on the floor of the American Law Institute. A gentleman from Massachusetts said in substance. "When we agreed to the Code, we understood that there could be purchase money priorities as to inventory, and I took it for granted that the priority would flow through to the receivables. My orientation is in favor of unsecured trade creditors, but it was on this assumption that I was willing to go along with the Code. Now you say that the inventory security interest does not carry through to receivables." His ultimate point was just like yours: "What good is the inventory financing if it doesn't carry through to the receivables." Now Bob Braucher and I answered him on the floor of the Institute, and I think the answer is still applicable and is sound. The answer is: "If you were right that your inventory financing carried through to the receivable, there wouldn't be any receivables financing and you wouldn't get paid until the receivable was paid. You'd have to extend your credit a great deal longer. By permitting receivables financing to occur, you're going to get paid when the sale occurs. You'll get paid a lot earlier, you're a trade creditor, you're not in the financing business, you need your own working capital, and you want to limit the duration of your own extensions of credit." Now, if the inventory parties are seriously concerned about the problem, they can, of course, insist on some kind of an arrangement with the receivables party that he pay them, or they'll refuse to do the inventory financing. I recall another meeting at which this question was thrashed out. Persons presently actively engaged in financing said that a number of Japanese trading companies are doing substantial amounts of inventory financing in the United States on the goods which they ship over here, knowing that others will be picking up the receivables financing and being content to lose their security interest when the goods are sold.

MR. HAYDOCK: I see that our time is up. Thank you very much.

————

Problem 12. *D* is a wholesaler of textiles whose business is like that described in Problems 7 and 11.

As in Problem 11, on June 1, when accounts receivable due *D* from retail stores amounted to $60,000, *D* applied to *SP*-1 for a loan. *SP*-1 extended *D* a loan of $50,000, and *D* executed to *SP*-1 a security agreement covering "all present and future accounts, and all inventory now owned or hereafter acquired." *SP*-1 promptly filed a financing statement covering "accounts receivable currently existing or arising hereafter, and all inventory now owned or hereafter acquired."

On July 1 *D* wanted to purchase $20,000 worth of additional stocks of textiles from manufacturer *M*. In response to *D*'s request *SP*-2 made a $20,000 loan to *D* by a check payable jointly to *D* and *M*; *D* indorsed the check to *M*. *D* executed a security agreement covering the new shipment. *SP*-2 immediately filed a financing statement covering "textiles, now owned or hereafter acquired." In addition, *SP*-2 immediately gave *SP*-1 written notice of the transaction. Shortly thereafter *M* delivered the textiles to *SP*-2.

In September *D* defaulted on the loans to *SP*-1 and *SP*-2. In the meantime, textiles purchased from *M* under the July transaction had been sold to retail stores, generating (i) unpaid accounts of $15,000; (ii) a separate deposit collateral account containing $5,000, which came from payments by retail stores of such accounts; and (iii) a check for $4,000 received as an advance payment for an order of textiles that were subsequently shipped to the buyer.

(a) Who has priority with respect to (i) the unpaid accounts of $15,000; (ii) the $5,000 in the deposit account; (iii) the $4,000 check? See UCC 9–312(3)–(6). What explains the result?

The proper resolution of the foregoing priority disputes was hotly contested under the 1962 version of Article 9. Although the drafters of the 1972 version addressed the problems, they communicated their solutions in a subtle fashion, through omission and innuendo. It may help to take the following steps: (a) Is the purchase-money priority under UCC 9–312(4) applicable to this case? (b) Does the purchase-money priority for inventory under UCC 9–312(3) carry through to proceeds in the form of accounts? (Note: "identifiable *cash* proceeds.") (c) As to the identifiable cash received from the payments of accounts, note: "cash proceeds received *on or before* the delivery of the inventory to a buyer." (d) Is any of the "special" rules of UCC 9–312 applicable to these proceeds? If not, what result follows from the general rule of UCC 9–312(5)?

(b) Would the priorities be resolved differently if *SP*–1 had taken a security interest only in inventory and not in accounts?

SECTION 2. BUYERS OF GOODS

Introduction. We have seen that UCC 9–201 provides secured lenders with powerful words of comfort: "Except as otherwise provided by this Act a security agreement is effective ... against *purchasers* of the collateral and against creditors." Of course, Article 9 does "otherwise provide[ ]" if the security interest is not perfected; certain good faith buyers of goods (and instruments, documents, and chattel paper) can prevail under UCC 9–301(1)(c). But when the security interest *is* perfected (usually by public filing), then UCC 9–201, especially when read in conjunction with UCC 9–306(2), stands as a serious threat to buyers. In many circumstances a buyer who fails to check the public records will have only itself to blame if its ownership interest is encumbered by a security interest.

(A) PERFECTED SECURITY INTERESTS AND BUYERS OF GOODS

This part deals with priority contests between buyers of goods and secured parties with *perfected* security interests.

Problem 1. Gadget Construction Co. is in the road construction business. Gadget has a line of credit with Wowsers State Bank ("Bank"), secured by all of Gadget's construction equipment. Bank's security interest is perfected by filing. The security agreement signed by Gadget strictly prohibits Gadget from selling, leasing, or otherwise disposing of any of the collateral without first obtaining Bank's written permission.

Gadget's business was slow during the winter months. On February 1 Gadget sold two of its front-end loaders to Penny, Inc., another construction company. Penny did not check the Code records and had no knowledge of Bank's security interest or Gadget's agreement not to dispose of the equipment. Gadget used the cash received from Penny to pay various unsecured creditors.

Gadget is in default and Bank has made demand on Penny to deliver the two loaders to Bank.

(a) Is Bank's security interest senior to Penny's interest in the loaders? See UCC 9–306(2).

(b) What result in part (a) if the security agreement permits Gadget to sell collateral free of the security interest "on the condition that, immediately following any such sale, Gadget remits the net proceeds of the sale to Bank." See National Livestock Credit Corp. v. Schultz, infra; Notes on Authorized and Unauthorized Dispositions, infra. Would your answer be different if Penny had *known* about the foregoing "condition"?

(c) What result in part (a) if the security agreement permits Gadget to sell collateral on the condition that Bank's security interest will continue in the collateral (i.e., sales are to be *subject to*, instead of *free of*, the security interest)? See PEB Commentary No. 3.

(d) What result in part (a) if, during the last two years, Gadget has sold unneeded equipment on several occasions and Bank, which was aware of those dispositions, raised no objection with Gadget? What difference, if any, would it make if Penny had been a party to several of these sales? See UCC 1–103; UCC 1–205; Note (3) on Authorized and Unauthorized Dispositions, infra.

(e) Assume that Bank's security interest continued in the loaders following the sale to Penny (i.e., that Penny bought the loaders *subject to* Bank's security interest). Does Bank's security interest continue to be perfected as against creditors of Penny? Is Bank under a duty to file a new financing statement against Penny? Should it be? If Bank is under no duty to refile, how can Penny's creditors discover that Penny owns the loaders subject to Bank's "secret" security interest? See UCC 9–402(7) (3d sentence); PEB Commentary No. 3; Note (2) on Authorized and Unauthorized Dispositions, infra.

(f) Assume that Bank's security interest continued in the loaders following the sale to Penny and that, on February 1 (the date of Penny's purchase), $25,000 was outstanding on the line of credit. Unaware of the sale, Bank extended an additional $5,000 on the line of credit on March 1 and an additional $10,000 on April 1. Can Bank enforce its security interest in the loaders to recover the entire $40,000? See UCC 9–307(3). (The equitable doctrine of "marshaling," discussed in Chapter 15, Section 3, infra, may affect the result.)

(g) What result in part (f) if Bank had learned of the sale to Penny on February 15?

Parts (f) and (g) concern the priority of "future advances." Section 1, Problem 2, supra, raises a similar priority dispute; however, the competing claimant in that Problem is not a buyer, but another secured party. Compare your answers to parts (f) and (g) with your answer to Problem 2(a), Section 1, supra. Can you explain any differences in result? (The 45–day periods in UCC 9–307(3) and 9–301(4) derive from the Federal Tax Lien Act. See Comment 7 to UCC 9–301.

NATIONAL LIVESTOCK CREDIT CORP. v. SCHULTZ[*]

Court of Appeals of Oklahoma, 1982.
653 P.2d 1243.

BRIGHTMIRE, JUDGE. The major question raised by this appeal is whether the terms of a cattle security agreement regarding sale of the cattle, designed for perfected lender's protection, were waived by the creditor's long-term course of conduct inconsistent with the protective provisions. A secondary issue is whether a secured party is estopped to deny authorization of the sale in a suit for conversion against the buyer based upon a detrimental reliance theory. The trial court resolved both issues against the loan company. We affirm.

I

The facts are not disputed. G.W. "Bill" Schultz and his son were the general and limited partners of Schultz Cattle Co., that ran and grazed cattle until 1973 when it began a so-called "fat cattle" operation.[1] Beginning in April 1964, Schultz Cattle Co. financed its operation with funds from loans obtained through National Livestock Credit Corporation. The financial arrangement was such that in April 1964 a note was executed in excess of $400,000 payable to National in one year. In each of the succeeding years a new note was executed representing the carry over indebtedness of the cattle company from the preceding year's operations. The last such note, and the one that forms the basis of the present suit, was executed on July 27, 1973, in the principal sum of $586,639.02, payable on July 1, 1974. G.W. Schultz signed the note as co-maker with Schultz Cattle Co. and both executed a security agreement to National giving it a security interest in the herd, including after-acquired cattle and proceeds. Also executed was a loan agreement that, among other things, allowed Schultz to draw whatever money he needed over the course of the year to operate his business. Through this type of arrangement there would be no

---

[* The court's citations are to the applicable pre–1972 version of the Code.]

1. That is, cattle were raised and fed at a feedlot and sold for slaughter at a higher rate of return.

need for Schultz to retain any portion of the proceeds received from sales of cattle to meet business expenses.

The security agreement also provided: "The Debtor will care for and maintain the crops and property herein described in a good and husbandlike manner and will not further encumber, conceal, remove or otherwise dispose of the same without the written consent of the Secured Party; however, permission is granted for the Debtor to sell the property described herein for the fair market value thereof, providing that payment for the same is made jointly to the Debtor and to the Secured Party . . . ."

The loan agreement contained no conditional consent provision, but did say that "Borrower agrees to remit all funds from sale of secured property directly to National" to apply toward the indebtedness.

Between 1973 and 1974, Schultz sold portions of the collateral cattle to various packers without the prior written consent or knowledge of National. In every instance, the check was made payable to Schultz Cattle Co. only. Schultz, in turn, either mailed the check to National or deposited the packer's check into the Cattle Co.'s account and then issued a new check to National to pay off the note indebtedness. National concedes that it never rebuked Schultz for ignoring the terms of the security agreement relating to sales of secured cattle. As a matter of fact, it admits this procedure was customarily followed by all its loan account clients and by the industry as a whole.

In 1974 and 1975, Schultz, along with the entire cattle industry, began experiencing severe financial problems. By a letter dated April 19, 1974, National's then manager, Harley Custer, informed Schultz that several loans would have to be "shaken down fairly well," including the Schultz Cattle Co. loan and that this loan would be discussed at the next board meeting. On June 20, 1974, Custer again wrote Schultz saying there would be no renewal of the loan, due July 1, 1974, because National's bank would approve no more loans and National could not carry the loan unless it were discounted. Custer told Schultz that the loan could be extended an additional 60 to 90 days if Schultz could reduce the loan amount by $200,000. National, however, agreed to a plan by Schultz to liquidate the herd as "fat cattle" over a period of several months instead of immediately selling the cattle as feeders—the expectation was that this plan would increase the value of the herd by $100,000.

It was anticipated, said Custer, that under this program cattle would be sold out of the feedlot to a packer buyer beginning in September 1974 and that National was leaving it solely up to Schultz to decide to whom he would sell the cattle. And, according to Custer, the procedure for handling the proceeds of the sales was to be the same as it had been in the past, i.e., packer would send check to Schultz Cattle Co. in its or Schultz' name and then the cattle company would forward the check to National.

Schultz could not sell the cattle during the fall of 1974 and this spawned weekly calls from Custer to Schultz expressing the lender's concern that no sales had been made. "We had fulfilled our part of the plan in advancing this money [additional money for feed, and extending the note's due date]," he once said, "and we did want him to get to selling these cattle ...."

Eventually, some sales were made to a small processing plant owned by Schultz (Schultz Farms), and the proceeds of these sales were remitted to National in the usual manner. On January 5, 1975, Wilson and Company bought 34 steers and 42 heifers from Schultz on a grade and yield basis[2] for a total fair market value of $29,089. Wilson acquired 42 more heifers on January 6 for which it paid a grade and yield price of $14,609. On January 8, Schultz sold 140 heifers to Iowa Beef Processors (IBP) for $50,330.24 and on January 19 sold another 148 head to IBP for $51,121.73. With the exception of the last draft paid by IBP,[3] all of the checks were made payable to Schultz Cattle Co. or Schultz Industries, as directed by Schultz. The proceeds, however, were not transmitted to National, but rather to some of Schultz' feed suppliers.

Upon learning of the sales and Schultz' application of the proceeds to grain bills, National liquidated the remaining herd and otherwise attempted to salvage what it could to reduce the loan balance. National also made demand of Wilson and IBP for payment, which demand, of course, was refused. Schultz, in the meantime, had filed bankruptcy. On March 3, 1976, National filed this action against Wilson and IBP claiming the unauthorized sales to them were in derogation of its security interest and filed financing statements and constituted conversion.

Defendants in their answer admitted the respective purchases of cattle and that they rejected National's demand for the purchase price, but denied they had converted the cattle. IBP also raised the affirmative defenses of waiver and estoppel. Wilson alleged, among other things, "that a pattern and practice of dealing was developed over many years whereby [National] allowed ... Schultz ... to keep possession of all [secured] cattle," sell them without National's knowledge or consent and remit the proceeds of the sale to National; therefore, National waived the consent terms in the security agreement, relinquished its security interest in the cattle and is estopped to assert any claim against Wilson. Both defendant buyers specifically asked for reasonable attorney's fees.

Cross-motions for summary judgment were filed by plaintiff and defendants. By letter order dated July 10, 1980, the trial court granted

---

2. The sales price for cattle bought on a grade and yield basis as opposed to live weight basis is not determined until after the cattle are slaughtered.

3. At this point in time, National had learned of the sales and Schultz' failure to pay it the proceeds. National instructed IBP to make the last check jointly payable to Schultz Cattle Co. and National, and IBP complied.

summary judgment in favor of the defendants after finding that National waived the sale restriction terms of the security agreement through a "course of performance" that allowed Schultz to remit only the proceeds of such sales to National. "Thus," the court said, "National authorized Schultz to sell the cattle to IBP and Wilson without restriction and they took title free and clear of National's security interest." Moreover, the court concluded, National was estopped to demand literal compliance with the payment provisions of its security agreement on a detrimental reliance theory on the authority of Poteau State Bank v. Denwalt, Okl., 597 P.2d 756 (1979). Finally, the trial judge denied the defendants' prayer for attorney's fees upon the theory that 12 O.S.1979 Supp. § 940(A) does not apply to conversion of property causes of action.

National timely filed its petition in error challenging the judgment. . . .

II

The arguments raised by National in its voluminous brief boil down to this: only the provisions of general Article One of the Uniform Commercial Code and of secured transactions Article Nine govern security agreements, and therefore, the trial court erred in finding that the course of performance and waiver provisions of Article Two can be invoked to undermine express terms of a security agreement. It further argues there were no transactions between National and defendant packing companies that could act to estop National from asserting its security interest in the cattle.

Since we affirm the trial court's order as to the waiver issue, it becomes unnecessary to address the detrimental reliance theory.

National concedes, as it must, that the uniform code expressly provides that its provisions shall be supplemented by principles of law and equity unless these principles have been displaced by particular provisions of the act. 12A O.S.1981 § 1–103. The code, too, explicitly provides that it is to be liberally construed and applied to promote its underlying purposes and policies, one of which is "to permit the continued expansion of commercial practices through custom, usage and *agreement of the parties.*" 12A O.S.1981 § 1–102(1) & (2)(b) (emphasis added).

The principal code provision having application to the present appeal is 12A O.S.1981 § 9–306, which provides in part:

> "(2) Except where this Article otherwise provides, a security interest continues in collateral, notwithstanding sale, exchange or other disposition thereof, *unless the disposition was authorized by the secured party in the security agreement or otherwise,* and also continues in any identifiable proceeds including collections received by the debtor." (emphasis added)

Clearly, the statute continues the secured party's security interest both in the collateral in the hands of a buyer as well as the proceeds received by the borrower from the unauthorized sale of the collateral. The security interest can be lost, however, and is lost if the sale is authorized by the secured party in the "security agreement or otherwise."

The trial court found the undisputed facts to be that National's prior conduct and its actions in regard to the sales at issue here constituted a waiver of its contractual rights. While National does not deny the facts are undisputed, it does disagree with the court's conclusion on the ground that the doctrine of waiver cannot be applied to a U.C.C. security agreement. More specifically National contends that the court impermissibly applied an Article Two concept to an Article Nine transaction, and in advancing this thesis it assumes that the only statutory basis for the decision is 12A O.S.1981 § 2–208.[5]

We think National misapprehends the basis of the trial court's decision and the effect the separate articles of the uniform code have on one another as well as the effect supplemental principles of law and equity have on commercial transactions. Another provision in Article One, which is applicable to all sections of the code, amply supports the trial court's legal conclusions.

As at least one court has quite correctly pointed out, the definitions in Article One (12A O.S.1981 § 1–201) are automatically made a part of each article in the code and thus a "security agreement" must first be an "agreement" as defined in § 1–201. And, since an agreement is defined by the code as "the bargain of the parties in fact as found in their language or by implication from other circumstances including ... course of performance as provided in this Act (Section ... 2–208)," this has to include security agreements. Therefore, a certain course of performance can result in the waiver of an express term in a security agreement.

There is yet another U.C.C. basis for the invocation of the waiver theory. Section 9–306(2) contemplates extinguishment of a security interest if disposition of collateral is authorized by a secured party "in the security agreement *or otherwise*." The italicized language cannot be considered as mere surplusage and, in fact, the connective "or" gives it at least as much substantive value as the express terms of a security agreement. National's course of conduct certainly has to be considered as an "otherwise" authorization of the sale that resulted in defendant purchasers taking the cattle free from National's security interest.

---

5. This section, entitled "Course of Performance or Practical Construction," provides:

"(1) Where the contract for sale involves repeated occasions for performance by either party with knowledge of the nature of the performance and opportunity for objection to it by the other, any course of performance accepted or acquiesced in without objection shall be relevant to determine the meaning of the agreement.

. . .

"(3) Subject to the provisions of the next section [2–209] on modification and waiver, *such course of performance shall be relevant to show a waiver* or modification *of any term inconsistent with such course of performance*." (emphasis added)

Finally, apart from the interconnections among the various articles and sections of the code, the previously mentioned §§ 1–103 and 1–102—which allow for supplementation of the code with principles of law and equity in determining rights of the parties—require the court to look not only at the words used by the parties but to analyze their conduct as well in determining what agreement they actually made and what the equities should be. Certainly the facts of this case lend themselves to the application of one time honored maxim of equity: "Where one of two innocent persons must suffer by the act of a third, he who has enabled such third person to occasion the loss must suffer." Pettis v. Johnston, 78 Okl. 277, 190 P. 681 (1920).

Assuming National is an innocent party, it made no effort to alter the customary financial practices of prosperous times after the cattle business turned sour. This "business as usual" attitude made it possible for Schultz to misapply the funds in question and, therefore, from an equitable standpoint National should bear the loss....

[Judgment affirmed.]

Notes on Authorized and Unauthorized Dispositions

(1) **"Authorized" Dispositions.** UCC 9–306(2) provides that "a security interest continues in collateral notwithstanding sale, exchange or other disposition thereof unless the disposition was authorized by the secured party in the security agreement or otherwise." The negative implication of that sentence is that a security interest does not continue in collateral whose disposition the secured party has authorized.

To apply the statutory language, one must answer at least two questions. First, what is the substance of an authorization that allows a disposition to cut off a security interest? In other words, precisely what must the secured party authorize? Consider the following answer:

> The intent underlying this exception [for authorized dispositions] is to permit a disposition of the collateral free and clear of the security interest when the secured party has authorized the disposition free and clear of its security interest in the security agreement or otherwise. In the case of such an authorized disposition, the general rule of survivability of the security interest set forth in § 9–306(2) will not apply and the security interest will terminate upon the disposition. However, this exception to the rule of survivability only applies if the secured party has authorized the disposition, by agreement or otherwise, *free and clear of the security interest.* The exception will not apply if the secured party did not authorize the disposition of the collateral or if the secured party authorized the disposition subject to its security interest.

PEB Commentary No. 3 (emphasis in original). Are you satisfied with that answer? Is it reasonable to require a transferee to investigate the details of any authorization given by its transferor's secured party? (Keep in mind that the transferee normally will be able to identify the secured party by searching the appropriate public records.)

Second, when a security agreement gives no authorization, under what circumstances is an authorization "otherwise" given? According to PEB Commentary No. 3, "[t]he questions of what facts will constitute an effective express or implied authorization for purposes of this Section [UCC 9–306(2)] and what standard of proof is applicable to this determination are not addressed in the Code but are instead left to other law." The following Notes consider this second question.

(2) **Consequences of an Unauthorized Disposition: Remedies Against Collateral and Proceeds; Continued Perfection.** A secured party whose security interest survives an unauthorized disposition is entitled to exercise its rights against the collateral, such as the right to take possession from the debtor, the purchaser, or any other junior party following the debtor's default. See UCC 9–503; see generally Chapter 15, infra. (Note that in the typical case the unauthorized disposition itself would constitute a default.) This is, of course, the clear implication of the continuation of the security interest. UCC 9–306(2) also makes it clear that the secured party is entitled not only to the continued security interest in the original collateral *but also* to the identifiable proceeds of that collateral. Does this give the secured party a "windfall"? A "double recovery"? Keep in mind that the secured party will be entitled to only one satisfaction of the secured debt.

A secured party's continuing security interest following an unauthorized disposition also will be effective against the purchaser's creditors and transferees. PEB Commentary No. 3 points out that under UCC 9–402(7) a financing statement continues to be effective following a disposition of collateral "even though the secured party knows of or consents to the transfer." UCC 9–402(7) (3d sentence). (Of course, if a secured party "consents" to a disposition *free of* the security interest, the security interest will not continue and the effectiveness of the financing statement will not matter. See Note (1), supra.) It follows that when a security interest is perfected by filing and it continues following a disposition, the security interest will remain perfected until and unless the financing statement lapses. The secured party is not obliged to file a new financing statement, even though no one searching against the purchaser's name would discover the filing against the original debtor. Earlier in these materials, in Chapter 11, Section 2, we noted Professor Westbrook's criticism of this rule and the operation of the second sentence of UCC 9–402(7) (insofar as a secured party need not refile against a new name following a debtor's name change.) See Westbrook, Glitch: Section 9–402(7) and the U.C.C. Revision Process, 52 Geo. Wash. L. Rev. 408 (1984); Chapter 11, Section 2, supra.

(3) Waiver, Estoppel, Course of Performance, and Course of Dealing. The breadth of the statutory formulation, "or otherwise," in UCC 9–306(2) openly invites a buyer of goods covered by a perfected security interest to assert that the disposition was "authorized" by the secured party. Even in the absence of the broad statutory language, a buyer could attempt to prove that the secured party had waived or subordinated its security interest. Cf. UCC 9–316. In many situations, however, the buyer will be unable to marshal evidence sufficient to establish, through UCC 1–103, a common-law waiver. See, e.g., Weidman v. Babcock, 241 Va. 40, 400 S.E.2d 164 (1991) (" 'Waiver is the voluntary, intentional abandonment of a known legal right, advantage, or privilege.' Essential elements of the doctrine are both knowledge of the facts basic to the exercise of the right and the intent to relinquish that right. A waiver of legal rights will be implied only upon clear and unmistakable proof of the intention to waive such rights; the essence of waiver is voluntary choice."). In a proper case a secured party also might be estopped from asserting that its security interest continues in collateral following a disposition. But, as with waiver, buyers often cannot prove the reasonable reliance on the secured party's actions or omissions that is necessary to establish an estoppel. "A well-established principle of estoppel doctrine provides that in order for silence and inaction to estop a person from pressing some right or claim, there must have been a timely opportunity for the person to speak or act and, in addition, an obligation to do so." Hillman, McDonnell & Nickles, Common Law ¶ 22.04[2][d], at 24–54 to 24–55 (citing 3 J. Pomeroy, Equity Jurisprudence § 808a (S. Symons 5th ed. 1941)).

Because buyers usually lack the clear evidence necessary to establish a true waiver or an estoppel, they often argue that an authorization should be inferred from a secured party's conduct. (Keep in mind that a buyer asserting that a disposition was authorized typically will not have known, at the time of sale, about the facts relevant to the issue of authorization; rather, the buyer will be making the assertion "after the fact.") Indeed, an alternative holding in the *Schultz* case, supra, is that the secured party's conduct—repeatedly failing to insist on the debtor's compliance with a requirement that checks for livestock sold be made jointly payable to the debtor and the secured party— constituted an "or otherwise" authorization under UCC 9–306(2). The *Schultz* court also pointed to the secured party's conduct as evidence of a "course of performance" sufficient to constitute a waiver of the offended provisions of the security agreement, citing UCC 2–208. The cases that have inferred authorizations from the secured party's conduct reflect the following common-sense approach: "A secured party deserves no protection from the terms of a security agreement that he himself ignores." Hillman, McDonnell & Nickles, Common Law ¶ 22.-02[1][b][iv], at 22–27.

A "course of dealing" may provide another rationale for finding an authorization. See Lisbon Bank & Trust Co. v. Murray, 206 N.W.2d 96 (Iowa 1973); UCC 1–205(1) ("A course of dealing is a sequence of previous conduct between the parties to a particular transaction which is fairly to be regarded as establishing a common basis of understanding for interpreting their expressions and other conduct."). But when a course of dealing and the "express terms of an agreement" cannot reasonably be construed "as consistent with each other," the express terms control. UCC 1–205(4). Consequently, courts have declined to allow a course of dealing to overcome an inconsistent provision of a security agreement, especially if the security agreement provides that a consent to a disposition must be in writing. See, e.g., Erlandson Implement, Inc. v. First State Bank, 400 N.W.2d 421 (Minn. App.1987).

What seems to be missing in the Code, the case law, and the commentary is a principled approach to putative "or otherwise" authorizations. Should a court stretch to find an authorization, thereby diluting the value of a security interest, or should it practice a contrary bias? It is important to note, here, that the case law construing "or otherwise" may be contaminated by the over-representation of cases in which the buyer was a *buyer in ordinary course of business* of *farm products.* See UCC 1–201(9) (definition of "buyer in ordinary course"); UCC 9–109(3) (definition of "farm products"). Buyers of inventory in ordinary course of business take free of security interests granted by their sellers. See UCC 9–307(1) (considered in more detail in Problem 2 and the Note on the "His Seller" Rule and the Interplay Between UCC 2–403(1) and 9–307(1), infra). However, buyers of farm products—even if in the ordinary course—are exempted from the cleansing benefits of UCC 9–307(1). See Note (5), infra. To the extent that reported cases involve sales of farm products in the ordinary course of business (excluded from the benefits of UCC 9–307(1)), they may not provide useful precedents for non-ordinary course dispositions of other types of collateral.[1]

(4) **Conditional Authorization of Sales.** Recall that the security agreement in the *Schultz* case gave the debtor permission "to sell [collateral] ... for the fair market value thereof, providing that payment for the same is made jointly to the Debtor and to the Secured Party." Implicit in the court's opinion is the belief that when a debtor fails to comply with the condition, a buyer acquires the goods subject to the security interest. Otherwise, the court's reliance on the secured party's conduct as authorizing the sale would not have been necessary.

The effectiveness (as against the debtor's transferee) of these "conditional authorizations" also was upheld in Southwest Washington Production Credit Association v. Seattle–First National Bank, 92 Wash.2d 30, 593 P.2d 167 (1979) (sale was not authorized because debtor failed to comply with condition of authorization requiring debtor to pay over proceeds of disposition to secured party). Consider the following critique of the result and reasoning of that case:

---

1. Most buyers of inventory from merchants need not rely on UCC 9–307(1) alone: Inventory financers often expressly authorize the debtor's ordinary-course sales of inventory free of the security interest. Agricultural lenders, however, normally insist on restricting the debtor's authority to sell farm products collateral.

The reasoning of the court in *Southwest* is problematic, however. First, the only unauthorized aspect of the debtor's disposition in such a case is the failure to remit the sale proceeds. The sale itself is authorized. Moreover, even if such a disposition is properly deemed unauthorized, the reasoning in *Southwest* runs counter to well-established principles of agency law that should apply directly to cases such as *Southwest*. The secured party's consent never is required for a debtor to sell his own rights in collateral. The true significance, therefore, of authorizing a debtor to dispose of collateral is to empower him to sell the secured party's own interest in the property. The debtor in effect becomes the secured party's agent for this purpose. When an agent acts for his principal, the rights acquired by one who deals with the agent are unaffected by the agent's failure to follow secret instructions of his principal even though the principal is disclosed. Further, the law is clear that when an agent is authorized to deal with chattels, the "interests of the principal are affected by an unauthorized transaction of the same kind as that authorized." [132] Professor Seavey wrote that for this reason, if an agent's authority to sell is conditioned on the agent holding the proceeds for his principal, "the rights of a transferee can not, of course, be taken away by his [the agent's] failure to perform the condition subsequent." [133]

The court's reasoning in the *Southwest* case also ignores the predicament of the debtor's transferee. As observed by the court in *First National Bank v. Iowa Beef Processors*,[134] when a secured party consents to a sale of collateral in the debtor's own name provided the debtor remits the proceeds to the secured party,

> such a condition makes the buyer an insurer of acts beyond its control. The ... [secured party] has made performance of the debtor's duty to remit proceeds ... a condition of releasing from liability a third party acting in good faith. [The buyer from the debtor] could not ascertain in advance whether this condition would be met ...; nor did [this buyer] ... have any control over the performance of the condition, as long as it paid ... [the debtor].[135]

These considerations led to the conclusion in *Iowa Beef* that "even though the secured party conditions consent on receipt of the proceeds, failure of this condition will not prevent that

---

132. [Restatement (Second) Agency] §§ 175(2) (disclosed principal), 201(2) (undisclosed principal) [1958].

133. W. Seavey, Handbook of the Law of Agency § 66 at 115 (1964).

134. 626 F.2d 764 (10th Cir.1980).

135. Id. at 769.

consent from cutting off the security interest under Section 9–306(2)." [136]

Hillman, McDonnell & Nickles, Common Law ¶ 22.02[2], at 22–28 to 22–29. A majority of the cases, like *Iowa Beef*, do not give effect to similar conditions placed on authorizations to dispose of collateral; they treat dispositions as being authorized even when the conditions are not satisfied.

Does UCC 9–306(2) admit of a construction that would render a conditional authorization effective to cut off a security interest when the transferee does not know of the condition but ineffective when the transferee knows of the condition? Should it be revised to provide for those results? Would it be reasonable to insist instead that prospective transferees identify secured creditors (by searching the financing statement records) and confirm the existence or nonexistence of (and any conditions on) the secured party's authorization of dispositions? (Again, the "ordinary course" nature of sales of farm products may engender additional sympathy for the plight of the farm products transferee.)

(5) Farmers and Farm Products: Amendments to UCC 9–307(1); The Food Security Act. We mentioned above that farm products are excluded from the general rule of UCC 9–307(1) that protects buyers in ordinary course of business. Responding to a large volume of litigation and widespread dissatisfaction with the farm products exception in UCC 9–307(1), several states repealed (or limited) the farm products exception.

In 1985 Congress intervened. Section 1324 of the Food Security Act of 1985, Pub. L. No. 99–198, § 1324, 99 Stat. 1535 (1985) (codified at 7 U.S.C. § 1631) preempts the farm products exception of UCC 9–307(1). Under the federal statute, ordinary course buyers take free of security interests in farm products—subject to two significant exceptions. (The Act also protects commission merchants and selling agents.) The first exception applies when (i) a buyer has received a notification that contains certain details (specified in the statute) concerning a security interest, including "any payment obligations imposed on the buyer by the secured party as conditions for waiver or release of the security interest" and (ii) "the buyer has failed to perform the payment obligations." The second exception applies to certain buyers who buy "a farm product produced in a State that has established a central filing system." (As of 1991, about one-third of the states had established such a system.) Why does the priority rule for buyers of farm products collateral warrant such a complicated (some might say, convoluted), federally imposed system? One answer is suggested by the inherent characteristics of agricultural production and marketing. Unlike inventory generally, many farm products are marketed only a few times each year—e.g., at harvest-time or after cattle are fattened. Moreover, sales frequently may involve a large proportion (sometimes all) of the

---

136. Id.

farm products owned by a debtor at the time. These factors indicate that the prospects for a secured lender to be left "high and dry" are materially greater in the case of agricultural financing. (Article 6 of the Code, which regulates "bulk sales" of a large proportion of a merchant's inventory, reflects similar concerns; however, Article 6 is primarily for the benefit of unsecured creditors. See generally Notes on Bulk Sales, infra.)

Problem 2. The Diapason Music Company is a retail store that sells electric organs, grand pianos and other expensive musical instruments. Diapason's inventory has been purchased with the aid of loans from Castle Finance Company. Diapason has executed in Castle's favor a security agreement covering its inventory, both existing and after-acquired. Castle filed a financing statement that described the collateral as "organs, pianos and other musical instruments."

(a) Diapason, without consulting Castle, sold and delivered an organ to Customer, a consumer, for $4,000 cash, and used the money to pay rent, utilities and other pressing bills. Promptly upon learning the facts, Castle brings a replevin action for the organ against Customer. What result? See UCC 9–306(2); UCC 9–307; UCC 1–201(9). (If you are not sure whether subsection (1) or subsection (2) of UCC 9–307 applies to this Problem, see Note on UCC 9–307(2), infra.) What considerations underlie the Code's rule on this point? Whose expectations does the rule reflect?

(b) Suppose that the security agreement in part (a) included the following covenant: "Diapason agrees that, under no circumstances, will it complete a sale of any of its inventory without Castle's prior approval. In the event of such approval, Diapason will immediately turn over to Castle any cash, chattel paper or other proceeds resulting from such sale." Suppose also that the financing statement added the sentence, "Sale of collateral not authorized without Castle's prior approval." Would the result change? Does the Code's rule make sense?

(c) Would the result in part (a) change if Diapason delivered the organ to Customer under a month-to-month lease? See UCC 2A–307(3).

(d) Clef, a similar music store in the same city, needed a particular model of organ in order to make prompt delivery to a customer. Diapason had such an organ in stock. In accordance with past arrangements between the two firms, Diapason sold the organ to Clef for $3,000 cash, which was slightly more than wholesale cost. Clef knew that Diapason had inventory financing with Castle. As in part (a), Diapason dissipated the cash received for the organ. Castle brings a replevir action against Clef. What result? See UCC 9–306(2); UCC 9–307(1); UCC 1–201(9). What difference, if any, would it make if the past arrangements between Clef and Diapason were highly unusual among music stores?

(e) Diapason owed $4,000 to Creditor, who was pressing for payment. Diapason delivered one of the organs in the store to Creditor in satisfaction of the debt. Castle brings a replevin action against Creditor. What result? What could the losing party have done to protect itself?

(f) Assume that, in part (e), Creditor also was in the business of selling organs. Before Castle learned that Creditor was in possession of the organ, Creditor sold and delivered the organ to Bass, who had no idea how Creditor acquired the organ. Castle brings a replevin action against Bass. What result? What could the losing party have done to protect itself?

(g) What result in part (f) if, several weeks before Creditor sold the organ to Bass, Castle had learned that Creditor was in possession of the organ but had raised no objection with Diapason or Creditor? See UCC 9–307(1) ("A buyer in ordinary course of business ... takes free of a security interest *created by his seller*"); UCC 2–403(2), (3); UCC 2–402(3); Note on the "His Seller" Rule and the Interplay Between UCC 2–403(1) and 9–307(1), infra.

Note on the "His Seller" Rule and the Interplay Between UCC 2–403(2) and 9–307(1)

UCC 9–307(1) contains a curious limitation: a buyer in ordinary course of business takes free only of security interests that are "created by his seller." This means that an inventory financer takes the risk that *its own debtor* will cut off the security interest by selling to a buyer in ordinary course of business, but does not risk losing its security interest if the collateral is sold by some other merchant. For example, assume that *A*, a merchant dealer in goods of that kind, sells inventory to *B*, another merchant, and that *B* is *not* a buyer in ordinary course of business (say, because the sale was in "bulk" and not in "ordinary course"). *B* then sells to *C*, who *is* a buyer in ordinary course of business. *C* would cut off *SP–B*, *B*'s inventory financer, but not *SP–A*, *A*'s inventory financer.

UCC 9–307(1) seems to be an analogue to UCC 2–403(2) in that an inventory financer typically can be said to have "entrusted" the collateral to the merchant-dealer. But what result obtains if *C*, in the example, could show that *SP–A* entrusted the goods to *B*? See UCC 2–403(3) ("'Entrusting includes ... any acquiescence in retention of possession[.]"). As the most straightforward example, imagine that a secured party takes possession of inventory after the debtor's default (UCC 9–503) and then delivers an item of the inventory to another merchant dealer for repairs. The non-debtor merchant dealer then sells to a buyer in ordinary course of business. If the sale would cut off the rights of an *owner*-entruster—and it would under UCC 2–403(2)— why should the secured party's rights remain intact?

Some courts have permitted buyers in ordinary course of business to cut off security interests under UCC 2–403(2) when the "his seller" requirement of UCC 9–307(1) was not satisfied, so long as it could be shown the secured party itself was an entruster to the selling merchant. See, e.g., In re Woods, 25 B.R. 924 (Bkrtcy.E.D.Tenn.1982). Other courts have insisted on strict observance of the "his seller" limitation in UCC 9–307(1). See, e.g., National Shawmut Bank v. Jones, 108 N.H. 386, 236 A.2d 484 (1967). There is support for the latter view in the statute and the Comments (even if not in logic or policy). See UCC 9–306(2) ("Except where this *Article* [9] otherwise provides" a security interest survives an unauthorized disposition); UCC 2–402(3) ("Nothing in this Article [2] shall be deemed to impair the rights of creditors of the seller (a) under the provisions of … Article 9"); UCC 2–403, Comment 2 ("As to entrusting by a secured party, subsection (2) is limited by the more specific provisions of Section 9–307(1)," giving the farm products limitation as an example).

Consider the majority recommendation of the PEB Article 2 Study Group: "The Study Committee recommends a revision that insures protection of the BIOCB [buyer in ordinary course of business] under § 2–403(2) if the secured party itself has entrusted the goods to a merchant, even though the security interest was created by another party [other than the seller]." PEB Article 2 Report 129–30 (1990).

Note on UCC 9–307(2)

UCC 9–307(2) has been drafted in a manner that confuses many readers. Its purpose and meaning, however, will be readily grasped once it is noted that it protects buyers of goods that are subject to a security interest that is "perfected" even though no financing statement has been filed. Security interests of this kind typically are purchase money security interests in consumer goods. See UCC 9–302(1)(d).

Suppose S retains a security interest in a television set sold to B for home use, but S does not file a financing statement. B sells the set to N, a neighbor. Under UCC 9–307(2), may S retake from N? Suppose B resells to D, a second-hand dealer? Who would prevail in these situations if S had filed?

Code mavens generally agree not only that UCC 9–307(2) applies to sales by consumer debtors to consumer buyers but also that it does not cover sales of inventory by dealers to consumer buyers. Can you point to specific language in UCC 9–307(2) that limits its application in this manner?

Problem 3. Manufacturer delivered mobile homes to Dealer on credit and, by filing, perfected a security interest in that inventory. Buyer agreed in writing to purchase one of the mobile homes and made a substantial down payment to Dealer. Before Buyer took possession, Dealer defaulted on its debt to Manufacturer and Manufacturer repossessed the trailers held by Dealer, including the trailer that Buyer had agreed to purchase.

(a) Does UCC 9–307 protect Buyer? See Tanbro Fabrics Corp. v. Deering Milliken, Inc., infra; Notes on Buyers Who Do Not Take Possession, infra. Could one disagree with *Tanbro* and yet hold for Buyer? (Hint: Did Buyer become a buyer in ordinary course of business *before* Manufacturer took possession?)

(b) Is there a basis other than Manufacturer's security interest for Manufacturer to attack Buyer's interest? See UCC 2–402(2); Uniform Fraudulent Transfer Act §§ 4(a)(1), 4(b)(2), 7, 8(a); Note 5 on Buyers Who Do Not Take Possession, infra.

(c) Suppose that Buyer made a substantial down payment to Dealer for a mobile home to be ordered from Manufacturer. The mobile home was delivered to Dealer but was seized by Manufacturer before Buyer took possession. Should this modification of the facts change the result?

(d) Would the result in part (b) change if the mobile home had been "specially" constructed to Buyer's specifications, such that if Buyer were to order a similar, specially constructed mobile home from another dealer, delivery to Buyer would be delayed at least six months? See UCC 2–716. Assuming that Buyer's right to take delivery (as against Dealer) is contingent on Buyer's payment of the remaining balance of the purchase price, could Buyer become a buyer in ordinary course of business before making the payment?

TANBRO FABRICS CORP. v. DEERING MILLIKEN, INC.[*]

Court of Appeals of New York, 1976.
39 N.Y.2d 632, 385 N.Y.S.2d 260, 350 N.E.2d 590.

BREITEL, CHIEF JUDGE. In an action for the tortious conversion of unfinished textile fabrics (greige goods), plaintiff Tanbro sought damages from Deering Milliken, a textile manufacturer. Tanbro, known in the trade as a "converter", finishes textile into dyed and patterned fabrics. The goods in question had been manufactured by Deering, and sold on a "bill and hold" basis to Mill Fabrics, also a converter, now insolvent. Mill Fabrics resold the goods, while still in Deering's warehouse, also on a bill and hold basis, to Tanbro.

Deering refused to deliver the goods to Tanbro on Tanbro's instruction because, although these goods had been paid for, there was an open account balance due Deering from Mill Fabrics. Deering under its sales agreements with Mill Fabrics claimed a perfected security interest in the goods.

At Supreme Court, Tanbro recovered a verdict and judgment of $87,451.68 for compensatory and $25,000 for punitive damages. The

[* The court's citations are to the applicable pre–1972 version of the Code.]

Appellate Division, by a divided court, modified to strike the recovery for punitive damages, and otherwise affirmed. Both parties appeal.

The issue is whether Tanbro's purchase of the goods was in the ordinary course of Mill Fabrics' business, and hence free of Deering's perfected security interest.

There should be an affirmance. Mill Fabrics' sale to Tanbro was in the ordinary course of business, even though its predominant business purpose was, like Tanbro's, the converting of greige goods into finished fabrics. All the Uniform Commercial Code requires is that the sale be in ordinary course associated with the seller's business (§ 9–307, subd. [1]). The record established that converters buy greige goods in propitious markets and often in excess of their requirements as they eventuate. On the occasion of excess purchases, converters at times enter the market to sell the excess through brokers to other converters, and converters buy such goods if the price is satisfactory or the particular goods are not available from manufacturers. Both conditions obtained here.

Tanbro and Mill Fabrics were customers of Deering for many years. Goods would be purchased in scale on a "bill and hold" basis, that is, the goods would be paid for and delivered as the buyers instructed. When the goods were needed, they were delivered directly where they were to be converted, at the buyers' plants or the plants of others if that would be appropriate. Pending instructions, the sold and paid for goods were stored in the warehouses of the manufacturer, both because the buyers lacked warehousing space and retransportation of the goods to be processed would be minimized.

Mill Fabrics, like many converters, purchased greige goods from Deering on credit as well as on short-term payment. Under the sales notes or agreements, all the goods on hand in the seller's warehouse stood as security for the balance owed on the account. Tanbro was familiar with this practice. It was immaterial whether or not particular goods had been paid for. If the goods were resold by Deering's customers, Deering obtained for a period a perfected security interest in the proceeds of resale for the indebtedness on the open account (Uniform Commercial Code, § 9–306, subds. [2], [3]).

Deering's sales executives advised Tanbro that it had discontinued production of a certain blended fabric. Upon Tanbro's inquiry, the Deering sales executives recommended to Tanbro that it try purchasing the blended fabric from Mill Fabrics, which Deering knew had an excess supply. Ultimately, Tanbro purchased from Mill Fabrics through a broker 267,000 yards at 26 cents per yard. Tanbro paid Mill Fabrics in full.

During October and November of 1969, approximately 57,000 yards of the blended fabric was released by Deering on Mill Fabrics' instructions and delivered to a Tanbro affiliate. There remained some 203,376 yards at the Deering warehouse.

In early January of 1970, Tanbro ordered the remaining fabric delivered to meet its own contractual obligation to deliver the blended fabric in finished state at 60 cents per yard. Deering refused.

By this time Mill Fabrics was in financial trouble and its account debit balance with Deering at an unprecedented high. In mid-January of 1970, a meeting of its creditors was called and its insolvency confirmed.

As noted earlier, under the terms of the Deering sales agreements with Mill Fabrics, Deering retained a security interest in Mill Fabrics' "property" on a bill and hold basis, whether paid for or not. This security interest was perfected by Deering's continued possession of the goods (Uniform Commercial Code, § 1–201, subd. [37]; § 9–305). Tanbro argued that if it had title by purchase its goods were excluded from the security arrangement which was literally restricted to the "property of the buyer", that is, Mill Fabrics. In any event, unless prevented by other provisions of the code, or the sale was not unauthorized, Tanbro took title subject to Deering's security interest.

Under the code (§ 9–307, subd. [1]) a buyer in the ordinary course of the seller's business takes goods free of even a known security interest so long as the buyer does not know that the purchase violates the terms of the security agreement. As defined in the code (§ 1–201, subd. [9]) "a buyer in ordinary course" is "a person who in good faith and without knowledge that the sale to him is in violation of the ownership rights or security interest of a third party in the goods buys in ordinary course from a person in the business of selling goods of that kind but does not include a pawnbroker. 'Buying' may be for cash or by exchange of other property or on secured or unsecured credit and includes receiving goods or documents of title under a preexisting contract for sale but does not include a transfer in bulk or as security for or in total or partial satisfaction of a money debt." Critical to Tanbro's claim is that it purchased the goods in the ordinary course of Mill Fabrics' business and that it did not purchase the goods in knowing violation of Deering's security interest.

Under the code whether a purchase was made from a person in the business of selling goods of that kind turns primarily on whether that person holds the goods for sale. Such goods are a person's selling inventory. (Uniform Commercial Code, § 1–201, subd. [9]; § 9–307, subd. [1]; Official Comment, at par. 2.) Note, however, that not all purchases of goods held as inventory qualify as purchases from a person in the business of selling goods of that kind. The purpose of section 9–307 is more limited. As indicated in the Practice Commentary to that section, the purpose is to permit buyers "to buy goods from a dealer in such goods without having to protect himself against a possible security interest on the inventory" (Kripke, Practice Commentary, McKinney's Cons.Laws of N.Y., Book 62 1/2, Uniform Commercial Code, § 9–307, p. 491, par. 1). Hence, a qualifying purchase is one made from a seller who is a dealer in such goods.

A former Mill Fabrics' employee testified that there were times when Mill Fabrics, like all converters, found itself with excess goods. When it was to their business advantage, they sold the excess fabrics to other converters. Although these sales were relatively infrequent they were nevertheless part of and in the ordinary course of Mill Fabrics' business, even if only incidental to the predominant business purpose. Examples of a nonqualifying sale might be a bulk sale, a sale in distress at an obvious loss price, a sale in liquidation, a sale of a commodity never dealt with before by the seller and wholly unlike its usual inventory, or the like. . . .

The combination of stored, paid for goods, on a hold basis, and the retention of a security interest by Deering makes commercial sense. Mill Fabrics' capacity to discharge its obligation to Deering was in part made possible because it sold off or converted the goods held at the Deering warehouse. Mill Fabrics, as an honest customer, was supposed to remit the proceeds from resale or conversion to Deering and thus reduce, and eventually discharge its responsibility to Deering. Thus, so long as it was customary for Mill Fabrics, and in the trade for converters, to sell off excess goods, the sale was in the ordinary course of business. Moreover, on an alternative analysis, such a sale by Mill Fabrics was therefore impliedly authorized under the code if its indebtedness to Deering was to be liquidated (see Official Comment to § 9–307, par. 2; Draper v. Minneapolis–Moline, 100 Ill.App.2d 324, 329, 241 N.E.2d 342).

All subdivision (1) of section 9–307 requires is that the sale be of the variety reasonably to be expected in the regular course of an on-going business. . . . This was such a case.

Hempstead Bank v. Andy's Car Rental System, 35 A.D.2d 35, 312 N.Y.S.2d 317, stands for no contrary principle. Rightly or wrongly, it was there held as a matter of law, unlike the situation here, that the selling of used rental cars was not in the ordinary course of business for an auto rental company (compare Bank of Utica v. Castle Ford, 36 A.D.2d 6, 9, 317 N.Y.S.2d 542, 544). It may be significant that the used cars were in no sense an "inventory" of a sales business, but the capital inventory of a leasing company, usually subject to extended term financing.

With respect to Tanbro's claim for punitive damages, the evidence was not clear that Deering was guilty of a wanton or willful obstruction to Tanbro's rights as a secondary buyer, let alone of fraud or a high degree of moral turpitude (cf. Walker v. Sheldon, 10 N.Y.2d 401, 404–405, 223 N.Y.S.2d 488, 490–491, 179 N.E.2d 497, 498–499). Deering could have believed in good faith that its security interest survived the sale by Mill Fabrics to Tanbro. Hence, the Appellate Division properly struck the award for punitive damages.

Accordingly, the order of the Appellate Division should be affirmed, with costs to plaintiff Tanbro.

———

KRIPKE v. TANBRO

KRIPKE, SHOULD SECTION 9–307(1) OF THE UNIFORM COMMERCIAL CODE APPLY AGAINST A SECURED PARTY IN POSSESSION?
33 Bus.Law. 153, 155–60 (1977).

The single point that I wish to discuss is the Court's holding [in *Tanbro*] that a buyer of goods may be a buyer in ordinary course of business under section 9–307(1) even though he knows that the goods are not in his debtor's possession, and are held by a secured party (pledgee) under a form of contract which does not permit the buyer to order the goods out unless the secured party agrees. The holding has attracted wide attention in the textile industry. I believe that it also has potentially wider applications and that the question is therefore worthy of serious consideration.

It must be admitted that section 9–307(1) does not by its terms exclude the situation in which the secured party is a pledgee in possession of the goods, and in which the debtor does not have and cannot exhibit the goods to a buyer. Nevertheless, in all the years that I was associated with the drafting and the Amendments of Article 9, almost from the very beginning when a first draft was made public, I do not remember a discussion of this subject. I believe that the explanation is that for me and perhaps for others involved in the drafting, it was so obvious that the buyer could not be protected as a buyer in ordinary course against a security interest when the seller does not have the goods that the limitation was never considered and expressly stated in section 9–307(1).

The difference between a possessory security interest perfected by virtue of the possession and a non-possessory security interest perfected by filing is more than a difference between alternate methods of perfecting the security interest, which methods Article 9 treats equally, in general. The fact of possession in the secured party, the pledge relationship, means that the secured party has taken the goods out of the hands of the debtor (or withheld them from the debtor) and thus has made it impossible for the debtor to take any advantage from his apparent ownership of the goods as evidenced by possession or to exhibit them or to deliver them upon sale. Until this case I believe that it was always assumed that possession of the secured party protected him from being surprised by a sudden devastation of his security through sales by the debtor to buyers in the ordinary course of business. For this reason, even though the Code facilitated perfection by filing of security interests on shifting inventories, some secured parties demanded warehouse arrangements through field warehousemen, thus exerting a physical control over the goods. Until this case, I believe it was thought that this precluded the debtor from selling the goods out to a buyer in ordinary course of business, thus leaving the secured party to try to recoup from the proceeds if he could find and obtain them from a debtor to whom the secured party had refrained from entrusting them. Field warehousing arrangements are widely used even though the lenders frequently perfect the security interests by filing. The possession of the goods by field warehousemen is not just a means of perfection, which can be accomplished by filing, but it adds something else. Or at least it was thought to do so until now.

It is, of course, true that when a buyer in ordinary course of business buys goods "from a person in the business of selling goods of that kind" (section 1–201(9)), the buyer's entitlement to the protection of section 9–307(1) cannot be precluded—so long as the debtor is in possession of the goods—by the secured party and debtor contracting, or purporting to contract, that the debtor does not have liberty of sale. It does not follow that the same result should apply when possession of the goods has been withheld from the debtor (and apparent ownership denied to him) for the very purpose of protecting the seller's normal right to payment before he surrenders the goods, sections 2–507, 2–511. It is believed that there was no case before *Tanbro* which weakened this right, in the absence of agreement otherwise.

Let us examine section 9–307(1) in the context of the whole scheme of the Code. It is important to note that section 9–307(1) protects the buyer in ordinary course only against the rights of a secured party claiming a *security interest* against the merchant-seller. It does not deal with the rights of the buyer in ordinary course as against the rights of someone else claiming *ownership* of the property as against the merchant-seller. That right is found in section 2–403(2), which protects a buyer in ordinary course in much the same fashion as section 9–307(1), but the protection is only against an entruster, i.e., a person who has entrusted possession of goods to a merchant who deals in goods of that kind (the same person mentioned in section 9–307(1)), and the susceptibility of the entruster to defeat clearly arises because he *entrusted possession of the goods to the merchant.* Section 2–403(3) says that "entrusting includes any delivery and any acquiescence in retention of possession." Since section 2–403(2) and section 9–307(1) are obviously intended to be parallel, and section 2–403(2) is limited to cases where the prior claimant has given the seller apparent ownership through possession, section 9–307(1) might reasonably have been construed by the Court of Appeals to be limited correspondingly. This is, after all, a Code which is being construed, not an isolated section of a statute.

Another point to be noted is that in the Code's system of priorities, the rights of a holder of a security interest and those of a buyer of goods (other than a buyer in ordinary course) are in general equated. The secured party, of course, is limited to his limited interest, but otherwise his priority role is the same as that of a buyer. For this purpose the term "purchase" is used in section 1–201(32) and (33) to include not only buyers but holders of security interests. The term "purchaser" is then used in a variety of sections. In section 2–403(1), which deals with the rights of "purchasers" when the transferor had less than perfect title, the term "purchaser" clearly includes both buyers and secured parties. The position of the latter is referred to in the language "... a purchaser of a limited interest acquires rights only to the extent of the interest purchased." Similarly, under section 2–702, a seller's right to reclaim goods when his immediate buyer was insolvent is limited in favor of a buyer in ordinary course or "other good faith purchaser." It has been held that "purchaser" in this context includes a secured party.

The same concept of "purchaser" appears in sections 9–308 and 9–309, as applied to property other than goods.

With this background, we can test the public policy behind the Court of Appeals' decision against a series of cases involving the buyer in ordinary course of business, on the one hand, and a prior buyer or a prior secured party in possession, on the other.

Note that I do not contend that a buyer must see the goods or receive delivery promptly in order to be a buyer in ordinary course of business. Admittedly, it is an everyday occurrence that buyers buy goods from a merchant's stock other than that which is on display in the showroom, and they even buy goods by telephone without ever being in the showroom. In all such cases, if the seller in fact has the goods, the buyer in ordinary course should prevail against a secured party under section 9–307(1). Similarly, when the seller in fact has the goods, the buyer in ordinary course should prevail against a prior buyer who may even have paid for the goods, but has left them in the seller's possession and thus has "entrusted" them to the seller under § 2–403(2). Thus, when the seller still has the goods, the rights of a buyer in ordinary course against a secured party under section 9–307(1) and against an earlier buyer-entruster under section 2–403(2) are identical.

But what if the seller does not have the goods? Let us take some cases:

Case 1: Suppose the seller never had the goods? Putting aside for the moment the rights of a secured party, a buyer may believe ever so much in good faith that he is a buyer of the goods in the ordinary course of business of a person engaged in selling goods of that kind, but he cannot prevail against the true owner if the seller never had any ownership rights in the goods described in the contract.

Case 2: Next, suppose that the seller once had the goods and owned them, but sold them last week to an earlier buyer and delivered them promptly to the earlier buyer. Does a second buyer prevail against the first buyer, because the second thinks that he is in the ordinary course of business? Obviously not. The second buyer takes the risk of his seller still owning the goods.

Case 3: Next comes the same question when the seller once did have the goods in his possession, but last week created a security interest in them in favor of a secured party who took the goods away with him in pledge. Should that secured party, because he is only a "purchaser with only a limited interest" fare any worse than the first purchaser in Case 2 who was a buyer and who took the goods away with him? There is no reason for a difference.

Let us take another set of examples. Assume that the security interest in the inventory was originally perfected by filing, and possession was left with the merchant-debtor. The secured party later found his loan to be in default and repossessed the goods and proceeded under Part 5 of Article 9 in order to vest title in himself.

Case 4: The first example is where the secured party has completed the procedures of Part 5 and has vested title in himself. He is now a buyer of some kind. Obviously, once he eliminates the merchant's title and has possession, there can be no later buyer who can prevail under section 9–307(1). This case is like Case 2.

Case 5: Suppose the repossessing secured party is waiting out the required period before he holds his sale under section 9–504 or before completing acceptance of title in lieu of sale under section 9–505. At this point, where the secured party has taken possession away from the merchant-debtor precisely to preclude him from being able to sell to a buyer in ordinary course, should the Code open up possibilities of fraud by letting the debtor sell them from his empty showroom or by telephone to alleged buyers in ordinary course?

It is irrelevant to argue that it is not commercially feasible for the law to require buyers to inspect the goods and ascertain that the seller has them, and that therefore the secured party as the person best able to bear the risk should bear it. Of course, I do not contend that every buyer should inspect the goods. Trust in fair dealing and honesty is the foundation of all forms of business, but when there is a mistaken reliance on the seller to have unseen goods, it is obvious that there is not always a likely victim to bail out the buyer who thinks that he is in ordinary course of business. As we have seen, the buyer who thinks that he is in ordinary course is out of luck if the seller never had the goods or if he has sold them or if a secured party has repossessed them and thus taken title in himself or another. Why should a secured party who has done everything that he could, namely, taken them into his possession and eliminated any apparent ownership by the merchant, be the one victim required to bail out the improvident or unlucky buyer?

When a secured party has taken possession in himself, he has done everything he could to preclude the existence of a buyer in ordinary course. In my opinion, the Code should not make it impossible to have a loan on goods which are not in fact available for exhibition, sale and delivery by the merchant, without running the risk of losing the security through sales to purported buyers in ordinary course, just because the goods are classified as inventory. The fact that the goods are not in the buyer's possession, but are held by the secured party

under an adverse claim of right, makes them very different from
ordinary inventory.

Case 6: The Court's reaction in the *Tanbro* case probably depended
on the fact that the particular inventory in question had been paid for.
But suppose it had been specially ordered and made by the mill to
order, but never paid for, and held by the mill under the contract until
payment and the buyer had never had possession of it. The buyer
would have had a "special property" under section 2–401 and an
insurable interest under section 2–501. Could the buyer, the converter,
pass unencumbered title to a buyer in ordinary course under those
circumstances? The Court's reasoning that the secured party could
look to the proceeds is equally applicable in this hypothetical case.
Indeed, section 9–307(1) has its normal application in the case where
the merchant has not paid for the goods, and the supplier has to look to
the proceeds for payment. And yet such a holding in Case 6 would be
clearly the wrong answer, because the supplier is in possession. Such a
holding would fly in the face of the basic policy of the UCC's Article on
Sales that a seller is entitled to be paid before he delivers possession.
Sections 2–507, 2–511. And yet such a holding would flow logically
from the Court's reasoning.

Notes on Buyers Who Do Not Take Possession

(1) **In General.** In Chapter 1, Section 1, supra, we asked whether
taking possession was necessary for protection, under UCC 2–403(1), as
a good faith purchaser for value from a seller with voidable title. In
that setting, the interest at risk was the general (or "beneficial")
ownership interest of a person who enjoyed a right to reclaim goods
that the person had sold to the seller. Our current concern is with a
putative buyer in ordinary course of business under UCC 9–307(1) as
against a secured party with a security interest in the goods. In
particular, we consider the role of possession in determining when a
buyer achieves the status of "buyer in ordinary course of business"
under UCC 1–201(9).

(2) **When a Buyer Becomes a "Buyer in Ordinary Course of
Business."** A primary issue raised in both the commentary and the
cases interpreting UCC 9–307(1) and 1–201(9) is the stage of the sale
transaction at which a buyer becomes eligible to be a buyer in ordinary
course of business. Some have suggested that one cannot be a buyer in
ordinary course of business until there has been a sale, i.e., until title
has passed. See UCC 2–106 ("A 'sale' consists in the passing of title
from the seller to the buyer for a price (Section 2–401)."). Others
suggest that the status may arise as soon as the buyer acquires an
interest in the goods—i.e., once the goods are identified to the contract
and the buyer acquires a "special property" in them. See UCC 2–501;
UCC 2–401; UCC 2–103(1)(a) (" 'Buyer' means a person who buys *or*

contracts to buy goods."). Some have argued that one cannot be a buyer in ordinary course of business until delivery of the goods. See UCC 1–201(9) (" 'Buying' ... includes receiving goods ... under a pre-existing contract for sale...."). See Frisch, Buyer Status Under the U.C.C.: A Suggested Temporal Definition, 72 Iowa L.Rev. 531, 568–75 (1987).

Consider the implications of permitting a putative buyer (*B*) of goods to become a buyer in ordinary course of business from Seller (*S*) *before* it obtains possessory rights against *S*. That normally would produce the anomalous result that *B* could cut off the rights of *S*'s secured party (*SP*) under UCC 9–307(1) even though *B* has no right to possession of the goods as against *S*! Article 2 would provide pre-delivery possessory rights to *B* only under very limited circumstances. See UCC 2–502 (reclamation right "if the seller becomes insolvent within ten days after receipt of the first installment on their price"); UCC 2–716(1) (right to specific performance of the sale contract "where the goods are unique or in other proper circumstances"); UCC 2–716(3) (right to replevin of goods identified to the contract in two limited circumstances). Even *S*'s *unsecured* creditors can obtain rights in the goods (e.g., by execution lien) that are senior to those of *B* until such time as *B* obtains possessory rights against *S*. See UCC 2–402(1). *SP*, on the other hand, does have a right to possession as against *S* (albeit a right that normally is contingent on *S*'s default). UCC 9–503.

Consider also the implications of permitting a buyer to become a buyer in ordinary course of business and take free of a security interest when the seller (Article 9 debtor) remains in possession of the goods. Can one reconcile such a result with one of Article 9's principal themes: that a secured party ordinarily must give public notice of its interest in order to prevail over competing claimants to the collateral? Should the Code be revised to provide that a buyer becomes a buyer in ordinary course of business only if it either removes the goods from the seller-debtor's possession or notifies the secured party of its purchase? The answer would seem to turn, at least in part, on whether inventory financers actually rely on the debtor's possession of particular items of inventory.

(3) The *Tanbro* Debate. The *Tanbro* case became a *cause celebre* that generated dispute among specialists in secured financing. Professor Kripke's article provoked replies. The PEB Article 2 Report specifically rejects the reasoning of the *Tanbro* case:

> (A) The case of *Tanbro Fabrics* apparently held that a BIOCB of goods from a seller took free of a security interest in the goods even though they were in the possession of the seller's secured party. Unless the secured party has authorized the disposition, we reject the rule of *Tanbro Fabrics* and recommend an appropriate revision of § 9–307(1) or § 1–201(9).

> (B) We recommend that the time when the status of BIOCB arises before delivery should be no earlier than the

time when the buyer has a right to possession of the goods under Article 2.

PEB Article 2 Report 27–28. Observe that one inference to be drawn from the Article 2 Report is that one need not take delivery of goods to qualify as a buyer in ordinary course.

(4) Buyer's Nonpayment. Assume that *B*, in a *cash sale* transaction, has a right to specific performance under UCC 2–716(1). Notwithstanding *B*'s right to specific performance, does *B* actually have a possessory right against *S* before *B* pays the price? See UCC 2–511(2); UCC 2–511(1). If not, and if *B*'s interest is (consequently) subordinate to *S*'s inventory financer, *SP*, what remedy does *B* have against *S*? See UCC 2–711; UCC 2–713.

(5) Fraudulent Transfer Implications of Seller's Retention of Possession; UCC 2–402(2). Recall the discussion of *Twyne's Case* and the "Fraud in Law" doctrine in Note (2) on Attachment and Perfection by Filing (Chapter 11, Section 2(A), supra). We noted there that modern fraudulent transfer law adopts the "fraud in fact" approach, whereby a seller's retention of possession of goods is merely a factor to be considered in determining whether the seller has made the transfer "with actual intent to hinder, delay, or defraud any creditor." Uniform Fraudulent Transfer Act §§ 4(a)(1), 4(b)(2). The Code generally leaves the matter of fraudulent transfers to non-UCC law. However, UCC 2–402(2) does provide a safe harbor for "retention of possession in good faith and current course of trade by a merchant-seller for a commercially reasonable time after a sale or identification." Detailed treatment of fraudulent transfers is beyond the scope of these materials.

Notes on Bulk Sales

(1) Regulation of Bulk Sales. According to the definition of "buyer in ordinary course of business," " '[b]uying' . . . does not include a *transfer in bulk*." UCC 1–201(9). The reference is to the pre–1988 Article 6. That Article defined "bulk transfer" as "any transfer in bulk and not in the ordinary course of the transferor's business of a major part of the materials, supplies, merchandise or other inventory (Section 9–109) of an enterprise subject to this Article." UCC 6–102(2) (pre–1988). "The enterprises subject to this Article are all those whose principal business is the sale of merchandise from stock, including those who manufacture what they sell." UCC 6–102(3) (pre–1988).

In 1988, the sponsors of the Code recommended that Article 6 be repealed and not replaced. The following excerpt from the Prefatory Note to the Repealer of Article 6 explains the history of bulk sales legislation and the reasons for eliminating Article 6 from the Code:

"**Background.** Bulk sale legislation originally was enacted in response to a fraud perceived to be common around the turn of the century: a merchant would acquire his stock in trade on credit, then sell his entire inventory ('in bulk') and abscond with the proceeds, leaving creditors unpaid. The creditors had a right to sue the merchant on the unpaid debts, but that right often was of little practical value. Even if the merchant-debtor was found, in personam jurisdiction over him might not have been readily available. Those creditors who succeeded in obtaining a judgment often were unable to satisfy it because the defrauding seller had spent or hidden the sale proceeds. Nor did the creditors ordinarily have recourse to the merchandise sold. The transfer of the inventory to an innocent buyer effectively immunized the goods from the reach of the seller's creditors. The creditors of a bulk seller thus might be left without a means to satisfy their claims.

"To a limited extent, the law of fraudulent conveyances ameliorated the creditors' plight. When the buyer in bulk was in league with the seller or paid less than full value for the inventory, fraudulent conveyance law enabled the defrauded creditors to avoid the sale and apply the transferred inventory toward the satisfaction of their claims against the seller. But fraudulent conveyance law provided no remedy against persons who bought in good faith, without reason to know of the seller's intention to pocket the proceeds and disappear, and for adequate value. In those cases, the only remedy for the seller's creditors was to attempt to recover from the absconding seller.

"State legislatures responded to this perceived "bulk sale risk" with a variety of legislative enactments. Common to these statutes was the imposition of a duty on the buyer in bulk to notify the seller's creditors of the impending sale. The buyer's failure to comply with these and any other statutory duties generally afforded the seller's creditors a remedy analogous to the remedy for fraudulent conveyances: the creditors acquired the right to set aside the sale and reach the transferred inventory in the hands of the buyer.

"Like its predecessors, [pre–1988] Article 6 ... is remarkable in that it obligates buyers in bulk to incur costs to protect the interests of the seller's creditors, with whom they usually have no relationship. Even more striking is that Article 6 affords creditors a remedy against a good faith purchaser for full value without notice of any wrongdoing on the part of the seller. The Article thereby impedes normal business transactions, many of which can be expected to benefit the seller's creditors. For this reason, Article 6 has been subjected to serious criticism.

"In the legal context in which [pre–1988] Article 6 ... and its nonuniform predecessors were enacted, the benefits to creditors appeared to justify the costs of interfering with good faith transactions. Today, however, creditors are better able than ever to make informed decisions about whether to extend credit.... A search of the public real estate and personal property records will disclose most encumbrances on a debtor's property with little inconvenience.

"In addition, changes in the law now afford creditors greater opportunities to collect their debts.... Moreover, creditors of a merchant no longer face the choice of extending unsecured credit or no credit at all. Retaining an interest in inventory to secure its price has become relatively simple and inexpensive under Article 9.

"Finally, there is no evidence that, in today's economy, fraudulent bulk sales are frequent enough, or engender credit losses significant enough, to require regulation of all bulk sales, including the vast majority that are conducted in good faith. ...

"**Recommendation.** The National Conference of Commissioners on Uniform State Laws and the American Law Institute believe that changes in the business and legal contexts in which sales are conducted have made regulation of bulk sales unnecessary. The Conference and the Institute therefore withdraw their support for Article 6 of the Uniform Commercial Code and encourage those states that have enacted the Article to repeal it.

"The Conference and the Institute recognize that bulk sales may present a particular problem in some states and that some legislatures may wish to continue to regulate bulk sales. They believe that [pre–1988] Article 6 has become inadequate for that purpose. For those states that are disinclined to repeal Article 6, they have promulgated a revised version of Article 6. The revised Article is designed to afford better protection to creditors while minimizing the impediments to good-faith transactions."

As of this writing, fourteen states are without a bulk sales law; four states have adopted revised Article 6; the remainder have retained the pre–1988 Article or a variant thereof. The revised Article, the decision to recommend repeal of its predecessor, and the revision process are discussed in Symposium: Article 6 of the Uniform Commercial Code, 41 Ala. L. Rev. 649 (1990). For an examination of some practical issues arising under pre–1988 Article 6 and a comparative overview of the revised Article, see Harris, Practicing Under Existing Bulk Sales Law—And a Look at the Future of Article 6, 22 UCC L.J. 195 (1990).

(2) Does a Buyer's Compliance With Article 6 Affect Its Rights? Bulk sales legislation was enacted primarily for the benefit of *unsecured* creditors of the seller. But for this legislation, these unsecured creditors would have no right to satisfy their claims against the seller from the property of the buyer (i.e., from the inventory sold in bulk). See generally Chapter 1, Section 1, supra (discussing the *nemo dat* principle).

In contrast, the seller's secured party (inventory financer) would seem to have little need for the protection Article 6 affords. Inasmuch as "buying" does not include a "transfer in bulk," UCC 1–201(9), a person who buys the seller's inventory at a bulk sale appears not to be a buyer in ordinary course of business and not to take free of perfected security interests in the inventory. See UCC 9–306(2); UCC 9–307(1). Nevertheless, one court suggested repeatedly, albeit in dictum, that compliance with the notice and other requirements of pre–1988 Article

6 would enable a non-ordinary course buyer to take free of perfected security interests. In re McBee, 714 F.2d 1316 (5th Cir.1983). For strong criticism of this, and other, aspects of the case, see Harris, The Interaction of Articles 6 and 9 of the Uniform Commercial Code: A Study in Conveyancing, Priorities, and Code Interpretation, 39 Vand. L.Rev. 179 (1986). For a somewhat less disapproving view of *McBee*, see Carlson, Bulk Sales Under Article 9: Some Easy Cases Made Difficult, 41 Ala. L. Rev. 729, 736–48 (1990).

Problem 4. Lender obtained a perfected security interest in all existing and after-acquired inventory of Poss.

(a) Poss is now in the process of assembling components into a finished widget that Nonposs has agreed to buy. Nonposs has made advance payments to Poss under the written sale contract. Is Lender's security interest in the components senior to the interest claimed by Nonposs? Can a judgment creditor of Poss acquire an execution lien on the components? If so, is the lien senior to the interest claimed by Nonposs in the goods? What, if anything, could Nonposs have done to ensure its seniority? See generally Notes on Buyers Who Do Not Take Possession, supra.

(b) Would the results in part (a) change if Nonposs had loaned funds to Poss, the seller, in order to enable Poss to acquire the components and complete the manufacture of the widget? See Note on the "Financing Buyer," infra.

(c) Instead of agreeing to buy a widget from Poss, Nonposs agrees to buy, directly from third-party suppliers, all of the raw materials and components necessary to build a widget. Under the terms of the purchase orders, Nonposs will advance funds directly to the suppliers of the materials and components, although the goods are to be delivered directly to Poss's factory. Poss and Nonposs enter into a "service agreement" under which Poss is to manufacture the widget using the supplies "bought and paid for" by Nonposs. Is there an economic difference between this arrangement and Nonposs's prepayment under a contract of sale and the use of those funds by Poss to buy the components? Would each transaction appear in the same fashion on Poss's balance sheet? Should the result here differ from the results in (a) and (b) above? See Note on Bailments for Processing, Chapter 12, Section 1(C), supra.

Note on the "Financing Buyer"

We have seen that a prepaying buyer is in a precarious position until it takes delivery or obtains pre-delivery possessory rights against a seller. See Notes on Buyers Who Do Not Take Possession, supra; UCC 2–402(1), (2); UCC 2–502; UCC 2–716.

There are many reasons why one who contracts to buy goods might be called upon to pay before delivery. The seller may require a down payment (or even prepayment of the price in full) in order to offset the risk that the seller will acquire or manufacture the goods only to discover that the buyer cannot or will not pay. But what of the situation where the buyer prepays in order to "finance" the seller's costs of manufacturing the goods to be sold to the buyer? (Among these costs might be the costs of labor, materials, rent, and utilities.) The buyer could achieve priority over subsequent lien creditors by taking and perfecting a security interest in the seller's relevant materials and in the work in process as manufacturing proceeds. The security interest could be made to secure all of the seller's obligations under the sales contract. But, assuming that there is an earlier-filed financing statement made by the seller's inventory financer (as often is the case), the buyer is left with two choices. One choice is to seek to obtain a subordination agreement from the seller's inventory financer. See UCC 9–316. The other alternative is to ensure that the security interest is a purchase money security interest (PMSI) and that all of the steps necessary for PMSI priority under UCC 9–312(3) are taken.

In many transactions the time and expense of obtaining a subordination agreement may make that alternative infeasible. Under current law, obtaining a PMSI also may be impractical; in addition, the PMSI may not provide the buyer with the protection it desires. For example, in order to comply with the strict tracing requirement of UCC 9–107(b), the buyer would be required to advance funds directly to the seller's suppliers. Even then, PMSI status would be available only to the extent of the cost of the raw components, and buyer's damages for the seller's non-delivery could exceed that amount. See generally Chapter 11, Section 1(B), supra. Problems also could arise from the commingling of PMSI-financed goods with other supplies and materials of the seller-debtor. See UCC 9–315.

Professors Jackson and Kronman recognized that the purchase money financer and the financing buyer perform a similar economic function and that Article 9 affords scant protection to the latter. The following excerpt reflects their proposed solution.

———

JACKSON & KRONMAN, A PLEA FOR THE FINANCING BUYER
85 Yale L.J. 1, 36–37 (1975).

The financing buyer may be elevated to parity with the purchase money lender in two ways. The first would simply be to abolish the strict tracing requirement of § 9–107(1)(b) by deleting the words "if such value is in fact so used." Although the elimination of the § 9–107(b) tracing requirement may be desirable, it is also certain to be controversial.

A more conservative solution would be to add a new subsection (c) to § 9–107 . . ., which would read as follows:

A security interest is a "purchase money security interest" to the extent that it is ...

(c) taken by a buyer who makes advances to a seller to enable the seller to manufacture, assemble or process goods for the buyer during the period of one year following the advance, and the collateral securing the advance consists of (i) materials acquired after the advance has been made which are necessary for the manufacture, assembly or processing of the contract goods, and (ii) goods manufactured, assembled, or processed after the advance has been made which could be used to satisfy the contract (whether or not in a deliverable state).[147]

No further change in the Code would be necessary; the new subsection would give the financing buyer a purchase money security interest in the goods he had contracted for, thereby making him eligible for the special priority of § 9–312(3). In this way, the financing buyer would be endowed with the rights and charged with the duties, of a purchase money lender.

Although the latter approach lacks simplicity and elegance, it achieves the same result, so far as the financing buyer is concerned, as the abolition of the strict tracing requirement. Whichever approach is preferred, the time has come to improve the status of the financing buyer. Indeed, as we have suggested, the elevation of the financing buyer is dictated by the Code's own policy of giving new money priority protection over old. By promoting the financing buyer to parity with the purchase money lender, the Code can cure a longstanding anomaly in commercial law and effectuate the fair and uniform application of one of its own underlying policies.

Professors Jackson and Kronman apparently have recanted as to the plausibility of eliminating generally the tracing requirement of UCC 9–107(b). See Jackson & Kronman, Secured Financing and Priorities Among Creditors, 88 Yale L.J. 1143, 1176 (1979) (arguing that eliminating the tracing requirement would result in a "last-in-time"

---

147. The proposed section limits the priority to materials received or manufacturing steps taken after the advance of the money. This is to ensure that the financing buyer is, indeed, a "financing," and not merely a prepaying, buyer. The ordinary prepaying buyer does nothing to allow the manufacturer to move forward in the completion of the contract, and should not receive a special priority in the completed goods.

The relevant test should be, not the strict tracing requirement itself, but rather a test that looks to see if the financing money has actually been used in a manner that arguably enabled the debtor to progress towards completion of its contract with the financing buyer. This test is, itself, a kind of "tracing" requirement. It looks to any manufacturing steps taken after the receipt of the money from the financing buyer that further the produc tion of goods that are for, or arguably could be for, the financing buyer. The existence of such a continuing manufacturing process signals that the money has been used in an "enabling" sense for that contract. The equities that attach to the purchase money lender, as a consequence, also attach here.

priority rule leading to all credit being unsecured credit); Note (5) on Purchase Money Priority and the Definition of "Purchase Money Security Interest," Section 1(B), supra.

Does their proposed UCC 9–107(c) have merit? Although it solves some of the commingling and tracing problems, it elevates the "new money" above the interest of first-to-file secured party as to *all* of the qualifying goods. Those goods might be of a value considerably in excess of the amount of the financing buyer's advances, thereby giving the financing buyer a greater "equity cushion" than the normal PMSI financer. Would this "last-in-time" priority rule have deleterious effects on the utility of secured credit similar to (even if not so significant as) those that the authors later argued would follow from generally eliminating the tracing requirements for PMSI's? Would the proposed solution exacerbate the problem of commingling in cases of multiple financing buyers who claim the same collateral? Is the plight of the financing buyer limited to so few transactions that the alternative of obtaining subordination agreements is more cost-effective than creating additional complexity in the statute?

(B) Unperfected Security Interests and Buyers of Goods

Problem 5. On June 1 *SP* loaned $50,000 to *D*. On the same day, in order to secure the loan, *D* granted a security interest to *SP* by signing a security agreement covering "all equipment now owned or hereafter acquired." Although *D* signed and gave to *SP* a proper financing statement, *SP* inadvertently failed to file the financing statement.

On July 1 *D* sold an item of equipment (a backhoe) to *B*–1, a competitor, for $5,000 cash. That same day *B*–1 came to *D*'s place of business and picked up the backhoe and took it away. *B*–1 knew nothing of *SP*'s security interest.

(a) Whose rights in the backhoe are senior, *SP*'s or *B*–1's? See UCC 9–301(1)(c); UCC 9–302(1).

(b) On July 15 *SP* discovered the error and filed the financing statement in the proper office. On August 1, *B*–1 sold the backhoe to *B*–2. Whose rights are senior, *SP*'s or *B*–2's? See Aircraft Trading and Services, Inc. v. Braniff, Inc., infra; Notes on Unperfected Security Interests, Buyers of Collateral, and the Shelter Principle, infra.

(c) Now assume that *SP* did not perfect the security interest. However, *SP* found out about the sale to *B*–1 as well as the imminent sale to *B*–2. On August 1, as *B*–2 was at *B*–1's place of business preparing to load the backhoe on *B*–2's truck, *SP* showed up and said to *B*–2, "Don't go through with that sale. I want the backhoe; I have a security interest in it!" *B*–2 ignored the demand and took the backhoe away. Whose rights are senior, *SP*'s or *B*–2's?

Problem 6. Your client, *B*, is interested in buying, for cash, a large quantity of used construction equipment from *S*, a contractor that is going out of business. What precautions would you take to ensure that your client gets good title to the equipment free of all Article 9 security interests? How would you structure the closing of the transaction (i.e., payment and delivery of the equipment)?

AIRCRAFT TRADING AND SERVICES, INC. v. BRANIFF, INC.

United States Court of Appeals, Second Circuit, 1987.
819 F.2d 1227.
Cert. denied, 484 U.S. 856, 108 S.Ct. 163, 98 L.Ed.2d 118 (1987).

MINER, CIRCUIT JUDGE: Plaintiff-appellant Aircraft Trading and Services, Inc. ("ATASCO") appeals from a judgment entered in the United States District Court for the Southern District of New York (Goettel, J.) in favor of defendants-appellees Braniff, Inc., William Condren, and International Air Leases, Inc. ("IAL"), following ATASCO's motion for summary judgment against IAL only and defendants' cross-motion for summary judgment. ATASCO's action arose out of its sale of a jet aircraft engine, subject to a chattel mortgage that secured the payment of the purchase price, to Northeastern Airlines. ATASCO failed to record the chattel mortgage with the Federal Aviation Administration ("FAA"), as required for perfection of its security interest under the Federal Aviation Act, 49 U.S.C. §§ 1403–1406 (1982 & Supp. III 1985) ("the Act"), until after the engine had been conveyed to Northeastern to Braniff, and then by Braniff to Condren, culminating in a lease from Condren to IAL with an option to purchase. IAL subsequently exercised its option to buy after ATASCO recorded its interest and after IAL had actual notice of ATASCO's security interest in the engine. ATASCO brought suit for conversion, replevin and forfeiture of the engine, claiming that its rights were superior to those of Braniff, Condren, and IAL.

The district court denied ATASCO's motion for summary judgment against IAL and granted defendant's cross-motion for summary judgment, finding that the intermediate transfers of the engine, prior to ATASCO's perfection of its security interest, extinguished ATASCO's security interest under 49 U.S.C. § 1403(c). On appeal, ATASCO asserts that its interest in the engine is superior to IAL's under U.C.C. Article 9. We find merit in ATASCO's claim and reverse the denial of ATASCO's motion for summary judgment against IAL. We affirm the grant of defendants' cross-motion for summary judgment as to Braniff and Condren, but reverse as to IAL.

BACKGROUND

In December 1982, ATASCO, a Panamanian company engaged in the business of selling and leasing aircraft and aircraft engines, sold a jet aircraft engine to Northeastern Airlines ("Northeastern"), a commercial airline carrier. The purchase price of the engine was $412,-344.00. The sales agreement provided that Northeastern would pay ATASCO $36,000.00 as a down payment, with the balance to be paid in 36 equal installments of $10,454.00, due monthly, beginning in March 1983. Northeastern's obligation to pay the debt was secured by a chattel mortgage dated December 31, 1982, held by ATASCO. The chattel mortgage provided that Northeastern would be in default if it (1) failed to pay any note when due; (2) disposed of the engine before all payments were made; or, (3) was subject to bankruptcy proceedings.

Northeastern paid the monthly installments on the engine through January 10, 1985, but has made no payments since then, and is now in bankruptcy. The balance due on the engine is $135,902.00 plus interest. ATASCO failed to record the chattel mortgage with the FAA, as required under 49 U.S.C. § 1403(c), until March 1985.

On November 28, 1984, Northeastern agreed to sell the aircraft containing the engine subject to ATASCO's chattel mortgage to Braniff, a commercial airline carrier. Northeastern, in its bill of sale to Braniff, represented that it was conveying good and marketable title for both the aircraft and the engine. Braniff, which was planning to sell this aircraft immediately to William Condren, a private individual, checked the FAA records for prior claims or liens upon the aircraft or its parts, and found no record of any incumbrances. After the sale of Braniff was consummated, Braniff filed the bill of sale with the FAA on November 30, 1984. On December 7, 1984, Braniff sold the aircraft to Condren after Condren also checked the FAA records for a prior claim. Condren subsequently filed his bill of sale.

In early February 1985, Condren leased the aircraft, with an option to buy, to IAL. The lease was not filed within the FAA as required by 49 U.S.C. § 1403. ATASCO finally filed its chattel mortgage with the FAA in March of 1985. In April of 1985, IAL learned of ATASCO's chattel mortgage when Condren notified IAL of ATASCO's interest by letter. Nevertheless, in late July or early August of 1985, after procuring a copy of ATASCO's chattel mortgage directly from the FAA, IAL exercised its option to buy the aircraft. That bill of sale was filed with the FAA on August 5th.

ATASCO brought suit for conversion, replevin, and forfeiture against Braniff, Condren and IAL. ATASCO's central contention before the district court was that its rights were superior to those of IAL because its chattel mortgage was filed prior to IAL's filing, and IAL had actual knowledge of the terms of the instrument when it exercised its option to purchase. The district court granted summary judgment in favor of IAL, Condren, and Braniff, noting that if the only transaction at issue were the sale to IAL, then ATASCO might prevail. However, the district court ruled that, because of the intermediate transfers to Braniff and Condren prior to ATASCO's filing of the chattel mortgage,

Braniff received good title and passed good title to Condren, who in turn passed good title to IAL.

DISCUSSION

A. The Federal Aviation Act

Under the Federal Aviation Act, an interest in aircraft or aircraft engines, including a chattel mortgage, see 49 U.S.C. § 1403(a), is not valid against an innocent third party [1] "until such conveyance or other instrument is filed for recordation in the office of the Secretary of Transportation." 49 U.S.C. § 1403(c). Federal law thus requires recordation with the FAA to perfect a security interest in an aircraft engine....

In the case before us, although both Braniff and Condren purchased the engine and filed with the FAA prior to the time that ATASCO filed and perfected its interest,[2] ATASCO eventually did file and perfect in March of 1985. Therefore, state law determines priority as between ATASCO and Braniff and Condren, and as between ATASCO and IAL. All parties concede that New York's Uniform Commercial Code applies to determine priority in this case. We therefore turn to an analysis of the New York U.C.C., particularly Article 9, to determine how ATASCO's late perfected security interest should be treated.

B. The Uniform Commercial Code

1. Buyer in the Ordinary Course of Business

Appellees contend that, under New York's Uniform Commercial Code section 9–307(1), Braniff was a buyer in the ordinary course of business who could subsequently convey the engine free of ATASCO's security interest. Section 9–307 provides:

> (1) A buyer in ordinary course of business ... takes free of a security interest created by his seller even though the security interest is perfected and even though the buyer knows of its existence.

N.Y.U.C.C. Law § 9–307(1) (McKinney 1964). It generally is recognized that the purpose of section 9–307(1) is to protect the buying public where the secured party finances inventory that is sold to the public by the debtor in the regular course of the debtor's business. J. White & R. Summers, Uniform Commercial Code § 25–13, at 1067 (2d ed. 1980); N.Y.U.C.C. Law § 9–307 practice commentary 1 (McKinney 1964).

---

1. Section 1403(c) invalidates an unfiled interest in an aircraft as against "any person other than the person by whom the conveyance or other instrument is made or given, his heir or devisee, or any other person having actual notice thereof...." 49 U.S.C. § 1403(c).

2. The date of perfection of a security interest in aircraft generally is held to coincide with the date that the security interest is filed for recordation. In re Gelking, 754 F.2d 778, 780 (8th Cir.), cert. denied, 473 U.S. 906, 105 S.Ct. 3529, 87 L.Ed.2d 653 (1985).

Under section 9–307(1), if Braniff were a buyer in the ordinary course of business, it would "take free" of the security interest created by its seller, Northeastern, extinguishing ATASCO's interest, whether or not ATASCO subsequently perfected. Section 9–307(1) thereby provides an exception to the general rule, codified in section 9–306(2), that "a security interest continues in collateral notwithstanding sale, exchange or other disposition thereof unless the disposition was authorized by the secured party." N.Y.U.C.C. Law § 9–306(2) (McKinney Supp. 1987).

A buyer in the ordinary course of business is defined as "a person who in good faith and without knowledge that the sale to him is in violation of the ownership rights or security interest of a third party in the goods buys in ordinary course from a person in the business of selling goods of that kind...." N.Y.U.U.C. Law § 1–201(9) (McKinney Supp. 1987) (emphasis added). This definition requires, inter alia, that the buyer in ordinary course buy from a seller who ordinarily sells similar goods. ATASCO argues that Northeastern, an airline carrier, was not in the business of selling airplanes, and therefore Braniff was not a buyer in the ordinary course of business. Appellees counter that it is a practice in the airline industry for airlines periodically to sell off airplanes and therefore Northeastern sold the plane to Braniff in the ordinary course of business.

Northeastern evidently was selling jets and engines to upgrade its fleet, which may be a practice in the industry. However, under New York law, whether a sale is an ordinary sale of similar goods turns on whether the goods sold are classified as capital equipment or as inventory. In Hempstead Bank v. Andy's Car Rental Sys., 35 A.D.2d 35, 312 N.Y.S.2d 317 (2d Dep't 1970), the court held that a rental company's used car sales were not in the ordinary course of business, even though such sales are common in the industry, because the used cars were capital equipment of the leasing company and not inventory. Accord Sindone v. Farber, 105 Misc.2d 634, 432 N.Y.S.2d 778 (Sup.Ct.1980). IAL's reliance on Tanbro Fabrics Corp. v. Deering Milliken, Inc., 39 N.Y.2d 632, 350 N.E.2d 590, 385 N.Y.S.2d 260 (1976), is misplaced. In Tanbro Fabrics the unfinished textiles sold off by a converter were inventory and not capital equipment. Therefore, the sale was in the ordinary course of business, a result that accords with the Hempstead Bank holding. See 69 Am. Jur. 2d Secured Transactions § 469, at 328 (1973) ("a buyer of collateral that is classified as equipment will rarely if ever be a buyer in ordinary course of business, even where the debtor makes it a regular practice to sell used or obsolescent equipment at regular intervals").

Northeastern's aircraft and engines clearly were capital equipment. See N.Y.U.C.C. Law § 9–109(2) (McKinney 1964). Therefore, we hold that the sale of Braniff was not in the ordinary course of business, and section 9–307(1) does not extinguish ATASCO's security interest. We note that neither Condren nor IAL attempts to establish status as a buyer in the ordinary course of business. Even if Condren or IAL qualified as a buyer in the ordinary course of business, however, they would be unable to avail themselves of section 9–307(1) protection because section 9–307(1) applies only to security interests created by the buyer's seller. Here, Northeastern created the security interest and therefore Braniff was the only party in a position to invoke section 9–307(1) in its own right.

2. Priority Between ATASCO and Braniff & Condren

We now turn to a determination of the strength of ATASCO's claim as against Braniff and Condren. Section 9–301(1) provides that:

> (1) an unperfected security interest is subordinate to the rights of
>
> > (b) a person who becomes a lien creditor before the security interest is perfected;
> >
> > (c) in the case of goods, instruments, documents, and chattel paper, a person who is not a secured party and who is a transferee in bulk or other buyer not in ordinary course of business ... to the extent that he gives value and receives delivery of the collateral without knowledge of the security interest and before it is perfected.

N.Y.U.C.C. Law § 9–301(1) (McKinney Supp. 1987) (emphasis added). Both Braniff and Condren bought without knowledge of ATASCO's security interest and before it was perfected. Therefore, as buyers not in the ordinary course of business, their respective rights to the engine were superior to ATASCO's, by application of section 9–301(1)(c).

It is critical to note for the discussion that follows that ATASCO's unperfected security interest, though subordinate, continued to exist. Section 9–301(1) explicitly provides that "an unperfected security interest is subordinate" to the rights of certain buyers and lien creditors. The language of subordination indicates that the secured party's rights live on, although junior to the buyer's rights. Contrast the language of section 9–307—"[a] buyer in ordinary course ... takes free of a security interest created by his seller"—which terminated the secured party's interest for all time. Some courts seemingly ignore the subordination language of section 9–301(1) and state that a senior buyer "takes free" of an unperfected security interest, see, e.g., United States v. Handy & Harman, 750 F.2d 777, 780–81 (9th Cir.1984); In re Miguel, 30 B.R. 896, 898 (Bankr.E.D.Cal.1983), but those cases do not involve subsequent buyers and apparently use the phrases "takes free" and "has priority over" interchangeably. One commentator has suggested that the U.C.C. drafters intended that an unperfected security interest terminates upon subsequent sale of the collateral to a buyer not in the ordinary course of business, but that an unperfected security interest subject to a senior lien continues. D. G. Carlson, Death and Subordination Under Article 9 of the Uniform Commercial Code: Senior Buyers and Senior Lien Creditors, 5 Cardozo L. Rev. 547, 553–57 (1984). We decline, however, to interpret section 9–301(1) in a manner that would give "subordinate" two different meanings in the same sentence depending upon the particular subsection that is relevant to the case at bar—section 9–301(1)(c) (buyers not in the ordinary course of business) or section 9–301(1)(b) (lien creditors). Rather, we are convinced that a plain reading of the statute requires that "subordinate" be given consistent meaning within section 9–301, and that the difference in phrasing between sections 9–301(1) ("is subordinate") and 9–307 ("takes free") is to be given effect, notwithstanding cases that use language of termination interchangeably with language of subordination.

3. Shelter Provision of Article 2, Sales

Appellees argue that if Braniff and Condren are buyers not in the ordinary course of business, their priority over ATASCO's security interest under section 9–301(1) would pass to IAL with the conveyance. Relying on the shelter provision of Article 2, Sales, section 2–403, appellees assert that Braniff conveyed title to Condren, and Condren conveyed that title to IAL, subject at most to ATASCO's subordinated unperfected security interest. Section 2–403 provides that:

(1)(a) purchaser of goods acquires all title which his transferor had or had power to transfer except that a purchaser of a limited interest acquires rights only to the extent of the interest purchased.

N.Y.U.C.C. Law § 2–403(1) (McKinney 1964). Appellees have directed us to no authority for their assertion that the shelter provision of Article 2 may be applied to immunize transferees from a buyer who is protected under section 9–301(1)(c). It is a novel theory that we believe must fail.

Appellees' reliance on In re Gary Aircraft Corp., 681 F.2d 365 (5th Cir.1982), is misplaced. In Gary Aircraft, the secured party contended that it was entitled to possession of an aircraft because the last purchaser in the chain of sale was not a purchaser for value without notice, and therefore could not escape the secured party's interest as a buyer in the ordinary course of business. Rejecting that analysis, the Fifth Circuit held that the last purchaser was not subject to the secured party's interest because an intervening purchaser qualified under section 9–307 as a buyer in the ordinary course of business. That special status of the intervening purchaser extinguished the security interest in the collateral such that a subsequent sale could not resurrect it, and the last purchaser therefore prevailed.

New York law is in agreement. See Marine Midland Bank, N.A. v. Smith Boys, Inc., 129 Misc.2d 37, 41, 492 N.Y.S.2d 355, 358 (Sup.Ct. 1985) (if any party in the chain of title takes free of the security interest under section 9–307, "all succeeding buyers likewise take free of the security interest"). However, this is a narrow exception to the general rule stated in section 9–306(2) that a security interest in collateral continues upon the sale of the collateral unless the sale was authorized by the secured party. Id. at 43, 492 N.Y.S.2d at 360. The case before us does not fall within this narrow exception because

ATASCO's security interest was not extinguished, but merely subordinated, by the sale to Braniff: Braniff did not "take free" of ATASCO's interest under section 9–307; it took subject to ATASCO's subordinated claim. See T. M. Quinn, Uniform Commercial Code Commentary and Law Digest para. 9–306[A][2], at 9–169 (1978) ("Anyone dealing with the collateral deals with it subject to the continuing security interest.").

As the Fifth Circuit recognized in Gary Aircraft, "the rule is that section [2–403(1)] is not available to save one who buys when the seller's title is subject to a security interest but who does not qualify under section [9–307]" for preferred status as a buyer in the ordinary course of business.[3] Gary Aircraft, 681 F.2d at 377. See Commercial Credit Equipment Corp. v. Bates, 159 Ga.App. 910, 285 S.E.2d 560 (1981). But see Executive Financial Services, Inc. v. Pagel, 238 Kan. 809, 715 P.2d 381 (1986) (buyer in the ordinary course of business may prevail on "entrustment" theory under section 2–403(2) and (3) even though he could not prevail under section 9–307(1)). Similarly, in National Shawmut Bank v. Jones, 108 N.H. 386, 388, 236 A.2d 484, 486 (1967), the court recognized section 9–307 as the only provision of Article 9 "under which a buyer of goods can claim to take free of a security interest where a sale, exchange or other disposition of the collateral was without consent of the secured party .... Article 9–306(2) gives the court no leeway to create any other exceptions to its dictates." Accord Matteson v. Harper, 297 Ore. 113, 117, 682 P.2d 766, 769 (1984). See J. White & R. Summers, Uniform Commercial Code § 25–15, at 1073 (2d ed. 1980).

We find further support for this rule in other sections of the U.C.C. Section 9–306(2) provides for continuance of a security interest upon sale of the collateral "except where this Article otherwise provides." We interpret this clause as expressly limiting exceptions to those found within Article 9. Moreover, section 2–402(3)(a) specifies that "nothing in this Article shall be deemed to impair the rights of creditors of the seller ... under the provisions of [Article 9]." We conclude that the general scheme of the U.C.C. contemplates that a security interest is to be governed by Article 9, unimpaired by Article 2. See National Shawmut, 108 N.H. at 389, 236 A.2d at 486; J. I. Case Credit Corp. v. Foos, 11 Kan.App.2d 185, 188–89, 717 P.2d 1064, 1067 (1986); Carlson, supra, at 550 n.9 & 556 ("section 2–403 does not contemplate the destruction of unperfected security interests"); Anderson, supra, § 9–102:9, at 453. Furthermore, the drafters of the U.C.C. explicitly provided shelter elsewhere in Article 9. See N.Y.U.C.C. Law § 9–302(2) (McKinney Supp. 1987) ("If a secured party assigns a perfected security interest, no filing under this Article is required in order to continue the perfected status of the security interest against creditors of and transferees from the original debtor."). "Their failure to do so in section 9–301(1)(c) should be taken as significant." Carlson, supra, at 558.

---

3. IAL purchased with knowledge of ATASCO's security interest after ATASCO filed and perfected its claim. Therefore IAL cannot invoke protection in its own right under section 9–301(1)(c).

Finally, we note that the U.C.C. does not require a security interest to be filed immediately or promptly, Anderson, supra, § 9–302:20, at 77–78, although it is the most prudent course for a cautious lender. Delay in perfection does not preclude perfected status at a later time upon filing. While the secured party's interest may be subordinated to interests of others arising prior to filing, "he can, of course, file, even after a delay, and protect himself against interests arising subsequent to such filing." 53 N.Y. Jur. Secured Transactions § 175, at 152 (1967); 69 Am. Jur. 2d Secured Transactions § 422, at 271 (1973); Anderson, supra, § 9–301:9, at 29–30. The rule appellees urge us to adopt effectively would freeze a secured party's priority status as of the time of the first intervening conveyance: If one failed to file a security interest the day of the sale, the buyer could, by immediately reselling, forever destroy the security interest. While appellees urge that their rule would result in an increment of certainty in such transactions, we believe that such an extreme result would discourage lenders from taking security interests and would thereby inhibit commerce. The U.C.C. does not attempt to remove all uncertainty from secured transactions. It provides automatic perfection in certain situations, see N.Y.U.C.C. Law §§ 9–302(1)(b) (10–day automatic perfection for documents, proceeds), 9–302(1)(d) (purchase money security interest in consumer goods), § 9–304(4) (21–day automatic perfection for certain instruments) (McKinney Supp. 1987), and allows a filing to relate back to the time of attachment in others, see N.Y.U.C.C. Law §§ 9–103(1)(d), 9–103(3)(e) (McKinney Supp. 1987) (in multistate transaction, secured party has four months to file in state to which collateral has been removed). The U.C.C. aims to balance the competing concerns of protection for secured lenders and encouragement of trade.

4. Priority Between ATASCO and IAL

Having determined that ATASCO's security interest was not extinguished by the subsequent conveyances to Braniff and Condren, we now address the priority in the engine as between ATASCO and IAL.

At the time the engine was conveyed from Northeastern to Braniff and then to Condren, ATASCO's claim was subordinate to Braniff's and Condren's under section 9–301 as discussed above, because it was unfiled and unperfected. However, ATASCO eventually did file and perfect its security interest, and therefore section 9–301, which determines priority where an interest is unperfected, has no bearing on the issue of priority as between ATASCO and IAL, who have competing perfected interests in the engine.

Section 9–312(5)(a), the catch-all priority section of Article 9, governs conflicts between competing perfected interests:

Conflicting security interests rank according to priority in time of filing or perfection. Priority dates from the time a filing is first made covering the collateral or the time the security interest is first perfected, whichever is earlier, provided that there is no period thereafter when there is neither filing nor perfection.

N.Y.U.C.C. Law § 9–312(5)(a) (McKinney Supp. 1987). As previously discussed, section 1403 of the Federal Aviation Act requires filing with the Secretary of the FAA to perfect an interest in an aircraft engine. Therefore, time of filing is identical to time of perfection in the case before us. Under section 9–312(5)(a), the first to file an interest with the FAA will rank first in priority. It is undisputed that ATASCO filed its chattel mortgage with the FAA in March 1985, and IAL filed its interests on August 5, 1985. Therefore, under the first to file or perfect rule of section 9–312(5)(a), ATASCO's security interest in the engine has priority over IAL's interest. We therefore reverse the district court's grant of summary judgment in favor IAL and the denial of ATASCO's motion for summary judgment as against IAL, and remand the case for a determination of damages.

C. Sanctions

Appellees request that we award double costs and attorney's fees against appellant for bringing an appeal "totally lacking in merit, framed with no relevant supporting law, conclusory in nature, and utterly unsupported by the evidence." As is clear from our discussion of appellant's claims, we are of the view that this appeal was highly meritorious and well supported by relevant law. But even if we are wrong, the issues are obviously not frivolous. Appellees' request for sanctions therefore borders on the frivolous, and we caution that we will not hesitate to impose appropriate penalties in the future for frivolous requests for sanctions.

CONCLUSION

For the reasons stated above, we reverse the district court's grant of summary judgment in favor IAL. We affirm the district court's grant of summary judgment for Braniff and Condren, on the grounds herein stated. We reverse the denial of ATASCO's summary judgment motion as against IAL, and remand for a determination of damages and entry of judgment.

Notes on Unperfected Security Interests, Buyers of Collateral, and the Shelter Principle

(1) **Reaction to the *Braniff* Case.** In Permanent Editorial Board Commentary No. 6, the Permanent Editorial Board rejected both the reasoning and the result of Aircraft Trading and Services, Inc. v. Braniff, Inc., supra. In *Braniff*, the Second Circuit made much of the fact that UCC 9–301(1)(c) purports to *subordinate* unperfected security interests but does not provide that qualifying good faith purchasers

"take free" of unperfected security interests. Is it plausible that the structure of UCC 9–301(1) is nothing more than a drafting "glitch" resulting from an operative rule that applies to both holders of limited interests (UCC 9–301(1)(a) & (b) (security interests and judicial liens)) and buyers of the whole (UCC 9–301(1)(c) & (d)) alike?

(2) UCC 9–301(1) and the Shelter Principle. Could the absence of a statement of the shelter principle in UCC 9–301(1) also be a "glitch"? A negative answer seems appropriate. UCC 9–301(1) serves to subordinate certain interests to unperfected security interests. Once these interests are subordinated, Article 9 leaves the matter of continued subordination (i.e., shelter) to other applicable law. For example, the Code codifies the shelter principle for goods, instruments, documents, and securities. UCC 2–403(1); 3–306; 7–504; 8–301. As to property that is not the subject of general codification in the Code, such as ordinary contract rights, the Restatement (Second) Contracts provides similar (but not identical) guidance.[2]

The *Braniff* court also drew support for its reasoning from UCC 2–402(3)(a), which provides that "[n]othing in this Article shall be deemed to impair the rights of creditors of the seller ... under the provisions of" Article 9. As explained in Permanent Editorial Board Commentary No. 6, however, it is the application of UCC 9–301(1) that subordinates an unperfected security interest, not the application of the shelter principle. The shelter principle actually *gives effect* to the subordination mandated by Article 9. What could it mean for a buyer to receive rights that are senior to an unperfected security interest if the buyer could never transfer those senior rights to another person? What kind of "seniority" is that? Why should one with senior rights in property have to keep the property forever in order to enjoy the benefits of seniority?

Professor David Carlson, one of whose articles features in the *Braniff* case, has taken issue with both the opinion and the Permanent Editorial Board Commentary. He concludes that "the PEB's invocation of the shelter provision in section 2–403 is poor theory. It is better to face up to the fact that section 9–301(1)(c) is a murderer. It kills off the security interest altogether—and that Judge Miner (sitting in diversity, mind you, and therefore merely *guessing* at the content of state law) simply made an error." Carlson, Bulk Sales Under Article 9: Some Easy Cases Made Difficult, 41 Ala. L. Rev. 729, 759 (1990) (emphasis in original).

---

2. See Restatement (Second) Contracts § 342:

§ 342. Successive Assignees From the Same Assignor

Except as otherwise provided by statute, the right of an assignee is superior to that of a subsequent assignee of the same right from the same assignor, unless

(a) the first assignment is ineffective or revocable or is voidable by the assignor or by the subsequent assignee; or

(b) the subsequent assignee in good faith and without knowledge or reason to know of the prior assignment gives value and obtains

   (i) payment or satisfaction of the obligation,

   (ii) judgment against the obligor,

   (iii) a new contract with the obligor by novation, or

   (iv) possession of a writing of a type customarily accepted as a symbol or as evidence of the right assigned.

(3) The "Delivery" Requirement. UCC 9–301(1) conditions a buyer's seniority to an unperfected security interest on both the giving of value and the receipt of delivery of the property "without knowledge of the security interest and before it is perfected." How can a buyer ensure its seniority? Consider the prospective buyer who searches, turns up no filed financing statements against the seller (or its predecessors in interest), and then pays the seller. What result if the buyer learns of the unperfected security interest, or if the secured party files, during the gap (which might be very short) between payment and delivery?

(4) Buyers of Accounts and General Intangibles: UCC 9–301(1)(d). UCC 9–301(1)(d) applies to certain transferees of accounts and general intangibles. For the most part, subsection (1)(d) parallels UCC 9–301(1)(c). Note, however, that the former provision contains no "delivery" requirement. Accounts and general intangibles, unlike the collateral covered by subsection (1)(c) (i.e., goods, instruments, documents, and chattel paper), cannot be delivered or possessed. Note also that subsection (1)(d) applies only to transferees who are not secured parties. Because the assignee of accounts normally is a secured party, see UCC 9–105(1)(m), a priority contest between the assignee and an unperfected security interest in the same accounts would be governed by the first-to-file-or-perfect rule of UCC 9–312(5)(a), not by UCC 9–301(1)(d). Consequently, subsection (1)(d) applies only to assignments of accounts excluded from Article 9 (UCC 9–104(f)) and to outright sales of general intangibles.

Chapter 14

SECURITY INTERESTS (INCLUDING THE "FLOATING LIEN") IN BANKRUPTCY

This Chapter discusses the rights of a secured party when the debtor enters bankruptcy. Although the debtor's insolvency is not a statutory prerequisite to the commencement of a bankruptcy case, the vast proportion of debtors who enter bankruptcy are insolvent. Unsecured creditors are likely to receive much less than the amount of their claims. Thus, bankruptcy is a time when a security interest may be of particular value.

SECTION 1. OVERVIEW OF BANKRUPTCY

The Bankruptcy Process. The nonbankruptcy law of creditors' rights is a race of diligence: every creditor for itself. Bankruptcy substitutes a collective debt-collection procedure for individual collection activity. The filing of a bankruptcy petition puts an immediate halt to the race. See BC 362(a) (discussed infra). Instead, all creditors must satisfy their claims only through the bankruptcy.

The filing of a bankruptcy petition creates an estate. The property of the estate generally includes "all legal or equitable interests of the debtor in property as of the commencement of the case." BC 541.

Some bankruptcy cases are commenced for the purpose of liquidating the property of the estate and distributing the proceeds to creditors. In these cases, which are filed under Chapter 7 of the Bankruptcy Code, a trustee is appointed to "collect and reduce to money the property of the estate for which such trustee serves, and close the estate as expeditiously as is compatible with the best interests of the parties in interest." BC 704(1). The bankruptcy court may authorize the trustee to operate the debtor's business, but only for a limited period and only if the operation is in the best interests of the estate and consistent with the orderly liquidation of the estate. See BC 721.

Cases filed under Chapter 11 (reorganization) contemplate that the debtor will continue to operate its business as debtor-in-possession ("DIP"). A trustee is not appointed in Chapter 11 cases, except in the relatively unusual circumstances set forth in BC 1104. Instead, the debtor-in-possession enjoys most of the rights and powers, and is charged with performing most of the functions and duties, of the trustee. See BC 1107; BC 1108; BC 1106(a). While the DIP operates the business, Chapter 11 affords creditors and the debtor (or, if the debtor is a corporation, its shareholders) the opportunity to determine what should be done with the assets so as to maximize the return. Should some or all of the assets be sold? Used to continue one or more lines of the prebankruptcy business? Used to enter into a new line of business?[1]

Where corporate debtors are concerned, the principal purposes of bankruptcy are to maximize the value of the corporation and to allocate the value among various claimants. Substituting a collective remedy (bankruptcy) for individual remedies promotes the former purpose. Nonbankruptcy law subjects businesses to piecemeal dissolution: each creditor is free to levy upon and sell whatever assets it chooses. In contrast, bankruptcy enables the assets to be sold together. The sale of a business as a package is likely to yield more than individual sales of each of the assets; a buyer typically will be willing to pay an additional amount to reflect the cost savings in gathering together the different assets needed to operate the business. A business whose assets not only are maintained intact but also are up and running is likely to command an even larger ("going-concern") premium. Moreover, sales conducted to enforce judicial liens are distress sales. The seller (the sheriff) must sell quickly and so is in no position to hold out for a higher price. In contrast, bankruptcy liquidation puts the seller (the trustee, who represents the creditors) in a somewhat better bargaining position by affording the trustee a little more time.

Bankruptcy not only affects the size of the corporate pie but also its distribution. Allocating the value of the corporation requires both a determination of who is entitled to share and a ranking of the entitlements relative to one another. Potential claimants include not only the prebankruptcy creditors but also the postbankruptcy creditors and the shareholders. In a Chapter 7 case, the distribution is fixed by statute. See BC 726. The statute generally (but not always) respects the nonbankruptcy ranking of various claims. Thus, holders of secured claims ordinarily will be entitled to the value of their collateral, see BC 725; holders of unsecured claims may share in the collateral's value only to the extent it exceeds the secured debt. Unsecured creditors are entitled to be paid in full before shareholders receive any distribution. See BC 726(a).

Chapter 11 permits the interested parties to fix the distribution in a "plan." See generally BC 1123 (contents of plan). A Chapter 11 plan divides creditors and holders of equity interests into classes and sets forth what (if anything) the members of each class will receive and when (if ever) they will receive it. See BC 1123(a). Most plans are

---

1. Chapters 13 (available only to individual debtors with "regular income") and 12 (available only to debtors who are "family farmer[s] with regular annual income") are similar to Chapter 11 in that the debtor remains in possession of the property of the estate and undertakes to pay prebankruptcy debts pursuant to a court-approved plan. But unlike in Chapter 11 cases, creditors in Chapters 12 and 13 cases do not vote on proposed plans. A trustee is appointed in every Chapter 12 and Chapter 13 case; however, the trustee's primary obligation is to serve as a disbursement agent for payments made pursuant to the plan.

compositions and **extensions**; that is, they provide (i) that the cash or other property (e.g., stock in the reorganized debtor) that creditors receive for their claims will be worth less than 100 cents on the dollar and (ii) that creditors will receive payment over time. The terms of any particular plan typically reflect extensive negotiations by representatives of shareholders and various creditor groups. Most claimants are afforded the opportunity to vote on the plan. Before their acceptances or rejections may be solicited, the court must approve a disclosure statement or summary of the plan as providing information sufficient to enable the voters to make an informed judgment about the plan. See BC 1125. Chapter 11 contains a number of protections for holders of claims in classes that reject the plan and for dissenting members of classes that approve the plan. See, e.g., BC 1129(a)(7), (a)(8); BC 1129(b).

Even when the debtor is an individual, bankruptcy may serve as a collective creditors' remedy. More often than not, however, there are few unencumbered assets available for distribution. For most individual debtors, bankruptcy affords a unique opportunity to begin financial life anew. This **fresh start** consists of three components. First, the individual debtor may keep certain prebankruptcy assets (**exempt property**) free of prepetition claims. See BC 522. Second, to the extent that the debtor's current, nonexempt assets do not suffice to pay prebankruptcy debts, the debts are **discharged**; that is, they no longer may be collected as personal liabilities of the debtor. The discharge has the effect of freeing the debtor's human capital (future earning potential) from the reach of prepetition creditors. See BC 727; BC 524; see also BC 541(a)(6) (property of the estate does not include earnings from services performed by individual debtors after commencement of bankruptcy case). Third, employers and governmental units are prohibited from discriminating against the debtor solely because the debtor was insolvent, was in bankruptcy, or received a discharge. See BC 525.

What Will the Secured Party Recover From the Bankruptcy? As a first approximation, it is fair to say that bankruptcy respects the value of nonbankruptcy property rights, including security interests. Thus, a secured party is entitled to receive from the bankruptcy its collateral or the value of its collateral up to the amount of its claim. See BC 506(b); BC 724; BC 1129(a)(7). As we explain below, the secured party may be compelled to wait quite some time before receiving this value; however, even with a substantial delay, a creditor usually is much better off to receive the value of its collateral than it would be if it were unsecured. Holders of general unsecured claims share pro rata in whatever unencumbered assets remain after payment of secured claims, expenses of administering the bankruptcy case, and unsecured claims entitled to priority of payment (priority claims include those for unpaid prebankruptcy wages and taxes). See generally BC 726(a); BC 507(a).

The following Problems demonstrate the desirability of having a security interest in bankruptcy.

Problem 1. Debtor files a petition under Chapter 7 and has two assets: (i) a piece of equipment worth $100,000, subject to a perfected security interest securing an $80,000 debt to Seller; and (ii) real estate worth $500,000, subject to a recorded mortgage securing a $400,000 debt to Bank. In addition, Debtor owes $300,000 to other (unsecured) creditors. How will the assets be distributed? (The effect of Seller's having perfected its security interest is discussed infra, Section 2(A).)

Problem 2. What result in Problem 1 if Debtor had purchased the equipment from Seller on an unsecured basis?

Problem 3. What result in Problem 1 if the equipment is worth only $70,000 at the time Debtor enters bankruptcy? Note that BC 506(a) would divide Seller's $80,000 claim into two parts: Seller would have a secured claim in the amount of the value of its collateral ($70,000); the balance of its claim ($10,000) would be an unsecured claim.

The Automatic Stay. Bankruptcy cases can be complex and time-consuming. Even the relatively simple consumer bankruptcy can take several months: The debtor's assets must be gathered together, the claims against the debtor must be assessed, and the value of the assets must be distributed among the claimants. Chapter 11 cases typically take much longer. Months, even years, may elapse before a plan is proposed. Approval of the disclosure statement, solicitation of acceptances and rejections, and the confirmation hearing extend the process even further.

To effect the orderly administration of the bankruptcy estate, creditors must be prevented from continuing the nonbankruptcy race to the assets while the bankruptcy case is proceeding. If creditors were free to ignore the pendency of the bankruptcy case, then much of the value of a collective proceeding would be lost: creditors would incur duplicative costs of collection and assets might be sold piecemeal at distress prices.

Under BC 362(a), the filing of a bankruptcy petition "operates as a stay, applicable to all entities," of all collection activity with respect to prebankruptcy claims. The following Problems address the scope of the automatic stay as it applies to secured parties. Note that any acts taken in violation of the automatic stay are void, and that parties who deliberately violate the stay may be held in contempt of court and fined.

Problem 4. Debtor is in the printing business. On November 1, Seller sold Debtor a press and retained a security interest in the press to secure its price. Debtor filed a Chapter 11 petition on November 25. Seller has yet to file a financing statement to perfect its security interest. May Seller do so? See BC 362(a)(4); BC 541(a) (defining property of the estate). The consequences of having a security interest that is unperfected at the time the debtor enters bankruptcy are discussed infra, Section 2(A).

Problem 5. Assume that, in Problem 4, Seller filed a financing statement on November 5. May Seller repossess the press? See BC 362(a)(3), (a)(5).

Problem 6. May Debtor continue to use the press if Seller cannot repossess it? See BC 363(c); BC 1108.

Problem 7. Seller is concerned that the case may last several years, and that the press will decline substantially in value during that time, whether because of depreciation caused by normal wear and tear, obsolescence resulting from technological improvements in presses, or unanticipated damage resulting from misuse or natural calamity. For these reasons, Seller would like to repossess the press and sell it now, rather than wait for a future distribution from the bankruptcy. What can Seller do? See BC 363(e); BC 362(d); BC 362(g); Note on Relief from the Automatic Stay, infra.

Note on Relief From the Automatic Stay

BC 362(d) sets forth two circumstances under which the bankruptcy court "shall grant relief from the stay." Under subsection (d)(2), the court shall grant relief from the stay if the debtor "does not have an equity in [the] property" and the property is "not necessary to an effective reorganization." As used in BC 362(d)(2)(A), the debtor's "equity" is calculated by deducting from the value of the collateral the amount of debt that it secures. (When the property secures more than one debt, the cases tend to calculate the debtor's "equity" by deducting the aggregate amount of the secured obligations from the value of the collateral. See, e.g., Stewart v. Gurley, 745 F.2d 1194 (9th Cir.1984); In re Royal Palm Square Associates, 124 B.R. 129 (Bkrtcy.M.D.Fla.1991). Accordingly, if Seller can prove that the press is worth $80,000 and secures a debt of $100,000, the first element of BC 362(d)(2) would be met. The court must grant relief from the stay unless the trustee (or DIP) proves that the property is "necessary to an effective reorganization." See BC 362(d)(2), (g)(2). According to a widely-cited dictum from the Supreme Court,

> [w]hat this requires is not merely a showing that if there is conceivably to be an effective reorganization, this property will be needed for it; but that the property is essential for an effective reorganization *that is in prospect*. This means ... that there must be "a reasonable possibility of a successful reorganization within a reasonable time."

United Savings Association v. Timbers of Inwood Forest Associates, Ltd., 484 U.S. 365, 375–76, 108 S.Ct. 626, 633, 98 L.Ed.2d 740, 751 (1988) (emphasis in original). Thus, the trustee will not succeed merely by proving that *if* Debtor is to continue in the printing business, continued use of the press would be essential.

The court also is required to lift the stay "for cause, including lack of adequate protection of an interest in property of [a] party in interest." BC 362(d)(1). BC 361 explains the term "adequate protection." To protect against an anticipated decline in the value of the press resulting from continued use by Debtor, the trustee might provide monthly payments to Seller in the amount of the anticipated decline. See BC 361(1). To protect against the risk of obsolescence, the trustee might secure Seller's claim with a lien on other property of the estate. See BC 361(2). Where there is a risk of destruction, the trustee might insure the collateral against loss. See BC 361(3).

But even if the trustee (or DIP) provides the described protection, Seller may be less than content. Seller has bargained for the right, upon Debtor's default, to repossess the collateral, sell it, and apply the proceeds toward its claim against Debtor. See UCC 9–503; UCC 9–504. Were the automatic stay not in place, Seller would receive the value of its collateral in a matter of weeks. Even if the trustee insures the press, makes periodic payments, and grants a supplemental lien, Seller will be worse off. Rather than have a certain $80,000 in the very near term, Seller has only part payment now and a promise of the balance when a distribution is made. Even if the promise is kept, Seller will receive the vast proportion of its claim in the future, perhaps years from now. Had the automatic stay been lifted, Seller would receive the money in a matter of weeks; by investing the money, Seller would have considerably more than $80,000 in a few years.

Consider the following statutory argument. Adequate protection of an interest of an entity in property (here, Seller's security interest) may be provided by "granting such other relief ... as will result in the realization by such entity [Seller] of the indubitable equivalent of such entity's interest in such property." BC 361(3). Receipt of periodic cash payments and a secured promise to pay the balance at an indefinite time in the future is not the "indubitable equivalent" of receiving $80,000 today. If payment is to be deferred, Seller should be entitled to recover an amount equal to $80,000 plus interest on that amount, in order to put Seller in the same position it would have been in had the stay not been in effect. To support the argument, Seller might cite the legislative history of BC 361, which contains the statement that "[s]e-cured creditors should not be deprived of the benefit of their bargain." H.R. Rep. No. 595, 95th Cong., 1st Sess. 339 (1977), reprinted in 1978 U.S.C.C.A.N. 5963, 6295; S. Rep. No. 989, 95th Cong., 2d Sess. 53 (1978), reprinted in 1978 U.S.C.C.A.N. 5787, 5839. The benefit of Seller's bargain is to turn the collateral into cash promptly upon Debtor's default.

The Supreme Court considered and unanimously rejected this argument in United Savings Association v. Timbers of Inwood Forest Associates, Ltd., 484 U.S. 365, 108 S.Ct. 626, 98 L.Ed.2d 740 (1988). The Court concluded that the "interest in property" that BC 362(d)(1) protects does not include a secured party's right to foreclose on the collateral. Thus the "value of such entity's interest" in BC 361 means the dollar value of the collateral and not the present value of the secured party's right to use the collateral as a means to satisfy its claim. Accordingly, as long as the trustee takes appropriate steps to protect Seller's ultimate recovery of $80,000, Seller has received "adequate protection" for its security interest and is not entitled to relief from the stay on that ground.

In *Timbers*, the Supreme Court distinguished the undersecured creditor, whose collateral is worth less than its claim, from the oversecured creditor, whose collateral is worth more. In holding that undersecured creditors are not entitled to recover interest as part of the adequate protection required by BC 362, the Court relied in part on BC 502(b)(2) and 506(b). Under the former section, interest that is unmatured at the time of the filing of the petition is not part of the creditor's allowed secured claim; i.e., it ordinarily will not be paid from the bankruptcy. Under BC 506(b), to the extent that a claim is secured by collateral having a value in excess of the claim (i.e., to the extent that the secured creditor is oversecured), "there shall be allowed to the holder of such claim, interest on such claim, and any reasonable fees, costs, or charges provided for under the agreement under which such claim arose." In other words, postpetition interest continues to accrue on oversecured claims. However, interest accruing postpetition becomes part of the allowed secured claim; nothing in the Bankruptcy Code requires that interest be paid as it accrues.

As you might expect from reading the foregoing, secured parties have incentives not to become enmeshed in a bankruptcy case. If they are undersecured, they ultimately will recover the value of their collateral but will lose the value of having received it promptly. Oversecured creditors will be entitled to recover accrued postpetition interest to the extent that the value of the collateral is large enough to cover it, but the rate at which interest accrues may be less than the rate to which the parties have agreed.[2] And even oversecured creditors must wait until the time of distribution before actually recovering interest that accrues postpetition.

Problem 8. Assume that, in Problem 5, Seller repossessed the press on November 10 (prior to bankruptcy) and scheduled a sale for December 10.

(a) May Seller conduct the sale? See BC 362(a)(5).

(b) Debtor's trustee demands that Seller return the press so that Debtor can use it during the bankruptcy case. Must Seller do so? See BC 542(a); BC 363(c); BC 541(a)(1); United States v. Whiting Pools, Inc.

---

2. Most—but not all—courts agree that the contract rate is the appropriate rate at which interest accrues under BC 506(b); however, when the contract contains two rates, the higher of which comes into effect upon the debtor's default, the courts disagree about which rate is appropriate under BC 506(b). Compare, e.g., In re Skyler Ridge, 80 B.R. 500 (Bkrtcy.C.D.Cal.1987) (restrictions on higher rate of interest after default must come from state law, not Bankruptcy Code) with, e.g., In re W.S. Sheppley & Co., 62 B.R. 271 (Bkrtcy. N.D.Iowa 1986) (listing five equitable factors to be considered in determining whether the default rate applies) and In re DWS Investments, Inc., 121 B.R. 845 (Bkrtcy.C.D.Cal.1990) (rejecting *Skyler Ridge* and following *W.S. Sheppley*; finding default rate of 25% to be inequitable, if not illegal under California law).

462 U.S. 198, 103 S.Ct. 2309, 76 L.Ed.2d 515 (1983) (turnover order was properly issued against IRS, which had seized property subject to federal tax lien before commencement of Chapter 11 case).

(c) Suppose Seller is concerned that, if Debtor uses the press, the value of its collateral will decline? See BC 363(e).

SECTION 2. THE BANKRUPTCY TRUSTEE'S AVOIDING POWERS

Introductory Note. Generally speaking, the holder of a security interest will receive a secured claim in bankruptcy. As we discussed above, the holder of a secured claim is entitled to the value of its collateral (up to the amount of its claim) from the bankruptcy estate. However, not all security interests are valid in bankruptcy. The Bankruptcy Code affords the trustee (or DIP) the power to avoid (i.e., undo) certain otherwise valid prebankruptcy transfers, including transfers of security interests. This Section discusses the **avoiding powers** as they apply to security interests.

For the most part, BC 544–548 define the scope of the avoiding powers. BC 550 sets forth the consequence of avoidance: "to the extent that a transfer is avoided under [one of the enumerated sections of the Bankruptcy Code], the trustee may recover, for the benefit of the estate, the property transferred, or, if the court so orders, the value of such property." In other words, if the trustee succeeds in avoiding the transfer of a security interest, the trustee may recover the property transferred (i.e., the security interest) for the benefit of the estate. Any interest in property that the trustee recovers under BC 550 becomes property of the estate, see BC 541(a)(3), and is preserved automatically for the benefit of the estate. See BC 551. As a practical matter, this means that the avoided security interest no longer encumbers the collateral, and that whatever portion of the collateral it previously encumbered becomes available for distribution to creditors generally. Among those creditors will be the (former) secured party.

(A) Unperfected Security Interests: The Strong Arm of the Trustee

Problem 1. Debtor files a petition under Chapter 7 and has two assets: (i) a piece of equipment worth $100,000, subject to an unperfected security interest securing an $80,000 debt to Seller; and (ii) real estate worth $500,000, subject to a recorded mortgage securing a $400,000 debt to Bank. In addition, Debtor owes $300,000 to other (unsecured) creditors. How will the assets be distributed? See UCC 9–203(1); BC 541(a)(1); BC 544(a)(1); UCC 9–301(1)(b); UCC 9–302(1); BC 550(a); BC 541(a)(3); Notes on Bankruptcy Code Section 544(a), infra. (This Problem is identical to Problem 1 in Section 1, supra, except that Seller's security interest is unperfected.)

Problem 2. On June 1 Devon bought a set of living-room furniture from Cellar Department Store and executed a security agreement, covering the furniture, to secure payment of the price. Cellar did not file a financing statement. On July 1 Devon went into bankruptcy. What are the rights of Cellar and the trustee?

Problem 3. On June 1 Dramco purchased pharmaceutical equipment from Supplier. Supplier, who retained a security interest to secure payment of the price, filed a financing statement on June 9. In the interim, on June 7, Dramco filed a bankruptcy petition.

(a) What are the rights of Supplier and the trustee? See BC 544(a)(1); BC 546(b); UCC 9–301(2).

(b) Did Supplier violate the automatic stay? See BC 362(b)(3).

Problem 4. Consider the facts of Problem 5 in Chapter 13, Section 1, supra: Bank took a security interest in D's equipment and filed a financing statement in only one of the two required offices; having seen the financing statement, Lender extended secured credit to D and immediately perfected its security interest in D's equipment by filing in both offices.

D enters bankruptcy owing Bank $20,000 and Lender $50,000. The equipment is worth $45,000. Is either or both of the security interests avoidable? If so, how is the value of the collateral to be allocated? See BC 544(a); UCC 9–301(1)(b); BC 550; BC 551; UCC 9–401(2).

Notes on Bankruptcy Code Section 544(a)

(1) **The Operation of BC 544(a).** The assets that will be available for distribution in the bankruptcy case are referred to as "property of the estate." Under BC 541(a)(1), property of the estate includes "all legal or equitable interests of the debtor in property as of the commencement of the case." When the bankruptcy case in Problem 1 was commenced, Debtor was the owner of the equipment, but its ownership interest was encumbered by Seller's security interest. As you know, Seller's failure to file or otherwise "perfect" its security interest does not impair Seller's rights to the collateral against Debtor. See UCC 9–203(1)(a). Hence, at first blush, it would appear that the property of Debtor's estate would not include Seller's unperfected security interest, which would be effective in bankruptcy.

The bad news for Seller is BC 544(a). This section derives from section 70(c) the old Bankruptcy Act of 1898, which sometimes was called the "strong-arm" clause because of the formidable powers it conferred on the bankruptcy trustee. BC 544(a)(1) affords to the trustee, as of the commencement of the case, the rights and powers of a creditor that extends credit to the debtor at the time of the commencement of the case, and that obtains, at that time and with respect to that credit, a judicial lien on all property on which a creditor on a simple contract could have obtained a judicial lien, whether or not such a creditor exists. In other words, BC 544(a)(1) asks us to *imagine* that a specified type of creditor has obtained a "judicial lien" on the property; it affords to the trustee the rights of that *hypothetical* lien creditor.

What is a "judicial lien"? Fortunately, the Bankruptcy Code gives us a definition that is short and relatively clear. The long list of definitions in BC 101 includes paragraph (36): " 'judicial lien' means lien obtained by judgment, levy, sequestration, or other legal or equitable process or proceeding." For personal property, the most significant illustration is a "lien obtained by ... levy," e.g., seizure of the property by a sheriff under a writ of execution. Thus, if an imaginary levy, on an imaginary judgment of unlimited amount, would have established a lien in favor of an imaginary creditor, the rights and powers that the lien would have afforded to the imaginary creditor are taken over by the very real trustee in bankruptcy.

What are those rights and powers? Under a broad reading of the Commerce Clause of the Constitution, Congress might have established unified national rules on the relative rights of lien creditors and holders of security interests. However, Congress has not done so: the basic rules must be derived from state law. You are familiar with the applicable state law; it is UCC 9–301(1)(b), in the form enacted by the relevant state. Under UCC 9–301(1)(b), at the "commencement of the [bankruptcy] case"—i.e., the filing of the bankruptcy petition—would a judgment creditor of Debtor who obtained an execution lien on the equipment have acquired rights superior to Seller's unperfected security interest? If so, then the trustee likewise will do so and render Seller unsecured.

(2) The Policy Behind BC 544(a). Why does the Bankruptcy Code invalidate certain otherwise valid security interests in bankruptcy? Consider the following explanations:

BC 544(a)(1) Mirrors the Nonbankruptcy Result. Outside of bankruptcy, who would have been entitled to the value of Debtor's equipment? Although Seller retained a security interest effective against Debtor, Seller was not guaranteed "first dibs" on the equipment. Any creditor or group of creditors that acquired a judicial lien on the equipment before Seller perfected its security interest would have taken priority over Seller. In the nonbankruptcy race to this asset, Seller was leading, but had not yet won when bankruptcy occurred. When the ultimate nonbankruptcy outcome has yet to be determined, BC 544 has the effect of creating a "tie": Seller and the competing, unsecured creditors share equally in the value of the equipment. For a fuller explication of this argument, see T. Jackson, The Logic and Limits of Bankruptcy Law 70–75 (1986).

A variation on this argument is as follows: Traditionally, upon the commencement of a bankruptcy proceeding at the behest of creditors (i.e., an **involuntary bankruptcy**), a trustee took possession of the debtor's assets; the creditors represented by the trustee thereby acquired a lien on the debtor's property. Although most bankruptcy petitions now are filed by debtors rather than creditors (i.e., most bankruptcies are **voluntary**), the result should be the same: a judicial officer has taken control over the debtor's property and the creditors (or their representative) thereby should acquire a lien. Like any other lien that arises through the judicial process or through the exercise of a collective creditors' remedy, the lien that arises on bankruptcy should take priority over an unperfected security interest. See UCC 9–301(1)(b); UCC 9–301(3).

BC 544(a)(1) Reflects a Bankruptcy Policy Against Secret Liens. Although phrased in general terms, the primary use of the strong-arm power historically has been the avoidance of unperfected security interests and other secret liens. As a normative matter, one might argue that bankruptcy distribution *should* mirror nonbankruptcy distribution; however, as a descriptive matter, BC 544(a) changes the distribution. Bankruptcy calls off the race to the assets. When the bankruptcy petition is filed, the secured party has an enforceable interest in the collateral; unsecured creditors do not. The secured party has won the race. BC 544(a) deprives the secured party of its victory because it has come at the expense of unsecured creditors, who may have been prejudiced by the secret lien. See McCoid, Bankruptcy, the Avoiding Powers, and Unperfected Security Interests, 59 Am. Bankr. L.J. 175 (1985).

(B) THE TRUSTEE'S POWER TO AVOID PREFERENCES

Note on Preference Law

Under nonbankruptcy law, each creditor is entitled to take all legal steps to be paid. If the debtor's assets do not suffice to pay all creditors, some creditors will succeed in obtaining payment; others will remain unpaid. The amount a particular creditor receives is likely to depend upon the leverage it enjoys. A trade creditor may threaten to withhold future supplies or services unless it is paid for past credit extensions. A secured creditor may threaten to repossess collateral unless it is paid. Collecting one's claims through persuasion or through the judicial process is perfectly appropriate conduct under nonbankruptcy law. Using unencumbered assets to pay some creditors rather than others typically does not violate any nonbankruptcy principle.

Consider the following scenario: Debtor is hopelessly insolvent, having incurred substantial trade debt as well as bank debt. Debtor has one remaining asset of value—a checking account containing $27,-128.50. Debtor withdraws $25,000 and gives it to *C*, a favored creditor, in satisfaction of *C*'s $25,000 claim. Although other, unpaid creditors may be chagrined to discover that *C* has beaten them to the assets, this fact alone is insufficient to enable them to cry "foul"; the other creditors ordinarily will have no right to deprive *C* of its payment.

Bankruptcy calls off the nonbankruptcy race to the assets. After bankruptcy has begun, payment of one creditor's claim at the expense of another creditor would violate the bankruptcy principle of pro rata distribution. Add to the foregoing scenario the additional fact that, immediately after paying $25,000 to *C*, Debtor files a bankruptcy petition. As before, *C* is overwhelmed with joy. Because Debtor preferred to pay *C* (for whatever reason or mix of reasons), *C* has been made whole. The other, unpaid creditors are not merely chagrined; they are outraged. Why, they ask, should *C* be paid in full when they receive a pittance? Had bankruptcy been filed 24 hours earlier, *C* would be sharing equally with them.

Preference law addresses prebankruptcy transfers that have the result of affording a particular creditor more than its pro rata share. BC 547 enables the bankruptcy trustee to avoid certain of these preferential transfers. Under BC 550, "the trustee may recover, for the benefit of the estate, the property transferred, or, if the court so orders, the value of [the] property." In the example, unless *C* has a defense to the preference action, see BC 547(c) (discussed infra), *C* would be required to return the property to the estate. *C*'s claim would be restored, and *C* would share pro rata with other holders of unsecured claims. See BC 502(h).

Traditional preference jurisprudence suggests that preference law is designed to promote equality of distribution among unsecured creditors: "the preference provisions facilitate the prime bankruptcy policy of equality of distribution among creditors of the debtor." H.R. Rep. No. 595, 95th Cong., 1st Sess. 177–78 (1977), reprinted in 1978 U.S.C.C.A.N. 5963, 6138. Without preference law, unsecured creditors would share pro rata in whatever property the debtor has when it enters bankruptcy. The pro rata shares would be based upon the actual size of the claims at the time of the commencement of the bankruptcy case. Avoiding preferential transfers puts the preferred creditor in the same position as the other creditors, who have not been preferred; all will share pro rata in the debtor's bankruptcy estate, which is enhanced by the preference recovery. Preference law thereby blunts the advantage that certain creditors otherwise would enjoy. It prevents some creditors from retaining payments and other transfers of property that otherwise would have been more widely shared.

Some argue that preference law ought to (and, at least to some extent, actually does) do more than protect the bankruptcy rule of pro rata sharing. They assert that preference law should deter creditors from obtaining payment whenever the debtor is approaching bankruptcy. In their view, preference law should be (and largely is) directed to "opt-out behavior"—acts by which creditors seek to remove themselves from an impending collective proceeding (bankruptcy) by "gun-jumping" and, in doing so, reduce the value of the property that is available for all creditors. See, e.g., T. Jackson, The Logic and Limits of Bankruptcy Law 123–138 (1986); Baird, Avoiding Powers Under the Bankruptcy Code, in The Williamsburg Conference on Bankruptcy 305 (1988).

The injurious effects of taking a preference are clearest when the creditor removes real estate or goods prior to bankruptcy. Loss, for example, of a printer's presses may diminish the value of the printer's business by an amount greater than the value of the presses themselves. A complete printing business worth, say, $1,000,000 may be worth only $500,000 without the presses, even though the presses would fetch only $250,000 if sold separately. When a preferred creditor receives cash, however, the detrimental effects on the value of the assets available for distribution to creditors are considerably smaller.

As we shall see, preference law in fact does not distinguish among events (including payments) on the basis of their detrimental effect on the total return to creditors. Indeed, the repossession and sale of collateral—an event that is likely to be particularly destructive to the going concern value of the debtor's business—often will not constitute a preference. In contrast, the delayed filing of a financing statement—an event whose principal consequence is distributional—often will result in the secured party losing its collateral and becoming unsecured in bankruptcy.

BC 547(b) describes those prebankruptcy transfers that the trustee may avoid as preferences. Subsection (c) excepts from avoidance certain otherwise preferential transfers. The following Problems address "eve of bankruptcy" transfers.

Problem 5. On June 1 Debtor borrowed $12,000 from Firstbank and repaid the debt when due on September 1. On October 1 Debtor filed a bankruptcy petition. May the trustee recover the payment from Firstbank? See BC 547(b). (For now, do not worry about the exceptions in subsection (c).)

Problem 6. What result in Problem 5 if on September 1, instead of paying Firstbank, Debtor granted Firstbank a perfected security interest in a piece of equipment worth in excess of $12,000? Has there been a prebankruptcy "transfer" to Firstbank? See BC 101(54).

To answer the foregoing Problems, one must read BC 547 carefully. Has there been a "transfer of an interest of the debtor in property"? Is each of the other elements of BC 547(b) met? Observe that many of the terms used in BC 547(b) are defined in BC 101, among them "transfer," "debt," "creditor," and "insolvent." BC 547(g) imposes upon the trustee the burden of proving each element of BC 547(b). BC 547(f) gives the trustee a bit of help: For purposes of BC 547, the debtor is presumed to have been insolvent on and during the 90 days immediately preceding the filing of the bankruptcy petition.[1]

---

1. Under Federal Rule of Evidence 301, "a presumption imposes on the party against whom it is directed [in Problems 5 and 6, Firstbank] the burden of going forward with evidence to rebut or meet the presumption, but does not shift to such party the burden of proof in the sense of the risk of nonpersuasion, which remains throughout the trial upon the party on whom it was originally cast [in Problems 5

The most difficult element of BC 547(b) to comprehend is subsection (b)(5). This complex language is designed to capture only those transfers that have a preferential effect, i.e., that enable a creditor to receive more than its pro rata share of the property of the estate. BC 547(b)(5) requires one to compare (a) what the creditor would receive if (i) the transfer is allowed to stand and (ii) the creditor receives a distribution on any remaining claim in the bankruptcy, with (b) what the creditor would have received in a Chapter 7 case if the transfer had not been made.

Recall that Chapter 7 of the Bankruptcy Code provides for liquidation of the debtor's property and pro rata distribution of the proceeds to holders of unsecured claims. Suppose that, had the payment to Firstbank not been made, liquidation would have given general creditors (including Firstbank) 50 cents on the dollar. The prebankruptcy transfer in Problem 5 enabled Firstbank to receive more than 50 cents on the dollar. Thus the requirement of subsection (b)(5) is satisfied. Would the same be true for the transfer of the security interest in Problem 6? How much would Firstbank receive if the transfer is not avoided? How much would Firstbank have received without the transfer in a Chapter 7 case? (Remember that holders of unavoided secured claims are entitled to receive the value of their collateral; general unsecured claims share pro rata in the unencumbered assets.)

Problem 7. On August 1 Debtor borrowed $12,000 from Firstbank and secured the loan with a piece of equipment worth in excess of that amount. Firstbank filed a financing statement covering the equipment shortly before the security agreement was signed. On October 1 Debtor filed a bankruptcy petition. May the trustee avoid the transfer of the security interest? Was there a transfer on account of an antecedent debt? See also BC 547(c)(1). What difference, if any, would it make if Firstbank took the security interest with knowledge that Debtor was insolvent?

Problem 8. What result in Problem 7 if Debtor repaid the debt when due on September 1? Did the payment enable Firstbank to receive more than it would have received had the payment not been made and Firstbank received a Chapter 7 distribution? See BC 547(b)(5); BC 547(c)(1); BC 547(a)(2); Note (1) on Prepetition Payments to Secured Parties, infra.

Problem 9. To alleviate Debtor's "cash flow" problem, Firstbank made a 90–day unsecured loan in the amount of $12,000 to Debtor on June 1. Debtor made no payment until September 20, when Debtor paid Firstbank only $8,000. The balance remained unpaid on October 1, when Debtor filed a bankruptcy petition. May the trustee recover the $8,000 payment?

and 6, the trustee]." Nevertheless, the debtor's solvency is an issue in preference litigation only infrequently.

Problem 10. On June 1 Debtor borrowed $12,000 from Firstbank and secured the loan with a piece of equipment worth only $7,000. Firstbank filed a financing statement covering the equipment shortly before the security agreement was signed. Debtor repaid the entire debt when due on August 1. On October 1 Debtor filed a bankruptcy petition. May the trustee recover the payment from Firstbank? See Note (1) on Prepetition Payments to Secured Parties, infra.

Problem 11. What result in Problem 10 if Debtor repaid only $5,000 when the debt was due? For purposes of BC 547(b) does it matter whether the $5,000 payment is applied to the $5,000 unsecured portion of Firstbank's claim or to the $7,000 secured portion? See BC 547(b)(2); BC 547(c)(1); BC 547(a)(2); Note (1) on Prepetition Payments to Secured Parties, infra.

Problem 12. On June 1 Firstbank made a one-year, unsecured installment loan in the amount of $12,000 to Debtor. Debtor was obligated to repay $1,000 in principal plus accrued interest on the first day of each month. Debtor made timely payments in July, August, and September. Debtor filed a bankruptcy petition on October 1. May the trustee recover the three payments? See BC 547(c)(2); Note (2) on Prepetition Payments to Secured Parties, infra.

Notes on Prepetition Payments to Secured Parties

(1) Allocating Payments Between the Secured and Unsecured Portions of Claims. BC 547 does not permit the trustee to avoid every prepetition payment to creditors. Rather, the trustee may avoid and recover only those payments that have the effect of enabling the creditor to receive more than it would have received in a Chapter 7 case had the transfer not been made. See BC 547(b)(5).

Whether a prepetition transfer will meet the test in 547(b)(5) may depend on whether, and the extent to which, the creditor's claim is secured. Payments to unsecured creditors almost invariably meet the test and are potentially preferential. An unsecured creditor who is permitted to keep a prepetition transfer receives 100 cents on the dollar for each dollar paid. Unless the creditor would have received 100 cents on the dollar in a Chapter 7 distribution (i.e., unless the bankruptcy debtor is solvent), the creditor always will do better by having received payment of even a portion of its claim prepetition.

On the other hand, perfected secured creditors are entitled to receive the value of their collateral from the bankruptcy estate. Theoretically, then, the claim of a fully-secured creditor (i.e., one whose claim is less than or equal to the value of its collateral) will be paid in full from the bankruptcy. Accordingly, it appears that prepetition payments to fully-secured creditors do not enable them to receive more than they would have received had no payment been made and had they received a Chapter 7 distribution. BC 547(c)(1) is consistent with this approach: to the extent that a fully-secured creditor is paid, the creditor has given "new value" to the debtor; i.e., the value of its collateral is freed up for application to the payment of unsecured claims.[2]

What about a payment to a creditor who, but for the payment, would have held two claims—one secured and one unsecured? This is the case presented by Problems 10 and 11. Problem 10 is the easier of the two. Did the payment meet the test in BC 547(b)(5)? Even if so, didn't Firstbank give "new value" in exchange for the payment?

Problem 11 is a bit trickier. *In theory*, whether the $5,000 payment is treated as a payment of the secured portion of the claim or the unsecured portion should make no difference; the amount of Firstbank's secured claim can be adjusted to make sure that it receives no more than it would have received in a Chapter 7 case had the transfer not been made. Thus, the payment could be treated as if it were a payment on account of the secured portion of the claim. If so, the payment would be unavoidable; Firstbank would retain the payment and hold a $7,000 bankruptcy claim secured by $2,000 in collateral. Alternatively, the payment could be treated as if it were on account of the unsecured portion of the claim. If so, then the payment would be avoidable; after recovery, Firstbank would hold a $12,000 claim secured by $7,000 of collateral.

As you might have realized, the theory and the practice diverge. Neither Firstbank nor the trustee can be expected to be indifferent about whether Firstbank must return the $5,000 prepetition payment, even though under either scenario Firstbank ultimately would receive $7,000 plus a distribution on a $5,000 unsecured claim. "Ultimately"— there's the rub! To fully appreciate the import of the word, see Note on Relief from the Automatic Stay, Section 1, supra. Given the Supreme Court's decision in *Timbers of Inwood Forest* (discussed in the Note on Relief, supra), Firstbank would be likely to choose to keep the $5,000 prepetition payment so that the funds can generate income while the bankruptcy case is pending. Conversely, the trustee probably would choose to treat the payment as a preference, so that the estate could recover the funds and enjoy the use of $5,000 interest-free. (Recall from Section 1, supra, that postpetition interest on unsecured claims is not allowable.)

The reported preference cases generally treat prebankruptcy payments on partially secured claims as having been applied first to the unsecured portion. See, e.g., Drabkin v. A.I. Credit Corp., 800 F.2d 1153 (D.C.Cir.1986); Barash v. Public Finance Corp., 658 F.2d 504 (7th Cir.1981); In re Paris Industries Corp., 130 B.R. 1 (Bkrtcy.D.Me.1991) This approach, which treats Firstbank as having received payment of

2. There is, however, a line of cases holding that for purposes of BC 547(b)(5) the collateral should be valued as of the date of the filing of the bankruptcy petition. Thus, if payments are made to a secured party whose collateral is declining in value, the payments may be preferential even though the value of the collateral exceeded the debt at the time the payments were made. See, e.g., In re Paris Industries Corp., 130 B.R. 1 (Bkrtcy. D.Me. 1991).

its $5,000 unsecured claim on August 1, is consistent with the position Firstbank probably would have taken had bankruptcy not been filed. (Suppose that, after paying Firstbank $5,000, Debtor had not entered bankruptcy. Instead, Firstbank repossessed the collateral and sold it for $7,000. Would Firstbank have applied only $2,000 to the debt and remitted the balance to Debtor or a junior lienor?) Under these cases, the payment to Firstbank in Problem 11 would be avoidable: Firstbank would be compelled to return $5,000 to the estate in exchange for a correspondingly larger secured claim.

(2) **"Ordinary Course" Payments.** BC 547(c)(2) contains an exception for certain "ordinary course" payments. As originally enacted, the exception shielded only those payments that were made within 45 days after the debt was incurred. The 1984 amendments to the Bankruptcy Code eliminated the 45–day limitation.

As originally written, the exception was of little use to secured parties; secured debts typically are outstanding for more than 45 days. Since the elimination of the 45–day limitation, secured parties who received timely payments on **term loans** and **revolvers** have argued that these payments qualify for BC 547(c)(2) even though they otherwise would be preferential. Some reported decisions took the view that the exception applies only to payments of trade debt and other current expenses, not to payment of longer-term debt. See, e.g., In re CHG International, Inc., 897 F.2d 1479 (9th Cir.1990) (timely interest payments on term loans held not to qualify for BC 547(c)(2)). But in Union Bank v. Wolas, 112 S.Ct. 527 (1991), the Supreme Court held that "payments on long-term debt, as well as payments on short-term debt, may qualify for the ordinary course of business exception." Unfortunately, the Court gave absolutely no guidance on the more difficult issues raised by BC 547(c)(2): What does it mean for a debt to be "incurred by the debtor in the ordinary course of business"? What are the characteristics of a payment "made in the ordinary course of business" and "according to ordinary business terms"?

(3) **Payments on Revolving Credit Facilities.** Assume the following, rather typical scenario: Bank agrees to make available to Debtor up to $1 million of credit under an unsecured, revolving **line of credit**. During the 90 days prior to bankruptcy, Debtor makes fifteen borrowings of $100,000 each and makes eleven payments of $100,000 each. Debtor's trustee seeks to recover $1,100,000 from Bank under BC 547(b). Bank is outraged, arguing that it never would have made all the advances unless Debtor had made the repayments; indeed, it took great care to insure that no more than $1 million was outstanding at any given time. Moreover, even though Bank has received $1,100,000 during the preference period, Bank has in effect replenished the bankruptcy estate by $1,500,000; accordingly, Bank argues that it should have no liability whatsoever under BC 547.

BC 547(c)(4) affords some relief to Bank under these circumstances, but sometimes not as much relief as Bank would wish. Under that section, the trustee may not avoid a transfer to the extent that, *after* the transfer, the creditor gave "new value" to or for the benefit of the debtor. Thus, to the extent that Bank can show that, after any one or more of the eleven payments, Bank extended additional credit to Debtor, Bank can use that additional credit to nullify the preference. It is as if Bank returned the preference to the estate. Bank may not, however, aggregate the new value and offset it against the aggregate amount of preferential payments. As in comedy, so with preferences: timing is everything!

Problem 13. On January 2 Creditor loaned $10,000 to Debtor. On that date, to secure the loan, Debtor executed a security agreement granting Creditor a security interest in a bulldozer that Debtor had previously purchased. Creditor did not file a financing statement until September 1. On September 2, Debtor filed a petition in bankruptcy. The trustee seeks to avoid the transfer of the security interest as a preference. What result? See BC 547(b); BC 547(e)(2); BC 547(e)(1); UCC 9–301(1)(b); UCC 9–203(1); Notes on Delayed Perfection, infra.

Notes on Delayed Perfection

(1) The Application of BC 547 to Delayed Perfection. Problem 13 poses this question: *When* did Debtor transfer an interest in property to Creditor? Clearly, Debtor transferred a property interest to Creditor that was fully effective as between these two parties on January 2. See UCC 9–203(1). If the date of transfer is January 2 for purposes of BC 547(b), then the transfer cannot be avoided for two reasons: the transfer was made for a concurrent, rather than for an "antecedent," debt, and the transfer was made more than 90 days before the filing of the bankruptcy petition. On the other hand, if we deem that the transfer was not made until the financing statement was filed on September 1, then the "antecedent debt" requirement is satisfied and the remaining elements for avoidance probably can be established with ease.

BC 547(e) provides the way to date the transfer. The structure of subsection (e), unhappily, forces us to start with paragraph (2) and then back-track to paragraph (1). Paragraph (2) tells us that "a transfer is *made* ... (B) at the time such transfer is *perfected*." (The exception in paragraph (2)(A) will be considered later.)

Having learned that the time when the transfer is "perfected" is the key, we move back to paragraph (1)(B), where we learn that a transfer of personal property is perfected "when a creditor on a simple contract cannot acquire a judicial lien that is superior to the interest of the transferee." We explored the meaning of "judicial lien" above in

connection with the "strong-arm" clause, BC 544(a). For present purposes we may assume that the quoted language of BC 547(e)(1)(B) refers,
inter alia, to the execution lien obtained by the holder of an ordinary
contract claim.

Thus, instead of giving us the *answer*, the preference rules of BC
547 provide us with a hypothetical *question*. (In this regard, BC 547 is
like the "strong-arm" clause of BC 544(a), discussed in Section 2(A)
above.) In the setting of Problem 13, the question is this: *Suppose* a
judgment creditor of Debtor had acquired a judicial lien on the bulldozer during the period leading up to September 1—the date on which
Creditor filed the financing statement: Would this lien have been (in
the language of BC 547(e)(1)(B)) "superior to the interest of the transferee" of the security interest? (Don't despair—we're almost home!)

Where can we find the answer to this hypothetical question that
the Bankruptcy Code has thrown at us? Not in the Bankruptcy Code
or in any other federal law! As in dealing with the strong-arm clause
we must look to state law—more precisely, to the Uniform Commercial
Code as enacted in the relevant jurisdiction. Prior to the filing on
September 1, could a creditor with a judicial lien have trumped the
security interest? UCC 9–301(1)(b) and 9–302(1) provide a clear answer.

Those who have followed the trail this far should be able to answer
these questions: (1) In Problem 13, when was the transfer of the
security interest made? (2) Can the trustee avoid the transfer? (If you
have any doubts about how to answer these questions, keep going
through the steps outlined above until the system is perfectly clear.
You will soon need to use this system in solving problems that are
much more difficult than Problem 13. As you probably now realize,
Problem 13 was a sitting duck.)

(2) The Policy Behind Applying BC 547 to Delayed Perfection.
On what basis might one argue in support of the result that the
transfer occurred upon the filing of the financing statement and not
earlier, when the transfer took effect between the debtor and the
secured party? Some have argued that delayed perfection is a "false
preference"—that preference law has been used to address indirectly an
entirely different problem: that of secret liens that operate to the
prejudice of unsecured creditors. See, e.g., R. Jordan & W. Warren,
Bankruptcy 475–76 (2d ed. 1989) ("There is no true preference ...
because the transfer of the security interest ... was not on account of
an antecedent debt. Rather, the problem of delayed perfection is the
evil of the secret lien."). Of course, this argument assumes that
bankruptcy law expresses a policy against secret liens that is more
stringent than the anti-secret-lien policies of Article 9 and other state
laws.

Others have argued that delayed perfection, at least in some cases,
implicates the "anti-last-minute-grab" policy that they believe underlies

preference law. As we have seen, a security interest that is unperfected at the time a bankruptcy petition is filed ordinarily will be avoidable by the bankruptcy trustee. A secured party who believes bankruptcy is imminent may review the loan files and discover that the security interest is unperfected. (Perhaps no financing statement ever was filed; perhaps the financing statement contained errors than made it ineffective; perhaps an effective financing statement became ineffective because the debtor's name or the location of the collateral changed). By perfecting before bankruptcy, an unperfected secured party improves its position relative to other creditors. Had no filing occurred, the secured party might have been rendered unsecured through the trustee's exercise of the strong-arm clause. By filing, the secured party immunizes the security interest from attack under BC 544(a). Is this not precisely the kind of opt-out behavior that preference law addresses? See Jackson, The Logic and Limits of Bankruptcy Law 138–46 (1986).

In assessing the explanations for using preference law to avoid security interests whose perfection has been delayed, one should consider the fact that the principal effect of delayed perfection is likely to be distributional. Delayed perfection is unlikely to affect the total value of the debtor's business; rather, it affects how the value of the business will be distributed among the creditors.

———

In working the following Problems, don't lose sight of the requirements of BC 547(b). In particular, be sure you can identify when the transfer was made and when the debt was incurred. You should also consider whether the outcome that the statute appears to compel is consistent with the policies that underlie preference law.

Problem 14. What result in Problem 13 if Creditor filed the financing statement on May 9? Would the result change if Debtor was a wholly-owned subsidiary of Creditor? See BC 547(c)(4); BC 101(31); BC 101(2).

Problem 15. What result in Problem 13 if Creditor filed the financing statement on January 9 and Debtor filed for bankruptcy on March 1? See BC 547(e)(2)(A). What is the reason for this refinement? Consider the technical attacks that might be made on security arrangements when there is a gap of one day (or one hour) between the loan and the filing.

Problem 16. What result in the immediately preceding Problem if Creditor mailed the financing statement to the filing office on January 5, but the financing statement did not arrive there until January 13? See BC 547(e)(2)(B); UCC 9–403(1). Can Creditor prevail under BC 547(c)(1)? See In re Arnett, 731 F.2d 358 (6th Cir.1984) (applicability of

BC 547(c)(1) to delayed perfection of security interests is limited to 10 days).

Problem 17. What result in Problem 13 if Creditor filed the financing statement on January 9 but bankruptcy fell on January 8? Note that, as in the other Problems in this set, Debtor owned the bulldozer before getting the loan from Creditor. Don't forget that the trustee is not confined to a preference attack but also enjoys the rights and powers of a judicial lien creditor under BC 544.

A quick glance at BC 546(b) may suggest that this provision gives effect to the postbankruptcy filing. Note, however, that BC 546(b) gives effect to such filing only when state law "permits perfection of an interest in property to be effective against an entity that acquires rights in such property *before* the date of such perfection." Does state law under the Uniform Commercial Code protect a non-purchase-money security interest from a levy that occurs before perfection? See UCC 9–301(1)(b).

What does the answer to this Problem suggest concerning the advisability of relying on the 10–day period in BC 547(e)(2)(A)?

Problem 18. Would the result in Problem 17 change if Creditor financed Debtor's purchase of a bulldozer that was delivered to Debtor on January 2? Recall Problem 3 above. What is the relationship between the answer to Problem 3 and the powers of the trustee in bankruptcy? See BC 544(a); UCC 9–301(2); BC 546(b); BC 362(b)(3).

Problem 19. On June 1 Bank made a $100,000 term loan to Debtor. The loan was secured by "all Debtor's existing and after-acquired equipment." On June 1 Debtor owned equipment worth $90,000. Bank "prefiled" a financing statement on May 28. On July 1 Debtor purchased and took delivery of an additional piece of equipment worth $12,000. Debtor files a bankruptcy petition on August 1. The trustee seeks to avoid Bank's security interest in all the equipment. What result? See BC 547(e)(2)(A); BC 547(e)(3).

Problem 20. What result in Problem 19 if Bank and Debtor agreed that Debtor would use $12,000 of the loan proceeds to acquire an additional piece of equipment, and the proceeds were so used? See BC 547(c)(3).

Observe that the exception in BC 547(c)(3) applies only if the security interest is perfected on or before ten days after the debtor receives possession of the property. A large number of states have enacted nonuniform amendments extending the ten-day periods in UCC 9–301(2) and 9–312(4) to twenty days. Does a creditor who perfects a purchase money security interest within the twenty-day period but outside the ten-day period escape preference liability? The cases are in disagreement. Compare In re Hamilton, 892 F.2d 1230 (5th Cir.1990) (10–day rule of BC 547(c)(3) controls; PMSI perfected on 11th day was avoidable), with In re Busenlehner, 918 F.2d 928 (11th Cir.1990) (where state law provided that perfection of security interest in automobile relates back to time of creation, transfer was "perfected" under BC

547(e)(1)(B) on the date of creation, notwithstanding that act of perfection did not occur until 13th day), cert. denied, 111 S.Ct. 2251 (1991).

Problem 21. On June 1 Creditor loaned $10,000 to Debtor and Debtor delivered to Creditor negotiable bonds in Company A worth $10,000. On September 1, at a time when Creditor knew Debtor to be insolvent, Creditor delivered the bonds in Company A to Debtor in exchange for bonds of the same value in Company B. The bonds of both companies continue to sell at par. On September 2 Debtor went into bankruptcy.

(a) May the trustee avoid the transfer of the Company B bonds as a preference? See BC 547(a)(2) & (c)(1).

(b) What difference, if any, would it make if on June 1 Debtor delivered bonds of Company A worth only $6,000, and on September 1 Debtor exchanged these bonds for bonds of Company B worth $10,000? What result if on September 1, instead of the exchange, Debtor delivered additional bonds in Company A worth $4,000?

(c) Would it make any practical difference if the bonds of Company A delivered on June 1 were worth $15,000 and these bonds were exchanged on September 1 for bonds in Company B worth $20,000? See BC 547(b)(5).

Problem 22. On June 1 C loaned $100,000 to D and at the same time, to secure the loan, D delivered to C stock in Company X worth $50,000. In July Company X announced the development of a new product; by the middle of August the stock had increased in value by 50 percent. On August 30 D entered bankruptcy. The trustee argues that C received a $25,000 preference. Do you agree? Was there more than one "transfer of an interest of the debtor in property"? If so, when did each transfer occur?

It is generally assumed that increases in the value of collateral shortly before bankruptcy do not constitute "transfers" giving rise to a voidable preferences. Is the conclusion that the "transfer" of the stock occurred on June 1 consistent with policies underlying the bankruptcy rules governing preferences? Does it violate the "anti-last-minute-grab" policy? Does it violate the "equality of distribution" policy? The latter arguably is directed toward recapturing transfers of the debtor's property that diminish the assets available for distribution to unsecured creditors. When, as in this Problem, the increase in the value of collateral is due to market forces, is the bankruptcy estate diminished within the preference period? See BC 101(5); BC 547(b)(5). As we shall see in Section 3 below, the answer is less clear-cut when the increase in value results from labor or other inputs supplied by the debtor.

SECTION 3. REPLENISHMENT AND ADDITIONS; THE "FLOATING LIEN"

———

(A) The "Floating Lien" Under the Uniform Commercial Code

———

Notes on the Development of the Law Governing the "Floating Lien"

(1) Security Interests in After–Acquired Property. In this Section we meet problems presented by the transitory character of some types of collateral. Before addressing the bankruptcy treatment of security interests in these types of collateral, we take a closer look at the nonbankruptcy treatment.

A merchant may think of inventory as a fairly constant unit. Inventory at the beginning of the year is compared with inventory at the end without regard to whether any of the items is the same. But, from another point of view, there is a fairly constant process of exhaustion and replenishment, as inventory flows in through a merchant's stockroom and out over the counter or through the shipping room. Consider a hardware store: Each day there may be hundreds of sales (large and small) that convert inventory into cash or accounts. Situations of this kind arise in a wide range of retail, wholesale, and manufacturing settings. Accounts receivable go through a similar cycle: Each time a debtor contracts to sell goods or provide services, a new account is generated; upon payment the account disappears.

Attempts to finance the flow of inventory and accounts have generated serious and important legal problems, both within and outside of bankruptcy. Underlying the legal doctrines are conflicting values: the utility of added operating capital versus the desire to hold assets in reserve for last-ditch financing and to meet the claims of unsecured creditors.

For better or for worse, Article 9 has eliminated most of the nonbankruptcy legal problems for those who take a "floating lien" on inventory and accounts. But life was not always so easy for inventory or accounts financers. As the following excerpt suggests, until the adoption of the Code, secured parties found it difficult (and sometimes impossible) to maintain an effective security interest in collateral that was subject to a constant process of exhaustion and replenishment.

"At common law property to be created or acquired in the future could not be transferred or encumbered prior to the creation or acquisition of the property. Illustrative of the constant striving to make future assets available for present purposes was the attempt of common-law lawyers to add to the conveyances of the day the words: 'Quae quovismodo in futurum habere potero.' But, as Littleton says, these words were 'void in law.' The reasoning upon which the rule was based was simple—'A man cannot grant or charge that which he hath not.' This infallible bit of syllogistic logic received its first breakdown in the famous case of Grantham v. Hawley, [K.B.1616] the parent of the fictitious doctrine of 'potential existence.' Briefly stated, this principle permits the sale or encumbrance of future personal property having a so-called potential existence arising from the fact that the processes of creation have already begun, with the limitation that the basic substance which yields the increment must be owned by the vendor or mortgagor. Typical examples would be crops already planted upon land of the vendor, or wool to be grown upon sheep owned by the mortgagor. As stated by the court: 'A parson may grant all the tithewool that he shall have in ... a year; yet perhaps he shall have none; but a man cannot grant all the wool, that shall grow upon his sheep that he shall buy hereafter; for there he hath it neither actually nor potentially.' The doctrine rests, of course, upon the fiction that a man may own something that is not yet in existence but which in the normal course of events will come into being; thereby the rule that 'a man cannot grant or charge that which he has not' is left inviolate. The refusal of the court to recognize the fictional quality of its rule prevented the satisfaction of more than a very small portion of the need for which the rule itself had been evolved. Grantham v. Hawley left us with little more than we had before; but it was the first step toward the solution of a problem, vexing even today—the problem of how to utilize future property for present credit.

The civil law had a simple device—a 'mortgage on an estate to come.' Therefore, it is not surprising that one of our greatest students of the civil law, Justice Joseph Story, should have been the first on the bench to establish the precedent in Anglo–American law that future property may be presently charged. The case is, of course, Mitchell v. Winslow [1843]. Cutlery manufacturers, in order to bolster their business, borrowed money, and as security therefor executed a deed of trust conveying the manufacturing plant 'together with all tools and machinery ... which we may at any time purchase for four years from this date, and also all the stock which we may manufacture or purchase during said four years.' The instrument was recorded and upon default the mortgagee took possession of some after-acquired tools. The mortgagor went into bankruptcy and thereupon perplexing questions arose. Did the trust instrument create a lien upon the after-acquired property? If it did, was such a lien good against creditors? The bankruptcy judge certified these two questions to Circuit Judge Story, and Story answered in the affirmative, stating that although it was true that future property could not be presently charged at common law, nevertheless equity would enforce the agreement. He pointed out that equity precedents existed, if authority was necessary, in the analogous cases of contracts to assign future claims and expectancies. His conclusion is the most frequently quoted passage in the field.

'It seems to me a clear result of all of the authorities, that wherever the parties, by their contract, intended to create a positive lien or charge, either upon real or upon personal property, whether then owned by the assignor or contractor, or not, or if personal property, whether it is then in esse or not, it attaches in equity as a lien or charge upon the particular property, as soon as the assignor or contractor acquires a title thereto, against the latter, and all persons asserting a claim thereto, under him, either voluntarily, or with notice, or in bankruptcy.'

"Mitchell v. Winslow was paralleled about twenty years later [1862] by the celebrated English case of Holroyd v. Marshall, decided by the House of Lords. Here, a deed of trust covering the machinery in a mill and containing the provision that 'all machinery, implements, and things which, during the continuance of this security, shall be ... placed in or about the said mill ... shall ... be subject to the trusts ...,' was executed and recorded. Subsequently, a creditor of the mortgagor levied on after-acquired property. The mortgagor then defaulted and possession of the property was taken by the mortgagees in disregard of the creditor's levy. The House of Lords upheld the claim of the mortgagees on the ground that 'immediately on the new machinery and effects being fixed or placed in the mill, they became subject to the operation of the contract, and passed in equity to the mortgagees' ....

"With such excellent precedents on the books it would have appeared that the problem was solved and that after-acquired property could be mortgaged and that recording of the mortgaging instrument would constitute notice to would-be purchasers and creditors. Yet, three years after Story's excellent decision the Massachusetts Supreme Judicial Court held [1845] that a recorded mortgage on after-acquired property (stock of goods) was not effective against creditors. The action was at law and left open the possibility that the result might be otherwise in equity. But then came Moody v. Wright [Mass.1847]. Here, the owner of a tanning business executed a purchase-money mortgage which included an after-acquired property clause. The mortgage was recorded. Subsequently an assignee for benefit of creditors was appointed under a state 'insolvent law' and the mortgagee contested his right to the after-acquired property. The court held that the assignee prevailed on the ground that nothing had been done by either the mortgagor or the mortgagee to perfect the lien attempted to be created by the after-acquired property clause."

"A cursory examination of the cases from a doctrinaire standpoint without consideration of the varying economic factors involved would reveal that some jurisdictions follow Story's Equity rule, others accept the Massachusetts doctrine, a few follow both, and still others have set up independent principles." Cohen & Gerber, The After–Acquired Property Clause, 87 U.Pa.L.Rev. 635, 635–38 (1939).

Notwithstanding "[t]he widespread nineteenth century prejudice against the floating charge," . . . "[i]n almost every state it was possible before the Code for the borrower to give a lien on everything he held or would have. ... Article [9], in expressly validating the floating charge, merely recognizes an existing state of things." UCC 9–204, Comment 2. Article 9 replaced the different rules described in the foregoing excerpt with a uniform legal regime that expressly validates the "floating lien." UCC 9–204(1) provides explicitly that "a security agreement may provide that any or all obligations covered by the security agreement are to be secured by after-acquired collateral." The filing of a single financing statement indicating the "type" of collateral is sufficient to perfect a security interest in inventory and accounts that the debtor acquires after the filing. See Chapter 11, Section 2, supra. Article 9 "decisively rejects" the "inarticulate premise" underlying pre-UCC hostility to the floating lien—that "a commercial borrower should not be allowed to encumber all his assets present and future, and that for the protection not only of the borrower but of his other creditors a cushion of free assets should be preserved"—"not on the ground that it was wrong in policy but on the ground that it was not effective." UCC 9–204, Comment 2.

(2) The Privilege to Dissipate Proceeds; Benedict v. Ratner. When a lender takes a security interest in inventory and accounts that are subject to rapid turnover and liquidation into cash, what is the borrower to do with the proceeds? When relatively few sales of expensive items are involved (e.g., automobiles and grand pianos), it would be feasible for the borrower to bring the proceeds to the lender and obtain fresh loans when new inventory is needed. But when individual transactions are small and numerous, both borrower and lender may prefer to cut short the paperwork involved in numerous repayments and fresh loans and allow the debtor to collect the proceeds and use them to run the business, replenish its stock of inventory, and generate new accounts.

Prior to Article 9, the arrangement just described was in grave danger. The operative rule was associated with Justice Brandeis and his opinion in the famous case of Benedict v. Ratner, 268 U.S. 353, 45 S.Ct. 566, 69 L.Ed. 991 (1925). The Hub Carpet Company, doing business in New York, obtained loans from Ratner and assigned to Ratner all its accounts, present and future. Under the arrangement (unless Ratner demanded otherwise) Hub Carpet "was not required to apply any of the collections to the repayment of Ratner's loan. It was not required to replace accounts collected by other collateral of equal value. ... It was at liberty to use the proceeds of all accounts collected as it might see fit." Hub Carpet went into bankruptcy, and Benedict, the trustee, challenged the validity of Ratner's security interest in all the accounts—including accounts that had not yet been paid by Hub's customers, and for which Ratner was, of course, now demanding direct payment.

The Supreme Court unanimously held that the attempted assignment was void as to all the accounts—including those in which no payment had been made to the debtor, Hub Carpet. Justice Brandeis's opinion, heavily documented by citations of New York authority, stated:

Under the law of New York a transfer of property as security which reserves to the transferor the right to dispose of the same, or to apply the proceeds thereof, for his own uses is, as to creditors, fraudulent in law and void. ...

[The rule rests] upon a lack of ownership because of dominion reserved. It does not raise a presumption of fraud. It imputes fraud conclusively because of the reservation of dominion inconsistent with the effective disposition of title and creation of a lien.

268 U.S. at 360–63, 45 S.Ct. at 568–69, 69 L.Ed. at 997–99.

Although the Supreme Court, in a bankruptcy setting, stated that it was applying the law of New York, the "doctrine of Benedict v. Ratner" was, with a few exceptions, followed in other states. 1 Gilmore, Security §§ 8.2—8.6, at 253–74. A substantial body of case law developed over how much "policing" by the lender of the debtor's accounting for proceeds was necessary to avoid the conclusion that the creditor lacked a property interest in the collateral that was effective against judicial liens obtained by competing creditors.

One of Article 9's steps toward facilitating the "floating lien" was a frontal attack on the doctrine of Benedict v. Ratner. UCC 9–205 provides: "A security interest is not invalid or fraudulent against creditors by reason of liberty in the debtor ... to use, commingle or dispose of proceeds, or by reason of the failure of the secured party to require the debtor to account for proceeds or replace collateral." Since the opinion in Benedict v. Ratner purported to apply state law, the revision of state law by UCC 9–205 should be effective to change the result.

For second thoughts about the Code's validation of the floating lien and its rejection of the rule of Benedict v. Ratner, see Gilmore, The Good Faith Purchase Idea and the Uniform Commercial Code: Confessions of a Repentant Draftsman, 15 Ga.L.Rev. 605, 621–27 (1981).

Note on Article 9's Treatment of Proceeds in Bankruptcy

A secured party who finances "revolving" types of collateral, such as inventory and accounts, is likely to be especially concerned about acquiring and maintaining a perfected security interest in the proceeds of the collateral. The Code's protection of security interests in proceeds extends beyond UCC 9–205 and its repeal of the rule of Benedict v. Ratner. As we saw in Chapter 11, Section 4, supra, UCC 9–306 gives a secured party a continuing security interest in the "identifiable proceeds" of its collateral, including the proceeds of the proceeds.

Ultimately, a secured party's proceeds are likely to find their way into a "deposit account." See UCC 9–105(1)(e) (definition of "deposit account"). Courts typically permit a secured party to use tracing rules to identify proceeds that have been commingled with non-proceeds in a deposit account. As the *Farmers Bank* case and related materials in Chapter 11, Section 4, supra, suggest, the process of tracing may be difficult.

Recognizing that this difficulty may be particularly acute when the debtor has filed bankruptcy (the likelihood of keeping complete and accurate financial records often seems correlated with a debtor's wealth), the drafters of Article 9 included a special provision that fixes the extent of a security interest in proceeds "[i]n the event of insolvency proceedings instituted by or against a debtor[.]" UCC 9–306(4). See also UCC 1–201(22) (definition of "insolvency proceedings").

Under UCC 9–306(4), in insolvency proceedings (including bankruptcy cases) "a secured party with a perfected security interest in proceeds has a perfected security interest only in" the four categories of proceeds set forth in UCC 9–306(4)(a)–(d). The first three categories are unremarkable. Together they consist of all identifiable proceeds other than "cash and deposit accounts of the debtor in which proceeds have been commingled with other funds."[1] UCC 9–306(4)(d). The fourth category, UCC 9–306(4)(d), which is designed to alleviate some of the burdens of tracing cash proceeds, presents a variety of interpretive problems.

Before parsing the text of the section, it is useful to understand its thrust. Under the normal proceeds rule of UCC 9–306(2), a secured party seeking to claim a security interest in commingled funds must utilize a tracing rule. The secured party not only must trace the proceeds into the fund (e.g., by showing that a check representing proceeds of inventory was deposited into a particular bank account) but also must show that the proceeds remain in the account notwithstanding subsequent withdrawals. See *Farmers Bank*, Chapter 11, Section 4, supra.

Compare UCC 9–306(4)(d): Once the secured party shows that "proceeds have been commingled with other funds" in a particular deposit account, the secured party apparently acquires a perfected security interest in the *entire* account, subject to the depositary bank's right of set-off (see UCC 9–306(4)(d)(i)) and the limitation in subsection (d)(ii).[2]

The qualifying deposit account having been identified, subsection (d)(ii) limits the security interest in the account to "the *amount* of any cash proceeds *received*" (*not* the amount deposited) by the debtor during the ten-day period prior to bankruptcy that cannot otherwise be

---

1. In determining whether "a separate deposit account contain[s] *only* proceeds," within the meaning of UCC 9–306(4)(a), may the secured party use the "lowest intermediate balance" rule? See First Nat'l Bank of Amarillo v. Martin, 48 B.R. 317 (N.D.Tex.1985) (application of UCC 9–306(4)(a) is limited to those accounts specifically created and used for the deposit of proceeds).

2. Authorities are divided on whether the phrase "subject to any right to set-off" in UCC 9–306(4)(d)(i) elevates rights of set-off that applicable law otherwise would subordinate to a security interest in the deposit account or whether it means only that the security interest remains subject to any setoff right that otherwise would be senior.

accounted for. The idea seems to be that, unless the cash proceeds received within the ten days prior to bankruptcy went somewhere else (e.g., they were paid to the secured party or were deposited in a separate deposit account containing only proceeds; see subparagraphs (d)(ii)(I) and (II)), they are conclusively presumed to have been deposited in the commingled account. (Perhaps they went to pay unsecured creditors; if so, one might argue that allowing the secured party to claim an interest in the deposit account to that extent is "only fair.")

Although the general thrust of UCC 9–306(4)(d) is relatively clear, the particular language chosen by the drafters is subject to differing interpretations. By way of example, consider the deceptively simple phrase, "deposit accounts ... in which proceeds have been commingled with other funds." What does it mean? All accounts in which proceeds have *ever*, in the history of the world, been commingled? Those accounts in which proceeds have often or customarily been mingled— but not necessarily during the final ten-day period? Those accounts in which at least some proceeds, no matter how small, were deposited during the final ten-day period? Those accounts in which proceeds that were received within the ten-day period were also deposited during that period? Those accounts to which proceeds can be traced (by whatever methods deemed appropriate) and which (based on those methods) actually contain proceeds on the date an insolvency proceeding is commenced? To date, no definitive answer has developed.

How do secured parties fare under UCC 9–306(4)(d)? That depends on when a debtor receives cash proceeds and what the debtor does with them. Suppose, for example, that the debtor deposited $100,000 in proceeds into a deposit account containing $500,000 in non-proceeds eleven days before bankruptcy. Suppose further that no withdrawals followed. Outside bankruptcy, under UCC 9–306(2) and (3), the secured party would be able to claim a perfected security interest in $100,000 from the account.

In bankruptcy, however, the secured party could claim a perfected security interest in the *entire* account, but only in "an *amount* not greater than the amount of any cash proceeds received by the debtor within ten days before the institution of the insolvency proceedings." If the debtor received only $100 in cash proceeds during the ten-day period, then the security interest in the account would be limited to $100; to the extent the $100 was paid to the secured party or falls within UCC 9–306(3)(a), (b), or (c), the secured party would be permitted to claim even less. But if the debtor received $400,000 in cash proceeds during the ten days, then the security interest in the account might be as large as $400,000 (again, the actual amount might be less once UCC 9–306(4)(d)(ii)(I) and (II) are applied).

To summarize, under the foregoing facts, a secured party would be able to claim $100,000 from the account had bankruptcy not intervened. Once a bankruptcy case commences, the secured party might be able to claim substantially more than $100,000 or as little as $0. One's initial response to this situation might be that it probably all evens out in the end. Secured parties often are repeat players; UCC 9–306(4)(d) may mean a bonus in one bankruptcy and a penalty in another. In any event, the secured party may avoid the application of UCC 9–306(4)(d) by taking steps to insure that the debtor does not commingle the proceeds of its collateral.

Even if, in the aggregate, secured parties are neither helped nor hindered by UCC 9–306(4), the section is problematic. What justifies having two different tracing rules—one for debtors in insolvency proceedings and another for other debtors? If the rule in UCC 9–306(4)(d) is easier to apply and yields fairer results, should not the drafters adopt it for all circumstances? On the other hand, if the "lowest intermediate balance" rule works well, why should its application be preempted in bankruptcy?

In any event, the preemption may not be effective. Suppose that, in the example above, application of UCC 9–306(4) results in the secured party's being able to enforce a security interest in an additional $300,000 in the deposit account. Has there been a "transfer of an interest of the debtor in property ... on account of an antecedent debt"? If so, does the transfer fall within BC 547(b)? See also BC 547(c)(5), discussed in Section 3(B), infra. The trustee also might attack the security interest under BC 545, which permits the avoidance of certain "statutory liens" (as defined in BC 101(53)). Whether the trustee would succeed on either of these grounds is unclear.

(B) AFTER-ACQUIRED COLLATERAL AND VOIDABLE PREFERENCES

Notes on the "Floating Lien" in Bankruptcy

(1) **The Problem.** Outside of bankruptcy, a security interest in incoming collateral covered by an appropriate security agreement and financing statement will be senior to a judicial lien acquired by the debtor's other creditors. UCC 9–201; UCC 9–301(1)(b); Chapter 11, Section 2, supra. Does this mean that new collateral acquired shortly before bankruptcy will be immune from attack as a preference under BC 547?

In the floating lien, the loan is made, the security agreement is signed, and a financing statement is filed at the beginning of the arrangement. When bankruptcy falls, the debtor may hold little or none of the original collateral. The trustee's attack will center on collateral that the debtor acquired within the 90 days before bankruptcy: *When* was this collateral transferred to the creditor? If the transfer occurred only when the debtor acquired the collateral, then the trustee can assert that the new collateral was transferred to the creditor for an "antecedent debt." If so, the trustee is well on the way to proving a voidable preference under BC 547(b).

BC 547 contains special provisions that address potential preference attacks on floating liens. One of those provisions, BC 547(c)(5), is quite complicated and may be understood more easily in its historical context.

(2) The Historical Background of BC 547(c)(5). BC 547(c)(5) derives from a proposal put forward in a report of a committee of the National Bankruptcy Conference [3] known as the "Gilmore Committee." National Bankruptcy Conference, Report of the Committee on Coordination of the Bankruptcy Act and the Uniform Commercial Code (1970) ("Gilmore Committee Report"), reprinted in H.R. Rep. No. 595, 95th Cong., 1st Sess. 204 (1977), reprinted in 1978 U.S.C.C.A.N. 5963, 6164. The report explains:

"In 1966 it appeared that security interests in personal property under Article 9 of the Uniform Commercial Code were in serious jeopardy in bankruptcy proceedings. At the time when the revision of [Bankruptcy Act] § 60 which was enacted in 1950 was being prepared, the drafting of Article 9 was in its early stages. The § 60 revision, of necessity, was written in what we may call pre-Code language; it reflected the pre-Code structure of personal property security law.... If the structure of security law had remained as it was, the compromise represented by the 1950 revision of § 60 would have worked perfectly well. With the general enactment of the Code, including Article 9, the situation was radically altered. Arguably, Article 9 contained little or nothing that was revolutionary, or even novel, as a matter of substance. The Article 9 terminology, on the other hand, represented a sharp break with the past. The difficulty of making the two statutes (§ 60 and Article 9) mesh or track with each other was immediately apparent. During the 1950's and continuing into the 1960's a quantitatively impressive amount of literature was devoted to the problem in the law reviews, specialized journals, and treatises. A considerable part of this literature seemed dedicated to the proposition that almost any Article 9 security interest could be turned into a voidable preference under § 60. The Article 9 security interest in after-acquired property (including inventory and receivables) was thought to be particularly vulnerable .... This literature, it is true, was, to start with, merely literature; there were no cases. Nevertheless, the holders of Article 9 security interests became understandably concerned about their fate." 1978 U.S.C.C.A.N. at 6167.

In the late 1960's two circuit court opinions addressing the avoidability of security interests in after-acquired property gave comfort to secured lenders. The Ninth Circuit proclaimed the most sweeping theory for protecting the floating lien in DuBay v. Williams, 417 F.2d 1277 (9th Cir.1969). The *DuBay* opinion reached its result in two steps. The first step invoked the strong protection that Article 9 gives security

---

3. The National Bankruptcy Conference is a nonprofit, unincorporated organization devoted to the improvement of bankruptcy law. Its members include bankruptcy judges, law professors, and practicing attorneys who specialize in bankruptcy and creditors' rights law.

arrangements that include a claim of after-acquired property. Under UCC 9–301(1)(b), once the secured party files a financing statement, the lien acquired by any creditor that levies on any property that might thereafter be acquired by the debtor would be junior to the perfected security interest. The second step integrated this rule of state law with section 60(a)(2) of the Bankruptcy Act, which governed the time when transfers shall be "deemed" to be made:

> a transfer of property . . . shall be deemed to have been made or suffered at the time when it became so far perfected that no subsequent lien upon such property obtainable by legal or equitable proceedings on a simple contract could become superior to the rights of the transferee.

As the Ninth Circuit applied the "levying-creditor" test, incoming property would be "deemed" to have been transferred to the debtor when it became immune from levy—the date of filing—even though at that time the debtor had no interest in the property; indeed, at the time of filing the property may not even have been in existence. (An admirer of "Man of La Mancha" has referred to this as the "impossible deem"; and Professor Countryman roundly condemned this approach as "The Abracadabra, or the Transfer Occurred before it Occurred, Theory." Countryman, Code Security Interests in Bankruptcy, 75 Com. L.J. 269, 277 (1970).) The sweeping theory of the *DuBay* case was as comforting to secured lenders as it was disturbing to others, for it set no controls over enlarging the protection given to the holder of the floating lien (at the expense of suppliers and other unsecured creditors) when the debtor purchased additional property shortly before bankruptcy.

During the same year, the Seventh Circuit applied preference law to a floating lien on accounts. In Grain Merchants of Indiana, Inc. v. Union Bank & Savings Co., 408 F.2d 209 (7th Cir.1969), cert. denied, 396 U.S. 827, 90 S.Ct. 75, 24 L.Ed.2d 78 (1969), the court used three alternative theories to immunize the floating lien from preference attack. First, using an analysis similar to that of the Ninth Circuit in *DuBay*, the court found that accounts that were generated during the preference period had been transferred to the secured party a year before bankruptcy, when the financing statement was filed.

Second, the court suggested that one ought to consider all accounts, existing and future, as a single entity that was given as collateral at the outset of the transaction, in a contemporaneous exchange for the loan. It quoted Professor Hogan with favor:

> The secured creditor's interest is in the stream of accounts flowing through the debtor's business, not in any specific accounts. As with the Heraclitean river, although the accounts in the stream constantly change, we can say it is the same stream.

Hogan, Games Lawyers Play with the Bankruptcy Preference Challenge to Accounts and Inventory Financing, 53 Cornell L. Rev. 553, 560 (1968). Although the "entity theory" is inconsistent with UCC 9–

203(1), the court observed that a contrary result—one that would immunize only those accounts that were taken in exchange for a new loan—would jeopardize the flexible methods of financing that UCC 9–205 made possible by abrogating the requirement that a secured party must maintain dominion over collateral in order to protect its security interest.

The court's third theory was grounded in the long-standing "substitution of collateral" doctrine: a prebankruptcy transfer of collateral is not preferential when the collateral is taken in exchange for a release of other collateral. (Problem 21, Section 2, supra, examines this doctrine.) Unlike other courts that had applied the doctrine, the Seventh Circuit found that "the newly arising accounts receivable may be considered as having been taken in exchange for the release of rights in earlier accounts and for a present consideration," without inquiring into either the timing of the supposed exchange (i.e., whether the release was substantially contemporaneous with or subsequent to the transfer of new collateral) or the relative value of the two items of collateral (i.e., whether the released collateral was worth at least as much as the new collateral). Rather, the court found that because the secured party no longer was required to assume dominion over individual accounts, "it is no longer appropriate to apply strict timing or value rules so long as at all relevant times the total pool of collateral, as here, exceeded the total debt."

The alternative grounds set forth in *Grain Merchants* were encouraging to lenders contemplating a floating lien but left nagging doubts as to the precise circumstances for protection. And, of course, one could not have safely predicted the approach of other federal courts. Nevertheless, as the Gilmore Committee reported, as of 1970:

> [T]he secured creditor bar (if there is such a thing) [was] basking happily in the warm glow of Judge Hufstedler's opinion in *DuBay* and, we may assume, [had] lost any interest it may once have had in reform of the Bankruptcy Act.
>
> What may be called the politics of the project of revising § 60 have thus come full circle during the past few years [ending in 1970]. What started out as a rescue mission for secured creditors may end up as a rescue mission for unsecured creditors.

1978 U.S.C.C.A.N. at 6168.

(3) The Bankruptcy Code and the Floating Lien. Drawing on the work of the Gilmore Committee, the drafters of the Bankruptcy Code addressed directly the problems raised by the floating lien, including the problem of determining the time when a transfer of a security interest in after-acquired property occurs. Section 547(e)(3) states that, for purposes of determining whether a transfer of a debtor's interest constitutes a preference, "a transfer is not made until the debtor has acquired rights in the property transferred." The avowed purpose of this provision was to overrule *DuBay* and *Grain Merchants*. S. Rep.

No. 989, 95th Cong., 2d Sess. 89 (1978), reprinted in 1978 U.S.C.C.A.N. 5787, 5875. Certainly, this language leaves no room for either the "Heraclitean river" or "Abracadabra" ("impossible deem") approach.

The rule of BC 547(e)(3) is far from the end of the story. To meet the practical difficulties of maintaining security interests in inventory and receivables, the Bankruptcy Code provides an important exception from the general preference rules of 547(b). That exception is BC 547(c)(5).

Please look at BC 547(c)(5) now. As you can see, the subsection is somewhat forbidding. Its language is easier to understand if one starts with a general idea of what the drafters were trying to accomplish. Their central idea was that the floating lien should be subject to attack only to the extent that the acquisition of additional collateral in the aggregate resulted in an improvement in the secured creditor's position during the 90–day period preceding bankruptcy. More specifically, BC 547(c)(5) focuses on whether the aggregate of preferential transfers of security interests caused a reduction in the secured party's unsecured claim (what the statute calls the "amount by which the debt secured by such security interest exceeded the value of all security interests for such debt"). BC 547(c)(5) does not take into account day-to-day fluctuations in collateral levels; rather, one measures the actual unsecured claim as of the date of the bankruptcy petition and compares it to the secured party's unsecured position at the start of the preference period.[4]

The language of BC 547(c)(5) is difficult to penetrate. The following Problems are designed to facilitate your understanding.

Problem 1. Debtor filed a Chapter 11 petition on March 31, 1992. At that time, Debtor owed $70,000 to Creditor. This debt was secured by a security interest in all Debtor's existing and after-acquired inventory, then valued at $75,000.

At the end of 1991, Debtor's inventory had a value of $75,000 and secured a debt of $70,000. During the first quarter of 1992, Debtor's entire inventory turned over completely; that is, all the inventory that Debtor held at the start of the year was sold.

(a) How much, if any, of the security interest in the $75,000 of new inventory constitutes a preference under BC 547(b)?

(b) How much, if any, of the security interest in the $75,000 of new inventory can the trustee avoid? See BC 547(c)(5). On the ninetieth day prior to bankruptcy, what was the "amount by which the debt ... *exceeded* the ... security interest[ ] ..."? Did subsequent transfers "cause[ ] a reduction" in that figure? Does the result surprise you?

4. In some cases, the secured party may not yet have extended any value to the debtor as of the start of the preference period. If so, then the secured party's actual unsecured claim as of the petition date must be compared to the secured party's unsecured position on the date on which new value was first given under the security agreement. See BC 547(c)(5)(B).

Problem 2. Debtor filed a Chapter 11 petition on March 31, 1992. At that time, Debtor owed $70,000 to Creditor. This debt was secured by a security interest in all Debtor's existing and after-acquired inventory. At the end of 1991, Debtor's inventory had a value of $55,000 and secured a debt of $70,000. During the first quarter of 1992, Debtor's entire inventory turned over completely. As of the time of the petition, Debtor's inventory is worth $60,000.

(a) How much, if any, of the security interest in the $60,000 in new inventory can the trustee avoid?

(b) What result in part (a) if Creditor was owed $65,000 at the time of the filing of the petition? Of what relevance, if any, are the facts surrounding the reduction in the amount of the debt? Suppose the $5,000 payment came from unencumbered funds? Suppose it represented proceeds from the sale of inventory? Would it make any difference if the payment was one of a series of monthly payments required under the terms of the credit agreement? See Notes on Prepetition Payments to Secured Parties, Section 2, supra.

Problem 3. Debtor filed a Chapter 11 petition on March 31, 1992. At that time, Debtor owed $70,000 to Creditor. This debt was secured by a security interest in all Debtor's existing and after-acquired inventory. At the end of 1991, Debtor's inventory had a value of $55,000 and secured a debt of $70,000. During the first quarter of 1992, Debtor was unable to sell any inventory, but because of market shifts the inventory was worth $60,000 at the time of the filing of the petition.

(a) How much, if any, of the security interest in the $60,000 in inventory can the trustee avoid? In what way, if any, does this Problem differ from Problem 2? Does this Problem implicate BC 547(c)(5)? If so, to what extent did "*transfers* to the transferee cause[ ] a reduction" in the unsecured portion of Creditor's claim?

(b) Would the result in part (a) change if, the day before bankruptcy, Debtor acquired some additional inventory worth $2,000?

Problem 4. Surf Advertising has a contract with Calvert Distillers, under which Calvert agreed to pay Surf $1,000 each month for two years, during which time Surf agreed to maintain certain advertising signs. Abrams made a loan to Surf and took a perfected security interest in Surf's rights under the unperformed contract with Calvert. During the 90 days prior to Surf's bankruptcy, Surf collected $3,000 from Calvert and paid those amounts to Abrams.

Did Abrams receive an avoidable preference? See BC 547(b); Rockmore v. Lehman, infra. Precisely what "transfer" would the trustee seek to avoid? How would the trustee distinguish this situation from that presented in Problem 3?

ROCKMORE v. LEHMAN [*]

United States Court of Appeals, Second Circuit, 1942.
129 F.2d 892.
Cert. denied, 317 U.S. 700, 63 S.Ct. 525, 87 L.Ed.2d 559 (1943).

[Proceedings were instituted for the reorganization of the Surf Advertising Corporation under Chapter X of the Bankruptcy Act. Abrams had advanced sums to Surf; in exchange, Surf assigned to Abrams Surf's rights to payment, still to be earned, under an existing contract to maintain advertising signs for Calvert Distillers Corporation. In an earlier opinion (here reversed on rehearing) the Court of Appeals had held that payment to Abrams of funds earned under these contracts constituted a preference.]

AUGUSTUS N. HAND, CIRCUIT JUDGE. ... In each of the cases before us, advances were made upon contracts whereby Surf in the first case and Fiegel Advertising Company in the second case were to furnish and maintain advertising signs for Calvert in return for which Calvert bound itself to pay fixed sums over a period of years for the furnishing and maintenance of the signs. The advances were not made upon a mere agreement to assign rights which might arise in the future and did not exist at the time contracts were made, but upon assignments of definite contractual obligations.

We are convinced that the New York Court of Appeals has differentiated assignments of existing contracts by way of pledge from agreements to assign rights that have not yet come into being, even as interests contingent upon counter-performance. The most recent decision is Kniffin v. State, 283 N.Y. 317, 28 N.E.2d 853, where a building contractor assigned his contract with the State of New York to a subcontractor as security for a pre-existing indebtedness, and then became bankrupt. The State made payments under the contract to the assignor, but the assignee was allowed to recover the amount of its claim in spite of the fact that the assignment embraced moneys "to become due" under the contract.

We cannot agree with appellant's contention that Section 60, sub. a, of the present Bankruptcy Act, 11 U.S.C.A. § 96, sub. a, affects our decision, and that there would be an unlawful preference as to any sums paid or payable after knowledge of insolvency. On the contrary we hold that the date of the assignments governed the imposition of the liens on any sums due from Calvert. This is because the contracts, and not the moneys accruing under them, were the subjects of the assignments. Section 60, sub. a, provides that: "a transfer shall be deemed to have been made at the time when it became so far perfected that no bona-fide purchaser from the debtor and no creditor could thereafter have acquired any rights in the property so transferred superior to the rights of the transferee therein." It has long been the New York law

[* Decided under the then-current version of the Bankruptcy Act of 1898.]

that such an assignment is good against a bona fide purchaser, even though the bona fide purchaser is the first to give notice to the obligor. The same thing is true of an execution creditor or a trustee in bankruptcy. ...

[The opinion also concluded that New York Lien Law § 230 did not require filing of the assignment.]

It follows from the foregoing that our former decision in this matter was erroneous and that the decision of the court below in both cases should have been affirmed.

Orders affirmed.

Problem 5. Suppose that, in order to perform the Calvert contract in Problem 4, Surf was required to hire Employee and purchase from Seller a piece of additional equipment. Surf's trustee makes the following argument: payments to Employee and Seller had the effect of exchanging Surf's unencumbered property for an increase in the value of Abrams's collateral, the Calvert account. Even if these payments were not transfers *to* a creditor (Abrams), they were transfers *for the benefit of a creditor* (Abrams) and thus potentially preferential under BC 547(b). See BC 547(b)(1). If the trustee can prove the other elements of BC 547(b), then BC 550(a)(1) enables the trustee to recover the property transferred (or its value) from "the entity for whose benefit such transfer was made." Thus, argues the trustee, Abrams is liable for payments made to Employee and Seller.

(a) Are you persuaded by the trustee's argument? As to the ability of the trustee to recover transfers that create preferences indirectly, see Note on Dean v. Davis, infra.

(b) Suppose Employee and Seller provided their services and goods to Surf on open credit and remained unpaid at the time of bankruptcy. Would the trustee's argument be stronger or weaker?

Problem 6. On June 1, Crystal Credit loaned $100,000 to the Dream Spinning Co. At the same time Dream granted Crystal a perfected security interest in bales of cotton then worth $60,000. The security interest also extended to after-acquired cotton and yarn. During June, July and August Dream processed this cotton into yarn. As a result of the processing, the yarn was worth $100,000 by August 30, when Dream went into bankruptcy. Can the trustee avoid Crystal's interest as a preference to the extent of the increase in value during the 90 days before bankruptcy? When did the "transfer" of the security interest in the yarn occur? See Note on "Prejudice of Other Creditors," infra.

Note on "Prejudice of Other Creditors"

At stake in Problems 4, 5, and 6 is nothing less than the continuing vitality of the leading case of Rockmore v. Lehman, supra. That decision rejected a trustee's attack on the secured party's receipt of amounts the debtor earned under a contract that had been assigned to the secured party, even though the debtor had earned those amounts by work performed shortly before bankruptcy.

Grappling with these Problems requires a bit of legislative history. As you know, the two-point test embodied in BC 547(c)(5) emerged from the work of the Gilmore Committee. The Gilmore Committee Report put a case where raw materials worth $10,000 are converted into finished products worth $20,000; the Gilmore Committee stated that under its proposal the $10,000 increase in value was not protected and would go to the trustee. It observed: "If the final holding in *Rockmore v. Lehman* [citation omitted] suggests the contrary conclusion, that holding is here overruled." 1978 U.S.C.C.A.N. at 6177–78.

This feature of the Gilmore Committee's recommendations encountered criticism. Professor Homer Kripke argued that any increase in the value of collateral due, e.g., to harvesting crops, completing work in progress, and sales of inventory, should redound to the benefit of the secured party "so long as it is not at the expense of other parties interested in the estate." H.R. Doc. No. 137, 93d Cong., 1st Sess. pt. 1, at 210 (1973) (quoting a letter from Professor Kripke to the Gilmore Committee). To implement this policy, Professor Kripke mentioned the formula used in Meinhard, Greeff & Co. v. Edens, 189 F.2d 792 (4th Cir.1951), which gave the secured creditor the entire value of the finished goods, less the costs expended in finishing them.

In response to this conflict in views, the provision that became BC 547(c)(5) was amended by inserting the qualifying phrase "and to the prejudice of other creditors holding unsecured claims." Does the meaning of this phrase become clear in the light of the legislative history? In Problem 6, what facts would show that Crystal's improvement in position resulted from "transfers to the transferee ... to the prejudice of other creditors holding unsecured claims"?

Could this provision jeopardize construction loans, crop loans, and other types of complex financing in which the secured party gives value before the debtor does the work that creates value in the collateral? Can (and should) the Bankruptcy Code be interpreted to avoid such dangers?

One interpretation that would give some comfort to secured parties would be to focus on the requirement that the improvement in position results from "transfers" that otherwise would be avoidable under BC 547(b). The line between an increase in the value of a given item of collateral (which does not constitute a "transfer") and an exchange of one item of collateral for another (which does) may be difficult to discern. Consider, for example, an account receivable. What happens when the debtor earns a right to payment by performing its contractual obligation? Like Rockmore v. Lehman, both BC 547(a)(3) and UCC 9–106 suggest that although the right to payment has increased in value, it is the same item of collateral. But under the pre–1972 version of UCC 9–106, only earned rights to payment were accounts; unearned rights to payment were a different type of collateral, "contract rights." Should nonbankruptcy law's characterization of the collateral determine whether a preference has occurred?

Note on *Dean v. Davis*

A favorite aphorism of many first-year law students is "One cannot do indirectly what one cannot do directly." In Dean v. Davis, 242 U.S. 438, 37 S.Ct. 130, 61 L.Ed. 419 (1917), the Supreme Court applied this principle to preference law under the Bankruptcy Act of 1898. Fearing that Bank would have him arrested for fraud, Debtor borrowed $1,600 from his father-in-law, Dean, and secured the debt with a mortgage on substantially all his property. Shortly thereafter an involuntary bankruptcy petition was filed against Debtor. The trustee sought to set aside the mortgage and was successful. The district court held the mortgage constituted a fraudulent conveyance; the court of appeals held it also was a voidable preference.

In affirming the district court, the Supreme Court (Brandeis, J.) rejected the preference attack as follows:

> The mortgage was not voidable as a preference under § 60b. Preference implies paying or securing a preexisting debt of the person preferred. The mortgage was given to secure Dean for a substantially contemporary advance. *The bank, not Dean, was preferred.* The use of Dean's money to accomplish this purpose could not convert the transaction into a preferring of Dean, although he knew of the debtor's insolvency. Mere circuity of arrangement will not save a transfer which effects a preference from being invalid as such. But a transfer to a third person is invalid under this section as a preference, only where that person was acting on behalf of the creditor ....

242 U.S. at 443, 37 S.Ct. at 131 (emphasis added).

Inasmuch as the trustee did not proceed against Bank, the court's observation that the Bank was preferred is dictum. The recodification of preference law in the Bankruptcy Code is consistent with the notion that an otherwise nonpreferential transfer to one person may result in a preference to a creditor who received the benefit of the transfer. Thus, BC 547(b)(1) refers to transfers "to *or for the benefit of* a creditor" and BC 550(a)(1) permits recovery of an avoided transfer from "the initial transferee of such transfer *or the entity for whose benefit the transfer was made.*"

A number of reported cases are consistent with this aspect of Dean v. Davis. See, e.g., In re Air Conditioning, Inc. of Stuart, 845 F.2d 293 (11th Cir.1988), cert. denied, 488 U.S. 993, 109 S.Ct. 557, 102 L.Ed.2d 584 (1988) (grant of security interest to issuer of letter of credit held preferential to beneficiary); In re Compton Corp., 831 F.2d 586 (5th Cir.

1987) (same), rehearing granted per curiam, 835 F.2d 584 (1988) (explaining what facts are to be considered on remand). A particularly interesting case is In re Prescott, 805 F.2d 719 (7th Cir.1986). In *Prescott,* transfers were made during the preference period to a partially secured senior creditor. Because the transfers had the effect of increasing the collateral available to a junior secured creditor (i.e., converting part of the unsecured portion of the claim into a secured claim), the court held that the transfers preferred the junior creditor.

Two other aspects of Dean v. Davis are also important. Although the dictum that Bank *was* preferred seems to have survived the enactment of the Bankruptcy Code, a highly controversial holding by the Seventh Circuit casts doubt on the continuing validity of the holding, that Dean *was not* preferred. In re V.N. Deprizio Construction Co., 874 F.2d 1186 (7th Cir.1989). *Deprizio* has been followed by other courts of appeals. See In re C–L Cartage Co., 899 F.2d 1490 (6th Cir.1990); In re Robinson Brothers Drilling Co., 892 F.2d 850 (10th Cir.1989). However, some lower courts were unpersuaded. See, e.g., In re Arundel Housing Components, Inc., 126 B.R. 216 (Bkrtcy. D.Md.1991) (*Deprizio* represents "an incorrect interpretation of the law whose application would subvert justice"); In re Performance Communications, Inc., 126 B.R. 473 (Bkrtcy.W.D.Pa.1991) (*Deprizio*'s analysis is "flawed"). The implications of the *Deprizio* case are beyond the scope of this book. Also beyond the scope of this book is whether Dean v. Davis continues as a part of the fraudulent conveyance law applicable in bankruptcy.

Note on Valuation of Collateral

As should be apparent by now, most of the issues we have discussed in this Chapter implicate issues of valuing the collateral. For example, one cannot work the two-point test of BC 547(c)(5) without valuing the collateral at each of the two points. Nor can one determine whether the debtor has any "equity" in the collateral for purposes of BC 362(d)(2) unless one knows the collateral's value.

Depending on the circumstances, appraisers apply different standards of valuation to any given piece of property. Among the most common are going-concern value (what the property is worth as part of an ongoing business; this standard requires that the total value of the business be allocated among its various assets), fair market value (what the property would yield at a sale by a willing seller to a willing buyer), and forced-sale (or quick liquidation) value (what would the property yield at an immediate sale by a seller who was compelled to sell).

The Bankruptcy Code does not define the applicable standard. Under BC 506(a), the value of a security interest in property "shall be determined in light of the purpose of the valuation and of the proposed disposition or use of such property, and in conjunction with any hearing on such disposition or use or on a plan affecting such creditor's interest." The legislative history suggests that courts will have to determine value on a case-by-case basis and that a valuation at one time for one purpose (e.g., adequate protection) would not be binding at a later time for another purpose (e.g., distribution). See S. Rep. No. 989, 95th Cong., 2d Sess. 68 (1978), reprinted in 1987 U.S.C.C.A.N. 5787, 5854; H.R. Rep. No. 595, 95th Cong., 1st Sess. 356 (1977), reprinted in 1978 U.S.C.C.A.N. 5963, 6312.

Detailed discussion of valuation issues is best left to the bankruptcy course. Among the articles discussing the issues are Cohen, "Value" Judgments: Accounts Receivable Financing and Voidable Preferences Under the New Bankruptcy Code, 66 Minn.L.Rev. 639 (1982); Queenan, Standards for Valuation of Security Interests in Chapter 11, 92 Com. L.J. 18 (1987); and Thomas, Valuation of Assets in Bankruptcy Proceedings: Emerging Issues, 51 Mont. L. Rev. 128 (1990).

Problem 7. On June 1, 1981, Castle Finance loaned $100,000 to Diggins Construction Company; Diggins executed an agreement granting Castle a security interest in "all of the construction equipment including bulldozers and other machinery, that Diggins now owns or may hereafter acquire." At the time of the agreement Diggins owned five bulldozers each worth $20,000. On June 9, Castle filed a financing statement, signed by Diggins, that referred to the collateral as "construction equipment."

On July 1 Diggins traded one of the bulldozers for a cement mixer that also was worth $20,000. On July 15 the construction business was slack, so Diggins sold two of its remaining four bulldozers for $40,000 and used these funds to pay workers and social security taxes. On August 1, Diggins received a $20,000 down payment from a new construction job and used this money to purchase a new $20,000 bulldozer.

On September 1 several creditors of Diggins threw Diggins into bankruptcy. Which assets of Diggins may Castle Finance claim against opposition by the trustee in bankruptcy? See Eisenberg, Bankruptcy Law in Perspective, 28 UCLA L. Rev. 953, 961–62 & n. 27 (1981) (discussing how BC 547(c)(5) distinguishes equipment from inventory and receivables).

References. For further illustrations of BC 547(c)(5) see Shanor, A New Deal for Secured Creditors in Bankruptcy, 28 Emory L.J. 587, 600–610 (1979). See also Justice, Secured Transactions—What Floats Can Be Sunk, 24 Vill.L.Rev. 867 (1979). For further analysis of the "floating lien" in bankruptcy see Breitowitz, Article 9 Security Interests as Voidable Preferences, 3 Cardozo L. Rev. 357 (1982); Breitowitz, Article 9 Security Interests as Voidable Preferences: Part II The Floating Lien, 4 Cardozo L. Rev. 1 (1982).

Note on Proceeds Arising After Bankruptcy

The filing of a bankruptcy petition does not necessarily coincide with the cessation of the debtor's business. Indeed, the debtor-in-possession may continue to operate the business in Chapter 11 unless the court orders otherwise. BC 1108. See also BC 721 (bankruptcy court may authorize Chapter 7 trustee to operate debtor's business).

In the course of operating the business, the DIP may acquire property that would be covered by an after-acquired property clause in a prepetition security agreement. Although the transfer of a security interest in property acquired postpetition ordinarily would not be avoidable under BC 547—the transfer would not have occurred *before* the date of the filing of the petition, see BC 547(b)(4)—a postpetition transfer of this kind might have the same effect as a voidable preference: the acquisition of additional collateral might improve the position of a secured creditor at the expense of other creditors.

BC 552 addresses this concern. The general rule, set forth in BC 552(a), is that property acquired by the bankruptcy estate after the commencement of the case is not subject to a security interest resulting from a prebankruptcy security agreement. In other words, BC 552(a) generally renders after-acquired property clauses ineffective as to property acquired after the commencement of a bankruptcy case.

Obviously, this rule is overbroad. It invalidates security interests not only in additional collateral but also in substitute collateral (e.g., an account that results from the postpetition sale of inventory collateral acquired by the debtor before bankruptcy). Subsection (b) cuts back on the general rule when a prepetition security agreement "extends to property of the debtor acquired before the commencement of the case and to proceeds, product, offspring, rents, or profits of such property." In that event, the security interest extends to such proceeds, etc., acquired by the estate after the commencement of the bankruptcy case to the extent provided by the security agreement and by applicable nonbankruptcy law. In other words, the filing of the bankruptcy petition does not invalidate a prepetition security agreement insofar as the secured party claims proceeds of prepetition collateral that the debtor acquires postpetition.

BC 552(b) uses two important terms that the Bankruptcy Code leaves undefined: "extends to" and "proceeds." As discussed in Chapter 11, Section 4, supra, Article 9 gives every secured party a security interest in "proceeds" (as defined in UCC 9–306(1)), even if the security agreement does not provide for one. See UCC 9–306(2). The legislative history makes clear that a security agreement that is silent nevertheless "extends to" proceeds, as the term is used in BC 552(b). See H.R.Rep. No. 595, 95th Cong., 1st Sess. 377 (1977), reprinted in 1978 U.S.C.C.A.N. 5963, 6333.

What constitutes "proceeds" within the meaning of BC 552(b)? In In re Bumper Sales, Inc., 907 F.2d 1430 (4th Cir.1990), the secured party claimed a security interest in inventory acquired by the debtor-in-possession during the bankruptcy case. The parties stipulated that the postpetition inventory was produced entirely with the proceeds of prepetition inventory. The Fourth Circuit held that "the UCC's definition and treatment of proceeds applies to Section 552 of the Bankruptcy Code" and covers "second generation proceeds" that are traceable to the prepetition collateral (e.g., inventory acquired with the proceeds of accounts generated postpetition from the sale of prepetition inventory).

The legislative history suggests that the term "proceeds" in BC 552 may encompass even more than the same term encompasses under the Uniform Commercial Code. "The term 'proceeds' is not limited to the technical definition of that term in the U.C.C., but covers any property into which property subject to the security interest is converted." H.R.Rep. No. 595, 95th Cong., 1st Sess. 377 (1977). However, the Fourth Circuit "believe[s] that Section 552(b)'s express reference to 'nonbankruptcy law' should take priority over a vague and isolated piece of legislative history. We also note that the judicial creation of a definition for 'proceeds,' broader post-petition than pre-petition, would produce arbitrary and potentially inequitable results."

BC 552(b) contains an important exception to the protection it affords to proceeds arising postpetition: the court may cut back on the security interest "based on the equities of the case." According to the legislative history, in the course of considering the equities, "the court may evaluate any expenditures by the estate relating to proceeds and any related improvement in position of the secured party." 124 Cong. Rec. 32400 (1978) (statement of Rep. Edwards; 124 Cong.Rec. 34000 (1978) (statement of Sen. DeConcini). See, e.g., In re Kain, 86 B.R. 506 (Bkrtcy.W.D.Mich.1988) (proceeds of sale postpetition offspring of prepetition livestock collateral "should be reduced by reasonable postpetition expenses validly and demonstrably paid or incurred by the Debtors to raise, preserve, enhance or market the livestock.") You should realize that the problem addressed by the exception to BC 552(b) also arises under BC 547(c)(5). (The former deals with postpetition activity; the latter, prepetition.)

SECTION 4. EFFECT OF BUYER'S BANKRUPTCY ON SELLER'S RIGHT TO RECLAIM GOODS

(1) **Introductory Note.** In Chapter 9, Sections 2 and 3, supra, we discussed the right of a seller to reclaim goods delivered to a buyer. You may recall that the Uniform Commercial Code contemplates two different rights to reclaim. The credit seller's right to reclaim goods arises when the seller discovers that the buyer has received goods on credit while insolvent. See UCC 2–702(2). The cash seller's right to reclaim goods arises when payment was due and demanded, but not received, upon delivery of the goods. See UCC 2–507(2).

Sellers commonly seek to exercise rights of reclamation when the buyer has entered bankruptcy. The buyer's entry into bankruptcy is the event most likely to cause the credit seller to "discover[ ] that the buyer has received goods on credit while insolvent." UCC 2–702(2). The cash seller may have delivered goods in exchange for a check that subsequently was dishonored, perhaps because the bank on which it was drawn had learned of the buyer's bankruptcy. See UCC 2–511(3) (payment by check is conditional and is defeated, as between the parties, by dishonor); BC 542(b), (c) (requiring those who owe debts to bankruptcy debtor and who have actual notice or knowledge of bankruptcy case to make payment to bankruptcy trustee).

(2) Reclamation Based on Buyer's Insolvency (UCC 2–702). Under the old Bankruptcy Act, attempts by sellers who had delivered goods on credit to reclaim the goods from the estate of a bankrupt buyer were subject to serious objections by the trustee. The trustee would argue that the right to reclaim under UCC 2–702 when "the seller discovers that the buyer has received goods on credit while insolvent" was inconsistent with various provisions of the Bankruptcy Act, particularly section 67c(1)(A), which invalidated as against a trustee "every statutory lien which first becomes effective upon the insolvency of the debtor."

As we saw in Sections 1 and 2, supra, in bankruptcy, the difference between recognizing an *in rem* remedy against specific goods and an *in personam* claim for damages against the bankruptcy estate is crucial. Successful reclamation is likely to make the seller whole (or close to it), even though it precludes the seller from asserting a damage claim against the estate. See UCC 2–702(3). In contrast, when a trustee avoids a seller's reclamation rights, the goods remain in the estate, and their value ordinarily will be distributed to unsecured creditors pro rata according to the size of their claims.

Suppose, for example, that UCC 2–702 affords Seller the right to reclaim $25,000 of goods delivered to Buyer before bankruptcy. If reclamation is successful, Seller will recover the goods, which Seller ordinarily can resell for about $25,000. But if the trustee can avoid the reclamation right, Seller would receive instead an unsecured claim against the estate. As the holder of an unsecured claim, Seller would share with all the other unsecured creditors in the proceeds of the sale of the goods. If, for example, unsecured creditors receive only ten percent of their claims, Seller would receive only $2,500. Although the balance of Seller's claim against Buyer ($22,500) would remain unpaid, Seller almost never will be entitled to recover any of this amount. To the extent a debt is not paid through the bankruptcy, it normally is discharged and cannot be collected as a personal liability of the debtor See BC 727; BC 1141; BC 524. For this reason, neither sellers nor trustees are indifferent between the exercise of reclamation rights and the assertion of a claim for damages.

Unlike its predecessor statute, the current Bankruptcy Code directly addresses sellers' reclamation rights. Although the Bankruptcy Code retains strong provisions for avoiding state statutory liens that first "become[ ] effective against the debtor ... when the debtor becomes insolvent," BC 545(1)(D), it also includes a provision limiting the trustee's attack on reclamations under UCC 2–702. This provision is BC 546(c). Please read it now.

Observe that, unlike UCC 2–702(2), BC 546(c)(2) gives the bankruptcy court the option to deny reclamation and instead grant the reclaiming seller a lien on property of the estate or a priority administrative claim. From the seller's perspective, reclamation is preferable to either a lien or an administrative claim. Recall that, generally speaking, holders of liens are entitled to receive their collateral or its value from the bankruptcy estate, but they run the risk that, by the time of distribution, the collateral will have diminished in value and no other assets will be available to satisfy the claims. To guard against this risk, secured claims may receive "adequate protection" under BC 361. See Section 1, supra. In some cases, however, the court-approved protection may prove inadequate and the secured party will receive an administrative claim of the highest priority. See BC 507(b). Administrative claims, including also the trustee's fees and expenses and other costs of maintaining and preserving the estate, are paid from unencumbered assets ahead of general unsecured claims. See BC 507(a)(1). However, bankruptcy estates have been known to be or become **administratively insolvent**. Of course, when the buyer is in bankruptcy, either a lien or an administrative claim is preferable to a general unsecured claim for the price of goods sold.

(3) Fraud, "Rubber" Checks, and the Bankruptcy Code. Important questions remain notwithstanding (or perhaps because of) the enactment of BC 546(c). The section is silent with respect to the exercise of a number of the reclamation rights that nonbankruptcy law provides. For example, the credit seller's demand may be sufficient for purposes of UCC 2–702(2) but not in conformity with BC 546(c)(1). That is, the seller might give an oral demand or, having received a written misrepresentation of solvency, might make demand more than ten days after delivery of the goods to the buyer. Or the seller may not have delivered the goods to the buyer on credit, but rather in exchange for a "rubber" check that "bounced." And a seller may have the right to recover goods obtained through active fraud unrelated to the buyer's solvency. See generally Chapter 9, Section 2(C), supra.

Does BC 546(c) provide the exclusive remedy for a seller attempting to reclaim goods from a bankruptcy trustee? In other words, does the inclusion of BC 546(c) mean that reclaiming sellers who do not fall within its scope automatically lose their reclamation rights in bankruptcy? Or does the section afford a safe harbor for certain reclamation rights and leave to the trustee the burden of proving the avoidability of other reclamation rights under other sections of the Bankruptcy Code, such as 544, 545, and 547? The following case addresses these questions.

————

IN RE CONTRACT INTERIORS, INC.

United States Bankruptcy Court, E.D. Michigan, 1981.
14 B.R. 670.

GEORGE BRODY, BANKRUPTCY JUDGE. This controversy involves the construction to be given to section 546(c) of the Bankruptcy Code, 11 U.S.C.A. § 546(c) (1979).

On December 24, 1980, B. Berger & Co. (the "plaintiff") shipped certain decorative goods to Contract Interiors, Inc. On February 6, 1981, Contract Interiors filed a petition for relief under chapter 11 of the Bankruptcy Code. The plaintiff made demand in writing for the return of the goods on February 20, 1981. When the defendant (the "debtor") failed to honor this request, the plaintiff instituted this action contending that it was induced to ship the goods in reliance upon a false financial statement submitted by the debtor and, therefore, it was entitled to reclaim them either by virtue of section 2–702 of the Uniform Commercial Code, M.S.A. § 19.2702 [M.C.L.A. § 440.2702], or based upon a theory of common-law fraud.

The parties agree that whether the plaintiff may prevail depends, at least initially, upon the construction to be given to section 546(c) of the Code.

"§ 546. *Limitations on avoiding powers*

. . .

(c) The rights and powers of the trustee under sections 544(a), 545, 547, and 549 of this title are subject to any statutory right or common-law right of a seller, in the ordinary course of such seller's business, of goods to the debtor to reclaim such goods if the debtor has received such goods while insolvent, but—

(1) such a seller may not reclaim any such goods unless such seller demands in writing reclamation of such goods before ten days after receipt of such goods by the debtor;

(2) the court may deny reclamation to a seller with such a right of reclamation that has made such a demand only if court—

(A) grants the claim of such a seller priority as an administrative expense; or

(B) secured such claim by a lien.

Based upon section 546(c), the debtor argues that a seller may reclaim the goods he was induced to sell by fraudulent representation only if the seller complies with the requirements set forth in section 546(c) and, since the plaintiff did not make a written demand within ten days of the receipt of the goods by the debtor no right to reclaim exists.

Counsel for the plaintiff, however, maintains that section 546 deals with the limitation of the trustee's avoiding powers and, therefore, subsection (c) of section 546 should be construed to mean that it merely prevents the trustee from relying upon sections 544(a), 546, 547 and 549 to defeat any statutory or common-law right of the seller to reclaim the goods sold in the ordinary course of business if the seller complies with the conditions set forth in section 546(c); but that a seller may still rely upon any statutory or common-law right that he may have to reclaim goods he has sold to a debtor even though he does not comply with the conditions set forth in section 546(c), but if a seller does so, the trustee may employ all of his avoiding powers to resist the seller's claim. In support of this construction of section 546(c), plaintiff relies on a law review article by Mann & Phillips analyzing section 546(c), entitled "Section 546(c) of the Bankruptcy Code: An Imperfect Resolution of the Conflict Between the Reclaiming Seller and the Bankruptcy Trustee," 54 Am.Bankr.L.J. 239 (1980). In that article, the writers concede that section 546(c) may be construed to mean that it is the "exclusive and conclusive bankruptcy provision governing [a seller] reclamation rights," and that the failure to comply with section 546(c) precludes any recovery by the seller. The writers then state:

> "Although this interpretation of section 546(c) cannot be dismissed peremptorily, it is unpersuasive for a number of reasons. First, section 546(c) does not expressly state the effect of a failure to comply with its requirements; nor does it directly state that consideration of the listed Reform Act sections is precluded in cases where the seller fails so to comply. Second, the only legislative history specifically addressing this point suggests that section 546(c) should not prevent the non-complying seller from contesting the trustee under other bankruptcy provisions. Third, the basic idea that seller reclamation rights outside of section 546(c)'s coverage are therefore ineffective in bankruptcy leads to entirely ludicrous results if extended to any degree. For example, this reasoning could deny the recovery to sellers exercising a right of stoppage in transit or even asserting a perfected Article 9 security interest. Finally, the view severely undermines any coherent reading of the Bankruptcy Reform Act as a whole, for it would dictate that the trustee's right to invalidate certain statutory liens or to assume the status of an ideal lien creditor is no longer dependent upon whether the reclamation right falls within the purview of these bankruptcy provisions but now is solely determined by the parameters of section 546(c)."

Based upon this analysis, the writers suggest that

> "... it is preferable to treat section 546(c) as providing the seller with a 'non-exclusive safe harbor' against a trustee proceeding under the Reform Act sections it lists. Thus, sellers complying with section 546(c) would be immune from attack under the listed sections, while those who did not

comply would be free to defend themselves against the trustee on the merits as defined by the Reform Act section used by the trustee."

A brief discussion of the background leading to the adoption of section 546(c) may be of aid in resolving this controversy. The common law recognized the right of a defrauded seller to rescind the contract of sale and to reclaim the goods sold. State law, however, differed as to what fact had to be established to give rise to this remedy. ... To the extent that the state law recognized the remedy of reclamation on a given set of facts, the remedy was available as against a trustee in bankruptcy. For whatever reason, the lack of state law uniformity did not cause any significant difficulties when the debtor filed a petition in bankruptcy.

The American Law Institute and the National Conference of Commissioners on Uniform State Laws proposed the first Official Draft of the Uniform Commercial Code in 1952. The Uniform Commercial Code was first adopted in Pennsylvania in 1954 and has since been adopted by every state except Louisiana. The Uniform Commercial Code became effective in Michigan in 1964. P.A. 174 (1962) ....

With the adoption of section 2–702 of the Uniform Commercial Code, relative stability was displaced by confusion and uncertainty. Attempts by sellers to reclaim goods from bankrupt estates was resisted by debtors in possession and trustees on various grounds. The areas of conflict have been summarized as follows:

> "Trustees claimed that the right of reclamation was a statutory lien triggered by the debtor's insolvency and voidable by former section 67c(1)(A); that it was a priority in conflict with former section 64; or that it was subordinate to the rights of a judicial lien creditor under former section 70c." 4 Collier on Bankr. ¶ 546.04 (15th ed. 1980), at 546–9.

This conflict "produced a body of case law notable for its intricacy, its profession of doctrinal approaches, and its general incoherence." Mann & Phillips, supra, at 239.

Section 546(c) was adopted in an attempt to resolve the problems created by section 2–702(2). The legislative history states that the purpose of section 546(c) is "to recognize, in part, the validity of section 2–702 of the Uniform Commercial Code which has generated much litigation, confusion, and divergent decisions in different circuits." H.R.Rep. No. 95–595, 95th Cong., 1st Sess. 372 (1977); S.Rep. No. 95–989, 95th Cong., 2d Sess. 87 (1978), U.S.Code Cong. & Admin.News 1978, pp. 5787, 5873, 6328. Section 2–702(2) permits a seller to reclaim goods if the buyer received the goods while insolvent if the seller made a demand for the goods within ten days after the receipt of the goods by the buyer. If the buyer induced the seller to ship goods based upon a written misrepresentation of solvency and the goods were shipped within three months of such misrepresentation, the ten-day limitation does not apply. The legislative history accompanying section 546(c), when read in conjunction with section 546(c), makes it clear that the drafters intended to retain only that part of the section 2–702 which permits reclamation if demand was made for the return of the goods within ten days after receipt and to make this right to reclaim exclusive in order to put an end to the disruptive litigation engendered by section 2–702(2).[3] The purpose set forth in the legislative history can be given effect only if it is held that section 546(c) provides the exclusive remedy for a reclaiming seller.

The Mann & Phillips article, supra, relied upon by the plaintiff is a scholarly and comprehensive analysis of section 546(c). However, the arguments marshalled by them to support the contention that section 546(c) should not be given exclusive effect, are not persuasive.

Admittedly, section 546(c) does not expressly state the effect of a failure to comply with its requirements, nor does it directly state that section 546(c) is an exclusive remedy for a seller who seeks to reclaim property. The mere failure to state the effect of noncompliance with section 546(c) does not, of itself, support the conclusion that section 546(c) is non-exclusive. Mann & Phillips' assertion that the only legislative history which addresses the exclusivity issue supports a "safe harbor" interpretation is based on a letter written to the Minority Counsel of the Committee on Improvement in the Judicial Machinery, United States Senate, by Professor Minahan of the University of Vermont Law School. The letter was written when the Senate was considering section 4–407, an earlier version of section 546(c)—a version essentially similar to that of section 546(c).[4] In the letter, Professor Minahan stated that the proposed section 4–407 should not be construed to provide the exclusive remedy for a defrauded seller but that whether a seller could reclaim property, if he did not comply with section 4–407,

---

3. This is actually the solution that was suggested by Weintraub & Edelman: "Seller's Right to Reclaim Property Under Section 2.702(2) of the Code Under the Bankruptcy Act: Fact or Fantasy," 32 Bus.Law 1165 (1977). This recommendation was based, in part, on the view that so limiting the right of seller to reclaim goods would eliminate costly, time-consuming litigation, enhance the likelihood of successful reorganization, and give relief in those cases in which there is an 'overwhelming aura of fraud' cases in which sellers were induced to deliver goods to a debtor on the eve of bankruptcy." Henson, "Reclamation Rights of a Seller Under § 2.702," 22 N.Y.L.F. 41, 49 (1975).

4. The proposed section 4–407 provided as follows:

"Sec. 4–407. *Right of Reclaiming Seller.*—A seller's right under state law to recover property sold upon subsequent

discovery that buyer received the property while insolvent or at a time when buyer had ceased to pay his debts in the ordinary course of business or had an inability to pay his debts as they became due shall not be defeated upon the commencement of a case under this Act by or against the buyer as debtor because of anything contained in section 4–405 or 4–406 provided:

(1) debtor received the property on credit or payment by draft which was subsequently dishonored; and

(2) within ten days of debtor's written receipt of property seller made a written demand of debtor that property be returned; and

(3) at the time of debtor's receipt of the property seller had no actual knowledge of the contemplation of the filing of a petition under this Act by or against the debtor."

"... should be left to the courts to decide in light of the particular circumstances of the case. Here the courts have discretion, absent notification within the ten-day period, to declare that the particular reclamation is a statutory lien or that it conflicts with the federal priorities. Section 4–407 merely gives a minimum of ten days worth of protection. Beyond the ten day period, the courts could go either way." Mann & Phillips, supra, at 265 n. 181.

Professor Minahan was not directly involved in the drafting of the Code. "[R]emarks other than by persons responsible for the preparation or the drafting of bill are entitled to little weight." Ernst & Ernst v. Hochfelder, 425 U.S. 185, 203 n. 24, 96 S.Ct. 1375, 1386 n. 24, 47 L.Ed.2d 668 (1976). The only pertinent legislative history that sheds light on the interpretation to be given to section 546(c) is that which accompanies section 546(c) and which, as previously stated, indicates that section 546(c) is to be given exclusive effect.

Mann & Phillips also maintain that if section 546(c) is held to be the exclusive remedy governing a seller's right to reclamation, it "could deny recovery to a seller exercising a right of stoppage in transit or asserting a perfected Article 9 security interest." A realistic reading of section 546(c) reveals that such fears are unjustified. A seller's right to stop goods in transit is governed by section 2–705 of the Uniform Commercial Code. This right continues until the buyer has either actually or constructively received the goods. § 2–705(2). It is only when the debtor either has actual or constructive possession that a seller is compelled to rely on section 546(c). There is nothing in section 546(c) that remotely indicates that it deprives a seller of any remedy that he may have had under the Bankruptcy Act by virtue of section 2.705. Nor does section 546(c) impact on the right of a seller who has a valid security interest in goods received by a debtor. If a seller has a valid security interest, he has no need to rely upon section 546(c). Section 546(c) does not invalidate any such interest.

Finally, the authors contend that if section 546(c) means that a seller can reclaim goods only if he complies with the conditions set forth in section 546(c), it leads to "the absurd conclusion that the seller's recovery rights included by section 546(c) *are not* statutory liens or rights subordinate to a lien creditor so long as the seller complies with the section's procedural requirements, but *would* be so designated if the seller fails to comply." Inquiry as to whether a seller's right to reclaim is a statutory lien or a priority or a preference is no longer pertinent. It is no longer necessary to characterize the seller's right. A seller has a remedy if he complies with the condition set forth in section 546(c); he does not have a remedy if he does not so comply. This is the result that the drafters of the Code intended.

It is evident from the tenor of their comments that Mann & Phillips' basic concern is that to hold that section 546(c) provides more than a "safe harbor" is ill-advised. The court recognizes that to give exclusive effect to section 546(c) permits a debtor, who either actively or passively defrauds a seller of goods in the ordinary course of business, to insulate such fraudulent transactions unless the seller complies with the conditions therein.[7] The court also recognizes that to limit the right of a defrauded seller to recover property only if he complies with the conditions set forth in section 546(c), for all practical purposes, makes the right meaningless. The event that generally triggers demand for reclamation is the filing of a petition in bankruptcy. Unless the filing of the petition is preceded by extensive publicity, a seller will ordinarily not be able to comply with the conditions set forth in section 546(c). A court, however, does not have the power to legislate; it must merely accept what the legislature has written. It is "not at liberty to revise while professing to construe." Sun Printing and Publishing Assoc. v. Remington Paper and Power Co., 235 N.Y. 338, 346, 139 N.E. 140 (1923).[8]

For the foregoing reasons, the complaint is dismissed.

An appropriate order to be submitted.

Note on *Contract Interiors*

The opinion in *Contract Interiors* observed that permitting a defrauded seller to reclaim only if the seller has given written notice within ten days after delivery "for all practical purposes, makes the right meaningless," but that a court "must merely accept what the legislature has written." This approach calls for a close look at the language of BC 546(c).

Does BC 546(c) say that a defrauded seller may reclaim goods only if the seller has given the ten-day written notice? Or does the section say that the trustee's right to avoid transfers of property under BC 544(a), 545, 547, and 549 does *not* apply if the ten-day notice has been given? The question is important, for under the latter reading one must first determine whether the trustee *has* the right to avoid the property interest of a defrauded seller under the sections of the Bankruptcy Code cited in BC 546(c).[1] If the answer to this inquiry is "no," then BC 546(c) becomes irrelevant.

Most of the reported decisions have read BC 546(c) to be the exclusive mode of reclamation once the debtor has entered bankruptcy, see J. White & R. Summers, Uniform Commercial Code (3d ed. 1988)

---

7. Not only is a defrauded seller unable to exercise the right of reclamation unless he complies with the conditions set forth in § 546(c), but he is also precluded—if the debtor is a corporation—from bringing an action to except his debt from discharge. § 1141.

8. It should be noted that the limitation of a defrauded seller to recover property applies only to sales which have been made in the ordinary course of business. The right of a seller to reclaim property based upon allegations of fraud is not limited by § 546(c) if the transaction is not in the ordinary course of business.

1. For example, UCC 2-702(3) was amended in 1966 to delete the words "or lien creditor," thereby suggesting that the credit seller's reclamation right would prevail over a judicial lien creditor. In states that have adopted this amendment, the reclamation right would not be avoidable under BC 544(a).

§ 23–10, notwithstanding the argument to the contrary in Mann & Phillips, The Reclaiming Seller Under the Bankruptcy Reform Act: Resolution or Renewal of an Old Conflict?, 33 Vand.L.Rev. 1 (1980). See also Mann & Phillips, The Reclaiming Cash Seller and the Bankruptcy Code, 39 Sw. L.J. 603 (1985).

SECTION 5. "FLOATING LIEN" VERSUS RECLAIMING SELLER

In Chapter 9, Section 3, supra, we considered the rights of a reclaiming cash seller and a reclaiming credit seller as against third parties—lien creditors of, buyers from, and secured creditors of the buyer. Now that we have seen the reach of a "floating lien" under Article 9, it is useful to revisit the priority contest between a reclaiming seller—as contrasted with a lien creditor or a trustee in bankruptcy— and a buyer's secured creditor claiming the sold goods as after-acquired collateral.

Problem. On June 1 Seller and Buyer tentatively agreed on a sale to Buyer of a load of cotton; the price was $4,000. Buyer then said, "I hope you can give me a week to pay." Seller replied, "I'm afraid I'll have to have your check within three days after delivery, with the understanding that you won't dispose of the cotton until the check clears." Buyer agreed. Buyer took delivery on June 2 and sent Seller the check on June 5. On June 10, Seller received word that the check had "bounced." On June 12, Seller brought a replevin action to recover the cotton.

Under these facts, Seller (a credit seller) will be entitled to reclaim the goods if it can show that Buyer received the goods while "insolvent." UCC 2–702; UCC 1–201(23).[1] You may assume that Buyer was insolvent on June 2.

Now suppose that before the transaction between Buyer and Seller took place, Buyer, a cotton dealer, had granted a security interest to Lender in all of Buyer's existing and after-acquired cotton inventory. Lender has intervened in Buyer's replevin action, claiming that its security interest is senior to the reclamation rights of Seller. Lender's security interest secures loans that remain unpaid.

What result? See UCC 2–702; UCC 2–403; House of Stainless, Inc. v. Marshall & Ilsley Bank, infra; Note on the Reclaiming Seller versus the "Floating Lien" Financer, infra.

----

1. A cash seller who delivers goods in exchange for a check that "bounces" also may be entitled to reclaim the goods. See UCC 2–507; UCC 2–511.

HOUSE OF STAINLESS, INC. v. MARSHALL & ILSLEY BANK

Supreme Court of Wisconsin, 1977.

75 Wis.2d 264, 249 N.W.2d 561.

FACTS

Plaintiff-respondent The House of Stainless Steel, Inc. (Stainless) commenced this action against defendant-appellant Marshall & Ilsley Bank (M & I) in regard to certain goods delivered by Stainless to Alkar Engineering Corporation, Lodi, Wisconsin. Stainless alleged priority of claim over these goods against M & I pursuant to sec. 402.702(2), Stats.

On November 1, 1971, Alkar Engineering entered into a general revolving loan and security agreement with M & I, the latter lending money to Alkar and taking back a security interest in " ... all Debtor's Inventory, documents evidencing Inventory, ... whether now owned or hereafter acquired, and all proceeds or products of any of them." (This security agreement was properly perfected by the timely filing of financing statements.)

In January, 1973, Stainless shipped certain stainless steel goods to Alkar on open account with an invoice value of $36,130.66. Subsequently Stainless discovered that Alkar had received such goods on credit while insolvent, and demanded in writing the return of said goods from Alkar. (This demand was within ten days of receipt of the goods pursuant to sec. 402.702(2), Stats. On January 17, 1973, notice of this demand was given to M & I.) On January 31, 1973, M & I sold the goods claimed by Stainless to DEC International, Inc.

On July 3, 1973, Stainless commenced this action for conversion against M & I. M & I interposed the following affirmative defenses: (1) That M & I had a perfected security interest in the goods superior to that of Stainless; and (2) that Stainless should not be permitted to maintain this action because it is transacting business in Wisconsin without a certificate of authority as required by sec. 180.847(1), Stats.[*]

Both parties moved for summary judgment, each filing supporting affidavits. The motion of plaintiff Stainless was granted and judgment was entered in its favor in the amount of $36,130.66, plus interest and costs (total $39,954.71). Defendant Marshall & Ilsley Bank appeals from this judgment and the denial by the trial court of the M & I motion for summary judgment ....

ROBERT W. HANSEN, JUSTICE. [The court found that Stainless was not required to secure a certificate of authority and was entitled to bring this action in Wisconsin.]

PRIORITIES AMONG CREDITORS.

M & I claims priority over Stainless via a perfected security interest in the after-acquired property of Alkar. Under its loan and

[* Discussion of the second issue is omitted.]

security agreement dated November 1, 1971, and the financing statements properly filed and recorded in connection therewith, M & I did
have a security interest in all of Alkar's inventory, then owned or
thereafter acquired.   There is no dispute as to the validity of this
perfected security interest.

M & I claims priority for its claim under sec. 409.312, Stats., which
determines priority among conflicting interests in the same collateral
. . . .

Stainless, as a supplier of goods on credit, claims priority for its
claim under sec. 402.702(2), Stats., providing for seller's remedies on
discovery of buyer's insolvency.   This statute provides a right to reclaim upon demand made within ten days after receipt of the goods.   It
is undisputed that Stainless delivered goods to Alkar and within ten
days sought reclamation of said goods.

However, Stainless did not secure possession or repossession of the
goods sold and shipped to Alkar.   The right to reclaim on discovery of
insolvency is subject to an exception where the rights of "a buyer in
ordinary course or other good faith purchaser" are involved.   Thus,
while possessing only voidable title to the goods transferred, Alkar here
could transfer title to a good faith purchaser.   The trial court here held
M & I not to be a "good faith purchaser" drawing a distinction between
"goods" and "future goods" and treating differently the M & I interest
under its security agreement as to then-held and after-acquired property of Alkar.   The issue as to applicability of the exemption to M & I as
a "good faith purchaser" is one of law, to be resolved by this court . . . .

Thus, Stainless' only basis of priority is sec. 402.702, Stats. The
second question of law raised on this appeal is whether M & I is a "good
faith purchaser" and thus within the exception to the right of reclamation granted by sec. 402.702, Stats. What cases there are dealing with
this narrow question appear to agree with the affirmative answer
sought by M & I on this appeal.

In re Hayward Woolen Co. [3 U.C.C. Rep. Serv. 1107 (Bkrtcy.
D.Mass.1967)] dealt with the opposing claims of a reclaiming seller on
credit and a secured party under provisions identical with those in our
Wisconsin law.   There, wool goods were delivered to a bankrupt buyer
and rights to reclaim these goods were asserted by the sellers, otherwise
unsecured, and their assignees.   The opposing claimant held a perfected security interest in the after-acquired wool inventory of the bankrupt buyer.

The court in *Hayward* reasoned as follows: Seller's right to reclaim
on the ground of buyer's insolvency is subject to the rights of a good
faith purchaser under U.C.C. 2–702(3).   U.C.C. sec. 2–403(1) provides "a
person with voidable title has power to transfer a good title to a good
faith purchaser for value."   Hayward, the insolvent buyer, is a party
having a voidable title.   Textile, the party with a security interest in
after-acquired collateral, qualifies as a purchaser under U.C.C. sec. 1–

201(32, 33). Textile's preexisting claim constitutes value under U.C.C. sec. 1–201(44)(b).

The *Hayward* court referred to the opinion of two commentators who have expressed the opinion that the seller's right of reclamation is inferior to a perfected security interest in the goods arising under an after-acquired property clause.[21]

The court held, therefore, "that Textile, as the holder of a security interest in the debtor's after-acquired inventory, acquired title to the goods remaining in Hayward's possession, as a good faith purchaser for value, and that Textile's rights to such goods are superior to those of the reclamation petitioners. It follows that the reclamation petitions must be denied ...."

Analyzing the result reached in *Hayward*, one commentator concluded that " ... it is hard to quarrel with the decision as an application of statutory provisions." [23] Stainless argues the 1969 amendment deleting "lien creditor" as one subject to the rights of reclamation mandates a contrary conclusion. But we do not find that amendment as intending or resulting in a changed definition of good faith purchaser under sec. 402.702, Stats. In part because uniform codes ought be interpreted uniformly, we follow *Hayward* and the decisions in other jurisdictions to hold that M & I here was a "good faith purchaser" and exempted by sec. 402.702(3) from the Stainless right of reclamation under that statute. . . .

It follows that the trial court order granting the Stainless motion for summary judgment must be reversed and set aside. It likewise follows that the trial court order denying the M & I motion for summary judgment must be set aside. Judgment is reversed and cause remanded with directions to the trial court to grant summary judgment in favor of the appellant, Marshall & Ilsley Bank, and against the respondent, The House of Stainless Steel, Inc.

Order and judgment reversed, and cause remanded for further proceedings consistent with this opinion. Costs are awarded to appellant. . . .

---

21. See: Hogan, The Marriage of Sales to Chattel Security in the UCC: Massachusetts Variety, 38 BU L.Rev. 571, 580, 581; Note, Selected Priority Problems in Secured Financing under the UCC, 68 Yale L.J. 751, 758.

23. Skilton, Security Interest in After-Acquired Property Under the Uniform Commercial Code, 1974 Wis.L.R. 925, 946, commenting further on *Hayward*: "Fireside equities may seem to favor the seller over the secured party who did not give new value in latching on to the after-ac-

quired property. The secured party with the after-acquired property clause may seem to get a windfall at the expense of the sellers, who provided the property. But it is hard to quarrel with the decision as an application of statutory provisions....

"The case illustrates the 'voidable title' area. Title passes to buyer, but seller has a right to rescind the title, until a bona fide purchaser for value intervenes—that is the general restitutionary rule. Section 2–702 merely tinkers with it."

Note on the Reclaiming Seller versus the "Floating Lien" Financer

In Chapter 9, Section 3(B), supra, we saw that the second sentence of UCC 2–403(1) distinguishes between a "good faith purchaser for value," who takes good title from a person with voidable title, and a "lien creditor," who does not. We examined in some detail whether the position of a secured party whose debtor has voidable title to goods more closely resembles that of a prototypcial good faith purchaser (i.e., buyer) or that of a lien creditor. We also examined the role of reliance in resolving competing claims to goods acquired by wrongdoers. See Notes on Reliance and Nonreliance Parties, Chapter 9, Section 3(B), supra. We now return to these inquiries in the context of the "floating lien."

As you know, unless an inventory financer takes a security interest in future inventory (and accounts), its collateral base will erode and the loan may become less and less secured. Sometimes a lender agrees to make recurring advances as the debtor continues to acquire inventory and generate accounts; sometimes not. In the former case, the secured party with a floating lien acts more like a buyer, giving value in exchange for an interest in particular property; in the latter, less so. But even when after-acquired property secures an antecedent debt, the secured party usually bargains for a security interest in the after-acquired property at the time it extends the credit. In this respect it is unlike a judicial lien creditor, who extends unsecured credit and acquires its lien only in conjunction with judicial collection procedures.

Most courts have subordinated reclamation claims of sellers based on fraud or UCC 2–702 to claims of creditors under after-acquired property clauses in security agreements. As in *House of Stainless*, the courts generally treat secured creditors as "good faith purchasers for value" (UCC 2–403) under literal applications of the definitions of "purchase" (UCC 1–201(32)) and "value" (UCC 1–201(44)(d)), without inquiring whether the secured creditor gave value subsequent to or in exchange for the property that the seller delivered to the buyer.

Most courts have reached the same result with regard to cash sellers, although the route to the result is somewhat more circuitous. Unlike UCC 2–702, which creates a reclamation right for credit sellers and provides explicitly that the right to reclaim is "subject to the rights of a ... good faith purchaser under this Article (Section 2–403)," UCC 2–507 does not even explicitly provide for reclamation, let alone purport to address priorities. Moreover, unlike a misrepresentation of solvency, which was considered a fraud at common law and gave rise to "voidable title," failure to abide by an agreement to pay for goods upon delivery was sometimes treated as theft, giving the buyer "void title." In protecting the secured party against a reclaiming cash seller, courts have looked to UCC 2–507, Comment 3. That Comment suggests that

2–507(2) addresses the cash seller's rights only as against the buyer, not against third parties who may be protected under "the bona fide purchase sections of this Article." Among those sections, clause (b) of UCC 2–403(1) supports the view that, at least when the cash seller took a "rubber check" upon delivery, the voidable title rule applies to cash sales. See also clause (d) (applying the voidable title rule to buyers who procure delivery through fraud punishable as larcenous under the criminal law). For extended discussions of whether a cash seller has a right to reclaim and, if so, whether the reclamation right takes priority over a security interest arising under an after-acquired property clause, see the opinion of the court en banc in In re Samuels & Co., 526 F.2d 1238 (5th Cir.1976), cert. denied, 429 U.S. 834 (1976), and the dissenting opinion of Judge Ainsworth in In re Samuels & Co., 510 F.2d 139 (5th Cir.1975).

One may wonder whether the committees and councils that prepared and reviewed the Code faced the problem that since has been exposed by cases like *Samuels* and *House of Stainless*. One also may wonder whether the Code's provisions on "after-acquired property" (UCC 9–204), "purchase" (UCC 1–201(32)), and "value" (UCC 1–201(44)(d)) were focused on saving "floating lien" financing from the threat of invalidity under state law (cf. Code 9–205) and in bankruptcy (cf. UCC 9–108), rather than on claims to specific goods obtained by fraud or other wrongdoing by the debtor. Suppose that the drafters had put the facts of *House of Stainless* to the Code's sponsors as part of their review of Articles 2 and 9. Would the reviewers have approved these consequences of the validation of the floating lien?

Consider in this regard an amendment to UCC 2–702(3) adopted by the Code's sponsors in 1966. Prior thereto, the credit seller's reclamation right was "subject to the rights of a buyer in ordinary course or other good faith purchaser *or lien creditor* under this Article (Section 2–403)." UCC 2–702, Comment 3, in a paragraph that was deleted in 1966, indicated that the rights of lien creditors may have priority over reclaiming sellers under non-Code law, which, according to UCC 1–103, may supplement the Code's rules. The Comment referred to In re Kravitz, 278 F.2d 820 (3d Cir.1960), in which the court held that the debtor's bankruptcy trustee defeated the seller's rights under UCC 2–702 because under the pre-Code law of Pennsylvania, the right of reclamation would have been subordinate to the rights of a lien creditor who extended credit to the debtor after the debtor received the goods. In proposing the deletion of the words "or lien creditor" from UCC 2–702(2), the Permanent Editorial Board noted that "[t]he result in Pennsylvania is to make the right of reclamation granted by this section almost entirely illusory. In most states the pre-Code law was otherwise, and the right of reclamation seems to be fully effective." Report No. 3 of the Permanent Editorial Board 3 (1967).[2]

---

2. It may seem odd that the drafters sought to protect the reclaiming seller's priority over a lien creditor by *deleting* three words ("or lien creditor") from UCC

How far does the solicitude of the Code's sponsors toward reclamation rights, evidenced by the 1966 amendment to UCC 2–702(3), extend? Is the Article 9 secured party with a floating lien more or less sympathetic than the lien creditor? Than the buyer's bankruptcy trustee? See Section 4, supra.

SECTION 6. IS SECURED CREDIT EFFICIENT?

Introduction. In recent years several legal scholars have debated whether the institution of secured credit is "efficient" (as that term is used by economists).[1] Now that we have studied many of the effects of secured credit under current law—in particular, the priority rules and the favored treatment afforded to secured claims in bankruptcy—we can consider these effects in the context of this debate.

The question whether security interests are efficient is a positive, not a normative, inquiry. However, the literature reflects strong undercurrents of a normative debate as well. In particular, whether a legal regime that respects—indeed, fosters—secured transactions should be retained if it is found to be inefficient clearly is a normative question. And that question lies at (or just below) the surface in much of the commentary. (Not surprisingly, some of the participants demonstrate a normative preference for economically efficient legal rules.)

The following excerpts from Professor Paul Shupack's article illustrate much of the flavor and substance of the debate.

——————

2–702(3) rather than by providing that the reclamation right is superior. The PEB appears to have chosen its drafting technique with care: "Six states have resolved the problem by deleting the words 'or lien creditor' from this section, and there seems to be no other practicable route to uniformity among the states." Report No. 3 of the Permanent Editorial Board 3 (1967).

1. See Buckley, The Bankruptcy Priority Puzzle, 72 Va.L.Rev 1393 (1986); Carlson, Rationality, Accident and Priority Under Article 9 of the Uniform Commercial Code, 71 Minn.L.Rev. 207 (1986); Jackson & Kronman, Secured Financing and Priorities Among Creditors, 88 Yale L.J. 1143 (1979); Jackson & Schwartz, Vacuum of Fact or Vacuous Theory: A Reply to Professor Kripke, 133 U.Pa.L.Rev. 987 (1985); Kripke, Law and Economics: Measuring the Economic Efficiency of Commercial Law in a Vacuum of Fact, 133 U.Pa.L.Rev. 929 (1985); Schwartz, A Theory of Loan Priorities, 18 J. Legal Stud. 209 (1989); Schwartz, The Continuing Puzzle of Secured Debt, 37 Vand.L.Rev. 1051 (1984); Schwartz, Security Interests and Bankruptcy Priorities: A Review of Current Theories, 10 J. Legal Stud. 1 (1981); Scott, A Relational Theory of Secured Financing, 86 Columbia L. Rev. 901 (1986); Shupack, Solving the Puzzle of Secured Transactions, 41 Rutgers L. Rev. 1067 (1989); Shupack, Defending Purchase Money Security Interests Under Article 9 of the UCC from Professor Buckley, 22 Ind.L.Rev. 777 (1989); White, Efficiency Justifications for Personal Property Security, 37 Vand. L.Rev. 473 (1984).

SHUPACK, SOLVING THE PUZZLE
OF SECURED TRANSACTIONS

41 Rutgers L. Rev. 1067–74, 1083–86, 1088, 1091–92, 1121–24 (1989).

I. A PARABLE

In the 1740's, visible cracks in the dome of Saint Peter's in Rome led Pope Benedict XIV to commission three mathematicians to write a report described as "the first attempt ... made to apply the methods of exact science to a practical building task." ... The report met with a storm of criticism ...

We now know that the conclusions reached by the mathematicians analyzing St. Peter's dome depended in part on the erroneous assumption that the various components of the dome would interact without friction. Calculations accounting for the force of friction would have to await the development, well into the next century, of statistical mechanics. The authors of the report did the best they could with the tools that were available, but their best efforts nevertheless resulted in an analysis that the skilled builders of the day recognized as absurd.

II. THE PROBLEM

This Article seeks to accomplish two things. It attempts to solve the puzzle of secured transactions as that question has been posed by legal academics using economic analysis. It also attempts to show that, much in the spirit of the 18th century analysis of St. Peter's dome, the economics-based model does not yet have the capacity to inform our legal practice.

In recent debate concerning the efficiency of secured transactions, legal academics using economic analysis have challenged the general community of lawyers and legal scholars to give what economists would call a rational account of secured credit. Their economic analysis begins with a model that excludes what might be characterized as the economic equivalent of friction—transaction costs.

The challengers have asked: How is it possible for a debtor to improve his position by assigning personal property to one of his creditors as collateral, that is, by entering a secured transaction? They argue that, to the extent creditors rely on collateral, the creditor to whom the collateral is assigned will reduce the charges made for a loan as a consequence of having special rights on default. Most members of the general community would agree. These economic analysts, however, pose a further question. Would not the other creditors, who are denied collateral, react by increasing the price of credit by an amount that exactly corresponds to the reduction in price made by secured creditors? The conclusion reached by the economic analysts surprises the general community: so long as creditors are knowledgeable, there is no obvious benefit to the debtor resulting from his issuance of secured debt. This leads to a further conclusion. To the extent that creditors are not knowledgeable, a debtor can impoverish them by issuing secured debt. Under this analysis, a leveraged debtor who issues secured debt improves his position, but only by means of transferring wealth from ignorant unsecured creditors to himself and his secured creditors.

In order to rescue secured transactions, legal academics using economic analysis ask for an account of secured debt that demonstrates its efficiency. These economic analysts ask whether, in the absence of that account, and regardless of any other functions served by secured transactions, we ought to consider whether we would all be better off if the law did not encourage the creation of security interests.

This Article will attempt to show that it is possible to answer these economic analysts' question, but that the answer has little value for public policy. . . .

As defined in the debate, any account of secured transactions demonstrating their efficiency would have to show how the debtor who offers security is able to borrow more (or at lower rates) than he would otherwise be able to, assuming that the same assets are available on default. Using Kaldor–Hicks criteria,[10] the standards apparently used by those in the debate, the efficiency of secured transactions will be demonstrated by creating a model showing that the availability of security interests enables debtors to increase wealth by an amount greater than is lost by others as a result of these transactions. Other models have shown that security interests are, in a sense, a good thing for debtors; but these models have also implied that debtors with assets will always collateralize loans to the fullest extent possible. Because our experience includes debtors with assets who have not collateralized all their loans, any successful model has to account for the existence of unsecured debt. Under the model developed here, debtors can profit by issuing secured debt to some creditors, but not all creditors will necessarily seek security interests. Establishing this model within the terms set by the debate, and using plausible assumptions, this Article demonstrates the theoretical efficiency of secured transactions. This demonstration suggests that previous attempts to frame a model have not been successful because they contain implicit assumptions which, on examination, make these models both implausible and unable to inform our understanding of everyday events.

One of these implicit assumptions is that the cost of secured debt always exceeds that of unsecured debt. Any model, however, which insists that secured debt is necessarily costly, as compared to unsecured debt, is unrealistic. Once this assumption concerning cost is removed,

---

10. *See generally* Kaldor, *Welfare Propositions and Interpersonal Comparisons of Utility,* 49 Econ. J. (1939); Hicks, *The Valuation of Social Income,* 7 Economica 105 (1940); Hicks, *The Foundation of Welfare Economics,* 49 Econ. J. 696 (1939). The Kaldor–Hicks efficiency criteria have a uti-litarian basis. For secured transactions to be efficient in the Kaldor–Hicks sense, the utility gains of the winners must exceed the disutilities of the losers, although there is no need for the winners to compensate the losers out of their gains. Kaldor–Hicks criteria are not easily applied.

two sensible propositions emerge. Security interests can be explained in part by: (1) the differing capacities of creditors to realize on the value of collateral; and (2) the likelihood that creditors will have significantly different information about their common debtor. These differences, though part of any plausible model of security interests, are not sufficient to provide a general efficiency explanation. A *general* efficiency explanation, as used in this Article, starts with perfect market assumptions and relaxes them one by one until security interests appear. This Article presents a general model, but also attempts to show why any model that can demonstrate the general efficiency of security interests offers little insight into their structures.

This Article does not argue that economic theory can never fully illuminate problems in the law of secured transactions. Rather, it argues that the theory offered in the debate over the efficiency of secured transactions is not yet sufficiently developed to permit it to be the basis of any policy prescription. The theory does have the capacity, however, to make the empirical propositions underlying an efficiency claim explicit. As this Article shows, those matters of fact which are necessary to sufficiently inform any policy prescription are, as a practical matter, unknowable. To rely on current economic theory as an adequate guide for formulating policy concerning secured transactions risks a repeat of Thomas Tredgold's complaint: We would all too likely find the stability of the legal structure governing our credit system to be inversely proportional to the science of its builders.

III. A BRIEF HISTORY OF THE CONTROVERSY

The secured debt puzzle first appeared in the law review literature in a 1979 article by Thomas Jackson and Anthony Kronman. It assumed its formal shape in a 1981 article by Alan Schwartz. There followed a series of attempts to convince Professor Schwartz that the puzzle had been solved. First, Saul Levmore and then James White attempted to make matters clear for Professor Schwartz, but he remained dissatisfied. "The secured debt puzzle remains," he wrote. Then, Homer Kripke told Professor Schwartz that his problem resulted from joining others who "practice economics in a vacuum of fact." Joined by Thomas Jackson, Schwartz sharply denied the relevance of the charge. Next came Robert Scott's relational theory, which argued that the Article 9 "floating lien" is a mechanism which brings about the type of creditor participation in the debtor's financial strategies that benefits all creditors—secured and unsecured alike. This theory met with objection from F.H. Buckley, who noted that although it may be advantageous for the debtor to enter a long-term relationship with a lender, it was not necessary to use security agreements to do so. Buckley argued that, although the granting of a security interest in a perfect market "seems puzzling," no market is perfect, and, in imperfect credit markets, firms will choose to issue secured debt. Buckley went on to argue that, although imperfections in the market do offer opportunities for creditors to use security devices as a means to transfer wealth from some creditors to others, these "distributional concerns about secured lending are in general not compelling."...

IV.   WHY THIS DEBATE NOW?

These various arguments do more than raise a question about the validity of a prominent social institution.   In the exchange between Jackson and Schwartz and Kripke, the underlying methodological issues become the debate.   The question of why this concern with social policy surfaces now deserves examination in its own right.

The more traditional legal community, concerned as it is with practice, not theory, was not prepared for the legal academics' use of economics.   Practicing lawyers tend to be pragmatic and see questions of public policy as problems to be solved.   With respect to personal property security interests, these lawyers have taken as true something they know from their practice: Some debtors must be prepared to offer security to receive loans.   Taking that truth as an immutable part of their world, practicing lawyers see issues about priorities and ostensible ownership as the only problems created by personal property security interests.   After more than one hundred years of case law and statutory development, Article 9 of the *UCC* has emerged as the latest and most successful attempt to solve those problems.   With ostensible ownership almost entirely solved, the rewriting of Article 9 in the form of the 1972 amendments refined priority concepts with respect to the priority of specific creditors to specified categories of collateral.   Within its own framework, the conceptual work of the secured transactions bar was essentially finished.   There remained, to be sure, nagging problems, but they can be solved as further refinements within the system.

For this broader community, adoption of the *UCC* was seen as a step that increased transactional efficiencies with respect to secured transactions.   Although the drafters thought they were merely simplifying transactions that were already permitted, the increases in transactional efficiencies may have changed the financial world more than the drafters intended.   Prior to the adoption of the *UCC*, at least some of the assets of a bankrupt debtor who had assets were highly likely to be available to general creditors.   No articulated policy rationalized this result.   It may simply have been an unintended consequence of a system in which creditors found security interests uncertain in legal effect and expensive to create.

Because Article 9 of the *UCC* permits creditors to encumber all of a debtor's assets easily, it creates this additional risk.   This fact has led to a common complaint concerning Article 9: It is unfair to unsecured creditors.   Economic analysts would have to say that the feeling of unfairness is based more on appearances than reality.   The economists' model assumes that knowledgeable creditors adjust their behavior by raising the costs of their loans to their debtors.   If so, then unsecured creditors, after a transition period, now receive compensation for their apparently unfair treatment in bankruptcy by means of higher charges made to all debtors.

Thus, economic analysis leads to the realization that transactional efficiency is not necessarily the same thing as welfare efficiency. Once one realizes that ignorant creditors exist who, by definition, will not adjust their claims in response to the new market created by Article 9's transactional efficiencies, the *UCC* can be seen as having a dark side.

A partial explanation of the intensity of the debate could well be an uneasy conscience on the part of its participants. The participants must know that the larger claims made for his side's method of analysis cannot be fully defended. Economic analysts, though often modest about moving from analysis to prescription, can often write as if that move is appropriate. Traditional scholars would probably agree that transactional efficiency is not itself a sufficient justification for statutory reform. Rather, one must examine the worth of the social institution itself prior to debating how to make it operate most efficiently. For example, one could have legitimately questioned measures that improved the transactional efficiency of slavery.

Obviously, economic analysis can describe a pattern that is common to all credit transactions. The serious intellectual issue is what value does that description have in evaluating and judging alternative social policies.

V.   THE PUZZLE OF SECURED TRANSACTIONS

Alan Schwartz described the puzzle of secured transactions by using an economic model that includes the following assumptions:

> [C]reditors (i) can learn of and react to the existence of security; (ii) can calculate risk of default reasonably precisely; (iii) are risk-neutral; and (iv) have homogeneous expectations respecting default probabilities.

His example, illustrating the consequences of these assumptions, tells of a firm with $100 in assets. The creditors assume this value to be stable over time. The firm "wants to borrow $200 from two risk-neutral creditors." The first $100 of the loan is backed by the assets, and for this neither creditor will charge a risk premium. As to the second $100 of the loan, whichever creditor lends it will charge a risk premium. Under these assumptions, the behavior of the creditors and debtor will not change, no matter how the creditors choose to divide either the stable assets or the risk premium between them. Should a third or a fourth or a hundredth creditor appear, the then-existing creditors will each costlessly and instantaneously readjust the terms of their loans so each retains a proportional claim to the $100 worth of assets and each will charge a risk premium for the revised percentage of the loan that is not secured by any claims to assets. The consequence of this model is that no matter how the debtor divides the collateral between or among creditors, he will pay the same total dollar amount of interest . . . .

VI. ONE SPECIAL SOLUTION TO THE PUZZLE

A common ground in the debate has been to assume that the transaction costs associated with secured transactions are higher than those of unsecured obligations. The assumption appears plausible; on examining actual security interests, one notices costs unique to secured transactions such as paying for lawyers' special fine print and filing fees. Establishing the existence of costs unique to secured transactions does not, however, prove that secured transactions are necessarily more costly to create than unsecured transactions. This conclusion requires an additional assumption: that the costs unique to secured credit will always exceed the costs unique to unsecured credit. This additional assumption appears implausible, upon examination, because the economic analysts assume that there are no costs unique to unsecured credit. Secured creditors, however, do not necessarily have the need for the same information as unsecured creditors, and therefore do not incur all of the information acquisition costs of unsecured creditors . . . .

[1.] Costs associated with secured lending are not simply the sum of the costs unique to secured transactions and the costs associated with unsecured loans. The costs of creating a loan in a world without security interests are not universally less than, or even equal to, the costs of a parallel system with both secured and unsecured loans. the best that can be said is that a system of unsecured loans involves costs different from those of a system with secured loans. A model insisting that security interests are inherently more costly than unsecured debt is implausible.

Previous attempts to introduce theoretical motivations for security interests have run into a common difficulty. If the explanation shows that debtors will profit by issuing security interests, then the explanation requires the prediction that rational debtors will always issue secured debt. Thus, the puzzle is not one of secured transactions, but one of unsecured debt. . . .

This puzzle of the general creditor can easily be solved by recognizing that nothing certain can be said concerning the relative costs of creating secured and unsecured debt. This uncertainty can explain why not all debtors will profit by issuing the maximum possible amount of secured debt. Saved costs of information acquisition provide an additional theoretical basis for the creation of security interests, especially purchase money security interests, by insolvent debtors . . . .

[2.] Creditors viewing the same collateral—even readily marketable collateral such as used cars—will not necessarily assign the same value to it. Each creditor will discount the collateral by the costs of its reacquisition and disposition. Creditors, each having different skills, knowledge, and talents, are likely to value the collateral differently. In Professor Schwartz's example of a debtor who wants to borrow $200 against collateral worth $100, there are substantial reasons to believe that, outside the assumptions of a perfect market, the collateral will not be worth $100 to each creditor, even if it does have a readily established market price of $100. To the extent that the creditor to whom the asset is assigned as collateral is the creditor who can obtain the best *net* price for the collateral after accounting for the costs of reacquisition and disposition, there is an additional justification for the existence of security interests.

VIII.   WHY AN EVEN MORE REALISTIC MODEL EXPLAINS LITTLE ABOUT SECURED TRANSACTIONS

The question that general theories have previously failed to answer is why any given debtor with assets available on default would have both secured and unsecured voluntary creditors. The most general answer is that each voluntary creditor does not know the same things about the debtor and the collateral. Differences among creditors, which have been offered and rightfully rejected as general explanations for security interests, begin to explain the more *limited* phenomenon of why different creditors behave differently with respect to the same debtor. Differences in a particular creditor's knowledge about different debtors can also account for differing treatment of debtors.

[If creditors have differences, it means that one is no longer operating within the assumptions underlying a perfect market model. These assumptions must be relaxed to permit two consequences: (i) as described in Part VI, it must be possible for unsecured credit to be either more or less costly than secured debt, and (ii) functional alternatives to security interests, such as insurance, must exist whose costs can be either greater or less than the cost of creating security interests. With these modifications, the model begins to mimic the behavior of actual creditors.] ... Debtors may now find risk premiums higher or lower than the costs of creating security interests, and may find that costly devices other than costly security interests will offer knowledgeable creditors enough protection to induce them to make loans without risk premiums. With this modification, the model ceases to be able to predict the general behavior of debtors and creditors.

The model, as now elaborated, is capable of predicting that every loan will be secured. All one needs to assume is that the costs of creating security interests are less than the costs of the risk premiums, insurance or other alternatives to security interests. The model is equally capable of predicting that all loans will be unsecured, because insurance, the risk premium, or other costs of unsecured debt can be less than the costs of creating security interests.

It is now possible to understand why the debate about the efficiency of secured transactions, which has included frequent arguments from example, has been so lacking focus. Because, in reality, situations exist in which the costs of risk premiums, insurance and other alternatives to security interests can either exceed or be less than the costs of creating security interests, models not allowing for these various possibilities cannot account for the examples cited. It is therefore not surprising that the entire discussion of the puzzle of secured debt has had a curiously indeterminate air.

Once one realizes that the most plausible assumption is that nothing *general* can be said about the relative costs of secured and unsecured debt, the model ceases to be able to predict the behavior of any debtor or creditor. The model explains, at a very general level, why security interests *can* be efficient, but still does not account for the behavior of most observed creditors and debtors. Explanatory theories for actual behavior must be derived from the particular situations of the specific debtors and creditors.

There are circumstances in which the best monitor of the debtor is likely to take a security interest, and there are circumstances in which the worst monitor will do the same. Under this view, it is by no means improbable that a particular debtor's worst and best monitor would simultaneously take security interests. Their reasons for so acting would have more to do with their unique characteristics than with any characteristic of creditors generally. These specific creditor character- istics, restated in general terms could explain why some debtors might issue secured debt to some creditors with definable characteristics. These explanations would not, however, necessarily apply to all credi- tors and all debtors.

A creditor with a portfolio of loans, for example, need not have but one institutional role with respect to all of her debtors. With respect to a particular debtor, the creditor may possess knowledge sufficient to enable her to make unsecured loans. Her institutional abilities (*i.e.,* a letter of credit department or accounts receivable financing capabili- ties) may enable her to offer secured loans to debtors less well known to her at prices below those she would charge the same debtors for unsecured loans. It is not surprising, therefore, to find creditors offering a mix of secured and unsecured loans.

The efficiency gain identified by the general theory, although always present, may well be of so little weight as not to influence specific transactions. [As one leaves the economists' model and intro- duces slightly more realistic assumptions, the security interests created by parties cannot be proven to be efficient.] ... If those who gain were forced to compensate the ignorant and involuntary creditors for their losses, there would be no reason to assume that any efficiency gain would remain to those who otherwise benefitted from the creation of the security interest. Under these circumstances, if compensation had to be paid to losers, only unsecured credit would appear.

In the absence of empirical data, the possibility of inefficient transactions prevents any certain conclusions as to the Kaldor–Hicks efficiency of secured transactions as a social institution. No one can deny the possibility that the losses of even one inefficient transaction could overwhelm the efficiency gains of all the other transactions put together. Such a denial necessarily requires the empirical data we lack.

IX. CONCLUSION

This Article has shown that there is a social gain from secured transactions, which must be set off against their social cost. Secured transactions have an economic function other than to act as conduits for the transfer of wealth from ignorant and involuntary creditors to shrewd debtors and creditors. Knowing whether that economic function outweighs the social harm that secured transactions can cause requires information, not only about the economy at large, but also about legal rules that have the effect of constraining secured creditors from taking full advantage of their capacity to use these normatively suspect transactions for their own benefit.

Solving the puzzle of secured transactions from the initial perspective of a perfect market does not tell us much about secured transactions. Identifying efficiency gains within the abstract model does not guarantee that those efficiency gains, though present in every secured transaction, are in reality the motivation for every secured transaction. This inability to move from the model to reality means that the explanation of how secured transactions are, and might be, efficient has little to say about the social structures built around secured transactions. Showing that secured transactions *can* be efficient justifies only that they *might* exist. The forms in which they exist depend upon a series of empirical claims, into which the model can give little insight. Solving the puzzle of secured transactions, therefore, offers surprisingly little help in answering the important public policy questions surrounding their creation and use in the real world.

––––––

Note on the Efficiency Debate and a
Proposal for Radical Change

In Chapter 10, Section 1, supra, we observed:

[F]actors such as disparities in bargaining power and information, the relative size and duration of credit extensions, the costs of creating secured financings, disparities among creditors in their ability to monitor the debtor's financial activities and use of collateral, and market competition all serve to explain current financing patterns, ... which involve a mix of secured and unsecured credit.

... A positive explanation of why debtors sometimes give and creditors sometimes take secured credit under current law does not provide a normative justification for the advantages the current legal regime affords to secured claims.

Given what Professor Shupack calls the "transactional efficiency" of current law that facilitates the creation of effective security interests, is it difficult to understand why debtors sometimes give security in order to obtain credit and sometimes do not? Remember that the question whether there is an efficiency (or other) "normative" justification for our system of secured transactions underlies and drives the efficiency debate. That question is quite different from the question of why security is in fact given under the current regime. (Some of the participants in the debate have failed, at times, to keep this distinction in mind.) Professor Shupack systematically relaxed the economists' "perfect market" assumptions until he discovered examples of secured transactions that were "Kaldor–Hicks efficient"—i.e., the gains of the winners exceed in the aggregate the losses of the losers. Do examples of efficient secured lending under current rules necessarily mean that those rules should be retained intact?

One also might consider searching for any efficiency gains in moving from current law to a world that would not honor consensual security interests in personal property. Consider how that world would look. Would judicial liens be retained? Presumably *sales* and *exchanges* of property would be allowed. But would a sale for cash and a lease-back of equipment be honored (perhaps with a public notice requirement)? Would abolishing security interests put too much strain on already fuzzy lines between secured transactions and other kinds of dispositions of interests in property? Does this exercise suggest that respecting secured transactions can be seen as merely one genre of a more general principle of respect for the alienability of property?

Do you find the indeterminacy of Professor Shupack's conclusions unsatisfying? Assuming, as he concludes, that there can be no "general theory" of secured credit that consistently predicts behavior, does that mean that the participants in the debate have wasted their time (and ours)?

Others also have recognized that "[i]t is unlikely that a single explanation can rationalize all of these various forms of security." Scott, A Relational Theory of Secured Financing, 86 Colum.L.Rev. 901, 912 (1986). However, theoretical explorations of legal institutions can accomplish much even if no general theory emerges. For example, the efficiency debate has served to identify areas in need of further empirical research and those where empirical research (even if "necessary") would be largely impossible. It has served to heighten sensitivities to the relationship between finance theory and the legal rules that regulate security interests and priorities in bankruptcy. And it has underscored the enormous variety of transactions (secured and unsecured) that are affected by Article 9.

Professor Schwartz seems to have been the most frequent participant in the efficiency debate. In his most recent offering, he steps beyond consideration of secured credit as we know it. Although he remains puzzled about why security is given under the current regime, he recommends that the decisionmakers consider making radical changes to the structure of the Article 9 priority scheme. Schwartz, A Theory of Loan Priorities, 18 J. Legal Stud. 209, 247 (1989). Professor

Schwartz acknowledges that "[t]ractability is not the same thing as moral acceptability," but he concludes that his proposal's "central results serve the most affected parties better in some cases, and as well in others, as existing law does, without contradicting the equality norm in obviously unacceptable fashion. There is a prima facie case for amending current law to realize such results." Id. at 260.

In his article Professor Schwartz makes three claims. First, he claims that the statutory priority scheme should mirror the priorities that would be reflected in a contract between a borrower and its "initial financer." (He defines "initial financer" as "the first creditor that made a substantial loan that would be outstanding for a nontrivial time period"—i.e., *not* a typical unsecured trade creditor who is supposed to be paid within 30 to 45 days.) Second, if borrowers and initial financers would agree to confer a first priority on the initial financer's claim, then Professor Schwartz argues that this should be the legal priority rule even if the initial financers are unsecured and even if they give no public notice of their claim. Third, he claims (and endeavors to demonstrate with an economic model) that "the optimal priority contract—the typical acceptable priority proposal—actually would rank the initial financer first, whether it is secured or not." Id. at 211.

Professor Schwartz's priority scheme would rank the creditors of an insolvent debtor as follows:

1. Secured purchase money lenders, if any exist, but only to the extent permitted in the loan contract between the debtor and initial financer. Later credit sellers should not be presumed to be secured but must actually take purchase-money security interests. This is because the parties to initial loan contracts would not subordinate the financer to all later sellers.

2. Financers in the order in which they appear, whether secured or not. This status should be a consequence of the enactment of the modified ... [first in time] rule as the legal priority scheme and thus should obtain unless the parties contract out.

3. Nonpurchase-money creditors who are not financers but who take security in particular assets rank ahead of later creditors with respect to these assets.

4. Trade and other small creditors take pro rata with each other and with any financers that appeared after these creditors' claims arose. The costs of ranking in order of appearance the numerous creditors of an insolvent debtor would probably exceed any gains. Consistent with this view, there is no evidence that actual trade and other creditors contract for particular priority positions (apart from the creditors who take purchase-money security interests).

Id. at 248.   Professor Schwartz also would abolish the priority for chattel paper purchasers under UCC 9–308 as well as the PMSI priority for inventory under UCC 9–312(3).   Id. at 250–54.   (The article never mentions real estate.   One wonders if the initial financers in Professor Schwartz's world would have claims senior to those of a first mortgagee of real estate.)

Note that Professor Schwartz's system creates a de facto "secret lien" in favor of earlier-in-time financers.   He dismisses the Article 9 filing system as unnecessary for providing information and ranking priorities, because a private information system—debtor disclosure—is cheaper; "good debtors" will be motivated to give an accurate account of their debts.   Of course, bad debtors would have the opposite motivation, but Professor Schwartz reasons that creditors will simply refuse credit until prospective debtors prove the negative—i.e., that there are no earlier-in-time financers.   Moreover, he argues, collateral does not seem to be all that important to secured lenders anyway and secured lenders make the same credit investigations as do unsecured creditors. Id. at 222.   However, he concludes that the filing system should be retained to protect *buyers* from earlier-in-time security interests and he also would allow buyers to take ahead of earlier-in-time financers.   Id. at 223.

In some ways Professor Schwartz's proposal is reminiscent of a proposal that the "public files should be scrapped," which was made by the original Reporters who drafted Article 9.   1 Gilmore, Security § 15.1, at 464.   Professor Gilmore wrote of this proposal:

> The key to the proposal was the imposition of a duty on a secured party to use due diligence to see that his debtor's financial statements made full disclosure of the security interest; ....   The details of the proposal were never reduced to statutory language since the Reporters were unable to convince anyone of the soundness of their position, and the proposal was shortly abandoned.

Id.   Professor Schwartz seems to have expanded the idea underlying the earlier proposal and dispensed with the need for a security agreement as well.

If, as Professor Schwartz believes, initial financers typically extract loan agreement covenants that restrict borrowers' rights to incur later indebtedness, and if borrowers in fact typically comply with those covenants, why adopt a new scheme?   Why worry about the "optimal priority contract" when the *actual* priority contract typically controls? Professor Schwartz has ventured a partial answer to these questions (which must be answered if his proposals are not to become unglued) in a footnote:

> If a later lender is aware of the earlier contract restrictions, the lender may be liable for inducing breach of contract if it lends.   Few such tort suits against later lenders are brought, apparently because knowledge of restrictive loan covenants is a

necessary but not sufficient condition for tort liability; the later lender also must *induce* the breach rather than lend to a debtor that had already decided to breach. Most debtors that approach later lenders have already made the breach decision. Accordingly, this article assumes that the threat of tort liability does not discourage later lenders from dealing with debtors that are violating loan covenants.

Id. at 210 n. 5.

Professor Schwartz provides no support for his assumptions about the behavior of lenders and borrowers and about the law of tortious interference with contractual relations. Perhaps the reason that few suits against subsequent lenders are brought is that few later lenders in their right minds would dream of walking into the trap that Professor Schwartz has hypothesized. Almost invariably the default in the first lender's agreement would give it a right to accelerate its debt. And that default (or the acceleration) would almost invariably constitute a default under the later lender's new loan agreement. What lenders knowingly would lend into a situation like that?

Consider, also, the applicable legal liability rules. Professor Schwartz's assertion that the later lender would have nothing to fear of tort liability if the debtor had "already made the breach decision" is questionable. See Restatement (Second) of Torts § 766, comment *h* ("The rule stated in this Section applies to any intentional causation whether by inducement or otherwise. The essential thing is the intent to cause the result."), comment *j* ("The rule applies ... to an interference that is incidental to the actor's independent purpose and desire but known to him to be a necessary consequence of his action.") (1977).

Chapter 15

DEFAULT; ENFORCEMENT OF
SECURITY INTERESTS

Introductory Note. The preceding chapters focused primarily on the acquisition and perfection of security interests and the priority of competing claims to the collateral. For the most part, these issues become moot if the debtor pays the secured obligation.[1] Secured credit typically is extended with the expectation that the debtor *will* pay and that the secured party will not need to recover its claim from the collateral. A creditor's need to enforce its security interest typically is an indication that the credit transaction has failed.

Of course, transactions do fail and secured parties do find the need to turn their collateral into cash. This Chapter examines the rights and duties of a secured party who enforces a security interest. Section 1 deals with the scope of the secured party's right to take possession of collateral when the debtor is in default. Section 2 considers the right of a secured party to dispose of (e.g., sell) collateral and to apply the proceeds to the secured obligation. It also covers the effect of a secured party's noncompliance with its duties under Part 5 of Article 9. Section 3 addresses the implications of enforcement for certain third parties—sureties (such as guarantors of the secured obligation), the holders of security interests and other liens, and purchasers from a secured party who disposes of collateral after default. Section 4, which deals with "redemption," examines the scope of the debtor's right to satisfy the secured obligation and recover the collateral before the secured party disposes of it. Section 5 then considers the enforcement of security interests in accounts and other rights to payment through "collections" from the obligors. Finally, Section 6 deals with a secured party's retention of collateral in satisfaction of the secured obligation, sometimes called "strict foreclosure."

The term "foreclosure" is commonly used to refer the process by which security interests are enforced against collateral, although the word is not used in the Code. Under pre-Code personal property security law (as well as current real estate law), the term "foreclosure" embraces the process by which the debtor's right to "redeem" the encumbered property is "foreclosed." (UCC 9–506 provides for the debtor's right to redeem collateral by paying in full the secured obligation "[a]t any time before the secured party has disposed of collateral or entered into a contract for its disposition under Section 9–504[.]")

---

1. Even if the debtor pays the secured obligation, questions of perfection and priority may be implicated if the debtor enters bankruptcy within the preference period. See BC 547; Chapter 14, Section 2, *supra*.

Consistent with common parlance, these materials sometimes refer to "foreclosure," "foreclosure sale," and the like.

Most of the issues we have considered heretofore involve three parties—the debtor, the secured party, and the holder of a competing claim to the collateral. Although the enforcement of a security interest sometimes affects the rights of third parties, more often only the debtor and secured party are involved. Questions of perfection and priority often are irrelevant; Part 5 of Article 9 (the 9–500's) takes center stage. And, as we shall see, important legislation intended to protect consumers often supplements and modifies the rules of the Code.

As you work through the materials in this Chapter, you would do well to keep in mind what is at stake. A security interest, you will recall, is a limited "interest in ... *property*." UCC 1–201(37). Unless the security interest has been perfected by possession, the secured party's right to exercise any control over collateral is contingent on the debtor's default. When the secured party does exercise control, it may do so only for the limited purpose of obtaining payment of the secured obligation. Indeed, the secured party's property interest is limited to the amount of the secured obligation (except in the cases of outright sales of accounts or chattel paper). These limitations on the interest that the secured party enjoys should not be overemphasized. Immediately upon the debtor's default, creditors who hold security interests can look to specific property to satisfy their claims; unsecured creditors cannot.

The debtor, too, holds a property interest, one that typically includes the right to possess, use, and control the collateral. The debtor also takes the risks and enjoys the benefits of changes in collateral value. Thus, enforcement implicates a delicate interplay of interests: Curtailing the secured party's control over the collateral can impair the security on which the transaction depends; taking the control of collateral away from the debtor can impair personal and economic well-being.

Perhaps for this reason, Part 5 of Article 9 departs from the Code's general emphasis on freedom of contract. See UCC 1–102(3) (the effect of Code provisions generally may be varied by agreement). Part 5 contains a number of rules that cannot be waived or varied, even by sophisticated debtors who are represented by counsel. See UCC 9–501(3). As you study these rules, you should consider whether the departures from freedom-of-contract principles are justified.

This Chapter focuses primarily on the rights and remedies of debtors and secured parties under Part 5 of Article 9—an important and frequently litigated area of legal regulation. However, you should keep in mind that there is a large body of other law that features prominently in the relationship between creditors and debtors. Two aspects of this other law are particularly noteworthy. First, during the last fifteen to twenty years a rapidly growing body of law, generally dubbed **lender liability**, has emerged. The courts have been developing myriad theories of liability, ranging from claims based on common-law fraud and duress to claims based on securities regulation statutes and claims based on the failure to observe duties of good faith and fair dealing.

Second, a secured creditor who engages in inequitable conduct in the course of enforcing its security interest runs the risk that its claim will be subordinated to claims of other creditors in bankruptcy. See BC 510(c). The doctrine of **equitable subordination** has developed through the case law of the past half century. Generally speaking, a creditor's claim will be equitably subordinated if the creditor has engaged in fraud or other inequitable conduct that resulted in an unfair advantage to the creditor or in harm to other creditors, provided that subordination would not be contrary to the principles of bankruptcy law.

As you work your way through the following materials, do not forget that much law other than the Code regulates a creditor's behavior. Before proceeding to the following Problems, cases and Notes, you may find it useful to peruse the brief overview of Article 9, Part 5, found in Chapter 10, Section 2(G), supra. Finally, please bear in mind that when a debtor enters bankruptcy *the rules change* (even if equitable subordination is not at issue). In particular, recall the broad sweep of the automatic stay under BC 362 and the bankruptcy trustee's turnover powers under BC 542, discussed in Chapter 14, Section 1, supra.

Note on Rights and Duties After Default

UCC 9–501 explains generally the rights and remedies of the secured party and the debtor. Subsection (1) makes clear that the secured party may proceed without judicial process under Article 9, may exercise the rights and remedies provided in the security agreement, and may enforce the security interest by any judicial procedure. Although the secured party's rights and remedies are cumulative, they are not entirely independent from one another. UCC 9–501(5) explains the interplay between enforcement by judicial process and the secured party's rights under Article 9.

The rights and remedies of the debtor and secured party arise upon "default." The Code neither defines the term nor explains the concept of default; rather, what constitutes a default generally is left to the agreement of the parties. The most common default is the debtor's failure to make a required payment on a secured obligation when it becomes due. Most security agreements specify several other events of default as well. See Form 2, ¶ 12, and Form 6, ¶ 5, Chapter 11, Section 1, supra. As we shall see in Section 4, infra, determining whether a payment or other default has occurred sometimes can be difficult.

SECTION 1. TAKING POSSESSION OF COLLATERAL AFTER DEFAULT

(A) In General

THEY'RE THE NIGHT STALKERS

On the prowl, silent and fast: Repo Men

By Edward Power

Inquirer Staff Writer

You are now entering Repo Reality:

Somewhere out on the dark side streets, or tucked away in the fringe neighborhoods of Philadelphia, there was a gold 1988 Hyundai Excel, parked by the curbside pretty as a trophy.

Two months ago, the car's owner had walked onto a dealer's lot and then signed a loan agreement with a Philadelphia bank. The value of the contract: $13,124.14.

Sixty days after driving away, the new owner had yet to make his first payment of $218.59 per month. "Never even got out of the gate," as Dick Harris put it.[*]

That was when Harris, 58, and Jim Carden Jr., 25, got involved. They are repo men.

So there, motoring along the 1400 block of Fanshawe Street in Northeast Philadelphia, at 12:20 a.m. Friday, Carden and Harris let their eyes roam the taillights and license plates.

"You develop a feel, almost smell it," Harris said of the hunt for such cars.

"A sixth sense," Carden agreed, nodding.

And then Carden's sixth sense kicked like a turbocharger. There was the gold Excel, three cars ahead, a loan officer's dream.

"We've got to break into it and move it back so we can tow it," Harris said as Carden got out a long silver wire with a hook on one end. The street was dark, but suddenly a single porch light flicked on.

The two men ignored it. Within 30 seconds, Carden had the door open and was silently rolling the Hyundai back, just enough so he could get the tow boom from his truck under the fender.

[* Mr. Harris, who is quoted in this article, is not related to any of the authors of this book.]

Less than four minutes after spotting the car, Carden gunned the tow truck's engine, and he and Harris were rolling again.

"That's the name of that tune," Harris said, and on into the Philadelphia night he and Carden went, looking for more of the repossessions they call "deals."

Cruising the streets a little earlier, Harris had remarked on the reason he and Carden spend their nights fending off crack dealers, narrowly escaping irate car owners and looking for a prize $50,000 BMW owned by a drug dealer who is wanted by the police for stealing the car, not to mention executing his enemies.

"We're adrenalin freaks," Harris said smiling.

Inside the North Philadelphia warehouse where his repossession business is based, Jim Carden Sr., president of East Coast Recovery Inc., was readying the crews to go out one night last week; among them was his son, Jim . . . .

"Because I'm a repossessor there's a stigma attached to me," Carden [Sr.] said. "It's difficult when you've always had acceptance and now you're looked at as a dirt bag or something."

"Picture yourself walking up somebody's driveway at 3 o'clock in the morning," the younger Carden said of the perils of the repo business.

"And King Kong comes out of the house," Harris added.

. . .

Find it. Hook it up. Hit the gas.

Repo man.

The Philadelphia Inquirer, Nov. 20, 1988, at 1–B, 3–B.

Problem 1. In the setting of the Prototype, Lee Abel purchased a new Pontiac and signed the Installment Sale Contract. See Form 6, Chapter 9, Section 1, supra. As in the Prototype, Main Motors assigned the contract to Firstbank.

Abel made five monthly payments from June 15 through October 15. At the end of October Abel was laid off work and was unable to continue the payments. Two weeks after missing the November 15 payment, an employee of Firstbank phoned to remind Abel that the payment was overdue. Firstbank wrote and phoned Abel several more times in November and December, and on December 10 Firstbank wrote to Abel stating that unless prompt payment was forthcoming, Firstbank would be required to repossess the car. Abel was still unable to find the money for the payments.

Abel kept the car at home, parked in the street. At around 11:00 P.M. on December 15, Abel saw a car stop in front of the house. Two people got out and approached Abel's car, inserted a key in the lock, and opened the door. Abel said to a friend who was visiting at the time: "Someone's messing around with my car. Call the police." Abel then rushed out the door. Before Abel got outside the two people had entered the Pontiac and closed and locked the car doors. Abel ran up to the car and shouted: "Get out of my car." One of the people said: "Sorry, but we're repossessing the car for Firstbank." The other started the motor and they drove off with the car.

Before the car reached the corner, a patrol car arrived in response to a radio message that relayed the call from Abel's friend. Abel pointed to the departing Pontiac; the patrol car caught up with the Pontiac and stopped the car. The driver and passenger in the Pontiac identified themselves as employees of a repossession firm retained by Firstbank, and showed the officers a copy of the Installment Sales Contract and a copy of the December 10 letter to Abel giving notice that the payment was overdue. The officers then allowed the repo team to proceed with the Pontiac.

(a) Abel sues Firstbank for conversion, for compensation for loss of the use of the car, and for punitive damages. What result? See UCC 9–503; Stone Machinery Co. v. Kessler, infra; Williams v. Ford Motor Credit Co., infra; Wade v. Ford Motor Credit Co., infra.

(b) Suppose that Abel jumped into another car and gave chase, leading to traffic violations. What result? See Jordan v. Citizens & Southern National Bank, 278 S.C. 449, 298 S.E.2d 213 (1982) (high speed chase involving traffic violations following repossession was not a breach of the peace in the repossession; conduct at a distance from the place of repossession (plaintiff's home) was not "conduct at or near and/or incident to the seizure of the property").

(c) Now suppose that Abel rushed outside, confronted the repo team *before* they entered the car, and demanded that they leave the car where it was. Without responding, the repo team jumped in the Pontiac and drove it away. What result?

(d) Suppose, instead, that, while still inside, Abel noticed that the repo team was armed with shotguns. Abel, being no fool, remained inside, did not confront the repo team, and watched as they drove away the Pontiac. (You may assume that their possession of the shotguns was legal under applicable law.) What result? Is this scenario or the one presented in part (c) above more likely to result in actual violence?

(e) Suppose that the police had arrived before the repo team entered the car. Would their presence alone have affected the outcome? See *Stone Machinery*, infra.

Problem 2. Misako Inaba bought a food freezer from Cellar Department Store pursuant to an installment sales contract that gave Cellar a security interest in the freezer. After making eight monthly payments, Inaba missed the next two installments. Cellar's employees phoned and sent written notices to Inaba; these messages warned

Inaba that, unless payments were made, Cellar would be required to repossess the freezer. Inaba failed to pay. One afternoon two people knocked on Inaba's door. When Inaba opened the door, one of them said, "We've come to repossess the freezer," and then walked in. Inaba responded, "I think that's a terrible thing to do. I'll pay you as soon as I can." The other replied, "I'm awfully sorry, but we have our orders." Inaba spoke further, with considerable feeling, of the personal and family hardship of losing the freezer. But they picked up the freezer and carried it away.

Inaba sued Cellar for wrongful repossession. What result from the courts that decided the *Stone Machinery*, *Williams*, and *Wade* cases, infra?

STONE MACHINERY CO. v. KESSLER

Court of Appeals of Washington, 1970.
1 Wash.App. 750, 463 P.2d 651, review denied, 77 Wash.2d 962 (1970).

Evans, Chief Judge. Plaintiff Stone Machinery brought this action in Asotin County to repossess a D–9 Caterpillar Tractor which plaintiff had sold to defendant Frank Kessler under conditional sales contract. Service of process was not made on the defendant but plaintiff located the tractor in Oregon and repossessed it. The defendant then filed an answer and cross-complaint in the Asotin County replevin action, alleging that the plaintiff wrongfully and maliciously repossessed the tractor, and sought compensatory and punitive damages under Oregon law. Trial was to the court without a jury and the court awarded defendant compensatory damages in the sum of $18,586.20, and punitive damages in the sum of $12,000 on defendant's cross-complaint.

The operative facts are not in serious dispute. Defendant Kessler purchased, by conditional sales contract, a used D–9 Caterpillar Tractor from the plaintiff Stone Machinery, for the sum of $23,500. The unpaid balance of $17,500 was to be paid in monthly installments, with skip payments.[*] The defendant's payment record was erratic and several payments were made late. However, payments of $3600 on March 29, 1966, and $1800 on July 18, 1966, put the contract payments on a current basis. The payment due on August 10, 1966 was not made and, on September 7, 1966, plaintiff's credit manager, Richard Kazanis, went to the defendant's ranch in Garfield, Washington, and demanded payment of the balance due on the contract or immediate possession of the tractor. At this time defendant had made payments on the purchase price totaling $17,200, including the trade-in. The defendant was unable to make full payment, or any payment at that time, and

[* A "skip payment" arrangement allows the debtor to skip a certain number of payments each year; these arrangements are seen most often in transactions involving debtors in seasonal lines of business, such as agriculture and construction.]

informed Mr. Kazanis that he would not relinquish possession of the tractor to him at that time, or at any time in the future, in the absence of proper judicial proceedings showing his right to repossess, and that "someone would get hurt" if an attempt was made to repossess without "proper papers." At that time the defendant informed Mr. Kazanis that he, the defendant, expected to be awarded a contract by the U.S. Bureau of Fisheries to do some work with the D–9 at their installation on the Grande Ronde River near Troy, Oregon, and that he would then be able to pay on the tractor.

On September 13, 1966, the plaintiff instituted this action in Asotin County, Washington, but the sheriff was unable to locate the tractor in that county. Thereafter, the plaintiff instituted another action in Garfield County, but the sheriff was unable to locate the tractor in that county. The evidence indicates that on September 24 Kessler took the tractor to Oregon to work the Bureau of Fisheries job.

On September 27, 1966, Mr. Kazanis, by use of an airplane, located the tractor on the Grande Ronde River, west of Troy, Wallowa County, Oregon. He then contacted the sheriff of Wallowa County and requested him to accompany them in the repossession of the tractor to prevent any violence by the defendant. The sheriff agreed to meet with Mr. Kazanis at Troy, Oregon, and on September 27, 1966, Mr. Kazanis in his private car, plaintiff's mechanic in a company pickup, and the plaintiff's truck driver in the company lo-boy truck, left Walla Walla, and the following morning met the Wallowa County Sheriff at Troy, where the sheriff was shown a copy of the conditional sales contract. The sheriff confirmed previous legal advice plaintiff had received that the plaintiff had the right to repossess the tractor (although not by the use of force) and thereupon the sheriff, in his official sheriff's car, followed by Mr. Kazanis in his private car, the mechanic in the pickup, and the truck driver in the lo-boy, proceeded to the scene where the defendant was operating the D–9 tractor in the Grande Ronde River approximately 7 miles west of Troy, pursuant to contract with the U.S. Bureau of Fisheries.

Upon arriving at the scene the sheriff, accompanied by Mr. Kazanis, walked to the edge of the river and motioned the defendant, who was working with the tractor in the river, to bring the tractor to shore. The sheriff was in uniform and wearing his badge and sidearms. The sheriff informed the defendant that the plaintiff Stone Machinery had a right to repossess the tractor, and stated, "We come to pick up the tractor." The defendant asked the sheriff if he had proper papers to take the tractor and the sheriff replied, "No." The defendant Kessler protested and objected to the taking of the tractor but offered no physical resistance because, as he testified, "he didn't think he had to disregard an order of the sheriff." The plaintiff's employee then loaded the tractor on the lo-boy and left for Walla Walla, Washington.

Within a few days the tractor was sold to a road contractor at Milton–Freewater, Oregon, for the sum of $7447.80 cash, on an "as is" basis. The sale price represented the balance due on the contract, plus the plaintiff's charges for repossession.

Plaintiff's first assignments of error are directed to the following findings of the trial court:

XII

That the plaintiffs actions in repossessing the defendant's tractor on September 28, 1966, and the actions of the Wallowa County Sheriff, in aid of the plaintiffs, amounted to constructive force, intimidation and oppression, constituting a breach of the peace and conversion of defendant's tractor.

XIV

That the plaintiffs failed to show just cause or excuse for the wrongful act of repossession of the defendant's tractor on September 28, 1966.

XV

That the wrongful act of repossession, done intentionally on September 28, 1966, was malicious and was so wanton and reckless as to show disregard for the rights of the defendant Frank Kessler.

. . .

Retaking possession of a chattel by a conditional seller, upon the default of the buyer, is governed by O.R.S. 79.5030 (U.C.C. 9–503):

Secured party's right to take possession after default. Unless otherwise agreed a secured party has on default the right to take possession of the collateral. In taking possession a secured party may proceed without judicial process *if this can be done without breach of the peace* or may proceed by action. * * *

(Italics ours.)

Defendant Kessler was admittedly in default for nonpayment of the August and September contract installments. By the terms of the above statute Stone Machinery had the right to take possession of the tractor without judicial process, but only if this could be done without a breach of the peace. The question is whether the method by which they proceeded constituted a breach of the peace.

No Oregon cases have been cited which define the term "breach of peace" so we must look to other authority. In 1 Restatement of Torts 2d, § 116 (1965), the term is defined as follows:

A breach of the peace is a public offense done by violence, or one causing or likely to cause an immediate disturbance of public order.

In the case of McKee v. State, 75 Okl.Cr. 390, 132 P.2d 173, breach of peace is defined (headnote 9, 132 P.2d 173), as follows:

> To constitute a "breach of the peace" it is not necessary that the peace be actually broken, and if what is done is unjustifiable and unlawful, tending with sufficient directness to break the peace, no more is required, nor is actual personal violence an essential element of the offense. * * *

In the instant case it was the sheriff who said that he had no legal papers but that "we come over to pick up this tractor." Whereupon, the defendant Kessler stated, "I told him I was resisting this; there was an action started and I wanted to have a few days to get money together to pay them off." At this point defendant Kessler had a right to obstruct, by all lawful and reasonable means, any attempt by plaintiff to forcibly repossess the tractor. Had the defendant offered any physical resistance, there existed upon both the sheriff and plaintiff's agents a duty to retreat. However, confronted by the sheriff, who announced his intention to participate in the repossession, it was not necessary for Kessler to either threaten violence or offer physical resistance. As stated by the court in Roberts v. Speck, 169 Wash. 613, at 616, 14 P.2d 33 at 34 (1932), citing from Jones on Chattel Mortgages (4th ed.), § 705:

> "The mortgagee becomes a trespasser by going upon the premises of the mortgagor, accompanied by a deputy sheriff who has no legal process, but claims to act *colore officii*, and taking possession without the active resistance of the mortgagor. To obtain possession under such a show and pretence of authority is to trifle with the obedience of citizens to the law and its officers."

Acts done by an officer which are of such a nature that the office gives him no authority to do them are "*colore officii*." See 7A Words & Phrases Perm.Ed. at 296.

In Burgin v. Universal Credit Co., supra, the conditional seller retook possession from the buyer, after default in payments, and in order to do so secured the presence of a police officer, without legal papers. The only act of the officer was to order the buyer to release the brakes and drive the car to the curb. The court said:

> "Because a party to a contract violates his contract, and refuses to do what he agreed to do, is no reason why the other party to the contract should compel the performance of the contract by force. The adoption of such a rule would lead to a breach of the peace, and it is never the policy of the law to encourage a breach of the peace. The right to an enforcement of this part of the contract must, in the absence of a consent on the part of the mortgagor, be enforced by due process of law, the same as any other contract." ...

In the case of Firebaugh v. Gunther, 106 Okl. 131, 233 P. 460 (1925), the defendant secured the services of a deputy sheriff to take possession of the property. The deputy sheriff, not having legal papers, stated "he was going to take the property and did not want to make any trouble." It was held that his conduct constituted intimidation amounting to force . . . .

In the instant case, when the sheriff of Wallowa County, having no authority to do so, told the defendant Kessler, "We come over to pick up this tractor," he was acting *colore officii* and became a participant in the repossession, regardless of the fact that he did not physically take part in the retaking. Plaintiff contends that its sole purpose in having the sheriff present was to prevent anticipated violence. The effect, however, was to prevent the defendant Kessler from exercising his right to resist by all lawful and reasonable means a nonjudicial take-over. To put the stamp of approval upon this method of repossession would be to completely circumvent the purpose and intent of the statute.

We hold there is substantial evidence to support the trial court's finding that the unauthorized actions of the sheriff in aid of the plaintiff amounted to constructive force, intimidation and oppression constituting a breach of the peace and conversion of the defendant's tractor . . . .

Plaintiff's final assignment of error relates to the trial court's award of punitive damages. The Oregon law regarding punitive damages has recently been set forth in the case of Douglas v. Humble Oil & Refining Co., 445 P.2d 590 (Or.1968):

> As a general rule, punitive damages will be allowed only when the proof supports a finding that the defendant acted with improper motives or with willful, wanton, or reckless disregard for the rights of others. * * *

> We held recently that it is only in those instances where the violation of societal interests is sufficiently great and of a kind that sanctions would tend to prevent that the use of punitive damages is proper. "Regardless of the nomenclature by which a violation of these obligations is described (grossly negligent, willful, wanton, malicious, etc.), it is apparent that this court has decided that it is proper to use the sanction of punitive damages where there has been a particularly aggravated disregard * * *" of the rights of the victim. Noe v. Kaiser Foundation Hospitals, Or., 435 P.2d 306 (1967).

Defendant Kessler was in default of his contract and had announced his intention to resist any attempted nonjudicial repossession. The words used in announcing his intention, namely, "someone would get hurt," were of such a nature as to justify the presence of a sheriff during any attempt at peaceable repossession although, as we have already held, this did not justify participation by the sheriff in the process of repossession. However, the fact that the sheriff did undertake to act *colore officii* in the repossession was not, under the circumstances, sufficient to support a finding that the plaintiff thereby displayed a particularly aggravated disregard for the rights of Kessler, within the meaning of Douglas v. Humble Oil & Refining Co., supra.

Judgment for compensatory damages is affirmed. Judgment for punitive damages is reversed.

WILLIAMS v. FORD MOTOR CREDIT CO.

United States Court of Appeals, Eighth Circuit, 1982.
674 F.2d 717.

BENSON, CHIEF JUDGE. In this diversity action brought by Cathy A. Williams to recover damages for conversion arising out of an alleged wrongful repossession of an automobile, Williams appeals from a judgment notwithstanding the verdict entered on motion of defendant Ford Motor Credit Company (FMCC). In the same case, FMCC appeals a directed verdict in favor of third party defendant S & S Recovery, Inc. (S & S) on FMCC's third party claim for indemnification. We affirm the judgment n.o.v. FMCC's appeal is thereby rendered moot.

In July, 1975, David Williams, husband of plaintiff Cathy Williams, purchased a Ford Mustang from an Oklahoma Ford dealer. Although David Williams executed the sales contract, security agreement, and loan papers, title to the car was in the name of both David and Cathy Williams. The car was financed through the Ford dealer, who in turn assigned the paper to FMCC. Cathy and David Williams were divorced in 1977. The divorce court granted Cathy title to the automobile and required David to continue to make payments to FMCC for eighteen months. David defaulted on the payments and signed a voluntary repossession authorization for FMCC. Cathy Williams was informed of the delinquency and responded that she was trying to get her former husband David to make the payments. There is no evidence of any agreement between her and FMCC. Pursuant to an agreement with FMCC, S & S was directed to repossess the automobile.

On December 1, 1977, at approximately 4:30 a.m., Cathy Williams was awakened by a noise outside her house trailer in Van Buren, Arkansas. She saw that a wrecker truck with two men in it had hooked up to the Ford Mustang and started to tow it away. She went outside and hollered at them. The truck stopped. She then told them that the car was hers and asked them what they were doing. One of the men, later identified as Don Sappington, president of S & S Recovery, Inc., informed her that he was repossessing the vehicle on behalf of FMCC. Williams explained that she had been attempting to bring the past due payments up to date and informed Sappington that the car contained personal items which did not even belong to her. Sappington got out of the truck, retrieved the items from the car, and handed them to her. Without further complaint from Williams, Sappington returned to the truck and drove off, car in tow. At trial, Williams testified that Sappington was polite throughout their encounter and did not make any threats toward her or do anything which caused her to fear any physical harm. The automobile had been parked in an unenclosed driveway which plaintiff shared with a neighbor. The neighbor was awakened by the wrecker backing into the driveway, but did not come out. After the wrecker drove off, Williams returned to her house trailer and called the police, reporting her car as stolen. Later, Williams commenced this action.

The case was tried to a jury which awarded her $5,000.00 in damages. FMCC moved for judgment notwithstanding the verdict, but the district court, on Williams' motion, ordered a nonsuit without prejudice to refile in state court. On FMCC's appeal, this court reversed and remanded with directions to the district court to rule on the motion for judgment notwithstanding the verdict. The district court entered judgment notwithstanding the verdict for FMCC, and this appeal followed.

Article 9 of the Uniform Commercial Code (UCC), which Arkansas has adopted and codified as Ark.Stat.Ann. § 85–9–503 (Supp.1981), provides in pertinent part:

> Unless otherwise agreed, a secured party has on default the right to take possession of the collateral. In taking possession, a secured party may proceed without judicial process if this can be done without breach of the peace....[4]

In Ford Motor Credit Co. v. Herring, 27 U.C.C.Rep. 1448, 267 Ark. 201, 589 S.W.2d 584, 586 (1979), which involved an alleged conversion arising out of a repossession, the Supreme Court of Arkansas cited Section 85–9–503 and referred to its previous holdings as follows:

> In pre-code cases, we have sustained a finding of conversion only where force, or threats of force, or risk of invoking violence, accompanied the repossession.

The thrust of Williams' argument on appeal is that the repossession was accomplished by the risk of invoking violence. The district judge who presided at the trial commented on her theory in his memorandum opinion:

> Mrs. Williams herself admitted that the men who repossessed her automobile were very polite and complied with her requests. The evidence does not reveal that they performed any act which was oppressive, threatening or tended to cause physical violence. Unlike the situation presented in Manhattan Credit Co. v. Brewer, supra, it was not shown that Mrs.

---

4. It is generally considered that the objectives of this section are (1) to benefit creditors in permitting them to realize collateral without having to resort to judicial process; (2) to benefit debtors in general by making credit available at lower costs; and (3) to support a public policy discouraging extrajudicial acts by citizens when those acts are fraught with the likelihood of resulting violence.

Williams would have been forced to resort to physical violence to stop the men from leaving with her automobile.

In the pre-Code case Manhattan Credit Co. v. Brewer, 232 Ark. 976, 341 S.W.2d 765 (1961), the court held that a breach of peace occurred when the debtor and her husband confronted the creditor's agent during the act of repossession and clearly objected to the repossession, 341 S.W.2d at 767–68. In *Manhattan*, the court examined holdings of earlier cases in which repossessions were deemed to have been accomplished without any breach of the peace, id. In particular, the Supreme Court of Arkansas discussed the case of Rutledge v. Universal C.I.T. Credit Corp., 218 Ark. 510, 237 S.W.2d 469 (1951). In *Rutledge*, the court found no breach of the peace when the repossessor acquired keys to the automobile, confronted the debtor and his wife, informed them he was going to take the car, and immediately proceeded to do so. As the *Rutledge* court explained and the *Manhattan* court reiterated, a breach of the peace did not occur when the "Appellant [debtor-possessor] did not give his permission but he did not object."

We have read the transcript of the trial. There is no material dispute in the evidence, and the district court has correctly summarized it. Cathy Williams did not raise an objection to the taking, and the repossession was accomplished without any incident which might tend to provoke violence.

Appellees deserve something less than commendation for the taking during the night time sleeping hours, but it is clear that viewing the facts in the light most favorable to Williams, the taking was a legal repossession under the laws of the State of Arkansas. The evidence does not support the verdict of the jury. FMCC is entitled to judgment notwithstanding the verdict.

The judgment notwithstanding the verdict is affirmed.

HEANEY, CIRCUIT JUDGE, dissenting. The only issue is whether the repossession of appellant's automobile constituted a breach of the peace by creating a "risk of invoking violence." See Ford Motor Credit Co. v. Herring, 267 Ark. 201, 589 S.W.2d 584, 586 (1979). The trial jury found that it did and awarded $5,000 for conversion. Because that determination was in my view a reasonable one, I dissent from the Court's decision to overturn it.

Cathy Williams was a single parent living with her two small children in a trailer home in Van Buren, Arkansas. On December 1, 1977, at approximately 4:30 a.m., she was awakened by noises in her driveway. She went into the night to investigate and discovered a wrecker and its crew in the process of towing away her car. According to the trial court, "she ran outside to stop them ... but she made no *strenuous* protests to their actions." (Emphasis added.) In fact, the wrecker crew stepped between her and the car when she sought to retrieve personal items from inside it, although the men retrieved some of the items for her. The commotion created by the incident awakened neighbors in the vicinity.

Facing the wrecker crew in the dead of night, Cathy Williams did everything she could to stop them, short of introducing physical force to meet the presence of the crew. The confrontation did not result in violence only because Ms. Williams did not take such steps and was otherwise powerless to stop the crew.

The controlling law is the UCC, which authorizes self-help repossession only when such is done "without breach of the peace * * *." Ark.Stat.Ann. § 85–9–503 (Supp.1981). The majority recognizes that one important policy consideration underlying this restriction is to discourage "extrajudicial acts by citizens when those acts are fraught with the likelihood of resulting violence." Despite this, the majority holds that no reasonable jury could find that the confrontation in Cathy Williams' driveway at 4:30 a.m. created a risk of violence. I cannot agree. At a minimum, the largely undisputed facts created a jury question. The jury found a breach of the peace and this Court has no sound, much less compelling, reason to overturn that determination.

Indeed, I would think that sound application of the self-help limitation might require a directed verdict in favor of Ms. Williams, but certainly not against her. If a "night raid" is conducted without detection and confrontation, then, of course, there could be no breach of the peace. But where the invasion is detected and a confrontation ensues, the repossessor should be under a duty to retreat and turn to judicial process. The alternative which the majority embraces is to allow a repossessor to proceed following confrontation unless and until violence results in fact. Such a rule invites tragic consequences which the law should seek to prevent, not to encourage. I would reverse the trial court and reinstate the jury's verdict.

WADE v. FORD MOTOR CREDIT CO.

Court of Appeals of Kansas, 1983.
8 Kan.App.2d 737, 668 P.2d 183.

SWINEHART, JUDGE: This is an appeal by defendant Ford Motor Credit Company (Ford) from a judgment against it and in favor of plaintiff Norma J. Wade, awarding her damages for conversion, loss of credit reputation, punitive damages and attorney fees in an action arising out of Ford's alleged breach of the peace in the repossession of Wade's car.

Wade entered into an automobile retail installment contract on August 9, 1979, for the purchase of a 1979 Ford Thunderbird automobile. The contract was assigned to Ford which advanced $6,967.75 to enable her to purchase the car. Pursuant to the terms of the contract, Ford had a security interest in the car which had been fully perfected. Wade contracted to pay Ford forty-eight equal monthly installments of $194.52 commencing September 8, 1979. Wade was late with these payments right from the start. The following illustrates her payment record:

Payment Due:	Payment Made:
September 8, 1979	September 17, 1979
October 8, 1979	October 23, 1979
November 8, 1979	January 18, 1980
December 8, 1979	February 14, 1980
January 8, 1980	March 4, 1980

No other payments were made.

On December 6, 1979, Ford mailed Wade a notice of her default and of her right to cure the default. The notice was mailed to Wade pursuant to K.S.A. 16a–5–110 and 16a–1–201(6), and was sent by certified mail to the address listed in Ford's records from the information provided by Wade. [Kansas had adopted legislation based on the Uniform Consumer Credit Code (U3C); the section-numbers of the Kansas legislation conform to those of the U3C, quoted infra.] It was returned to Ford several days later marked "Return to sender, moved, left no address." Wade had moved and not notified Ford of a new address. K.S.A. 16a–1–201(6) provides:

> "For the purposes of K.S.A. 16a–1–101 through 16a–9–102, and amendments thereto, the residence of a consumer is the address given by the consumer as the consumer's residence in any writing signed by the consumer in connection with a credit transaction. Until the consumer notifies the creditor of a new or different address, the given address is presumed to be unchanged."

The trial court found that Ford had complied with the statutory notice requirements precedent to repossession. That finding stands since Wade has not appealed from it.

Collection efforts continued after the mailing of the above notice. After communication with Wade, a payment was received and promises of additional payments were made. With the account still in arrears, Ford assigned it on February 4, 1980, to the Kansas Recovery Bureau, a subsidiary of Denver Recovery Bureau, as independent contractors to repossess the car.

On or about February 10, 1980, in the early afternoon, David Philhower, an employee of Kansas Recovery Bureau, located the car in the driveway of Wade's residence. He had a key for the car, so he unlocked the door, got in and started it. Philhower then noticed an apparent discrepancy between the serial number of the car and that listed in his papers. He shut the engine off, got out and locked the car door. At that time Wade appeared at the door of her house. Philhower told her that he had been sent there by Ford to repossess the car, and she replied that he was not going to take it because she had made the payments on it. She invited him in the house to prove her claim, but was unable to locate the cancelled checks and receipts for the payments made. Philhower told her of the serial number discrepancy, and stated that he was not going to take the car until he confirmed the number, and advised her to contact Ford to straighten out the problem.

Wade then told him that if he came back to get the car that she had a gun in the house, which she had obtained because of several burglaries in the area, and she would not hesitate to use it. She then called a representative of Ford and stated she had a gun and that if she caught anyone on her property again trying to take her car, that "I would leave him laying right where I saw him."

Ford then received two more payments, the last being received March 4, 1980. On March 5, 1980, Ford reassigned the account to Kansas Recovery Bureau for repossession. In the early morning hours of March 10, 1980, at around 2:00 a.m., Philhower made another attempt to repossess the car from the driveway of Wade's residence. This time he was successful. Wade heard a car "burning rubber" at around 2:00 a.m., looked out the window, and discovered her car missing. There was no confrontation between Wade and Philhower, since Wade was not even aware of the fact her car was being repossessed until after Philhower had safely left the area in the car. Upon calling the police, Wade was informed that her car had been repossessed. Philhower had informed the police just prior to the repossession that he was going to recover the car in case they received reports of a prowler.

Wade subsequently brought an action against Ford for wrongful repossession, conversion and loss of credit, and sought both actual and punitive damages, along with attorney fees. Ford filed a counterclaim for breach of contract, seeking the deficiency of $2,953.44 remaining after the car was sold at public auction.

After a trial to the court, the trial court found Ford had breached the peace in repossessing the car and found in favor of Wade. The trial court also found for Ford on its counterclaim. Wade was awarded damages and attorney fees.

Ford appeals, raising the following two issues: (1) Did the trial court err in finding that Ford breached the peace on March 10, 1980, when it repossessed Wade's car? (2) Did the trial court err in assessing damages against Ford?

Defendant Ford contends that the trial court erred in finding that Ford breached the peace on March 10, 1980, when its agent repossessed Wade's car. The issue presented can be stated as follows: Does the repossession of a car, when there is no contract or confrontation between the repossessor and the debtor at the time and place of repossession, constitute a breach of the peace when there has been a prior threat of deadly violence if repossession is attempted? This particular set of facts has not been addressed by the courts before.

The trial court found that Ford had breached the peace in repossessing Wade's car. In its findings and conclusions made at the conclusion of the trial, the trial court emphasized Wade's lack of consent to the repossession and stated: "It's this Court's view that the Legislature, when it permitted self-help repossession, it was meant to cover amicable situations where there was no dispute as there apparently was in this particular case." At the hearing on defendant's motion to alter the judgment, the trial court stated:

"[I]n no way did she consent at no time did she consent to the peaceful recovery of the security, namely, one automobile that she kept and maintained on her private property, namely, that of her residence. The plaintiff, having threatened Mr. Philhower, the recovery agent, with bodily harm through the use of a lethal weapon known as a revolver, having informed Mr. Philhower never to enter her property again, otherwise she would shoot him. So, that being the last communication between Philhower and the plaintiff, at a later date when it was a month or so later, I don't recall since this hearing was seven months ago, Mr. Philhower, after that initial confrontation at 2:00 o'clock in the morning, 1:00 in the morning, quietly entered this private property, in effect, in this Court's opinion, taking the law in its own hands, come what may.

"Now, fortunately, no harm resulted from his entry on this private property. He was willing to assume that risk and that danger, knowing full-well that had he awakened the plaintiff, violence could very well have occurred and ensued. He knowingly and willfully brought that situation about in our community.

"I am reminded in some ways of the old frontier Wichita, Kansas in where firearms were used as a settlement of personal differences. Fortunately, the law and the courts have supplemented that mode or method of settling private differences.

"We have in this state the replevin action, which provides for an orderly process for the recovery of personal property held under a security for a debt and under oath, the parties are privileged to come into the court and expose through the witnesses and their evidence to the court, their claims such as in this case, the defendant claimed that the plaintiff was past due on her note involving the automobile involved here. Then, likewise, in that same hearing, the plaintiff in a replevin action would have had the right and the privilege to be heard by a judge or a jury to determine and make the finding as to whether or not she was in fact delinquent and in violation of her promise to pay thus providing for her being relieved of the security of the automobile in this case . . . .

"These facts violate every principle of civilized procedures that is understood as to why we have the courts and why we have the law to avoid confrontations between parties to avoid dangers to life, limb, and property. It's an orderly process that we seek to serve in this case.

"The Court is very grateful that no violence did ensue, result from the ultimate repossession of the car by Mr. Philhower, but nevertheless, is of the view that such action as came out in this court, done by Mr. Philhower was a breach of the peace.

"The Court is convinced that the purpose of permitting creditors to obtain a peaceful repossession, recovery of their securities such as an automobile in this case, would apply to instances where the recovery is freely done without threats of violence with consent of the parties and in view of the facts, this Court feels that the threat of firearms that this was a breach of the peace and will affirm the decision made in October, 1981, after hearing the evidence. The motion of the defendant is denied."

It appears that the trial court put a great deal of emphasis on Wade's lack of consent and the great potential for violence involved in the second repossession attempt.

K.S.A. 16a–5–112 [U3C 5.112] provides:

"Upon default by a consumer, unless the consumer voluntarily surrenders possession of the collateral to the creditor, the creditor may take possession of the collateral without judicial process only if possession can be taken without entry into a dwelling and without the use of force or other breach of the peace."

K.S.A. 84–9–503 provides in part:

"Unless otherwise agreed a secured party has on default the right to take possession of the collateral. In taking possession a secured party may proceed without judicial process if this can be done without breach of the peace or may proceed by action."

The statutes do not define the term "breach of the peace." The courts are left with that job. There are few Kansas cases doing so, but numerous cases from other jurisdictions. The leading Kansas case is Benschoter v. First National Bank of Lawrence, 218 Kan. 144, 542 P.2d 1042 (1975), where the court found that the self-help repossession provisions of K.S.A. 84–9–503 do not violate constitutional due process. The court also held:

"A creditor may repossess collateral without judicial process if this can be done without breach of the peace. Standing alone, stealth, in the sense of a debtor's lack of knowledge of the creditor's repossession, does not constitute a breach of the peace." Syl. ¶ 2 ....

An extensive search of the cases in other jurisdictions does not reveal a case on point which involved an initial confrontation with a threat of future violence, an intervening period of time with communication between the parties, and a subsequent successful repossession without incident.

In Morris v. First Natl. Bank & Trust Co., 21 Ohio St.2d 25, 254 N.E.2d 683 (1970), the court considered a case involving a self-help repossession statute similar to Kansas'. The facts included a confrontation at the time of repossession. The court noted:

> "While we leave the question of conversion to be determined in future proceedings below, we are constrained to hold that when appellee's agents were physically confronted by appellant's representative, disregarded his request to desist their efforts at repossession and refused to depart from the private premises upon which the collateral was kept, they committed a breach of the peace within the meaning of Section 1309.46, Revised Code, lost the protective application of that section, and thereafter stood as would any other person who unlawfully refuses to depart from the land of another." p. 30, 254 N.E.2d 683
>
> . . . .

In Census Federal Credit Union v. Wann, Ind.App., 403 N.E.2d 348 (1980), the court also considered self-help repossession under U.C.C. 9–503 and what constitutes breach of the peace. There the creditor made demand on the debtor for possession of the secured car. The debtor refused to give possession of it to the creditor. Unlike the present case, there were no threats of future violence. Thereafter, the creditor, through its agents and without benefit of any judicial process, took possession of the car at approximately 12:30 a.m. by taking it from the parking lot of the apartment building where the debtor lived. During this second, successful, repossession attempt, no contact whatever was had by the creditor's agents with the debtor or any other person in the immediate control of the car. The court provided the following discussion on breach of the peace:

> "In Deavers v. Standridge, (1978) 144 Ga.App. 673, 242 S.E.2d 331, the court held that blocking the movement of the defaulting debtor's automobile after his oral protest to the secured party's repossession attempt was a breach of the peace
>
> . . . .

> "Cases in other jurisdictions have held that absence of consent of the defaulting party to repossession is immaterial to the right of a secured party to repossess without judicial process. This, of course, is a necessary result, for contrary to the argument of plaintiff, Ind.Code 26–1–9–503, by its very existence, *presupposes that the defaulting party did not consent.* Should the defaulting party consent, no statutory authority would be required for a secured party to repossess, with or

without judicial process. To hold otherwise would emasculate that statute."

We find it is clear from a survey of the cases dealing with self-help repossession that the consent of the debtor to the repossession is not required. K.S.A. 16a–5–112 even presupposes the lack of consent: "Upon default by a consumer, unless the consumer *voluntarily surrenders* possession...." (Emphasis supplied.) The trial court's emphasis on the lack of consent by Wade in the present case and its view that "the Legislature, when it permitted self-help repossession ... meant to cover amicable situations where there was no dispute...." are not found in case law. Repossession, without the consent of the debtor, absent more, does not constitute a breach of the peace by the creditor.

The trial court also emphasized the potential for violence brought on by Wade's threats made during the first repossession attempt. A breach of the peace may be caused by an act likely to produce violence. The facts presented in this case do not, however, rise to that level. A period of one month elapsed between the repossession attempts. During that period, Wade and Ford were in communication and two payments were made. We find the potential for violence was substantially reduced by the passage of this time. Moreover, the actual repossession was effected without incident. The time of the repossession was such that in all likelihood no confrontation would materialize. In fact, Wade was totally unaware of the repossession until after Philhower had successfully left the premises with the car. We therefore find that as a matter of law there was no breach of the peace in the repossession of Wade's car.

The trial court's judgment finding a breach of the peace is reversed, and the case is remanded for a modification of the award of damages in accordance with this opinion.

Wade's motion for attorney fees on appeal is denied.

Reversed and remanded with directions.

Notes on Wrongful Repossession

(1) Measure of Damages for Wrongful Repossession. In the *Stone Machinery* case the court concluded that only "compensatory damages" would be awarded. How does one compute such damages for repossession by a secured party who (as in *Stone Machinery*) had a legal right to obtain possession by the use of appropriate procedures? (The *Stone Machinery* opinion does not explain how the trial court computed the "compensatory damages" of $18,586.20.) If damages are based on the interruption of the debtor's use of the collateral, should the relevant period of interruption be limited to the time that would have been required to repossess by judicial proceedings? In the *Stone Machinery* case, would it have been wrong for a judge to defer repossession of the tractor until Kessler, the debtor, could complete his current job—at least if Kessler would assign to the plaintiff the sums to become payable under the contract? Even if that approach would be sensible, how could a judge overcome the fact that UCC 9–503 confers upon Stone Machinery the unequivocal right to possession?

In *Stone Machinery* the court upheld the debtor's judgment for conversion. According to the Restatement (Second) of Torts, "[c]onversion is an intentional exercise of dominion or control over a chattel which so seriously interferes with the right of another to control it that the actor may justly be required to pay the other the full value of the chattel." Restatement (Second) of Torts § 222 A(1) (1965). Consider also Comment *c* to that section:

> The importance of the distinction between trespass to chattels and conversion . . . lies in the measure of damages. In trespass the plaintiff may recover for the diminished value of his chattel because of any damage to it, *or for the damage to his interest in its possession or use.* Usually, although not necessarily, such damages are less than the full value of the chattel itself. In conversion the measure of damages is the full value of the chattel, at the time and place of the tort. [Emphasis added.]

Is there any plausible justification for the debtor, who is in default, to recover the full value of the collateral from the secured party? If a worthwhile compensatory measure of damages cannot be found (e.g., where the wrongful possession did not interrupt profitable use of the equipment), should further thought be given to the assessment of punitive damages? For a useful discussion of recovery in conversion for wrongful repossession and a collection of the cases, see Hillman, McDonnell & Nickles, Common Law ¶ 26.01[2], at 26–4 to 26–7.

Consider *Stone Machinery* from another perspective. It was undisputed that Kessler, the debtor, was in default. It follows that, as between Kessler and Stone Machinery, the latter was entitled to possession. UCC 9–503. Notwithstanding that Kessler was not (and did not claim to be) entitled to possession, Kessler refused to deliver the tractor to Stone Machinery and even made a threat of physical injury if a non-judicial repossession were to be attempted. Does it seem anomalous that it is Kessler, and not Stone Machinery, that is entitled to a judgment for conversion?

(2) Procedural Aspects of the Breach–of–the–Peace Exception to Self–Help. Perhaps the results of cases like *Stone Machinery* can be understood best by viewing the breach of peace exception to self-help repossession as *procedural* in nature. The secured party is entitled to possession if, in fact, the debtor is in default. But the debtor can prevent self-help, and force the secured party to recover the collateral through judicial proceedings, *if* the debtor is able to control the circumstances so that self-help would constitute a breach of the peace. As illustrated by the *Williams* and *Wade* cases, sometimes the debtor may find it difficult to challenge a successfully completed, self-help repossession on the basis that the secured party breached the peace.

Might this procedural conceptualization also explain why courts generally treat unauthorized involvement by law enforcement officials ("*colore officii* ") as a breach of the peace? It seems highly unlikely that the involvement of a peace officer will result in an actual breach of the peace. But the appearance of authority that the officer conveys is likely to deprive the debtor of the opportunity to protest and to insist on a judicial recovery.

Problem 3. In the factual setting of Problem 1(a), supra, Abel sued Firstbank for wrongful repossession, alleging both a breach of the peace and a violation of her rights under the Fourteenth Amendment of the United States Constitution under color of state law. See 42 U.S.C. § 1983 (1988).[1] At trial, the court directed a verdict for Firstbank.

(a) Assuming that the supreme court of the state upholds the repossession as proper under state law (i.e., not a breach of the peace), how should it rule on the Section 1983 claim? See Note on Replevin, Due Process, and State Action, infra.

(b) Now suppose that Firstbank's employees repossessed the Pontiac with assistance from the police that was essentially identical to the assistance provided in the *Stone Machinery* case. What result on the Section 1983 claim?

Note on Replevin, Due Process, and State Action

The traditional requirements for obtaining a writ of replevin (a procedure for recovering possession of personal property) were an *ex parte* application by the plaintiff, accompanied by an affidavit affirming the plaintiff's right to possession and a bond to assure compensation for the defendant if seizure under the writ was unjustified. The Supreme Court invalidated these procedures in Fuentes v. Shevin, 407 U.S. 67, 92 S.Ct. 1983, 32 L.Ed.2d 556 (1972). See also North Georgia Finishing, Inc. v. Di–Chem, 419 U.S. 601, 95 S.Ct. 719, 42 L.Ed.2d 751 (1975) (holding invalid the *ex parte* garnishment of an industrial corporation's bank account).[2]

Fuentes concerned the seizure of property by sheriffs who had acted pursuant to state legislative authority. The Supreme Court held that this procedure violated the following provision of the Fourteenth

1. 42 U.S.C. § 1983 (1988) provides in relevant part as follows:

Every person who, under color of any statute ... of any State ... subjects, or causes to be subjected, any citizen of the United States or any other person within the jurisdiction thereof to the deprivation of any rights, privileges, or immunities secured by the Constitution and laws, shall be liable to the party injured

in an action at law, suit in equity, or other proper proceeding for redress.

2. State procedural rules generally have been revised to require judicial supervision of replevin actions. These rules generally provide an opportunity for the defendant to be heard before seizure of property unless a court finds that emergency action is justified, in which case a hearing is held immediately after seizure.

Amendment: "[N]or shall *any State* deprive any person of life, liberty, or property without due process of law." Does the *Fuentes* doctrine apply to *self-help* repossession of collateral by a private person? Does the *state* violate the Due Process Clause when, as in UCC 9–503, it authorizes repossession by the creditor?

The *Fuentes* decision led to widespread litigation challenging the constitutionality of self-help repossession by Article 9 secured parties. Several Courts of Appeals rejected Due Process attacks on self-help repossession. The prevailing view (in brief) has been that, although UCC 9–503 permits self-help in some circumstances, the creditor's action is based on the creditor's property right rather than on the "state action" contemplated by the Fourteenth Amendment. Nothing would seem to impair the effectiveness of a *contractual* right to self-help repossession. The prevailing view received support in the 1978 decision of the Supreme Court that a warehouse's sale of goods for unpaid storage fees, although permitted by UCC 7–210, was not "state action" in violation of the Due Process Clause. Flagg Brothers v. Brooks, 436 U.S. 149, 98 S.Ct. 1729, 56 L.Ed.2d 185 (1978). Unlike the typical self-help repossession, the participation of a sheriff *colore officii*, as in the *Stone Machinery* case, clearly seems to implicate state action.

(B) CONSUMER PROTECTION LEGISLATION

Problem 4. In the setting of the Prototype, Lee Abel purchased a new Pontiac and signed the Installment Sale Contract. See Form 6, Chapter 11, Section 1, supra. As in the Prototype, Main Motors assigned the contract to Firstbank. Paragraph 2 (on the reverse side) of the contract provides, in part:

> "I agree ... not to sell, assign or encumber, without your prior written consent, any of my rights under the Contract or in the Vehicle ... to notify you promptly of all changes in the place where the Vehicle is permanently kept (and I represent that until further notice, the Vehicle will be kept at the address I have given you on the face of the Contract) ...."

Paragraph 5 (on the reverse side) of the contract provides, in part:

> "The occurrence of any of the following shall, at your option, constitute an event of default under the Contract: ... my failure to make any payment under the Contract in full punctuality on or before its due date; my failure to comply with any other provision of the Contract ...."

The monthly payments were due on the 15th of the month; Abel made the first seven payments (through December 15). On January 10 Abel was in desperate need of cash, took the Pontiac to a used car dealer in another city, and offered it for sale. Dealer's manager asked to see the certificate of title; Abel said that the certificate was at home and that Dealer could have it as soon as Dealer bought the car. (In fact, Firstbank held the certificate, as in the Prototype, Chapter 11, Section 1, supra.) The manager indicated the price that Dealer would be willing to pay, but added that there could be no deal without a clean certificate of title. Abel agreed to bring in the car and certificate the next day in order to close the deal.

Dealer's manager took note of the number of the car's license and, as soon as Abel left, Dealer phoned the Bureau of Motor Vehicles to inquire about ownership and liens. Later that afternoon the Bureau reported by telephone that their records showed that Firstbank held a security interest in the Ford. Dealer phoned Firstbank to inquire if the lien had been discharged. That night, employees of Firstbank found the Ford parked at the curb three blocks from Abel's residence and towed it away.

(a) Abel sued Firstbank for compensatory and punitive damages. Does the Installment Sale Contract authorize the repossession? If not, is Firstbank aided by UCC 1–208? Does UCC 2–609 apply to the seller's *assignee* of a security interest, such as Firstbank? If so, are its provisions adequate for the current situation?

(b) Suppose that Abel (promising to bring in the certificate of title the next day) actually sold the Pontiac to the out-of-town dealer on January 10. That clearly would be a default under the terms of the Installment Sales Contract and UCC 9–503 would permit repossession. The state has enacted the Uniform Consumer Credit Code (1974) (U3C). In this case, Firstbank has not given Abel the notice specified in U3C 5.110. Does the U3C bar repossession? See U3C 5.109(2), 5.110(1), 5.111(1); Notes 2 and 3 on Legislation Limiting Self–Help Repossession Against Consumers, infra.

(c) Now suppose that Abel failed to make the payments due on October, November, and December 15. The U3C remains applicable. Does the U3C bar repossession? If the court concludes that the repossession was improper under U3C, what judgment should be entered?

(d) On the morning after Firstbank's repossession of the Pontiac (January 11), Firstbank concluded that its repossession was inconsistent with the provisions of the U3C. What can Firstbank do to extricate itself with a minimum of difficulty and liability?

Notes on Legislation Limiting Self-Help
Repossession Against Consumers

(1) **Article 9.** As you know, the Code contains only a few provisions specifically addressing consumer transactions. A few of these concern enforcement of security interests. See, e.g., UCC 9–505(1)

(discussed in Section 6, infra); UCC 9–507(1) (discussed in Section 2, infra). Article 9 contains no special rules regulating repossession of collateral from consumers, despite the widespread belief that such repossessions may have particularly disruptive and destructive effects. In the face of Article 9's silence, regulation has come from other sources.

(2) **The Uniform Consumer Credit Code.** One of the Code's sponsors, the National Conference of Commissioners on Uniform Commercial State Laws, has dealt with repossession in another of its products, the Uniform Consumer Credit Code. As initially promulgated in 1968, the U3C did not significantly restrict repossession. Experience with the 1968 version and pressure from consumer groups (including the National Consumer Law Center) led to the promulgation in 1974 of a second version that strengthens the rights of debtors.

Neither version of the U3C has been widely adopted. (By 1991 one or the other version was in force in ten states.) However, the U3C has been an influential model for states enacting legislation dealing with consumer credit. Provisions of the U3C that relate to default and repossession include U3C 5.109–5.112.

(3) **Consequences of Violating the U3C's Default and Repossession Rules.** What are the consequences of a creditor's noncompliance with the foregoing provisions of the U3C? A court may have some difficulty in finding the answer. U3C 5.201(1) lists 22 provisions of the U3C and states that if any of these provisions is violated the consumer may "recover actual damages and also a right in an action other than a class action, to recover from the person violating this Act a penalty in an amount determined by the court not less than $100 nor more than $1,000." The list of the 22 duties for which the U3C imposes a penalty does *not* include U3C 5.109–5.112.

Do U3C 5.109–5.112 specify legal consequences of failing to comply with the requirements set forth in these provisions? See U3C 5.111(1). Should one conclude that the *only* legal consequences of these provisions are those that are specified therein? U3C 1.103, in language closely comparable to UCC 1–103, states that "the principles of law and equity" and the Uniform Commercial Code supplement the provisions of the U3C, unless displaced by its "particular provisions."

It should be noted that U3C 5.201, after a series of limited remedial provisions (including the listing in subsection (1) of the 22 provisions mentioned above), ends with the following subsection that seems to be of general applicability:

> (8) In an action in which it is found that a creditor has violated this Act, the court shall award to the consumer the costs of the action and to his attorneys their reasonable fees. In determining attorney's fees, the amount of the recovery on behalf of the consumer is not controlling.

(4) Other Approaches to the Problem. The Model Consumer Credit Act (1973) (MCCA), drafted by the National Consumer Law Center, gives short shrift to self-help repossession. Under Section 7.202 of the MCCA:

> No person shall take possession of collateral by other than legal process pursuant to this Part, notwithstanding any provision of law or term of a writing.

Wisconsin has taken a less extreme, but still restrictive, approach. Under the Wisconsin Consumer Act a secured creditor may repossess only after obtaining a court determination that the creditor is entitled to the collateral; following such a determination the creditor may repossess by self-help, provided there is no breach of the peace. Wis. Stat. Ann. §§ 425.203–.206 (West 1988 & Supp. 1991).

SECTION 2.   DISPOSITIONS OF COLLATERAL; DEFICIENCY; CONSEQUENCES OF NONCOMPLIANCE

Introductory Note. Taking possession of collateral following a debtor's default only begins the process of enforcing a security interest in collateral. A secured party in possession of tangible collateral following a default typically wishes to sell the collateral and then to apply the net proceeds of the sale to the secured obligation. If the proceeds are insufficient to satisfy the secured obligation, the secured party may wish to pursue the debtor to collect the remaining, unsecured portion of the debt (the "deficiency"). If a disposition yields proceeds sufficient to satisfy the secured obligation, the secured party will pay over any excess funds (the "surplus") to the debtor (or, in some circumstances, to junior claimants).

UCC 9–504 regulates dispositions of collateral after default. That section provides for the secured party's disposition of the collateral (UCC 9–504(1), (3)), application of the proceeds (UCC 9–504(2)), and pursuit of a deficiency claim (UCC 9–504(2)); it also addresses the right of a debtor to any surplus (UCC 9–504(2)) and the rights that a disposition transfers to a purchaser of the collateral (UCC 9–504(4)).

When a secured party opts to "sell, lease or otherwise dispose of . . . collateral" under UCC 9–504, "every aspect of the disposition including the method, manner, time, place and terms must be commercially reasonable." UCC 9–504(1), (3). In addition, a secured party is required to give a debtor "reasonable notification" of a disposition (subject to narrow exceptions). UCC 9–504(3). This Section of the book deals with the strict, albeit general, standards imposed by UCC 9–504. It also considers how the secured party's failure to comply with UCC 9–504 when disposing of collateral affects the rights of the secured party and the debtor. Before continuing on to the Problem, cases, and Notes that follow, please read carefully UCC 9–504(1)—(4).

Problem. Schmelli Services, Inc. is an Arkansas-based personnel agency that provides temporary office employees to businesses. It has offices in twenty-four cities in several eastern and southeastern states. Schmelli owes your client, Atlanta Industrial Bank (AIB), approximately $4,500,000 under a **line of credit** facility, secured by a perfected, first priority security interest in Schmelli's accounts receivable and a first priority real estate mortgage on Schmelli's home office building (located in Little Rock, Arkansas). The security agreement covering the accounts provides that the collateral secures not only Schmelli's $6,000,000 note executed pursuant to the line of credit facility, but also "all other obligations of Borrower to Bank now existing or hereafter incurred, whether (i) contingent or noncontingent, (ii) liquidated or unliquidated, (iii) disputed or undisputed, (iv) contemplated or uncontemplated, or (v) of the same or different type as the indebtedness evidenced by the Note."

Schmelli also owes AIB about $2,500,000, secured by a perfected, first priority security interest in a Learjet Model 35A–596. (Schmelli's flamboyant CEO, Telli Schmelli, uses the Learjet to fly from city to city while making monthly visits to each office.) There are about 1,500 hours on the airframe and engines, and Schmelli has maintained the aircraft in accordance with applicable Federal Aviation Administration regulations. The security agreement covering the Learjet provides that it secures the purchase-money loan (originally, $3,300,000) and also other obligations, using language identical to that in the line of credit security agreement, quoted above. Each security agreement provides that it is "governed by the law of the State of Georgia."

Schmelli is in default under both the line of credit facility and the aircraft loan. AIB has not yet "pulled the plug" on Schmelli; it continues to make discretionary advances against Schmelli's accounts receivable. However, yesterday a repo team retained by AIB peacefully took possession of the Learjet at the Pine Bluff, Arkansas airport. AIB stored the aircraft with an aircraft dealer located at that airport.

The loan officer assigned to Schmelli wants to "turn the Learjet into cash as soon as possible." The officer, who has little experience with repossessions and enforcement, has asked you for advice on how to proceed.

(a) Which state's law will govern a disposition of the Learjet by AIB? See UCC 1–105; UCC 9–103. Will you recommend that AIB remove the Learjet from Arkansas before disposing of it? Compare Emmons v. Burkett, infra, with First State Bank of Morrilton v Hallett, infra; Note (4) on Commercially Reasonable Dispositions and Reasonable Notification, infra.

(b) Do you recommend a "public" or "private" disposition of the aircraft? What considerations bear on what approach to take? See Notes on Commercially Reasonable Dispositions and Reasonable Notification, infra. You may assume that Georgia law applies.

(c) After settling on a general approach, what specific steps will you recommend? Assume, alternatively, that (i) Schmelli is very cooperative, being grateful for the continued financing, and (ii) shortly after the repossession AIB cut off Schmelli's financing, and now Schmelli and AIB are "not on speaking terms." (Telli Schmelli's ride in a crowded bus from Pine Bluff to Little Rock following the "surprise" repossession did not help matters!) You may continue to assume that Georgia law applies.

(d) Would you change any of your recommendations under part (b) or (c) if Arkansas law were applicable? Would you consider taking any additional steps? See UCC 9–501(5); UCC 9–507(2); Note 1 on Commercially Reasonable Dispositions and Reasonable Notification, infra.

(e) Would your answers in part (d) be different if Schmelli were hopelessly insolvent, leaving no chance for AIB to recover any deficiency? If there were no other collateral (i.e., the accounts and real estate)?

(f) What provisions might the security agreement have included that would have made your advice, at the disposition stage, more definite and easier to give? See UCC 9–501(3); Note 3 on Commercially Reasonable Dispositions and Reasonable Notification, infra.

(g) Suppose that, three weeks after the repossession, while en route from Pine Bluff to Atlanta, the Learjet crashed and was destroyed. The loan officer has just told you that the insurer under Schmelli's policy (AIB is the loss payee on the policy) has denied AIB's claim for loss because the policy does not cover loss or damage incurred when the Learjet is flown by anyone other than an agent or employee of Schmelli. Are there any *additional* steps that you *wish* you had recommended in part (b) above? See UCC 9–501(3); UCC 9–207(1) & (2)(b); Note 5 on Commercially Reasonable Dispositions and Reasonable Notification, infra.

EMMONS v. BURKETT

Supreme Court of Georgia, 1987.
256 Ga. 855, 353 S.E.2d 908.

BELL, JUSTICE. We granted certiorari in this case to determine whether the Court of Appeals correctly concluded that the appellee creditor, who had sold a small portion of the debtor's collateral without the notice required by OCGA § 11–9–504(3), was not barred from obtaining an in personam judgment against or selling the other collateral of the debtor. Emmons v. Burkett, 179 Ga.App. 838(1) (348 S.E.2d 323) (1986).

The facts of this case are well-stated in the Court of Appeals' opinion, see Emmons v. Burkett, supra, 179 Ga.App. at 838–840, and will be reiterated here only when necessary to a discussion of the issues presented.

1. In Gurwitch v. Luxurest Furniture Mfg. Co., 233 Ga. 934 (214 S.E.2d 373) (1975), this court adopted the rule that, if a creditor sells collateral of a debtor without the notice required by OCGA § 11–9–504(3), the creditor is barred from proceeding to obtain a personal judgment against the debtor to recover the difference between the amount obtained from the sale of the collateral and the amount the court determines is due on the note. In Reeves v. Habersham Bank, 254 Ga. 615(2) (331 S.E.2d 589) (1985), this court was presented with the question whether the Gurwitch rule barring a deficiency recovery should be applied to cases in which a creditor attempted to recover a deficiency against the collateral of a guarantor. We answered this question in the affirmative, and have reiterated that answer in United States v. Kennedy, 256 Ga. 345 (348 S.E.2d 636) (1986).

In the instant case, relying on Gurwitch, Reeves, and Kennedy, Emmons, the debtor, argues that Burkett, the creditor, should be barred from proceeding against his remaining collateral or from obtaining a personal judgment against him, to satisfy the deficiency remaining on his note following the sale of the collateral.

The Court of Appeals concluded that, because Burkett filed a suit for recovery on the note before selling the collateral in question,[1] this was not a deficiency action and the effect of Burkett's noncompliance with OCGA § 11–9–504(3) was not the same as if he had first sold the collateral and then sued to recover a deficiency. We disagree with this conclusion.

We do so because we see no reason to distinguish between a situation where the creditor first sues on the note and then sells collateral, and a situation where the creditor first proceeds against collateral and then sues on the note. In both situations, the creditor must obtain a judgment on the note and must attempt to recover the deficiency between the amount obtained on the sale of the collateral and the amount determined to be due on the note.

Moreover, the fact that a creditor may have proceeded to judgment on a note before selling collateral without notice does not in any manner satisfy the ultimate purposes of OCGA § 11–9–504(3), which are to enable the debtor to exercise his right of redemption under OCGA § 11–9–506, if he or she so chooses, and, if not, to minimize any possible deficiencies remaining after the sale. Reeves, supra, 254 Ga. at 619; Kennedy, supra, 256 Ga. at 347. As is readily apparent, the debtor has the same interest in the disposition of the collateral whether the creditor first obtains a judgment on the note and then sells the collateral or first sells the collateral and then obtains a judgment on the note. Since OCGA § 11–9–504(3) is designed to protect the debtor, the effect of the creditor's noncompliance with that code section should be the same in either instance, and we now so hold.

---

1. When we refer to the sale of collateral in this opinion, we refer to a sale carried out pursuant to the creditor's rights under the security agreement and the UCC, and not to a sale carried out by judicial process following a judgment on the note.

2. Having determined that the effect of a creditor's noncompliance with the notice provision of OCGA § 11-9-504(3) should be the same whether the creditor first obtains a judgment on the note or first sells the collateral, we must now examine the effect of the creditor's noncompliance.

As previously noted, in Gurwitch v. Luxurest Furniture Mfg. Co., supra, 233 Ga. 934, 214 S.E.2d 373, this court adopted the "absolute-bar" rule, holding that the failure of the creditor to comply with the notice requirements of OCGA § 11-9-504(3) when selling collateral operates as an absolute bar to the recovery of a deficiency. This rule has been followed since its inception without reanalysis of its merits. See, for example, Reeves v. Habersham Bank, supra, 254 Ga. 615, 331 S.E.2d 589, and United States v. Kennedy, supra, 256 Ga. 345, 348 S.E.2d 636, in which the primary issues involved the application of the rule rather than the wisdom of it. We are now convinced, however, that the harshness of the absolute-bar rule of Gurwitch should be reevaluated.

An alternative rule which we find merits our consideration has been termed the "rebuttable-presumption" rule. In fact, in Farmers Bank v. Hubbard, 247 Ga. 431, 276 S.E.2d 622 (1981), we carved out an exception to the absolute-bar rule of Gurwitch, and adopted the rebuttable-presumption rule for cases in which the only issue is whether, concerning the commercial reasonableness of the sale, see OCGA § 11-9-504(3), the sale price of the collateral was adequate.

Under the rebuttable-presumption rule, if a creditor fails to give notice or conducts an unreasonable sale, the presumption is raised that the value of the collateral is equal to the indebtedness. To overcome this presumption, the creditor must present evidence of the fair and reasonable value of the collateral and the evidence must show that such value was less than the debt. If the creditor rebuts the presumption, he may maintain an action against the debtor or guarantor for any deficiency. Any loss suffered by the debtor as a consequence of the failure to give notice or to conduct a commercially reasonable sale is recoverable under § 11-9-507 and may be set off against the deficiency. For example, if a creditor has conducted a commercially unreasonable sale, the debtor may suffer a loss, in that he will not receive as much of a credit from the sale of the collateral as he should have. In such an instance, the debtor is entitled to be awarded an additional credit equalling the difference between the fair market value of the collateral and the amount for which the collateral was sold.

In examining the merits of the absolute-bar rule of Gurwitch and of the rebuttable-presumption rule outlined above, we conclude that the fairer rule and the rule most consistent with the intent of the Uniform Commercial Code is the rebuttable-presumption rule. First, we note that OCGA § 11-9-504(2) expressly states that the creditor has a right to recover any deficiency from the debtor. Significantly, the code provisions concerning a debtor's default nowhere provide that a lack of notice bars a deficiency judgment or that proper notice is a condition precedent to the bringing of a deficiency action. Moreover, OCGA § 11–9–507 explicitly provides a remedy for a creditor's noncompliance with the requirements of OCGA § 11–9–504(3). Under § 11–9–507(1), "[i]f the [creditor's] disposition has occurred the debtor or any person entitled to notification or whose security interest has been made known to the secured party prior to the disposition has a right to recover from the secured party any loss caused by a failure to comply with the provisions of this part." OCGA § 11–9–507 does not provide that a failure to comply with § 11–9–504 bars the creditor from bringing an action to recover any deficiency. Based on the foregoing we conclude that the code provisions themselves do not require the imposition of an absolute-bar rule.

In addition, and most importantly, we find that the absolute-bar rule is contrary to the intent of the Uniform Commercial Code. OCGA § 11–1–106 expressly prohibits penal damages, and provides that the remedies provided by the UCC should be liberally administered so that the aggrieved party "may be put in as good a position as if the other party had fully performed." Yet, by absolutely barring a deficiency action, even if the debtor has suffered no damage from a lack of notice or a commercially unreasonable sale, the debtor receives a windfall and the creditor is arbitrarily penalized. This is so despite the fact that it is the debtor's default on his obligation which necessitated the sale of the collateral.

We conclude that the rebuttable-presumption rule, by placing the burden on the creditor to show the propriety of the sale and making him liable under § 11–9–507 for any injury to the debtor, provides an adequate deterrent to an improper sale on the part of a creditor, and adequately protects the debtor's interest, without arbitrarily penalizing the creditor. This is consistent with the conclusion reached in many, if not most, jurisdictions which have considered the question. We therefore now adopt the rebuttable-presumption rule, both for situations in which the creditor fails to give notice of a sale, and for situations in which the creditor fails to conduct a commercially reasonable sale.

3. Because of our adoption of the rebuttable-presumption rule, this case must be remanded for further consideration consistent with this rule. In this regard, we note that, pursuant to Reeves v. Habersham Bank, supra, 254 Ga. 615, 331 S.E.2d 589, and United States v. Kennedy, the rebuttable-presumption rule should be applied to this creditor's efforts to collect a deficiency either from the debtor's collateral or by way of a personal judgment.

All the Justices concur, except SMITH, J., who dissents.

FIRST STATE BANK OF MORRILTON v. HALLETT

Supreme Court of Arkansas, 1987.
291 Ark. 37, 722 S.W.2d 555.

HOLT, CHIEF JUSTICE. The appellant, First State Bank (FSB), concedes it failed to give the appellee, Edith Hallett, proper notice before it sold her collateral which it repossessed when she defaulted on a promissory note. FSB nevertheless sought a deficiency judgment against Hallett for the balance owed on the note. The trial court granted Hallett's motion for summary judgment, dismissing the FSB claim. The issue on appeal is whether the failure of FSB as a secured party, to give proper notice to debtor Hallett of the time and place of the sale of repossessed collateral, as required by Ark. Stat. Ann. § 85–9–504(3) (Supp. 1985), absolutely bars FSB's right to a deficiency judgment. We hold that it does and affirm the trial court. ...

Hallett gave FSB a promissory note in the amount of $11,342.90, secured in part by a security interest in a 1983 pickup truck. Hallett defaulted. FSB repossessed the truck and sold it without written notice to Hallett of the sale date. A deficiency of $4,057.40 remained on the note. The trial court granted Hallett's motion for summary judgment because FSB had not complied with § 85–9–504(3)'s guidelines for the disposition of repossessed collateral. That section states in pertinent part:

> Unless collateral is perishable or threatens to decline speedily in value or is of a type customarily sold on a recognized market, reasonable notification of the time and place of any public sale or reasonable notification of the time after which any private sale or other intended disposition is to be made shall be sent by the secured party to the debtor, if he has not signed after default a statement renouncing or modifying his right to notification of sale.

The trial court's ruling complies with our most recent decision, Rhodes v. Oaklawn Bank, 279 Ark. 51, 648 S.W.2d 470 (1983). In Rhodes, we reversed a deficiency judgment in favor of the secured party, and held:

> When a creditor repossesses chattels and sells them without sending the debtor notice as to the time and date of sale, or as to a date after which the collateral will be sold, he is not entitled to a deficiency judgment, unless the debtor has specifically waived his rights to such notice.

FSB does not attempt to distinguish Rhodes, but rather argues that it should be overruled in favor of an earlier line of cases which took a different approach to this issue. Those cases did not bar a deficiency judgment altogether, but instead "indulg[ed] the presumption in the first instance that the collateral was worth at least the amount of the debt, thereby shifting to the creditor the burden of proving the amount that should reasonably have been obtained through a sale conducted according to law." Norton v. Nat'l Bank of Commerce, 240 Ark. 143, 398 S.W.2d 538 (1966). We think Rhodes represents the right approach and, although it did not expressly overrule these cases, its effect was to change our law.

Creditors are given the right to a deficiency judgment by Ark. Stat. Ann. § 85–9–502(2) (Supp. 1985): "If the security agreement secures an indebtedness, the secured party must account to the debtor for any surplus, and unless otherwise agreed, the debtor is liable for any deficiency." As stated, § 85–9–504(3) requires the creditor to send reasonable notification to the debtor before he disposes of this type of collateral. If the creditor does not dispose of the collateral in accordance with the code provisions, Ark. Stat. Ann. § 85–9–507 (Supp. 1985) gives the debtor "a right to recover from the secured party any loss caused by a failure to comply with the provisions of this Part [§§ 85–9–501—507]."

There is a split of authority nationwide on the correlation of these provisions of the code. A group of cases follows the position that § 85–9–507 gives the debtor a defense to a deficiency judgment when the creditor has failed to give proper notice, and that the deficiency judgment is reduced by the damages the debtor can prove. Our previous cases, as represented by Norton, supra, followed this approach with the presumption in favor of the debtor that the collateral and the debt were equal and the burden placed on the creditor to prove a deficiency. The apparent majority position, however, with which we concur, is that § 85–9–507 is not applicable to the creditor's action to recover a deficiency judgment, but is separate affirmative action by the debtor to recover damages. The creditor's right to a deficiency judgment is not merely subject to whether the debtor has a right to damages under § 85–9–507, but instead depends on whether he has complied with the statutory requirements concerning disposition and notice.

This view was explained in Atlas Thrift Co. v. Horan, 27 Cal.App. 3d 999, 104 Cal.Rptr. 315 (1972), quoting Leasco Data Processing Equip. Corp. v. Atlas Shirt Co., 66 Misc.2d 1089, 323 N.Y.S.2d 13 (1971):

> "The plaintiff's contention that a secured creditor's right to a deficiency judgment under the described circumstances is limited only by the remedies set forth in 9–507 seems to me a tenuous one indeed, apart from the fact that no such effect was ever accorded the corresponding section in the Uniform Conditional Sales Act....

> "Preliminarily, it may be noted that Section 9–507 makes no direct allusion to the circumstances under which a right to a deficiency judgment may arise.

> "More significant is the special nature of the language used: 'the debtor or any person entitled to notification ... has a right to recover from the secured party any loss caused by a failure to comply with the provisions of this Part.' If this were

intended to authorize a defense to action for a deficiency judgment, it is hard to envisage language less apt to that purpose. The words used plainly contemplate an affirmative action to recover for a loss that has already been sustained—not a defense to an action for a deficiency. The distinction between an affirmative action and a defense is a familiar one, phrases that articulate the different concepts are familiar in the law, and it is unlikely that the experienced authors of the [Uniform Commercial Code] intended by the above language to provide a limited defense to an action for a deficiency judgment based on a sale that had violated the simple and flexible statutory procedure.

"It seems far more probable that this latter section has nothing whatever to do with defenses to an action for a deficiency, since it was never contemplated that a secured party could recover such a judgment after violating the statutory command as to notice."

The Horan court concluded: "The rule and requirement are simple. If the secured creditor wishes a deficiency judgment he must obey the law. If he does not obey the law, he may not have his deficiency judgment."

When the code provisions have delineated the guidelines and procedures governing statutorily created liability, then those requirements must be consistently adhered to when that liability is determined. Here, FSB failed to comply with the code's procedures for disposition of collateral, and is therefore not entitled to a deficiency judgment under the code.

Affirmed.

GLAZE, JUSTICE, dissenting. The majority court decision overrules Norton v. National Bank of Commerce, 240 Ark. 143, 398 S.W.2d 538 (1966) and its progeny as those cases have interpreted and applied Arkansas's Uniform Commercial Code §§ 85–9–504 and 9–507 during the past twenty years. Because I believe the rule established in Norton to be a fair one and the one adopted in this cause to be punitive, I am obliged to dissent.

Unlike the court's holding here, the Norton court rejected the debtor's contention that the bank's failure to give him notice of the intended sale completely discharged his obligation. Instead, that court, Justice George Rose Smith writing, held that, because the bank disposed of the debtor's car without notice, the just solution is:

to indulge the presumption in the first instance that the collateral was worth at least the amount of the debt, thereby shifting to the creditor the burden of proving the amount that should reasonably have been obtained through a sale conducted according to law.

Id. at 150, 398 S.W.2d 538.

As one can readily see, our court in Norton wrestled with the same situation as presented in the instant case, and it derived a most workable and equitable solution which was designed to treat both debtors and creditors fairly. Frankly, I am unaware of any serious problems or criticisms that have arisen in the application of the Norton rule, especially that would demand or warrant this court's changing the "rules-of-the-game" at this late date. The rule this court adopts today is a drastic and punitive one, and no public policy argument has been offered to support it.

Finally, I note the majority court seems to premise its holding, in part, on the California case of Atlas Thrift Co. v. Horan, 27 Cal.App. 3d 999, 104 Cal.Rptr. 315 (1972) which, in turn, quotes from Leasco Data Processing Equip. Corp. v. Atlas Shirt Co., 66 Misc.2d 1089, 323 N.Y.S.2d 13 (1971). While California may have adopted the same "no notice-no deficiency" rule now embraced by this court, the New York courts have since overruled the Atlas Shirt Co. case, thereby rejecting that punitive rule. The New York courts, I might add, have adopted Arkansas's rule as set out in Norton. See Leasco Computer v. Sheridan Industries, 82 Misc.2d 897, 371 N.Y.S.2d 531 (1975) and Security Trust Co. of Rochester v. Thomas, 59 A.D.2d 242, 399 N.Y.S.2d 511 (1977) (citing Universal C.I.T. Credit Co. v. Rone, 248 Ark. 665, 453 S.W.2d 37 (1970)).

I would reverse.

HAYS and NEWBERN, JJ., join in this dissent.

Notes on Commercially Reasonable Dispositions and Reasonable Notification

(1) What Is a "Commercially Reasonable" Disposition? A secured party who is enforcing a security interest faces considerable uncertainty as to whether a proposed disposition will be "commercially reasonable," as required by UCC 9–504(3). How will a court or a jury view the circumstances in an after-the-fact examination? The potentially disastrous consequences of failing to dispose of collateral in a commercially reasonable manner, discussed in Note (4), infra, underscore the importance of taking the proper approach. Professors White and Summers highlight one source of the secured party's dilemma:

> We suspect that, after the fact, courts are unduly optimistic about the value of the goods or about the debtor's evidence of comparatively higher prices, and that there is a tendency to overestimate the ease of sale and to underestimate the cost and difficulty. Courts should have skepticism about hired experts' testimony concerning the value of the collateral, about facile assertions concerning the ease of its resale and the large price that the collateral "could" bring.

J. White & R. Summers, Uniform Commercial Code (3d ed. 1988) § 25.14, at 1234.

It should be apparent that predicting what is "commercially reasonable" in a given context is an enormously subjective enterprise. What is "reasonable" leaves much to the imagination. A review of the case law and commentary often can leave a student or lawyer confused and uncertain about a given, specific set of facts. Might a more principled approach emerge from examining the *purpose* or *function* of the commercial reasonableness requirement?

A secured party who desires enhanced certainty of compliance can obtain court approval of the terms of a disposition, in which case the disposition will "conclusively be deemed to be commercially reasonable." UCC 9–507(2). (The second sentence of UCC 9–507(2) offers useful guidance on what constitutes a commercially reasonable disposition, but hardly provides a sharply delineated "safe harbor.") A secured party also could obtain a judgment on the secured debt, levy execution on the collateral, and have the collateral sold at a sheriff's sale, thereby obviating the need to comply with Part 5's notice and commercial reasonableness requirements. See UCC 9–501(5). Either route, however, is likely to be more expensive and time-consuming than non-judicial enforcement. Moreover, the judgment, levy, and execution sale approach may be vulnerable to attack in a subsequent bankruptcy of the debtor if the value of the collateral is substantially higher than the sales price.[1]

A secured party also may achieve a high level of comfort if the debtor is cooperative. Absent circumstances suggesting coercion or unfair advantage, a debtor's post-default agreement that particular procedures will constitute a commercially reasonable disposition can do much to reduce the risk of a contrary assertion by the debtor down the road. Even if the debtor is not cooperative, a secured party sometimes will be well-advised to communicate the proposed disposition procedures to the debtor; the debtor's failure to object or to make a reasonable counter-proposal may weigh heavily in favor of the secured party in a later dispute concerning commercial reasonableness.

The requirement of a commercially reasonable disposition must be applied in a wide variety of circumstances. Smith v. Daniels, 634 S.W.2d 276 (Tenn.App.1982), provides useful guidance as to factors to consider. Among specific factors, such as adequate advertising and display, the court emphasized the relevance of customary commercial practices for selling a particular type of asset (the collateral, there, was amusement equipment). What will do for thoroughbred horses may not do for a Learjet aircraft and vice versa.

Some lenders and their counsel may develop substantial expertise concerning market practices for certain collateral—automobiles being a good example. But in many situations neither the staff of a secured

---

1. In theory, even a disposition in compliance with UCC 9–504 could be vulnerable under BC 548 in the face of a very large disparity between value and sales price. The Uniform Fraudulent Transfer Act is more forgiving; a "regularly conducted, noncollusive foreclosure sale or execution" generally is protected. Uniform Fraudulent Transfer Act § 3(b).

creditor nor its lawyer will have sufficient expertise, and it will be necessary to retain or consult with experts. Nevertheless, the creditor and the lawyer responsible for conducting a commercially reasonable disposition must know the right kinds of questions to ask the experts.

The following excerpt identifies various factors that courts most often consider when determining whether a disposition was commercially reasonable.

RUDOW, DETERMINING THE COMMERCIAL REASONABLENESS OF THE SALE OF REPOSSESSED COLLATERAL
19 UCC L.J. 139, 140–58 (1986).

Conduct of Sale

The reasonableness of the conduct of the sale is a factor that could tip the scale in a court's determination of whether the sale, itself, was consummated in a commercially reasonable manner. Many factors have been considered in determining the reasonableness of the conduct of sale. For instance, ... the fact that the collateral was not present at the time of the sale. ...

Estoppel or Waiver

Sometimes creditors claim that debtors waive or are estopped from claiming that the collateral was not disposed of in a commercially reasonable manner. However, the right to a commercially reasonable disposition of repossessed property *can not* be waived. [See Note (3), infra.]

Method of Sale as a Factor (Public or Private)

Whether a sale is public or private might conclusively affect the commercial reasonableness of that sale.[*] In Section 9–504(3), "disposition of the collateral may be by public or private proceedings, and may be made by way of one or more contracts...." Official Comment 1 to Section 9–504 helps clarify the choice. "Although public sale is recognized, it is hoped that private sale will be encouraged where, as is frequently the case, the private sale through commercial channels will result in higher realization on collateral for the benefit of all parties." The purpose of allowing a private sale of collateral is to allow the

---

[* You may find the "public" and "private" sale concepts confusing; the Code does not speak directly to how the two forms of dispositions are to be distinguished. The paradigmatic public sale is an auction. See UCC 9–504, Comment 1; UCC 2–706, Comment 4. But an auction will not be a public sale unless the general public (or an appropriately broad and interested segment) is invited to attend. A public sale, by its nature, is held at a particular time and place. A private sale, on the other hand, is one negotiated between the secured party and the buyer, and may not occur at a predetermined place and time.]

secured party more flexibility.... Most courts weigh this factor as a factor (it is considered as one in many), but some courts hold that the decision to sell in a public or private sale causes the sale to be presumed irrebuttably to be in a noncommercially reasonable manner if [the decision is] improperly made. ...

The place of sale must be commercially reasonable too.

Price

Price is a major factor in determining the commercial reasonableness of a sale under Section 9–504(3). It is probably the most common contention ... The weight of the price as a factor varies between [sic] the courts ....

Many courts explain that if the creditor has access to both wholesale and retail markets, it must sell in the higher retail market. [Other c]ourts play down price as a factor because of Section 9–507(2) and because they recognize that repossession sales rarely bring the market price, inherently opening the door for the debtor to legitimately claim that any sale brought too small a price for the good. ...

Approval by Judicial Scrutiny

Some sales or dispositions of collateral are approved by judicial proceedings.... [See UCC 9–507(2), discussed supra.]

The issue in determining the commercial reasonableness of the sale that is approved in a prior judicial proceeding is to determine if the judicial body allowed all the parties involved to have a fair chance to challenge the commercial reasonableness. ...

Advertising (Notice to the Public)

The courts use the adequacy of the advertisement as a key factor in determining the commercial reasonableness of a public sale. This is sometimes referred to as "notice to the public." Be aware that courts often confuse notice to the public with notice to the debtor. [See Note (2), infra.]

Courts hold that the purpose for notice, or advertisement, is to assure such publicity that the collateral will bring the best possible price from the competitive bidding of a lively concourse of bidders....

Courts want this advertising to be genuinely effective. Although 1,000 flyers can be dropped over a crowded city by a helicopter announcing the sale of the helicopter, the advertising will most likely be insufficient since it probably will not reach the class of potential helicopter buyers. However, merely five flyers sent to potential bidders who all show up at the sale and bid can make the sale a commercially reasonable one. ... To be effective, the notice must accurately state the time, place, and type of collateral sold. It must include any special features such as radar on an aircraft or a plow attachment on a truck.

The Secured Party as a Purchaser

Another factor that is often the cause of litigation, despite its clear enumeration in the Code, is the secured party as a purchaser of the repossessed collateral. In Section 9–504(3), "the secured party may buy at any public sale and, if the collateral is of a type customarily sold in a recognized market, or is of a type which is the subject of widely distributed standard price quotations, he may buy at a private sale." The purpose of limiting the secured party's purchase of the collateral is to restrict the secured party's participation in the purchase process to a manner that is reasonably calculated to assure that the disposition of the collateral will bring the *best possible price*. This is not accomplished if the secured party can repurchase the collateral below market price, creating a large deficiency against the debtor, while keeping a windfall on his resale of the collateral later on for the much higher market price . . . .

Preparation of Collateral Prior to Resale

Although Section 9–504(1) clearly states that "the secured party after default may sell, lease, or otherwise dispose of any or all of the collateral *in its then condition*, or following any commercially reasonable preparation or [processing]," the courts consider the preparation or absence of it to the collateral prior to the sale a factor of the commercial reasonableness. . . . The courts look at the cost in money and time needed to prepare the goods, and weigh these factors against the difference in the amount received from a sale of similar, fully prepared goods. . . .

Auctioneer or Expert Salesperson

Another factor, considered as one in many . . ., is the use of an auctioneer or technical expert at an auction sale. Here, the courts weigh the costs of hiring a technical expert against the sophisticated nature of the equipment sold. They also weigh the effectiveness of the auctioneer or expert in his or her ability to consummate a sale for the highest sale [price] possible. . . . Usually, creditors do not need to hire experts to sell the collateral. If they had to, an expensive burden would be placed on them. . . .

Notice to Debtor

Notice to the debtor is sometimes a factor in determining the commercial reasonableness of the sale of collateral. [See Note (2), infra.] . . . The danger resulting from not notifying the debtor of the sale is that the property may be sold for an amount unreasonably below its market value. . . . Additionally, the notice requirement acts to the secured party's advantage if the debtor helps secure a higher sales price since the prospect of recovering any deficiency is dubious. . . .

Time Between Repossession and Sale

Another factor . . . is the amount of time between the repossession of the collateral and the sale. The official comments to the UCC help explain what a commercially reasonable time is. [Mr. Rudow here quotes UCC 9–504, Comment 5, which deals with the requirement of reasonable notification; see Note (2), infra.] This will allow the debtor to get more people to go to the seller to bid and cause a higher sale price . . . .

Goods Sold as Units or Individually

Another factor . . . is whether goods are sold as a unit or individually. . . .

----

(2) What Is a "Reasonable Notification"? UCC 9–504(3) provides that "reasonable notification of the *time and place* of any *public sale* or reasonable notification of the *time after which* any *private sale* or other intended disposition is to be made shall be sent by the secured party to the debtor." It excepts from this notification requirement collateral that "is perishable or threatens to decline speedily in value or is of a type customarily sold on a recognized market."

Why require reasonable notification to the debtor of a proposed disposition? Mr. Rudow observed that courts sometimes confuse notification to the debtor with the advertising that may be a necessary component of a commercially reasonable disposition. He also explained that inadequate notification to the debtor could bear on the issue of commercial reasonableness. That relationship, however, normally is quite attenuated; the notification requirement is separate and independent from the commercially reasonable disposition requirement. The requirement of commercial reasonableness encourages secured parties to dispose of collateral in a manner that is likely to bring a good price. The notification requirement is a procedural safeguard intended to aid the debtor in protecting its own interests. See UCC 9–504, Comment 5 (" 'Reasonable notification' is not defined . . .; at a minimum it must be sent in such time that persons entitled to receive it will have sufficient time to take appropriate steps to protect their interests by taking part in the sale or other disposition if they so desire.").

What interests can a debtor protect by virtue of a reasonable notification? UCC 9–504, Comment 5 refers to "taking part in the sale"; a debtor may wish to attend a public sale in order to observe, first-hand, the procedures that are followed. Knowing the time of a public sale and the time after which a private sale may take place also may permit a debtor to arrange for a third-party buyer who otherwise would not have been attracted to the collateral. Moreover, the act of disposition (or contracting for a disposition) cuts off the debtor's right to pay the secured obligation in full and thereby "redeem" the collateral. See UCC 9–506. Reasonable notification informs the debtor of the earliest date on which redemption rights could be lost. (Redemption is considered in Section 4, infra.)

As Comment 5 to UCC 9–504 indicates, timeliness is an important element of the reasonableness of a notification. How much time between giving a notification and a disposition is sufficient? A survey of the cases indicates that the secured party should feel safe in giving 10 days' notice. But this question of fact may turn on considerations such as the type, value, and location of the collateral; the knowledge and sophistication of the debtor; and general market conditions. Moreover, it should be answered in the context of the underlying purposes of the notification requirement, discussed above.

What are the contents of a reasonable notification? UCC 9–504(3) indicates that a notification need only state "the time and place of any public sale or ... the time after which any private sale or other intended disposition is to be made." Does the notice need to state explicitly whether the disposition is to be "public" or "private"? Most, but not all, courts have said "no." What if the secured creditor does specify a "public" disposition, but then conducts a private sale, or vice versa? According to the weight of authority, the notification would fail the test of reasonableness. (Note that consumer protection legislation may require additional information in a notification of disposition. See Form 9, Chapter 11, Section 1, supra.)

UCC 9–504(3) does not require that the debtor actually *receive* a notice; it provides only that "reasonable notification ... shall be *sent* by the secured party to the debtor." Consider the secured party who sends a notification to a debtor's last known address, only to have the letter returned by the Postal Service: "Addressee unknown." Can the secured party comfortably proceed with a disposition? Must the secured party undertake at least "reasonable efforts" to locate the debtor's current address, taking into account what information is readily available to the secured party (e.g., telephone book, knowledge of the debtor's place of employment, etc.)? Some courts have found that the secured party may need to "keep trying," at least for a while.

Finally, can a reasonable notification be given orally? Relying on the requirement that a notification be "sent" and the definition of "send" in UCC 1–201(38), some cases have held oral notifications to be ineffective. Others uphold oral notification, especially when it is clear that the debtor had actual knowledge of all information that a written notification would have contained. Should courts be concerned about the reliability of proof of the "contents" of an oral notification? Should oral notifications be upheld only when the debtor's actual knowledge of the required information can be shown by clear and convincing evidence?

(3) Pre- and Post–Default Debtor Waivers; Agreed Standards of Compliance. When the duties that a legal rule imposes are uncertain, the parties to a transaction may wish to eliminate the uncertainty through contract. For example, a secured party might seek the debtor's agreement that the secured party need not notify the debtor of a proposed disposition and need not dispose of the collateral in a commercially reasonable manner. Notwithstanding that the Code generally promotes freedom of contract, see UCC 1–102(3), Article 9 provides that the parties may not waive or vary any right or duty that UCC 9–504(3) imposes. See UCC 9–501(3)(b). UCC 9–504(3) itself contains a narrow exception that validates a debtor's post-default, written "statement renouncing or modifying his right to notification of sale"; the section makes no mention of any other waivers. It follows that waivers of other UCC 9–504(3) rights of debtors and duties of secured parties, such as the requirement that dispositions be commercially reasonable and the limitation on sales in which the enforcing secured party can be a buyer (i.e., only at public sales), are not permitted. (UCC 1–102(3) also would bar waivers of the reasonableness requirement.)

Article 9 permits a debtor to encumber *all* its assets simply by signing a single piece of paper; yet the statute prohibits the debtor from agreeing as part of the same transaction to waive the right, for example, to notification of a disposition upon default. What explains Article 9's solicitude for debtors? Professor Gilmore's treatise gives one the impression that the original drafters of the Code did not examine this issue anew.

> Since the beginnings of mortgage law, *it has never been questioned* that the mortgagor's equity is entitled to absolute protection and cannot be frittered away. No agreement, we have long been told, will be allowed to "clog the equity of redemption." And not even the most drastic of pledge agreements has ever purported to free the pledgee from his inescapable duties of accounting to the pledgor for the value of the pledged property and of remitting any surplus. *Article 9, therefore, merely reflects history* when it provides that the debtor's rights and the secured party's correlative duties following default "may not be waived or varied."

2 Gilmore, Security § 44.4, at 1228–29 (emphasis added). Is it time for a reexamination of this hoary principle?

Although it is hostile to waivers, UCC 9–501(3) goes on to provide that "the parties may by agreement determine the standards by which the fulfillment of these rights and duties is to be measured if such standards are not manifestly unreasonable." Security agreements that contain standards concerning the timeliness of notifications of disposition appear to be widely used, based on the reported cases.

Agreed standards concerning what constitutes a commercially reasonable disposition seem to be comparatively rare. One explanation for this phenomenon may be the widespread use of standard printed forms that normally are intended to cover many types of collateral. And in large business financings involving highly negotiated documentation, perhaps the anticipated result of a default is bankruptcy, not repossession; negotiating elaborate standards may not be considered worthwhile. On the other hand, might there be many kinds of repetitive transactions in which agreed standards may be advisable (e.g., secured financings of automobiles, trucks, farm equipment, horses)? Consider the types of standards that might be utilized (e.g., agreements as to the names and locations of publications where advertisements should be placed; the number of issues or days or weeks of advertising; whether the sale is to be public or private; specified auctioneer; maximum amount of sale-preparation expenses).

(4) **Effects of Noncompliance: Three Approaches.** Reported decisions reflect three sharply conflicting approaches to whether, and, if so, how a secured party's noncompliance with the foreclosure procedures prescribed by UCC 9–504 affects the right to a deficiency.

UCC 9–507 is entitled "Secured Party's Liability for Failure to Comply With This Part." Subsection (1) provides that the debtor "has a right to recover from the secured party any loss caused by a failure to comply with the provisions of this Part." One might understand that section to limit the debtor's remedy for noncompliance to the assertion of a cause of action: If the noncomplying secured party does not claim a deficiency, then the debtor would be entitled to an affirmative recovery; if the secured party does claim a deficiency, then the debtor would be entitled to set off its damages for noncompliance against the deficiency claim. (The third sentence of UCC 9–507(1) affords the debtor a minimum recovery for noncompliance when the collateral is consumer goods. See Note 7, infra.)

Some courts have adopted this reading of UCC 9–507(1). But most courts have adopted either the "rebuttable presumption" rule, as did *Emmons v. Burkett, supra,* or the "absolute bar" or "loss of deficiency" rule, which the court in *First State Bank of Morrilton v. Hallett, supra,* approved. As those opinions indicate, a substantial body of authority has developed in support of each point of view. However, we doubt the accuracy of the Arkansas Supreme Court's statement in *First State Bank* that the absolute bar rule is the "apparent majority position." For a survey of the cases, see Clark, Secured Transactions ¶ 4.12[4], at 4–182 to 4–194.

In any event, the battle lines are drawn. It seems likely that a statutory solution will emerge, whether in a revised Article 9 or in state-by-state nonuniform amendments.

Application of the Absolute Bar Rule: Impact on Other Collateral; Partial Dispositions. Consider the following scenario: Debtor gives Lender a security interest in collateral worth $10,000 to secure a loan of $100,000. On Debtor's default, Lender sells the collateral in a commercially unreasonable manner or without reasonable notification to Debtor. Application of the absolute bar rule would prohibit Lender from recovering the balance of the debt, even if Debtor were solvent and able to pay.

Are you persuaded by the opinion in *First State Bank* that this result is desirable? As the foregoing scenario suggests, the rule is blatantly penal: any correlation between the harm done a debtor by the secured party's noncompliance and the sanction imp⸱sed on the secured party is entirely fortuitous. Why should a secured party's noncompliance put a debtor in a better position than would have been the case had the secured party complied? Indeed, UCC 1–106(1) makes clear that the Code disapproves of such results.

The absolute bar rule has other penal aspects. For example, under the facts set forth above, assume that Lender sold (again, employing defective procedures) only one item of collateral, worth $5,000; another item, also worth $5,000, remains unsold. Logically, having stripped Lender of its right to recover a deficiency (i.e., the remaining balance of the debt), the absolute bar rule would deprive Lender of any further right to recover on the remaining item. One court, however, permitted a secured party to recover on an *in rem* claim against the remaining collateral in this context. See In re Gerber, 51 B.R. 526 (Bkrtcy. D.Neb.1985).[2] Other secured parties have not been so fortunate, even when the remaining collateral was real estate.

Arguably, the absolute bar rule has a proper domain in certain contexts, such as PMSI's in consumer goods, where some equivalence between the secured debt and the collateral might be expected. Distinguishing among various contexts would require legislative action, of course. Indications are that such "consumer carve-outs" will be inspired more by political necessity than by thoughtful policy analysis. See the description of the California amendments, infra.

Significance of the Nature of Noncompliance: Unreasonable Notification or Commercially Unreasonable Disposition. Several of the early cases that adopted the absolute bar rule involved defective notification, not commercially unreasonable dispositions. There is some judicial support for applying the absolute bar rule to the failure to give the required notification while applying the rebuttable presumption rule to noncompliance consisting of the failure to dispose of collateral in a commercially reasonable manner. There also is some authority for the converse: applying the rebuttable presumption rule to cases of improper (or missing) notification and the absolute bar rule to commercially unreasonable dispositions. Do you see any reason to treat noncompliance consisting of defective notification differently from that consisting of a commercially unreasonable disposition? The *Emmons* court makes it clear that the rebuttable presumption rule applies in the case of either defect. Although less explicit, the court's broad language in *First State Bank* indicates that it would apply the absolute bar rule in either case.

2. The same result would obtain if the secured debt were discharged in bankruptcy.

Application of the Rebuttable Presumption Rule. As noted by the court in the *Emmons* case, "[u]nder the rebuttable-presumption rule, if a creditor fails to give notice or conducts an unreasonable sale, a presumption is raised that the value of the collateral is equal to the indebtedness." However, compliance with Part 5 will not necessarily result in the recovery of the "value" of collateral. See UCC 9–507(2) (1st sentence). Perhaps a better, more precise formulation of the rule would create a rebuttable presumption that compliance with Part 5 would have yielded an amount sufficient to satisfy the secured debt. Stated otherwise, the noncomplying secured party has the burden of proving the amount that would have been recovered had the secured party complied with Part 5, and the secured party's deficiency recovery is limited to the difference between that amount and the amount of the secured debt.

(5) Rights and Duties of Secured Parties Under UCC 9–207. When we considered perfection of security interests by possession we noted the rights and duties of secured parties under UCC 9–207. See Note on Rights and Duties of Secured Party in Possession of Collateral, Chapter 11, Section 2(B), supra. The most significant duty, of course, is the requirement of "reasonable care in the custody and preservation of collateral" when it is in the secured party's possession. UCC 9–207(1). UCC 9–207 also applies when a secured party has taken possession after a debtor's default. UCC 9–501(1) (4th sentence).

(6) Restrictions on Deficiency Recoveries in Consumer Transactions. Under Massachusetts legislation, in consumer credit transactions involving $2,000 or less that are secured by "a non-possessory security interest in consumer goods," the debtor is entirely excused from any deficiency liability once the secured party takes or accepts possession. In consumer credit transactions involving $2,000 or more (at the time of default), the deficiency is calculated by deducting from the outstanding secured obligation the "fair market value" of the collateral, *not* by deducting the net sale proceeds as provided by UCC 9–504(2). Mass. Ann. Laws ch. 255B, § 20B(d) & (e) (Law. Co-op 1980). (If the debt is *exactly* $2,000, *both* rules seem to apply!)

The Massachusetts legislation reflects an approach to deficiencies in consumer transactions that is a throwback to pre-Code rules and that has gained some support nationally. In the classical conditional sale, the conditional seller was required to elect between alternative remedies when the buyer defaulted: The seller could (i) repossess the goods sold *or* (ii) sue for the price (i.e., the remaining balance due). If the seller repossessed the goods, it had no further claim against the buyer. A claim for a "deficiency" was an attribute of a "mortgage" and not permitted in the setting of a conditional sale. See Gilmore, Security §§ 3.2, 43.1.

Before the Code, most experts on the law of conditional sales concluded that the election doctrine was awkward and harsh; it was generally assumed that the Uniform Conditional Sales Act made a significant contribution to the law by permitting the seller, on repossession, to establish a deficiency (usually by a public sale) for which the buyer would be liable. See Uniform Conditional Sales Act § 22 (1918) (superseded).

With that background, one can appreciate the sensation of *deja vu* in encountering the election doctrine in the 1974 version of U3C 5.103, set out at the end of this Note. The 1968 version similarly restricted deficiency judgments with respect to consumer credit sales of goods or services. Although neither version of the U3C has been widely adopted, several states have adopted election-of-remedies statutes modeled, to a greater or lesser extent, on U3C 5.103.

Would Lee Abel, in the Prototype transaction, and most other buyers of automobiles have protection from deficiency judgments under the U3C? What types of transactions and what buyers typically would receive protection under U3C 5.103? Would this provision provide some assistance when goods prove to be shoddy? Does it afford sufficient protection to the secured party when the goods are abused?

The denial of deficiency claims when the creditor repossesses has been characterized as self-defeating. Apart from cars, most consumer goods have little resale value; a creditor could avoid losing a claim for deficiency by not repossessing and pressing for collection of the debt. Perhaps the only consequence of this reform "is to leave the poor with the dissatisfaction of his merchandise." See Kripke, Gesture and Reality in Consumer Credit Reform, 44 N.Y.U.L.Rev. 1, 32–34 (1969). Professor Kripke suggests that a logical extension of the thinking behind the denial of deficiency judgments is a proposal to limit the creditor's recourse to the *collateral*. But such proposals to restrict the creditor's remedies, he suggested, could result in withdrawal of credit from the poorest credit risks, or in raising of the price level of merchandise "thus taxing the poor who struggle through their payment requirements with an added cost absorbing the losses of others who do not pay." For material that supports restricting the remedies of the secured party, see Consumer Credit in the United States: Report of the National Commission on Consumer Finance 29–31 (1972).

(7) **The Debtor's "Minimum Recovery."** Any injury caused by a secured party's noncompliance with Part 5 normally is limited by the monetary value of the disposed collateral. Inasmuch as the value of most consumer goods is small and the cost of litigation often is high, one might expect that consumers would be unwilling or unable to avail themselves of a remedy under UCC 9–507(1). Perhaps for this reason, the last sentence of UCC 9–507(1) affords what Comment 1 calls a "minimum recovery" as follows:

> If the collateral is consumer goods, the debtor has a right to recover in any event an amount not less than the credit service charge plus ten per cent of the principal amount of the debt or the time price differential plus 10 per cent of the cash price.

Observe that, like the absolute bar rule, this remedy for noncompliance in the case of consumer goods need not bear any relationship to the injury resulting from the secured party's misconduct. Indeed, there may have been no injury at all. Isn't the "minimum recovery" more property called a "civil penalty"?

SECTION 3. RIGHTS OF THIRD–PARTY CLAIMANTS

Introduction. Sections 1 and 2 of this Chapter dealt with the enforcement rights of the secured party and the duties it owes to the debtor. This Section deals with the rights of certain third parties when a secured party enforces a security interest in collateral. Part (A) considers the rights of sureties for secured obligations, such as guarantors of payment; Part (B) addresses competing secured parties and other lienholders, both senior and junior to the enforcing secured party, and the position of a purchaser of collateral at a disposition conducted under UCC 9–504.

(A) Sureties (Including Guarantors)

Introductory Note: The Elements of Suretyship. Secured lenders and sellers frequently bargain for (perhaps more accurately, insist on) a third-party **guaranty of payment**. Under a guaranty, a third party (the "guarantor") undertakes to pay an obligation of the debtor (the borrower or buyer). If the debtor defaults in payment of the obligation, then the guarantor must step up and pay it (or an agreed portion thereof). Most guaranties provide that the guarantor "unconditionally guarantees the punctual payment when due" of the debtor's obligations; they normally do not condition liability on the debtor's default. In practice, however, a guarantor usually will not be prepared to pay the guaranteed obligation unless it is informed that the debtor has failed to pay. Guaranties are given in transactions that span the spectrum of secured and unsecured credit. Examples abound: Large corporations guaranty payment of debts incurred by their subsidiaries; parents guaranty payment by young daughters and sons who do not have an established credit rating; principal shareholders of closely-held corporations guaranty the corporate borrowings.

A guaranty of payment is governed by the law of **suretyship.** There are many other kinds of suretyship contracts. A common example is the **performance bond**, under which an insurance company "surety" agrees to complete the performance of a construction contract if the contractor fails to perform as agreed. Before focusing specifically on the guaranty of payment in the context of secured credit, the chief area of concern here, it will be useful to have a nodding acquaintance with the elements of suretyship law.

Although the obligation of a third party who acts as a surety is not "collateral" (UCC 9–105(1)(c)) subject to a "security interest" (UCC 1–

201(37)), the obligation nevertheless is classified within the general category of "security" by the Restatement of Security: "Suretyship is included in the general field of Security because the obligation of a surety is an additional assurance to the one entitled to the performance of an act that the act will be performed." Restatement of Security, Scope Note to Division II (1941).

What Is "Suretyship"? Fortunately, we need not attempt here a hair-splitting definition of "surety" or "suretyship"; the materials here are in the mainstream, and far from the penumbra, of suretyship law. The Restatement of Security § 82 gives a satisfactory working definition: "Suretyship is the relation which exists where one person has undertaken an obligation and another person is also under an obligation or other duty to the obligee, who is entitled to but one performance, and as between the two who are bound, one rather than the other should perform." The Restatement uses "guaranty" as a synonym for suretyship. (Considerable confusion surrounds the scope of these two terms, and if there is any sense in attempting to dispel it, the task is best left for another time and place.)

Take a simple example. Suppose that *P* wishes to borrow $5,000 from *C*. In order to induce *C* to make the loan, *P* has *S* join with *P* in promising to repay. As further security, *P* pledges $30,000 worth of corporate bonds to *C*. Both *P* and *S* are under an obligation to *C*; *C* is entitled to but one performance; and as between *P* and *S*, *P* rather than *S* should perform. This relationship clearly fits the Restatement definition of suretyship. *P* is the *principal,* *S* is the *surety,* and *C* is the *creditor.* If *S* engages in the business of executing surety contracts for a premium determined by a computation of risks spread over a large number of transactions, *S* is a *compensated surety,* using Restatement terminology, and typically is subject to state law regulation as an insurance company. A compensated surety may not be discharged from liability as readily as an uncompensated surety.

C's rights against *P* are governed basically by contract law: Absent peculiar circumstances (e.g., *C*'s fraud upon *P*; *P*'s infancy), *C* will have the right to enforce the obligation against *P*.

The Creditor's Rights Against the Surety. In the alternative, *C* may proceed against *S*, the surety. If *P* defaults, generally *C* need not attempt to collect from *P* nor to satisfy the debt from the corporate bonds before enforcing *S*'s liability. Immediate recourse against *S* upon *P*'s default was one of the advantages that *C* expected from *S*'s suretyship contract. Even if *C*'s lack of diligence in pursuing *P* causes loss, *S* is not discharged.[1] In a number of states this rule is subject to an exception under which *C*'s failure to sue *P* at *S*'s request discharges

---

1. It is, of course, possible for the surety to limit its engagement to a guaranty of *collection* of the principal's obligation. Such a **guarantor of collection** is, by the nature of the undertaking, discharged to the extent of any loss caused by the creditor's lack of diligence in proceeding against the principal. See Restatement, Security § 130(2). Understandably, guaranties of collection are rare in the credit markets.

$S.^2$ (Compare the engagement of secondary parties to negotiable instruments under UCC 3–414(b), (e); UCC 3–415(a), (b); UCC 3–419.)

S, who is subject to an action by *C* should *P* default, has in turn three major remedies against *P*: exoneration, subrogation, and reimbursement. *S*'s right of **exoneration** is an equitable one. Basically it allows *S*, upon *P*'s default, to compel *P* in a suit in equity to pay *C*. It is reasoned that without this remedy *S* might undergo considerable hardship in raising the money to pay *C*, even though *S* could afterwards recover over from *P*. However, sureties rarely assert the right to exoneration, probably because most principal debtors who *do not* pay probably *cannot* pay. Rather, the surety usually will pay the creditor and then attempt to recover from the principal under the right to subrogation or reimbursement.

When *S* pays in full *P*'s debt to *C*, *S* is subrogated to the rights of *C*. See Restatement, Security § 141. **Subrogation** may be viewed as equitable assignment. *S* would therefore succeed, as by assignment, to *C*'s rights (as holder of the secured debt and as pledgee of the corporate bonds) against *P* and to the priority of *C*'s security interest as against third parties. Since the right is an equitable one, it is subject to equitable limitations.[3] An important qualification is that if the debt has not been paid *in full*, the surety ordinarily has no right of subrogation. Thus in the usual case if *S* should pay *C* only $40,000, leaving a balance of $10,000 due, *S* would not thereby be entitled to any part of *C*'s security interest in the bonds. This is to insure that the benefits of *P*'s collateral are applied first to the satisfaction of *P*'s debt to *C*.

S would, however, have the right to **reimbursement** (sometimes called **indemnification**) from *P* to the extent of $40,000. See Restatement, Security § 104. Because *S* became bound as surety at the request of *P*, *S*'s right to reimbursement can be spelled out from *P*'s implied request to *S* to pay the debt at maturity if *P* does not and from *P*'s implied promise to reimburse *S* for any such payment. (Well-drafted suretyship contracts explicitly provide for a right to reimburse-

---

2. The exception was laid down in Pain v. Packard, 13 Johns. (N.Y. Sup. Ct.) 174 (1816). In that case the surety, when sued by the creditor, pleaded that he had requested the creditor to proceed immediately to collect from the principal; that the creditor had not done so; and that although the principal could have then been compelled to pay, he later became insolvent and absconded. The court held that his plea stated a good defense; since the defendant was known to be a surety, the principal, was "bound to use due diligence against the principal in order to exonerate the surety." A number of other states have adopted some form of the rule in Pain v. Packard, in most instances by statute. It was rejected by the Restatement of Secu-

rity § 130 and by the great majority of courts that have faced the issue without statutory guidance. The reason given by the Restatement is that, "[s]ince the surety may pay the claim of the creditor and himself proceed against the principal for exoneration in advance of payment …, the creditor's non-action generally affords no equitable basis for a claim of discharge by the surety." Pain v. Packard was overruled by statute in New York in 1968. See N.Y. Gen. Oblig. Law § 15–701 (Consol. 1977).

3. This is particularly true where the surety attempts to enforce a right that the creditor would have had against a third party.

ment.) Of course, the right to reimbursement is only a right *in personam* against *P* and may be, for this reason, less satisfactory to *S* than subrogation, particularly if *S* must compete with other creditors of *P*.

The Surety's Defenses. Exoneration, subrogation and reimbursement, then, are the three principal remedies of *S* against *P*. An elementary understanding of them is necessary to answer the next question: In what circumstances will an agreement between *C* and *P* to *modify P*'s obligation to *C* operate to *discharge S* from its obligation as surety?[4] Suppose that *C* and *P* were to modify their original agreement so as to increase the interest rate from eight to nine per cent. *S* would be discharged. The modification has increased the burden on *P* and made it more likely that *P* will default. However, should the modification decrease the interest rate from eight to seven per cent, it is difficult to justify discharge of the surety because the surety is not prejudiced. Nevertheless, there is authority for the proposition that since a suretyship contract is *strictissimi juris,* the surety will be discharged whether the modification increases or decreases the burden of the principal's performance! Under the Restatement of Security § 128, however, the surety is not discharged if "the modification is of a sort that can only be beneficial to the surety." Under either view, since a compensated surety not only has been paid for the undertaking but usually also has supplied the form setting forth the express terms, it is less likely to be discharged because of a modification. See Restatement, Security § 128(b).

Consider two other common types of modification—*C*'s release of *P* and *C*'s extension of the time for *P* to perform. It is hardly surprising that release of *P* generally discharges *S*. Two reasons suggest themselves. One rests upon concern for *S*; if *C* released *P*, then *C* would have no rights to which *S* could be subrogated should *S* be required to pay. The other rests upon concern for *P*; should *S* be required to pay *C*, *S* still would be entitled to reimbursement from *P*, thus accomplishing indirectly the enforcement of *P*'s debt to *C*, contrary to *P*'s expectations upon discharge.

There are two exceptions to the general rule discharging the surety upon release of the principal: consent of the surety and reservation of rights by the creditor against the surety. Suppose that a fourth party, upon *P*'s default, agrees to make good $30,000 of *P*'s debt to *C* in consideration for *P*'s release. If *C* releases *P* but obtains *S*'s consent to remain bound, *S*'s liability to pay *C* the balance of $20,000 will be unaffected by the release. *S* has consented to the loss of the remedy of subrogation and is deemed to have relinquished the right to reimbursement. *S* has, in effect, become principal debtor.

---

4. This discussion of discharge of a surety is premised upon the assumption that the creditor has knowledge of the suretyship relationship of *S*. See Restatement, Security § 114.

More startling is the doctrine that *C*, *without* obtaining *S*'s consent, can preserve *S*'s liability merely by reserving *C*'s rights against *S* at the time of *P*'s release. The reasoning runs as follows. Concern for *S* does not require *S*'s discharge, because *S* has not lost the remedy of subrogation. The release of *P* with reservation of rights against *S* is construed as a covenant by *C* not to sue *P*. It does not deprive *C* of the power to enforce *P*'s liability, although it places *C* under a duty not to do so. Concern for *P* does not require the discharge of *S* because when *P* accepted a release with the reservation, *P* assumed the risk that the liability might be enforced against *P* by *S*. But has not the release of *P* made it almost inevitable that *S* will now be called upon to perform? Does this not unfairly increase *S*'s burden? It may be an answer to say that *S*'s expectation that *P* will pay and discharge the obligation is a matter solely between *S* and *P*, and of no concern to *C*. Certainly it would seem that *S*'s remedy of exoneration would be unaffected. Perhaps a more satisfactory answer is one suggested by the Restatement of Security § 122: it may encourage **compositions**. The Restatement suggests that should *P* propose a composition to creditors, *C* could accept the composition, releasing *P* but reserving rights against *S*. If *S* pays *C*, then *S* has a right of reimbursement against *P*.

A binding agreement between *C* and *P* extending the time for *P*'s performance also will discharge *S*. See Restatement, Security § 129. It is reasoned that *S* would be precluded by the extension from paying *C* at maturity and proceeding against *P*.[5] Here, too, an exception is made where *S* consents or where *C* reserves its rights against *S*. If *C* has reserved its rights against *S*, then *S* may avoid any prejudicial effect of the extension by paying at maturity and proceeding against *P* in spite of the extension.

Finally, if *C* "impairs" collateral, as by releasing the security interest in the bonds that *C* holds to secure *P*'s debt, the general rule is that the *S* is discharged to the extent of the value of collateral released. See Restatement, Security § 132. Discharge is based on the impairment of the surety's right of subrogation and the right to enforce the security interest. Thus, if *C* should release the security interest in the $30,000 worth of bonds, *S* would be discharged to the extent of $30,000. *C*'s failure to perfect the security interest also could constitute an impairment of collateral if a buyer or other conflicting claimant were to prevent *S* from receiving the benefit of the collateral. For a sampling of the case law, see Clark, Security Interests ¶ 4.03[3][b], at 4–39 to 4–41.

UCC 3–605 (the successor to pre–1990 UCC 3–606) deals explicitly with issues of discharge of a surety who is an "accommodation party" to a negotiable instrument. See UCC 3–419(a) (defining "accommodation

---

5. The rule is not without its critics. "How many would hold that a surety is released, irrespective of resulting damage, if by agreement between principal and creditor the time of payment of the debt is extended for a single day?", Cardozo, A Ministry of Justice, 35 Harv.L.Rev. 113, 117 (1921). Under Restatement, Security § 129, a compensated surety is discharged only to the extent that it is harmed by the extension.

party"). Extensions of time, other material modifications of terms, and impairment of collateral will discharge an accommodation party only to the extent that the accommodation party suffers loss thereby. UCC 3–605(c), (d), (f), & (g). Moreover, an accommodation party is not discharged if it gives consent to the event or conduct involved or waives in advance its suretyship defenses. UCC 3–605(i).

The Future Restatement of Suretyship. Although the suretyship provisions in UCC 3–605 represent the most recent expression of consensus, there is a wide range of transactions to which Article 3 does not apply. Moreover, as we shall see, there is considerable tension between UCC 3–605 and Article 9's restrictions on waivers of rights by debtors. See Note (2) on Rights of Guarantors of Secured Obligations, infra. For these reasons, and others (including the advanced age of the Restatement of Security), The American Law Institute has begun work on a new Restatement of Suretyship. See The American Law Institute, Annual Reports 7 (1991).

Surety vs. Secured Party: A Brief Excursus. One additional aspect of the relationship between suretyship law and Article 9 should be mentioned. Assume that a debtor (*P*) has a contract to build a building for the owner of land (*C*). As is customary, *P* obtains a performance bond, under which a third-party surety (*S*) undertakes to complete the building if *P* should default in its performance. In addition, a secured party, *SP*, has a security interest in *P*'s accounts, including *P*'s right to payment from *C*. Following *P*'s default and *S*'s completion of the contract, both *S* and *SP* claim the remaining amounts owing by *C* to *P*. The source of *S*'s claim is the law of suretyship: Having completed the contract, *S* is subrogated to *P*'s rights against *C*, which include the right to be paid for a completed building. *S*'s claim may include the right to funds earned by *P*'s pre-default performance but withheld by *C* pursuant to the contract. This right is premised on the notion that *S* is subrogated to *C*'s rights.

Although *SP* has perfected its security interest by filing, *S* has not filed. Whose claim is senior? The law has become well-settled since the leading case of National Shawmut Bank v. New Amsterdam Casualty Co., 411 F.2d 843 (1st Cir.1969). *S* wins. *S*'s rights do not derive from a consensual security interest under Article 9, but instead are born of suretyship law. See UCC 9–102(2) (Article 9 applies to security interests created by contract). Accordingly, the priority rules of UCC 9–312 are inapplicable.

UCC 9–201 has been construed to award priority to a security interest over a conflicting non-Article 9 interest (the right of setoff). What accounts for the near unanimity of judicial opinion in favor of sureties? An intuitive approach might be to ask, what would the value of *SP*'s collateral have been had *S* not performed? Is it fair to pay *S* for the value its performance created? Alternatively, one might (but courts generally have not) rank the competing claims by reference to UCC 9–318(1). The secured party ordinarily takes its rights subject to "all the terms of the contract between the account debtor [C] and assignor [P] and any defense or claim arising therefrom." Wouldn't P's breach have given C a defense to payment, or at least a partial setoff? S, having performed the contract, simply steps into C's shoes as against SP.

Problem 1. Under the facts of the Problem in Section 2, supra, suppose that Telli Schmelli, the CEO, had executed in favor of the bank (AIB) an absolute, unconditional guaranty of payment, whereby Telli, individually, guaranteed to AIB the punctual payment when due of all existing and future indebtedness of Schmelli Services, Inc., to AIB. The guaranty thus covers the outstanding indebtedness on the line of credit facility as well as the Learjet indebtedness. Under the terms of the guaranty Telli waived all possible suretyship defenses and all rights (including rights to notice) relating to any collateral.

You are counsel for both Schmelli Services and Telli. The Learjet has been sold by AIB for an amount that left a substantial deficiency on the Learjet debt. AIB has accelerated the line of credit indebtedness and is in the process of collecting the accounts receivable, but Telli expects a deficiency on that loan as well.

Prior to selling the Learjet AIB sent a notification of private sale (by certified mail, return receipt requested) addressed to:

Schmelli Services, Inc.

1000½ E. Markham

Little Rock, Arkansas 72206

Attention: Telli Schmelli, Pres. & CEO

When the envelope containing the notice was delivered to Schmelli's headquarters, Telli's private secretary, Melli Vanelli, signed for it. Telli saw the notice the next day, while reading the mail, and immediately faxed a copy to you.

(a) AIB has sued Telli on his personal guaranty of payment for an amount equal to the outstanding balance on all Schmelli corporate debt. Assume that the Learjet security agreement was governed by the law of a jurisdiction that has adopted the absolute bar rule. See Note (4) on Commercially Reasonable Dispositions and Reasonable Notification, Section 2, supra. What, if any, defenses will you raise? See Notes on Rights of Guarantors of Secured Obligations, infra.

(b) Now assume that the law of a jurisdiction that has adopted the rebuttable presumption rule controlled the Learjet secured transaction. What, if any, defenses will you raise?

Notes on Rights of Guarantors of Secured Obligations

(1) Treatment of a Guarantor of a Secured Obligation as a "Debtor" Under UCC 9–504(3). Suppose that a secured party fails to send reasonable notification of a disposition to a guarantor of secured debt or that the secured party disposes of collateral in a commercially unreasonable manner. Does the secured party owe these duties to a guarantor? If so, does Article 9 afford the guarantor a remedy for noncompliance?

UCC 9–504(3) requires the secured party to send reasonable notification of the disposition "to the debtor." Can the guarantor successfully argue that it is a "debtor"? If so, then the secured party was obliged to give the guarantor reasonable notification. Moreover, under UCC 9–507(1) the right to recover loss for noncompliance with Article 9 extends to (i) the debtor, (ii) any person entitled to notification of the disposition, and (iii) any person whose security interest has been made known to the secured party. Thus it would appear that, if the guarantor is "the debtor," then it would be entitled to a remedy for the secured party's failure to give notification of the disposition and to dispose of the collateral in a commercially reasonable manner. This argument is especially attractive to guarantors when applicable law embraces the absolute bar rule. See Note (4) on Commercially Reasonable Dispositions and Reasonable Notification, Section 2, supra. Because the secured party would lose any right to a deficiency, the guarantor-debtor could escape entirely all liability on the guaranty!

A substantial number of reported cases address whether a guarantor is a "debtor," as the term is used in UCC 9–504(3). The vast majority decide in favor of the guarantor. See Annotation, Construction of Term "Debtor" as Used in UCC § 9–504(3), Requiring Secured Party to Give Notice to Debtor of Sale of Collateral Securing Obligation, 5 A.L.R.4th 1291 (1981). Most of these cases recognize that a disposition may affect the size of the deficiency claim against the guarantor in much the same way as it affects the size of the claim against the principal obligor. Many of the cases also focus on the definition of "debtor":

> "Debtor" means the *person who owes payment* or other performance *of the obligation secured*, whether or not he owns or has rights in the collateral .... Where the debtor and the owner of the collateral are not the same person, the term *"debtor" means* the owner of the collateral in any provision of the Article dealing with the collateral, *the obligor in any provision dealing with the obligation*, and *may include both* where the context so requires.

UCC 9–105(1)(d) (emphasis added).

(2) Waiver of Debtor's Rights and Secured Party's Duties by a Guarantor "Debtor": Suretyship Law and Article 3 versus Article 9, Part 5. UCC 9–501(1) provides that the rules in UCC 9–504(3) "may not be waived or varied." We already have seen that UCC 9–504(3) itself permits only post-default waivers consisting of a debtor's "statement renouncing or modifying his right to notification of sale." On the other hand, we also have seen that traditional suretyship law and UCC 3–605(i) (as well as the pre–1990 UCC 3–606 that it replaced) recognize the enforceability of pre-default waivers of suretyship defenses, *including impairment of collateral*.[6] Does Article 9's limitation on waiver override suretyship law and UCC 3–605? Does UCC 3–605 control when the secured debt is evidenced by a negotiable instrument, leaving Article 9 to control in other cases?

A substantial number of reported cases address whether a guarantor who is entitled to notice under UCC 9–504(3) nevertheless may make an effective pre-default waiver of the right to receive notice. These cases are fairly evenly divided between those enforcing the waiver and those refusing to do so. See Note, Guarantors as Debtors Under Uniform Commercial Code § 9–501(3), 56 Fordham L. Rev. 745, 749 & n.35 (1988).

The frequency with which these issues—whether a guarantor is a debtor and the efficacy of a guarantor's waivers—have been litigated and the nonuniformity of results, particularly as regards the waiver issue, suggest that clarification may be in order. Should Article 9 be amended so as to state affirmatively the extent to which a guarantor's pre-default waiver is enforceable? So as to leave the waiver issue entirely to suretyship law (including any new Restatement of Suretyship that may be forthcoming)?

Note that application of the rebuttable presumption rule (or the offset rule) to a secured party's noncompliance goes far to reduce the importance of these issues. By reducing a deficiency claim only to the extent that noncompliance has harmed the principal debtor or a guarantor, the risk of a solvent guarantor's escape from liability based on a harmless technicality is removed. On the other hand, UCC 3–605 likewise provides for an accommodation party's discharge on account of suretyship defenses only to the extent of actual loss and *also* validates pre-default waivers.

(3) Security Interests in One Debtor's Collateral Securing Obligations of Another Debtor. There are means other than giving a guaranty by which a third party can lend support to an obligation of another. Sometimes a third party (**hypothecator**) will give a security interest in property that it owns to support another's obligation. For example, Telli's stock might be used to secure Schmelli Services' debt. It is clear that the hypothecator is a "debtor," as defined in UCC 9–105(1)(d), whether or not the third party also guaranties the obligation. If no guaranty exists, of course, the third party would not become liable for any deficiency. The obligation for a deficiency mentioned in UCC

---

6. Although noncompliance with UCC 9–504(3) is the focus of attention here, that is not the only way that a secured creditor might impair collateral so as to give rise to suretyship defenses. See UCC 3–605(g).

9–504(2) must be considered a "provision dealing [only] with the obligation." See UCC 9–105(1)(d). On the other hand, if disposition of the non-obligor-debtor's collateral yields a surplus, that debtor (not the obligor) would be entitled to the surplus.

(B) Competing Secured Parties and Lienholders; Purchasers of Collateral in Dispositions Under UCC 9–504

We now leave (for a brief time) the paradigm of enforcement of security interests against obligors on secured indebtedness and owners of the collateral. The Problems and Notes in this part consider some of the difficulties and questions that can arise when collateral is subject to multiple security interests and other liens and one or more of the claimants seeks to enforce a security interest. Most of the issues that have arisen over the duties that are or should be imposed upon an enforcing secured party in favor of a competing claimant concern (a) whether and under what circumstances the foreclosing secured party should be required to afford notice of a foreclosure sale to a competing claimant and (b) the appropriate allocation of the proceeds of the sale.

Problem 2. Under the facts of the Problem in Section 2, supra, suppose that AIB's security agreement covering accounts also covers all equipment at any time owned by Schmelli Services. AIB has perfected that security interest by filing in all states where Schmelli has offices.

You now represent Tuleight Co., one of Schmelli's trade creditors. Several months ago Tuleight's president was pressing Schmelli's treasurer for payment of past due invoices. To "buy some time," the treasurer offered Tuleight a security interest in all of Schmelli's office equipment located in Arkansas (where Tuleight's sole office is located). Tuleight agreed. To "save time and money," Tuleight did not consult you or any other lawyer. Tuleight's president bought a form security agreement and financing statement at a stationery store, completed the documents (properly, as luck would have it), obtained Schmelli's execution of the documents, and filed the financing statement in the proper office in Arkansas. Also as luck would have it, Tuleight's president did not think to search the filings and was (and remains) ignorant of AIB's earlier filing and senior security interest.

Tuleight now asks for your advice about how to take possession of and sell the equipment. The outstanding balance that Schmelli owes Tuleight is $50,000.

(a) If Tuleight can recover possession of the equipment, to whom should Tuleight give notification of a disposition? See UCC 9–504(3). Will you request a search of the UCC filing office in Arkansas? See Note (1) on Duties Owed by an Enforcing Secured Party to a Competing Secured Party or Lienholder and Rights of Purchasers, infra.

(b) Assume, for the time being, that AIB has *no other collateral* for the Schmelli debt (i.e., assume that AIB already has liquidated the accounts, the equipment in other states, and the Learjet, and that a deficiency remains unpaid). Under which, if any, of the following scenarios will Tuleight be liable to AIB? See Note (4) on Duties Owed by an Enforcing Secured Party to a Competing Secured Party or Lienholder and Rights of Purchasers, infra.

(i) Tuleight takes possession of the equipment.

(ii) After Tuleight takes possession, AIB demands that Tuleight deliver the equipment to AIB and Tuleight refuses. Does it matter whether AIB's loan is in default?

(iii) After Tuleight takes possession, Tuleight sells the equipment. Does it matter whether the buyer at the sale disappears with the equipment?

(iv) Tuleight sells the equipment at a public sale following two days' advertising in a "throw-away" newspaper.

(v) Tuleight sells the equipment at a commercially reasonable sale for $30,000 and keeps the money. Does it matter whether Tuleight gave reasonable notification of the disposition to AIB?

(vi) Tuleight sells the equipment at a commercially reasonable sale for $90,000, keeps $55,000 (including $5,000 costs of sale), and gives $45,000 to Schmelli.

Problem 3. How would the existence of the other collateral for the AIB debt affect any of the results in Problem 2(b)? See Note (6) on Duties Owed by an Enforcing Secured Party to a Competing Secured Party or Lienholder and Rights of Purchasers, infra.

Problem 4. Under the facts of the Problem in Section 2, supra, assume that Schmelli Services enters bankruptcy. See Note (6) on Duties Owed by an Enforcing Secured Party to a Competing Secured Party or Lienholder and Rights of Purchasers, infra.

(a) If AIB wishes to satisfy its claim first from the Arkansas equipment, can Tuleight compel AIB to satisfy its claim first from the other collateral instead? See Note (6) on Duties Owed by an Enforcing Secured Party to a Competing Secured Party or Lienholder and Rights of Purchasers, infra.

(b) If AIB wishes to satisfy its claim first from the other collateral, can the bankruptcy trustee compel AIB to satisfy its claim first from the Arkansas equipment instead?

Problem 5. Assume the facts of the Problem in Section 2, supra. Assume also that Schmelli Services did not enter bankruptcy. You now represent Bonzo Co. Bonzo has reached tentative agreement with Tuleight to buy, in a private sale, various office equipment that Tuleight has repossessed from Schmelli. What steps do you take to protect Bonzo? See Note (4) on Duties Owed by an Enforcing Secured Party to a Competing Secured Party or Lienholder and Rights of Purchasers, infra. What, if any, special provisions will you insist on in the sale agreement?

Notes on Duties Owed by an Enforcing Secured Party to a Competing Secured Party or Lienholder and Rights of Purchasers

(1) Duties of Senior Secured Parties to Junior Claimants: Notification Requirements. We have seen that UCC 9–504(3) requires an enforcing secured party to send "reasonable notification" of a disposition to the debtor. It provides further:

> In the case of consumer goods no other notification need be sent. In other cases notification shall be sent to any other secured party from whom the secured party has received (before sending his notification to the debtor or before the debtor's renunciation of his rights [to receive notice]) written notice of a claim of an interest in the collateral.

Prior to the 1972 amendments to Article 9, UCC 9–504(3) required the foreclosing secured party to send reasonable notification of the sale "except in the case of consumer goods to any other person who has a security interest in the collateral and who has duly filed a financing statement indexed in the name of the debtor in this state or who is known by the secured party to have a security interest in the collateral." To comply with the pre–1972 text, a foreclosing secured party not only had to search the Code filings for financing statements showing a competing security interest but also had to review its own records to discover whether some communication, perhaps informal, had given the secured party knowledge of another security interest. In the view of the Article 9 Review Committee, "[t]hese burdens of searching the record and of checking the secured party's files were greater than the circumstances called for because as a practical matter there would seldom be a junior secured party who really had an interest needing protection in the case of a foreclosure sale." Review Committee for Article 9, Final Report, UCC 9–504, Reasons for 1972 Change. Accordingly, UCC 9–504(3) was revised to require a secured party to send notice of a foreclosure sale only to those secured parties "from whom the secured party has received ... written notice of a claim of an interest in the collateral."

The decision to eliminate the knowledge test for the duty to notify competing secured parties is consistent with certain other rules in Article 9. See, e.g., UCC 9–312(5); Notes on the Role of Knowledge in Priority Contests, Chapter 13, Section 1(A), supra. Are you persuaded by the drafters' explanation for eliminating the requirement that all secured parties of record be notified? Note that requiring the enforcing secured party to give notice to others of record would delay the sale by the amount of time necessary to search the public record and determine whether other secured parties are on file. In an ideal world, this delay would be trivial; in the real world it may not be.

(2) Duties of Senior Secured Parties to Junior Claimants: Allocation of Proceeds. UCC 9–504(1) specifies how the proceeds of a foreclosure sale are to be applied. After payment of (a) the reasonable expenses of sale and (b) any reasonable attorney's fees and legal expenses incurred by the secured party (to the extent provided for in the agreement and not prohibited by law), the proceeds are to be applied first to the satisfaction of the indebtedness secured by the security interest under which the disposition is made and, if any proceeds remain, then to "the satisfaction of indebtedness secured by any subordinate security interest in the collateral if written notification of demand therefor is received before distribution of the proceeds is completed." UCC 9–504(1)(c). This rule has the effect of requiring a junior secured party who wishes to share in the proceeds of a senior's foreclosure sale to make written demand upon the senior.

Suppose that a junior secured party makes demand and receives payment from a senior under circumstances giving rise to an objection by the debtor. (For example, the debtor may claim that the junior's purported security interest is invalid (perhaps the security agreement contains a defective collateral description) or that the junior's loan is not in default.) Would the *senior* face liability to the debtor for having complied with the statute in good faith? Presumably not. Any recovery from the *junior* to which the debtor may be entitled would be governed by the law of restitution.

Now suppose that three secured parties (in order of priority, *SP*–1, *SP*–2, and *SP*–3) claim a security interest in the same collateral. If *SP*–3 makes demand and receives payment under UCC 9–504(1)(c) but *SP*–2 does not, what rights, if any, does *SP*–2 have against *SP*–1 or *SP*–3? Once again, *SP*–1 should face no liability and any recovery against *SP*–3 by *SP*–2 should be governed by the law of restitution.

Can one derive these results readily from Article 9? If not, should the statute be amended to reflect these results? Would clarification in the Comments be sufficient?

(3) Non–Article 9 Lienholders. UCC 9–504(1)(c) entitles the holder of a "subordinate security interest" to receive excess net proceeds of a disposition of collateral by a senior secured party. Similarly, UCC 9–504(3) requires that notice be given to "any other secured party" who has given timely notice to the enforcing secured party. By their terms, then, neither of these provisions works to the benefit of lienholders other than holders of Article 9 security interests. See UCC 9–105(1)(m) (defining "secured party"); UCC 1–201(37) (defining "security interest").

Because these non-Article 9 liens might be hard to find, it is understandable that UCC 9–504 places no duty on enforcing secured parties to uncover them. Under the current regime, an enforcing secured party has duties to other *secured parties* from which it has received notice. Is there any good reason why non-Article 9 *lienholders* who give notice to an enforcing secured party should not be entitled to receive notification of an intended disposition or to share in a surplus? Professor Gilmore thought that the benefits conferred on a non-enforcing "secured party" under UCC 9–504(3) (as well as under UCC 9–505 and UCC 9–506) do extend to a non-Article 9 lienor, blaming the more narrow statutory grant on "drafting inadvertence." 2 Gilmore, Security § 44.2, at 1217–18, § 44.3, at 1225, § 44.6, at 1240; cf. UCC 9–504(4) (a disposition under UCC 9–504 "discharges the security interest under which it is made and any security interest *or lien* subordinate thereto.").

(4) **Dispositions of Collateral by Junior Secured Parties Pursuant to UCC 9–504.** The notice provisions of subsection (3), if not the entire section, appear to have been written with sales by a senior in mind. See Review Committee for Article 9, Final Report, UCC 9–504 Reasons for 1972 Change. Although they are not entirely problem-free (the major issue concerns the appropriateness of the notice requirement), the rules seem to work reasonably well in that context.

Article 9 clearly contemplates the existence of multiple security interests in collateral. UCC 9–311 explicitly recognizes a debtor's ability to create junior interests, although creation of a competing security interest (even if junior) may cause a default as to a senior. By its terms, Part 5 of Article 9 applies to all security interests, regardless of priority. Unlike the enforcement of security interests by seniors, however, questions abound concerning foreclosure sales conducted by juniors. The remainder of this Note raises some of those questions.

Junior's Right to Take Possession of and Dispose of Collateral. Inasmuch as Article 9 recognizes junior security interests in collateral, it would be odd indeed if the Article did not permit a junior secured party to enforce its security interest by taking possession of and disposing of collateral. See UCC 9–503; UCC 9–504. There is nothing in Article 9 to suggest that the holder of a junior secured party does not have the right to enforce its security interest.

Senior's Right to Take Possession From Junior. What are the rights of a senior secured party when a junior has taken possession of collateral after default? In most cases the debtor also will be in default as to the senior security interest (by virtue of the creation of the junior interest, the debtor's default under the junior secured obligation (a **cross-default**), or the junior's taking possession). Is it a reasonable implication from a senior's senior status that its right to possession after default is superior to that of a junior?

Senior's Right to Control the Junior's Proposed Disposition. Assuming a senior secured party rightfully takes possession of collateral from a junior secured party, may the senior pick up where the junior left off? For example, may the senior avail itself of any advertisements concerning the proposed disposition and any notifications sent by the junior to the debtor and other secured parties? Or must the senior start the process all over again? On the other hand, is the senior necessarily *entitled* to begin anew? Perhaps the senior is concerned that the junior's planned procedures would not be commercially reasonable. But, could the debtor later argue successfully that the delay caused by the senior's starting all over again rendered the senior's (otherwise commercially reasonable) disposition commercially unreasonable?

Senior's Right to Notification From Junior. In specifying the class of secured parties entitled to notification of a disposition, UCC 9–504(3) does not distinguish between junior and senior creditors. It follows that if a junior secured party receives a written notice of a senior's interest, the junior would be obliged to give notification of a disposition to the senior. Do you find it anomalous to require juniors to notify seniors of a disposition? If the notification is intended to afford parties an opportunity to protect their interests, arguably the senior does not need notification. Unlike a security interest that is junior to the interest being enforced, the senior's interest will not be cut off by the disposition. UCC 9–504(4). Nevertheless, the disposition in fact may affect the senior adversely. In some cases, the senior may be unable to locate the collateral after sale and so in effect will have become unsecured. Even if the senior can locate the collateral, the senior will have incurred the costs of searching for it as well as the costs of repossessing it from the purchaser, who may be less cooperative than the debtor would have been. (A purchaser who did not take account of the senior's security interest when calculating the purchase price is likely to be particularly ornery.) Moreover, when the senior has a security interest in all the assets of a debtor's business, the proceeds the senior will receive from the resale of a single item of collateral upon repossession from a purchaser are likely to be less than the allocable portion of proceeds that the senior would have received upon a foreclosure sale of all the assets of the debtor's business.

Senior's Right to Recover Collateral From Purchaser at Junior's Sale. Even if the senior has the right to control a disposition, in any given case it might not do so. Assume that the junior proceeds with its disposition of the collateral (because, for example, neither the junior nor the senior secured party is aware of the other's interest). One of the few issues, in this context, on which Article 9 does speak with clarity is the rights of a purchaser in a disposition under UCC 9–504. As already mentioned, the purchaser cuts off only "the security interest under which it is made and any security interest or lien *subordinate thereto.*" UCC 9–504(4). If the senior did not authorize the disposition and if its security interest is perfected, the senior's security interest would continue notwithstanding the junior's disposition; the senior would be entitled to take possession of the collateral from the junior's purchaser. See UCC 9–306(2); UCC 9–301(1)(b); Chapter 13, Section 2, supra.

What can a buyer do to protect itself against claims of a senior? As with any sale out of the ordinary course of business, the prudent buyer must undertake Code searches and investigate the seller's source of title. However, there is an additional risk for a purchaser in a disposition under UCC 9–504. Many non-ordinary course buyers fear little for hidden conflicting interests because they are satisfied with the creditworthiness of their seller and the seller's warranty of title. In a foreclosure sale, it is likely that the seller makes no warranty of title. See UCC 2–312, Comment 5. Might the purchaser from the junior assert a common-law warranty? What about mutual mistake? In the typical case it is fair to assume that neither the selling junior secured party nor the buyer knows about the senior.

Rights to Proceeds Received Upon Junior's Disposition; Liability of Junior to Senior. Suppose that a junior secured party takes possession of collateral and sells it to a buyer pursuant to UCC 9–504. The buyer then flees with the collateral and cannot be found. The senior secured party then sues the junior, asserting that the junior converted the collateral by (alternatively) (i) taking possession of it in the first place, (ii) selling it, or (iii) failing to turn over the proceeds to the senior. What result?

One case (citing UCC 9–503) held that a junior in a similar situation acted properly and within its rights in taking possession of the collateral. The court implicitly came to the same conclusion about the junior's right to dispose of the collateral. However, the court went on to hold that "once [the junior] achieved repossession, ... the junior secured party ... had an obligation to turn proceeds of the sale of the collateral over to ... the senior secured party. Failure to so act is a conversion." Consolidated Equipment Sales, Inc. v. First State Bank & Trust Co., 627 P.2d 432, 438 (Okl.1981). If *Consolidated Equipment* were correct, how could a junior *ever* effectively enforce its security interest? Would it be forced to wait for the senior's disposition and hope for a distribution under UCC 9–504(1)(c)? For a cogent argument that the result in *Consolidated Equipment* is wrong, based in part on the negative implication of the provision for subordinate security interests in UCC 9–504(1), see Hillman, McDonnell & Nickles, Common Law ¶ 25.02[4], at 25–68 to 25–79. See also PEB Commentary No. 7 (secured party with a junior security interest in receivables who collects cash proceeds may achieve a senior security interest in the cash proceeds either as a holder in due course of a negotiable instrument or under analogous rules applicable to currency).

Note that the rights conferred on a junior secured party under UCC 9–503 and 9–504 ought to protect it from liability for conversion as a result of its taking possession and disposing of collateral. However, if upon the senior's demand and before a disposition has taken place, the junior refuses to give possession to the senior, or if the disposition *in fact* renders the collateral unavailable to the senior, liability for conversion may be appropriate. As to conversion liability, see Note (1) or Wrongful Repossession, Section 1, supra.

(5) Enforcement by Junior Secured Parties: Some Proposals for Reform. Although these interpretive problems rarely have given rise to reported decisions, one state has attempted a partial solution. Louisiana's version of UCC 9–306(1) makes it clear that "proceeds" does not include what is received in a disposition of collateral under UCC 9–

504 or in a judicial sale. La. Rev. Stat. Ann. § 9–306(1) (West Supp. 1992). That was thought to solve the problem of whether a junior can be forced to remit to the senior whatever the junior receives from a UCC 9–504 disposition. On the other hand, if these receipts are not proceeds, on what does the enforcing secured party base its claim to a security interest in them?

These problems also have not escaped academic attention. In the most recent proposal for reform, Professor Starnes argues for amendment of UCC 9–504 to require notice to all secured parties of record, both senior and junior. Starnes, U.C.C. Section 9–504 Sales by Junior Secured Parties: Is a Senior Party Entitled to Notice and Proceeds?, 52 U.Pitt.L.Rev. 563 (1991). In addition, she would amend UCC 9–504 to provide more clearly for the senior's right to take possession from a junior and pursue disposition itself. If the notified senior failed to respond within a reasonable time, the junior could dispose of the collateral and retain all of the proceeds. Under her proposal the senior's security interest would follow the collateral, however, as under current law.

Two other calls for reform also recognize that many problems derive from the absence of notification to a senior secured party; like Professor Starnes, they also would reinstate something like the notification requirements under the pre–1972 Article 9. See Byrne, Murphy, & Vukowich, Junior Creditors' Realization on Debtors' Equity Under U.C.C. Section 9–311: An Appraisal and a Proposal, 77 Geo. L.J. 1905 (1989); Wechsler, Rights and Remedies of the Secured Party After an Unauthorized Transfer of Collateral: A Proposal for Balancing Competing Claims in Repossession, Resale, Proceeds, and Conversion Cases, 32 Buff.L.Rev. 373 (1983). The proposal made by Professors Byrne, Murphy, and Vukowich goes farther than that of Professor Starnes. They argue that if the notified senior fails to act by taking over the disposition, the junior should be entitled to sell the collateral free of the senior interest. Professor Wechsler argues for a similar result.

(6) Determining Who Is Senior: Herein of Marshaling. In Problem 3, supra, both AIB and Tuleight held security interests in the Arkansas equipment. AIB's security interest was senior. AIB held a security interest in other collateral as well. Is AIB entitled to look to the Arkansas equipment, thereby leaving Tuleight with no collateral? Tuleight's counsel will, no doubt, invoke the doctrine of "marshaling of assets."

As explained by the Supreme Court, " '[t]he equitable doctrine of marshalling rests upon the principle that a creditor having two funds to satisfy his debt, may not by his application of them to his demand, defeat another creditor, who may resort to only one of the funds.' " Meyer v. United States, 375 U.S. 233, 236, 84 S.Ct. 318, 321, 11 L.Ed.2d 293, 297 (1963), quoting Sowell v. Federal Reserve Bank, 268 U.S. 449, 456–57, 45 S.Ct. 528, 530–31, 69 L.Ed.2d 1041, 1049 (1925). The purpose of the doctrine is "to prevent the arbitrary action of a senior lienor from destroying the rights of a junior lienor or a creditor having less security." Id. at 237, 84 S.Ct. at 321, 11 L.Ed.2d at 297. Because it is an equitable doctrine, marshaling is applied only when it can be equitably fashioned as to all of the parties having an interest in the property. In order to successfully invoke marshaling, there must be two creditors of a common debtor and two separate assets or funds of that debtor. In addition, one of the creditors must have a lien on only one of the funds and the other a lien on both of the funds. Tuleight's situation presents a classic case for marshaling. And case law supports the availability of marshaling where an Article 9 security interest is involved. See, e.g., Shedoudy v. Beverly Surgical Supply Co., 100 Cal.App.3d 730, 161 Cal.Rptr. 164 (1980). See also UCC 9–311, Comment 3 (suggesting, in a somewhat different factual setting, that marshaling "may be appropriate").

Now assume that all the collateral is sold in Schmelli's bankruptcy and that the proceeds of the other collateral are sufficient to repay AIB in full. Which would be fairer to Tuleight: to pay AIB's claim, in part, from the proceeds of the Arkansas equipment and give Tuleight nothing, or to pay Tuleight's claim from the proceeds of the Arkansas equipment and pay AIB from the proceeds of the other collateral? Which approach would be fairer to AIB?

Over the past decade or so, a number of cases have raised questions concerning the applicability of marshaling to secured claims in bankruptcy. Under the guise of marshaling, efforts have been made to require a secured party to seek recovery from sources other than the bankruptcy estate (e.g., from secured or unsecured guaranties). The cases are conflicting. Compare In re Jack Green's Fashions for Men— Big & Tall, Inc., 597 F.2d 130 (8th Cir.1979) (upholding marshaling order that compelled secured party to look first to secured guaranties instead of collateral owned by debtor) with In re Computer Room, Inc., 24 B.R. 732 (Bkrtcy.N.D.Ala.1982) (rejecting Jack Green and declining to require secured creditor to look first to guarantor). In other cases, the bankruptcy trustee has attempted, with mixed success, to impose what may be called "reverse marshaling," i.e., to require a senior to look first to collateral in which a junior has a security interest, so as to reduce the size of secured claims against the bankruptcy estate. Compare In re Center Wholesale, Inc., 759 F.2d 1440 (9th Cir.1985) (denying junior secured party's request for marshaling order because the order would prejudice rights of trustee in bankruptcy, as hypothetical lien creditor under BC 544(a)(1), leaving less property in estate for general creditors) with Computer Room, supra (applying marshaling doctrine, senior secured creditor was required to look first to collateral not claimed by junior secured creditor).

SECTION 4. REDEMPTION

Introductory Note. UCC 9–506 gives "the debtor or any other secured party" a right to redeem collateral by "tendering fulfillment of all obligations secured by the collateral" together with related expenses incurred by the secured party. UCC 9–506.

> [I]f the agreement contains a clause accelerating the entire balance due on default in one installment, the entire balance would have to be tendered. "Tendering fulfillment" obviously means more than a new promise to perform the existing promise; it requires payment in full of all monetary obligations then due and performance in full of all other obligations then matured.

UCC 9–506, Comment. The right of redemption must be exercised "before the secured party has disposed of collateral or entered into a contract for its disposition under Section 9–504 or before the [secured] obligation has been discharged under Section 9–505(2)." UCC 9–506. Upon disposition (or a contract for disposition) the debtor's "equity of redemption" is *foreclosed*. Although UCC 9–501(3)(d) prohibits waiver of redemption rights before default, UCC 9–506 explicitly permits waiver after default if so "agreed in writing."

Redemption is an ancient common law right. Professor Gilmore saw the right of redemption preserved by UCC 9–506 as a "ghostly remnant of the seventeenth century right":

> Three centuries ago ... the equity courts deduced the post-default right to redeem out of the mortgagor's pre-default equity .... To our ancestors the principal thing must have seemed to be not so much the fair resolution of a debtor-creditor relationship as it was the maintenance of stability in land tenure. Whatever could be done to keep the land in the ownership of the mortgagor and his family was a good thing.

2 Gilmore, Security § 44.2, at 1216. As described by Mr. Clark, the right to redeem gives "the debtor one last opportunity to recover the collateral. The debtor may desire to scrape the redemption money together—perhaps through a refinancing—because he fears that the collateral will not be sold for a good price, or because there is sentimental attachment irrespective of price." Clark, Secured Transactions ¶ 4.11, at 4–167. It appears that debtors infrequently exercise the right of redemption—probably because defaulting debtors typically cannot, to repeat Mr. Clark's words, "scrape the redemption money together."

Problem 1. In the setting of the Prototype, Lee Abel purchased a new Pontiac and signed the Installment Sale Contract (Form 6, Chapter 11, Section 1, supra). As in the Prototype, Main Motors assigned the contract to Firstbank.

Abel made five monthly payments from June 15 through October 15. At the end of October Abel was laid off work and was unable to continue the payments. Two weeks after missing the November 15 payment, an employee of Firstbank phoned to remind Abel that the payment was overdue. Firstbank wrote and phoned Abel several more times in November and December, and on December 10 Firstbank wrote to Abel stating that unless prompt payment was forthcoming, Firstbank would be required to repossess the car. Abel was still unable to find the money for the payments. On the night of December 15 the repo team repossessed the Pontiac. (These are the facts of Problem 1, Section 1, supra, omitting the details of the repossession.)

On December 17 Firstbank sent Abel a Notice of Repossession (Form 9, Chapter 11, Section 1, supra). On December 20 Abel met with one of Firstbank's loan officers and offered to pay the November and December payments ($288.79 for each month) plus the default charges specified in the agreement (including the costs of repossession and storage). The loan officer pointed to provisions in paragraph V on the reverse of the Installment Sales Contract that provide for acceleration of payments; the officer explained that the Pontiac would be returned to Abel only on payment of the full unpaid balance and other charges specified in the Notice of Repossession.

Abel has sued Firstbank for recovery of the Pontiac and for damages. The only applicable legislation is the Code. What result? See UCC 9–506; Williams v. Ford Motor Credit Co., infra; Dunn v. General Equities of Iowa, Ltd., infra; Notes on Acceleration and Redemption of Collateral, infra.

Problem 2. The facts are the same as in Problem 1, except that the U3C is in force. See U3C 5.111(1). What result?

WILLIAMS v. FORD MOTOR CREDIT CO.[*]

Supreme Court of Alabama, 1983.
435 So.2d 66.

MADDOX, JUSTICE. Although several issues are presented for review, the issue which is dispositive of this appeal involves the question of whether a security agreement can be modified either orally or by waiver if the security agreement requires that all modifications be in writing. The directed verdict of the trial court is affirmed.

On November 1, 1976, Curtis Williams, plaintiff-appellant, entered into a contract to purchase a 1974 Oldsmobile from Joe Meyers Ford in Houston, Texas. The contract was financed through Ford Motor Credit Company (FMCC), the defendant-appellee. Thirty payments of $136.40 were to be made, commencing December 7, 1976, with subsequent payments to be made on the like day of each month thereafter.

The payment which was due on February 7, 1977, was not timely made, but on March 4, 1977, Mrs. Williams mailed two money orders to FMCC, one in the amount of $151.40 to include payment, plus late charges, for February, and another in the sum of $136.40 to be applied

[* The court's citations are to the applicable pre–1972 version of the Code.]

on the March 7, 1977, payment. On March 5, 1977, the vehicle was repossessed.

Mr. James Osbourn testified on behalf of FMCC that the two payments in question were received by FMCC on March 7, 1977, which was Monday after the unit was repossessed on Saturday. The deposition testimony of Samuel Wright, who was employed by the Houston West Branch of FMCC, indicated that as Customer Account Supervisor, he had custody and control of Williams's file. On March 4, 1977, Wright initiated action to repossess the car and accelerated the contract balance by means of a mailgram. He did so, he stated, after reviewing Williams's account and ascertaining that Williams was located in Mobile, and seeing that Williams was past due and that default in the March payment was imminent. FMCC had tried to contact Williams by phone, but his telephone was not in service. Williams stated that he had moved from Houston to Mobile on about the 11th or 12th of February, 1977, but he did not notify FMCC of his change in address. An independent contractor was employed by FMCC to repossess the vehicle.

By affidavit and by deposition, Mrs. Williams stated that she made a long distance telephone call to FMCC on or about March 3 or 4. She stated that the substance of the call was that a representative of FMCC told her if the Williamses sent in two payments plus the $15.00 late charge, there would be no problem with the account. FMCC's motion in limine to suppress this evidence was granted over objection. The trial court sustained objection to Mrs. Williams's testifying that she made the call to FMCC.

After repossessing the automobile, FMCC, by letter dated March 11, 1977, sent Williams a notice of private sale. This notice informed Williams he had 10 days in which to redeem the automobile. It also stated that Williams would be liable for any deficiencies. Williams's attorney, on March 7, 1977, contacted FMCC by telephone and demanded return of the automobile because of the two payments submitted. FMCC denied that any employee of FMCC ever received a letter confirming the call.

Williams commenced this action against FMCC and other named defendants who were later dismissed from the case. The complaint, as amended, contained five counts seeking damages for the wrongful detention and conversion of a vehicle and the two money orders, and for fraud and misrepresentation. Williams sought $50,000 in damages under each of the first four counts, and $1,000,000 under the fifth count.

At the close of the plaintiff's evidence, FMCC submitted a written motion for directed verdict. After lengthy argument, this motion was later granted as to counts 3, 4, and 5. At the close of all the evidence, FMCC filed a further motion for directed verdict, which was granted as to the remaining two counts in the complaint. Williams's motion for

J.N.O.V. or in the alternative a new trial was denied. This appeal followed.

We think our decision in Hale v. Ford Motor Credit Co., 374 So.2d 849 (Ala.1979), in which this Court delineated the rights and obligations of the parties under the terms of a security agreement containing both a non-waiver acceleration clause and a non-modification clause, is controlling here. In *Hale*, supra, this Court ruled that the secured party is not required to give notice to the debtor prior to repossession, even though past-due payments have been accepted on previous occasions. Further, this Court concluded that a security agreement is effective according to the terms expressed in the agreement and that the inadvertence of the debtor in failing to make timely payments cannot raise an estoppel against the contractual interest of the creditor under the express terms of the security agreement, when there has been no written modification as required by the terms of the agreement.

Assuming, *arguendo*, that Mrs. Williams's telephone conversation on March 3 or 4, 1977, was admissible to show that the contract between the Williamses and FMCC had been modified to extend the time for payment, that testimony would not change the outcome of this case since the security agreement expressly provided that any modification of its terms must be in writing. Likewise, the acceptance of the late payment could not, without a writing evidencing the modification, operate as a waiver of default. Thus, we need not decide whether the trial court erred by granting the motion in limine as to Mrs. Williams's testimony concerning the telephone call.

Mr. Wright testified that he exercised FMCC's right to accelerate the contract on March 4, 1977, by mailgram, because the appellant was in default on his February 7, 1977, payment. Paragraph 19 of the security agreement provides in pertinent part:

> "Time is of the essence of this contract. In event [sic] Buyer defaults in any payment ... Seller shall have the right to declare all amounts due or to become due hereunder to be immediately due and payable and Seller shall have the right to repossess the property wherever the same may be found with free right of entry, and to recondition and sell the same at public or private sale. Seller shall have the right to retain all payments made prior to repossession and Buyer shall remain liable for any deficiency. Buyer agrees to pay ... expenses incurred by Seller in effecting collection, repossession or resale hereunder. Seller's remedies hereunder are in addition to any given by law and may be enforced successively and concurrently. Waiver by Seller of any default shall not be deemed waiver of any other default."

The evidence shows that FMCC received on March 7, 1977, subsequent to the acceleration and repossession, two money orders which, acceleration and repossession aside, would have made the appellant's account current through March 1977; however, in repossessing the automobile, FMCC incurred expenses of $323.50, which it was also entitled to recover.

We agree with FMCC that under the terms of the security agreement, its right to repossess the vehicle due to the default of the appellant existed independently of any right to accelerate the indebtedness due to that default. Consequently, the acceptance by FMCC of the late payment for February and the timely payment for March did not nullify the acceleration nor the remainder of the indebtedness; rather the payments received on March 7 must be considered as payments on the full indebtedness due on the appellant's account immediately after repossession on March 5. Had the appellant paid the entire contract balance, plus expenses incurred by FMCC in retaking the collateral, he would have been entitled to redeem the vehicle. The facts indicate, however, that the appellant did not redeem the automobile.

In a directed verdict case, such as the one here, the function of this Court is to view the evidence most favorably to the non-moving party; and if, by any interpretation, the evidence can support any inference supportive of a conclusion in favor of the non-moving party, we must reverse. After a review of the record, we conclude that there was no factual dispute requiring the trial court to submit the case to the jury; therefore, the trial court did not err in granting the directed verdict.

Affirmed.

DUNN v. GENERAL EQUITIES OF IOWA, LTD.[*]

Supreme Court of Iowa, 1982.
319 N.W.2d 515.

McCormick, Judge. The question here is whether the trial court erred in holding that the payees of two promissory notes waived their right to invoke acceleration clauses by accepting late payments on several prior occasions. We must decide if acceleration clauses can be waived by a previous course of dealing between the parties and, if so, whether the finding of waiver in this case is supported by substantial evidence. Because we give affirmative answers to each of these issues, we affirm the trial court.

Plaintiffs W.A. and Lola Dunn are payees on separate notes executed by defendant General Equities of Iowa, Inc., on March 31, 1974. The notes are identical except for the payees' names. Each provides for payment of $121,170 with seven percent annual interest. They are payable over a period of ten years, with annual installments due on or before March 31 of each year starting in 1975. Delinquent installments draw interest of nine percent. The acceleration clauses provide:

[* The court's citations are to the applicable pre–1972 version of the Code.]

"Upon default in payment of any interest, or any installment of principal, the whole amount then unpaid shall become due and payable forthwith, at the option of the holder without notice."

The parties agree that the 1979 payments were not made until April 10, 1979. Plaintiffs returned defendant's single check for both 1979 installments and demanded payment of the entire unpaid balance, with interest, in accordance with the acceleration clause. Defendant refused payment, and this suit resulted.

The determinative issue at trial was whether defendant established its defense that plaintiffs had waived their right to invoke the acceleration clause by accepting late payments in the past. The case was tried to the court at law, and the court found for defendant on the basis of its defense. This appeal followed.

I. *Waiver by course of dealing.* This court has not previously decided whether the right to enforce an acceleration clause can be waived by a course of dealing of accepting late payments on prior occasions. The issue is not affected by statute and therefore must be decided under common law principles.

The court has long held that acceleration clauses are subject to principles governing contracts generally:

> Stipulations such as are found in these notes and in the mortgage under consideration are not regarded in the nature of a penalty or forfeiture, and, for that reason, viewed with disfavor by the courts, but as agreements for bringing the notes to an earlier maturity than expressed on their face, and are to be construed and the intention of the parties ascertained by the same rules as other contracts.

Swearingen v. Lahner and Platt, 93 Iowa 147, 151, 61 N.W. 431, 433 (1894).

Contract rights, of course, can be waived, and an option to accelerate a debt is one such waivable right. Acceleration provisions are not self-executing, and "the holder of an instrument ... must take some positive action to exercise his option to declare payments due under an acceleration clause. ..." Weinrich v. Hawley, 236 Iowa 652, 656, 19 N.W.2d 665, 667 (1945). A failure to exercise the option or an acceptance of late payment will establish waiver:

> The notes did not become absolutely due on default in payment of the interest installment. Appellee had the right or "option" to so consider them, and to proceed at once to bring suit upon them, but was under no obligation so to do. It could waive the default and permit the notes to run without payment of any interest until they fell due on July 5, 1912, and the statute of limitations would not begin to run against the principal debt before that date. If, the interest installment being past due, its payment was tendered or offered by the defendant, and plaintiff received and accepted the same as interest, or if,

knowing that defendant paid it, understanding that it was being received in satisfaction of the past-due interest, it will be held to have waived the default, and can not thereafter make it a ground for declaring the whole debt due.

Farmers' & Merchants' Bank v. Daiker, 153 Iowa 484, 487, 133 N.W. 705, 705–06 (1911).

Moreover, this court has recognized that one way to prove waiver of contract provisions is "by evidence of a general course of dealing between the parties." Livingston v. Stevens, 122 Iowa 62, 69, 94 N.W. 925, 927 (1903). The court has held, for example, that a prior "course of dealing," as defined in the Uniform Commercial Code, "may overcome express terms in [a] security agreement and translate into an authorization for sale free of lien." Citizens Savings Bank v. Sac City State Bank, 315 N.W.2d 20, 26 (Iowa 1982). As defined in the UCC, "course of dealing" means "a sequence of previous conduct between the parties to a particular transaction which is fairly to be regarded as establishing a common basis of understanding for interpreting their expressions and other conduct." § 554.1205(1), The Code. This definition is similar to the definition of course of dealing in Restatement (Second) of Contracts § 223 (1979):

> (1) A course of dealing is a sequence of previous conduct between the parties to an agreement which is fairly to be regarded as establishing a common basis of understanding for interpreting their expressions and other conduct.
>
> (2) Unless otherwise agreed, a course of dealing between the parties gives meaning to or supplements or qualifies their agreement.

It is obvious, therefore, that waiving an acceleration option on prior occasions may constitute a course of dealing sufficient to establish waiver of the right to exercise the option on a subsequent occasion. This court has previously applied the rule in the context of real estate contract forfeitures:

> There is another reason why we think it should be held that appellees could make payment at the time the tender was made. The entire record shows a course of dealings between the buyer and the seller wherein the seller accepted payments made on dates other than those fixed by the contract. In so doing, we hold that the seller waived [its claim that payments could be made only at the time fixed in the contract].

Westercamp v. Smith, 239 Iowa 705, 717, 31 N.W.2d 347, 353 (1948). Because the rule is applicable to contract rights generally, the forfeiture context is not of controlling significance. Consequently we hold that the holder of an installment note who has engaged in a course of dealing of accepting late payments waives the right to accelerate the obligation upon a subsequent late payment unless the holder has notified the obligor that future late payments will not be accepted.

Other courts that have considered the issue have reached a similar conclusion.

The right to withdraw a waiver of time for performance upon reasonable notice to the other party has been recognized previously by this court.

The trial court was correct in holding that acceleration options in installment notes can be waived by a course of dealing of accepting late payments.

II. *Sufficiency of evidence.* Because the case was tried to the court at law, the court's findings of fact have the force of a jury's special verdict. They are binding on us if supported by substantial evidence. When reasonable minds could differ, a waiver issue is for the trier of fact.

The evidence here showed that plaintiff accepted late payments on at least three of the four prior occasions. The 1975 payments were made by a single check dated April 1, 1975. The 1976 payments were made in two installments, one on April 13 and the other on June 16 of that year. Although letters from plaintiffs following the partial payments in April demanded payment of the installment balance with interest, they did not invoke the acceleration clause or demand timely payment of future installments. The 1977 payments were made on April 11, 1977, and the 1978 payments were made by a check dated March 31, 1978.

This evidence provides a substantial basis for the trial court to find a course of dealing demonstrating waiver of timely payment of the 1979 installments. An issue of fact was presented. Therefore the trial court's finding of waiver has sufficient evidentiary support.

Affirmed.

Notes on Acceleration and Redemption of Collateral

(1) **The Value of the Right of Redemption.** One often hears of, or reads references to, the great value attributed to a debtor's right of redemption. As a practical matter, however, debtors infrequently are in a position to pay in full the secured obligation. Although the court in the *Williams* case observed that "[h]ad the appellant paid the entire contract balance, plus expenses incurred by FMCC in retaking the collateral, he would have been entitled to redeem the vehicle[,]" neither that case nor the *Dunn* case directly involved an issue of redemption under UCC 9–506. As the *Dunn* case illustrates, however, a debtor may have better luck by arguing that no default occurred or that the default was cured.

(2) **Acceleration and Cure.** The Code does not regulate generally the powerful right of acceleration. For the most part it leaves acceleration and the issue of cure to the parties' agreement. It does contain limitations on the use of "at will" or "insecurity" acceleration clauses,

however.   UCC 1–208 limits the effectiveness of these provisions to
situations where the accelerating party "in good faith believes that the
prospect of payment or performance is impaired."   Moreover, do not
infer that the absence of specific regulation in the Code is the end of
the matter.   A creditor's right to accelerate and a debtor's right to cure
are matters of considerable regulation in the case of consumer credit
transactions.   See U3C 5.110; U3C 5.111.   Other statutes in effect in
numerous states also provide a grace period following a default and a
right to cure.

(3) **Who Is Entitled to Redeem Collateral?**   UCC 9–506 confers
the right to collateral on the "debtor."   Remember that the debtor may
include more than one party—the party who owes payment of the
obligation and the party who owns the collateral, when they are not the
same.   See UCC 9–105(1)(d).   A guarantor of the secured obligations
also should be considered a debtor for purposes of UCC 9–506.   See
Note 1 on Rights of Guarantors of Secured Obligations, Section 3(A),
supra.

If an owner of collateral who is not obligated on the secured debt or
a guarantor of the debt exercises the right of redemption, the redeeming party should be subrogated to the secured party's claim against the
principal obligor, including the benefits of the redeemed collateral in
the case of a guarantor's redemption.   If the principal obligor redeems
collateral owned by a third party, the owner should be entitled to the
collateral free of the security interest and any claims of the redeeming
principal obligor.

UCC 9–506 also extends the right of redemption to "any other
secured party."   Note that the class of secured parties entitled to
redeem is larger than the class entitled to notice of disposition.   See
UCC 9–504(3).   But, as we saw when considering the parties who are
entitled to notification of a disposition under UCC 9–504(3), the right of
redemption under UCC 9–506 also appears to be limited to Article 9
"secured parties."   Although UCC 9–506 does not, by its terms, appear
to extend to other lienors, recall that Professor Gilmore took the
position that the right of redemption does extend to non-Article 9
lienors.   See Note (3) on Duties Owed by an Enforcing Secured Party to
a Competing Secured Party or Lienholder and Rights of Purchasers,
Section 3(B), supra.   Would granting all lienors a redemption right
work any particular hardship on secured parties whose collateral is
redeemed?

UCC 9–506 does not provide a statutory right of redemption to a
buyer of collateral subject to a senior security interest.   Consider the
potential plight of Bonzo Co. in Problem 5, Section 3(B), supra.   Assume
that Bonzo fails to discover AIB's senior security interest and buys the
office equipment from Tuleight for $50,000.   Even if Bonzo had a right
to redeem the equipment, under UCC 9–506, Bonzo would be required
to pay several million dollars to AIB because the equipment secures all
Schmelli indebtedness to AIB!   But, would AIB have any incentives *not*

to accept the fair value for the collateral instead? For an argument that a junior buyer should be entitled to redeem collateral by paying to the senior secured party the fair market value of the collateral, *not* the entire amount of the secured debt, see Wechsler, Rights and Remedies of the Secured Party After an Unauthorized Transfer of Collateral: A Proposal for Balancing Competing Claims in Repossession, Resale, Proceeds, and Conversion Cases, 32 Buff. L. Rev. 373, 381–84 (1983).

(4) Is There a Duty to Give Notice of Redemption Rights?
UCC 9–506 does not, by its terms, require a secured party to notify the debtor or any other secured party of a right to redeem. Should Article 9 require an enforcing secured party to give notice of redemption rights? If it is thought that certain classes of debtors, such as consumers, should be given notice of a right to redeem collateral, that protection can be afforded by statute or regulation outside the Code. See, e.g., Pennsylvania Motor Vehicle Sales Finance Act, Pa. Stat. Ann., tit. 69 § 623D (Supp. 1991).

Although notice of redemption rights is not required by UCC 9–506, an incorrect statement of the debtor's rights in a notice may violate UCC 9–506. If, for example, a debtor is notified that redemption of collateral by payment in full must be made earlier than the time specified in UCC 9–506, or may be made only by payment of a sum greater than that necessary to redeem, then the secured party may be liable for failure to proceed in accordance with Part 5. See Clark, Security Interests ¶ 4.11, at S4–30 (1992 Supp. No. 1) ("[A]n incorrect statement of the debtor's redemption rights is probably fatal. For example, the creditor should not notify the debtor that the collateral must be redeemed within 10 days, since UCC 9–506 allows redemption until foreclosure sale.").

SECTION 5. COLLECTIONS FROM ACCOUNT DEBTORS AND OBLIGORS ON INSTRUMENTS

Introductory Note. This book examines rights in and concerning receivables in many and varied contexts. This Section deals with collections by secured parties from account debtors and obligors on instruments. As between a debtor and a secured party, the rights and duties of the secured party concerning these collections are governed by UCC 9–502. (The rights and duties of the account debtor are, of course, the subject of UCC 9–318.) UCC 9–502(1) entitles a secured party to undertake direct collections from account debtors and obligors on instruments "[w]hen so agreed and in any event on default[.]" The following materials focus primarily on the rights and duties of secured parties who elect to undertake collections following a debtor's default. As to the debtor's agreement to the assignee's collections on the collateral before default, recall Mr. Kupfer's discussion of the distinction between "notification" receivables financing, where account debtors are notified and instructed at the inception of the transaction to remit payments to the assignee, and "non-notification" financing, where the debtor is permitted to collect the receivables—at least until a default occurs. See Chapter 12, Section 2, supra. See also UCC 9–502, Comment 1.

Problem. Under the facts of the Problem in Section 2, supra, you now represent AIB once again. AIB has ceased making new advances against Schmelli's accounts and has demanded payment of the $4,500,-000 owed on the line of credit facility. The loan officer fears that the lagging economy and Schmelli's more aggressive collection efforts are combining to shrink Schmelli's pool of accounts receivable; the officer has asked you for advice on how to collect Schmelli's accounts as soon as possible.

(a) What alternatives are available? What do you recommend? Would your advice be different if AIB had bought the accounts from Schmelli "outright," on a non-recourse basis? See UCC 9–502 & Comments 2 & 3; Notes on Collections by Secured Parties, infra.

(b) After AIB notified Schmelli's account debtors, instructing them to remit all payments directly to AIB, a "funny" thing happened: the account debtors quit paying Schmelli and many of them *also* have not paid AIB. The loan officer has written letters to the delinquent account debtors. What else, if anything, should be done? See UCC 9–502(2); Note (1) on Collections by Secured Parties, infra.

(c) The loan officer has informed you that Fractured Factors, Inc. (FFI), has made an offer to buy all of Schmelli's accounts—on a non-recourse basis and at a very steep discount. However, considering how long it may take to collect the accounts, and considering the interest charges that continue to run (at the default rate) on Schmelli's loans, the officer thinks that selling to FFI "may be just about the best thing for us and for Schmelli as well." What advice do you give? What steps should be taken? See UCC 9–504; Note (3) on Collections by Secured Parties, infra.

(d) One of the largest accounts, about $50,000, is disputed. The account debtor, Gravilumps Corp. (GC), has demanded a credit of $18,000 because of "grossly unqualified personnel" supplied by Schmelli. (One of Schmelli's temps caused GC's computer to "eat" the payroll records.) GC refuses to pay anything until the matter is resolved. Schmelli adamantly denies GC's claims. The loan officer thinks that the matter could be settled by offering a $10,000 credit. What do you recommend? Would you give different advice if the amount involved were $180? $180,000? Will your advice be affected by whether applicable law has adopted the absolute bar rule for a secured creditor's noncompliance? See Note (1) on Collections by Secured Parties, infra. What, if anything, might have been provided in the security agreement that would make your advice more certain?

(e) Another of the largest accounts involves a financially troubled customer, Nodough Co. (NC). Last year Schmelli took a negotiable note from NC evidencing NC's two-year installment obligation; NC is current on the note and is willing and able to make this month's payment. Schmelli refuses to deliver the note to AIB. Is AIB entitled to collect the payment from NC? See Note (5) on Collections by Secured Parties, infra.

Notes on Collections by Secured Parties

(1) **Commercially Reasonable Collections; Surplus and Deficiency.** A secured party who has "full or limited recourse against the debtor and who undertakes to collect from the account debtors or obligors must proceed in a commercially reasonable manner." UCC 9–502(2). And if the "security agreement secures an indebtedness," the debtor is entitled to any surplus and liable for any deficiency. Most of the factors and issues relating to commercially reasonable dispositions under UCC 9–504(3), considered in Section 2, supra, are equally applicable to the determination of whether collections are commercially reasonable; the rules also share a common rationale. A secured party's failure to proceed in a commercially reasonable manner exposes the secured party to the same sanctions that can result from conducting a commercially unreasonable disposition. See Note (4) on Commercially Reasonable Dispositions and Reasonable Notification, Section 2, supra.

The issue of whether collections are commercially reasonable has not been a frequent and major point of litigation, unlike the issue of commercially reasonable dispositions under UCC 9–504(3). Although foreclosure sales typically are out-of-the-ordinary transactions, collections normally are routine, whether undertaken by the debtor or an assignee. When an account debtor or obligor fails to pay, however, the reasonableness of the collecting assignee's response may be put to the test.

Note that UCC 9–502(2) differs in one important respect from its analogue for dispositions of collateral, UCC 9–504(3). There is no requirement in UCC 9–502(2) that notification be given to the debtor or any other secured parties. What justifications are there for the absence of a notification requirement in UCC 9–502(2)? Is the interest of a debtor in commercially reasonable collections any less than in the case of dispositions? Perhaps the distinction results from the drafters' perception that a debtor is more likely to be able to increase the price that collateral fetches at a disposition (e.g., by finding potential buyers) than to increase the amount that an account debtor pays on a receivable.

Nothing in Article 9 would seem to impose a *duty* on an assignee of a receivable to undertake collection. The obligations in UCC 9–502(2) are triggered only when and if a secured party "undertakes to collect." If a secured party endeavors to collect one receivable, is it obliged to attempt collection of *all* receivables in which it has a security interest? What actions constitute an undertaking to collect that triggers UCC 9–502(2)? The statutory language is less than clear on these issues. See

DeLay First National Bank & Trust Co. v. Jacobson Appliance Co., 196 Neb. 398, 243 N.W.2d 745 (1976) (secured creditor that took possession of all of debtor's records concerning its accounts, wrote two letters to some account debtors, and then took no further action failed to meet its burden of proof as to commercially reasonable collections).

The last sentence of UCC 9–502(2) makes explicit what is implicit in the preceding sentences—when there is a *sale* of accounts or chattel paper the debtor (seller) is neither entitled to any surplus nor (absent agreement to the contrary) liable for a deficiency. With the exception of this provision and the corresponding provision in UCC 9–504(2), Article 9 provides identical treatment for secured transactions consisting of sales of accounts or chattel paper and those where accounts or chattel paper secure an indebtedness.

(2) Sale versus Security for Indebtedness. As mentioned in the preceding Note, when the right to a surplus or the liability for a deficiency is at stake it will be necessary to distinguish a sale of accounts or chattel paper from a security interest that secures an indebtedness. At the extremes the distinction is easy to make. For example, a putative sale pursuant to terms that unconditionally require the assignor to repurchase the receivable upon default of the account debtor, for a price equal to the outstanding balance of the account, is the functional equivalent of a loan and would be treated as such. On the other hand, where the assignee has absolutely no recourse whatsoever against the assignor, regardless of whether the account debtor performs, characterization as an outright sale seems appropriate. Other arrangements may be much less clear.

Unlike its treatment of leases, the definition of "security interest" in UCC 1–201(37) provides no explicit guidance as to when the assignment of an account or chattel paper constitutes a "sale." "[T]he cases [dealing with the sale-secured loan dichotomy] are not easily harmonized, and different readers can argue as to which factors are relevant and which are entitled to greater weight." S. Schwarcz, Structured Finance 19 (1990). Mr. Schwarcz identifies the following factors as relevant: the existence and nature of recourse against the transferor, the extent to which the transferor retains rights (including the right to surplus collections), the nature of the pricing mechanism, and the arrangements for administration and collection.

The leading case is Major's Furniture Mart, Inc. v. Castle Credit Corp., 602 F.2d 538 (3d Cir.1979). Finding that virtually all of the account-debtor-related credit risks were placed on the assignor, the court concluded that the transaction was not an outright sale and that the assignor was entitled to a surplus.

(3) Dispositions of Receivables as an Alternative to Collection. Is a secured party entitled to sell a receivable in lieu of collection under UCC 9–502? The references to accounts and chattel paper in UCC 9–504(2) clearly indicate that receivables can be the subject of a disposition under UCC 9–504. Of course, the disposition must itself be commercially reasonable, and one could imagine circumstances where the ease and certainty of collection would render unreasonable any disposition for a price less than the full present value of the receivable.

(4) "Lockbox" Arrangements. Collection of a debtor's receivables by a secured party following the debtor's default typically, and understandably, reflects poorly on the debtor's continued economic viability. Account debtors who fear that the debtor may be unable to perform future contracts may be tempted to withhold payments for goods or services that the debtor previously provided. Additionally, the account debtors' uncertainty about whether to pay a notifying secured party and their requests for evidence of the assignment (see UCC 9–318(3)) frequently disrupt and delay the collection of the receivables.

To avoid these problems and to facilitate the secured party's collections following a default, the parties sometimes enter into a **lockbox** arrangement at the inception of a transaction. A typical lockbox arrangement involves a special **cash collateral deposit account** that is under the control of the secured party. The debtor is required to change its billing practices by instructing all account debtors to remit their payments to a particular post office box that is controlled by the depository bank. The bank then deposits all receipts into the cash collateral account. The secured party typically agrees that the debtor may make withdrawals from the account, provided that no default has occurred. If a default does occur, collection efforts are facilitated and (unless the debtor wrongfully changes the payment instructions on its bills) the secured party need not disclose the fact of the default to the account debtors.

(5) Collections on Negotiable Instruments. A secured party's collection rights also extend to collections from obligors on instruments. See UCC 9–502(1); UCC 9–105(1)(i) (defining "instrument"). However, as we have seen, a secured party cannot generally enforce an obligation evidenced by a negotiable instrument governed by Article 3 unless the secured party is in possession of the instrument. See Chapter 2, Section 3(A) supra. This does not present a problem when the instruments involved are delivered to the secured party at the inception of a financing transaction. As to after-acquired instruments, on the other hand, the secured party must rely on the debtor's compliance with covenants to deliver them for the purpose of perfection (UCC 9–305) as well as for the purpose of collection in the event of a default.

SECTION 6. RETENTION OF COLLATERAL: "STRICT FORECLOSURE"

Introductory Note. After a debtor's default a secured party may propose to retain the collateral in full satisfaction of the debtor's secured obligations pursuant to UCC 9–505(2). This remedy is commonly known as "strict foreclosure."

The requirements for an effective strict foreclosure under UCC 9–505(2) are as follows:

(i) The secured party must be in possession of the collateral.

(ii) The secured party must send to the debtor (and to any other secured party from which the secured party has received written notice of a claim to an interest in the collateral) a written proposal to retain the collateral in satisfaction of the obligations, unless the debtor has renounced that right after default.

(iii) The secured party may retain the collateral in satisfaction of the secured obligations only if the secured party does not receive, within 21 days after the proposal was sent, written objection from a party entitled to notice of the proposal. If no objection is made, "the secured party is bound by his notice" and must retain the collateral in satisfaction of the secured obligations. UCC 9–505(2), Comment 2. If a timely objection is received, the secured party must dispose of the collateral under UCC 9–504.

When the collateral is consumer goods and the debtor has paid 60% or more of the secured loan or the cash price (i.e., the price of the goods, without taking into account finance charges and other amounts included in the secured obligations), UCC 9–505(1) prohibits strict foreclosure unless the debtor has signed after default a statement modifying or waiving the right to insist upon a disposition under UCC 9–504.

Problem. You continue to represent AIB under the facts of the Problem in Section 2, supra. As in the Problem in Section 5, supra, AIB has ceased making new advances against Schmelli's accounts and has demanded payment of the $4,500,000 owed on the line of credit facility. So far AIB has not disposed of any of the collateral or collected any of the receivables.

The loan officer met today with Telli Schmelli. Although relationships remain strained, AIB and Schmelli have agreed in principle that the bank will accept ownership of the Learjet in full satisfaction of the $2,500,000 balance on the Learjet loan and in satisfaction of $600,000 of the line of credit debt. Both Schmelli and AIB recognize that the market for corporate aircraft is poor right now. Schmelli believes that it will receive a credit on the debts approximately equal to the fair market value of the Learjet. The loan officer is pleased not to be faced with the hassles and risks of a foreclosure sale.

(a) The loan officer has asked you to "draft the papers as soon as possible." How do you respond? See Note (2) on Retention of Collateral, infra.

(b) If you see problems with the proposal, what modifications, if any, to the relevant agreements could be made now that would solve those problems?

Notes on Retention of Collateral

(1) Requirement That Collateral Be in Secured Party's Possession. UCC 9–505(2) provides that a secured party must be "in possession" of collateral in order to propose a retention. Professor Hawkland has explained that the requirement of possession means "actual possession." In his view, "[i]f a secured party does not possess the collateral, either because it is incapable of possession, such as an account receivable, or because the collateral is left in the possession of the debtor after default under section 9–503, the secured party may not propose a strict foreclosure." W. Hawkland, Uniform Commercial Code Series § 9–505:04 (1991). There is substantial support for this interpretation. See, e.g., Sprangers v. Fundamental Business Technology, Inc., 412 N.W.2d 47 (Minn.App.1987) (secured party that does not have possession of collateral may not exercise remedy of strict foreclosure; debtor cannot waive possession requirement); Lakin, Default Proceedings Under Article 9: Problems, Solutions, and Lessons to be Learned, 8 Akron L. Rev. 1, 12 (1974) ("[W]hen collateral is intangible personal property, such as accounts receivable and chattel paper, the secured party has nothing tangible to take into his possession. Therefore, his ability to realize on intangible collateral depends on his right to collect the proceeds of such intangible property.").

Why should a secured party's possession of collateral be a necessary condition for strict foreclosure? Mr. Clark has argued for a more flexible interpretation of the seemingly "inflexible language" of UCC 9–505(2): "[A] good argument could be made that the term 'possession' really means 'possession where possible.'" Clark, Secured Transactions ¶ 4.10[3], at 4–160. But he notes that the secured party who attempts strict foreclosure on intangible collateral should be prepared for later objections from the debtor or competing secured parties.

Professor Gilmore speculated that the secured party's possession might be thought to give notice to interested third parties, but he suggested that it would be more effective to require notice by *publication* in order to alert competing parties to a pending strict foreclosure. 2 Gilmore, Security § 44.3, at 1223–24. Nevertheless, some may be troubled by the prospect that a secured party could become the *owner* of all of a debtor's inventory and equipment, for example, while allowing the debtor to remain in possession. If the possession requirement in UCC 9–505(2) for collateral that can be possessed were eliminated, and if intangible collateral were made eligible for strict foreclosure, would those changes warrant expansion of the notification requirement in UCC 9–505(2)? See Note (3) infra.

(2) Retention in Partial Satisfaction; Waiver of Debtor's Rights. Strict foreclosure can be advantageous to both secured parties and debtors. "Experience has shown that the parties are frequently better off without a resale of the collateral[.]" UCC 9–505, Comment 1.

Through strict foreclosure, a secured party can avoid the time and expense of a disposition under UCC 9–504, can protect itself from later objections by the debtor to the commercial reasonableness of the disposition, and can eliminate the obligation to account to the debtor for any surplus. Because deficiencies probably arise more often than surpluses, a debtor also may be advantaged by a strict foreclosure because its secured obligations are deemed satisfied in full.

The 1972 revisions to Article 9 amended UCC 9–505(2) in order to of facilitate its use. The waiting period was reduced from 30 days to 21 days, to be measured from the time when the secured party sends a written proposal instead of from the time the debtor receives the proposal. And, unlike the 1972 version, the pre–1972 UCC 9–505(2) contained no provision for the debtor's post-default waiver of rights and required the secured party to discover and notify competing secured parties that had filed financing statements. See Note (3) infra.

The commentary and reported judicial decisions generally agree that UCC 9–505(2) does not permit a secured party to propose to retain collateral in *partial* satisfaction of the secured obligations. There is disagreement, however, concerning the effectiveness of post-default agreements by debtors to modify, renounce, or waive rights under Part 5 so as to result in a retention in partial satisfaction. Note that the effect of a retention in partial satisfaction would be equivalent to the purchase by a secured party at a private sale, which (except in limited circumstances) is prohibited by UCC 9–504(3). It seems clear that a debtor cannot effectively waive that prohibition. See Note (3) on Commercially Reasonable Dispositions and Reasonable Notification, Section 2, supra. It follows that permitting retention in partial satisfaction would enable the parties to accomplish indirectly what they could not accomplish directly under UCC 9–504(3).

Notwithstanding this reasoning, some have argued that the reference in UCC 9–505(1) to modification of "rights under this Part" and the reference in UCC 9–505(2) to modification of "rights under this subsection" can be read to permit valid post-default agreements for the retention of collateral in partial satisfaction of secured indebtedness. Mr. Coogan found in UCC 9–505 an implicit right of a debtor to require a secured party to abandon any claim for a deficiency judgment following a strict foreclosure. Coogan, The New UCC Article 9, 86 Harv.L.Rev. 477, 522 (1973). (Indeed, Comment 1 to UCC 9–505 observes that, "[i]n lieu of resale or other disposition, the secured party may propose under subsection (2) that he keep the collateral as his own, thus discharging the obligation and abandoning any claim for a deficiency.") Because he believed that UCC 9–505(2) makes that implicit right to be relieved of liability for a deficiency *waivable*, Mr. Coogan argued that a secured party (with the debtor's consent) effectively can retain collateral in partial satisfaction of the secured obligations while reserving an enforceable claim for the unsatisfied portion of those obligations.

Putting aside the question whether post-default agreements for partial satisfaction are effective under current law, *should* proposals to retain in partial satisfaction or post-default agreements be permitted? One alternative would be to allow a secured party to purchase at a private sale with the debtor's post-default consent. At least that approach would impose on a secured party the burden of proceeding in a commercially reasonable manner. But it would not protect a secured party who fails to undertake any advertising whatsoever, thereby reducing the savings thought to inhere in a strict foreclosure. It also would undercut the controlling effect of the agreement of the debtor and secured party. Another alternative would be to permit private sales to secured parties when the amount of the obligations forgiven are not disproportionately small in comparison with the net amount that would have been received in a commercially reasonable disposition. That approach would have an effect similar to the application of the rebuttable presumption rule for a secured party's noncompliance.

A more modest approach would be to permit proposals to retain in partial satisfaction when the collateral is of the type that a secured party is permitted to buy at a private sale. See UCC 9–504(3) ("[I]f collateral is of a type customarily sold in a recognized market or is of a type which is the subject of widely distributed standard price quotations," then the secured party is permitted to "buy at [a] private sale."). If Article 9 is revised to permit such proposals, should it require that the amount of the obligations satisfied be at least the amount that would have been realized at a commercially reasonable private sale? Or would the debtor's right to object to the proposal provide sufficient protection?

(3) Notice to Competing Secured Parties and Lienholders; Effect of Retention on Junior Secured Parties and Lienholders. UCC 9–505(2) requires a secured party proposing a strict foreclosure to send notice of the proposal "to any other secured party from whom the [proposing] secured party has received (before sending his notice to the debtor or before the debtor's renunciation of his rights) written notice of a claim of an interest in the collateral." The secured parties to be notified are the same ones entitled to receive notification of a disposition under UCC 9–504(3). Professor Hawkland has observed that UCC 9–505(2) contemplates that only Article 9 secured parties are within the class of creditors entitled to receive notice of a proposed strict foreclosure. See W. Hawkland, Uniform Commercial Code Series § 9–505:06 (1991). But implicit in Professor Gilmore's view (as with the notice provisions of UCC 9–504 and UCC 9–506) was that non-Article 9 lienholders are entitled to notice. 2 Gilmore, Security § 44.3, at 1225.

Curiously, UCC 9–505(2) is silent as to the effect of a strict foreclosure by a senior secured party on the claims to the same collateral of junior secured parties and other junior lienholders. In contrast, UCC 9–504(4) is explicit: a "disposition ... discharges the security interest under which it is made and any security interest or lien subordinate thereto."

Professor Gilmore, while noting that UCC 9–505(2) fails to mention junior claimants, nonetheless took the position that strict foreclosure should have the same effect (discharge of junior parties) as a disposition under UCC 9–504(3). See 2 Gilmore, Security § 44.3, at 1225–26. See also W. Hawkland, Uniform Commercial Code Series § 9–505:10 (1991) (secured party who retains collateral should take free of all subordinate security interests and liens but subject to any senior security interests or liens). Consistent with this view, one court has held that a "merger"—resulting in the junior interests rising to the top—does not occur when a senior secured creditor retains the collateral in satisfaction of the indebtedness. Food City, Inc. v. Fleming Companies, 590 S.W.2d 754 (Tex.Civ.App.1979).

Strict foreclosure would be much less attractive if subordinate security interests and liens were not discharged. But consider the potentially harsh effects of strict foreclosure on discharged junior secured parties and lienholders. Junior claimants not included in the narrow class that is "entitled to receive notification" are not entitled to object to a proposal under UCC 9–505(2). Consequently, an ill-informed judgment by a debtor or a debtor's neglect could deny junior claimants access to collateral value substantially in excess of the obligations satisfied in a strict foreclosure. By way of contrast, the "commercially reasonable" standard applicable to dispositions under UCC 9–504 affords greater protection for a junior party's interest in reaching an excess value.[1]

Even if one agrees with the designation of parties entitled to notice of a disposition under UCC 9–504(3), the potentially more severe impact on junior claimants might provide a plausible basis for broader notice requirements in UCC 9–505(2). And even if the notice requirements in UCC 9–505(2) remain unchanged, the class of parties entitled to object to a proposed retention could be broadened to include all junior secured parties and lienholders. Cf. UCC 9–504(3) & (4) (notice of disposition is to be given only to certain secured parties, although disposition discharges all junior security interests and liens).

(4) Retention of Collateral Under UCC 9–505 Followed by Immediate Sale. Nothing in UCC 9–505 prohibits a secured party from retaining collateral under UCC 9–505 and then selling it immediately. However, one court has held a sale under these circumstances to be impermissible. In Reeves v. Foutz & Tanner, Inc., 94 N.M. 760, 617 P.2d 149 (1980), the secured party proposed to retain jewelry that was worth much more than the secured obligation. After the debtor (an individual) failed to make a timely objection, the secured party placed

---

1. If, however, there is a substantial disparity between the obligations satisfied and the actual value of the collateral, a strict foreclosure may be vulnerable as a fraudulent transfer. The "safe harbor" provided by Uniform Fraudulent Transfer Act § 3(b) for "a regularly conducted, non-collusive foreclosure sale or execution of a power of sale for the acquisition or disposition of the interest of the debtor" does not, by its terms, seem to apply to a strict foreclosure. Moreover, termination of the debtor's equity of redemption in a strict foreclosure would constitute a "transfer" as defined in BC 101(54), thereby exposing the transfer to avoidance under BC 548.

the jewelry in its inventory and promptly sold it. The court relied in part on UCC 9–505, Statement of Reasons for 1972 Changes in Official Text: "Under subsection (2) of this section the secured party may in lieu of sale give notice to the debtor and certain other persons that he proposes to retain the collateral *in lieu of sale.*" (Emphasis added.) The court also relied on a Federal Trade Commission decision interpreting the cited Statement for the proposition that a waiver of surplus or deficiency rights is appropriate only when the creditor does not contemplate the prompt resale of the repossessed collateral in the ordinary course of business. See *Reeves*, 617 P.2d at 151 (citing and quoting In the Matter of Ford Motor Company, Ford Motor Credit Co., and Francis Ford, Inc., 94 F.T.C. Rep. 564, 3 Trade Reg. Rep. (CCH) 21756, 21767 (1979)). Mr. Clark argues that *Reeves* repeals UCC 9–505 and is "obviously wrong." Clark, Secured Transactions ¶ 4.10[1], at 4–156 to 4–157.

(5) Compulsory Disposition of Consumer Goods—Subsection (1). When a debtor in default has paid sixty percent or more of the indebtedness secured by consumer goods, UCC 9–505(1) requires the secured party to dispose of the goods under UCC 9–504 if the debtor "has not signed after default a statement renouncing or modifying his rights under this Part [5]." Although Article 9 explicitly permits these post-default waivers, the case law and commentary agree that a debtor cannot and should not be allowed to renounce or modify rights to a compulsory disposition before default.

Professor Gilmore observed that UCC 9–505(1) was designed for the protection of consumers and was part of an abandoned plan for Article 9 to address comprehensively secured consumer finance problems. He questioned whether that subsection, "which happened more or less by accident to survive to the final draft," is useful and whether the problems of consumer protection would be better left to the Retail Instalment Sales Acts. See 2 Gilmore, Security § 44.3, at 1221.

(6) "Constructive" Strict Foreclosure. A number of courts have held that a secured party's conduct in retaining possession of collateral without disposition for an unusually long period of time can constitute a retention in satisfaction within the scope of subsection 9–505(2), whether or not the secured party intended to invoke that remedy. See generally Clark, Secured Transactions ¶ 4.10[5], at 4–162. These decisions deny the secured party any right to a deficiency judgment. Of course, courts are not likely to find an involuntary strict foreclosure when it is the creditor, instead of the debtor, who advances the implied election argument. There also exists a line of decisions that refuses to find an involuntary strict foreclosure in cases of delay. See, e.g., *Warnaco, Inc. v. Farkas*, 872 F.2d 539 (2d Cir.1989). Mr. Clark argues in support of these decisions because "strict foreclosure under § 9–505(2) expressly requires a voluntary written proposal coming from the secured party"; an unreasonably long retention of collateral instead should be treated as a violation of UCC 9–504(3), thereby exposing the secured party to liability under UCC 9–507(1). Clark, Secured Transactions ¶ 4.10[5], at 4–162 to 4–163.

*

INDEX

References are to Pages

†